Cases and Text on
PROPERTY

EDITORIAL ADVISORY BOARD

Cases and Text on
PROPERTY

Third Edition

A. James Casner
Austin Wakeman Scott Professor of Law, Emeritus
Harvard University

W. Barton Leach
Late Story Professor of Law
Harvard University

Assisted by
Donald S. Snider, Esquire
In Part VI

 ASPEN LAW & BUSINESS
Aspen Publishers, Inc.

Library of Congress Catalog Card No. 83-082695

ISBN 0-7355-0617-5

Fifteenth Printing

MV-NY

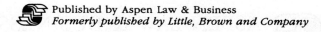 Published by Aspen Law & Business
Formerly published by Little, Brown and Company

Printed in the United States of America

SUMMARY OF CONTENTS

v

PART III

BONA FIDE PURCHASERS OF PERSONAL PROPERTY   137

PART IV

ESTATES IN LAND   183

PART V

BEFORE AND AFTER THE STATUTE OF USES   285

PART VI

LANDLORD AND TENANT   353

PART VII

THE MODERN LAND TRANSACTION   663

PART VIII

LAND USE PLANNING
AND DEVELOPMENT   937

PART IX

RIGHTS INCIDENT TO
OWNERSHIP OF LAND   1193

PART X

TAXATION   1243

TABLE OF CONTENTS

ix

CHAPTER 11

CHAPTER 12

CHAPTER 13

CHAPTER 14

CONCURRENT OWNERSHIP   251

PART V
BEFORE AND AFTER THE STATUTE OF USES 285

CHAPTER 15

CONVEYANCING AND FUTURE INTERESTS
BEFORE THE STATUTE OF USES   287

CHAPTER 16

THE STATUTE OF USES AND ITS CONSEQUENCES (INCLUDING THE RULE AGAINST PERPETUITIES AND SOME OTHER RULES RESTRICTING THE CREATION OF PROPERTY INTERESTS)   317

CHAPTER 18

MEANS AVAILABLE TO ASSURE LEASE
PERFORMANCE

CHAPTER 19

WHEN PARTIES ARE EXCUSED FROM PERFORMANCE 459

CHAPTER 22

CHAPTER 23

PART VII
THE MODERN LAND TRANSACTION 663

CHAPTER 24

THE STATUTE OF FRAUDS   693

CHAPTER 25

THE CONTRACT FOR THE SALE OF LAND (HEREIN THE LAW OF VENDOR AND PURCHASER)   699

CHAPTER 26

THE MORTGAGE 739

CHAPTER 27

THE DEED 755

CHAPTER 28

RECORDING (HEREIN BONA FIDE PURCHASER OF REAL PROPERTY)   801

CHAPTER 29

TITLE EXAMINATION IN MASSACHUSETTS
by Richard B. Johnston

CHAPTER 30

CHAPTER 31

PART VIII
LAND USE PLANNING AND DEVELOPMENT

CHAPTER 32

CHAPTER 33

PUBLIC LAW DEVICES   1115

PREFACE

The late Professor Leach and I sought to attain the following objectives when we conceived the first edition of Cases and Text on Property in 1951: (1) to give the first-year law student basic training in property law and in the handling of legal materials generally; and (2) to provide such student with a practical grasp of the law governing commercial transactions in land. In the second edition of the casebook, which we presented in 1969, we stated our objectives as follows: (1) to give the first-year law student basic training in property law; (2) to provide such student with material that would enable him or her to judge how well property law copes with significant modern social problems; and (3) to start the student along the road of becoming a lawyer and then to move him or her onward with celerity.

I have prepared this third edition of the casebook without the personal help of my partner, the distinguished scholar W. Barton Leach, former Story Professor of Law at the Harvard Law School, whose untimely death occurred in 1971. But his intellectual qualities pervade the third edition because of his contributions to the first and second editions, and that is why I have continued to use the pronoun "we" when referring to the authors of this book. I have tried to carry forward in the third edition the objectives we announced for the casebook in the Preface to the second edition.

Prior to the 1950s, law schools offered various separate courses in property law: Personal Property; Possessory Estates in Land; Future Interests; Conveyancing; Wills; Landlord and Tenant; and Rights in the Land of Another. In addition, there were property-related courses in areas such as mortgages and trusts. These various aspects of property law have been brought together in this book and can be divided into two topics: (1) commercial transactions in land, with an introduction to commercial transactions in personal property (Bona Fide Purchasers of Personal Property, Part III; Landlord and Tenant, Part VI; Conveyancing, Part VII; Land Use Planning, Part VIII; and Rights Incident to Ownership of Land, Part IX); and (2) donative transfers of real and personal property (generally referred to as estate planning). This book is designed to cover in detail commercial transactions in land and to provide a foundation in the field of donative transfers.

In the interim between the second and the third editions of this casebook, I served as Reporter for the Restatement (Second) of Property (Landlord and Tenant), a work that was published in two volumes in 1977. As might be expected, I have drawn heavily on the Restatement in reworking Part VI, on Landlord and Tenant. In the development of Part VI, I have been extensively assisted by Donald S. Snider, an active practitioner in the field of landlord and tenant and one of my advisors on the Restatement.

The material on commercial transactions in land, which includes Part VI, Landlord and Tenant, offers the student an opportunity to consider deeply the extent to which the law in this area has contributed to or helped to provide relief from the social problems created by housing conditions in this country, including discrimination in housing on the ground of race, color, religion, sex, or national origin.

The material in Chapter 23 on the negotiation and drafting of a commercial lease and the material in Part VIII on the development of an exclusive residential area as it might evolve in the office of a lawyer who represents the developer are designed to give the student two practical experiences in what it is like to be a lawyer. It is hoped that these experiences will further the objective of starting the student along the road of becoming a lawyer.

The foundation for donative transfers of real and personal property is laid in Parts II (Gifts of Personal Property), IV (Estates in Land), V (Before and After the Statute of Uses) and Part X (The A-B-C of Taxes For Property Lawyers).

Part I, Problems in Possession, is designed to introduce the student to the study of law by confronting him or her with the dangers of trying to solve legal problems by using general concepts such as "possession." It is an enlightening and challenging experience to understand the changing meaning of this word as it comes to the forefront in different contexts.

I repeat here what we said at the end of the Preface to the second edition: "We find it exciting to strive to attain the objectives we have stated at the beginning of this Preface. We wonder why all of our colleagues are not fighting to get a chance to teach the first-year property course. We can only surmise that they want to live more sheltered lives. We do not envy them."

A few words need to be said about the mechanics of the casebook. Authors' footnotes and footnotes from quoted material are numbered sequentially per chapter; thus the numbers of footnotes from quoted material have been changed. Further, to keep the text uncluttered, the omission of footnotes or citations from quoted material has not been noted.

s/ *A. James Casner*
s/ *W. Barton Leach*
   by A. James Casner
   under a durable power
   of attorney that not
   even W. Barton Leach's
   death could terminate

April 1984

ACKNOWLEDGMENTS

The authors gratefully acknowledge the permissions granted to reproduce the following materials.

American Bar Association, Special Committee on Residential Real Estate Transactions, Residential Real Estate Transactions: The Lawyer's Proper Role-Services-Compensation, 14 Real Prop., Prob. & Tr. J. 581, 581-607 (1979). Copyright © 1978 American Bar Association. Reproduced with permission.

American Law Institute, Restatement (Second) of Property (Donative Transfers) §1.4, comments c–o. Restatement (Second) of Property (Landlord and Tenant, blackletter of §6.2; Introductory Note to Chapter 5; blackletter of §11.1 (rent abatement); blackletter of §11.2; blackletter of §11.3; blackletter of §8.1; blackletter of §12.1(3); blackletter of §17.6; §5.6; comment e under §5.6; §15.2(2). Copyright © 1977 by The American Law Institute. Reprinted with the permission of The American Law Institute.

American Law Institute, Restatement (Second) of Torts §358 comment b. Copyright © 1965 by The American Law Institute. Reprinted with the permission of The American Law Institute.

Chafee, The Music Goes Round and Round: Equitable Servitudes and Chattels, 69 Harv. L. Rev. 1250, 1262-1263 (1956). Copyright © 1956 by the Harvard Law Review Association.

Clark, Real Covenants and Other Interests Which Run With the Land, various short quotations and paraphrases (2d ed. 1947). Reprinted with permission of Callaghan & Co., 3201 Old Glenview Road, Wilmette, Illinois 60091.

8 Criminal Law Quarterly 137 (1965). Reprinted with permission of Canada Law Book Limited.

Geist, Friends of Hunted Unite to Sabotage Hunters, N.Y. Times, Mar. 1, 1983, at 1, col. 3. Copyright © 1983 by The New York Times Company. Reprinted with permission.

Greater Boston Real Estate Board, standard form purchase and sale agreement. Copyright © 1978. Reproduced Courtesy of the Greater Boston Real Estate Board.

New York Times, Jan. 16, 1964, at 46, col. 2. Copyright © 1964 by The New York Times Company. Reprinted with permission.

Rundell, Judge Clark on the American Law Institute's Law of Real Covenants: A Comment, 53 Yale L.J. 312, 314 (1944). Reprinted with permission of the Yale Law Journal Company and Fred B. Rothman and Company.

INTRODUCTION

CHAPTER 1

THE LEGAL PROFESSION, LAWYERS, AND THE STUDY OF PROPERTY LAW

We, the authors of this book,[1] will be with you in spirit for some considerable time. It is well that you should know how we feel about our profession and yours, what we think a law school can do for you, and in what manner we hope this book will help you along the road of learning that leads to a useful and satisfying career. So let us talk to you for a few pages on subjects related to your future.

Necessarily this chapter is general. You may find it worthwhile to read it again in three or four months, after you have acquired reference points in the law.

The Area of Responsibility of the Legal Profession

You and others who are being trained as lawyers must be prepared to perform three tasks during the productive years of your professional lives.

1. *To assume direction of all phases of the areas of personal conflict inherent in a complex society and economy.* You will be advisers, negotiators, advocates, judges, arbitrators—and frequently administrators and executives having a large amount of quasi-legislative power. This scope of activity would have seemed revolutionary and presumptuous to an eighteenth century solicitor, but it has become traditional lawyers' work in our

---

1. The late Professor Leach is regarded as one of the authors of this edition because many ideas of his that went into prior editions have been retained in one form or another in this edition.

1

time. The number and complexity of the conflict areas increase, and pari passu the need increases for lawyers who can farsightedly advise their clients, ably represent their clients' causes, and wisely administer the organizations and wield the powers of decision through which government exercises its authority. There are a lot of big words in this paragraph, but we do not want to be understood to limit these remarks to the stratosphere of human controversy. The small issues between people who never make the headlines—the action for a broker's commission, the boundary dispute between neighbors, the personal injury claim, the troubles of a partnership in a garage business—these are a primary responsibility of our profession, serving also as a training ground in which lawyers by doing smaller tasks well can learn to perform greater tasks when they come.

2. *To provide a very large proportion of national leadership at all levels of authority.* Naturally, this field of activity has a tendency to overlap that of the previous paragraph; the distinction we draw lies between those tasks in which membership in the bar is a prerequisite and those in which a journalist, a stockbroker, or a haberdasher is equally eligible. It is an observable fact that through some combination of chromosomes and professional training lawyers tend to come to the top of the barrel in the shaking and jolting of competition for authority.

3. *To serve, at little or no compensation, the needs of indigent criminal defendants and to participate, so far as a lawyer can, in the "war on poverty."* The dimensions of this task are not altogether clear; but it is obvious that the task is large, that it will require a rethinking of the economics of the professions, that it will require constant cooperation with social workers, and that it will impose large demands upon the lawyer's professional time. It might be thought that if one is capable of handling the large affairs of affluent clients, it should be easy to handle the smaller affairs of the poverty-stricken. This is true only to a limited extent. The problems are often different in kind, not only in degree. Psychiatry, sociology, and a maze of legislation and regulations at all levels of government suddenly become relevant. But the job must be done.

The Basic Qualities of a Good Lawyer

The best way to describe a good lawyer in a phrase is to call him or her a professional in versatility. This is another way of saying that a good lawyer has acquired certain abilities that enable him or her to operate effectively in any enterprise, familiar or unfamiliar, to diagnose its difficulties, and to contribute substantially to the solution of its problems. A lawyer's usual field of operation is one in which the legal ingredient is large, and to this ingredient the lawyer brings professional knowledge as well as the basic abilities; but the fact that the nonlegal ingredient is frequently dominant and the further fact that the situations in which a lawyer's help is solicited are many and varied give the lawyer the habit of tackling new problems with confidence and skill, regardless of their nature.

Our listing of the basic qualities is the following:

1. *Fact consciousness.* An insistence upon getting the facts, checking their accuracy, and sloughing off the element of conclusion and opinion.

2. *A sense of relevance.* The capacity to recognize what is relevant to the issue at hand and to cut away irrelevant facts, opinions, and emotions which can cloud the issue.

3. *Comprehensiveness.* The capacity to see all sides of a problem, all factors that bear upon it, and all possible ways of approaching it.

4. *Foresight.* The capacity to take the long view, to anticipate remote and collateral consequences, to look several moves ahead in the particular chess game that is being played.

5. *Lingual sophistication.* An immunity to being fooled by words and catch phrases; a refusal to accept verbal solutions which merely conceal the problem.

6. *Precision and persuasiveness of speech.* That mastery of the language which involves (a) the ability to state exactly what one means, no more no less, and (b) the ability to reach others with one's own thought, to create in their minds the picture that is in one's own.

7. And finally, pervading all the rest, and possibly the only one that is really basic: *self-discipline in habits of thoroughness,* an abhorrence of superficiality and approximation.

These are not qualities which spring naturally from family background plus a liberal arts education. You will be shocked at your deficiencies in all of them as your professors will point them out. But be not dismayed, for the qualities can be acquired and developed; and the law schools of this country are in the business of doing precisely that. The important thing is that you realize that this is what they are striving for — this, even more than "teaching law."

Beyond this list of rather earthy qualities, transmissible from teacher to student, lie insight, ingenuity, imagination, and judgment — native qualities which distinguish the artist from the artisan, genius from competence. And above all stands character — that indispensable resource in a profession which is charged with maintaining equal justice under law. In our law schools there is a tradition of "teaching law greatly" which should assist you to germinate and develop these attributes. It is important that you should realize that these are among your objectives.

No specific reference is made above to social consciousness as a basic quality of a lawyer. The issue is one of relevance. If a member of the bar litigates the validity of a clause in a deed which restricts the use of land without considering the consequences to the community of this type of restriction, the lawyer will be giving the client very bad representation. On the other hand, if the lawyer draws a will for a Rockefeller, or cross-examines a lying witness in a tort case, while reflecting on the inequalities of the distribution of wealth, the lawyer is not likely to do the best job of which he or she is capable.

Professional Knowledge Which a Lawyer Should Have in the Property Field

In any problem where a lawyer is called upon, the lawyer must provide the law ingredient. Others may have a mastery of the economics of business, of the various fields of expertness relevant to the issue, of the important facts of the current problem; but no one else will have a grasp of the applicable statutes, regulations, and decisions and a sound basis for judgment as to how governmental authority will react. It therefore follows that there is some body of doctrine — legislative, administrative, and judicial — with which the working lawyer must be familiar.

In the property field we think that two major areas must be covered in order to make a reasonably well-rounded lawyer. The first, with which this casebook principally deals, is the land law — the body of doctrine which governs the ownership, commercial transfer, and use of the one basic resource of any society. The second, with which this casebook deals only occasionally, is the law of the transmission of wealth — the body of doctrine which governs wills, trusts, and other gifts by which persons with assets varying from small means to great fortunes seek to provide for their families.

In dealing with the land law you make take one course covering the bulk of this book, or you may take several courses dealing with such segments as conveyances, mortgages, landlord and tenant, rights in land of another, and the like. But you will observe a functional unity in the land law — by which we mean that, however much and however properly courses may compartmentalize the subject for teaching purposes, any given transaction in which you as a practitioner engage on behalf of a client may well include a conveyance, a mortgage, a lease, or a right of way. Thus we think there is something to be said for dealing with all of these subjects within the same covers and in relationship to each other.

This Course (or These Courses) on Commercial Transactions in Land

First as to objectives. These can be listed under (1) professional equipment, and (2) basic discipline.

We hope to give you a professional equipment which will enable you to perform the real estate side of a general law practice. Upon leaving law school you will familiarize yourself with the particularities of the law of your chosen state, chiefly in preparation for the bar examination. If you enter a medium-to-large office you will engage in an apprenticeship proportionate to the degree of your specialization in real estate matters. If you practice alone or nearly so, you will tread cautiously and seek help often. But we will consider that we have failed if you do not feel that you have a solid grasp of the main body of real estate law and if you do not have a sense of being on familiar ground in representing vendors, purchasers, mortgagors, mortgagees, lessors, and lessees. In the many incidental ways in which real estate problems crop up in a general practice we should expect you to form initial judgments which would prove acceptably close to the mark when there is time to consult the authorities.

In the matter of basic training and discipline we feel that the first year property course bears a heavy responsibility. We trust you will not feel injured if we tell you that students come to the law schools with habits of skim-reading; they understand, reason, and use language by approximation. There are college courses in which precision of thought is required, but in most of them expression is in mathematical or chemical formulae, not in words and sentences. Students coming to law school are verbally unsophisticated, accepting and using expressions which conceal, rather than solve, a problem. The standard of performance they set for themselves is relatively low.

The property course has many advantages as an instrumentality for correcting these initial deficiencies without creating other deficiencies equally undesirable. In some areas, as you will find, there is one answer to a problem, and only one; if you understand the issue, master the terminology, and think straight, you can get the answer and know that you have gotten it with the precision of solution of a chess problem. Side by side with such areas are others where the issues are subtle and complex; you are furnished with the means of developing a capacity to probe through superficial mechanical solutions, of which the courts have provided a gratifying supply. Usage has sown through this field an adequate number of boobytrap terms—"constructive possession," "delivery," and "estoppel," to mention only some of the worst offenders you will meet; you will probably undergo the caution-breeding experience of having one or more of these explode in your face.

If this course is to perform its disciplinary function, you will doubtless agree with us that (1) it must be hard; it must stretch your abilities; (2) the problems must not be beyond your capacity; when the discussion is finished, and your review completed, you must comprehend the problem fully, see where you went off (or were pushed off) the track, and believe that you can solve the next one; and (3) approximation and superficiality must never be accepted. So expect to be extended, have confidence that intelligent effort will enable you to master the subject, and take the traditional academic buffets in good grace.

You ought to enjoy this course. We have devoted our professional lives to property law because we like it. We are challenged by it and find amusing its wealth of human interest. If there is any rule that requires a property book to be dull, it has been our aim to violate it.

PART I

PROBLEMS IN POSSESSION

C H A P T E R 2

ACQUIRING TITLE TO WILD ANIMALS

This chapter is designed to introduce you to the careful, analytical, and thoughtful study of case law. A subject is chosen which is small enough in extent to permit you to grasp it in its entirety — the manner in which title to non-domesticated animals is acquired. You should realize that, in examining and discussing these cases, we are not concerned with some abstract proposition of law but with determining the principles governing an activity which has always been a major concern of mankind. In seriousness, the cases range from a petulant sportsmen's row over a fox on Long Island (Pierson v. Post) to the claims of rival groups of Cornish fishermen to 2,000,000 herring in the Bay of St. Ives (Young v. Hichens).

In this chapter there will be a considerable emphasis on the procedural aspects of the cases. As you will discover, it makes a great deal of difference whether the issue in a case arises upon a demurrer or motion in arrest of judgment (both of which test the sufficiency of the plaintiff's allegations in his declaration or complaint), or upon a motion for a directed verdict (which tests the sufficiency of the evidence presented at the trial), or otherwise. You should be alert to observe the procedural differences between cases and to analyze their effects upon the decisions.

You may or may not ever take a formal course in legal history. But you should begin at once to acquire a historical sense which will enable you to make proper use of the various types of legal materials that will come to your hand. In this book you are given, where it seems useful, historical notes to enable you to put a case in its setting and to build up gradually a familiarity with the lore which is the common heritage of the bar. This chapter contains several such notes.

You also may or may not ever take a formal course in jurisprudence. If you do, you will be able to discourse learnedly upon determinism, sociological jurisprudence, realism, and the functional approach; and you will become familiar with Jhering, Austin, Pound, Hohfeld, and a group of incipient savants, none of whom anyone in the position of the editors would

9

dare name for fear of offense to those omitted. However, jurisprudence —
the examination into the method by which law is derived and the forces by
which it is affected — is the essential grist of your intellectual mill for the
entire period of your law study, and that means from now until the end of
your professional career. It must be clear that we would not ask you to study
wild animal cases for a few precious hours in order to prepare you to try wild
animal cases or advise upon them, any more than the neophyte in medicine
is given a cadaver to dissect in order to learn how to dissect cadavers. No,
both you and the medical student are given these things to work on in order
to see how they are put together. And, in the law, this is the essence of
jurisprudence. What considerations moved this court to this result? Were
the true factors in the situation properly urged upon the court by counsel? Is
the law doing a good job for the community in establishing the rule in this
case? These are some of the questions upon which you should constantly be
reflecting. The cases in this chapter raise problems of this nature which
should not be beyond your powers.

There have been many foxes in song and fable — the masticator of the
abdomen of the Spartan boy, Aesop's grape swindler, Uncle Remus's sly
friend so useful as a soporific for the very young, to mention a few — but
none has the sterling utility of the quarry in Pierson v. Post. For more than
half a century law students have teethed upon this particular mammal. He is
to the law of property what "Gallia est omnis divisa . . ." is to Latin; it is
conceivable that a student might start somewhere else, but it would hardly
seem right.

PIERSON v. POST
3 Cai. R. 175 (N.Y. Sup. Ct. 1805)

This was an action of trespass on the case, commenced in a justice's court
by the present defendant against the now plaintiff.

The declaration stated that Post, being in possession of certain dogs and
hounds under his command, did, "upon a certain wild and uninhabited,
unpossessed and waste land, called the beach, find and start one of those
noxious beasts called a fox," and whilst there hunting, chasing and pursuing
the same with his dogs and hounds, and when in view thereof, Pierson, well
knowing the fox was so hunted and pursued, did, in the sight of Post, to
prevent his catching the same, kill and carry it off. A verdict having been
rendered for the plaintiff below, the defendant there sued out a certiorari,
and now assigned for error, that the declaration and the matters therein
contained were not sufficient in law to maintain an action.[1]

---

1. When the defendant in this case "sued out a certiorari," the various steps which were
taken were substantially as follows:
   a. The defendant, the losing party in the trial court, petitioned the supreme court to issue a
   writ of certiorari, directed to the trial court, ordering the trial court to certify its record
   and transmit the same to the supreme court for review;

TOMPKINS, J., delivered the opinion of the court. This cause comes before us on a return to a certiorari directed to one of the justices of Queens county.

The question submitted by the counsel in this cause for our determination is, whether Lodowick Post, by the pursuit with his hounds in the manner alleged in his declaration, acquired such a right to, or property in the fox, as will sustain an action against Pierson for killing and taking him away?

The cause was argued with much ability by the counsel on both sides, and presents for our decision a novel and nice question. It is admitted, that a fox is an animal ferae naturae, and that property in such animals is acquired by occupancy only. These admissions narrow the discussion to the simple question of what acts amount to occupancy, applied to acquiring right to wild animals?

If we have recourse to the ancient writers upon general principles of law, the judgment below is obviously erroneous. Justinian's Institutes, lib. 2, tit. I, sect. 13, and Fleta, lib. III, c. II, page 175, adopt the principle, that pursuit alone, vests no property or right in the huntsman; and that even pursuit accompanied with wounding, is equally ineffectual for that purpose, unless the animal be actually taken. The same principle is recognised by Bracton, lib. II, c. I, page 8.

Puffendorf, lib. IV, c. 6, sec. 2, §10, defines occupancy of beasts ferae naturae, to be the actual corporal possession of them, and Bynkershoek is cited as coinciding in this definition. It is indeed with hesitation that Puffendorf affirms that a wild beast mortally wounded, or greatly maimed, cannot be fairly intercepted by another, whilst the pursuit of the person inflicting the wound continues. The foregoing authorities are decisive to show that mere pursuit gave Post no legal right to the fox, but that he became the property of Pierson, who intercepted and killed him.

It therefore only remains to inquire whether there are any contrary principles, or authorities, to be found in other books, which ought to induce a different decision. Most of the cases which have occurred in England, relating to property in wild animals, have either been discussed and decided upon the principles of their positive statute regulations, or have arisen between the huntsman and the owner of the land upon which beasts ferae naturae have been apprehended; the former claiming them by title of occupancy, and the latter ratione soli. Little satisfactory aid can, therefore, be derived from the English reporters.

---

b. The supreme court granted the petition and issued the writ;

c. The trial court, in compliance with the writ, prepared a copy of the proceedings before it, certified that this copy was accurate, and forwarded the certified copy to the supreme court.

At the time of this case the supreme court was not, and is not now, the highest court in New York. In 1805 the court of errors was the highest court; its presiding officer was the president of the state senate, and it comprised the senators, the chancellor, and the judges of the supreme court. Since 1846 the court of appeals has been the highest court; all its members are judges. The supreme court now comprises both trial courts (special term and trial term) and intermediate appellate courts (appellate division of the supreme court). — EDS.

Barbeyrac, in his notes on Puffendorf, does not accede to the definition of occupancy by the latter, but, on the contrary, affirms that actual bodily seizure is not, in all cases, necessary to constitute possession of wild animals. He does not, however, *describe* the acts which, according to his ideas, will amount to an appropriation of such animals to private use, so as to exclude the claims of all other persons, by title of occupancy, to the same animals; and he is far from averring that pursuit alone is sufficient for that purpose. To a certain extent, and as far as Barbeyrac appears to me to go, his objections to Puffendorf's definition of occupancy are reasonable and correct. That is to say, that actual bodily seizure is not indispensable to acquire right to, or possession of, wild beasts; but that, on the contrary, the mortal wounding of such beasts, by one not abandoning his pursuit, may, with the utmost propriety, be deemed possession of him; since thereby, the pursuer manifests an unequivocal intention of appropriating the animal to his individual use, has deprived him of his natural liberty, and brought him within his certain control. So, also, encompassing and securing such animals with nets and toils, or otherwise intercepting them, in such a manner as to deprive them of their natural liberty, and render escape impossible, may justly be deemed to give possession of them to those persons who, by their industry and labor, have used such means of apprehending them. . . . The case now under consideration is one of mere pursuit, and presents no circumstances or acts which can bring it within the definition of occupancy by Puffendorf, . . . or the ideas of Barbeyrac upon that subject. . . .

We are the more readily inclined to confine possession or occupancy of beasts ferae naturae within the limits prescribed by the learned authors above cited, for the sake of certainty, and preserving peace and order in society. If the first seeing, starting or pursuing such animals, without having so wounded, circumvented or ensnared them, so as to deprive them of their natural liberty, and subject them to the control of their pursuer, should afford the basis of actions against others for intercepting and killing them, it would prove a fertile source of quarrels and litigation.

However uncourteous or unkind the conduct of Pierson towards Post, in this instance, may have been, yet his act was productive of no injury or damage for which a legal remedy can be applied. We are of the opinion the judgment below was erroneous, and ought to be reversed.

LIVINGSTON, J. (dissenting). . . . This is a knotty point, and should have been submitted to the arbitration of sportsmen, without poring over Justinian, Fleta, Bracton, Puffendorf, Locke, Barbeyrac or Blackstone, all of whom have been cited; they would have had no difficulty in coming to a prompt and correct conclusion. . . . But the parties have referred the question to our judgment, and we must dispose of it as well as we can, from the partial lights we possess, leaving to a higher tribunal the correction of any mistake which we may be so unfortunate as to make. By the pleadings it is admitted, that a fox is a "wild and noxious beast." Both parties have regarded him as the law of nations does a pirate, "hostem humani generis," and although "de mortuis nil nisi bonum" be a maxim of our profession, the memory of the deceased has not been spared. His depredations on farmers and on barn yards, have not been forgotten; and to put him to death wherever found, is allowed to be meritorious, and of public benefit. Hence it follows, that our decision should have in view the greatest possible encouragement to the destruction of an animal so cunning and ruthless in his career. But who would keep a pack of hounds; or what gentleman, at the sound of the horn and at peep of day would mount his steed, and for hours together, "sub jove frigido" or a vertical sun, pursue the windings of this wily quadruped, if, just as night came on, and his stratagems and strength were nearly exhausted, a saucy intruder, who had not shared in the honors or labours of the chase, were permitted to come in at the death, and bear away in triumph the object of pursuit? Whatever Justinian may have thought of the matter, it must be recollected that his code was compiled many hundred years ago, and it would be very hard indeed, at the distance of so many centuries, not to have a right to establish a rule for ourselves. In his day, we read of no order of men who made it a business, in the language of the declaration in this cause, "with hounds and dogs to find, start, pursue, hunt, and chase," these animals, and that too, without any other motive than the preservation of Roman poultry; if this diversion had been then in fashion, the lawyers who composed his institutes, would have taken care not to pass it by without suitable encouragement. If any thing, therefore, in the digests or pandects shall appear to militate against the defendant in error, who, on this occasion, was the fox hunter, we have only to say tempora mutantur; and if men themselves change with the times, why should not laws also undergo an alteration? . . .

Now, as we are without any municipal regulations of our own, . . . we are at liberty . . . [to hold] . . . that property in animals ferae naturae, may be acquired without bodily touch or manucaption, provided the pursuer be within reach, or have a *reasonable* prospect (which certainly existed here) of taking, what he has *thus* discovered [with] an intention of converting to his own use.

When we reflect also that the interest of our husbandmen, the most useful of men in any community, will be advanced by the destruction of a beast so pernicious and incorrigible, we cannot greatly err in saying that a pursuit like the present, through waste and unoccupied lands, which must inevitably and speedily have terminated in corporal possession, or bodily seisin, confers such a right to the object of it as to make anyone a wrong doer who shall interfere and shoulder the spoil. The *justice's* judgment ought therefore, in my opinion, to be affirmed.

Note: *Authorities, Civil Law and Common Law, and That Fox*

Get the habit of identifying cases in your mind by court and approximate date. These factors are important in determining what authority the case has and how much you can rely on it. This particular case was decided by the Supreme Court of New York in 1805. Chief Justice James Kent, better known as Chancellor Kent and the author of Kent's Commentaries (the American opposite number of Blackstone), presided over this court and, being a leading character in the development of American law, gave its judgments an authority which is considerable.

One very outmoded characteristic of the opinion is the citation of the Institutes of Justinian (sixth century) and the views of the civil law jurisconsults Puffendorf (1632-1694) and Barbeyrac (1674-1744). The separation of the Anglo-American common law from the Roman law and its successor, the continental civil law, is now a completed process (but keep in mind that Louisiana law is based on the civil law). Justice Livingston, as evidenced by his dissent, was willing to make the separation complete in the early nineteenth century.

Bracton and Fleta, also cited by the court, stand on somewhat different ground, since these are both English books. Henry Bracton, a judge who was the greatest early English legal scholar, undertook to write a comprehensive treatise on English law. He never quite finished; but when he stopped working in 1256 he had compiled a work which assured him of immortality. "Fleta" was an imitator of Bracton some forty years later. The book was written in the Fleet prison—hence the book's name, the identity of the author being unknown.

Livingston, J., plainly showed by his dissent that he was impatient with this petty squabble between country squires—the stubborn affronted Dutchman and the English-descended violator of the fox hunter's code—and disapproved the pomposity of Tompkins, J., in dealing with it. But you should not permit his facetiousness of expression, which must have caused some tongue clucking at that time, to obscure the trend of his thought.

"Acceptance" of English law in the United States. As of 1783 (perhaps retroactive to 1776) the 13 original states were free from political subordination to the British Crown. It is of interest, but little else, what English authorities thought about disputes of who gets that fox pelt, and it is of no interest at all what the Code of Justinian provided. We should have been developing an *American* law suited to our needs and based upon our own situation—geographic, political, social. But lawyers and judges at the time of Pierson v. Post were a conservative lot, having been brought up principally on Blackstone. Livingston, J., hit the matter on the head when he said that this matter "should have been submitted to the arbitration of sportsmen." But cases of this type are all too few. Since feudalism never existed in this country, none of the legal buttresses of feudalism should have been "received," but mirabile dictu nearly all of them were, and some of them remain to this day, and even have been extended.

That fox. Wouldn't you think that this silly litigation over a fox pelt would have been given a decent burial, never to be heard of again? Not a bit of it. It is learnedly discussed by Professor Reich in 73 Yale L.J. at 778 (1964) and Professor Michelman in 80 Harv. L. Rev. at 1165 (1967). Each party to the litigation spent more than £1,000 on the case, which caused the family of one litigant to sell his home to the family of the other to get out of debt. J. T. Adams, Memorials of Old Bridgehampton 166 et seq. (1916). A photocopy of the deed has been deposited in the Harvard Law School Library. See also Lund, Early American Wildlife Law, 51 N.Y.U.L. Rev. 703 (1976).

Note: Friends of Hunted Unite to Sabotage Hunters

In a recent New York Times article, William E. Geist discussed opposition to the hunting of wild animals:

NEPTUNE, N.J., Feb. 26 — When Susan Russell strolls through the woods playing classical music on her tape player, the deer, muskrats and other wildlife of the forest run the other way. A muskrat may linger momentarily over a few notes of Chopin, but John Philip Sousa always sends them crashing through the brush.

Miss Russell is one of tens of thousands of animal lovers who patrol the woods during hunting and trapping seasons, blaring everything from Sousa marches to recorded wolf howls in a nationwide campaign to set animals running for their lives before hunters arrive. She has found that the hunter has no more appreciation for her music than the muskrat.

A growing number of confrontations between hunters and these protectors of wildlife has led a New Jersey legislator to introduce a bill that would make it illegal to "interfere or attempt to interfere with the lawful hunting, pursuit, killing or taking of an animal, bird or freshwater fish." Violators would be fined.

The legislator, Assemblyman Joseph W. Chinnici, Republican of Bridgeton, himself a hunter, said his legislation was needed to protect both the hunters from harassment and the animal protectors from reprisals. Such legislation recently became law in Arizona and is under consideration in several other states in response to the growing militance of animal protectionists.

"There's a war going on," said Miss Russell, a spokesman for Friends of Animals, a national organization with headquarters here and in New York that distributes "Tips for Hunt Saboteurs" to its 120,000 members. The tips range from lobbying for changes in the law with local, state and national officials to such guerrilla tactics as taking a female dog in heat into the field to turn the heads of male hunting dogs, and scattering rotten eggs and cow dung in duck blinds.

Miss Russell sees nothing extreme in any of this. "Wildlife belongs to everybody," she said. "We think it is audacious of hunters to say they can shoot animals but we cannot protect them."

"If this isn't stopped immediately," Assemblyman Chinnici said, "someone is going to get hurt."

Implicit in his warning, and those voiced by concerned hunters throughout the state, is that the side carrying the tape players is at a distinct disadvantage in confrontations with those carrying rifles and shotguns.

Mr. Chinnici said he had received reports of "antisportsmen's groups" blaring car horns and firing weapons to scare off game and in one instance even flying a helicopter over a hunting area.

His bill has been referred to the Assembly's Agriculture and Environment Committee, where four of the five committee members are co-sponsors. Both opponents and proponents believe the bill has substantial support in the Legislature.

Bob Busnardo, host of the weekly radio program "Sportsmen's Hot Line" on a Bridgeton station, said "these antis" (one of the more pleasant terms that hunters use to describe those opposed to hunting) had disrupted his hunting excursions by playing radios, honking car horns, letting air out of tires and swerving their automobiles toward him as he stood on country roads.

"The confrontations have been verbal so far," he said, "but when you harass someone long enough and hard enough, eventually there are going to be serious problems."

Disruptive Goose Used

Opponents charge that Mr. Chinnici's bill would infringe on their rights of speech and assembly. "Whenever there is a protest of anything," said Miss Russell, "whether it be civil rights or women's rights or whatever, there is the chance of confrontation. But someone cannot just do away with our right to speak out on things we disagree with. If they do, I believe that in good conscience we would have to continue to protest as we are now."

Miss Russell told of excursions in boats equipped with loudspeakers before duck and geese hunting seasons and of "the star spangled goose" that a member uses in Connecticut to scare geese away from hunting areas. Painted red, white and blue, the goose-shaped object motors through the water playing the National Anthem.

"Tips for Hunt Saboteurs" also recommends: giving animals early warning of human presence by collecting hair from local barber shops and scattering it about in the woods; spreading deer repellent; applying for restricted permits to hunt rare species or to use particular duck blinds and then not using the permits; removing bait, such as piles of apples, that hunters set out for deer; and even setting out old stuffed animals that hunters might shoot, scaring off live wildlife.

All of this, the tip sheet said, "serves to anger them, and angry hunters do not stalk so quietly, their aim is not so precise."

"Emotions can play heavily in the success of a hunt," the tip sheet continues, "and the most effective killers are cool and methodical. Disrupt!"

Marc Lanzim, a spokesman for the New Jersey Federation of Sportsmen's Clubs, said: "The antis may even have a perfect right to drive around blasting their car horns, but they are setting the stage for terrible tragedy."

"Our position," said Nina Austenberg, regional director of the Humane Society of the United States, "is that we want to see sport hunting and trapping stopped, but within the law. This confrontation is dangerous. It is, however, born of understandable frustration. The positions of groups trying to protect animals have been uniformly disregarded."

"We consider wildlife a natural resource," said Miss Russell, "and we cannot reconcile this policy of their right to kill animals while saying we cannot protect them with other public policy concerning resources. If you pick a flower or cut a tree on state lands, you can be arrested, but it's all right to kill animals with guns and smash their bones in steel traps."

"This is a group," said Assemblyman Chinnici, "determined not to let a deer be killed. And, of course, they are wrong." [N.Y. Times, Mar. 1, 1983, at 1, col. 3.]

KEEBLE v. HICKERINGILL

11 East 574; *sub nom.* Keeble v. Hickeringall,
Cas. t. Holt 14, 17, 19; *sub nom.*
Keble v. Hickringill, 11 Mod. 74, 11 Mod. 130;
sub nom. Keeble v. Hickeringhall, 3 Salk. 9
(K.B. 1707)

[This was an action of trespass on the case. The plaintiff's declaration alleged that in November, 1704 he was possessed of a close of land called Minnott's Meadow containing a decoy pond to which wildfowl used to come; that the plaintiff had prepared decoy ducks, nets, etc., for taking the wildfowl, and enjoyed the benefit of taking them; that the defendant, with knowledge of these facts, and intending to drive away the wildfowl which used to resort thither and to deprive the plaintiff of the yearly profit which he made from his said decoy, did, on the eighth, eleventh, and twelfth of November, resort to the head of the said pond and discharge guns laden with gunpowder and with the noise and stink of the gunpowder did drive away the wildfowl then being in the pond, causing the wildfowl to forsake the said pond. The defendant pleaded not guilty. A verdict was rendered for the plaintiff for £20. The defendant made a motion in arrest of judgment on the ground that the declaration was insufficient to support the action. This motion was heard by all the judges of the King's Bench. It was twice argued, first in Easter Term, then in Hilary Term. The opinion denying the motion follows.]

HOLT, C.J. This decoy is a benefit to the plaintiff, and in the nature of a trade; and there is the same reason that he should be repaired in damages for his decoy as for any other trade. It is true, there may be a damnum sine injuria. If a man set up the same trade as mine in the same town, this is a damage to me, but it is sine injuria, for it is lawful for him to set up the same trade if he please. But this action is brought for disturbing the wild ducks coming to his decoy and so is in the nature of disturbing him from exercising his trade. Where a violent or malicious act is done to a man's occupation, profession or way of getting livelihood, there an action lies in all cases. But if a man doth him damage by using the same employment; as if Mr. Hickeringill had set up another decoy on his own ground near the plaintiff's, and that had spoiled the custom of the plaintiff, no action would lie, because he had as much liberty to make and use a decoy as the plaintiff. This is like the case of Y.B. 11 H. IV, 47. One schoolmaster sets up a new school to the damage of an ancient school, and thereby the scholars are allured from the old school to come to his new [school]. The action was held there not to lie. But suppose Mr. Hickeringill should lie in the way with his guns, and fright the boys from going to school, and their parents would not let them go thither, sure that schoolmaster might have an action for the loss of his scholars. This action is not brought for his property, but is brought for hindering him to take his profit. Judgment for the plaintiff.[2]

Note: Early English Reporters

As appears above from the notation under the title of this case, it is reported in four different volumes of reports. The facts given above constitute a restatement derived from all four reports. The opinion of Holt, C.J., is a composite of what will be found at 11 East 576, Cas. t. Holt 19, and 11 Mod. 130. This raises another problem concerning the authority of cases as precedents. In modern times judicial opinions are written out, handed to an official reporter of decisions, and printed as written. But in England, up to the nineteenth century, reporting of decisions was done on a private enterprise basis in a quite haphazard fashion. Some reports were accurate and some very bad. The four different reports of Keeble v. Hickeringill represent what four different persons got out of the case.

It follows from the foregoing that in determining the authority of one of the old cases you must evaluate not only the standing of the judges but also the accuracy of the report. The best guide to this matter is Wallace, The Reporters (4th ed. 1882). Wallace, himself a reporter of decisions for the Supreme Court of the United States, undertook to collect data on the English reporters. Here are his views on the reporters who concerned themselves with Keeble v. Hickeringill.

Cas. t. Holt (which means, of course, cases in the time of Chief Justice

---

2.   For a case presenting a reverse twist of the *Keeble* situation, see Andrews v. Andrews, 242 N.C. 382, 88 S.E.2d 88 (1955). The case reached the Supreme Court of North Carolina on demurrer to a complaint which alleged that the defendant had set up a decoy pond (in which he used live, but lame, geese as decoys) on a lot adjoining the plaintiff's farm; that the pond attracted wild geese, who wintered there in increasing numbers each year; and that the geese used the pond as a base from which to set upon and destroy the plaintiff's growing crops. The court held that an action would lie in nuisance: "Surely the arm of the law is neither too short nor too weak to reach out to the pond and take away the wild geese maintained as prisoners there to attract their kind in ever increasing numbers." The dissent argued that the case should be dismissed on the ground that the defendant did not have ownership of the geese, or even possession of them, as to make him responsible for their delicts.—Eds.

Holt, as distinguished from Holt's Reports, an early nineteenth century collection of common pleas cases by a barrister named Holt):

> Giles Jacob—immortalized by Pope as "blunderbuss of law"—is reputed to be the collector or at least the publisher of these cases. The greater number of them are abridged from other books of reports; the remaining ones—not a few of which were taken by Mr. Farresly—are printed at large from MSS. Farresly was the author of [another] book of but indifferent authority. The merits of the present work, I believe, are in a concatenation accordingly.

Salkeld: "The first two volumes . . . their general accuracy has not been questioned. The third . . . has never been considered as of any authority."

Modern: "The volume is said to be of 'no authority.' . . . Although Mr. Green speaks of the book as 'execrable,' without reference to editions, a distinction may perhaps deserve to be made between the two." Wallace then goes on to point out that the 1796 edition by a Mr. Leach (no relative) is "the latest and in most volumes the best."

East is a much later report (1815). Keeble v. Hickeringill appears in East as a note, but there is every reason to give this report prime importance because the reporter states that the opinion as he prints it "is taken from a copy of Lord C.J. Holt's own MS. in my possession."

It therefore appears that Keeble v. Hickeringill did not fare very well from contemporaneous reporting and that the only report which approaches trustworthiness did not become available until 1815—a factor which may have influenced the advocacy and the decision in Pierson v. Post.

Lest you get a false general impression about the English reporters, let it be said that there were some very fine ones. The most celebrated was Sir Edward Coke, Queen Elizabeth's savage prosecutor (Essex, Southampton, Raleigh, the Gunpowder Plot conspirators) and the first man to bear the title of Lord Chief Justice of England. The British pronounce his name "Cook," but this is not compulsory in the United States. Coke's 13 volumes of reports of cases from 1572 to 1616 have such a standing that they are usually referred to as the Reports (Rep. or Co. Rep.). The Reports contain not only reports of cases but also Coke's commentaries and statements as to historical background. They are definitely not light reading. However, before too long, you should know what they look like, and you should get acquainted with their author. He lived in a time when English law was in a state of upheaval, and he guided its destiny to a degree equaled by no other individual. Whereas Coke's American counterparts, Marshall and Holmes, led relatively quiet and secluded lives during their mature years, Coke was in the thick of political battle from adolescence to the grave. His retort to James I, "Non sub homine sed sub Deo et lege," ranks among the great utterances in the history of liberty. An acceptable short sketch appears in the Britannica. Any book on legal history will have much on Coke. An excellent biography is Lyon & Block, Edward Coke (1929).

"Y.B. 11 H. IV, 47," referred to in the opinion of the court, is the Year Book for the eleventh year of the reign of King Henry IV (1410), page 47. In some reports this reference is cut down to "11 H. 4.47." The Year Books run from 1283 to 1535 and comprise anonymous notes of cases which are uneven in quality. They are important sources of legal history, but it would be a very rare case in which you could cite a Year Book today without evoking the wrong kind of smile. For further detail, see Plucknett, Concise History of the Common Law 268-273 (5th ed. 1956).

YOUNG v. HICHENS
1 Dav. & Mer. 592, 6 Q.B. 606 (1844)

[This was an action of trespass. The first count of the declaration alleged that the plaintiff had enclosed by a net and taken into his possession 2,000,000 mackerel, worth £2,000; that the defendant by force, for 20 days, prevented the plaintiff from dipping and taking the fish out; that the defendant drove away 1,000,000 of said fish and caused others to die or escape, whereby the fish were completely lost to the plaintiff; and further that the defendant caused the plaintiff to be put to great expense by hiring 50 men to watch, protect, and save the fish. The second count alleged that the defendant took the said 2,000,000 fish of the plaintiff and converted and disposed of them to his own use. The defendant pleaded not guilty and that the fish did not belong to the plaintiff.

The plaintiff in this action represented a group of fishermen who called themselves The Victoria Company; the defendant represented another group who called themselves The Hichens Company.

The case was tried before a jury, presided over by Atcherley, Serjt., at the Spring Assizes, 1843, in Bodmin, Cornwall. The evidence was as follows. On the day in question, a very large shoal of mackerel came into the Bay of St. Ives. The plaintiff's boat, the Wesley, put out and shot her sean. The sean, nearly 140 fathoms long, was drawn in a semicircle completely around the shoal, with the exception of a space of seven fathoms, according to the plaintiff's witnesses, ten fathoms according to the defendant's, which was not filled up. In this opening, according to the plaintiff's witnesses, the fishermen in the plaintiff's boat were splashing with their oars and disturbing the water in such a manner that, as they affirmed, the mackerel within effectually would have been prevented from escaping. At this juncture, before the plaintiff could draw his net closer, the Ellen, the defendant's boat, rowed in through the opening thus made, shot her sean, enclosed the fish, and captured the whole of them.[3]

---

3. One is tempted to speculate why this maritime hijacking produced only litigation in the civil courts and no indictments for murder and mayhem. These Cornishmen are certainly entitled to some sort of award for self-restraint. Perhaps a hint as to the answer can be found in 4 & 5 Vict., ch. 57 (Local and Personal Acts), which indicates that the fishery in the Bay of St. Ives is a very highly regulated affair with the most detailed rules as to technique, covering 24

It was argued for the defendant at the trial that the evidence did not show such a possession by the plaintiff as would entitle him to maintain trespass and that there was, therefore, no case to go to the jury. The learned serjeant left to the jury the question of whether the fish were the fish of the plaintiff and in his possession when the defendant took them. The jury found that they were. On the answer, the learned serjeant directed the verdict to be entered for the plaintiff for £569, the agreed value of the fish, with leave for the defendant to move to have the verdict entered for him if the full Court of Queen's Bench should be of opinion that the question of the plaintiff's possession of the fish should not have been left to the jury. Counsel obtained a rule nisi for entering a verdict for the defendant on this ground. This was argued before the full Court of Queen's Bench, which thereupon entered a rule absolute, rendering the opinions which follow.[4]]

LORD DENMAN, C.J.: It does appear almost certain that the plaintiff would have had possession of the fish but for the act of the defendant; but it is quite certain that he had not possession. Whatever interpretation may be put upon such terms as "custody" and "possession," the question will be whether any custody or possession has been obtained here. I think it is impossible to say that it had, until the party had actual power over the fish. It may be that the defendant acted unjustifiably in preventing the plaintiff from obtaining such power: but that would only shew a wrongful act, for which he might be liable in a proper form of action.

PATTESON, J.: I do not see how we could support the affirmative of these issues upon the present evidence, unless we were prepared to hold that all but reducing into possession is the same as reducing into possession. Whether the plaintiff has any cause of action at all is not clear; possibly there may be a remedy under the statutes.

WIGHTMAN, J.: I am of the same opinion. If the property in the fish was vested in the plaintiff by his partially inclosing them but leaving an opening in the nets, he would be entitled to maintain trover for fish which escaped through that very opening.

(COLERIDGE, J., was absent.)

Rule absolute for reducing the damages to 20s., and entering the verdict for defendant on the second and third issues.[5]

---

large pages of the statute book. There are indications in the report that the crew of the Ellen believed that the Wesley was not abiding by the rules, and the Wesley seems to have been none too sure of her ground. However, the jury appears to have found that the Wesley was behaving properly.—EDS.

4. The statement of facts here given is a synthesis taken from the two reports.

If this case were presented under modern American practice, the following steps would probably be taken: (a) a motion by the defendant in the trial court, at the close of the evidence, that a verdict be directed in his favor; (b) a denial of this motion by the trial judge; (c) an exception by the defendant to this ruling; (d) a verdict for the plaintiff; (e) a motion by the defendant for judgment notwithstanding the verdict; (f) a denial of this motion by the trial judge; (g) an exception by the defendant to this ruling; (h) an appeal by the defendant, assigning as error the denial of his motions; (i) a reversal by the appellate court and an entry of judgment notwithstanding the verdict, under an appropriate statute authorizing such judgments.—EDS.

5. The opinions are those reported in 6 Q.B.—EDS.

Problems

2.1. Judge Wightman in Young v. Hichens thought that if the plaintiff had become the owner of the fish, his ownership would have continued even though the fish escaped through the opening. Mullett v. Bradley, 24 Misc. 695, 53 N.Y.S. 781 (1898), contains the following quotation from Blackstone: "These [animals ferae naturae] are no longer the property of a man, than while they continue in his keeping or actual possession; but if at any time they regain their natural liberty, his property instantly ceases; unless they have animus revertendi, which is only to be known by their usual custom of returning." Why should the ownership acquired by the capture of an animal ferae naturae cease when it escapes and regains its natural liberty? Why should it be relevant whether the escaped animal has the animus revertendi? In Mullett v. Bradley, O was in the business of capturing wild animals for display. He invested time and money in this activity. It was his livelihood. He captured a sea lion in the Pacific Ocean (its natural habitat) and took it across the country. It escaped into the Atlantic Ocean. (Sea lions are not normally found in the Atlantic Ocean.[6]) What policy justifies denying to O the return of his sea lion when someone else captures it? Suppose an elephant in a circus owned by O escapes in a metropolitan area and it is captured by A. Should A be entitled to retain the elephant against the claim of O, the owner of the circus? A fox bred in captivity by O and branded with O's brand escapes and is captured by A in the woods. Does A's claim to the fox as against O rest on a more solid foundation than A's claim to the elephant? See Stephens & Co. v. Albers, 81 Colo. 488, 256 P. 15 (1927). If an animal ferae naturae is domesticated and escapes, what should

---

6. The following is a quotation from a newspaper clipping that a former student of ours sent to us:

> A sea lion with oil-matted fur and the inquisitiveness of any normal 2-year-old sniffed through a fence at some equally curious arctic seals at the Coney Island Aquarium yesterday but refused, as some 2-year-olds do, to eat.
>
> The 69-pound female, who cocks her head at the grunts of neighboring walruses and is "soothed like a dog by the sound of a human voice," is something of a mystery.
>
> So far known only as a rather sickly specimen of Zalophus californianus, the four-foot-long, dark brown mammal jumped into a dredging barge 10 miles off Coney Island on Saturday.
>
> "It seems quite obvious she's used to human company although I don't believe she's a performer," said Dr. Paul L. Montreuil, the Aquarium director. He said that no calls had been received claiming ownership but that she probably was an escaped pet.
>
> The animal has declined all offers of smelt and herring. Dr. Montreuil said that if her appetite didn't pick up by this morning she would be given antibiotic and vitamin injections.
>
> She has rings of oil around her neck and midsection and several minor sores that Dr. Montreuil believes are a result of swimming in the polluted water around New York.
>
> "She seems to have been in these waters for a week or two," he said, noting that the breed was native to California waters.
>
> He said it was "virtually impossible" that she could have swum all the way around South America. "It would be like a polar bear swimming from the North Pole to Hawaii," he said.

be the result? See Conti v. ASPCA, 77 Misc. 2d 61, 353 N.Y.S. 288 (New York City Civ. Ct., Queens County, 1974).

2.2. O was the owner of Blackacre, and by drilling he had exhausted the natural gas beneath his land. He pumped natural gas which he had acquired elsewhere into the space below his land for storage purposes. This gas escaped into subterranean areas under the adjoining land of A. A withdrew the gas under his land. In a suit by O against A for the value of the gas thus removed, would you, as counsel for A, refer to Mullett v. Bradley? See Hammonds v. Kentucky Central Natural Gas Co., 255 Ky. 685, 75 S.W.2d 204 (1934).

2.3. O owns swamp land, through which runs the Little River, a stream occasionally used by inhabitants of the vicinity for floating logs and rafts. O owns the bed of the stream. O has just discovered that A has taken out of the bed of the stream over a period of years some 307 tons of mussels, boiled them to get the shells, and made "pearl" buttons out of the shells, to his very substantial profit. O consults you.

    a.   You discover a case holding that where a person owns both banks and the bed of a stream he still cannot recover the value of trout taken from the stream by a trespasser, for they are ferae naturae. Beach v. Morgan, 67 N.H. 529, 41 A. 349 (1893). Can you distinguish this case from your own?

    b.   You discover a case holding that, even in an enclosed pond entirely owned by one person, in sparsely populated areas it is the custom of the country that anyone can fish there unless notice to the contrary is given and that therefore salmon caught by a person fishing on the weekend are owned by him or her and not by the owner of the pond. Marsh v. Colby, 39 Mich. 626 (1878). Can you distinguish this case?

    c.   If O was the owner of the mussels, can he maintain replevin against A for two tons of buttons that A has manufactured out of the mussel shells? See McKee v. Gratz, 260 U.S. 127, 43 S. Ct. 16 (1922).

2.4. O owns land in a city which has a zoning law. O's land is located in what is termed an R-1 zone, in which land may be used for "the raising of poultry, rabbits and chinchillas and the keeping of domestic animals in conjunction with the residential use of a lot." O desires to keep bees on his lot. He requests your advice as to whether such action on his part is permitted under the zoning law. What advice would you give him? See People v. Kasold, 153 Cal. App. 2d 891, 314 P.2d 241 (1957).

Note: Statutory Construction

As an introduction to statutory construction in the context of a statute relating to animals and to prevent the material involved from being lost in the mass of legal literature, the following memorandum prepared by the late

W. Barton Leach is reproduced:

MEMORANDUM   19 January 1970

TO: Harvard Law Faculty and Teaching Fellows

I have recently come across a Canadian case which merits the attention of each of you. It is not officially reported but appears in 8 Criminal Law Quarterly 137 (Toronto, 1965) (permission to reproduce granted by Criminal Law Quarterly) and is reprinted in a volume entitled Legislation and the Courts at page 512. The case is Regina v. Ojibway. If it had a headnote, which it does not, it would be something like this:

> *Is a pony, fortuitously saddled with a feather pillow, a "small bird" within the meaning of the Ontario Small Birds Act?*

I here reproduce the Opinion in full as above reported.

(IN THE SUPREME COURT)
REGINA v. OJIBWAY

Blue, J.   August, 1965

Blue, J.: — This is an appeal by the Crown by way of a stated case from a decision of the magistrate acquitting the accused of a charge under the Small Birds Act, R.S.O., 1960, c. 724, s. 2. The facts are not in dispute. Fred Ojibway, an Indian, was riding his pony through Queen's Park on January 2, 1965. Being impoverished, and having been forced to pledge his saddle, he substituted a downy pillow in lieu of the said saddle. On this particular day the accused's misfortune was further heightened by the circumstance of his pony breaking its right foreleg. In accord with Indian custom, the accused then shot the pony to relieve it of its awkwardness.

The accused was then charged with having breached the Small Birds Act, s. 2 of which states: "2. Anyone maiming, injuring or killing small birds is guilty of an offence and subject to a fine not in excess of two hundred dollars." The learned magistrate acquitted the accused holding, in fact, that he had killed his horse and not a small bird. With respect, I cannot agree.

In light of the definition section my course is quite clear. Section 1 defines "bird" as "a two legged animal covered with feathers." There can be no doubt that this case is covered by this section.

Counsel for the accused made several ingenious arguments to which, in fairness, I must address myself. He submitted that the evidence of the expert clearly concluded that the animal in question was a pony and not a bird, but this is not the issue. We are not interested in whether the animal in question is a bird or not in fact, but whether it is one in law. Statutory interpretation has forced many a horse to eat birdseed for the rest of its life.

Counsel also contended that the neighing noise emitted by the animal could not possibly be produced by a bird. With respect, the sounds emitted by an animal are irrelevant to its nature, for a bird is no less a bird because it is silent.

Counsel for the accused also argued that since there was evidence to show accused had ridden the animal, this pointed to the fact that it could not be a bird but was actually a pony. Obviously, this avoids the issue. The issue is not whether the animal was ridden or not, but whether it was shot or not, for to ride a pony or a bird is of no offence at all. I believe counsel now sees his mistake.

Counsel contends that the iron shoes found on the animal decisively disqualify it from being a bird. I must inform counsel, however, that how an animal dresses is of no concern to this court.

Counsel relied on the decision in Re Chicadee, where he contends that in similar circumstances the accused was acquitted. However, this is a horse of a different colour. A close reading of that case indicates that the animal in question there was not a small bird, but, in fact, a midget of a much larger species. Therefore, that case is inapplicable to our facts.

Counsel finally submits that the word "small" in the title Small Birds Act refers not to "Birds" but to "Act," making it The Small Act relating to Birds. With respect, counsel did not do his homework very well, for the Large Birds Act, R.S.O. 1960, c. 725, is just as small. If pressed, I need only refer to the Small Loans Act, R.S.O. 1960, c. 727 which is twice as large as the Large Birds Act.

It remains then to state my reason for judgment which, simply, is as follows: Different things may take on the same meaning for different purposes. For the purpose of the Small Birds Act, all two-legged, feather-covered animals are birds. This, of course, does not imply that only two-legged animals qualify, for the legislative intent is to make two legs merely the minimum requirement. The statute therefore contemplated multi-legged animals with feathers as well. Counsel submits that having regard to the purpose of the statute only small animals "naturally covered" with feathers could have been contemplated. However, had this been the intention of the legislature, I am certain that the phrase "naturally covered" would have been expressly inserted just as 'Long' was inserted in the Longshoreman's Act.

Therefore, a horse with feathers on its back must be deemed for the purposes of this Act to be a bird, and a fortiori, a pony with feathers on its back is a small bird.

Counsel posed the following rhetorical question: If the pillow had been removed prior to the shooting, would the animal still be a bird? To this let me answer rhetorically: Is a bird any less of a bird without its feathers?

Appeal allowed.

Reported by: *H. Pomerantz*
              S. Breslin

GHEN v. RICH
8 F. 159 (D. Mass. 1881)

NELSON, D.J. This is a libel to recover the value of a fin-back whale. The libellant lives in Provincetown and the respondent in Wellfleet. The facts, as they appeared at the hearing, are as follows:

In the early spring months the easterly part of Massachusetts Bay is frequented by the species of whale known as the fin-back whale. Fishermen from Provincetown pursue them in open boats from the shore and shoot them with bomb-lances fired from guns made expressly for the purpose. When killed they sink at once to the bottom, but in the course of from one to three days they rise and float on the surface. Some of them are picked up by vessels and towed into Provincetown. Some float ashore at high water and are left stranded on the beach as the tide recedes. Others float out to sea and are never recovered. The person who happens to find them on the beach usually sends word to Provincetown, and the owner comes to the spot and removes the blubber. The finder usually receives a small salvage for his services. Tryworks are established in Provincetown for trying out the oil. The business is of considerable extent, but, since it requires skill and experience, as well as some outlay of capital, and is attended with great exposure and hardship, few persons engage in it. The average yield of oil is about twenty barrels to a whale. It swims with great swiftness, and for that reason cannot be taken by the harpoon and line. Each boat's crew engaged in the business has its peculiar mark or device on its lances, and in this way it is known by whom the whale is killed.

The usage on Cape Cod, for many years, has been that the person who kills a whale in the manner and under the circumstances described, owns it, and this right has never been disputed until this case. The libellant has been engaged in this business for ten years past. On the morning of April 9, 1880, in Massachusetts Bay, near the end of Cape Cod, he shot and instantly killed with a bomb-lance the whale in question. It sank immediately, and on the morning of the 12th was found stranded on the beach in Brewster, within the ebb and flow of the tide, by one Ellis, seventeen miles from the spot where it was killed. Instead of sending word to Provincetown, as is customary, Ellis advertised the whale for sale at auction, and sold it to the respondent, who stripped off the blubber and tried out the oil. The libellant heard of the finding of the whale on the morning of the 15th, and immediately sent one of his boat's crew to the place and claimed it. Neither the respondent nor Ellis knew the whale had been killed by the libellant, but they knew or might have known, if they had wished, that it had been shot and killed with a bomb-lance, by some person engaged in this species of business.

The libellant claims title to the whale under this usage.[7] The respondent insists that this usage is invalid. It was decided by Judge Sprague, in Taber v. Jenny, 1 Sprague, 315, that when a whale has been killed, and is anchored and left with marks of appropriation, it is the property of the captors; and if it is afterwards found, still anchored, by another ship, there is no usage or

---

7. Lewis and Clark recount that on December 7, 1804, 15 men of their party joined a group of friendly Mandan Indians in a buffalo hunt. The Indians hunted with bow and arrow, the white men with guns. The whites killed ten buffalo and brought five of them into their fort. But "those we did not get in was taken by the indians under a Custom which is established amongst them, i.e. any person seeing a buffalow lying without an arrow Sticking in him or some purticular mark takes possession." The Journals of Lewis and Clark 71 (DeVoto ed. 1953). —EDS.

principle of law by which the property of the original captors is diverted, even though the whale may have dragged from its anchorage. The learned judge says:

> When the whale had been killed and taken possession of by the boat of Hillman (the first taker) it became the property of the owners of that ship, and all was done which was then practicable in order to secure it. They left it anchored, with unequivocal marks of appropriation. . . .

In Swift v. Gifford, 2 Low. 110, Judge Lowell decided that a custom among whalemen in the Arctic seas, that the iron holds the whale, was reasonable and valid. In that case a boat's crew from the respondent's ship pursued and struck a whale in the Arctic Ocean, and the harpoon and the line attached to it remained in the whale, but did not remain fast to the boat. A boat's crew from the libellant's ship continued the pursuit and captured the whale, and the master of the respondent's ship claimed it on the spot. It was held by the learned judge that the whale belonged to the respondents. It was said by Judge Sprague, in Bourne v. Ashley, an unprinted case referred to by Judge Lowell in Swift v. Gifford, that the usage for the first iron, whether attached to the boat or not, to hold the whale was fully established; and he added that, although local usages of a particular port ought not to be allowed to set aside the general maritime law, this objection did not apply to a custom which embraced an entire business, and had been concurred in for a long time by every one engaged in the trade. . . .

I see no reason why the usage proved in this case is not as reasonable as that sustained in the case cited. Its application must necessarily be extremely limited, and can affect but a few persons. It has been recognized and acquiesced in for many years. It requires in the first taker the only act of appropriation that is possible in the nature of the case. Unless it is sustained, this branch of industry must necessarily cease, for no person would engage in it if the fruits of his labor could be appropriated by any chance finder. It gives reasonable salvage for securing or reporting the property. That the rule works well in practice is shown by the extent of the industry which has grown up under it, and the general acquiescence of a whole community interested to dispute it. It is by no means clear that without regard to usage the common law would not reach the same result. That seems to be the effect of the decisions in Taber v. Jenny and Bartlett v. Budd. If the fisherman does all that it is possible to do to make the animal his own, that would seem to be sufficient. Such a rule might well be applied in the interest of trade, there being no usage or custom to the contrary. Holmes, Com. Law, 217. But be that as it may, I hold the usage to be valid, and that the property in the whale was in the libellant.

The rule of damages is the market value of the oil obtained from the whale, less the cost of trying it out and preparing it for the market, with interest on the amount so ascertained from the date of conversion. As the question is new and important, and the suit is contested on both sides, more for the purpose of having it settled than for the amount involved, I shall give no costs.

Decree for the libellant for $71.05, without costs.

Note: Whales

The whaling industry long ago disappeared from Cape Cod, but not the whales. They are periodically washed up on the beach, where they first attract and later repel the tourist trade. The disposal problem is traditionally solved by waiting until a curious New Yorker approaches near enough to the whale to be charged with possession, and hence title, thereof and then requiring the New Yorker as owner to give the whale a decent burial under the public health laws. According to the folklore of the locality, the whales usually come ashore in the summer at Wellfleet but in the winter choose Cohasset because, it is believed, they like to be nearer town. This subject is explored in Dahl, What, More Dahl! (1944), and Dahl's Boston (1946).

But do not take Ghen v. Rich lightly. It is not just another case. It has very serious analytical problems which you should be able to spot. Among other factors here, note that the respondent is not the man who found the whale but one who paid the finder good money for it and is now being compelled to pay again. See Chapter 9.

CHAPTER 3

TYPES OF POSSESSION

The difference between Chapter 2 and this chapter is the difference between concentration and distribution. There you were giving intensive study to a single problem of limited scope where possession was a dominant factor; here you are roaming around among a considerable group of problems where possession has more or less relevance. Your purposes should be three: (1) to notice how differently a concept, such as possession, acts in different settings; (2) to develop agility in handling different types of situations, in recognizing their common or differing ingredients, and in spotting the changes in circumstances which produce essential changes in the nature of the problems; (3) to pick up, as you go, at least an introductory understanding of the various fields of law into which this chapter leads you.

SECTION 1. UNCONSCIOUS POSSESSION

Unconscious possession is the term used to describe those situations where you are completely unaware that a particular item is in your control, or where you are aware that some item is in your control but you have no idea what it is, or where you know an item is under your control and think it is one thing whereas in fact it is something else. This section will explore the legal rights and liabilities of one who is in control of a particular item under these circumstances.

HANNAH v. PEEL
1 K.B. 509 (1945)

Action tried by BIRKETT, J. On December 13, 1938, the freehold of Gwernhaylod House, Overton-on-Dee, Shropshire, was conveyed to the defendant, Major Hugh Edward Ethelston Peel, who from that time to the end of 1940 never himself occupied the house and it remained unoccupied until October 5, 1939, when it was requisitioned. In August, 1940, the plaintiff, Duncan Hannah, a lance-corporal, serving in a battery of the Royal Artillery, was stationed at the house and on the 21st of that month, when in a bedroom, used as a sick-bay, he was adjusting the black-out curtains when his hand touched something on the top of a window frame, loose in a crevice, which he thought was a piece of dirt or plaster. The plaintiff grasped it and dropped it on the outside window ledge. On the following morning he saw that it was a brooch covered with cobwebs and dirt. Later, he took it with him when he went home on leave and his wife having told him it might be of value, at the end of October, 1940, he informed his commanding officer of his find and, on his advice, handed it over to the police, receiving a receipt for it. In August, 1942, the owner not having been found the police handed the brooch to the defendant, who sold it in October, 1942, for £66, to Messrs. Spink & Son, Ltd., of London, who resold it in the following month for £88. There was no evidence that the defendant had any knowledge of the existence of the brooch before it was found by the plaintiff. The defendant had offered the plaintiff a reward for the brooch, but the plaintiff refused to accept this and maintained throughout his right to the possession of the brooch as against all persons other than the owner, who was unknown. By a letter, dated October 5, 1942, the plaintiff's solicitors demanded the return of the brooch from the defendant, but it was not returned and on October 21, 1943, the plaintiff issued his writ claiming the return of the brooch, or its value, and damages for its detention. By his defense, the defendant claimed the brooch on the ground that he was the owner of Gwernhaylod House and in possession thereof.

BIRKETT, J. There is no issue of fact in this case between the parties. As to the issue in law, the rival claims of the parties can be stated in this way: The plaintiff says: "I claim the brooch as its finder and I have a good title against all the world, save only the true owner." The defendant says: "My claim is superior to yours inasmuch as I am the freeholder. The brooch was found on my property, although I was never in occupation, and my title, therefore, ousts yours and in the absence of the true owner I am entitled to the brooch or its value." . . .

[Bridges v. Hawkesworth, 21 L.J. 75, 15 Jur. 1079 (Q.B. 1851), was] an appeal against a decision of the county court judge at Westminster. The facts appear to have been that in the year 1847 the plaintiff, who was a commercial traveller, called on a firm named Byfield & Hawkesworth on business, as he was in the habit of doing, and as he was leaving the shop he picked up a small parcel which was lying on the floor. He immediately showed it to the shopman, and opened it in his presence, when it was found to consist of a quantity of Bank of England notes, to the amount of £65. The defendant, who was a partner in the firm of Byfield & Hawkesworth, was then called, and the plaintiff told him he had found the notes, and asked the defendant to keep them until the owner appeared to claim them. Then various advertisements were put in the papers asking for the owner, but the true owner was never found. No person having appeared to claim them, and three years having elapsed since they were found, the plaintiff applied to the defendant to have the notes returned to him, and offered to pay the expenses of the advertisements, and to give an indemnity. The defendant refused to deliver them up to the plaintiff, and an action was brought in the county court of Westminster in consequence of that refusal. The county court judge decided that the defendant, the shopkeeper, was entitled to the custody of the notes as against the plaintiff, and gave judgment for the defendant. Thereupon the appeal was brought which came before the court composed of Patteson, J. and Wightman, J. Patteson, J., said:

> . . . The general right of the finder to any article which has been lost, as against all the world, except the true owner, was established in the case of Armory v. Delamirie, 1 Str. 505, which has never been disputed. This right would clearly have accrued to the plaintiff had the notes been picked up by him outside the shop of the defendant and if he once had the right, the case finds that he did not intend, by delivering the notes to the defendant, to waive the title (if any) which he had to them, but they were handed to the defendant merely for the purpose of delivering them to the owner should he appear. . . . The case, therefore, resolves itself into the single point on which it appears that the learned judge decided it, namely, whether the circumstance of the notes being found inside the defendant's shop gives him, the defendant, the right to have them as against the plaintiff, who found them. . . . If the discovery had never been communicated to the defendant, could the real owner have had any cause of action against him because they were found in his house? Certainly not. The notes never were in the custody of the defendant, nor within the protection of his house, before they were found, as they would have been had they been intentionally deposited there; and the defendant has come under no responsibility, except from the communication made to him by the plaintiff, the finder, and the steps taken by way of advertisement. . . . We find, therefore, no circumstances in this case to take it out of the general rule of law, that the finder of a lost article is entitled to it as against all persons except the real owner, and we think that that rule must prevail, and that the learned judge was mistaken in holding that the place in which they were found makes any legal difference. Our judgment, therefore, is that the plaintiff is entitled to these notes as against the defendant. . . .

With regard to South Staffordshire Water Co. v. Sharman, [1896] 2 Q.B. 44, the first two lines of the head note are: "The possessor is generally entitled, as against the finder, to chattels found on the land." I am not sure that this is accurate. The facts were that the defendant Sharman, while cleaning out, under the orders of the plaintiffs, the South Staffordshire Water

Company, a pool of water on their land, found two rings embedded in the mud at the bottom of the pool. He declined to deliver them to the plaintiffs, but failed to discover the real owner. In an action brought by the company against Sharman in detinue it was held that the company were entitled to the rings. Lord Russell of Killowen, C.J., said, [1896] 2 Q.B. 46:

> . . . The principle on which this case must be decided, and the distinction which must be drawn between this case and that of Bridges v. Hawkesworth, is to be found in a passage in Pollock and Wright's "Essay on Possession in the Common Law," p. 41: "The possession of land carries with it in general, by our law, possession of everything which is attached to or under that land, and, in the absence of a better title elsewhere, the right to possess it also. . . . And it makes no difference that the possessor is not aware of the thing's existence."

. . . It has been said that it [South Staffordshire Water Co. v. Sharman] establishes that if a man finds a thing as the servant or agent of another, he finds it is not for himself, but for that other, and indeed that seems to afford a sufficient explanation of the case. The rings found at the bottom of the pool were not in the possession of the company, but it seems that though Sharman was the first to obtain possession of them, he obtained them for his employers and could claim no title for himself.

The only other case to which I need refer is Elwes v. Brigg Gas Co., 33 Ch. D. 562, in which land had been demised to a gas company for ninety-nine years with a reservation to the lessor of all mines and minerals. A prehistoric boat embedded in the soil was discovered by the lessees when they were digging to make a gasholder. It was held that the boat, whether regarded as a mineral or as part of the soil in which it was embedded when discovered, or as a chattel, did not pass to the lessees by the demise, but was the property of the lessor though he was ignorant of its existence at the time of granting the lease. Chitty, J., said (33 Ch. D. 568):

> The first question in this case is whether the boat belonged to the plaintiff at the time of the granting of the lease. I hold that it did, whether it ought to be regarded as a mineral, or as part of the soil, or as a chattel. If it was a mineral or part of the soil, then it clearly belonged to the owners of the inheritance as part of the inheritance itself. But if it ought to be regarded as a chattel, I hold the property in the chattel was vested in the plaintiff. . . . The plaintiff, then, had a lawful possession, good against all the world, and therefore the property in the boat. In my opinion it makes no difference, in these circumstances, that the plaintiff was not aware of the existence of the boat.

. . . It is fairly clear from the authorities that a man possesses everything which is attached to or under his land. Secondly, it would appear to be the law from the authorities I have cited, and particularly from Bridges v. Hawkesworth, that a man does not necessarily possess a thing which is lying unattached on the surface of his land even though the thing is not possessed by someone else. . . .[1]

There is no doubt that in this case the brooch was lost in the ordinary meaning of that term, and I should imagine it had been lost for a very considerable time. But the moment the plaintiff discovered that the brooch might be of some value, he took the advice of his commanding officer and handed it to the police. His conduct was commendable and meritorious. The defendant was never physically in possession of these premises at any time. It is clear that the brooch was never his, in the ordinary acceptation of the term, in that he had the prior possession. He had no knowledge of it, until it was brought to his notice by the finder. A discussion of the merits does not seem to help, but it is clear on the facts that the brooch was "lost" in the ordinary meaning of that word; that it was "found" by the plaintiff in the ordinary meaning of that word, that its true owner has never been found, that the defendant was the owner of the premises and had his notice drawn to this matter by the plaintiff, who found the brooch. In those circumstances I propose to give judgment in this case for the plaintiff for £66.[2]

Problems

3.1. Suppose that you represent the man who previously owned Gwernhaylod House, lived in it from 1932 to 1938, and sold it to Major H. E. Peel. What would you advise your client as to his rights:

    a. Before the action was brought in Hannah v. Peel?

    b. After satisfaction of the judgment in Hannah v. Peel?

1. Corporation of London v. Appleyard, [1963] 2 All E.R. 834, refers to Hannah v. Peel and also discusses *Bridges, Elwes,* and *South Staffordshire.* In the *Appleyard* case, the contents of an old wall safe found in the basement of a building being demolished were held to belong to the owner of the fee, as against the demolition company and the lessee of the property. The situation was simplified somewhat by the existence of a contract providing that as between the demolition company and fee owner, the fee owner was to be awarded possession of any curiosities, antiquities, or articles of value discovered during demolition.—EDS.

2. As a caricature of the functioning of the judicial mind, compare Rex v. Haddock, Misl. Cas. C. Law 31 (Herbert ed. 1927). In this case, the defendant, having had one or two beers and being on the Hammersmith Bridge on Regatta Day, bet a bystander that he would jump in for a swim, and did. He was accused of (a) causing an obstruction, (b) being drunk and disorderly, (c) attempting suicide, (d) conducting the business of a street bookmaker, and (e) endangering the lives of mariners. He was convicted in the police court. The following is an excerpt from the opinion of Frog, L.J., in the Court of Criminal Appeal:

> It is a principle of English law that a person who appears in a police court has done something undesirable, and citizens who take it upon themselves to do unusual actions which attract the attention of the police should be careful to bring these actions into one of the recognized categories of crimes and offences, for it is intolerable that the police should be put to the pains of inventing reasons for finding them undesirable. I have come to the conclusion that this appeal must fail. It is not for me to say what offence the appellant has committed, but I am satisfied that he has committed some offence, for which he has been most properly punished.

—EDS.

3.2. In McAvoy v. Medina, 93 Mass. (11 Allen) 548 (1866), the plaintiff, who was a customer in the defendant's barber shop, saw and took up a pocketbook which was lying on a table there, and said, "See what I have found." The plaintiff permitted the defendant to keep the pocketbook, so that it could be given to the owner if he returned to claim it. Subsequently, the owner not having appeared, the plaintiff demanded the pocketbook and the defendant refused to give it to him. The plaintiff sued to recover the amount of money contained in it. It was agreed that the pocketbook was placed upon the table by a transient customer of the defendant, and accidentally left there. The court held for the defendant, stating in part as follows:

> In the case of Bridges v. Hawkesworth the property, although found in a shop, was found on the floor of the same, and had not been placed there voluntarily by the owner, and the court held that the finder was entitled to the possession of the same, except as to the owner. But the present case more resembles that of Lawrence v. The State, 1 Humph. (Tenn.) 228, and is indeed very similar in its facts. The court there take a distinction between the case of property thus placed by the owner and neglected to be removed, and property lost. It was there held that "to place a pocket-book upon a table and to forget to take it away is not to lose it, in the sense in which the authorities referred to speak of lost property."
>
> We accept this as the better rule, and especially as one better adapted to secure the rights of the true owner. [93 Mass. (11 Allen) at 549.]

If you represented the defendant in Hannah v. Peel, what argument, if any, would you make based on McAvoy v. Medina?

3.3. In Barker v. Bates, (13 Pick.) 30 Mass. 255 (1832), the defendants trespassed on the plaintiff's land, discovering some timber which had washed ashore. The court held that the plaintiff was entitled to the timber as against the defendants, stating in part as follows:

> Considering it as thus established, that the place upon which this timber was thrown up and had lodged, was the soil and freehold of the plaintiff, that the defendants cannot justify their entry, for the purpose of taking away or marking the timber, we are of opinion that such entry was a trespass, and that as between the plaintiff and the defendants, neither of whom had or claimed any title except by mere possession, the plaintiff had, in virtue of his title to the soil, the preferable right of possession, and therefore that the plaintiff has a right to recover the agreed value of the timber, in his claim of damages. [30 Mass. (13 Pick.) at 261.]

If you represented the defendant in Hannah v. Peel, what argument, if any, would you make based on Barker v. Bates?

On the rights of a trespasser who finds property, see also Hibbert v. McKiernan, [1948] 1 All E.R. 860.

3.4. "Treasure-trove" is gold or silver or paper money which is intentionally concealed in the earth or in a house or some other private place and which is then found by someone other than the owner, the owner being unknown. In England, at common law, the finder has to turn the treasure over to the Crown. In this country, however, it is generally held that the finder may keep the treasure so long as the owner does not appear.

In state X, a statute provides that "if any person shall find any money or goods of the value of three dollars or more and if the owner thereof be unknown" notices must be posted in public places and that "every finder of lost goods of the value of $10 or more" shall also advertise in a local newspaper. It also provides that "if any finder of lost money or goods of the value of three dollars or upward" shall fail to comply with the provisions above, "he shall be liable for the full value of such money or goods, one-half to the use of the town and the other half to the person who shall sue for the same, and shall also be responsible to the owner for such lost money or goods."

A church in state X founds a "Carpet Rag Committee," which collects rags and then parcels them out to women who are paid to weave them into rugs. Mrs. Zech gets a bundle of rags rolled into a ball for these purposes. She finds $2,100 concealed in the center of the ball. She hands the money over to the rag rug committee for safekeeping, and the committee then refuses to give the money back. Is the committee liable to her for the money? See Zech v. Accola, 253 Wis. 80, 33 N.W.2d 232 (1948), noted in 47 Mich. L. Rev. 718 (1949) and 1949 Wis. L. Rev. 393; see also Willsmore v. Oceola Township, 106 Mich. App. 671, 308 N.W.2d 746 1981, involving the right to $383,840 in a suitcase buried on vacant land.

3.5. Mrs. Lillian Irene Nelson, owner of a rooming house, made a bid of $1.90 for a box of odds and ends at a charity auction. This particular box, one of several, was furnished by the First National Bank of Seattle from certain apparently worthless effects of one George Lee Baber, deceased, of whose will the bank was executor. The box contained some partly used cans of cleaning powder, soot remover, and soap flakes. When Mrs. Nelson began using the cleaning powder, she discovered, buried in it, $7,800 in currency. The find was disclosed by two roomers, who have since ceased to be such. The bank now claims the fund. You represent Mrs. Nelson. What additional facts would you like to be able to establish? How much, if anything, would you offer the bank in settlement of its claim?[3]

3. See the following for a discussion of the law applicable to finders: Riesman, Possession and The Law of Finders, 52 Harv. L. Rev. 1105 (1939); Note, 46 Mich. L. Rev. 235 (1947).

THE QUEEN v. ASHWELL
16 Q.B.D. 190 (1885)

Case stated by DENMAN, J.

At the assizes for the County of Leicester in January, 1883, Thomas Ashwell was tried for larceny of a sovereign, the moneys of Edward Keogh.

Keogh and Ashwell met in a public-house on the evening of the 9th of January. At about 8 P.M., Ashwell asked Keogh to go into the yard, and when there requested Keogh to lend him a shilling, saying that he had money to draw on the morrow, and that he would then repay him. Keogh consented, and putting his hand in his pocket pulled out what he believed to be a shilling, but what was in fact a sovereign, and handed it to Ashwell, and went home leaving Ashwell in the yard. About 9 the same evening, Ashwell obtained change for the sovereign at another public-house.

At 5:20 the next morning, Keogh went to Ashwell's house and told him that he had discovered the mistake, whereupon Ashwell falsely denied having received the sovereign, and on the same evening he gave false and contradictory accounts as to where he had become possessed of the sovereign he had changed at the second public-house on the night before. But he afterwards said, "I had the sovereign and spent half of it, and I shan't give it him back because I only asked him to lend me a shilling." . . .

I declined to withdraw the case from the jury, thinking it desirable that the point raised should be decided by the Court of Criminal Appeal.

The jury found that the prisoner did not know that it was a sovereign at the time he received it, but said they were unanimously of opinion that the prosecutor parted with it under the mistaken belief that it was a shilling, and that the prisoner having, soon after he received it, discovered that it was a sovereign could have easily restored it to the prosecutor, but fraudulently appropriated it to his own use, and denied the receipt of it, knowing that the prosecutor had not intended to part with the possession of a sovereign but only of a shilling. They added that if it were competent to them consistently with these findings and with the evidence to find the prisoner guilty, they meant to do so.

A verdict of guilty was entered, but the prisoner was admitted to bail, to come up for judgment at the next assizes if this court should think that upon the above facts and findings he could properly be found guilty of larceny.

SMITH, J. . . .

To constitute the crime of larceny at common law, in my judgment there must be a taking and carrying away of a chattel against the will of the owner, and at the time of such taking there must exist a felonious intent in the mind of the taker. If one or both of the above elements be absent there cannot be larceny at common law. The taking must be under such circumstances as would sustain an action of trespass. If there be a bailment or delivery of the chattel by the owner, inasmuch as, among other reasons, trespass will not lie, it is not larceny at common law. In Hawkins's Pleas of the Crown, book I, chap. 33, sect. 1, it is stated:

It is to be observed that all felony includes trespass; and that every indictment of larceny must have the words felonice cepit as well as asportavit; from whence it follows, that if the party be guilty of no trespass in taking the goods, he cannot be guilty of felony in carrying them away. . . .

In the present case it seems to me, in the first place, that the coin was not taken against the will of the owner, and if this be so, in my judgment it is sufficient to shew that there was no larceny at common law; and secondly, it being conceded that there was no felonious intent in the prisoner when he received the coin, this in my judgment is also fatal to the act being larceny at common law.

. . . The contention, however, of the Crown was that, although the above might be correct, yet the present case was to be likened to those cases in which finders of a lost chattel have been held guilty of larceny. The principle upon which a finder of a lost chattel has been held guilty of larceny is, that he has taken and carried away a chattel, not believing that it had been abandoned, and at the time of such taking has had the felonious intent. . . . Then it was argued by the counsel for the Crown, that the prisoner in this case was on the same footing as a finder of a chattel. In my judgment the facts do not support him.

Keogh, in the present case, intended to deliver the coin to the prisoner, and the prisoner to receive it. The chattel, namely the coin, was delivered over to the prisoner by its owner, and the prisoner received it honestly. He always knew he had the coin in his possession after it had been delivered to him. The only thing which was subsequently found was that the coin delivered was worth 240d. instead of 12d., as had been supposed. This argument, as it seems to me, confounds the finding out of a mistake with the finding of a chattel. In some cases, as above pointed out, the finder of a chattel may be guilty of larceny at common law; but how does that shew that the finder out of a mistake may also be guilty of such a crime? A mistake is not a chattel. The chattel (namely the coin) in this case never was lost; then how could it be found? In my judgment the argument upon this point for the Crown is wholly fallacious and fails. . . .

. . . Merry v. Green, 7 M. & W. 623, which was . . . the case of a purse in a secret drawer of a bureau which had been purchased at a sale, was clearly decided by Baron Parke, who delivered the judgment of the court, upon the principles applicable to a case of finding. The learned Baron says:

It seems to us, that though there was a delivery of the secretary, and a lawful property in it thereby vested in the plaintiff, there was no delivery so as to give a lawful possession of the purse and money. The vendor had no intention to deliver it, nor the vendee to receive it; both were ignorant of its existence: and when the plaintiff discovered that there was a secret drawer containing the purse and money, it was a case of simple finding, and the law applicable to all cases of finding applies to this.

I understand the learned Baron when he says "the law applicable to all cases of finding applies," to mean the law applicable to the cases of finding a chattel, for there are no cases extant as to finding out a mistake to which his remark could apply. That, too, is the distinction between the present case and that before Baron Parke. No intention to deliver the chattel (namely, the purse and money) at all ever existed, whereas in the present case there was every intention to deliver the chattel (namely the coin), and it was delivered and honestly received.

In my judgment, a man who honestly receives a chattel by delivery thereof to him by its true owner, cannot be found guilty of larceny at common law, and in my opinion the prisoner in this case is not guilty of that offence. . . .

LORD COLERIDGE, C.J. . . .

I assume it also to be settled law that where there has been a delivery — in the sense in which I will explain in a moment — of a chattel from one person to another, subsequent misappropriation of that chattel by the person to whom it has been delivered will not make him guilty of larceny, except by statute, with which I am not now concerned. But then it seems to me very plain that delivery and receipt are acts into which mental intention enters, and that there is not in law any more than in sense a delivery and receipt, unless the giver and receiver intend to give and to receive respectively what is respectively given and received. It is intelligent delivery, as I think, which the law speaks of, not a mere physical act from which intelligence and even consciousness are absent. . . . In this case, therefore, it seems to me there was no delivery of the sovereign to the prisoner by Keogh, because there was no intention to deliver, and no knowledge that it had been delivered.

Applying the same principles of reasoning, it appears to me that the sovereign was received by the prisoner and misappropriated by him at one and the same instant of time. In good sense it seems to me he did not take it till he knew what he had got; and when he knew what he had got, that same instant he stole it. According to all the cases, if at the very moment of the receipt of a chattel the receiver intends to misappropriate and does misappropriate it, he is guilty of larceny. I think for the reasons I have given, and in the sense I have defined, the prisoner did so here: and this seems to me, with great deference to my brother Smith, to be the answer to the exceedingly able and ingenious passage in his judgment in which he says that it is a fallacy to confound two things so utterly different as the discovery of a mistake and the stealing of a chattel, I do not shrink from the conclusion, which seems to me good sense, that sometimes the discovery of a mistake and the stealing of a chattel may be the same or rather may be two forms of words equally descriptive of the same facts, if, as here, the chattel is really discovered and stolen at one and the same instant of time.

. . . I think we cannot reverse this conviction without practically overruling . . . the Court of Exchequer in Merry v. Green. . . . I can see no sensible or intelligible distinction between the delivery of a bureau not known to contain a sum of money or a purse and the delivery of a piece of metal not known to contain in it 20s. . . .

In the judgment I have pronounced I am desired to say that my learned Brothers Grove, Pollock, and Huddleston concur. There are, therefore, seven for affirming the conviction and seven for quashing the conviction, and by the well-known rule of this Court, *praesumitur pro negante*, the conviction stands.[4]

Note: *Bailments and the Obligations of a Bailee*

Williston defines a bailment as "the rightful possession of goods by one who is not the owner." 9 Williston on Contracts §1030 (Jaeger 3d ed. 1967). Thus, when you borrow a book, keep your friend's cat for a week while he is away, or rent a drive-yourself car, you are a bailee. Railroads carrying freight, warehousemen storing commodities, persons working in checkrooms, pawnbrokers, garagemen, watch repairmen, and banks which hold stocks and bonds as security for repayment of loans—all these make a business of being bailees.

In earlier times, the law of bailments was a matter of great importance. Joseph Story, Marshall's brilliant lieutenant on the Supreme Court of the United States and the intellectual founder of the Harvard Law School, devoted his first scholarly attention to the subject. Story on Bailments (1840) was one of the great textbooks of the early nineteenth century. At the present time, however, the operation of the law of bailments has been squeezed into narrow compass by the encroachments of (1) standard forms of contract for the routine business bailments, and (2) statutes and regulations, which, as in the case of the railroads, have practically prescribed the liabilities of the bailee.

The common-law rule is well established that any one of the usual types of bailees who delivers the bailed chattel to the wrong person has converted the chattel and is liable to the bailor in an action of trover. Restatement of Torts (Second) §§234, 235. Proof of negligence is not required, and proof of due care on the part of the bailee is no defense. As in other actions of trover, the bailor may recover the full value of the chattel and, upon satisfaction of the judgment, the bailee acquires title to the chattel, for what it is worth, and

---

4. The opinions of Cave, Mathew, Stephen, Hawkins, Manisty, Denman, and Field, JJ., are not presented here.

Queen v. Ashwell is discussed in Russell v. Smith, [1957] 2 All E.R. 796. There the driver of a delivery lorry was held not to have had possession of some bags of feed mistakenly put into his lorry until he discovered them and decided to sell them, thereby converting them to his own use.—EDS.

may pursue it in the hands of the person to whom it has been misdelivered. Damage to the bailed chattel, or loss through means other than misdelivery, is the basis for an action by the bailor only if negligence is proved, the required degree of negligence varying from slight to gross depending on the type of bailment involved.

PEET v. ROTH HOTEL CO.
191 Minn. 151, 253 N.W. 546 (1934)

Action in the district court for Ramsey county to recover judgment against defendant for the value of a ring belonging to plaintiff, valued at $2,500, which became lost after plaintiff had left it with defendant's cashier to be delivered to a guest in its hotel. The case was tried before Richard A. Walsh, Judge, and a jury. Plaintiff recovered a verdict of $2,140.66. Defendant appealed from an order denying its alternative motion for judgment or a new trial. Affirmed.

STONE, J. After an adverse verdict, defendant moved in the alternative for judgment notwithstanding or a new trial. That motion denied, defendant appeals.

The record is the story of a ring. Defendant operates the St. Paul Hotel in St. Paul. Mr. Ferdinand Hotz is a manufacturing jeweler. For 20 years or more he has visited St. Paul periodically on business, making his local headquarters at the St. Paul Hotel. He had long been one of its regular patrons, personally known to the management. Plaintiff's engagement ring, a platinum piece set with a large cabochon sapphire surrounded by diamonds, was made to order by Mr. Hotz. One of its small diamonds lost, plaintiff had arranged with him to have it replaced and for that purpose was to leave it for him at the St. Paul Hotel. November 17, 1931, he was a guest there on one of his seasonal visits. About four P.M. of that day plaintiff went to the cashier's desk of the hotel, wearing the ring. The cashier on duty was a Miss Edwards. At this point plaintiff may as well tell her own story, for upon it is based the jury's verdict. She thus testified:

> "I had it [the ring] on my finger and took it off my finger. The cashier—I told the cashier that it was for Mr. Ferdinand Hotz. She took out an envelope and wrote 'Ferdinand Hotz.' I remember spelling it to her, and then I left. . . . I handed the ring to the cashier, and she wrote on the envelope. . . . The only instructions I remember are telling her that it was for Mr. Ferdinand Hotz, who was stopping at the hotel."

Plaintiff's best recollection is that Miss Edwards told her that Mr. Hotz was registered but was not in at the moment. Miss Edwards frankly admitted, as a witness, that the ring had been delivered to her. It is conceded that it was immediately lost, doubtless stolen, probably by an outsider. Miss

Edwards herself is beyond suspicion. But the ring, where she placed it upon its delivery to her by plaintiff, was on her desk or counter and within easy reach of anyone standing or passing just outside her cashier's window.

The loss was not then reported either to plaintiff or Mr. Hotz. About a month later he was again in St. Paul, and then plaintiff was advised for the first time that her ring had never reached him. Upon inquiry at the hotel office, it was learned that it had been lost. The purpose of this action is to recover from defendant, as bailee of the ring, its reasonable value, fixed by the jury at $2,140.66. The reasonableness of that figure is not questioned.

1. The jury took the case under a charge that there was a bailment as a matter of law. Error is assigned upon the supposition that there was at least a question of fact whether the evidence showed the mutual assent prerequisite to the contract of bailment which is the sine qua non of plaintiff's case. The supporting argument is put upon the cases holding that where the presence or identity of the article claimed to have been bailed is concealed from the bailee he has not assented to assume that position with its attendant obligation, and so there is no bailment. Samples v. Geary (Mo. App.) 292 S.W. 1066 (fur piece concealed in coat checked in parcel room); U.S. v. Atlantic C.L.R. Co., 206 F. 190 (cut diamonds in mail package with nothing to indicate nature of contents); Riggs v. Bank of Camas Prairie, 34 Idaho, 176, 200 P. 118, Anno. 18 A.L.R. 83 (bailee of locked box supposed to contain only "papers and other valuables" not liable for money therein of which it had no knowledge).

The claim here is not that plaintiff perpetrated fraud upon defendant but that she failed to divulge the unusual value of her ring when she left it with Miss Edwards. The latter testified that at the moment she did not realize its value. Taking both facts and their implications as favorably as we may for defendant, the stubborn truth remains that plaintiff delivered and defendant accepted the ring with its identity and at least its outward character perfectly obvious.

The mutual assent necessary to a contract may be expressed as well by conduct as by words; or it may be manifested by both. Restatement, Contracts, Sec. 21. The latter is the case here. The expression of mutual assent is found in what passed between plaintiff and Miss Edwards. The former delivered and the latter accepted the ring to be delivered to Mr. Hotz. Below that irreducible minimum the case cannot be lowered. No decision has been cited and probably none can be found where the bailee of an article of jewelry, undeceived as to its identity, was relieved of liability because of his own erroneous underestimate of its value.

If there was mistake with legal effect worth while to defendant, it must have been of such character as to show no mutual assent and so no contract. There was no such error here. Identity of the property and all its attributes, except only its value, were as well known to defendant as to plaintiff. The case is identical in principle with Wood v. Boynton, 64 Wis. 265, 25 N.W. 42, 54 Am. R. 610. There the plaintiff had sold to defendant, for one dollar, a stone which she supposed was at best a topaz. It turned out to be an uncut diamond worth $700. Neither its true character nor value was known to either buyer or seller at the time of the sale. There being neither fraud nor mistake as to identity, the mutual mistake as to value was held no obstacle to completion of the contract. Plaintiff was denied recovery. . . .

Defendant's liability, if any, is for negligence. In that field generally the legal norm is a care commensurate to the hazard, i.e. the amount and kind of care that would be exercised by an ordinarily prudent person in the same or similar circumstances. The character and amount of risk go far, either to decrease or increase the degree of care required. The value of the property, its attractiveness to light-fingered gentry, and the ease or difficulty of its theft have much to say with triers of fact in determining whether there has been exercised a degree of care commensurate to the risk, whether the bailment be gratuitous or otherwise. However unsatisfactory it may be, until legal acumen has developed and formulated a more satisfactory criterion, that of ordinary care should be followed in every case without regard to former distinctions between slight, ordinary, and great care. Even the courts which adhere to the former distinctions will be found in most cases to be demanding no other degree of care than one commensurate to the risk and other relevant circumstances; e.g. in Ridenour v. Woodward, 132 Tenn. 620, 179 S.W. 148, 149, 4 A.L.R. 1192, it was held that a gratuitous bailee was answerable only for his gross negligence or bad faith. But, as the court proceeded to say, the care to be taken was (132 Tenn. 623) "to be measured, however, with reference to the nature of the thing placed in his keeping." The defendant was relieved of liability because it was held as matter of law that he had (132 Tenn. 628) "acted with a fairly commensurate discretion" in handling the bailed property. . . .

Order affirmed.

Problems

3.6. The defendant runs the ladies' checkroom concession in a night-club. The plaintiff wore a cloth coat and silver fox fur piece to the club, stuck the fur piece into the sleeve of the coat, folded the coat around it, and handed the coat (with fur piece inside) to the defendant for checking. The plaintiff received a check. When the plaintiff presented her check, the fur piece was no longer in the coat. The plaintiff brings action to recover the value of the fur piece. If you represent the defendant, what contentions will you make and how do you evaluate your chances of success? See Samples v. Geary, 292 S.W. 1066 (Kansas City, Mo., Ct. App. 1927).

3.7. Colonial Auto Parks, Inc., operates an open-air parking space adjacent to a ballpark. Shortly before the beginning of a ballgame, the plaintiff entered the space, paying 50 cents to the attendant at the gate. Another attendant directed him where to place his car. The plaintiff locked the car and took the keys with him. At the time the 50 cents was paid, the attendant tied a check to the handle of the plaintiff's car and gave him the stub of this check, reading as follows: "No. 2367. Parking privilege check. Colonial Auto Parks, Inc., assumes no responsibility for lost or stolen property or damage to property while parking in this parking space." When the plaintiff returned for his car, it was gone. The plaintiff complained to the attendants, who professed no knowledge of what had happened to it. The plaintiff now sues for the value of the car. It is settled law in the jurisdiction that one may not by contract exonerate oneself from liability for one's own negligence in the performance of duties one has assumed. If you represent Colonial Auto Parks, Inc., what additional facts will you seek to establish and what contentions will you make on your client's behalf? Ex parte Mobile Light & R.R., 211 Ala. 525, 101 So. 177 (1924); Galowitz v. Magner, 208 A.D. 6, 203 N.Y.S. 421 (1924).

3.8. A bellboy in a hotel was in the act of transporting the baggage of a hotel guest to the guest's hotel room when he was stopped by a police officer with a warrant to search the baggage for narcotics. The search revealed that the baggage contained a substantial quantity of narcotics. A statute in the state provides as follows: "It shall be unlawful for any person to receive, import, possess, transport, deliver, manufacture, sell, give away or barter, any narcotics within this state." The bellboy is indicted under this statute for transporting and possessing narcotics. You are appointed by the court to defend him. What would be your defense? See State v. Cox, 91 Or. 518, 179 P. 575 (1919). Also consider footnote 9 *infra* this chapter.

SECTION 2. INVOLUNTARY POSSESSION

You may find yourself in control of a particular item when you had nothing to do with bringing this about or when it occurred contrary to your desires. We are now concerned with the responsibilities you may be under with respect to such item in these cases of involuntary possession, keeping in mind the general rule referred to in the Note on Bailments, at page 39 *supra* that the bailee is absolutely liable for misdelivery.

COWEN v. PRESSPRICH

117 Misc. 663, 192 N.Y.S. 242 (Sup. Ct. App. Term),
reversed, 202 A.D. 796, 194 N.Y.S. 926 (1922)

[The plaintiffs, a firm of stockbrokers, sued the defendants, another firm of stockbrokers, for conversion of a $1,000 bond of the Oregon & California

R.R. Co. The complaint alleged that the plaintiffs, Cowen and his partners, were under contract to deliver a bond of the Oregon Short Line R.R. Co. to the defendants, Pressprich and his partners; that by mistake they delivered a bond of the Oregon & California R.R. Co.; that Pressprich notified Cowen that he would not accept the bond delivered; that, by reason of these facts, Cowen is entitled to the return of the Oregon & California R.R. Co. bond; and that, although the plaintiffs have demanded the bond, the defendants have neglected and refused to deliver it to them (192 N.Y.S. at 249-250).

The case was tried before a judge of the Municipal Court, Borough of Manhattan, sitting without jury.

The plaintiff's evidence showed the following facts. ("Cowen" is used to designate the plaintiffs, "Pressprich" to designate the defendants.) Cowen sent a runner, Goldberg, aged 17, to make delivery of an Oregon Short Line bond which had been sold to Pressprich. By mistake, he took an Oregon & California R.R. bond. For receiving deliveries of securities, Pressprich had a small room into which the delivery boys entered; in one wall of the room was a slot for depositing the securities and above it a ground-glass window, which could be opened from the inside; securities pushed through the slot fell on the desk of Pressprich's clerk, whose job it was to receive deliveries. All deliveries were accompanied by slips describing the item delivered. Goldberg came into the small room and pushed through the slot the Oregon & California bond and a slip describing an Oregon Short Line bond and then left to make other deliveries. Pressprich's clerk noticed the discrepancy between the bond and the slip. He opened the ground-glass window and called "Cowen." A boy who was there stepped up. (The boy was not Goldberg or any representative of Cowen. Pressprich's clerk knew none of the runners.) The clerk said, "Make your statement agree with the bond" and handed the boy the bond and the slip. The boy took them and left. The bond was negotiable and was never recovered.

At the close of the evidence, the defendants requested a ruling that the evidence was not sufficient to sustain a cause of action. The court denied this ruling and found for the plaintiffs, giving no statement as to the basis of decision. The defendants appealed to the Supreme Court, Appellate Term.]

MULLAN, J. . . .

The defendants have refused to make good the plaintiffs' loss, contending that they were chargeable only with due diligence, and that, accepting the version of the plaintiffs as given by Goldberg, it appears that they exercised all the care required of them. The plaintiffs contend that there was an absolute obligation on the part of the defendants to redeliver the bond to the plaintiffs, and that no question of negligence enters into the case. They also argue that, if the negligence question does enter, there was sufficient evidence to warrant a finding that the defendants did not, in fact, exercise due care. The learned trial judge did not state the ground of his decision in plaintiffs' favor.

A person who has been put, through no act or fault of his own, in such a situation as that in which the defendants were put upon the delivery to them of the wrong bond, has come to be known as "involuntary bailee," (1 Halsbury Laws of Eng. 528; Heugh v. L. & N.W.R.R. Co., L.R. 5 Ex. 51 (1870); 5 Cyc. 166, n.27; Story Bailm. (7th ed.) Secs. 44a, 83a), or bailee by casualty (T. J. Moss Tie Co. v. Kreilich, 80 Mo. App. 304) or constructive or quasi bailee (Schouler Bailm. (3d ed.) para. 3).

In the field of voluntary bailments, whether they be for hire or be otherwise coupled with an interest on the part of the bailee, or whether they be merely gratuitous, no rule is better settled than that it is the duty of the bailee to deliver the bailed article to the right person, and that delivery to the wrong person is not capable of being excused by any possible showing of care or good faith or innocence.

Such distinctions as have been drawn between the duties of voluntary bailees for compensation and voluntary gratuitous bailees relate solely to the degree of care the bailee should exercise in respect of the *custody* of the thing bailed. In respect of *delivery* to the proper person, no such distinction is drawn; the duty in both cases is absolute.

What, then, is the difference, if any, between the duty of a voluntary gratuitous bailee and that of a wholly involuntary bailee? There is an astonishing paucity of decision and text opinion upon the subject. I think, however, that all that can be found upon it points to the conclusion that the involuntary bailee, as long as his lack of volition continues, is not under the slightest duty to care for or guard the subject of the bailment, and cannot be held, in respect of custody, for what would even be the grossest negligence in the case of a voluntary bailment, but that, in case the involuntary bailee shall exercise any dominion over the thing so bailed, he becomes as responsible as if he were a voluntary bailee. . . .

[Here the learned court discussed Hiort v. Bott, 9 L.R.-Ex. 86 (1874). In this case, Hiort, a grain dealer, received a telegram from Grimmett, a grain broker, directing him to ship 83 quarters of barley to Bott. Hiort shipped the barley by the L.N.W. Ry. and sent to Bott a letter stating that the barley was sold to him through Grimmett as broker; the letter enclosed a delivery order, issued by the railroad, which made the barley deliverable to the order of Hiort or Bott. Bott, who had ordered no barley, got in touch with Grimmett. Grimmett said it was a mistake of Hiort and asked Bott to endorse the delivery order to Grimmett to save trouble and expense in clearing up the matter. Bott endorsed the order. Grimmett got the barley, sold it, and absconded. Hiort brought an action of trover against Bott. The Court of Exchequer gave judgment for the plaintiff. Bramwell, B. said:

> If the defendant had done nothing at all [the barley] would have been delivered to the plaintiff. By means of this order so endorsed Grimmett got the barley and made away with it. Thus, by an unauthorized act on the part of the

defendant, the plaintiff has lost his barley. This was assuming control over the disposition of these goods, and causing them to be delivered to a person who deprived the plaintiff of them. The conversion is therefore made out.]

I have reached the conclusion that while, at first blush, it may seem to be imposing upon the defendants an unduly severe rule of conduct to hold them to an absolute liability, the rule is no more severe than the occasion calls for. . . . The defendants could easily have protected themselves by telephoning the plaintiffs that the wrong bond had been delivered, or they could have sent the bond back to the plaintiffs by one of their own messengers. Instead, they chose to take the chance of delivering it to the wrong messenger. As the delivery window was closed when the bond was dropped through the slot, and remained closed for an appreciable time, they could not have known what messenger had made the delivery. . . .

The plaintiffs, as has already been mentioned, urge that, if the defendants are not to be held in conversion, they are, at least, liable in negligence. The action, however, was brought in conversion, and both sides insist that it was tried as a conversion action. The judgment therefore may only be sustained, if at all, upon that theory. . . .

Judgment affirmed, with $25 costs, with leave to defendants to appeal to the Appellate Division.[5]

LEHMAN, J.,[6] dissenting. . . .

It is unnecessary now to consider whether the complaint sufficiently sets forth any cause of action; for no motion was made by the defendants to dismiss the complaint on the ground of insufficiency, and no such point is raised on this appeal. It is to be noted, however, that the complaint does not allege any negligence on the part of the defendants, and I agree with Mr. Justice Mullan that no such issue was litigated, and that the judgment can be sustained only if, as a matter of law, the defendants' mistake in returning the bond to the wrong messenger constituted a conversion of the bond or at least a breach of an implied agreement on their part to return the bond only to the plaintiffs.

. . . The defendants had not consented to accept the bond as a deposit, they claimed no title to it, and they were not subject to any trust or obligation as bailees, for a bailment arises only through an express or implied contract. They were put in possession of the bond without any agreement on their part, express or implied, to accept the deposit of the

5. The concurring opinion of Burr, J., is not present here.— EDS.
6. This is Irving Lehman, who in 1924 became a judge of the court of appeals and in 1940 became chief judge. He is a brother of Herbert H. Lehman, governor of New York from 1932 to 1942, later director general of United Nations Relief and Rehabilitation Administration, then elected U. S. Senator in 1949. The Lehman family business is Lehman Brothers, investment bankers. Governor Lehman was a partner of this firm for years; it does not appear that Judge Lehman was ever officially connected with it. However, some practical understanding of the brokerage business can be inferred.— EDS.

bond; and, though persons who come into possession of the property of others without their consent are sometimes for convenience called "involuntary" or "quasi bailees," they incur no responsibility to the true owner in respect thereof. It is only where they commit some "overt act" of interference with the property that an implied contract of bailment is created. Halsbury's Laws of England, vol. 1, §1078.

. . . In other words, an implied contract of bailment with its consequent obligations arises only where a person in possession of the property of another does some act which is inconsistent with the view that he does not *accept* the possession which has been thrust upon him. . . .

. . . In the present case the defendants were put in possession of the bond by mistake; they discovered the mistake promptly, and thereafter they committed no "overt act" of interference with the bond except that they attempted to divest themselves of this possession by delivering the bond to a person whom they believed to be the messenger of the plaintiffs. That act was not only consistent with the continued title and right of dominion in the plaintiffs, but was an honest attempt to restore possession to the true owners. . . . An attempt to return the bond to the true owner or to the person who delivered it cannot be considered as inconsistent with a recognition of the complete ownership and right of dominion by the true owner, and certainly shows no intent to accept the possession thrust upon the defendants by plaintiffs' mistake, and I fail to see how, in the absence of such elements, any implied contract of bailment can arise. If in making an attempt to return the goods, which was lawful and proper in itself, the defendants used means which were not reasonable and proper, and as a result thereof the goods were lost or misdelivered, then the defendants would be liable for negligence or possibly for conversion, for every man is responsible for his own acts; but, if the defendants had a right to divest themselves of possession and attempt to return the goods, then, in the absence of some obligation resting upon contract to deliver the goods only to the true owner or upon his order, I do not see how the mere fact that through innocent mistake the defendants handed the bond to the wrong messenger could constitute a conversion. . . .

Even if under these pleadings we could consider the question of negligence, I find no evidence upon this question to sustain a judgment in favor of the plaintiffs. There is no doubt that the defendants acted in good faith and in the honest belief that they were handing back the bond to the messenger who delivered it. They had assumed no obligation of any kind to the plaintiffs; any act they performed was for the plaintiffs' benefit, and it was through plaintiffs' mistake that they were called upon to act at all in the premises. Doubtless, if they had foreseen the possibility of mistake, they would not have delivered the bond to the wrong messenger; but it was not unreasonable to suppose that the messenger might be waiting or that, if he had left, no thief would be in the office who would claim to represent the plaintiffs. They probably committed an error of judgment, but for such error they cannot be held liable. Since they owed no obligation to the plaintiffs and acted in good faith under the reasonable belief that they were returning the bond to the messenger who delivered it, I see no ground for imposing upon them liability for the loss of a bond which would never have been lost but for the plaintiffs' mistake, due apparently to the plaintiffs' negligence. . . .

For these reasons, it seems to me that the judgment should be reversed with costs, and the complaint dismissed, with costs.

[On appeal to the appellate division of the supreme court, the judgment of the appellate term was reversed on the basis of the dissenting opinion of Lehman J., and judgment was ordered for the defendants (202 A.D. 796, 194 N.Y.S. 926).]

Problems

3.9. One of the hoariest swindles still working is the false order game; and it is very difficult to stop.

The basic version is this. S, the swindler, telephones to M, a manufacturer of ladies' dressing gowns, saying that he is an assistant buyer in the A. B. Brown Co., a reputable local department store; that they need 15 of M's dressing gowns; and will M send them over right away? M delivers the dressing gowns to Brown's receiving room. S then telephones to Brown's receiving room, stating that he is M's delivery manager; that the parcel of 15 dressing gowns was delivered to Brown by mistake, since it was another Brown who gave the order; and that he will send over a man right away to pick them up. Thereupon S appears at Brown's receiving room, states that he is M's man, and picks up the dressing gowns. The gowns disappear. M brings action against A. B. Brown Co. to recover their value. Should he recover? Krumsky v. Loeser, 37 Misc. 504, 75 N.Y.S. 1012 (1902).[7]

3.10. O leaves a package in a railroad coach. The conductor finds it and turns it in to the railroad's lost-and-found department. A appears at the lost-and-found department, describes the package and its contents with accuracy, and receives the package. O brings an action against the railroad for conversion of the package. O's counsel argues as follows:

> The company was a bailee of the package. It is the duty of a finder to return the article to the person who lost it. "The law always implies an agreement to do what a man's legal duty requires him to do." Smith v. Nashua & Lowell R.R., 27 N.H. 86, 97 (1853). Therefore the two vital elements of a bailment exist in this case, viz. possession by the railroad, and a contract to return the

---

7. The principal variant of the basic swindle is as follows: C, a customer, can telephone an order for merchandise to a store; then, after the merchandise is delivered, C can *say* that he did not order the goods and that someone who said he was from the store picked the goods up after a telephone call in which C was informed that there had been a misdelivery.

chattel. The obligation of a bailee to return a chattel is absolute, and the bailee is absolutely liable in trover for a misdelivery. There is no question of negligence. It follows that the plaintiff is entitled to recover.

Reply to this argument. See Morris v. Third Ave. R.R., 1 Daly 202 (N.Y. Ct. C.P. 1862).

3.11. O was the owner of a farm abutting on the right of way of the X Railway Company. By reason of a wreck on the right of way at a point near O's farm, coal belonging to the X Company was thrown on O's land. O refused to grant permission to the X Company to remove the coal unless he was paid $35. The X Company brought an action against O for conversion of the coal. If you represented O, what contentions would you make? See Chicago, I. & L. Ry. v. Pope, 99 Ind. App. 280, 188 N.E. 594 (1934); American Law of Property §28.9 (Casner ed. 1952).[8]

SECTION 3. "CONSTRUCTIVE POSSESSION"

Note: "Constructive" This and That, and Other Fictions

Here you find a group of cases where "possession" is being used in a Pickwickian sense, signalized by the word "constructive." As you go further, you will discover that "constructive possession" is one of a rather large family. For example:

1. In this course you will find that where O, the owner of land, conveys to A by a deed which A records in the registry of deeds, and then O conveys the same land to B, B has "constructive notice" of A's deed even though, as a matter of actual fact, he knew nothing about it at all.

2. Also, in this course, you will find that, where a landlord allows premises to get into a very bad state of disrepair, he has "constructively evicted" his tenant, even though he desperately implores the tenant to stay on and could not possibly rent the premises to anyone else.

3. When you deal with trusts and wills, you will discover that, in many circumstances where A has defrauded B, he thereby automatically becomes "constructive trustee" for B, even though he loathes the

---

8. For general reading on the subject of possession, see Bingham, The Nature and Importance of Legal Possession, 13 Mich. L. Rev. 535, 623 (1915); Shartel, Meanings of Possession, 16 Minn. L. Rev. 611 (1932). On the subject of bailments, see Laidlaw, Principles of Bailment, 16 Cornell L.Q. 286 (1931).

ground B walks on and would not voluntarily have any relationship with him.

Elsewhere you will discover other oddities. In applying the rule against perpetuities the courts solemnly assert that a woman of 80 can have children. In actions of ejectment, the courts forbid the defendant to call attention to the obvious fraud when the plaintiff appears repeatedly as "John Doe," a lessee, despite the fact that there has been no lease of the land for decades; and, until stopped by statute, the courts followed this notion to its logical conclusion in allowing a plaintiff in ejectment to bring as many successive actions as he had money to support through the expedient of alleging a different fictitious lease each time and thereby bringing suit in the name of a new plaintiff not barred by prior defeats. In a celebrated case involving an action upon a contract made on the island of Minorca, the English court refused to allow the defendant to deny the plaintiff's allegation that Minorca was within the city of Westminster. In the law "husband and wife are one," and it is presumed that everything a wife does in her husband's presence is done at his direction — which gets us back to Dickens (Oliver Twist) where this particular presumption prompted the assertion that "the law is a ass, a idiot."

These and other legal fictions have performed various functions. It is important that you recognize them when they arise, and that you diagnose the ends they seek to attain and the methods by which they operate. At some time — perhaps during the vacation after your first year of law study — you will want to read a searching analysis of this subject in Professor Fuller's trilogy, Legal Fictions, 25 Ill. L. Rev. 363, 513, 877 (1930-1931).

GILLESPIE v. DEW
1 Stew. 229 (Ala. 1827)

In Greene Circuit Court, James Gillespie declared in trespass against Duncan Dew, that the defendant broke and entered his close, and cut down and carried away sundry timber trees, etc. General issue. Verdict and judgment for defendant. On the trial the plaintiff proved title to the land, and that the defendant had cut timber thereon and carried it away, while the plaintiff was so entitled. It was proved that the plaintiff resided about twenty miles from the land. It did not appear that any one was in actual possession when the timber was cut, etc. The Circuit Court charged the jury that, unless the evidence shewed that the plaintiff by himself or agent was in actual possession of the land, when the trespass was committed, they must find for the defendant. To which the plaintiff excepted, and there assigned this matter as error.

WHITE, J., delivered the opinion of the court.

The charge was in accordance with the English authorities, and with the decisions in some of the States of the Union. But in North Carolina, New

York and Connecticut, it has been held that, where there is no adverse possession, he who has title, though he has never been in actual possession, may maintain the action of trespass.

The situation of our country requires this modification of the English doctrine. In England, almost all the lands are occupied; but here, the proprietor often lives at a great distance from some of his lands which are not occupied by tenants, and unless they can maintain this action, they must be denied an important remedy for injuries to their property. Their right to this remedy is sustained by the strong argument of convenience, and by the respectable authorities referred to by the counsel for the plaintiff.

We are of opinion that, where there is no adverse possession, the title draws with it constructive possession, so as to sustain the action of trespass. Let the judgment be reversed and the cause be remanded.

STATE v. SCHINGEN
20 Wis. 79 (1865)

On Exceptions from the Circuit Court for Winnebago County.

The defendant was indicted for larceny of two horses and a set of harness, the property of one Buhler; and the jury having found him guilty, a new trial was refused. The principal questions presented by the defendant's exceptions, arose upon instructions asked for by him and refused; the character of which will sufficiently appear from the opinion, infra.

COLE, J. The first instruction asked for on the trial by the defendant, however true as an abstract proposition of law, yet, without some explanation, was calculated to mislead the jury. The evidence shows most clearly that the defendant was in the employ of Buhler, and had been sent from Berlin with the team to take some beer to Omro and Waukau, with instructions to bring back the kegs and money, returning by the way of Eureka the same day. It appears that, after disposing of most of the beer at Omro, the defendant threw the empty kegs and two full ones remaining unsold over the fence into a field at that place, and instead of returning to Berlin, drove off with the wagon and horses to Oshkosh, where he offered the horses for sale, and did actually sell the harness. By the instructions above referred to, the court was asked to charge the jury that without the commission of a trespass there could be no larceny, and that there could be no trespass unless the goods were taken by the accused while in the possession of the owner. The court gave this instruction with the additional remark, that if the accused was at work for the owner of the property, and the property was put into the prisoner's hands to go to Omro and other places, it remained in the owner's possession; and if the prisoner took it beyond the places he was to go, for the purpose of converting it to his own use, this was a trespass. Now we think the explanatory remarks were very proper, in view of the facts of the case. For the evidence was most distinct and positive upon the point, that the defendant was in the employ of Buhler, and had been sent away by him with the wagon, horses, harness, beer, etc., for the purpose just stated. He was therefore the servant of Buhler, having only a bare charge or custody of the property, while the legal possession was in the owner. The relation of master and servant thus existing between the parties when the property was entrusted to the care of the defendant for a special purpose, in contemplation of law the possession was in the master, and the defendant might be guilty of a trespass and larceny in fraudulently converting it to his own use. . . .

By the Court: The exceptions in this case are overruled, and the judgment of the circuit court affirmed.[9]

SECTION 4. ADVERSE POSSESSION

Note: *Statutes of Limitations — Their Purpose and Operation*

In all states there exist statutes which limit the time within which certain types of actions may be brought — for example, the controlling law may provide six years for actions upon ordinary contracts, 20 years for actions upon contracts under seal, two years for actions for wrongful death, one year for death claims based on the employer's liability act.

Among statutes of limitations, those which deal with the recovery of possession of land have a peculiar standing because the running of this statute has not only a procedural, but a proprietary, significance. That is, if the statute prescribes that an action to recover possession of land must be commenced within 20 years from the time the action accrues (the usual provision), and the owner of the land of which someone else is in possession allows the 20-year period to go by without commencing his action, the right of action is dead, the owner loses his title to the land, and the possessor acquires title.

Thus, the statute of limitations is a means of acquiring title to lands and suppressing long dormant claims. This is not a byproduct of the statute but its very purpose, for one finds in the original general Statute of Limitations (21 Jac. 1, ch. 16, (1623)) a preamble stating that it is designed "for quieting

---

9. If you were the prosecuting attorney and a person indicted for illegal "possession" of narcotics contended he was the servant of another and therefore only had "custody" of the narcotics, not "possession," how would you reply?

In regard to the distinction that a servant has custody and the master possession, see Melli & Remington, Theft, A Comparative Analysis of Present Law and the Proposed Criminal Code, 1954 Wis. L. Rev. 253 (Wisconsin Criminal Code), and Baldwin, Criminal Misappropriation in Wisconsin — Part I, 44 Marq. L. Rev. 253 (1961). — EDS.

of men's estates." It is natural, then, that this branch of the law should receive a name—"adverse possession"—which adopts the point of view of the possessor whose claim is being ripened rather than the point of view of the suitor whose cause of action is being lost.

EWING v. BURNET
36 U.S. (1 Pet.) 41 (1837)

In Error from the circuit court of the district of Ohio.

The plaintiff in error instituted an action of ejectment in the circuit court of Ohio, at December term 1834, against the defendant, to recover a lot of ground in the city of Cincinnati. Both the plaintiff and the defendant claimed title under deeds from John Cleves Symmes, the original grantee of the United States for all the land on which the city of Cincinnati is erected. The deed from Symmes, under which the plaintiff asserted his title, was executed June 11th, 1798, to Samuel Forman; the deed from Symmes to the defendant, for the same lot, was dated May 21st, 1803.[10] [Forman conveyed to Williams later in 1798; Williams died in 1824; and Ewing succeeded to Williams' title either as heir or devisee.] An adverse possession for twenty-one years and upwards, was relied on, as constituting a sufficient legal title, under the statute of limitations of Ohio. . . .

[The Ohio statute of limitations applicable to this type of proceeding is as follows: "An action to recover the title to or possession of real property shall be brought within twenty-one years after the cause thereof accrued, but if a person entitled to bring such action, at the time the cause thereof accrues, is within the age of minority, of unsound mind, or imprisoned, such person, after the expiration of twenty-one years from the time the cause of action accrues, may bring such action within ten years after such disability is removed." (Ohio Rev. Code Ann. §2305.04).[11]]

BALDWIN, J. . . .

---

10.   John Cleves Symmes was a Revolutionary War veteran who secured from the federal government in 1792 the Miami Purchase, running northward from the Ohio River between the Miami and Little Miami Rivers. This included the site of Losantiville, later renamed Cincinnati. Washington appointed Symmes a judge of the Northwest Territory. Symmes maintained a constant state of warfare with the territorial governor, St. Clair. Symmes sold to settlers large tracts of land which were not within the Federal grant to him; and, as this case indicates, he sold some land twice. St Clair issued proclamations warning the settlers against him. Sued by numerous settlers to whom he had purported to make sales, Symmes tried to get Congress to bail him out by making further grants; but this effort, though supported by Symmes' son-in-law, William Henry Harrison, failed. Washington, Hamilton, and Jefferson were continually pestered by this business; finally some relief was given to the settlers, but not to Symmes, by preemption rights. The conclusion has been drawn that Symmes was "a far-sighted pioneer, somewhat careless in details, but not intentionally dishonest." Bond, The Civilization of the Old Northwest 85 (1934). — EDS.

11.   The Ohio statute in effect in 1834 was substantially equivalent to the section quoted above.

It was in evidence that the lot in controversy is situated on the corner of Third and Vine streets; fronting on the former one hundred and ninety-eight feet, on the latter ninety-eight feet; the part on Third street is level for a short distance, but descends towards the south along a steep bank, from forty to fifty feet, to its south line; the side of it was washed in gullies, over and around which the people of the place passed and repassed at pleasure. The bed of the lot was principally sand and gravel, with but little loam or soil; the lot was not fenced, nor had any building or improvement been erected or made upon it, until within a few years before suit brought; a fence could have been kept up on the level ground on the top of the hill on Third street, but not on its declivity, on account of the deep gullies washed in the bank; and its principal use and value was in the convenience of digging sand and gravel for the inhabitants. Third street separated this lot from the one on which the defendant resided from 1804, for many years, his mansion fronting on that street; he paid the taxes upon this lot from 1810, until 1834, inclusive; and from the date of the deed from Symmes, until the trial, claimed it as his own. During this time, he also claimed the exclusive right of digging and removing sand and gravel from the lot; giving permission to some, refusing it to others; he brought actions of trespass against those who had done it, and at different times made leases to different persons, for the purpose of taking sand and gravel therefrom, besides taking it for his own use, as he pleased. This had been done by others without his permission, but there was no evidence of his acquiescence in the claim of any person to take or remove the sand or gravel, or that he had ever intermitted his claim to the exclusive right of doing so; on the contrary, several witnesses testified to his continued assertion of right to the lot; their knowledge of his exclusive claim, and their ignorance of any adverse claim for more than twenty-one years before the present suit was brought. They further stated, as their conclusion from these facts, that the defendant had, from 1806, or 7, in the words of one witness, "had possession of the lot"; of another, that since 1804, "he was as perfectly and exclusively in possession, as any person could possibly be of a lot not built on or enclosed"; and of a third, "that since 1811, he had always been in the most rigid possession of the lot in dispute; a similar possession to other possessions on the hill lot." It was further in evidence, that Samuel Williams, under whom the plaintiff claimed, lived in Cincinnati, from 1803, till his death in 1824; was informed of defendant having obtained a deed from Symmes, in 1803, soon after it was obtained, and knew of his claim to the lot; but there was no evidence that he ever made an entry upon it, demanded possession, or exercised or assumed any exercise of ownership over it; though he declared to one witness, produced by plaintiff, that the lot was his, and he intended to claim and improve it when he was able. This declaration was repeated often; from 1803 till the time of his death, and on his deathbed; and it appeared that he was, during all this time, very poor; it also appeared in evidence, by the plaintiff's witness, that the defendant was informed that Williams owned the lot before the deed from Symmes, in 1803, and after he had made the purchase.

This is the substance of the evidence given at the trial, . . . : whereupon the plaintiff's counsel moved the court to instruct the jury that on this evidence the plaintiff was entitled to a verdict; also, that the evidence offered by the plaintiff and defendant was not sufficient, in law, to establish an adverse possession by the defendant; which motions the court overruled. . . .

Before the court could have granted the first motion, they must have been satisfied, that there was nothing in the evidence, or any fact which the jury could lawfully infer therefrom, which could in any way prevent the plaintiff's recovery; if there was any evidence which conduced to prove any fact that could produce such effect, the court must assume such fact to have been proved; for it is the exclusive province of the jury to decide what facts are proved by competent evidence. It was also their province to judge of the credibility of the witnesses, and the weight of their testimony, as tending, in a greater or less degree, to prove the facts relied on; as these were matters with which the court could not interfere, the plaintiff's right to the instruction asked must depend upon the opinion of the court on a finding by the jury in favor of the defendant on every matter which the evidence conduced to prove, giving full credence to the witnesses produced by him, and discrediting the witness for the plaintiff. . . .

An entry by one man on the land of another, is an ouster of the legal possession arising from the title, or not; according to the intention with which it is done: if made under claim and colour of right, it is an ouster; otherwise it is a mere trespass, in legal language the intention guides the entry, and fixes its character. That the evidence in this case justified the jury in finding an entry by the defendant on this lot, as early as 1804, cannot be doubted; nor that he claimed the exclusive right to it under colour of title,[12] from that time till suit brought. There was abundant evidence of the intention with which the first entry was made, as well as of the subsequent acts related by the witnesses, to justify a finding that they were in assertion of a right in himself; so that the only inquiry is, as to the nature of the possession kept up. It is well settled that to constitute an adverse possession, there need not be a fence, building, or other improvement made: 10 Pet. 442: it suffices for this purpose, that visible and notorious acts of ownership are exercised over the premises in controversy, for twenty-one years, after an entry under claim and colour of title. So much depends on the nature and situation of the property, the uses to which it can be applied, or to which the owner or claimant may choose to apply it; that it is difficult to lay down any precise rule adapted to all cases. But it may with safety be said, that where

12. See Kalo, The Doctrine of Color of Title in North Carolina, 13 N.C. Cent. L. Rev. 123 (1982). — Eds.

acts of ownership have been done upon land, which from their nature indicate a notorious claim of property in it, and are continued for twenty-one years, with the knowledge of an adverse claimant without interruption, or an adverse entry by him, for twenty-one years; such acts are evidence of an ouster of a former owner, and an actual adverse possession against him: if the jury shall think, that the property was not susceptible of a more strict, or definite possession than had been so taken, and held. Neither actual occupation, cultivation, or residence, are necessary to constitute actual possession; 6 Pet. 513; when the property is so situated as not to admit of any permanent useful improvement: and the continued claim of the party has been evidenced by public acts of ownership, such as he would exercise over property which he claimed in his own right, and would not exercise over property which he did not claim. Whether this was the situation of the lot in question, or such was the nature of the acts done, was the peculiar province of the jury; the evidence in our opinion was legally sufficient to draw the inference that such were the facts of the case; and if found specially, would have entitled the defendant to the judgment of the court in his favor; they, of course, did not err in refusing to instruct the jury that the evidence was not sufficient to make out an adverse possession. . . .

The judgment of the circuit court is therefore affirmed.

Problems

3.12. Observe that in Ewing v. Burnet the plaintiff did not acquire a right of action until the death of Williams in 1824, ten years before commencement of the action. And Williams had a right of action only from 1804 (on the evidence most favorable to Burnet) until his death in 1824 — which was one year less than the period of the statute of limitations in Ohio. How, then, can there be any contention that the statute has run in Burnet's favor? Consider the following cases under a 21-year statute:

a. A (adverse possessor) enters against O (owner) in 1970. In 1980 O conveys all his right, title and interest to O-2. In 1984 A, having continuously adversely possessed, conveys all his right, title and interest to A-2. How long must A-2's adverse possession continue for him to acquire title? See American Law of Property §15.10 (Casner ed. 1952).

b. T (testator) devises land to L (life tenant) for life, remainder to R (remainderman) in fee. T dies in 1949. Thereafter in 1950 A enters adversely. In 1980 L dies. How long must A continue his adverse possession to get title? See American Law of Property §15.8 (Casner ed. 1952). For an extreme case, see White v. Summers, [1908] 2 Ch. 256.

c. A enters against O in 1960. In 1970 O dies, devising the land to L for life remainder to R in fee. L dies in 1984. A has been in continuous adverse possession. R now brings ejectment against A. What judgment? See American Law of Property §15.8 (Casner ed. 1952).

3.13. Read with utmost care the provisions of the Ohio statute in Ewing v. Burnet. Then apply it to the following cases. O is the owner in 1960; A then enters adversely on July 1, 1960, and continues in adverse possession. The question in each case is: On what date does A acquire title?

  a. O is insane on July 1, 1960. He dies intestate in 1970. H is his heir and has no disability.
  b. O is insane on July 1, 1960. He dies intestate in 1980. H is his heir and has no disability.
  c. O has no disability in 1960. He dies intestate in 1960. H is his heir and is 6 years old.
  d. O is insane on July 1, 1960. He dies intestate in 1980. H is his heir and is 6 years old.
  e. O is 10 years old on July 1, 1960. In 1970 he is convicted of a felony and is imprisoned until 1984.

See generally American Law of Property §15.12 (Casner ed. 1952).

3.14. O owns Blackacre. In 1945 A, an adverse possessor, enters. He remains in adverse possession for 20 years. The statute of limitations in actions of ejectment is 20 years; in actions for trespass and recovery of mesne profits, six years. In 1966 O brings actions against A for (1) damage to the land inflicted by him between 1960 and 1965, (2) profits realized from the land by A between 1960 and 1965. Can O recover? Restatement of Property §224 comment c; ibid., §465.

3.15. O owned some riparian land on the Mississippi River. A acquired title to O's land by adverse possession. During the period of the adverse possession, an island (Tow-Head) formed by accretion in such a way that it would become the property of the owner of the land on the shore. A never occupied the island. Who owns the island, A or O? Davis v. Haines, 349 Ill. 622, 182 N.E. 718 (1932).

3.16. A school district, having a school building on district land, erected a necessary outbuilding on land which district officials believed also to be district land, but which actually belonged to Benson. The outbuilding thus remained for the period of the statute of limitations. Benson then discovered the error and called it to the attention of district officials. They expressed regret and removed the outbuilding to district land at the expense of $25. New district officials, wishing to erect still another outbuilding, brought an action of ejectment against Benson for the land on which the first outbuilding had stood. What judgment? Inhabitants of School District No. 4 v. Benson, 31 Me. 381 (1850); Statute of Frauds §1, page 695 *infra.* See American Law of Property §15.14 (Casner ed. 1952).

3.17. Is B's possession "adverse" to A under the following circumstances? A and B are next-door neighbors, members of the same club, and good friends. B decides he wants to put an ornamental white picket fence around his garden. He tells A that he wants to be sure to put the fence in the proper place; so A and B together measure off the two lots and agree as to where the dividing line is. B puts his fence on the agreed line, cultivates his garden up to the fence, and continues doing this for 20 years. (The controlling statute of limitations is 20 years.) B then dies intestate and it appears from an accurate survey that B's fence and garden encroach on A's land by six feet. At all times during the 20 years B believed the fence was on the correct boundary and would have moved the fence back if the true situation had been called to his attention. Who owns the six feet of ground, as between A and B's heirs? Grube v. Wells, 34 Iowa 148 (1871); Daily v. Boudreau, 231 Ill. 228, 83 N.E. 218 (1907); Joiner v. Janssen, 85 Ill. 2d 74, 421 N.E.2d 170 (1981); Boyer v. Noirot, 97 Ill. App. 3d 636, 423 N.E.2d 274 (1981); American Law of Property §§15.4,15.5 (Casner ed. 1952).

3.18. New York-Kentucky Oil & Gas Co. v. Miller, 187 Ky. 742, 220 S.W. 535 (1920), points out that in determining the extent of an adverse possession which can ripen into title under the statute of limitations, the deed under which the possessor claims title is relevant. If the possessor occupies adversely a portion of the land, the balance of the area covered by the deed is also considered to be adversely possessed even though the adverse possessor never actually goes on the rest of the land. This is sometimes referred to as the doctrine of "constructive adverse possession." Dills v. Hubbard, 21 Ill. 328 (1859); American Law of Property §15.11 (Casner ed. 1952). Under this doctrine, consider the following case:

a. There are adjoining lots, X and Y. A owns lot X and B owns lot Y. A executes a conveyance of both lots to C. C enters upon lot X, claiming both lots under A's deed. He continues thus to occupy for the period of the statute of limitations. At the end of the period, who owns lot Y? Bailey v. Carleton, 12 N.H. 9 (1841).

b. Lot X is located in Boston and lot Y is located in Chicago. Both lots are owned by O. A executes a conveyance of both lots to B. B enters upon lot X, claiming both lots under A's deed. He continues thus to occupy for the period of the statute of limitations. At the end of the period, who owns lot Y?

BRUMAGIM v. BRADSHAW
39 Cal. 24 (1870)

[This action of ejectment was originally brought by Robert Dyson against T. T. Bradshaw and others. Dyson died after the action was brought, and Brumagim, his administrator, was substituted as plaintiff. The plaintiff alleged that he was in possession of a tract of land known as the Potrero and had been in possession thereof for several years; that the defendants, being trespassers without title, had entered upon the said land; and that defendants were remaining upon said land without right. The answer was a general denial.

After a judgment for the plaintiff the defendants appealed. The instruction of the court to the jury, to which the defendants objected and upon which they base their appeal, appears in the opinion.]

CROCKETT, J. . . .

At the instance of the plaintiff, the court gave twelve instructions to the jury, the second of which is in the following words: —

If the jury are satisfied from the evidence given in this cause, that George Treat entered upon the inclosed the Potrero in the year 1850, and are further satisfied that he then made a complete inclosure of the same, and that such inclosure was sufficient to turn and protect stock, and that he actually used such inclosure for that purpose up to the time of the alleged conveyance to Dyson, and that he deeded the same to Dyson, and that the land was used by Dyson subsequent thereto, for the purpose of pasturage, and that the land was suitable for pasturage; and that the defendants, or either of them who have answered, or those under whom they claim, entered adversely and subsequent to the completion of said inclosure, and while the said land was being so used by said Treat prior, and, by said Dyson, after said conveyance, you will find for the plaintiff against such defendant, or defendants, provided such defendant, or defendants, was occupying the premises at the time of the commencement of this suit.

This instruction is objected to by the defendants as wholly unauthorized by the testimony, and calculated to mislead the jury.

There is no contrariety in the evidence as to the natural features of the Potrero, nor as to the acts performed by Treat or Dyson, which, it is claimed amounted, in law, to an inclosure and to the actual possession of the land. The testimony shows the Potrero to be a peninsula, containing about one thousand acres; bounded on the north by Mission creek and bay, on the east by the bay of San Francisco, on the south by the same bay and Precita creek, and on the west by a stone wall and ditch, running from Mission creek on the north to Precita creek on the south, across the neck of the peninsula. It further appears that the wall and ditch were ancient works, probably built by the priests of the adjoining Mission of Dolores at an early day; and that in 1850 they had become considerably dilapidated, so as no longer to prevent the ingress and egress of cattle; that John Treat, or George Treat, or the two jointly, in the summer or autumn of 1850, repaired the wall and ditch, so as that, thereafter, it was sufficient to turn cattle; that they erected a gate in the wall, through which admission was had to the Potrero, and a small corral, for herding cattle, inside the wall, together with a shanty, in which the gate-keeper resided; that, immediately after the wall was repaired and the gate erected, they commenced to receive horses for pasturage and used the Potrero for the purpose — having, at times, several hundred head of horses pasturing there for hire; that, whilst the land was being thus used, John Treat relinquished to George Treat all his interest in the premises, who thereafter continued to use the land for pasturage, as it had before been used, until February, 1852, when he conveyed, by deed, to Dyson, all his interest in the property; and thereafter Dyson used the land for pasturage up to the time when the defendants entered; that the wall and ditch, together with the creeks and bay, formed an inclosure sufficient to protect and turn cattle; that, in 1850, and for several years hereafter, the Potrero afforded grass suitable for pasturage.

If the fact does not sufficiently appear in proof, the Court will take judicial notice that the Potrero in the year 1850 was separated from the City of San Francisco, as it then was, only by Mission creek and bay, and that it is now a portion of the city, divided into lots, blocks and streets. . . .

. . . It is clearly established, both by reason and authority, that the acts of ownership and dominion over land, which may be sufficient to constitute an actual possession, vary according to the condition, size and locality of the tract. If it contain but one acre, and have upon it a valuable quarry of stone or marble, and be not adapted to any other use than as a quarry, and if it be openly claimed and actually and notoriously used for that purpose, for a reasonable time, this might be such an act of dominion over it as to establish an actual possession, even though there was no inclosure or residence upon it. So if it be a small parcel, containing a mine, the working of the mine, in the usual manner, might establish an actual possession at common law, without the aid of our mining laws and in the absence of any inclosure. But if the tract contain one thousand acres, with a mine or a quarry on one margin of it, no one would maintain that the mere working of the mine or quarry, without other acts of ownership, would establish a possession of the whole tract. . . .

. . . The general principle which underlies all this class of cases is, that the acts of dominion must be adapted to the particular land, its condition, locality and appropriate use. The philosophy of the rule is, that by such acts the party proclaims to the public that he asserts an exclusive ownership over the land, and the acts which he performs are in harmony with his claim of title. . . .

. . . If, for example, a tract be inclosed on three of its sides by a substantial fence, and the fourth side front upon the ocean, or a deep river, or a precipitous cliff, the erection of the fence would, doubtless, clearly enough indicate to the public that the land was appropriated; or, if there be a small peninsula, containing but a few acres, a fence across the neck of it might accomplish the same result. But it is evident that where natural barriers form much the greater portion of the inclosure, the rule to which we have adverted is not of universal application, but must be varied according to the circumstances of each particular case. . . .

. . . The general principle pervading all this class of cases, where the inclosure consists wholly or partially of natural barriers, is, that the acts of dominion and ownership which establish a possessio pedis must correspond, in a reasonable degree, with the size of the tract, its condition and appropriate use, and must be such as usually accompany the ownership of land similarly situated. But, in such cases, it is the peculiar province of the jury, under proper instructions from the court, to decide whether or not the acts of dominion relied upon, considering the size of the tract, its peculiar condition and appropriate use, were of such a character as usually accompany the ownership of lands similarly situated. . . . The Court should have instructed the jury, that, if all the facts hypothetically stated in the second instruction were true, it was the province of the jury to decide, considering the quantity, quality and character of the land, whether or not these acts of dominion were sufficient and had the effect, upon the facts proved, to give notice to the public that Treat, first, and Dyson, as his successor in interest, had appropriated the land and claimed the exclusive dominion over it; and if this be answered in the affirmative, then, that there had been established in Treat, first, and, afterwards in Dyson, an actual possession. . . .

For these reasons, the judgment should be reversed and a new trial ordered.

MENDONCA v. CITIES SERVICE OIL CO.
354 Mass. 323, 237 N.E.2d 16 (1968)

KIRK, J.

This bill in equity was brought to enjoin the defendant from entering upon a strip of land (the strip) which the plaintiffs claim to have acquired by adverse possession and to recover damages for trespass. Annexed to the plaintiffs' bill is a copy of an affidavit, signed by them and recorded in the registry of deeds on July 17, 1964, claiming title to the strip by adverse possession. In its answer the defendant asked for affirmative relief against the claim and the acts of the plaintiffs.

The defendant appeals from a decree that the plaintiffs acquired the strip by adverse possession. The plaintiffs appeal because no damages were awarded. The judge made a statutory report of material facts. The evidence is reported. It consists of stipulations made at the trial, of exhibits including deeds, a plan and photographs, and the entire transcript of testimony. . . .

The parties own adjacent lots in New Bedford. It is undisputed that record title to a parcel of land including the disputed strip has been in the defendant since 1936 and that taxes on the whole parcel have been assessed to it and paid by it to the city since 1936. The defendant's predecessor, Cities Service Refining Company, had purchased the property in 1927. The defendant's parcel is at the southwest corner of the intersection of Emma Street and Brock Avenue. Emma Street runs east to west; Brock Avenue runs generally north to south. Since 1936 the defendant has operated a gasoline station on the property. It is also undisputed that the plaintiffs hold title as tenants by the entirety to the lot adjoining the defendant's on Emma Street by virtue of a deed dated February 14, 1957; that the deed to the plaintiffs and the deeds to their predecessors in title, dating back to 1923, were all warranty deeds, and that none of them purported to convey the disputed strip to the grantee. All of the deeds in the plaintiff's chain of title define or describe the north (Emma Street) and south boundaries of the plaintiffs' lot as forty-one feet long.

It is the plaintiffs' position that by adverse possession the north (Emma Street) and south boundaries of their property have been extended approximately twenty-four feet easterly into the property of the defendant, encompassing a strip ninety feet long, for a total of 2,187 square feet. They contend that they and their predecessors in title have occupied the strip (twenty-four feet wide and ninety feet long) adversely to the defendant for more than twenty years and now own it under G.L. c.260, §21.

There was no finding and there was no evidence to warrant a finding of adverse use prior to 1936. The plaintiffs' case must stand or fall on events commencing with that year. We have considered all of the evidence in the case and have weighed and measured it with due regard to the findings of the judge. We conclude for purposes of this decision that it is unnecessary to recount the evidence in detail or to embark upon a dissertation on the propriety of the legal significance or nonsignificance given to the evidence by the judge. There is no doubt that the defendant erected and maintained a fence parallel to and more than twenty-four feet from its ninety foot west boundary until 1951. There is no doubt that the plaintiffs and some of their predecessors made use of the strip for various purposes without protest or objection by the defendant, nor is there any doubt that a chain link fence was erected in 1941 by one of the plaintiffs' predecessors in title on the Emma Street side of the strip. But there likewise is no doubt as the judge found, and his finding is firmly supported by the evidence, that "[i]n 1951 the defendant rebuilt the gas station renovating the small building and adding thereto a large lubrication bay which extended the building both toward Emma Street and back in the direction of the disputed area. During this renovation work the contractor used the disputed area for the storage of building materials and equipment for a period of three or four weeks without protest from the then current owner of the plaintiffs' land. As part of the work, the contractor tore down both of the fences . . . [which the defendant had erected and] which were then in poor repair. A new wooden fence was erected across the lot parallel to and about twenty-four feet from the boundary line between the parcels."

The judge concluded his findings of fact with the statement, "On all the evidence I find as a matter of fact that plaintiffs and their predecessors in title had actual open, continuous possession of the disputed area under a claim of right or title for a period of over twenty years." We think this ultimate finding is plainly wrong. "Acquisition of title through adverse possession is a fact . . . to be proved by the one asserting the title. The burden of proof extends to all of the necessary elements of such possession and includes the obligation to show that it was actual, open, continuous, and under a claim of right or title." Holmes v. Johnson, 324 Mass. 450, 453, 86 N.E.2d 924, 926, and cases cited. If any of these elements is left in doubt, the claimant cannot prevail. Gadreault v. Hillman, 317 Mass. 656, 661, 59 N.E.2d 477; Holmes v. Johnson, 324 Mass. 450, 453, 86 N.E.2d 924.

The plaintiffs cannot prevail here because the use of the strip by the defendant in 1951 broke the requisite element of continuity of possession. Any adverse use subsequent to 1936 was interrupted before twenty years had lapsed; and any adverse use since 1951 falls short of the required twenty years. The removal of the fences and the use of the strip during the remodeling of the station were acts of dominion by the defendant consistent with its title of record.

The final decree must be reversed. A decree is to be entered (1) confirming the title of Cities Service Oil Company to the area described as the second parcel in the deed to it dated December 23, 1936, recorded with Bristol South District registry of deeds, book 788, page 81; (2) declaring the plaintiffs' affidavit recorded in the same registry on July 17, 1964, book 1452, page 345, to be null and void; (3) enjoining permanently the plaintiffs and the members of their family, tenants, agents or servants from trespassing on any part of the defendant's premises as described above in clause (1); and (4) dismissing the plaintiffs' bill.

So ordered.[13]

Note: Adverse Possession of Chattels

O'Keefe v. Snyder, 83 N.J. 478, 416 A.2d 862 (1980), involved some paintings that were stolen from a New York art gallery in 1946. Georgia O'Keefe was the artist and owner of the paintings. O'Keefe did not discover who had the paintings until 1975 when she learned that they had been purchased by Snyder for $35,000 from a person named Frank who acquired them as a result of the death of his father in 1968. The statute of limitations pertaining to an action of replevin is six years. Does the statute of limitations begin to run during the period O'Keefe did not know who held the paintings? The court concluded that the so-called discovery rule applied to an action for replevin of a painting. "O'Keefe's cause of action accrued when she first knew, or reasonably should have known through the exercise of due

---

13. See generally on the subject of adverse possession the following: Ballantine, Claim of Title in Adverse Possession, 28 Yale L.J. 219 (1918); Ballantine, Title by Adverse Possession, 32 Harv. L. Rev. 135 (1918); Bordwell, Mistake and Adverse Possession, 7 Iowa L. Bull. 129 (1922); Sternberg, The Element of Hostility in Adverse Possession, 6 Temp. L.Q. 207 (1932); Taylor, Titles to Land by Adverse Possession, 20 Iowa L. Rev. 551, 738 (1935); Taylor, Actual Possession in Adverse Possession of Land, 25 Iowa L. Rev. 78 (1939); Walsh, Title by Adverse Possession, 16 N.Y.U.L.Q. Rev. 532 and 17 N.Y.U.L.Q. Rev. 44 (1939); Helmholz, Adverse Possession and Subjective Intent, 61 Wash. Uni. L.Q. 331 (1983); American Law of Property §§15.1-15.16 (Casner ed. 1952). — Eds.

diligence, of the cause of action, including the identity of the possessor of the paintings."

The court in the *O'Keefe* case regarded the "discovery rule" as fulfilling the purposes of the statute of limitations as applied to personal property that is lost or stolen and specifically overruled a prior New Jersey case to the extent it held that the doctrine of adverse possession applies to chattels. The following is quoted from the court's opinion:

> The considerations are different with real estate, and there is no reason to disturb the application of the doctrine of adverse possession to real estate. Real estate is fixed and cannot be moved or concealed. The owner of real estate knows or should know where his property is located and reasonably can be expected to be aware of open, notorious, visible, hostile continuous acts of possession on it.
>
> Our ruling not only changes the requirements for acquiring title to personal property after an alleged unlawful taking, but also shifts the burden of proof at trial. Under the doctrine of adverse possession, the burden is on the possessor to prove the elements of adverse possession. [citation omitted] Under the discovery rule, the burden is on the owner as the one seeking the benefit of the rule to establish facts that would justify deferring the beginning of the period of limitations. [83 N.J. at 499-500, 416 A.2d at 873.]

The defendant in the *O'Keefe* case is one who is a bona fide purchaser of the paintings. This should be kept in mind when you examine the material in Chapter 9.

CHAPTER 4

REMEDIES OF A POSSESSOR WHO HAS LESS THAN COMPLETE OWNERSHIP

Note: *The Relativity of Title*

Here we meet the concept of the relativity of title—the notion that A can have title as against B, but not as against C. To put it differently, what we call "title" to land or a chattel is not so much a relationship to the thing as it is a relationship to a multitude of other people with reference to the thing. Some say that an owner has a bundle of rights against various people. Yale's great legal analyst, Professor Wesley N. Hohfeld, refined this notion further by describing ownership as an aggregate of rights, powers, privileges, and immunities, and minutely defining and analyzing each of these.[1]

We also meet here a three-party problem where one of the parties is absent, and where, therefore, we must consider (1) the impact of any decision upon the absent person, and (2) the impact upon the present parties of future action the absent third party may take. The problem is not a simple one. The realities of any given situation are not easily apparent. History has a tendency to confuse rather than to assist. Tempting analogies are deceptive. Yet a workable body of law, self-consistent to the extent judicial tradition requires, must be developed. This is our task.

We deal here with four types of possessors who have something less than full title—a finder (Armory v. Delamirie), a bailee (The Winkfield), a life tenant (Zimmerman v. Shreeve and the *Rogers* case), and one who, as far as the proof goes, has no legal right at all beyond his or her possession (the rest of the cases).

---

1. Hohfeld's doctrine is found in Fundamental Legal Conceptions (1923), a book expanding articles in 23 Yale L.J. 16 (1913) and 26 Yale L.J. 710 (1917). Hohfeld's gift of expression was not felicitous, but his ideas were restated with great effect by Professor Corbin in Legal Analysis and Terminology, 29 Yale L.J. 163 (1919), and Rights and Duties, 33 Yale L.J. 501 (1924).

ARMORY v. DELAMIRIE
1 Str. 505 (K.B. 1722)

The plaintiff being a chimney sweeper's boy found a jewel and carried it to the defendant's shop (who was a goldsmith) to know what it was, and delivered it into the hands of the apprentice, who under pretense of weighing it, took out the stones, and calling to the master to let him know it came to three halfpence, the master offered the boy the money, who refused to take it, and insisted to have the thing again; whereupon the apprentice delivered him back the socket without the stones. And now in trover against the master these points were ruled:

1. That the finder of a jewel, though he does not by such finding acquire an absolute property or ownership, yet he has such a property as will enable him to keep it against all but the rightful owner, and consequently may maintain trover.

2. That the action well lay against the master, who gives a credit to his apprentice, and is answerable for his neglect.

3. As to the value of the jewel several of the trade were examined to prove what a jewel of the finest water that would fit the socket would be worth; and the Chief Justice (Pratt, C.J.) directed the jury that unless the defendant did produce the jewel and show it not to be of the finest water, they should presume the strongest against him and make the value of the best jewels the measure of their damages: which they accordingly did.

Note: The Sweep and the Pawnbroker

Armory v. Delamirie is a celebrated case, though the reason for this is something of a mystery: it is a nisi prius decision on a point which hardly seems global in its implications. Yet the saga of the Sweep and the Pawnbroker appears in Smith's Leading Cases (Vol. 1, p. 385) and is rendered into parody verse by Sir Frederick Pollock in Leading Cases Done Into English (1892). For an illustrated version, see Harvard Law School Year Book, 1940-1941, at 25.

The result seems fair enough until you realize that the Sweep didn't own the jewel. What happens now when the owner appears and demands the jewel from Delamirie? Or, to put it differently, if you represented Delamirie after the rendition of judgment in this case, what would you advise your client as to the dangers of his or her position and what he or she should do to avoid them? In considering this question, note the following sentence which appears in the Winkfield case which follows: "The wrongdoer, having once paid full damages to the bailee, has an answer to any action by the bailor."

Problems

4.1. O owns a bag of cement. It falls off his truck onto the road. A picks it up. Then it falls off A's truck and B finds it. Can A recover from B the bag of cement or its value?

4.2. Reexamine the distinction made between lost and mislaid property in McAvoy v. Medina referred to in Problem 3.2 *supra*. Is this distinction relevant in solving the issue presented in Armory v. Delamirie?

THE WINKFIELD
[1900-1903] All E.R. 346 (P. 1901)

[On April 5, 1900, the Winkfield collided with and sank the Mexican off the coast of Cape Colony, South Africa. The owners of the Winkfield admitted liability for one half of the damage done to the Mexican and her cargo and obtained a decree (under §503 of the Merchant Shipping Act, 1894) limiting their liability to £8 per ton and paid into court £32,514. Against this fund, claims by the owners of the Mexican, passengers, crew, and cargo owners were filed totaling £90,085.

A substantial amount of mail was lost on the Mexican, and the postmaster general filed three classes of claims therefor:

1. £105 for mail bags and parcels which were Crown property,

2. £5,041 for parcels of which the owners had given the postmaster general written authority to represent them, and

3. £1,726, the estimated value of letters and parcels in respect of which no claim had been made by, or instructions received from, the senders or addressees, but which the postmaster general undertook to distribute amongst them. The postmaster general undertook to indemnify the fund in court against any claims put forward by the actual owners of these parcels.

The president of the Probate, Divorce and Admiralty Division (Sir F. H. Jeune) allowed claims (1) and (2) but disallowed claim (3) on the ground, conceded by all parties, that the postmaster general was not liable to the senders or addressees of these parcels for their loss. The postmaster general appealed from the disallowance of claim (3).]

COLLINS, M.R. . . .

The case was dealt with by all parties in the court below as a claim by a bailee who was under no liability to his bailor for the loss in question. . . .

It seems to me that the position, that possession is good against a wrongdoer and that the latter cannot set up the jus tertii unless he claims under it, is well established in our law, and really concludes this case against the respondents. . . . And the principle being the same, it follows that he can equally recover the whole value of the goods in an action on the case for their loss through the tortious conduct of the defendant. I think it involves this also, that the wrongdoer who is not defending under the title of the bailor is quite unconcerned with what the rights are between the bailor and bailee, and must treat the possessor as the owner of the goods for all purposes quite irrespective of the rights and obligations as between him and the bailor. . . .

. . . It cannot be denied that since the case of Armory v. Delamirie, 1 Stra. 524, not to mention earlier cases from the Year Books onward, a mere finder may recover against a wrongdoer the full value of the thing converted. That decision involves the principle that as between possessor and wrongdoer the presumption of law is, in the words of Lord Campbell in Jeffries v. Great Western Ry. Co., 5 E. & B. 802, at p. 806, "that the person who has possession has the property." In the same case he says (at p. 805):

> I am of opinion that the law is that a person possessed of goods as his property has a good title as against every stranger, and that one who takes them from him, having no title in himself, is a wrongdoer, and cannot defend himself by shewing that there was title in some third person, for *against a wrongdoer possession is title.* The law is so stated by the very learned annotator in his note to Wilbraham v. Snow, [2 Wms. Saund. 47 f.].

Therefore it is not open to the defendant, being a wrongdoer, to inquire into the nature or limitation of the possessor's right, and unless it is competent for him to do so the question of his relation to, or liability towards, the true owner cannot come into the discussion at all; and, therefore, as between those two parties full damages have to be paid without any further inquiry. The extent of the liability of the finder to the true owner not being relevant to the discussion between him and the wrongdoer, the facts which would ascertain it would not have been admissible in evidence, and therefore the right of the finder to recover full damages cannot be made to depend upon the extent of his liability over to the true owner. To hold otherwise would, it seems to me, be in effect to permit a wrongdoer to set up a jus tertii under which he cannot claim. But, if this be the fact in the case of a finder, why should it not be equally the fact in the case of a bailee? Why, as against a wrongdoer, should the nature of the plaintiff's interest in the thing converted be any more relevant to the inquiry, and therefore admissible in evidence, than in the case of a finder? It seems to me that neither in one case nor the other ought it to be competent for the defendant to go into evidence on that matter. . . .

. . . As between bailee and stranger, possession gives title — that is, not a limited interest, but absolute and complete ownership, and he is entitled to receive back a complete equivalent for the whole loss or deterioration of the thing itself. As between bailer and bailee the real interests of each must be inquired into, and, as the bailee has to account for the thing bailed, so he must account for that which has become its equivalent and now represents it. What he has received above his own interest he has received to the use of his bailor. The wrongdoer, having once paid full damages to the bailee, has an answer to any action by the bailor. See Com. Dig. Trespass B. 4, citing Roll. 551, 1.31,569, 1.22, Story on Bailments, 9th ed. s. 352, and the numerous authorities there cited. . . .

STIRLING and MATHEW, L.JJ., concurred.

Appeal allowed.[2]

Problems

4.3. In the *Winkfield* case, the bailors were unknown at the time of the litigation. The true owner was also unknown at the time of the litigation in Armory v. Delamirie. In the normal bailment case, the bailee will know who the bailor is and the bailee will have to account to the bailor for any damages recovered by the bailee. In this situation, what is the justification, if any, in allowing the bailee to recover damages from the wrongdoer?

4.4. O owned a watch. O lost the watch, and A found it. A loaned the watch to B. The watch was wrongfully taken from B by C. If B sues C and recovers the value of the watch, will C have title to the watch as against A? As against O? In answering this question, consider the applicability of the statement in The Winkfield that "the wrongdoer, having once paid full damages to the bailee, has an answer to any action by the bailor."

4.5. George owned an automobile. He loaned it to his sister, Emily, for the day. While Emily was driving the car on her own business, Forsyth negligently ran his car into it. Emily was badly injured, and the car was smashed up to the extent of $570. Emily brought an action of tort against Forsyth and in her declaration alleged her personal injuries only. On the same day, and by the same attorneys, George brought an action of tort against Forsyth and in his declaration alleged the damage to the car. Forsyth settled with Emily, paying her $3,500. Emily signed a release reading:

> I, Emily Belli, for myself, my executors, administrators, and assigns, hereby release and discharge Albert C. Forsyth from all claims and demands of whatsoever nature which I now have against him, or hereafter shall have against him by reason of any thing which has occurred from the beginning of the world to the date of this instrument, and particularly from all claims for personal injury and/or property damage arising out of an automobile accident while I was driving my brother's car.

Forsyth's original answer in George's action for property damage was a general denial and allegation of contributory negligence. Cf. Nash v. Lang, 268 Mass. 407, 167 N.E. 762 (1929). After Emily signed the release, Forsyth amended his answer, alleging that George's claim had been released. At this point George concludes that new counsel would be desirable and retains

2. See Note, Bailment: The Winkfield Doctrine, 34 Cornell L.Q. 615 (1949).—EDS.

you. What steps do you take, what evidence do you offer, and what arguments do you make on George's behalf? Belli v. Forsyth, 301 Mass. 203, 16 N.E.2d 656 (1938); Associates Discount Corp. v. Gillineau, 322 Mass. 490, 78 N.E.2d 192 (1948).

4.6. An automobile operated by O's bailee, A, is in collision with one owned and operated by X. X sues A for damages to X's car, alleging that A was negligent and that X was not. X prevails. The next day, O sues X for damages to O's car, alleging that X was negligent. X argues that it has already been adjudicated that X was not negligent, and that therefore judgment should go for X. What judgment? See Hudson Transit Corp. v. Antonucci, 137 N.J.L. 704, 61 A.2d 180 (1948).

4.7. An automobile operated by O's bailee, A, is in collision with one owned and operated by X. O sues X for damages to O's car, alleging that X was negligent. O prevails. The next day, X sues A for damages to X's car, alleging that A was negligent. A argues that it has already been adjudicated that X was negligent, and that judgment should go for A. What judgment? See Hornstein v. Kramer Brothers Freight Lines, 133 F.2d 143 (3d Cir. 1943).

Note: *Effect if the Plaintiff-Possessor Obtains Possession Wrongfully*

If the plaintiff by theft obtained possession of the property wrongfully damaged by another, is he or she to be given the same access to the courts to protect his or her wrongfully obtained possessory interest as a finder or bailee? Anderson v. Gouldberg, 51 Minn. 294, 53 N.W. 636 (1892), provides as follows:

> One who has acquired the possession of property, whether by finding, bailment, or by a mere tort, has a right to retain the possession as against a mere wrongdoer who is a stranger to the property. Any other rule would lead to an endless series of unlawful seizures and reprisals in every case where property had once passed out of the possession of the rightful owner. [51 Minn. at 296, 53 N.W. at 637.]

ZIMMERMAN v. SHREEVE
59 Md. 357 (1882)

[Mary E. Shreeve died in 1866 owning an outlying, unenclosed mountain lot. She devised this in her will to her children for their respective lives; upon the death of any child, his or her share was to go to his or her issue in fee simple. The plaintiff, one of the children of Mary E. Shreeve, bought up the interests of his brothers and sisters and took conveyances of those interests.

The defendant cut timber on this land and carried away considerable quantities of rails, posts, logs, tan bark, etc. These facts were undisputed.

The plaintiff-appellee brought an action of trespass quare clausum fregit against the defendant-appellant for the damage thus caused. At the trial, the court instructed the jury that the plaintiff could recover the full amount of the damage done. The defendant excepted to this instruction and appealed from the judgment rendered upon the jury's verdict.]

ALVEY, J. . . .

The gist of the action of trespass quare clausum fregit is the injury to the plaintiff's possession, and therefore, to maintain the action, it is essential that he be either in the actual or constructive possession of the locus in quo, at the time of the injury done. Gent v. Lynch, 23 Md. 58. The damages will vary, and must be measured, according to the interest of the plaintiff in the locus in quo. This rule of damages is founded upon obvious principles of justice, as otherwise the plaintiff might get extravagant recompense for the injury to the land, when his interest therein was limited, or upon the eve of expiring, and the defendant might be made liable for the same damages to different persons. It is well settled that the same acts of trespass may inflict injuries upon different rights, for which the defendant may be liable in several actions, to different persons, according to the nature and extent of the injury inflicted. In the case of a tenant, whether for life or for years, he may sue and recover for the injury to his possession and right of enjoyment, and the reversioner or remainder-man may sue and recover for any injury sustained to the estate in reversion or remainder. And where there are several entitled in succession, as tenants for life, in tail, or in fee, they can recover only damages commensurate to the injury done to their respective estates. The damages, therefore, must be assessed with reference to the extent of the several interests affected.

In the case of a tenant for life, he is entitled of right, to take reasonable estovers from the land, that is, wood for fuel, fences, agricultural erections, and other necessary improvements and repairs. But, under this right of estovers, the tenant cannot destroy or dispose of the timber, nor do any other permanent injury to the estates in reversion or remainder; for that would subject him to the action and penalties of waste. Co. Litt., 41, b, and 73, a; 4 Kent Com., 73; 1 Washb. R. Pro., 115, 116, (3rd Ed.). The tenant must cut only such wood and timber as he may need for immediate use, and not in anticipation; and he must cut only such timber as is fit for the use for which he is allowed to take it. And, as a general principle, whatever wood or timber he is allowed to cut, he must use upon the premises, and not elsewhere. 1 Washb. R. Pro., (3rd Ed.) 116, and the cases there cited. If, therefore, this right of estovers, thus limited and restricted, be disturbed or impaired by a trespasser, the tenant for life is entitled to recover for the injury he may have sustained in respect of that right.

But in the present case, the lot trespassed upon was an outlying, unenclosed mountain lot, used exclusively for its wood and timber, and which constituted its main value. Such timber lots are generally used in connection with separate farm land, and as means of supplying the necessary wood and timber to the farm. In such case, the injury to the possessory right, by cutting and carrying away the wood and timber, consists in the damage done to the right to use such wood and timber by the life tenant, according to the customary mode of user; such user to be reasonable, and confined to such wood and timber as could be taken for ordinary estovers; and any trespass that disturbs and impairs such beneficial user by the tenant for life is an injury for which he may recover.

By the instruction, however, . . . no reference whatever is made to the several interests or estates of the tenant for life and that of the parties entitled in remainder; and though the cutting of trees, and the hauling away of rails, cross-ties, or other articles made of trees cut upon the premises, may have occasioned serious damage to the estate in remainder, yet, according to the instruction given, the whole amount of damage is required to be rendered to the plaintiff, the tenant for life. This, we think, was error. The jury should have been instructed with reference to the interest or estate of the plaintiff, and the injury thereto by the trespass of the defendant; and not have been allowed to award compensation to the plaintiff for an injury done to the estate of another. . . .

We shall reverse the judgment and award a new trial.

Judgment reversed, and new trial ordered.

ROGERS v. ATLANTIC, GULF & PACIFIC CO.
213 N.Y. 246, 107 N.E. 661 (1915)

Appeal from a judgment of the Appellate Division of the Supreme Court in the third judicial department, entered October 14, 1912, affirming a judgment in favor of plaintiff entered upon a verdict.

The nature of the action and the facts, so far as material, are stated in the opinion.

MILLER, J. The plaintiff, a life tenant, has recovered a judgment for all of the damages, both to the life estate and to the inheritance, caused by a fire set by the defendant, a canal contractor, on adjoining lands of the state, and negligently allowed to spread to the lands of the plaintiff. The single question involved in this appeal is whether the recovery should have been limited to the damages to the life estate. The right of the plaintiff to recover all of the damages has thus far been maintained on the ground that she is liable to the remaindermen for any injury to the inheritance not caused by them, the act of God or the public enemy. . . .

[Here the learned judge examined the question whether a life tenant is liable to a remainderman for damage caused by the negligence of a third person but without negligence by the life tenant. The following is a summary of this portion of the opinion:

The obligations of life tenant to remainderman or reversioner are governed by the law of waste. *Voluntary waste* consists of the commission of some destructive act, such as pulling down a house; the life tenant is liable for such acts. *Permissive waste* consists of neglect or omission to do what will prevent injury, such as allowing a house to fall into disrepair. The type of injury caused in the present case, i.e., by negligence of a third person, is permissive waste if it is waste at all. Lord Coke believed that the Statute of Gloucester, 6 Ed. I, c. 5, made the life tenant liable for permissive waste, including the type here in question. 2 Inst. 145, 303. However, it is not clear that the English law has followed Coke, and it is clear that the reasons given by Coke no longer exist today. In New York there has been no case which imposes upon a life tenant liability for this type of damage. However, there are cases—e.g., Cook v. Champlain Transportation Co., 1 Denio 91—in which it is *said* that the life tenant would be liable to the remainderman and that for that reason he is able to recover full damages from the wrongdoer.]

The doctrine has only been invoked in this state to permit the tenant to recover from the wrongdoer. And it may well be that a rule so long recognized may be adhered to without adopting the reason originally assigned to it. . . . Notwithstanding the removal of the impediments of the ancient common law, there will be many cases in which, for practical reasons, the tenant alone can compel redress from the wrongdoer, and it should not be open to the latter to escape liability by asserting the rights of a third party under whom he does not claim. The tenant has not only possession, but an interest in the premises, in this case a life estate, and there is equal, if not greater, reason for allowing a full recovery by him as for allowing a depositary, who has no interest, but only possession, to recover for the conversion of, or an injury to, the deposit. A bailee, though not liable to the bailor, may recover for the wrongful act of a third party resulting in the loss of, or injury to, the subject of the bailment. If the bailee recovers, he holds the recovery as trustee for the bailor. . . .

The recovery in this case might be treated as a substitute pro tanto for the land damaged, as would be the case of the proceeds of a sale (see Ackerman v. Gorton, 67 N.Y. 63), the plaintiff being entitled to the life use of it and becoming trustee of the principal for the remaindermen. (See Smith v. Van Ostrand, 64 N.Y. 278; Leggett v. Stevens, 185 N.Y. 70, at page 76.) The recovery might be apportioned between life tenant and remaindermen according to their respective interests and the court might require the life tenant, if intrusted with the principal, to give security. (See Matter of Cant, 126 N.Y. 377; Matter of McDougall, 141 N.Y. 21.) It is for the court to make proper provision for the protection of the rights of remaindermen. The wrongdoer is only concerned in being protected from a second suit, and we are of the opinion that it must be held, as a necessary corollary to the proposition that the life tenant may recover all the damages, that such a recovery will bar an action by the remaindermen.

The judgment should be affirmed, with costs.

WERNER, HISCOCK, CHASE, COLLIN, HOGAN and CARDOZO, J.J., concur. Judgment affirmed.

Note: *Valuation of Life Interests*

Section 118 of the Restatement of Property adopts the rule of Zimmerman v. Shreeve as follows:
"The measure of the damages recoverable by the owner of the estate for life is the difference between the value of the estate for life before and its value after the violation. . . ."
The method of making this evaluation is illustrated as follows:

> X, wherein Blackacre is located, utilizes the American Experience Table of Mortality in computing the value of estates for life and computes such value on the basis of a 5 per cent return to the life beneficiary. At age 48, a 5 per cent annuity for life is worth 12.13275 years' annual income. A, owning Blackacre in fee simple absolute, transfers Blackacre "to B for life, remainder to C and his heirs." Blackacre is a city lot improved with a residence. If vacant it would have value as a site for a gasoline dispensing station. On the day when B is 48 years of age, D negligently causes the structure on Blackacre to be consumed by fire. Prior to this destruction an estate in fee simple absolute in Blackacre was worth $10,000 and after this destruction such estate is worth $4,000. By calculation, B's estate for life was worth $6,066,37 before the fire and $2,426.55 after the fire. B's damages are the difference between these two sums, namely, $3,639.82." [Restatement of Property §118 illustration 1.]

As to valuation of life estates generally, see Restatement of Property, at 214-224 (Tent. Draft No. 3); Milner, Evaluating Life Estates and Other Calculations, 7 Ala. Law. 5 (1946); American Law of Property §2.25 (Casner ed. 1952).

Quite frequently it becomes necessary in the tax field to place a value on a life interest or on a remainder interest in order to calculate the tax due. For example, O transfers a residence or a farm "to A for life remainder to the X Charity." O may claim a federal income tax deduction for the value of the remainder gift to charity in the year the transfer is made and the value of the remainder gift is deductible in calculating the value of the gift made by O for federal gift tax purposes. The federal income tax regulations and the federal gift tax regulations provide tables which enable the remainder interest to be valued for tax purposes. See section 25.2512-5 of the federal gift tax regulations. If O's transfer of a remainder interest to charity is made in a will, the charitable remainder will have to be valued to ascertain the charitable deduction available for federal estate tax purposes.

Problems

4.8. Section 118 of the Restatement of Property was favored by the Reporter but strenuously contested by some of his advisers — Dean Fraser of Minnesota, Circuit Judge Clark, Professor Aigler of Michigan, and Mr. Charles C. White of the Cleveland bar. Suppose that, in a debate on this subject, those who approve the Restatement rule make the following argument:

> Take the typical case: A devises property to B for life, remainder to C. Then X, a wrongdoer negligently damages the property — for example, by burning down the structure that makes the property valuable as a gasoline service station. You have two claimants, B and C. Each has been damaged. Each should recover the value of his or her interest. No one suggests that C should recover the whole amount and then leave B to recover against C. Why should B be able to recover the whole amount and then leave C with nothing but a right of action against B?
>
> By letting B recover the whole amount you do not reduce litigation; for you have two suits just the same, one by B against X and one by C against B.

Reply to this argument.[3] (For an extensive debate on this issue, see Restatement of Property, at 193-199, 224-236 (Tent. Draft No. 3.)

4.9. If the damage to the land in which the life estate exists relates to property which the life tenant could not use without committing waste, such as timber or minerals in the ground, what should be done with the income from the money recovered by the life tenant for the loss of such property under the rule of the Rogers case? Will the value of the life estate be unaffected by the damage to the land in such case for the purpose of applying the rule in Zimmerman v. Shreeve? In answering these questions, keep in mind that though the life tenant was not entitled to the property damaged by the wrongdoer, the life tenant had the right to exclude the remainderman from access to such property as long as the life estate lasted. See Restatement of Property §138 comment e.

TAPSCOTT v. COBBS
52 Va. (11 Gratt.) 172 (1854)

[Action of ejectment brought in 1846 by lessees of Mrs. Cobbs against Tapscott.

The following was the evidence produced at the trial. Anderson owned the lot in question. Upon his death his executors, to whom the land had been

---

3. Professor Joseph H. Beale (1861-1945) of Harvard, sometime dean of University of Chicago Law School, was a master dialectician. Among his students it was common talk that you could occasionally beat Beale in an argument, but never if you let him state the question. This footnote is designed to be helpful with reference to the problem above.

devised by Anderson with a power of sale, contracted to sell to Mrs. Lewis in about 1820 and at a later date contracted to sell to Rives. It did not appear that either Mrs. Lewis or Rives paid the full purchase price or that either of them got a deed from the executors. Deed or no deed, Mrs. Lewis entered upon the land shortly after making her contract to buy the land; she built upon the land and remained in possession until she died in 1835. Mrs. Cobbs, the plaintiff's lessor, is Mrs. Lewis's heir. There is no evidence that she was in possession of the land after Mrs. Lewis's death. Tapscott took possession of the land in 1842 without any pretense of title.

The defendant demurred to the evidence. Judgment was given for the plaintiff upon the demurrer. The defendant appealed to and obtained a supersedeas from the court of appeals.]

DANIEL, J. It is no doubt true, as a general rule, that the right of a plaintiff in ejectment to recover, rests on the strength of his own title, and is not established by the exhibition of defects in the title of the defendant, and that the defendant may maintain his defense by simply showing that the title is not in the plaintiff, but in someone else. And the rule is usually thus broadly stated by the authorities, without qualification. There are, however, exceptions to the rule as thus announced, as well established as the rule itself. As when the defendant has entered under the title of the plaintiff he cannot set up a title in a third person in contradiction to that under which he entered. . . .

Whether the case of an intrusion by a stranger without title, on a peaceable possession, is not one to meet the exigencies of which the courts will recognize a still further qualification or explanation of the rule requiring the plaintiff to recover only on the strength of his own title, is a question which, I believe, has not as yet been decided by this court. And it is somewhat remarkable that there are but few cases to be found in the English reporters in which the precise question has been decided or considered by the courts.

The cases of Read & Morpeth v. Erington, Croke Eliz. 321; Bateman v. Allen, ibid. 437; and Allen v. Rivington, 2 Saund. R. 111, were each decided on special verdicts, in which the facts with respect to the title were stated. In each case it was shown that the plaintiff was in possession, and that the defendant entered without title or authority; and the court held that it was not necessary to decide upon the title of the plaintiff, and gave judgment for him. In the report of Bateman v. Allen, it is said that Williams, Serjeant, moved, "that forasmuch as in all the verdict it is not found that the defendant had the *primer* possession, nor that he entered in the right or by the command of any who had title, but that he entered on the possession of the plaintiff without title, his entry is not lawful," and so the court held.

And in Read & Morpeth v. Erington, it was insisted that for portion of the premises the judgment ought to be for the defendant, inasmuch as it appeared from the verdict that the title to such portion was outstanding in a third party; but the court said it did not matter, as it was shown that the plaintiff had entered, and the defendant had entered on him. . . .

. . . In this country the cases are numerous, and to some extent conflicting, yet I think that the larger number will be found to be in accordance with the earlier English decisions. I have found no case in which the question seems to have been more fully examined or maturely considered than in Sowden, etc. v. McMillan's heirs, 4 Dana's R. 456. The views of the learned judge (Marshall) who delivered the opinion in which the whole court concurred, are rested on the authority of several cases in Kentucky, previously decided, on a series of decisions made by the Supreme Court of New York, and on the three British cases of Bateman v. Allen, Allen v. Rivington, and Read & Morpeth v. Erington, before mentioned.

> These three cases [he says] establish unquestionably the right of the plaintiff to recover when it appears that he was in possession, and that the defendant entered upon and ousted his possession, without title or authority to enter; and prove that when the possession of the plaintiff and an entry upon it by the defendant are shown, the right of recovery cannot be resisted by showing that there is or may be an outstanding title in another; but only by showing that the defendant himself either has title or authority to enter under the title.
>
> It is a natural principle of justice, that he who is in possession has the right to maintain it, and if wrongfully expelled, to regain it by entry on the wrong-doer. When titles are acknowledged as separate and distinct from the possession, this right of maintaining and regaining the possession is, of course, subject to the exception that it cannot be exercised against the real owner, in competition with whose title it wholly fails. But surely it is not accordant with the principles of justice, that he who ousts a previous possession should be permitted to defend his wrongful possession against the claim of restitution merely by showing that a stranger, and not the previous possessor whom he has ousted, was entitled to the possession. The law protects a peaceable possession against all except him who has the actual right to the possession, and no other can rightfully disturb or intrude upon it. . . .

In Delaware, North Carolina, South Carolina, Indiana, and perhaps in other states of the Union, the opposite doctrine has been held.

In this state of the law, untrammeled as we are by any decisions of our own courts, I feel free to adopt that rule which seems to me best calculated to attain the ends of justice. The explanation of the law (as usually announced) given by Judge Marshall in the portions of his opinion which I have cited, seems to me to be founded on just and correct reasoning; and I am disposed to follow those decisions which uphold a peaceable possession for the protection as well of a plaintiff as of a defendant in ejectment, rather than those which invite disorderly scrambles for the possession, and clothe a mere trespasser with the means of maintaining his wrong, by showing defects, however slight, in the title of him on whose peaceable possession he has intruded without shadow of authority or title. . . .

. . . An apparent difficulty in the way of a recovery by the plaintiff arises
from the absence of positive proof of their possession at the time of the
defendant's entry. It is to be observed, however, that there is no proof to the
contrary. Mrs. Lewis died in possession of the premises, and there is no proof
that they were vacant at the time of the defendant's entry. In Gilbert's
Tenures 37 (in note) it is stated as the law that as the heir has the right to the
hereditaments descending, the law presumes that he has the possession also.
The presumption may be rebutted, but if the possession be not shown to be
in another the law concludes it to be in the heir.[4] . . .

Judgment affirmed.

Problem

4.10. Mrs. Lewis entered upon the land in question in Tapscott v.
Cobbs after executing a contract to buy the land. If the time of occupancy by
her between the time of her entry and the time of her death exceeded the
period of the controlling statute of limitations, would she have acquired title
to the land in question by adverse possession? Could the heir of Mrs. Lewis
tack the period of time between Mrs. Lewis' death and the date of the
defendant's entry to the period of possession by Mrs. Lewis to make out the
period of the controlling statute of limitations?

WINCHESTER v. CITY OF STEVENS POINT
58 Wis. 350, 17 N.W. 3 (1883)

[The plaintiff's declaration alleged that she was the owner of certain
described lots in Stevens Point, Wisconsin, and had been in actual possession thereof for more than one year before commencement of this action;
that in 1881 the defendant city, as a flood control measure, so built a dike
that the plaintiff's ingress and egress were seriously impaired and water of
the Wisconsin River was backed up on her land; and that "by means
whereof the said premises are greatly diminished in value and the plaintiff
has sustained damage in the sum of $700."

The answer was a general denial and that the dike had been built and
maintained for more than twenty years.

It appeared from the evidence given at the trial that the dike was
originally built in 1855; that it was rebuilt in 1880 and made considerably
higher; and that its height was again increased in 1881. The jury found

---

4. What do you think of the quality of the advocacy which left this issue open on the
record?

Are you aware that the principal issue in this case has already been decided sub silentio in a
prior case in this book? Which one? — Eds.

specially that the premises were damaged by such increased height in the amount of $225. The plaintiff undertook to trace her title from an original United States patent to herself. Two deeds in this chain of title were actually recorded but were not entitled under the statutes to be recorded because they were attested by only one witness. When certified copies of the registry copies of these deeds were offered in evidence the defendant objected to them;[5] one was excluded, the other admitted. Thus the plaintiff was not able to prove a complete chain of title. The defendant offered no evidence of title in any other person.

The trial judge at one time told the jury that the plaintiff had to prove title in order to recover; but at another time he told them that she might recover

5. The problem of the law of evidence here involved is somewhat intricate but should be mastered.

To establish a deed of conveyance for purposes of showing the title to a parcel of real estate, it is necessary to show (a) that the deed was executed, and (b) what its contents were. The normal way to do this with regard to any writing is (a) to prove that it was executed by calling to the witness stand the person who executed it and have him state that he signed it, or a person who saw him sign it and have this witness testify that he saw the deed signed, or a person who knows the grantor's signature and have him testify that the signature on the deed is the grantor's; and (b) to prove the contents by producing the deed itself.

The foregoing method is obviously cumbersome where a large number of instruments, executed at various times by various grantors, have to be placed in evidence. It is much simpler to get a certified copy of the recorded copy of the instrument from the registry of deeds and produce this. (Of course, the original deed is returned by the recording official to the grantee of the deed after the deed has been copied into the record books; thus the instrument produced in court is a copy of a copy of the deed.) However, the use of such a certified copy runs afoul of two basic rules of evidence:

a. *The best evidence rule.* The best evidence rule requires that in proving the contents of a document the document itself must ordinarily be produced. There is an exception to this rule for properly recorded documents, at least where the grantee of the deed is not a party to the action. 4 Wigmore, Evidence §§1224, 1225.

b. *The hearsay rule.* Observe that the copy of a deed in the registry of deeds is nothing more than a statement by some registry official, usually not identified, that the registry copy is a true copy. Since this is not subject to cross-examination, it is hearsay. It can escape the objection of the hearsay rule only if it comes under the exception in favor of official statements — i.e. only if it is an act done in pursuance of official duty. 5 Wigmore, Evidence §§1648 et seq.

If the deed is recorded but is not entitled by law to be recorded (as, in this case, where there is only one witness to the deed whereas the statute permits recording only of deeds with two witnesses), the entire basis for permitting the certified copy of the record to be introduced is destroyed and the certified copy, or the record itself for that matter, is inadmissible. 5 Wigmore, Evidence §1653; Wis. Stat. §889.17.

The fact that the registry copy is inadmissible does not mean that the deed cannot be proved, but only that it cannot be proved through the registry copy. As to other available means of proof, see 5 Wigmore, Evidence §1653.

As to other serious consequences which may follow from the fact that a recorded deed was not entitled to be recorded, see Graves v. Graves, 72 Mass. (6 Gray) 391 (1856).

Section 235.20 of Wisconsin Statutes provides:

Any instrument in writing affecting the title to real property in this state, which . . . is not properly witnessed . . . shall, after the same has been recorded in the office of the proper register of deeds for 10 years, have the same force and effect as though such instrument had been originally . . . witnessed . . . according to law.

This statute also covers other defects of a formal nature; but it was not in force at the time of Winchester v. City of Stevens Point. Such curative statutes are fairly common, e.g., Mass. Ann. Laws ch.184, §24 — EDS.

if she was in possession under claim of paper title. After a verdict for the plaintiff, the defendant appealed, alleging as error the court's instructions and the denial of the defendant's motion for new trial.]

COLE, C.J. . . .

The action is not for the mere injury to the possession, but is to recover damages for an injury to the freehold. That being the case, it was essential for the plaintiff to show a title beyond what would be necessary to maintain trespass; for the question of title was made a material issue by the pleadings. There was no dispute about plaintiff's possession. But she attempted to prove a good paper title and failed. Nevertheless, she recovered for the permanent depreciation in the value of the property. The question is, Can the recovery be sustained upon the evidence given?

It seems to be assumed that damages for a permanent injury to the freehold — that is, an injury which not only affects the present use and enjoyment of the property, but its value for all future time — are recoverable in this action, though it is apparent the embankment may be removed any day, or so reduced in height as to restore the property to its condition when she acquired it. There doubtless may be an injury to the freehold which is permanent in its character; but was this such an one? The suggestion is made without deciding the point.

But what proof of title was it necessary for the plaintiff to make in order to maintain the action on the theory upon which it was tried? Her counsel contends it was sufficient for her to show she was in actual possession under claim of title. He also says that she established a good paper title; but this certainly is a mistake. Not to dwell on other defects in her claim of title, it will be noticed that the deeds from Kingston to Fay, and from Solomon Smith to William Randall, each had but one subscribing witness. The former was excluded; the latter was admitted in evidence against objection. Neither of the deeds was entitled to be recorded, and could not be proven by the record as the last one was.

There are authorities which hold that the seizin of the plaintiff in any real action is proved, prima facie, by evidence of his actual possession under claim of title. Ward's Heirs v. McIntosh, 12 Ohio St. 231; Gulf R.R. Co. v. Owen, 8 Kan. 410. Prof. Greenleaf so states the rule. 2 Greenl. on Ev. §555. See, also, Rau v. M.V.R.R. Co., 13 Minn. 442; St. P. & S.C.R.R. Co. v. Matthews, 16 Minn. 341. That is, these facts afford presumptive evidence of seizin in fee simple, until the contrary appears. But that rule would not save the plaintiff's case, because she offered evidence which disproved or over-came the presumption arising from these facts. She was not content to show actual possession under claim of title, but she undertook to prove title and failed. The evidence was probably offered to prove an adverse possession, under paper title, for ten years. That would have been sufficient had she established the fact of such adverse possession for the requisite time. But she did not; so the question returns, Was not the plaintiff bound, under the circumstances, to prove her title? We think she was. For if she was not the owner of the premises, why should she recover damages for a permanent injury to them? She saw fit to put her title in issue, to rely upon it, and sought to recover as owner. The case is much like condemnation proceedings, and should be governed by the same rule as to proof of title. Since the early case of Robbins v. M. & H.R.R. Co., 6 Wis. 636, it has been understood that the plaintiff must show title, and that title will not be presumed from evidence of possession under claim of title. . . .

The judgment is reversed and a new trial ordered.

TAYLOR, J. . . .

The question lying at the basis of the controversy is this: Can a party in the actual possession of real estate recover for an injury to the freehold, against a mere wrongdoer who neither has nor claims any title to the premises or to the possession thereof, nor sets up any justification of the acts complained of under the authority of some third person who claims under a title paramount to the plaintiff's, without showing a perfect title to the premises? By the opinion of the court filed in this case this question would seem to be answered in the negative. . . .

. . . It seems to me well settled, if anything can be settled in the law, that a mere trespasser, having no title and not claiming under a third person having a title, who intrudes upon the actual peaceable possession of one claiming title, cannot defend by questioning such possessor's title. . . .

In the case at bar it is said the plaintiff ought not to recover her damages to the freehold because one of the deeds in her chain of title was witnessed by but one witness, and so was not entitled to record, and the record was not good evidence. She was in possession and claiming title under this deed. Supposing the grantor in this deed had brought ejectment, or an action against the plaintiff for some injury to the freehold, would it not be perfectly clear that she would have a good defense in equity, and I think in the law, to such action? The deed so imperfectly executed would, as we have just decided in the case of Dreutzer v. Lawrence, 58 Wis. 594, be in equity a good contract to convey the land to the plaintiff, and on its face would prove the payment of the consideration for the lands, as well as the right to the possession of it under such contract. Yet this defect, which would be of no avail to the grantor in the deed, is permitted to be set up by a mere wrongdoer as a defense to an action for a willful injury to the plaintiff's lands. . . .

The only cases which are relied upon as supporting the opinion of the court in this case are Robbins v. M. & H.R.R. Co., 6 Wis. 636, and Diedrich v. N.W.U. Ry. Co., 42 Wis. 248. These were both cases under the statute to have assessed the plaintiff's damages for lands taken by a railroad company under the statute. The railroad company was not a wrongdoer in any sense. It was taking the plaintiff's land as it had the right to do; and in such case it might be very just to compel the plaintiff to show his title before he should be entitled to charge the company with the price of the lands taken. The rule established in such cases ought to have no application where the plaintiff is proceeding against a mere trespasser who makes no claim of rights as against the plaintiff.

I am inclined to think the judgment of the circuit court ought to be reversed, but for a reason not discussed, though referred to in the opinion of the court. It seems to me that the acts complained of by the plaintiff are in the nature of a continuing trespass or nuisance, and that the rule as to the damages which the plaintiff may recover in such actions is not the damages the plaintiff may sustain in the future, but such as he has sustained at the time the action was commenced. See Carl v. S. & F. du L. R.R. Co., 46 Wis. 625; Blesch v. C. & N.W. Ry. Co., 43 Wis. 183; Cumberland & O. Canal Corp. v. Hitchings, 65 Me. 140; and other cases cited in Carl v. S. & F. du L. R.R. Co. If the reversal of the judgment had been placed upon that ground, I should have concurred in the opinion of the court. The judgment should be reversed, not because the plaintiff did not show sufficient title to the locus in quo to entitle her to recover damages for the injury done to her freehold estate, but because she was permitted to recover damages to which she would not have been entitled, even though she had established a perfect title in herself by a chain of conveyances from the United States to herself.[6]

Problem

4.11. In the opinion of Judge Cole, in referring to the plaintiff's attempt to prove title, he states: "The evidence was probably offered to prove an adverse possession, under paper title, for ten years. That would have been sufficient had she established the fact of such adverse possession for the requisite time." Do you see anything wrong with this statement?

LASALLE COUNTY CARBON COAL CO. v. SANITARY DISTRICT
260 Ill. 423, 103 N.E. 175 (1913)

[Prior to 1900, Chicago drew all its drinking water from, and dumped all its sewage into, Lake Michigan. To remedy this situation, the Sanitary District of Chicago constructed a channel and other works which made the Chicago River run backward and caused Chicago's sewage to flow into the Desplaines River, thence into the Illinois River, and thence into the Mississippi. The Great Lake states and the United States and Canadian governments sought an injunction against excessive withdrawals of water from Lake Michigan, alleging an impediment to navigation in lowering the water level of Lake Michigan and the eastern Great Lakes. Chicago was supported

---

6. The opinion of Cassoday, J., concurring in the result, is not presented here. — EDS.

by the river states, which liked the increased flow of water and didn't care what came along with it. The bill in equity was heard before District Judge Kenesaw Mountain Landis of Chicago; he kept the case under advisement for eight years "because I like to drink clean water" and left it for a successor to give a final decision when he stepped down from the bench to become the "czar" of big league baseball. The Supreme Court of the United States confirmed the War Department's veto power over the project (266 U.S. 405, 45 S. Ct. 176 (1925)), but the Chicago River still flows backward.

An Illinois statute (1889 Ill. Laws, p. 133, §19) provided that:

> Every sanitary district shall be liable for all damages to real estate which shall be overflowed or otherwise damaged by reason of the construction, enlargement or use of any channel or other improvement. And in case judgment is rendered against such district for damages the plaintiff shall also recover his reasonable attorney's fees, to be taxed as costs of suit. [Superfluous words omitted.]

The plaintiff coal company had held adverse possession of certain lands for 15 years when the sanitary district caused the lands to be flooded in 1900, doing permanent damage. In 1905, the plaintiff's adverse possession ripened into title under the Illinois 20-year statute of limitations. Immediately thereafter the plaintiff brought this action to recover damages for permanent injuries to the real estate. The evidence of damage was that the works of the sanitary district caused the land to be overflowed in each year to such an extent that it could not be farmed. Prior to 1900, the land had been used as farm land. A verdict for the plaintiff was rendered in the amount of $35,000, plus a $5,009 counsel fee.]

FARMER, J. . . .

At the request of the plaintiff the court gave to the jury the following instruction:

> While the plaintiff must prove, by a preponderance of the evidence in this case, that it had the legal title to the land in question, yet you are charged that if the plaintiff has proven, by the greater weight of all the evidence in this case, that it was in the open, peaceable, notorious and exclusive possession, either by itself or tenant, of the real estate described in the declaration in this case on and prior to the 17th day of January, 1900, and up to and including the trial of this suit, during that time paid all taxes due thereon, then there is sufficient proof of its title for the purposes of this suit, in the absence of evidence tending to show that it does not have the legal title to said land.

The cause of action accrued to the owner of the land in January, 1900, when the sanitary district channel was opened and the water turned into the Illinois river. At that time plaintiff had not been in the possession of this land twenty years. This suit was brought in 1905, and counsel contend that the plaintiff's title by prescription was complete before the action was brought.

In our opinion the plaintiff could not rely upon title by prescription unless its possession had ripened into title before the cause of action accrued. When the right of action accrued the then owner of the land had a right to sue and recover for any permanent damages caused by the acts of the defendant complained of, but the grantee of such owner after the cause of action accrued could not maintain a suit for damages for permanent injury. Plaintiff was not in the adverse possession of the tract of land referred to, for twenty years before January, 1900, when the water from the sanitary district channel was turned into the Illinois river, and did not at that time have title to the land, by adverse possession or otherwise. That its title became complete by prescription after the cause of action accrued places it in no different position from what it would have been in if it had not been in possession but had acquired title by conveyance after the right of action accrued. If the owner of real estate injuriously affected or damaged by a permanent structure, and who had not brought an action to recover damages, conveys the land to another, the cause of action does not pass with the title nor inure to the benefit of the grantee, but the grantee takes the land as he finds it, the presumption being that he has the benefit of the depreciation in value in the price paid. This has been so frequently held by this court that it is unnecessary to do more than cite some of the cases.

Counsel for the defendant moved to exclude from the consideration of the jury all question of damages to the tract of land referred to, on the ground that the plaintiff had not proved title thereto, but the court overruled the motion. This action of the court, and the giving of the instruction above set out, we think were such errors as to require a reversal of this judgment. Plaintiff alleged in its declaration that it was the owner of the land, and this meant that it was the owner in fee. It sought to recover for permanent depreciation in the value of the land, and to authorize it to do so it was necessary for it to prove such ownership. . . .

. . . As the case must go back for another trial we have not determined whether the amount allowed as counsel fees is so large as to require our disapproval, but we think it not improper to say that we would have been better satisfied with the allowance for attorney's fees if the amount had been materially less.

Reversed and remanded.

ILLINOIS & ST. LOUIS RAILROAD & COAL CO. v. COBB
94 Ill. 55 (1879)

[The line of the bank of the Mississippi at Cahokia, Illinois, was subject to substantial changes by accretion and erosion. After a period of erosion which moved the line of the river about half a mile eastward, a period of accretion began shortly before 1865. An island formed east of the center line of the river. When the island was large enough to take a house, Francis H.

Cobb took possession of it and built a small house. (It was clear, by Illinois law, that the island belonged to the owners of the Illinois shore, who appear to have made no claim, whose names are not given, and who are strangers to the present action.) The island grew very substantially and finally joined with the mainland at both its north and south ends. During all of this period, Cobb leased the premises to a tenant, claiming the ownership of the island, and the tenant remained in possession under the lease from Cobb. In 1871 Cobb fenced in a part of the land for pasturage.

In January, 1872, the Illinois & St. L.R.R. & Coal Co., the defendant-appellant, broke down Cobb's fence, laid a switch and track across the land, and began to remove sand and soil therefrom. On March 6, 1872, Cobb brought an action of trespass against the railroad for damages between January and March, 1872, and got a judgment for $600, which was paid.

Early in 1873 Cobb put up the fence again, and the railroad tore it down. On March 6, 1873, Cobb brought a second action to recover damages for the previous 12 months. Later on the same day (March 6, 1873) Cobb put up the fence again and the railroad again broke it down. In August, 1873, Cobb brought a third action to recover damages from March 6, 1873, to August, 1873.

The second and third actions were consolidated for trial. A judgment for the plaintiff for $5,000 was rendered, from which the railroad appealed. The Supreme Court of Illinois reversed on the ground that the railroad was rightfully on the land by virtue of a lease to it of Lot 301 on the original river bank. Counsel for Cobb petitioned for rehearing on the ground that the record showed clearly that the land in question was outside the boundaries of the lease. The basis of the petition was incontestable, but the court reversed anyway on the ground that the damages were excessive.[7] The case was tried again, resulting in a jury verdict for the plaintiff for $4,379. The present appeal is from the judgment entered upon this verdict.[8]]

---

7. That judges are human is demonstrated by the frequent fate of successful petitions for rehearing: The court finds some other way to reach the same result. There seems to be a feeling that the greater judicial turpitude lies in mistaking the result, the less in mistaking the reason. The ancient maxim cessante ratione, cessat ipsa lex yields to one less ancient: cessante ratione, alia inveniatur. For other cases in point, see Frank L. Young Co. v. McNeal-Edwards Co., 35 F.2d 829 (D. Mass), *on rehearing,* 42 F.2d 362, *reversed,* 283 U.S. 398, 51 S. Ct. 538, *on further rehearing,* 51 F.2d 699 (1929-1931); Ginn v. W. C. Clark Coal Co., 143 Mich. 84, 106 N.W. 867 (1906).

The search for the applicable maxim was greatly facilitated by Dean Pound, who provided the Roman law reference to the digest: L. 1, D. "de div. reg. jur. nov." (50.18). He suggests that the reader compare Horace, Fifth Book (Kipling trans.). Judge Arnold Raum of the Tax Court prefers a simpler maxim to explain these cases: stare decisis.

Dean Pound reports that William Jennings Bryan, arguing before the Supreme Court of Nebraska, was told from the bench that the court was clearly against him on the point he was arguing. Bryan replied, "If the court is against me on this point I have three others equally conclusive." And Lord Campbell, as attorney general, is said to have remarked, "There are cases in which, good points having been overruled, it becomes necessary to take bad ones for the sake of justice."

8. The rephrasing of the facts is based on 82 Ill. 183, which is the report of this case when it was before the Supreme Court at a former term.

WALKER, C.J. . . .

Another ground is urged, in reference to the question of damages for a reversal. Appellant gave evidence tending to prove an outstanding title to the property in controversy in the village of Cahokia. And appellant asked, but the court refused to give, this instruction:

> If the defendant has shown that the title to the land described by the declaration, at the time when the trespass is said to have been committed, was outstanding, that is to say, not in the plaintiff, the plaintiff cannot recover damages for an injury that may have been done to the freehold or to the land, soil or sand, but only such injury, if any have been shown, that was done to the possession or property of the plaintiff.

This raises the question whether a mere trespasser may justify his wrong to all but the actual damage done to the possession, by showing a title in a third person. Or to state the proposition differently, can he mitigate the damages so as to prevent a recovery for all damages beyond the actual injury to this mere possession. . . .

To hold that a wrongdoer may put a plaintiff in peaceable possession upon the proof of his title, to enable him to a recovery, would be a harsh rule. If there should be any technical objection to any link in his chain of title he would fail, although no other person was claiming title and might never claim. His title might be clearly equitable, unclaimed and unchallenged by the person holding the legal title, and yet, if such a rule should prevail, the equitable owner and occupant might have his property destroyed and only recover nominal damages. Many titles are defective in the want of proper acknowledgments or other mere technical defects, and yet no one claims or challenges the title of the occupant claiming to be the owner, and shall it be said, that he shall not be protected against a reckless, lawless wrongdoer? The wrongdoer should in justice make recompense to someone for the wrong and loss he has inflicted upon the property and no reason is perceived why he should have a choice as to whom he will pay the damages. A recovery by the occupant is a bar to all future recoveries, and it in nowise concerns him who shall have the benefit of that recovery. Benjamin v. Stumph, 13 Ill. 466; Lyle v. Baker, 5 Binn. 457; Chamberlin v. Shaw, 18 Pick. 278; and White v. Webb, 15 Conn. 302, show a recovery as against a wrongdoer may be had of the full value when a recovery is had.

The judgment of the Appellate Court is affirmed.

Note: *Homily on Minimum Pain and Maximum Profit in Reading Cases*

You have just read Illinois R.R. v. Cobb. Were you annoyed by the complexities of the litigation? Did you simply read the opinion as you would a textbook and ignore the facts because the opinion seemed intelligible enough without them? Or did you get the flavor of the case — the dogged persistence of the litigious Cobb, the railroad trying to wear him down, the red-faced Supreme Court having to eat its first opinion, reversing on the ground of "excessive damages," and having another jury (of Cobb's neighbors) slap the case right back at them at substantially the same figure? Cobb must have been quite a power locally. His island property, now joined to the mainland, is obviously quite valuable, if only as a basis for victimizing the railroad; yet the riparian owners are neither making claims themselves nor yet selling out to the railroad which, at this point, must have been making fairly attractive offers for any rights that would give them the whip hand over Cobb. The smoke of battle finally clears away leaving Cobb with a very neat annuity levied on the railroad for no more trouble than putting up his fence some night each spring, contentedly watching the section gang tear it down, and walking down to the court house to file his next action. When this case was finally decided in November, 1879, more than six years had passed since Cobb's third action had been commenced in August, 1873; undoubtedly Cobb had half a dozen more actions against the railroad on file, each going through its lucrative rhythm of trial, verdict, and judgment.

And as you considered this case, did you compare the skill of the plaintiff's lawyer with that of Mrs. Winchester's attorney in the Winchester case? One did very well for his client, the other very badly. Basically Mrs. Winchester seems to have had the better case of the two, but she didn't get the better result. Are you sure you understand why? And have you assimilated the lesson into your store of professional wisdom?

Each appellate opinion that you are offered for reading has two characteristics which can be overlooked unless they are emphasized:

1.   The opinion is the end product of a row that sent people to their attorneys, a battle of witnesses and lawyers in a court room, probably a lengthy wrangling in the jury room, and two appellate briefs and arguments. The winning party and his or her lawyer will regale their friends with details of the triumph for years; the losers will say as little about it as possible. If you sense the humanity and drama of the conflict, while still focusing principal attention on the matters of legal significance, you will enjoy it more and, for that reason, get more out of it.

2.   Each case should be to you an item of vicarious experience. If you could only live long enough, you would find the apprentice system the best method of learning law. Twenty or thirty years of a broad general practice under the tutelage of a master practitioner would be the ideal education. There is no teacher like experience, and in twenty or thirty years you would get a sufficiently broad basis of personal experience. Next best is vicarious experience — and this is what the reading of cases offers to you. Two other lawyers have lived through each case, and each has learned much in the process. It should be your purpose to get out of the case as much as possible of the benefits which accrued to the actual participants. Naturally the

percentage will not be large, because you are given too little detail as to the development of the case; but if you keep in mind that you are assessing the professional excellence of the lawyers in these cases and determining to imitate the good and shun the bad, you will derive much benefit. Ask yourself "What kind of situation might arise in my practice where this case would be significant? What does this teach me that I should do or avoid doing?"

Of course it would not be realistic to give this degree of consideration to each case you read in every course. But if you keep in mind that these are your objectives when appropriate and practicable, you will increase the effectiveness of this part of your education. You will soon develop a sound judgment as to which cases to lean upon and which to skim over lightly.

P A R T I I

GIFTS OF PERSONAL PROPERTY

Note: ***Types of Donative Transactions
and the Problems They Raise***

In this part you are introduced to the legal difficulties involved when you get generous and want to give away some of the property which you own. Donative transactions may take many different forms, and in order to understand the types of donative transactions with which we shall be concerned at this time, it is necessary to outline briefly the various forms which donative transactions may take.

First, there is the apparently simple situation where I have a watch and I want to give it to you now, so that henceforth you will have the complete ownership of the watch. In other words, I want to make an inter vivos, absolute, and unqualified gift which is to be operative immediately. In this part we meet this situation, and you are expected to become fully cognizant of what is necessary to accomplish such desire.

The effectuation of my desire to make an absolute gift to you that is immediately operative may be relatively simple when the subject matter of the gift is a tangible article such as a watch. If, however, I have such desire with respect to stock in a corporation, government bonds, or money I have on deposit in a savings bank, the nature of the subject matter of the gift may well introduce additional complexities. The material in this part is designed to acquaint you with the special problems which may arise as a result of the nature of the subject matter of the gift.

My desire may be that your enjoyment of the subject matter of the gift will not begin until I die. The standard method of accomplishing such desire is by making what we call a will. My will has no legally operative effect until I die, so that if I change my mind about giving the property to you at any time before I die, I can revoke the will or amend it so as to eliminate you as a beneficiary. Various rigid formalities have been established by statute in the various states for the making of a will in order to avoid the possibility of people making fraudulent claims as to my property after I am dead and unable to testify as to my intentions. In a course in estate planning or in a separate course on wills you will develop in detail the formalities required for the execution of a will.[1] Here the will is touched on only incidentally in order to distinguish it from similar situations.

I may want to make an arrangement now that will assure you of getting the enjoyment of some of my property at the time of my death but which will be binding on me, so that I cannot change my mind. From what has been said above, it is obvious that the will does not do this. In this part we do develop the requirements for the making of an irrevocable arrangement which will be effective to pass the enjoyment of certain property to you on my death.

In between the irrevocable arrangement, which is to pass the enjoyment of the property to you on my death, and the ambulatory arrangement, which results from the making of a will and which is completely revocable by me until I die, there are many variations of intentions which I may have. I may want you to get the property if, and only if, certain events occur; I may want your interest in the property to terminate if specified events occur; I may want you to have some kind of joint control with me over the property while I am alive and have you entitled to what is left at the time of my death; etc. The principal problem with which we shall be concerned is to ascertain when my desires are such that they can be effectuated only by complying with all the formalities that have been established for the creation of a will. The gift causa mortis is the technical name of the gift that looks very much like the arrangement that normally requires a will in order to make it effective. A considerable part of our attention will be devoted to this kind of gift.

My desire may be to confer on you the beneficial enjoyment of certain property of mine but not to entrust you with the management of that property, which management will produce the benefits to be enjoyed. This situation will be presented normally only when the subject matter of the gift is income-producing property which requires certain managerial experience as to the type of property involved in order that the maximum income will be produced. Stocks and money form the principal examples of property of this type. The most significant device which the law has provided to carry out such a desire is what is called a trust, where the legal title to the property in question rests in the trustee and a duty is imposed on the trustee pursuant to the terms of the trust to manage the property and pay the income to the designated beneficiaries. The interest of the beneficiary under the trust is what we call an equitable interest because it is in a court applying equitable principles that protection is given to the beneficiary in the event the trustee

1. The execution of wills is dealt with in Casner, Estate Planning ch. 3 (4th student ed. 1979, Supp. 1982; 4th lawyer's ed. 1980, Supp. 1983).

does not perform the trust. In your course in estate planning[2] or in a separate course on trusts you will consider in detail the ramifications of the trust device. It is touched on in this part only to make you aware of the difference in requirements for passing a legal interest by way of gift and an equitable interest by way of gift.

Sooner or later you will hear about the revocable trust. A transfer is made that passes the legal title to the designated trustee and the beneficial rights under the trust are described, but the entire arrangement is revocable by the transferor. This arrangement is similar to a will in many respects, but technically it differs in that it is legally operative during the lifetime of the transferor, whereas the will, as has been noted, has no legally operative effect until the testator dies.[3]

Lifetime transfers of property by gift may be subject to the federal gift tax (and in some states to a state gift tax) and deathtime transfers (or what is considered their equivalent) may be subject to the federal estate tax (or to a state death tax). Chapter 37 examines the significant aspects of the federal estate and gift tax laws.

2. The use of trusts in estate planning is explored in Casner, Estate Planning chs. 5, 6 (4th ed.).

3. The revocable trust is discussed in Casner, Estate Planning ch. 5 (4th student ed. 1979, Supp. 1982; 4th lawyer's ed. 1980, Supp. 1983).

CHAPTER 5

BASIC REQUIREMENTS: "DELIVERY," DONATIVE INTENT, AND ACCEPTANCE

IRONS v. SMALLPIECE
2 B. & Ald. 551, 106 Eng. Rep. 467 (K.B. 1819)

Trover for two colts. Plea, not guilty. The defendant was the executrix and residuary legatee of the plaintiff's father, and the plaintiff claimed the colts, under a verbal gift made to him by the testator twelve months before his death. The colts however continued to remain in possession of the father until his death. It appeared further that about six months before the father's death, the son having been to a neighbouring market for the purpose of purchasing hay for the colts, and finding the price of that article very high, mentioned the circumstance to his father; and that the latter agreed to furnish for the colts any hay they might want at a stipulated price, to be paid by the son. None however was furnished to them till within three or four days before the testator's death. Upon these facts, Abbott, C.J., was of opinion, that the possession of the colts never having been delivered to the plaintiff, the property therein had not vested in him by the gift; but that it continued in the testator at the time of his death, and consequently that it passed to his executrix under the will; and the plaintiff was therefore non-suited.

ABBOTT, C.J. I am of opinion that by the law of England, in order to transfer property by gift there must either be a deed or instrument of gift, or there must be an actual delivery of the thing to the donee. Here the gift is merely verbal, and differs from a donatio mortis causa only in this respect, that the latter is subject to a condition, that if the donor live the thing shall be restored to him. Now it is a well established rule of law, that a donatio mortis causa does not transfer the property without an actual delivery. The possession must be transferred, in point of fact; and the late case of Bunn v. Markham, 2 Marsh. 532, where all the former authorities were considered, is a very strong authority upon that subject. There Sir G. Clifton had written upon the parcels containing the property the names of the parties for whom they were intended, and had requested his natural son to see the property delivered to the donees. It was therefore manifestly his intention that the property should pass to the donees; yet as there was no actual delivery, the Court of Common Pleas held that it was not a valid gift. I cannot distinguish that case from the present, and therefore think that this property in the colts did not pass to the son by the verbal gift: and I cannot agree that the son can be charged with the hay which was provided for these colts three or four days before the father's death; for I cannot think that that tardy supply can be referred to the contract which was made so many months before.

HOLROYD, J. I am also of the same opinion. In order to change the property by a gift of this description, there must be a change of possession: here there has been no change of possession. If indeed it could be made out that the son was chargeable for the hay provided for the colts, then the possession of the father might be considered as the possession of the son. Here however no hay is delivered during a long interval from the time of the contract, until within a few days of the father's death; and I cannot think that the hay so delivered is to be considered as delivered in execution of that contract made so long before, and consequently the son is not chargeable for the price of it.

BEST, J., concurred.

Note: Reasons for the Requirement of Delivery

In the case of Cochrane v. Moore, 25 L.R.-Q.B.D. 57 (1890), the court reviewed all the English cases on the subject of delivery in connection with gifts and concluded as follows:

> This review of the authorities leads us to conclude that according to the old law no gift or grant of a chattel was effectual to pass whether by parol or by deed, and whether with or without consideration unless accompanied by delivery: that on that law two exceptions have been grafted, one in the case of deeds, and the other in that of contracts of sale where the intention of the parties is that the property shall pass before delivery: but that as regards gifts by parol, the old law was in force when Irons v. Smallpiece was decided: that that case therefore correctly declared the existing law. [25 L.R.-Q.B.D. at 72-73.]

Lord Esher, M.R., in his concurring opinion, advances his reasons for the necessity of a delivery:

> Up to the time of Irons v. Smallpiece, and afterwards, I have no doubt the Courts did require proof of an actual delivery in such a case. Upon long consideration, I have come to the conclusion that actual delivery in the case of a "gift" is more than evidence of the existence of the proposition of law which

constitutes a gift, and I have come to the conclusion that it is a part of the proposition itself. It is one of the facts which constitute the proposition that a gift has been made. It is not a piece of evidence to prove the existence of the proposition; it is a necessary part of the proposition, and, as such, is one of the facts to be proved by evidence. The proposition is not—that the one party has agreed or promised to give, and that the other party has agreed or promised to accept. In that case, it is not doubted but that the ownership is not changed until a subsequent actual delivery. The proposition before the Court on a question of gift or not is—that the one gave and the other accepted. The transaction described in the proposition is a transaction begun and completed at once. It is a transaction consisting of two contemporaneous acts, which at once complete the transactions, so that there is nothing more to be done by either party. The act done by the one is that he gives; the act done by the other is that he accepts. These contemporaneous acts being done, neither party has anything more to do. The one cannot give, according to the ordinary meaning of the word, without giving; the other cannot accept then and there such a giving without then and there receiving the thing given. After these two things are done, the donor could not get possession of the chattel without bringing an action to force the donee to give it back. Short of these things being done, the donee could not get possession without bringing an action against the donor to force him to give him the thing. But if we are to force him to give, it cannot be said that he has given. Suppose the proposing donor offers the thing saying, "I give you this thing—take it"; and the other says, "No, I will not take it now; I will take it tomorrow." I think the proposing donor could not in the meantime say correctly to a third person, "I gave this just now to my son or my friend." The answer of the third person would (I think rightly) be: "You cannot say you gave it him just now; you have it now in your hand." All you can say is: "That you are going to give it to him tomorrow, if then he will take it." I have come to the conclusion that in ordinary English language, and in legal effect, there cannot be a "gift" without a giving and taking. The giving and taking are the two contemporaneous reciprocal acts which constitute a "gift." They are a necessary part of the proposition that there has been a "gift." They are not evidence to prove that there has been a gift, but facts to be proved to constitute the proposition that there has been a gift. That being so, the necessity of their existence cannot be altered unless by Act of Parliament. For these reasons, I think that the decision in Irons v. Smallpiece cannot be departed from. [25 L.R.-Q.B.D. at 75-76.]

Summarize Lord Esher's position.[1]

These reasons have been advanced in support of the requirement of delivery in making of parol gifts:

1. It makes vivid and concrete to the donor the significance of the act performed;
2. The act of manual tradition is unequivocal to actual witnesses of the transaction; and

---

1. See also in regard to the English law of gifts Stoljar, A Rationale of Gifts and Favours, 19 Mod. L. Rev. 237 (1956); Stoljar, The Delivery of Chattels, 21 Mod. L. Rev. 27 (1958). —Eds.

3. The fact of delivery gives the donee, subsequent to the act, prima facie evidence in favor of the alleged gift.[2]

NEWELL v. NATIONAL BANK
214 A.D. 331, 212 N.Y.S. 158 (1925)

Appeal by the defendant, The National Bank of Norwich, as executor, etc., from a judgment of the Supreme Court in favor of the plaintiff, entered in the office of the clerk of the county of Broome on the 24th day of November, 1924, upon the decision of the court, rendered after a trial at an adjourned Trial and Special Term before the court without a jury, the jury having been waived.

COCHRANE, P.J. Emory S. Reynolds, the defendant's testator, was a childless widower. For many years he had been an intimate friend of plaintiff. About March 1, 1918, he was seriously ill with pneumonia and expected to die. He sent for the plaintiff and gave him a diamond ring the title to which is the question to be determined herein. He caused the ring to be delivered to plaintiff. The circumstances are described as follows by a nurse in attendance:

"He told Mr. Newell why he sent for him that morning. He had everything seen to and was ready to go. Had all his affairs seen to with the exception of handing over the ring to him. He was ready to go, or was ready to die, and that his other business was all straightened up."

Mr. Reynolds recovered from his illness and lived more than four years thereafter.

Viewed as a gift causa mortis the gift cannot be sustained because it is well established that the recovery to health of the donor works per se a revocation of the gift. Curtiss v. Barrus, 38 Hun 165; Grymes v. Hone, 49 N.Y. 17, 20; Williams v. Guile, 117 N.Y. 343, 348, 22 N.E. 1071; Basket v. Hassell, 107 U.S. 602, 2 S. Ct. 415; Ridden v. Thrall, 125 N.Y. 572, 579, 580, 26 N.E. 627.

The trial court has found that there was a gift inter vivos. Such a gift may exist although at the time of making it the donor was under the apprehension of death. In 28 Corpus Juris (p. 622) the rule is stated as follows:

The test whether the gift is one inter vivos or one causa mortis is not the mere fact that the donor is in extremis, and expects to die, and does die of that illness, but whether he intended the gift to take effect in praesenti, irrevocably and unconditionally, whether he lives or dies.

---

2. See Mechem, 21 Ill. L. Rev. 341, 348 (1926). Also examine Rohan, The Continuing Question of Delivery in the Law of Gifts, 38 Ind. L. Rev. 1 (1962); Rohan, Some Problems of Constructive Delivery, Agency and Proof in Gift Litigation, 38 Ind. L.J. 470 (1963).

In Hatcher v. Buford (60 Ark. 169, 29 S.W. 641; 27 L.R.A. 507) it is said: "But it must not be forgotten that an absolute gift—one inter vivos—may be made by one upon his deathbed, and who is aware of the near approach of death from his then ailment. Thornton, Gifts & Advancements (Sec. 21, p. 24) and authorities cited." There can be no doubt that the expectation of death is frequently the inducement for a gift inter vivos.

The question then is does the evidence sustain the finding that a gift inter vivos was intended. We approach that question with the rule in mind that the presumption is otherwise and that the burden is on the plaintiff to establish such a gift. We have already alluded to the testimony of the nurse. There is also some testimony given by her tending to show that the testator wanted the plaintiff to have the ring regardless of whether the testator lived or died. It clearly appears that after the restoration of the testator to health plaintiff did not want to wear the ring and was willing to return it to the testator for his use as long as he lived. He so expressed himself orally and by letter. The testator was equally insistent that plaintiff should retain the ring. Finally several months after he got well the testator summoned a witness to the office of plaintiff and speaking to this witness in the presence of the plaintiff said:

> "Frank [the plaintiff] wants me to wear this ring, but I don't think I should do it. I gave him that ring and I want him to have it, but he insists upon my wearing it now that I am able to be around again. Under only one consideration will I agree to wear it and I want it thoroughly understood that this ring belongs to Frank and when I die I want it understood that it belongs to him and that he shall have it."

Thereafter the testator had the ring in his possession and wore it until his death. Other witnesses testify to substantially the same statement at different times by the testator. The transaction in the office of the plaintiff is insufficient to constitute a gift to him by the testator because it left the donor in possession of the property, but we think it reflects the mental attitude of the testator at the time when during his illness he delivered the ring to the plaintiff. He had no near relatives. The most of his property at that time had been willed to charitable purposes as the evidence discloses. His business and social relations with plaintiff were very intimate. The circumstances surrounding the transaction and his attitude thereafter and subsequent declarations indicate quite clearly that when during his illness he gave the ring to the plaintiff he did so irrespective of whether he lived or died, although at the time he was apprehensive of death. If that was his purpose, absolute title then vested in the plaintiff and the subsequent possession and use thereof by the testator was that merely of a bailee. We think the findings of the trial court are fairly sustained by the evidence.

The judgment should be affirmed, with costs.

Judgment unanimously affirmed, with costs. The court disapproves the eighth and thirteenth findings contained in the defendant's requests for findings.

Problems

5.1. O had a diamond ring on her finger, and she took it off and handed it to A, saying: "I will give this ring to you." A tried the ring on, and it was too small; but both agreed that A could have it enlarged at a jewelry store. O then said, "Let me take it and wear it until I am through with it, but the ring is yours." A turned over the ring to O, and she wore it until she died, several years later. On O's death, A demanded the ring from O's administrator. Is A entitled to it? See Garrison v. Union Trust Co., 164 Mich. 345, 129 N.W. 691 (1910). Suppose O had been on her deathbed when the above transpired and had died a few days later; would the result be the same? See Dunbar v. Dunbar, 80 Me. 152, 13 A. 578 (1888).

5.2. O, who was planning to go to the hospital to have an operation performed which O had reason to believe might be fatal, delivered to A certain jewelry, stating at the time that if O did not survive the operation, the jewelry was to be kept by A. The operation was performed successfully, and a week after the operation, while O was convalescing in the hospital, O had a heart attack and died. O's administrator demands the jewelry from A. As A's attorney, what would you advise A to do? See Ridden v. Thrall, 125 N.Y. 572, 26 N.E. 627 (1891).

5.3. In Allen v. Hendrick, 104 Or. 202, 206 P. 733 (1922), the court said:

> A gift causa mortis is made subject to three conditions implied by law, the occurrence of any one of which will defeat the gift: (1) the recovery of the donor from the sickness or his delivery from the peril; (2) revocation by the donor before his death; (3) death of the donee before the death of the donor. [104 Or. at 219, 206 P. at 737-738.]

Suppose O, in apprehension of death, delivers to A money and securities, with the following letter: "Dear Son, will send you two deposit checks you will keep safely for me in case I come to need any part or all of them and if I never need them they are all yours when I am done with them." Shortly thereafter A undertakes to drive O to the hospital. On the way there they have an accident, and both O and A are killed instantly. O's administrator demands the money and securities from A's administrator, and the latter refuses to give up the property. Which administrator is entitled to the property?

5.4. O, in apprehension of death, delivers to A a valuable diamond ring with the intention that A shall keep it if O dies from O's present illness. The next week and just prior to O's death from the illness, O executes a will in which O specifically bequeaths the diamond ring to B. Who is entitled to the ring, A or B? See Jayne v. Murphy, 31 Ill. App. 28 (1889), and Lumberg v. Commonwealth Bank, 295 Mich. 566, 295 N.W. 266 (1940).

5.5. O has a safe deposit box at the X bank. O gives the keys to the box to A with instructions to go "and get a package in the box that was in the box with A's name on it." A did not open the safe deposit box during O's lifetime. After O's death, the safe deposit box was opened and the envelope with A's name on it was contained therein. The envelope contained a number of gold debenture bonds, payable to bearer; shares of common stock issued in the name of O and endorsed in blank by O in the presence of a witness. If you represented A, what would be your position in claiming for A the contents of the envelope? See In re Stevenson's Estate, 79 Ohio App. 315, 69 N.E.2d 426 (1946).

5.6. O bought a grand piano and placed it in the living room of his home. Shortly thereafter O said to his wife, "Dear, I give you the piano." The piano remained where it was in the living room of their home. On O's death, should the piano be included as part of his estate? See Robinson v. Hoalton, 213 Cal. 370, 2 P.2d 344 (1931); In re Cole ex parte Trustee v. Cole, [1963] 3 All E.R. 433.

5.7. What is the basis of determining the ownership of property used jointly by a husband and wife during their marriage when (a) it was received as a wedding present, (b) it was acquired with the husband's funds, or (c) it was acquired with the wife's funds? See Avnet v. Avnet, 204 Misc. 760, 124 N.Y.S.2d 517 (Mun. Ct. 1953).

5.8. O recorded a cattle brand in the name of O's daughter, A. O then branded some of O's own cattle with A's brand with the avowed purpose of making a gift to A. O kept the cattle so branded with O's own cattle and made no further effort to turn them over to A. On O's death, is A entitled to the cattle branded with her brand? Hillebrant v. Brewer, 6 Tex. 45 (1851).

5.9. O and A had lived together for 15 years. O became depressed as a result of injuries suffered in an automobile accident. She committed suicide by jumping from the roof of the apartment building in which they lived. On the morning of her death, she received a check in the amount of $17,400 in satisfaction of her claim arising out of the automobile accident. She endorsed the check in blank and placed it on the kitchen table with a handwritten note that she "bequeathed" everything she owned, including the check, to A and asked him to forgive her "for taking the easy way out." Is A entitled to the amount of the check? Is A entitled to other property O may have owned at her death? See Scherer v. Hyland, 75 N.J. 127, 380 A.2d 698 (1977).

5.10. O delivered to A for safekeeping $1 million in bearer bonds. One month later O said to A in the presence of a witness that "I hereby give to you the bearer bonds you have been safekeeping for me." O dies, and you are O's executor. Are you as executor of O's estate entitled to recover the bonds and include them as part of O's estate for disposition under O's will? See In re

Mills, 172 A.D. 530, 158 N.Y.S. 1100, *aff'd,* 219 N.Y. 642, 114 N.E. 1072 (1916).

Note: Requirement of Acceptance

The completion of a gift requires the acceptance of the gift by the donee. Miller v. Herzfeld, 4 F.2d 355 (3d Cir. 1925), recognizes the acceptance requirement but states as follows:

> It has long since been firmly established in England, that, while a man may not be made to accept a gift which he does not desire to possess, yet, when the gift has been made, it vests in him, subject to his repudiation, and remains vested until he repudiates it. [4 F.2d at 356.]

Scherer v. Hyland, 75 N.J. 127, 380 A.2d 698 (1977), comments as follows on the acceptance requirement:

> Although the issue of acceptance is rarely litigated, the authority that does exist indicates that, given a valid delivery, acceptance will be implied if the gift is unconditional and beneficial to the donee. The presumption of acceptance may apply even if the donee does not learn of the gift until after the donor's death. A donee cannot be expected to accept or reject a gift until he learns of it and unless a gift is rejected when the donee is informed of it the presumption of acceptance is not defeated. [75 N.J. at 135-136, 380 A.2d at 702.]

C H A P T E R 6

DELIVERY TO A THIRD PERSON

GRYMES v. HONE
49 N.Y. 17 (1872)

Appeal from judgment of the General Term of the Supreme Court in the third judicial department, affirming a judgment in favor of plaintiff, entered upon the report of a referee.

The action is brought to recover twenty shares of the stock of the Bank of Commerce of the city of New York, or its value, claimed by plaintiff as a gift mortis causa by Federal Vanderburgh, defendant's testator. The facts sufficiently appear in the opinion. The referee directed judgment that defendant, as executor, permit the transfer of the twenty shares of stock on the books of the bank, and, for that purpose, surrender the certificate; that he account for dividends received after the testator's death, and in case the stock was sold that he pay its value out of the estate. Judgment was entered accordingly.

PECKHAM, J. On the 19th August, 1867, the alleged donor being the owner of 120 shares of stock, included in one certificate, in the Bank of Commerce of New York city, made an absolute assignment in writing, transferable on the books of the bank on the surrender of the certificate, under seal and witnessed, of twenty shares thereof to this plaintiff, his favorite granddaughter, for value received, as the assignment purports, and appointed her his attorney irrevocable to sell and transfer the same to her use. After this paper had been signed, "he kept it by him for awhile" (how long, nowhere appears), and afterward handed it to his wife to put with the will and other papers in a tin box she had. When he gave to his wife the paper so drawn, he said: "I intend this for Nelly. If I die, don't give this to the executors; it isn't for them, but for Nelly; give it to her, herself." She asked, "why not give it to her now?" "Well," he said, "better keep it for the present; I don't know how much longer I may last or what may happen, or whether we may not need it." This is the statement, as given by the widow of donor. It was admitted that, at the time of executing said instrument, the donor was

101

from seventy-eight to eighty years of age, was in failing health, and so continued till his death, January 23d, 1868. Upon these facts was there a valid gift mortis causa?

Upon the question as to what constitutes such a gift, the authorities are infinite, not always consistent. But at this time it is generally agreed that, to constitute such a gift, it must be made with a view to the donor's death from present illness or from external and apprehended peril. It is not necessary that the donor should be in extremis, but he should die of that ailment. If he recover from the illness or survive the peril, the gift thereby becomes void; and until death it is subject to his personal revocation. 2 Kent, 444, and cases cited; 2 Redfield on Wills, 299 et seq.; 1 Story's Eq., Sec. 606, etc., notes and authorities.

In the next place there must be a delivery of it to the donee or to some person for him, and the gift becomes perfected by the death of the donor.

Three things are necessary. 1. It must be made with a view to donor's death. 2. The donor must die of that ailment or peril. 3. There must be a delivery. The appellant insists that the gift in this case fulfills neither requisite.

Was this gift made with a view to the donor's death? It is so found by the referee as a question of fact. What the witness intended to convey by the term "failing health" is not clear; but intendments are against the appellant where the fact is left uncertain. There is nothing in the case inconsistent with the idea that the testator, when he signed this assignment, was confined to his bed, and so continued till his death; though I do not wish to be understood as saying that such confinement was necessary to validate the gift. It seems that he died, as the referee finds, from this failing health, in five months thereafter; so that the terms, as used, indicated a very serious ailment.

True, he did not, and of course could not, know when death would occur when he executed this assignment, but he was in apprehension of it. His age and his "failing" told him death was near, but when it might occur he had no clear conviction. An ailment at such an age is extremely admonitory.

From these facts, can this court say, as a matter of law, that this testator was not so seriously ill when he executed this assignment as to be apprehensive of death; that he was not legally acting "in view" of death; that he was not so ill as to be permitted to make this sort of gift? True, the donor died five months thereafter; but we are referred to no case or principle that limits the time within which the donor must die to make such a gift valid. The only rule is that he must not recover from that illness. If he does the gift is avoided. The authorities cited by the appellant's counsel, of Weston v. Hight (5 Shep., Me., 287), and Staniland v. Willott (3 McN. & Gor. Ch. R. 664), are both instances of recovery, and the gifts, on that ground, declared void. In the latter the donor and his committee recovered back the stocks given, because of his recovery. The first case is improperly quoted in 2 Red. 300, note 11, as not originally authorizing the gift.

The declaration of the donor, that his wife should keep the assignment and not hand it over till after his death, as he did not know what might happen, nor but that they might need it, was simply a statement of the law, as to such a gift, whether the declaration was or was not made. Clearly he could not tell whether he should die or recover from that ailment. If he did recover, the law holds the gift void.

The transaction as to such a gift is, the donor says, I am ill, and fear I shall die of this illness; wherefore I wish you to take these things and hand them to my granddaughter after my death; but do not hand them to her now, as I may recover and need them. A good donatio mortis causa always implies all this. If delivered absolutely to the donee in person, the law holds it void in case the donor recovers, and he may then reclaim it. (Staniland v. Willott, *supra.*)

To make a valid gift mortis causa, it is not necessary that there should be any express qualification in the transfer or the delivery. It may be found to be such a gift from the attending circumstances, though the written transfer and the delivery may be absolute. See the last case.

I think this donor made this gift "with a view to his death," within the meaning of the rule on that subject.

2d. This also settles the second requisite, as it is admitted that he did not recover, but died of this "failing health," as it is expressed.

3d. Was there a delivery? The assignment was delivered to his wife for the donee. She thus became the agent of the donor [*sic*]. So far as the mere delivery is concerned, this is sufficient. (See the elementary writers before cited; also Drury v. Smith, 1 P.W., 404; Sessions v. Moseley, 4 Cush. 87; Coutant v. Schuyler, 1 Paige, 316; Borneman v. Sidlinger, 8 Shep., Me., 185; Wells v. Tucker, 3 Binn. 366; Hunter v. Hunter, 19 Barb. 631.) Such a delivery to be given to the grantee after the grantor's death, is good as to a deed of real estate. Hathaway v. Payne, 34 N.Y. 92.

It is urged that this gift was not completed; that the stock was not transferred on the books of the bank, and could not be until the certificate held by the donor was surrendered, and that equity will not aid volunteers to perfect an imperfect gift.

Within the modern authorities this gift was valid, notwithstanding these objections. The donor, by this assignment and power, parted with all his interest in the stock assigned as between him and the donee, and the donee became the equitable owner thereof as against every person but a bona fide purchaser without notice. Delivery of the stock certificate without a transfer on the bank's books would have made no more than an equitable title as against the bank (N.Y. and N.H.R.R. Co. v. Schuyler, 34 N.Y. 80, and cases cited), though it would give a legal title as against the assignor. McNeil v. Tenth Nat. Bank (46 N.Y. 325), just decided, and according to the case of Duffield v. Elwes, 1 Bligh., N.S., 497, 530, decided in the house of lords [*sic*]. The representatives of the donor were trustees for the donee by operation of law to make the gift effectual. (See also to the same effect Ex parte Pye, 18

Ves., 140; Kekewich v. Manning, 1 DeG., M. & G., 176; Richardson v. Richardson, 3 Eq. Ca. 686.) This trust, like this species of gift, is peculiar. The trust, like the gift, is revocable during the donor's life, and is perfected and irrevocable by his death.

This extended the law as laid down by Lord Hardwicke, in Ward v. Turner (2 Ves., Sr., 431, 442), upon this subject and our courts have gone in the same direction with Duffield v. Elwes. Where notes payable to the donor's order and not indorsed, and other things of similar character, have been given mortis causa, courts compel the representatives of the donor to allow the donee to sue in their name, though the legal title has not passed. (See last case; Grover v. Grover, 24 Pick., 261; Chase v. Redding, 13 Gray, 418; Bates v. Kempton, 7 id., 382; and see also Westerlo v. DeWitt, 36 N.Y., 340; Walsh v. Sexton, 55 Barb., 251.)

The equitable title to this stock is thus passed by the assignment, and it was not necessary to hand over the certificate. A court of equity will compel the donor's representatives to produce the certificate, that the legal title to the stock may be perfected.

As there is great danger of fraud in this sort of gift, courts cannot be too cautious in requiring clear proof of the transaction. This has been the rule from the early days of the civil law (which required five witnesses to such a gift) down to the present time. In this case the proof of the assignment, etc., is entirely clear, the question being as to its effect. The judgment should be affirmed, with costs to be paid out of the estate.

All concur; ALLEN, J., not voting.

Judgment affirmed.

Problems

6.1. O delivered to A for safekeeping $1 million in bearer bonds. One minute later O said to A in the presence of a witness that "I hereby give to your sister the bearer bonds you have been safekeeping for me." O dies before A delivers the bonds to his sister, and you are O's executor. Are you as executor of O's estate entitled to recover the bonds and include them as part of O's estate for disposition under O's will? See Problem 5.10 *supra* and the *Mills* case, cited there.

6.2. O owned some United States registered bonds, on the back of which appeared the statement that the bonds could be transferred only by a written assignment which was witnessed before one of certain named officials. O delivered these bonds to A with the request that A deliver them to B, without complying with the statement on the back of them as to the method of assignment. O, at the time O delivered the bonds to A, was contemplating suicide. O voluntarily drowned within an hour after delivering the bonds to A. Should O deliver the bonds to B or turn them over to O's administrator? Suppose O decides not to commit suicide — is O entitled to recover the bonds from A? See In re Estate of Stockham, 193 Iowa 823, 186 N.W. 650 (1922); Ray v. Leader Federal Savings & Loan Association, 292 S.W.2d 458 (Tenn. Ct. App. 1953).

MEYERS v. MEYERS
99 N.J. Eq. 560, 134 A. 95 (1926)

BACKES, V.C. Isador Meyers while ill, and about to undergo a serious surgical operation, signed and acknowledged a deed assigning to his fifteen-year-old son his two-third interest in a bond and mortgage, and, retaining the bond and mortgage, left the deed of assignment with the lawyer, who had just drawn it, with instructions to put it on record if anything happened to him. He had informed the lawyer of his illness and impending operation, and he died following the operation. The administratrix of the deceased attacks the assignment on the ground that there was no complete gift, in that there was no delivery of the subject-matter, and that the assignment was testamentary in character and invalid for non-compliance with the statute of wills.

The gift is typically causa mortis. The legal requirements of this form of gift are the same as a gift inter vivos. The two are alike in composition and legal effect, differing only in their consummation. Both are between living persons; the former is made under apprehension of death, the latter is not, and while both gifts must be presently operative, causa mortis is conditional, inter vivos is absolute. A more nearly accurate statement, perhaps, would be, that in both classes the donee must be completely vested of the title, the gift causa mortis being subject to divestment by the donor revoking it in his lifetime, or automatically if he escapes the peril. It is, of course, essential to the validity of a gift of personal property that the donor deliver the subject-matter to the donee with intent to make a gift and part with all dominion and control over it. The delivery is good if made to another for the donee. The gift is valid if made by deed and the deed delivered with donative intent, though the subject does not accompany the deed. The delivery of the deed is equivalent to a delivery of the subject. It has been held that a deed, delivered, operates as an estoppel, because of our ancient reverence for sealed instruments, but the weight of authority is that the delivery of the deed is an effective symbolical delivery of the thing given. For instructive discussion of gifts causa mortis see Basket v. Hassell, 107 U.S. 602, 2 S. Ct. 415, and Emery v. Clough, 63 N.H. 552, 4 A. 796, and the authorities sustaining the foregoing fundamental propositions collected in 21 L.R.A. 694; Dilts v. Stevenson, 17 N.J. Eq. 407; Ruckman v. Ruckman, 33 N.J. Eq. 354.

It is not questioned that the deceased executed the deed of assignment and left it with the lawyer with donative intent, but it is contended that he did not deliver it to him for his son, intending to then strip himself of all ownership and control of his interest in the bond and mortgage, and that this is indicated by his retention of the bond and mortgage. The donor's mental attitude must be determined by his acts, of which we have a clear expression in the absolute and disposing language of the deed assigning the interest to the donee, and in putting it into effect by delivering it to the lawyer, without reservation or qualification, save the instructions, perfectly consistent with a gift causa mortis, to put on record if anything happened to him, meaning death. The fact that the donor had, or the supposition that he believed he retained the right to revoke the gift, are not incongruous. The right to revoke is a condition of a gift causa mortis. The direction to record the deed was the equivalent of a direction to deliver it to the donee, and the delivery of the deed to the lawyer for the purpose of a second delivery to the donee was in perfect harmony with the situation, for the son was an infant and the deed could not very well have been given to him to hold during the precarious period. The argument that the donor did not intend absolutely to deliver the deed as a then present gift, because he took away with him the bond and mortgage, reacts to the inference that if he did not intend the legal effect of the deed delivered, he would have taken that too. No rational conclusion can be drawn from all the circumstances other than that the donor intended to make the deed presently operative subject to being defeated if death did not overtake him. Persuasive reasoning for sustaining the gift is to be found in the opinion of Vice-Chancellor Leaming in Rowley v. Bowyer, 75 N.J. Eq. 80, 71 A. 398, in which he upheld as legally delivered deeds executed by father to son, and left with the lawyer, who drew them with instructions to "deliver these to my son after my death." The learned vice-chancellor restated the true principle of gifts in respect of delivery, as again he did in Watson v. Magill, 97 A. 43, affirmed 85 N.J. Eq. 592, and pointed out that Schlicher v. Keeler, 67 N.J. Eq. 635, 61 A. 434, affirmed the principle to which he adhered, but was decided on the finding of fact that the deed in that case was not delivered with intent to pass the title to the subject of the gift. Williams v. Guile, 117 N.Y. 343, 22 N.E. 1071, is very much like the present case. There the donor, aged and paralytic, executed an assignment of a life insurance policy and handed it with the policy to his attorney with directions to deliver it to the donee if anything happened to him. Judge Gray, upon principle and authority, upheld the transfer as a gift causa mortis. The delivery of the policy with the assignment, wherein the facts differ, was not dwelt upon as a factor.

The bill will be dismissed.

Problems

6.3. William W. Cole was the owner of a steam yacht. He wrote a letter to Frank Hawkins as follows:

I have just been talking to your mother and given you my boat which she asked me to write and tell you about. Call when you are over this way and I will tell you more about it. If necessary, I will assist you to establish yourself, if you think you would care to take this way of making a living up. With your knowledge of mechanics I feel you could make something out of it. You will remember this is my birthday. In celebration of this fact I give you my boat. Take care of your health and your mother.

Yours truly,

W. W. Cole

Mr. Cole delivered this letter to Frank Hawkins's mother, and she in turn delivered it to Frank Hawkins. The yacht was in storage somewhere not far from New York City, where Cole and Hawkins lived. Shortly after the delivery of the letter, Cole died. Hawkins brings an action against the executor of Cole to recover possession of the steam yacht. Is he entitled to recover? See Hawkins v. Union Trust Co., 187 A.D. 472, 175 N.Y.S. 694 (1919).

6.4. O, about to undergo a serious operation, wrote and mailed to her husband a letter telling him the location of certain caches of money and securities secreted about the house which she and her husband had occupied. Part of the letter was as follows:

My Dearest Papa,

In the kitchen, in the bottom of the cabinet, where the blue frying pan is, under the wine bottle, there is one hundred dollars. Along side the bed in my bedroom, in the rear drawer of the small table, in the corner of the drawer, where my stockings are, you will find about seventy-five dollars. In my purse there is six dollars. Where the coats are, in a round tin box, on the floor, where the shoes are, there is two hundred dollars. This is Dianna's. Please put it in the bank for her. This is for her schooling.

The building loan book is yours, and the bank book, also the money that is here. . . .

My will is in the office of the former lawyer Anekstein, and his successor has it. There you will find out everything. . . .

The will had been made some years earlier when the couple had been separated and left O's estate to her children and one dollar to her husband. O was unconscious from the time of the operation to the date of her death eight days later. What is the effect of the letter? See Foster v. Reiss, 18 N.J. 41, 112 A.2d 553 (1955); Ireton, Survey of New Jersey Law — Personal Property, 10 Rutgers L. Rev. 300 (1956).

Note: Objectives Attainable by One Type of Gift Which Are Not Attainable by Another Type

Personal property owned outright by you at the time of your death is subject to the claims of your creditors, but your will can establish the order in which your property shall be used to pay your debts. In many states such property cannot be disposed of by you in your will so as to deprive your spouse of a statutory share in your property. Furthermore, generally such property cannot be disposed of by your will so as to deprive a child who is born after the execution of the will of a right to take an intestate share against your will, unless the will clearly shows the afterborn child was intentionally excluded. Personal property retained by you until you die, of course, may be subject to both federal and state death taxes as it passes on to your intended beneficiaries.

You should now stop to consider the extent to which you may be able to accomplish desires with respect to the disposition of your personal property by a gift causa mortis which you cannot accomplish by your will. You should consider the following questions:

1. In what way are the formalities which must be observed for the execution of a will different from the formalities for the completion of a gift causa mortis? Examine the statute in your state relating to execution of wills.

2. Are you as free to revoke a gift causa mortis as you are to revoke your will? Examine the statute in your state relating to the revocation of wills.

3. Can you remove your property from the claims of your creditors by making a gift causa mortis to a greater extent than you can by disposing of your property by your will? See Casner, Estate Planning ch. 5, E.3 (4th ed.).

4. Can you avoid federal and state death taxes through the medium of a gift causa mortis to a greater extent than you can by disposing of your property by your will? See Casner, Estate Planning ch. 5, E.3.1, 2 (4th ed.).

5. Can you deprive your spouse of a statutory share in your property by a gift causa mortis to a greater extent than you can by disposing of your property by your will? See Casner, Estate Planning ch. 5, B (4th ed.).

6. Can a child born after the making of a gift causa mortis claim an intestate share against the subject matter of the gift to the same extent that such child can claim such share against a will executed before the child's birth? See McCoy v. Shawnee Building & Loan Association, 122 Kan. 38, 251 P. 194 (1926).

In addition to appreciating the similarity and differences between disposing of property by a gift causa mortis and disposing of it by a will, you should be aware of the results obtainable by a gift inter vivos as distinguished from a gift causa mortis. It is generally recognized that an absolute gift inter vivos of personal property is effective to deprive your spouse and children of any rights in the subject matter of the gift. Furthermore, your creditors cannot reach such property unless they can show the transfer was in fraud of them.

CHAPTER 7

RETENTION OF RIGHTS BY THE DONOR

INNES v. POTTER
130 Minn. 320, 153 N.W. 604 (1915)

Action in the district court for Aitkin county by the administrator with the will annexed of the estate of Warren Potter, deceased, to recover possession of certain personal property or $100,000 the value thereof. The case was tried before Wright, J., who made findings and ordered judgment in favor of defendant. From the judgment entered pursuant to the order for judgment, plaintiff appealed. Affirmed.

HALLAM, J. 1. Warren Potter was the owner of 1370 shares of stock, of the par value of $100 a share, in the Potter-Casey Co. a business corporation of Aitkin county. In 1910 he was a man advanced in years. He had made a will some years before. In the meantime his business associate, Mr. Casey, had died and his estate had been probated. There was "considerable noise" about the amount of his property, and a substantial inheritance tax had been paid. On December 27, 1910, after some talk with J. A. Casey, son of his former associate, in which deceased stated that he wanted to leave a certain amount of property to his daughter, he took a certificate of 1,000 shares of stock of the Potter-Casey Co., indorsed upon it an absolute assignment to the defendant, and wrote a letter addressed to her in which he stated that he had transferred this stock to her, and making certain requests. The certificate, with the indorsement upon it, and this letter he inclosed in an envelope, securely sealed it, and indorsed thereon the following:

The certificate No. 1 for 1,000 shares to be sent by registered letter to H. Marcia Potter if not present or handed to her, taking her receipt for the same. . . .

The certificates to be held by J. A. Casey and delivered to the above parties only in case of the death of

12—27—10   *W. Potter*

109

This he then delivered to J. A. Casey, and Casey held it until Mr. Potter's death. Deceased never mentioned the matter to Casey again, and never exercised nor attempted to exercise any control over the stock. Warren Potter died in February, 1914. After his death, J. A. Casey delivered the envelope and its contents to the defendant. She opened the envelope and took therefrom the letter and the certificate. Potter's will was admitted to probate, and plaintiff was appointed administrator with the will annexed. He commenced this action to recover possession of the certificate of stock or its value. The trial court found that defendant owned the stock; that deceased intended to and did relinquish all control over the stock and all rights in it; that he intended to and did give the stock to defendant, and intended that the gift take effect at once on the delivery to Casey, but that the right of defendant to the beneficial enjoyment thereof was postponed until the death of deceased.

2.   The first question is this: Is it competent for a person to make a gift of personal property by delivery of the subject of the gift to a trustee where delivery by the trustee to the donee and beneficial enjoyment by the donee are postponed until the death of the donor?

As to deeds of real estate the law in this state is well settled. Where a grantor executes a deed and deposits it with a third person, to be delivered by him to the grantee after the death of the grantor, and reserves to himself no right to control or recall the instrument, the transaction is a valid one and full and complete title is vested in the grantee after death of the grantor. Haeg v. Haeg, 53 Minn. 33, 5 N.W. 1114; Wicklund v. Lindquist, 102 Minn. 321, 113 N.W. 631; Dickson v. Miller, 124 Minn. 346, 145 N.W. 112. This is true, even though the enjoyment of the estate granted is postponed until the death of the grantor, and even though the deed thereof expressly reserves a life estate in the grantor (Ekblaw v. Nelson, 124 Minn. 335, 144 N.W. 1094), and even though the grant is subject to the contingency that the grantee survive the grantor, or to any contingency, as long as it is one over which the grantor has no control. Thomas v. Williams, 105 Minn. 88, 117 N.W. 155.[1]

3.   Anciently there was no such thing recognized in law as an expectant estate in personal property. This was because of the perishable nature of such property, its movable characteristics, and its insignificance. An exception was early made in favor of chattels real. Manning's Case, 8 Co. (Eng.) 94b; Lampet's Case, 10 Co. (Eng.) 46b; but in that case only as to interests created by will, and when merely the use of the chattel was given to the first legatee. 2 Bl. Com. 398. The exception was later extended from chattels real to chattels personal under like restrictions. 2 Bl. Com. 398; 1 Eq. Cas. Abr. (Eng.) 360. These limitations one by one dropped away. In chancery before the close of the seventeenth century it was settled that a bequest of an

---

1.   For a consideration of the problems involved in the delivery to a third person of a deed to land with instructions to deliver it to the grantee after the death of the grantor, see Chapter 27, Section 2. — EDS.

expectant estate in goods to another was good, whether the goods or the use of the goods were given to the first legatee. Hyde v. Parrat, 1 P. Wms. (Eng.) 1. And in recent times it has not been necessary in England that limitations of this sort be made by will. They are equally good when made by deed of trust. Child v. Baylie, Cro. Jac. (Eng.) 459; 2 Bl. Com. 398.

Perishable chattels are said to constitute an exception to the rule, particularly chattels the use of which consists in their consumption. But the reason given is one of construction, the theory being that the gift of such articles for life must have been intended as an absolute gift, since one could not use without consuming the property. Andrew v. Andrew, 1 Col. C.C. 686; Randall v. Russell, 3 Meriv. 190; Evans v. Iglehart, 6 Gill & J. (Md.) 171; Henderson v. Vaulx, 10 Yerg. (Tenn.) 30; German v. German, 27 Pa. 116, 67 Am. Dec. 451.

The doctrine that personal property may be limited by way of remainder after a life interest created at the same time was early recognized in the United States. 2 Kent. Com. (13 ed.) 352, 353, and notes; Executors of Moffat v. Strong, 10 Johns. (N.Y.) 12; Langworthy v. Chadwick, 13 Conn. 42. The disposition of the later cases has been to dispense with all fictitious distinctions between transfers of real and personal property, and to apply the same rules to both, except where distinctions are founded upon some substantial principle of law or are required by some statutory enactment. In this state expectant interests in personal property are recognized. State ex rel. Tozer v. Probate Court of Washington County, 102 Minn. 268, 291, 113 N.W. 888. Since it is competent for a person to create an expectant interest in personal property, we see no ground for saying that he may not do so either by will, by sale or by gift. Nor do we see any reason why the rules as to delivery to a third person, with direction to deliver to the donee on the death of the donor, should not apply to personal as well as to real property. Delivery is of course necessary to give effect to a gift, but so it is to give effect to a deed. If valid delivery may be made to a trustee in case of a gift of a deed of real property, why not in case of a gift of personal property? Not only do we think there should be no distinction between the two classes of property in this respect, but we are equally convinced that it is the settled law in most of the states of the Union that no such distinction does exist.

We accordingly hold that the owner of personal property may make a valid gift thereof with the right of enjoyment in the donee postponed until the death of the donor, if the subject of the gift be delivered to a third person with instruction to deliver it to the donee upon the donor's death, and if the donor parts with all control over it, reserves no right to recall, and intends thereby a final disposition of the property given.[2]

4. The next question is, did this transaction constitute such a gift? Plaintiff's contention is that the transaction was not a gift at all, but that it is

---

2. Legal future interests in personal property are discussed in Casner, Estate Planning ch. 11, C.6 (4th ed.). — EDS.

testamentary in character and void. The gift, if sustainable at all, must be sustained as a gift inter vivos. It was in no sense a gift causa mortis. Effect should be given to the transaction if possible. Thomas v. Williams, 105 Minn. 88, 117 N.W. 155. If, as plaintiff claims, the documents were testamentary in character the transaction was void, for the formalities required for the execution of a will were not followed. It is only by construing the transaction as an executed gift that effect can be given to it at all. It is not always easy to determine whether or not an instrument is testamentary in character. It depends upon the intention of the maker. The fact that the instrument postpones the enjoyment of the subject matter until after the death of the grantor, is not decisive that the instrument is testamentary in character. The test is whether the maker intended the instrument to have no effect until after the maker's death, or whether he intended it to transfer some present interest. If some interest vests at once in right, though the enjoyment of it be postponed, the instrument is not a will, and it is irrevocable. Thomas v. Williams, 105 Minn. 88, 117 N.W. 155. We think the evidence sustains the finding of the trial court that the transaction constituted an absolute and irrevocable gift from deceased to defendant.

5.   Plaintiff contends that the direction to deliver "only in case of the death" of the donor signifies a condition attached to the delivery and an intent that the gift shall become operative only in the event that the donee survived the donor. There is some authority sustaining plaintiff's contention. Sterling v. Wilkinson, 83 Va. 791, 3 S.E. 533. We do not, however, agree as to this effect of the words "in case of the death." If the donor were at the time suffering with some illness, as in the case of Basket v. Hassell, 107 U.S. 602, 2 S. Ct. 415, 27 L. Ed. 500, such language might well be construed to imply a condition that the gift should be operative only in the event of death from such illness, and the survival of the donee. But Warren Potter was not ill, nor was there anything that suggested impending death. Under the circumstances, we think the language "in case of the death," which was certain sooner or later to occur, meant nothing more or less than that delivery should be made upon the death of the donor. And this is sustained by authority. Small v. Marburg, 77 Md. 11, 19, 25 A. 920; Goodell v. Pierce, 2 Hill (N.Y.) 659; Ewing v. Winters, 34 W. Va. 23, 11 S.E. 718.

Plaintiff lays much stress upon the fact that J. A. Casey testified that, if Potter had in his lifetime demanded a return of the envelope and its contents, he would have returned it to him. It is not certain that this expressed anything more than Casey's mistaken view of the law applicable to such a case or his submission to Potter's judgment. But in any event the evidence is not decisive. The intention of Potter, not of Casey, controls.

Nor do we attach great importance to the statement of Casey that Potter said he wanted to "leave" a certain amount of property to his daughter Marcia. The word "leave" is often used in reference to property left by will, but the word is often loosely used and its use should not be given controlling importance.

Plaintiff also urges strongly that deceased was endeavoring by this transaction to evade the payment of the inheritance tax. We are not sure that he did not have such a purpose. But we cannot see that it is important whether he did or not. It seems to be conceded that he did not succeed and that his property is subject to tax whether this be construed as a gift or not. If the construction of this as a gift would result in a fraud upon the state, that circumstance might be a reason for not adopting that construction, but this is not such a case.

Judgment affirmed.

Problems

7.1. O delivered to her daughter, who is the mother of A, some silver candlesticks, stating "here are the silver candlesticks that have been in the family since the Revolutionary War. I would like you to give these to A when she marries." What are the possible legal consequences of O's action?

7.2. O was engaged to marry A. O sent A $5,000 to buy a ring, pay for a wedding gown, and pay the expenses of the contemplated marriage. Thereafter A broke the engagement and married someone else. O desires to recover the $5,000 from A and seeks your advice. What would you tell him? See Williamson v. Johnson, 62 Vt. 378, 20 A. 279 (1890); Splendore v. Guglielmo, 205 Misc. 941, 129 N.Y.S.2d 374 (1954). If O broke the engagement, would this fact affect the result? See Coconis v. Christakis, 70 Ohio Misc. 29, 435 N.E.2d 100 (1981).

Does the following statute (a so-called heart balm act) have any bearing on the problem? "Breach of contract to marry shall not constitute an injury or wrong recognized by law, and no action, suit, or proceeding shall be maintained thereon." See Gikas v. Nicholis, 96 N.H. 177, 71 A.2d 785 (1950).

Consider the following statute:

Where either party to a contemplated marriage in this State makes a gift of money or property to the other on the basis or assumption that the marriage will take place, in the event that the donee refuses to enter into the marriage as contemplated or that it is given up by mutual consent, the donor may recover such gift or such part of its value as may, under all of the circumstances of the case, be found by a court or jury to be just.

See Steinbeck v. Halsey, 115 Cal. App. 2d 213, 251 P.2d 1008 (1953).

7.3. O informs A that if A will name an expected child after O, O will give A $5,000 for the child's education. A names the child after O and then requests the money. O refuses. If you were A's attorney, what arguments would you advance in favor of A's claim to the money? See Gardner v. Denison, 217 Mass. 492, 105 N.E. 359 (1914).

TYGARD v. McCOMB
54 Mo. App. 85 (1893)

GILL, J. On September 5, 1888, and for years prior thereto, Alexander Wilson resided at Rich Hill, Missouri. He was then married to the second wife and had four living children, all by his first wife. Two of these children were of age, and two, the above named plaintiffs, Isabella and Anna, were minors.

On said September 5, 1888, Wilson went to the Rich Hill Bank, where he did business, and transferred the entire balance of his account, to-wit, $1,302.97, to the joint credit of his two minor daughters, Isabella and Anna. He got from the bank a pass-book, made out in the names of these children, wherein was entered the above deposit. He retained this in his own possession till his death in January, 1890. In addition to this other smaller sums were deposited, and he checked out from time to time different amounts, in every instance signing the names of the two girls by Alexander Wilson. The last check on the account made by him was in August, 1889, and this was on account of a loan of $600 that day made to one Hill. For this he took Hill's note payable to himself. Hill's note was renewed from time to time always made payable to Alexander Wilson, and the same, together with the bank book, was found among Wilson's papers at his death in January, 1890.

The above facts have given rise to two suits; this one being brought by the guardian and curator of the two minor children seeking to have the court declare them entitled to the Hill note, on the ground that the money thus loaned by the father belonged to them, and the second suit was brought by the administrator against the guardian of the two infant children, asking that the balance left in the bank ($724.97), and to the nominal credit of Isabella and Anna, be decreed and held as assets of the estate of said Alexander Wilson.

Both suits are in equity, and the court below decided each case in favor of the administrator and against the infants, and their guardian appealed.

When we have settled the character of the transaction of September 5, 1888, where Alexander Wilson drew his money out of the bank at Rich Hill and replaced it to the credit of his two minor children, the determination of both these cases becomes easy. If that was a valid and effective gift, then the two children were vested with a title to the money thus deposited; and they are entitled not only to the $724.97, balance to their credit, but as well to the Hill note given for the loan of the $600.

The trial judge in terms declared, in his finding and judgment, "that the moneys so deposited by Alexander Wilson in the names of his said minor children, Isabella and Anna Wilson, was not a complete gift to them during his life, as contended for by plaintiff herein, but that the same was deposited by said Alexander Wilson subject to his own order and control, and was not intended to vest in said minors until his death." The correctness of this holding is the question here.

This was in no sense a gift causa mortis; it was not made if at all "in his last illness and in contemplation and expectation of death" as is necessary to constitute a gift causa mortis. 2 Kent's Commentaries, 444. Hence, much that is said in briefs of counsel may be eliminated. If anything, it was a gift inter vivos. Mr. Wilson made this deposit some eighteen months before his death and while in perfect health, it seems. His death was from an accident in a mine.

As to what will constitute a gift, or such as the courts recognize, has been so often declared that repetition is tiresome. We had occasion to say in Keyl v. Westerhaus, 42 Mo. App. 49, 57, that "a gift inter vivos is a parting with the title of personal property in praesenti absolutely and irrevocably. As said by Chancellor Kent, 'gifts inter vivos have no reference to the future, and go into immediate and absolute effect.' In order to constitute a valid gift there must be a complete and irrevocable transmutation of title and possession, perfect in all things at the time the gift is made, dependent on no circumstances or condition in the future. 1 Parsons on Contracts, 234." There must be a complete delivery of the thing given; such a delivery of possession as works an immediate change of dominion over the property. Gartside v. Pahlman, 45 Mo. App. 160, and cases cited. There must be an absolute and unequivocal intention by the donor to pass the title and possession at once over to the donee. To constitute a valid gift it will not do to have it go into effect on the happening of some event in the future or at the death of the donor. In the latter case the gift would be testamentary in character and would violate the wise provisions of the statute of wills.

In view now of these well established principles, I would state the law as applicable to this case to be this: If, when Alexander Wilson placed this money in the Rich Hill bank to the credit of his minor children, he intended thereby to make an absolute gift in praesenti, intended to part with the money at once, and vest the title thereto in said Isabella and Anna, and no longer to retain dominion thereof on his own account, then it became a valid gift, absolute and irrevocable. But if when such deposit was made said Wilson did not intend at once to part with the title and possession, and simply placed the money to the credit of the children to take effect as a kind of post mortem benefaction, to be his while he lived and theirs at his death, then it was not an executed and valid gift, and the courts will not give it effect.

No importance is attached to the mere fact that he kept the pass-book and never gave it over to the children, never notified them of the deposit to their credit, and that therefore no such delivery for these reasons as would answer the purpose of a valid gift. For as the transaction was clearly for the benefit of the children their assent and acceptance of the gift would be assumed. And besides a delivery of the pass-book to their father, who was their natural guardian, would be a delivery to them. A delivery therefore to the father on their account was, under the circumstances of the case, all that could be expected. If then we were to decide this case, looking alone to the deposit in the bank and retention by the donor of the evidence of such deposit, we should not hesitate to award the money to these minor children. The following well considered adjudications would warrant the decision.

But the question arises, what was Alexander Wilson's intention in the matter of this deposit in the names of his minor children. Did he intend thereby to transfer the property to his infant children at once, or was it a mere attempted testamentary disposition? The intention is the important element in determining the character of such transactions, and such intention may be manifested by acts or words or both. Sneathen v. Sneathen, *supra,* 210; Standiford v. Standiford, 97 Mo. 231, 10 S.W. 836; Ells v. Railroad, 40 Mo. App. 165. After a careful consideration of the evidence adduced at the trial, we conclude with the trial court that Alexander Wilson did not make a complete gift of that money to said minor children during his life, "but that the same was deposited by him subject to his own order and sole control and was not intended to vest in said minors until his death." Wilson stated to the bank officers, when he transferred the money to the credit of the girls, that he wanted it so fixed that the money would be theirs if anything happened to him. He stated also to his daughter, Mrs. Watson, that the money was so placed that the stepmother should not handle it and that if anything happened to him, the girls would get it. Witness Hill, speaking of the loan represented by the note in controversy (and which loan was clearly from this deposit in the names of the minor children) testified:

> "When Mr. Wilson came over to the club rooms, and gave me the $588 in money, he said, this is some of the money that I checked out of the girls' account. Says I, what do you mean? Well, he says, just this, there is quite a number of persons here after me all the time wanting to borrow, and, in order to get rid of them, I tell them that I have no money, and what surplus funds I have on hand I just deposit to the credit of my girls."

The testimony shows conclusively too that he treated this money all the time as if his own, checking on it at pleasure. In short, the circumstances all the way through show that when he placed the deposit in the bank to the credit of the children he still regarded it as his money, but that it was his desire, if anything happened to him, to have it go to the said minor children. At most then Mr. Wilson attempted a noncupative [*sic*] will under circumstances by law not permitted, and it is not in the power of the courts to give it effect. In addition to cases *supra* the following are in point: Geary v. Page, 9 Bosw. (N.Y.) 290; Sherman v. Bank, 138 Mass. 581.

The judgment of the circuit court will be affirmed. All concur.

Problem

7.4. O, desiring to make a gift to A, gives A a personal check in the amount of $1,000, writing in the bottom lefthand corner thereof the words "at my death." O dies shortly thereafter. Three months later, A presents the check to the bank on which it is drawn and requests the payment of $1,000. O's account in the bank exceeds $1,000. Should the bank honor the check? See Burks v. Burks, 222 Ark. 97, 257 S.W.2d 369 (1953).

In re TOTTEN
179 N.Y. 112, 71 N.E. 748 (1904)

Appeal from an order of the Appellate Division of the Supreme Court in the second judicial department, entered December 30, 1903, which reversed a decree of the Kings County Surrogate's Court rejecting certain claims of the respondent herein against the estate of Fanny Amelia Lattan, deceased.

This is a controversy between the administrator of Fanny Amelia Lattan, deceased, and Emile R. Lattan, who presented a claim against the estate of said decedent which was duly rejected by the representative thereof. The claim was for the sum of $1,775.03, besides interest, alleged to be due "by reason of certain deposits made by" the decedent "in the Irving Savings Institution, as trustee for the said Emile R. Lattan, the moneys so deposited having been subsequently withdrawn by the said decedent." Upon the final accounting of the administrator the justice of said claim, in accordance with the stipulation of all concerned, was determined by the surrogate after a referee had reported the evidence, the facts and his conclusion. The surrogate confirmed the report and dismissed the claim upon the merits, but the decree entered accordingly was reversed by the Appellate Division "upon the law and the facts" and the claim was allowed with costs. The administrator and certain heirs and next of kin of the decedent appealed to this court.

VANN, J. . . .

Beginning in 1886 the decedent and her sister Angelica each had numerous accounts in the Irving Savings Institution, the greater part in the name of the former individually, or as trustee. At various times there were sixteen of the latter class. While no single account in the name of the decedent ever exceeded $3,000 the aggregate amount of all her accounts always exceeded that sum and occasionally by several thousand dollars. At the same time many accounts were kept by her in other savings institutions, some in her own name simply and others with the addition of "trustee for" or "in trust for" some person named. It was her practice to draw from all these accounts at will, whether they were kept in her name as trustee or otherwise, and to close them and open others as she saw fit. She kept the pass books and no beneficiary named in any account ever drew therefrom except upon drafts signed by her. When she died intestate in March, 1900, accounts were outstanding in her name as trustee in favor of Emile R. Lattan and three other persons and they had the benefit thereof without controversy.

On the 2nd of January, 1886, the decedent opened an account in the Irving Savings Institution by depositing the sum of $355. A rule of the bank required the depositor to give the name of the person for whom he wished to place the money in trust, but the one making the deposit had absolute control of the account so long as he retained possession of the pass book. The pass book was numbered 42,728 and the deposit was entered thereon as well as on the books of the bank as an account with Fanny A. Lattan, trustee for Emile R. Lattan, depositor. At some time, but it does not appear when except that it was prior to May 1893, the words "Trustee for Emile R. Lattan" were canceled by rulings in red ink. As at first entered in the ledger of the bank the account stood as at first entered on the pass book, but when carried forward to a new ledger in 1892 it stood as an account with the decedent individually. When she opened this account she had between $6,000 and $7,000 standing in her name individually and as trustee on the books of the same bank. Two other deposits were made in this account, the first of $5.10 on July 1st, 1886, and the second of $740, September 21st, 1886. Twelve drafts were drawn against it at various times. The first, dated January 27th, 1886, for $100 in favor of Lewis H. Lattan, was signed by the decedent as trustee, but all the rest commencing with September 19th, 1890, were signed by her individually. July 8th, 1898, the account was closed by her individual draft for $1,104.06 and the pass book was surrendered. With the amount thus drawn she opened two new accounts in the same bank, the first No. 66,807 in favor of Fanny A. Lattan in trust for Rosalie M. Beam for the sum of $552.03, and the other No. 66,808 in favor of Fanny A. Lattan in trust for Emile R. Lattan for the same amount. Both of these accounts remained open at the time of the decedent's death and the pass books were delivered by her administrator to the parties named who drew the money accordingly. During the existence of account No. 42,728 the decedent at all times had possession of the pass book and Emile R. Lattan received no part of the moneys deposited to the credit of that account except as already mentioned.

On the 19th of September, 1890, the decedent had ten accounts amounting to between $8,000 and $9,000 standing in her name, individually or as trustee, on the books of the Irving Savings Institution. On that day she opened account No. 51,556 in that bank by depositing $462.03 in her name as trustee for Emile R. Lattan. Said amount was largely made up of sums drawn from other accounts in her name as trustee. She retained possession of the pass book, and no one, except herself and the officers of the bank, appears to have known of the existence of the account until after her death. September 19th, 1892, she deposited $100 in that account and September 13th, 1893, the further sum of $80.60. When it was closed on the 15th of November, 1894, it amounted with interest to $733.30, which she drew out and deposited in another account, in her name as trustee for Lewis H. Lattan, who after her death drew the amount thereof.

Emile R. Lattan was the son of Lewis H. Lattan, a spendthrift, who in 1884 turned over to his sisters Angelica Lattan and the decedent all his property, worth about $20,000, for their management, but without instructions as to their course in managing the same. No accounting was ever made to him with reference thereto, although he survived them both.

There was no evidence that the decedent ever spoke to any one about any of these accounts or stated what her intention was in opening them. The accounts in question were opened with her own money and no part thereof came from her brother Lewis. Out of thirty-one accounts in seven savings banks she paid over to the alleged beneficiaries the balance left when two thereof were closed, but in both of these instances, as well as in all other cases, she treated the accounts as her own, drawing against them and making new deposits from time to time as she thought best. All the pass books with a trust heading, containing accounts which had not been closed when the decedent died, were delivered to the respective beneficiaries who drew the balance on hand. Emile R. Lattan did not know of the existence of any accounts on which he relies in this proceeding until more than a year after the decedent died. Angelica Lattan, who was appointed and qualified as administratrix, died on the 10th of April, 1901, leaving the administrator as the sole representative of the estate. The personal property of Fanny A. Lattan was inventoried at the sum of $32,950.08, but owing to increase in values the amount on hand at the date of the final decree of distribution was more than $40,000.

The most favorable view of these facts and others of like character not mentioned does not permit the inference as matter of fact that the decedent in making the deposits in question intended to establish an irrevocable trust in favor of the respondent. Aside from what took place when the deposits were made, every act of the decedent, with one exception, is opposed to the theory of a trust. That exception is the closing of one account after the words of trust had been canceled and the deposit of part of the proceeds in the same form as the original. This is not enough when considered with the other facts to establish an irrevocable trust. Cunningham v. Davenport, 147 N.Y. 43, 41 N.E. 412. No connection was shown between any deposit and the sum held in trust by the decedent and her sister Angelica for Lewis H. Lattan, who is still living and was sworn as a witness at the trial. A deposit in favor of the son would not have satisfied the claim of the father in the absence of a request from the latter, of which there was no evidence. In view of the practice of the decedent in doing business with savings banks, the custom of many other persons in that regard, the various objects which people have in making deposits in the form of a trust, the retention of the pass book with the corresponding control of the deposits according to the rules of the bank, the subsequent history of the various accounts with the frequent withdrawals and changes, we think that the form of the deposits as they appear upon the books was not strengthened by the other evidence. There was no question of fact in the case and the Appellate Division had no power to reverse upon the facts. We find no exception in the record warranting a reversal upon the law, unless the exception to the conclusion of the referee and surrogate that the claim should be dismissed upon the merits raises reversible error. This involves the question whether upon the conceded facts as matter of law, an irrevocable trust was established.

Savings bank trusts, as they are sometimes called, have frequently been before the courts during the past few years. When we considered the pioneer case but few instances of deposits in trust were known and a liberal rule was laid down without the limitations which later cases required. After a while when it became a common practice for persons to make deposits in that form, in order to evade restrictions upon the amount one could deposit in his own name and for other reasons, the courts became more conservative and sought to avoid unjust results by adapting the law to the customs of the people. A brief review of the cases will show how the subject has been gradually developed so as to accord with the methods of the multitude of persons who make deposits in these banks. . . .

While we have considered we do not cite the numerous cases decided by the Supreme Court bearing upon the question, owing to the conflict in the opinions of learned justices in different appellate divisions. It is necessary for us to settle the conflict by laying down such a rule as will best promote the interests of all the people in the state. After much reflection upon the subject, guided by the principles established by our former decisions, we announce the following as our conclusion: A deposit by one person of his own money, in his own name as trustee for another, standing alone, does not establish an irrevocable trust during the lifetime of the depositor. It is a tentative trust merely, revocable at will, until the depositor dies or completes the gift in his lifetime by some unequivocal act or declaration, such as delivery of the pass book or notice to the beneficiary. In case the depositor dies before the beneficiary without revocation, or some decisive act or declaration of disaffirmance, the presumption arises that an absolute trust was created as to the balance on hand at the death of the depositor. This rule requires us to reverse the order of the Appellate Division and to affirm the decree of the surrogate, with costs to the appellants in all courts.

MALONE v. WALSH

315 Mass. 484, 53 N.E.2d 126 (1944)

LUMMUS, J. Mary A. Ryan, late of Lynn, died intestate on December 25, 1939, leaving her husband, Patrick J. Ryan, a sister, Catherine Reigle of Cleveland, Ohio, and three brothers, Patrick, Peter and James Walsh, of Lettermoghera in Ireland. The petitioner was appointed administrator of her estate. In 1939 Mary A. Ryan made three joint deposits in different savings banks in Massachusetts, substantially in the names of Mary A. Ryan and Patrick Walsh (her brother) payable to either or the survivor. This petition is brought under G.L. (Ter. Ed.) c. 215, Sec. 6, as amended by St. 1939, c. 194, Sec. 2, to determine the title to these deposits and to recover them for the estate. Walsh v. Mullen, 314 Mass. 241. The probate judge found that Mary A. Ryan did not intend that the deposits should pass into the control of her brother Patrick or that any part of the funds should become his property until her death, and found that she did not intend to make a present completed gift. He entered a decree ordering the respondent savings banks to pay the funds represented by the bank books standing in the joint names as hereinbefore described, to the petitioner. The respondent Patrick Walsh appealed. The judge found the material facts, and all the evidence is reported.

The law on this subject of joint deposits was stated in Goldston v. Randolph, 293 Mass. 253, 256, 257, 199 N.E. 896, 898. It was there said that a change in a deposit to the joint account of the former owner and another " 'would operate as a present and complete gift in joint ownership if she [the former owner] clearly intended such a result.' . . . Such a present gift could be made even though the donor retained the exclusive right to the income of the deposit during her life. . . . A present gift of an interest in the deposit would be effected on the principle of Chippendale v. North Adams Savings Bank, 222 Mass. 499, 111 N.E. 371, and cases following it, by a contract to which the bank, the deceased and the . . . [donee] were parties if the requisite intention on the part of the deceased existed. Delivery of the bank book would not be essential since the contract takes the place of the delivery ordinarily required. . . . Furthermore, a transfer of this nature is not a gift of the deposit as such, but rather a gift of the interest therein created by the contract. . . . And such a gift made in the lifetime of the deceased of an interest in the deposit, though ripening into full ownership of the deposit by the . . . [donee] on the death of the deceased, is not testamentary in character." In Ball v. Forbes, 314 Mass. 200, 203-204, 49 N.E.2d 898, 900, it was said:

> It is settled that, while the contract of deposit is conclusive as between the parties and the bank, and that the contract with the bank takes the place of delivery ordinarily required, and that a present gift could thus be made if that result was intended even though the deceased retained control of the books evidencing the deposits, nevertheless, as between the survivor and the representative of the estate of the deceased, it is still open to the latter to show by attendant facts and circumstances that the deceased did not intend to make a present completed gift of a joint interest in the account, and that the mere form of the deposits does not settle the matter.

These statements of the law are supported by other recent cases.

There was evidence of the following facts. Mary A. Ryan was born in Ireland on June 24, 1871, and came to this country in 1900. On March 2, 1902, she married Patrick J. Ryan. Two children were born, who died in infancy. A third child, Veronica, was born in 1905 and died in February, 1914. In 1908 Mary A. Ryan and Veronica went to Ireland and remained nine months. Mary was displeased because her husband would not go with her, and also because he was working nights. She left her husband in 1914, when she sold his boats, dogs, hens, guns and fishing tackle without his knowledge. They went to living together again within a year, and parted again in 1915. She had him placed on probation in a District Court with an order for her support. They began to live together again in 1924, but lived together only a few weeks. Though living apart thereafter they were not unfriendly, and sometimes went to a theatre or a restaurant together or spent weekends together. The judge found as follows: "The decedent during her lifetime was not a generous woman, but rather close and penurious, and of a suspicious nature. She insisted to her close associates and friends that she was without funds, and received favors and gratuities from those friends who supposed her to be living in poverty."

The amount of the savings bank deposits in question is approximately $15,000. They were originally established in the name of Mary A. Ryan, the first in a Quincy bank in October, 1915, the second in a Charlestown bank on December 1, 1920, and the third in a Lynn bank on September 13, 1929. There were other deposits in other savings banks, but in May, 1935, they were withdrawn and the money was deposited in one of the three accounts just mentioned.

About April 23, 1935, Mary A. Ryan consulted a lawyer in Lynn about her savings bank deposits. She wished to make provision for the disposition of her money so that her husband would not get any of it. She showed the lawyer her will, but he told her that her husband could waive the will and take his statutory interest. She destroyed the will in the presence of the lawyer. Then she talked with the lawyer about making a trust agreement, and decided to make one. She told him exactly who were to be the beneficiaries. They were her brothers and sisters, the children of one of her sisters, some cousins, and charities. When the trust instrument was drawn, she decided not to sign it. This was on May 17, 1935. Finally she decided to transfer her deposits to herself and her sister Catherine Reigle jointly. The three deposits already described were transferred into new accounts in the names of Mary A. Ryan and Catherine Reigle, payable to either or the survivor. She told the lawyer that the money had been earned by her own labor. The lawyer drew, and she signed, instructions to Catherine Reigle as to the distribution of the money after her death. The beneficiaries named in those instructions were much the same, and the gifts to them were in much the same amounts, as in the proposed trust agreement. Catherine Reigle was included to the extent of $500 only, though her three brothers in Ireland were to receive $4,000 each. Relatives named Coyne were included for amounts not exceeding $500 each. These written instructions were given to Catherine Reigle on May 20, 1935. Mary A. Ryan retained possession of the bank books at all times, and made withdrawals from the accounts for her own purposes. No withdrawals were made by Catherine Reigle.

Beginning with the summer of 1938 the relations between Mary A. Ryan and Catherine Reigle became unfriendly. The former thought the latter too grasping for money. On December 5, 1938, Mary A. Ryan wrote to her brother Patrick Walsh in Ireland, whom she had not seen since 1908 but with whom she corresponded, saying among other things this:

> Now Pat I am going to send papers to you to fill out and sign your name to them and whatever is left if anything should happen to me you would get whatever is left. There is Michael Coyne and John Coyne and Kate and her good for nothing crowd wishing me to pass away. . . . I know your prayers are helping me. [Spelling corrected.]

The "papers" referred to evidently were cards for the transfer of the savings bank deposits into the names of Mary A. Ryan and Patrick Walsh jointly. She wrote Patrick that when the cards had been signed "then they cannot touch anything belonging to me if I died in [the] morning and the Coynes don't get even my old shoes. This doesn't mean anything more than a protection so safety first. Don't say anything to James or his family or to anyone. Keep this to yourself. This is just been for fear the Coynes might try to put me in a place where I could not hear from you and I am not trusting Kate or her daughter either." (Spelling corrected.) On February 28, 1939, she wrote Patrick that she was sending him some more cards to be filled out and returned to her so that she could have them by the first of April. She added, "[If] I don't have it by the first of April I shall make other plans." (Spelling corrected.) On April 4, 1939, the deposit in the Quincy bank was transferred into a new account in the names of Mary A. Ryan and Patrick Walsh jointly. On April 20, 1939, the deposit in the Charlestown bank was so transferred. On May 1, 1939, the deposit in the Lynn bank was so transferred. There was no evidence that Catherine Reigle participated in or knew about this change, and it is to be inferred that she knew nothing about it. But as the judge found, Mary A. Ryan impliedly reserved a power of revocation of any trust created by the joint deposits in 1935 and the instructions to Catherine Reigle, and exercised that power by the transfers in 1939. Mary A. Ryan retained possession of the bank books at all times, and made withdrawals for her own purposes. No withdrawals were made by Patrick Walsh.

On February 3, 1940, the respondent Patrick Walsh wrote from Ireland to the Lynn bank as follows:

> In December 1938 I understand that the amount was placed in the joint names of Mrs. Ryan (who was my sister) and myself for the purpose of the money belonging to the person who outlived the other, and as such person I now wish to have the account placed solely in my name as no other persons has [*sic*] any claim to it.

A letter from the respondent Patrick Walsh in Ireland to the probate judge contained the following:

> The said monies were in the joint names of my deceased sister Mary A. Ryan and myself and it was understood that upon her death the money would be mine. In the year 1938 & 1939 I signed the necessary papers to have the money put in our joint names and claim that I am entitled to the monies now standing to that account absolutely.

The transactions in 1935 were relevant to show the nature of the transactions in 1939. It could be inferred that the motives and intentions of Mary A. Ryan in 1935 still actuated her in 1939. The judge found that "the decedent at all times reserved to herself the right to revoke the transfer to her sister and the later one to the respondent, Patrick Walsh, and that she never intended that the deposits made by her should pass into her brother Patrick's control, or that any part of the funds would become his property until her death." He added, "I further find that the decedent did not intend a present completed gift on either occasion."

We assume in favor of the decree below that the judge believed every piece of testimony in favor of the decree. We accept all such testimony as true. With that assumption the decree has the full benefit of the rule that findings of fact depending upon the credibility of oral evidence made by the judge who saw and heard the witnesses will not be reversed unless plainly wrong. Inferences from the basic facts shown by such testimony, however, are open for our decision, and the inferences drawn by the trial judge are entitled to no weight in this court.

The purpose of Mary A. Ryan to prevent her husband from taking as distributee of her estate was not unlawful. Redman v. Churchill, 230 Mass. 415, 418, 119 N.E. 953. Roche v. Brickley, 254 Mass. 584, 588, 150 N.E. 866. Her reservation of a right to withdraw both income and principal and to revoke the joint tenancy was not inconsistent with a perfected creation inter vivos of a joint tenancy. Coolidge v. Brown, 286 Mass. 504, 507, 190 N.E. 723; Batal v. Buss, 293 Mass. 329, 331, 199 N.E. 750; National Shawmut Bank v. Joy, 315 Mass. 457, 53 N.E.2d 113. Neither was her exclusive control of the deposits and deposit books. Perry v. Leveroni, 252 Mass. 390, 393, 147 N.E. 826; Goldston v. Randolph, 293 Mass. 253, 257, 199 N.E. 896; Castle v. Wightman, 303 Mass. 74, 20 N.E.2d 436.

The statement of Mary A. Ryan in a letter to her brother Patrick that "if anything should happen to me you would get whatever is left" (spelling corrected), his statement in a letter to the Lynn bank that the purpose of the joint deposit was to cause the money to belong "to the person who outlived the other," and his statement in a letter to the probate judge that "it was understood that upon her [Mary's] death the money would be mine," may well refer to the time of enjoyment rather than to the time of vesting in interest, and are not inconsistent with the creation inter vivos of a present

interest in Patrick as joint tenant which would ripen into complete ownership and enjoyment on the death of Mary before his death. Batal v. Buss, 293
Mass. 329, 199 N.E. 750 ("after I am gone this money is yours").

It is evidence in favor of the creation of a present interest in Patrick that
without it the purpose of his sister Mary to keep the deposits out of her estate
and to defeat any inheritance by her husband or Catherine Reigle could not
be accomplished. Castle v. Wightman, 303 Mass. 74, 78, 20 N.E.2d 436;
Kaufman v. Federal National Bank, 287 Mass. 97, 100, 101, 191 N.E. 422.
The transaction is taken at its face value unless the evidence shows that it
was not so intended. Ball v. Forbes, 314 Mass. 200, 203-204, 49 N.E.2d 898.

The only fact that has any considerable tendency to negative an intent to
create a present interest in Patrick is the statement of his sister Mary in a
letter to Patrick that "this doesn't mean anything more than a protection so
safety first." (Spelling corrected.) That ambiguous statement has little weight
when balanced against the considerations already mentioned. A majority of
the court think that on all the evidence the right conclusion is that Patrick
took during the life of his sister Mary a valid interest as joint tenant, and now
is entitled to the deposits by survivorship.

Decree reversed.

Petition dismissed.[3]

Problem

7.5. Would arrangements like the ones in Malone v. Walsh and In re
Totten stand up against the claims asserted by the following:

a. A creditor of the decedent?

b. A spouse of the decedent?

---

3. See the following articles dealing with bank account problems: Bogert, The Creation of
Trusts by Means of Bank Deposits, 1 Cornell L.Q. 159 (1915); Havighurst, Gifts of Bank
Deposits, 14 N.C.L. Rev. 129 (1936). — Eds.

CHAPTER 8

ORAL TRUSTS COMPARED

SMITH'S ESTATE
144 Pa. 428, 22 A. 916 (1891)

On May 15, 1890, the second account of the Pennsylvania Company for Insurances on Lives and Granting Annuities, executor of the will of Thomas Smith, deceased, was called for audit in the court below, before Ashman, J. The subject of the account was a fund composed of $13,000 in coupon bonds of the Pensacola & Atlantic Railroad Company, and interest collected thereon. The fund was claimed by Henry S. Parmalee, guardian of Thomas Smith Kelly.

The facts found in the adjudication of the auditing judge, and in the opinion of the court in banc, were in substance as follows:

The testator, Thomas Smith, died May 20, 1883. Then living with him, as a member of his family, was a nephew, Thomas Smith Kelly, about thirteen years of age, who had resided with and been maintained by him during the preceding ten years. The nephew continued to reside with the surviving members of the testator's family, after his death, until 1887.

In January, 1882, the testator purchased the coupon bonds, embraced in this account. About that time he informed the father of the minor that he had laid by or appropriated some bonds for the boy. After his death, his box in the trust company's vault was opened, and an envelope was found therein endorsed as follows:

13 bonds, $1,000 each, held for Tom Smith Kelly.
T.S.

Pensacola & Atlantic Railroad Mortgage bonds.

The envelope contained the bonds in question. In the account-book of the decedent, in his own handwriting, appeared an account relating to the bonds, copied at length in the opinion of the court, *infra*. The M. E. Smith mentioned in the latter part of the entries, was the testator's wife. He also kept a pocket memorandum book, in which he jotted down his monetary transactions as they took place, and in January of each year made a summary of his investments. In the latest statement of this character in the book, dated shortly before his death, the sum total was $1,000,000, and included in the items making up that total was "$13,000 Pensacola & Atlantic Bonds." Under the head of income for 1883, in the same book, was noted $390 interest on these securities. Opposite to the entry of the bonds was the word "Tom," in testator's handwriting. The entry had a red line drawn through it, which line was afterwards scratched out by the testator, and the entry was written in again by him. It was explained that the half brother of the minor had drawn the line through at the testator's request, because the testator had intended to enter the item elsewhere.

The will of the testator bequeathed his residuary estate to his executor, to be held upon certain trusts. At the audit, all technical objections to the capacity of the accountant to object to the claim, were waived by the claimant.

The auditing judge . . . adjudged that a valid declaration of trust had been established in favor of the claimant, and awarded the bonds and accrued income thereon to the guardian of Thomas Smith Kelly.

Exceptions to the adjudication, after argument thereof, were dismissed, and the adjudication confirmed. . . .

Opinion, CLARK, J.: The appellant is the Pennsylvania Company for Insurances on Lives and Granting Annuities, trustee under the will of Thomas Smith, deceased; the appellee, Henry S. Parmalee, guardian of Thomas Smith Kelly, a minor. The proceeding was the adjudication of an account, filed by the trustee under the will of Thomas Smith, of the principal and income of thirteen thousand dollars of Pensacola & Atlantic Railroad Company's coupon bonds, which the said trustees claimed were part of the estate of decedent and passed to them under his will. . . .

The owner of personal property, in order to make a voluntary disposition of it, may, by a proper transfer of the title, make a gift of it direct to the donee, or he may impress upon it a trust for the benefit of the donee. It is well settled, however, that whether a gift or a trust is intended, if the transaction still remains imperfect . . . , equity will not aid in its enforcement. The expression of a mere intention to create a trust, therefore, without more, is insufficient; like a promise to give, it will not be enforced in equity: Dipple v. Corles, 11 Hare 183; Helfenstein's Est., 77 Pa. 328. . . .

Nor, in such case, if it appear that the intention of the donor was to adopt either one of these methods of disposition, will a court resort to the other for the purpose of carrying it into effect. What is clearly intended as a voluntary assignment or a gift, but is imperfect as such, cannot be treated as a declaration of trust. If this were not so, an expression of present gift would in all cases amount to a declaration of trust, and any imperfect gift might be made effectual simply by converting it into a trust. There is no principle of equity which will perfect an imperfect gift, and a court of equity will not impute a trust where a trust was not in contemplation: Milroy v. Lord, 4 DeGex, F. & J. 264-274; Flanders v. Blandy, 45 Ohio St. 108. . . . Although the cases may not be altogether consistent, the rule is now, we think, well settled in accordance with the doctrine declared in Richards v. Delbridge, *supra,* that, if the transaction is intended to be affected by gift, the court will not give it effect by construing it as a trust. It is well settled that nothing can take effect as an assignment or gift which does not manifest an intention to relinquish the right of dominion on one hand and to create it on the other. If the donor has perfected his gift as he intended, and has placed the subject beyond his power or dominion, the want of consideration is immaterial; the donee's right will be enforced. A gift can only be effectual after the intention to make it has been accompanied by delivery of possession or some equivalent act; if it is not, the transaction is not a gift, but a contract merely.

If a trust is intended, it will be equally effectual whether the donor transfer the title to the trustee, or declare that he himself holds the property for the purposes of the trust. "It is well settled that the owner of personal property may impress upon it a valid present trust, either by a declaration that he holds the property in trust, or by a transfer of the legal title to a third party upon certain specified trusts. In other words, he may constitute either himself or another person trustee. If he makes himself trustee, no transfer of the subject-matter of the trust is necessary; but if he selects a third party, the subject of the trust must be transferred to him in such mode as will be effectual to pass the legal title." . . . If the donor makes a third party a trustee, he must transfer to him the subject of the trust in such mode as will be effectual to pass the title. The transaction, as in the case of a gift, to be effectual must be accompanied by delivery of the subject of the trust, or by some act so strongly indicative of the donor's intention as to be tantamount to such a delivery; but, where the donor makes himself the trustee, no transfer of the subject-matter is necessary. Ex parte Pye, 18 Ves. 140; Donaldson v. Donaldson, Kay, 711; and Crawford's App., 61 Pa. 52, are illustrations of trusts in this form. In such cases, no assignment of the legal title is required, for the nature and effect of the transaction is that the legal title remains in the donor for the benefit of the donee. It is conceded that, as the bonds of the Pensacola & Atlantic Railroad Company, the bonds in question, were not delivered to Thomas Smith Kelly by Thomas Smith, the transaction cannot be sustained as a gift. It is clear that a gift was not in contemplation, and the only question for our determination is, whether or not a complete and valid trust was created, for a trust would seem to have been contemplated.

There is no certain form required in the creation of a trust. In the case of personal property or choses in action, trusts may be proved by parol. If the declaration be in writing, it is not essential, as a general rule, that it should be in any particular form. It may be couched in any language which is sufficiently expressive of the intention to create a trust. "Three things, it has been said, must concur to raise a trust; sufficient words to create it, a definite subject, and a certain or ascertained object; and to these requisites may be added another, viz., that the terms of the trusts should be sufficiently declared:" Bispham's Eq., 65, citing Cruwys v. Colman, 9 Ves. 323; Knight v. Boughton, 11 C. L. & F. 513. The intention must be a complete one, and this requisite is especially appliable to trusts created by voluntary dispositions. "A mere inchoate and executory design is not enough, and unless there is some distinct equity, as fraud, for example, it cannot be enforced:" Bispham's Eq., 65. The intention must be plainly manifest, and not derived from loose and equivocal expressions of parties, made at different times and upon different occasions; but any words which indicate with sufficient certainty a purpose to create a trust will be effective in so doing. It is not necessary that the terms "trust" and "trustee" should be used. The donor need not say in so many words, "I declare myself a trustee," but he must do something which is equivalent to it, and use expressions which have that meaning; for, however anxious the court may be to carry out a man's intention, it is not at liberty to construe words otherwise than according to their proper meaning. . . .

In the case at bar, the subject of the alleged trust is certain; the cestui que trust is particularly designated by name and identified, whilst the terms are specific, and sufficiently shown. The contention is, however, that a trust upon these terms was not sufficiently declared; that the whole matter rested in the undeclared and unexecuted intention of the donor, and was, therefore, wholly without effect.

Thomas Smith, although a married man, had no children. He was the owner of a large estate, the personalty alone aggregating about $1,000,000. Thomas Smith Kelly was his nephew, his godson and namesake; and, although his father and mother were both living, he lived with and was maintained and educated by his uncle from the age of three years until the time of the decedent's death on the twentieth of May, 1883, when he was about thirteen years of age. His uncle admittedly stood in loco parentis, which would seem to furnish a sufficient motive for making this disposition of the bonds, and would have like effect generally to that which attends the relation of parent and child: Ex parte Pye, 18 Ves. 146. The bonds were purchased the twenty-eighth of January, 1882, and the death of the decedent occurred on the twentieth of May, 1883. A year or more before his decease, which was presumably near the time when the bonds were purchased, Thomas Smith, in a conversation with John H. Kelly, the father of Thomas Smith Kelly, stated "he had laid by or appropriated some bonds for Tom." After his death, when his box in the trust company's vaults was opened, the bonds in question were found amongst his assets. The envelope in which they were contained was indorsed: "13 bonds, $1,000 each, held for Tom Smith Kelly.   [Signed] T.S.   Pensacola & Atlantic R.R. mortgage bonds."

The envelope contained bonds of that description and amount. In the decedent's account-book was an entry in his own handwriting, as follows:

Account Thomas Smith Kelly.
Pensacola and Atlantic Railroad Company Mortgage Bonds.
Dr.

1882.
Jan. 28.   To cash paid E. W. Clark & Kimball for $16,000
bonds at 95 and interest from August 1st, 1881 $15,189.33
Less Nos. 1223, 1224, 1225, $3,000, sold William Simpson,
Jr., same day at same price, $3,000 $2,850.00

Balance $13,000, cost $12,339.33

$13,000 of these bonds I bought for, and are the property of, my nephew and godson, Thomas Smith Kelly and belong to him.

Thomas Smith.
Philadelphia, January 28th, 1882.

Cr.

1881.
August 1.   Due and payable August 1st, 1921, coupons due August 1st and February 1st, six per cent per annum on New York. Principal and interest guaranteed by the Louisville Railroad Company. Bonds, $16,000, $1,000 each, Nos. 1223-1238, both inclusive.

1882.
Aug. 10.   Thomas Smith Kelly, interest collected for him. $390.00

1883.
Feb. 1.   Cash coupons paid M. E. Smith for Tom.   S.K. $390.00

It also appears that the decedent kept a pocket memorandum-book, in which he jotted down his monetary transactions as they took place, and in January of each year made a summary of his investments. In the latest statement of this character in the book, dated shortly before his death the sum total was $1,000,000, and, included in the items making up that total, was, "$13,000 Pensacola & Atlantic bonds." Under the head of income for 1883, in the same book, was noted $390 interest on the securities. Opposite to the entry of the bonds was the word "Tom," in testator's handwriting. The entry had a red line drawn through it, which line was afterwards scratched out by the testator, and the entry was written in again by him. It was explained that a nephew had drawn the line through at testator's request, because the testator had intended to enter the item elsewhere. Was not all this, taken together, a sufficient and clear declaration of trust in favor of the nephew? The decedent, as we have seen, in his lifetime, in his own handwriting, and over his own initials and signature declared that these bonds, thus set apart and "appropriated or laid by" for his nephew, not only were the "property of his nephew," and "belonged to him," but they were "bought for" and "held for him." In the absence of the precise terms "in trust," it is difficult to suggest words more expressive of a trust than the words thus employed. Their meaning is so obvious and certain that there can be no doubt of the decedent's intention.

But it is said that this intention was not properly declared; that the words were written upon the envelope and in the private account-book of the decedent, and it is not shown that these entries and indorsements were witnessed by or were ever exhibited to any one; that they were mere private memoranda which were wholly within the power of the donor, and which in his lifetime he might have revoked, canceled, or destroyed. The argument of appellant's counsel is that a "declaration" of trust involves the idea that the donor must declare his assumption of the trust; in other words, that he must say something, or write something or exhibit something, to some other person, or to the world at large. "If he stands alone," say the learned counsel, "in a room, and repeats his intention to himself, that is not a declaration. If he writes a memorandum, not intended to be shown to any one during his lifetime, that is not a declaration. It may be a testamentary disposition, if he looks forward to its discovery and inspection after death; but it cannot be a declaration of trust, if he does not intend to communicate it in his lifetime. As in gifts there must be a delivery, so in declarations of trust there must be something equivalent to a delivery, to wit, a declaration made to some other person or to the world at large, which constitutes the donor at once a trustee and conveys to the cestui que trust an immediate equitable interest."

It is admitted that the declaration need not be made to the cestui que trust; that, if made to other persons, under circumstances indicating the intention of the donor to make a declaration, it is sufficient. It is conceded, also, that but little publicity is required, and that the donor may retain the paper in his possession; but it is contended that the declaration must of necessity be made to some one besides himself.

It may be conceded that if a man, being alone, merely repeat his purpose to himself, that would not be a declaration, for it is obvious that, as his utterance was not intended for other ears than his own, it was merely the expression of an intention. It may also be conceded that if, under such circumstances, he were to have written his purpose formally upon paper, and added his signature and seal, he might the next moment have destroyed it. The trust, in such case, would take effect whenever it appeared that the instrument was executed as the deliberate expression of his purpose, and this may be shown by his acts or declarations respecting it, or by circumstances tending to establish the fact.

The purpose of Thomas Smith, with reference to these bonds, was not only written and authenticated by his initials or signature, but the writing was carefully preserved until the time of decedent's death. The envelope containing the bonds in question had an informal declaration indorsed thereon that the bonds were held for Tom Smith Kelly; the account-book showed, not only that they were bought for his nephew, but that they belonged to him,—they were his property. For whose inspection were those written declarations intended? Certainly not for the inspection of the donor, but for those who might have occasion at any time in the future to investigate his affairs. The doctor was advanced in years, and was subject to the ordinary ills, accidents, and misfortunes of life, both physically and mentally. He was liable, although living, to be incapacitated for all business affairs, or he might be removed by death. In any event, his purpose would seem to have been to leave a memorandum for the eyes of others, exhibiting his intention and purpose with respect to these bonds. It is unnecessary for us to consider whether or not the donor might have revoked the declaration. He did not revoke it; he put it away with the bonds themselves, and carefully preserved it. He collected the interest semi-annually, and, in recognition of the existing trust, placed the several amounts to the credit of the donee. It is not essential to the validity of a trust of personal property that it should be irrevocable; indeed, a right of revocation may be expressly reserved: Dickerson's App., 115 Pa. 198, 8 A. 64; Lines v. Lines, 142 Pa. 149, 21 A. 809. The question in such case is not so much whether in the lifetime of the decedent the declaration was actually exhibited to the inspection of others, as whether, under all the circumstances of the case, it would appear to have been written and preserved for the inspection of others. If the declaration had been a formal one, under the hand and seal of the declarant, upon proof of its execution we think its effectuality would not have been questioned, even though it never had been exhibited to the cestui que trust or to any other person; and we cannot see that the informal nature of the writing could alter its effect, if the donor's intention is otherwise clearly established.

There was no provision for the assignment of the bonds of the Pensacola & Atlantic Railroad Company on the books of the company. They were simply ordinary coupon bonds, transferable by delivery. A formal assignment was unnecessary to transfer the title. The rights of creditors do not intervene. The appellants stand in the shoes of the testator, and their rights do not rise superior to his. Whilst a gift, in its proper legal acceptation, was not contemplated by Thomas Smith, it is plain that his purpose was to vest the equitable ownership of these bonds in his nephew, and to apply the interest for his benefit. In the language of the president judge of the Orphans' Court, his "declarations and subsequent acts, evidenced by his admissions and solemn entries in his books, and the indorsement upon the envelope containing the bonds, furnish incontrovertible proofs of his intention to hold them as a trustee." . . .

We are of opinion that the trust is fully established and the decree of the Orphans' Court is affirmed, and the appeal dismissed at the costs of the appellant.

Note: *Imperfect Gift as a Trust*

In Young v. Young, 80 N.Y. 422 (1880), certain bonds were found among the papers of Joseph Young on his death. These bonds were enclosed in two envelopes, upon which were endorsed memoranda, signed by Joseph Young, which described the bonds enclosed by numbers and stated that certain of the bonds belong to William H. Young and others to John N. Young, "but the interest to become due thereon is owned and reserved by me for so long as I shall live, at my death they belong absolutely and entirely to them and their heirs." The court held that this was an imperfect gift which could not be upheld as a trust. An excerpt from the opinion follows:

> The words of the donor in the present case are that the bonds are owned by the donees, but that the interest to accrue thereon is owned and reserved by the donor for so long as he shall live, and at his death they belong absolutely to the donees. No intention is here expressed to hold any legal title to the bonds in trust for the donees. Whatever interest was intended to be vested in them, was transferred to them directly, subject to the reservation in favor of the donor during his life, and free from that reservation at his death. Nothing was reserved to the donor, to be held in trust or otherwise, except his right to the accruing interest which should become payable during his life. It could only be by reforming or supplementing the language used, that a trust could be created, and this, as has been shown, will not be done in case of a voluntary settlement without consideration. There are two English cases, where indeed the circumstances were much stronger in favor of the donees than in the present case, which tend to sustain the position that a settlement of this description may be enforced in equity by constituting the donor trustee for the donee. They are Morgan v. Malleson (L.R. (10 Eq. Cas.) 475), and Richardson v. Richardson (L.R. (3 Eq. Cas.) 686). In the first of these cases, Morgan v. Malleson (L.R. (10 Eq. Cas.) 475), the intestate signed and delivered to Dr. Morris a memorandum in writing: "I hereby give and make over to Dr. Morris one India bond," but did not deliver the bond. Sir John Romilly sustained this gift as a declaration of trust. The case is referred to by Church, Ch. J., in Martin v. Funk, as an extreme case. In Richardson v. Richardson an instrument purporting to be an assignment, unsupported by a valuable consideration was upheld as a declaration of trust. In speaking of these cases in Richards v. Delbridge (L.R. (18 Eq. Cas.) 11), Sir Geo. Jessel, M.R. says: "If the decisions of Lord Romilly (in Morgan v. Malleson), and of V.C. Wood (in Richardson v. Richardson) were right, there never could be a case where the expression of a present gift would not amount to an effectual declaration of trust." And it may be added that there never could be a case where an intended gift, defective for want of delivery, could not, if expressed in writing, be sustained as a declaration of trust. Both of the cases cited are now placed among overruled cases. Fisher's Ann. Digest (1873 and 1874) 24, 25. In Moore v. Moore (43 L.J. Ch. App. (N.S.) 623), Hall V.C. says:
>
>> I think it very important indeed to keep a clear and definite distinction between these cases of imperfect gifts, and cases of declarations of trust;

and that we should not extend beyond what the authorities have already established, the doctrine of declarations of trust, so as to supplement what would otherwise be mere imperfect gifts.

If the settlement is intended to be effectuated by gift, the court will not give effect to it by construing it as a trust. If it is intended to take effect by transfer, the court will not hold the intended transfer to operate as a declaration of trust, for then every imperfect instrument would be made effectual by being converted into a perfect trust. Milroy v. Lord, 4 DeG. F. & J. 264.

The case of Martin v. Funk and kindred cases cannot aid the respondent. In all those cases there was an express declaration of trust. In the one named the donor delivered the money to the bank, taking back its obligation to herself in the character of trustee for the donee; thus parting with all beneficial interest in the fund, and having the legal title vested in her in the character of trustee only. No interposition on the part of the court was necessary to confer that character upon her; nor was it necessary by construction or otherwise to change or supplement the actual transaction. None of the difficulties encountered in the present case stood in the way of carrying out her intention. It was capable of being executed in the form in which it was expressed. [80 N.Y. at 438-440.]

PART III

BONA FIDE PURCHASERS OF PERSONAL PROPERTY

CHAPTER 9

WHEN A BONA FIDE PURCHASER ACQUIRES A BETTER TITLE THAN THE VENDOR HAD

Note: Conflicting Policy Considerations

Here we meet the eternal triangle of the law: an honest person (O), a rascal (A), and another honest person (B). Typically the rascal imposes upon both of them—for example, steals from O, then sells to B—and leaves to the law the problem of deciding which of them shall bear the loss.

The cases call attention to certain common variations in the facts which may be decisive:

1. In many cases O has entrusted the goods to A and given A certain indicia of ownership which have enabled A to deceive B. How are O's rights vis-à-vis B affected by such conduct?
2. In some cases A obtains a voidable legal title from O; in others A obtains only possession. If O's rights against A can be asserted only in a court applying equitable principles, should that fact result in the shifting of the burden of loss between O and B?
3. In some cases tangible chattels are the subject matter of A's wrongdoing and O's and B's undoing; in others, various types of commercial documents—e.g., currency, promissory notes, stock certificates, bills of lading. Should this difference in subject matter produce a difference in result?

In these cases O and B are demanding protection as individuals. But also they personify important social interests. O represents the demand of owners to be protected in their ownership. B represents the demand of the commercial community for the security of transactions, which in turn requires that an honest, careful purchaser be able to rely upon the appearance of title in buying goods. These demands are often in conflict, and this chapter shows how the conflict has been resolved.

HESSEN v. IOWA AUTOMOBILE MUTUAL INSURANCE CO.

195 Iowa 141, 190 N.W. 150 (1922)

Action to recover on policy of insurance covering an automobile against theft. Verdict of the jury finding for plaintiff. Defendant appeals. Reversed.

DE GRAFF, J. On the 13th day of October 1920 a policy of insurance was issued by the defendant company to the plaintiff insuring against theft a certain Buick touring automobile, Model 1919, factory number 321311. The policy was issued for a term of one year and it is alleged by plaintiff that the automobile therein described was stolen on the 9th day of October, 1921 resulting in a loss to plaintiff in the sum of $1,350. The defendant in answer inter alia alleged that the plaintiff never had an insurable interest in the automobile referred to in plaintiff's petition. . . .

Upon the conclusion of the testimony defendant moved for a directed verdict and again upon its motion for new trial urged the following . . . that the automobile claimed to have been owned by the plaintiff was a stolen automobile and the plaintiff did not and could not have acquired ownership thereof by reason of his purchase of the same from anyone other than the true owner and that at the time the policy of insurance issued plaintiff had no insurable interest in the automobile described in said policy. . . .

An insurable interest is necessary to the validity of a policy regardless of its subject-matter. If no insurable interest exists the contract is void, and no recovery can be had thereon in case of loss either by the insured or his assignee and notes given for the premium upon such insurance are void for want of consideration. In the instant case the defendant tendered to plaintiff the premium paid on the policy and deposited same in the hands of the clerk of the district court for his benefit.

Did the insured have an insurable interest in the automobile described in the policy of insurance in suit? It is unnecessary to detail the evidence in relation to the history of the insured automobile. Sufficient to state our conclusion that the automobile when purchased and insured by the plaintiff was a stolen car. This is unmistakably shown by the evidence. By the terms of the contract of insurance it is provided that the entire policy shall be void if the interest of the insured in the property be other than "unconditional and sole ownership."

If a person has no interest, legal or equitable, in the thing insured it is viewed in law as a mere wager and the courts will not enforce such a contract Warren v. Davenport Fire Ins. Co., 31 Iowa 464; Bartling v. German Mut. L. & T. Ins. Co., 154 Iowa 335, 134 N.W. 864. A person has no insurable interest in a thing where his only right arises under a contract which is void or unenforceable either at law or in equity.

Whatever interest plaintiff had in the insured property must have been derived under his contract of purchase. His vendor is not shown to have had anything more than the possession of a stolen car. Through his purchase plaintiff acquired no title and clearly never had such ownership as was required and defined by the terms of the policy. No one can convey a valid title to goods or chattels unless the vendor is the owner thereof or lawfully represents the owner. It is the duty of a vendee to determine whether he is securing good title to the thing purchased, and if title fails and loss ensues, the purchaser must look to his vendor. In general no one can transfer a better or higher title to a chattel than he himself has. Boulden v. Gough, 4 Pen. (Del.) 48, 54 A. 693; Godwin v. Taenzer, 122 Tenn. 101, 119 S.W. 1133; Tuttle v. White, 46 Mich. 485, 9 N.W. 528; Turnbow v. Beckstead, 25 Utah 468, 71 P. 1062.

The burden was upon the plaintiff to establish his insurable interest in the property described in the policy, and that burden required that he establish the interest which was defined in said policy.[1] The recital of ownership is a valid provision, and by the very terms of the policy the insurance was void if the insured was other than the unconditional and sole owner. This the evidence failed to establish.[2] . . .

---

1.   If a person in good faith thinks he or she owns a particular item of property, that person will naturally be as concerned about the care of such item as would be one who in fact had the right to the property against everyone else. Consequently, such person is not making a "mere wager" when entering into a contract of insurance.

The court in the *Hessen* case seemed to say that in order to have an insurable interest the ownership must be complete in all respects. This view of insurable interest has not been followed by some courts. Scarola v. Insurance Co. of North America, 31 N.Y.2d 411, 292 N.E.2d 776 (1972), involved an innocent purchaser of a stolen car and in holding that such purchaser had an insurable interest in the car, the court stated: "Plaintiff had a right to possession of the car against any contrary assertion except that of the true owner. This right under general principles, ought to be regarded as an insurable interest." Phillips v. Cincinnati Insurance Co., 60 Ohio St. 2d 180, 398 N.E.2d 564 (1979), also held that the innocent purchaser of a stolen car had an insurable interest. The court observed:

> One view holds that, since even a bona-fide purchaser cannot acquire good title from a thief, such buyer has no insurable interest in the vehicle. However a contrary theory bases an insurable interest on the economic interest a purchaser has in protecting his investment in the vehicle, or on the insured's right to possession of the vehicle against all the world except the true owner. Primarily on public policy grounds, to discourage trading in stolen property, these latter courts have usually required the insured to be an innocent, bona fide purchaser of the stolen vehicle. [60 Ohio St. 2d at 181-182, 398 N.E.2d at 566.]

—EDS.

2.   To the effect that a bona fide purchaser of personal property, whose title is good against all the world except the rightful owner, may recover on a policy of insurance even though the policy contains a provision invalidating it if the insured's interest is other than "unconditional and sole ownership," see Savarese v. Hartford Fire Insurance Co., 1 N.J. Misc. 315, 123 A. 762 (1924); Barnett v. London Assurance Corp., 138 Wash. 673, 245 P. 3 (1926).

If the reason for the sole and unconditional ownership clause in the policy is to assure that the insured will be interested in preserving the insured property, a bona fide purchaser of property will meet the test and *ought* to be a sole and unconditional owner within the meaning of such policy provision.

A reason for the sole and unconditional ownership clause may be to enable the insurance company to have a worthwhile right of subrogation to the rights of the insured against the wrongdoer on payment to the insured of the insured's loss. Is there such a worthwhile right if

For the reasons indicated the judgment entered must be and is — Reversed.

STEVENS, C.J., WEAVER and PRESTON, JJ., concur.

Note: The Tribulations of Charles Hessen

Reading the *Hessen* case, one wonders what story lies behind the bare recital of facts. Was Hessen a member of an auto-theft ring with a new twist, i.e., cashing in twice on a stolen auto, first from the insurance company and next from the innocent purchaser of the hot car?

With the aid of students from Iowa we got access to the original papers in the files of the supreme court. In law, as in science, when you look for something you may find something else even more interesting. The record provides no scintilla of evidence to support our cynical suspicions about Hessen, but it does tell quite a tale and provides useful instruction on everyday aspects of insurance law and trial practice.

The Buick in question was sold to a man in Roanoke, Virginia, and stolen from him. Hessen had bought it in 1919 from a corporation doing a used car business in Sioux City, Iowa; the corporation has since been dissolved. Hessen paid $900 for the car and testified that he put $400 or $500 into fixing it up. It was stolen from him once before in connection with a bank robbery; but it was recovered, somewhat damaged, and again fixed up. So this ill-favored vehicle was stolen, not twice, but three times. The policy valued the car at $1,350 but provided that only actual value could be recovered in case of loss.

Hessen worked in the Sioux City Bottling Works; and at the time of the theft here in question he also ran a dance hall, in front of which the car was parked when it was stolen from him. The car was later found by the police; it had been completely and deliberately destroyed, "picked to pieces."

The doctrinal message of the *Hessen* case in the law of bona fide purchasers is absurdly simple: a BFP from a thief does not acquire title as against the owner from whom the chattel was stolen. But it certainly does not follow that the BFP has no insurable interest. Couldn't the chimney sweep in Armory v. Delamirie, page 66 *supra,* have effectively insured that jewel? If not, it is indeed strange that he had a sufficient interest to enable him to recover full value from a converter. Yet the chimney sweep *knew* he

---

the insured's claim to the insured property is subordinate to that of another? If payment by the insurance company is the equivalent of the settlement by the *insured* with the wrongdoer, then such settlement may bar the true owner from action against anyone but the insured, so that the subrogation of the insurance company to the rights of the insured against the wrongdoer would be worthwhile (see Problem 4.4, at page 69 *supra*). If this is so, the purpose of the sole and unconditional ownership clause may be fulfilled by recognizing the bona fide purchaser as a sole and unconditional owner within the meaning of those words in the policy.—EDS.

had only a finder's title — valid against all the world except one person, as in the case of Hessen. The Iowa court surely neglected the principle of relativity of title, page 65 *supra*. The remark of the learned court at page 141 that "if title fails and loss ensues, the purchaser must look to his vendor" is small comfort to Hessen even if it is true that he could recover the consideration paid to his vendor without surrendering the automobile (which he obviously cannot do), for his vendor was a corporation which has since been dissolved.

Further, it is by no means axiomatic that the "sole and unconditional ownership" clause defeats Hessen's claim under the policy. See the comment in footnote 2 at page 141 *supra*.

The court had two other grounds, not included in our excerpt from the opinion, for denying recovery to Hessen:

1. The policy covered a 1919 model Buick, factory number 321311. The court held that such a policy did not cover Hessen's car, which was a 1916 model, with factory number 249114, engine number (apparent) 321311. The factory number, appearing on a plate on the front of the frame, remained as it was when it came from the factory. The motor number originally stamped on the cylinder block of this car was 221311. This had been changed by erasing the first digit and substituting "3." The manufacturer provides lists of factory and motor numbers showing dates at which a frame or engine bearing a certain number was manufactured; these lists are available to anyone who knows enough to ask for them. According to the Buick list, the higher (changed) engine number showed the spring of 1917 as the date of manufacture; the lower (original) number showed a date about one year earlier, and this coincided with the date of the factory number on the frame. All parties — Hessen, the insurance broker, the home office of the insurance company — had the means of knowing that a car with those numbers could not be a 1919 model. By the simplest process of comparison they also could determine that the factory number and the (changed) motor number did not coincide as to date; the inference that the car had been stolen was routine. The insurance company was in this business and knew about these lists, but *Hessen could not read or write English.* Hessen had twice registered the car, giving the correct factory number and the higher (changed) engine number, describing the car as a 1917 model, which would have been right for that engine number but wrong for the factory number. The application had been made out for Hessen by "the fellow" in the office of his vendor, signed by Hessen and taken to the appropriate state office. Hessen did not know what was on the application he signed. "The fellow" also arranged the first insurance policy, placing it with a company other than the defendant. When that policy expired, Hessen, at the solicitation of a friend in the insurance business who had seen him riding around in the Buick, placed the new policy with the defendant company; the friend, who was probably a broker but also possibly an agent for the defendant company, copied the data from the former policy. All evidence showed that Hessen signed papers put before him without having ability to read them. (Repre-

senting Hessen, what would you have done to meet the defense that the car was misdescribed in the policy?)

2. All insurance policies require, as a condition of the company's liability under the policy, that the insured provide (a) *notice of loss* within a very short period after the loss is discovered and (b) written *"proof of loss"* under oath within some longer period, e.g., 60 days. Hessen did not comply with either of these requirements. He testified that he promptly told "the company," orally, that the car was stolen. Someone told him they would send an agent to see him. The agent came the next day and told him, "You have 60 days to wait." The company sent to him by mail a form of proof of loss and directed him to fill it out; but, not being able to read English, he did nothing about it. (Representing Hessen, what would you have done to meet the defense based on Hessen's failure to give proof of loss?)

The policy expired October 13, 1921. On direct examination Hessen testified that the theft occurred in October, 1921 but that he didn't remember the date. Then, after a recess, he testified that the loss occurred on October 9. The following ensued on cross-examination:

> *Q.* What has refreshed your memory during the recess as to the date when you say this car was stolen from you?
> *A.* I just called up a fellow working for me and asked him what date and he told me.

The defendant moved to strike this answer. How should the judge rule? Do you approve of the form of the question asked by defendant's attorney?

The jury found for the plaintiff after denial of defendant's motion for a directed verdict. But all Hessen had at the finish was a lawyer's bill. Do we, who pride ourselves on being the "melting pot," adjust our legal system to the circumstances of those of our citizens who are unable to read and write the English language?

MORGAN v. HODGES
89 Mich. 404, 50 N.W. 876 (1891)

Trover. Plaintiff brings error. Reversed. The facts are stated in the opinion of Grant, J.

GRANT, J. This is an action of trover to recover the value of a horse.

In November, 1888, defendants purchased two horses, harness, buggy, robes, and whip of one Seaman. Seaman had hired one of the horses, harness, and the other property from plaintiff, at Traverse City, to drive to Frankfort. He drove them to Grand Rapids, and sold them to defendants. Defendants had known Seaman, and had no occasion to doubt his statement that he owned the property. No question is raised of the good faith of the defendants. In the following March plaintiff traced his property into the possession of the defendants. They had sold the horse, but still had the other property.

The defendants pleaded the general issue, and gave notice of a settlement. The only question arises upon this settlement. The settlement was denied by the plaintiff, but, to present the question properly the testimony of the defendants alone is material. Plaintiff, who was a stranger to defendants, went to their stable, and, finding Frank E. Hodges there, informed him of the loss of his property, and asked if they had bought such property of Mr. Seaman. Mr. Hodges informed him that they had bought two horses, harness, buggy, and robes of Mr. Seaman; that they had sold the horses; and that the other property was in his brother's barn. Mr. Hodges went with plaintiff to see the property. Plaintiff recognized it as his. Plaintiff and Frank went back to defendants' barn and found defendant Chester there. Frank introduced plaintiff to his brother, and told him of his claim. A conversation ensued between them, in which plaintiff stated how Mr. Seaman obtained the property, and Mr. Hodges stated how they came in possession of it, and what they had done with it. Mr. Hodges testified that plaintiff then said:

"If you will return me the buggy, robe, harness, and things, I will let the horse go, and we will call it square. You got him in good faith."

To which Mr. Hodges replied, "All right," and immediately telephoned to his employees at the other barn to let plaintiff have the property. He took the property away, and subsequently brought this suit.

It is urged on behalf of plaintiff that, even if this arrangement was made, it was void for want of consideration, because there was nothing in dispute, and no controversy had arisen. The learned circuit judge instructed the jury that, if this was so, and if the defendants conceded at the outset that the property belonged to the plaintiff, then there was no consideration for the settlement, and plaintiff must recover; but, if the defendants did not concede that the plaintiff was the owner, and before any determination was reached upon this point,— viz., whether the property should be surrendered or not,— plaintiff made the offer above given, as a settlement of the matter, that would be binding upon the parties. This instruction was correct if the facts were sufficient to warrant it. Under the defendants' evidence plaintiff had made no demand for the unconditional surrender of his property. The horse was not very valuable. He might well think it wise to gain possession of the remainder of his property without litigation or trouble. No misrepresentations were made to him by the defendants, nor any fact concealed from him. They had not offered to surrender the property prior to the offer made by him. They said nothing which can be construed into a recognition of plaintiff's title. Their silence upon this point cannot, under the circumstances, be legally construed as a recognition by them of plaintiff's title. The law favors settlements of this character. Bish. Cont. 57. I do not think it was the province of the court to decide that there was no valid agreement under these circumstances. The question was properly submitted to the jury.

Judgment should be affirmed.

MORSE, J., concurred with GRANT, J.

LONG, J.: I think the court below was in error in his charge, as it appears that the defendants only did that, in surrendering the property, which in law they were compelled to do, and therefore there was no consideration for the promise on the part of the plaintiff not to reclaim the horse.

Judgment must be reversed, with costs, and a new trial ordered.

CHAMPLIN, C.J., and MCGRATH, J., concurred with LONG, J.

Problems

9.1. If the defendant's attorney in Morgan v. Hodges had claimed that the plaintiff made a gift of the horse in question, what arguments would you have made as attorney for the plaintiff against such a claim?

9.2. O delivers a wristwatch to the A Jewelry Company to have it repaired. The A Jewelry Company sells new and secondhand watches and also repairs watches. B purchases O's watch from the A Jewelry Company without knowledge that the A Jewelry Company is not the owner and is not authorized by the owner to sell the watch. O learns that the watch is in the possession of B and brings an action of trover against B without making any demand for the return of the watch. Judgment for whom? See Restatement (Second) of Torts §229; cf. Gillet v. Roberts, 57 N.Y. 28 (1874). See also Uniform Commercial Code §2-403(2).

Note: Security Transactions Involving Personal Property — Liens, Pledges, Conditional Sales, and Chattel Mortgages

It is desirable at this point to give you some appreciation of various types of commercial security transactions with respect to personal property.

1. *Common-law liens.* Where O owns a chattel and A (an improver) improves it at O's order, A can retain the chattel until A receives payment. But A must improve the chattel, not merely store it, to acquire a lien. Thus a watch repairer has a lien. A garage-keeper has a lien for repairs but not for storage. Does an agister (one who feeds cattle) have a lien? Some of the class debated this hotly in our law school days; but, being city boys, we didn't much care. Aside from improvers, common carriers and innkeepers had common-law liens. The right of the common-law lienholder was to retain possession of the chattel until the bill was paid; a "worrying asset," nothing more. The lienholder could not sell the chattel, i.e., foreclose the lien. Certain aspects of the common law of liens were pretty silly (e.g., limiting the lien to improvers, providing no foreclosure rights) and generally have been corrected by statute; but the law still falls considerably short of giving to the person-on-the-street the right to take retaliatory and compensatory

action against chattels of the debtor which are in his or her hands. Moreover, the law imposes the stringent penalties of the action of trover (a judgment for the full value of the chattel) upon one who wrongfully withholds or disposes of another's goods. So, in such cases as a client may be astute enough to ask your advice, you should be astute enough to take a careful look at the books before recommending action, however apparently reasonable.

2. *Pledges.* O borrows $1,000 from A and hands over to A O's diamond necklace as security. This is the old-fashioned or Queen Isabella pledge. Nowadays the security is usually stocks and bonds, and A is the collateral loan department of a commercial bank. The pledge is a type of lien, using that word in the broader sense. If O, the pledgor, pays back the money, O gets back the pledged property; if O defaults, the pledgee can foreclose by a bill in equity praying for sale of the pledge. But the common law of pledge is almost unused since nearly all commercial pledges are governed by form contracts which the pledgor signs on borrowing the money. The contract normally requires the pledgor to provide additional security if the value of the collateral falls below a certain margin of safety; it also specifies a foreclosure procedure. Where O opens a margin account with A, a broker, O is engaging in a pledge transaction; O buys through A 100 shares of GE, putting up a percentage of the purchase price; thus O is a debtor of A for the unpaid portion of the price, and A holds the 100 shares as security. A normally carries customers' margin accounts by repledging their shares to a bank to secure a "call" loan, i.e., a loan payable on demand. When the market breaks, when the broker or the bank or both fail, and when O's 100 shares of GE have been mingled with the securities of several hundred of A's other customers, some rightfully and some wrongfully, it is clear that a field day for the legal fraternity is in prospect.

3. *Pawns.* These are not security transactions at all since there is no debt. O delivers a watch to A, receives from A $25, and also acquires the right to recover the watch within 30 days by paying back the $25 plus interest. If A fails to pay within the prescribed period, A's rights in the watch are gone. O is under no obligation to A to repay the $25, even though the watch proves to be worth less than $25.

4. *Chattel mortgages.* O, owning an automobile, wants to borrow $200 from A, using the car as collateral. O receives the $200 and gives to A (1) a note for $200, payable in an agreed period with interest, and (2) a document conveying to A a security interest in the car. To protect creditors and subsequent purchasers, it is usually provided by statute that a chattel mortgage is valid against them only if it is recorded in the appropriate public repository, normally the city hall. A holds both a personal claim against O on the note and a security title in the car. If O does not pay the note at maturity, A can foreclose by selling the car. If more than $200, plus interest, plus the expense of foreclosure, is realized, O gets the balance; if less, O is liable for the deficiency.

5. *Conditional sales.* A wants to buy a $100 radio but has only $30; A

wants to pay the rest in installments. O takes the $30 as a down payment and delivers the radio to A. O gives A possession of the radio but retains title. The contract establishes a debt from A to O and declares that title will pass to A only when A has completed the specified number of payments, which include "finance charges." Frequently the conditional-sale contract is called a "lease" and declares that the payments by A are rental payments and that title will pass to A at the end of a specified rental period as a sort of bonus. When, as frequently happens, A defaults in the payments, O "repossesses" the radio. The principal question is whether various forms of conditional-sale contracts can bring it about that the conditional vendee forfeits all payments upon repossession in spite of the fact that the radio has a saleable value in excess of the balance due. The courts are astute to prevent this result.

In those situations in which the creditor has possession of property as security for what is owing (the common law lien and the pledge), what are the rights of one who paid full value for the property in purchasing it from the creditor, thinking in good faith that the creditor was the unqualified owner of the purchased property? If the possession of the property that is security for the debt is in the debtor (the conditional sale and chattel mortgage), will a bona fide purchaser from the debtor defeat the security rights of the creditor in the purchased property? Statutes have invaded this area; the principal statute to keep in mind is the Uniform Commercial Code, about which you will learn in your course on commercial law.

DONALD v. SUCKLING
1 L.R.-Q.B. 585 (1866)

Declaration. That the defendant detained from the plaintiff his securities for money, that is to say, four debentures of the British Slate Company, Limited, for £200 each, and the plaintiff claimed a return of the securities or their value, and £1000 for their detention.

Plea. That before the alleged detention, the plaintiff deposited the debentures with one J. A. Simpson, as security for the due payment at maturity of a bill of exchange, dated 25th August, 1864, payable six months after date, and drawn by the plaintiff, and accepted by T. Sanders, and endorsed by the plaintiff to and discounted by Simpson, and upon the agreement then come to between the plaintiff and Simpson, that Simpson should have full power to sell or otherwise dispose of the debentures if the bill was not paid when it became due. That the bill had not been paid by the plaintiff nor by any other person, but was dishonoured; nor was it paid at the time of the said detention or at the commencement of this suit; and that before the alleged detention and the commencement of this suit, Simpson deposited the debentures with the defendant to be by him kept as a security for and until the repayment by Simpson to the defendant of certain sums of money advanced and lent by the defendant to Simpson upon the security of the debentures, and the defendant had and received the same for the purpose and on the terms aforesaid, which sums of money thence hitherto have been and remain wholly due and unpaid to the defendant; wherefore the defendant detained and still detains the debentures, which is the alleged detention.

Demurrer and joinder.

BLACKBURN, J. [after stating the pleadings]: The plea does not expressly state whether the deposit with the defendant by Simpson was before or after the dishonour of the bill of exchange; and as against the defendant, in whose knowledge this matter lies, it must be taken that it was before the bill was dishonoured, and consequently at a time when Simpson was not yet entitled by virtue of his agreement with the plaintiff to dispose of the debentures. We cannot construe the plea as stating that Simpson agreed to transfer to the defendant, as indorsee of the bill, the security which Simpson had over the debentures, and no more. We must, I think, as against the defendant, construe the plea as stating that Simpson deposited the debentures, professing to give a security on them for repayment of a debt of his own, which may or may not have exceeded the amount of the bill of exchange, but was certainly different from it. And it is quite clear that Simpson could not give the defendant any right to detain the debentures after the bill of exchange was satisfied, so that a replication that the plaintiff had paid, or was ready and willing to pay the bill would have been good. The defendant could not in any view have a greater right than Simpson had. But there is no such replication; and so the question which is raised on this record, and it is a very important one, is, whether the plaintiff is entitled to recover in detinue the possession of the debentures, he neither having paid nor tendered the amount for which he had pledged them with Simpson. In detinue the plaintiff's claim is based upon his right to have the chattel itself delivered to him; and if there still remain in Simpson, or in the defendant as his assignee, any interest in the goods, or any right of detention inconsistent with this right in the plaintiff, the plaintiff must fail in detinue, though he may be entitled to maintain an action of tort against Simpson or the defendant for the damage, if any, sustained by him in consequence of their unauthorized dealing with the debentures.

The question, therefore, raised on the present demurrer is, whether the deposit by Simpson of the debentures with the defendant, as stated in the plea, put an end to that interest and right of detention till the bill of exchange was honoured, which had been given to Simpson by the plaintiff's original contract of pledge with him.

There is a great difference in this respect between a pledge and a lien. The authorities are clear that a right of lien, properly so called, is a mere personal right of detention; and that an unauthorized transfer of the thing does not transfer that personal right. The cases which established that, before the Factors Acts, a pledge by a factor gave his pledgee no right to retain the goods, even to the extent to which the factor was in advance, proceed on this ground. In Daubigny v. Duval [5 T.R. at p. 606], Buller, J., puts the case on the ground that, "a lien is a personal right and cannot be transferred to another." In M'Combie v. Davies [7 East at p. 6], Lord Ellenborough puts the decision of the Court on the same ground, saying that "nothing could be clearer than that liens were personal and could not be transferred to third persons by any tortious pledge of the principal's goods." Story in his Treatise on Bailments, ss. 325, 326, and 327, is apparently dissatisfied with these decisions, thinking that a factor, who has made advances on the goods consigned to him, ought to be considered as having more than a mere personal right to detain the goods, and that a pledgee from him ought to have been considered entitled to detain the goods until the lien of the factor was discharged. This is a question which can never be raised in this country, for the legislature has intervened, and in all cases of pledges by agents, within the Factors Acts, the pledge is now available to the extent of the factor's interest.

But, on the facts stated on the plea, Simpson was not an agent within the meaning of the Factors Acts; and we have to consider whether the agreement stated to have been made between the plaintiff and him did confer something beyond a mere lien properly so called, an interest in the property, or real right, as distinguished from a mere personal right of detention. I think that both in principle and on authority, a contract such as that stated in the plea, pledging goods as a security, and giving the pledgee power in case of default to dispose of the pledge (when accompanied by an actual delivery of the thing), does give the pledgee something beyond a mere lien; it creates in him a special property or interest in the thing. . . .

In England there are strong authorities that the contract of pledge, when perfected by delivery of possession, creates an interest in the pledge, which interest may be assigned. . . .

It is laid down by Lord Holt in his celebrated judgment in Coggs v. Bernard [2 Ld. Raym. at p. 916], that a pawnee "has a special property, for the pawn is a securing to the pawnee that he shall be repaid his debt, and to compel the pawnor to pay him," language certainly seeming to indicate an opinion that he has an interest in the thing, or real right, as distinguished from a mere personal right of detention. And Story in his Treatise on Bailments, s. 327, says: "But whatever doubt may be indulged as to the case of a factor, it has been decided," that is, in America, "that in case of a strict pledge, if the pledgee transfers the same to his own creditor, the latter may hold the pledge until the debt of the original owner is discharged."

In Whitaker on Liens, published in 1812, p. 140, the law is laid down to be, that the pawnee has a special property beyond a lien. I do not cite this as an authority of great weight, but as shewing [showing] that this was an existing opinion in England before Story wrote his treatise. But there is a class of cases in which a person having a limited interest in chattels, either as hirer or lessee of them, dealing tortiously with them, has been held to determine his special interest in the things, so that the owner may maintain trover as if that interest had never been created. But I think in all these cases the act done by the party having the limited interest was wholly inconsistent with the contract under which he had the limited interest; so that it must be taken from his doing it, that he had renounced the contract. . . . Such is the case where a hirer of goods, who is not to have more than the use of them, destroys them or sells them; that being so wholly at variance with the purpose for which he holds them, that it may well be said that he has renounced the contract by which he held them, and so waived and abandoned the limited right which he had under that contract. It may be a question whether it would not have been better if it had been originally determined that, even in such cases, the owner should bring a special action on the case, and recover the damage which he actually sustained, which may in such cases be very trifling, though it may be large, instead of holding that he might bring trover, and recover the whole value of the chattel without any allowance for the special property. But I am not prepared to dissent from these cases, where the act complained of is one wholly repugnant to the holding, as I think it will be found to have been in every one of the cases in which this doctrine has been acted upon. But where the act, though unauthorized, is not so repugnant to the contract as to shew [show] a disclaimer, the law is otherwise. . . . Now I think that the subpledging of goods, held in security for money, before the money is due, is not in general so inconsistent with the contract, as to amount to a renunciation of that contract. There may be cases in which the pledgor has a special personal confidence in the pawnee, and therefore stipulates that the pledge shall be kept by him alone, but no such terms are stated here, and I do not think that any such term is implied by law. In general all that the pledgor requires is the personal contract of the pledgee that on bringing the money the pawn shall be given up to him, and that in the meantime the pledgee shall be responsible for due care being taken for its safe custody. This may very well be done though there has been a subpledge; at least the plaintiff should try to experiment whether, on bringing the money for which he pledged those debentures to Simpson, he cannot get them. . . .

But the latest case, and one which I think is binding on this Court, is that of Johnson v. Stear [15 C.B. (n.s.) 330, 33 L.J. 130 (C.P.)]; and I think that the decision of the majority of the Court of Common Pleas in that case is an authority, that at all events there remains in the pawnee an interest, not put an end to by the unauthorized transfer, such as is inconsistent with a right in the pawnor to recover in detinue. In that case the goods had been pledged as a security for a bill of exchange, with a power of sale if the bill was not paid at maturity. The pledgee sold the goods the *day before* he had a right to do so. The assignees of the bankrupt pledgor brought trover, and sought to recover the full value of the goods without any reduction. Williams, J., thought that they were so entitled, giving as his reason, "that the bailment having been terminated by the wrongful sale, the plaintiff might have resumed possession of the goods freed from the bailment, and might have held them rightfully when so resumed, as the absolute owner against all the world." And if this was correct, the present plaintiff is entitled to judgment. But the majority of the Court decided that "the deposit of the goods in question with the defendant to secure repayment of a loan to him on a given day, with power to sell in case of default on that day, created an interest and a right of property in the goods which was *more* than a mere lien; and the wrongful act of the pawnee did not annihilate the contract between the parties, *nor the interest* of the pawnee in the goods under that contract." . . . The fact that they differed from Williams, J., shews [shows] that after consideration they *meant* to decide, that the pledge gave a special property, which still continued; and though I have the highest respect for the authority of Williams, J., I think we must, in a court of co-ordinate jurisdiction, act upon the opinion of the majority, even if I did not think, as I do, that it puts the law on a just and convenient ground. And as already intimated, I think that unless the plaintiff is entitled to the uncontrolled possession of the things, he cannot recover in detinue.

For these reasons, I think we should give judgment for the defendant.[3]

SHERER-GILLETT CO. v. LONG
318 Ill. 432, 149 N.E. 225 (1925)

Appeal from the Second Division of the Appellate Court for the First District; — heard in that court on appeal from the Municipal Court of Chicago; the Hon. John Richardson, Judge, presiding.

THOMPSON, J., delivered the opinion of the court:

The sole question presented for decision in this case is whether under the law of this State in effect April 5, 1924, a reservation of title by the seller is good against a bona fide purchaser from a buyer in possession under a contract of conditional sale. The question arises out of the following transactions: April 3, 1924, appellee, the Sherer-Gillett Company, entered into a contract of conditional sale with H. C. Taylor for the sale of a display counter to be used by Taylor in his grocery store, by which Taylor agreed to pay $10 in cash and $10 each month until the full purchase price was paid, the title to remain in appellee until full payment of the purchase price had been made. Two days later Taylor sold the counter to appellant, J. W. Long, for $100, Long then having no notice of the reservation of title under the contract of conditional sale and no notice of any rights of appellee. The Appellate Court for the First District reversed a judgment of the municipal court entered in favor of appellant in an action of replevin brought by appellee and granted a certificate of importance allowing this appeal.

---

3. The concurring opinion of Cockburn, C.J., and Mellor, J., are not presented here; the dissenting opinion of Shee, J., also is not presented.— EDS.

Before sales became a subject of uniform legislation it was settled by an overwhelming weight of authority that the seller is not estopped by his conduct in delivering the possession of goods to the buyer upon a contract of conditional sale from asserting his title against one who purchases from the buyer, relying upon the apparent title of the latter (1 Williston on Sales 2d ed., sec. 324; Harkness v. Russell & Co., 118 U.S. 663, 7 Sup. Ct. 51; Arnold v. Chandler Motors, 45 R.I. 469, 123 A. 85); but in this State we had held that a delivery of personal property to the purchaser upon a contract of conditional sale, with a retention of title in the seller, amounts to constructive fraud, which postpones the right of the real owner in favor of those who have dealt without notice with the conditional vendee, who has been given the indicia of ownership. Gilbert v. National Cash Register Co., 176 Ill. 288, 52 N.E. 22; Brundage v. Camp, 21 Ill. 329. Uniformity in the law of the several States pertaining to sales being deemed essential to the commercial welfare of the country, leaders of the American bar prepared and submitted to the legislatures of the several States a uniform sales act and a uniform conditional sales act. The former was adopted in this State in 1915 and is the law to-day. By section 20 of the act the validity of a contract of conditional sale is recognized. Section 23 declares the law of this State respecting the transfer of title to be that theretofore declared by the great majority of the courts of this country. It provides:

> Subject to the provisions of this act, where goods are sold by a person who is not the owner thereof, and who does not sell them under the authority or with the consent of the owner, the buyer acquires no better title to the goods than the seller had, unless the owner of the goods is by his conduct precluded from denying the seller's authority to sell.[4]

It is a general, well-established principle that no one can transfer a better title than he has. Drain v. LaGrange State Bank, 303 Ill. 330, 135 N.E. 780; Williams v. Merle, 11 Wend. 80, 25 Am. Dec. 604. Nemo plus juris ad alium transferre potest quam ipse habet. Section 23 declares, in harmony with the settled law of estoppel, that the owner of the goods may by his conduct be precluded from denying the seller's authority to sell. In order to give rise to an estoppel, however, it is essential that the party estopped shall have made by act or word a representation, and that the person setting up the estoppel shall have acted on the faith of this representation in such a way that he cannot without damage withdraw from the transaction. 1 Williston on Sales, 2d ed., sec. 312. What representation has appellee made upon which appellant has relied to his damage? What conduct of appellee precludes it from denying the seller's authority to sell? It did not clothe Taylor with indicia of title. Clothing another person with indicia of ownership does not mean simply giving him possession of a chattel. Possession is one of the

---

4. For the comparable provision in the Uniform Commercial Code, see §2-403.— EDS.

indications of title, but possession may be delivered by the owner to a lessee, a bailee, an agent or a servant. Owners of chattels must frequently entrust others with their possession, and the affairs of men could not be conducted unless they could do so with safety, so long as the possession of the chattel is not accompanied by some indicium of ownership or the right to sell. Drain v. LaGrange State Bank, *supra*. Whether the legislature should adopt the companion act, which provides for the recording of contracts of conditional sale, is not for this court to decide. The Uniform Sales act recognizes the validity of such contracts and specifically provides that no title can be passed by the purchaser of goods under such a contract "unless the owner of the goods is by his conduct precluded from denying the seller's authority to sell." There is no basis for the operation of an estoppel in this record.

In National City Bank v. National Bank, 30 Ill. 103, 132 N.E. 832, after discussing the purpose of uniform legislation, the court, in laying down a rule of construction to be followed in the consideration of a uniform law, said:

> The court must take the act as it is written and should give to the words used their natural and common meaning. The law was enacted for the purpose of furnishing in itself a certain guide for the determination of all questions covered thereby, . . . and, so far as it speaks without ambiguity as to any such question, reference to case law as it existed prior to the enactment is more likely to be misleading than beneficial. If the provisions of the act harmonize with the general principles of commercial law in force before its enactment those principles should be followed, but if the language of the act conflicts with statutes or decisions in force before its enactment the courts should not give the act a strained construction in order to make it harmonize with earlier statutes or decisions. If this is done the very purpose of the act is defeated. In order to keep the law as nearly as may be uniform, the courts of all the States should keep in mind the spirit and object of the law and should give to the language of the act a natural and common construction, so that all might be more likely to come to the same conclusion.

To the same effect is the statement of the Supreme Court of the United States in Commercial Nat. Bank v. Canal-Louisiana Bank and Trust Co., 239 U.S. 52, 36 S. Ct. 194.

The judgment of the Appellate Court is affirmed.

Judgment affirmed.

O'CONNOR, ADMINISTRATRIX v. CLARK
170 Pa. 318, 32 A. 1029 (1895)

Replevin for a horse and wagon. Before Pennypacker, J.

At the trial evidence for the defendant tended to show that in September, 1890, John O'Connor, who was engaged in the business of keeping wagons for hire, had in his employ George Tracy, who had formerly been in business for himself as a piano mover. At this time, O'Connor was having a wagon built, and he directed the builder to print on the wagon the words "George Tracy, Piano Mover." The apparent object of this was to retain the business which Tracy had built up for himself. In April, 1891, Tracy attempted to sell the wagon at a bazaar but was not successful. He subsequently encountered the defendant, who agreed to buy the horse and wagon for $125, but before paying the money, he went with Tracy to a police station and a saloon, where Tracy was identified as the George Tracy whose name was on the wagon. There was evidence that Tracy was intoxicated at the time of the sale.

[The court charged the jury that the undisputed testimony established that the wagon belonged to plaintiff's testator, and that he was the owner of it, and that Tracy, without permission, took it off and sold it, or attempted to sell it. Thus, no title was conveyed to the defendant, and if the jury believed the testimony, a verdict must be returned for the plaintiff. The defendant assigned as error number one the granting of this charge.

The defendant assigned as error number two the refusal of the court to instruct that "[i]f the jury believe from the evidence that the plaintiff's decedent allowed Tracy, who sold the team to the defendant, to exercise such control and possession as to imply a right to sell, then the evidence must be for the defendant."

The defendant assigned as error number three the refusal of the court to instruct that "[i]f the jury find from the evidence that the plaintiff's decedent allowed Tracy to put his name on the wagon, and made no effort to efface it, and thereby allowed the defendant to be misled, their verdict must be for the defendant."]

Opinion by STERRETT, C.J.

If there were nothing more in this case than the facts recited by the learned trial judge in the excerpt from his charge quoted in the first specification of error, the instructions therein given to the jury to find for the plaintiff, if they believed the testimony, would be substantially correct. The only facts on which this instruction is predicated are, (1) that the wagon in question was the property of John O'Connor the original plaintiff, and (2) that Tracy, without his permission, took it and sold it or attempted to sell it to the defendant as his own. But, these are not the only facts of which there was evidence before the jury. On defendant's behalf, it is contended that the testimony tended to prove, and the jury, if they had been permitted, would have been warranted in finding that defendant purchased the property in question from Tracy in the honest belief that he was in fact the owner thereof; that the name and occupation of Tracy, viz: "George Tracy, Piano Mover," were on the wagon when he offered it for sale, and that fact was referred to as indicating his ownership of the property etc.; that Tracy being a stranger, defendant was specially careful to inquire and inform himself that the person, who was in possession of and offering to sell the wagon, was the George Tracy whose name and occupation were painted thereon; that Tracy's name and occupation were put upon the wagon with the knowledge of O'Connor, the original plaintiff, and himself, and by direction of the former, for the purpose of creating the impression and inducing the public to believe that the property belonged to Tracy, and was being used by him in his business, as a "piano mover," in which he had theretofore been engaged.

Without attempting to summarize the testimony relied on by the defendant, it is sufficient to say that it tends to prove substantially the state of facts above outlined, and especially that the original plaintiff, for his own gain and benefit, was a party to the arrangement whereby Tracy's name was put on the wagon for the purpose of misleading the public into the belief that the property was his, and that defendant, acting with due caution and in good faith, was thus misled as to the ownership of the property and purchased the same from Tracy.

While the soundness of the general rule of law that a vendee of personal property takes only such title or interest as his vendor has and is authorized to transfer, cannot for a moment be doubted, it is not without its recognized exceptions. One of these is where the owner has so acted with reference to his property as to invest another with such evidence of ownership, or apparent authority to deal with and dispose of it, as is calculated to mislead and does mislead a good faith purchaser for value. In such cases the principle of estoppel applies and declares that the apparent title or authority, for the existence of which the actual owner was responsible, shall be regarded as the real title or authority, at least so far as persons acting on the apparent title or authority and parting with value are concerned. Strictly speaking, this is merely a special application of the broad equitable rule that where one of two innocent persons must suffer loss by reason of the fraud or deceit of another, the loss should fall upon him by whose act or omission the wrongdoer has been enabled to commit the fraud. Assuming in this case that a jury under the evidence should find, as we think they would be warranted in doing, that such marks of ownership were placed on the property by direction of O'Connor, the real owner, as were not only calculated to deceive, but actually intended to deceive the public, and that by reason thereof, and without any fraud or negligence on his part, the defendant was misled into the belief that Tracy was the real owner, and he accordingly bought and paid him for the property, can there be any doubt, as between the real owner and the innocent purchaser, that the loss should fall upon the former by whose act Tracy was enabled to thus fraudulently sell and receive the price of the property? We think not.

In Bannard v. Campbell, 55 N.Y. 456, and 58 N.Y. 73—a well considered case involving substantially the same principle—it was held that to create an estoppel by which an owner is prevented from asserting title to and is deprived of his property by the act of a third person, without his assent, two things must concur:

1st. The owner must have clothed the person, assuming to dispose of the property, with the apparent title to or authority to dispose of it. 2d. The person alleging the estoppel must have acted and parted with value upon the faith of such apparent ownership or authority, so that he will be the loser if the appearances to which he trusted are not real.

Without further consideration of the questions involved we think the testimony, to which reference has been made, tended to prove facts which, if found by the jury, would have brought the case within the principle of estoppel above stated, and that the learned judge, by the instructions above complained of, virtually withdrew the effect of that testimony from the consideration of the jury. In defendant's second point, he was requested to charge: "If the jury find from the evidence that the plaintiff's intestate allowed Tracy to put his name on the wagon, and made no effort to efface it and thereby allowed the defendant to be misled, their verdict must be for the defendant." This was refused with the remark that he had already instructed them that their verdict ought to be for the plaintiff in the event of their believing the testimony.

It follows from what has been said that the first and third specifications should be sustained. The second specification is dismissed. As presented, defendant was not entitled to an affirmance of the point therein recited.

Judgment reversed and a venire facias de novo awarded.[5]

Note: A Sale in a Market Overt and a Sheriff's Sale

1.   *Market overt.* The English Sales of Goods Act of 1893 provides: "Where goods are sold in market overt according to the usage of the market, the buyer acquires a title to the goods provided he buys them in good faith and without notice of any defect or want of title on the part of the seller."

Bouvier's Law Dictionary (Rawle's third revision), Volume 2, defines a market overt as follows: "an open or public market; that is, a place appointed by law or custom for the sale of goods and chattels at stated times in public." See further as to what amounts to a sale in market overt Clayton v. LeRoy, 2 K.B. 1031 (1911), and Bishopsgate Motor Finance Corp. v. Transport Brakes, Ltd., [1949] 1 K.B. 322.

---

5.   Uniform Commercial Code §1-103 is as follows:

§1-103. Supplementory General Principles of Law Applicable.
Unless displaced by the particular provisions of this Act, the principles of law and equity, including the law merchant and the law relative to capacity to contract, principal and agent, estoppel, fraud, misrepresentation, duress, coercion, mistake, bankruptcy, or other validating or invalidating cause shall supplement its provisions.

—Eds.

The market overt is still very much alive in England. For a case involving the sale of an automobile and a comment which suggests that the market overt is not adapted to the modern commercial transaction, see 12 Mod. L. Rev. 371 (1949).

The following quotation is from Griffith v. Fowler, 18 Vt. 390 (1846):

> It seems to be considered in Massachusetts, and in New York, and in many of the other states, that nothing, analogous to *markets overt* in England exists in this country. Dame v. Baldwin, 8 Mass. 518. Wheelwright v. DePeyster, 1 Johns. 480, 2 Kent, 324 and cases there cited. Nothing of that kind, surely, exists in this state, unless it be a sheriff's sale. And if the practice of holding sales in *market overt* conclusive upon the title existed in any of the states, it would be readily known. I conclude, therefore, that Chancellor Kent is well founded in his opinion when he affirms that the law of *markets overt* does not exist in this country. [18 Vt. at 393-394.]

2.   *Sheriff's sale.* In Griffith v. Fowler, 18 Vt. 390 (1846), a sheriff levied on certain property as property of the debtor and sold the same at a sheriff's sale. In considering the rights of the purchaser at such sale, the court said:

> It seems probable to me, that the idea of the conclusiveness of a sheriff's sale upon the title is derived from the effect of sales under condemnations in the exchequer, for violations of the excise or revenue laws, and sales in prize cases, in the Admiralty courts, either provisionally, or after condemnation. But these cases bear but a slight analogy to sheriff's sales in this country, or in England. Those sales are strictly judicial, and are merely carrying into specific execution a decree of the court in rem, which, by universal consent, binds the whole world. . . .
>
> But with us nothing of this character exists in regard to sheriff's sales. . . . It is plain, then, that a sheriff's sale is not a judicial sale. If it were, no action could be brought against the sheriff, for selling upon execution property not belonging to the debtor. [18 Vt. at 394.]

Problems

9.3.   O, being the owner of a shearing machine, lent it to A to use in A's business as a clothier. A was to pay a yearly rent for the use thereof. Five years later the machine was sold at a sheriff's sale, on execution, as the property of A. B purchased it at the sheriff's sale without any knowledge of O's claim to the machine. O took the machine from the possession of B. B brings an action of trespass against O. Judgment for whom? See Griffith v. Fowler, 18 Vt. 390 (1846).

9.4.   A vessel, with a cargo owned by O, was captured on the high seas, on August 20, 1809, by a French privateer. The vessel and cargo were condemned by the court of prize, sitting at Guadaloupe, a part of the French empire, professedly for a violation of the Milan decree for trading with a dependence of England. The cargo was purchased by B and sent to B in Philadelphia. The cargo was claimed by O on its arrival in Philadelphia. Is O entitled to the cargo? See Williams v. Armroyd, 11 U.S. (7 Cranch) 423 (1813).

Note: Factors Acts

Statutes, commonly called factors acts, have been adopted in many states. Bouvier's Law Dictionary (Rawle's third revision), Volume 1, defines a factor as "an agent employed to sell goods or merchandise consigned or delivered to him, by or for his principal, for a compensation, commonly called factorage or commission." The purpose of the factors acts is summarized in the following quotation from H. A. Prentice Co. v. Page, 164 Mass. 276, 41 N.E. 279 (1895): "If the goods have been properly intrusted to an agent for sale, a party afterwards dealing in good faith with the agent will be protected, though the latter may violate his instructions, or, in disposing of or dealing with the goods, conduct himself fraudulently towards his principal."

Problems

9.5. O, the owner, consigns merchandise to A in town X. A is instructed to ship the goods to Smith in town Y. A sells the goods to B, a bona fide purchaser. Can O recover the merchandise from B? See Wilson v. Nason, 4 Bosw. 155 (N.Y. Sup. Ct. 1859); Hellings v. Russell, 33 L.T.R. (n.s.) 380 (C.P. 1875).

9.6. O, the owner, consigns merchandise to A, a factor, who is to sell it. After A has received the merchandise, O wires to A revoking the authority to sell. A then sells to B, a bona fide purchaser. May O recover the merchandise from B? See Fuentes v. Montis, 3 L.R.-C.P. 268 (1868).

Note: Voidable Titles

Section 2-403 of the Uniform Commercial Code provides that a person with a voidable title has power to transfer a good title to a good faith purchaser for value. Why should this be so?

In Part V you will learn about the historical development of equitable interests in property and become familiar with the maxim that the bona fide purchaser of the legal title cuts off outstanding equities. If, however, you desire to pursue the development of this maxim at this time, we suggest you read Ames, Purchase for Value Without Notice, 1 Harv. L. Rev. 1 (1887).

PHELPS v. McQUADE
220 N.Y. 232, 115 N.E. 441 (1917)

Appeal from a judgment, entered November 28, 1913, upon an order of the Appellate Division of the Supreme Court in the first judicial department, reversing a judgment in favor of plaintiffs entered upon a decision of the court on trial at Special Term and directing judgment for the defendant.

The nature of the action and the facts, so far as material, are stated in the opinion.

ANDREWS, J. One Walter J. Gwynne falsely represented to the appellants that he was Baldwin J. Gwynne, a man of financial responsibility, residing at Cleveland, Ohio. Relying upon the truth of this statement the appellants delivered to him upon credit a quantity of jewelry. Gwynne in turn sold it to the respondent, who bought it without notice express or implied of any defect in title, and for value. Learning of the deception practiced upon them, the appellants began an action in replevin to recover the goods.

The only question before us is whether under such circumstances, the vendor of personal property does or does not retain title thereto after he has parted with possession thereof.

The learned Appellate Division rested their decision upon the definition of common-law larceny, holding that where such larceny had been committed the thief acquired no title by his crime; where it had not, at least a voidable title passed.

We agree with that statement of the law. But we should prefer to define the rule in another form. Where the vendor of personal property intends to sell his goods to the person with whom he deals, then title passes, even though he be deceived as to that person's identity or responsibility. Otherwise it does not. It is purely a question of the vendor's intention.

The fact that the vendor deals with the person personally rather than by letter is immaterial, except in so far as it bears upon the question of intent.

Where the transaction is a personal one the seller intends to transfer title to a person of credit, and he supposes the one standing before him to be that person. He is deceived. But in spite of that fact his primary intention is to sell his goods to the person with whom he negotiates.

Where the transaction is by letter the vendor intends to deal with the person whose name is signed to the letter. He knows no one else. He supposes he is dealing with no one else. And while in both cases other facts may be shown that would alter the rule, yet in their absence, in the first title passes; in the second it does not.

Two cases that illustrate the distinction are Edmunds v. Merchants' Despatch Transportation Company, 135 Mass. 283, and Cundy v. Lindsay, L.R. (3 App. Cas.) 463.

In Edmunds v. Merchants' D. Transportation Company a swindler, representing himself to be one Edward Pape, personally bought goods of the plaintiff on credit. The court held that the title passed.

The minds of the parties met and agreed upon all the terms of the sale, the thing sold, the price and the time of payment, the person selling and the person buying. The fact that the seller was induced to sell by fraud of the buyer made the sale voidable, but not void. He could not have supposed that he was selling to any other person; his intention was to sell to the person present, and identified by sight and hearing; it does not defeat the sale because the buyer assumed a false name, or practiced any other deceit to induce the vendor to sell.

Cases of the same type are Perkins & Gray v. Anderson, 65 Iowa 398, 21 N.W. 696, and Hickey v. McDonald Bros., 151 Ala. 497, 44 So. 201.

In Cundy v. Lindsay one Blenkarn, signing himself Blenkiron & Co., bought goods by letter of Lindsay & Co. The latter shipped the goods to Blenkiron & Co. They knew of the firm of Blenkiron & Son; believed the letter came from that firm and that the goods were shipped to it. Blenkiron & Son were the persons with whom Lindsay & Co. intended to deal and supposed they were dealing. Under those circumstances it was held that although Blenkarn obtained possession of the goods he never acquired title thereto.

A similar case is Mercantile Nat. Bank, N.Y., v. Silverman, 148 App. Div. 1, 132 N.Y.S. 1017, *affirmed,* 210 N.Y. 567, 104 N.E. 1134, on opinion below.

Another class of cases such as Hentz v. Miller, 94 N.Y. 64 and Consumers Ice Company of Buffalo v. Webster, Son & Co., 32 App. Div. 592, 53 N.Y.S. 56, illustrate the rule under different circumstances. In them, persons falsely stating that they are the agents or representatives of others, fraudulently obtained possession of goods under a pretense of sale to such others. There is no intention on the part of the vendor to sell to the pretended agent or representative and no title passes.

In indictments for larceny, before the definition of that crime was changed by statute, this question of the passing of title was material; and, therefore, discussions as to whether an indictment or conviction could be sustained were relevant in cases where the question was whether or not the title had in fact passed. But in cases of each class the intention of the person having title to the goods and delivering them to another was the ultimate matter to be decided. And although it might be said in the one class of cases that where title did not [*sic*] pass there was no larceny; and in the other that where there was larceny the title did not pass, yet in both the test to be applied was this same intention on the part of the owner of the property.

The judgment of the Appellate Division must be affirmed, with costs.

HISCOCK, Ch. J., CHASE, COLLIN, CARDOZO and POUND, J., concur; McLAUGHLIN, J., not sitting.

Judgment affirmed.

Problems

9.7. A bought 70 tons of iron from O, paying for the iron by giving 83£ in cash and giving a bill of exchange for 113£ 14s. for the balance of the purchase price, which bill purported to be accepted by X, who was, in fact, a fictitious person. A then sold the iron to B, a bona fide purchaser, and the iron was delivered directly to B by O pursuant to A's direction. O then discovered that the supposed acceptor of the bill of exchange was a fictitious person and retook possession of the iron from B. B brings an action of trover against O for the iron. Judgment for whom? See White v. Garden, 10 C.B. 919 (C.P. 1851).

9.8. A procured a diamond ring from O on the basis of a fraudulent representation that A had a prospective purchaser of the ring and wanted to show it. A then sold the ring to B, a bona fide purchaser, and A absconded with the purchase money. O brought an action of replevin against B. Judgment for whom? See Baehr v. Clark, 83 Iowa 313, 49 N.W. 840 (1891).

9.9. O owns a radio. A informs O that A desires to buy it and will pay $50 for it. O delivers the radio to A, and A gives O a check in the amount of $50. Later the same day, A sells the radio to B, who pays value therefor without any knowledge of A's transaction with O. The next day, O presents the check for payment, but it is not honored by the bank because of insufficient funds in A's account. O learns that B has the radio and requests it of B. What advice would you give to B? See Corman, Cash Sales, Worthless Checks and the Bona Fide Purchaser, 10 Vand. L. Rev. 55 (1956); Gilmore, The Commercial Doctrine of Good Faith Purchase, 63 Yale L.J. 1057 (1954); U.C.C. §2-403.

Note: Negotiable Instruments, Bills of Lading, and Warehouse Receipts

The Uniform Commercial Code contains provisions regarding various so-called negotiable documents, which are designed to protect bona fide purchasers of such documents against defenses that otherwise might be available. The check you write is a negotiable instrument.

CHAPTER 10

WHEN A PERSON IS A BONA FIDE PURCHASER

In Chapter 9, we learned that there are many situations in which the bona fide purchaser of personal property will prevail over all other claimants. In view of this fact, it is necessary to be able to determine when a person is a purchaser and is a taker in good faith.[1] The purpose of this chapter is to aid us in making such determinations.

HURD v. BICKFORD
85 Me. 217, 27 A. 107 (1892)

On Exceptions.

This was an action of trover for one horse and sleigh. Demand was proved.[2] Pleadings were the general issue with brief statement of title in defendant. Verdict was for the plaintiff, with special findings of value of horse and sleigh. Defendant was a physician.

The evidence tended to show that the property was owned by the plaintiff, who subsequently sold and delivered it with other livery stock, to one Reuben G. Gross, and that the purchase by said Gross was fraudulent as to plaintiff.

It also tended to show that said Gross was, at the time of said pretended purchase indebted to the defendant for medical services, and after said pretended purchase gave defendant his note on time for such debt. That after such pretended sale, defendant purchased said horse of said Gross and gave in payment therefor said note before it was due.

---

1. See Gilmore, The Commercial Doctrine of Good Faith Purchase, 63 Yale L.J. 1051 (1954); Swartz, The Bona Fide Purchaser Revisited: A Comparative Inquiry, 42 B.U.L. Rev. 403 (1962).
2. What is the significance of this statement that demand was proved? — EDS.

It also tended to show that defendant at the time of his purchase of said horse was ignorant of any fraud by Gross in his purchase of the said livery stock of said Hurd.

The court instructed the jury that if they found the purchase by Gross was fraudulent as to Hurd, the defendant would not be an innocent purchaser, and they would find the defendant guilty and assess the damages at the value of the horse and sleigh as they shall find it to be.

The jury found for the plaintiff and the defendant excepted.

HASKELL, J. . . .

The horse was used to pay a pre-existing debt of Gross. The payment of that debt by his own note after he purchased the horse did not change the relation of the defendant to him, from prior to subsequent creditor. The same debt existed all the time. The note was but a new evidence of it. The time of payment may have been extended, but no new debt was created, no new credit given; simply further credit for the payment of an old debt.

The doctrine in favor of innocent purchasers is, that they have a right to rely upon the apparent title of their debtors to chattels in their possession, and deal with them as if the property were really their own. So it was held in Gilbert v. Hudson, 4 Me. 345, that chattels fraudulently purchased by a debtor, might be held on attachment, by his creditor, to the extent of an indebtedness contracted between them subsequent to the fraudulent purchase, but not for a debt contracted prior to that time. Gilbert v. Hudson, *supra;* Buffington v. Gerrish, 15 Mass. 156. This distinction between the rights of prior and subsequent creditors does not seem to have been always recognized. Jordan v. Parker, 56 Me. 557; Wiggin v. Day, 9 Gray 97; Atwood v. Dearborn, 1 Allen 483; Thaxter v. Foster, 153 Mass. 151, 26 N.E. 434; Donaldson v. Farwell, 93 U.S. 631. But property so purchased, and sold for a valuable consideration to a bona fide purchaser not conusant of the fraud, cannot be reclaimed. Trott v. Warren, 11 Me. 227; Neal v. Williams, 18 Me. 391; Sparrow v. Chesley, 19 Me. 79; Tourtellott v. Pollard, 74 Me. 418.

The discharge of an antecedent debt has always been held in our State a valuable consideration for the transfer of negotiable paper not due, so as to shut out equitable defenses. Homes v. Smith, 16 Me. 177; Norton v. White, 20 Me. 175; Railroad v. Bank, 102 U.S. 14. In many jurisdictions, such transfer, in good faith, as security merely, has also been held to so operate; Goodwin v. Massachusetts Loan Co., 152 Mass. 189, 199, 25 N.E. 100; Swift v. Tyson, 16 Pet. 1; Railroad v. Bank, 102 U.S. 14. Our decisions are to the contrary; Smith v. Bibber, 82 Me. 34, 19 A. 89. Does the same rule apply to the sale or pledge of chattels? . . .

The right of a vendee, depends upon whether the re-sale was made to a purchaser, ignorant of the fraud, and for a valuable consideration. Tourtellott v. Pollard, *supra.* And a valuable consideration, in such cases, means something more than the discharge of a debt that revives, when the consideration for its discharge fails. It means the parting with some value that cannot be actually restored by operation of law, leaving the purchaser in a changed condition, so that he may lose something beside his bargain. Barnard v. Campbell, 58 N.Y. 73; Stevens v. Brennan, 79 N.Y. 258; Hyde v. Ellery, 18 Md. 496, 501; McGraw v. Henry, 83 Mich. 442; George v. Kimball, 24 Pick. 234-240. The same rule applies to chattels pledged. Goodwin v. Massachusetts Loan Co., *supra.*

True, the discharge of an antecedent debt, in one sense, is a valuable consideration; but, if the title of the vendee fails, the discharge of his debt fails also, and he has lost nothing by the transaction. It is said that the vendor might pay his debt, and the vendee purchase the property with the proceeds. That is true, if the vendors have the means to do so, but all vendors are not solvent; if they were, there would be no occasion of reclaiming property fraudulently purchased by them, no occasion to rescind the sale. Other remedies would afford adequate redress. Or, if the property be reclaimed after they had sold it in payment of their existing debts, those debts could be easily collected, and no one would suffer from the transaction; whereas, if, perchance, they are insolvent and can, by fraud, purchase property, and apply it to their old debts, so as to leave their vendors without the power of reclaiming it, they, by defrauding one man, can thereby pay the debts of another, manifestly to the shame of honest dealing and even and exact justice among men. The authorities sustain the ruling at nisi prius.

Exceptions overruled.

PETERS, C.J., VIRGIN, LIBBEY, FOSTER AND WHITEHOUSE, JJ., concurred.

Problems

10.1. A, by fraudulent representations, induced O to sell to A an automobile that O owned. A gave B, who had no knowledge of the fraud, a chattel mortgage on the automobile as security for a pre-existing debt that A owed B. A later defaults on the mortgage and B desires to foreclose, but learns of A's fraud. B requests your advice. What advice would you give B?

10.2. A, by fraudulent representations, induced O to sell to A some timber on credit. The purchase price was $500. A, shortly after taking possession of the timber, sold it to B for $200, B giving A two negotiable notes, each for $100, and due, respectively, 90 and 120 days after date. A immediately sold and transferred B's two notes to the X Bank for value. O then learned of A's fraud and upon ascertaining that B had the timber, O notified B of the facts and demanded the return of the timber. What would you advise B to do? See Beebe Stave Co. v. Austin, 92 Ark. 248, 122 S.W. 482 (1909).

HIGGINS v. LODGE

68 Md. 229, 11 A. 846 (1888)

Appeal from the Superior Court of Baltimore City.

The case is stated in the opinion of the court.

Exception.— The plaintiffs offered three prayers, the third of which was as follows:

3.   That the plaintiffs are not precluded from recovering in this action by reason of any advances made to Hirsch Levy, or expenses incurred by the defendant upon the goods replevied, if the jury shall find that at the time said goods were delivered to him, the defendant had knowledge of circumstances calculated to put a man of ordinary prudence and caution upon inquiry as to whether said Levy was not perpetrating a fraud in selling off his stock at auction at that time, and the defendant failed to make inquiry into the character of the transaction in which said Levy was so engaged.

The defendant offered the two following prayers:

1.   That if the jury find that the defendant was, at the time of the transactions mentioned in the evidence, an auctioneer in the City of Baltimore, and that in the ordinary course of the business of the defendant, he did in good faith make advances to Hirsch Levy upon the security of goods consigned to him by said Levy for sale, and that among the goods so consigned, and upon the security of which the advances were made, were the goods replevied in this case, and that no advance was made upon the security of any part of the goods consigned, including the goods replevied, but that the advances were made upon the security of the whole amount of goods so consigned, and if they further find that said advances were made by the defendant without notice or knowledge of the circumstances under which said Levy had purchased said goods, then their verdict must be for the defendant.

2.   That if the jury find that the defendant made advances on the goods consigned to him by Levy for sale, as set forth in the defendant's first prayer, the plaintiffs are not entitled to recover even if the jury find that the defendant had knowledge of circumstances calculated to put a man of ordinary prudence and caution upon enquiry as to whether said Levy was not perpetrating a fraud in selling off his goods at the time the same were sold.

The court (Phelps, J.,) refused the plaintiffs' first and second prayers, and granted their third prayer, and refused the defendant's second prayer and granted his first prayer, and gave also the following instruction:

If you find that Hirsch Levy bought on credit from the plaintiffs the goods replevied in this case, but at the time of doing so had no reasonable expectation of paying for them and no intention to do so, and that he afterwards sent goods to the warehouse of the defendant to be sold at auction for the account of said Levy, and that before said goods had been so sold, the defendant was notified by the plaintiff, Lodge, or his attorney, of the fraudulent manner in which said goods had been obtained from plaintiffs by Levy, and demand was made of him for said goods, then the plaintiffs are entitled to recover, unless you shall further find that prior to such demand the defendant had, in good faith, advanced money to said Levy upon the security of said goods, or incurred expenses in relation thereto.

The defendant excepted to the refusal of his second prayer, to the granting of the plaintiffs' third prayer, and to the instruction given by the court. The verdict and judgment were in favor of the plaintiffs, and the defendant appealed.

The cause was argued before ALVEY, C.J., YELLOTT, MILLER, IRVING, and BRYAN, J.

BRYAN, J., delivered the opinion of the court.

Lodge and others replevied certain goods from Higgins. The evidence tended to show that one Hirsch Levy had made a fraudulent purchase of these goods from the plaintiffs; and that he had sent them for public sale to the defendant, who was an auctioneer. The defendant had made advances of money on them.

On the supposition that the purchase of the goods from the plaintiffs had been accomplished by the fraud of Levy, it is not questioned that it was void at the election of the sellers, and that they could have reclaimed their property from him. But if he sold them to a bona fide purchaser without notice of the fraud, a good title would be passed which could not be impeached by the original vendor. Ordinarily a purchaser cannot acquire a title from a vendor who has none. But the authorities show without dissent that there is an exception under the circumstances which we have just supposed. In Powel v. Bradlee, 9 G. & J., 278, it is said: "In such a case, good faith, and a valuable consideration would be essential constituents of a good title." If these features do not appear in the transaction, we take it that the title fails. An interest in the goods acquired by making advances on them when placed in the hands of an auctioneer for sale, would be protected under the same circumstances which would make a purchase valid.

The Court instructed the jury that if Levy's purchase was fraudulent, the defendant's title would be defeated, unless they found he had in good faith advanced money to Levy upon the security of the goods, or incurred expenses in relation to them. On the prayer of the defendant the Court ruled that the plaintiff could not recover, if the jury found that the advances were made by the defendant, without notice or knowledge of the circumstances under which Levy purchased the goods. On the prayer of the plaintiffs it was ruled that they were not precluded from recovering by these advances, if the jury found that at the time the goods were delivered to the defendant, he had knowledge of circumstances calculated to put a man of ordinary prudence on inquiry as to whether Levy was perpetrating a fraud in selling the goods by auction, and that he failed to make inquiry into the character of the transaction. Taking these instructions together it seems to us that they laid the case properly before the jury. Higgins could not deduce title to the goods through a fraudulent vendee, unless he showed that his advances were made in good faith. If he knew that Levy was selling these goods for the purpose of carrying into effect a fraud, his advances could not be considered as made in good faith; and if the circumstances were such as reasonably to call for inquiry, and if inquiry would have given him this knowledge, he is responsible in the same way as if he had obtained it. It has been held that if in any purchase "there be circumstances which in the exercise of common reason and prudence, ought to put a man upon particular inquiry, he will be presumed to have made that inquiry, and will be charged with notice of every fact which that inquiry would give him." Baynard v. Norris, 5 Gill 483. To the same effect are Green v. Early, 39 Md. 229; Abrams v. Sheehan, 40 Md. 446. The evidence showed that Levy rented a basement room about the fifteenth of June, 1885, and commenced business as a jobber; that between that time and September the seventh he purchased a large quantity of goods; six thousand dollars worth being purchased from these plaintiffs; that in the latter part of June, 1885, he commenced sending goods to the defendant to be sold by auction, the defendant making advances on them; that he continued to send goods for this purpose, and to receive advances from the defendant until September the fifth; that the amount of these auction sales was more than sixty-four hundred dollars; that on September the fifth, Levy had in his store only four or five hundred dollars worth of goods; that the week before he had fifteen thousand dollars worth; that he had opened a bank account on the eleventh of July, and on the seventh of September he drew out the balance to his credit with the exception of a small sum; that after that day he was regarded as utterly insolvent, that he purchased the goods in question from the plaintiffs on the twenty-first of August on credit, the time fixed for payment being October the tenth; that the small balance to his credit in the bank was attached by creditors, and that after September his business was conducted in his wife's name. The evidence certainly warranted the jury in finding that when Levy purchased these goods he did not intend to pay for them, and that he was engaged in a deliberate scheme of fraud, which he was effecting by purchasing large quantities of goods on credit, selling them by auction, and putting the proceeds beyond the reach of his creditors. Notwithstanding fraud on the part of Levy in making the purchase in question in this case, the title of Higgins would be good if the matters within his knowledge did not reasonably suggest to him the propriety of inquiring into the transactions in which Levy was engaged, and if this inquiry would not have discovered his fraudulent courses. It was the province of the jury to determine this question on the evidence in the cause.

Judgment affirmed.[3]

3. You should undertake to summarize exactly what misrepresentations Levy made which give the basis for concluding that he procured the goods by fraud. Furthermore, ask yourself what evidence there was that Higgins knew anything which should put him on inquiry. — EDS.

Problems

10.3. A obtains the title to some furniture owned by O by fraud. A sells the furniture to B. B paid A $1,000 at the time of the sale and promised to pay A another $1,000 within 30 days. Before the 30-day period had expired and before B had paid the balance of the purchase price, B learned of A's fraud. Which of the following solutions do you think is preferable and why?
   a. O may take back all the furniture on paying B $1,000.
   b. B may keep all the furniture on paying O $1,000.
   Assume B paid A the entire purchase price of $2,000 before learning of A's fraud but the furniture was worth $4,000 at the time B bought it from A. What would be your position as attorney for O?

10.4. A obtains title to some furniture owned by O by fraud. A sells the furniture to B, who knows that it was obtained from O by fraud. B sells the furniture to C, a bona fide purchaser. Later B buys the furniture from C. Is O entitled to obtain the furniture from B? See Pierce v. Carlton, 184 N.C. 175, 114 S.E.2d 13 (1922).

CHAPTER 11

DAMAGES RECOVERABLE FROM A BONA FIDE PURCHASER

If the bona fide purchaser prevails, the purchaser is not subject to a suit for damages for having asserted dominion over the personal property in question. We have seen though that frequently the purchaser's claims are subordinate to those of another. In such case, the purchaser has committed a wrong by asserting dominion over the personal property in question and is answerable in damages. Shall we apply to him or her the same measure of damages as is applied to a willful wrongdoer, or shall we be more lenient because the purchaser has acted innocently? We shall see.

WOODEN-WARE CO. v. UNITED STATES
106 U.S. 432, 1 S. Ct. 398 (1882)

Error to the Circuit Court of the United States for the Eastern District of Wisconsin.

The facts are stated in the opinion of the court.

MILLER, J., delivered the opinion of the court.

This is a writ of error, founded on a certificate of division of opinion between the judges of the Circuit Court.

The facts, as certified, out of which this difference of opinion arose appear in an action in the nature of trover, brought by the United States for the value of two hundred and forty-two cords of ash timber, or wood suitable for manufacturing purposes, cut and removed from that part of the public lands known as the reservation of the Oneida tribe of Indians, in the State of Wisconsin. This timber was knowingly and wrongfully taken from the land by Indians, and carried by them some distance to the town of Depere, and there sold to the E. E. Bolles Wooden-ware Company, the defendant, which

171

was not chargeable with any intentional wrong or misconduct or bad faith in the purchase.

The timber on the ground, after it was felled, was worth twenty-five cents per cord, or $60.71 for the whole, and at the town of Depere, where defendant bought and received it, three dollars and fifty cents per cord, or $850 for the whole quantity. The question on which the judges divided was whether the liability of the defendant should be measured by the first or the last of these valuations.

It was the opinion of the circuit judge that the latter was the proper rule of damages, and judgment was rendered against the defendant for that sum.

We cannot follow counsel for the plaintiff in error through the examination of all the cases, both in England and this country, which his commendable research has enabled him to place upon the brief. In the English courts the decisions have in the main grown out of coal taken from the mine, and in such cases the principle seems to be established in those courts, that when suit is brought for the value of the coal so taken, and it has been the result of an honest mistake as to the true ownership of the mine, and the taking was not a wilful trespass, the rule of damages is the value of the coal as it was in the mine before it was disturbed, and not its value when dug out and delivered at the mouth of the mine. Martin v. Porter, 5 Mee. & W. 351; Morgan v. Powell, 3 Ad. & E.N.S. 278; Wood v. Morewood, 3 Id. 440; Hilton v. Woods, Law Rep. 4 Eq. 432; Jegon v. Vivian, Law Rep. 6 Ch. App. 742.

The doctrine of the English courts on this subject is probably as well stated by Lord Hatherley in the House of Lords, in the case of Livingstone v. Rawyards Coal Co., 5 App. Cas. 25, as anywhere else. He said:

> There is no doubt that if a man furtively, and in bad faith, robs his neighbor of his property, and because it is underground is probably for some little time not detected, the court of equity in this country will struggle, or I would rather say, will assert its authority to punish the fraud by fixing the person with the value of the whole of the property which he has so furtively taken, and making him no allowance in respect of what he has so done, as would have been justly made to him if the parties had been working by agreement.

But "when once we arrive at the fact that an inadvertence has been the cause of the misfortune, then the simple course is to make every just allowance for outlay on the part of the person who has so acquired the property, and to give back to the owner, so far as is possible under the circumstances of the case, the full value of that which cannot be restored to him in specie."

There seems to us to be no doubt that in the case of a wilful trespass the rule as stated above is the law of damages both in England and in this country, though in some of the State courts the milder rule has been applied even in this class of cases. Such are some that are cited from Wisconsin. Weymouth v. Chicago & Northwestern Railway Co., 17 Wis. 550; Single v. Scheider, 24 Wis. 299.

On the other hand, the weight of authority in this country as well as in England favors the doctrine that where the trespass is the result of inadvertence or mistake, and the wrong was not intentional, the value of the property when first taken must govern; or if the conversion sued for was after value had been added to it by the work of the defendant, he should be credited with this addition.[1]

Winchester v. Craig, 33 Mich. 205, contains a full examination of the authorities on the point. Heard v. James, 49 Miss. 236; Baker v. Wheeler, 8 Wend. (N.Y.) 505; Baldwin v. Porter, 12 Conn. 484.

While these principles are sufficient to enable us to fix a measure of damages in both classes of torts where the original trespasser is defendant, there remains a third class, where a purchaser from him is sued, as in this case, for the conversion of the property to his own use. In such case, if the first taker of the property were guilty of no wilful wrong, the rule can in no case be more stringent against the defendant who purchased of him than against his vendor.

But the case before us is one where, by reason of the wilful wrong of the party who committed the trespass, he was liable, under the rule we have supposed to be established, for the value of the timber at Depere the moment before he sold it, and the question to be decided is whether the defendant who purchased it then with no notice that the property belonged to the United States, and with no intention to do wrong, must respond by the same rule of damages as his vendor should if he had been sued.

It seems to us that he must. The timber at all stages of the conversion was the property of plaintiff. Its purchase by defendant did not divest the title nor the right of possession. The recovery of any sum whatever is based upon that proposition. This right, at the moment preceding the purchase by defendant at Depere, was perfect, with no right in any one to set up a claim for work and labor bestowed on it by the wrong-doer. It is also plain that by purchase from the wrong-doer defendant did not acquire any better title to the property than his vendor had. It is not a case where an innocent purchaser can defend himself under that plea. If it were, he would be liable to no damages at all, and no recovery could be had. On the contrary, it is a case to which the doctrine of caveat emptor applies, and hence the right of recovery in plaintiff.

On what ground, then, can it be maintained that the right to recover against him should not be just what it was against his vendor the moment before he interfered and acquired possession? If the case were one which concerned additional value placed upon the property by the work or labor of the defendant after he had purchased, the same rule might be applied as in case of the inadvertent trespasser.

---

1. For a critical evaluation of the various positions courts have taken in this matter, and a suggestion that an innocent converter and the original owner should share in the ownership of the converted and improved property in an equitable proportion, see Cross, Another Look at Accession, 22 Miss. L.J. 138 (1951). — EDS.

But here he has added nothing to its value. He acquired possession of property of the United States at Depere, which, at that place, and in its then condition, is worth $850, and he wants to satisfy the claim of the government by the payment of $60. He founds his right to do this, not on the ground that anything *he* has added to the property has increased its value by the amount of the difference between these two sums, but on the proposition that in purchasing the property he purchased of the wrong-doer a right to deduct what the labor of the latter had added to its value.

If, as in the case of an unintentional trespasser, such right existed, of course defendant would have bought it and stood in his shoes; but as in the present case, of an intentional trespasser, who had no such right to sell, the defendant could purchase none. . . .

The case of Nesbitt v. St. Paul Lumber Co., 21 Minn. 491, is directly in point here. The Supreme Court of Minnesota says:

> The defendant claims that because they [the logs] were enhanced in value by the labor of the original wrong-doer in cutting them, and the expense of transporting them to Anoka, the plaintiff is not entitled to recover the enhanced value; that is, that he is not entitled to recover the full value at the time and place of conversion.

That was a case, like this, where the defendant was the innocent purchaser of the logs from the wilful wrong-doer, and where, as in this case, the transportation of them to a market was the largest item in their value at the time of conversion by defendant; but the court overruled the proposition and affirmed a judgment for the value at Anoka, the place of sale.

To establish any other principle in such a case as this would be very disastrous to the interest of the public in the immense forest lands of the government. It has long been a matter of complaint that the depredations upon these lands are rapidly destroying the finest forests in the world. Unlike the individual owner, who by fencing and vigilant attention, can protect his valuable trees, the government has no adequate defence against this great evil. Its liberality in allowing trees to be cut on its land for mining, agricultural, and other specified uses has been used to screen the lawless depredator who destroys and sells for profit.

To hold that when the government finds its own property in hands but one removed from these wilful trespassers, and asserts its right to such property by the slow processes of the law, the holder can set up a claim for the value which has been added to the property by the guilty party in the act of cutting down the trees and removing the timber, is to give encouragement and reward to the wrong-doer, by providing a safe market for what he has stolen and compensation for the labor he has been compelled to do to make his theft effectual and profitable.

We concur with the circuit judge in this case, and the judgment of the Circuit Court is
Affirmed.

Problems

11.1.   In Wooden-ware Co. v. United States, what would be the effect of the establishment of any one of the following facts?
   a.   The timber was removed from the land by the Indians innocently.
   b.   The timber was removed from the land by the Indians innocently, but the Wooden-ware Company at the time of the purchase of the timber knew that the Indians had no right to remove it.
   c.   The Wooden-ware Company at the time of the purchase of the timber knew that the Indians had no right to remove it.

11.2.   O delivered one hundred bushels of corn to A pursuant to an agreement whereby A was to store the corn and redeliver it to O on demand. One week later A without O's knowledge sold the one hundred bushels of corn to B at $1 a bushel, the market price on the day of the sale, and B purchased the corn without knowledge of O's ownership of it. One month later when O learned of A's wrongful act, the market price of corn was $1.25 a bushel. The price of corn rose steadily during the course of the next two weeks reaching a peak at one time of $1.50 a bushel during the two-week period. O without making any demand of B for the return of the corn brings an action of trover against B for the conversion of the corn. The value of the corn at the date of the trial is $1.60 a bushel. How much should O recover from B in this action? See Restatement (Second) of Torts §927 comment e. Suppose that O demanded of B the return of the corn when the market price of the corn was $1.60 a bushel and B refused to return the corn to B and O then instituted his action of trover for the conversion of the corn. How much would O be entitled to recover from B? See Restatement (Second) of Torts §927 comments h and i.

Note: Accession

A converter who has changed the specie of the converted property (corn changed into whiskey) or who by work and labor has measurably improved the value of the converted property (lumber made into furniture) may under some circumstances thereby acquire the title to the converted property. This situation is generally referred to as the acquisition of title by accession. If the original converter acquires title by accession and then sells the property in its changed or improved form, the purchaser from him acquires a clear title and consequently is not liable in damages to the person from whom the property in its original form was taken. See Arnold, The Law of Accession of Personal Property, 22 Colum. L. Rev. 103 (1922).

Note: Confusion

"Confusion of goods results when personal property belonging to two or more owners becomes intermixed to the point where the property of any of them no longer can be identified except as part of a mass of like goods." Johnson v. Covey, 1 Utah 2d 180, 264 P.2d 283 (1953).

The goods may be of the same kind or quality or not, and the respective amounts may be known or not. The confusion may be intentional on the part of all concerned, or it may occur without the consent of one or more owners, or without the consent of any of them. One or more of the owners may willfully cause the confusion or may negligently cause it, or it may be caused by a third party or by an act of God. There are a great many possible combinations of these variables, and out of them "arises much of the law of confusion." The issue is the ownership of the mixture when the ingredients contributed by each owner cannot be identified and separated from the mixture. If a person willfully and wrongfully mixes his or her grain with the grains of another, should the entire mixture belong to the innocent party?

RICHTMYER v. MUTUAL LIVE STOCK COMMISSION CO.
122 Neb. 317, 240 N.W. 315 (1932)

Appeal from the district court for Douglas county: Charles E. Foster, Judge. Reversed.

Heard before Goss, C.J., DEAN, EBERLY and PAINE, J.J., and BLACK-LEDGE, District Judge.

BLACKLEDGE, J. This action is by the plaintiff, appellee, for the conversion of certain cattle which were stolen from his ranch in Cherry county; and its object, to recover the value of the cattle from the defendant, which as a live stock commission merchant, some seven days after the theft, received the cattle at Omaha on shipment from the thief, and sold them in the usual course on the market.

In the briefing and submission of the case in this court, all assignments of error are eliminated except the one which involves the proper measure of damage to be applied in the case.

The defendant contends that, the jury having found for plaintiff upon the identity of the cattle, it is liable to plaintiff in some amount, as having handled and disposed of the stolen property, but insists that the value for which it may be held to account is that in Omaha where it received and dealt with the property. It claims to have acted innocently and in good faith, without knowledge of the prior theft and conversion; and this fact is conceded by plaintiff, who states in his brief: "We wish to make it clear that we do not charge the defendant with any culpability."

The plaintiff contends, and the trial court adopted the theory, that the proper measure of damage was the value of the cattle in Cherry county at the time of the original taking by the thief, with interest from that date. Evidence was either received or excluded in the trial in accordance with that theory, and the jury were so instructed.

The cattle were pure bred registered Herefords, valuable for breeding purposes. They were sold on the market as ordinary beef cattle, netting the shipper some $1,000. Their value as pure breds in Cherry county is amply sustained by the evidence at $3,500, which the jury found. The defendant was not permitted to show the value of such cattle at Omaha.

Both parties concede that the general rule for the measure of damages for conversion is the value of the property at the time and place of conversion, with interest from that date. Here they part company, however, and each seeks to apply that statement, as an unbending and all-inclusive rule, to the facts of his own case. Plaintiff urges that his loss occurred at the original taking, and that this unalterably fixes the time and place governing the value to be allowed, regardless of the remoteness of time or place when and where they came into possession of defendant, or of the innocence or culpability of the defendant, who had no part in the original taking and became liable solely by having, in the usual course of business, handled and disposed of the stolen property, and regardless also of the condition or value of the property at the time defendant came into possession.

Plaintiff further urges that, in receiving the cattle consigned to it by the thief, defendant became the agent of the thief and so liable in the same measure as would be the original taker as principal; and that the taking of the cattle by Gross, his shipment of them to defendant at Omaha, and their subsequent sale and remittance of the proceeds were all consecutive steps in the conversion, the sale by defendant being merely the completion of the acts that constituted the conversion. The infirmity in this argument so far as concerns plaintiff's case is that it proves too much to result in any strengthening of plaintiff's position. For, if these were successive steps in the one conversion and the final sale the completion thereof, it necessarily follows that it, being made in Omaha, the time and place of that act, as well as the acts in Cherry county, must be considered in the application of the rule of damage. There is some merit in defendant's argument that it should not, as agent, be chargeable with acts of which it knew nothing, and which took place before any agency was, or under the facts in this case could have been, created.

That the general rule hereinbefore stated of the measure of damages for conversion is the law of this state, there can be no doubt. [Citations omitted.]

It does not follow, however, that it is so unyielding and all inclusive that no account should be taken of the facts attendant upon the conversion, the entrance of defendant into the zone of liability, or the location or condition of the property at that time. Courts have often considered the condition of the converted property as it came into the hands of the defendant, and, upon comparison with its condition when originally taken, modified the measure of damage as it is hereinbefore stated. This has generally occurred in cases wherein the property had been increased in value by some process of trade or manufacture. In some instances the plaintiff was awarded the value as increased, upon the ground that it was made by the wrong-doer himself who should not be permitted to thus profit by his own act and in effect compel an involuntary sale by plaintiff. Wooden-ware Co. v. United States, 106 U.S. 432, 1 S. Ct. 398. In Pine River Logging & Improvement Co. v. United States, 186 U.S. 279, 2 S. Ct. 920, it is said: "The cases involving this distinction and in line with the Wooden-Ware case are abundant, both in the federal and state courts, and are too numerous even for citation."

In many cases the courts rest a distinction upon the ground that the defendant, not being an intentional wrong-doer, came innocently into possession of the property, and allow the defendant credit for any increase in value contributed by him, although holding him to account for the condition of the property as it came into his hands. . . .

This court, as stated in the opinion by Letton, J., in Clay v. Palmer, 104 Neb. 476, 177 N.W. 840, has adopted a slight modification of the rule in Wooden-ware Co. v. United States, 106 U.S. 432, 1 S. Ct. 398, and follows that of Carpenter v. Lingenfelter, 42 Neb. 728, 60 N.W. 1022, to the effect that the original value only is to be given the owner, regardless of whether the increase was made by a wilful wrong-doer or by one in good faith.

In Potter v. United States, C.C.A. Minn., 122 F. 49, Sanborn, J., in discussing the matter of damages and the bad or good faith of the purchaser who had been sued, says: "The measure of damages for the conversion by an innocent purchaser from a wilful trespasser is the value of the property converted at the time of the purchase."

A number of Nebraska cases, in addition to those herein noted, have been cited in the briefs of counsel. None of them determine a situation as between the owner and an unintentional wrong-doer. They all were suits against the original wilful trespasser. No case has been cited to us which involves a decrease in the value of the property after the taking or at the time it reached the hands of defendant who is called upon to account, and a rather diligent search has failed to discover any judicial determination of that question.

Examination of the precedents does disclose, however, that the inquiry as to the value of the converted property is by no means limited to the immediate time or place of the original taking, but is to be governed largely by the facts of the particular case on trial. Whatever distinctions may be drawn by or from the Wooden-ware case, and later adjudications by that court, they do approve inquiry as to value at a time and place more or less remote from the original taking. . . .

The court must consider here the rights of the two parties, each without culpability, in relation to the facts upon which the case rests. The plaintiff should of course have full recovery for the loss at the time sustained; and so he would if his suit ran against the original taker. The original taker is not a party to this action. The defendant became unwittingly involved by the circumstance of having dealt with and disposed of the property. If the property was of less value when and where defendant got it, one of two innocent parties must suffer loss. A fixed rule of law for the protection of property owners puts upon one so dealing with stolen property the duty, no matter how innocently he dealt, to account to the true owner for its value. Upon what theory of substantial justice can either of these be entitled to preferential treatment at the hands of the court? Upon what theory of right shall the defendant, without culpability itself, but bound nevertheless to render to the true owner the value of the property in which it dealt, be required to submit to an additional penalty for the wrongful act of another in which it had no part? It is presumed of course to know the value of the property in which it dealt at the time and place it got it, and to take the risk of dealing with the lawful owner; but by what just means can it be held further chargeable with knowledge of, or liability for, an additional value that it could not see and did not know, and which was not in fact then in the property?

This all leads to the conclusion that in such cases "the time and place of conversion" to be considered, and which controls on the question of value, is that fixed by the acts of the defendant in its dealing with the property, rather than the original taking in which defendant had no part. The trial court was in error in excluding evidence as to the value of the property at Omaha, and in instructing the jury that the value in Cherry county on the date of the theft was the only value to be considered. This gives to the plaintiff full compensation for his loss in so far as the defendant had any connection with it, holds defendant responsible for the full value of that in which it dealt, without attaching additional penalty for the acts of another, and seems to us a just and salutary rule.

It is not to be understood, however, that the value of the property in Cherry county, so recently before the conversion by defendant, becomes immaterial in the case. The limits of the inquiry should not in this case be so confined. The value there at that time might well tend to show the value on shipment to Omaha. Also whether the cattle in question were pure breds or only beef cattle was one of the issues in the case. We judicially know the relative location of the counties and cities in the state and approximate distances and the general routes of travel, and that Omaha is the principal live stock market in the state and probably the one most accessible from Cherry county. It seems reasonable that in this investigation the values at either place would be relevant in fixing the actual value of the property at the time and place of the acts of the defendant in relation thereto.

For the reasons stated, the judgment of the district court is reversed and a new trial awarded.

Reversed.

Problem

11.3. O transfers the possession of a watch to A to hold until O requests its return. B, who is a friend of A, sees the watch in A's possession and claims ownership of it. B recently had lost a watch and the one A held looked to B like the one B had lost. A turned the watch over to B on demand from B. A few days later B realized the watch was not the one B had lost and B returned the watch to A. O learned of these facts and sued B for the value of the watch. Should O recover? See Whittler v. Sharp, 43 Utah 419, 135 P. 112 (1913).

Note: Selection of Remedy, Selection of Person To Be Sued, and Effect of Obtaining a Judgment

If you have not been deprived of your rights in personal property by a sale to a bona fide purchaser, you have a choice of remedies. You may seek to obtain the return of your property in specie (replevin, detinue, and when the property is unique, relief in a court applying equitable principles; under some circumstances you may even employ self-help) or you may sue for damages. In selecting the remedy to pursue, an important factor is whether the damages recoverable equal the present value of the property. In addition to having a choice of remedies, you may have a choice of persons to sue because ordinarily the one who makes the sale to the bona fide purchaser will also be liable to you. In view of the fact that such seller will no longer have possession of your property, you will be able to sue such seller only for damages. In determining whether to sue such seller for damages or to sue the bona fide purchaser for damages or to recover the property in specie, an important factor is the amount recoverable against each possible defendant.

If you elect to sue the one who sold your property to the bona fide purchaser and obtain a judgment against such person, which judgment is satisfied, it is clear that you are barred thereafter from maintaining any action against the bona fide purchaser. The satisfaction of the judgment ends your title to the property. Suppose, however, you have obtained a judgment against such seller but it has not yet been satisfied. In such case, are you barred from suing the bona fide purchaser? This question is raised in the problems which follow. Do you see the arguments for and against allowing a suit against the bona fide purchaser when the outstanding judgment has not been satisfied? See Comment, Judgment or Satisfaction as Passing Title, 30 Yale L.J. 742 (1921).

Problems

11.4.   O through an agent, A, purchased a horse, and A retained possession of it. Several months later O demanded the horse of A and A refused to deliver it, claiming ownership of the horse. A then sold the horse to B who purchased it in good faith. Thereafter O brought an action of trover against A for the conversion of the horse and obtained a judgment. O was unable to collect on the judgment against A because A was financially worthless. O then brought an action of trover against B for conversion of the horse.

Judgment for whom? See Miller v. Hyde, 161 Mass. 472, 37 N.E. 760 (1894).

11.5. O was the owner of a truck valued at $2,000. A wrongfully took the truck and converted it to her own use. O brought an action of trover against A for the conversion of the truck, and judgment was entered against A in favor of O for $2,000. Six days after the rendition of the judgment A sold the truck to B for $1,700. O was unable to collect on the judgment against A and therefore O now brings an action against B for the conversion of the truck. Should O be allowed to recover and, if so, how much? See Hodur v. Cutting, 248 Ill. App. 145 (1928).

Note: *Implied Warranty of Title as Basis of Suit by a Bona Fide Purchaser*

When a sale of personal property is made to a bona fide purchaser, in the absence of a contrary manifestation of intention, there is an implied warranty of title. Thus if the bona fide purchaser is deprived of the property by one having a superior title or is made to pay damages to such a person, the bona fide purchaser may recover from his or her vendor for the breach of the implied warranty of title. See Argens v. Whitcomb, 20 Wash. 2d 371, 147 P.2d 501 (1944).

P A R T   I V

ESTATES IN LAND

Introduction

We are now interested in examining the various ways in which two or more people may have interests in the same piece of land. We want to see what their respective rights are as against one another and as against third persons. This knowledge is the foundation of a real estate practice in which the legal profession plays a dominant role. A lawyer who undertakes to do estate planning for a client will, to a considerable extent, be arranging for the beneficial enjoyment of land and things other than land moving from the client who controls the family wealth to multiple members of the client's family. The knowledge gained from understanding the options available with respect to dispositions of land often may be applicable to interests in things other than land. Hence, this material is essential background for the lawyer engaged in estate planning.

In determining the title to land, one must search backward through the various prior dispositions of the land. The legal effect of those dispositions normally will be governed by the law in effect at the time they were made. Thus, it is often important that the lawyer understand the earlier law as well as what the legal effect would be of the same dispositions if made today. This is why an examination of history is so critical to the study of land law.

Interests in land in two or more people may be either successive or concurrent in relation to enjoyment in possession. A devise by O to O's son *or* daughter for life, with remainder to the son's or daughter's issue, creates a successive interest. On the other hand, if O devises land to his son *and* daughter, each to own an undivided one-half interest, their interests are concurrent.

Individuals may also have interests in land that give them rights of enjoyment with respect to the land but not the possession of any part of it. Such is the case when O owns land and O's neighbor has the right to pass over a designated portion of it to get to the neighbor's land.

Finally, interests in land may exist in two or more persons when the land is possessed by a person who has no beneficial rights in it but manages it for

183

the benefit of another. The modern trust is an example of this situation. Generally, the manager (the trustee) will have the legal title to the land, and the beneficiary will have the equitable title to the land. The equitable nature of the beneficiary's title is significant because the remedies to protect the beneficiary's rights usually are provided by a court applying equitable principles.

We hope that you will find this study of estates in land as fascinating as we have. It is a very vital and significant part of the law.

CHAPTER 12

HISTORICAL BACKGROUND OF REAL PROPERTY LAW

Note: Up From Feudalism

Pusey Manor, near the Berkshire-Oxfordshire border, between Faringdon and Oxford, came to the Pusey family in the eleventh century and there continued for nearly nine hundred years. Over the great fireplace a bas-relief, depicting the legend of the founding of the estate, shows a knight receiving a hunting horn from a regal figure. But Pusey Manor is no longer owned by the Pusey family.

In some degree the story of the Puseys and their manor epitomizes the history of English land ownership and land law. The bas-relief commemorates an episode of the wars in which Canute and his Danes contested the mastery of England with Edmund Ironside and his Saxons. In 1016 the Saxons were encamped at nearby Cherbury, where the remains of their earthworks can still be seen. It is told that William Pusey, a supporter of Canute, went through the Saxon lines in disguise, brought back information which enabled his master to carry the day, and received from Canute the gift of the horn and all the lands over which he could make the horn heard from the battlefield.

Until well into the twentieth century the Pusey land remained in the family — no small achievement when it is realized that, in the Wars of the Roses and the Stuart upheavals, the winners made a practice of confiscating the lands of the losers. The Pusey horn was extant and acted as the title deed to the property. In 1684 an issue arose as to whether, upon the death of a Pusey, it passed as personalty to his executor or as realty to his heir. Lord Guilford came to the conclusion that it remained with the land. Pusey v. Pusey, 1 Vern. 273 (Ch. 1684).

Of course, the land was the source of the family fortune. In the middle nineteenth century the estate was thriving. It was devoted chiefly to wool-raising, with a "home farm" of some 400 acres of level fields which was a model of progressive, practical agriculture. In 1933 the entire 1800 acres of

Pusey Manor was sold, for reasons which, though undisclosed, may fairly be guessed to have some relationship to taxes. In their desecrating professional jargon the real estate agents pointed out that this magnificent relic of a millennium of history comprised "a Georgian residence, woodlands and farms, and is a good sporting property." It was also pathetically noted in The Times that "the Sheraton and Chippendale furniture, which was originally made for the house and which has never been removed from it, is now being taken away to the sale rooms." [1]

---

1. The Times, August 2 and 17, 1933. For other material on the Pusey land and family see 4 Victoria History of the County of Berkshire 471 (1924); 1 Liddon, Life of E. B. Pusey 449 (1893); 47 Dict. Nat. Biog. 53; 12 Archaeologia 397 (1790); Pusey, The Pusey Family (1883); Camden, Britannia 163 (1722).

In company with the volumes above, one of the editors and Mr. Arthur L. Eno, Jr., Harvard Law School '48, wallowed pleasantly in antiquity for a spell and have the following to report.

The Canute episode. By the weight of evidence, it is fiction. Domesday Book shows that immediately prior to the Conquest one Alvred held the land of the Abbot of Abingdon. Berkshire was a county which was strongly pro-Harold, and nearly all Berkshiremen were deprived of their holdings and superseded by Normans. Alvred was replaced by Gilbert the Norman, who took the name of the estate for his own, possibly to rid himself of the stigma of being an invader. Gilbert appears to be the ancestor of the Pusey line.

The name. A little stream, finding its way into the Ock, runs around the Pusey land and justifies the early name of Peo's (or Peot's) Island. Peo is an early Saxon name, and it is surmised that its original bearer was a hermit who had found a safe retreat in the "island" surrounded by marshes. The name was already ancient at the date of the Conquest. Down through the centuries the name ran through variations: Peise, Peseia, Petsia, Pewsey, finally Pusey.

The family. It is not to be inferred from the continuance of the Pusey name that the Puseys succeeded in procreating a continuous male line from the Conquest to 1933. In the eighteenth century the male line ran out, followed shortly by the female line. This difficulty was solved by the surviving sister's devising the estate to a nephew by marriage, Philip Bouverie, on condition that he assume the name of Pusey. He complied with the condition and took possession of the estate in 1789; so the family name is now usually given as Bouverie-Pusey. If you have wondered where the British get those double-barreled names, this is one explanation.

The land. At the time of Domesday the manor comprised two hides (240 acres). There is no evidence of change in size until 1749, when John Allen Pusey acquired, by common recovery, two adjoining manors: Mansell's Court, which had been held by Roger of Ivrey at the time of Domesday, and Bishop's Manor, which had come from the Abbot of Super Dive (St. Pierre-sur-Dives).

The horn. This heirloom is an ancient ox horn with a silver gilt mounting of the fifteenth century bearing the inscription "KYNG KNOWDE GEVE WYLLYAM PEWSE THYS HORNE TO HOLDE BY THY LONDE." It is, of course, just possible that a soldier of the time of King Canute received the Pusey land from him and adopted its name and that the fifteenth century engraver had sources of information denied to us of the present day; but this seems highly unlikely, especially in view of the fact that the name William nowhere else appears with reference to the Pusey land until the fifteenth century. However, Lord Guilford believed the legend, and if we choose to do so, the matter is at least not actionable. It is fairly common for a horn to be closely associated with the tenure of land, in one of two ways. First, a horn (or other distinctive chattel, such as a sword, cup, or spur) could act as a token or memorandum of the transfer at a time when the ability to read and write was limited to the clergy. (3 Archaeologia 7.) Second, the service by which land was held could consist of an obligation to sound a horn in warning of the approach of "Scots or other enemies"; this was known as tenure by cornage. (Littleton, Tenures s. 156.)

Miscellany. As one might expect, there are many sidelights to this story which may interest and amuse those who, like the editors of this book, are amateurs of the irrelevant. For example,

As above suggested, the Pusey Manor cycle of feudal domain to country manor to auctioneer is typical of the development of the status of land ownership in the English political and economic system. Very briefly to summarize:

1. *In feudal times land was power.* The king conferred estates upon his faithful retainers (such as William Pusey) and they in turn upon theirs. In the absence of a centralized administration of the kingdom, order and discipline were maintained through this series of lord-and-vassal relationships.

2. *In post-feudal times land was family wealth.* Land ownership was no longer essentially a series of political responsibilities to an overlord and claims upon a group of tenants. Instead land ownership was a private and proprietary matter, like the ownership of jewels. It differed from jewels in that it was productive; and for centuries it was the only important source of income. The family estate was the means of supporting the family and maintaining family cohesion. This was the era of the peerage and the landed gentry — of whom the Puseys were typical.

3. *At the present day land is a basic commodity of commerce.* In this country, land has never had feudal characteristics (though Pennsylvania and Maryland were nominally feudal domains) and has never been tied up in families on a large scale (though the Van Rensselaers approached a family empire in New York State, and the Parker Ranch in Hawaii is probably a greater land holding than any subject of the Crown ever controlled). Within the last 30 years it has come about that the situation in England is not significantly different from the situation here. Pusey Manor was sold to the

---

the Dictionary of National Biography shows Philip Pusey (1799-1855) to have been a fairly colorful character. He entered Christ Church, Oxford, in 1817, "but left without taking a degree." He then wished to marry Lady Emily Herbert, who, we are assured, was "a lady unusually accomplished, sympathetic and earnest-minded," but his father would not approve. Still hoping for paternal approval, Philip took a European tour, in the course of which he passed through Catalonia and fell into the hands of insurgent guerillas. Returning from the Continent, he married the lady anyway but had to live abroad until his father died in 1828. At this point he came into possession of the entailed estates and devoted himself wholeheartedly to their development. He was the first user of a McCormick reaper in England. He rebuilt the cottages of his laborers, and on Midsummer Day, 1851, brought some five hundred of them to London to see the Great Exhibition. He wrote articles on agriculture, became an M.P., received an honorary D.C.L. from Oxford, and on his death was eulogized by Disraeli as "one of the most distinguished country gentlemen who ever sat in the House of Commons." But, lest it be thought that he had become stodgy, he "was one of the best whips in England, once driving a four-in-hand over the Alps."

Apart from Canute's G-2, the most famous Pusey was Edward Bouverie-Pusey (1800–1882), who was Regius Professor Hebrew at Oxford, a leader of the (original) Oxford movement, an intimate of Cardinal Newman, and an author of "Tracts for the Times." He is also the translator of The Confessions of Saint Augustine, as this appears in the Harvard Classics.

The following is quoted from The Times: "The beer that was formerly brewed at Pusey House was famed for its strength, and the story is still told there of how the austere wife of a famous Oxford Don of the last century, after having drunk some, protested in an uncertain voice, 'But I see two staircases.'"

highest bidder and in the course of time will be sold again in smaller and smaller parcels.

It is inevitable that these essential changes in the place that land ownership holds in the national life should be reflected in the land law. You will find, for example, that the dominant characteristic of the feudal period was the relationship of *tenure* between lord and man; that the dominant institution of the intermediate period was the *fee tail* and its development into the *strict settlement;* and that the dominant features of modern land law are the *recording act,* with its emphasis upon protection of commercial transactions in land, and land use development.

You will study the recording acts, title registration, and title insurance; these institutions provide the machinery designed to give title security to the purchaser of land. We now proceed to sketch for you the history out of which these modern institutions have grown. This will not only give depth to your understanding of the land law but will also provide a starting point for your study of the transmission of wealth from one generation to the next, which is the subject matter of the course in estate planning and the courses in wills, trusts, and future interests.

As a starting point 1066 is an obvious date; and as the end of the first historical phase 1660 is at least plausible. Between these dates the land law took a general form which it still retains — and which is so different from the law of other countries that the study of comparative law in this field is extremely difficult. During this period arose a certain number of specific rules and doctrines which still persist; though these feudal vestiges are rapidly disappearing, they continue to plague us because a title search looks backward to what has been the law in determining the current state of the title.[2]

2.   *FROM WILLIAM THE CONQUEROR*
                        TO QUEEN VICTORIA

First William the Norman, then William his son,
Henry, Stephen and Henry, then Richard and John.
Then Henry the Third, Edwards One, Two and Three,
And again after Richard, three Henrys we see.
Two Edwards, third Richard, if rightly I guess
Two Henrys, sixth Edward, Queen Mary, Queen Bess,
Then Jamie the Scotchman, and Charles whom they slew,
Yet received after Cromwell another Charles too.
Then Jamie the Second ascended the throne,
Then William and Mary together came on.
Queen Anne, Georges four, fourth William all past,
God gave us Victoria, may she long be the last.

Source unknown

SECTION 1. THE FEUDAL SYSTEM

In the 21 years given to William the Conqueror to organize his kingdom, he imposed feudalism in England to whatever extent it did not already exist. Then at the end of his reign he directed the cataloging of the land holdings of the kingdom and its feudal structure; and this catalog, Domesday Book, completed in 1086, became the first basic document of English constitutional history.[3]

It was a basic concept of the feudal system that the king was the personal owner of all land in the kingdom. He granted vast lands to his tenants-in-chief (tenants-in-capite) not as owners but literally as tenants, i.e., persons who had a continuing relationship to their lord, the king, and who had to render continuing services in order to satisfy the terms of their tenancy. The tenants-in-chief then granted parts of their lands to various persons, again as tenants, requiring from each of them lesser continuous services proportionate to his holding. Thus was created a hierarchy of which the apex was the king; the base comprised relatively small landowners who were actually working the land. The bestowal of rights in the land moved down the pyramid; and a constant flow of various services moved up. A person in the middle reaches of the pyramid was tenant of the person next higher and lord of the persons next lower — a mesne lord.

You will, of course, realize that this picture is oversimplified. Some of the complexities will later appear.

The feudal system was not entirely, or even primarily, a system of land ownership. In a kingdom where there was no administrative organization it was a means of exercising authority; but the difficulty was, as King John discovered, that when the tenants-in-capite, the barons, made up their minds that they would not obey, there were no means of compelling obedience. In a kingdom where the king had no army larger than a body

---

3. For the understanding of property law you have no need to know more about Domesday Book than appears in the text. But as a matter of general culture we suggest that you at least skim through some of the literature. For exhaustive scholarship by the greatest legal historian of his period, see Maitland, Domesday Book and Beyond (1897). For a more recent work, see Ballard, The Domesday Inquest (2d ed. 1923). Your law school library will also contain translations of all or part of the book, possibly with photographs of the text. (In reading a translation you will be helped by knowing that the recurrent letters T.R.E. mean *tempore Regis Edwardi,* i.e., in the time of King Edward, who died in January, 1066. *Hide, virgate,* and *ferling* are units of land assessment on the basis of which *geld* was paid.)

There was but one copy of Domesday Book, and it still exists, together with the chest originally designed to contain it. By an oddity of coincidence, when Wigmore requested a photograph of a sample page of Domesday Book for use in his Panorama of the World's Legal Systems, the page to which the book happened to be opened in its locked glass case in the Records Office, London, showed the status of Wigmore Castle in Herefordshire. This was the page fortuitously photographed for Wigmore's book. See Wigmore, Panorama 1057, 1111 (library ed. 1936).

guard, the feudal system was a means of raising troops. And in a kindgom where the treasury was still kept in the king's bedchamber several hundred years after the Conqueror's death, the feudal system provided an elementary type of fiscal organization. Domesday Book was basically an assessor's list, designed to facilitate the collection of revenue by feudal lords who, thus enriched, would be able the better to support the royal structure.

We now think of the land law as being designed to carry out the legitimate intentions of owners and purchasers, and we evaluate it as good or bad to the extent that it succeeds or fails in carrying out these intentions. But this was not the attitude of the feudal law. It gave only secondary concern to the desires of the "owner" of land; its primary concern lay in protecting the rights of the owner's lord and assuring to him a continuity of those services and payments upon which the performance of his feudal obligations might depend. It is inevitable, therefore, that many rules growing out of the political and military character of feudal tenure should prove anomalies in modern law. Few of them are left; but it is a reproach that there are any at all.

Problem

12.1. "Under the feudal system the Crown was the universal landlord. It is the modern socialist dream to make the state the universal landlord. Hence, William the Conqueror is the ideological founder of the Socialist Party." What is your reaction to this quoted statement?

SECTION 2. TENURE

The essential idea of tenure exists today in the landlord-tenant relationship. L, owning Blackacre in fee simple, leases to T for one year. T holds *(teneo)* of L; T is the tenant, i.e., the holder. L, the landlord, owes to T the duty of protecting him in his holding; and this is evidenced by the warranty of quiet enjoyment, which is implied in the tenancy. T owes to the landlord the service of providing a periodic rent. In these aspects the landlord-tenant relationship is similar to feudal tenure.

But in another aspect feudal tenure was far different. The landlord-tenant relationship is now wholly impersonal and proprietary; it is only rarely that one party to the relationship is persona grata to the other and so remains. Each habitually avoids the other as far as is humanly possible. But in feudal times the lord-tenant relationship was essentially personal and only incidentally proprietary. It was created by the ceremony of homage, at which the tenant placed his hands between those of the lord and swore fealty to him.[4] The breach of this oath was treason — petit treason, as distinguished from high treason, which involved disloyalty to the king.[5] Certain acts which implied a renunciation of the feudal relationship caused the estate to be forfeited; for example, if a life tenant purported to convey a fee simple by certain methods, the life tenancy was automatically forfeited — a rule which made sense in the twelfth century but was still operative in the nineteenth.

SECTION 3. SERVICES AND INCIDENTS

The service of a particular tenure was the duty of the tenant owed to the lord. This was specified at the time he received the land, usually in a charter of feoffment. (As we shall see, the feoffment — the standard common-law conveyance — was a ceremonial proceeding not involving any writing. The charter of feoffment was merely evidence as to what took place in the ceremony. Therein the charter differed from the modern deed which *is* the conveyance.) Originally the services were mostly military, tenure by knight service, and involved fixed obligations as to furnishing knights and squires for specified periods. Some services involved no great exertion; for example, *cornage,* which was the tenure of Pusey Manor, required the tenant to wind a horn on the approach of the king's enemies.[6] In the lower reaches of the hierarchy the services tended to be less dignified — for example, ploughing the lord's land and making his hedges — and were classified

---

4. The terms of the oath of homage underscore the personal nature of the relationship created:

> I become your man from this day forward of life and limb and of earthly worship, and unto you shall be true and faithful, and bear to you faith for the tenements that I claim to hold of you, saving the faith that I owe unto our sovereign lord the king.

The last clause is the result of William the Conqueror's decision to require direct oaths of allegiance to himself in addition to the homage which most subjects owed to mesne lords. He was unwilling to rely upon indirect loyalties.

5. Petit treason also included a wife killing her husband and a servant his master. Petit treason was abolished as a crime in 1828 in England; it never existed in the United States.

The Treason Act has somewhat expanded the concept of high treason. The net result was put into verse by Sir Frederick Pollock:

> Thou shalt not encompass the death of the King,
> The Queen or his eldest son.
> To be intimate too with his wife is a thing
> That is much better left undone.

6. In Pusey v. Pusey, 1 Vern. 273 (Ch. 1684), it is said that Pusey Manor was held by cornage; but the context indicates that the learned Lord Keeper (Guilford) who decided the case may have confused the method of determining the extent of the tenement with the service by which it was held.

as *villeinage.* (By an obvious transposition of ideas the ancient word *villein*, meaning a person in a servile status, developed, during centuries when thieves were more likely to resemble Jean Valjean than Ivar Krueger, into the *villain* of current English.)

The notion of tenure, with its requirement of continuous services to the lord, was so deep-seated that, even when a person wanted to make a gift of land, he felt obliged to require some nominal and picturesque service. Thus if a father was parceling out an estate to his daughter or younger son he would impose the rent of a peppercorn annually or the delivery of a rose at midsummer.[7]

There were always some tenures which required a money service only, and as the feudal system declined these increased. Old tenures requiring personal services of various types were gradually transformed into money types. Finally, in 1660, the Statute 12 Car. 2, ch. 24, changed practically all existing tenures into free and common socage, of which the only required service was an annual rent.

Besides the services, which were individual to each tenure, the lord was entitled to "incidents." These were of substantial importance, and, as the feudal system declined, came to be more valuable than the services. The incidents were as follows:[8]

1. *Homage.* This ceremonial pledge of personal loyalty was vital in feudal days but gradually deteriorated into a quaint relic. In later days it was important only when the tenant broke it by making a type of conveyance which indicated that he had renounced the tenure. Then the tenant's estate was forfeited — with consequences later described.

2. *Relief.* In the early feudal period, when a tenant died, the lord customarily took his heir as succeeding tenant, but he was under no obligation to do so. The heir would make a payment to the lord for the privilege of retaining his ancestor's rights. It later became a matter of right for the heir to inherit; but the payment of a relief to the lord continued. Reliefs were the inheritance taxes of ancient days. Then as now, some ingenuity was expended in avoiding them; and then as now, the courts and the legislature undertook to frustrate the avoidance. The Rule in Shelley's Case and the doctrine of worthier title, of which more later, seem to have arisen out of this conflict.

3. *Wardship and marriage.* When a tenant died leaving an infant heir the lord was entitled to the *wardship* of the infant. This permitted him to

---

7. The owners of the Red Rose Inn in West Grove, Pa., solemnly went through the yearly ceremony stipulated by a 216-year-old deed and handed over one red rose to the heir of William Penn. The heir: Amy Penn-Gaskell Hall II, a tenth direct descendant of Penn. Time, Sept. 15, 1947, at p. 27.

8. The incidents described are those attached to military tenure, which existed chiefly among the nobility. The lower classes normally held by way of socage tenure. The incidents of wardship and marriage did not apply to such tenure, and the other incidents in general existed in a much modified and less burdensome form. Religious organizations held by way of frankalmoign tenure, which carried no feudal incidents.

take the rents and profits during the heir's minority with no obligation except to support, educate, and protect the child. In the unruly early days the protection given to the child against stepfathers, marauders, murderers, and assorted spalpeens may have been a fair consideration for the use of the lands. But after the kingdom quieted down the wardship was an unjustified and very profitable windfall.

Marriage was closely connected with wardship. It was an obvious application of the feudal theory that if land descended to an unmarried woman, the lord should have something to say in the choice of her husband; otherwise he might find that he had a tenant (the woman's husband, who would come into control of her lands upon marriage) who was his enemy. So the lord was given the power to choose the female heir's husband. There never was any substantial justification for extending this privilege to choosing a wife for a male heir, but it was so extended. Overlords, especially the king, also had some claim to the marriage of widows who were their tenants.[9]

Wardships and marriages were the gilt-edged investments of feudal times. They were bought and sold freely. If the lord died the wardship and marriage passed to his estate and could be bequeathed in his will. The striking thing is that the relationship of feudal guardian and ward was considered as a privilege of the guardian, not a duty to the infant; the fiduciary aspect of modern guardianship was almost wholly lacking. If the ward married without the lord's assent, the lord's investment was protected by the rule that the tenant forfeited twice the value of the marriage. If the ward declined a suitable marriage offered by the lord, the ward forfeited the value of the marriage. The fact that the king was the individual principally profiting from wardships and marriages tended to keep these anomalous rights alive much longer than would naturally have been the case.

4. *Aids.* The lord called upon his tenants for financial help from time to time. These calls, originally discretionary with the lord, were finally reduced to ransoming the lord when captured and making fixed payments for knighting his eldest son and marrying his eldest daughter.

5. *Escheat.* When the tenant died without heirs (i.e., without children, brothers, sisters, or any other relatives who could inherit) the tenancy became vacant and escheated to the lord.

It rarely happens, in modern times, that a person of any considerable property dies without heirs; the general rule is the more property, the more heirs. However, in ancient times the elimination of an entire blood line appears to have occurred, or to have been engineered, more frequently. Many prominent landholders were bastards—the prevalence of the name Fitzroy was a living commentary on the morals of the monarch—and only

---

9. Any simplified statement on the feudal incident of marriage is difficult because (a) the nature of the common-law right varied from time to time, (b) statutes dealt extensively with it in various ways and were variously avoided, (c) the king had some peculiar rights with regard to tenants-in-capite.

descendants could inherit from them; hence if a bastard died childless, there was an escheat. Until 1540 land could not be devised (i.e., given by will) except by local custom; after that date the ability to devise lands greatly diminished the number of escheats, since a person dying without heirs could, by making a will, prevent the tenancy from becoming vacant.

If the tenant breached a feudal obligation or committed a felony, the tenancy ended; this was another type of escheat.

Forfeiture for high treason was a prerogative of the king as such; it was not a tenurial right. Thus when a person committed treason — which was very easy during the dynastic struggles — his lands were forfeited to the king; they did not escheat to the traitor's feudal lord.

Problems

12.2. In feudal times (say 1250) the king conveys Blackacre to A in fee simple. Of whom does A hold? Who takes the land if A dies without heirs, and by what process?

12.3. In feudal times the king conveys Blackacre to A in fee simple. A then makes the same type of conveyance to B. Of whom does B hold? Who takes the land if B dies without heirs, and by what process? Who takes the land if B commits high treason, and by what process? What happens if A dies without heirs?

12.4. Suppose A's conveyance in Problem 12.3 is to B and his heirs as long as the property is used for agricultural purposes. Of whom does B hold? Who takes the land if B dies without heirs, and by what process? Who takes the land if B ceases to use it for agricultural purposes, and by what process? Who takes the land if B commits high treason, and by what process? Does the land remain subject to the qualification that it can be used only for agricultural purposes?

Note: Tenure in the United States

In some states in this country it is held that lands in fee simple are owned allodially — that is, in the same way a book is owned, with no notion of holding of anyone. In other states it is held that an owner in fee simple holds of the state in a tenurial relationship. And in some states this issue is not determined because it rarely makes any difference.

Where land is owned allodially, what happens when the owner in fee simple dies intestate and without heirs? The state takes it, as it takes a book under the same circumstances. In the case of a book this right of the state is called the doctrine of *bona vacantia*. In the case of land it is frequently called *escheat*, but there is an obvious difference between this process and feudal escheat. Where there is tenure, the conception is that the grantor has given to his grantee a limited estate which may be less than the grantor had and which, expiring through failure of heirs, causes the grantor to be revested of the land by reason of his original estate. Where there is no tenure "escheat" merely means that the state is the ultimate successor where no other successors exist.[10]

Of course, where one owns less than a fee simple — say a life estate — one holds of the fee simple owner. Thus, where O owns Blackacre in fee simple and conveys to A an estate to last for A's life, A has a life estate which A holds of O. And where L owns Blackacre in fee simple and leases to T for two years, T has a term of years which T holds of L.

By way of probing into the nature of tenure, let us consider some questions of inheritance taxation. All the following problems arise in a state which has a statute which reads as follows: "All property within this state which shall pass by will or by intestate succession shall be subject to a tax of five per cent payable to the county in which said property lies."

Problems

12.5. O, owner of Blackacre in fee simple, dies intestate (i.e., without a will), leaving as his heir his son, S. Is a tax due under the statute above?

12.6. O, owner of Blackacre in fee simple, conveys to A an estate in Blackacre for the life of A. A dies intestate, leaving as her heir her son, S. Who is entitled to possession of Blackacre? Is a tax due under the statute above?

12.7. The state has a further statute which provides:

Upon the death intestate of any person owning real property in this state, the same shall pass as follows:

(a) If such person leaves a widow or widower and issue, one-third to said widow or widower, and two-thirds to said issue. . . .

[Here follow several clauses disposing of the property successively to parents if the intestate leaves no widow, widower, or issue; and to brothers and sisters and their issue, if the intestate also leaves no parents; and to more remote kindred, if these are all who survive the intestate.]

(g) If such person leaves no widow, widower, issue, parents, brothers, sisters, issue of brothers and sisters, or other kindred, to the state.

---

10. Matthews v. Ward's Lessee, 10 G. & J. 443 (Md. 1839). And see N.Y. Rev. Stat. part 2, ch. 1, tit. 1, §3 (1827-1828): "All lands within this state are declared to be allodial, so that, subject only to the liability to escheat, the entire and absolute property is vested in the owners. . . ." A similar provision now appears in the New York Constitution, art. I, §10:

The people of the state, in their right of sovereignty, possess the original and ultimate property in and to all lands within the jurisdiction of the state. All lands shall forever remain allodial so that the entire and absolute property is vested in the owners, according to the nature of their respective estates. All lands the title of which shall fail, from a defect of heirs, shall revert, or escheat to the people.

In regard to the abandonment of this provision of the New York Constitution in the 1938 revision, see Sutherland, The Tenantry on the New York Manors, 41 Cornell L.Q. 620 (1956).

At a sale of state lands, O buys Blackacre from the state and takes a conveyance in fee simple. Then O dies, leaving no spouse or relatives. It is agreed by all parties that the state is now owner of Blackacre. The county claims that it is entitled to an inheritance tax upon Blackacre. The state claims that no tax is due. There has been no decision by the state supreme court as to whether ownership in fee simple is allodial or tenurial.

    a.   If you are county attorney, will you contend that land ownership is allodial or that it is tenurial?

    b.   If you are the state attorney general will you contend that land ownership is allodial or that it is tenurial? What will be your contention as to the effect of clause g of the statute, quoted above in this problem?

See Estate of O'Connor, 126 Neb. 182, 252 N.W. 826 (1934); People v. Richardson, 269 Ill. 275, 109 N.E. 1033 (1915).[11]

12.8.   When an owner of land dies intestate and without heirs, it is clear that the land will escheat to the state in which the land is located. To what state will other assets pass? In considering this question, assume the decedent maintained a savings account in a bank in New York; owned shares of stock in a Delaware corporation; owned bonds issued by a Maine corporation; had furniture in a house in Florida and in a house in Massachusetts; and spent six months of each year living in the house in Florida and six months living in the house in Massachusetts. See Note, 65 Harv. L. Rev. 107, 152 (1951).

SECTION 4. THE STATUTE QUIA EMPTORES

When T (tenant) held a fee simple of L (his lord) and wanted to make G (grantee) tenant in fee simple of the land, there were two possible courses of action:

1.   T could substitute G in his place as L's tenant. This clearly required the assent of L, for he could not be forced to accept and rely on a tenant not of his own choice.

2.   T could create a new tenurial relationship with G, in which T was lord and G tenant. This was known as subinfeudation — i.e., creating a new feudal relationship in fee simple under an old one. There was a doubt whether the assent of L was necessary to this transaction.

Subinfeudation was very common, and it hugely complicated the feudal structure. It did not diminish the *services* which L could get from the land,

---

11.   It is not to be inferred that the question whether ownership in fee simple is allodial or tenurial is the only issue that would be argued by counsel in this case. There would also be minute examination of the statutes and their legislative history.

but it could seriously diminish the *incidents*. (Perhaps you can figure out how this would work. Suppose T, who holds of L by substantial services, subinfeudates to his daughter, D, upon service of a rose at midsummer. The solution is spelled out in Plucknett, Concise History of the Common Law 538 (5th ed. 1956).)

In 1290, in the reign of Edward I, the Statute Quia Emptores (taking its name from its first two Latin words) was passed. The following is the text with considerable omissions:

> Forasmuch as purchasers of lands of the fees of great men and other lords have many times heretofore entered into their fees to be holden in fee of their feoffers and not of the chief lords of the fees, whereby the same chief lords have many times lost their escheats, marriages, and wardships, which thing seems very hard and extreme unto those lords and other great men, our lord the king, at the instance of the great men of the realm, ordained that it should be lawful for every freeman to sell at his own pleasure his lands so that the feoffee shall hold the same of the chief lord of the same fee, by such service and customs as his feoffer held before. [Here is a provision for division of the services due upon partial alienation.] This statute extendeth but only to lands holden in fee simple [the Latin phrase is in feodo simpliciter].

There are several things to observe about Quia Emptores. First, the preamble is definitely not reminiscent of modern social legislation. There is no talk about the common man or the rights of the people. Second, the statute gives a tenant in fee simple the right to substitute another in his place without the permission of the lord of the fee; in this aspect it was a long step forward toward modern real property law. Third, the statute was construed to forbid future subinfeudations, though the prohibition is certainly not clear in the text; the result was that, as mesne lordships disappeared, the feudal structure tended to be simplified, though it never reached the point where all tenure was direct from the king. Fourth, the statute did not prevent a tenant in fee simple from creating new tenurial relationships by granting estates less than a fee simple; thus, if T, tenant in fee simple, granted to G an estate tail, a life estate, or a term of years, G held of T, not of T's lord. Fifth, the statute was held to permit the king to give to his immediate tenants the right to subinfeudate; and this right to subinfeudate was in fact given in the charters by which the Crown granted Maryland to Lord Baltimore and Pennsylvania to William Penn.[12]

---

12. But for this the rose-at-midsummer tenure from the Penn family to the Red Rose Inn (footnote 7, *supra*) would have been impossible.

The following are the relevant terms of the 1632 Maryland charter from Charles II to Lord Baltimore, some repetitious words being omitted:

> We do by these presents, for us, our heirs and successors, make, create, and constitute him, the now Baron of Baltimore, and his heirs, the true and absolute lords and proprietaries of the region aforesaid, saving always the faith and allegiance and sovereign dominion due to us, our heirs, and successors; to have, hold, possess, and

In most states which recognize tenure Quia Emptores is a common-law statute — i.e., it is part of the law brought with the colonists to this country and is incorporated into the law of the state. However, this is not universally true.

Problems

12.9. Assume that prior to 1290 the chain of conveyances with respect to Blackacre was king to A and his heirs, and A to B and his heirs. Point out the disadvantages from A's standpoint if B made any one of the following conveyances of Blackacre in 1300 (assume each conveyance would be effective as written).

  a.   B conveys to C and his heirs.

  b.   B conveys to C and his heirs as long as the land is used for agricultural purposes.

  c.   B conveys to C and his heirs, but if the land is ever used for other than agricultural purposes B or his heirs may re-enter and take possession.

  d.   B conveys to C and his heirs but if C dies childless to D and his heirs.

  e.   B conveys to C and his heirs from and after B's death if B dies childless.

  f.   B conveys to C and the heirs of his body.

  g.   B conveys to C for life.

  h.   B conveys to C for life, then to D and his heirs.

  i.   B conveys to C for life, then to D and his heirs if D marries E.

12.10. In state A the courts hold that ownership of land is allodial. In state B the courts hold that there is tenure and that Quia Emptores is in force

---

enjoy the aforesaid region, unto the aforesaid now Baron of Baltimore, and to his heirs and assigns. To hold of us, our heirs and successors, kings of England, as of our Castle of Windsor, in our County of Berks, in free and common soccage, by fealty only for all services, and not in capite, nor by knight's service, yielding therefore unto us, our heirs and successors two Indian arrows of those parts, to be delivered at the said Castle of Windsor, every year, on Tuesday's in Easter week: And also the fifth part of all gold and silver ore, which shall happen from time to time, to be found within the aforesaid limits.

And furthermore, of our special grace, we do give, grant and confirm, unto the aforesaid now Baron of Baltimore, his heirs, and assigns, full and absolute license, power and authority, that he, may assign, alien, grant, demise, or enfeoff such parcels of the premises, to any person or persons to have and to hold to the same person or persons in fee simple, or fee tail, or for term of life, lives, or years; to hold of the aforesaid now Baron of Baltimore, his heirs and assigns, by such services, customs, and rents of this kind, as to the same now Baron of Baltimore, his heirs, and assigns, shall seem fit and agreeable, and not immediately of us, our heirs and successors . . . the statute made in the parliament of Lord Edward, son of King Henry, late King of England, our progenitor, commonly called the "Statute Quia Emptores Terrarum," or any other statute to the contrary notwithstanding.

The feudal service attached to the grant of Pennsylvania was the delivery of two beaver skins annually.

as a common-law statute. In state C the courts hold that there is tenure but that Quia Emptores is not in force. The above-stated doctrines of two of these states are, for most practical purposes, the same. Which two?

SECTION 5. MANOR LANDS AND COPYHOLD

The words "manor" and "domain" (original form: "demesne") are used as words of ordinary speech with no very specific significance; but they have a technical meaning, which we now consider.

When the king enfeoffed L, a great lord, and L split up his fief by enfeoffing several lesser lords, he retained a choice and extensive parcel for his castle and for the farmlands, pasturage, and woodlots necessary to provide the necessaries for himself and his household. These were the demesne lands of the manor, and he was lord of the manor.

The manor lands were worked by an agrarian population. The lord provided housing for them and made available small plots of land for their own farming needs. In very early times this arrangement was essentially peonage, and the workers occupied their cottages and worked their gardens at the will or whim of the lord. But as time went on it became usual to make a notation on the manor rolls, kept as a record of the manorial court which decided petty disputes, that such and such a peasant held such and such a parcel under specific obligations as to labor for the lord. The peasant was given a copy of the manor records which set forth his rights and duties and thus came to be known as a copyholder.

Then came a gradual process of elevation of the rights of the copyholder. In the thirteenth century the tenant was given some measure of protection by the customary law of the manor. In the fourteenth century the Black Death, by establishing a scarcity market for agricultural labor, improved the bargaining position of the copyholders, so that they obtained greater and more certain rights. In the fifteenth century the king's courts undertook to protect the copyholder against a lord of the manor who violated his rights. The next step can readily be guessed: commutation of labor services by substituting a fixed rent payment. In the sixteenth century the gold and silver mines of the western hemisphere did the next favor for the copyholder by reducing the value of money and pari passu reducing the burden of the fixed rent. The final step, achieved by private agreement or ultimately by statutory compulsion, was the redemption of the rent by a lump-sum payment.

Even as far back as Queen Elizabeth I's time Coke could justifiably say that "time hath dealt very favourably with Copyholders in divers respects." A comparative view of European history suggests that the development of the copyhold is encouraging evidence of the Anglo-American instinct for self-government. In the time of the Conqueror there was little to distinguish the lot of the English manor worker from that of the French peasant or the Russian serf. The latter two achieved acceptable status only by the explosions of '93 and '17. The English farmer achieved a higher status than either of them by a centuries-long evolutionary process in which the copyhold played no inconsiderable role.[13]

Two technical points about a copyhold. First, the copyholder (like the tenant for years) did not have *seisin,* that ceremonial type of possession which was reserved for estates of feudal dignity; the lord of the manor had seisin and the copyholder had possession. We shall see that whether or not an owner has seisin seriously affects the application of some of the old technical rules. Second, if a copyholder wanted to convey, surrender and admission was the method of doing so; that is, the grantor surrendered the copyhold to the lord of the manor, and the latter then admitted the grantee into the copyhold.

SECTION 6.　FEUDALISM IN THE UNITED STATES[14]

The relationship between the English government and the colonies was essentially feudal. From the Crown's point of view the colonies stood in much the same position as the County Palatine of Durham and the County Palatine of Chester, which were quasi-independent states organized as military bulwarks against the Scots and the Welshmen respectively. The Maryland charter expressly gave palatine powers to the proprietors. The powers of James, Duke of York, in New York were substantially regal.[15]

Within several of the colonies the problem faced by the proprietors was not unlike that which faced William the Conqueror in 1066. In New York, for example, there was a Dutch population essentially hostile to the British; the Indians were rugged and warlike compared with the tribes with which the Pilgrims and the Puritans had to deal; the French threatened; the New

---

13. See Plucknett, Concise History 310. For general information on the copyhold, see Williams & Eastwood, Real Property 37 et seq. (1933); Holdsworth, Historical Introduction to the Land Law 39 et seq. (1927). The incidents of copyhold were fully effective through 1925. By the Law of Property Act, 1922, 12 & 13 Geo. 5, ch. 16, certain incidents were abolished as of 1926, others were abolished as of 1936, and others (including any tenants' rights of common, e.g., to pasture beasts on the wasteland of the manor) were preserved indefinitely. See Megarry, Manual of Real Property Law 24-25 (1946).

14. See American Law of Property §§1.40-1.50 (Casner ed. 1952).

15. For the charter from Charles II to his brother, who was later James II, see Fowler, History of Real Property in New York 179 (1895). To indicate the breadth of the powers: the duke was given authority to "correct, punish, pardon, govern and rule . . . according to such laws, orders, ordinances, directions and instruments as by our said dearest brother or his assigns shall be established" (spelling modernized).

Englanders were showing dangerously democratic leanings; distances were considerable and communications bad. There was a need for building up a class upon whose loyalty the duke could count, giving that class the means of imposing its will and requiring from it financial support and the mainte- nance of order. The van Rensselaer manor on the upper Hudson was confirmed as a bulwark against the Indians after assurances of van Rensse- laer loyalty were given. The manors of Pell and Fordham were established in Westchester as a buffer in the direction of New England. Other similar manors were established on the periphery. In those days a manor meant a working feudal unit, not a quaint name given to a land development.[16]

The revolutionary period produced legislation designed to transfer the rights of the proprietors to the states and to eliminate the principal feudal institutions. However, noteworthy vestiges survived, and we now proceed to examine briefly three of these.

The Manor of Rensselaerwyck. The patroon system on the upper Hudson was established by the Dutch. The original patroon (1629) of the van Rensselaer family called himself the Lord Kiliaen and required shipping on the Hudson to strike colors as it passed his manor. After the Revolution the van Rensselaer estate was still intact and flourishing. Stephen van Rensse- laer III, known as the Good Patroon, retained Alexander Hamilton to devise legal methods by which the manor could continue under the new regime as it had functioned under the Dutch and the British. Hamilton drafted a form of deed which was used in all grants to farmers on the van Rensselaer properties. Its principal provisions were the following:

1. The patroon conveyed the land to the farmer "forever" but upon a yearly rent of a certain number of bushels of wheat (say 15) and a certain number of fat fowls (say 4) and one day's service with horse and wagon;
2. If the rent was not paid the patroon could seize crops and animals on the land to the value of the amount owed or could re-enter on the land and terminate the farmer's estate;
3. The obligation to pay rent was stated to be binding on any assignee of the farmer and was to run in favor of any assignee of the patroon;
4. The land was not to be sold until it had first been offered for 21 days to the patroon at the contemplated sale price; and if it were thereafter sold the patroon should receive one-quarter of the price received.

Under the sons of the Good Patroon, who divided the estate into the East Manor and the West Manor, the rents were exacted to the full and evictions took place. There was extensive recourse to the courts, which, apart from holding the restrictions on sale invalid, ruled consistently in favor of the patroons. The farmers then set up a resistance organization containing

---

16. See generally Sutherland, The Tenantry on the New York Manors, 41 Cornell L.Q. 620 (1956); Goebel, Some Legal and Political Aspects of the Manors of New York (1928); Fowler, History of Real Property in New York 29 et seq. (1895).

about equal ingredients of the Boston Tea Party and the rising of the clans under Roderick Dhu. An elusive figure known as "Big Thunder" (actually a country doctor named Boughton) led the farmers into increasingly violent action. The anti-renters, seeking relief through the ballot, became enough of a political force to play a considerable role in the rise of William H. Seward. They got some help through legislation, but in the last analysis the anti-renters won out simply through wearing down the patroons by their stubborn resistance. Little by little the manors were liquidated by discharging the rent for relatively small cash payments.[17]

Problem

12.11. In 1796 the Good Patroon conveyed to Dietz a certain farm by the type of deed described above. The Good Patroon died in 1839, devising to plaintiff all rights under the deed. In 1840 Dietz assigned and conveyed to Hays, the defendant, all Dietz's right, title, and interest in the said farm, and Hays took and retained possession of the farm.

You represent Hays. What contention will you make as to the effect of the Statute Quia Emptores on the rights of the plaintiff? van Rensselaer v. Hays, 19 N.Y. 68 (1859).

Pennsylvania ground rents. In Pennsylvania deeds in fee simple may provide for a perpetual annual rent instead of a lump-sum purchase price. By statute all ground rents created since 1885 have to be redeemable by a lump-sum payment; but there still exist some ground rents, created prior to 1885, which are perpetual unless the parties can agree upon a figure by which the holder of the rent will release it. The fact that Pennsylvania courts recognize tenure unhampered by Quia Emptores creates a congenial atmosphere for such rents; but far more important is the fact that this device makes it possible for a buyer bent on developing property to obtain the land without a large initial cash outlay or the threat of a future lump-sum obligation.[18]

17. For a popularized version of the story, see Christman, Tin Horns and Calico (1945). (When a rent collector or sheriff appeared, the horns sounded the warning through the Helderberg. A calico robe was the disguise of Big Thunder.) For the legal issues, see Bingham & Colvin, Rents Real and Personal Covenants and Conditions (1857), which is a brief by anti-renter lawyers. And see Vance, The Quest for Tenure in the United States, 33 Yale L.J. 248, 269 (1923). By constitutional amendment, passed in 1846, future agricultural leases in New York were limited to 12 years. Const. 1846 art. I, §14. But the 1938 constitutional revision omitted this provision.

18. See Nicholson, Pennsylvania Law of Real Estate §§49-68 (3d ed. 1929). The feudal flavor of these rents is illustrated by the following. Before the Revolution they were called quit-rents—i.e., rents which were paid as a substitute for feudal services, "that the tenant might be quit of his service." In 1779 the Divesting Act abolished quit-rents as "badges of slavery." However, the Penn family had made two kinds of deeds with reservation of rent: (a) many such

Maryland ground rents. In Baltimore and neighboring counties it is common to find leases for 99 years, renewable forever, with a fixed rent reserved. As in Pennsylvania, these were the outgrowth of fee simple conveyances upon a quit-rent made by the colonial proprietor. However, the Maryland post-revolutionary legislation abolished all fee simple quit-rents of the Calverts, not merely those made in their capacity as proprietors. Legislation makes the leases redeemable and thereby gives the tenant a means of getting an unencumbered title; but there are still some irredeemable leases from the early days of the Republic. As a means of financing home-building and home-purchasing the Baltimore system has the great advantage that it seldom results in default and eviction, even during depressions such as that of the 1930s.[19]

Long-term leases of business property are not uncommon today. The land on which Rockefeller Center in New York City was built is under a long-term lease.[20]

Problem

12.12. To what extent can it properly be said that the van Rensselaer or Pennsylvania or Maryland rent systems are feudal?

---

deeds in their capacity of proprietors of the colony, i.e., feudal lords, (b) other deeds out of their manor lands, which they owned in their private right. Rents issuing out of these latter deeds were not affected by the Divesting Act; and these became the precedents for the present ground rent system. See Nicholson, §50. And see Chesnut, Effect of Quia Emptores on Pennsylvania and Maryland Ground Rents, 91 U. Pa. L. Rev. 137 (1942).

19.   For a thorough and searching analysis, see Kaufman, The Maryland Ground Rent — Mysterious but Beneficial, 5 Md. L. Rev. 1 (1940).

20.   See 48 Yale L.J. 1400 (1939).

CHAPTER 13

THE TYPES OF ESTATES IN LAND

Note: The Estate Concept

The *estate concept* of Anglo-American land law is not duplicated in any other system of law, but it seems natural to us by reason of its familiarity. At the present time, if L owns a house lot and leases it to T for a year, it is apparent that both L and T have rights in that property. T is entitled to exclusive possession of the property for one year, and T can assert this against L as well as against anyone else. L, though not entitled to possession during the year, is entitled to possession at the end of the year; and we conceive of this as a present right to future possession, for in common parlance we speak of L as being the "owner." T must not abuse the property so that it will be less valuable at the end of the year. If T does so abuse it, L can recover damages, sometimes get an injunction against the abuse, and under the usual form of lease terminate the lease by re-entry.

In the landlord-tenant situation the fact that the tenant pays a periodic rent and that the landlord may have a continuing obligation as to repairs makes it easy to realize that both the landlord and the tenant have interests in the property at the same time. If you eliminate the periodic obligation as to rent, relieve the landlord of all duty to repair, and substantially lengthen the lease, the simultaneous interests of the two parties in the property still exist, but they are less apparent to the eye. Thus if O, owner of Blackacre in fee simple, grants vacant land to A for 20 years with no rent, both O and A have estates in Blackacre; O has a future estate which is called a reversion, and A has an estate for 20 years. The same is true if O grants to A "for A's life" or if a good churchgoer grants to his or her church "so long as the premises are used for church purposes."

The estates which have gained recognition through the years are the following:

1. The *fee simple.* This is absolute ownership so far as our law knows it.
2. The *fee tail.* This is an estate which is designed to pass from the

205

grantee to the grantee's descendants. Whereas the fee simple can be sold or devised by the grantee outside of the family, the intent of the grantor of a fee tail is to keep the property in the grantee's line of issue. As we shall see, this intent can be frustrated.

3. The *life estate*. This is an estate to last during some person's life, usually the life of the grantee.

4. The *estate for years*. This is the usual lease; it may be for a very short period (one week) or a very long period (a hundred years).

5. The *tenancy from year to year* or other period. This provides a tenancy for one of the specified periods with automatic successive renewals unless terminated. Thus a tenancy from month to month is a firm commitment for one month with successive renewals for one month each until one party or the other calls a halt.

6. The *tenancy at will*. T is on O's land by permission with either party being free to terminate the arrangement at any time.

The first three of these are *freehold estates;* the last three are *less than freehold estates*. The distinction derives from considerations of feudal dignity. The fee simple, fee tail and life estate were normal tenures in the feudal hierarchy. The term of years seems originally to have been a money-lender's device; in any event it never attained feudal stature.

What difference does it make whether an estate is or is not a freehold? Most of the differences flow from the fact that the freeholder has *seisin,* whereas the less-than-freeholder has only *possession*.

Volumes have been written in the attempt to explain the concept of seisin, but for practical purposes it suffices to point out its consequences. The feudal reliance of lord upon vassal caused great emphasis to be placed upon the person who was seised of the land, and who therefore could produce the services required. To preserve continuity of seisin quite a series of rules arose:

1. A present freehold could be created or transferred only by livery of seisin, i.e., physical delivery of possession of the land, both grantor and grantee going to the land and the one symbolically delivering a twig to the other.

2. From this first rule there followed a corollary: A freehold could not be created to commence in futuro. If livery of seisin were made at a particular date, the freehold would commence at that date; if no livery of seisin were made, there could be no estate at all.

3. No abeyance of the seisin was permissible. There always had to be some person responsible to the lord for the performance of the services.

4. If the owner of a fee simple, O, was disseised (i.e., dispossessed) by A, the latter (the disseisor) became the holder of the fee simple, and O (the disseisee) had only a right of entry. A's fee simple was tortious and was subject to being cut short by O's entry or O's assertion of O's rights through the courts; but until this happened A was the one who, as regards third persons, was entitled.

None of these rules applied to the term of years or the person who owned one; and this was a great blessing, as will appear. Indeed it is interesting to observe the freehold estates, striding along in their topheavy feudal dignity, trying to take advantage of the simple and flexible rules and procedures that were available to the plebeian term of years. You are already familiar with the action of ejectment — a remedy, originally developed for the tenant for years, which proved so much more effective than the ancient real actions that freeholders used it by alleging a fictitious lease. And we shall discover instances in which a grantor, wishing to create a life estate in A but being unwilling to accept the feudal incrustations of a freehold estate, makes the conveyance "to A for 100 years if A so long live" — thus creating a term of years terminable upon A's death.

Problems

13.1. The Statute of Uses (1536) provides: "Where any person be seised of any lands to the use of any other person, such person that have such use shall from henceforth be deemed in lawful seisin and possession of the same lands in such like estates as he had in use." (Many words are omitted. The phrase "to the use of" means "for the benefit of.") Does the Statute of Uses apply to the following cases?

    a.   O conveys to A in fee simple to the use of B for life.

    b.   O conveys to A in fee simple to the use of B for ten years.

    c.   O conveys to A for ten years to the use of B.

13.2. Anne was the owner of Blackacre in England in 1865. Mary, claiming title under a forged will, entered upon Blackacre. Anne died shortly thereafter, leaving a will in which she provided: "All real estate of which I shall die seised I devise to my beloved brother John." Anne's heir is Henry. Who gets Blackacre? Leach v. Jay, 9 Ch. D. 42 (1878).

13.3. In which of the following conveyances of Blackacre is the grantor undertaking to make a conveyance that will cause the seisin to move from the grantor to another at a future date, if the conveyance is allowed to take effect in accordance with its terms?

    a.   O conveys to A for life, then to B and her heirs.

    b.   O conveys to A for life, then to B and her heirs if B marries C.

    c.   O conveys to A for life, then to B and her heirs if B writes a complete biography of A.

    d.   O conveys to A for life, then to B and her heirs if B gives A a suitable burial.

    e.   O conveys to A for life and one day after A dies to B and her heirs.

    f.   O conveys to A for one day, then to B and her heirs.

    g.   O conveys to A for ten years, then to B and her heirs if B marries C.

    h.   O conveys to A and her heirs from and after the death of O.

    i.   O conveys to A and her heirs, but if A dies childless then to B and her heirs.

SECTION 1.   THE FEE SIMPLE

A fee simple is created by a conveyance "to A and his heirs" or "to A and her heirs." (Henceforward in this discussion the words "and his heirs" should be understood to include "and her heirs" and "his" to include "hers.") It used to be considered that nothing other than this formula would do; for example, it was formerly held that a conveyance "to A" or "to A forever" or even "to A in fee simple" created only a life estate because the magic words "and his heirs" were missing. At the present time, however, any form of words which indicates an intention to give an unlimited estate will suffice.[1]

Words of purchase and words of limitation. In the phrase "to A and his heirs," the words "to A" are words of purchase; the words "and his heirs" are words of limitation. To explain this distinction let us return for a moment to the Statute Quia Emptores. That statute deals with *purchasers* (emptores). This does not mean persons who buy land as distinguished from persons to whom land is given. It does mean persons to whom land is granted or devised as distinguished from persons who take land as heirs by descent. Thus the word "purchaser" means "one who takes land by grant or devise." And words of purchase are words which designate the person who is to take by grant or devise. Thus "to A" are words of purchase. Words of limitation are words which define the extent or limits of the estate which is taken by the purchaser. Thus the words "and his heirs" are words of limitation because they establish the extent of the estate given to A; they show that it is a fee simple. Do A's heirs take any estate by a conveyance? Certainly not. The phrase "and his heirs" is the legalistic equivalent of "in fee simple." It is true that A's heirs *may* get this property at some later time, but if they do they will take a title which derives from A, not a title which was given to them by A's grantor; and they will take as heirs only if A does not grant the land away during his lifetime or devise it to someone else by will.

Problem

13.4.   Select the words of purchase and the words of limitation in the following conveyances:

   a.   O conveys "to A for ten years, remainder to B for life, remainder to

---

1.   The Restatement of Property §27 states the old rule. This has been the subject of no little raillery at American Law Institute meetings, chiefly by the late Circuit Judge (formerly Dean) Charles E. Clark. The sponsors of this section agree that it is no longer law anywhere except South Carolina, and there is a suspicion that if the issue now arose in South Carolina the courts would reject it.

The words "and his heirs" have never been necessary in a will. (Restatement §37). But some manifestation of an intent to create a fee simple had to be present or only a life estate would be created.

the First Baptist Church, its successors and assigns, so long as the premises shall be used for church purposes."

b. O conveys "to A for life, remainder to the heirs of B."

c. O conveys "to A and his heirs, but if A shall die without issue living at his death, to B and his heirs."

Words of inheritance. The words "and his heirs" or in the usual formula for creating a fee simple are also words of inheritance, i.e., they indicate that the estate is inheritable, not merely a life estate. They are words of *general inheritance,* as distinguished from the words of special inheritance which bring it about that an estate tail can be inherited only by descendants.

Descent of a fee simple. If the owner of a fee simple dies intestate, to whom does the estate go? We must distinguish various phases of English law from current American law.

1. *Primogeniture.* Until 1925 nearly all land in England descended under the doctrine of primogeniture according to certain fixed Canons of Descent. The system is complex, but the following will indicate its principal applications. The eldest surviving son, if any, took all freeholds. (Less-than-freeholds passed as personalty; they were chattels real.) If there were daughters but no sons or issue of sons, the daughters took equally. If the owner left no issue, the property went to brothers, sisters, and other collaterals according to an order of seniority which was designed to keep the land in the hands of one male if possible, to prefer the father's line to the mother's, and, lacking an available male, to distribute the property equally among females of equal degree. The widow or widower did not participate as heir, but was given dower or curtesy as discussed below.

2. *Local custom.* According to the custom of *gavelkind* (applicable chiefly in Kent) land descended to all sons equally. By the custom of *Borough English* (applicable in the English part of Nottingham and some few other places) land descended to the youngest son. But no custom allowed the daughters to have anything if there were sons or issue of sons.

3. In the *United States* (and in England since 1925) land descends generally the same as personalty. There are variations from state to state, but the following represents the usual pattern. If the owner leaves a spouse and children, the spouse takes one-third, the children two-thirds. If the owner leaves children but no spouse, the children take all. Issue of a deceased child take the same share the child would have taken had the child lived, i.e., they take by right of representation. If the owner leaves a spouse but no issue, the spouse takes half, and the owner's blood relatives take half. If the owner leaves no spouse or issue, the owner's blood relatives take it all. The order of

priority among blood relatives is specified, but it is not worth examining in detail.[2]

4. The *blood of the first purchaser* and *ancestral property*. It will be recalled that under the Canons of Descent, collaterals of the father's line were preferred to all collaterals of the mother's line. Where an intestate died owning property inherited from the intestate's mother this rule would have produced an indefensible result had it not been for the additional rule that inherited property passing to collaterals goes only to those who are "of the blood of the first purchaser." Thus, if O dies intestate owning property which O's mother had bought and which O inherited from her, only persons who are of O's mother's blood can inherit from O. O's mother is the "first purchaser" within the rule. In the United States this doctrine exists in only a few states. Where it exists, it is known as the doctrine of "ancestral property"; its terms are governed by the various statutes of descent and distribution, and these usually differ in some particulars from the common-law rule.

Problems

13.5. The following is a chart of a famous current family, somewhat simplified:

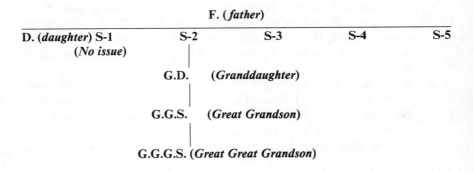

Under the system of primogeniture:
  a. Father dies. Who takes?
  b. S-1 renounces. Who takes?
  c. S-4 is killed while serving in the military. S-2 dies. Who takes?

---

2. An examination of the local statute on descent and distribution of a decedent's property in the state in which you are interested will give you a picture of the order of priority among blood relatives. The subject is dealt with in Casner, Estate Planning ch. 2 (4th ed.).

d. As a result of the recital of events, do you recognize the family and what is at stake in determining who takes?
e. If property should be left to "the eldest lineal male descendant of F.," would that be G.G.S.? See Thellusson v. Rendelsham, 7 H.L.C. 429 (1859).

13.6. In Massachusetts, the doctrine that to take land by descent a person must be of the blood of the first purchaser is abolished; for example, when a person dies intestate, Massachusetts property which the decedent has received by inheritance from the decedent's mother passes to paternal cousins if they are the nearest relatives at the decedent's death. The rule is also in force that new kinds of inheritance cannot be created. Co. Litt. 27.

Royal Whiton devised Massachusetts land "to my grand-daughter Sarah and her heirs on her father's side."

a. Sarah conveys "to Albin Johnson and his heirs." What estate does Johnson have? Johnson v. Whiton, 159 Mass. 424, 34 N.E. 542 (1893).
b. Sarah dies intestate, leaving as her nearest relatives a paternal aunt and a maternal aunt. Who takes the property?
c. In drafting Royal Whiton's will, could the attorney have carried out his client's intention so that there would be no question of the validity of the provision?

Further comment on "to A and his heirs." This is an odd phrase for the law to fix upon to express the simple idea of full ownership. It naturally raises several questions, which we now discuss. (1) How did this phrase come to be used? In early feudal times when the hand-picking of tenants had real importance to the lord, no estate could be transferred without the lord's assent; and when the tenant died the lord could accept or reject as successor the tenant's heir. Thus when a lord enfeoffed to a person and such person's heirs, this form of conveyance gave in advance an undertaking to accept the heir — an assent to descent, if you like word play. (2) Who are the "heirs" referred to in the phrase? Remember that primogeniture is in force so that only one heir takes when an owner dies.[3] Obviously, then, the plural word "heirs" cannot refer to contemporaneous heirs; it must refer to successive heirs. So the phrase means to A, then to A's heir, then to the heir's heir, and so on ad infinitum. (3) How accurately descriptive was the phrase in the days of its origin? Very accurately descriptive indeed. In a state of the law where the estate could not be conveyed inter vivos and could not be devised by will a fee simple was an estate which passed from heir to heir in successive generations indefinitely. So, in those days, if you were asked whether the words in the phrase were words of purchase or words of limitation, you

---

3. If descent is to females all those of equal degree take equally as co-parceners, but they are considered in law as a single heir.

could properly answer that it made no difference because the heirs were bound to take in any event. However, when the owner of a fee simple acquired the right to convey it and devise it,[4] the significance of the phrase became wholly artificial; at that stage these words simply meant "in fee simple." (4) What is the duration of an estate "to A and his heirs"? Certainly in early times, before a fee owner could convey or devise, it was an estate which was to last as long as A's line of heirs continued. But suppose that, at some time after Quia Emptores, O enfeoffs "A and his heirs," A enfeoffs "B and his heirs," and then A dies without heirs. You might think that the estate would terminate for the reason that A had an estate limited to the duration of his line of heirs, that A's conveyance to B could only transfer what A had, and that the original estate had reached its limit by the failure of A's heirs. But it was not so held; B's estate produced an escheat only when B's heirs failed. Thus, in a sense, a conveyance of a fee caused the grantee to have a different estate than the grantor had — perhaps greater, perhaps smaller.

Determinable fees. If O conveys "to the X Church, its successors and assigns, so long as the premises shall be used for church purposes," the X Church has a fee simple determinable (or determinable fee). John Chipman Gray argued that determinable fees were impossible after Quia Emptores, but no court has adopted that view. (Can you make an argument against Gray on the basis of the fact that the last sentence of Quia Emptores declares that the Statute applies only to lands held *in feodo simpliciter?* It has been done.[5]) If the Church ceases to use the premises for church purposes, the property reverts to O. O's interest during the continuation of the determinable fee is called a *possibility of reverter.* Just as a fee simple can be determinable on the happening of a stated event, so also can a life estate or term of years be determinable before the end of the life or of the stated term; these variations are taken up under Life Estates and Terms of Years.

Fees subject to a condition subsequent. If O conveys "to A and his heirs, but if the premises shall be used for the sale of intoxicating liquors then O and his heirs may re-enter and repossess the premises as of their former estate," A has a fee simple subject to a condition subsequent, and O has a *right of entry for condition broken.* Note that there is a difference between the determinable fee and the fee subject to a condition subsequent: the former expires of its own force when the stated event occurs, whereas the latter continues until it is cut short by the exercise of the right of entry by O. This distinction between interests which expire and interests which are cut short is a fundamental one. You will meet it again.

4. Quia Emptores (1290) gave the tenant in fee simple the right to substitute another in the tenant's place, but this may have merely confirmed a development which had already taken place in the courts. The Statute of Wills (1540) gave the right to devise, but for some time before this date owners had enjoyed the substantial equivalent of the right to devise through a dexterous use of a reserved power of appointment. O would convey inter vivos to A to the use of such persons as O should name in O's will, and, until O's death and in default of persons being named in the will, to the use of O.

5. Powell, Determinable Fees, 23 Colum. L. Rev. 207, 212 (1923).

SECTION 2. THE FEE TAIL

In old England the ancestral estate, not commerce, was normally the basis of the family fortune. It was also the focus of family pride. These factors provided the motivation for attempts to keep the land in the family as long as the family lasted. The estate tail was the basic instrumentality designed for that purpose.

By way of contrast we in America have, generally speaking, no such attachment to the land. In the cities we start our married lives in an apartment, then rent a small house, then buy a larger house which we occupy until the children have married and moved away, and usually end up in an apartment again because the house in which we now rattle around alone has become too much trouble to keep up. In the country the life of a farmer is not so attractive that children habitually follow in the steps of their parents — at least not those children who, through educational or marital opportunity, have a choice of doing something else. There are a few exceptional cases of attachment to the land — in the Old South, in New York's Dutchess County — but not many. Hence, the estate tail has never been a major factor in American land law. However, our law incorporates certain vestigial traces of the estate tail which lay traps for the unwary. The subject cannot be ignored as a foreign historical curiosity.

The fee simple conditional. Before 1285 it was common for O, an owner in fee simple, to convey "to A and the heirs of A's body." This normally took place as part of a marriage settlement, and the form of conveyance was designed to require that upon A's death the property should pass to A's lineal descendants or, if there were no descendants, revert to O. In passing upon such conveyances the courts seem to have held that

1. If A had issue born alive, A could then convey a fee simple, thus cutting off the inheritance of A's issue and O's reversion.
2. If A had no issue, A could make no conveyance which would cut off the reversionary interest; and, at A's death, the property would revert to O.

The estate with these characteristics was called a fee simple conditional. (N.B.: When referring to this estate call it a "fee simple conditional" and nothing else. There are so many similar names for other estates — fee simple determinable, fee simple subject to a condition, etc. — that the danger of confusion is substantial.)[6]

The Statute De Donis Conditionalibus (1285). A Petition of the Barons in 1258 called attention to the manner in which the intention of grantors was being frustrated by allowing tenants in fee simple conditional to convey a fee simple absolute after birth of issue. But it was not until 1285 that a statute

---

6. For the lore on fee simple conditional, see Restatement of Property §§68–77; Plucknett, Concise History of the Common Law 549 (5th ed. 1956).

was passed on the matter. Then De Donis, after reciting that issue ought not to be disinherited or grantors deprived of their reversions, provided:

> The will of the giver according to the form in the deed of gift manifestly expressed shall be from henceforth observed, so that they to whom the land was given under such condition shall have no power to alien the land so given, but that it shall remain unto the issue of them to whom it was given after their death, or shall revert unto the giver or his heirs if issue fail, either by reason that there is no issue at all, or if any issue be, it fail by death, the heir of such issue failing. [Many words omitted.]

The statute gave writs to protect the issue (formedon in descender) and the reversioner (formedon in reverter).[7] The estate given to A "and the heirs of A's body" came to be known as a fee tail — from the French "tailler," meaning "to carve," the thought being that the grantor has carved an estate precisely to the grantor's liking.[8] You will observe that the statute does not in terms forbid the issue of the tenant in tail from conveying a fee simple. However, when this question arose, Bereford, C.J., solved the matter with the chummy informality of the time by saying, "he that made the statute meant to bind the issue in fee tail as well as the feoffees . . . , and it was only through negligence that he omitted to insert express words to that effect in the statute"[9]; so he held that the issue were forbidden to convey.

Problem

13.7.   Assume you are in a state where there is no constitutional or statutory provision dealing with estates given "to A and the heirs of his body," and the courts have held that the Statute De Donis is not a common-law statute and is, therefore, not in force. In such a state what type of estate is created by such a conveyance? Restatement of Property, Chapter 5, Introductory Note, Special Note 1.[10]

---

7.   "Formedon" is a corruption of "forma doni."
8.   See Plucknett, Concise History of the Common Law 551.
9.   Y.B. Edw. II 5 (Selden Soc.), i, 177; ii, 226.
10.   In 1941 Nebraska adopted the Uniform Property Act which contains a provision prohibiting fees simple conditional. The Nebraska statute reads in part as follows:

> The use in an otherwise effective conveyance of property, of language appropriate to create such a fee simple conditional or a fee tail, creates a fee simple in the person who would have taken a fee simple conditional or a fee tail. Any future interest limited upon such an interest is a limitation upon the fee simple and its validity is determined accordingly. [Neb. Rev. Stat. §76.10.]

The Nebraska statute does not apply to conveyances which became effective before it was enacted. Prior to 1941 Nebraska had recognized the fee simple conditional; so that estate will be a matter of concern in that state for years to come.

Expressions which create an estate tail. The standard formula is "to A and the heirs of A's body." Some variation of the formula is accepted in some jurisdictions—e.g., "to A and A's issue"—and in wills considerable latitude is allowed for informal expression of intent. Observe that "heirs of the body" must mean successive generations of issue, not several "heirs of the body" in the same generation, for there could be only one heir at a time under the system of primogeniture. In an estate tail the essential requirement for the words of limitation is that a *line of inheritance,* restricted to descendants, be specified; therefore "To A and A's children" will not create an estate tail unless you give "children" a wholly artificial meaning.[11] If a remainder is created after a fee tail the standard formula runs as follows: "To A and the heirs of A's body, but if A dies without issue then to B and his [or her] heirs."

Problems

13.8. O conveys Blackacre "To A and A's issue, but if A die without issue then to B and her heirs." What is the meaning of the phrase "die without issue?" What is the state of the title to Blackacre?

13.9. O conveys Blackacre "To A and A's heirs, but if A die without issue then to B and her heirs." What is the meaning of the phrase "die without issue?" What is the state of the title to Blackacre? Restatement of Property §61. Machell v. Weeding, 8 Sim. 4 (Ch. 1836).

Types of estates tail. The *estate tail general,* which is the type we have heretofore assumed, permits the property to pass to all descendants, male or female, by any spouse, according to the rules of descent. The *estate tail male* ("To A and the heirs male of his body") limits descent to males. The *estate tail female* exists but is rarely found. The *estate tail special* ("To A and the heirs of his body begotten upon the body of his present wife, W") limits the descent to issue of a particular marriage.[12]

Problem

13.10. Thomas conveys "to Richard and his issue of the body of Elizabeth, his present wife." Elizabeth dies childless. What estate does

11. See Restatement of Property §283 for the meaning that is given. Note particularly the Rule in Wild's Case, stated in Comment a. See also, Casner, Construction of Gifts "To A and His Children" (Herein The Rule in Wild's Case), 7 U. Chi. L. Rev. 438 (1940).

12. For the episode of "a grave and honest gentleman" who created in himself seven estates in special tail, the spouses designated being the wives of seven of his close friends and professional associates, see Williams, The Limitations in Chudleigh's Case, 13 L.Q. Rev. 4 (1897).

Richard have? And what difference does it make? Restatement of Property §79, Comment d.

Disentailing conveyances. From 1285 until 1472 the estate tail seems to have functioned as planned by the sponsors of De Donis—and 187 years is well above the life expectancy of legal institutions. In 1472 Taltarum's Case, Y.B. 12 Edw. IV, 19, decided that a tenant in tail in possession could convey a fee simple by suffering a common recovery. A common recovery was a type of conveyance by means of a collusive law suit. It represented an all-time high in legalistic hocus-pocus; but, in a country where there was no recording system, it did have the by-product advantage of making the conveyance a matter of public record.[13]

Very much simpler forms of disentailing conveyances are now available wherever estates tail are recognized. But note that the disentailing conveyance did not bring it about that a fee tail was the same thing as a fee simple, for

1.   Only a tenant in tail *in possession* could make a disentailing conveyance—and this fact was the basis upon which the English con-

---

13.   By far the best statement we have found on common-law disentailing conveyances is in Williams & Eastwood, Real Property 143 et seq. (1933). The following is a brief statement on the subject.

Common recovery. The rule of law which made disentailment possible proceeded in two steps: (a) it was first held that a tenant in tail could convey a fee simple provided that lands of equal value were substituted for those conveyed; (b) it was next held that a *judgment* for the recovery of lands of equal value could be substituted for the entailed lands. With such a rule, plus a complacent blindness of the goddess of Justice, the rest was easy. Suppose A, tenant in tail of Blackacre, wanted to convey a fee simple to B. B brought a writ of right (the highest form of real action) against A, claiming title to Blackacre, and demanding that a judgment be awarded that B recover the same. A alleged (falsely) that A had acquired title from C and that C had warranted the title, wherefore A "vouched C to warranty," i.e., called upon C to defend the title to Blackacre and demanded that if C should fail in the defense of the title, A should be given judgment to recover from C lands equal in value to Blackacre. C admitted (falsely) that C had warranted as A alleged. Then C allowed judgment to go in favor of B by default. Under the judgment B recovered Blackacre from A, and A was given a judgment against C to recover lands of the same value as Blackacre. The catch, of course, was that C was carefully chosen as a person who owned no lands at all; so the judgment against C was worthless. (C was usually the court crier and was known as the "common vouchee"—whence the judgment was called a *common* recovery.)

Of course, after B got the fee simple, B could convey it directly back to A; thus, more frequently than not, B as well as C was a straw who was brought into the picture merely to turn A's fee tail into a fee simple. With a genius for complication seldom equalled, the English conveyancers next conceived a method of inserting a fourth party into the proceeding, a *tenant to the praecipe,* who also had no real connection with the land and also suffered a judgment founded on false allegations.

Fine. The final concord, or fine, was another means of conveying land by a collusive law suit. If O owned Blackacre and wanted to convey to A, A would bring action against O, O would allege a defense, the parties would obtain leave to compromise, and they would then enter into a "final concord" agreeing that A should have the land. This compromise was approved by the court and thereby became a judgment. O was said to *levy a fine* (compare *"suffering* a recovery") and the operative compromise was called the *foot of the fine.* The foot of the fine was a tripartite indenture, one copy staying in the Records Office, one part going to O

veyancers succeeded in working out the system of "strict settlement" by which land was effectively tied up for generations, as will appear;

2. If the tenant in tail in possession did not execute a disentailing conveyance, the tenant could not devise the property, and upon the tenant's death it could not pass to the general heirs but only to the lineal heirs, and in default of them it would pass to the remainderman or reversioner.

Estates tail in the United States. An estate "to A and the heirs of his body" is treated in different ways in various states:

1. As already indicated, there are some states (e.g., South Carolina) in which the old law of fee simple conditional is applicable.
2. Some states (e.g., Massachusetts) still have the estate tail but permit a simple type of disentailing conveyance.
3. Some states (e.g., Illinois) have statutes giving a life estate to A with a remainder in fee simple to A's issue.
4. Some states (e.g., New York) have statutes which declare that A has a fee simple.

And there are variations and sub-classes of these four types of treatment, specified in elaborate detail in Chapter 5 of the Restatement of Property.

Problems

13.11. In a state like Massachusetts, where a disentailing conveyance can be made only by a tenant in tail in possession, under what circum-

---

and one part going to A. In regard to a fee tail, the levy of a fine cut out the rights of the fee tail owner's issue but not the rights of remaindermen or reversioners; thus the grantee under the fine got an estate, known as a base fee, which would last as long as the line of issue of the original grantee in tail continued.

Comment on the hardihood of institutions. The fine was a standard method of conveyance from at least as early as 1195, and the recovery considerably antedates Taltarum's Case. Yet both persisted until 1833. Why all this mumbo jumbo of collusive law suits, fictitious parties, and patently false allegations when much simpler means could have been devised to attain the same ends? The first report of the commissioners appointed by George IV to inquire into the English law of real property may suggest to the cynical a clue:

> In addition to the essential acts to be done, either in court or before a Judge, or a serjeant, or commissioners, in levying a fine, or suffering a recovery in that court, documents must be obtained at the following offices; viz. for a fine, two at the Cursitor's Office, one at a Judge's chambers, one at the Alienation Office, one at the Return Office, one at the Warrant of Attorney Office, one at the Custos Brevium Office, one at the King's Silver Office, and one at the Chirographer's Office; and for a recovery, two at the Cursitor's Office, one at the Alienation Office, four at the office of the Clerk of the Recoveries, and one at the Seal Office. In every stage of the numerous proceedings in a fine and recovery, expenses are incurred in official fees and stamps; these, together with the professional charges of the attorney, come to a considerable sum.

If you really want to get the smell of an English solicitor's office in Dickens's time and feel the clammy handshake of Uriah Heep, read the itemized solicitor's bill for a common recovery at pages 666-667 of the commissioners' report. Dickens inveighed against the Chancery counterpart of this sort of thing in Bleak House.

stances, if any, would you advise O, the owner of Blackacre in fee simple, to convert his holding into a fee tail estate or to create by inter vivos gift or devise a fee tail estate in a grantee or devisee?

13.12.   In Ohio the fee tail estate is preserved as a fee tail for the lifetime of the original grantee. What is the difference in the legal position of the original grantee of a fee tail estate in Ohio and in Illinois? See Long v. Long, 45 Ohio St. 2d 165, 343 N.E.2d 100 (1976).

SECTION 3.   THE LIFE ESTATE

You will be pleased and surprised to know that a grant or devise "to A for life" creates exactly what you would expect, a life estate in A. This is a freehold estate; but obviously it is not an estate of inheritance. Complexities arise in the matter of its termination. It must terminate on A's death, but it may terminate at an earlier period by forfeitures or merger. This matter is discussed at a later point.

Determinable life estates. These can exist, the most common type being a gift to a woman "for life so long as she shall remain a widow." A gift also may be made to a man "for life so long as he shall remain a widower."

Infrequency of legal life estates in modern practice. The lack of attachment of Americans to family land militates against the creation of life estates and remainders. Where O, owner of Blackacre, devises to A for life, remainder to some other person or persons, O is creating a very inflexible interest in A. If A wants to live on the land, well and good. But suppose the property is too big or too small, too expensive to maintain or too far from town, what does A do then? If A can get the cooperation of the remaindermen A can sell the property; but if the remaindermen are stubborn or if they are unborn or unascertained (e.g., "to A for life, remainder to A's children who survive A"), sale is impossible — in the absence of appropriate statutory provisions.[14]

Problem

13.13.   O devises Blackacre "to A for life, remainder to such of A's issue as survive him." A advertises the property for rent. You have a client, B, who desires to rent the property for a year with four yearly options to renew at the same rental. Advise B as to what she should do.

---

14.   See Casner, Legal Life Estates and Powers of Appointment Coupled with Life Estates and Trusts, 45 Neb. L. Rev. 342 (1966).

These difficulties bring it about that legal life estates, if used, must be drafted carefully.[15] Of course, giving property to a trustee in trust for A for life, remainder to others, is quite a different matter, because the trustee is given a power of sale of the fee as a matter of course and can therefore dispose of the property if that seems the wise thing to do; or, to put it differently, the objections that apply to *legal* life estates in land do not apply to *equitable life* interests under a trust.

Estates pur autre vie. One can be given an estate for the life of another — e.g., "to A for the life of B." Or this same situation can arise by the creation of a life estate plus a conveyance — e.g., "to B for life," then B conveys B's interest to A. In either event A is a tenant pur autre vie; B is the cestui que vie. If B dies first, there is no problem: the estate ends. But suppose A dies intestate during the life of B. In that case the estate has not expired, and yet it is not inheritable. This situation produced in the old law a quaint rule:

1. If the conveyance to A was simply "to A for the life of B," then on A's death intestate, the first person to enter the land could stay there as *general occupant.* A's heirs were not entitled because the estate was not inheritable; and the remainderman or reversioner could not come in because B was still alive. So the old law simply quit in this situation and let the first entrant stay in.

2. If the original conveyance to A was "to A and A's heirs for the life of B" (or if B had conveyed his life estate "to A and A's heirs") then on A's death intestate A's heir came in as *special occupant.* The heir was considered to take because of the grantor's designation, not by inheritance — an odd anomaly.

At the present time, however, various types of statutory change have brought it about that an unexpired estate pur autre vie descends like other interests in land. Such interests have been devisable at least since 1677.[16]

SECTION 4. HUSBAND AND WIFE

We select this as the place to discuss marital rights by way of underscoring the fact that the characteristic common-law doctrines of *dower* and *curtesy* give to the surviving spouse a life estate only. But dower and curtesy constitute only a fraction of the problem. Seisin *jure uxoris,* statutes modify-

---

15. For an example of a legal life estate coupled with various powers in the life tenant which eliminate the difficulties that would otherwise be present in the life-estate-and-remainder arrangement. See 5 Casner, Estate Planning (5th ed.).

16. For the learning on this, see Restatement of Property §151. See Collins v. Held, 174 Ind. App. 584, 369 N.E.2d 641 (1977), which decided this issue for the first time in Indiana. The court rejected the doctrine of general occupancy and adopted the Restatement's position that the owner's heirs took by descent.

ing the husband's dominant rights, statutes modifying or abolishing dower and curtesy, statutes creating heirship and forced heirship in the surviving spouse, and the adoption of the Spanish institution of community property introduce complications which we try to sort out here and which you must succeed in keeping sorted out in your mind. In any system of rules as to marital rights the following questions, among others, arise:

During the joint lives of the spouses,

1. Who has power to convey?
2. Who receives the income?

When a spouse dies,

1. What does the surviving spouse receive if the deceased spouse leaves no will?
2. To what extent can the deceased spouse's will cut off the surviving spouse's rights?

In studying this subject we suggest that you keep these questions in mind as a check on your understanding.

At common law it was a man's world. Husband and wife were one, and the one was the husband. The married woman had little control over her property. She could not make a will. She could bring no actions except in conjunction with her husband, even in cases of personal assault upon her.[17] Her husband could collect her choses in action and keep the proceeds. Property-wise her position was one of almost complete dependence on the male — her husband, her son, and others — the most striking manifestation being the ability of her deceased husband's collateral relatives to protect their inheritances by subjecting her person to the indignities of the writ de ventre inspiciendo.[18] However, let it be remembered that in the rough-and-tumble of feudal times the husband's function of protector involved something more than a hand under the elbow at street crossings and a scowl at too appreciative glances. Yet, after all is said and done, the husband was given more control than was necessary to exercise his protective function and the control persisted long after any possible justification had disappeared.

During the joint lives of husband and wife, the husband was seised of his wife's freeholds jure uxoris — which meant that he was entitled to exclusive possession or to the entire rents and profits. He could sell his interest and it was reachable by his creditors. As to his wife's leaseholds he had even greater rights; not only was he entitled to the rents and profits but he could dispose of the entire leasehold if he wished. By the sixteenth century courts of equity had whittled away at this male empire by holding that property could be so given that the wife retained control of it and received its profits — an

---

17. For example, I. de S. et ux. v. W. de S., Y.B. Lib. Assisarum, fol. 99, pl. 60 (1348), a case featured in most torts casebooks.
18. See 1 Blackstone, Commentaries 456 n.48 (Lewis ed. 1897). On the succeeding page you can discover, if you care, how a child can be "more than ordinarily legitimate." The editor of the 1897 edition of Blackstone is William Draper Lewis, then dean of the University of Pennsylvania Law School, later director of the American Law Institute during the period when the original Restatements were being prepared and published.

institution known as the *wife's separate estate in equity.* In the nineteenth century, statutes, usually referred to as the Married Woman's Property Acts, eliminated or greatly reduced the husband's control of the wife's real estate.[19]

Dower. Heirship followed the blood line only; the wife was not an heir of her husband. However, she had dower in all lands of which her husband was seised during coverture and which were inheritable by her issue[20]—and when her husband died she thereby became a *dowager,* a word which common parlance has corrupted into meaning any strong-willed and austere matron who wears Queen Mary hats. Under her right of dower the widow had a life estate in one-third of the lands of which her husband had been seised at any time during their marriage. The husband could not defeat dower either by inter vivos conveyance or by will; but, by declaring in his will that his provisions for his wife therein were "in lieu of dower" he could compel her to elect whether to take dower or the testamentary gifts. Ordinarily, in the large estates like Pusey Manor, there was a Dower House on the premises, into which the widow moved when her eldest son succeeded to the fee tail and took up residence in the manor house; prior to the death of his father the eldest son and his family might well have been using the Dower House themselves.

In early times dower was optional with the husband. He could endow his wife at the time of the marriage or not, as he chose. Hence the antique importance of including in the marriage ceremony the words, "and with all my worldly goods I thee endow." But at the present time this clause represents a hollow tradition. It does not apply to personal property; and as to real property the wife is either endowed or not according to the local law, regardless of the form of the ceremony.

In a state of society where the family fortune was the family land and the family life centered upon the family estates, dower gave to the widow dignity, security, and proximity to her children and grandchildren. But at the present time in this country, where the family estate, if any, consists of stocks, bonds, and life insurance, and where there is no family land, dower is an anachronism. American legislation has given two rights to the widow not allowed by the common law:

1. In case the husband dies intestate, the widow is an heir as to real estate as she has always been one of the next-of-kin as to personal property. She is usually given one-half of the estate if there are no issue, one-third if there are issue.
2. In case the husband leaves a will, she may renounce her claims

19. On the rights of the husband in the wife's property at common law, in equity, and under the statutes, see Haskins, The Estate by the Marital Right, 97 U. Pa. L. Rev. 345 (1949); American Law of Property §§5.1-5.56 (Casner ed. 1952).

20. See Haskins, The Development of Common Law Dower, 62 Harv. L. Rev. 42 (1948). The wife had dower in fees simple, and also in fees tail with the exception of fees tail special by some spouse other than herself. The Restatement declares that in the United States the dower right is less extensive than under English law where the husband's estate is less than a fee simple absolute. Restatement of Property §§54, 75, 84, 93, and Appendix.

thereunder—"waive the will"—and take a statutory share (usually her intestate share) in all property comprising her husband's estate at the time of his death.[21]

Many states have abolished dower as a part of the reform in which the widow was given the rights just described. However, there are still a number of states which retain dower, and in these a very complex situation may exist. You should examine your local law.[22] In all states the wife can release dower by joining in the deed.

The following problems are given for the purpose of checking your understanding of the subject matters just discussed.

Problems

13.14. In a state that still recognizes common-law dower you are counsel for P (Purchaser) who has contracted to buy Blackacre from V (Vendor) upon production by V of a good marketable title. In searching the title you find the following transactions in V's chain of title. The grantor's wife did not join in any of these deeds. The question in each case is whether the transaction constitutes a defect in the title by reason of dower rights.

    a. In 1976 L conveyed to M, the deed stating that L is unmarried. You ascertain from P that P has no knowledge or reason to know that L was ever married.

    b. In 1913 C conveyed to D. There is no indication in the deed whether C was married and you cannot discover any information on this point.

    c. In 1964 F conveyed to Charles R. Gorman, Inc., a corporation all of whose stock (other than qualifying shares for directors) is owned by Charles R. Gorman, a married man. In 1966 Charles R. Gorman, Inc., conveyed to H by a deed signed by Charles R. Gorman as President.

    d. In 1970 I conveyed to J, an unmarried man, for a stated consideration of $25,000. On the same date J mortgaged the property to K, a married man, to secure payment of a demand note for $50,000 which contains a clause providing that J shall not be liable for any amount in excess of the amount for which the land is sold at a mortgagee's sale. You discover that K really put up the $25,000 purchase price for J, that J is K's bookkeeper, that K occupied the land and J never did, and that K was on bad terms with his wife and has since separated from her, both being still living.

    e. In 1982 M contracted in writing to convey the land to Q, a married

---

21. The intestate share of a wife is discussed in Casner, Estate Planning ch. 2 (4th ed.); and the right of the wife to renounce her husband's will and claim a statutory share is considered id., ch. 3.

22. In checking your local law, ascertain whether dower attaches to all the land of which the husband was seised during marriage, or only to the land he was seised of on his death.

man, on February 1, 1983, and Q contracted to pay $22,000 therefor on that date. This contract is recorded. There also is recorded an instrument dated January 15, 1983, in which M and Q mutually release each other from the 1982 contract.

13.15. In a state in which a widow can renounce her husband's will and elect either common-law dower or a statutory forced share equal to her intestate share, you represent W, a widow, aged 42. The widow is entitled to her statutory share in the personal property even though she elects dower on the renunciation of a will. W was the second wife of her deceased husband; he had a daughter, D, by his former marriage, and D is still living. The deceased husband owned at the time of his death Greenacre (value $15,000) and $30,000 in excess of debts, taxes, and administration expense. During his lifetime and after his marriage to W he had engaged in the following transactions:

a. He conveyed to D Blackacre (value $9,000), which he had received under the will of his former wife.

b. He conveyed to D Whiteacre (value $30,000), which he bought after his marriage to W.

c. He gave D $50,000 par value of U.S. government bonds which he bought after his marriage to W.

His will provides, "I leave everything I own to my daughter, D." Advise W as to what she should do.

13.16. If the husband is seised of an estate of inheritance which is inheritable by the issue of the marriage, will the dower right of the wife survive the termination of the husband's estate? Consider this question in connection with the following situations:

a. O conveys Blackacre to A and the heirs of his body. Blackacre is located in a jurisdiction where such a conveyance creates in A a fee simple conditional. A has a child. The child dies. A dies survived by his wife, W.

b. The same as part a above only Blackacre is located in a jurisdiction where such a conveyance creates in A a fee tail.

c. O conveys Blackacre to A and his heirs as long as the property is used for residential purposes. A dies survived by his wife, W. After A's death, the heirs of A who take Blackacre subject to W's right of dower use their portion of the land for other than residential purposes. O claims Blackacre free and clear of any dower right in W.

d. O conveys Blackacre to A and his heirs, but if the land is ever used for commercial purposes, O or his heirs may re-enter and take possession. A uses the land for commercial purposes. A dies survived by his wife, W. O asserts his right of entry.

e. O conveys Blackacre to A and his heirs, but if A dies without a child surviving him, then to B and his heirs. A dies childless survived by his wife, W.

13.17. H desires to purchase Blackacre. He wants to be able to deal with the property after the purchase without any interference from his wife. In what way should he take title to Blackacre in a jurisdiction which has common law dower?

13.18. Should the wife's right of dower be abolished where it still exists?

Curtesy. After the wife's death the husband was entitled to a life estate in all her freeholds, legal or equitable, provided issue was born alive capable of inheriting the freeholds. It made no difference that the infant did not survive, but he or she must be born alive "and heard to cry within the four walls"—a requirement imposed so that the husband's curtesy would be established by the testimony of males, who were not allowed within the bedroom where the mother lay (an unusual display of consideration by the standards of the times) but were waiting outside to hear the wail so important to the husband. Even after married women were permitted to make wills, the wife could not by will defeat her husband's curtesy; but she could, of course, make a testamentary gift "in lieu of curtesy" and thereby compel an election by her husband. Observe the differences from dower:

1. Curtesy extends to all of the wife's inheritable freeholds, whereas dower extends only to one-third of the husband's.
2. If no issue is born alive the husband gets no curtesy.
3. Curtesy extends to equitable interests though dower does not.[23] Curtesy has been abolished in all states which have abolished dower, and in those that have not abolished dower, the husband usually is given dower instead of curtesy. You should examine your local law. The husband has been given additional statutory rights, similar to those given the wife: (1) He has been made an heir—generally one-half if no issue, one-third if issue; (2) he has been given the right to waive the will and take a statutory forced share in the estate, real and personal, which his wife owned at her death.

The following cases consider the extent to which lifetime arrangements a spouse (whether husband or wife) may make will have the effect of depriving the surviving spouse of rights in the deceased spouse's estate.

STRONG v. WOOD
306 N.W.2d 737 (Iowa 1981)

Larson, J.

Sometime in 1976 Philander L. ("Mike") Strong and the plaintiff, then Ruby Esterley, became acquainted. At that time Mike was a 76-year-old

---

23. In some states dower has been extended by statute to equitable interests. There were some other differences at common law, and these are discussed in American Law of Property §§5.57-5.74 (Casner ed. 1952). For example, curtesy initiate (i.e., the husband's interest during the wife's life) was considered an estate which vested in the husband at once upon the birth of issue, although this had little practical importance with regard to legal estates of which he was seised jure uxoris anyway. Inchoate dower (i.e., the wife's interest during the husband's life) was considered only an expectancy, like the interest of an expectant heir.

farmer who had lived by himself in rural Pocahontas County since the death of his wife Velma in 1968; Ruby was a 66-year-old widow living in Minneapolis, Minnesota. Their relationship progressed to the point where Mike proposed to her in October, 1976; Ruby, however, did not "make up her mind" to marry him until December, 1976.

In late November and early December, 1976, Mike vacationed in Hawaii. When he returned to Iowa before the Christmas holidays he wrote to Ruby saying that he was "looking forward to the day we are going to be married. I can't wait much longer. . . . I'll be glad when we can live together all the time." During this period, Mike contacted the defendants, children from the marriage to his deceased wife, requesting that they meet at the office of his attorney, R. L. Hudson, over the upcoming holidays. The purpose of the meeting was not disclosed, and the children did not question their father on the matter.

On December 29, the family met at Hudson's office in Pocahontas where, according to Hudson, the following conversation took place:

[A.] I said, "Mike, what can I do for you?" And he said, "Well, the children were all home, and I've been reading about this new revenue act," and he said, "I thought I better — we better come in and I better find out what to do to save myself taxes." . . .

I think I told him that, well, I know I did, that anything that was done, would have to be done on or before December 31, because the new law became effective January 1. . . .

Q. Did he eventually, then, on that day, direct you to draft a deed conveying the —
A. Well, after discuss[ing] it back and forth, he said — he said this: He said, "Well, I think I better deed the land and whatever there is could be some there is going to be some change in the rules." He said, "I think I better do that," and he instructed me to do it. . . .

Mike said that the children are all home the 29th or just a few days after Christmas, and Dean was here, and he wanted to come over and talk about it — his estate. And thought something was necessary to be done, because of what was going to happen under the new law.

After some discussion between Mike and his attorney, it was agreed that Hudson would draw up a warranty deed which, after reserving to Mike a life estate, would transfer Mike's interest in an 80-acre farm to his three children in return for "$1.00 and other consideration." Mike did not indicate to the others at this conference that he was considering marriage, and in fact, they testified they did not know of Mike's relationship with Ruby. The deed which Hudson executed was recorded on the same day, December 29.

On January 26, 1977, nearly one month after this meeting in Hudson's office, Mike and Ruby were married, without prior notice to their children. Retiring to the 80-acre farm, the couple lived there until Mike died, intestate, on December 3, 1978.

This action in equity was commenced by Ruby against Mike's children, Naomi Strong Wood and Carol Strong Shimon, as administrators of Mike's estate, and against these same defendants and Dean L. Strong as individual grantees of Mike's interest in the farm. She alleged that she had entered into an oral contract of marriage with Mike prior to December 29, 1976; that she had not been aware of the transfer of the farm to his children prior to the marriage; that only after his death did she learn of the conveyance; and that as a result of her reliance on a statement by Mike that "she would be well provided for, both before and after his death," the transfer of the farm to his children fraudulently deprived her of her marital interest, §633.211(1), The Code 1977. She requested that the deed be cancelled and annulled, and that she be granted her one-third share in the farm under the provisions of chapter 633. The matter was tried to the district court which found that Ruby failed to prove (1) that she relied on any representation as an inducement to marry and (2) that Mike intended to deceive or defraud her. Accordingly, the court entered judgment in favor of the defendants, from which Ruby now appeals.

We have reviewed the record de novo since the action was tried to the district court sitting in equity. See Iowa R. App. P. 4.

I. *Elements of Claim.* The parties do not dispute whether the plaintiff may bring an action for fraudulent or secret conveyances in contemplation of marriage; rather, they dispute the elements required to be proven for recovery under such a claim. Our earlier cases involving such claims have not been consistent in defining the elements of recovery or the applicable presumptions. See e.g. In re Estate of Mann, 201 Iowa 878, 208 N.W. 310 (1926) (conveyance four months prior to marriage but during period of engagement; plaintiff required to show (1) existing contract of marriage at time of conveyance and (2) no knowledge of conveyance prior to marriage); Bell v. Dufer, 142 Iowa 701, 121 N.W. 500 (1909) (conveyance nine days prior to marriage but during "two month courtship"; plaintiff required to show (1) want of knowledge of the conveyance, and (2) reliance on her prospective rights in the property); Wallace v. Wallace, 137 Iowa 169, 114 N.W. 913 (1908) (conveyance two days prior to marriage; defendant conceded deed executed in contemplation of marriage without plaintiff's actual knowledge; recovery for plaintiff since "[i]t is well settled that a secret conveyance in contemplation of marriage is fraudulent as to the spouse, the intent to deprive her of the marital rights which she would otherwise have acquired being *presumed* from the circumstances") (emphasis added); Beechley v. Beechley, 134 Iowa 75, 108 N.W. 762 (1906) (conveyance eight months prior to offer of matrimony; "[f]raudulent intent will *not* be presumed"; judgment for plaintiff reversed) (emphasis added). See generally D. McCarthy, Iowa Probate §1665, at 454-56 (1965); 4 G. Thompson, Real Property §1917, at 121-37 (1961).

This conflict in authority is not limited to cases within our own jurisdiction. One authority has noted: "There has been some conflict of authority over the fraudulent character of a voluntary conveyance of property by one engaged to marry where the conveyance is merely not revealed, no resort being made to any active expedient to mislead or keep the intended spouse ignorant with respect to the conveyance. One view is that the conveyance is actually fraudulent; at least, if by a woman it is actually fraudulent against the common-law marital rights of her intended husband. That view has likewise been followed with respect to a secret antenuptial conveyance by a husband, regarding it as actually or at least constructively fraudulent. Another view is that such a conveyance, though prima facie good, must be judged by its own particular surroundings, purposeful concealment, however, being evidence of purposeful fraud. Still a different view is that such a conveyance is prima facie fraudulent, but the parties holding thereunder may show that no fraud was intended or practiced on the party complaining. Again, it has been said simply that the mere failure of a grantor to inform his intended wife of a conveyance by him just before marriage is not of itself sufficient to make it fraudulent against her." 41 Am. Jur. 2d Husband and Wife §198, at 174 (1968) (footnote omitted).

Upon analysis of the various authorities we conclude the establishment of such a claim should turn on proof of the following elements: (1) a transfer made during a contract to marry or under such other circumstances, including its proximity to the marriage, indicating it was made in contemplation of marriage; (2) lack of adequate consideration for the transfer; (3) lack of knowledge of the transfer on the part of the prospective spouse; (4) fraudulent intent on the part of the transferor and (5) reliance by the prospective spouse upon the transferor's interest in the transferred property as an inducement to marriage. Proof of fraudulent intent understandably raises troublesome evidentiary problems, especially where, as here, the transferor is deceased. We believe the preferable rule is that which creates a presumption of fraudulent intent on the part of the transferor upon establishment of the first three elements, i.e., a transfer during the contract to marry or in contemplation of marriage, a lack of adequate consideration, and a lack of knowledge on the part of the prospective spouse. The burden of overcoming such presumption would be upon the proponents of the transfer to show a lack of such fraudulent intent. See 41 Am. Jur. 2d, supra §198, at 174.

II. *Application of the principles to this case.* Despite the existence of some evidence tending to show Mike's intent to defraud Ruby, including his failure to reveal the transfer prior to marriage and its proximity in time to the marriage, the existence of an engagement or contract of marriage at the time of the transfer was not established. Although Ruby testified she "made up her mind" in December 1976, to accept Mike's marriage proposal there was no evidence that this decision had been conveyed to Mike. Whether the proximity of the transfer to the actual marriage is sufficient, alone, to establish that it was made in contemplation of marriage presents a difficult question. However, it need not be decided in this case; nor is it necessary to decide whether, if the presumption of fraudulent intent was thus established, the proponents' estate-planning explanation was sufficient to rebut the presumption. We do not reach these issues because, even assuming the existence of a fraudulent intent, Ruby's claim suffers from another failure of proof: there is no showing that she relied on her prospective property rights as an inducement to marriage. In regard to her reliance, Ruby was asked this question: "Prior to Christmas of 1976, did you know about Mr. Strong's farm?" She replied: "Just that [he] said it was his farm, and—I mean we never really discussed it, except that he said that he had a farm." There was no evidence that Ruby was induced to marry Mike by his ownership of the land nor that she was even informed as to any details of Mike's interest, whether he was full or part owner, what equity he had in it, the size of the farm, or even its approximate value. Fraudulent intent alone is insufficient to establish a claimant's rights in the transferred property; it is the fraudulent *effect* of the transferor's actions which we must consider. A complaining spouse cannot claim such effect if no reliance is shown. See Bell v. Dufur, 142 Iowa 701, 703, 121 N.W. 500 (1926), 41 C.J.S. *supra* §20, at 420.

We conclude the district court properly denied Ruby's claim.

Affirmed.

KERWIN v. DONAGHY
317 Mass. 559, 59 N.E.2d 299 (1945)

LUMMUS, J.

The widow of William J. Kerwin, late of New Bedford, brought this petition in equity in the Probate Court under G.L. (Ter. Ed.) c.230, §5, as amended (Walsh v. Mullen, 314 Mass. 241, 50 N.E.2d 1), against his daughter Gladys M. Donaghy and the executors of his will (the executors having refused to bring suit) to recover for the estate a large number of stocks, bonds and deposits in banks, standing in the name of or held by the respondent Gladys M. Donaghy, but owned, it was alleged, by the estate of William J. Kerwin. One of his two sons, Ernest W. Kerwin, intervened, and joined with the widow in seeking relief against Gladys M. Donaghy. The Probate Court, on May 28, 1943, entered a decree ordering the respondent Gladys M. Donaghy to transfer and deliver the stocks, bonds and bank deposits in question to the executors of the will of William J. Kerwin. She appealed. The case comes here upon a report of the evidence, with a finding of material facts.

William J. Kerwin died on April 20, 1941, leaving as his widow his second wife, Lillian A. Kerwin, whom he had married on February 15, 1926, when he was fifty-seven years old and she was thirty-nine. They had no children. She was a widow with a young son when they married. William J. Kerwin left three adult children by his first marriage, Harold E. Kerwin, Gladys M. Donaghy, and Ernest W. Kerwin. The eldest son, William J.

Kerwin, Junior, had died about a year before his father, leaving a widow, Estelle C. Kerwin, but no issue. Gladys was unmarried when her father married the second time, and lived with her father and his second wife until she herself married one Paul A. Donaghy in July, 1926.

At that time William J. Kerwin was worth, according to his own judgment, half a million dollars. He had been superintendent of the Beacon Manufacturing Company for twenty-five years, and his annual income from that company alone amounted to $25,000. He retired from business in June, 1927, and thereafter had no regular occupation. Although his property evidently diminished in value afterwards, he always seemed to have plenty of money for his needs and those of his family, until his last illness.

On December 12, 1928, William J. Kerwin executed his will,[24] which after his death was duly proved and allowed. On November 12, 1941, his widow filed a waiver of the will, and claimed the interest in the estate that she would have taken had he died intestate.

The judge found in substance that from a time as early as 1923 William J. Kerwin was addicted to the folly of carrying most of his property in the names of some of his children, with the understanding that it should remain his and should be turned back to him at his request. His purpose was to defraud the Federal government by pretending to divide his income so as to avoid large surtaxes. The parts of his property held by his children other than Gladys were conveyed either to Gladys or back to him. In 1929 and thereafter the bulk of his property was held by and in the name of Gladys, and was kept in a safe deposit box of which she was the proprietor, although he had access to the box and kept the key to it in his desk. Many of the stock certificates, standing in her name, bore and still bear her indorsement in blank. In 1934, apparently with his consent, she cancelled his right of access, but that, the judge found, "was entirely consistent with a desire on Mr. Kerwin's part to make it appear, in case it should be questioned, that Gladys and not he was the owner of the contents of the box. He would have no difficulty in having Gladys go to the box with him and he kept the key to the box in his desk. It was customary when Mr. Kerwin wanted money to telephone Gladys to put it in his bank account which she promptly did whenever he called, excepting towards the last" of his life, during his last illness. During 1940 she paid him at his request about $15,000. It is hard to see how the surtaxes could be lessened by holding the bulk of his property in

---

24. In the will he used the adjective "beloved" in speaking of his wife and his children as well. He appointed his children Gladys and Harold, and Thomas M. Quinn, Esquire, as executors. He divided the household effects among his wife and children. He gave pecuniary legacies to grandchildren, but those were revoked by a codicil executed on November 28, 1936, which also was proved and allowed. He spoke of gifts made to residuary legatees, and declared that "all of said gifts were complete and outright and not advancements." He provided that any gifts to any legatee made after the execution of the will shall be on account of the legacy. The seventeenth paragraph of the will divided the residue into five equal parts, and gave one part to each of the following: his widow, his daughter Gladys, and his sons William, Harold and Ernest. The codicil ratified and confirmed the will except as changed by the codicil.

the name of Gladys after he ceased in 1927 to earn money, unless upon the tax returns the income was divided between him and Gladys. Whether it was or not does not appear.

Nothing in the relations of William J. Kerwin with his children made it likely that he would wish at any time to give all his property to Gladys and cut the others off. The judge found that "Mr. Kerwin and his wife got along well excepting for occasional times when there were some disagreements, but not very serious, and towards the last of his life they were very close to each other and he was solicitous for her welfare." Nevertheless the judge found that "he told Harold that he had put stock in Gladys' name because Mrs. Kerwin made so many demands for money he was going to see when he passed on that his children were going to have the money." It was, the judge found, "as a result of a temporary disagreement between William J. Kerwin and his wife" that he executed two trust agreements in August, 1936

At that time William J. Kerwin consulted John D. Kenney, Esquire, a lawyer in New Bedford. Kerwin came alone at the first visit to the lawyer, but on later occasions Gladys accompanied him. He told the lawyer that he wished to make sure that at his death Gladys would own the property that she was holding for him. The lawyer advised him that a will would be ineffective, for his wife could waive the will. The lawyer advised a trust, and two formal trust agreements were drawn, and were executed by William J. Kerwin and by Gladys. One agreement dealt with the stocks and bonds, the other with the bank deposits. The agreements were substantially identical in their terms.

In these agreements Gladys declared herself trustee of a large number of specified stocks, bonds and bank deposits "to pay the net income therefrom to said William J. Kerwin, for and during the term of his natural life . . . and upon the decease of said William J. Kerwin to hold said fund, together with any undistributed income therefrom, to her own use and behoof absolutely forever." He reserved the right during his life "to alter, amend or revoke this agreement in whole or in part, by giving written notice thereof to said Gladys M. Donaghy." He covenanted, agreed and declared that he had no interest in the trust property except that set forth in the agreements. It was provided that "this trust agreement shall be binding upon the heirs, executors and administrators of the parties hereto." It was provided that the trustee "shall not be obligated to disclose the existence of this trust to any person, nor shall she be required to have said securities registered or recorded in her name as trustee, nor shall she be forbidden to mingle said securities or the income therefrom with her own funds. . . ."

The stocks, bonds and bank deposits to which the trust agreements related were in the main the same as those which the decree ordered Gladys M. Donaghy to transfer to the executors.[25]

25.   But in addition to the stocks specified in the trust agreements, Gladys M. Donaghy held certificates for three hundred fifty shares of the stock of Beacon Manufacturing Company, one hundred fifty of them in her name, one hundred fifty of them in the name of Harold E. Kerwin, indorsed by him in blank, and fifty of them in the name of Ernest W. Kerwin, indorsed

The property covered by the two trust agreements comprised substantially all the property that William J. Kerwin had, except a comparatively small amount that he transferred to Lillian A. Kerwin in 1940 and 1941, and that forms the subject matter of the companion case which is hereinafter dealt with. Late in 1940 he was disturbed about the condition of his affairs, and was trying to reach Gladys for the purpose of arranging his affairs so that what he considered his property would form part of his estate if he should die, to the end that his wife and all his children would be protected. Gladys apparently avoided any considerable talk with him. He was in bad health, and entirely dependent on Gladys for money. On October 9, 1940, he got Gladys and Harold together, and asked them whether they would do the "right thing" by his wife. When they said they would, he fell on his knees and said "Thank God for that." He apparently rested content with that vague assurance, and did not then remember or appreciate the fact that under the trust agreements he had reserved a power of revocation of the trusts. Not unlikely he was then too ill to take decisive action, and still trusted Gladys, although he was beginning to doubt her. When he died there was little if anything remaining in his hands.

The judge had the task of discovering the truth in the tangled web of deceit that had been woven about the ownership of the property. As to the basic facts dependent upon the credibility of the witnesses, his findings are entitled to great weight, and we see no reason to disagree with them. But his inferences of fact from those basic facts, and his conclusions of law, are fully open to review by this court. Malone v. Walsh, 315 Mass. 484, 490, 53 N.E.2d 126; New England Trust Co. v. Commissioner of Corporations & Taxation, 315 Mass. 639, 644, 53 N.E.2d 1001; Swinford v. Welch, 316 Mass. 112, 117, 54 N.E.2d 932; MacLennan v. MacLennan, 316 Mass. 593, 595, 55 N.E.2d 928; Cooperstein v. Bogas, 317 Mass. 341, 58 N.E.2d 131; Jurewicz v. Jurewicz, 317 Mass.—, 58 N.E.2d 832.

Those inferences and conclusions are as follows:

> Said securities and bank accounts were at no time given to Gladys by her father to have as her own property. Said pretended trust instruments were made as a result of a temporary disagreement between William J. Kerwin and his wife . . . they were never intended to be carried out according to their terms but constituted an illusive device to deprive the widow of any substantial interest in her husband's estate as his widow. It was not intended thereby to give the property all to Gladys upon her father's death, or to deprive his sons

---

by him in blank. She held also a certificate for eighty-seven shares of the probably worthless stock of Dexdale Hosiery Mills in the name of Harold E. Kerwin but indorsed by him in blank. She testified that she held the Beacon stock on the terms stated in the trust agreements, but that she intended to turn over to Harold and Ernest the shares standing in their names. The judge found that there was no understanding that these stocks should belong to Gladys, subject to a life interest in her father, to the exclusion of the widow and the other children. Accordingly the final decree included these stocks in the property which Gladys was ordered to transfer to the executors.

of any share therein as heirs or legatees of William J. Kerwin. Said trusts are collusive and invalid and the securities and bank accounts . . . are the property of the estate of William J. Kerwin.

The main question before us is whether these inferences of fact and conclusions of law are correct.

Up to the time of the execution of the trust agreements, it could have been shown by oral evidence that there had been no beneficial gift of the property to Gladys because of the absence of a deed, or of proof of donative intent coupled with delivery (Rock v. Rock, 309 Mass. 44, 47, 33 N.E.2d 973; Reardon v. Whalen, 306 Mass. 579, 29 N.E.2d 23; Murphy v. Smith, 291 Mass. 93, 195 N.E. 912; Bedirian v. Zorian, 287 Mass. 191, 195, 191 N.E. 448), or because of proof that she took title to the property upon an oral trust in favor of her father and his estate. Rock v. Rock, 309 Mass. 44, 47, 33 N.E.2d 973; Russell v. Meyers, 316 Mass. 669, 672, 56 N.E.2d 604. And even after the trust agreements were executed a third person not a party to them nor claiming under them, whose rights might be affected by them — for example, the Federal taxing authorities — could show by extrinsic evidence that they were false and illusory and did not express the real transaction between Gladys and her father. Kellogg v. Tompson, 142 Mass. 76, 6 N.E. 860; Guaranty Security Corp. v. Eastern Steamship Co., 241 Mass. 120, 123, 134 N.E. 364; Tripp v. National Shawmut Bank, 263 Mass. 505, 511, 161 N.E. 904; Commonwealth v. Weinfield's Inc., 305 Mass. 108, 25 N.E.2d 198; Lamson & Co., Inc., v. Abrams, 305 Mass. 238, 243, 244, 25 N.E.2d 374; Wanders' Case, 308 Mass. 157, 31 N.E.2d 530; Commonwealth v. Hayes, 311 Mass. 21, 28, 40 N.E.2d 27; Williston, Contracts (Rev. ed. 1936) §647; Rice v. Cunningham, 116 Mass. 466, 469.

But in this case Lillian A. Kerwin and Ernest W. Kerwin claim under William J. Kerwin. They stand in his shoes. If title passed to Gladys as against William J. Kerwin, it passed to her as against his legatees. When the trust agreements were executed, the property to which they related was already in the possession of Gladys, and most if not all of it stood in her name. Those agreements contemplated the holding by her of the legal title. Under those circumstances no formal delivery of the property itself was necessary to vest the legal title in her. Creeden v. Mahoney, 193 Mass. 402, 79 N.E. 776; Blackwell v. Blackwell, 196 Mass. 186, 189, 81 N.E. 910, 12 Ann. Cas. 1070; Sullivan v. Hudgins, 303 Mass. 442, 447, 22 N.E.2d 43; 24 Am. Jur., Gifts, §26.

The trust agreements furnish incontrovertible internal evidence that they were intended to express the whole transaction between Gladys and her father. He covenanted, agreed and declared under seal that he had no right, power or interest in the trust property except such as was set forth in the trust agreements. The beneficial interest was completely disposed of by giving him an equitable life estate and Gladys the remainder "to her own use and behoof absolutely forever." His apparent purpose to render a will practically unnecessary, and his reserved power to alter, amend or revoke the trust, did not make the trust testamentary in its nature. National Shawmut Bank v. Joy, 315 Mass. 457, 469, 475, 477, 478, 53 N.E.2d 113. The reserved power could be exercised only according to its terms and since there was never even an attempt to exercise it there was no impairment of the rights in remainder given to Gladys. Kelley v. Snow, 185 Mass. 288, 298, 70 N.E. 89; Coates v. Lunt, 210 Mass. 314, 96 N.E. 685; Clune v. Norton, 306 Mass. 324, 28 N.E.2d 229; National Shawmut Bank v. Joy, 315 Mass. 457, 462, 474, 475, 53 N.E.2d 113. There was no mistake in drafting the trust agreements. Plainly they conformed to the purpose of William J. Kerwin at the time, that of disinheriting his wife. He could hardly have been so obtuse as to fail to see that they disinherited his sons also in plain words.

As matter of law the trust instruments must be taken as intended to accomplish the very purpose of the so called "parol evidence rule," that of fixing beyond all question the rights of the parties to those agreements in accordance with their terms, and to preclude resort to extrinsic evidence apart from exceptional and strictly limited instances of need that are not applicable to this case.[26] As to trusts, a learned author has said:

> Under the parol evidence rule, if the manifestation of intention of the settlor is integrated in a writing, that is, if a written instrument is adopted by him as the complete expression of his intention, extrinsic evidence, in the absence of fraud, duress, mistake or other ground for reformation or rescission, is not admissible to contradict or vary it. [Scott, Trusts (1939) §§38, 164.1.]

That statement finds support in our decisions. Moore v. Stinson, 144 Mass. 594, 597, 12 N.E. 410; Crawford v. Nies, 224 Mass. 474, 484, 485, 113 N.E. 408; Coolidge v. Loring, 235 Mass. 220, 126 N.E. 276; Gorey v. Guarente, 303 Mass. 569, 573, 574, 22 N.E.2d 99; O'Brien v. Holden, 104 Vt. 338, 345, 346, 160 A. 192. Though often stated in terms of the admissibility of evidence, the so called "parol evidence rule" is really a rule of substantive law. Extrinsic evidence, even though admitted, cannot control the words of a document that purports to express the whole transaction.[27] O'Malley v.

26.   Glackin v. Bennett, 226 Mass. 316, 115 N.E. 490; Boston Consolidated Gas Co. v. Folsom, 237 Mass. 565, 567, 130 N.E. 197; Kilroy v. Schimmel, 243 Mass. 262, 267, 137 N.E. 366; Snider v. Deban, 249 Mass. 59, 61, 144 N.E. 69; Ernest F. Carlson Co. v. Fred T. Ley & Co., Inc., 269 Mass. 272, 276, 277, 168 N.E. 812; Whitty Manuf. Co., Inc., v. Clark, 278 Mass. 370, 374, 180 N.E. 315; Hirsch v. Fisher, 278 Mass. 492, 495, 180 N.E. 230; Kennedy Bros., Inc., v. Bird, 287 Mass. 477, 482, 192 N.E. 73; Graustein v. H. P. Hood & Sons, Inc., 293 Mass. 207, 216, 200 N.E. 14; Bellows v. Worcester Storage Co., 297 Mass. 188, 189, 190, 7 N.E.2d 588; Norfolk County Trust Co. v. Green, 304 Mass. 406, 24 N.E.2d 12; Bates v. Southgate, 308 Mass. 170, 172, 31 N.E.2d 551, 133 A.L.R. 1349; State Street Trust Co. v. Hall, 311 Mass. 299, 306, 41 N.E.2d 30; Wigmore, Evid. (3d Ed. 1940) §2425.

27.   "It is not surprising that confusion results from a rule called 'the parol evidence rule' which is not a rule of evidence [and] which relates to extrinsic proof whether written or parol." Zell v. American Seating Co., 2 Cir., 138 F.2d 641, 643. For the history of the rule, see Wigmore, Evid. (3d Ed. 1940) §2426.

Grady, 222 Mass. 202, 204, 109 N.E. 829; Glackin v. Bennett, 226 Mass. 316, 320, 115 N.E. 490; Pelonsky v. Wattendorf, 255 Mass. 558, 562, 152 N.E. 337; Paulink v. American Express Co., 265 Mass. 182, 185, 163 N.E. 740, 62 A.L.R. 506; Kidder v. Greenman, 283 Mass. 601, 609, 187 N.E. 42, 88 A.L.R. 1370; Kesslen Shoe Co., Inc., v. Philadelphia Fire & Marine Ins. Co., 295 Mass. 123, 129, 3 N.E.2d 257; Higgs v. De Maziroff, 263 N.Y. 473, 189 N.E. 555, 92 A.L.R. 807.

It is true that a written contract or other instrument may be invalidated by extrinsic proof that it was executed as a joke or even in some instances as a pretence, with no intention on the part of either party that it should create any legal right or obligation.[28] Williston, Contracts (Rev. ed. 1936) §21; Beaman-Marvell Co. v. Gunn, 306 Mass. 419, 422, 423, 28 N.E.2d 443; Zell v. American Seating Co., 2 Cir., 138 F.2d 641, 644.[29]

We need not decide whether that rule can be extended to sealed instruments, in view of the common law theory that the obligor in such an instrument is conclusively bound by its terms. Williston, Contracts (Rev. ed. 1936) §205; Goode v. Riley, 153 Mass. 585, 587, 28 N.E. 228; Mahoney v. Emergency Fleet Corp., 253 Mass. 234, 148 N.E. 454. "Where a seal [is] not required for the validity of a contract [it] has been treated as surplusage in order to carry out the expressed intention of the parties through resort to the rules applicable to simple contracts." Johnson-Foster Co. v. D'Amore Construction Co., 314 Mass. 416, 421, 50 N.E.2d 89, 92, 148 A.L.R. 353. The reason why we need not decide that question is that in our opinion an inference of fact could not properly be drawn that the trust agreements were intended merely as shams. The evident purpose at the time was to disinherit the wife. The husband was careful to reserve the right to revoke the trusts, and revest the trust property in himself. The correct conclusion, we think, is that the trust agreements express the actual intention of the parties at the time.

---

28. It has also been held that a written contract, though duly executed and delivered to the obligee, may be shown by oral evidence not to have become effective because of the nonperformance of some condition precedent orally attached to its taking effect. Wilson v. Powers, 131 Mass. 539; Marr v. Washburn & Moen Manuf. Co., 167 Mass. 35, 38, 44 N.E. 1062; Elastic Tip Co. v. Graham, 185 Mass. 597, 600, 601, 71 N.E. 117; Hill v. Hall, 191 Mass. 253, 265, 77 N.E. 831; Diebold Safe & Lock Co. v. Morse, 226 Mass. 342, 344, 115 N.E. 431; Levene v. Crowell, 243 Mass. 441, 138 N.E. 9; Hallett v. Moore, 282 Mass. 380, 395, 185 N.E. 474, 91 A.L.R. 572; Exchange Realty Co. v. Bines, 302 Mass. 93, 95, 96, 18 N.E.2d 425. Apart possibly from deeds of conveyance (Ward v. Lewis, 4 Pick, 518; Browning v. Haskell, 22 Pick, 310, 312; Hubby v. Hubby, 5 Cush. 516, 519, 52 Am. Dec. 742; Buszozak v. Wolo, 125 Misc. 546, 211 N.Y.S. 557; Reed v. Reed, 117 Me. 281, 104 A. 227), it has been held in other jurisdictions that the same rule applies to sealed instruments. Blewitt v. Boorum, 142 N.Y. 357, 37 N.E. 119, 40 Am. St. Rep. 600; Whitaker v. Lane, 128 Va. 317, 104 S.E. 252, 11 A.L.R. 1157. In Diebold Safe & Lock Co. v. Morse, 226 Mass. 342, 344, 115 N.E. 431, the original papers show that the lease was under seal. See also Daley v. Carney, 117 Mass. 288; Bromley v. Mitchell, 155 Mass. 509, 511, 512, 30 N.E. 83; Crowley v. Holdsworth, 264 Mass. 303, 309, 162 N.E. 334; Williston, Contracts (Rev. ed. 1936) §§210, 212.

29. The Zell case was reversed in 322 U.S. 709, 64 S. Ct. 1053, by a divided court, two justices voting to affirm, four justices holding that recovery by the plaintiff upon the oral addition to the written contract was precluded by the parol evidence rule, and three justices holding the oral addition contrary to public policy.

Even if, notwithstanding the terms of the trust agreements, the remainder passing to Gladys under those agreements might be subjected to a trust in favor of her brothers and Lillian A. Kerwin by proof of an oral promise by Gladys to share the remainder with them (Ham v. Twombly, 181 Mass. 170, 172, 173, 63 N.E. 336; Beals v. Villard, 268 Mass. 129, 132, 133, 167 N.E. 264; compare Scott, Trusts [1939] §38), the difficulty in this case would be that there is little evidence of such an oral promise. The trust agreements themselves, and all that was said when they were drawn and executed, negative any promise that would benefit Lillian A. Kerwin, for the plain purpose was to disinherit her. Neither was there anything said or done at that time to show a promise to hold for the other children. If there had been such a promise, it would not support the present petition which is brought for the benefit of the estate generally. The only conduct of Gladys that might be thought to recognize the claim of Lillian A. Kerwin was her promise, jointly with Harold who had no property in his hands, made on October 9, 1940, when their father was in his last illness and mentally disturbed, to "do the right thing" by Lillian. Such a promise by Harold could hardly have reference to a money settlement out of property of his father in his hands, for there was no such property. The promise by Gladys was in identical words. We cannot find that such a vague promise amounted to an understanding to hold for the distributees of the father's estate the remainder given to Gladys by the trust agreements.

At various times after the trust agreements were executed William J. Kerwin made statements indicating that he considered that all the stocks, bonds and bank deposits held by Gladys were really his and would form part of his estate. For example, in 1934 and again in 1938 Ernest told his father that he thought it was unfair to put only fifty shares of the Beacon stock into his name while Gladys and Harold held one hundred fifty shares each. His father denied any unfairness, saying that the stock was all his, and "if anything happened to him we were all to be treated alike." He said that the way the stock was held "didn't mean a thing." In 1940, when William J. Kerwin and his wife opened his safe deposit box and found in it only twenty-five shares of Beacon stock, he told his wife that everything else he owned was in the safe deposit box which was in the name of Gladys, and about the same time he gave his wife a memorandum of securities of the value of about $64,000 that he said he owned. Those securities must have been among those held by Gladys, for he himself held no such amount. Besides, there is his act on November 28, 1936, of ratifying and confirming his will after the bulk of his property had been covered by the trust agreements. A simple explanation of most of this testimony is that Kerwin knew that he had reserved the power to alter, amend or revoke the trust agreements, and concluded that that reserved power left him substantially the master of the trust property. Very likely he intended sooner or later to make an equitable division of it among his wife and children. But we cannot infer from this testimony any promise on the part of Gladys.

The judge found that the trust agreements "constituted an illusive device to deprive the wife of any substantial interest in her husband's estate as his widow." It has been shown already that that "device" was not "illusory," but was one that fixed the rights of the parties to those agreements. The judge found further that William J. Kerwin, if the trust agreements were intended to be effective, "intended to cheat his wife." He could not "cheat" her in any legal sense by means of those agreements unless she had rights that were paramount to his right to do what he pleased in his lifetime with his own personal property.

The right of a wife to waive her husband's will, and take, with certain limitations, "the same portion of the property of the deceased, real and personal, that . . . she would have taken if the deceased had died intestate" G.L. (Ter. Ed.) c. 191, §15, does not extend to personal property that has been conveyed by the husband in his lifetime and does not form part of his estate at his death. Fiske v. Fiske, 173 Mass. 413, 419, 53 N.E. 916; Shelton v. Sears, 187 Mass. 455, 73 N.E. 666. In this Commonwealth a husband has an absolute right to dispose of any or all of his personal property in his lifetime, without the knowledge or consent of his wife, with the result that it will not form part of his estate for her to share under the statute of distributions, G.L. (Ter. Ed.) c. 190, §§1, 2, under his will, or by virtue of a waiver of his will. That is true even though his sole purpose was to disinherit her. Leonard v. Leonard, 181 Mass. 458, 63 N.E. 1068, 92 Am. St. Rep. 426; Kelley v. Snow, 185 Mass. 288, 299, 70 N.E. 89; Redman v. Churchill, 230 Mass. 415, 418, 119 N.E. 953; Roche v. Brickley, 254 Mass. 584, 588, 150 N.E. 866; Malone v. Walsh, 315 Mass. 484, 490, 491, 53 N.E.2d 126; Beirne v. Continental-Equitable Title & Trust Co., 307 Pa. 570, 161 A. 721; Rynier's Estate, 347 Pa. 471, 32 A.2d 736; Scott, Trusts (1939) §57.5; 26 Am. Jur., Husband & Wife, §198. So far as it may conflict with the foregoing decisions, the case of Brownell v. Briggs, 173 Mass. 529, 54 N.E. 251, is no longer controlling. The right of a wife as distributee stands no higher than the similar right of a child. Chase v. Redding, 13 Gray 418, 422; Marshall v. Berry, 13 Allen 43, 47; Rolfe v. Clarke, 224 Mass. 407, 113 N.E. 182; Harding v. Bailey, 306 Mass. 108, 27 N.E.2d 687.

The limitation found in some of our cases upon the right of a husband to disinherit his wife by a conveyance or gift of personal property inter vivos, that the conveyance or gift must not be "colorable" (Kelley v. Snow, 185 Mass. 288, 299, 70 N.E. 89; Roche v. Brickley, 254 Mass. 584, 588, 150 N.E. 866), means merely that the conveyance or gift must be one legally binding on the settlor or donor, accomplished in his lifetime, and not testamentary in its effect. In other words, it must be an actual conveyance or gift. Potter Title & Trust Co. v. Braum, 294 Pa. 482, 144 A. 401, 64 A.L.R. 463. In Newman v. Dore, 275 N.Y. 371, 9 N.E.2d 966, 112 A.L.R. 643, complete control of the trustee, reserved to the settlor, was held to make testamentary and invalid a settlement designed to disinherit his wife. See also Krause v. Krause, 285 N.Y. 27, 32 N.E.2d 779; Brown v. Crafts, 98 Me. 40, 45, 56 A. 213. The soundness of that ground was recently left open by us in National

Shawmut Bank v. Joy, 315 Mass. 457, 476, 53 N.E.2d 113. In the present case no such control was reserved.

Cases are not in point that hold invalid a conveyance by a husband to defeat a possible decree for the support of his wife. Shepherd v. Shepherd, 196 Mass. 179, 81 N.E. 897; Doane v. Doane, 238 Mass. 106, 112, 130 N.E. 484; Caines v. Sawyer, 248 Mass. 368, 374, 143 N.E. 326; 26 Am. Jur., Husband & Wife, §197. Neither are cases holding invalid a gift made by a husband for the purpose of reducing the share of his estate to which his wife is entitled under an antenuptial contract. Eaton v. Eaton, 233 Mass. 351, 369, et seq., 124 N.E. 37, 5 A.L.R. 1426. Nor are cases in which a woman married a man of supposed means in ignorance of the fact that on the eve of marriage he had conveyed away all his property for the purpose of defeating her expectations. Gedart v. Ejdrygiewicz, 305 Mass. 224, 25 N.E.2d 371; LeStrange v. LeStrange, 242 App. Div. 74, 273 N.Y.S. 21; Collins v. Collins, 98 Md. 473, 57 A. 597, 103 Am. St. Rep. 408, 1 Ann. Cas. 856; Kirk v. Kirk, 340 Pa. 203, 16 A.2d 47; Hanson v. McCarthy, 152 Wis. 131, 139 N.W. 720; 26 Am. Jur., Husband & Wife, §§185-195.

The judge was right in ordering, upon the petition brought by Lillian A. Kerwin, a conveyance to the executors of the Beacon and Dexdale stocks. Even if the actually innocent wife could be affected by the fraudulent purpose of her late husband in holding these stocks in the name of his daughter Gladys, the wife has made out her case without reliance upon any fraud. Harvey v. Varney, 98 Mass. 118; Stillings v. Turner, 153 Mass. 534, 27 N.E. 671; Lufkin v. Jakeman, 188 Mass. 528, 74 N.E. 933; Murphy v. Moore, 228 Mass. 565, 568, 117 N.E. 918; O'Gasapian v. Danielson, 284 Mass. 27, 34, 187 N.E. 107, 89 A.L.R. 1159; Paula v. Soares, 304 Mass. 450, 23 N.E.2d 1006; Zak v. Zak, 305 Mass. 194, 25 N.E.2d 169; Levy v. Levy, 309 Mass. 486, 491, 35 N.E.2d 659; Braga v. Braga, 314 Mass. 666, 673, 51 N.E.2d 429.

But the other findings and orders contained in the final decree upon that petition are to be stricken out. As so modified that decree is affirmed. There was no error in the final decree dismissing the petition brought by Gladys M. Donaghy and others, executors. Discussion of that petition is unnecessary. The final decree dismissing it is affirmed.

So ordered.[30]

30. The Massachusetts Supreme Judicial Court, in Sullivan v. Burkin, 390 Mass. 864, —N.E.2d—(1984), stated as follows:

For the future, however, as to any inter vivos trust created or amended after the date of this opinion, we announce that the estate of a decedent, for the purpose of G.L. c. 191, §15, shall include the value of assets held in an inter vivos trust created by the deceased spouse as to which the deceased spouse alone retained the power during his or her life to direct the disposition of those trust assets for his or her benefit, as, for example, by the exercise of a power of appointment or by revocation of the trust. [390 Mass. at 867, —N.E.2d at—.]

New York, by statute, has taken a position quite different from that taken in Massachusetts in Kerwin v. Donaghy. New York Estates, Powers and Trusts Law §5-1.1 provides that the

Community property. Eight states—Arizona, California, Idaho, Louisiana, Nevada, New Mexico, Texas, and Washington—borrowed from the Civil Law of Spain and France the system of community property in delimiting rights as between husband and wife. With the enactment of income tax laws and the adoption of a steeply graduated surtax, it became clear that the rules of community property—which, among other things, causes one-half of a spouse's earnings to be the spouse's income and the other half to be the non-earning spouse's income—had enormous tax advantages. These tax advantages were eliminated by the split-income provisions of the Revenue Act of 1948 (see Chapter 37) so that now husbands and wives in non-community-property states are given approximately the same tax advantages as were available formerly to husbands and wives only in community-property states. Prior to the action taken by the Federal government under the Revenue Act of 1948, various states under-

---

following transactions, whether benefiting the surviving spouse or any other person, shall be treated as testamentary provisions, and the capital value thereof, as of the date of the deceased spouse's death, shall be included in the net estate in working out the surviving spouse's right of election:

    a.   gifts causa mortis;
    b.   savings accounts in the name of deceased spouse in trust for another;
    c.   joint bank accounts in the name of deceased spouse and another, with right of survivorship;
    d.   joint tenancy, or tenancy by the entirety, in the name of deceased spouse and another;
    e.   transfers with power to revoke or to invade retained by deceased spouse alone or in conjunction with another.

The Uniform Probate Code §2-202 has adopted the statutory approach of New York in regard to the rights of an electing surviving spouse to reach assets in a revocable inter vivos trust created by the deceased spouse.

The Restatement (Second) of Property (Donative Transfers) considers the position taken in Kerwin v. Donaghy in §13.7. The Reporter's Note to that section collects the cases that support the position taken in the *Kerwin* case and the cases that reach an opposite result. The Reporter's Statutory Note to §13.7 lists the various statutes which have been enacted to deal with the problem.

Massachusetts and some other states have enacted statutes providing for an equitable division of property on divorce. The Massachusetts statute, Mass. Gen. Laws Ch. 208, §34, provides as follows:

> Upon divorce or upon a complaint in an action brought at any time after a divorce, whether such a divorce has been adjudged in this commonwealth or another jurisdiction, the court of the commonwealth, provided there is personal jurisdiction over both parties, may make a judgment for either of the parties to pay alimony to the other. In addition to or in lieu of a judgment to pay alimony, the court may assign to either husband or wife all or any part of the estate of the other. In determining the amount of alimony, if any, to be paid, or in fixing the nature and value of the property, if any, to be so assigned, the court, after hearing the witnesses, if any, of each party, shall consider the length of the marriage, the conduct of the parties during the marriage, the age, health, station, occupation, amount and sources of income, vocational skills, employability, estate, liabilities and needs of each of the parties and the opportunity of each for future acquisition of capital assets and income. The court may also consider the contribution of each of the parties in the acquisition, preservation or appreciation in value of their respective estates and the contribution of each of the parties as a homemaker to the family unit. [Amended by 1982, 642, §1, approved January 4, 1983, effective 90 days thereafter.]

—Eds.

took to obtain this tax advantage for their citizens by changing from a common-law system of property rights to the community-property system. The shift had been made by Hawaii, Michigan, Nebraska, Oklahoma, Oregon, and Pennsylvania, by the time the Revenue Act of 1948 was passed. However, in 1947 Pennsylvania's shift was nullified by a decision of the Supreme Court of Pennsylvania holding the statute unconstitutional.[31] The case evoked some talk at the bar about "strong arm decisions" and "courts making themselves third houses of the legislature." But the prescience of the Pennsylvania court is attested by the fact that the Revenue Act of 1948 was passed, and, as a consequence, Hawaii, Michigan, Nebraska, Oklahoma, and Oregon all repealed — legislatively — their community-property laws.

Problem

13.19. The Michigan legislature passed a community-property law; later the legislature repealed it. The Pennsylvania legislature passed a community-property law; later the Pennsylvania Supreme Court declared the law unconstitutional. What different legal consequences flow from these two methods of eliminating community-property laws?

In describing briefly the functioning of community property it must first and foremost be pointed out that the entire system is statutory and that between the states there are variations, more or less substantial, in nearly all the particulars hereafter dealt with. Subject to this caveat the following represents the basic structure of the community-property system:
1. What is community property?
   Property acquired through the earnings of either spouse during marriage. Also income from community property, and property acquired as a result of the sale of community property.
2. What is separate property?
   Property owned by either spouse before marriage belongs to him or her separately. Also property acquired by gift, inheritance, or devise after marriage. Also the income from separate property (except in Idaho, Louisiana, and Texas where, with some exceptions, it is community property). But it is a characteristic of the system that all property is presumed to be community property until shown to be separate.

---

31. Willcox v. Penn Mutual Life Insurance Co., 357 Pa. 581, 55 A.2d 521 (1947). It was held that so far as the statute caused future income of a spouse from property owned by that spouse at the date of the statute to belong in part to the other spouse, it deprived the former of property without due process of law. But it was also held that the statute was so "vague, indefinite, uncertain . . . incomplete, conflicting and inconsistent in its provisions" as to be "incapable either of rational interpretation or of judicial enforcement" and consequently was "inoperative and void." These are right harsh words. Many law reviews commented, e.g., 9 U. Pitt. L. Rev. 105 (1947), 23 N.Y.U.L.Q. Rev. 346 (1948), and 46 Mich. L. Rev. 422 (1948).

Problems

13.20. H, prior to his marriage to W, owned all the stock in the X Corporation. He gets a salary from the corporation and dividends on the corporate stock. The dividends as well as the money used to pay his salary are the result of his energy and skill in managing the corporation. After H's marriage, the stock in the corporation will be separate property and his salary will be community property. What about the dividends on his stock? See Van Camp v. Van Camp, 53 Cal. App. 17, 199 P. 885 (1921).

13.21. W, prior to her marriage to H, was the sole proprietor of a business. Her investment in fixtures and inventory in the business at the time she married H was $40,000. After her marriage, will W be entitled to treat that portion of the net profits as separate property that is equivalent to the interest rate on a $40,000 investment? See Pereira v. Pereira, 156 Cal. 1, 103 P. 488 (1909).

3. Who controls community property during the joint lives of the spouses?
   In the early law the husband had full power to manage and dispose of community assets — a situation not unlike the early common law — but statutes now give the wife substantial rights. For example, in most states a deed or mortgage of community property is not binding on the wife unless she joins in it.

4. What happens to community property on the death of one spouse?
   By will either spouse can devise his or her half of community property but no more. On intestacy the local statute must be consulted as to the disposition of the deceased spouse's share of the community property.

5. What happens to community property upon a divorce?
   The community property is divided equally. Beyond this the court may make adequate provision for the spouse who is seeking the divorce.

6. What is the status of separate property?
   Either spouse has full power to convey his or her separate property. Either spouse also has the right to devise the same, subject to the right of the other spouse (if given by statute) to waive the will and take a statutory forced share. Upon intestacy, the local statute must be consulted as to division of separate property.

7. Does the community property that is moveable (such as stocks and bonds) remain community property when the spouses move from a community-property state to a non-community-property state? To the extent the answer to this question is yes, one practicing in a

non-community-property state must be familiar with the community-property system.

In leaving this subject we wish to warn you that this is an extremely complicated matter and that the foregoing does nothing more than sketch major outlines for your general information. The subject is thoroughly developed in the current literature.[32]

Note: Uniform Marital Property Act

A Uniform Marital Property Act (UMPA), developed by the National Conference of Commissioners on Uniform State Laws, has been completed and recommended for adoption in the various states. The UMPA is designed to move husband and wife ownership of property in the direction of the result that obtains in community property states. An announcement by ULC dated July 28, 1983, contains the following statement: "UMPA's theme is 'sharing'; the Uniform Act recognizes each spouse has a vested ownership right in all property acquired by the personal efforts of either. The drafting committee believes this 50-50 relationship during marriage would lessen the trauma at divorce or death."

The Uniform Law Commissioners also have developed a Uniform Premarital Agreements Act (UPAA) which enables couples to "opt out" of UMPA's property division provisions and to handle other pre-marital contract problems.

Note: Cohabitation Without Marriage — Property Rights Acquired

Cohabitation without marriage exists on an increasing scale. The cohabitation may result in the accumulation of property in a manner quite similar to the way in which married couples accumulate wealth. When one cohabitant dies, should there be a recognition of property rights in the survivor that would be similar to the rights of a surviving spouse? If so, on what basis?

A leading case considering the respective property rights in property acquired during the cohabiting period when the cohabitation ends before either one has died is Marvin v. Marvin, 18 Cal. 3d 660, 557 P.2d 106, 134 Cal. Rptr. 815 (1976). The court in this case stated as follows:

---

32. If you are interested in a particular community-property state, you should check the literature to ascertain the most recent consideration of the subject in that state. For a general review of community property, see American Law of Property, §§7.1-7.36 (Casner ed. 1952).

We conclude: (1) The provisions of the Family Law Act do not govern the distribution of property acquired during a nonmarital relationship; such a relationship remains solely subject to judicial decision. (2) The courts should enforce express contracts between nonmarital partners except to the extent that the contract is explicitly founded on the consideration of meretricious sexual services. (3) In the absence of an express contract, the courts should inquire into the conduct of the parties to determine whether that conduct demonstrates an implied contract, agreement of partnership or joint venture, or some other tacit understanding between the parties. The courts may also employ the doctrine of quantum meruit or equitable remedies such as constructive or resulting trusts, when warranted by the facts of the case. [18 Cal. 3d at 665, 557. P.2d at 106, 134 Cal. Rptr. at 819.]

In considering the acquisition of property rights when there is cohabitation without marriage, keep in mind the situation of a person who has cohabited with a member of the opposite sex to whom the person is not married in the honest but erroneous belief that a marriage exists between them. Such person is referred to as a putative spouse. It should be easier in such case to find an implied agreement as to property rights and such agreement should not be found to rest on the consideration of meretricious sexual services.

If a divorced spouse is receiving alimony from a former spouse which alimony will end on remarriage, there is an inducement not to remarry but rather to cohabit without marriage and to continue enjoying the alimony payments of the former spouse. Allgood v. Allgood, 626 P.2d 1323 (Okla. 1981), considered the request of the former spouse who was paying the alimony to be relieved of that obligation when the alimony recipient cohabited without marriage with another. If the continuation of alimony is required until death or remarriage, the Oklahoma court recognized that cohabitation without marriage cannot affect the obligation to continue the alimony payments. If the alimony obligation is reviewable from time to time to determine whether the recipient's situation has changed so that it is not needed to the same extent for support, the fact that the recipient is cohabiting with another may be relevant in determining whether the payments are necessary to provide the support.

If O in O's will devises the family residence to O's spouse for life as long as the spouse remains unmarried, the spouse's interest will terminate if the spouse remarries. The spouse realizes that the interest in the residence will be lost on remarriage but cohabits with another on a permanent basis in the house without marriage. The remainderman seeks to have the spouse's estate terminated on the basis that the spouse's cohabitation is the equivalent of no longer remaining unmarried. What result would you expect a court to reach? Try to draft a provision that you might insert in O's will to cause the spouse's interest in the devised property to terminate if the spouse cohabited with another without remarriage.

Note: Wife's (or Husband's) Investment in Spouse's Career

It is not uncommon for wives or husbands to work and to provide the funds that enable their spouses to complete an education that will be the basis of a long-term income-earning power. The wife who works as a secretary to earn the funds needed to enable her husband to acquire a legal education and the husband who provides the funds for his wife to go through medical school are but two examples of this situation.

What happens? The spouse completes his or her education with the funds provided by the working spouse, and then finds someone else more attractive. Under these circumstances, does the working and now discarded spouse have a property interest in the educated spouse's career? If the answer to this question is yes, how is this property interest to be valued? For a discussion of these questions, see Sullivan v. Sullivan, 134 Cal. App. 3d 484, 184 Cal. Rptr. 796 (1982). See also the article by Georgia Dullea entitled Setting a Diploma's Value in Divorce in N.Y. Times, Nov. 21, 1982, at 72, col. 2.

SECTION 5. THE TERM OF YEARS

The term of years began life in disreputable company. It was the device commonly used by moneylenders to evade the Church's prohibition of usury. L, a landowner in need of money, would sell a term of years to T upon a lump-sum consideration; the length of the term was so determined that the rents and profits would pay back to T not only the lump sum but also a handsome profit. In a word, the term of years was used and thought of as an instrument of extortion, and it thereby became the victim of hostile discrimination by the courts. The consequences of this discrimination still persist, though they have long since ceased to be undesirable.

Thus when a conveyance is made "to T for 5 years," T has an interest which is not real estate at all but a "chattel real." Upon T's death it passes to T's executor or administrator as personal property rather than to T's heir as real property. T has a less-than-freehold interest. T has possession during the term; but T does not have seisin, which is reserved for freehold estates. Under the old common-law procedure the termor did not have the benefit of the real actions (writ of right, writ of entry, novel disseisin, mort d'ancestor, etc.), a circumstance which was a serious handicap in the twelfth century but which was remedied by the creation of the action of ejectment. These slights which the law heaped upon the term soon turned out to be substantial benefits, and we soon discover that a strange situation has come to pass:

freeholders, impatient with the rigid and cumbersome technicalities of the feudal substantive law and procedure, are seeking to place themselves in the position of termors — for example, by alleging a fictitious lease for the purpose of asserting their rights by ejectment rather than in a real action.

An estate is a term of years if it must end at or before a fixed date. Thus the following are terms of years:

"To T for one day."

"To T for a thousand years."

Problem

13.22. L, owner of Blackacre in fee simple, conveys "to T for 100 years if T so long live."
  a. What estate does T have?
  b. Who has seisin of Blackacre?

There is one vitally important characteristic of the lease for years that must be kept in mind: It is a continuing relationship. The obligations of the parties during the term are fixed by the covenants of the lease, and the drafting of those covenants is a matter requiring very substantial skill, ingenuity, and foresight. Whereas a deed in fee simple transmits the grantor's whole title to the grantee and is mainly judged by the effectiveness with which it severs all connection of the grantor with the property, the instrument of lease undertakes to create in the lessor and lessee simultaneous interests which will prove beneficial to both for a considerable period during which all manner of things may happen — destruction of the property by fire, partial taking by eminent domain, bankruptcy of the lessee, accidents on the premises, and many others. Hence, although a deed in fee simple is characteristically a very short document, a lease of substantial property is normally a very long one. (The complexities of the law of landlord and tenant are dealt with in Part VI of this book.)

Observe that the lessee's covenants perform a double function: (1) they determine the obligations of the tenure by which the lessee holds of the lessor, and (2) they constitute promises by the lessee to the lessor.

SECTION 6.   PERIODIC TENANCIES

Where property is leased "to T from month to month," T holds for one month and for successive months thereafter until one party terminates the lease by an appropriate notice. The same holds true for leases for other periodic terms — e.g., from year to year, from week to week.

Most periodic tenancies, however, are created, not by an express lease, but by implication. The following are examples:

1. L leases to T without specification of the term of the lease. This creates a tenancy at will. Then T pays rent to L on a monthly basis. In most states this transforms the tenancy into one from month to month.[33]

2. L leases to T for one year. At the end of the year T holds over and sends L a check for the usual monthly rent. L cashes the check. In most states T is a tenant from year to year.[34]

To terminate a periodic tenancy the notice must be given with some precision. As to the length of the notice: (1) A tenancy from year to year requires one-half year's notice unless, as is sometimes the case, a shorter notice is permitted by statute; (2) a tenancy for any less period than from year to year requires notice equal to the length of the period — e.g., a tenancy from month to month can be terminated only by one month's notice. As to the time of termination: The notice must terminate the tenancy at the end of a period not in the middle of a period.

Problem

13.23. L leased to T on January 15, 1980, from month to month. On May 1, 1983, T wrote and mailed to L a letter as follows: "I hereby notify you that I elect to terminate my present tenancy one month from this date."

T moved out on June 1, 1983. L notified T that L proposed to hold T for the rent. T then consulted a friend who had once been to law school and as a result thereof, on June 15, 1983, T wrote and mailed to L another letter as follows:

Without prejudice to the former notice of termination given to you by my letter of May 1, 1983, but insisting on the effectiveness thereof, I hereby notify

33. See American Law of Property §§3.25, 3.31 (Casner ed. 1952). Massachusetts and Maine hold that the statute of frauds, providing that any lease not in writing creates an estate at will only, prevents this implication of periodic tenancies. Hence, in these states, T continues to be a tenant at will.

In most states the statute of frauds has an exception for leases for one year or less, i.e., it gives full effect to an oral lease for one year. Among those states which have no short-term exception in the statute, all but Massachusetts and Maine hold that periodic tenancies-by-implication do not fall within the statute and hence are valid although not in writing.

34. See American Law of Property §§3.22-3.26 (Casner ed. 1952). Of course, Massachusetts and Maine do not follow this rule for the reason stated in the preceding footnote.

As to tenants remaining in possession after the term is over, note the severe rule, applied in many states, that the landlord has the option to hold such a tenant for another full tenancy identical with the original one, whether or not the tenant wants to renew the tenancy. Thus if T, tenant for one year, holds over for a few days with no intention of continuing longer or of paying L any rent if T can help it, L can hold T for an entire further year. But see New York Real Property Law §232-c.

you that, if any tenancy shall exist at the present time, I elect to terminate the same on July 15, 1983.

L notified T that L intended to continue to hold T for the rent. On Oct. 1, 1983, L brings an action against T for rent accruing up to September 15. T retains you as counsel.

    a.   For how much rent is T liable?

    b.   What action, if any, should you take?

    Sanford v. Harvey, 65 Mass. (11 Cush.) 93 (1853); May v. Rice, 108 Mass. 150 (1871).[35]

SECTION 7.   TENANCIES AT WILL

If L leases to T with a provision that either may terminate the arrangement at will, this is a tenancy at will. So also is any other arrangement whereby T takes possession of L's land with L's permission, express or implied. The statute of frauds usually provides that "an estate or interest in land created without an instrument in writing signed by the grantor or by his attorney shall have the force and effect of an estate at will only," and this provision results in quite a number of tenancies at will.[36]

At common law an estate at will could be terminated at any time by either party without notice. However, statutes now commonly provide that notice equivalent to the period between rent payments is required to terminate a tenancy at will.[37] Upon nonpayment of rent special provisions for termination are ordinarily made.[38] The tenancy at will is automatically terminated if

---

35.   While we are being technical about dates, on what day does a lease end which describes the term as "for the term of three years from the first day of July, 1968?" Atkins v. Sleeper, 89 Mass. (7 Allen) 487 (1863).

36.   The statute here quoted is Mass. Gen. Laws ch. 183, §3. As noted in a previous footnote many states give full effect to oral leases for 1 year or less.

37.   E.g., Mass. Gen. Laws ch. 186, §12. It has been noted above that the Massachusetts Statute of Frauds has no exception for short-term leases and that the Massachusetts courts have ruled that, by reason of this, tenancies at will cannot be transformed into tenancies from month to month by implication from the payment of a monthly rent. It will be observed that G.L. ch. 186, §12, effectively cancels out this ruling of the Massachusetts courts. Thus, if L makes an oral lease to T for two years at $100 per month, which T starts paying:

    a.   In most states, the payment of rent at a monthly rate causes T to be a tenant from month to month. T can be evicted only upon the giving of one month's notice, maturing on a day of rent payment.

    b.   In Massachusetts, T remains a tenant at will, but by this statute T's tenancy can be terminated only by a procedure which is identical with that required in case of a tenancy from month to month. T, too, can be evicted only upon the giving of one month's notice, maturing on a day of rent payment.

38.   E.g., Mass. Gen. Laws ch. 186, §12, provides for 14 days' notice to quit for non-payment of rent; but if the tenant has not received a similar notice in the previous 12 months, T can retain the estate if T pays the rent within 5 days of receiving the notice.

either party dies or if the landlord conveys the landlord's interest, but statutes frequently provide that in this situation the tenant cannot be evicted for some stipulated period.[39]

Problems

13.24. In Massachusetts, L orally offers to lease Blackacre to T for one year at $100 per month. On July 1, 1983, T telephones to L that T will take the place for a year beginning immediately. L suggests a written lease, but T says it isn't necessary since they understand and trust each other. T occupies for a year and moves out on June 30, 1984. The premises remain vacant. L dies in October 1984. In December 1984, L's executor and devisee demands that T pay rent at $100 per month for the period July-December. Is T liable? Mass. Gen. Laws ch. 183, §3, is quoted above in the text; ch. 186, §12, provides:

> Estates at will may be determined by either party by three months' notice in writing for that purpose given to the other party; and, if the rent reserved is payable at periods of less than three months, the time of such notice shall be sufficient if it is equal to the interval between the days of payment. . . .

See Creech v. Crockett, 59 Mass. (5 Cush.) 133 (1849).[40]

13.25. O, the owner of Blackacre and Whiteacre in fee simple, makes the following conveyances:

a. Blackacre to A as long as A lives on the land.

b. Whiteacre to A as long as O wills.

What estate does A have in Blackacre? What estate does A have in Whiteacre?

13.26. The X Hotel is located in Massachusetts. T registers at the hotel and takes a single room, nothing being said about the duration of T's stay at the time of registering. The hotel renders a bill at the end of the first week which T pays. In the middle of the second week the hotel requests T to leave the next day stating that the room has been engaged for the following day and that, because of the arrival of a convention, no other rooms are available. T, finding it extremely inconvenient to leave, consults you. Advise T. See White v. Maynard, 111 Mass. 250 (1872); Roberts v. Casey, 36 Cal. App. 2d Supp. 767, 93 P.2d 654 (1939).

---

39. E.g., Mass. Gen. Laws ch. 186, §13, allows the tenant to remain for the period between rent payments. This section also provides that a tenancy at will of property occupied for dwelling purposes shall not be terminated by operation of law by the conveyance, transfer, or leasing of the premises by the owner or landlord thereof.

40. In Creech v. Crockett, you will find that the court uses the expression "tenant at sufferance." Such a tenant is one who entered under a lawful lease but has wrongfully stayed on after his lease has terminated. Further consideration is given to the tenant at sufferance in Part VI.

SECTION 8. INTERESTS THAT ARE LESS THAN ESTATES

As the last problem indicates, an owner may give rights in the owner's real estate to another person without creating an "estate"—even as slight an estate as a tenancy at will. These rights in land of another are cataloged here:

1. *Easement.* O, owner of Blackacre, grants to A, owner of Whiteacre a right of way over a specified portion of Blackacre for passage to and from Whiteacre. A has an easement over Blackacre appurtenant to Whiteacre. The right of way is the most common easement, but there are many others: an easement of flowage over Blackacre for surface waters needed on Whiteacre, a right to flood Blackacre by waters backed up by a dam on Whiteacre, a right to have the soil on Blackacre retained in such condition that it continues to support the soil or buildings on Whiteacre—in a word, a right to *use* Blackacre for specified purposes, as distinguished from a right to *possess* Blackacre.

2. *Profit à prendre*—usually called simply a *profit.* O, owner of Blackacre, grants to A a right to come on Blackacre and cut and remove timber. A has a profit in Blackacre—i.e., a right of severance which will result in his acquiring title to the severed thing. (The Restatement of Property (§450) defines the term "easement" so that it includes profits.)

3. *License.* This is a very broad term covering a multitude of permissive uses of land which, unless permitted, would be trespasses. Thus a guest who comes to your house to dinner is a licensee. So also is a shopper in a grocery store.

4. *Restrictive covenant.* Blackacre and Whiteacre are adjoining parcels. Their owners mutually covenant that these parcels will not be used for any non-residential purpose for twenty years. Such covenants limiting the use of land are essential features of most residential developments.[41]

Many arrangements concerning land do not fall clearly within any category. Frequently these arrangements are set up by the unlearned, in and out of the legal profession. The more peculiar and unspecific the arrangement, the more intricate the problems it creates.

Take the share cropper, for instance. The share cropper works land under an agreement with the owner by which the crops are to be divided. The arrangement may produce several types of legal relationships:

1. The cropper may be tenant of the owner.
2. The cropper may be the employee of the owner, having no estate in the land.
3. Whether or not the cropper has an estate in the land, the cropper and the owner may be tenants in common of the crop.

The rights of the parties may be substantially different in these various relationships.

---

41. Restrictive covenants are dealt with in detail in Part VIII. In Part VIII consideration is also given to easements and licenses.

Problem

13.27. O owned a parcel of corn and cotton land in Sumter County, South Carolina. O made an arrangement as to this land with A, B, and C, which was contained in the following document signed by all four parties (the last three signing by mark):

> This deed witnesseth: That the undersigned croppers are to have the South Farm to work for the year; that, in consideration of O furnishing the land and mules, the croppers will furnish the labor to make a crop; that O will have one-half of the crop for rent; that O will advance up to 300 lbs. of bacon and up to 6 bushels of corn and that the croppers will pay back the price of this before any of the crop is moved off the place; that the planting, cultivating, and manuring will be done according to O's agent's directions; that the croppers will house the crops in the best possible condition; that the croppers will be of good moral behavior while on the place, will see that there is no disorderly conduct, and will be respectful to the proprietor, the proprietor's family and agent.

Under this arrangement the croppers farm the land; O advances 300 pounds of bacon and six bushels of corn; the crops are gathered and housed.

    a. A creditor of the croppers attaches the crops in the barn. Does the creditor prevail over O?

    b. O goes into bankruptcy. What are the rights of the croppers?

    c. A fire destroys the crops. Can the croppers recover from O one-half the value of the crops, less the advance for bacon and corn?

See McCutchen v. Crenshaw, 40 S.C. 511, 19 S.E. 140 (1893); Appling v. Odom, 46 Ga. 583 (1872); Harrison v. Ricks, 71 N.C. 7 (1874).

And consider the following situation — a legal classic which we state in the language of the English report. This case arose in 1834, immediately before Victoria ascended the throne. The ladies of the day still costumed themselves in the high-bosomed Grecian-classic gowns of the Regency; the men wore tall hats and varicolored tail coats of the design of our modern evening clothes. The Adelaide must have made a gay and colorful picture in the May sunshine that morning on the Thames. One can sense the consternation of the ladies and the indignation of the gentlemen at the horrid intrusion to which they were subjected.

Problem

13.28. The defendant hired a steamboat for a party of pleasure to Richmond, upon the terms disclosed in the following letter from the owner: "I note the Adelaide is engaged to you for Richmond or Twickenham for Tuesday the 28th of May, at the hire for the day of 5 £, 10s., your party not exceeding fifty persons." The vessel was navigated by a captain and crew, employed and paid by the owner. Just as she was about to start from a quay in London, the plaintiff, an attorney, a stranger to the defendant, stepped on board, not being aware that the vessel had been hired for the day. The plaintiff was not long in discovering that he had intruded into a private party, and expressed to someone near him his readiness to quit the vessel when an opportunity should present itself; but the person so addressed rather counselled him to stay. However, by the time the Adelaide had reached Battersea, it was generally bruited about that a stranger was on board. The ladies became alarmed; defendant in an imperious tone ordered him to quit the vessel. The plaintiff, irritated by what appeared to him a harsh manner of making a lawful request, refused to go; whereupon the defendant, after calling on the captain to remove the plaintiff, with considerable violence shoved him into a boat alongside, and, in so doing, tore off the skirts of his coat. For this assault, the plaintiff now sued in trespass.

At the trial the defendant requested the following instruction: "If the defendant ejected the plaintiff from the Adelaide with no more force than was necessary to get him off the vessel, you should find for the defendant." Should this instruction be granted? Dean v. Hogg, 10 Bing. 345 (1824).

What rights are created by a *"mineral lease"?* O owns Blackacre, which holds substantial deposits of coal; and O and A make an arrangement by which A can mine the coal and pay to O either a fixed sum or a "royalty" on each ton taken out. This arrangement can create several types of interests of which the following are the most common:

1. O can convey the fee simple in the coal to A. In that case there is an implied easement over the rest of Blackacre to take out the coal.[42] Interesting questions arise as to who owns the hole that is left when the coal is removed — and the question is important.[43]

2. O can lease Blackacre to A for a specified period and exempt A from liability for waste so that A is privileged to take out any coal that A can extract during the period.

3. O can create in A a profit à prendre, i.e., a right to sever coal from the land and thereby become its owner. Here also A gets an implied easement to take out the minerals as severed.

Oil and gas "leases" raise similar problems as to the nature of the transaction. Additional complexities arise because of the facts that (1) oil and gas are migratory, and (2) the exploratory and drilling expense is substantial and the investment highly speculative.[44]

42. 5 Restatement of Property §513 illustration 1 (1944); American Law of Property §§8.32, 8.38, 8.39, 10.1 (Casner ed. 1952).
43. See Vance, Interests Created by Grants of Coal Apart From the Surface, 31 Yale L.J. 747 (1922).
44. See American Law of Property §§10.1 to 10.137 for an analysis of oil and gas problems.

CHAPTER 14

CONCURRENT OWNERSHIP

SECTION 1. TYPES OF CONCURRENT OWNERSHIP—PLANNING FACTORS

The situations are very numerous indeed in which two or more persons participate concurrently in the same property. Some of these are commercial arrangements and some donative transactions. Here are a few:

1. O dies, leaving a will which bequeaths all her household furniture and furnishings, china and glassware, silverware, jewelry, automobiles, and other tangible personal property to her two children, John and Ellen.

2. O creates an inter vivos trust of stocks, bonds, and cash valued at $50,000 in which the trustee is directed to pay the income to his two sisters, Sarah and Amelia, for their lives and upon the death of either to pay to that one's issue the principal of the share upon which the decedent was receiving income.

3. O creates a testamentary trust to pay the income to her widower for life and upon her death to distribute the principal per stirpes to her issue surviving the widower.

4. O dies intestate, owning Blackacre, and leaving as his only heirs two daughters.

5. O establishes a joint savings bank account for herself and her spouse, "payable to either or the survivor."

6. O buys a residence for his family, taking the deed in the name of himself and his spouse "as tenants by the entirety."

7. Two partners, A and B, purchase with partnership funds a building in which to conduct the partnership business.

8. Three persons, desiring to go into the business of buying, selling, and managing real estate, form a corporation, Acme Real Estate, Inc., each taking one-third of the stock in the corporation. Then the corporation buys Blackacre and takes a 20-year lease on Whiteacre.

Which of these arrangements are desirable and which undesirable? Or, to put it differently, when counsel is brought into the picture at the outset and can guide the choice of method, which should he or she advise? It must be obvious that no categorical answer can be given, that one method is adapted to some situations and another to others. The adviser must analyze the needs of the parties, know the characteristics and possibilities of the various methods available, foresee the problems that may arise in the future, and make a choice accordingly. At the least counsel should ask the following questions about any method of concurrent participation that is being considered.

1. A time will come when the property should be sold. Is a convenient method provided for (a) arriving at a decision to sell, and (b) giving a deed to a purchaser?

2. The property will incur expenses: taxes, insurance, repairs, etc. Is a fund provided for paying these expenses? Is a convenient method available for dividing the expenses and seeing that each participant pays his or her share?

3. The property may produce an income. Is a method available for paying current expenses out of income, for setting up appropriate reserves for future expense, for dividing the net income as it is received, and for protecting the share of such income of each participant?

4. One participant may actually occupy the property, whereas another may have no desire to. Is there a method by which the former makes appropriate adjustment with the latter?

5. One participant may want to get cash for his or her interest. Is it desired that he or she should be able to do so? If so, is a convenient method provided which does not upset the rest of the arrangement?

6. One participant may have or acquire creditors. What rights will they have with reference to the property?

7. When a participant dies, what happens to such participant's interest? Does it go to such participant's heirs or devisees, or does it survive to the other participants? If the latter, is it desired that a participant should be able to eliminate this quality of survivorship by action taken during life or upon death?

8. And finally, and far from least important, what are the tax consequences of the choice of the various possible methods? Income taxes, estate taxes, and gift taxes may all be, and usually are, relevant.[1]

Clearly the problem is complex. With the questions above in mind let us consider a few of the available devices.

The corporation. This is the only one of the methods enumerated above where the participants are not "owners" of the real estate, in the language of property; title is in the corporation, and the shareholders are not considered

---

1. The tax aspects of concurrent interests are dealt with in Chapter 37.

as having any property interest, legal or equitable, in the real estate. (It is for this reason that we have used the rather heavy word "participants." To designate as "co-owners" of real estate shareholders of a corporation which owns real estate would not be an acceptable classification.) Taking up the issues in order: (1) Title is in the corporation. A decision to sell can be made by majority vote of the directors, and a directors' meeting can be called easily. The corporation's deed to the purchaser, supported by the vote of the directors, will give to the purchaser the full title owned by the corporation. (2) The expenses incurred by the corporation will be charged against income or will reduce the net worth of the corporation. In either event the burden will be borne by the shareholders ratably. (3) Income will be received by the corporation. Current expenses will be paid, and future expenses can be provided for by the establishment of appropriate reserves. Net income will be available for dividends, which will be distributed ratably. (4) If one shareholder occupies the land, he or she will do so as lessee of the corporation, and the rent due to the corporation will be distributed ratably among the shareholders as dividends. (5) If one shareholder wants to get out, he or she sells shares of stock to whoever wishes to buy. There is no dislocation of the interests of the other shareholders and no change in the title to the real estate, which is always in the corporation. Subject to some restrictions, the other shareholders can be given options to purchase the shares if any one shareholder wants to sell out. (6) Creditors of a shareholder can reach the shareholder's shares of stock and thereby become shareholders in his or her stead. (7) When a shareholder dies, the shares owned by the decedent go to the decedent's next of kin or, if the decedent leaves a will, the decedent's legatees. (8) But, ah me, the tax situation is not so good. The corporation's net income from rents is taxable to it at the applicable corporate rate. Dividends are paid out of what is left over after this corporation income tax is paid. Then each shareholder pays an income tax on the dividends received by him or her. In a word, the use of a corporation results in double income taxation.[2] Of course, the shareholders will be officers of the corporation and as such will take salaries; these salaries will be deductible from the corporation's gross income in computing its net income, but will be taxable income to the shareholder-officer; in a word, as to these amounts there will be only a single income tax. But there are limitations, imposed by the tax authorities, on what can be taken out in salaries; and as to any excess the double tax liability is incurred. When a shareholder dies, his or her shares of stock are, of course, included in his or her estate for estate tax purposes.

Without going into the same degree of detail as to each of the other situations, we should like to make a few comments — the numbers corresponding to those which appear at page 251 *supra*.

1. *The testamentary gift of tangible personalty.* This requires the execu-

---

2. The double taxation of corporate income can be avoided if what is termed a subchapter S corporation is involved.

tor of O's will to divide the property between the two children. A realistic method of division should be required or at least suggested in the will.[3]

2. *The trust for the life of two sisters.* This keeps a fund of investment securities in the hands of a trustee. Division of the income is made by the trustee. Powers are given to the trustee by the will which permit the trustee to invest and reinvest.[4] There is no double income taxation; each of the sisters pays a tax on income received by her, but the trustee pays no tax on income payable to the sisters. The testator usually does not want to permit a sister to anticipate her income or sell her right to it, and the testator usually wishes to make her rights immune to the claims of creditors; in most states this can be accomplished by a "spendthrift clause."[5] Note that, by the conceptions of our property law, each sister holds an equitable property interest in the assets of the trust — this in contrast to the situation of the shareholder of a corporation.

3. *The trust remainder to several persons.* It is expected that the trustee will divide the property and distribute it. The will should give appropriate discretion to the trustee in this matter.[6]

4, 5, and 6. *The tenancy in common, joint tenancy, and tenancy by the entirety.* These we consider in some detail below. Observe one characteristic that distinguishes them from Nos. 1-3: interests 4-6 are usually created by only a phrase, the incidents of the tenancy and the rights of the owners being left to legal doctrine rather than being provided for in the creating instrument. The will, the inter vivos trust, and the testamentary trust normally make specific provision for the various events that can happen during the time the two owners have interests in the property. But the tenancy in common, the joint tenancy, and the tenancy by the entirety normally have to function without benefit of such provisions. Hence the great importance of the incidents which the law attaches to these various types of interests.[7]

7. *The partnership.* The tenancy in partnership is governed by partnership principles as codified, in many states, in the Uniform Partnership Act.[8] The partnership agreement is controlling as to many matters, and such agreements vary widely in different circumstances. As to taxes, the significant factor is that there is no double levy on the income as in the case of a corporation, the income being taxable on the individual returns of the partners.

3. For an example, see 5 Casner, Estate Planning, Will of Richard Harry Black III (5th ed.).

4. For examples of the trustee's powers, see 5 Casner, Estate Planning, various sample documents (5th ed.).

5. 3 Casner, Estate Planning ch. 11, C.7.

6. 5 Casner, Estate Planning, various sample documents (5th ed.).

7. Recall that in Part II the joint bank account ran into difficulties. Was it a gift? If so, was it testamentary and therefore a violation of the statute of wills?

8. In general, partnership realty is treated as if the partnership were a separate entity like a corporation. Thus, a partner's interest in the realty cannot be assigned except as a part of the partner's interest in the partnership; it cannot be reached by a partner's individual creditors; and on death it passes to the surviving partner, but for partnership purposes.

SECTION 2. CHARACTERISTICS OF CONCURRENT INTERESTS

Tenants in common are owners of undivided shares in the land. There is no survivorship between them, i.e., when one dies that person's share in the property passes to the decedent's heirs or devisees. When two or more persons take real estate by descent by reason of the owner's dying intestate, these persons were formerly called *parceners* or *coparceners* and their estate was called *coparcenary*. However, they are now called tenants in common, since their interests are identical with those of tenants in common, and the terminology of coparcenary is disappearing from the law.[9]

Joint tenants are also owners of undivided shares in the land. But there *is* survivorship between them, i.e., when one dies the other is sole owner. Note that we do *not* say that his or her share in the property passes to the other. That is not the conception of the common law. Each joint tenant is thought of as owning the whole, subject to the equal rights of the other. When one dies, the estate of the other is "simply . . . freed from participation by him [or her]."[10] This follows, it is said, from the fact that each joint tenant is seised *per my et per tout* — and if this helps you to get the idea, so much the better.

A joint bank account is sometimes referred to as a joint tenancy, and this is also true of a Series E government bond that is payable to A or B or the survivor. In the typical joint bank account, however, either one of the joint owners may draw out the entire amount in the account. Either joint owner of the government bond may cash it. But the true joint tenant of real property may only pull out that joint tenant's undivided share.

Problems

14.1. A and B are joint tenants of Blackacre. A dies intestate. The inheritance tax statute provides that on death a tax shall be assessed upon property "which shall pass by will or by laws regulating intestate succession." Is a tax payable on a one-half interest in Blackacre? Attorney General v. Clark, 222 Mass. 291, 110 N.E. 299 (1915).[11]

The survivorship feature of a joint tenancy is destructible by either party or, to put it differently, the *joint tenancy can be severed* and thereby changed

---

9. However, in an odd situation now and then the old learning may become important. Gilpin v. Hollingsworth, 3 Md. 190 (1852).

10. Palmer v. Treasurer, 222 Mass. 263, 110 N.E. 283 (1915).

11. This issue is not left open by estate and inheritance tax laws at the present time. See Chapter 37.

into a tenancy in common. Severance occurs when one joint tenant transfers his or her interest, voluntarily or involuntarily, to another. This follows, according to common-law dogma, because the conveyance destroys two of *the four unities* which must exist in any joint tenancy:

    a.   Unity of time — i.e., the interests of the joint tenants must vest at the same time.

    b.   Unity of possession — i.e., the joint tenants must have undivided interests in the whole, not divided interests in separate parts.

    c.   Unity of title — i.e., the joint tenants must derive their interests by the same instrument.

    d.   Unity of interest — i.e., the joint tenants must have estates of the same type and duration.[12]

14.2. In which of the following conveyances of Blackacre is a joint tenancy created?

    a.   O conveys to A and B for their joint lives as joint tenants.

    b.   O conveys an undivided one-half to A for A's life and an undivided one-half to B for B's life as joint tenants.

    c.   O conveys to A and B (brothers) and the heirs of their bodies as joint tenants.

14.3. O conveys Blackacre to A and B and their heirs as joint tenants.

    a.   A dies, survived by his wife, W. Is W entitled to dower in Blackacre?

    b.   A conveys his interest in Blackacre to C. A dies, survived by his wife, W, who did not join in his deed to C. Is W entitled to dower in Blackacre?

14.4. O conveys Blackacre to A, B, and C and their heirs as joint tenants. A conveys her interest in Blackacre to X. B dies intestate, leaving H as his heir. Describe ownership of Blackacre.

14.5. O devises Blackacre to "A and B and their heirs as joint tenants." A borrows $5,000 from M, giving to M a demand note for $5,000 secured by a mortgage of "all my right title and interest in Blackacre." Six months later A pays back the loan and M surrenders the note and executes a discharge of the mortgage. Shortly thereafter A dies intestate, her heir being H. Who owns Blackacre? See Hardin v. Wolf, 318 Ill. 48, 148 N.E. 868 (1925); Wilkins v. Young, 144 Ind. 1, 41 N.E. 68 (1895). If A had leased A's interest in Blackacre to T for five years and had died during the five-year period, would T's lease be good against B for the balance of the five-year period? See Tenhet v. Boswell, 18 Cal. 3d 150, 554 P.2d 330 (1976). Would T be entitled to possess Blackacre with B during the five-year period while A is alive? See Swartzbaugh v. Sampson, 11 Cal. App. 2d 451, 54 P.2d 73 (1936).

---

12. On the unities, see Blackstone, Commentaries 180 et seq. See generally on joint interests the following: Moss & Siebert, Classification and Creation of Joint Interests, 1959 Ill. L.F. 883; Reichelderfer, Severance of Joint Interests, 1959 Ill. L.F. 932; Mamer, Legal Consequences of Joint Ownership, 1959 Ill. L.F. 944.

The *tenancy by the entirety* is a form of co-ownership limited to husband and wife. Its characteristics are said to flow from the following cabialistic dogma: tenants by the entirety are seised per tout et non per my and do not take by moieties but by entireties,[13] for the estate comprises an additional unity—the unity of husband and wife. As a practical matter what this means is that there is survivorship between tenants by the entirety and that neither one can sever the tenancy and thereby destroy the survivorship feature. Of course, the two together can convey a fee simple. During the joint lives of H and W, tenants by the entirety, H is entitled at common law to sole possession and control and takes all the rents and profits. (It is not clear how far this is an individual characteristic of a tenancy by the entirety and how far it is an application of the common-law rule that a husband was seised of his wife's freeholds jure uxoris. This can become important where the doctrine of seisin jure uxoris is abolished by a married women's property act with no mention of tenancies by the entirety.) There is no unanimity as to the power of the husband to convey his present possessory right and his right of survivorship, or of the wife to convey her right of survivorship, or of the ability of creditors of either to reach these interests.

Statutes and judicial divergences have dealt variously with tenancies by the entirety. Somewhat more than half the states do not recognize them at all. A few — New York and New Jersey among them — recognize tenancies by the entirety as to real estate but not as to personalty, which creates some complications when the realty is changed into personalty by various kinds of forced sale, such as foreclosure of a mortgage or a taking by eminent domain. Some give the whole rents and profits to the husband during the joint lives of the spouses; some divide the rents and profits equally. Some make the estate immune to creditors; some make it practically immune by allowing levy only upon an unsalable type of interest; and some give creditors broader rights. This kind of conflict between the states is bound to occur when you have a doctrine based upon ancient social and legal realities which have now fundamentally changed. Some states will discard the doctrine; others will modify it; and still others, either through inertia or through finding that it justifies itself on pragmatic grounds, will retain it.

SECTION 3.   CREATION OF CONCURRENT INTERESTS

As between a tenancy in common and a joint tenancy a common-law presumption favored the latter. Thus at common law a conveyance "to A and B and their heirs" created a joint tenancy in A and B in fee simple. The

---

13. See Palmer v. Treasurer, 222 Mass. 263, 110 N.E. 283 (1915). By contrast, joint tenants "take by moieties."

reason for this is the same as the reason for primogeniture—the feudal desirability of keeping the land in the hands of one tenant, if possible, so that the lord would have one responsible person from whom to receive the services and incidents and not find things complicated by a lot of minor landholders. Still the determination of the type of tenancy remained a question of construction, and if the grantor clearly specified a tenancy in common this would be created.

As the feudal system waned the presumption of a joint tenancy lost its validity. Courts of equity first broke away from it. Then statutes nullified it, substituting a presumption in favor of tenancies in common. Such statutes are standard items of legislation. Several states declare that there shall be no joint tenancy unless the right of survivorship is expressly provided for in the instrument.

At common law a conveyance to husband and wife was presumptively a tenancy by the entirety. Thus a grant or devise "to A and B and their heirs" created a tenancy by the entirety in fee simple if A and B were husband and wife. Where these tenancies are still permitted, the statutes may or may not alter the common-law presumption.

What of a grant or devise "to A, B, and C and their heirs," A and B being husband and wife? A and B took one-half as tenants by the entirety; and after the presumption in favor of joint tenancies was abolished, C took one-half as a tenant in common.

Personalty. Joint tenancies in personalty are permitted. The same was true at common law as to tenancies by the entirety; but the laws of the several states now vary on this matter.

Statutes. In any given jurisdiction you will probably discover that the statutes on the effect of conveyances to two or more persons have been several times amended. Thus a deed or will taking effect at one date may produce a quite different result from an identical deed or will taking effect at a later date.

Problems

14.6. O conveys Blackacre to A and B "as tenants by the entirety." A and B had gone through a marriage ceremony and believed they were husband and wife. It turned out that a previous marriage of A had not been properly dissolved, and consequently A and B were not husband and wife when the conveyance to them was made. What estate is held by A and B? See Fuss v. Fuss, 373 Mass. 445, 368 N.E.2d 276 (1977).

14.7. H and W own real property as tenants by the entirety. The land is taken in a condemnation proceeding. What disposition should be made of the proceeds received if the land is located in a state which allows a tenancy by the entirety in personal property? See Ronan v. Ronan, 339 Mass. 460, 159 N.E.2d 653 (1959); Smith v. Tipping, 349 Mass. 590, 211 N.E.2d 231

(1965). If the land is located in a state where a tenancy by the entirety in personal property is not provided for in the statute? Should the result in such state differ if the buildings on the land are destroyed by fire and the disposition of the proceeds of the fire insurance is involved? See Hawthorne v. Hawthorne, 13 N.Y.2d 82, 192 N.E.2d 20 (1963).

14.8. Massachusetts General Laws Annotated ch. 184, §7, provides in substance that a conveyance or devise of land to two or more persons shall create a tenancy in common unless the intention to create a joint tenancy or tenancy by the entirety is manifested. This statute, however, excepts from its operation "a mortgage or a devise or conveyance in trust." What is the reason for these exceptions?

SECTION 4. PARTITION BETWEEN CO-OWNERS[14]

It is of the essence of a *tenancy by the entirety* that the spouses should not have partition — until a divorce occurs, which usually changes the estate to a tenancy in common.[15]

Joint tenants and tenants in common are normally entitled to partition. (Grantors may, in some states, impose limitations on the right to partition; and in some peculiar situations — e.g., a burial lot with corpse — partition is obviously inappropriate.) The usual proceeding is a bill in equity by one co-tenant against the others praying the court to appoint commissioners to divide the land equitably or, if that proves impracticable, to sell it and divide the proceeds. As you would expect, the procedure in partition varies considerably from state to state. If the land is physically divided, it frequently happens that exact equality is unattainable; and in that case the court orders the favored co-owner to compensate the others by a cash payment, called *owelty*.

Of course, if the co-owners can agree on a division, they can accomplish partition by an exchange of deeds.

---

14. In regard to partition, see American Law of Property §§6.16, 6.19-6.26 (Casner ed. 1952), and see particularly the material on restraints on partition, §§26.72-26.80.

15. If a tenancy by the entirety is involved, a divorce terminates it and a tenancy in common is the normal result, so that when one dies the survivor does not become the owner of the whole. If a husband and wife own property as joint tenants, a divorce does not disturb such form of ownership and the survivor may become the owner of the whole. In Witzel v. Witzel, 386 P.2d 103 (Wyo. 1963), the court decided a transfer to husband and wife "as joint tenants" created a joint tenancy and not a tenancy by the entirety. Consequently, the divorce did not affect the form of ownership and the former wife as survivor became the sole owner of the property, much to the distress of the former husband's second wife.

SECTION 5.   A FEW CASES AND PROBLEMS

SAWADA v. ENDO
57 Hawaii 608, 561 P.2d 1291 (1977)

MENOR, J. This is a civil action brought by the plaintiffs-appellants, Masako Sawada and Helen Sawada, in aid of execution of money judgments in their favor, seeking to set aside a conveyance of real property from judgment debtor Kokichi Endo to Samuel H. Endo and Toru Endo, defendants-appellees herein, on the ground that the conveyance as to the Sawadas was fraudulent.

On November 30, 1968, the Sawadas were injured when struck by a motor vehicle operated by Kokichi Endo. On June 17, 1969, Helen Sawada filed her complaint for damages against Kokichi Endo. Masako Sawada filed her suit against him on August 13, 1969. The complaint and summons in each case was served on Kokichi Endo on October 29, 1969.

On the date of the accident, Kokichi Endo was the owner, as a tenant by the entirety with his wife, Ume Endo, of a parcel of real property situate at Wahiawa, Oahu, Hawaii. By deed, dated July 26, 1969, Kokichi Endo and his wife conveyed the property to their sons, Samuel H. Endo and Toru Endo. This document was recorded in the Bureau of Conveyances on December 17, 1969. No consideration was paid by the grantees for the conveyance. Both were aware at the time of the conveyance that their father had been involved in an accident, and that he carried no liability insurance. Kokichi Endo and Ume Endo, while reserving no life interests therein, continued to reside on the premises.

On January 19, 1971, after a consolidated trial on the merits, judgment was entered in favor of Helen Sawada and against Kokichi Endo in the sum of $8,846.46. At the same time, Masako Sawada was awarded judgment on her complaint in the amount of $16,199.28. Ume Endo, wife of Kokichi Endo, died on January 29, 1971. She was survived by her husband, Kokichi. Subsequently, after being frustrated in their attempts to obtain satisfaction of judgment from the personal property of Kokichi Endo, the Sawadas brought suit to set aside the conveyance which is the subject matter of this controversy. The trial court refused to set aside the conveyance, and the Sawadas appeal.

I

The determinative question in this case is, whether the interest of one spouse in real property, held in tenancy by the entireties, is subject to levy and execution by his or her individual creditors. This issue is one of first impression in this jurisdiction.

A brief review of the present state of the tenancy by the entirety might be helpful. Dean Phipps, writing in 1951,[16] pointed out that only nineteen states and the District of Columbia continued to recognize it as a valid and subsisting institution in the field of property law. Phipps divided these jurisdictions into four groups. He made no mention of Alaska and Hawaii, both of which were then territories of the United States.

In the Group I states (Massachusetts, Michigan, and North Carolina) the estate is essentially the common law tenancy by the entireties, unaffected by the Married Women's Property Acts. As at common law, the possession and profits of the estate are subject to the husband's exclusive dominion and control. Pineo v. White, 320 Mass. 487, 70 N.E.2d 294 (1946);[17] Speier v. Opfer, 73 Mich. 35, 40 N.W. 909 (1888); Johnson v. Leavitt, 188 N.C. 682, 125 S.E. 490 (1924). In all three states, as at common law, the *husband* may convey the entire estate subject only to the possibility that the wife may become entitled to the whole estate upon surviving him. Phelps v. Simons, 159 Mass. 415, 34 N.E. 657 (1893); Arrand v. Graham, 297 Mich. 559, 298 N.W. 281 (1911); Hood v. Mercer, 150 N.C. 699, 64 S.E. 897 (1909). As at common law, the obverse as to the wife does not hold true. Only in Massachusetts, however, is the estate in its entirety subject to levy by the husband's creditors. Splaine v. Morrissey, 282 Mass. 217, 184 N.E. 670 (1933). In both Michigan and North Carolina, the use and income from the estate is not subject to levy during the marriage for the separate debts of either spouse. Dickey v. Converse, 117 Mich. 449, 76 N.W. 80 (1898); Hood v. Mercer, *supra.*

In the Group II states (Alaska, Arkansas, New Jersey, New York, and Oregon) the interest of the debtor spouse in the estate may be sold or levied upon for his or her separate debts, subject to the other spouse's contingent right of survivorship. Pope v. McBride, 207 Ark. 940, 184 S.W.2d 259 (1945); King v. Greene, 30 N.J. 395, 153 A.2d 49 (1959); Hiles v. Fisher, 144 N.Y. 306, 39 N.E. 337 (1895); Brownley v. Lincoln County, 218 Or. 7, 343 P.2d 529 (1959). Alaska, which has been added to this group, has provided by statute that the interest of a debtor spouse in any type of estate, except a homestead as defined and held in tenancy by the entirety, shall be subject to his or her separate debts. Pilip v. United States, 186 F. Supp. 397 (D. Alaska, 1960).

In the Group III jurisdictions (Delaware, District of Columbia, Florida,

16. Phipps, Tenancy by Entireties, 25 Temple L.Q. 24 (1951).

17. On November 13, 1979, by an amendment to Massachusetts General Laws Annotated ch. 209, §1, effective 90 days thereafter, Massachusetts changed the characteristics of a tenancy by the entirety, as follows: a husband and wife shall be equally entitled to the rents, products, income, or profits and to the control, management, and possession of property held by them as tenants by the entirety. The interest of a debtor spouse in property held as tenants by the entirety shall not be subject to seizure or execution by a creditor of such debtor spouse so long as such property is the principal residence of the non-debtor spouse, provided, however, both spouses shall be liable jointly or severally for debts incurred on account of necessaries furnished to either spouse or to a member of their family.— EDS.

Indiana, Maryland, Missouri, Pennsylvania, Rhode Island, Vermont, Virginia, and Wyoming) an attempted conveyance by either spouse is wholly void, and the estate may not be subjected to the separate debts of one spouse only. Citizens Savings Bank Inc. v. Astrin, 5 Terry 451, 44 Del. 451, 61 A.2d 419 (1948); Golden v. Glens Falls Indemnity Co., 102 U.S. App. D.C. 106, 250 F.2d 769 (1957); Hunt v. Covington, 145 Fla. 706, 200 So. 76 (1941); Sharp v. Baker, 51 Ind. App. 547, 96 N.E. 627 (1911); McCubbin v. Stanford, 85 Md. 378, 37 A. 214 (1897); Otto F. Stifel's Union Brewing Co. v. Saxy, 273 Mo. 159, 201 S.W. 67 (1918); O'Malley v. O'Malley, 272 Pa. 528, 116 A. 500 (1922); Bloomfield v. Brown, 67 R.I. 452, 25 A.2d 354 (1942); Citizens' Savings Bank & Trust Co. v. Jenkins, 91 Vt. 13, 99 A. 250 (1916); Vasilion v. Vasilion, 192 Va. 735, 66 S.E.2d 599 (1951); Ward Terry and Company v. Hensen, 75 Wyo. 444, 297 P.2d 213 (1956).

In Group IV, the two states of Kentucky and Tennessee hold that the contingent right of survivorship appertaining to either spouse is separately alienable by him and attachable by his creditors during the marriage. Hoffmann v. Newell, 249 Ky. 270, 60 S.W.2d 607 (1933); Covington v. Murray, 220 Tenn. 265, 416 S.W.2d 761 (1967). The use and profits, however, may neither be alienated nor attached during coverture.

It appears, therefore, that Hawaii is the only jurisdiction still to be heard from on the question. Today we join that group of states and the District of Columbia which hold that under the Married Women's Property Acts the interest of a husband or a wife in an estate by the entireties is not subject to the claims of his or her individual creditors during the joint lives of the spouses. In so doing, we are placing our stamp of approval upon what is apparently the prevailing view of the lower courts of this jurisdiction.

Hawaii has long recognized and continues to recognize the tenancy in common, the joint tenancy, and the tenancy by the entirety, as separate and distinct estates. See Paahana v. Bila, 3 Haw. 725 (1876). That the Married Women's Property Act of 1888 was not intended to abolish the tenancy by the entirety was made clear by the language of Act 19 of the Session Laws of Hawaii, 1903 (now HRS §509-1). See also HRS §509-2. The tenancy by the entirety is predicated upon the legal unity of husband and wife, and the estate is held by them in single ownership. They do not take by moieties, but both and each are seized of the whole estate. Lang v. Commissioner of Internal Revenue, 289 U.S. 109, 53 S. Ct. 534, 77 L. Ed. 1066 (1933).

A joint tenant has a specific, albeit undivided, interest in the property, and if he survives his cotenant he becomes the owner of a larger interest than he had prior to the death of the other joint tenant. But tenants by the entirety are each deemed to be seized of the entirety from the time of the creation of the estate. At common law, this taking of the "whole estate" did not have the real significance that it does today, insofar as the rights of the wife in the property were concerned. For all practical purposes, the wife had no right during coverture to the use and enjoyment and exercise of ownership in the marital estate. All she possessed was her contingent right of survivorship.

The effect of the Married Women's Property Acts was to abrogate the husband's common law dominance over the marital estate and to place the wife on a level of equality with him as regards the exercise of ownership over the whole estate. The tenancy was and still is predicated upon the legal unity of husband and wife, but the Acts converted it into a unity of equals and not of unequals as at common law. Otto F. Stifel's Union Brewing Co. v. Saxy, *supra;* Lang v. Commissioner of Internal Revenue, *supra.* No longer could the husband convey, lease, mortgage or otherwise encumber the property without her consent. The Acts confirmed her right to the use and enjoyment of the whole estate, and all the privileges that ownership of property confers, including the right to convey the property in its entirety, jointly with her husband, during the marriage relation. Jordan v. Reynolds, 105 Md. 288, 66 A. 37 (1907); Hurd v. Hughes, 12 Del. Ch. 188, 109 A. 418 (1920); Vasilion v. Vasilion, *supra;* Frost v. Frost, 200 Mo. 474, 98 S.W. 527 (1906). They also had the effect of insulating the wife's interest in the estate from the separate debts of her husband. Jordan v. Reynolds, *supra.*

Neither husband nor wife has a separate divisible interest in the property held by the entirety that can be conveyed or reached by execution. Fairclaw v. Forrest, 76 U.S. App. D.C. 197, 130 F.2d 829 (1942). A joint tenancy may be destroyed by voluntary alienation, or by levy and execution, or by compulsory partition, but a tenancy by the entirety may not. The indivisibility of the estate, except by joint action of the spouses, is an indispensable feature of the tenancy by the entirety. Ashbaugh v. Ashbaugh, 273 Mo. 353, 201 S.W. 72 (1918); Newman v. Equitable Life Assur. Soc., 119 Fla. 641, 160 So. 745 (1935); Lang v. Commissioner of Internal Revenue, *supra.*

In Jordan v. Reynolds, *supra,* the Maryland court held that no lien could attach against entirety property for the separate debts of the husband, for that would be in derogation of the entirety of title in the spouses and would be tantamount to a conversion of the tenancy into a joint tenancy or tenancy in common. In holding that the spouses could jointly convey the property, free of any judgment liens against the husband, the court said:

> To hold the judgment to be a lien at all against this property, and the right of execution suspended during the life of the wife, and to be enforced on the death of the wife, would, we think, likewise encumber her estate, and be in contravention of the constitutional provision heretofore mentioned, protecting the wife's property from the husband's debts.
>
> It is clear, we think, if the judgment here is declared a lien, but suspended during the life of the wife, and not enforceable until her death, if the husband should survive the wife, it will defeat the sale here made by the husband and wife to the purchaser, and thereby make the wife's property liable for the debts of her husband. [105 Md. at 295, 296, 66 A. at 39.]

In Hurd v. Hughes, *supra,* the Delaware court, recognizing the peculiar nature of an estate by the entirety, in that the husband and wife are the owners, not merely of equal interests but of the whole estate, stated:

The estate [by the entireties] can be acquired or held only by a man and woman while married. Each spouse owns the whole while both live; neither can sell any interest except with the other's consent, and by their joint act; and at the death of either the other continues to own the whole, and does not acquire any new interest from the other. There can be no partition between them. From this is deduced the indivisibility and unseverability of the estate into two interests, and hence that the creditors of either spouse cannot during their joint lives reach by execution any interest which the debtor had in land so held. . . . One may have doubts as to whether the holding of land by entireties is advisable or in harmony with the spirit of the legislation in favor of married women; but when such an estate is created due effect must be given to its peculiar characteristics. [12 Del. Ch. at 190, 109 A. at 419.]

In Frost v. Frost, *supra,* the Missouri court said:

Under the facts of the case at bar it is not necessary for us to decide whether or not under our married women's statutes the husband has been shorn of the exclusive right to the possession and control of the property held as an estate in entirety; it is sufficient to say, as we do say, that the title in such an estate is as it was at common law; neither husband nor wife has an interest in the property, to the exclusion of the other. Each owns the whole while both live and at the death of either the other continues to own the whole, freed from the claim of any one claiming under or through the deceased. [200 Mo. at 483, 98 S.W. at 528, 529.]

We are not persuaded by the argument that it would be unfair to the creditors of either spouse to hold that the estate by the entirety may not, without the consent of both spouses, be levied upon for the separate debts of either spouse. No unfairness to the creditor is involved here. We agree with the court in Hurd v. Hughes, *supra:*

But creditors are not entitled to special consideration. If the debt arose prior to the creation of the estate, the property was not a basis of credit, and if the debt arose subsequently the creditor presumably had notice of the characteristics of the estate which limited his right to reach the property. [12 Del. Ch. at 193, 109 A. at 420.]

We might also add that there is obviously nothing to prevent the creditor from insisting upon the subjection of property held in tenancy by the entirety as a condition precedent to the extension of credit. Further, the creation of a tenancy by the entirety may not be used as a device to defraud existing creditors. In re Estate of Wall, 142 U.S. App. D.C. 187, 440 F.2d 215 (1971).

Were we to view the matter strictly from the standpoint of public policy, we would still be constrained to hold as we have done here today. In Fairclaw v. Forrest, *supra,* the court makes this observation:

The interest in family solidarity retains some influence upon the institution [of tenancy by the entirety]. It is available only to husband and wife. It is a convenient mode of protecting a surviving spouse from inconvenient administration of the decedent's estate and from the other's improvident debts. It is in that protection the estate finds its peculiar and justifiable function. [130 F.2d at 833.]

It is a matter of common knowledge that the demand for single-family residential lots has increased rapidly in recent years, and the magnitude of the problem is emphasized by the concentration of the bulk of fee simple land in the hands of a few. The shortage of single-family residential fee simple property is critical and government has seen fit to attempt to alleviate the problem through legislation. When a family can afford to own real property, it becomes their single most important asset. Encumbered as it usually is by a first mortgage, the fact remains that so long as it remains whole during the joint lives of the spouses, it is always available in its entirety for the benefit and use of the entire family. Loans for education and other emergency expenses, for example, may be obtained on the security of the marital estate. This would not be possible where a third party has become a tenant in common or a joint tenant with one of the spouses, or where the ownership of the contingent right of survivorship of one of the spouses in a third party has cast a cloud upon the title of the marital estate, making it virtually impossible to utilize the estate for these purposes.

If we were to select between a public policy favoring the creditors of one of the spouses and one favoring the interests of the family unit, we would not hesitate to choose the latter. But we need not make this choice for, as we pointed out earlier, by the very nature of the estate by the entirety as we view it, and as other courts of our sister jurisdictions have viewed it, "[a] unilaterally indestructible right of survivorship, an inability of one spouse to alienate his interest, and, importantly for this case, a broad immunity from claims of separate creditors remain among its vital incidents." In re Estate of Wall, *supra,* 440 F.2d at 218.

Having determined that an estate by the entirety is not subject to the claims of the creditors of one of the spouses during their joint lives, we now hold that the conveyance of the marital property by Kokichi Endo and Ume Endo, husband and wife, to their sons, Samuel H. Endo and Toru Endo, was not in fraud of Kokichi Endo's judgment creditors. Cf. Jordan v. Reynolds, *supra.*

Affirmed.

KIDWELL, J., dissenting. This case has been well briefed, and the arguments against the conclusions reached by the majority have been well presented. It will not materially assist the court in resolving the issues for me to engage in an extensive review of the conflicting views. Appellants' position on the appeal was that tenancy by the entirety as it existed at common law, together with all of the rights which the husband had over the property of his wife by virtue of the common law doctrine of the unity of the person, was recognized by the early decisions, Paahana v. Bila, 3 Haw. 725 (1876); Von Hasslocher v. Executors of Robinson, 3 Haw. 802 (1877); Cummins v. Wond, 6 Haw. 69 (1872); Kuanalewa v. Kipi, 7 Haw. 575 (1889); that the Married Women's Act of 1888 (now Ch. 573, HRS) destroyed the fictional unity of husband and wife, First National Bank v. Gaines, 16 Haw. 731 (1905); that the legislature has recognized the continuing existence of the estate of tenancy by the entirety, but has not defined the nature or the incidents of that estate, HRS §509-1, 509-2; that at common law the interest of the husband in an estate by the entireties could be taken by his separate creditors on execution against him, subject only to the wife's right of survivorship, Kuanalewa v. Kipi, *supra;* and that the Married Women's Act merely eliminated any inequality in the positions of the spouses with respect to their interests in the property, thus depriving the husband of his former power over the wife's interest, without thereby altering the nature and incidents of the husband's interest.

I find the logic of Appellant's analysis convincing. While the authorities are divided, I consider that the reasoning of the cases cited by Appellant best reconciles the Married Women's Act with the common law. Hiles v. Fisher, 144 N.Y. 306, 39 N.E. 337 (1895); Pope v. McBride, 207 Ark. 940, 184 S.W.2d 259 (1944); Branch v. Polk, 61 Ark. 388, 33 S.W. 424 (1895); King v. Greene, 30 N.J. 395, 153 A.2d 49 (1959); Buttlar v. Rosenblath, 42 N.J. Eq. 651, 9 A. 695 (1887); Brownley v. Lincoln County, 218 Or. 7, 343 P.2d 529 (1959); Ganoe v. Ohmart, 121 Or. 116, 254 P. 203 (1927); Hoffmann v. Newell, 249 Ky. 270, 60 S.W.2d 607 (1932); Cole Mfg. Co. v. Collier, 95 Tenn. 115, 31 S.W. 1000 (1895); Raptes v. Cheros, 259 Mass. 37, 155 N.E. 787 (1927).

The majority reaches its conclusion by holding that the effect of the Married Women's Act was to equalize the positions of the spouses by taking from the husband his common law right to transfer his interest, rather than by elevating the wife's right of alienation of her interest to place it on a position of equality with the husband's. I disagree. I believe that a better interpretation of the Married Women's Acts is that offered by the Supreme Court of New Jersey in King v. Greene, 30 N.J. 395, 412, 153 A.2d 49, 60 (1959):

> It is clear that the Married Women's Act created an equality between the spouses in New Jersey, insofar as tenancies by the entirety are concerned. If, as we have previously concluded, the husband could alienate his right of survivorship at common law, the wife, by virtue of the act, can alienate her right of survivorship. And it follows, that if the wife takes equal rights with the husband in the estate, she must take equal disabilities. Such are the dictates of common equality. Thus, the judgment creditors of either spouse may levy and execute upon their separate rights of survivorship.

One may speculate whether the courts which first chose the path to equality now followed by the majority might have felt an unexpressed aversion to entrusting a wife with as much control over her interest as had previously been granted to the husband with respect to his interest. Whatever may be the historical explanation for these decisions, I feel that the resultant restriction upon the freedom of the spouses to deal independently with their respective interests is both illogical and unnecessarily at odds with present policy trends. Accordingly, I would hold that the separate interest of the husband in entireties property, at least to the extent of his right of survivorship, is alienable by him and subject to attachment by his separate creditors, so that a voluntary conveyance of the husband's interest should be set aside where it is fraudulent as to such creditors, under applicable principles of the law of fraudulent conveyances.

Problems

14.9. Alfred and Blanche Leney owned an apartment house as tenants by the entirety in a jurisdiction where such property is controlled by the husband during the joint lives of the husband and wife. Wingrove rented an apartment for one year and received a lease signed by both Alfred and Blanche. A common stairway fell into disrepair. Blanche's father did the repairs, and Blanche helped him. When another tenant asked them why they didn't get a carpenter, Blanche said, "We can't afford it." The repair was not adequate to hold the weight of Wingrove, a heavy man. He fell and was seriously injured. Is Blanche Leney liable to him in tort? Wingrove v. Leney, 312 Mass. 683, 45 N.E.2d 837 (1942).

14.10. If a state has an equal rights amendment to its constitution, does it necessarily follow that the rights of a husband and wife in a tenancy by the entirety cannot be unequal? See West v. First Agricultural Bank, 382 Mass. 534, 419 N.E.2d 262 (1981). If a state recognizes and enforces unequal spousal rights in a tenancy by the entirety, is that state action that violates the equal protection clause of the fourteenth amendment to the federal Constitution?

14.11. Section 7403 of the Internal Revenue Code provides that in any case where there has been a refusal or neglect to pay any tax, or to discharge any liability in respect thereof, a civil action may be filed in the district court to enforce the lien of the United States with respect to such tax or liability or "to subject any property, of whatever nature, of the delinquent, or in which he has any right, title or interest, to the payment of such tax or liability." In a jurisdiction that takes the position of the Hawaii court, if one of the tenants by the entirety has a tax liability owing the United States, can the district court order a sale of all interests in the tenancy by the entirety to obtain funds to satisfy the tax liability if some portion of the sales proceeds are paid to the non-debtor spouse to satisfy such spouse for the loss of the interest in the tenancy by the entirety? See United States v. Rodgers, —U.S.—, 103 S. Ct. 2132 (1983).

PICO v. COLUMBET
12 Cal. 414 (1859)

[Bill in equity for accounting. A demurrer to the bill was overruled. Then, after trial, the bill was dismissed on the merits. The complainant appealed. The Supreme Court of California affirmed the decree, pointing out that the demurrer should have been sustained. The opinion follows.]

FIELD, J., delivered the opinion of the court — TERRY, C.J., and BALDWIN, J., concurring.[18]

This action is brought by one tenant in common against his cotenant, who is in the sole possession of the entire premises, to recover a share of the profits received from the estate. The case was argued upon the demurrer to the complaint, which, by stipulation of the parties, was admitted to have been taken on the ground that the complaint does not state facts sufficient to constitute a cause of action. The complaint avers a tenancy in common between the parties; the sole and exclusive possession of the premises by the defendant; the receipt by him of the rents, issues and profits thereof; a demand by the plaintiff of an account of the same, and the payment of his share; the defendant's refusal; and that the rents, issues and profits amount to $84,000. These averments, and not the form in which the prayer for judgment is couched, must determine the character of the pleading. The complaint is designated a bill in equity, but the designation does not make it such. There are no special circumstances alleged which withdraw the case from the ordinary remedies at law, and require the interposition of equity. The action is a common law action of account, and, viewed in this light, the complaint is fatally defective. It does not aver that the defendant occupied the premises upon any agreement with the plaintiff, as receiver or bailiff of his share of the rents and profits. It is essential to a recovery that this circumstance exist, and equally essential to the complaint that it be alleged.

---

18. Two of the trio who occupied the bench in this case made headlines in a way which is denied most of those who choose the cloistered life of the judiciary. Not to put too fine a point upon it, Terry, C.J., was shot dead by a United States Marshal in the railroad station restaurant at Lathrop, California, at breakfast on the morning of August 14, 1889, while committing a physical assault on Field, J.

The transition between the decorous bench of 1859 and the breakfast gunplay thirty years later is a great tale unaccountably neglected by Hollywood. The center of the action is, as it ought to be, a woman — Sarah Althea Hill, good to gaze upon by contemporaneous accounts, and not to be trifled with by necessary inference from the story itself. She married (or did not marry — the issue was disputed) one Senator Sharon, then conducted a series of lawsuits against him and his estate. Terry retired from the bench. In the very year of Pico v. Columbet he killed another senator in a duel. Six feet three inches tall and weighing two hundred and fifty pounds, Terry was just the man for Sarah. He first became her attorney, then her husband. Field was appointed to the United States Supreme Court. Sitting on circuit in California, he decided an issue against Mrs. Sarah Althea Hill (Sharon?) Terry. She pulled a gun. Terry knocked out the teeth of a bailiff who sought to restrain her, then pulled a knife on the crowd. Field sent both to jail for contempt. When the Terrys got out, David Neagle was appointed a United States Marshal to protect Field. The paths of Field, Neagle, and the Terrys crossed definitively in the station restaurant at Lathrop, California. For the story, see Swisher, Life of Stephen J. Field 321-361 (1930). — EDS.

By the common law, one tenant in common has no remedy against the other who exclusively occupies the premises and receives the entire profits, unless he is ousted of possession when ejectment may be brought, or unless the other is acting as bailiff of his interest by agreement, when the action of account will lie. The reason of the doctrine is obvious. Each tenant is entitled to the occupation of the premises; neither can exclude the other; and if the sole occupation by one cotenant could render him liable to the other, it would be in the power of the latter, by voluntarily remaining out of possession, to keep out his companion also, except upon the condition of the payment of rent. The enjoyment of the absolute legal right of one cotenant would thus often be dependent upon the caprice or indolence of the other. 1 Co. Lit. 200; 5 Bacon's Abrid. 367; Willes, 209.

The statutes of 4 and 5 Anne, 16, gave a right of action to one joint tenant, or tenant in common, against the other as bailiff, who received more than his proportional share of the profits. At common law the bailiff was answerable, not only for his actual receipts, but for what he might have made from the property without willful neglect (Co. Lit. 172, a. Willes, 210), but as bailiff under the statute of Anne, he was responsible only for what he received beyond his proportionate share. That statute only applied to cases where one tenant in common received from a third person money, or something else, to which both cotenants were entitled by reason of their cotenancy, and retained more than his just share according to the proportion of his interest. This was held in Henderson v. Eason in the Exchequer Chamber, 9 Eng. Law and Eq. 337. In that case it was decided, that if one of two tenants in common solely occupies land, farms it at his own cost, and takes the produce for his own benefit, his cotenant cannot maintain an action of account against him as bailiff for having received more than his share and proportion.

The statute of Anne has never been adopted in this State, nor have we any similar statute. The case at bar must therefore be determined upon the principles of the common law. By them, as we have observed, the action cannot be maintained against the occupying tenant unless he is by agreement a manager or agent of his cotenant. The occupation by him, so long as he does not exclude his cotenant, is but the exercise of a legal right. His cultivation and improvements are made at his own risks; if they result in loss he cannot call upon his cotenant for contribution, and if they produce a profit his cotenant is not entitled to share in them. The cotenant can at any moment enter into equal enjoyment of his possession; his neglect to do so may be regarded as an assent to the sole occupation of the other. . . .

We have treated this case as an action of account at law, but to the same result we should come if the proceeding were in equity. There is no equity in the claim asserted by the plaintiff to share in profits resulting from the labor and money of the defendant, when he has expended neither, and has never claimed possession, and never been liable for contribution in cases of loss. There would be no equity in giving to the plaintiff, who would neither work himself, or subject himself to any expenditures or risks, a share in the fruits of another's labor, investments and risks.

McKNIGHT v. BASILIDES
19 Wash. 2d 391, 143 P.2d 307 (1943)

[Charles Basilides, the appellant here, married Alice in 1901. By a former marriage Alice Basilides had two children, whose names are now Alice McKnight and Fred W. King. Charles and Alice Basilides had one child, whose name is now Ruth Allison. Charles bought two parcels with houses on them in 1907 — the "big house" and the "little house."

Alice Basilides died intestate November 20, 1929, and the estate has never been probated. Appellant has been in possession of both pieces of property since the death of his wife and has paid all the taxes and assessments levied against the property. In addition, he made certain improvements upon the real estate. He rented the "little house" and occupied the "big house" as his home. During the time from the death of his wife, Alice, until a few days prior to the beginning of this action, appellant never made any claim to respondents that he was the sole owner of the property; nor did respondents make any claim to the property during the same period of time.

Alice McKnight and Fred W. King brought a bill in equity against Charles Basilides and Ruth Allison, claiming that each of the plaintiffs owned $\frac{1}{6}$ of the two parcels[19] and praying (1) partition, and, against Charles Basilides only, (2) an accounting for the rents received from the "little house" up to the time it was sold in 1938 and for its fair rental value thereafter, (3) an accounting for the fair rental value of the "big house," (4) that any sums due from Basilides should constitute a lien on his share of the property. The trial court entered a decree for the plaintiffs substantially as prayed.

The assignments of error present three questions for consideration:
1. Did appellant obtain title to the real estate by adverse possession?
2. Should appellant be compelled to make an accounting of income from the property?
3. Were respondents entitled to a lien upon appellant's interest in the property for the amount found due after accounting?

The opinion discusses the questions, in the order set out above.]

SIMPSON, C.J. . . .

Appellant contends that the evidence shows him to have been in actual, uninterrupted, open, notorious, hostile and exclusive possession of the property under claim of right since November 20, 1929, and for that reason he has acquired title by adverse possession.

---

19. How do the two plaintiff children of Alice Basilides (not children of Charles) get any interest in the property? Can you deduce what the Washington statutes must provide? Wash. Rev. Code ch. 117 (1974) amended the Washington intestacy laws to provide that the surviving spouse takes all the community property even if there is issue.

The general rule relative to securing title to property owned in common by adverse possession is found in the following comprehensive statements:

> Since acts of ownership which, in case of a stranger, would be deemed adverse and per se a disseisin, are, in cases of tenancies in common, susceptible of explanation consistently with the real title, they are not necessarily inconsistent with the unity of possession existing under a cotenancy. For this reason, whether the acts of ownership will be such as to break and dissolve the unity of possession, constitute an adverse possession as against the cotenants, and amount to a disseisin, depends upon the intent with which they are done, and upon their notoriety and essential character. Accordingly, it is a general rule that the entry of a cotenant on the common property, even if he takes the rents, cultivates the land, or cuts the wood and timber without accounting or paying for any share of it, will not ordinarily be considered as adverse to his cotenants and an ouster of them. Rather, such acts will be construed in support of the common title. Mere exclusive possession, accompanied by no act that can amount to an ouster of the other cotenant, or give notice to him that such possession is adverse, will not be held to amount to a disseisin of such cotenant. Mere intention, unannounced, is not sufficient to support a claim of adverse title although the exclusive taking of the profits by one tenant in common for a long period of time, with the knowledge of the other cotenant and without any claim of right by him, may raise a natural presumption of ouster upon which the jury may find the fact to exist, if it satisfies their minds, yet the law will not, from this fact, merely raise a presumption of such ouster.
>
> Generally, a cotenant's sole possession of the land becomes adverse to his fellow tenants by his repudiation or disavowal of the relation of cotenancy between them, and any act or conduct signifying his intention to hold, occupy, and enjoy the premises exclusively, and of which the tenant out of possession has knowledge, or of which he has sufficient information to put him upon inquiry, amounts to an ouster of such tenant. In other words, where one cotenant occupies the common property notoriously as the sole owner, using it exclusively, improving it and taking to his own use the rents and profits, or otherwise exercising over it such acts of ownership as manifest unequivocally an intention to ignore and repudiate any right in his cotenants, such occupation or acts and claim of sole ownership will amount to a disseisin of his cotenants, and his possession will be regarded as adverse from the time they have knowledge of such acts or occupation and of the claim of exclusive ownership. A writing is unnecessary, but the claimant must show a definite and continuous assertion of an adverse right by overt acts of unequivocal character clearly indicating an assertion of ownership of the premises to the exclusion of the right of the other cotenants. [1 Am. Jur., Adverse Possession §54.]

> It is a general rule that an entry upon real property by a tenant in common claiming an adverse possession against his cotenants can never become the foundation of such a title until such cotenants first have had actual knowledge of the repudiation of their rights. The law deems the possession to be amicable until the tenant out of possession has in some way been notified that it has become hostile. [1 Am. Jur., Adverse Possession §56.]

In the following cases this court has adhered to the rule of law just quoted.

In Cox v. Tompkinson, 39 Wash. 70, 80 P. 1005, 1006, Hiram Muzzy made a homestead entry on land near Spokane Falls in 1880, and lived on the property for some time with his family. His wife died, January 6, 1886, leaving as heir one child. Immediately after receiving his final receiver's receipt, Muzzy platted a part of the land into streets, alleys, lots and blocks as an addition to the city of Spokane Falls. The streets and alleys were dedicated to the public use. Thereafter he placed a mortgage upon a portion of the lots and blocks. The mortgage was thereafter foreclosed and the property purchased by the mortgagee, who went into possession at once and thereafter paid taxes and assessments. Many of the lots were sold and improved for business and residential purposes. The streets were used and improved by the city. The daughter of Muzzy and wife lived with her father until 1887, and thereafter for many years lived near the property and was acquainted with the actions of her father and those who succeeded him as owners of the property. In upholding a decree establishing title by an adverse possession in the purchaser at the foreclosure sale, this court said:

> As the possession of land, held by a common title by one tenant in common does not imply hostility, as does possession by a stranger to the title, stronger evidence is required to show an adverse holding by a tenant in common than by a stranger, but the evidence need not differ in kind. Actual verbal or written notice is not necessary to start the statute running in such a case. If there be outward acts of exclusive ownership by the tenant in possession, of such a nature as to preclude the idea of a joint ownership, brought home to the cotenant, or of so open and public a character that a reasonable man would discover it, it is sufficient. 1 Cyc. 1071 et seq. The facts in the case before us, we think, show conclusively that the possession of Hiram Muzzy of the homestead property was at all times adverse to the appellant. He not only had and maintained exclusive control and dominion over it as long as he retained the title, but his outward acts with reference thereto were inconsistent with any other idea than that of sole ownership. We think, too, they were of sufficient publicity and notoriety to put the appellant upon notice of his claim. It would be difficult to give more publicity to one's claim of ownership and title to real property than to plat the same into lots and blocks as an addition to a city, and sell and convey such lots by deeds of warranty.

The facts in Graves v. Graves, 48 Wash. 664, 94 P. 481, 482, show that husband and wife owned two pieces of real property. The husband, Norris Graves, obtained a decree of divorce which did not dispose of the real estate. Graves retained exclusive possession of the property for over thirteen years, collected rents, paid taxes and made some slight improvements. In deciding the case, we said:

> The decree, therefore, left them tenants in common of that property. Ambrose v. Moore, 46 Wash. 463, 90 P. 588, 11 L.R.A., N.S., 103. It is true she has made no effort to enforce her interest in the property since that time, and it is

also true that he has collected the rents and paid the taxes, but there was no communication between the parties until about 1906, when an effort was made by the respondent to purchase the interest of appellant, and, not being able to agree upon the price, the respondent then notified the appellant that she had no interest in the lots, and then the appellant brought this action. There can be no doubt that during all the years since the divorce was granted in 1893 the property was joint property, and has been held by the respondent who was a co-tenant with the appellant. The general rule in regard to adverse possession by one co-tenant against another is stated in 1 Cyc. 1071, as follows: "The entry and possession of land under the common title by one co-tenant will not be presumed to be adverse to the others, but will ordinarily be held to be for the benefit of all."

Following a quotation from Cox v. Tompkinson, *supra,* the court continued:

In this case the outward act of ownership consisted in possession, the collection of rents, and the payment of taxes by the respondent. "The mere receipt and retention by one co-tenant in possession of all the rents and profits does not of itself constitute an adverse possession, and will not ripen into title as against the others, though continued for the statutory period." 1 Cyc. 1076. The property appears to have been improved property, consisting of two dwelling houses. It was not shown that the rents and profits do not meet the taxes and other necessary expenses, or that respondent had refused to account for rents, or that appellant had ever requested an accounting. In fact, the appellant appears to have made her home in places distant from Spokane, and had no communication with respondent from 1893 until about 1906. We think she had a right to assume that the rents would meet all the expenses and that the respondent was holding the property as co-tenant, because there were no outward acts which would put her on notice of an adverse claim. We do not think the appellant was guilty of laches. The record shows no improvements to have been made on the property since the separation of appellant and respondent. There has been no change of condition and no platting or mortgages or sales of any part of the property, as was the case in Cox v. Tompkinson, *supra. . . .*

When we apply the rules just set out to the facts present in the case at bar, we find that they are like those present in the *Graves* . . . case and dissimilar to those in the *Cox* . . . case. We therefore hold that the evidence in this case was not sufficient to establish the claim that appellant made any adverse claim to the property, and that the facts indicate that his actions in living in the "big house" and collecting rents from the "little house" were not such outward acts as would amount to adverse possession.

Appellant argues, however, that the action was not commenced within the time limited by law. There is no merit in this contention. The statute of limitations does not begin to run in cases of this character until notice has been made of an adverse holding or claim on the part of one seeking title by adverse possession, and there has been an ouster. Hicks v. Hicks, 69 Wash.

627, 125 P. 945. Accord: Adams v. Hopkins, 144 Cal. 19, 77 P. 712; Ludey v. Pure Oil Co., 157 Okl. 1, 11 P.2d 102; Fowler v. Hardee, Tex. Civ. App., 16 S.W.2d 154.

It is next claimed that respondents were guilty of laches which estopped them from claiming an interest in the property. Appellant argues that respondents deliberately delayed their action for fourteen years and concealed their claim in the hope of profiting by the delay and the ignorance of the claim on the part of appellant. He argues that the intent to delay on the part of respondents is proven by certain testimony given by Mrs. McKnight. About a year after appellant re-married in 1933 and after appellant had asked her to sign a quitclaim deed to the properties, Mrs. McKnight consulted a lawyer concerning her interest in the property. Her testimony relative to the visit to the attorney was as follows:

> A. Yes, and I went to him and I says,— After he looked it up to see if he had probated anything and there wasn't anything probated at all, he says, "They can't do a thing. There won't be anything done until it is probated." And he says, "I wouldn't worry a thing about it until it is probated," he says, "Let them start probating and then it is time for you to start in."

He presents figures to prove that, if the estate had been probated, he would have received over $4,000 and the respondents about $400 each, but that, under the present judgment, he will receive approximately $200 and respondents over $3,000.

"Laches is a doctrine of equity. It does not arise from mere lapse of time alone, but arises upon lapse of time together with some intervening change in the condition or relation of the parties adversely affecting the rights of the party sought to be charged. To constitute laches, not only must there have been delay in the assertion of the claim, but some change of condition must have occurred which would make it inequitable to enforce the claim." Lindblom v. Johnston, 92 Wash. 171, 158 P. 972, 974. . . .

The situation is best explained by the trial judge in his oral decision made at the close of the trial, when he said:

> That brings me to the question raised here of laches. Now, suppose these girls, a month after the mother died, when they found the father had not taken out letters of administration, had taken out letters of administration, had this estate probated, this father would have been worse off today than their silence has left him. He is worth more today by their not asserting that right than if they had asserted it and left him with only half of the property. So laches does not put him in any worse position. The only effect of it is that he is today in a better position by reason of what is called laches than he would have been, in a much better position. So that disposes of the doctrine of laches.

The lapse of time did not obscure any evidence in this case. All of the witnesses who could have testified relative to the situation and condition of the property in 1929 were available at the trial of this case, and there is no showing that any material documents were lost or destroyed. Appellant's argument that he would have received more from the property had the estate been probated promptly loses its force when we call to mind that he could have himself probated the estate immediately after the death of his wife in 1929. If there was any undue delay, he was a party to that delay and cannot now urge the defense of laches against his cotenants.

We hold that respondents were not estopped by their delay in instituting this action.

The trial court compelled appellant to make an accounting. In so doing, appellant was given credit for repairs, improvements, taxes and insurance in the amount of $4,753.46. He was then charged for the use of the properties between November 20, 1929, and May, 1943, in the total sum of $8,001. Respondents were given a judgment in the sum of $1,083.18 for their share of the rental use of the two properties, and the judgment was made a lien upon the interest that appellant owned in the properties. A portion of the income received consisted of rentals for the "little house," which was sold, April 1, 1938, on a partial payment sales contract. Since the date of the sale, appellant was charged a reasonable value for its use. The charge for the use of the "big house" was fixed at an amount which the court found from testimony to be the reasonable rental value thereof. The record discloses that the income was at all times sufficient to pay the taxes and other expenses. The improvements were of a minor nature and did not to any appreciable extent enhance the rental or sales value of the property.

Appellant was responsible for and was properly held to an accounting of the rents he received from the "little house." Thompson on Real Property (Perm. Ed.), vol. 4, p. 431, §1908.

The charge for the occupancy of the "big house" and the reasonable rental value of the "little house" subsequent to its sale presents a more difficult problem.

The general rule is stated as follows in 62 C.J., Tenancy in Common, p. 446, §64:

While there is some authority in the United States to the contrary, based apparently upon the assumption that the Statute of Anne has become a part of the common law of the particular jurisdiction and upon an interpretation of that statute at variance with that adopted by the English courts, the generally accepted rule is that at common law one tenant in common who occupies all or more than his proportionate share of the common premises is not liable, because of such occupancy alone, to his cotenant or cotenants for rent or for use and occupation. He may become liable therefor, however, because of an express or implied agreement or if he stands in a fiduciary relationship to his cotenant, or where he has ousted his cotenant and, in some jurisdictions, liability is placed on him by virtue of express statute or because of the interpretation placed upon statutes similar in their terms to that of the Statute of Anne. Notwithstanding the rule may prevail in the particular jurisdiction that a cotenant may be charged for the use and occupancy of more than his proportionate share of the common premises, the circumstances of the particular case may require a denial of the application of the rule as inequitable, as where the occupancy has been with the acquiescence of the cotenants or the other cotenants have abandoned the occupancy of the property and declined to occupy it.

If common property was unoccupied without the fault of any of the tenants in common then, on an accounting between them, none of them should be charged for the use of the property.

Accord: Thompson on Real Property (Perm. Ed.), vol. 4, p. 434, §1911. . . .

The last expression of this court upon the question under discussion is found in In re Foster's Estate, 139 Wash. 224, 246 P. 290, 292. The facts in that case were that one John Foster was the owner of an undivided one-half interest in real estate upon which he made his home. The other half was owned by his children. After the death of his wife, Foster remarried and subsequently died. The surviving spouse brought an action against the children for taxes, insurance and improvements made upon the property. The evidence showed that the taxes and insurance had been paid by Foster, and that his widow had made a number of improvements on the property. The trial court denied the right to show the rental value of the use of the premises occupied by the widow from the time of the death of Foster. This court reversed the case and in so doing stated:

Objection is also made that the court refused to allow recovery for the rental value of the premises occupied by Adeline Foster from the time of decedent's death. If it is sought to render a money judgment in favor of Adeline Foster for improvements made from her separate funds, there should be offset against this one-half of the reasonable rental value of the premises from the time of decedent's death. The court was of the opinion that the claim for rent should be filed in the matter of the estate. But the occupancy by Adeline Foster of the premises in question was not an occupancy as administratix; it was personal. As to the one-half belonging to the estate she may be required at the time of her final account as administratix to render an account as to its rental value if the circumstances justify, but, as to the one-half belonging to the other cotenants, her use is a personal one, which can be offset against any claim that she has against the cotenants.

The cause is reversed, with instructions (1) to ascertain if the improvements made upon the premises were necessary, or to what extent they enhanced the value thereof; (2) to ascertain the reasonable value of the rental of the premises, and allow recovery for one-half of that amount.

. . . We are not disposed to follow the general rule laid down in 62 C.J., *supra,* for the reason that it is not an equitable one. There is no sound basis for the general rule of law. No practical or reasonable argument can be advanced for allowing one in possession to reap a financial benefit by occupying property owned in common without paying for his personal use of that part of the property owned by his cotenants. The fairest method in cases in which the cotenant occupies and uses common property, instead of renting it out, is to charge him with its reasonable rental value. Of course there would be an exception to this holding in cases where the income resulted from improvements placed upon the property by the cotenant in possession. Appellant used the "big house" as a home for many years, and it was proper that he be charged with the reasonable rental value of that use and made to account to his cotenants for their share of that rental value. However, appellant should not be charged with the rental value of the "little house" after its sale, for the reason that he did not receive any rent, nor did he occupy or use it in any way. . . .

The judgment will be modified by striking therefrom the charge for use of the "little house" subsequent to the time it was sold. In all other particulars the judgment will be affirmed.

MILLARD, BLAKE, ROBINSON, JJ. concur.

MALLERY, J. (dissenting).

"The generally accepted rule is that at common law one tenant in common who occupies all or more than his proportionate share of the common premises is not liable, because of such occupancy alone, to his cotenant or cotenants for rent or for use and occupation." 62 C.J. Tenancy in Common, p. 446, Sec. 64.

This rule accords well with the rule that in the absence of an ouster the cotenant's possession is not adverse. In the face of the presumption of permission, the hostile character of the possession must fail. Therefore the majority opinion rightly holds that appellant's claim to title by adverse possession cannot prevail.

By the same token, since the adverse possession failed by reason of the permissive nature of his possession, he cannot be held liable for rent for the use of the "big house." His cotenants deliberately let him "carry the burden" during the depression years. They cannot now deny their permission without establishing his hostile possession. Of course the rentals for the "little house" were received in trust for his cotenants.

Appellant has been charged in the accounting with his share of $8,001 of the rental value on the "big house" for the period beginning November 20, 1929, and ending May, 1943, which is over thirteen years. Rem. Rev. Stat., §157 . . . limits an action for the rents and profits or for the use and occupation of real estate to a period of six years. He should have been charged nothing. Even a stranger to the title could have been held for only six years. I dissent.[20]

20. Commented on in 19 Wash. L. Rev. 218 (1944). On the incidents of concurrent interests, see American Law of Property §§6.10-6.18 (Casner ed. 1952).—EDS.

Problems

14.12.   A and B are tenants in common of oil and gas lands. A occupies the lands and, without objection by B, produces oil and gas therefrom. B brings a bill for an accounting in a state which follows Pico v. Columbet and does not follow McKnight v. Basilides. Can B get an accounting? Harrigan v. Lynch, 21 Mont. 36, 52 P. 642 (1898); 29 L.R.A. (n.s.) 224, 226 (1911).

14.13.   The real estate tax normally does not create a personal liability; it creates a lien upon the land as of the date upon which it is assessed.[21] A and B are tenants in common of Blackacre. A refuses to make any payment for taxes. B pays the taxes in full. Then A goes into bankruptcy. You represent B. What will be your contention on B's behalf? See 54 Harv. L. Rev. 521 (1941).

14.14.   A and B are tenants in common of Blackacre. They give to M a mortgage on Blackacre to secure their note of $25,000. M forecloses by sale; A purchases the property for $21,000 at the foreclosure sale. A conveys to V. V contracts to sell to P, the contract calling for "a good marketable and clear record title," with exceptions as to easements and restrictions of record and local zoning laws. P refuses to accept the title and sues for return of P's deposit. What judgment? Salter v. Quinn, 334 Mass. 220, 134 N.E.2d 749 (1956).

14.15.   Eighteen acres of land were conveyed "to George and Martha Zeigler, husband and wife."

Martha Zeigler died, survived by George and three adult children. George and the children all thought that title to the land vested in him at Martha's death; but, under the local statutes, this was erroneous. In reality the land was owned as tenants in common by George (a one-half share) and his children (a one-sixth share each).

George executed an oil and gas lease to Seybert for three years and so long thereafter as oil should be produced and royalties paid, Seybert to have the exclusive right to drill for and produce oil and gas on the premises. The royalty was one-eighth of the product. Seybert drilled on the land in full view of George and his children, who made no comment. Seybert struck oil in about six weeks, then began drilling another well.

Someone suggested to the children that they should have a lawyer look into the title. The children thereupon discovered that they owned a half interest in the land. They told Seybert to stop drilling. He refused.

George and the three children then executed an oil and gas lease of the property to Rapp, who went upon the premises and erected a derrick. The royalty was one-sixth of the oil produced. Seybert tore down the derrick.

What are the rights of Seybert and Rapp?

Zeigler v. Brenneman, 237 Ill. 15, 86 N.E. 597 (1908); Prairie Oil & Gas Co. v. Allen, 2 F.2d 566 (8th Cir. 1924); 16 Chi.-Kent L. Rev. 301 (1938).

---

21.   For a statute which does create a personal liability, see Mass. Gen. Laws Ann. ch. 60, §35.

14.16. James C. Peyton had spent most of his business life developing the National Stoker Company, a corporation with a net worth of about $2,000,000. Peyton owned 70 percent of the stock; the balance was owned by others. At Peyton's death he was childless and a widower. He bequeathed his stock to five men who had worked closely with him in the National Stoker Company

> as joint tenants and not severally nor as tenants in common, with the right of survivorship expressly vested in said joint tenants. Acceptance of this gift by the five above named shall be deemed an agreement among them to hold such gift without severance of the joint tenancy to the end that this stock may be administered as a unit by them and their survivors only. . . . It is my wish to so dispose of my interest in the National Stoker Company as to leave the control and direction thereof concentrated in the hands of those who have been associated with me in its development and to evidence to them my appreciation and gratitude for their cooperation with me in the development of this enterprise.

The effect of this clause was litigated before the Connecticut courts. The following passages are quoted from the opinion of the supreme court of errors:

> This [will] unmistakably expresses an intent that the defendants should take the estate as joint tenants with right of survivorship. Such an estate is not favored in this jurisdiction, but where the intent to create it is plainly manifested by the terms of a will we give effect to it. An incident of such an estate is that it may be severed by a voluntary conveyance of his interest by one of the tenants, by partition, or by appropriation under process of law of the interest of a tenant to satisfy his debts.
>
> The testator did not seek directly to impose upon the estate he created a prohibition against the alienation of his interest by any of the defendants. He left the matter of the prevention of a severance to agreement between them. He had the right to place any legal condition upon his gift, and, if the defendants accepted, that condition would become binding upon them. . . . [U]pon their accepting the fund an agreement not to sever would be implied in fact from their act in so doing. An agreement by joint tenants that they will not sever the estate does not affect the legal title to the property but is binding only upon them personally, and it would not destroy the right of creditors of any of them to reach their interests any further than would any agreement of an owner of property with reference to the disposition of the title to it. . . .
>
> It remains to consider the claim of the plaintiff that the acceptance of the gift by the defendants upon this condition and the consequent implied agreement that they would not sever their interests was in violation of the rules forbidding restraints upon alienation. . . .
>
> It is generally held that a condition imposed by a testator that property bequeathed or devised shall not be partitioned after his death or any agreement between joint owners that they will not partition the property for some reasonable period is not invalid as constituting an illegal restraint upon

alienation. . . . [A]greements restricting the sale of stock in corporations made to assure a continuous and harmonious administration of the property are sustained as serving rather than interfering with its beneficial use. . . .

In this instance the restraint resulting from an agreement among the defendants not to sever their interests in the fund would be calculated to secure a skilled and harmonious conduct of the enterprise; it could not extend beyond a life or lives in being, which we have held to be the limit beyond which, even when incident to a trust, restraints on alienation cannot extend; and at most it went no farther than to restrain the alienation of particular property except as the defendants might as joint owners agree to its disposition. The agreement against the severance of the interests of the defendants is not invalid as offensive to public policy. [Peyton v. Wehrhane, 125 Conn. 420, 436-439, 6 A.2d 313, 319-320 (1939).]

a. Was the testator's plan of disposition a sensible one?
b. Did he use the best method available to carry out the plan he had?
c. What method would you use to carry out any different plan that would have better carried out testator's basic purpose?

With *Peyton*[22] compare 54 Harv. L. Rev. 1081 (1941).

14.17. Lloyd and Martha Dean were husband and wife. She had a safe deposit box in the Bank of America containing stock certificates, bonds, and jewelry, worth $12,000. Mrs. Dean went to the hospital and was told by her physician that she could not get well. She wrote a letter to the Bank of America asking that Lloyd be given access to her box, and she asked Lloyd to bring its contents to her. Lloyd took the letter to the bank, but they refused to turn over the property on the basis of such a letter. "But," the clerk added, "if she wants to have it put in joint tenancy then you could enter the box." The clerk gave Lloyd a form of signature card which would be accepted by the bank. Lloyd repeated the conversation to Martha. Martha said, "All right. Give me the card. I'll sign it" and did so. Lloyd also signed. The card read in part as follows:

Joint Tenants (One Signature Required — Right of Survivorship)
The undersigned jointly and severally agree with each other and with the said Bank that in the event of the death of either renter, the survivor will for every purpose be the sole renter of said box, with the exclusive right of access thereto and possession of the contents thereof.

Lloyd took the card to the bank and brought the contents to Martha. Martha took out certain jewelry, which she gave to her sister. Then she asked Lloyd to put the property back into the box, which he did. Shortly thereafter Martha died.

---

22. The facts are slightly changed to eliminate other issues that arose in the actual case. In view of the change of facts the names of the testator and of his company have also been slightly changed.

Who is entitled to the contents of the box as between Lloyd and the executor of Martha's will? In re Dean's Estate, 68 Cal. App. 2d 86, 155 P.2d 901 (1945); 32 Calif. L. Rev. 301 (1944); 33 Calif. L. Rev. 328 (1945).

Note: *Simultaneous Death of Joint Owners*

Uniform Simultaneous Death Law

> §3. Joint tenants or tenants by the entirety. Where there is no sufficient evidence that two joint tenants or tenants by the entirety have died otherwise than simultaneously the property so held shall be distributed one half as if one had survived and one half as if the other survived. Where more than two joint tenants have died and there is no sufficient evidence that they died otherwise than simultaneously the property so held shall be divided into as many equal shares as there were joint tenants and the share allocable to each shall be distributed as if he had survived all the others.

For a case which discusses the simultaneous death problem where no statute is involved, see In re Strong's Will, 171 Misc. 445, 12 N.Y.S.2d 544 (1939).

Problem

14.18. H and W own real property as tenants by the entirety. He shoots his wife and then shoots himself, but the order of their deaths cannot be established by proof. H's will gives all his property to his son, S, and W's will gives all her property to her daughter, D. In a state which has adopted the Uniform Simultaneous Death Law, what disposition should be made of the real property? If it is established that H did survive W by a short period of time, should that change the result? See In re Bobula, 25 A.D.2d 241, 269 N.Y.S.2d 599 (1966), *remitted for further proceedings,* 19 N.Y.2d 818, 227 N.E.2d 49 (1967). See also In re Cox's Estate, 141 Mont. 583, 380 P.2d 584 (1963).

SECTION 6. PROBATE CONSIDERATIONS

When a person of property dies, the decedent's estate is normally administered under the direction of a probate court. An executor (if there is a will) or an administrator (if there is no will) collects the assets, pays the debts, pays the taxes, pays his or her fee and that of the lawyer for the estate, and distributes the balance of the property according to the will or the intestate law.

In small estates where there are no complicating factors, joint tenancies of land, bank accounts, government bonds, and the like cause the survivor to take the whole automatically and thereby eliminate the necessity of probate. This saves trouble and money in most cases.

Even in large estates, where the complexities are such that probate is necessary, joint tenancies can perform useful functions. For one thing a joint tenancy can cause the title to the family residence to be located in a surviving relative immediately. Then again, a joint bank account can provide for the survivor resources of immediate ready cash — a commodity which is often lacking due to the fact that upon death all assets of the deceased pass at once to his or her executor or administrator. This official cannot be expected to pay out funds to the family until it is known for sure that creditors will not wipe out the estate.

Of course, both of these advantages also attach to tenancies by the entirety. But, by way of cynical caution, ponder well the divorce and separation statistics before creating for your clients a form of estate which, in the case of estrangement, gives to an embittered spouse a veto power over sales and mortgages of the property.[23]

Note: Condominiums and Cooperatives

Multi-party living accommodations may be worked out in what are called condominiums or cooperative housing arrangements. Condominiums and cooperative housing are dealt with as an aspect of the general problem of land use and development in Part VIII.

Note: Time-Sharing Arrangements

Multi-party living accommodations may be worked out which involve each party's being entitled to exclusive rights in specified living accommodations for some specified period of time during each year. These time-sharing arrangements are particularly useful in a year-round resort area. Each party can plan his or her vacation at the time of the year his or her exclusive use of the accommodation is available. In this regard, see the Model Real Estate Time Share Act. See also The Law and Business of Time-Share Resorts (1982), by Mark E. Henze, which includes the texts of various time-share acts.

---

23. The pros and cons of avoiding probate are examined in Casner, Estate Planning — Avoidance of Probate, 60 Colum. L. Rev. 108 (1960).

Probate and Property, Vol. 12, No. 2, Fall 1983, published by the Section of Real Property, Probate and Trust Law, American Bar Association, contains an article by Robert E. Dungan entitled Right-to-Use Timeshare Contracts Rejected in Bankruptcy Proceedings. In footnote 5 to this article, it is pointed out that there are two principal ways to create a time-share fee and that the time-share fee arrangement is to be compared with the non-ownership time-share plans. A right-to-use time-share contract is a non-ownership time-share plan. As the name of the article indicates, it is concerned with right-to-use time-share contracts. The case the article examines is In re Sombrero Reef Club Inc., 18 B.R. 612 (S.D. Fla. Bankr. Ct. 1982), which held that the right-to-use contracts in a time-share development are executory contracts and can be rejected by the debtor in possession or by the trustee.

PART V

BEFORE AND AFTER THE STATUTE OF USES

CHAPTER 15

CONVEYANCING AND FUTURE INTERESTS BEFORE THE STATUTE OF USES

Modern real estate law commences with the Statute of Uses (1536). To understand it we must dip into the background of common-law conveyancing and the common-law rules as to future interests.

You will find this background irritating unless you consider it in historical perspective. It comprises a set of rules which had no certain foundation in reason, even feudal reason, and which were rigidly adhered to with utter disregard of their practical effects long after any possible utility had vanished. Many of these rules received their definitive formulation in the period during which Coke (1552-1634) dominated English legal thinking; and Coke in turn was dominated by his antiquarian interest in Littleton (1407-1481). It was not the temper of the times to re-examine premises and basic assumptions; people were burned alive for this in the field of religion, and law was close to religion. When Lord Mansfield, even a century later, undertook to loosen up the old rules in the name of practicality and common sense, he evoked two statements which epitomized the temper of the English courts and the conveyancing bar. Justice Blackstone, severely reversing Lord Mansfield, announced the conveyancer's creed when he said: "The law of real property in this country is now formed into a fine artificial system, full of unseen connections and nice dependencies, and he that breaks one link of the chain, endangers the dissolution of the whole."[1] "Junius," a controversialist uninhibited by the limitation of the bench, added:

> Instead of those certain positive rules by which the judgments of a court of law should invariably be determined, you [Lord Mansfield] have fondly intro-

---

1. Perrin v. Blake, reported in Hargrave, Tracts Relative to the Law of England 489 (1787).

duced your own unsettled notions of equity and substantial justice. . . . By such treacherous arts the noble simplicity and free spirit of our Saxon laws were first corrupted.[2]

If you can adjust yourself to the spirit of the eras of Littleton and Coke, you will be able to recapture some measure of the satisfaction which they obviously took in the esoteric formalism of their legal system. If you cannot, prepare yourself to be unhappy for a space.

SECTION 1. COMMON-LAW METHODS OF CREATING AND TRANSFERRING ESTATES

A freehold in possession could be created or transferred only by livery of seisin (feoffment). If O owned Blackacre in fee simple and wanted to transfer it to A, both of them went on the land and O handed A a twig, uttering appropriate words to indicate an intent to transfer title.[3] A charter of feoffment usually accompanied the ceremony, but it had only evidential value and was not necessary to the effectiveness of the transfer. Why this rule? One can speculate: (1) The rule arose in a period when only the clergy could read and write—indeed, anyone who could read and write was automatically a cleric and entitled to "benefit of clergy," i.e., important exemptions from criminal process and punishment—but anyone at all

---

2. 3 Campbell, Lives of the Chief Justices 337. The Perrin v. Blake controversy, with Fearne's ironic letter of "apology" and the disclosure of the fact that Mansfield had previously represented *both* sides in a case which he decided from the bench, is detailed in Leach & Logan, Future Interests and Estate Planning 122 (1961).

3. Just the right things had to be said and/or done. Coke set this forth in all its lush detail for the conveyancers of his day:

> And there be two kinds of livery of seisin, viz., a livery in deed, and a livery in law. A livery in deed is when the feoffor taketh the ring of the door, or turf or twig of the land, and delivereth the same upon the land to the feoffee in name of seisin of the land.
>
> A seised of an house in fee, and being in the house, saith to B: I demise to you this house for term of my life; this is a good beginning to limit the estate, but here wanteth livery. A livery in deed may be done two manner of ways. By a solemn act and words; as by delivery of the ring or hasp of the door, or by a branch or twig of a tree, or by a turf of the land, and with these or like words, the feoffor and feoffee both holding the deed of feoffment, and the ring of the door, hasp, branch, twig, or turf, and the feoffor saying, Here I deliver you seisin and possession of this house, in the name of all the lands and tenements contained in this deed, according to the form and effect of this deed. Or by words without any ceremony or act; as, the feoffor being at the house door, or within the house, Here I deliver you seisin and possession of this house, in the name of seisin and

could grasp the significance of the ceremonial transfer; (2) all semi-primitive law, including the early feudal system, places great significance on physical possession.

A freehold not in possession — a remainder or reversion — could be transferred by grant, i.e., an instrument under seal. "All lands lie in livery or in grant; and they do not lie in livery where the party intending to convey cannot give immediate possession."[4] Until 1705 (4 & 5 Anne ch. 16, §9) the holder of the present estate had to give assent to the transfer before the new tenurial relationship was established. This assent was known as *attornment.*

A leasehold estate could be created or transferred by an agreement between the parties, plus a taking of possession by the lessee or transferee. After the agreement, but before the taking of possession, the lessee had an *interesse termini.*

Surrender and release. Where there is a present interest and a future interest, a conveyance by the owner of the former to the owner of the latter is a surrender (if the future interest is the next vested estate); a conveyance by the latter to the former is a release. These are principally important with regard to terms of years. Thus, where L has leased to T for one year, T can surrender T's leasehold to L (and the law of landlord and tenant has much to do with surrenders, express and implied) or L can release L's reversion to T (and you will shortly observe how the lease and release became a common form of conveyance of a fee simple). A release had to be made by grant, i.e., instrument under seal. Originally no formalities were required for a surrender, but the Statute of Frauds (1677) required that surrenders be in writing except those which took place "by operation of law."

---

possession of all the lands and tenements contained in this deed; et sic de similibus: or, Enter you into this house or land, and have and enjoy it according to the deed; or, Enter into the house or land, and God give you joy; or, I am content you shall enjoy this land according to the deed; or the like. For if words may amount to a livery within the view, much more it shall upon the land. But if a man deliver the deed of feoffment upon the land, this amounts to no livery of the land, for it hath another operation to take effect as a deed; but if he deliver the deed upon the land in name of seisin of all the lands contained in the deed, this is a good livery; and so are other books intended that treat hereof, that the deed was delivered in name of seisin of that land. Hereby it appeareth, that the delivery of any thing upon the land in name of seisin of that land, though it be nothing concerning the land, as a ring of gold, is good.

A livery in law is, when the feoffor saith to the feoffee, being in the view of the house or land: I give you yonder land to you and your heirs, and go enter into the same, and take possession thereof accordingly, and the feoffee doth accordingly in the life of the feoffor enter, this is a good feoffment. . . . But if either feoffor or the feoffee die before entry the livery is void. And livery within the view is good where there is no deed of feoffment. [Co. Litt. 48a, b.]

If this seems to you too, too quaint, take note that the formal requirements for making a will at the present date are every bit as precise, and any deviation from them is penalized by rendering the will invalid. See Casner, Estate Planning ch. 3 (4th ed.).

4. Doe v. Cole, 7 B. & C. 243 (1827).

SECTION 2. COMMON-LAW FUTURE INTERESTS

Once you conceive of the possibility of an estate which is less than infinite in duration, you must necessarily conceive of a future interest to occupy some or all of the balance of infinity.

Reversionary Interests

Where the only interest conveyed is a present interest of limited duration, the grantor has, as a future interest, the balance of the original estate. Hence arise the following correlatives:

1. Fee simple determinable: possibility of reverter.
2. Fee tail: reversion.
3. Life estate: reversion.
4. Term of years: reversion.

Two comments on the foregoing are called for:

a. The word "estate" has had a changing content through the centuries. A possibility of reverter is now called an estate—for example, in the Restatement; but our grandfathers would have called it, not an estate, but a possibility of becoming an estate. A reversion has always been considered an estate.

b. A reversion after a term of years is unlike a reversion after a freehold in this respect: the reversioner after a term has the seisin, since the termor has only possession. Thus, where O, owner of Blackacre in fee simple, conveys to A for ten years, it is probably more accurate to describe the state of the title as "Fee simple in O, subject to a term of ten years in A." But in common parlance one describes it as "Term of ten years in A, reversion in O."

Problems

15.1. Would it be proper to add to the four reversionary correlatives listed above "Fee simple: escheat"—

a. before Quia Emptores?
b. after Quia Emptores?

15.2. What is the name of the reversionary interest retained by O in each of the following conveyances of land?

a. O conveys to A for life, then if B marries C, to B and her heirs as long as the land is used for residential purposes.

   i. Before B marries C.
   ii. After B marries C.

b.   O conveys to A as long as A lives on the land.
c.   O conveys to A for A's life; A then conveys to B for B's life.
d.   O conveys to A for A's life. A then conveys to B for the life of A as long as the property is used for residential purposes.

Rights of Entry for Condition Broken

In the case of a well-drafted right of entry for condition broken (1) O conveys an estate to A, (2) the conveyance stipulates that the estate is given upon condition that something be done or not done, and (3) the conveyance stipulates that upon breach of the condition the grantor and his or her heirs may re-enter as of his or her former estate. For example, "to A and his [or her] heirs upon condition that the land be not used for industrial or commercial purposes, and if the land shall ever be so used then the grantor and his [or her] heirs may re-enter as of their former estate."

Reversionary interests await the termination of preceding interests before they become possessory. They have, as Professor Edward H. Warren used to say, the quality of patient politeness; and he could say it in such a way that your mind's eye was filled with an Alice-in-Wonderland picture of a reversion stepping aside and bowing low as a life estate preceded it. Not so the right of entry, which unceremoniously cuts off the existing estate and re-establishes the grantor in possession. It can be reserved only in the grantor; "a condition cannot be reserved in a stranger." (But, as we shall see, a reasonable facsimile — shifting executory interest — was made possible by the Statute of Uses.)

Distinguish clearly between the following:

1.   Rights of entry for condition broken *incident to a reversion.* They are very common indeed. Nearly every lease contains one or more. They pass with the landlord's interest to any person to whom the landlord sells the reversion. They are the means by which the landlord retains an effective means of enforcing performance of the tenant's covenants. They are a part of the law of landlord and tenant and are not further considered at this point.

2.   Rights of entry for condition broken *not incident to a reversion.* These are quite rare. Ordinarily when O sells Blackacre to A, A has no obligation to O other than payment of the purchase price. But in some cases O wishes to require or forbid some use of the land — e.g., to require a passageway to be kept in repair, to forbid sale of intoxicating liquors, to forbid non-residential building, etc. In such a case O can provide that the conveyance is upon condition that such and such a thing be done (or not done) and upon breach of the condition O shall have the right to re-enter as of his or her former estate.

This latter type of right of entry has an obviously close relationship to the possibility of reverter after a determinable fee. Indeed it is sometimes called a possibility of reverter — but we suggest that this leads to confusion. The difference between the two estates is that the possibility of reverter arises when the preceding determinable fee expires by the terms of its own limitation, whereas the right of entry cuts short a fee simple which would otherwise continue indefinitely. This distinction between estates which expire and estates which are cut short is one that the old law took very seriously; and significant vestiges still persist.

The fact that the right of entry is optional, whereas the possibility of reverter is automatic, is emphasized in the Restatement by calling the right of entry a "power of termination."

Effect of attempt to assign. In Rice v. Boston & Worcester R.R., 94 Mass. (12 Allen) 141 (1866), it was held that an attempt to assign inter vivos a right of entry not incident to a reversion destroyed the right of entry. It is well established that such a right of entry cannot be assigned inter vivos unless this is specifically permitted by statute. But there was no sound basis in either precedent or logic for holding that the attempt to assign caused a destruction. The court pointed out that the unassignability of rights of entry arose out of the law's abhorrence of maintenance and champerty (obsolete common-law offenses involving stirring up litigation and trading in lawsuits). It then went on:

> Neither party to a conveyance which violates the rule of law can allege his own unlawful act for the purpose of securing an advantage to himself. The grantor of a right of entry cannot be heard to say that his deed was void, and that the right of entry still remains in him, because this would be to allow him to set up his own turpitude in engaging in a champertous transaction as the foundation of his claim. . . . The grantor cannot aver the invalidity of his own deed, nor can the grantee rely on its validity. Both being participators in an unlawful transaction, neither can avail himself of it to establish a title in a court of law. [94 Mass. (12 Allen) at 144.[5]]

Though the rule is unsound it must be reckoned with.[6]

Problem

15.3. In 1950, O granted to A, B, and C a certain parcel of waterfront real estate "to have and to hold to them and their heirs, successors and

---

5. Oak's Oil Service, Inc. v. Massachusetts Bay Transportation Authority, 15 Mass. App. 593, 447 N.E.2d 27 (1983), held that the *Rice* case was no longer the law in Massachusetts as a result of the enactment of Mass. Gen. Laws ch. 184A, §3.

6. Accord Halpin v. Rural Agricultural School District No. 9, 224 Mich. 308, 194 N.W. 1005 (1923); but see Potter, J., dissenting (42 pages), in Dolby v. State Highway Commissioner, 283 Mich. 609, 278 N.W. 694 (1938). Contra Jones v. Oklahoma City, 193 Okla. 637, 145 P.2d 971 (1943). The Restatement of Property (§160, comment c) originally felt compelled to follow Rice v. Boston & W.R.R. but in 1947 voted to change this position on the basis of Jones v. Oklahoma City. See Restatement of Property 415 (1948 Supp.). See American Law of Property §§4.68, 4.69 (Casner ed. 1952).

assigns, so long as the same shall be used for a tee totaling yacht club and no longer, and if the grantees or their successors shall cease to operate a yacht club or shall permit intoxicating liquor to be sold on the premises, the said O and O's heirs shall have the right to re-enter and retake the premises."

In 1980 O died and left a will devising and bequeathing all real and personal property to a close friend, X. The officers of the club, successors to A, B, and C, come to the conclusion that they cannot balance the club's budget unless they operate a bar. They ask your advice. Advise them. Compare Attorney General v. Merrimack Manufacturing Co., 80 Mass (14 Gray) 586, 612 (1860).[7]

Remainders

In addition to reversionary interests (reversions and possibilities of reverter), which exist simply because the grantor has given away less than the grantor had, the common law permitted the creation of certain future interests in strangers. These were called remainders. Thus O, owner of Blackacre in fee simple, could convey:

1. to A for life, remainder to B and his heirs.
2. to A for life, remainder to B for life. (In this case O would have a reversion after the two life estates.)
3. to A for life, remainder to B and the heirs of his body, remainder to C and her heirs.

---

7. Possibilities of reverter and rights of entry are not subject to the rule against perpetuities (see discussion of rule against perpetuities at page 339 *infra*). Statutes have been enacted in a number of states which place a limit on the duration of these future interests. Massachusetts General Laws Annotated ch. 184A, §3, is as follows:

> A fee simple determinable in land or a fee simple in land subject to a right of entry for condition broken shall become a fee simple absolute if the specified contingency does not occur within thirty years from the date when such fee simple determinable or such fee simple subject to a right of entry becomes possessory. If such contingency occurs within said thirty years the succeeding interest, which may be an interest in a person other than the person creating the interest or his heirs, shall become possessory or the right of entry exercisable notwithstanding the rule against perpetuities.

These interests, when valid, only appear of record in the year they are created, and the title examiner has to search the land records back to the beginning if he or she is to be certain there is no possibility of reverter or right of entry outstanding with respect to the land he or she is concerned with. Statutes have been enacted that are designed to ease the title search for these interests. Massachusetts General Laws Annotated ch. 260, §31A, is as follows:

> No proceeding based upon any right of entry for condition broken or possibility of reverter, to which a fee simple or fee simple determinable in land is subject, created before the second day of January, nineteen hundred and fifty-five, shall be maintained either at law or in equity in any court after the first day of January, nineteen hundred and sixty-four, unless on or before the first day of January, nineteen hundred and sixty-four, (a) the condition has been broken or the reverter has occurred, and a person

4. to A for ten years, remainder to B and his heirs. (In this case B was the owner of the present freehold, subject to A's term, a less-than-freehold estate.)

And so on.

But O could not create a remainder after a fee simple determinable. There could be no remainder after any fee simple. Why not? Well, just because there couldn't be, and stop asking impertinent questions.[8]

Remainders are classified as *vested* or *contingent*. Tracing the line of distinction between these two is a very intricate business in some situations; but most cases are not difficult, and the following will serve as a workable

---

or persons having the right of entry or reverter shall have taken possession of the land, and in case of entry made after January first, nineteen hundred and fifty-seven, shall have filed a certificate of entry pursuant to section nineteen of chapter one hundred and eighty-four, or (b) a person or persons having the right of entry, or who would have it if the condition were broken, or would be entitled if the reverter occurred, or one of them if there be more than one, shall by himself, or by his attorney, agent, guardian, conservator or parent, have filed in the registry of deeds, or in the case of registered land, in the registry of the land court, for the district in which the land is situated, a statement in writing, duly sworn to, describing the land and the nature of the right and the deed or other instrument creating it, and where it may be found if recorded or registered, and, in case of registered land, naming the holder or holders of the outstanding certificate of title and stating the number of said certificate, and, in case of land not registered, naming the person or persons appearing of record to own the fee subject to such right or possibility, or shown by the records of the tax assessors at the last prior assessment date to be the owner or owners thereof.

Such statement shall be received and recorded or registered upon payment of the fee required by law, and shall be indexed in the grantor index under the person or persons so named, and in case of registered land, noted on the certificate of title. The register and assistant recorder shall also keep a separate list of such statements.

This section shall apply to all such rights whether or not the owner thereof is a corporation or a charity or a government or governmental subdivision, or is under any disability or out of the commonwealth, and it shall apply notwithstanding any recitals in deeds or other instruments heretofore or hereafter recorded, unless a statement is filed as above provided. Nothing in this section shall be construed to extend the period of any other applicable statute of limitations or to authorize the bringing of any proceeding to enforce any right which has been or may be barred by lapse of time or for any other reason.

It is to be noted that the last paragraph quoted above from section 31A made the statute applicable even though the owner of the right of entry or possibility of reverter was "a government or governmental subdivision." This language was amended in 1968 to read "a government or governmental subdivision other than the Commonwealth." In 1974 a further clarifying amendment was made that stated that the exemption of the commonwealth applied to rights of entry and possibilities of reverter whether created before or after the 1968 amendment. Economic Development & Industrial Corp. v. United States, 546 F. Supp. 1204 (D. Mass. 1982), involved a case where the commonwealth retained a possibility of reverter in land granted to the United States prior to 1968 and the commonwealth failed to comply with the recording requirement. Nevertheless, the court held the possibility of reverter was enforceable as a result of the 1968 amendment.

See also the material on marketable title statutes at page 680 *infra* and page 840 *infra*.

8. The Restatement says that, after the Statute of Uses, an interest can be created in a stranger after a determinable fee and that it is an executory interest. Restatement of Property §25(1)(b). But the point has no substantial importance.

definition at the outset, subject to later amplification and refinement. A remainder is vested if (1) it is given to a born and ascertained person, and (2) no condition precedent is attached to it. A remainder is contingent if (1) it is given to a person who is unborn or unascertained, or (2) it is subject to a condition precedent.[9] Consider the following examples:

1. "To A for life, remainder to B and her heirs." Vested. This means that if B dies in the life of A, the remainder will pass to any person to whom B has devised it in her will or, if she has not devised it, to her heirs. Of course, if B conveys the remainder during her lifetime, the person to whom she conveys it becomes the owner thereof from the moment of the conveyance.

2. "To A for life, remainder to B and her heirs if B survives A." Contingent. The remainder is subject to a condition precedent — viz., that B survive A.

3. "To A for life, remainder to such children of A as shall survive A and their heirs." Contingent. The children to take are not ascertained until it is determined which ones survive A.

4. "To A for life, remainder to A's eldest son and his heirs." A is childless. The remainder is contingent since the remainderman is unborn. But when A has a son, the remainder becomes vested. If the son then dies in the life of A, the remainder passes to any person to whom he conveyed it during his lifetime, or to anyone to whom he devised it in his will, or, if he did neither of these, to his heirs.

5. "To A for life, remainder to the heirs of B," a living person. Contingent. Since nemo est haeres viventis, the remaindermen are unascertained. If B dies in the life of A, the remainder becomes immediately vested in those persons who are B's heirs.

6. "To A for life, remainder to B and her heirs, but if B does not survive A, then to C and his heirs." B's remainder is vested. It is subject to a condition *subsequent* and is thus distinguishable from case 2 above. Yes, the difference is only in the form of expression, and this doesn't make very good sense. But the disposition of millions of dollars of property has turned upon this type of verbal distinction and continues to do so. In this case B's remainder is usually called "vested

9. A tremendous amount of scholarship and printer's ink have been poured at one time and another into working out an exact definition of vested and contingent remainders. In Gray's Rule Against Perpetuities §9 (4th ed. 1942) appears one classic solution:

A remainder is vested if, at every moment during its continuance, it becomes a present estate, whenever and however the preceding freehold estates determine. A remainder is contingent if, in order for it to become a present estate, the fulfillment of some condition precedent, other than the determination of the preceding freehold estates, is necessary.

The Restatement of Property §157 separates vested remainders into three subcategories, renames contingent remainders "remainders subject to a condition precedent," and defines these four classifications in 23 pages, 24 comments, and 26 illustrations of rugged verbal mountaineering.

subject to divestment"; the Restatement calls it "vested subject to total defeasance," which comes to the same thing.[10]

7.   "To A for life, remainder to B and her heirs if B survives A, remainder to C and his heirs if B does not survive A." B and C both have contingent remainders. Observe that one contingency is the reverse of the other; these are called "alternative contingent remainders" or "contingent remainders upon a double aspect" and are quite common.

Does the grantor have a reversion in any of these cases? Of course he or she does. Not in case 1, because there the grantor has given away to A and B all the grantor had. But in case 2 the grantor has a reversion which will become possessory if B dies and then A dies; the reversion will be cut off if A dies, survived by B. A similar situation exists in case 3. In case 4 the grantor has a reversion which is cut off when A has a son. In case 5 the grantor has a reversion which is cut off when B dies in the life of A, thus designating B's heirs. In case 6 there is no reversion, since the remainder in fee to B is vested and can be cut short only by C's interest, which is also a fee; there is no hole in this sequence of estates for a grantor's reversion to fill. Case 7 is the famous case of Egerton v. Massey, 3 C.B. (n.s.) 338 (1857), in which it was held that there was a reversion in the grantor.[11]

You have now met the vested remainder (case 1), the vested remainder subject to divestment (case 6), and the contingent remainder (case 2 and others). You should also now meet in a preliminary way the "vested remainder subject to partial divestment" or, in Restatement language, the "vested remainder subject to open." This is a phenomenon occurring in connection with gifts to classes, which are very common. Suppose there is a conveyance to A for life, remainder to A's children. The remainder is a gift to a class, the class being composed of children. If none of the class is living, the remainder is contingent. But if one or more is living, it is vested in the living children subject to opening to receive any children who may later be born. Thus if two children, C1 and C2, are living, they have vested remainders as co-owners, each having a half interest. When C3 is born, the interests of C1 and C2 are reduced from one-half to one-third each, and C3 also takes one-third. And so on.[12]

10.   Probably case 6 could not exist prior to the Statute of Uses (1536), but this case must be inserted here to emphasize the important distinction between remainders on conditions precedent and remainders on conditions subsequent. The really intricate cases on this distinction are dealt with in Casner, Estate Planning ch. 11 (4th ed.).

11.   For the explanation see Gray, Perpetuities §113.1 (4th ed. 1942). The key to the solution lies in the fact that the life estate in A can end before A dies — e.g., by A committing a breach of feudal obligation which causes A's estate to be forfeited. If this happens, it is clear that neither the estate of B nor the estate of C can come into possession, since the contingency upon which either will take can only be determined at A's death. Hence, the grantor comes into possession upon A's forfeiture by virtue of a reversion.

12.   The common-law rule against perpetuities operated with particularly devastating effect on a class gift in that it defeated the entire class gift if the interest of one member of the class might vest too remotely. See the discussion of the rule against perpetuities, page 335 infra.

Problems

15.4. O conveys to A for life, remainder to A's widower for his life, remainder to B and her heirs. A is living and married to X. B is living. What interests are vested and what contingent? As to any contingent interest, when will it vest, if at all?

15.5. O conveys to A for life, remainder to A's children and their heirs. A is living and has a child, C1. Another child, C2, is born. C1 dies. A dies one year later. Who owns what interests in the property?

SECTION 3.   COMMON-LAW TECHNICAL
RULES AS TO FUTURE INTERESTS

We come now to a series of legal taboos which the early artificers of the land law worked out. Individually they are pretty hard to justify, and in many cases they frustrated the reasonable plans and clear intentions of property owners; but in total they succeeded in simplifying transactions in real estate and in imposing a crude check upon the tendency of the landed rich to tie up the surface of Great Britain in family meshes. When some of these rules were nullified by the Statute of Uses, the courts had to invent a new type of check on this tendency; this was the rule against perpetuities.[13]

At the end of the discussion of each of these rules you will find a note on modern law. This will indicate to you how much of this chapter, which is chiefly historical in function, deals with rules which still survive. (With some sense of shame we must announce that *all* the old rules have been abolished in England, the last of them disappearing in the general property legislation of 1925. But you must become accustomed to learning that we in America adhere to English anomalies and anachronisms long after the British have thrown them down the drain. Even when we do abolish a property rule, the abolition is prospective in operation, and thus the old rule continues in the picture for title examination purposes as the title search delves into past conveyances.)

1.   No Freeholds to Commence In Futuro
(Springing Interests)

Rule 1: A freehold could not be created to commence in futuro. Thus, if O owned Blackacre and wanted presently to transfer it to A so that A's estate would begin when A married B, O could not do it. It can readily be seen that

---

13. The rule against perpetuities is considered at page 335 *infra.*

this would be inconvenient in the case of marriage settlements. B's family, on the basis of the usual highly commercial deal, would be willing to convey the agreed lands to their daughter's intended husband; but they obviously would not care to run the risk that A would leave B waiting at the church.

This rule prohibited what are called *springing* freehold interests, i.e., freeholds which spring out of the estate of the grantor at some future date.

The justification given for the rule was that it was a corollary of the requirement that present freeholds be transferred by livery of seisin. If O made livery of seisin to A, then A had title as of that moment. If O did not make livery of seisin to A, then A got nothing.

How about a conveyance to A for ten years, remainder to B? This was all right. O made livery of seisin to A for the benefit of B. B then had a *present* freehold subject to A's term.

Suppose O owned a valuable portrait and executed a deed of gift declaring that he gave the portrait to A commencing one year from the date of the deed. There was no objection to this since the notion of seisin related only to freehold land. So also there was no objection to creating less-than-freehold interests in land to commence in futuro, or to transferring leasehold interests in such a way that the transfer operated in the future.

Problem

15.6.   Was there a rule that there could be no contingent remainder after a term of years? Consider this question with reference to the following cases, which are assumed to arise in 1500:

a.   O, owner of Blackacre in fee simple, conveys to A for 100 years if A so long live, remainder to A's children who shall survive A and their heirs.

b.   O, owner of a term of 999 years in Blackacre, conveys to A for 100 years if A so long live, remainder to A's children who shall survive A.

c.   O, owner of Blackacre in fee simple, conveys to A for ten years, remainder for ten years to A's eldest daughter living at the end of A's term, remainder to B and her heirs.

Note on modern law. The Statute of Uses (1536) authorized the creation of legal springing interests if the proper formula of words was used. The Statute of Wills (1540) was construed to permit the creation of legal springing interests by will without regard to the form of words. At the present time there is no obstacle to the creation of legal springing interests.

2.   No Conditions in Strangers (Shifting Interests)

Rule 2: A condition could not be reserved in a stranger; that is, the grantor could not give to any grantee an estate which would cut another estate short and thus supersede it. The grantor could reserve to himself or herself a right of entry for condition broken but could not create an estate of this type in anyone else.

This rule prohibits what are called *shifting* freehold interests, i.e., interests which shift from one grantee to another. Thus if O enfeoffed A and his heirs but if A should use the land for non-residential purposes, to B and her heirs, B would get nothing and A would have a fee simple absolute.

Note on modern law. Legal shifting interests were authorized by the Statute of Uses if the proper words were used. The Statute of Wills authorized these interests in wills without any verbal formalities. There is now no obstacle to creating legal shifting interests.

Problem

15.7. The following conveyances of land take place in 1500. Describe the state of the title after each conveyance.
  a. O to A and his heirs as long as the property is used during the next 20 years for agricultural purposes, and then to B and his heirs.
  b. O to A for life and then to B and his heirs, but if B dies without issue, then to C and his heirs.
  c. O to A for life and then to B and his heirs, but if B marries C before A's estate ends, then to D and his heirs.
  d. O to A for life and then to B for ten years, but if B uses the land for non-residential purposes, then to C for the balance of the term.

3. Destructibility of Contingent Remainders

Rule 3: A contingent remainder is destroyed unless it vests at or before the termination of the preceding freehold estates. In that case the next vested estate comes into possession; this is usually the reversion. For example, if O conveys to A for life, remainder to the first son of A who reaches 21, then A dies, leaving a son aged 16, the contingent remainder is destroyed; O's reversion becomes possessory. When the son reaches 21, he still takes nothing.

The justification given for this rule was that the feudal system could not tolerate an "abeyance of the seisin," and it was pointed out that, in the case supposed, the seisin would be in abeyance for the five years between A's death and A's son's majority. Of course there was nothing to this; O's reversion would be possessory during this five-year period, and O would have the seisin and thus be liable for the feudal obligations incident to the estate. However, if the law allowed the son to take when he reached 21, it would seem that he would take by way of a springing interest (i.e., a freehold springing out of the grantor's estate in reversion), and if there is a rule forbidding springing interests it is at least logical to apply it in this case. In any event the rule was well settled and was treated as an article of faith to such an extent that, as late as 1695, a judge who acquiesced in a minor exception to the rule brought down upon himself the severe censure of his brethren.[14]

Artificial destruction of contingent remainders. A life estate ends when the life tenant dies, but it can end in at least two ways while the life tenant is living: (1) by forfeiture, or (2) by merger. Life tenants frequently found it worthwhile to terminate their estates artificially, so that contingent remainders were destroyed; naturally they would take precautions in advance to see to it that they controlled the estates which would become possessory on the termination of the life estates. Let us now describe the two artificial methods of terminating life estates:

1. *Forfeiture.* If a life tenant renounced the fealty to the life tenant's lord which was at the basis of the feudal tenurial relationship the life estate was forfeited. There were certain types of conveyance which a life tenant could make which constituted such renunciation, for, by making them, the life tenant impliedly claimed the fee simple and thereby rejected the tenure by which the life tenant held. Thus if A, a life tenant, enfeoffed B and his heirs, or suffered a common recovery in favor of B and his heirs, or levied a fine on B and his heirs, this conveyance was "tortious" and A's life estate was forfeited. This meant that any remainders which were still contingent failed. The next vested estate came into possession; this was usually the reversion.

2. *Merger.* Suppose O conveys Blackacre to A for life, remainder to B in fee; then A conveys A's life estate to B. B now has a present fee simple; the life estate has merged in the remainder in fee and has thus disappeared. This makes good sense. But now suppose that O conveys to A for life, remainder to A's first son in tail, remainder to B in fee. While A is childless A conveys the life estate to B. Again the life estate merges in the fee simple and thus disappears. Since the remainder in tail to A's first son has not vested at the time the life estate ends, it is destroyed; thus, when a son is born he takes nothing. This does not make good sense; but it was settled law that where a life estate and the next vested estate of freehold came into the same hands,

---

14.   In Reeve v. Long, 3 Lev. 408 (1695), the conveyance was to A for life, remainder to A's first son and his heirs. No son was born to A in his lifetime, but at his death his wife was pregnant. A son was born a few months later. The House of Lords held that the son could take, despite the obvious fact that the remainder had failed to vest before the preceding estate of freehold had determined. Baron Turton of the Court of Exchequer was present in the House at the time, and the Reporter notes that "all the judges . . . very much blamed Baron Turton for permitting it to be found specially where the law was so clear and certain." Mr. Donald G. McNeil, Harvard Law School '38, after reading this case and the appropriate passages in Charles Fearne's great work on contingent remainders, reduced the matter to verse as follows:

> Let's fill the cups to Baron Turton
> Who, though the law was clear and certain,
> Would rather help a little foetus
> Than round out Charlie Fearne's dull treatise.

the life estate was destroyed by merger along with any contingent remainders which were dependent upon it. There are two exceptions to this doctrine of merger which you should master:

a. An estate tail does not merge in a fee simple. Life estates merge, estates for years merge, but not estates tail. Thus, if property is held by A in tail, remainder to B in fee simple, and B conveys B's remainder in fee simple to A, A has a fee tail and also a remainder in fee simple. The rights of A's issue are not cut off. (However, as we know, A can cut off the rights of A's issue by suffering a common recovery or, in later times, by other simpler types of disentailing conveyance.)

b. If a life estate and the next vested estate are created in the same person simultaneously, they do not merge in such a way as to destroy contingent remainders. However, if the person who holds them then conveys the two estates to some other person, the contingent remainders are destroyed. To illustrate: O dies, devising Blackacre to A (who has no son) for life, remainder to A's first son in fee. A is also O's heir and therefore takes the reversion by descent. At this point no merger takes place; thus, if a son is born to A, the son acquires a vested remainder in fee. However, if, before birth of a son, A conveys A's life estate and reversion to B, the contingent remainder is destroyed. B can then convey back to A, who will thus acquire a present fee simple.

Problems

15.8. O conveys to A for life, remainder to the heirs of B. A dies. Then B dies. Who owns the land?

15.9. O conveys to A for life, remainder to B for life, remainder to B's first daughter who shall reach 21 and her heirs. B dies, leaving a daughter aged 19. What is the state of the title?

15.10. O conveys to T and his heirs in trust to pay the income of the land to A for life and then in trust to convey the land to the son of A who shall first reach 21. A dies, leaving a son aged 19. Two years later the son reaches 21. What are his rights?

15.11. O conveys to A a term of 999 years. A dies, bequeathing the term to B for life, remainder to B's first daughter who shall reach 21. B dies, leaving a daughter aged 19. Two years later the daughter reaches 21. What are her rights?

15.12. O conveys to A for life, remainder to A's first son who shall reach 21 and the heirs of his body. Before A marries, O dies intestate. A is O's heir. What is the state of the title?

15.13. O conveys to A and the heirs of her body. O dies intestate, and A is her heir. What is the state of the title?

15.14. O conveys to A for life, remainder to A's first son and the heirs of his body, remainder to B and his heirs. While A is still childless O dies intestate, and A is his heir. What is the state of the title?

Note on modern law. It is clear enough that the courts should have held that the Statutes of Uses and Wills abolished the destructibility of contingent remainders; but it was not so held. Decisions have generally nipped at the heels of this ancient feudal relic without going for the jugular. Statutes have abolished it in many states and restricted it in a few others. The Restatement (§240) declares the rule to be nonexistent in the United States — a declaration which is sound as a desideratum of policy but at least dubious as a statement of fact.[15]

4. Rule in Shelley's Case

Rule 4: If an instrument creates a freehold in A and purports to create a remainder in A's heirs (or the heirs of A's body) and the estates are both legal or both equitable, the remainder becomes a fee simple (or fee tail) in A.

To illustrate with the recurring simple example: O conveys Blackacre to A for life, remainder to A's heirs. Observe that all the requirements are met: (1) the two estates are created by the same instrument, (2) there is a freehold in A, i.e., the life estate, (3) there is a remainder in A's heirs, (4) both estates are legal. Therefore the remainder becomes a remainder to A in fee simple, making the state of the title: To A for life, remainder to A in fee simple. *Note well: this is all that the Rule in Shelley's Case does.* However, in the case here considered, the doctrine of merger now steps in, destroys the life estate, and causes the state of the title to be: To A in fee simple.

You can readily guess the probable reason for the rule: it tended to increase the number of times that land passed by descent and thereby caused reliefs, wardships, and marriages to accrue to the lord of the fee. Take the illustration given in the preceding paragraph. If there were no Rule in Shelley's Case, on A's death the property would pass to A's heirs *by purchase,* and no relief, wardship, or marriage would accrue to the lord of the fee. However, under the rule, since A has a fee simple, if A dies intestate A's heir takes *by descent;* and a relief accrues (and also, if military tenure is involved, a wardship and marriage if there is an infant heir). So, as usually explained, the Rule in Shelley's Case was a crude device for preventing owners from avoiding their feudal obligations (which were the medieval

---

15. See, for example, Blocker v. Blocker, 103 Fla. 285, 137 So. 249 (1931), which established the doctrine of destructibility in Florida, there being no previous Florida authority on the subject one way or the other. A decision which has completely nullified the rule without aid of statute is Hayward v. Spaulding, 75 N.H. 92, 71 A. 219 (1908), which declares that trustees to preserve contingent remainders will be implied to prevent defeat of the intention of the grantor or testator.

equivalent of our present inheritance taxes). We say a crude device because (1) for the purpose of protecting the lord it makes it possible for A to defeat the rights of A's heirs and, if A does this, the feudal rights of the lord are defeated too; (2) the rule applies in one class of situations where there are no feudal rights of the lord to be protected; and (3) the rule is ridiculously easy to circumvent by anyone who puts his or her mind to it. You should be sure that you understand why the things stated in the last sentence are true.

The truth is that the reasons for the rule, as so frequently happens, were confused at the outset, misunderstood in the course of development down through the centuries, and unhistorically simplified in modern times. In the early books the rule is spoken of as a rule of construction of the grantor's intention. Do you see why, shortly after the Conquest, a grantor who made a grant "to A for life, remainder to A's heirs" would mean just the same thing as one who made a grant "to A and his heirs"? Do you also see why it can be stated that "the modern justification for the rule is that it makes land alienable one generation earlier"?

In dealing with the Rule in Shelley's Case it is very easy to become antiquarian. The deeper you go into it, the more tantalizing its puzzles become; indeed, one can foresee, and perhaps envy, the scholar who some day will escape from a troubled world and devote his life to writing the definitive work on the rule. Done with insight and imagination it could be as great as Gibbon's Decline and Fall of the Roman Empire.

One of the charming anomalies of the rule is that it was christened more than two hundred and fifty years after it was born. The earliest case on the rule thus far uncovered is Abel's Case, Y.B. 18 Edw. 2, 577 (1324); but Shelley's Case, 1 Co. Rep. 93b, was decided only in 1581. Another oddity is that three points were at issue in Shelley's Case, and the so-called Rule in Shelley's Case which has resounded down the centuries was merely the fourth reason given by the court for the conclusion on the third point. Still another is that the classic statement of the rule is not contained in the court's opinion but is found in Coke's argument for the defendant, which was presented much more fully than any other aspect of the case by the reporter — who was, by happy chance, Coke. Coke's statement is as follows:

> It is a rule of law, when the ancestor by any gift or conveyance takes an estate of freehold, and in the same gift or conveyance an estate is limited either mediately or immediately to his heirs in fee or in tail, that always in such cases "the heirs" are words of limitation of the estate and not words of purchase.

Do you observe that the danger in this statement lies in a misunderstanding of the words "of the estate" which appear nearly at the end?

Epic battles of words have been fought over Shelley's Case. Friendships have been shattered and reputations blasted. The repercussions of Perrin v. Blake, 1 Bl. W. 672 (1769), drove one judge from the bench and would certainly have resulted in the impeachment of Lord Chief Justice Mansfield if modern standards of ethics had prevailed. Perhaps the greatest English book on real property law, Fearne's Contingent Remainders, was a philippic directed at the decision in Perrin v. Blake and is the classic exposition of the Rule in Shelley's Case. In Tennessee the rule was considered "a Gothic column found among the remains of feodality, . . . preserved in all its strength to aid in sustaining the fabric of the modern social system," whereas in North Carolina it is "the Don Quixote of the law, which, like the last knight errant of chivalry, has long survived every cause that gave it birth and now wanders aimlessly through the reports, still vigorous, but equally useless and dangerous."[16]

Turning from eulogy and denunciation to analysis and contemplation, let us consider the elements of the rule:

1.   There must be a freehold in A. Usually this is a life estate, but it may be an estate tail. The rule does not apply if the present estate in A is a term of years.

2.   There must be a remainder. Prior to the Statute of Uses (1536) the only future interests which could be created in strangers were remainders; but after the statute springing and shifting executory interests were permitted. You should bear it in mind, when you study these executory interests, that they could not invoke the Rule in Shelley's Case.

3.   The remainder must be limited to A's heirs or the heirs of A's body. If the remainder is limited "to A's children" the rule does not apply, even though the children turn out to be A's heirs. Here a refinement must be mentioned:

    In any English statement of the rule you will find it specified that the remainder to heirs must be to them "in an indefinite line of succession." The word "heirs" must mean heirs taking in succession in infinite generations, not several heirs taking simultaneously. This distinction was by far the greatest source of litigation over Shelley's Case in the English courts, and the subrules and sub-subrules that were developed on this point were extremely esoteric. The distinction is so difficult to grasp that many American courts simply have not grasped it. The result is that the distinction is progressively ignored. Thus the Restatement declares (§312, comments f and g) that in the United States a remainder complies with the requirements of the rule if it is to "heirs" in the usual sense, i.e., those persons who would, immediately upon A's death, take A's real estate if A should die intestate. Communis error facit jus.

4.   The present freehold in A and the remainder to heirs may be separated by another estate; the rule still applies. This is often

---

16.   Polk v. Faris, 17 Tenn. (9 Yer.) 209, 233 (1836); Stamper v. Stamper, 121 N.C. 251, 28 S.E. 20 (1897).

indicated by the statement that the rule is invoked by a freehold in A and then "mediately or immediately" a remainder to A's heirs.
5. Freehold and remainder must be both legal or both equitable.

CITY BANK & TRUST CO. v. MORRISSEY
— Ill. App.—, 454 N.E.2d 1195 (1983)

NASH, J.

Plaintiff, City Bank and Trust Company, as trustee of the Margaret Tyne Trust (Trust), brought this action seeking instruction as to the proper disposition of the assets remaining in the Trust following the death of the life beneficiary, William Tyne. The circuit court found the Rule in Shelley's Case applicable to the provisions of the Trust and ordered the real assets of the Trust distributed to appellees, Julia Appleman, Jane Morrissey, JoAnn Hademan, William Morrissey, Pat Donaldson and Kathleen Muldoon, as the residuary legatees under William Tyne's will. The personal assets of the Trust were ordered distributed to the appellees and appellants, Margaret Henry, Edward Tyne, Patricia Tyne and Margaret Tyne (non-beneficiaries of William Tyne's will), as the heirs at law of William Tyne. Appellants contend that the trial court erred in applying the Rule in Shelley's Case and that the realty of the trust should have been distributed in the same manner as the personalty.

The parties submitted this cause to the circuit court upon an agreed statement of facts. The record reflects that on January 2, 1952, Margaret Tyne died leaving a last will and testament which was admitted to probate on February 14, 1952. The will established the Trust pursuant to its fifth paragraph which provides:

FIFTH: I GIVE, DEVISE, and BEQUEATH all the rest, residue and remainder of my property now owned by me or hereafter acquired, whether the same be real, personal, or mixed, or wherever situated, one-third part thereof to my son Thomas Tyne, one-third part thereof to my daughter Frances Tyne, and the remaining one-third I GIVE, DEVISE, and BEQUEATH to my daughter Margaret Henry, in the trust for the following uses and purposes to wit:

To lease, manage, control, sell, or operate all real estate; to collect the income from all property of any kind or nature whatsoever; to pay all taxes and assessments levied thereon; to sell and invest the proceeds in other real estate or appropriate securities; to become a party to the agreements for operating all real estate which may be of the nature of an undivided interest with the co-owners; to bring all suits and actions necessary to preserve and protect said property; to distribute the net income to my son, William Tyne, at least quarterly or more often as my trustee shall deem best, and to retain such part thereof as may be necessary to preserve and protect said estate.

Said trustee shall have the right to encroach on principal and expend the same for the purpose of the welfare, health, and maintenance of the said William Tyne and I further DIRECT that the income from said trust and the principle thereof shall be payable to the persons entitled thereto only upon their own individual receipt and shall not be subject to assignment, transfer, or any legal process of any kind or nature. *I further DIRECT that upon the death of the beneficiary, William Tyne, that all the assets of the trust be converted into cash or distributed in kind to the heirs at law of the said William Tyne who survive him.* [Emphasis added.]

In 1974, Margaret Henry resigned as trustee of the Trust and was succeeded by the plaintiff, City Bank and Trust Company.

On November 13, 1980, the life beneficiary of the Trust, William Tyne, died testate and appellees were the residuary legatees of his will; however, William Tyne's heirs at law included both the appellants and appellees. As a result, plaintiff brought this action seeking instructions as to the distribution of the assets of the Trust.

The trial court found that the fifth paragraph of Margaret Tyne's will which created the Trust invoked the application of the Rule in Shelley's Case. Thus, at the time the Trust was created in 1952, William Tyne received an equitable fee simple interest in the realty of the Trust and its proceeds; this interest was fully alienable by William Tyne pursuant to the provisions of his will. Conversely, since the Rule does not apply to personalty, William Tyne received only a life estate in those assets which upon his death passed to his heirs at law pursuant to the fifth paragraph of Margaret Tyne's will. Accordingly, the court ordered plaintiff to distribute the realty and its proceeds to appellees as legatees under William Tyne's will and the personalty was ordered distributed to appellees and appellants as the heirs at law of William Tyne. The sole issue on appeal is whether the Rule in Shelley's Case applies to the fifth paragraph of Margaret Tyne's will which created the Trust.

Initially, we note that although the Rule was abolished by statute in 1953 (Ill. Rev. Stat. 1981, ch. 30, par. 186), the statute has no retroactive application and the rule must be given effect to instruments executed and delivered prior to the enactment of the statute. (Ill. Rev. Stat. 1981, ch. 30, par. 187; Arnold Baker (1962), 26 Ill. 2d 131, 134, 185 N.E.2d 844, 846; Orme v. Northern Trust Co. (1962), 25 Ill. 2d 151, 160, 183 N.E.2d 505, 510; see also, Evans v. Giles (1980), 83 Ill. 2d 448, 47 Ill. Dec. 349, 415 N.E.2d 354.) The Rule in Shelley's Case provides that if an estate of freehold is granted by any instrument and the remainder is limited by the same instrument, either mediately or immediately, to the heir or heirs of the body of the person taking the freehold as a class, without explanation, the person taking the freehold also takes the remainder, thus vesting him with a fee simple interest. (Churchill v. Marr (1921), 300 Ill. 302, 308, 133 N.E. 335, 337; Seymour v. Heubaum (1965), 65 Ill. App. 2d 89, 95-96, 211 N.E.2d 897, 900, *leave to appeal denied*.) There are three requisites for the application of the Rule: (1) a freehold estate must be granted to the ancestor; (2) a remainder must be limited to his heirs, general or special; and (3) the two estates, freehold and remainder, must both be of the same quality, either legal or equitable. (Sutlif v. Aydelott (1940), 373 Ill. 633, 636, 27 N.E.2d 529, 531; Seymour v. Heubaum (1965), 65 Ill. App. 2d 89, 95-96, 211 N.E.2d 897, 900, *leave to appeal denied.*) The Rule has been applied to the equitable interests in trusts (Sutliff v. Aydelott (1940), 373 Ill. 633, 636, 27 N.E.2d 529, 531; Wilson v. Harrold (1919), 288 Ill. 388, 393-94, 123 N.E. 563, 565), however, it does not apply to trusts insofar as the trust contains personal property. Sutliff v. Aydelott (1940), 373 Ill. 633, 638, 27 N.E.2d 529, 532; Lord v. Comstock (1909), 240 Ill. 492, 505, 88 N.E. 1012, 1018.

The Rule in Shelley's Case is a rule of law and not of construction. (Lord v. Comstock (1909), 240 Ill. 492, 499, 88 N.E. 1012, 1015; McFall v. Kirkpatrick (1908), 236 Ill. 281, 296, 86 N.E. 139, 143; Restatement of Property §312, comment (k) at 1759 (1940, 1982 Supp.).) Thus, if the requirements for the application of the Rule are present, the Rule will be applied regardless of the intent of the grantor. (Cahill v. Cahill (1949), 402 Ill. 416, 421, 84 N.E.2d 380, 384; Lord v. Comstock (1909), 249 Ill. 492, 499, 88 N.E. 1012, 1015.) When applied the Rule operates on the remainder alone, taking it from the heirs and vesting it in the ancestor thus giving the ancestor, through the doctrine of merger, a fee simple interest. Lydick v. Tate (1942), 380 Ill. 616, 623, 44 N.E.2d 583, 589; Seymour v. Heubaum (1965), 65 Ill. App. 2d 89, 96-97, 211 N.E.2d 897, 900-01, *leave to appeal denied.*

When the foregoing authority is applied to the instrument before us, it is clear that the trial court correctly applied the Rule in Shelley's Case. The appellants do not contest that the first two elements necessary for the application of the Rule are present in the instant case, i.e., that William Tyne received a freehold estate and that the remainder was to his heirs at law. No contrary conclusion is possible since the word "heirs" is a technical word which is presumed to have been used in its strict legal sense absent clear and affirmative language to the contrary. (Lydick v. Tate (1942), 380 Ill. 616, 625, 44 N.E.2d 583, 589; Seymour v. Heubaum (1965), 65 Ill. App. 2d 89, 97, 211 N.E.2d 897, 901, *leave to appeal denied.*) Since no such language is used in the Margaret Tyne will, the first two elements for the application of the Rule are satisfied.

Appellants contend, however, that the third element necessary for the application of the Rule in Shelley's Case is missing since the estate conveyed to William Tyne and the estate conveyed to his heirs are not of the same quality. Initially, appellants contend that the interest of William Tyne was in realty whereas the heirs' interest was in personality. They assert that the portion of the will which states that upon the death of William Tyne, the assets of the Trust are to be "converted into cash or distributed in kind" creates an equitable conversion of the realty in the Trust thus making their interest in personality rather than realty. Since William Tyne's interest is in realty, they contend the estates are not of equal quality and the Rule does not apply.

While a direction to convert land into cash may result in an equitable conversion, that direction must be clear and mandatory; if the trustee is given any option, choice or discretion as to whether the property is sold, then an equitable conversion does not occur because there is no duty to sell. (Rehbein v. Norene (1954), 2 Ill. 2d 363, 370, 118 N.E.2d 287, 291-92; Young v. Sinsabaugh (1930), 342 Ill. 82, 86, 173 N.E. 784, 786; In re Estate of Achilli (1979), 71 Ill. App. 3d 473, 476, 27 Ill. Dec. 580, 582, 389 N.E.2d 644, 646.) In the instant case, a plain reading of the will reveals that the trustee has complete discretion to either distribute the assets in kind or convert them into cash. Accordingly, no equitable conversion occurs and the two estates, freehold and remainder, are of equal quality as interests in realty.

In the alternative, appellants contend that the two estates are not equal in that William Tyne had an equitable interest in the realty whereas the heirs' interest was legal. They argue that title to the real property vested in the heirs immediately upon the death of William Tyne since the Trustee's legal title ended upon the death of William Tyne and the immediate vesting makes their interest legal, not equitable.

Under the terms of a will, the trustee will take whatever legal estate is necessary for him to carry out the purpose of the trust and his duties thereunder and a devise to a trustee which grants the power to sell, convey, rent or mortgage necessarily vests the fee in the trustee. (Lord v. Comstock (1909), 240 Ill. 492, 502, 88 N.E. 1012, 1016; Seymour v. Heubaum (1965), 65 Ill. App. 2d 89, 98-99, 211 N.E.2d 897, 901-02, *leave to appeal denied.*) If the trustee is vested with fee simple title in the residuary, the life estate in the ancestor and the remainder in the heirs are both equitable since the duties of the trustee would not be completed until after a conveyance is made to the heirs upon the death of the ancestor, thus there can be no legal vested remainder in the heirs. (Lord v. Comstock (1909), 240 Ill. 492, 503, 88 N.E. 1012, 1016; Seymour v. Heubaum (1965), 65 Ill. App. 2d 89, 101-02, 211 N.E.2d 897, 901-02, *leave to appeal denied.*) In the case at bar, it is apparent that the will gave the trustee power to convey, manage and sell, which powers lasted after the life of William Tyne. As such, the heirs' interest in the Trust was equitable as was that of the life tenant.

As a result of the foregoing, all three of the elements necessary for the application of the Rule are present and once the Rule is applied it does not matter that the quality or nature of one of the estates is altered at a later date. (Seymour v. Heubaum (1965), 65 Ill. App. 2d 89, 103-04, 211 N.E.2d 897, 904, *leave to appeal denied;* Restatement of Property §312, comment (h) at 1756 (1940, 1982 Supp.).) Thus, William Tyne received a fee simple interest in the realty of the Trust at the time of its original conveyance and that interest continued even though the realty may later have been converted into personalty. Accordingly, the trial court was correct in applying the Rule to the realty of the Trust and its proceeds and distributing them to the appellees as legatees of William Tyne's will. The court was also correct in not applying the Rule to the personalty which was ordered distributed to the appellants and appellees as William Tyne's heirs at law.

For the foregoing reasons the judgment of the circuit court of Lee County is affirmed.

Affirmed.

SEIDENFELD, P.J., and VAN DUESEN, J., concur.

Problems

15.15.   O conveys to A for life, remainder to A's first son and the heirs of his body, remainder to A's heirs.
a.   If A has no son, what is the state of the title?
b.   If A has a son, what is the state of the title?
c.   In either a or b, can A convey a present fee simple?
Provost of Beverley's Case, Y.B. 40 Edw. 3, 9 (1366).

15.16.   O devises to A for life, remainder to A's heirs. A dies, leaving H as her heir. O then dies. What is the state of the title? Belleville Savings Bank v. Aneshaensel, 298 Ill. 292, 131 N.E. 682 (1921).

15.17.   O conveys to A for life, remainder to the heirs of B. What is the state of the title (a) if B is living? (b) if B is dead?

15.18.   O conveys "to A for life, remainder to A's heirs in such shares as A, their father, shall appoint, and if he makes no appointment to A's heirs equally." Does the Rule in Shelley's Case apply? Jordan v. Adams, 9 C.B. (n.s.) 483 (1861).

15.19.   O conveys land in Illinois "to A for life, remainder to those persons who, according to the statutes of Illinois, would take A's real estate if A should die intestate." What is the state of the title? People v. Emery, 314 Ill. 220, 145 N.E. 349 (1924).

15.20.   O conveys land to A for life, remainder to A's heirs, and adds in the instrument of conveyance, "It is my intention that A shall take no more than a life estate and that A's heirs shall take a remainder as purchasers." What is the state of the title? Perrin v. Blake, 1 Bl. W. 672 (1769); Havely v. Comerford, 343 Ill. 90, 174 N.E. 830 (1931); Slemmer v. Crampton, 50 Iowa 302 (1878).

15.21.   O conveys land to T for the life of A, in trust to collect the rents and profits and pay them to A, remainder to the heirs of A. What is the state of the title?

15.22.   O conveys land to T, a trustee, with a direction to sell the same and hold the proceeds in trust to pay the income to A for life and upon A's death to pay the principal to A's heirs. What interests are created? Engel v. Mades, 25 Wash. L. Rep. 229 (D.C. 1897); Restatement of Property §312(3).

15.23. O conveys to A for life, remainder to B and his heirs if B survives A, but to A's heirs if B does not survive A.

    a.   What is the state of the title?

    b.   P wants to purchase the land. Who must execute the deed in order to give P a fee simple?

15.24. Nye conveyed to Joseph and Mora as tenants in common for their respective lives, remainder to the heirs of Joseph.

    a.   What is the state of the title?

    b.   P wants to purchase the land. Who must execute the deed in order to give P a fee simple?

Bails v. Davis, 241 Ill. 536, 89 N.E. 706 (1909).

15.25. O conveys to A for life, remainder to B for life, remainder to B's heirs.

    a.   What is the state of the title?

    b.   A dies. What is the state of the title?

15.26. O conveys to A for the life of B, remainder to B's heirs. A conveys all A's interest to B. What is the state of the title?

15.27. O conveys to A for life, remainder to B for life, remainder to the heirs of A ascertained on the death of the survivor of A and B.

    a.   What is the state of the title?

    b.   B dies. What is the state of the title?

15.28. O devises to A for life, remainder to B and her heirs, but if B dies without issue living at her death, to C for life, and then to C's heirs.

    a.   What is the state of the title?

    b.   B dies without issue. What is the state of the title?

15.29. O conveys to A for life, remainder to B for life if B marries C, remainder to B's heirs whether B marries C or not.

    a.   What is the state of the title?

    b.   B marries C. What is the state of the title?

See Restatement of Property §312, particularly comments o and q.

Note on modern law. The Restatement of Property §313 comment a, Special Note (1948 Supp.), lists various American jurisdictions which have abolished the Rule in Shelley's Case "wholly or partially" by statute and two which have abolished it by decision. Illinois abolished the rule by statute in 1953; Texas did the same in 1963. Keep in mind, however, that the statutory abolition of the rule does not affect prior transfers.

5.   Doctrine of Worthier Title

Rule 5a: If a will devises to a person a freehold estate of the same quality and quantity which such person would have taken by descent if the testator had died intestate, then such estate passes by descent and not by devise.

Rule 5b: If a grantor who is an owner in fee simple purports to create a life estate or estate tail, with remainder to the grantor's heirs, the remainder is void and the grantor has a reversion.

To illustrate Rule 5a: O dies, leaving a will in which a clause provides, "I devise Blackacre to my son, Charles." At O's death Charles proves to be O's only heir. Charles takes Blackacre by descent, not by devise. As you consider this illustration two questions ought to arise in your mind:

1. How can this question arise before 1540, for was it not in that year that freeholds first became devisable by virtue of the Statute of Wills? In general yes; but prior to 1540 land was devisable by local custom. It is true that the doctrine of worthier title had much greater applicability after 1540 than before.

2. What difference does it make whether the land passes by devise or by descent? In ancient times the answer to this was easy: a descent entitled the lord to a relief and (if the heir was an infant) a wardship and marriage, whereas these incidents would not accrue upon a devise. In modern times the difference between a passage by descent and a passage by devise should only very rarely be significant; it has been the characteristic of the modern cases to give this rule several unjustifiable applications.[17]

To illustrate Rule 5b: O conveys to A for life, remainder to O's heirs. Or a more usual case: O conveys to a trustee in trust to pay the income to O for O's life and then to convey the premises to O's heirs. In either case O has a reversion (legal in the first case, equitable[18] in the second) and the heirs have nothing. This means that O can convey away this reversion during O's lifetime, that O can devise it by O's will, and that O's creditors can reach it at any time. Thus you will observe that whereas Rule 5a merely deals with the manner in which the heir gets the property, Rule 5b takes it away from the heir and gives it to the ancestor — a much more serious matter.

The basis for these rules was, of course, the desire to preserve the incidents of tenure which accrued upon a descent. It was said, with reference to Rule 5a, that the heir took by descent because it was the "worthier title"; hence the name of this rule. Rule 5b probably cannot be correctly called by the same name; it is generally referred to as the rule forbidding remainders to the grantor's heirs.[19]

Observe that in Rule 5b, as in the Rule in Shelley's Case, the remainder to

---

17. Consider the following questions. (a) If there is a devise to an heir, does this gift rank as devised property or intestate property in determining which property shall be sacrificed to creditors? Ellis v. Page, 61 Mass. (7 Cush.) 161 (1851); Biederman v. Seymour, 3 Beav. 368 (Ch. 1840). (b) If there is a devise to an heir, is the heir a "devisee" within the terms of an anti-lapse statute? Estate of Warren, 211 Iowa 940, 234 N.W. 835 (1931). (c) If the local doctrine of ancestral property applies to land received by descent and not to land received by devise, does such doctrine apply in the case where a person has made a devise to an heir? Hurst v. Earl of Winchelsea, 1 Bl. W. 187 (1759); Gilpin v. Hollingsworth, 3 Md. 190 (1852). In regard to these questions, see Restatement of Property §314.

18. In some jurisdictions, this reversion would be legal, too. But don't worry about this yet.

19. See 3 Simes & Smith, Future Interests §§1601-1613 (2d ed. 1956).

heirs must be to them by that designation — that is, neither of these rules is invoked where there is a remainder to a named person who turns out to be the heir. But Rule 5a applies if the devise is either to heirs by that designation or to a named person who turns out to be the heir at death.

Note on modern law. These rules have been abolished by statute in some states.[20] As above indicated, Rule 5a lost its significance when feudal incidents ceased to exist; the rule now survives only in some few applications, most of which should never have been made. Rule 5b, however, is considerably more of a vital force. Some courts — illustrated by the leading case of Doctor v. Hughes, 225 N.Y. 305, 122 N.E. 221 (1919) — have diluted the rule into a principle of construction *and have extended its constructional application to personalty.* Thus, in states following this view where O creates a trust of stocks and bonds for himself or herself for life, remainder to O's own heirs, O holds the reversion after his or her own life estate and the heirs have nothing, unless the instrument shows a contrary intent. This means that O can revoke the trust at any time and that at O's death the property passes under the residuary clause of O's will, not to O's heirs.[21]

ESTATE OF ANNIE I. KERN
274 N.W.2d 325 (Iowa 1979)

UHLENHOPP, J.

This appeal involves an attack upon the testamentary branch of the worthier title doctrine in the context of the antilapse statute, §633.273, Iowa Probate Code.

Testatrix Annie I. Kern and her predeceased husband had but one descendant, their son Ralph Kern. Testatrix made a will giving all of her property to Ralph, who thereafter died unmarried. Testatrix died subsequent to Ralph's death, and her will was admitted to probate.

The collateral heirs of testatrix' deceased husband claim that testatrix' property is to be divided among Ralph's heirs. If so, half of the property would go to the collateral heirs of Ralph's father and half to the collateral heirs of Ralph's mother, testatrix, pursuant to the antilapse statute. That statute provides: "If a devisee dies before the testator, his heirs shall inherit the property devised to him, unless from the terms of the will, the intent is clear and explicit to the contrary."

Testatrix' collateral heirs contend that the property is to be divided entirely among them under the judicially-created worthier title doctrine, citing In re Estate of Warren, 211 Iowa 940, 234 N.W. 835. Under that

20. The Tennessee statute abolishing both aspects of the doctrine of worthier title became effective in 1983. Keep in mind that these statutes do not apply to prior transfers.

21. See Restatement of Property §314.

doctrine a devise in the same quantity and quality as the devisee would take by descent is void. If the devisee survives the testator he takes as heir. If he does not so survive, the property goes as though the devise had never been made. As a result the worthier title doctrine sometimes nullifies application of the antilapse statute.

Application of the doctrine here would give all of testatrix' property to her collateral heirs, rather than to her heirs and her predeceased husband's heirs. The probate court held that the property passed entirely to testatrix' heirs, applying the *Warren* case. Ralph's heirs on his father's side appealed.

The present case is a classic one for application of the worthier title doctrine, and the *Warren* decision controls the result if we adhere to it. But Ralph's heirs on his father's side mount a frontal attack on the doctrine. The time has arrived for us to reexamine the doctrine as applied in cases involving the antilapse statute. We leave other types of cases involving the doctrine to future consideration.

I.   The scholars have little good to say about the doctrine. They assert that it is purely a technical principle, it frustrates testamentary intent and antilapse enactments, and it creates confusing and contradictory results in application. Morris, The Wills Branch of the Worthier Title Doctrine, 54 Mich. L. Rev. 451; Harper & Heckel, The Doctrine of Worthier Title, 24 Ill. L. Rev. 627; Johanson, Reversions, Remainders, and the Doctrine of Worthier Title, 45 Texas L. Rev. 1 (inter vivos application). Iowa commentators are similarly unenthusiastic about the doctrine. Comment, 16 Iowa L. Rev. 559 ("This so-called rule of 'worthier title,' though it may often be restated, seems obsolete"); Comment, 39 Iowa L. Rev. 199, 202 ("It is hoped that the Iowa court will eliminate this antiquated doctrine from the Iowa law"). See also Note, 46 Harv. L. Rev. 993, 998. Professors Harper and Heckel cite undesirable results and say of the doctrine on page 655 of their article:

> Obviously the real pragmatic considerations which occasioned its development have long since ceased to exist. But a vestige, a survival of ancient legal theory, it serves no genuine social purpose, if accurately applied. So long as courts continue to pay it lip service, in blind and complacent adulation, we may expect many such incongruous and unsatisfactory situations.

Morris says of the wills branch of the doctrine in his article in 54 Michigan Law Review 451, 495:

> What meritorious arguments can be made in favor of the wills branch of the worthier title doctrine? The writer can think of none. The rule invites litigation, ensnares the unwary draftsman and frustrates the wary draftsman. As a rule of law it applies to devises made to people who are the most natural objects of the testator's bounty. To the writer's knowledge, every man who has taken up the pen to write on the policy aspects of the rule has concluded that it has no place in our law.

In rejecting the doctrine in Kentucky, the Court of Appeals of that state concluded: "After a careful consideration we are convinced that the doctrine of worthier title serves to hinder, rather than aid, in the ascertainment of the intention of a testator, which is the cardinal purpose in the construction of wills, and that it has no place in our jurisprudence." Mitchell v. Dauphin Deposit Trust Co., 283 Ky. 532, 538, 142 S.W.2d 181, 184.

The American Law Institute, expressing the statutory and decisional trend in this country, has taken the position that the worthier title doctrine applies to inter vivos conveyances but not to testamentary devises. Restatement, Property, §314(2) and Comment j. England abolished the testamentary worthier title doctrine by statute in 1833. 3 & 4 Will. IV, ch. 106, §3. See also Lucas v. Parsons, 24 Ga. 640, 659 ("The reason of the rule in England . . . does not apply in this state"); Bunting v. Speek, 41 Kan. 424, 21 P. 288; Besche v. Murphy, 190 Md. 539, 59 A.2d 499; In re Sewart's Estate, 342 Mich. 491, 70 N.W.2d 732; Stone v. Bucklin, 69 R.I. 274, 32 A.2d 614; Estate of Pfaff, 41 Wis. 2d 159, 163 N.W.2d 140.

II. The doctrine originally had a practical purpose: under the feudal system, if real property passed by law the lord retained benefits which were lost if the property passed by will. As stated in Restatement, *supra,* comment j, "This rule originated under the feudal system to preserve the feudal incidents of relief, wardship and marriage. These incidents were preserved only if the new tenant of land acquired his interest by descent from the former tenant, rather than by purchase under the terms of a devise." The Institute adds, "The reason which caused the origin of this rule no longer exists." This court itself stated in Beem v. Beem, 241 Iowa 247, 251-252, 41 N.W.2d 107, 110:

> The common-law rule originated under the old feudal system in England. It was for the protection or preservation of certain benefits flowing to the overlord which would be lost if grantor's title passed to his heirs by purchase, that is, by any method other than inheritance. A rule was accordingly developed that heirs could only take from their ancestor by inheritance. A title thus acquired was considered a "worthier title." . . . The rule was abolished by statute in England in 1833. . . . But in the meantime it had gained some foothold in American common law.

III. The Iowa decisions illustrate the frustrating effect of the doctrine when applied to negate application of the Iowa antilapse statute. Conscious of this effect, this court has drawn minute distinctions to remove cases from the operation of the doctrine. The principal cases involving the doctrine in the antilapse statute setting are Tennant v. Smith, 173 Iowa 264, 155 N.W. 267 (inter-spousal devise; doctrine applied); Herring v. Herring, 187 Iowa 593, 174 N.W. 364 (similar); In re Will of Watenpaugh, 192 Iowa 1178, 186 N.W. 198 (devise and inheritance found not identical; doctrine not applied); In re Estate of Davis, 204 Iowa 1231, 213 N.W. 395 (same); In re Estate of Warren, 211 Iowa 940, 234 N.W. 835 (facts similar to present case; doctrine applied); Wehrman v. Farmers' & Merchants' Savings Bank, 221 Iowa 249, 259 N.W. 564 (will and inheritance not identical, daughter to receive $50 for care of cemetery lot in addition to regular share; doctrine not applied); In re Estate of Schroeder, 228 Iowa 1198, 293 N.W. 492 (devise and descent not identical; doctrine not applied); In re Estate of Everett, 238 Iowa 564, 28 N.W.2d 21 (same); Beem v. Beem, 241 Iowa 247, 41 N.W.2d 107 (will gave devisees exactly what they would have received under statute but verbiage of will and statute not same; doctrine not applied); In re Estate of Coleman, 242 Iowa 1096, 49 N.W.2d 517 (devise and descent not identical; doctrine inapplicable); and In re Estate of Miller, 243 Iowa 920, 54 N.W.2d 433 (doctrine applied on facts similar to *Beem* case).

IV.   In support of the worthier title doctrine, testatrix' heirs argue that since testatrix outlived Ralph, she would likely have desired to have her property remain with her side of the house, rather than go half to her side and half to her deceased husband's side. But how do we know this? The husband's heirs can argue plausibly that testatrix and her husband may have accumulated this property together and therefore may have wanted it divided between the two sides. If Ralph had survived testatrix by as little as a day and died intestate, the property would have gone to both sides. Testatrix' heirs are really arguing against the policy of the antilapse statute itself, wherein the legislature abolishes the common-law lapse rule and presumes that a testator normally desires the gift to go to the devisee's heirs.

Testatrix' heirs also present the familiar argument that blood is thicker than water: a testator would rather have his property stay with those of his own blood than go to the heirs of the predeceased devisee. One illustration demonstrates that this argument contradicts the policy of the antilapse statute favoring the devisee's heirs: if the predeceasing devisee is not an heir of the testator, the worthier title doctrine does not apply, the antilapse statute does, and the property goes to the devisee's heirs—who may be complete strangers to the testator's blood. Yet, according to testatrix' heirs, if the predeceasing devisee happens to be an heir of the testator, the devisee's heirs may be cut off by the doctrine. Here again testatrix' heirs are really arguing against the policy of the antilapse statute.

V.   Our most difficult problem with the worthier title doctrine is in trying to square it with the strong language of the antilapse statute. The statute makes no express exception for the case of the devisee who is an heir of the testator. To uphold the worthier title doctrine in that framework we must read the doctrine into the only exception which the statute contains: the predeceasing devisee's heirs take "unless from the terms of the will, the intent is clear and explicit to the contrary." (See also §§633.271 and 633.274.) We must say, merely from the circumstance the devise happens to be the same as the inheritance, that the will is "clear" and "explicit" the testator intended the predeceased devisee's heirs not to take. We are no longer able to make that long leap successfully. We thus abrogate the worthier title doctrine in antilapse statute situations.

VI.   The worthier title doctrine is a rule of property, and we abrogate it prospectively only. See Great Northern Ry. v. Sunburst Oil & Refining Co., 287 U.S. 358, 53 S. Ct. 145, 77 L. Ed. 360; State v. Martin, 217 N.W.2d 536 (Iowa); 20 Am. Jur. 2d Courts §233 at 562; 21 C.J.S. Courts §194 at 327. Today's holding thus applies only to the present will, to wills in cases now pending in which the issue is properly raised, and to wills executed after the day we file this opinion. The worthier title doctrine, if otherwise applicable under our prior pronouncements, applies to other wills.

In the present case testatrix' property passes under her will and the antilapse statute to Ralph's heirs.

Reversed.

Problems

15.30.   On the marriage of Thomas and Sarah, Sarah conveyed lands to trustees in trust for Thomas and Sarah for their joint lives, then for the survivor of them for life, then for the children of the marriage, if any, and their heirs, but if there should be no children of the marriage, then for the heirs of Sarah. When, some years later, it became clear that Sarah was going to have no children, Thomas examined the trust deed carefully for the first time and concluded that if Sarah predeceased him he would only have a life estate and upon his death Sarah's brothers and sisters would take a substantial part of the property as her heirs. He took this matter up with Sarah, and she agreed with him that this was not the intention of either of them at the time of the trust deed. They then went to a lawyer, and the lawyer advised them to bring a bill in equity to reform the trust deed so that it conformed to their intentions. Comment on the soundness of this advice. King v. Dunham, 31 Ga. 743 (1861); Wilson v. Pharris, 203 Ark. 614, 158 S.E.2d 274 (1941).

15.31.   Same facts as Problem 15.30, but the land in question is located in a state that has abolished the Rule in Shelley's Case but has not abolished Rule 5b. Is your answer the same as the one you gave to Problem 15.30? See Restatement of Property §314 comment i.

CHAPTER 16

THE STATUTE OF USES AND ITS CONSEQUENCES
(Including the Rule Against Perpetuities and Some Other Rules Restricting the Creation of Property Interests)

SECTION 1. POLITICAL BACKGROUND OF THE STATUTE

In 1536, in words of one syllable, Henry VIII was broke. But perhaps this manner of statement is too undignified. We shall rephrase it in Holdsworth's measured language: "Some years before the passing of the Statute of Uses fiscal necessities led Henry VIII to reflect upon the depletion of his feudal revenues." [1] The House of Commons was in no mood to grant him supply out of respect and good will, for these two qualities were notably lacking in the attitude of the populace toward the Crown. Henry divorced Catherine of Aragon in 1533; he promptly married Anne Boleyn, about whom rude remarks were freely spoken; he was in a running fight with the Catholic Church; and he was backing the ruthless Thomas Cromwell against such popular and revered antagonists as Bishop Fisher of Rochester and Sir Thomas More, both of whom were finally sent to the block.

The Crown still retained the right to the feudal incidents of reliefs, wardships, and marriages, but this right had been of merely nominal value for some time. The reason was that landowners had learned that all manner of happy consequences followed upon placing the legal title to the land in the

---

1. Holdsworth's History of English Law 450 (1937). The account herein given of the political background of the Statute of Uses is based upon Holdsworth.

hands of several joint tenants who would hold this title "to the use of" (i.e., in trust for) the real parties in interest. Through this method of transforming what would normally be legal estates in the beneficial owners of the land into equitable estates (1) the land was made devisable, since the chancery courts recognized a declaration of use in a will, (2) remainders were made indestructible, (3) feudal incidents otherwise payable to the king or other lord of the fee were avoided, (4) the property was made substantially immune to the claims of creditors, (5) the widow's dower was eliminated, (6) an alien could be a cestui que use — i.e., beneficiary — although an alien could not hold a legal title, (7) the proprietary penalties of treason and felony tended to be avoided, and (8) generally the fruits of secrecy were made available to those who would benefit from secrecy.[2]

Henry's sole interest was in item (3) of this list. He realized that he could expect to enlist no support for a project which benefited only himself; so he sought to tie in his own interests with those of some dominant force in the House of Commons. This he found (after two false starts) in the common-law lawyers who, then as now, were numerically strong and vocally active in the legislature. Uses were unpopular with the lawyers since they resulted in locating the principal litigation over land in the Chancery court which was served by a small specialized bar. Henry conceived the notion that a measure which would change the equitable uses into the corresponding legal estate would at once (1) restore his feudal revenues,[3] and (2) restore the land-law business to the common-law courts, thereby enlisting the support of the lawyers in Parliament.

This is precisely what the Statute of Uses did, and Parliament duly approved it in 1535 to take effect on May 1, 1536. Its operative words for our purposes are the following — and you would do well to master these: "If any person be seised of any lands to the use of any other person, such person that have such use shall henceforth be deemed in lawful seisin and possession of the same lands in such like estate as he had in use."[4]

---

2. At an earlier date there had been another advantage, which may have provided the original reason for creating uses. The conveyance of land in mortmain, i.e., to religious organizations, was forbidden in Magna Carta (1215), and this was confirmed by the Statute of Mortmain (1279), which formed a part of the legislation of Edward I. These enactments prevented the Church from receiving *legal* title to lands; but this was evaded by conveyances to the use of the Church, thus giving the Church equitable title. This practice was forbidden in 1391 by 15 Rich. 2, ch. 5.

3. The Court of Wards and Liveries and its relationship to the Statute of Uses is discussed in Bell, An Introduction to the History and Records of the Court of Wards and Liveries 1-13 (1953).

4. From the full text, given below, of that part of the statute in which we are interested you will see that the fourth and sixth words from the end of our compressed version are given by us in the singular number whereas they are in the plural in the original. Otherwise our compressed version is a quotation from the statute with many words, mostly redundant, omitted. But you may want to read this full text both for color and for certain specifications of detail. Here it is:

Where by the common laws of this realm, lands, tenements and hereditaments be not devisable by testament, (2) nor ought to be transferred from one to another, but by solemn livery and seisin, matter of record, writing sufficient made bona fide, without

SECTION 2. BASIC EFFECT OF THE STATUTE

The statute did not abolish uses, i.e., equitable estates. It recognized them, but immediately transformed certain of them into the corresponding legal estates.

covin or fraud; (3) yet nevertheless divers and sundry imaginations, subtle inventions and practices have been used, whereby the hereditaments of this realm have been conveyed from one to another by fraudulent feoffments, fines, recoveries and other assurances craftily made to secret uses, intents and trusts; (4) and also by wills and testaments, sometime made by nude parolx and words, sometime by signs and tokens, and sometime by writing, and for the most part made by such persons as be visited with sickness, in their extreme agonies and pains, or at such time as they have scantly had any good memory or remembrance; (5) at which times they being provoked by greedy and covetous persons lying in wait about them, do many times dispose indiscreetly and unadvisedly their lands and inheritances; (6) by reason whereof, and by occasion of which fraudulent feoffments, fines, recoveries and other like assurances to uses, confidences and trusts, divers and many heirs have been unjustly at sundry times disherited, the lords have lost their wards, marriages, reliefs, harriots, escheats, aids pur fair fits chivalir, & pur file marier, (7) scantly any person can be certainly assured of any lands by them purchased, nor know surely against whom they shall use their actions or executions for their rights, titles and duties; (8) also men married have lost their tenancies by the curtesy, (9) women their dowers, (10) manifest perjuries by trial of such secret wills and uses have been committed; (11) the King's highness hath lost the profits and advantages of the lands of persons attainted, (12) and of the lands craftily put in feoffments to the uses of aliens born, (13) and also the profits of waste for a year and a day of lands of felons attainted, (14) and the lords their escheats thereof; (15) and many other inconveniences have happened, and daily do encrease among the King's subjects, to their great trouble and inquietness, and to the utter subversion of the ancient common laws of this realm; (16) for the extirping and extinguishment of all such subtle practised feoffments, fines, recoveries, abuses and errors heretofore used and accustomed in this realm, to the subversion of the good and ancient laws of the same, and to the intent that the King's highness, or any other his subjects of this realm, shall not in any wise hereafter by any means or inventions be deceived, damaged or hurt, by reason of such trusts, uses or confidences: (17) it may please the King's most royal majesty, That it may be enacted by his Highness, by the assent of the lords spiritual and temporal, and the commons, in this present parliament assembled, and by the authority of the same, in manner and form following; that is to say, That where any person or persons stand or be seised, or at any time hereafter shall happen to be seised, of and in any honours, castles, manors, lands, tenements, rents, services, reversions, remainders or other hereditaments, to the use, confidence or trust of any other person or persons, or of any body politick, by reason of any bargain, sale, feoffment, fine, recovery, covenant, contract, agreement, will or otherwise, by any manner means whatsoever it be; that in every such case, all and every such person and persons, and bodies politick, that have or hereafter shall have any such use, confidence or trust, in fee-simple, fee-tail, for term of life or for years, or otherwise, or any use, confidence or trust, in remainder or reverter, shall from henceforth stand and be seised, deemed and adjudged in lawful seisin, estate and possession of and in the same honours, castles, manors, lands, tenements, rents, services, reversions, remainders and hereditaments, with their appurtenances, to all intents, constructions and purposes in the law, of and in such like estates as they had or shall have in use, trust or confidence of or in the same; (19) and that the estate, title, right and possession that was in such person or persons that were, or hereafter shall be seised of any lands, tenements or hereditaments, to the use, confidence or trust of any such person or persons, or of any body politick, be from henceforth clearly deemed and adjudged to be in him or them that have, or hereafter shall have, such use, confidence or trust, after such quality, manner, form and condition as they had before, in or to the use, confidence or trust that was in them.

The person who would have held the legal estate under the law prior to the statute, still got the legal estate for an instant and then lost it to the cestui que use. This is neatly illustrated by Pimbe's Case, Moore 196 (1585), which is as follows. Throckmorton committed treason. Then land was conveyed to Throckmorton to the use of Scudamore, who conveyed his rights to Pimbe. Throckmorton was thereafter convicted of high treason, thus causing to be forfeited to the Crown any lands of which he was seised at the time of his treason or thereafter. It was held that the land in question was forfeited; but Queen Elizabeth I granted the land to Pimbe as an act of grace. How long was Throckmorton seised of the land? A scintilla juris — not absolute zero (one minus one) but relative zero (one over infinity) — a period of time shorter than any period you can mention, but still a period of time, witness Pimbe's Case.[5]

Since the effect of the statute was to transform equitable estates (uses) into legal estates, it becomes relevant to consider how equitable estates could be created just prior to 1536. There is much learning on the rise of the use in earlier times, but for any present utility 1536 is the relevant date. As of that date two common methods of raising uses (i.e., creating equitable estates) existed, and a third was soon thereafter established as follows:

1.   *The feoffment to uses.* O enfeoffed T and his (or her) heirs to the use of A and his (or her) heirs. T held a legal fee simple, but A held an equitable fee simple; that is, a court of equity would require T to devote T's legal estate solely to A's benefit, either by allowing A to occupy the land or take its rents and profits or, if A demanded it, by conveying the legal title to A. Again, O could enfeoff T and his (or her) heirs to the use of O and his (or her) heirs; and, as the preamble to the Statute of Uses indicates, there were many reasons why an owner would rather hold an equitable estate than a legal one.[6] In such case T held the legal fee simple and O the equitable fee simple.

---

5.   Our mathematical friends tell us that "relative zero" and one-over-infinity are old hat, pre-atomic and perhaps anti-democratic. Now they just call it zero. When we object that it is hard to see how the Queen got anything in Pimbe's Case if Throckmorton got zero, they answer that we would do better to go at it geometrically instead of arithmetically — it's like the point at which two lines intersect, which has a length of zero — or, better still, the point at which a tangent touches an arc, which also has a length of zero. "Gosh," they say, "is this what you lawyers spend your time on?" And we say, "Sure, especially at Harvard. All our time."

For a translation of Pimbe's Case, see Scott & Scott, Cases on Trusts 286 (5th ed. 1966).

6.   This practice became so common that if O enfeoffed A and his (or her) heirs and there was no consideration or recital of consideration and no declaration of a use, it was implied that there was a use in favor of O and his (or her) heirs. O's interest was called a *resulting use.* This process of implying a resulting use in the grantor in an outright conveyance where no use at all is declared has no modern counterpart and is therefore dealt with only in this footnote. In all later discussions and problems in this book it is assumed that appropriate factors exist to prevent this type of resulting use from arising.

Quite different is the resulting use which arises where O gives an estate to T and then declares a use which is less in extent than T's estate. For example,

a.   O conveys to T and his (or her) heirs to the use of A for life.

b.   O conveys to T and his (or her) heirs to the use of A and his (or her) heirs after the death of O.

2. *The bargain and sale.* O for a consideration would "bargain and sell" the land to A and his (or her) heirs by an instrument in writing. Of course, this could not transfer the legal title, because there was no livery of seisin. But equity would treat this instrument much as modern equity courts treat a contract to sell land; that is, the court would require O to treat the land as belonging beneficially to A and would require O, if requested, to convey the legal title to A. In modern times we say that equity grants specific performance of the contract, and the fact that A can get specific performance gives A equitable title. In the older terminology it was said that the bargain and sale raised a use in A.

3. *The covenant to stand seised.* If O and A were relatives by blood or marriage and O executed an instrument under seal declaring that O "covenants to stand seised to the use of A and his [or her] heirs," this raised a use in A in fee simple.

In these three simple standard cases the operation of the Statute of Uses is obvious. By the three methods enumerated above a use could be raised (i.e., an equitable estate created). The statute transformed these equitable estates into legal estates. Thus, after 1536

1. if O enfeoffed T and his (or her) heirs to the use of A and his (or her) heirs, the result was a legal fee simple in A. (The feoffment to uses raised a use in A; the statute executed the use.)[7]

2. if O bargained and sold to A and his (or her) heirs, A obtained a legal fee simple. (The bargain and sale raised a use in A which was executed by the statute.)

3. if O covenanted to stand seised to the use of O's son, A, and his heirs, A obtained a legal fee simple. (The covenant to stand seised raised a use in A and the statute executed the use.)

SECTION 3. EFFECT OF THE STATUTE ON METHODS OF CONVEYANCING

The *bargain and sale* was already in wide use before the statute, but it created only an equitable estate. It was a foregone conclusion that it would be used even more widely after the statute. Do you quickly observe why it would be preferred to a feoffment as a means of passing legal title? The

---

In each of these cases a use in O is implied, the extent of the implied use being the difference between the estate conveyed to T and the use declared in A. For example, in case (a) there is a resulting use in O in fee after A's life estate; in case (b) there is a resulting use in O in fee to take effect immediately, but to be cut short by A's springing use in fee. This type of use has a very common counterpart in the modern resulting trust.

7. The verb "execute" is the standard expression to indicate the process by which a use is changed by the Statute of Uses into a legal estate.

reason is, of course, that this new method did not require the parties to go to the land, as was required in the old-fashioned feoffment with all its charming symbolic passing of a twig or clod on the premises. Thus a conveyance of a manor in Cornwall could be comfortably — and secretly — arranged in a solicitor's chambers in London. In days of horse travel this was very important.

The popularity of the bargain and sale was foreseen by Parliament. In 1536 the Statute of Enrollments was enacted (27 Hen. 8 ch. 16) which provided that no bargain and sale of a freehold should be effective unless the document were enrolled — i.e., recorded. This was a tremendous step in the direction of modern conveyancing. But, alas, it was tainted with avarice, for a substantial tax was imposed upon the enrollment process; and besides the attendant publicity was abhorrent to the landed gentry. So a method was devised for taking advantage of the Statute of Uses while yet avoiding the Statute of Enrollments. This method, worthy of some of our more ingenious modern tax counsel, nullified the Statute of Enrollments. We now proceed to describe it.

The lease and release. Suppose O wants to convey Blackacre to A in fee simple, does not want to go to the land, and does not want to incur the publicity or the tax of the Statute of Enrollments. O makes a bargain and sale to A of a lease for one year. This gives A a legal estate for one year with reversion in O. (The bargain and sale raises a use for one year in A; the Statute of Uses executes the use.) Now O releases O's reversion in fee simple to A by a common-law release. (You will recall that a future freehold could be conveyed by grant at common law, and that when it is conveyed to the holder of the present estate it is called a release.) A's estate for one year merges in the reversion in fee simple and A therefore has a present fee simple, which is what O started out to accomplish. No enrollment of the lease is required because the Statute of Enrollments applies only to bargains and sales of *freeholds;* no enrollment of the release is required because it operates at common law and not under the Statute of Uses. This method of conveyance by lease and release became standard procedure.[8]

Problems

16.1. In most states, the statute of uses is a common-law statute, i.e., it was brought over as part of the common law.[9] The statute of enrollments is not a common-law statute because it was a revenue measure.[10] Many old deeds, particularly in New York, are found in the form of a lease and release.

---

8. You could also have a release to uses, as part of this transaction, and thus raise uses which the statute would execute so that they became legal estates. For example, O bargains and sells to T for one year; then O releases O's reversion to T and his (or her) heirs to the use of A for life and upon A's death to the use of B and his (or her) heirs. The legal title ends up in A for life, remainder to B in fee.

9. 4 Kent Commentaries 299.

10. Givan v. Doe, 7 Blackf. 210 (Ind. 1844).

Comment upon the professional skill of the attorneys responsible for these deeds.

16.2. Thomas Kirby leased to his brother Christopher for one year. Then he "granted, released and confirmed" the premises "after the death of the said Thomas" to Christopher and the heirs of his body and thereafter to his cousin John Wilkinson and his heirs. Who gets what and by what method? Roe v. Tranmer, 2 Wils. K.B. 75 (1757).[11]

The new methods of conveying were cumulative to the old, not substitutional. Thus, after 1536 as before, O could convey to A in fee simple by a common-law feoffment; and no writing was required, though a charter of feoffment was desirable for evidential purposes.

You will observe that the Statute of Uses was the second phase of a five-phase development in the law of conveyancing from the Conquest to the present day:

Phase One: The Era of Livery of Seisin. Physical transfer of the land was required; no document could take the place of this.

Phase Two: The Era of the Statute of Uses (1536). Documents were permitted to take the place of physical transfer, but documents were still not required.

Phase Three: The Era of the Statute of Frauds (1677). All transfers were required to be in writing. (See Chapter 24.)

Phase Four: The Era of the Recording Acts. Facilities are made available for recording instruments of conveyance, and unrecorded instruments are made ineffective against certain later claimants of the land. (See Chapter 28.)

Phase Five: The Era of the Torrens System. Titles are adjudicated by a court, and the purchaser gets a certificate of title from that court. (See Chapter 30.)

SECTION 4. NEW LEGAL INTERESTS MADE POSSIBLE BY THE STATUTE

Courts of equity never paid any attention to two of the common-law restrictive rules as to the creation of future interests, viz., (1) the rule that you

---

11. In this famous case Willes, C.J., said,

Judges have been astuti to carry the intent of the parties into execution, and to give the most liberal and benign construction to deeds ut res magis valeat quam pereat. . . . Certainly it is more considerable to make the intent good in passing the estate, if by any legal means it may be done, than, by considering the manner of passing it, to disappoint the intent and principal thing, which was to pass the land.

This very modern approach was a surprising phenomenon in the period of Blackstone. It was not uniformly adhered to by later generations of judges.

could not create a freehold to commence in futuro — i.e., a springing interest, and (2) the rule that you could not create a condition in favor of a stranger, i.e., a shifting interest. Springing and shifting interests, generically called "executory interests," were freely allowed in equity. Thus, prior to the Statute of Uses,

1. if O enfeoffed T and his (or her) heirs to the use of A and his (or her) heirs when A should marry B, the state of the legal title was "Fee simple in T" and the state of the equitable title was "Fee simple in O (by resulting use) subject to a springing executory interest in A in fee simple to take effect when A marries B."

2. if O enfeoffed T and his (or her) heirs to the use of A and his (or her) heirs, but if A dies without having had children, then to the use of B and his (or her) heirs, the state of the legal title was "Fee simple in T" and the state of the equitable title was "Fee simple in A subject to a shifting executory interest in B in fee to take effect if A dies without having had children."

This, then, was the situation which existed when the Statute of Uses took effect on May 1, 1536. That statute provided, as you will recall, that the person who had a use should henceforth be deemed to have a legal interest in the land "in such like estate as [such person] had in use." Thus were imported into the law of legal estates the springing and the shifting interest. In example (1) immediately above, A had an equitable springing interest before the statute; the statute changed this interest into the "like estate" at law; and A therefore had a legal springing interest after the statute. In example (2) above, B had an equitable shifting interest before the statute; the statute changed this interest into the "like estate" at law; and B therefore had a legal shifting interest after the statute.

Problem

16.3. In 1600 O enfeoffed A and his heirs under a charter of feoffment which provided that "if A shall die without ever having had children, then B shall have the said estate to him and his heirs." What is the state of the title?

The foregoing problem is designed to bring out the fact that, while the Statute of Uses enabled a grantor to create springing and shifting interests by raising a use which the statute would execute, the statute had no effect on the common-law rules applicable to the common-law methods of conveyancing. If a grantor wished to create a springing or a shifting legal interest in a freehold, the grantor had to employ the machinery of the Statute of Uses. By contrast, the Statute of Wills, passed four years later in 1540, was construed to permit springing and shifting executory devises to be created without declaration of a use. Thus, if O left a will declaring, "I devise Blackacre to A and his heirs, but if A shall die without having had children, then to B and his heirs," the gift took effect as expressed and B had an effective shifting executory devise in fee. In modern times no declaration of a use is necessary to create springing and shifting interests.

Heretofore we have spoken of springing interests as comprising the type of estate that was traditionally created in a marriage settlement — that is, where O owning Blackacre desires to make a present conveyance so that A will become the owner on a future event. However, there can also be a springing interest upon a reversion. Thus, if O bargains and sells to A for life and one year after A's death to B and her heirs, B has a springing interest. It works this way. The bargain and sale raises a use in A for life; then there is a resulting use (an equitable reversion) in O in fee; then one year later there is a springing use in B in fee. All these uses are changed by the Statute of Uses into the corresponding legal estates; so the state of the legal title is, "A for life, reversion in O in fee, subject to a springing interest in B in fee to take effect one year after A's death."

Problems

16.4. In 1600 O bargains and sells to A for 100 years if A so long live, then to A's heirs. What is the state of the title? Why would this form of conveyance be made?

16.5. In 1600 O bargains and sells to A for life and one day after A's death to A's heirs. What is the state of the title? Why would this form of conveyance be made?

16.6. In 1600 O enfeoffs A for 100 years if A so long live, thereafter to A's heirs. What is the state of the title? Comment on the professional competence of the conveyancer.

Let us now consider the status of the rule of destructibility of contingent remainders after the Statute of Uses. Before the statute there could be no legal springing interests, including a legal springing interest upon a reversion. Thus, before 1536, where O conveyed to A for life and then to A's first son who should reach 21 and his heirs, and where A died leaving only a minor son, the estate of the son failed; if it were to take effect it would operate as a legal springing interest on O's reversion, and there could be no such springing interest. However, the Statute of Uses changed the basic situation by legitimizing legal springing interests, including a springing interest on a reversion; it authorized "abeyance of the seisin," if anyone chooses thus to designate the situation where a reversion becomes possessory to be later divested. Now suppose that, after 1536, O bargains and sells to A for life, remainder to A's first son who shall reach 21, and A dies leaving only a minor son. One might expect the courts to say:

The Statute of Uses constitutes a legislative declaration that springing interests upon a reversion are acceptable and that there is no longer any objection to abeyance of the seisin. Since considerations of seisin are basically feudal in character, this legislative declaration is thoroughly in accord with the nonfeudal nature of the present land law. In the conveyance under consideration it is clear that O intends A's first son to take at 21 whether the son reaches that age before or after the death of A. There is no longer any legal objection to carrying out this intention. So we give it effect. Upon A's death O takes possession under O's reversion, and at such time as A's first son shall reach 21, the son will take the property in fee by virtue of his springing executory interest.

But the courts said no such thing. Instead they said:

No limitation capable of taking effect as a contingent remainder shall, if created inter vivos, be held to be a springing use under the Statute of Uses, or, if created by will, be held to be an executory devise under the Statute of Wills.

This is known as the Rule of Purefoy v. Rogers (1670).[12] Thus contingent remainders created by way of use or devise were destructible after the Statutes of Uses and Wills just as they were before. (We have already pointed out the modern state of the law on this matter: destructibility exists except as abolished by "contingent remainder acts" which have been enacted in England and many states.) The great Professor Kales of Northwestern University remarked that "the rule that a future interest which can take effect as a common law remainder must do so or fail entirely and can never take effect as a springing executory devise or use is no more than a circumlocution announcing the rule of destructibility."[13] Do you follow this?

Problems

16.7. After Purefoy v. Rogers, O bargains and sells Blackacre to A for 100 years if A so long live, and after the death of A to A's first son who shall reach the age of 21 and his heirs. What is the state of the title? What is the reason for this odd form of conveyance?

16.8. After 1670 O bargains and sells Blackacre to A for life and one day after A's death to A's first son who shall reach 21 and his heirs. What is the state of the title? Why this form of conveyance?

The ruling that contingent remainders were destructible despite the Statute of Uses was bad news for the landed gentry and their attorneys.

---

12. The quotation is from White v. Summers, 2 L.R.-Ch. D. 256, 262 (1908), but the rule was first announced in Purefoy v. Rogers, 2 Wms. Saund. 380 (1670). See American Law of Property §4.60 (Casner ed. 1952).
13. Kales, Cases on Future Interests 121 (1917).

Where part of the family estates had, according to custom, been given to S, a son, for life with remainder to his eldest son in tail male, the remainder was at the mercy of S until a son was born in whom the remainder could vest. To protect such remainders the most common and ingenious devise was the creation of an intermediate estate in *trustees to preserve contingent remainders,* an invention of Sir Orlando Bridgman.[14] This device worked as follows.[15] The land was conveyed to S for life, remainder to trustees "for the life of S in trust for S for life and to preserve contingent remainders," remainder to S's first son in tail male. Observe the cleverness of the scheme. The danger was that S might become the reversioner or, in collusion with the reversioner (who might be an untrustworthy member of the family if one or more deaths should occur), might extinguish his life estate by forfeiture or merger and thereby destroy the contingent remainder. To prevent this, a *vested* estate in trustees is created; if S is a good member of the family and does nothing in the way of forfeiture or merger, the estate of the trustees never becomes possessory since it expires at the same instant as S's life estate; if S becomes the reversioner or conveys his life estate to the reversioner, the vested estate in the trustees blocks a merger; if S forfeits his estate by a tortious conveyance, the vested estate in the trustees becomes possessory, and they hold this in trust for S, so that he does not even hurt himself by his foolishness. Cannot S make a deal with the trustees to bring them into a merger scheme? No, equity will nullify any such breach of trust by the trustees. But how is it that the equitable estate of S is not transformed by the Statute of Uses into the corresponding legal estate? Ah, *that* is a very good question, and if you have asked yourself this before reading the question on this page, take a bow to deafening scholarly applause. By way of answer we shortly point out that the statute did not execute all uses, only some; and the ones that it left unexecuted are very important indeed.

Problems

16.9. O devised to Sarah for 100 years if she should so long live, then to her husband John for life, then to trustees for the life of John in trust for John for life and to preserve contingent remainders, then in fee simple to the

---

14. Bridgman was an outstanding ornament of the legal profession in his day. He obviously had most of the great and wealthy of the land among his clientele, and his practice was characterized by daring and ingenuity rather than the standard counselor's virtues of conservatism and adherence to precedent. Among his clients Bridgman counted the family of the Duke of Norfolk, then as now the first peer of the realm, and for this family he drew an instrument to meet a situation involving insanity of the eldest son. The validity of this instrument was finally litigated in The Duke of Norfolk's Case, 3 Ch. Cas. 1 (1682), one of the leading decisions of all time, in which the foundations of the rule against perpetuities were laid. Bridgman set up a whole series of future interests in this instrument; the most important one was held valid; others were held void. Bridgman became Lord Keeper, but never was raised to the dignity of Lord Chancellor.

15. For further detail see Kales, Estates and Future Interests in Illinois §78 (1920).

children of John and Sarah who should survive John and Sarah. The remainder is not safe from destruction. Here is an example of a conveyancer who knew the two common ways of protecting contingent remainders, used them both, and failed. Do you see why? Cunliffe v. Brancker, 3 Ch. D. 393 (1876).

16.10. O devised to A for life, then if at or before A's death a son of A has reached 21 to such son and his heirs, but if at A's death no son of A has reached 21, then to the first son of A who reaches 21 after A's death and his heirs. What is the effect of this devise? See White v. Summers, 2 L.R.-Ch. D. 256 (1908).

16.11. O devised to A for life, remainder in fee to such son of A as shall reach 21 before or after A's death. A dies leaving only a minor son. Can the son take when he reaches 21? In re Lechmere & Lloyd, 18 Ch. D. 524 (1881); Simonds v. Simonds, 199 Mass. 552, 85 N.E. 860 (1908); Kales, Estates and Future Interests in Illinois §103 (1920).

The Strict Settlement

We are now in a position to appreciate the deftness of the strict settlement, the method by which the estates of the landed families were so tied up in legal meshes, over the period roughly from 1650 to 1925, that it was quite unlikely that they would stray out of the family circle. The settlement provided for wives, daughters, and younger sons, and therein became very complex[16]; but its central core comprised the provisions for assuring that the freehold passed down through, and stayed in, the male line. Let us assume that F, a father, has a son, S, who is about to marry and for whom he wants to set up an estate. He conveys the property to S for life, remainder to trustees for the life of S to preserve contingent remainders, remainder in tail male to the first son of S, with successive remainders in tail male to the other sons of S. As we have seen, the estate in the trustees effectively blocks any attempt on the part of S to break up the settlement by destroying the contingent remainders in his sons. When a son is born, whom we will call G, his remainder in tail vests. When G reaches 21, S has reached his forties or fifties and feels himself the guardian of the family honor, tradition and estates. G may be rebellious and undisciplined, but he cannot disentail and thereby acquire a fee simple in remainder, because disentailment is possible only for a tenant in tail in possession; so, no matter what wild and radical ideas G may have at the age of 21, he can do the family estates no damage. It was at this point that, traditionally, S called G in for a chat. He explained to him that, having arrived at manhood's threshold, G would be wanting to

---

16. For the whole story, if you are interested, see Chapter 14 of Radcliffe, Real Property Law (1933).

make the grand tour of the continent, and present himself at the London season; this would take money, but there were family funds, controlled by S, available for members of the family who showed that they had the family interests at heart. S further explained that one of the important interests of the family was the continuation of the family estates and that there were a few papers to be signed to that end, now and at once. Thus gently nudged, it was traditional for G to sign as requested and thus make available to himself those advantages which flow from a generous parental allowance. The resettlement which would be created at this point comprised the following steps:

1. S, the life tenant, and the trustees surrendered their estates to G, the remainderman in tail. This made him a tenant in tail in possession.
2. G suffered a recovery in favor of the family solicitor, thus making the solicitor owner of the fee simple.
3. The family solicitor conveyed to S for life, remainder to G for life, remainder to trustees for the lives of S and G to preserve contingent remainders, remainders to the first and other sons of G in tail male, remainders to the second and other sons of S in tail male.

Thus the basic pattern was pushed forward one generation. S could now rest easy in the confident belief that G would have no power to put the estates out of the family until he had a son 21 years old; and by that time G in his turn would be settled down, devoted to a shire life of farming and fox hunting, and determined to see that the family estates were preserved. You will, of course, realize that this little narrative is a simplification and to some extent a fictionalization and that for various family contingencies other devices were required; but this was the fundamental process. By this method thousands of estates like Pusey Manor were kept substantially intact for centuries; if you care to get a notion of the extent to which this went, look at copies of Burke's Peerage and Burke's Landed Gentry for any period during the nineteenth century.

SECTION 5. UNEXECUTED USES: THE MODERN TRUST

In the modern trust T, trustee, holds the legal title while the trust beneficiaries, the cestuis que trust, hold equitable title. How can this be after the Statute of Uses? Why does not the statute execute the uses, thus giving the beneficiaries legal estates and putting the trust companies out of business? The answer is: The Statute of Uses does not execute all uses, and the modern trust is simply an unexecuted use that falls outside the operation of the statute. Unexecuted uses are of three types.

Type 1:   A Use on a Use

Suppose O enfeoffs T and her heirs to the use of A and his heirs to the use of B and her heirs. The statute executes A's use and makes him the owner of the legal estate. It would now seem that he in turn falls within the provisions of the statute and that B's use should be executed, thus depriving A of any interest. But no, the statute (as Professor Warren used to say) gets tired after executing one use (and, to illustrate this, he would let his arms drop to his side and let his fine white head fall forward limply on his chest in a posture of utter exhaustion). The historical reasons for the rule have been carefully developed,[17] but the Warren fatigue demonstration has yet to be equaled as a graphic expression of the result. This means that where O bargains and sells to A and his heirs to the use of B and her heirs, B has an equitable estate. The bargain and sale raises a use in A, which the statute executes by giving to A the legal estate. But the statute does not undertake the second operation of executing the use in B. So also a covenant by O to stand seised to the use of A and his heirs to the use of B and her heirs puts legal title in A and equitable title in B.

Do not confuse a use-on-a-use with a use-after-a-use. For example, if O enfeoffs T and her heirs to the use of A for life and on A's death to the use of B and her heirs, both uses are executed. This is a two-story structure, like this

A for life, remainder to B in fee (*use*)

T in | **fee (*legal title*)**

It is to be contrasted with the case where O enfeoffs T and her heirs to the use of A and his heirs to the use of B and her heirs. This creates a three-story structure, like this

B in fee   (*use on a use*)

A in fee   (*use*)

T in | **fee (*legal title*)**

When the statute has operated on these two conveyances, the results are, respectively, (1) legal title in A for life, legal remainder in B in fee, and (2) legal title in A in fee, equitable title in B in fee.

---

17.   Ames, Lectures on Legal History 243 (1913); 1 Scott on Trusts §71 (3d ed. 1967).

Type 1a: Doe v. Passingham

The rule that a use-on-a-use was valid and was not executed was established at least as early as 1634.[18] It had no justification in the statute and plainly defeated the statute's purpose of eliminating equitable interests. At a much later date, in Doe v. Passingham, 6 B. & C. 305 (1827), it was held that where O made a common-law conveyance to T and his heirs "to T's own use to the use of A and his heirs," the use in A was not executed. This brought it about that the Statute of Uses had succeeded not in prohibiting a person from creating equitable interests, but only in compelling the addition of four more words to the conveyance, viz., "to T's own use."

Type 2:   Active Duties Imposed on the Trustee

The characteristic of the modern trust is the separation of management from benefit. The trustee manages the property for the benefit of the cestui que trust. If the property is real estate, this means keeping the premises rented and in repair, collecting the rents and profits, and paying over the net proceeds to the cestui. It was determined at an early date that if management duties of this nature were imposed upon the holder of the legal title, the use would not be executed by the statute.[19]

Type 3:   Holder of Legal Title Not "Seised"

You will recall that the Statute of Uses applies where "any person be *seised* of any lands to the use of any other person." This language plainly excludes the case where one holds a term of years to the use of another (though it includes the case where one holds a fee simple to the use of another for a term of years). Also, of course, the statute has no application where the subject matter of the conveyance comprises chattels personal; and most modern trusts consist of stocks, bonds, and cash.

Problems

16.12.   O, owner in fee simple, bargains and sells to A for 99 years to the use of B. Is B's estate legal or equitable, and for what reason or reasons?

16.13.   O, owner in fee simple, bargains and sells to A and her heirs to the use of B for 20 years and thereafter to the use of C and his heirs. Is B's estate legal or equitable and for what reason or reasons?

18.   Sambach v. Dalston, Toth. 188 (1634).
19.   See Note, The Statute of Uses and Active Trusts, 17 Mich. L. Rev. 87 (1918).

16.14. O, owner in fee simple, devises to T and his heirs to the use of A for life and then to the use of A's heirs, T to collect the income during A's life and pay it over to A in quarterly installments. What is the state of the title?

16.15. O, owner in fee simple, devises to T and her heirs to the use of A for life and then to the use of A's heirs, T to collect the income during A's life and pay it over to A in quarterly installments and on A's death to convey the premises to A's heirs. What is the state of the title? See Ayer v. Ritter, 29 S.C. 135, 7 S.E. 53 (1888).

SECTION 6. RECAPITULATION AND APPRAISAL

The Statute of Uses was designed to eliminate the system of uses by which most of the land of England was held beneficially by equitable titles. In this it signally failed; and, although we have made no search of the fiscal records of the Crown, we infer that Henry VIII failed to reap the pecuniary harvest which motivated his sponsorship of the statute.

The Statute of Enrollments also signally failed to attain its double objective. It did not succeed in establishing an effective recording system for deeds; and it did not succeed in bringing in the revenues expected from the tax on enrollment.

However, the Statute of Uses did accomplish two notable reforms in the land law. First, it established the effectiveness of conveyance by document, regardless of transfer of possession; and the bargain and sale, the lease and release, and the covenant to stand seised became the standard forms of deed. Second, it removed the old feudal shackles from the law of future interests, and made it possible to create springing and shifting interests at law. (The fact that the courts held that remainders were still destructible should not overshadow the major accomplishment of the statute in validating executory interests.)

The Statute of Uses was repealed in England in 1925 as part of an entire statutory recasting of the law of property. Oddly enough, the statutory changes of 1925 back-tracked on the Statute of Uses by changing many legal estates into equitable estates — a step which tended to re-establish the status quo ante 1536 though for entirely different reasons.[20]

Commentary on the lack of bulldog qualities in Parliament and the courts. You must have been struck by the consistency with which important acts of Parliament were ignored or circumvented. Consider the list:

1. De Donis declared that where an estate tail was established the rights of the issue of the tenant in tail and of remaindermen and rever-

---

20. See Bordwell, The Repeal of the Statute of Uses, 39 Harv. L. Rev. 466, 480 (1926); Bordwell, Property Reform in England, 11 Iowa L. Rev. 1 (1926).

sioners were inviolable. Yet Taltarum's Case held that, by a common recovery, the tenant in tail could cut off these rights. And Parliament took no corrective steps.

2. The Statute of Uses undertook to abolish equitable estates. The conveyancers invented the use on a use, and frustrated the statute. Doe v. Passingham simply added insult to injury.

3. The Statute of Enrollments undertook to establish a recording system and raise a tax. The lease and release checkmated both aims and made the statute a dead letter.

All these evasions could easily have been prevented by corrective legislation; but no steps in that direction were taken. This seems strange to us. We are used to a running battle between Congress and various groups upon which Congress is seeking to impose its will. The most notable is the contest between Congress and its taxpayers, the latter continually inventing devices to take advantage of loopholes in the revenue laws and the former plugging up the loopholes as discovered and, as likely as not, laying the lash over the backs of the discoverers. The antitrust laws and the labor laws are other notable examples. But Parliament simply did not react in that manner in the old days.[21]

The courts likewise allowed their doctrines to be pushed around. They announced that estates tail could be enlarged into fees simple and that contingent remainders after life estates were destructible. They then supinely approved Bridgman's slick device of trustees to preserve contingent remainders, thereby providing the basic ingredient of the strict settlement which, as a practical matter, made estates tail incapable of enlargement and contingent remainders incapable of destruction. It is true that the courts developed the Rule against Perpetuities to keep indestructible future interests within limits; but even the rule was nearly helpless against the strict settlement. The fact is that the courts did not think then as we think now. We are conscious of the function of courts as lawmakers and their resultant obligation to look at the practical political and social consequences of their decisions; but we must not forget that the term "sociological jurisprudence" is a fairly recent invention and that the frame of mind described by that term is a very modern development. In the old days the law was thought of as essentially a logical system. If an ingenious fellow like Bridgman could turn the logic of the law against itself—as a judo wrestler throws his opponent by using his own weight against him—the courts acknowledged defeat in sportsmanlike fashion and left it at that.

---

21. The time lag between each of these statutes and the judicial approval of the device which frustrated it may be cited as an extenuating circumstance. De Donis (1285) was frustrated by Taltarum's Case (1472); The Statute of Uses (1536) by Sambach v. Dalston, Toth. 188 (1634); The Statute of Enrollments (1536) by Lutwich v. Mitton, Cro. Jac. 604 (1620). Perhaps the shady political deal back of the Statute of Uses had no appeal in the succeeding century; but whatever reasons of policy lay behind De Donis and the Statute of Enrollments were equally valid one or two centuries later.

The result was that the English land law was replete with prohibitory rules which prohibited only the uninformed. Almost anything that a person might want to do with his or her property could be done, but it frequently had to be done by circuitous methods studded with traps for the unskillful. This is hardly a situation to excite admiration; but, in view of the fact that much of this law is the background of the law in the United States, it is a situation which the prudent will take pains to understand.

SECTION 7. THE STATUTE OF USES IN THE UNITED STATES

In most of the United States it is held that the Statute of Uses is a common-law statute and therefore is in force unless it has been repealed.[22] Some states (e.g., New York) have expressly repealed the statute and others (e.g., Illinois) have expressly confirmed it. But all states have legislation which accomplishes the two basic reforms of the statutes, viz. permitting deeds to take effect without transfer of possession, and permitting springing and shifting interests to be created.

An issue concerning the statute can still arise in this way. O executes a home-made deed in which O declares that O "gives and makes over for due consideration" to T certain lands to be held in trust for A. The question is whether A has an equitable or a legal estate — which may affect the rights of creditors, the right of A's spouse to dower, and other rights. If the deed is considered as a feoffment, then A's right is legal, since the statute will execute the use in A. If the deed is considered as a bargain and sale, then A's right is equitable, since the statute exhausted itself in executing the use in T; A's use-on-a-use is not executed.[23] The situation is usually complicated by various local statutes — for example, a statute declaring that a recorded grant can take effect as a feoffment without any livery of seisin.

These cases now arise very rarely, though they were an essential part of the learning of the last century. The Statute of Uses was an important factor in the development of the land law but it is no appreciable part of its present substance.[24]

22. For example, French v. French, 3 N.H. 234 (1825); Jackson v. Alexander, 3 Johns. 484 (N.Y. 1808). Contra, Farmers' & Merchants' Insurance Co. v. Jensen, 58 Neb. 522, 78 N.W. 1054 (1899).

23. The case supposed is a combination of Matthews v. Ward's Lessee, 10 G. & J. 443 (Md. 1839), and Jackson v. Alexander, 3 Johns. 484 (N.Y. 1808).

24. For extensive treatment of the American cases on the Statute of Uses, see 1 Scott on Trusts §§67-73.1 (3d ed. 1967).

Problem

16.16.   In which of the following conveyances does it make any difference whether the instrument of conveyance is a bargain and sale or a common-law feoffment?

a.   O conveys Blackacre "to A for life then if B marries C to B and his [or her] heirs." A dies. Then B marries C. You represent B.

b.   O conveys Blackacre "to A for life and if B sends flowers to A's funeral, to B and his [or her] heirs." You represent B.

c.   O conveys Blackacre "to T and his [or her] heirs for the use of A and his [or her] heirs but if A dies without a child of A living at A's death to the use of B and his [or her] heirs." A dies childless. B dies survived by a spouse. You represent the spouse.

d.   O conveys Blackacre "to T and his [or her] heirs for the use of A for life." You represent O.

e.   O conveys Blackacre "to A and his [or her] heirs but if A dies without issue to B and his [or her] heirs." You represent B.

f.   O conveys Blackacre "to A for life then to B and his [or her] heirs, B's interest to be held for the use of A's heirs." You represent A.

g.   O conveys Blackacre "to T and his [or her] heirs for the use of H and W [husband and wife] and their heirs." You represent W.

h.   O conveys Blackacre "to A and B for their lives then to A's heirs." You represent A's son, S.

i.   O conveys Blackacre "to A and his [or her] heirs from and after O's death." You represent A.

SECTION 8.   THE RULE AGAINST PERPETUITIES

The What-Might-Happen Test

The need for a rule against perpetuities arose when indestructible remotely vesting future interests became possible, because such future interests fetter the alienability of the complete title to property and remove such property from the channels of commerce. The stagnation with respect to transfers of land during the period of the fee tail estate from 1285 to the development of a method that enabled the owner of the fee tail to bar the entail and convey a fee simple interest is an early example of the social need to end at some time the division of ownership into present and future interests. The common law rule against perpetuities, a judicially developed rule, invalidated future interests that might vest beyond the period of the rule.

The original common-law rule against perpetuities requires that an interest in property, in order for it to be valid, must be certain to vest, if it ever vests, not later than 21 years after a life or lives in being at the date the period of the rule begins to run. The fact that the interest might vest within the required time is not enough. It had to be certain to vest, if it ever vested, within the required time.

An interest does not violate the common-law rule against perpetuities just because it is one that may never vest. Every contingent future interest is one that may never vest because the contingency may never occur. The issue is whether or not it will be definitely known within the required period of time whether or not the interest will vest in the light of what conceivably might happen.

The question you should ask yourself with respect to any contingent interest is whether the interest must vest, if it ever is going to vest, within 21 years after some life or lives in being when the period of rule begins to run. If you can find such a life or lives, the interest does not violate the rule, and if you cannot, the interest is invalid under the what-might-happen test of the common-law rule against perpetuities.

We present to you at this point a leading case that is designed to test your imagination of what might happen in applying the what-might-happen test.

JEE v. AUDLEY
1 Cox 324 (Ch. 1787)

Edward Audley, by his will, bequeathed as follows:

> Also my will is that £1000 shall be placed out at interest during the life of my wife, which interest I give her during her life, and at her death I give the said £1000 unto my niece Mary Hall and the issue of her body lawfully begotten, and to be begotten, and in default of such issue I give the said £1000 to be equally divided between the daughters then living of my kinsman John Jee and his wife Elizabeth Jee.

It appeared that John Jee and Elizabeth Jee were living at the time of the death of the testator, had four daughters and no son, and were of a very advanced age. Mary Hall was unmarried and of the age of about 40; the wife was dead. The present bill was filed by the four daughters of John and Elizabeth Jee to have the £1000 secured for their benefit upon the event of the said Mary Hall dying without leaving children. And the question was, whether the limitation to the daughters of John and Elizabeth Jee was not void as being too remote; and to prove it so, it was said that this was to take effect on a general failure of issue of Mary Hall; and though it was to the daughters of John and Elizabeth Jee, yet it was not confined to the daughters living at the death of the testator, and consequently it might extend to after-born daughters, in which case it would not be within the limit of a life or lives in being and 21 years afterwards, beyond which time an executory devise is void.

On the other side it was said, that though the late cases had decided that on a gift to children generally, such children as should be living at the time of the distribution of the fund should be let in, yet it would be very hard to adhere to such a rule of construction so rigidly, as to defeat the evident intention of the testator in this case, especially as there was no real possibility of John and Elizabeth Jee having children after the testator's death, they being then 70 years old; that if there were two ways of construing words, that should be adopted which would give effect to the disposition made by the testator; that the cases, which had decided that after-born children should take, proceeded on the implied intention of the testator, and never meant to give an effect to words which would totally defeat such intention. . . .

MASTER OF THE ROLLS [Sir Lloyd Kenyon]. Several cases determined by Lord Northington, Lord Camden, and the present Chancellor, have settled that children born after the death of the testator shall take a share in these cases; the difference is, where there is an immediate devise, and where there is an interest in remainder; in the former case the children living at the testator's death only shall take; in the latter those who are living at the time the interest vests in possession; and this being now a settled principle, I shall not strain to serve an intention at the expense of removing the land marks of the law; it is of infinite importance to abide by decided cases, and perhaps more so on this subject than any other. The general principles which apply to this case are not disputed: the limitations of personal estate are void, unless they necessarily vest, if at all, within a life or lives in being and 21 years or nine or ten months afterwards. This has been sanctioned by the opinion of judges of all times, from the time of the Duke of Norfolk's case to the present: it is grown reverend by age, and is not now to be broken in upon; I am desired to do in this case something which I do not feel myself at liberty to do, namely to suppose it impossible for persons in so advanced an age as John and Elizabeth Jee to have children; but if this can be done in one case it may in another, and it is a very dangerous experiment, and introductive of the greatest inconvenience to give a latitude to such sort of conjecture.[25] Another thing pressed upon me, is to decide on the events which have happened; but I cannot do this without overturning very many cases. The

25. The New Hampshire court repudiated the idea that a man or woman was capable of having issue as long as he or she lived, in a case where the termination of a trust depended on the possibility of the birth of additional issue. In this case the man was 63 and the woman was 45. There was medical evidence that neither one was capable of having children. See In re Bassett's Estate, 104 N.H. 504, 190 A.2d 415 (1963). For a comment on the Bassett case, see Leach, Perpetuities: New Hampshire Defertilizes the Octogenarians, 77 Harv. L. Rev. 279 (1963). — EDS.

single question before me is, not whether the limitation is good in the events which have happened, but whether it was good in its creation; and if it were not, I cannot make it so. Then must this limitation, if at all, necessarily take place within the limits prescribed by law? The words are "in default of such issue I give the said £1000 to be equally divided between the daughters then living of John Jee and Elizabeth his wife." If it had been to "daughters now living," or "who should be living at the time of my death," it would have been very good; but as it stands, this limitation may take in after-born daughters; this point is clearly settled by Ellison v. Airey, and the effect of law on such limitation cannot make any difference in construing such intention. If then this will extended to afterborn daughters, is it within the rules of law? Most certainly not, because John and Elizabeth Jee might have children born ten years after the testator's death, and then Mary Hall might die without issue 50 years afterwards; in which case it would evidently transgress the rules prescribed. I am of opinion therefore, though the testator might possibly mean to restrain the limitation to the children who should be living at the time of the death, I cannot, consistently with decided cases, construe it in such restrained sense, but must intend it to take in after-born children. This therefore not being within the rules of law, and as I cannot judge upon subsequent events, I think the limitation void. Therefore dismiss the bill, but without costs.[26]

26. In Bowen v. Campbell, 344 Mass. 24, 181 N.E.2d 342 (1962), it was held that a period measured by lives in being at the time of the probate of the will creating the interests plus 21 years was a period that might exceed that of the rule against perpetuities, because the probate of the will might take place a long time after the death of the testator, and thus the measuring lives might not all be in being on the testator's death.

Medical science has made it possible for a person to have a child long after his death by preserving his sperm and using it in artificial insemination. Suppose that O makes a transfer in trust under which the income is to be paid to O's son S for life and the corpus is to pass after S's death to S's children who attain age 21. The gift to S's children has been regarded as valid under the common-law rule against perpetuities because each child of S who attains age 21 must do so within 21 years (plus any period of actual gestation) after S's death and S is a life in being when O establishes the trust. Is such a gift now to fail as a result of medical science's achievement, because it is now possible for a child of S to attain age 21 more than 21 years after S's death by the process of artificial insemination? The answer to this question should be a resounding no. How can this answer be reached? It is submitted that it should be reached on one of the following grounds:

1. A judicial wait-and-see rule under which a determination would be made at S's death as to whether it is possible for a child of S (that could conceivably be in the class) to be born by artificial insemination after S's death (if no sperm of S had in fact been preserved, this possibility would not exist); or

2. A rule of construction which would exclude from a class gift to S's children any child of S born after S's death by the process of artificial insemination.

The second ground would uphold all such gifts to S's children in the absence of affirmative evidence that children of S produced by artificial insemination after his death were to be included. The first ground would uphold practically all such gifts to S's children because of the unlikelihood that sperm of S would in fact be available to produce a child of his by artificial insemination after his death. See Leach, Perpetuities in the Atomic Age: The Sperm Bank and the Fertile Decedent, 48 A.B.A.J. 942 (1962).

The historical background of the development of the rule against perpetuities is reexamined in Haskins, Extending the Grasp of the Dead Hand: Reflections on the Origins of the Rule Against Perpetuities, 126 U. Pa. L. Rev. 19 (1977). —Eds.

The Wait-and-See Test

The complexity of the common-law rule against perpetuities is largely due to the application of the what-might-happen test. Some judicial decisions in recent years have substituted for the what-might-happen test a wait-and-see test under which the possibility that an interest may vest too remotely is ignored and invalidity results only if in fact the interest does not vest within the period of the rule against perpetuities. Restatement (Second) of Property (Donative Transfers) §1.4 adopts the wait-and-see test. Wait-and-see statutes in one form or another have been adopted in many states. We present for your examination the following material from the Restatement (Second) of Property (Donative Transfers) §1.4 comments c through o, reproduced here with the permission of the American Law Institute.

RESTATEMENT (SECOND) OF PROPERTY (DONATIVE TRANSFERS)
§1.4 comments c–o (1977)

c. *Reversionary interest.* A reversionary interest is what remains in a transferor who owns a vested interest and has made a transfer that does not exhaust the transferor's interest in the property transferred, so that an interest in the transferred property may return to the transferor at some future date. If the interest the transferor had in the transferred property before the transfer was not subject to the rule against perpetuities because it was vested, the reversionary interest is equally protected from the rule against perpetuities. If the interest the transferor had in the transferred property before the transfer was an interest subject to an unfulfilled condition precedent, the transferor will have had either a remainder or an executory interest and any interest retained in such non-vested interest after a transfer will continue to be either a remainder or an executory interest that is subject to an unfulfilled condition precedent and hence will be subject to the rule against perpetuities to the same extent as it was before the transfer.

Reversionary interests that are not subject to the rule against perpetuities are either reversions, possibilities of reverter, or rights of entry. Possibilities of reverter and rights of entry may be outstanding with respect to a piece of property for a long period of time, thereby hindering the full utilization of the property that is subject to one or the other of such interests. This has led to statutory enactments in some states which cause their elimination after the passage of some stated term of years. See Statutory Note to this section.

Illustrations:

1. O, owning Blackacre in fee simple absolute makes an otherwise effective devise thereof "to A for life, then to A's daughter B if B attains the age of 25." A and B survive O, and B is under the age of 25 at O's

death. The interest in B is subject to an unfulfilled condition precedent, namely the attainment of the age of 25. B is certain to attain 25, if she ever attains 25, in her own lifetime. Hence, her interest cannot vest more than 21 years after lives in being at the time the period of the rule begins to run and it will not fail under the rule of this section, regardless of her age at the death of O. If B does not live to attain 25, her interest will fail because the condition precedent to her interest is unfulfilled. Consequently, there is a reversion in O's estate that will pass under other provisions of O's will (or on intestacy if no other provision in O's will disposes of such reversion). Such reversion is not subject to the rule against perpetuities.

2.   O, owning Blackacre in fee simple absolute, makes an otherwise effective deed thereof "to A and his heirs as long as Blackacre is used for residential purposes." O retains a reversionary interest in Blackacre which is a possibility of a reverter. This reversionary interest is not subject to the rule against perpetuities.

3.   O, owning Blackacre in fee simple absolute, makes an otherwise effective deed thereof "to A and his heirs, but if A or his heirs or assigns ever use Blackacre for other than residential purposes, O or his heirs or assigns may reenter and take possession." O retains a reversionary interest in Blackacre which is a right of entry. This reversionary interest is not subject to the rule against perpetuities.

4.   O transfers property by will to T in trust. The terms of the trust direct T "to pay the income to A for life, then to pay income to A's children who are living from time to time, until no child of A is living who is under 21 years, at which time, the trustee shall pay the trust property to A's children then living, and if no child of A is then living, the trustee shall pay the trust property to the X Church." A survives O, A having no children at O's death. The unfulfilled condition precedent with respect to the interest of each child of A in the final distribution of the trust property is that the child be born and survive until no child of A is living who is under 21 years. Consequently, each child has an interest in the trust property that is subject to unfulfilled conditions precedent. The measuring life for purposes of the rule against perpetuities is A (see §1.3), because it is not possible for the unfulfilled condition precedent to the interest of each child of A in the trust property to be performed, if it is ever performed, more than 21 years after the death of A. Hence, the interest in a child of A will not fail because of the rule against perpetuities.

5.   O, owning Blackacre in fee simple absolute, makes an otherwise effective devise thereof "to A for life, then to A's first-born son for life, then to the issue then living of A's first-born son, such issue to take per stirpes." A survives O, but has no son born at the time of O's death. The

life interest in A's first-born son is subject to the unfulfilled condition precedent of his birth. His interest is vested as soon as he is born even though his interest might expire before he ever comes into possession of Blackacre, which would be the case if he should die before A. The interests in the issue of A's first-born son are subject not only to the unfulfilled condition precedent of their births, but also to the unfulfilled condition precedent of their surviving the survivor of A and A's first-born son. A reversionary interest is in O's estate which is not subject to the rule against perpetuities. The measuring life is A with respect to the interest in A's unborn son, but the measuring lives with respect to the interest in the issue of A's unborn son are A, the individuals to whom the reversionary interest passed on O's death, and any parents or grandparents who are alive on O's death of all beneficiaries of the devise (see §1.3). The unfulfilled condition precedent to the interest in A's first-born son will be performed, if it is ever performed, by the time A dies. The unfulfilled conditions precedent to the interests in the issue of A's first-born son may be performed within twenty-one years after the measuring lives. However, it is possible that such unfulfilled conditions precedent may not be performed within that time, which would be the case if A's first-born son should survive the measuring lives by more than twenty-one years. Under the what-might-happen approach, the interests in the issue of A's first-born son would fail regardless of what happens. Under the wait-and-see approach adopted by this section 1.4, the interests in the issue of A's first-born son will fail only if their interests in fact do not vest in time.

d. *Vesting of interest in child in gestation.* A child in gestation who is later born alive is considered a life in being during the period of gestation in determining whether such child's interest in property meets the vesting requirement of the rule against perpetuities. (For a comparable rule in regard to the measuring lives, see §1.3, Comment h.)

Illustration:

6. O transfers property by will to T in trust. The terms of the trust direct T "to pay the income to my children who are living from time to time, and on the death of my surviving child, to accumulate the income until the youngest grandchild of mine attains 21 years, or would have attained 21 had such grandchild lived, at which time, to distribute the trust property to my grandchildren then living and the issue then living of any deceased grandchild of mine, such issue to take per stirpes the share the deceased grandchild would have taken had such grandchild lived, and if no grandchild is then living and no issue of a deceased grandchild is then living, to distribute the trust property to the X Church." At O's death he has no grandchildren, but he has two

children, A and B, and his wife is pregnant and the child in gestation is born seven months after O dies and is named C. The accumulation period begins to run on the death of the survivor of A, B and C, but on the death of such survivor, the survivor, who is C, leaves his wife pregnant, and seven months after he dies, a child is born who is a grandchild of O and is O's youngest grandchild. Though that grandchild actually attains 21, 21 years and seven months after the death of the survivor of the measuring lives (the measuring lives are A, B and C, see §1.3), his interest is deemed to vest within the 21-year period after the death of the survivor of the measuring lives. Furthermore, if that grandchild should die just before he attains 21, leaving his wife pregnant and such child in gestation is born seven months after the grandchild dies, the interest in such child in gestation would be deemed vested during the period of gestation and hence would have vested in time for purposes of the rule against perpetuities.

e.   *Interest in property which cannot possibly vest within the period of the rule.* The vesting of an interest in property may be postponed under the terms of the instrument of transfer to a date that cannot possibly occur within 21 years after lives in being when the period of the rule begins to run. In such case, such interest fails at once because waiting and seeing cannot produce a vesting in time. The consequence of the failure of such interest is considered in §1.5.

Illustration:

7.   O transfers property by will to T in trust. The terms of the trust direct T "to pay the income to A for life, then to accumulate the income until 25 years after the death of the survivor of A and A's parents and grandparents living on O's death and the parents and grandparents living on O's death of A's issue, at which time to pay the accumulated income and principal to A's issue then living, such issue to take per stirpes, and if no issue of A is then living, to pay the same to the X Charity." A survives O and at O's death, A has no issue living. The measuring lives are A and the parents and grandparents of A and A's issue, which parents and grandparents are living on O's death (see §1.3). It is not possible for the non-vested interest in A's issue to vest within 21 years after the measuring lives. Hence, the non-vested interest in A's issue fails.

f.   *Interest in property which may vest, but is not certain to vest, if it ever vests, within the period of the rule.* Under the rule against perpetuities as it originally developed, a non-vested interest in property failed unless it was certain to vest, if it ever vested, within the period of the rule. This represented the so-called what-might-happen approach in applying the rule against perpetuities. The non-vested interest that might not vest within the period of the rule failed no matter how unlikely it was that events would so happen as to cause the interest to vest too remotely. The rule against perpetuities adopted by this section, however, is that what-does-happen approach, usually referred to as the wait-and-see approach, under which it is not possible to determine whether an interest fails under the rule against perpetuities as of the date the period of the rule begins to run, unless on such date it is impossible under all circumstances for the interest to vest in time (see Illustration 7). Under the wait-and-see approach, many interests in property that would fail under the what-might-happen approach will not fail, but in each such case, the instrument of transfer could have been drafted so as to allow the same amount of time for vesting under the what-might-happen approach. See §1.3, Comment a. Thus, the wait-and-see approach eliminates a trap into which the unwary tend to fall, but in which the skilled seldom get caught.

g. *Interest in property which is certain to vest, if it ever vests, within the period of the rule.* The adoption of the wait-and-see approach will never invalidate a non-vested interest in property that would have been valid under the what-might-happen approach. Consequently, if the non-vested interest is certain to vest, if it ever vests, within the period of the rule, the wait-and-see approach is not applicable to such non-vested interest.

h. *Fertile octogenarian case.* Under the what-might-happen approach in applying the rule against perpetuities, it was always assumed that an individual, whether male or female, was capable of having a child regardless of such individual's age, because who was to say with absolute assurance that such possibility did not exist as long as the individual was alive? Under the wait-and-see approach, the failure of an interest that may occur as a result of the birth of another child will not result if in fact another child is not born. Even if another child is born, by waiting and seeing, the vesting of the non-vested interest in question may occur in time.

Illustration:

8. O transfers property by will to T in trust. The terms of the trust direct T "to pay the income to O's brother A for life, then to pay the income to A's children living from time to time, until the death of his surviving child, then to distribute the trust property to A's issue then living, such issue to take per stirpes, and if no issue of A is then living, to distribute the trust property to the X Charity." A survives O and is 80 years old at O's death. The measuring lives are A and A's issue living at O's death and parents and grandparents alive on O's death of A and A's issue (see §1.3). If A does not have another child after O dies, the interest in A's issue living on the death of the survivor of A's children will in fact vest, if it ever vests, not later than lives in being when O dies, well within the period allowed by the rule against perpetuities, and under the wait-and-see approach of this section, there will be no failure of an

interest under the rule. Under the what-might-happen approach, however, the interest in A's issue living on the death of the survivor of A's children would fail because A might have another child, that child might survive by more than 21 years any life in being when O died, so that conceivably the interest in A's issue living at the death of A's surviving child might not vest until more than 21 years after lives in being at O's death. Under the wait-and-see approach of this section, even if A did in fact have another child after O died (or adopted a child not alive when O died), the interest in A's issue living on the death of A's surviving child would not fail unless that child in fact became the surviving child of A and in fact lived more than 21 years after the death of the measuring lives.

i.   *Unborn widow case.* The unfulfilled condition precedent to an interest in property may be the survivorship of a life beneficiary who is a measuring life and his widow. The word "widow" describes the person who in fact turns out to be the widow of the life beneficiary and it is possible that the life beneficiary may marry someone who was not alive at the time his life interest is created. If that in fact happens, and such widow lives more than 21 years after the death of the survivor of the measuring lives, an interest that will be subject to an unfulfilled condition precedent until the widow dies may vest too remotely. Under the what-might-happen approach, such non-vested interest in property fails, no matter how unlikely it is that the life beneficiary's widow would turn out to be a person unborn when the life interest was created. Under the wait-and-see approach of this section, such non-vested interest in property will fail only if it in fact turns out that it does not vest within the period of the rule.

Illustration:

9.   O transfers property by will to T in trust. The terms of the trust direct T "to pay the income to his brother A for life, then to pay the income to A's widow for life, then to distribute the trust property to A's issue then living, such issue to take per stirpes, and if no issue of A is then living, to distribute the trust property to the X Church." A survives O and at O's death he is 80 years old and is married to his wife W who is 78 years old. A dies survived by W. As events have turned out, W is A's widow and she is a measuring life as she was alive when the period of the rule began to run on O's death (see §1.3). The interest in A's issue living on the death of the survivor of A and W will vest, if it ever vests, within the period of the rule. Thus under the wait-and-see approach of this section an interest does not fail that would have failed under the what-might-happen approach. If W had predeceased A, and A had married someone else who was alive when O died, that someone else

would become a measuring life and the result would be the same under the wait-and-see approach of this section as if W had survived A. If, however, W had died after O, and A had in fact married a person who was not alive on O's death, and such person became A's widow, such widow would not be a measuring life and the interest in A's issue would fail under the wait-and-see approach of this section, unless such widow died within 21 years after the death of the survivor of the measuring lives, who are A, the issue of A living on O's death, and parents and grandparents alive at O's death of all beneficiaries.

j. *The age-contingency case.* The unfulfilled condition precedent may be the attainment of a certain age by the designated beneficiary of an interest in property. If the individual who must satisfy the age contingency is not one of the measuring lives, that is, is not a life in being when the period of the rule against perpetuities begins to run, the non-vested interest may fail under the what-might-happen approach, where the wait-and-see approach may not result in the failure of the interest.

Illustration:

10. O transfers property by will to T in trust. The terms of the trust direct T "to pay the income to A for life, then to accumulate the income until A's first-born daughter attains the age of 25 years, at which time the trust property shall be distributed to her, and if A's first-born daughter does not attain the age of 25 years, the trust property shall be distributed to the X Church." At O's death A has no daughter born to him. Under the what-might-happen approach, the interest in A's first-born daughter fails because it is possible that she might not attain the age of 25 until more than 21 years after any life in being when O died. Under the wait-and-see approach of this section, the interest in A's first-born daughter does not fail unless she in fact does not attain the age of 25 within 21 years after the death of the survivor of the measuring lives. If A's first-born daughter is at least four years old on the death of such survivor, her interest will vest in time if it ever vests.

k. *The class gift case.* The recipients of an interest in property under a donative transfer are frequently described not by name but by some class designation such as "children," "grandchildren," "issue," "next of kin," or "heirs." The interest of a class member is always contingent on the class member's birth and the interest may be subject to a condition precedent of attaining a designated age or of surviving to some future date. Under the what-might-happen approach, bearing in mind the assumption that there is always the possibility of an additional member of the class being born (see Comment h), the interests of some, if not all, of the class members conceivably might vest too remotely. Under the wait-and-see approach of this section, in most of these cases, the interest of each class member will in fact vest in time.

Illustrations:

11.   O transfers property by a deed of gift to T in trust. The terms of the trust direct T "to pay the income to A for life, then to distribute the trust property to A's children who attain 25 years." On the date the deed takes effect, A has three children, B age 20, C age 18, and D age 16. Each of these children will necessarily attain the age of 25 in the child's own life-time if the child ever attains that age. An after-born child of A, however, might not attain 25 until more than 21 years after the death of any life in being on the date of the transfer by O. Thus under the what-might-happen approach, the interest of any afterborn child of A fails under the rule against perpetuities (the effect of the failure of the interest of one member of the class on the interests of other members of the class is considered in §1.5). Under the wait-and-see approach of this section, the after-born child's interest will not fail unless in fact such child does not attain 25 years within 21 years after the death of the survivor of the measuring lives. It is to be noted that if no child of A has attained 25 years when A dies, or if some, but not all of A's children have attained 25 years, the trustee has not been given adequate guidance by the terms of the trust instrument as to what to do with the trust property pending a final determination of the number of A's children who attain 25 years. The trust instrument, if properly drafted, would provide for the disposition of the trust property during this gap.

12.   O transfers property by will to T in trust. The terms of the trust direct T "to pay the income to A for life, and on A's death, if issue of A are then living, to divide the trust property into as many equal shares as there are children of A then living and children of A then deceased with issue then living, and to allocate one such equal share to each deceased child of A who has issue then living and to distribute each such share so allocated to the issue then living of such deceased child, such issue to take per stirpes, and to allocate one such equal share to each living child of A and to hold each such share so allocated in a separate trust for such child of A as follows: to pay the income to such child for life, and then to distribute the trust property of such child's trust to such child's issue then living, such issue to take per stirpes, and if no issue of such child is then living, to distribute the trust property of such child's trust to A's issue then living, such issue to take per stirpes, and if no issue of A is then living, to distribute the trust property of such child's trust to the X Church." The trust also provides for a distribution of the trust property to the X Church if no issue of A is living on A's death. A survives O and at O's death A has three children, B, C, and D, and no other issue. The measuring lives are A, B, C, and D and the parents and grandparents

alive on O's death of all beneficiaries (see §1.3). Under the what-might-happen approach, the separate trust for an after-born child of A which is established on A's death will necessarily be valid as to such after-born child's life interest, but the interests under such trust that are contingent on the beneficiaries' surviving such after-born child of A conceivably might vest too remotely and fail (see §1.5 for the consequences of the invalidity of some but not all of the subclasses of the issue of each child of A). Under the wait-and-see approach of this section, the non-vested interest in the subclass of the issue of an after-born child of A will fail only if the after-born child of A survives the survivor of the measuring lives by more than 21 years.

13. O transfers property by will to T in trust. The terms of the trust direct T "to pay $10,000 to each child of A when and if the child attains 25, such payment to be made to a child of A whenever born if such child attains 25." The interest in a child of A born after O's death fails under the what-might-happen approach (see §1.5 for the consequences of the failure of a gift of a specific sum to each class member when the interests of some but not all class members may vest too remotely). Under the wait-and-see approach of this section the interest in an after-born child will fail under the rule against perpetuities only if the after-born child does not in fact attain 25 within 21 years after the death of the survivor of the measuring lives. The measuring lives with respect to the non-vested $10,000 gift to an afterborn child are the beneficiaries alive at O's death of such child's $10,000 gift in the event such child does not attain 25 and the parents and grandparents alive on O's death of all beneficiaries of the $10,000 gift to an afterborn child (see §1.3).

1. *Interests created by exercise of power of appointment or that take in default of exercise of power of appointment.* Interests in property that are created by the exercise of a power of appointment, or that take effect in default of the exercise of a power of appointment, present no special problem in applying the rule of this section, if the period of the rule against perpetuities does not begin to run until the power is exercised or until the power is no longer exercisable due to its release or the death of the power-holder (see §1.2, Comment d). Where, however, the power of appointment has no effect on when the period of the rule against perpetuities begins to run, as is the case when the power of appointment is a general power to appoint by will, or a limited power to appoint by deed or by will, the "second look" doctrine has been applicable under the what-might-happen approach. This has meant that in determining what might happen, the determination has been made by taking into account what in fact happened between the date the power was created and the date it was exercised or the date on which it was no longer exercisable; a limited wait-and-see rule. The rule of this section, which adopts a full wait-and-see rule, incorporates the limited wait-and-see rule of the "second look" and goes beyond it to permit the

wait-and-see to continue after the date the power is exercised or is no longer exercisable.

Illustrations:

14.   O transfers property by will to T in trust. The terms of the trust direct T "to pay the income to A for life, then to dispose of the trust property as A may appoint by his will to anyone, including A's estate, and in default of the exercise by A of the power to appoint by will, to accumulate the trust income until A's youngest child attains the age of 30 years, or would have attained such age had such child lived, then to distribute the trust property to A's issue then living, such issue to take per stirpes, and if no issue of A is then living, to distribute the trust property to the X Charity." A does not exercise the power to appoint by will. Even under the what-might-happen approach, what might happen is determined in the light of what has happened by the time of the death of A, the so-called "second look" doctrine, so that if by that time the youngest child of A is nine years of age, or older, the interests in default of appointment would necessarily vest, if they ever vested, within 21 years after the death of A, a life in being when O died. Under the wait-and-see approach of this section, even if at A's death, A's youngest child is under nine years of age, if such child in fact attains 30 years of age, or would have done so had such child lived, within 21 years after the death of the survivor of the measuring lives, the interests in default of appointment will not fail. The measuring lives are A, the issue of A alive when O dies, and parents and grandparents alive when O dies of all beneficiaries (see §1.3).

15.   Same facts as in Illustration 14, except that A exercises the power to appoint by will by appointing the trust property to A's issue living twenty-one years after the death of the survivor of C, D, E and F, individuals who were alive on O's death. By this appointment, A has in effect filled in a blank in O's will so that C, D, E, and F become the measuring lives specifically selected (see §1.3) and the interest in A's issue created by the exercise of the power to appoint by will in A cannot vest too remotely.

16.   Same facts as in Illustration 14, except that A exercises the power to appoint by will by appointing the trust property "to A's children who attain 25." If O's will had designated the takers of the trust property on A's death as the children of A who attain 25, it would be possible for a child of A born after O's death to attain 25 more than 21 years after any life in being at O's death. When A fills in the blank in O's will by the exercise of the power of appointment by will, even under the what-might-happen approach, the validity of the interest in the children of A who attain 25 is judged on the basis of what has happened by

the time of A's death, the "second look" doctrine. If at that time A had no child born after O's death, or if any after-born child A had is at least four years of age, no child of A could attain 25 more than 21 years after a life in being at O's death. If however, an after-born child of A is under four years of age at A's death, under the what-might-happen approach, such child might not attain 25 until more than 21 years after any life in being at O's death, even with the help of a "second look," and such child's interest would fail. Under the wait-and-see approach of this section, the interest in A's after-born child who is under four years of age will not fail if in fact such child attains 25 within twenty-one years after the death of the survivor of the measuring lives; the measuring lives are A and any of A's issue alive when O dies and the parents and grandparents alive when O dies of all beneficiaries (see §1.3).

m. *The executory interest case.* An executory interest that is subject to an unfulfilled condition precedent has to be certain to vest, if it ever vests, within the period of the rule against perpetuities or fail from the beginning under the what-might-happen approach. Under the rule of this section, such interest will be given the opportunity of vesting within the period of the rule against perpetuities and only if it does not vest in time, after waiting and seeing what happens, will it fail.

Illustrations:

17. O, owning Blackacre in fee simple absolute, makes an otherwise effective deed thereof "to A and his heirs but if A or his heirs or assigns ever use Blackacre for other than residential purposes, Blackacre shall pass to B and his heirs." Under the what-might-happen approach, B's executory interest fails because the cessation of residential use might not occur until more than 21 years after any life in being on the date of O's transfer. Under the rule of this section, B's interest will not fail unless residential use is in fact continuing 21 years after the death of the survivor of O, A and B and the parents and grandparents alive when the conveyance is made of A and B (see §1.3).

18. O, owning Blackacre in fee simple absolute makes an otherwise effective deed thereof "to A and his heirs 30 years from and after the death of O." The executory interest in A is vested from the date of the deed and hence does not violate the rule against perpetuities under the what-might-happen approach or under the rule of this section.

19. O, owning Blackacre in fee simple absolute, makes an otherwise effective deed thereof "to A and his heirs as long as Blackacre is used for residential purposes, then to B and his heirs." The executory interest in B is not a vested interest, and under the what-might-happen approach, since it is not certain to vest, if it ever vests, within the period

of the rule against perpetuities, it fails. Under the rule of this section, B's interest will not fail if Blackacre ceases to be used for residential purposes within 21 years after the death of the survivor of the measuring lives, who are O, A, and B and the parents and grandparents alive when the conveyance is made of A and B (see §1.3). If no cessation of residential use occurs in that period of time, B's interest will fail and the effect of this failure is dealt with in §1.5.

n.   *Survival of probate of will or administration of estate case.* A devise or bequest to a class, where after-born persons may satisfy the class description, which is subject to a requirement of survival to the "probate of my will" or to the date the "administration of my estate is completed" will fail as to after-born class members under the what-might-happen approach, unless such disposition is construed to require survival for only a reasonable time which time is less than 21 years after the testator dies. Under the wait-and-see approach of this section, such disposition will fail as to after-born persons only if the will is not in fact probated, or the administration of the testator's estate is not in fact completed, within 21 years after the death of the survivor of the measuring lives.

o.   *Alternate conditions precedent case.* A non-vested interest in property may be subject to two or more separate unfulfilled conditions precedent, with vesting to take place if any one of these conditions precedent occurs. These conditions precedent may be such that one will occur, if it ever occurs, within the period of the rule against perpetuities, and the other one that may or may not occur within the period of the rule. In such case, under the what-might-happen approach, the interest in property subject to such alternate conditions precedent does not fail if the condition that in fact occurs is the one that necessarily will occur, if it ever occurs, within the period of the rule; a wait-and-see approach built into the what-might-happen approach. Under the rule of this section, the interest in property that is subject to alternate conditions precedent does not fail if either condition precedent in fact occurs within the period of the rule.

Illustrations:

20.   O transfers property by will to T in trust. The terms of the trust direct T "to pay the income to A for life, then to distribute the trust property to the children of A who attain 25 years, but if A should have no children, or if all A's children should die under the age of 25 years, to distribute the trust property to B and his heirs." A has no child when O dies. The interest in B is subject to alternative unfulfilled conditions precedent. Under one condition precedent, B's interest is to vest at A's death, if A has no children. That condition precedent will occur, if it ever occurs, within the period of the rule against perpetuities. Under the other condition, B's interest is to vest if A has children and all of them

die under the age of 25 years. That condition precedent might occur beyond the period of the rule. Under the what-might-happen approach, B's interest does not fail if A never has a child, but fails if A has a child. Under the rule of this section, B's interest will not fail even if A has children, if in fact all of A's children die under 25 years within 21 years after the survivor of the measuring lives. The interest in A's children who attain 25 years also fails as to any child of A born after O's death under the what-might-happen approach, but such after-born child's interest does not fail under the wait-and-see approach of the rule of this section, unless in fact such child does not attain 25 years within 21 years after the death of the survivor of the measuring lives.

21. Same facts as in Illustration 20, except the condition precedent to B's interest is stated as a single condition, "to distribute the trust property to the children of A who attain 25 years, but if no child of A attains the age of 25 years, to distribute the trust property to B and his heirs." Though a single condition precedent is stated, it is implicit within it that if A has no children, B's interest is to vest. Under the what-might-happen approach, this single condition is not broken into its separate parts and B's interest fails even if A dies without ever having had a child. Under the rule of this section, the result is the same as in Illustration 20.

Drafting to Avoid Any Possibility of Violating the Rule Against Perpetuities

Every instrument under which present and future interests are created should contain what is called a "savings clause." In substance, a "savings clause" provides as follows: "Any interest under the dispositive instrument that has not vested within 21 years after death of the survivor of [name a reasonable number of individuals now in being] shall terminate and the property in which such interest existed shall be indefeasibly vested in [name takers]."

Other Rules Restricting the Freedom of Making Dispositions of Property

The Restatement (Second) of Property (Donative Transfers) develops, in addition to the rule against perpetuities, other social restrictions imposed upon the creation of property interests in donative transactions. Familiarity with these other rules is essential in order to do effective family estate planning, but they do not have the pervasive effect of the rule against perpetuities on family dispositions.

P A R T V I

LANDLORD AND TENANT[1]

Note: *The Diversity of Modern Landlord-Tenant*
Relationships and Problems as They Come to
the Lawyer

In Chapter 13, Sections 5 through 7, we have described the term of years,
the periodic tenancy, and the estate at will as common-law estates in land.
The present part deals with these estates as instrumentalities for modern
commercial dealings, including residential transactions of great disparity
(compare the rental of luxury apartments, particularly the proprietary
lease,[2] with the leasing of low income rental property, particularly to the
indigent tenant).

The origins and history of the early common law—like the Platonists'
search for universal ideas—is best understood by appreciating the human
need for and the mind's struggle to find and apply perfect principles which
would (or should) always govern the interrelations of people and property,
regardless of time and individual circumstances. This intellectual insensitiv-
ity to factual differences, in large part caused by an overweening desire for
the universality of rules, is perhaps nowhere better typified than in the
common law of landlord and tenant relations.

As you read the material which follows, you should ask yourself at least
the following question: Should the particular rule of law being articulated
(by either the court or the authors) apply to all landlord and tenant relations
regardless of:

---

1. Donald S. Snider, Esq.—a former student of the authors and a magna cum laude
graduate of the Harvard Law School, now a partner in the law firm of Finley, Kumble, Wagner,
Heine, Underberg, Manley & Casey, greatly assisted the authors in the preparation of Part VI,
Landlord and Tenant, in the second edition. He has graciously continued that assistance in the
preparation of this third edition, and his invaluable contribution in this regard is noted on the
title page of the casebook. Although the organization of Part VI and the selection of material for
the part are largely the work of Mr. Snider, the authors take full responsibility for it.
2. A purchaser of a cooperative apartment acquires not only shares of stock in the
cooperative corporation owning the building but also a long-term renewable occupancy
agreement, customarily called a "proprietary lease," under which the cooperative corporation
is the landlord and the apartment "owner" is the tenant.

1. the type, nature, or extent of the use to be made of the "leased premises," e.g., compare a lease involving land only with that involving residential or commercial space; also, compare the rental of an entire building with the rental of a part of a building; and

2. the type, nature, extent or duration of the "tenancy," e.g., compare the situation where the relationship is contemplated to be short-term (weekly, monthly, or seasonal) with the situation where the relationship is intended to be long-term (1, 5, 10, 25, 50, or 99 years); also, compare the leasing transaction which is a form of financing ownership (the sale/leaseback or the proprietary lease) with the sublease or sandwich lease.[3]

At the same time, you should also carefully consider the consequences of treating any of the foregoing as juridically significant and what principle(s) justify differing, anomalous, and at times inconsistent landlord and tenant results. Is there any single unifying principle? As many of you know, currently there is considerable controversy surrounding the question of whether a landlord impliedly warrants to the tenant the fitness of the leased premises. Should such a covenant be implied in each of the following illustrations?

1. Robert Slumlord rents a first floor flat to Ivan Indigent for $11.25 per week, payable on Friday night. After moving in, Mr. Indigent discovers that some of the walls have peeling lead paint, which has been determined to be poisonous to young children who consume it. (Does this matter if Mr. Slumlord did not know that Mr. Indigent had young children?)

2. Avaricious Apartmenthouse Owner leases a four-bedroom, two and one-half-bath duplex penthouse apartment to Luxury Lessee, who after moving in discovers that the central air conditioning is inoperative for most of the summer months. (Does it matter that vandalism and not owner neglect is the cause?)

3. Orville Office Building Owner leases the entire fifty-fifth floor suite of offices to the Sweat Shop Law Firm, which, after moving in, discovers that the central air conditioning is totally inoperative after 6 P.M. on weekdays and all weekend. (Does it matter if building-supplied air conditioning is available during the "off hours" but only at prohibitively expensive rates, e.g., $400 an hour?)

4. Freddy Farmer leases his 100-acre tract of land to David Developer for 99 years. During the third year of the ground lease, after completing his environmental impact studies and being granted the necessary rezoning as well as obtaining the required construction loan commitment, David Developer discovers that a critical 20-acre portion of the tract has a subterranean stream leading to an important

---

3. A sandwich lease is a lease which is "sandwiched" between the owner and the occupant's lease, usually for financing purposes.

aquifer, precluding the building of the contemplated regional shopping center. (Does it matter if Freddy Farmer knew of the underground stream/aquifer?)

5. Olivia Office Building Owner, widow of Orville Office Building Owner, net leases an entire 100-year-old, six-story loft building to the Precision Printing Press Company for a 25-year term. After the heavy printing presses and other commercial equipment are moved in, during its first week of operation, the Precision Printing Press Company discovers that the entire building begins to shake when the printing presses are operating and, upon investigation, learns that the building foundation, structural steel, and rated floor load capacities are totally insufficient to allow its printing press operation. (Does it matter if Orville knew of this limitation prior to his death?)

As instrumentalities for sophisticated commercial dealings or modern residential transactions, the common law estates in land are bedeviled by their antiquity, for the law of real estate (including the law applicable to landlord and tenant) has lagged behind the law of commerce in recognizing the needs of modern society. The following two cases provide but one dramatic illustration of this:

1. O owns a theater and A operates a traveling stock company. O contracts to pay A $2,400 a week for performances of Lady Windermere's Fan by A's company for four weeks. A contracts to provide the actors, scenery, and costumes and to have new costumes, new scenery, and a specified new leading lady of national reputation after the second week. Both parties realize that this change is of great importance to O. A does not provide the new costumes, scenery, and leading lady after the second week. We know that O can refuse to present the play with the old equipment and actress and can recover against A for any loss O has suffered as a result of A's breach of contract. O can excuse O's own non-performance of the promise to pay $2,400 a week by showing a material breach of A's promise.

2. L owns an office building and leases a suite of offices to T for four years at a rent of $1,000 per month. In the lease L promises to redecorate the suite at the end of two years with paint and wallpaper selected by T. Both parties realize that this redecoration is of great importance to T. At the end of two years L refuses to redecorate. T cannot, on account of L's breach, terminate T's liability for the rent. T is entitled to recover from L the difference between the fair rental value of a redecorated suite and an unredecorated suite, but that is T's only remedy.

The only reason for the difference of result in these two cases is historical. In case 2 T has an estate in the land and the rent is considered a tenurial service of this estate; historically a vassal could not excuse non-performance of services because of some default of the lord unless that default consisted of evicting the vassal from the land. Hence, the only case in which a landlord's default will permit a tenant to quit is where the landlord actually evicts the tenant from occupancy or where the landlord's conduct makes the premises untenantable or uninhabitable, which is called a "constructive eviction." A constructive eviction is treated the same as the case where the landlord sends someone around to actually evict the tenant. On the other hand, in case 1 the courts are faced with no ancient dogma of the law of estates; they are dealing with commercial arrangements which are entirely promissory. Lord Mansfield in the late eighteenth century developed the doctrine of dependent promises, declaring that, normally, where O and A are to perform promises concurrently, a substantial breach by A will excuse non-performance by O. But this doctrine of the law of contracts never was integrated into the law of estates. As you would expect, many courts have a tendency to expand the concept of "constructive eviction" to the point where it approaches the concept of "substantial breach"; but, at least in the older states, such courts find themselves blocked by earlier decisions.

Does this mean that T in case 2 cannot be protected? Certainly not. It means that T has to know the odd limitations on T's automatic rights and expressly provide in the lease for such additional rights as T desires and can negotiate. To be specific, T should insist upon a provision that "in the event that O does not redecorate as herein provided, T may perform the redecoration and deduct the cost thereof from later installments of rent or, at T's election, T may terminate the lease. In the event of such termination, rent shall be apportioned as of the date T quits the premises, and T shall be liable for no rent after such date." Whether T will be able to get such a clause from O depends upon the strength of T's bargaining position. When incomes are low and rental properties are going begging, landlords will sign anything. In a period of high incomes and a housing shortage, tenants say, "Yes sir. Thank you, sir" and do not have the ability to insist upon any protective clauses. It depends on who is in the driver's seat. One of the qualities you may acquire only after years of experience is the ability to judge who is in the driver's seat and how far he or she can drive.

The non-dependence of covenants in a lease is only one of a long list of rules of the law of landlord and tenant which you may find distasteful. For example, you will find that the obligation to repair, as between landlord and tenant, is an aspect of the law of waste; as a result, the landlord is under no obligation at all and the tenant may be stuck for repairs. Again, although in the law of contracts a defaulting promissor can expect the promisee to minimize damages — in default of which the law will reduce the recovery by the amount which "should have been mitigated" — a defaulting tenant may have no such expectation or entitlement; the landlord may be permitted to sit complacently still after the tenant has quit, make no attempt to get a new tenant, let the rent continue to accrue against the tenant, and then sue the tenant for it. As in the decoration case above discussed, the basic reason is that a lease primarily creates an estate, to which the covenants are promissory appendages.

So, in large part, the practice of the law of landlord and tenant requires the skillful preparation and negotiation of leases in order to eliminate ancient anomalies and provide realistically for the needs of the parties. As you go through this part, your pattern of thought should be: (1) What is this rule? (2) Is it working a fair result in this case? (3) Should it have been provided for in the lease, and if so, how?

Leases are individual instruments, adapted to the property, the term, the contemplated uses, the circumstances of the parties, the local law, and anticipated changes. You will find printed forms of leases, but they are unlikely to meet the exact needs of any particular situation. Most of them are strongly oriented in the landlord's favor. Some of you are tenants under such a form, and the mathematical chance is less than one in ten you read the form before you signed it — and there is no chance at all that you understood it. Read it now, we suggest, and recoil in horror from what you find. You will probably discover among other things that if you have put a nail or a tack into a wall or woodwork — and you know perfectly well that you have — you can be thrown out at any time and still be held for the rent for the rest of the term. Probably your only protection is the pressure your law school can put on the landlord to treat you fairly, which is a rather ignominious position for a law student, isn't it?

The law of landlord and tenant grew up with reference to fairly standardized transactions in agricultural land in England. No great difficulty was encountered in adapting this law to simple transactions in urban real estate. But at the present day in this country the same set of rules has to act as the basic doctrine for governing a staggering variety of transactions. In addition to the illustrations given earlier in this Note, here are some typical ones:

1. Henry Homeowner rents his entire furnished house in a suburb, with surrounding land and buildings (including a garage and a henhouse), for one year to Frederick and Frances Fertile and their six small children.

2. Rick Realty Co., owner of a downtown building in the shopping district, rents the first floor for five years with renewal privilege to Elite Plumbing Supply Co., which plans to use the premises for a showroom and salesroom for bathroom equipment.

3. The Trustees of the Capitol Theater, owners of the Capitol Theater building, lease it for 20 years to Consolidated Pictures, Inc., upon a net lease (i.e., the lessee pays taxes, insurance, and repairs), at a rent equal to $17\frac{1}{2}$ percent of the gross receipts of the theater.

4. The Creative Finance Co. purchases the Union Grand Hotel from Charlie Cashier for $10,000,000 and leases it back for a net annual rental equal to $1,440,000, payable at $12,000 per month, with an option to re-purchase exercisable at any time after 25 years for $10,000,000.

Our professional friends in the trial department look upon each one of these situations as a breeder of profitable litigation. They see Freddy Fertile tearing down the henhouse to build a "clubhouse" back in the woods; Elite Plumbing Supply Co. leaving the premises after five years with eight model bathrooms uselessly cemented into the structure; Consolidated Pictures, Inc., rigging the films it shows at the Capitol Theater so that Capitol patrons are drawn away to the nearby Plaza Theater, which Consolidated Pictures, Inc., owns outright; Charlie Cashier, finding that the Union Grand Hotel is outdistanced by newer structures, desiring to raze the hotel and put up a bigger, better, and newer one and being refused permission by the Creative Finance Co. It is our more exacting job to foresee these events — and hundreds more — before they happen, know what rights and duties the law establishes, provide for the maximum protection of our clients in any eventuality, and thereby leave our associates in the trial department in a state of impoverished frustration.

CHAPTER 17

The Landlord-Tenant Relation and the Condition of the Premises

**SECTION 1.   THE LANDLORD'S
                RESPONSIBILITIES**

A.   Duty to Deliver Possession

TEITELBAUM v. DIRECT REALTY CO.
172 Misc. 48, 13 N.Y.S.2d 886 (Nassau Cty. Sup. Ct. 1939)

Lockwood, J.

This action tried by the Court without a jury, is to recover $25,000, plaintiff's alleged damages for defendant's failure to deliver possession of the store at 61 Main Street, Hempstead, N.Y., under a written lease dated February 10, 1938.

At the time the lease was made, the store was occupied by Abe and Dorothy Fergang under a lease expiring June 30, 1938. For many years, plaintiff had operated a drugstore a few doors away from the leased premises.

Plaintiff was to take possession on July 1, 1938, make the necessary alterations and installations and open his new drugstore on August 1, 1938.

On July 1, 1938, the Fergangs refused to move out claiming a renewal of their lease by an alleged oral agreement. Defendant brought a summary proceeding in the District Court and the jury rendered a verdict in favor of the Fergangs. Defendant appealed to the Appellate Term, which reversed the order, and directed a new trial. On the retrial, the Fergangs defaulted. They vacated the premises in January 1939.

Upon the undisputed facts, the Fergangs wrongfully withheld possession of the premises from the plaintiff. Defendant did not refuse to put plaintiff in possession, nor was plaintiff's possession withheld or hindered by any act of the defendant. In fact, defendant did more than it was legally required to do. It attempted to dispossess the Fergangs and was finally successful after the appeal to the Appellate Term, and Fergangs' default on the new trial.

Plaintiff was not kept out of possession by anyone holding under authority of the defendant, landlord, or by one having a title paramount to his.

Plaintiff places great reliance upon Friedland v. Myers, 139 N.Y. 432, 34 N.E. 1055, where plaintiff-lessee was refused possession because the tenant then in possession was entitled to remain under a lease made by the landlord prior to the making of plaintiff's lease. It had previously been held in a dispossess proceeding that the tenant's possession was rightful.

However, the present case is not one where the landlord covenanted to give possession when he had no authority to do so. Plaintiff could have had possession but for the wrongful act of the Fergangs.

It is said in "New York Law of Landlord and Tenant," Vol. 1, Sec. 316, page 639:

> On the other hand, contrary to the view taken in England and in many jurisdictions in this country, it is held in our state in a number of cases in the lower courts, that the extent of the landlord's implied agreement is that he has a good title and can give a free and unincumbered lease for the term demised, and that if, at the time of the commencement of the term, the possession is held by a trespasser, not holding with the sanction of the landlord there is no implied obligation on the part of the landlord to oust such trespasser to enable the tenant to enter, and that consequently his failure to do so does not render him liable in damages to the lessee. And, on principle, this would seem to be true, though the lease is for such a short term that the lessee may not be able to avail himself of his remedies to recover the possession from the wrongdoer. In the above connection, Wilson, Ch. J., speaking for the Supreme Court in a leading case, says:
>
>> It is not the duty of the landlord, when the demised premises are wrongfully held by a third person, to take the necessary steps to put his lessee in possession.
>>
>> The latter being clothed with the title by virtue of the lease, it belongs to him to pursue such legal remedies as the law provided for gaining it, whether few or many.
>
> Gardner v. Keteltas, 3 Hill 330, 38 Am. Dec. 637; approved in United Merchants' Realty & Improvement Co. v. Roth, 193 N.Y. 570, 86 N.E. 544.
>
> The same view is taken where a prior tenant of the landlord or a sublessee of such tenant, after the expiration of his term, wrongfully and without the sanction of the landlord, retains the possession. This was also held true where a prior tenant of premises used for dwelling purposes held over under the right conferred by the Emergency Rent Laws (repealed); as in such a case the continued possession of the tenant was not by virtue of any right or authority given by the landlord. Where a prior tenant, at the request of the landlord, is permitted by the lessee to retain possession, such retention of possession imposes no liability on the landlord. Proof merely that a third person was in possession of the demised premises at the commencement of the term, with-

out further proof of his right to retain possession does not show a breach of the landlord's implied obligation to give possession. . . .

Furthermore, plaintiff's most substantial claim of damage is based upon the fact that he got his present landlord to release him from the unexpired term, which had a few months to run, and obtained a new tenant whose lease he agreed to buy for $2,500, but it appears that the $2,500 is payable only out of any recovery which he may make in this action.

Admittedly, plaintiff is a month-to-month tenant in his old place at $200 a month and could have moved into the new place when it was vacated last January and could have used the new fixtures which he now claims are a total loss. It might well be that on reflection, he found the rent he agreed to pay for the new property too high.

Defendant's motion for judgment is granted and judgment shall be entered in favor of the defendant, dismissing the complaint.[1]

Problems

17.1. L rents an apartment to T_2, the term to begin at the expiration of T_1's term, and T_1 wrongfully holds over. In a jurisdiction which has adopted the American rule (implied covenant to deliver "legal" possession only) as compared with the English rule (implied covenant to deliver actual possession), T_2 sues T_1 for rent. Judgment for whom? See United Merchants' Realty & Improvement Co. v. Roth, 193 N.Y. 570, 86 N.E. 544 (1908).

17.2. Assume the same facts as in Problem 17.1. L sues T_1 to recover possession of the apartment, and T_1 defends on the ground that since L has executed a lease with T_2, L is no longer entitled to possession of the apartment and therefore L does not have the legal capacity to maintain the proceeding. What decision? See Eells v. Morse, 208 N.Y. 103, 101 N.E. 803 (1913).

Note: The Landlord's Duty to Deliver Possession

In New York, where the American rule received some of its strongest support, the legislature had some second thoughts about the wisdom of the rule. In 1962 it enacted N.Y. Real Prop. Law §223-a:

In the absence of an express provision to the contrary, there shall be implied in every lease of real property a condition that the lessor will deliver possession at the beginning of the term. In the event of breach of such implied condition the lessee shall have the right to rescind the lease and to recover the consideration

---

1. See also Snider v. Deban, 249 Mass. 59, 144 N.E. 69 (1924), to the same effect.— Eds.

paid. Such right shall not be deemed inconsistent with any right of action he may have to recover damages.

What are the reasons, if any, for permitting the tenant to waive the protection of this statute by "express provision to the contrary"? The notion of "freedom of contract" pervades the whole area of landlord and tenant, and you should consider its wisdom and validity — especially with respect to the indigent tenant.[2]

Note: The Restatement's Position on Duty of the Landlord to Deliver Possession

§6.2   Third Person Improperly in Possession of Leased Property on Date Tenant Entitled to Possession

Except to the extent the parties to the lease validly agree otherwise, there is a breach of the landlord's obligations if a third person is improperly in possession of the leased property on the date the tenant is entitled to possession and the landlord does not act promptly to remove the person and does not in fact remove him within a reasonable period of time. For that breach, the tenant may:

(1)   terminate the lease in the manner prescribed in §10.1 and recover damages to the extent prescribed in §10.2; or
(2)   affirm the lease and obtain equitable and legal relief including:
    (a)   the recovery of damages to the extent prescribed in §10.2;
    (b)   an abatement of the rent to the extent prescribed in §11.1;
    (c)   the use of the rent to cover the costs of eliminating the possession of the third person to the extent prescribed in §11.2; and
    (d)   the withholding of the rent in the manner and to the extent prescribed in §11.3.

During the period of time following the date the tenant is entitled to possession and before the time the landlord is in default, the tenant is entitled to appropriate relief from his obligations under the lease and is entitled to recover from the third person damages sustained by him during that period. Before or after the landlord's default the tenant may recover the possession of the leased property from the third person improperly in possession.[3]

---

2.   See Chapter 19, Section 2.E., *infra,* on onerous terms in leases. In Reitmeyer v. Sprecher, 431 Pa. 284, 243 A.2d 395 (1968), the court observed: "If our law is to keep in tune with our times we must recognize the present day inferior position of the average tenant vis-à-vis the landlord when it comes to negotiating a lease."

3.   Copyright © American Law Institute. Reproduced with permission. All references to the Restatement in Part VI, unless otherwise noted, are to the Restatement (Second) of Property (Landlord and Tenant) (1977).

Problem

17.3. L rents retail business premises to T_2 for a ten-year term to commence September 1 at a minimum rent of $5,000 per month ($60,000 per year), plus 5 percent of gross sales in excess of $1,200,000 per year. The term is to begin at the expiration of T_1's lease (on August 31); T's fixed monthly rent was only $3,000 per month. In a jurisdiction which has adopted §6.2 of the Restatement, assume T_1 wrongfully holds over and L promptly commences a summary proceeding to evict T_1 from possession. Assume further that T_1 defends (in order to protect and preserve possession through the back-to-school and Christmas retail selling seasons, a four-month period that customarily accounts for 60 percent of T_1's sales and profits) and thus the summary proceeding is not finally decided in L's favor (pursuant to which T_1 is actually evicted by the marshal) until December 29. Assume further that T_2 purchased $200,000 of seasonal inventory (which by January 1 would be virtually useless) and spent $20,000 in advertising his grand opening at the new location.

   a. May L sue T_1 for damages, and if so, on what theories and for what amounts?

   b. May T_2 sue T_1 for damages, and if so, on what theories and for what amounts?

   c. May T_2 sue L for damages, and if so, on what theories and for what amounts?

B. Duty to Deliver the Premises in a Tenantable, Fit, or Suitable Condition

Having won the right to actual possession, as compared with the right to legal possession, the tenant's victory may prove to be a Pyrrhic victory. Consider the following case.

FRANKLIN v. BROWN
118 N.Y. 110, 23 N.E. 126 (1889)

Appeal from a judgment of the general term of the superior court of the city of New York, affirming a judgment in favor of the plaintiff entered upon the report of a referee.

This action was brought to recover the rent reserved by a lease of a furnished dwelling-house. The answer pleaded a counter-claim for damages alleged to have been sustained by the defendant on account of a breach of an implied covenant that said house was fit for immediate and permanent occupation. The referee found that on the 14th of September, 1883, the parties entered into a written agreement whereby the plaintiff leased to the defendant the dwelling-house known as "No. 6 West Seventeenth Street," in the city of New York, for the term of one year, at the annual rental of $3,100, and that the defendant covenanted to pay said sum in equal monthly payments, commencing on the 1st day of November thereafter. He also found due performance on the part of the plaintiff, and a failure to perform on the part of the defendant, who omitted to pay the rent which became due for the months of July, August, and September, 1884, the last three months of the term. Upon the request of the defendant, the referee further found that said house was leased to her to be used as a private residence; that the furniture therein was a large and important element in determining the amount of rent to be paid; that, during the time covered by the lease, noxious gases, and strong, unhealthy, and disagreeable odors, "existed generally, and in very large quantities, throughout said furnished dwelling-house," making the defendant sick, and rendering the house unhealthy and unfit for human habitation, and that she incurred certain expenses as the immediate and necessary result of occupying said premises. The referee, however, added to these requests, as found, that said gases, odors, etc., did not arise in or from any part of said house, but that they came from the adjoining premises, which were used for a livery stable, and that neither party knew of their existence when the lease was executed.

VANN, J. [*after stating the facts as above*]: It is not claimed that any deceit was practiced or false representations made by the plaintiff as to the condition of the house in question, or its fitness for the purpose for which it was let. The defendant thoroughly examined the premises before she signed the lease, and she neither ceased to occupy nor attempted to rescind until the last quarter of the term. Neither party knew of the existence of the offensive odors when the contract was made. They were not caused by the landlord, and did not originate upon his premises, but came from an adjoining tenement. The lease contained no covenant to repair, or to keep in repair, and no express covenant that the house was fit to live in. The defendant, however, contends that, as the demise was of a furnished house for immediate use as a residence, there was an implied covenant that it was reasonably fit for habitation. It is not open to discussion in this state, that a lease of real property only, contains no implied covenant of this character, and that, in the absence of an express covenant, unless there has been fraud, deceit, or wrong-doing on the part of the landlord, the tenant is without remedy, even if the demised premises are unfit for occupation. Witty v. Matthews, 52 N.Y. 512; Jaffe v. Harteau, 56 N.Y. 398; Edwards v. Railroad Co., 98 N.Y. 245; Cleves v. Willoughby, 7 Hill, 83; Mumford v. Brown, 6 Cow. 475; Westlake v. De Graw, 25 Wend. 669; Tayl. Landl. & Ten. (8th Ed.) §382; Wood, Landl. & Ten. §379.

But it is argued that the letting of household goods for immediate use raises an implied warranty that they are reasonably fit for the purpose, and that, when the letting includes a house furnished with such goods, the warranty extends to the place where they are to be used. This position is supported by the noted English case of Smith v. Marrable, 11 Mees. & W. 5, which holds that, when a furnished house is let for temporary residence at a watering place, there is an implied condition that it is in a fit state to be habited, and that the tenant is entitled to quit upon discovering that it is greatly infested with bugs. This case has been frequently discussed, and occasionally criticised. It was decided in 1843, yet during that year it was distinguished and questioned by two later decisions of the same court. Sutton v. Temple, 12 Mees. & W. 52; Hart v. Windsor, Id. 68. It was approved and followed in 1877 by Wilson v. Finch Hatton, L.R. 2 Exch. Div. 336, in which, however, there was an important fact that did not appear in the earlier case, as before the lease was signed there was a representation made in behalf of the landlord that she believed "the drainage to be in perfect order," whereas it was in fact defective, and the contract was promptly rescinded on this account. The principle that there is an implied condition or covenant in a lease that the property is reasonably fit for the purpose for which it was let, as laid down in Smith v. Marrable, has been frequently questioned by the courts of this country, and has never been adopted as the law of this state. Edwards v. Railroad Co., 98 N.Y. 248; Howard v. Doolittle, 3 Duer, 475; Carson v. Godley, 26 Pa. St. 117; Dutton v. Gerrish, 9 Cush. 89; Chadwick v. Woodward, 13 Abb. N.C. 441; Coulson v. Whiting, 14 Abb. N.C. 60; Sutphen v. Seebass, Id. 67; Meeks v. Bowerman, 1 Daly, 99. We have been referred to no decision of this court involving the application of that principle to the lease of a ready-furnished house, and it is not necessary to now pass upon the question, because the case under consideration differs from the English cases above mentioned in two significant particulars: (1) It involves a lease for the ordinary period of one year, instead of a few weeks or months during the fashionable season. (2) The cause of complaint did not originate upon the leased premises, was not under the control of the lessor, and was not owing to his wrongful act or default. It was simply a nuisance arising in the neighborhood, but neither caused nor increased by the house in question. Hence we are not called upon in this case to decide whether a lease of a furnished dwelling contains an implied covenant against inherent defects either in the house or in the furniture therein, but simply whether the lease under discussion contains an implied covenant against external defects, which originated upon the premises of a stranger, and were unknown to the lessor when he entered into the contract.

It is uniformly held in this state that the lessee of real property must run the risk of its condition, unless he has an express agreement on the part of the lessor covering that subject. As was said by the learned general term when deciding this case: "The tenant hires at his peril, and a rule similar to that of caveat emptor applies, and throws on the lessee the responsibility of examining as to the existence of defects in the premises, and of providing against their ill effects." 53 N.Y. Super. Ct. 479. In Cleves v. Willoughby, 7 Hill, 83, 86, Mr. Justice Beardsley, speaking for the court, said:

The defendant offered to show that the house was altogether unfit for occupation, and wholly untenantable. The principle on which this offer was made, however, cannot, I think, be maintained. There is no such implied warranty on the part of the lessor of a dwelling-house as the offer assumes. It is quite unnecessary to look at the common-law doctrine as to implied covenants and warranties, or to its modification by statute. 3 Rev. St. 594. That doctrine has a very limited application, for any purpose, to a lease for years, and in every case has reference to the title, and not to the quality or condition, of the property. The maxim caveat emptor applies to the transfer of all property, real, personal, and mixed, and the purchaser generally takes the risk of its quality and condition, unless he protects himself by an express agreement on the subject.

In O'Brien v. Capwell, 59 Barb. 504, the court declared that, "as between landlord and tenant, . . . when there is no fraud or false representations or deceit, and in the absence of an express warranty or covenant to repair, there is no implied covenant that the demised premises are suitable or fit for occupation, or for the particular use which the tenant intends to make of them, or that they are in a safe condition for use." In Edwards v. Railroad Co., 98 N.Y. 249, it was said in behalf of this court:

If a landlord lets premises, and agrees to keep them in repair, and he fails to do so, in consequence of which any one lawfully upon the premises suffers injury, he is responsible for his own negligence to the party injured. . . . If he creates a nuisance upon his premises, and then demises them, he remains liable for the consequences of the nuisance, as the creator thereof. . . . But where the landlord has created no nuisance, and is guilty of no willful wrong or fraud or culpable negligence, no case can be found imposing any liability upon him for any injury suffered by any person occupying or going upon the premises during the term of the demise, and there is no distinction stated in any authority between cases of a demise of dwelling-houses and of buildings to be used for public purposes. The responsibility of the landlord is the same in all cases. If guilty of negligence or other delictum which leads directly to the accident and wrong complained of, he is liable; if not so guilty, no liability attaches to him.

These quotations illustrate the strictness with which the courts have refused to imply covenants on the part of the lessor as to conditions under his control. What sound reason, then, is there for claiming that the law will imply a covenant as to conditions not under his control, and with reference to which neither lessor nor lessee can reasonably be supposed to have contracted, as they knew nothing about them? The fact that personal property was in part the subject of the lease can have no bearing upon this question, because neither the furniture, nor the place provided for its use, was the cause of the unpleasant odors. They were not a part of the leased property, either real or personal, but were independent of it in origin, and accidental in their effect. If smoke from a neighboring manufactory had blown through the windows, or gas had escaped from a leaky main in the street and entered the house, could the lessee have abandoned the premises, or have called upon the lessor to respond in damages? If any nuisance had existed in the vicinity without the landlord's agency or knowledge, but which materially lessened the value of the lease, upon whom would the loss fall? These questions suggest the danger of departing from the established rule as to implied covenants with reference to the condition of leased real property, simply because personal property is included in the lease. The furniture was not the basis of the contract, but a mere incident, and in law the rent is deemed to issue out of the realty. 1 Wood, Landl. & Ten. (2d Ed.) 128; Newman v. Anderton, 2 Bos. & P. (N.R.) 224; Emott's Case, 2 Dyer, 212b. The difficulty is still more serious when the effort is made to extend the contract of the lessor, by implication only, to causes having only an accidental connection with the property leased, whether real or personal. We do not think that there was any covenant in the lease in question, implied either by common law or from the acts or relations of the parties, that extended to the grievance of which the defendant complains. The judgment should therefore be affirmed, with costs. All concur.[4]

Problems

17.4.   L rents L's summer cottage to T for a term of three months at a monthly rental of $250. T does not inspect the cottage. On arriving at the cottage, T finds the windows broken, the roof leaky, and the furniture in total disrepair. What are T's rights? See Ingalls v. Hobbs, 156 Mass. 348, 31 N.E. 286 (1892), and Young v. Povich, 121 Me. 141, 116 A. 26 (1922).

17.5.   L negotiated a lease with T relating to an apartment in an uncompleted apartment house. The building was completed six months later, and on moving in T discovered that the plaster was falling and none of the kitchen appliances worked. What are T's rights? Compare J. D. Young Corp. v. McClintic, 26 S.W.2d 460 (Tex. Civ. App. 1930), *rev'd on basis of improper conduct of counsel,* 66 S.W.2d 676 (Tex. Commn. App. 1933), with Oliver v. Hartzell, 170 Ark. 512, 280 S.W. 979 (1926).

17.6.   L received authorization from the Civilian Production Administration to build factories to be used for food processing, with no other use of the buildings being permitted. While the buildings were in the construction stage, L executed a lease with T, L knowing that T intended to use the premises for the manufacture of perfume. After the lease was executed, the CPA rejected T's application to complete the building and T sued to cancel the lease. What result? L counterclaimed for termination of the lease. What result? See Ph. Chaleyer, Inc. v. Simon, 91 F. Supp. 5 (D.N.J. 1950).

---

4.   This case illustrates the strong common-law rule against an implied covenant on the part of the landlord as to fitness of the leased premises for contemplated use by the tenant. —EDS.

*Note: Implied Warranty of Fitness — Recent
         Developments*

The Introductory Note to Chapter 5 of the Restatement states:

In recent years, the definite judicial trend has been in the direction of increasing the responsibility of the landlord, in the absence of a valid contrary agreement, to provide the tenant with property in a condition suitable for the use contemplated by the parties. The judicial trend has been supported by the statutes that deal with this problem. This judicial and statutory trend reflects a view that no one should be allowed or forced to live in unsafe or unhealthy housing.

Discussion of more recent cases finding an implied warranty of fitness is reserved for subsequent treatment (Chapter 19, Section C).

C.   Duty to Protect the Tenant in His Quiet Enjoyment of the Premises

MILHEIM v. BAXTER
46 Colo. 155, 103 P. 376 (1909)

GABBERT, J. Appellee, plaintiff below, brought suit against appellant to recover damages claimed to have been sustained as the result of having been evicted from premises which she had leased from the defendant. The trial of the case resulted in a verdict and judgment for the plaintiff, from which the defendant appeals.

The first point made on behalf of defendant is that the complaint does not state a cause of action. In her complaint plaintiff alleged, in substance, that she rented of defendant for the term of one year the premises known as 818 Twenty-Second street, in the city of Denver, for a boarding and lodging house; that defendant was then the owner of the adjoining premises, No. 816; that these premises were then, and for a long time prior thereto had been, and thereafter were, used and occupied, with the knowledge and consent of defendant, as an assignation house, where immoral men and women were constantly meeting for immoral purposes; that she was not aware of the character of such premises when she leased those adjoining, and that she was greatly annoyed by the vulgar and indecent conduct of the tenants in No. 816. It is urged that these averments are insufficient, in that the lessee runs the risk of the condition of the premises, unless there is an express agreement to the contrary, for the reason that except in the case of furnished apartments, there is no implied covenant by the landlord that the leased premises are tenantable, or fit for the purpose for which they are let. Plaintiff is not complaining of the physical condition of the leased premises, but that defendant was guilty of acts which prevented her from the free use and enjoyment thereof. Unless expressed to the contrary, a lease contains, of necessity, an implied covenant for the quiet enjoyment of the leased premises. Pickett v. Ferguson, 45 Ark. 177, 55 Am. Rep. 545; Field v. Herrick, 10 Ill. App. 591; Avery v. Dougherty, 102 Ind. 443, 2 N.E. 123, 52 Am. Rep. 680. Any act willfully done by a landlord which justifies the tenant vacating the leased premises, and he vacates them on this account, amounts to, and may be treated as, an eviction; and, where the tenant has leased premises for a lawful purpose, and has been driven therefrom before the expiration of his lease by the conduct of persons occupying adjacent premises for immoral purposes, which the landlord owns and controls, and which he knowingly permits to be occupied for such purpose, a case is made within this rule. Lay v. Bennett, 4 Colo. App. 252, 35 Pac. 748; Dyett v. Pendleton, 8 Cow. (N.Y.) 727. The complaint, so far as considered, is sufficient.

It is next urged that there was no evidence of an eviction. In support of this claim it is contended that there was no evidence tending to prove that the defendant had actual knowledge of any improper conduct on the part of the tenants of No. 816, or that plaintiff was injured or disturbed by such conduct, and that it appears that plaintiff, without any complaint or request to the landlord to suppress the illegal conduct of the occupants of No. 816, abandoned the premises she had leased. From the evidence submitted there is no doubt regarding the character of the premises known as No. 816. The evidence discloses beyond all question that they were occupied for immoral purposes. It is also apparent from the testimony that the plaintiff was injured and disturbed by the conduct of the persons occupying such premises. It is probably true the evidence fails to disclose that plaintiff notified defendant of the character of the persons occupying No. 816, or requested the landlord to compel the persons occupying such premises to vacate or cease their unlawful conduct. We do not believe that plaintiff was required to take any such steps; at least counsel for defendant have cited no authorities holding that she was required to do so. It appears from the testimony that No. 816 had long been occupied for immoral purposes under circumstances which would justify the jury in finding that defendant had full knowledge that they were so occupied. When the lessor, by an illegal act, materially disturbs the possession of his tenant, which he should protect and defend, the latter may abandon the premises leased. Lay v. Bennett, *supra.*

Over the objection of defendant plaintiff was permitted to testify that she proposed occupying the premises rented as a rooming and boarding house; that the house contained 10 rooms; that she only required two for her own use; that she could have rented 8 at $12 per month each, and could have accommodated from 15 to 25 boarders; that the profit on each boarder would be about $1 a week. At the time she vacated the premises she had occupied them about two weeks. She further testified that the loss to her business was about $1,638. The court instructed the jury to the effect that, if they found for plaintiff, she was entitled to recover damages in such sum as they might believe from the evidence she suffered by reason of the defendant failing to give her a quiet, peaceable, and undisturbed possession of the leased premises for the term for which they were leased. The jury returned a verdict in the sum of $1,180. In the circumstances of this case the evidence admitted and the instructions given were erroneous. It appears that she had not established a business in the premises rented. The only roomers she had were guests. She says she never had any applications for roomers or boarders, but felt confident she would have secured all she could accommodate had it not been, as we infer, for the character of the premises next door. The business in which she intended to engage was a new one. Hence there was no basis upon which to estimate a loss of profits. They were remote, speculative, and incapable of ascertainment. She might have secured all the boarders and roomers she could accommodate, and she might not. The profits she claimed to have lost were purely conjectural, and embraced too many elements of uncertainty to form a just basis upon which to measure damages on this account. The tenant cannot recover, as damages for eviction, anticipated profits on a business not established. 1 Sedgwick on Damages, §185; Greene v. Williams, 45 Ill. 206; Engstrom v. Merriam, 25 Wash. 73, 64 Pac. 914. Except such special damages as plaintiff might have been entitled to recover, her recovery should have been limited to the actual rental value of the premises, over and above the rent she agreed to pay, from the time she was evicted. Sedgwick on Damages, *supra;* Greene v. Williams, *supra;* 3 Sutherland on Damages, 149; Engstrom v. Merriam, *supra.*

The judgment of the county court is reversed, and the cause remanded for a new trial.

Reversed and remanded.

Note: Constructive Eviction[5]

Dyett v. Pendleton, 8 Cow. 727 (N.Y. 1826), the first American case which recognized the doctrine of "constructive eviction" as a remedy for a landlord's breach of the covenant of quiet enjoyment, is remarkably similar to Milheim v. Baxter in its facts. There T leased two rooms on the second and third floor of L's house. In L's action for rent, T offered to prove that L brought various lewd women to the house, often with other men, who stayed all night, making a great deal of noise. T "being a person of good and respectable character, was compelled, by the repetition of the said indecent practices and proceedings, to leave the said premises." The Supreme Court had refused to receive this evidence, holding that an actual physical eviction must be proved to bar L's recovery of the rent. Senator Spencer, writing the main opinion, said:

---

5.   This subject of "constructive eviction" and the landlord's breach of the covenant of quiet enjoyment, as well as the implied warranty of fitness/habitability, are more fully treated in Chapter 18, Section 2, and in Chapter 19, Section 2.

. . . [T]he principle on which a tenant is required to pay rent, is the beneficial enjoyment of the premises, unmolested in any way by the landlord. It is a universal principle in all cases of contract, that a party who deprives another of the consideration on which his obligation was founded, can never recover damages for its non-fulfilment. The total failure of the consideration, especially when produced by the act of the plaintiff, is a valid defence to an action, except in certain cases, where a seal is technically held to conclude the party. This is the great and fundamental principle which led the courts to deny the lessor's right to recover rent where he had deprived the tenant of the consideration of his covenant, by turning him out of the possession of the demised premises. It must be wholly immaterial by what acts that failure of consideration has been produced; the only enquiry being, has it failed by the conduct of the lessor? This is a question of fact, and to establish it, the proof offered in this case was certainly competent. I do not feel called upon to say that those facts would have been alone sufficient. Of that the jury were to judge, at least, in the first instance; and the question whether they amounted to a full and complete legal defence, might have been presented in another shape. The only question for our decision is, whether that testimony ought to have been received at all? Believing that it tended to establish a constructive eviction and expulsion against the consent of the tenant; that it tended to prove a disturbance of his quiet possession, and a failure of the consideration on which only the tenant was obliged to pay rent, I am of opinion that it ought to have been received; and that therefore the judgment of the supreme court should be reversed, with directions to issue a venire de novo. [8 Cow. at 732-733.]

While it is usual for a formal lease to contain an express covenant by the landlord that he will protect the tenant in the latter's peaceful and quiet enjoyment of the demised premises, leases of a less formal nature frequently make no provision for the tenant's protection. However, this does not mean that such a tenant is without protection in this regard, for as the principal case notes, "unless expressed to the contrary, a lease contains, of necessity an implied covenant for the quiet enjoyment of the leased premises."[6]

The landlord's covenant, either express or implied, that the tenant shall have the peaceful and quiet enjoyment of the leased premises is probably the single most important clause in the whole lease — from the tenant's point of view. We will consider the possible remedies available to the tenant for the landlord's breach in later chapters,[7] but you should consider at this point whether the quotation from Senator Spencer's opinion is based upon a contract theory of "failure of consideration," or upon a property theory of

---

6. Although N.Y. Real Prop. Law §251 provides that "a covenant is not implied in conveyance of real property," this statute has been held inapplicable to leases. Fifth Avenue Building Co. v. Kernochan, 178 A.D. 19, 165 N.Y.S. 122, aff'd, 221 N.Y. 370, 117 N.E. 579, rehearing denied, 222 N.Y. 525, 118 N.E. 1057 (1917). Leases of more than three years are frequently deemed "conveyances," e.g., Wis. Stat. §706.01 (now a "conveyance" if the lease is for more than one year), but since it is in the short-term lease that the implied covenant is most needed, this limitation is rarely significant. New Jersey seems to be the only state which refuses to imply a covenant of quiet enjoyment, see e.g., Ellis v. McDermott, 7 N.J. Misc. 757, 147 A. 236 (Dist. Ct. 1929).

7. See Chapter 18 and Chapter 19, Section 2.

"constructive eviction," and what difference, if any, it makes.[8] A frequently litigated question is whether the landlord's failure to control other tenants' behavior constitutes a breach of the covenant. Compare Phyfe v. Dale, 72 Misc. 383, 130 N.Y.S. 231 (App. Term 1911), with Stewart v. Lawson, 199 Mich. 497, 165 N.W. 716 (1917).

BLACKETT v. OLANOFF
371 Mass. 714, 358 N.E. 2d 817 (1977)

WILKINS, J. The defendant in each of these consolidated actions for rent successfully raised constructive eviction as a defense against the landlords' claim. The judge found that the tenants were "very substantially deprived" of quiet enjoyment of their leased premises "*for a substantial* time" (emphasis original). He ruled that the tenants' implied warranty of quiet enjoyment was violated by late evening and early morning music and disturbances coming from nearby premises which the landlords leased to others for use as a bar or cocktail lounge (lounge). The judge further found that, although the landlords did not intend to create the conditions, the landlords "had it within their control to correct the conditions which . . . amounted to a constructive eviction of each [tenant]." He also found that the landlords promised each tenant to correct the situation, that the landlords made some attempt to remedy the problem, but they were unsuccessful, and that each tenant vacated his apartment within a reasonable time. Judgment was entered for each tenant; the landlords appealed; and we transferred the appeals here. We affirm the judgments.

The landlords argue that they did not violate the tenants' implied covenant of quiet enjoyment because they are not chargeable with the noise from the lounge. The landlords do not challenge the judge's conclusion that the noise emanating from the lounge was sufficient to constitute a constructive eviction, if that noise could be attributed to the landlords,[9] nor do the landlords seriously argue that a constructive eviction could not be found as matter of law because the lounge was not on the same premises as the tenants' apartments. See 1 American Law of Property §3.51 at 281 (A. J. Casner ed. 1952). The landlords' principal contention, based on the denial of certain requests for rulings, is that they are not responsible for the conduct of the proprietors, employees, and patrons of the lounge.

Our opinions concerning a constructive eviction by an alleged breach of

----

8.   See Bennett, The Modern Lease—An Estate or a Contract, 16 Tex. L. Rev. 47 (1937); The California Lease—Contract or Conveyance? 4 Stan. L. Rev. 244 (1952).

9.   There was evidence that the lounge had amplified music (electric musical instruments and singing, at various times) which started at 9:30 P.M. and continued until 1:30 A.M or 2 A.M., generally on Tuesdays through Sundays. The music could be heard through the granite walls of the residential tenants' building, and was described variously as unbelievably loud, incessant, raucous, and penetrating. The noise interfered with conversation and prevented sleep. There was also evidence of noise from patrons' yelling and fighting.

an implied covenant of quiet enjoyment sometimes have stated that the landlord must perform some act with the intent of depriving the tenant of the enjoyment and occupation of the whole or part of the leased premises. See Katz v. Duffy, 261 Mass. 149, 151-152, 158 N.E. 264 (1927), and cases cited. There are occasions, however, where a landlord has not intended to violate a tenant's rights, but there was nevertheless a breach of the landlord's covenant of quiet enjoyment which flowed as the natural and probable consequence of what the landlord did, what he failed to do, or what he permitted to be done. Charles E. Burt, Inc. v. Seven Grand Corp., 340 Mass. 124, 127, 163 N.E.2d 4 (1959) (failure to supply light, heat, power, and elevator services). Westland Housing Corp. v. Scott, 312 Mass. 375, 381, 44 N.E.2d 959 (1942) (intrusions of smoke and soot over a substantial period of time due to a defective boiler). Shindler v. Milden, 282 Mass. 32, 33-34, 184 N.E. 673 (1933) (failure to install necessary heating system, as agreed). Case v. Minot, 158 Mass. 577, 587, 33 N.E. 700 (1893) (landlord authorizing another lessee to obstruct the tenant's light and air, necessary for the beneficial enjoyment of the demised premises). Skally v. Shute, 132 Mass. 367, 370-371 (1882) (undermining of a leased building rendering it unfit for occupancy). Although some of our opinions have spoken of particular action or inaction by a landlord as showing a presumed intention to evict, the landlord's conduct, and not his intentions, is controlling. See Westland Housing Corp. v. Scott, *supra,* 312 Mass. at 382-383, 44 N.E. 959.

The judge was warranted in ruling that the landlords had it within their control to correct the condition which caused the tenants to vacate their apartments. The landlords introduced a commercial activity into an area where they leased premises for residential purposes. The lease for the lounge expressly provided that entertainment in the lounge had to be conducted so that it could not be heard outside the building and would not disturb the residents of the leased apartments. The potential threat to the occupants of the nearby apartments was apparent in the circumstances. The landlords complained to the tenants of the lounge after receiving numerous objections from residential tenants. From time to time, the pervading noise would abate in response to the landlords' complaints. We conclude that, as matter of law, the landlords had a right to control the objectionable noise coming from the lounge and that the judge was warranted in finding as a fact that the landlords could control the objectionable conditions.

This situation is different from the usual annoyance of one residential tenant by another, where traditionally the landlord has not been chargeable with the annoyance. See Katz v. Duffy, 261 Mass. 149, 158 N.E. 264 (1927) (illegal sale of alcoholic beverages); DeWitt v. Pierson, 112 Mass. 8 (1873) (prostitution).[10] Here we have a case more like Case v. Minot, 158 Mass.

10. The general, but not universal, rule in this country is that a landlord is not chargeable because one tenant is causing annoyance to another (A. H. Woods Theatre v. North American Union, 246 Ill. App. 521, 526-527 (1927) (music from one commercial tenant annoying another commercial tenant's employees)), even where the annoying conduct would be a breach of the landlord's covenant of quiet enjoyment if the landlord were the miscreant. See Paterson

577, 33 N.E. 700 (1893), where the landlord entered into a lease with one tenant which the landlord knew permitted that tenant to engage in activity which would interfere with the rights of another tenant. There, to be sure, the clash of tenants' rights was inevitable, if each pressed those rights. Here, although the clash of tenants' interests was only a known potentiality initially, experience demonstrated that a decibel level for the entertainment at the lounge, acoustically acceptable to its patrons and hence commercially desirable to its proprietors, was intolerable for the residential tenants.

Because the disturbing condition was the natural and probable consequence of the landlords' permitting the lounge to operate where it did and because the landlords could control the actions at the lounge, they should not be entitled to collect rent for residential premises which were not reasonably habitable. Tenants such as these should not be left only with a claim against the proprietors of the noisome lounge. To the extent that our opinions suggest a distinction between nonfeasance by the landlord, which has been said to create no liability (P. Hall, Massachusetts Law of Landlord and Tenant §§90-91 (4th ed. 1949)), and malfeasance by the landlord, we decline to perpetuate that distinction where the landlord creates a situation and has the right to control the objectionable conditions.

Judgments affirmed.

Problems

17.7. T_1 and T_3 occupy apartments on the same floor in a multiple-unit dwelling owned by L. T_2 moves into the apartment situated between T_1 and T_3. Unknown to L, T_2 has a colicky infant who cries loudly most of the night, preventing the families of T_1 and T_3 from getting any sleep. After receiving several complaints from both T_1 and T_3 about the intolerable noise from T_2's apartment, L warns T_2 that eviction will follow upon any future

---

v. Bridges, 16 Ala. App. 54, 55, 75 So. 260 (1917); Thompson v. Harris, 9 Ariz. App. 341, 345, 452 P.2d 122 (1969), and cases cited; 1 American Law of Property §3.53 (A. J. Casner ed. 1952); Annot., 38 A.L.R. 250 (1925). Contra Kesner v. Consumers Co., 255 Ill. App. 216, 228-229 (1929) (storage of flammables constituting a nuisance); Bruckner v. Helfaer, 197 Wis. 582, 585, 222 N.W. 790 (1929) (residential tenant not liable for rent where landlord, with ample notice, does not control another tenant's conduct).

The rule in New York appears to be that the landlord may not recover rent if he has had ample notice of the existence of conduct of one tenant which deprives another tenant of the beneficial enjoyment of his premises and the landlord does little or nothing to abate the nuisance. See Cohen v. Werner, 85 Misc. 2d 341, 342, 378 N.Y.S.2d 868 (N.Y. App. T. 1975); Rockrose Associates v. Peters, 81 Misc. 2d 971, 972, 366 N.Y.S.2d 567 (N.Y. Civ. Ct. 1975) (office lease); Home Life Ins. Co. v. Breslerman, 168 Misc. 117, 118, 5 N.Y.S.2d 272 (N.Y. App. T. 1938). But see comments in Trustees of the Sailors' Snug Harbor in the City of New York v. Sugarman, 264 App. Div. 240, 241, 35 N.Y.S.2d 196 (N.Y.1942) (no nuisance).

A tenant with sufficient bargaining power may be able to obtain an agreement from the landlord to insert and to enforce regulatory restrictions in the leases of other, potentially offending, tenants. See E. Schwartz, Lease Drafting in Massachusetts §6.33 (1961).

disturbance. Nevertheless, T_2's colicky infant continues to cry almost every subsequent evening and L promptly commences an eviction proceeding against T_2; however, during the pendency of the proceeding, T_1 moves out and T_3 ceases paying rent.

   a.   Should T_2 be evicted for the colicky infant's uncontrollable crying when there exists a critical housing shortage and a pediatrician testifies that the colic will probably disappear in a month or so? Is T_2 in any event liable to L for any lost rent from either T_1 or T_3? Is T_2 liable on any theory to T_1 or T_3?

   b.   May T_1 sue L for damages measured by the increased rent T_1 is paying for T_1's new apartment? May L counterclaim and collect rent from T_1 for the balance of T_1's term?

   c.   May T_3 properly withhold part of T_3's rent on the ground of a "constructive eviction"? On any other ground?

17.8. T_1 and T_3 are commercial tenants occupying retail space on the ground floor of an old inner-city loft building recently purchased by L. L has determined that the building's highest and best use would be to demolish it and construct a new high-rise office building. T_1, occupying approximately two thousand square feet and having 10 years left on a 15-year lease, is prohibited from using the leased premises for any purpose other than the sale of religious books and other items of a religious nature. T_3, occupying approximately four thousand square feet and having 8 years left on a 10-year lease, operates a discount high-fashion dress shop catering to young women, but T_3's lease permits any lawful use. T_2, occupying approximately twenty thousand square feet of space located between T_1 and T_3, whose month-to-month lease was entered into shortly after L's acquisition of the building, operates a very successful high-volume adult entertainment complex for single men with a recently installed neon-lit sign offering surrogate sexual therapy and a boutique containing a broad array of sexually kinky equipment — all of which is, however, perfectly legal. Because of the disreputable nature of T_2's establishment and large numbers of male customers frequently loitering in front of it, the previously successful businesses of T_1 and T_3 are reduced to virtually nothing. What are the remedies and the legal grounds of action available to T_1 and T_3?

D.   The Landlord's Tort Liability Based Upon the Condition of the Premises

Just as the doctrine of caveat emptor (tenant) shaped the common law with respect to the condition of the premises at the commencement of the tenancy, so too did the doctrine shape the common law with respect to the condition of the premises during the tenancy. The landlord had no obligation to put the premises in repair at the commencement of the term and no obligation, in the absence of an express covenant, to make any repairs during the term's continuance. The process by which these rules have been adapted to modern conditions has involved the building up of exception upon exception, and you are warned at the outset not to lose sight of the general rule.[11]

JOHNSON v. O'BRIEN
258 Minn. 502, 105 N.W.2d 244 (1960)

GALLAGHER, J.

Two appeals from an order denying defendants' motion for judgment notwithstanding the verdict or for a new trial in two personal injury actions which were tried together.

The cases were submitted to the jury for a special verdict under Rule 49.01, Rules of Civil Procedure, and arose out of the following fact situation.

Defendants owned a two-story building in Deerwood, Minnesota. The first floor was rented and used as a grocery store, the second floor was divided into two apartments, front and back. Both apartments were served by an inside stairway and the back apartment was served by an outside stairway of wooden construction which was built sometime prior to 1923.

On July 10, 1955, an agent of the defendants rented the back apartment to a Mrs. Elletson, age 70, on an oral month-to-month tenancy. There was no covenant to repair by the defendants. The outside stairway was leased as part of the back apartment and was not used in common by the other tenant.

On October 3, 1955, Mrs. Elletson's son and his wife, the plaintiffs, came to visit her. While they were using the back stairway, one of the treads, second from the top, gave way and the son's wife fell to the ground and sustained a fracture of the anterior border of the sixth cervical vertebra. . . .

Defendants contend first that the rule of law applied by the court as to the liability of a landlord is incorrect. In that connection the court instructed the jury as follows:

> In the absence of agreement, he is under no obligation to repair things damaged or deteriorating after the start of the lease. He has no responsibility to persons on the land for conditions developing after the start of the lease. The owner is, however, under obligation to disclose to the lessee, Mrs. Elletson in this case, concealed, dangerous conditions existing when the possession is transferred, when he has information which would lead a reasonable prudent owner, exercising due care, to suspect that the danger exists and that the tenant, exercising due care, would not discover it for himself and which conditions are not open to the observation of the tenant then he must at least disclose such information to the tenant or be found lacking in due care.

In the memorandum accompanying its order denying defendants' motion for a new trial, the court relied on Breimhorst v. Beckman, 227 Minn.

---

11. See generally Restatement (Second) of Torts §§355-362.

409, 418, 419, 35 N.W.2d 719, 726, where we stated that the liability of a landlord "is not restricted to those instances where the lessor has actual knowledge of the dangerous condition of the premises, but includes those cases where he has information which would lead an ordinarily reasonable man to suspect that danger exists," and that "The liability for concealing or failing to disclose a dangerous condition unknown to the lessee is based on the theory of negligence." This rule was applied in the *Breimhorst* case in determining whether the trial court erred in directing a verdict for the landlord and in denying plaintiff's motion for a new trial. There was no evidence in that case from which a jury could justifiably have found that the lessor ought reasonably to have suspected that a dangerous condition existed.

Defendants contend that the authorities cited in the *Breimhorst* case do not support the rule therein followed. They contend that in Murphy v. Barlow Realty Co., 214 Minn. 64, 7 N.W.3d 684, actual knowledge of the defect was present and that Anderson v. Winkle, 213 Minn. 77, 5 N.W.2d 355, involved a situation in which an injury occurred on a stairway used in common with other tenants.

We find in 1 Tiffany, Landlord and Tenant, §96b, also cited by the court in the *Breimhorst* case, that a lessor is liable to persons rightfully on the premises for injuries caused by defects or dangerous conditions existing at the time of the leasing, which, while not apparent to the lessee, were known to the lessor and of which he failed to inform the lessee, "And his liability extends not only to dangerous conditions of which he actually knows, but also to those the existence of which he has reasonable ground to suspect." . . .

In Prosser, Torts (2d ed.) §80, we find the following comment:

> Some courts apparently require that the lessor have actual knowledge of the existence of the condition before he is under a duty in regard to it. *The greater number have held, however, that it is sufficient that he has information which would lead a reasonable man to suspect that the danger exists, and that he must at least disclose such information to the tenant.* Tennessee has gone even further, and has imposed upon the lessor an affirmative duty to use reasonable care to inspect the premises before transfer; but the decision has not been followed in other jurisdictions, where it is generally agreed that there is no obligation to inspect or investigate in the absence of some reason to believe that there is a danger. There is of course no duty to disclose conditions which are known to the tenant, or which are so open and obvious that he may be expected to discover them when he takes possession. [Italics supplied.]

It would serve no useful purpose to analyze in detail the authorities cited by the defendants in support of their contention. We believe that the rule established in the *Breimhorst* case, as embodied in the instructions of the present case, is correct and well founded in reason and justice.

Accordingly, where a landlord has information which would lead a reasonably prudent owner exercising due care to suspect that danger exists on the leased premises at the time the tenant takes possession, and that the tenant exercising due care would not discover it for himself, then he must at least disclose such information to the tenant. Under the circumstances here a question of fact was properly presented for the jury.

We agree with the trial court that "To require one to use that care which an ordinarily prudent person would exercise under the same or similar circumstances can hardly be onerous, unreasonable or oppressive." . . .

Affirmed.

KNUTSON, J., dissenting.

I cannot agree with the majority in this case. At least since Harpel v. Fall, 63 Minn. 520, 524, 65 N.W. 913, 914, we have followed the rule that—

> . . . where there is no agreement to repair leased premises by the landlord, and he is not guilty of any fraud or concealment as to their safe condition, and the defects in the premises are not secret, but obvious, the tenant takes the risk of their safe occupancy; and the landlord is not liable to him or to any person entering under his title, or who is upon the premises by his invitation, for injuries sustained by reason of the unsafe condition of the premises. . . .

DELL, Ch. J., dissenting.

I certainly cannot agree with the majority either. I concur with everything that has been said in the dissent written by Mr. Justice Knutson.[12]

Note: The Landlord's Knowledge of Defective Condition

The original Restatement of Torts §358 (1934) provided that for a landlord to be liable for a dangerous condition existing at the time of the leasing there must be both (1) an absence of knowledge on the part of the tenant and (2) knowledge by the landlord with reason to expect that the danger would not be discovered by the tenant. The comments to this section made it clear that only "actual" knowledge would suffice. Under the Restatement of Torts (Second), the liability of the landlord is greatly expanded. Comment b under §358 now provides:

> It is not, however, necessary that the [landlord] have actual knowledge of the condition. . . . It is enough that he has reason to know that the condition exists . . . that is, that he has information from which a person of reasonable intelligence, or of his own superior intelligence, would infer that the condition

---

12. See the annotation Modern Status of Rule Requiring Actual Knowledge of Latent Defect in Leased Premises as Prerequisite to Landlord's Liability to Tenant Injured Thereby, 88 A.L.R.2d 586 (1963).—EDS.

exists, or would govern his conduct on the assumption that it does exist, and in addition would realize that its existence will involve an unreasonable risk of physical harm to persons on the land.

Problem

17.9. L and T entered into a written lease of certain described premises. There was a communicating door between the premises leased to T and the adjoining premises, which were also owned by L. This communicating door was not visible from the premises leased by T because it had been papered over, and L never notified T of the existence of the door. L thereafter leased the adjoining premises to A. A entered T's premises one night through the above mentioned door, knocked T out, and carried away a substantial amount of T's property. A has not been seen or heard from since that time. On what possible theory could T sue L to recover the loss sustained by the theft of A? See McIntyre, Ltd. v. Chandler Holding Corp., 172 Misc. 917, 16 N.Y.S.2d 642 (Sup. Ct. 1939), *aff'd,* 259 A.D. 710, 19 N.Y.S.2d 149 (1940). Could T sue L in order to recover for personal injuries resulting from A's assault and battery on the ground that T would have taken self-protective steps against an intruder if T had known of the door and that T's failure to know of the door was L's fault?

BOWLES v. MAHONEY
202 F.2d 320 (D.C. Cir. 1952), *cert. denied.,* 344 U.S. 935 (1953)

MILLER, J.

[A seven-year-old child, Ralph Mahoney, the nephew of the named tenant, Luke Gaither, was badly injured when a dilapidated retaining wall collapsed and fell on him while he was playing on an adjoining parking lot. The retaining wall had been built several years earlier by the owner-landlord (Mrs. Bowles) in the parking lot adjacent to the leased premises, which parking lot was owned by the District of Columbia. The court noted that "[t]he lease, a copy of which is in the record, did not obligate the landlord to make repairs. There is no statute imposing that duty on a landlord."]

[T]he plaintiff's theory is seen to be this: Mrs. Bowles, having constructed the wall in the parking for the benefit of her property, was under a duty to maintain it in a safe condition; she violated her duty by negligently failing to keep the wall in repair; as a result of her negligence the wall collapsed and injured tenant's invitee; she is therefore liable in damages to the invitee. The District of Columbia, says the complaint, permitted the structure to be erected, and negligently failed to keep it in repair. . . .

As to Mrs. Bowles. Judge Groner, speaking for this court in Harrison v. Mortgage Inv. Co., 1932, 61 App. D.C. 155, 156, 58 F.2d 881, 882, said, "before the owner of the premises can be held liable [for injuries due to a defect therein], there must be a failure on his part to perform a duty which the law imposes." We must therefore ascertain whether Mrs. Bowles owed the child the duty of maintaining the wall in good repair.

The plaintiff, Ralph Mahoney, was living in the house at the invitation of his uncle, who was Mrs. Bowles' tenant, so he was using the appurtenant passageway as the tenant's invitee. The rule is that the duties and liabilities of a landlord to persons on the leased premises by the invitation of the tenant are those owed to the tenant himself. Fraser v. Kruger, 8 Cir., 1924, 298 F. 693. It follows that Mrs. Bowles is not liable for the child's injuries unless she would have been liable to her tenant, Luke Gaither, had he been injured under similar circumstances.

We have seen that Mrs. Bowles had not agreed to repair or maintain the demised premises. It is not suggested that she fraudulently concealed from Gaither, at the time the lease was executed, a defect in the retaining wall which was known to her and not to him; in fact it is not suggested that the wall was defective when the lease was made in 1936. The first indication of a defective condition was the crack in the wall which Mrs. Armstrong noticed in 1946. So, if the crack indicated a defective condition, it was one which arose during the term of the lease. Absent any statutory or contract duty, the lessor is not responsible for an injury resulting from a defect which developed during the term. Johnson v. Kurn, 8 Cir., 1938, 95 F.2d 629, 632. . . .

In the foregoing, we have treated the case as though the accident had occurred on the premises owned by Mrs. Bowles and leased to Gaither. That the child was injured in the parking area and not on the premises proper, we regard as immaterial for the reason that Mrs. Bowles owed Gaither no greater duty with regard to maintaining the wall in the parking than with respect to keeping the actual premises in repair. As to the latter, we have seen she owed him no duty at all. . . .

As to the District of Columbia. The District had control of the publicly owned parking which was servient to the private easement therein enjoyed by the owner of 2320 H Street. The local authorities permitted the owner to erect the wall at his own expense. As between the owner of the premises and the District, there can be no doubt that the former had the duty of maintaining the retaining wall in good repair. When Mrs. Bowles conveyed the property and its appurtenances to Gaither, she transferred to him, and he assumed, that primary duty of keeping the wall safe. So, if Gaither had been injured by the collapse of the wall due to his own negligent failure to repair it, it would hardly be said he could recover from the District. The child had no greater right against the District than Gaither would have had in similar circumstances. The trial judge should have peremptorily instructed the jury to return a verdict in favor of the District of Columbia.

This conclusion makes it unnecessary for us to consider whether it was the District's duty to make regular inspections of the wall, and whether it had constructive notice of the defect in time to have caused repairs which would have prevented the accident. Nor is it material that the court erroneously included in its charge to the jury an instruction on res ipsa loquitur.

The cases will be remanded to the District Court with instructions to set aside the verdict and the judgment entered thereon, and to enter judgment in favor of both defendants.

Reversed and remanded.

BAZELON, J. (dissenting).

The key to the decision of the court, relieving both the landlord and the District of Columbia from liability, lies in its adherence to the rule at common law that "[a]bsent any statutory or contract duty, the lessor is not responsible for an injury resulting from a defect which developed during the term." I think that rule is an anachronism which has lived on through stare decisis alone rather than through pragmatic adjustment to "the felt necessities of [our] time." I would therefore discard it and cast the presumptive burden of liability upon the landlord. This, I think, is the command of the realities and mores of our day.

Courts have gradually recognized, at least in part, that the exalted position which the landlord held at early common law is discordant with the needs of a later day. At early common law a lessee was regarded as having merely a personal right against the lessor. But as a result of several remedies that were created in the lessor's favor, he came to be regarded as having rights in rem, and the lease "was regarded as a sale of the demised premises for the term." Upon this thesis, the courts held that a lease was "like the sale of specified personal property to be delivered" and applied the same concept of caveat emptor that prevailed generally in that day with respect to the sale of all chattels. As a corollary of this concept, courts generally held that the "destruction or any depreciation of [the] value [of the leased premises], other than such depreciation occasioned by a fault of the lessor, was entirely the loss of the lessee."

"[B]oth the English and the American law have broken almost entirely away from the ancient rule of caveat emptor," with respect to the sale of chattels generally. To some extent this development has been reflected in the law governing landlord and tenant relations. For example, now "the lessor, like a vendor, is under the obligation to disclose to the lessee [not only] concealed dangerous conditions existing when possession is transferred, of which he has knowledge . . ." but also any "information [in his possession] which would lead a reasonable man to suspect that the danger exists. . . ." But with respect to the landlord's responsibility for the condition of the premises during the term of the lease, courts have failed to reflect this development. As a result, the common law in this respect still lags behind the modern notion that in general one who sells an article is presumed to warrant that it is good for the purpose for which it is sold. In order to keep pace, the law should recognize that when one pays for the temporary use of a dwelling, the parties contemplate that insofar as reasonable care on the part of the owner can assure it, the dwelling will be safe and habitable, not only at the time possession is delivered but throughout the period for which payment is made. It is fair to presume that no individual would voluntarily choose to live in a dwelling that had become unsafe for human habitation. The community's enlightened self-interest requires the same presumption. It follows that, at least in the absence of express provision to the contrary, a landlord who leases property should be held to a continuing obligation to exercise reasonable care to provide that which the parties intended he should provide, namely, a safe and habitable dwelling. Applying this view to the circumstances of the present case, the landlord would be liable for the injuries to little Ralph Mahoney as the tenant's invitee. For the lease did not expressly make the tenant responsible for repairs and there is no doubt that the owner of this dilapidated dwelling failed to exercise reasonable care to prevent the collapse of the cracked retaining wall. And since the court's reason for excusing the District of Columbia from liability is that the tenant, and not the landlord, had the duty to repair, that reason would no longer be valid. . . .

Two reasons have been advanced to justify perpetuation of the rule at common law under modern day conditions. First, it is said that the tenant should bear the responsibility for repair during the term of the lease because his control and possession of the premises give him the opportunity to know their condition, whereas the landlord has no such opportunity. This reason might have some validity if the landlord had no right to go upon the premises. But if the landlord is presumed to have the duty to repair, then the concomitant right to enter upon the premises for inspection and repair would be necessarily implied. And, in any case, the landlord can always reserve the right to enter the premises in order to inspect and repair them. Indeed, the case at bar shows that the landlord did enter to make repairs from time to time, not that he was ever refused such entry. And insofar as "notice" is the reason for the rule, it bears emphasis that the landlord had specific notice of the defect which caused the injuries in this case.

The second and a more sophisticated reason for relieving the landlord from liability is the hypothesis that "it is still socially desirable not to discourage investment in and ownership of real estate, particularly private dwellings." This objective may well be desirable. But it is a fallacious oversimplification to suppose that the common law rule has much to do with the rate of investment in real property. On the other hand, it seems clear to me that the rule operates to defeat the interests of utility and justice. "Upon whom is the loss to be placed, more justly than upon the landlord? Upon the tenant who, because of his poverty . . . risks his own neck to live in the house? Upon the tenant's equally poor guest, the mailman, the visiting nurse, etc.?" Courts are not impervious to the unequal bargaining position of the parties in interpreting their agreements. For, as Mr. Justice Cardozo said, "Rules derived by a process of logical deduction from preestablished conceptions of contract and obligation have broken down before the slow and steady and erosive action of utility and justice." This court illustrated that in Kay v. Cain, where we said that ". . . it is doubtful whether a clause which did undertake to exempt a landlord from responsibility for such negligence would now be valid. The acute housing shortage in and near the District of Columbia gives the landlord so great a bargaining advantage over the tenant that such an exemption might well be held invalid on grounds of public policy." There is no reason to adopt an inconsistent view where, as here, the dwelling constitutes the entire premises and there is no clause expressly exempting the landlord from liability.

In a great many states, the common law rule to which the court adheres in this case has been changed by statutes based upon a recognition of its social and economic undesirability. For example, in explanation of the statute changing the rule in California, the Commissioner's note states,

> This section changes rule upon this subject to conform to that which, notwithstanding steady judicial adherence for hundreds of years to adverse doctrine, is generally believed by unprofessional public to be law, and upon which basis they almost always contract. The very fact that there are repeated decisions to the contrary, down to the year 1861, shows that the public do not and cannot understand their justice, or even realize their existence. So familiar a point of law could not rise again and again for adjudication were it not that the community at large revolt at every application of the rule.

. . . There is no fixed line dividing the sphere of action as between the legislature and the courts for effecting needed change of a common law rule. The line should not be marked in accordance with "metaphysical conceptions of the nature of judge-made law, nor by the fetish of some implacable tenet, such as that of the division of governmental powers, but by considerations of convenience, of utility, and of the deepest sentiments of justice." "Change of this character should not be left to the Legislature." "If judges have woefully misinterpreted the mores of their day, or if the mores of their day are no longer those of ours, they ought not to tie, in helpless submission, the hands of their successors."

It is undoubtedly true that many landlords have shaped their conduct in reliance upon the rule which I would discard. This consideration is entitled to some weight. But, in my view, it cannot outweigh the social and economic need for shifting the distribution of the risk. To those landlords who have acted in good faith there may undoubtedly be some hardship. But in our realistic experience, they are possessed of the better means to discharge this burden. We need give slight consideration to other landlords who would employ the rule to press their advantage to the extent of permitting a known hazard to exist in callous disregard of the safety of fellow human beings who are obviously without the means to protect themselves.

Note: Bowles v. Mahoney

Whetzel v. Jess Fisher Management Co., 282 F.2d 943 (D.C. Cir. 1960), contains the following statement:

> In Bowles v. Mahoney, this court adhered to the common-law rule that "absent any statutory or contract duty, the lessor is not responsible for an injury resulting from a defect which developed during the term." Since that case was decided, the commissioners of the District of Columbia have promulgated regulations concerning maintenance and repair of residential property. The primary question here presented is whether these regulations impose a "statutory . . . duty" on the lessor not presented in Bowles v. Mahoney. We conclude that they do. [282 F.2d at 944.]

Note: Tort Liability of the Landlord if Required by Statute to Repair

Compare the view of Bowles v. Mahoney with the following view of the New York courts as illustrated by Moore v. Bryant, 27 Misc. 2d 22, 83 N.Y.S.2d 365 (Sup. Ct. 1948):

> Although at common law there was no duty on a landlord to repair rooms demised to tenants and his liability in that respect was limited to the parts of the premises used in common by all the tenants, the Multiple Dwelling Law, formerly the Tenement House Law, has made the landlord liable for failure to make repairs within leased apartments as well as repairs in portions of the premises used in common. Altz v. Leiberson, 223 N.Y. 16, 134 N.E. 703 [1922]. The statute has also placed an obligation upon the landlord to make repairs even though he has leased the entire premises and is out of possession and although at common law there was no such liability. [Citation omitted.] It was the evident purpose of the statute in the case of a failure of the landlord to repair any part of a multiple dwelling to impose a liability upon him for the benefit of tenants and their families and also persons lawfully on the premises as invitees. In Altz v. Leiberson, *supra,* 233 N.Y. at page 19, 134 N.E. at page 704, Judge Cardozo declared that the right to seek redress was not limited to the city or its officers but extended to all whom there was a purpose to protect. The cases cited by him are cases dealing with violations of similar statutes which were held to give rise to a statutory action for resulting injuries. [27 Misc. 2d at 22-23, 83 N.Y.S.2d at 366.]

Problem

17.10.   N.Y. Mult. Dwell. Law §78 provides:

Every multiple dwelling, including its roof or roofs, and every part thereof and the lot upon which it is situated, shall be kept in good repair. The owner shall be responsible for compliance with the provisions of this section; but the tenant also shall be liable if a violation is caused by his own wilful act, assistance or negligence or that of any member of his family or his guest.

L, the owner of a multiple dwelling in New York City, leased an apartment to T. T notified L that a ceiling in one of the rooms in the apartment needed repairing. Four days after L received notice of the dangerous condition of the ceiling, L sold the multiple dwelling to A. The day after this sale the ceiling fell, injuring T. T sues L to recover the damage T sustained, and L defends on the ground that A was the "owner" of the multiple dwelling at the time the injury was sustained. Is this a good defense? See Pharm v. Lituchy, 283 N.Y. 130, 27 N.E.2d 811 (1940).

FABER v. CRESWICK
31 N.J. 234, 156 A.2d 252 (1959)

FRANCIS, J.

[The plaintiffs, a husband and wife, sued the defendants, a husband and wife who jointly owned a one-family house. The plaintiff-husband rented the entire house for a summer under a written lease which provided that the defendants would "have the house thoroughly clean and in good order and repair at the beginning of this lease." Sometime prior to the summer rental, the defendant-husband undertook to improve the attic as a do-it-yourself project, as a result of which a portion of the stairwell was dangerously covered over with a section of plasterboard. A few days after moving in, the tenant's wife went up to the attic for the first time; when she stepped upon the dangerous section of plasterboard, it collapsed, causing her to fall down the stairwell and suffer serious permanent injuries.]

At the close of the plaintiffs' case, the trial court granted the defense motion for dismissal. He declared that the rights and duties of the parties were controlled by the written lease between Edwin Creswick and E. Corning Faber. Despite the inclusion of an agreement to have the premises in good repair, he held, on the authority of Clyne v. Helmes, 61 N.J.L. 358, 39 A. 767 (Sup. Ct. 1898), that Mrs. Faber, not being a party to the instrument, could not recover for damages resulting from a breach of the covenant. And Mr. Faber's claim for consequential losses was denied because, as a derivative cause of action, its legal efficacy depended upon the right of his wife to recover.

At early common law, when an owner leased premises, there was no implied covenant of habitability, no implied warranty that they were fit or suitable for any particular purpose. The doctrine of caveat emptor was applied, the transaction being likened to a sale of an interest in land. No duty on the part of the lessor to repair or maintain the premises arose out of the relationship of the parties. If such a duty came into existence, it was because of express provision in the instrument of rental. In the absence of an agreement to this effect, the obligation to maintain and to repair devolved upon the tenant.

Originally, even where the lease or rental agreement contained a covenant by the landlord to repair, judicial construction in the majority of jurisdictions sharply limited the remedy afforded for disregard of the undertaking. The action against the defaulting landlord was treated strictly as one for breach of contract. The ex contractu measure of damages was applied and recovery was confined to the cost of making the particular repair. The law took no cognizance of the fact that injuries might have resulted, even to the tenant himself, from the failure of performance.

A number of years ago New Jersey recognized the obvious fact that if a compact to repair is not honored by the landlord, injury is likely to result to the tenant. And our courts espoused the legal concept that where such failure eventuates in injury, a cause of action arises in tort. That is, where there is a negligent omission to perform the duty thus assumed, liability arises for proximate consequential injuries suffered by the tenant. Smith v. Cruse, 2 N.J. Misc. 350, 128 A. 377 (Sup. Ct. 1924), *affirmed* 101 N.J.L. 82, 128 A. 379 (E. & A. 1925); Pabst v. Schwarzstein, 101 N.J.L. 431, 128 A. 879 (Sup. Ct. 1925); Colligan v. 680 Newark Ave. Realty Corp., 131 N.J.L. 520, dissent at page 544, 37 A.2d 206, at page 217 (E. & A. 1944); Michaels v. Brookchester, Inc., *supra.* The Restatement of Torts, §357, adopted this view in 1934. In more recent years, many jurisdictions joined the movement toward the theory of responsibility in tort and in 1946, when the Annotation at 163 A.L.R. 300, 315, was written, it was regarded as doubtful that a majority of the states still limit the action to one in contract and deny recovery for personal injuries.

Once the restrictive contract thesis was put aside, it was held generally that third persons, such as members of the tenant's family, his invitees, and all those on the premises under his right of possession, were entitled to the benefit of the cause of action. Mariotti v. Berns, 114 Cal. App. 2d 666, 251 P.2d 72 (Dist. Ct. App. 1952); Scibek v. O'Connell, 131 Conn. 557, 41 A.2d 251 (Sup. Ct. Err. 1945); Alaimo v. DuPont, 4 Ill. App. 2d 85, 123 N.E.2d 583 (App. Ct. 1955); Page v. Ginsberg, 345 Ill. App. 68, 102 N.E.2d 165 (App. Ct. 1951); Miles v. Boston, R.B. & L.R. Co., 274 Mass. 87, 174 N.E. 200, 202 (Sup. Jud. Ct. 1931); Annotation, 163 A.L.R., *supra* at p. 313. The Restatement of Torts proclaimed this as the rule which best serves the interests of a modern society. Section 357 states it as follows:

> A lessor of land is subject to liability for bodily harm caused to his lessee *and others* upon the land with the consent of the lessee or his sub-lessee by a condition of disrepair existing before or arising after the lessee has taken possession, if
>   (a) the lessor, as such, has agreed by a covenant in the lease or otherwise, to keep the land in repair, and

(b) the disrepair creates an unreasonable risk to persons upon the land which the performance of the lessor's agreement would have prevented. [Emphasis added.]

Although New Jersey had been in the advance guard of the proponents of the tort concept, it declined to abandon the rule of privity. Clyne v. Helmes, *supra*. This doctrinal limitation expressed in 1898 reflected the view announced more than 50 years earlier in the English case of Winterbottom v. Wright, 10 M. & W. 109, 152 Eng. Rep. 402 (Ex. 1842), and widely followed thereafter. That was before the distinction between contract and tort came into clear focus and before the recognition of negligence as an independent basis of responsibility. 2 Harper and James, The Law of Torts 1039 (1956). Under modern social conditions, the precept of privity is sterile and no longer serves the interests of justice. And this apart from other influences, for the obvious reason that it is utterly unrealistic to say that when the head of a family leases premises and bargains for an agreement on the part of the lessor to maintain them in good repair, the parties do not recognize that the pact is in the interest and for the protection of members of his household and others who enter thereon in his right. It is likewise inconsistent with reality to suggest that the parties do not accept their mutual engagements with a full awareness that if the necessary repairs are not made, the safety of such persons will be endangered.

In recent years, there have been many claims that Clyne v. Helmes is archaic and should be abrogated. The last such instance in the highest court of this State occurred in Colligan v. 680 Newark Ave. Realty Corp., *supra*. The proposal was rejected by an evenly divided court and the conflicting views on the subject were set forth forcefully in separate opinions. In our judgment, the present case amply demonstrates that the interests of justice are not served by the doctrine. See Collopy v. Newark Eye and Ear Infirmary, 27 N.J. 29, 141 A.2d 276 (1958); Colligan v. 680 Newark Ave. Realty Corp., *supra,* dissent 131 N.J.L. at pages 546-548, 37 A.2d at pages 218-219. Accordingly, the doctrine of Clyne v. Helmes is overruled and no longer may be considered as the law of this State.

Moreover, even in England, birthplace of the requirement that only persons who are parties to a rental contract can sue on account of a breach, Parliament has abolished it. Salmond, *supra,* at p. 530. In that country, because of the hybrid nature of its Parliament and highest court, once a common law doctrine has been established, only Parliament by the exercise of the lawmaking function can alter its fundamental character. Great Western Railway Co. v. Owners of S.S. Mostyn, 1928 App. Cas. 57, 82 (H.L. 1927); London Street Tramways Company v. London County Council, 1898 App. Cas. 375 (H.L. 1898); 22 Halsbury's Laws of England (3d ed. 1958) 798. In this State, the Judiciary suffers from no such limitation. Revision of an outmoded common law rule is within its competence as well as that of the Legislature. Collopy v. Newark Eye and Ear Infirmary, *supra*.

It is not necessary to be concerned at this time with some of the problems which have perplexed the courts of other states and to some extent our own, with respect to the administration of the concept of liability in tort arising out of breach of a contract to repair. In a number of states responsibility has been placed upon the express or implied retention of the right of re-entry to inspect and maintain the demised premises; others have construed the undertaking to signify the assumption of an obligation to repair only within a reasonable time after the landlord has received notice or acquired knowledge of the dangerous or defective condition. See Michaels v. Brookchester, Inc., *supra;* Prosser, *supra,* 474, 475; 163 A.L.R., *supra* at p. 314. In the present case, the express agreement was that the lessor would have the house "in good order and repair at the beginning of this lease." The hazardous condition was known to the defendants while they were in possession and control, and prior to the lessee's entry. Thus, on the facts liability is not dependent upon any consideration of subsequent control by them or further notice to them of the need for repair. . . .

The judgment is reversed and the cause is remanded for a new trial. Costs to abide the event.[13]

SARGENT v. ROSS
113 N.H. 388, 308 A.2d 528 (1973)

KENISON, C.J.

The question in this case is whether the defendant landlord is liable to the plaintiff in tort for the death of plaintiff's four-year-old daughter who fell to her death from an outdoor stairway at a residential building owned by the defendant in Nashua. The defendant resided in a ground-floor apartment in the building, and her son and daughter-in-law occupied a second story apartment serviced by the stairway from which the child fell. At the time of the accident the child was under the care of the defendant's daughter-in-law who was plaintiff's regular baby-sitter.

Plaintiff brought suit against the daughter-in-law for negligent supervision and against the defendant for negligent construction and maintenance of the stairway which was added to the building by the defendant about eight years before the accident. There was no apparent cause for the fall except for evidence that the stairs were dangerously steep, and that the railing was insufficient to prevent the child from falling over the side. The jury returned

---

13.   Accord Restatement (Second) of Torts §357 (1965). But see Comment a, which admits that "the rule stated in this section has thus far been adopted by only a minority of the courts . . . which have considered it." See generally Annot., Breach of Lessor's Agreement as Ground of Liability for Personal Injury to Tenant or One in Privity with Latter, 78 A.L.R.2d 1238 (1961). See also Reitmeyer v. Sprecher, 431 Pa. 284, 243 A.2d 395 (1968), which held the landlord liable for injuries sustained by the tenant. The landlord had made an agreement to repair the premises.— EDS.

a verdict for the daughter-in-law but found in favor of the plaintiff in her action against the defendant landlord. The defendant seasonably excepted to the denial of her motions for a nonsuit, directed verdict, judgment n.o.v., and to have the verdict set aside, and all questions of law were reserved and transferred to this court by Dunfey, J.

Claiming that there was no evidence that the defendant retained control over the stairway, that it was used in common with other tenants, or that it contained a concealed defect, defendant urges that there was accordingly no duty owing to the deceased child for the defendant to breach. This contention rests upon the general rule which has long obtained in this and most other jurisdictions that a landlord is not liable, except in certain limited situations, for injuries caused by defective or dangerous conditions in the leased premises. E.g., Black v. Fiandaca, 98 N.H. 33, 93 A.2d 663 (1953); Towne v. Thompson, 68 N.H. 317, 44 A. 492 (1895); 2 Powell, Real Property ¶234 (rev. ed. 1971); Prosser, Torts §63 (4th ed. 1971); 1 Tiffany, Real Property §§104, 107 (3d ed. 1939). The plaintiff does not directly attack this rule of nonliability but instead attempts to show, rather futilely under the facts, defendant's control of the stairway. She also relies upon an exception to the general rule of nonliability, to wit, that a landlord is liable for injuries resulting from his negligent repair of the premises. Hunkins v. Amoskeag Mfg. Co., 86 N.H. 356, 169 A. 3 (1933); Rowan v. Amoskeag Mfg. Co., 79 N.H. 409, 109 A. 561 (1920); Prosser, *supra* at 410-12; 1 Tiffany, *supra* at §105; Restatement (Second) of Torts §362 (1965). The issue, as framed by the parties, is whether the rule of nonliability should prevail or whether the facts of this case can be squeezed into the negligent repair or some other exception to the general rule of landlord immunity.

General principles of tort law ordinarily impose liability upon persons for injuries caused by their failure to exercise reasonable care under all the circumstances. Fitzpatrick v. Public Serv. Co., 101 N.H. 35, 131 A.2d 634 (1957); Fissette v. Boston & Maine R.R., 98 N.H. 136, 96 A.2d 303 (1953); Restatement (Second) of Torts §283 (1964). A person is generally negligent for exposing another to an unreasonable risk of harm which foreseeably results in an injury. Quint v. Porietis, 107 N.H. 463, 225 A.2d 179 (1966); State v. Dodge, 103 N.H. 131, 166 A.2d 467 (1960); Restatement (Second) of Torts §282 (1965). But, except in certain instances, landlords are immune from these simple rules of reasonable conduct which govern other persons in their daily activities. This "quasi-sovereignty of the landowner" (2 Harper and James, Law of Torts 1495 (1956)) finds its source in an agrarian England of the dark ages. Kline v. Burns, 111 N.H. 87, 276 A.2d 248 (1971); Clarke v. O'Connor, 140 U.S. App. D.C. 300, 435 F.2d 104, 111 (1970); Harkrider, Tort Liability of a Landlord, 26 Mich. L. Rev. 260, 261 (1928). Due to the untoward favoritism of the law for landlords, it has been justly stated that "the law in this area is a scandal." Quinn and Phillips, The Law of Landlord-Tenant: A Critical Evaluation of the Past with Guidelines for the

Future, 38 Ford. L. Rev. 225 (1969). "For decades the court persistently refused to pierce the hardened wax that preserved the landlord-tenant relationship in its agrarian state." Note, 59 Geo. L.J. 1153, 1163 (1971). But courts and legislatures alike are beginning to reevaluate the rigid rules of landlord-tenant law in light of current needs and principles of law from related areas. See Kline v. Burns *supra;* Lemle v. Breeden, 51 Haw. 426, 462 P.2d 470 (1969); Kline v. 1500 Massachusetts Ave. Apt. Corp., 141 U.S. App. D.C. 370, 439 F.2d 477 (1970); 2 Powell, Real Property ¶220, at 17-75 (rev. ed. 1971); 1970/71 Am. Survey of American Law 365; Note, 121 U. Pa. L. Rev. 378 (1972). "Justifiable dissatisfaction with the rule" of landlord tort immunity (2 Harper and James, *supra* at 1510) compels its reevaluation in a case such as this where we are asked either to apply the rule, and hold the landlord harmless for a foreseeable death resulting from an act of negligence, or to broaden one of the existing exceptions and hence perpetuate an artificial and illogical rule. See Note, Lessor's Duty to Repair: Tort Liability to Persons Injured on the Premises, 62 Harv. L. Rev. 669 (1949).

One court recognized at an early date that ordinary principles of tort liability ought to apply to landlords as other persons. "The ground of liability upon the part of a landlord when he demises dangerous property has nothing special to do with the relation of landlord and tenant. It is the ordinary case of liability for personal misfeasance, which runs through all the relations of individuals to each other." Wilcox v. Hines, 100 Tenn. 538, 548-549, 46 S.W. 297, 299 (1898). Most courts, however, while recognizing from an early date that "the law is unusually strict in exempting the landlord from liability" (Bowe v. Hunking, 135 Mass. 380, 386 (1883)), sought refuge from the rigors of the rule by straining other legal principles such as deceit (Cummings v. Prater, 95 Ariz. 20, 23 n.1, 386 P.2d 27, 29 n.1 (1963); Note, Landlord and Tenant: Defects Existing at the Time of the Lease, 35 Ind. L.J. 361 (1960)) and by carving out exceptions to the general rule of nonliability. 2 Harper and James, *supra* at 1510. Thus, a landlord is now generally conceded to be liable in tort for injuries resulting from defective and dangerous conditions in the premises if the injury is attributable to (1) a hidden danger in the premises of which the landlord but not the tenant is aware, (2) premises leased for public use, (3) premises retained under the landlord's control, such as common stairways, or (4) premises negligently repaired by the landlord. See generally 2 Powell, Real Property ¶234 (rev. ed. 1971); Prosser, Torts §63 (4th ed. 1971); Restatement (Second) of Torts §§358-62 (1965).

As is to be expected where exceptions to a rule of law form the only basis of liability, the parties in this action concentrated at trial and on appeal on whether any of the exceptions applied, particularly whether the landlord or the tenant had control of the stairway. 1 Tiffany, Real Property §109 (3d ed. 1939). The determination of the question of which party had control of the defective part of the premises causing the injury has generally been considered dispositive of the landlord's liability. E.g., Black v. Fiandaca, 98 N.H.

33, 93 A.2d 663 (1953); Flanders v. New Hampshire Sav. Bank, 90 N.H. 285, 7 A.2d 233 (1939). This was a logical modification to the rule of nonliability since ordinarily a landlord can reasonably be expected to maintain the property and guard against injuries only in common areas and other areas under his control. A landlord, for example, cannot fairly be held responsible in most instances for an injury arising out of the tenant's negligent maintenance of the leased premises. Manning v. Leavitt Co., 90 N.H. 167, 5 A.2d 667 (1939). But the control test is insufficient since it substitutes a facile and conclusive test for a reasoned consideration of whether due care was exercised under all the circumstances. See Clarke v. O'Connor, 140 U.S. App. D.C. 300, 435 F.2d 104, 111-113 (1970).

There was evidence from which the jury could find that the landlord negligently designed or constructed a stairway which was dangerously steep or that she negligently failed to remedy or adequately warn the deceased of the danger. A proper rule of law would not preclude recovery in such a case by a person foreseeably injured by a dangerous hazard solely because the stairs serviced one apartment instead of two. But that would be the result if the control test were applied to this case, since this was not a "common stairway" or otherwise under the landlord's control. See generally Annot., 26 A.L.R.2d 468 (1952). While we could strain this test to the limits and find control in the landlord (Gibson v. Hoppman, 108 Conn. 401, 143 A. 635 (1928)), as plaintiff suggests, we are not inclined to so expand the fiction since we agree that "it is no part of the general law of negligence to exonerate a defendant simply because the condition attributable to his negligence has passed beyond his control before it causes injury. . . ." 2 Harper and James, Law of Torts §27.16, at 1509 (1956); see id. at 207 (Supp. to vol. 2 1968).

The anomaly of the general rule of landlord tort immunity and the inflexibility of the standard exceptions, such as the control exception, is pointedly demonstrated by this case. A child is killed by a dangerous condition of the premises. Both husband and wife tenants testify that they could do nothing to remedy the defect because they did not own the house nor have authority to alter the defect. But the landlord claims that she should not be liable because the stairs were not under her control. Both of these contentions are premised on the theory that the other party should be responsible. So the orthodox analysis would leave us with neither landlord nor tenant responsible for dangerous conditions on the premises. This would be both illogical and intolerable, particularly since neither party then would have any legal reason to remedy or take precautionary measures with respect to dangerous conditions. In fact, the traditional "control" rule actually discourages a landlord from remedying a dangerous condition since his repairs may be evidence of his control. Hunkins v. Amoskeag Mfg. Co., 86 N.H. 356, 169 A. 3 (1933); see Flanders v. New Hampshire Sav. Bank, 90 N.H. 285, 7 A.2d 233 (1939). Nor can there be serious doubt that ordinarily the landlord is best able to remedy dangerous conditions, particularly where a substantial alteration is required. See Kline v. Burns, 111 N.H. 87, 276 A.2d 248 (1971); Note 62 Harv. L. Rev. 669 (1949).

In Wiggin v. Kent McCray, Inc., 109 N.H. 342, 252 A.2d 418 (1969), which involved an injury from a defective door in a shopping center, we considered the control question but analyzed the problem in ordinary negligence terms. In fact, the issue of control is relevant to the determination of liability only insofar as it bears on the question of what the landlord and tenant reasonably should have believed in regard to the division of responsibility for *maintaining* the premises in a safe condition. The basic claim in this case involves only the design or construction of the steps; the maintenance of the stairs was not seriously in issue, except perhaps concerning the lack of precautions, since the evidence was clear that the stairway was dry and free of debris. The inquiry should have centered upon the unreasonableness of the pitch of the steps and the unreasonableness of failing to take precautionary measures to reduce the danger of falls.

Similarly, the truly pertinent questions involved in determining who should bear responsibility for the loss in this case were clouded by the question of whether the accident was caused by a hidden defect or secret danger. E.g., Clark v. Sharpe, 76 N.H. 446, 83 A. 1090 (1912). The mere fact that a condition is open and obvious, as was the steepness of the steps in this case, does not preclude it from being unreasonably dangerous, and defendants are not infrequently "held liable for creating or maintaining a perfectly obvious danger of which plaintiffs are fully aware." 2 Harper and James, *supra* at 1493; Williamson v. Derry Elec. Co., 89 N.H. 216, 196 A. 265 (1938) (slippery floor); Cummings v. Prater, 95 Ariz. 20, 386 P.2d 27 (1963). Additionally, while the dangerous quality of the steps might have been obvious to an adult, the danger and risk would very likely be imperceptible to a young child such as the deceased. See Dorais v. Paquin, 113 N.H. 187, 304 A.2d 369 (1973). The obviousness of the risk is primarily relevant to the basic issue of a plaintiff's contributory negligence. See Williamson v. Derry Elec. Co. *supra.* Here, the trial court properly withdrew the issue of the contributory negligence of the deceased from the jury because of the child's very young age. See Dorais v. Paquin *supra.*

Finally, plaintiff's reliance on the negligent repairs exception to the rule of nonliability (Hunkins v. Amoskeag Mfg. Co., 86 N.H. 356, 169 A. 3 (1933)) would require us to broaden the exception to include the negligent construction of improvements to the premises. We recognize that this would be no great leap in logic (see Bohlen, Landlord and Tenant 35 Harv. L. Rev. 633, 648 (1922)), but we think it more realistic instead to consider reversing the general rule of nonliability (Note, 62 Harv. L. Rev. 669 (1949)) since "[t]he exceptions have . . . produced a twisting of legal concepts which seems undesirable." Id. at 676. And "it appears to us that to search for gaps and exceptions in a legal doctrine . . . which exists only because of the somnolence of the common law and the courts is to perpetuate further judicial fictions when preferable alternatives exist. . . . The law of landlord-tenant relations cannot be so frail as to shatter when confronted with modern urban realties and a frank appraisal of the underlying issues." Lemle v. Breeden, 51 Haw. 426, 435, 462 P.2d 470, 475 (1969) (establishing an implied warranty of habitability in dwelling leases). The emphasis on control and other exceptions to the rule of nonliability, both at trial and on appeal, unduly complicated the jury's task and diverted effort and attention from the central issue of the unreasonableness of the risk.

In recent years, immunities from tort liability affording "special protection in some types of relationships have been steadily giving way" in this and other jurisdictions. 2 Harper and James, *supra* at 1508. See Hurley v. Town of Hudson, 112 N.H. 365, 296 A.2d 905 (1972) (sovereign tort immunity disapproved); Dean v. Smith, 106 N.H. 314, 211 A.2d 410 (1965) and Briere v. Briere, 107 N.H. 432, 224 A.2d 588 (1966) (parental tort immunity abolished); Derby v. Public Serv. Co., 100 N.H. 53, 119 A.2d 335 (1955) (real estate vendor's immunity discarded and ordinary negligence principles applied) (see Annot., 48 A.L.R.3d 1027, 1039 (1973)); Welch v. Frisbie Memorial Hosp., 90 N.H. 337, 9 A.2d 761 (1939) (charitable tort immunity not adopted); Gilman v. Gilman, 78 N.H. 4, 95 A. 657 (1915) (husband's tort immunity from wife declared abolished by married woman's act). "Considerations of human safety within an urban community dictate that the landowner's relative immunity, which is primarily supported by values of the agrarian past, be modified in favor of negligence principles of landowner liability." Recent Development, Abrogation of Common-Law Entrant Classes of Trespasser, Licensee, and Invitee, 25 Vand. L. Rev. 623, 640 (1972). "In modern times the immunities have rightly though gradually, been giving way to the overriding social view that where there is foreseeability of substantial harm landowners, as well as other members of society, should generally be subjected to a reasonable duty of care to avoid it." Taylor v. New Jersey Highway Auth., 22 N.J. 454, 463, 126 A.2d 313, 317 (1956). We think that now is the time for the landlord's limited tort immunity to be relegated to the history books where it more properly belongs.

This conclusion springs naturally and inexorably from our recent decision in Kline v. Burns, 111 N.H. 87, 276 A.2d 248 (1971). *Kline* was an apartment rental claim suit in which the tenant claimed that the premises were uninhabitable. Following a small vanguard of other jurisdictions, we modernized the landlord-tenant contractual relationship by holding that there is an implied warranty of habitability in an apartment lease transaction. As a necessary predicate to our decision, we discarded from landlord-tenant law "that obnoxious legal cliché, caveat emptor." Pines v. Perssion, 14 Wis. 2d 590, 596, 111 N.W.2d 409, 413 (1961). In so doing, we discarded the very legal foundation and justification for the landlord's immunity in tort for injuries to the tenant or third persons. See Marston v. Andler, 80 N.H. 564, 122 A. 329 (1923); Clark v. Sharpe, 76 N.H. 446, 83 A. 1090 (1912); Wilcox v. Hines, 100 Tenn. 538, 46 S.W. 297 (1898); Comment, 45

N.Y.U.L. Rev. 943, 951 n.54 (1970); Notes, 62 Harv. L. Rev. 669 (1949); 35 Ind. L.J. 361 (1960). "Judicial discarding of the sale concept [and, hence, of caveat emptor] would leave the courts with an easy recourse to established principles of law; the lessor would fall within the general proposition underlying many areas of tort law that he who owns or is in a position to control or is responsible for things or persons has the duty to prevent their harming others. And the large body of negligence principles which have developed in other fields would bound this duty." Note, 62 Harv. L. Rev. 669, 678-79 (1949).

To the extent that Kline v. Burns did not do so, we today discard the rule of "caveat lessee" and the doctrine of landlord nonliability in tort to which it gave birth. We thus bring up to date the other half of landlord-tenant law. Henceforth, landlords as other persons must exercise reasonable care not to subject others to an unreasonable risk of harm. Scott v. Simons, 54 N.H. 426 (1874); Wilcox v. Hines *supra;* see Cummings v. Prater, 95 Ariz. 20, 386 P.2d 27 (1963); Presson v. Mountain States Properties, Inc., 18 Ariz. App. 176, 501 P.2d 17 (1972); Harkrider, Tort Liability of a Landlord, 26 Mich. L. Rev. 260 (1928). A landlord must act as a reasonable person under all of the circumstances including the likelihood of injury to others, the probable seriousness of such injuries, and the burden of reducing or avoiding the risk. See Quint v. Porietis, 107 N.H. 463, 225 A.2d 179 (1966); Flynn v. Gordon, 86 N.H. 198, 165 A. 715 (1933); Smith v. Arbaugh's Restaurant, Inc., 152 U.S. App. D.C. 86, 469 F.2d 97, 100 (1972); Conway v. O'Brien, 111 F.2d 611, 612 (2d Cir. 1940) (L. Hand, J.). See generally Note, 121 U. Pa. L. Rev. 378 (1972). We think this basic principle of responsibility for landlords as for others "best expresses the principles of justice and reasonableness upon which our law of torts is founded." Dowd v. Portsmouth Hosp., 105 N.H. 53, 59, 193 A.2d 788, 792 (1963) (on rehearing). The questions of control, hidden defects and common or public use, which formerly had to be established as a prerequisite to even considering the negligence of a landlord, will now be relevant only inasmuch as they bear on the basic tort issues such as the foreseeability and unreasonableness of the particular risk of harm. Cf. Clarke v. O'Connor, 140 U.S. App. D.C. 300, 435 F.2d 104, 111-113 (1970). The Massachusetts Supreme Judicial Court recently made the following pertinent remarks in a case abolishing the distinction in the standards of care owed by land occupiers to licensees and invitees: "In the absence of legislative action, we believe that this 'reasonable care in all the circumstances' standard will provide the most effective way to achieve an allocation of the costs of human injury which conforms to present community values." Mounsey v. Ellard, Mass., 297 N.E.2d 43, 52 (1973).

The abiding respect of this court for precedent and stability in the law is balanced by an appreciation of the need for responsible growth and change in rules that have failed to keep pace with modern developments in social and juridical thought. When we abolished the tort immunity of a parent from suit by his child, another artificial and inequitable exception to the general rules of tort liability, we made the following observation which is equally pertinent to this case:

> If after thorough examination a prior judicial decision seems manifestly out of accord with modern conditions of life, it should not be followed as a controlling precedent. 37 Harv. L. Rev. 409, 414. Finding no supportable rationale upon which this judicially created exception to the ordinary rules of liability can be predicated, justice demands and reason dictates that a change be made from the previous holding in such a situation.

Dean v. Smith, 106 N.H. 314, 318, 211 A.2d 410, 413 (1965); see In re Frolich Estate, 112 N.H. 320, 295 A.2d 448 (1972).

Our decision will shift the primary focus of inquiry for judge and jury from the traditional question of "who had control?" to a determination of whether the landlord, and the injured party, exercised due care under all the circumstances. Perhaps even more significantly, the ordinary negligence standard should help insure that a landlord will take whatever precautions are reasonably necessary under the circumstances to reduce the likelihood of injuries from defects in his property. "It is appropriate that the landlord who will retain ownership of the premises and any permanent improvements should bear the cost of repairs necessary to make the premises safe. . . ." Kline v. Burns, 111 N.H. 87, 92, 276 A.2d 248, 251 (1971).

Although the trial court's instructions to the jury in the instant case were cast according to the traditional exceptions of control and hidden danger, the charge clearly set forth the elements of ordinary negligence which were presented by the court as a prerequisite to a finding of liability on either issue. Thus, the jury could find that the defendant was negligent in the design or construction of the steep stairway or in failing to take adequate precautionary measures to reduce the risk of injury. We have carefully reviewed the record and conclude that there is sufficient evidence, on the basis of the principles set forth above, to support the verdict of the jury which had the benefit of a view. See Vezina v. Amoskeag Realty Co., 110 N.H. 66, 260 A.2d 115 (1969); Manning v. Freeman, 105 N.H. 272, 198 A.2d 14 (1964); Dowd v. Portsmouth Hosp., 105 N.H. 53, 193 A.2d 788 (1963); Blados v. Blados, 151 Conn. 391, 198 A.2d 213 (1964). Both plaintiff and the wife tenant testified that the stairs were too steep, and the husband tenant testified that his wife complained to him of this fact. While the defendant landlord did not testify, the jury could find that she knew that this steep stairway was frequently used by the young children for whom her daughter-in-law was the regular, daily babysitter. In any event, the use of these steps by young children should have been anticipated by the defendant. Saad v. Papageorge, 82 N.H. 294, 133 A. 24 (1926); see Manning v. Freeman, 105 N.H. 272, 198 A.2d 14 (1964).

The verdict of the jury is sustained, and the order is

Exceptions overruled; judgment on the verdict.

GRIMES, J., did not participate; DUNCAN, J., concurred in the result; the others concurred.[14]

Problem

17.11. L is the owner of an apartment building. A, a guest of one of the tenants in L's building, was leaving the apartment building about nine o'clock one rainy evening. The walkway leading to the street was slippery because of ice which formed as the rain fell. The day had been cold and dreary, and rain had been falling since morning. No sand or ashes had been placed on the walkway. A slipped and fell and was injured. Is L liable? See Pessagno v. Euclid Investment Co., 112 F.2d 577 (D.C. Cir. 1940).

SECTION 2.   THE TENANT'S RESPONSIBILITIES

A.   Duty to Refrain from Disturbing Other Tenants

LOUISIANA LEASING CO. v. SOKOLOW
48 Misc. 2d 1014, 266 N.Y.S.2d 447
(City of New York Civ. Ct., Queens County, 1966)

FITZPATRICK, J.

This is a proceeding to remove the respondents from the premises of the petitioner upon the ground that they are objectionable tenants. The applicable clauses in the lease between the parties contain the following:

> 15.   No Tenant shall make or permit any disturbing noises in the building by himself, his family, servants, employees, agents, visitors and licensees, nor do or permit anything by such persons that will interfere with the rights, comforts or convenience of other tenants.

Paragraph 9 of said lease states in part as follows:

> 9.   Tenant and Tenant's family, servants, employees, agents, visitors, and licensees shall observe faithfully and comply strictly with the Rules and Regulations set forth on the back of this lease. . . . Tenant agrees that any violation of any of said Rules and Regulations by Tenant or by a member of Tenant's family, or by servants, or employees, or agents, or visitors, or licensees, shall be deemed a substantial violation by Tenant of this lease and of the Tenancy.

---

14.   See Restatement (Second) of Property (Landlord and Tenant) chs. 17-19.—EDS.

The landlord alleges that the noise from respondents' apartment is destroying the peace and quiet of the new tenants immediately underneath them. The claim is and the proof attempted to establish that the noise is of such a character as to constitute a violation of the provisions of the lease set out above. The respondents have been in possession over two and one-half years and their lease runs until December 31, 1966. It is significant that the respondents over that period gave no evidence of being objectionable until the new tenants, the Levins, moved in last October. From the court's opportunity to observe them, both the respondents and the tenants below seem to be people who under other circumstances would be congenial and happy neighbors. It is unfortunate that they have had to come to court to face each other in an eye-ball to eye-ball confrontation.

The respondents are a young couple with two small children, ages 4 and 2. It was admitted by them that the children do run and play in their apartment, but they say that they keep shoes off their feet when at home. The father says that he does walk back and forth at various times when at home, particularly to the refrigerator during the TV commercials and, also, to other areas of the apartment as necessity requires, but denies that he does this excessively or in a loud or heavy manner. They maintain that whatever noises emanate from their apartment are the normal noises of everyday living.

The tenants below, the Levins, are a middle-aged couple who go to business each day. They are like many others of our fellow citizens, who daily go forth to brave the vicissitudes of the mainstream of city life. At the end of the toilsome day, like tired fish, they are only too happy to seek out these quiet backwaters of the metropolis to recuperate for the next day's bout with the task of earning a living. They have raised their own child and are past the time when the patter of little feet overhead is a welcome sound. They say they love their new apartment and that it is just what they have been looking for and would hate to have to give it up because of the noise from above. Mrs. Levin is associated with the publisher of a teen-age magazine and realizes that she is in a bind between her desire for present comfort and the possible loss of two future subscribers. She consequently hastens to add that she loves children and has no objection to the Sokolows because of them — that it is solely the noise of which she complains. So we have the issue.

The landlord's brief states that in its "view, the conduct that is even more objectionable than the noise, is the uncooperative attitude of the Tenants." This observation is probably prompted by testimony to the effect that Mr. Sokolow, one of the upstairs tenants, is reported to have said "This is my home, and no one can tell me what to do in my own home." This is a prevalent notion that stems from the ancient axiom that a man's home is his castle.

The difficulty of the situation here is that Mr. Sokolow's castle is directly above the castle of Mr. Levin. That a man's home is his castle is an old

Anglo-legal maxim hoary with time and the sanction of frequent repetition. It expressed an age when castles were remote, separated by broad moors, and when an intruder had to force moat and wall to make his presence felt within. The tranquillity of the King's Peace, the seclusion of a clandestine romance and the opportunity, like Hamlet, to deliver a soliloquy from the ramparts without fear of neighborly repercussions were real. Times however change, and all change is not necessarily progress as some sage has perceptively reminded us. For in an era of modernity and concentrated urban living, when high-rise apartment houses have piled castle upon castle for some twenty or more stories in the air, it is extremely difficult to equate these modern counterparts with their drawbridged and turreted ancestors. The builders of today's cubicular confusion have tried to compensate for the functional construction by providing lobbies in Brooklyn Renaissance that rival in decor the throne room at Knossos. They have also provided built-in air-conditioning, closed circuit television, playrooms and laundromats. There are tropical balconies to cool the fevered brow in the short, hot northern summer; which the other nine months serve as convenient places to store the floor mop and scrub pail. On the debit side they also contain miles of utility and sanitary piping which convey sound throughout the building with all the gusto of the mammoth organ in the Mormon Tabernacle at Salt Lake City. Also, the prefabricated or frugally plastered walls have their molecules so critically near the separation level that they oppose almost no barrier at all to alien sounds from neighboring apartments. This often forces one into an embarrassingly auditory intimacy with the surrounding tenants. Such are the hazards of modern apartment house living. One of my brother justices, the Honorable Harold J. Crawford, has opined that in this day in our large cities it is fruitless to expect the solitude of the sylvan glen. (Twin Elm Mgt. Corp. v. Banks, 181 Misc. 96, 46 N.Y.S.2d 952.) In this we concur. Particularly so, when we consider that all of us are daily assaulted by the "roaring traffic's boom," the early-morning carillon of the garbage cans and the determined whine of homing super-sonic jets. Further, children and noise have been inseparable from a time whence the mind of man runneth not to the contrary. This Court, therefore, is not disposed to attempt anything so schizophrenic at this late date.

Weighing the equities in this difficult controversy, the court finds that the Sokolows were there first, with a record as good tenants. The Levins underneath seem to be good tenants also. This was attested to by the superintendent who was called upon to testify. He made the understatement of the year when he said. "I kept out of the middle of this fight. It's near Christmas and this is no time for me to fight with tenants"—a piece of homely pragmatism which would have gladdened the heart of William James.

In his own crude way the superintendent may have suggested the solution to this proceeding. This is a time for peace on earth to men of good will. As the court noted above, they are all nice people and a little mutual forbearance and understanding of each other's problems should resolve the issues to everyone's satisfaction.

The evidence on the main question shows that in October the respondents Sokolow were already in a fixed relationship to the landlord. The Levins, on the other hand, were not — their position was a mobile one. They had the opportunity to ascertain what was above them in the event they decided to move in below. They elected to move in and afterwards attempted to correct the condition complained of. Since upon the evidence the overhead noise has been shown to be neither excessive nor deliberate, the court is not constrained to flex its muscles and evict the respondents. Upon the entire case the respondents are entitled to a final order dismissing the petition.

Problem

17.12. Suppose in the principal case the Levins had vacated the apartment and ceased paying rent claiming that the "noise" of the Sokolows constituted a "constructive eviction." Would this be a good defense in a suit brought by the landlord against the Levins for the rent due after they vacated the apartment? Suppose the Levins had moved in first. Do you believe Judge Fitzpatrick would (should) have ruled differently?

B. Duty to Make Repairs, in the Absence of a Covenant to Repair

KING v. COONEY-ECKSTEIN CO.
66 Fla. 246, 63 So. 659 (1913)

WHITFIELD, J. In an action to recover compensatory damages for personal injuries alleged to have been caused by the negligence of the defendant corporation, the court directed a verdict for the defendant; and to a judgment rendered on the verdict, the plaintiff took writ of error.

It appears that the defendant was the lessee of a wharf or dock, which the lessor covenanted "to keep in usual repair"; that the lessor reserved "the right to discharge at said dock one or more vessels each year" and also the privilege of "loading or unloading its lighter over said leased premises without charge"; that more than two years after the lease began a decayed plank in the dock gave way under a truck containing lumber, thereby injuring the plaintiff who was carrying the lumber to a ship being loaded at the dock; that the defect in the plank was not patent to casual observation, but could have been seen by a reasonably careful inspection.

It does not appear that any one other than the lessee was in control of or occupied the wharf or dock at the time of the injury, even though the loading of the vessel may not have been under the direction of the defendant lessee. The occupancy and control of the dock and the liabilities incident thereto were apparently that of the lessee in possession under the lease.

For the defendant in error it is contended that the lessor and not the lessee is liable for injuries caused by the defective condition of the wharf or dock. This contention ignores the fact that both the lessor and the lessee may be liable under certain circumstances and the prima facie liability rests primarily upon the one in actual occupancy and control of the premises.

At common law the tenant and occupier of premises is bound, as between himself and the public, to keep the premises in such condition that they will be reasonably safe for persons who go lawfully upon the premises by express or implied invitation; and such tenant or occupier is prima facie liable for damages caused by defects in or dangers on the premises that reasonably could have been avoided by appropriate care taken by the tenant or occupier. This is the law even though the lessor covenanted to keep the premises in repair.

The liability of the lessee is grounded upon his duty in being the occupant to keep the premises in reasonably safe condition for those who go thereon by express or implied invitation. See 1 Thompson on Neg. Sec. 1154 et seq.; Keeler v. Lederer Realty Corp. 26 R.I. 524, 59 A. 855; Hussey v. Ryan, 64 Md. 426; Abbott v. Jackson, 84 Me. 449, 24 A. 900; 24 Cyc. 1125.

The common law rule of liability of lessees who have control or occupancy of premises, for injuries caused by the defective or dangerous condition of the premises where such defective or dangerous condition reasonably should have been known to and remedied by the occupying tenant, is in force in this State. . . .

The plaintiff did not assume the risks incident to the negligence of the lessee in not having the dock in safe condition, when the danger was not obvious and was unknown to the plaintiff. Assumption of risk and contributory negligence when available are affirmative defenses; and neither appears in the evidence.

The injuries sustained by the plaintiff are apparently a natural and proximate result of the defendant's negligence in not exercising due care to keep the dock in a reasonably safe condition.

A verdict for the plaintiff on the evidence would not have been unlawful; and for the error in directing a verdict for the defendant the judgment is reversed.

Problem

17.13. L and T entered into a written lease of a building abutting on a street. The lease contained no covenants to repair, but T convenanted to keep the sidewalk free of snow and ice. The roof on the building pitched toward the street, and the eaves and gutters were out of repair at the time the lease was made. When it rained, water was discharged upon the sidewalk. Not long after the lease was made, water falling from the defective gutters formed into ice on the sidewalk and A, who was passing along the sidewalk, slipped and fell and was severely injured. On what basis, if any, is L liable to A? On what basis, if any, is T liable to A? Compare Bixby v. Thurber, 80 N.H. 411, 118 A. 99 (1922), with Lee v. McLaughlin, 86 Me. 410, 30 A. 65 (1894).

SUYDAM v. JACKSON
54 N.Y. 450 (Commn. App. 1873)

Appeal from judgment of the General Term of the Court of Common Pleas for the city and county of New York, affirming a judgment in favor of plaintiffs entered on a verdict.

This action was brought to recover a quarter's rent alleged to be due under a lease of certain premises situate in the city of New York.

On the 30th of March, 1866, the plaintiffs leased to the defendant the store known as No. 48 Front street, in the city of New York, for the term of three years from the 1st of May, 1866, at the yearly rental of $2,600, payable quarterly. The lease contained no covenant to repair on the part of the landlord, but that the Croton water and gas-pipes were to be kept in repair by the lessee. The demised premises consisted of a store five stories high, the main floor being about seventy feet long; in the rear of the first floor there was an extension, about eight or nine feet in width, and extending no higher than the first story; the roof of the extension was of glass; it was occupied as an office. On the 1st day of May, 1868, the defendant left, at the plaintiff's office, a notice that the premises were untenantable and unfit for occupancy, and that he surrendered possession of the same. The alleged untenantableness specified was that the roof, etc., had become "so injured, corroded and worn out by the action of the elements and by age, as to leak" in such a manner that the same were unfit for occupancy. In support of these allegations, the defendant's witnesses testified that after the tenants had been in possession nearly a year, the glass roof over the extension, in the rear of the first floor, began to leak in the beginning of 1867, when the snow broke up, about March of that year; that it began to leak a little at first, and afterward, during the ensuing summer and winter it leaked some, and leaked badly when it rained, rendering the office damp and admitting the water. That the glass roof of the extension was dilapidated and was decayed at the joining of the glass and the frame, and the crossing of the extension, where the leakage took place. Neither the defendant nor his sub-tenants repaired the glass roof when it began to leak from said decay, nor made any repairs. No proof was given as to any injury or damage to the premises during the term, except such as arose from natural decay, and no leakage, except that above noticed from the roof, over the extension in the rear.

At the conclusion of his evidence the court directed a verdict for the plaintiff; exceptions were ordered to be heard in the first instance at the General Term.

EARL, C. The sole defence to this action is based upon the statute (Laws of 1860, chap. 345) which provides "that the lessees or occupants of any building, which shall, without any fault or neglect on their part, be destroyed or be so injured by the elements or any other cause as to be untenantable and unfit for occupancy, shall not be liable or bound to pay rent to the lessors or owners thereof, after such destruction or injury, unless otherwise expressly provided by written agreement or covenant; and the lessees or occupants may thereupon quit and surrender possession of the leasehold premises, and of the land so leased or occupied." [15]

The roof of the small extension, in the rear of the main building, became gradually out of repair so as to leak badly, and the sole question for us to determine is, whether the demised premises were thus "injured" within the meaning of the statute. The leaking was not caused by any sudden, unusual, or fortuitous circumstance, but seems to have been caused by gradual wear and decay. The courts below held that the case was not within the statute, and that the lessee remained liable for the rent.

To be able properly to understand this statute, it is well to see what the common law was before it was enacted, and to ascertain, if we can, the mischief it was intended to remedy. At common law the lessor was, without express covenant to that effect, under no obligation to repair, and if the demised premises became, during the term, wholly untenantable by destruction thereof by fire, flood, tempest or otherwise, the lessee still remained liable for the rent unless exempted from such liability by some express covenant in his lease. (Walton v. Waterhouse, 3 Saund., 422; Hallett v. Wylie, 3 John., 44; Graves v. Berdan, 26 N.Y. 498; 3 Kent's Com., 465.) But the lessee was under an implied covenant, from his relation to his landlord, to make what are called "tenantable repairs." Comyn, in his work on Landlord and Tenant, at page 188, states the implied covenant or obligation of a lessee growing out of the relation of landlord and tenant to be "to treat the premises demised in such manner that no injury be done to the inheritance, but that the estate may revert to the lessor undeteriorated by the willful or negligent conduct of the lessee. He is bound, therefore, to keep the soil in a proper state of cultivation, to preserve the timber and to support and repair the buildings. These duties fall upon him without any express covenant on his part, and a breach of them will, in general, render him liable to be punished for waste." (To the same effect, see Taylor's Land. & Ten., 163, and 1 Wash. on Real Prop., 429.) The lessee was not bound to make substantial, lasting or general repairs, but only such ordinary repairs as were necessary to prevent waste and decay of the premises. If a window in a

---

15. The present version of this statute is N.Y. Real Prop. Law §227.—EDS.

dwelling should blow in, the tenant could not permit it to remain out and the storms to beat in and greatly injure the premises without liability for permissive waste; and if a shingle or board on the roof should blow off or become out of repair, the tenant could not permit the water, in time of rain, to flood the premises, and thus injure them, without a similar liability. He being present, a slight effort and expense on his part could save a great loss; and hence the law justly casts the burden upon him. I am not aware that it was ever claimed that it was unjust that he should bear this burden, or that any complaint was ever made of the rule of law which cast it upon him. It cannot, therefore, be presumed that the statute of 1860 was passed to shift this burden from the lessee to the lessor.

But it was considered a hard rule that the tenant who had from ignorance or inadvertence failed to protect himself by covenants in his lease, should be obliged to pay rent in cases where, from fire, flood or other fortuitous causes, the premises were destroyed or so injured as to be untenantable, and I am of opinion that it was to change this rule and cast the misfortune upon the owner of the demised premises that the law was enacted. The statute provides for two alternatives when the premises are "destroyed" or "injured." The first alternative, evidently, has reference to a sudden and total destruction by the elements, acting with unusual power, or by human agency. The latter has reference to a case of injury to the premises, short of a total destruction, occasioned in the same way. If the legislature had intended to provide that the tenant should cease to be liable for rent when the premises from any cause became so damaged or out of repair as to be untenantable, it would have been easy to have expressed the intent in apt and proper language. The terms "destroyed" and "injured" do not, to my mind, convey the idea of gradual deterioration from the ordinary action of the elements in producing decay, common to all human structures.

I am, therefore, of the opinion that the courts below did not err in the construction which they gave to this statute, and this conclusion is not without the support of learned judges. (Bloomer v. Merrill, 1 Daly 485; Austin v. Field, 7 Abb. (N.S.) 291.)

The judgment must be affirmed with costs.

KENNEDY v. KIDD
557 P.2d 467 (Okla. Ct. App. 1976)

Box, J. This cause is before us on a petition for writ of certiorari pursuant to 12 O.S. 1971, Ch. 15, App. 2, Rules 1.50-1.67. Petitioner, Administrator of the estate of Dafford O. Kennedy, deceased, seeks review of a certified interlocutory order overruling her demurrer to the petition of Neona S. Kidd, respondent. We grant certiorari, reverse the trial court's order and remand with instructions to dismiss respondent's action.

I

Some time in 1974 the decedent, Dafford O. Kennedy, rented an apartment from the respondent pursuant to an oral agreement. It is agreed that a month to month tenancy was thereby established. On June 1, 1974, while alone in his apartment, the decedent died of an apparent heart attack. His partially decomposed body was not discovered until a week later. According to respondent, the putrid odors associated with the decedent's body necessitated the complete refurbishing of the apartment.

Respondent presented petitioner, the decedent's administrator, with a timely claim for payment of rent and reimbursement of her expenses in renovating the apartment. This claim was disallowed except for some $90.00 in unpaid rent. Respondent then brought suit to enforce the claim, seeking more than $4,000 in expenses and rental fees for the two month period during which the apartment was being renovated. Petitioner filed a general demurrer to respondent's petition. The trial judge overruled the demurrer but upon petitioner's motion, certified the order for purposes of interlocutory review.

II

Petitioner contends that under no theory of recovery, equitable or legal, may a decedent's estate be held responsible for loss of the kind which respondent claims to have suffered. In order for respondent to recover from the estate, petitioner maintains, it would have to be shown that respondent's loss was caused by some act or omission of the decedent or that the loss became in some other way an indebtedness of the decedent during his lifetime. Respondent is unable to allege either of these circumstances here, petitioner contends, because the loss was in fact only an unfortunate consequence of the decedent's death. And losses of that nature, petitioner asserts, ought to be considered damnum absque injuria. That is to say, respondent's loss is one which gives rise to no cause of action and for which the law affords no remedy. See, e.g., Alabama Power Co. v. Ickes, 302 U.S. 464, 58 S. Ct. 300, 82 L. Ed. 374.

Respondent concedes much of petitioner's argument. She agrees that she would have no cause of action in tort, or in waste, and she disclaims any intent to rely upon any acts or omissions of the decedent during his lifetime. Her claim is predicated solely upon the landlord-tenant relationship which existed between the decedent and respondent. Respondent puts forth two theories for holding the estate liable: (1) the decedent, and his estate after him, was bound by a common law duty to return the leasehold in the same general condition in which it was at the time of letting, and, as a consequence, the estate was liable for all damages to the apartment over and above ordinary "wear and tear"; and (2) public policy demands that the tenant's estate, rather than the landlord, bear losses of the kind at issue here. We consider the merits of each of respondent's theories of recovery below.

III

Respondent contends that the common law imposes an implied covenant upon the tenant to redeliver the premises at the end of the term in the same general condition in which they were in at the time of the letting. Because there was no written lease providing otherwise, respondent maintains, the decedent was bound by this implied covenant. The decedent's estate, moreover, assumed this obligation at his death because a month to month tenancy is not terminated by the death of the tenant; the estate simply steps into the decedent's shoes and may terminate the tenancy only by giving the statutorily required notice. 41 O.S. 1971, §4. Petitioner should be held liable for the breach of this implied covenant, respondent argues, because the damages to the apartment resulting from the decedent's death are precisely the kind of damages for which a tenant ought to be held legally responsible.

As we have noted, both parties agree that a month to month (or periodic) tenancy was created by the oral agreement between respondent and the decedent. The month to month tenancy, which is of course a creature of the common law, is recognized by statute in Oklahoma, 41 O.S. 1971, §3. Like its common law predecessor, a chief attribute of the statutory month to month tenancy is that it continues in force until proper notice of termination is given. 41 O.S. 1971, §4. It would seem, then, that like the common law tenancy, the statutory tenancy could not be terminated merely by the death of either the lessor or the lessee; the appropriate notice would still be required. See generally Annot., 68 A.L.R. 590, 594 (1930). The estate of the deceased landlord or tenant would therefore assume the decedent's obligations under the tenancy until the notice to terminate was given. See, e.g., Baum v. Tazwell, 26 N.J. Misc. 292, 61 A.2d 12; Dorfman v. Barnett, 24 N.J. Misc. 212, 48 A.2d 217. Applying these principles here leads to the conclusion that the decedent's estate assumed, at least for some short period of time, the decedent's obligations under the month to month tenancy, including any implied covenant of the nature described by the respondent. Whether there is such an implied covenant and, if there is, whether the estate would be liable for the respondent's damages, are questions which we must consider.

It is clear that the common law imposed upon the tenant, independent of express agreement, a general and somewhat undefined obligation to treat the premises in such a way that no substantial injury would be done to the property during the tenancy. See generally United States v. Bostwick, 94 U.S. 53, 24 L. Ed. 65; G. Thompson, 3A Real Property §1273 (1959). It is doubtful, however, that this obligation was ever as all-embracing as the kind of implied covenant described by respondent. Respondent would have us believe that the tenant is responsible for any form of damage to the premises not resulting from ordinary "wear and tear," unless the damage is attributable to certain limited circumstances wholly beyond the tenant's control — such as the acts of the reversioner, an unavoidable accident, the misdeeds of a public enemy, or natural causes (the so-called "Acts of God"). Under this line of reasoning it is not necessary, in order to hold petitioner liable, to prove some wilful misconduct or misfeasance on the part of the decedent; it is necessary only to show the fact of loss and the inapplicability of any of the narrowly circumscribed exceptions to the tenant's liability. And in the present case, respondent maintains, the damage to the apartment was neither the result of ordinary wear and tear nor the consequence of the kinds of unavoidable circumstances for which a tenant or his estate may not be held responsible; hence the liability of the decedent's estate logically follows.

One obvious flaw in the respondent's argument is that the implied covenant, thus viewed, virtually has the effect of making the tenant the landlord's insurer. We think it clear that the common law stopped short of placing so burdensome a duty upon the tenant. The essence of the common law duty was to exercise reasonable care with respect to the premises so that they reverted to the landlord at the end of the tenancy unharmed by any acts of negligence, waste, or nuisance on the part of the tenant. See, e.g., Hill v. McKay, 1 W.W. Harr. 213, 31 Del. 213, 113 A. 804; Thompson, *supra* §1273. The landlord could thus hold the tenant responsible for any injuries to the premises resulting from the tenant's negligence, wilful misconduct, waste or nuisance. See Thompson, *supra;* 49 Am. Jur. 2d Landlord and Tenant §922 (1970). But when the injury to the premises could clearly not be shown to have been caused by some culpable conduct of the tenant, the landlord could not invoke the covenant in order to force the tenant to respond in damages. Sheer v. Fisher, 27 Ill. App. 464; Stultz v. Locke, 47 Md. 562; Thompson, *supra,* §1273. Respondent concedes, as he must, that there was no culpable conduct on the part of the decedent and it therefore seems an inescapable conclusion that the decedent's estate may not be held liable for breach of implied covenant.

Even if we were to accept the argument that the tenant is liable under an implied covenant for any permanent injury over and above ordinary wear and tear, it is difficult to perceive how the decedent's estate could be held responsible for the kind of loss suffered by respondent. Even under this theory it seems quite apparent that the damages occurred as a result of precisely the kind of unavoidable circumstances for which the tenant was never responsible even under the ancient common law. See Attersoll v. Stevens, 1 Taunt. 183; 4 Kent's Comm. 77; Thompson, *supra,* §1273. As respondent concedes, the implied covenant doctrine has never been employed to justify holding a tenant liable for damage caused by acts of nature which he could not have foreseen and was powerless to prevent. See, e.g., Pollard v. Shaaffer, 1 U.S. (1 Dall.) 210, 1 L. Ed. 104; United States v. Bostwick, 94 U.S. 53, 24 L. Ed. 65. It is difficult to imagine a more clear cut example of just such an occurrence than the death of a tenant by natural causes. Accordingly, even if we view the month to month tenancy as continuing past the death of the decedent and even if we accept the contention that this implied covenant was assumed by the estate upon decedent's death, the estate could not be held liable for damages of the kind involved here.

As petitioner forcefully argues, another deficiency in respondent's argument is that the implied covenant doctrine, to the extent that it imposes strict liability upon the tenant for all injuries not attributable to either ordinary wear and tear or unavoidable circumstances, is clearly contrary to 41 O.S. 1971, §31. That statute provides:

> The lessor of a building intended for the occupation of human beings must, in the absence of an agreement to the contrary, put it into a condition fit for such occupation, and repair all subsequent dilapidations thereof, except that the lessee must repair all deteriorations or injuries thereto occasioned by his ordinary negligence.

Section 31 is of course declaratory of the common law implied covenant doctrine in one sense: the tenant is liable for injuries to the premises occasioned by his ordinary negligence. But the statute clearly abrogates any common law duty, assuming arguendo that there was one, to pay for any damages to the premises that were not caused by the tenant's culpable conduct. That would seem to be the only logical conclusion in view of the affirmative duty of the landlord to repair all dilapidations not caused by the tenant's own negligence.

IV

We turn to respondent's contention that public policy dictates holding the estate liable for her loss. Respondent's argument, in essence, is that even if she has no cause of action against the estate under an implied covenant theory, she should be allowed to recover on public policy grounds because she is the more innocent of the parties. Because the damage to her apartment was the result of the decedent's death, respondent urges, it is the estate to whom the damage is most fairly attributable, and it is thus the estate which should bear the loss. We find this contention unacceptable.

The damage to the respondent's apartment, it must be emphasized, was not caused by the acts or omissions of the decedent, his estate, or anyone else. What caused the damage was the decomposition of the decedent's body — the inexorable process of biological decay. Since no one "caused" the damage, and no one could have prevented it without knowing of decedent's death, it is inappropriate to view respondent's claim in terms of relative fault or innocence. Both respondent and petitioner are equally innocent parties and when viewed as such it is difficult to justify shifting the loss from one to the other.

Even if we were to accept the contention that on general public policy grounds the decedent's estate ought to bear the loss, we could not legally compel it to do so without expanding the liability of a decedent's estate beyond that contemplated by statute. An administrator may pay a claim against the estate only if the claim is either (1) for a debt incurred by or for the decedent during his lifetime or (2) for an indebtedness which the administrator is clearly authorized by statute to pay. In re Goodin's Estate, 198 Okl. 9, 174 P.2d 375. Respondent's claim does not fall within either category. Clearly respondent's claim is not for any valid obligation incurred by the decedent during his lifetime. And respondent concedes, as she must, that her claim is not for the kind of indebtedness which the statutes authorize the administrator to pay out of the decedent's estate.

We must therefore conclude that respondent's petition fails to state a cause of action against the estate under either theory urged on appeal. We must also conclude that the losses for which respondent seeks compensation must be borne by her alone, for we are unable to perceive any legal or equitable theory under which respondent may recover her losses from the decedent's estate. That respondent has suffered an unfortunate loss cannot be denied. But this fact alone does not entitle respondent to obtain recompense from the assets of the estate. She must also show that the decedent, or his estate, invaded her legal rights or that they are in some other way chargeable with the injury. This she cannot do. The loss that respondent sustained is no different from the loss that the unrequited plaintiff suffers at the hands of a public enemy, 4 Kent's Comm. 77, a natural disaster, Gulf Oil Corp. v. Lemmons, 198 Okl. 596, 181 P.2d 568, or an unavoidable accident, Wilson v. Roach, 101 Okl. 30, 222 P. 1000; there is simply no liability for the loss. Respondent's loss, then, is damnum absque injuria.

We accordingly reverse the trial court's certified interlocutory order and remand this case with directions to dismiss.

Reversed and Remanded.

REYNOLDS, P.J., and ROMANG, J., concur.

Note: "Ordinary Wear and Tear"

Suydam and *Kennedy* noted that at common law the tenant is not responsible for "ordinary wear and tear"; however, the precise meaning of this often-used expression is elusive. For example, does a landlord who leases a home to a childless couple have different rights than a landlord who leases the same house to a family with six children and two dogs? What if the landlord didn't know of the children or the pets? May a lease prohibit pets? Children?

The problem of defining what constitutes "ordinary wear and tear" may be financially even more significant for business or commercial leases than for residential leases, where there presumably is a hypothetical standard against which to measure the tenant's behavior. What standard factors are appropriate to consider in the commercial context? For example, T leases a new warehouse for ten years. Is T liable to L if at the end of the ten-year term all the floors in the warehouse need to be replaced, in part because of the tenant's ordinary and routine use of heavy forklift vehicles, which are necessary for his storage business? What if this need for replacement first occurred during the lease term? Fortunately, in most long-term business or commercial transactions, the parties are represented by competent, experienced lawyers whose responsibility it is to anticipate and expressly provide in the lease document answers to these and to numerous other questions which history (and reported cases) has shown will arise.

C. Duty Under a General Covenant to Repair

POLACK v. PIOCHE
35 Cal. 416 (1868)

Appeal from the District Court, Fourth Judicial District, City and County of San Francisco.

On the 17th day of October, 1859, the plaintiff demised to the defendant, for the term of three years, a residence and tract of land on which the same was built, in the City of San Francisco, on the road leading from the Mission Dolores to the San Souci, receiving therefor a monthly rent of one hundred dollars, payable monthly, in advance. The defendant recovered judgment, and the plaintiff appealed.

The other facts are stated in the opinion of the court.

By the court, SANDERSON, J.

This is an action to recover damages for the nonperformance of a covenant to repair. By the terms of the covenant "damages by the elements or acts of Providence" are excepted from its operation.

The case was tried by the Court below without a jury, and has been brought here upon the findings only, it being claimed that the conclusions of law, which were in favor of the defendant, are erroneous.

The facts upon which the case turns were found by the Court below substantially as follows: During the term the demised premises were damaged to the amount of six thousand dollars by "A torrent of water overflowing and sweeping through" them. The torrent was produced by the accumulation of waters from the unusual rains of 1862, which were collected in a natural reservoir in the vicinity of the premises, upon lands of some other person than the plaintiff or defendant, and separated from the demised premises by lands in the possession of and belonging to persons other than the plaintiff or defendant. In ordinary seasons the natural embankment of the reservoir was sufficient to confine the water, or to prevent it from overflowing or breaking through, but was not sufficient for that purpose in the Winter of 1862, which was remarkable for extraordinary rains and floods. Prior to the torrent which caused the damages in question, however, the embankment had been strengthened by the labor of the adjacent land owners, among whom was the defendant, so as to make it sufficient to withstand even the rains and floods of that Winter; but "some persons or persons unknown to the defendant, and without his knowledge or consent, interfered with the natural embankment of the reservoir, and through their agency and their interference the embankment was made to give way, and the whole body of water in the reservoir was suddenly precipitated upon the premises," causing the damages in question.

A general covenant to repair is binding upon the tenant under all circumstances. If the injury proceeds from the act of a stranger, from storms, floods, lightning, accidental fire, or public enemies, he is as much bound to repair as if it came from his own voluntary act. Such has been the settled rule since the time of Edward III. (2 Platt on Leases, 186, 187, and cases there cited.) If the tenant desires to relieve himself from liability for injuries resulting from any of the causes above enumerated, or from any other cause whatever, he must take care to except them from the operation of his covenant. (Id. 186, 187.) So the defendant in the present case is liable, unless, in the language of the exception contained in his covenant, the damages were caused by "the elements or the acts of Providence."

What acts are to be regarded in the legal sense as "acts of God" is well settled. Upon that question the case of Forward v. Pittard, 1 T.R. 27, is a leading authority. The plaintiff's goods, while in the possession of the defendant as a common carrier, were destroyed by fire not caused by lightning or the negligence of the defendant. The question was, whether the fire was, in a legal sense, caused by the "act of God." The Court of King's Bench ruled that it was not, and Lord Mansfield said:

> Now, what is the act of God? I consider it to mean something in opposition to the act of man; for everything is the act of God and happens by his permission; everything by his knowledge, . . . such acts as could not happen by the intervention of man, as storms, lightnings, and tempests.

To the same effect are all the cases. (McArthur v. Sears, 21 Wend. 190; Ewart v. Street, 2 Bailey, 157; Fish v. Chapman, 2 Geo. 349; Merritt v. Earle, 29 N.Y. 115; Turner v. Tuolumne Water Co., 25 Cal. 403.) The expression excludes the idea of human agency, and if it appears that a given loss has happened in any way through the intervention of man, it cannot be held to have been the act of God, but must be regarded as the act of man.

Can a different rule be applied to the interpretation of the expression "the act of the elements"? Is it more comprehensive than the former? Does it include acts which the former does not? The answer is not material to the present purpose; for be that as it may, for the purpose of determining the cause of a particular event, the same test must be resorted to in the one case as in the other. If an act to which human agency has in any way contributed, cannot be considered as the act of God, but must be held to be the act of man, how does it become less the act of man if we substitute the elements in the place of God? The elements are the means by which God acts, and we are unable to perceive why "damages by the elements" and "damages by the acts of God" are not convertible expressions in the law of leases.

The act could not have happened in the one case more than in the other, had not the agency of man intervened. It follows that before an act can be considered the act of the elements it must appear that no human agency intervened, for if it did, the elements cannot be regarded as the cause, but only as the means. Had the waters in question broken through the embankment of the natural reservoir in which they had accumulated without the agency of man, the loss would have fallen within the exception contained in the defendant's covenant. The case shows, however, that they would not have broken through the embankment but for the help of man. The damages in question were, therefore, caused by the act of some stranger. Against the acts of strangers the defendant might have protected himself by excepting them from the operation of his covenant. Not having done so, however, he is liable, as we have seen, by force of his covenant.

Upon the findings, the plaintiff is entitled to judgment for the sum of six thousand dollars. The judgment is, therefore, reversed, and the Court below directed to enter a judgment for the sum of six thousand dollars, together with the costs below and here.[16]

Problems

17.14. L and T entered into a written lease of certain described premises. The term of the lease was 20 years. The lease contained the following covenant:

> T covenants to keep all of the buildings and structures situated upon said leased premises in as good repair as they were at the time of said lease until the expiration thereof and during the life of said lease to keep the same properly insured against loss or damage by fire and to replace any of the structures on said premises as of the date of said lease that are destroyed or injured by fire during the life thereof.

During the second year of the lease, a building on the leased premises was destroyed by fire, and T collected the insurance. Within what time must T

16. See American Law of Property §3.79 (Casner ed. 1952).—EDS.

replace the building destroyed by fire if T is to avoid a violation of the covenant? See Campbell v. Kanawha & Hocking Coal & Coke Co., 122 W. Va. 231, 9 S.E.2d 135 (1940).

17.15. T wishes to lease an entire 10-year-old, 40,000-square foot building for 10 years, with two 5-year renewal options, for use as a discount retail outlet. The rent is $3 per foot or $120,000 per year, payable in installments of $10,000 per month. L presents T's counsel with a proposed lease containing the following clause:

> T has carefully and independently inspected the entire building and based thereon is fully satisfied with and agrees to lease the demised premises in their "as is" condition. During the lease term (including any renewal) T shall make or pay for all necessary repairs in, on, or to the demised premises, whether interior or exterior, structural or nonstructural, ordinary or extraordinary, regardless of cause.

After much negotiation, the second sentence is rewritten, so that in the executed lease it merely provides: "During the lease term (including any renewal) T shall make or pay for interior, non-structural, ordinary repairs caused by T's use and occupancy of the demised premises." T's business becomes so successful that during the third year of operations T turns down a million-dollar purchase offer, the lease being freely assignable and, because of increased commercialization and other beneficial changes in the surrounding neighborhood, the stipulated lease rent by that time being significantly below market. T's business continues to prosper, and during the latter part of the seventh year of T's lease term, again in negotiating a purchase offer (this time for $1.35 million, $150,000 payable as a down payment and the balance payable ratably over the 12 remaining years of the lease term, including renewals), T discovers the following conditions based upon an inspection paid for by the proposed purchaser-assignee: The roof is decaying (requiring its almost total replacement); the sprinkler and air conditioning systems are inoperative (requiring substantial repairs); and the structural steel beams have badly weakened (requiring the installation of additional support columns to make the premises safe for occupancy). Assume that the reasonable cost of making the necessary repairs is approximately two hundred and fifty thousand dollars, which the proposed purchaser-assignee insists be totally deducted from the cash down payment and the first year's deferred portion of the purchase price. Assume further that an expert witness would testify that given the age of the building and T's normal use of the demised premises all of these items are properly considered exterior, structural, or extraordinary repairs from tenant's point of view — i.e., none were necessitated by T's normal use and occupancy of the demised premises. What are T's remedies?

D. *Duty Not to Commit Waste*

MELMS v. PABST BREWING CO.[17]
104 Wis. 7, 79 N.W. 738 (1899)

Appeal from a judgment of the circuit court for Milwaukee county: CLEMENTSON, J.; Affirmed.

This is an action for waste, brought by reversioners against the defendant, which is the owner of an estate for the life of another in a quarter of an acre of land in the city of Milwaukee. The waste claimed is the destruction of a dwelling-house upon the land, and the grading of the same down to the level of the street. The complaint demands double damages, under sec. 3176, Stats. 1898.

The quarter of an acre of land in question is situated upon Virginia street, in the city of Milwaukee, and was the homestead of one Charles T. Melms, deceased. The house thereon was a large brick building built by Melms in the year 1864, and cost more than $20,000. At the time of the building of the house, Melms owned the adjoining real estate, and also owned a brewery upon a part of the premises. Charles T. Melms died in the year 1869, leaving his estate involved in financial difficulties. After his decease, both the brewery and the homestead were sold and conveyed to the Pabst Brewing Company, but it was held in the action of Melms v. Pabst B. Co., 93 Wis. 140, that the brewing company only acquired Mrs. Melm's life estate in the homestead, and that the plaintiffs in this action were the owners of the fee, subject to such life estate. As to the brewery property, it was held in an action under the same title, decided at the same time, and reported in 93 Wis. 153, that the brewing company acquired the full title in fee. The homestead consists of a piece of land ninety feet square, in the center of which the aforesaid dwelling house stood; and this parcel is connected with Virginia street on the south by a strip forty-five feet wide and sixty feet long, making an exact quarter of an acre.

It clearly appears by the evidence that after the purchase of this land by the brewing company the general character of real estate upon Virginia street about the homestead rapidly changed, so that soon after the year 1890 it became wholly undesirable and unprofitable as residence property. Factories and railway tracks increased in the vicinity, and the balance of the property was built up with brewing buildings, until the quarter of an acre homestead in question became an isolated lot and building, standing from twenty to thirty feet above the level of the street, the balance of the property

---

17. As you read this case, you will notice that a life tenant (actually, a tenant for the life of another) is involved, not a tenant for years. The law of waste becomes significant whenever two or more persons have estates in the same land, either successive or concurrent. Recall Rogers v. Atlantic, Gulf & Pacific Co., Chapter 4, page 72.

having been graded down in order to fit it for business purposes. The evidence shows without material dispute that, owing to these circumstances, the residence, which was at one time a handsome and desirable one, became of no practical value, and would not rent for enough to pay the taxes and insurance thereon; whereas, if the property were cut down to the level of the street, so as to be capable of being used as business property, it would again be useful, and its value would be largely enhanced. Under these circumstances, and prior to the judgment in the former action, the defendant removed the building and graded down the property to about the level of the street, and these are the acts which it is claimed constitute waste.

The action was tried before the court without a jury, and the court found, in addition to the facts above stated, that the removal of the building and grading down of the earth was done by the defendant in 1891 and 1892, believing itself to be the owner in fee simple of the property, and that by said acts the estate of the plaintiffs in the property was substantially increased, and that the plaintiffs have been in no way injured thereby. Upon these findings the complaint was dismissed, and the plaintiffs appeal.

WINSLOW, J. Our statutes recognize waste, and provide a remedy by action and the recovery of double damages therefor (Stats. 1898, sec. 3170 et seq.); but they do not define it. It may be either voluntary or permissive, and may be of houses, gardens, orchards, lands, or woods (Id. sec. 3171); but, in order to ascertain whether a given act constitutes waste or not, recourse must be had to the common law as expounded by the text-books and decisions. In the present case a large dwelling house, expensive when constructed, has been destroyed, and the ground has been graded down by the owner of the life estate, in order to make the property serve business purposes. That these acts would constitute waste under ordinary circumstances cannot be doubted. It is not necessary to delve deeply into the Year Books, or philosophize extensively as to the meaning of early judicial utterances, in order to arrive at this conclusion. The following definition of waste was approved by this court in Bandlow v. Thieme, 53 Wis. 57:

> It may be defined to be any act or omission of duty by a tenant of land which does a lasting injury to the freehold, tends to the permanent loss of the owner of the fee, or to destroy or lessen the value of the inheritance, or to destroy the identity of the property, or impair the evidence of title.

In the same case it was also said: "The damage being to the inheritance, and the heir or the reversioner having the right of action to recover it, imply that the injury must be of a lasting and permanent character." And in Brock v. Dole, 66 Wis. 142, it was also said that "any material change in the nature and character of the buildings made by the tenant is waste, although the value of the property should be enhanced by the alteration."

These recent judicial utterances in this court settle the general rules which govern waste, without difficulty, and it may be said, also, that these rules are in accord with the general current of the authorities elsewhere. But, while they are correct as general expressions of the law upon the subject, and were properly applicable to the cases under consideration, it must be remembered that they are general rules only, and, like most general propositions, are not to be accepted without limitation or reserve under any and all circumstances. Thus the ancient English rule which prevented the tenant from converting a meadow into arable land was early softened down, and the doctrine of meliorating waste was adopted, which, without changing the legal definition of waste, still allowed the tenant to change the course of husbandry upon the estate if such change be for the betterment of the estate. Bewes, Waste, 134 et seq., and cases cited. Again, and in accordance with this same principle, the rule that any change in a building upon the premises constitutes waste has been greatly modified, even in England; and it is now well settled that, while such change may constitute technical waste, still it will not be enjoined in equity when it clearly appears that the change will be, in effect, a meliorating change which rather improves the inheritance than injures it. Doherty v. Allman, 3 App. Cas. 709; In re McIntosh, 61 Law J.Q.B. 164. Following the same general line of reasoning, it was early held in the United States that, while the English doctrine as to waste was a part of our common law, still the cutting of timber in order to clear up wild land and fit it for cultivation, if consonant with the rules of good husbandry, was not waste, although such acts would clearly have been waste in England. Tiedeman, Real Prop. (2d ed.), Sec. 74; Rice, Mod. Law Real Prop. Sec. 160, 161; Wilkinson v. Wilkinson, 59 Wis. 557.

These familiar examples of departure from ancient rules will serve to show that, while definitions have remained much the same, the law upon the subject of waste is not an unchanging and unchangeable code, which was crystallized for all time in the days of feudal tenures, but that it is subject to such reasonable modifications as may be demanded by the growth of civilization and varying conditions. And so it is now laid down that the same act may be waste in one part of the country while in another it is a legitimate use of the land, and that the usages and customs of each community enter largely into the settlement of the question. Tiedeman, Real Prop. (2d ed.), Sec. 73. This is entirely consistent with, and in fact springs from, the central idea upon which the disability of waste is now, and always had been, founded, namely, the preservation of the property for the benefit of the owner of the future estate without permanent injury to it. This element will be found in all the definitions of waste, namely, that it must be an act resulting in permanent injury to the inheritance or future estate. It has been frequently said that this injury may consist either in diminishing the value of the inheritance, or increasing its burdens, or in destroying the identity of the property, or impairing the evidence of title. The last element of injury so enumerated, while a cogent and persuasive one in former times, has lost most, if not all, of its force at the present time. It was important when titles were not registered, and descriptions of land were frequently dependent upon natural monuments or the uses to which the land was put; but since the universal adoption of accurate surveys and the establishment of the system of recording conveyances, there can be few acts which will impair any evidence of title. Doherty v. Allman, 3 App. Cas. 709; Bewes, Waste, 129, 130, et seq. But the principle that the reversioner or remainderman is ordinarily entitled to receive the identical estate, or, in other words, that the identity of the property is not to be destroyed, still remains, and it has been said that changes in the nature of buildings, though enhancing the value of the property, will constitute waste if they change the identity of the estate. Brock v. Dole, 66 Wis. 142. This principle was enforced in the last-named case, where it was held that a tenant from year to year of a room in a frame building would be enjoined from constructing a chimney in the building against the objection of his landlord. The importance of this rule to the landlord or owner of the future estate cannot be denied. Especially is it valuable and essential to the protection of a landlord who rents his premises for a short time. He has fitted his premises for certain uses. He leases them for such uses, and he is entitled to receive them back at the end of the term still fitted for those uses; and he may well say that he does not choose to have a different property returned to him from that which he leased, even if, upon the taking of testimony, it might be found of greater value by reason of the change. Many cases will be found sustaining this rule; and that it is a wholesome rule of law, operating to prevent lawless acts on the part of the tenants, cannot be doubted, nor is it intended to depart therefrom in this decision. The case now before us, however, bears little likeness to such a case, and contains elements so radically different from those present in Brock v. Dole, 66 Wis. 142, that we cannot regard that case as controlling this one.

There are no contract relations in the present case. The defendants are the grantees of a life estate, and their rights may continue for a number of years. The evidence shows that the property became valueless for the purpose of residence property as the result of the growth and development of a great city. Business and manufacturing interests advanced and surrounded the once elegant mansion, until it stood isolated and alone, standing upon just enough ground to support it, and surrounded by factories and railway tracks, absolutely undesirable as a residence and incapable of any use as business property. Here was a complete change of conditions, not produced by the tenant, but resulting from causes which none could control. Can it be reasonably or logically said that this entire change of condition is to be completely ignored, and the ironclad rule applied that the tenant can make no change in the uses of the property because he will destroy its identity? Must the tenant stand by and preserve the useless dwelling-house, so that he may at some future time turn it over to the reversioner, equally useless? Certainly, all the analogies are to the contrary. As we have before seen, the cutting of timber, which in England was considered waste, has become in this country an act which may be waste or not, according to the surrounding conditions and the rules of good husbandry; and the same rule applies to the change of a meadow to arable land. The changes of conditions which justify these departures from early inflexible rules are no more marked nor complete than is the change of conditions which destroys the value of residence property as such and renders it only useful for business purposes. Suppose the house in question had been so situated that it could have been remodeled into business property; would any court of equity have enjoined such remodeling under the circumstances here shown, or ought any court to render a judgment for damages for such an act? Clearly, we think not. Again, suppose an orchard to have become permanently unproductive through disease or death of the trees, and the land to have become far more valuable, by reason of new conditions, as a vegetable garden or wheat field, is the life tenant to be compelled to preserve or renew the useless orchard, and forego the advantages to be derived from a different use? Or suppose a farm to have become absolutely unprofitable by reason of change of market conditions as a grain farm, but very valuable as a tobacco plantation, would it be waste for the life tenant to change the use accordingly, and remodel a now useless barn or granary into a tobacco shed? All these questions naturally suggest their own answer, and it is certainly difficult to see why, if change of conditions is so potent in the case of timber, orchards, or kind of crops, it should be of no effect in the case of buildings similarly affected.

It is certainly true that a case involving so complete a change of situation as regards buildings has been rarely, if ever, presented to the courts, yet we are not without authorities approaching very nearly to the case before us. Thus, in the case of Doherty v. Allman, 3 App. Cas. 709, before cited, a court of equity refused an injunction preventing a tenant for a long term from changing storehouses into dwelling-houses, on the ground that by change of conditions the demand for storehouses had ceased and the property had become worthless, whereas it would be productive when fitted for dwelling houses. Again, in the case of Sherrill v. Connor, 107 N.C. 630, which was an action for permissive waste against a tenant in dower, who had permitted large barns and outbuildings upon a plantation to fall into decay, it was held that, as these buildings had been built before the Civil War to accommodate the operation of the plantation by slaves, it was not necessarily waste to tear them down, or allow them to remain unrepaired, after the war, when the conditions had completely changed by reason of the emancipation and the changed methods of use resulting therefrom; and that it became a question for the jury whether a prudent owner of the fee, if in possession, would have suffered the unsuitable barns and buildings to fall into decay, rather than incur the cost of repair. This last case is very persuasive and well reasoned, and it well states the principle which we think is equally applicable to the case before us. In the absence of any contract, express or implied, to use the property for a specified purpose, or to return it in the same condition in which it was received, a radical and permanent change of surrounding conditions, such as is presented in the case before us, must always be an important, and sometimes a controlling, consideration upon the question whether a physical change in the use of the buildings constitutes waste.

In the present case this consideration was regarded by the trial court as controlling, and we are satisfied that this is the right view. This case is not to be construed as justifying a tenant in making substantial changes in the leasehold property, or the buildings thereon, to suit his own whim or convenience, because, perchance, he may be able to show that the change is in some degree beneficial. Under all ordinary circumstances the landlord or reversioner, even in the absence of any contract, is entitled to receive the property at the close of the tenancy substantially in the condition in which it was when the tenant received it; but when, as here, there has occurred a complete and permanent change of surrounding conditions, which has deprived the property of its value and usefulness as previously used, the question whether a life tenant, not bound by contract to restore the property in the same condition in which he received it, has been guilty of waste in making changes necessary to make the property useful, is a question of fact for the jury under proper instructions, or for the court where, as in the present case, the question is tried by the court.

By the Court.— Judgment affirmed.[18]

Problem

17.16.   L and T enter into a written lease of certain described premises. The term of the lease is 50 years. Under the provisions of the lease, T is given an option to buy the fee in the leased premises for the sum of $10,000 at any time during the term of the lease by giving L notice of election to purchase at least 60 days prior to the date fixed for the consummation of the sale. Thirty years before the termination of the lease, T demolishes the building on the leased premises in order to establish a parking lot thereon, although the premises could be used profitably for purposes which would not require the demolition of the building. L sues T to recover for the damage to the leased premises resulting from T's acts. What defense would you advance for T? See Keogh v. Peck, 316 Ill. 318, 147 N.E. 266 (1925). See also American Law of Property §3.84 (Casner ed. 1952); id. §11.81.

Note: Statutory Permission to Make Changes in Leased Premises

N.Y. Real Prop. Acts. Law §803 provides as follows:

1.   When a person having an estate for life or for years in land proposes to make an alteration in, or a replacement of a structure or structures located

---

18.   See Niehuss, Alteration or Replacement of Buildings by the Long-Term Lessee, 30 Mich. L. Rev. 386 (1932). See also American Law of Property §2.16 (Casner ed. 1952) and 5 American Law of Property §20.11 and authorities cited therein.— EDS.

thereon, then the owner of a future interest in such land can neither recover damages for, nor enjoin the alteration or replacement, if the person proposing to make such alteration or replacement complies with the requirements hereinafter stated as to the giving of security and establishes the following facts:

a. That the proposed alteration or replacement is one which a prudent owner of an estate in fee simple absolute in the affected land would be likely to make in view of the conditions existing on or in the neighborhood of the affected land; and

b. That the proposed alteration or replacement, when completed, will not reduce the market value of the interests in such land subsequent to the estate for life or for years; and

c. That the proposed alteration or replacement is not in violation of the terms of any agreement or other instrument regulating the conduct of the owner of the estate for life or for years or restricting the land in question; and

d. That the life expectancy of the owner of the estate for life or the unexpired term of the estate for years is not less than five years; and

e. That the person proposing to make such alteration or replacement, not less than thirty days prior to commencement thereof, served upon each owner of a future interest, who is in being and ascertained, a written notice of his intention to make such alteration or replacement; specifying the nature thereof, which notice was served personally or by registered mail sent to the last known address of each such owner of a future interest.

2. When the owner of a future interest in the affected land demands security that the proposed alteration or replacement, if begun, will be completed and that he be protected against responsibility for expenditures incident to the making of the proposed alteration or replacement, the court in which the action to recover damages or to enjoin the alteration or replacement is pending, or if no such action is pending, the supreme court, on application thereto, on such notice to the interested parties as the court may direct, shall fix the amount and terms of the security reasonably necessary to satisfy such demand. The furnishing of the security so fixed shall be a condition precedent to the making of the proposed alteration or replacement.

3. This section applies only to estates for life or for years created on or after September 1, 1937. [See 38 Colum. L. Rev. 532 (1938) for a comment on N.Y. Real Prop. Acts. Law §803.]

SIGSBEE HOLDING CORP. v. CANAVAN

39 Misc. 2d 465, 240 N.Y.S.2d 900

(City of New York Civ. Ct., Bronx County, 1963)

The landlord seeks a final order of eviction on the ground that the tenant replaced old, used cabinets with new ones, and contends that this constitutes waste and a violation of a substantial obligation of the tenancy. The importance of this matter cannot of course be disregarded. Countless tenants would be affected by the decision in this case, for if this were a basis for eviction of tenants the door would be opened to evictions in almost every case where a landlord refuses to permit the tenant to improve the apartment, perhaps even to drive nails into the wall to hang shelves, pictures, curtains or medicine cabinets. The law obviously cannot permit such a reductio ad absurdum. Nor is this the law.

"It is the well-settled rule that a tenant, in the absence of restrictions contained in a lease, may occupy and use the demised premises in any lawful way not materially different from the way in which they are usually employed, to which they are adapted and for which they were constructed. The right to exclusive occupation granted to a tenant by a lease entitles him to use the premises in the same manner that the owner might have used them. However, the tenant must not do anything that injures the inheritance or which constitutes waste." (Rasch, Landlord and Tenant, Vol. 1, Section 354, pages 334 and 335, and cases therein cited.) The real inquiry in all cases involving alterations made by the tenant is whether there is damage done which injures the reversion (Agate v. Lowenbein, 57 N.Y. 604, 614). If a lessee make extensive alterations, takes down and removes a number of partitions and doors, gas fixtures, chandeliers, and plumbing in order to convert the premises into a hotel, causing serious injury to the reversion and substantially diminishing the value of the property he commits waste (Agate v. Lowenbein, *supra*). At common law if he materially and permanently changes the nature and character of the building, as where he completely changes the interior arrangement of a portion of the premises by removing some partitions and erecting others, by placing the wooden framework for a store frame in the place where brick piers had previously stood, it is waste even if the value of the property is enhanced (McDonald v. O'Hara, 117 Misc. 517, 192 N.Y.S. 545), particularly where such alterations "render it impossible for him to restore the same premises substantially at the expiration of the term." (Winship v. Pitts, 3 Paige 259.) But if a tenant leases a factory and requires an engine in good working order to run the machinery, and without the owner's consent removes the old, worn-out and dangerous engine, and installs a new one, he does not commit waste and does not violate the clause of the lease prohibiting alterations without the consent of the landlord if such replacement is done without injury either to the foundation or to the building, or to the old engine. (Andrews v. Day Button Co., 132 N.Y. 348, 30 N.E. 831.) For in such a case "no substantial alteration was made in the situation, condition, or nature of the premises, but . . . on removal of the new engine the old one could be restored to the foundation from which it was taken." (132 N.Y. page 354, 30 N.E. page 833.) See also Brooklyn Properties, Inc. v. Cargo Packers, Inc. (2nd Department, 1956) 1 A.D.2d 1040(7), 152 N.Y.S.2d 359. . . .

Accordingly, petition is dismissed on the merits.

Note: Removal of Timber or Minerals as Constituting Waste[19]

An important source of quarrels between landlords and tenants has been the removal of timber or minerals from leased land. When such action on the part of the tenant amounts to waste, so that the tenant may be enjoined or sued for damages, is revealed in the excerpts which follow:

"In England the right of a tenant for life or for years to reasonable estovers is implied from the mere leasing of farm land. Such estovers are of three kinds: housebote, or a sufficient amount of timber for the repair of buildings and for fuel; plowbote, for the making and repair of implements of husbandry, and haybote, for repairing hedges and fences. This common-law right of estovers is generally recognized in this country, and the right of the tenant to cut down trees for this purpose upheld." 16 R.C.L. 748. In this State it is declared by the Code, §61-109: "The tenant has no right beyond the use of the land and tenements rented to him, and such privileges as are necessary to the enjoyment of his use. He may not cut or destroy growing trees, remove permanent fixtures, or otherwise injure the property. He may use other timber for firewood and the pasturage for his cattle." It appears that in some cases there would exist the right of the tenant to clear land for the purposes of cultivation. Woodward v. Gates, 38 Ga. 205(5). Thus, while as a general rule it may be true that a tenant may, when it is good husbandry and "necessary to the enjoyment of his use" to clear off the timber and prepare land for cultivation, sell the timber so cut, as a rule he cannot cut timber merely to sell or dispose of for profit. This applies to both tenants for life and to tenants for years. [Higgins v. State, 58 Ga. App. 480, 481, 199 S.E. 158, 158 (1938).]

It seems to be universally recognized that it is waste to open up new mines or quarries on demised premises and take rock, oil, minerals, etc., therefrom. It is equally well settled that as between the life tenant and the remainderman, or as between the landlord and tenant, the tenant has the right to use mines already opened up at the time the relation is created, and that a mortgagor has the right to continue the operation of a mine being operated when the mortgage is given. This is on the theory that when the estate is created, or the mortgage executed, it will be expected that the tenant or mortgagor will continue to operate the property as theretofore. Courts have not hesitated, however, to restrain the mortgagor from opening up new mines. This is on the ground that the removal of the ore from the ground constitutes an impairment of the security, a sale of a part of the mortgaged property, and in no sense constitutes rents and profits. [Kremer v. Crase, 209 Wis. 183, 185, 244 N.W. 596, 597 (1932).]

19. See generally American Law of Property §§20.1-20.6 (Casner ed. 1952).

Problem

17.17. L, as the owner of a tract of land, had carried on coal-mining operations thereon. The mining of coal from the land became unprofitable, and all mining operations ceased. Thereafter, L and T entered into a written lease of the tract of land. The term of the lease was ten years. T had planned to use the leased premises for farming purposes, but no provision in the lease restricted T to such use. During the fifth year of the lease, T undertook coal-mining operations on the land in order to increase the financial return from it. L desires to prevent T from mining coal or recover from T the value of the coal taken from the leased premises. What would you tell L? See Restatement of Property §144 illustrations 1, 2 (1934).[20]

---

20. The first Restatement of Property, sections 138-146, develops in detail the law of waste as applied to life tenants. What difference does it make, in considering the law of waste, whether the tenant is one for life, or for 100 years, or for a short term? Note that N.Y. Real Prop. Acts. Law §803, set out at pages 418–419 *supra,* applies to both life estates and an estate for years as long as the estate for years is not less than 5 years. See generally Restatement (Second) of Property (Landlord and Tenant) §12.2.

CHAPTER 18

MEANS AVAILABLE TO ASSURE LEASE PERFORMANCE

SECTION 1. REMEDIES AVAILABLE TO THE LANDLORD

Over the years many special devices, procedures, and rules have evolved to assure the landlord of the full benefit of the landlord's original agreement, especially those needed for short-term urban leases and long-term commercial leases.[1] Sometimes a tenant is required to provide, as additional "security" for the tenant's performance, some specific chattels, such as the fixtures used by the tenant on the rented premises.[2] However, the more usual device for assuring performance is the "security deposit."

A. *The Security Deposit*

MALLORY ASSOCIATES, INC. v. BARVING REALTY CO.
300 N.Y. 297, 90 N.E.2d 468 (1949)

Conway, J. In November, 1946, the plaintiff, Mallory Associates, Inc., leased from defendant, Barving Realty Co., Inc., the Atlantic Hotel, located in Norfolk, Virginia, for a period of fifteen years. The lease provided:

---

1. See Chapter 23 for a discussion of the special problems involved in negotiating and drafting a long-term commercial lease.
2. See, e.g., Kimball v. Lincoln Theatre Corp., 125 Neb. 677, 251 N.W. 290 (1933), where the landlord attached personal property of a theater tenant which had been pledged with the landlord as security.

> The Tenant has this date deposited with the Landlord the sum of Sixty-Five Thousand ($65,000.) Dollars, receipt of which is hereby acknowledged, without interest as security for the full and faithful performance by the Tenant of all the terms, covenants and conditions of this lease upon the Tenant's part to be performed. . . . The Landlord shall return to the Tenant upon condition that the Tenant shall be in no wise in default under any of the terms of this lease, the sum of Three Thousand ($3,000.) Dollars on December 1st of each year commencing with December 1, 1950, until the expiration of this lease, at which time the unpaid balance of the security will be returned to the Tenant provided the Tenant has fully and faithfully carried out all of the terms, covenants and conditions on the Tenant's part to be performed, less any amount to cover all damages sustained by the terms or conditions of this lease. . . .

Both the landlord and the tenant are New York corporations with offices in New York. The individual defendants are officers and directors of defendant Barving Realty Co., Inc. The lease was executed in the city of New York and, pursuant to it, the $65,000 deposit of security was paid over to defendant Barving Realty Co., Inc., in the city of New York on November 15, 1946.

Alleging that the defendants did "on or about the said 15th day of November, 1946, in the City and State of New York, mingle and cause to be mingled" the $65,000 security deposit "with the personal moneys of the said defendant Barving Realty Co., Inc.," and that they did "wrongfully and unlawfully, convert and appropriate the said sum . . . to the use of the defendant Barving Realty Co., Inc.," the plaintiff-tenant commenced this action to recover the security deposit, with interest from November 15, 1946.

Prior to the enactment of section 233 of the Real Property Law, Consol. Laws, c. 50, L. 1935, ch. 581, and in the absence of facts from which a contrary intention could be inferred, Matter of Atlas, 217 App. Div. 38, 216 N.Y.S. 490, it was uniformly held that a deposit of security by a tenant under a lease created a debtor-creditor relationship and that the landlord had the right to use such moneys until the date specified for repayment.

The Legislature changed that rule in 1935 by adding a new section 233 to the Real Property Law, which reads as follows:

> Whenever money shall be deposited or advanced on a contract for the use or rental of real property as security for performance of the contract or to be applied to payments upon such contract when due, such money, with interest accruing thereon, if any, until repaid or so applied, shall continue to be the money of the person making such deposit or advance and shall be held in trust by the person with whom such deposit or advance shall be made and shall not be mingled with the personal moneys or become an asset of the person receiving the same, but may be disposed of as provided in section thirteen hundred and two-a of the penal law. Any provision of such a contract whereby

a person who so deposits or advances money waives any provision of this section is absolutely void.[3]

Defendants moved to dismiss the instant complaint on the ground that it did not state facts sufficient to constitute a cause of action. Special Term indicated that the complaint did state a cause of action in conversion under the above-quoted provisions of section 233, but held that the statute was inapplicable because the deposit of security in the case at bar was made under a lease relating to real property located outside of the State of New York. The court stated that, during the depression, the financial standing of many landlords became impaired or destroyed, that in the resulting insolvencies, the tenant frequently suffered not only the loss of his leasehold but also the loss of his security deposit, that this evil was one of great gravity, particularly in the city of New York, and that the Legislature, in enacting section 233 to remedy this evil, was concerned solely with conditions existing here and not elsewhere.

The provision in the lease for the deposit of security is a personal covenant between the contracting parties, creating rights in personam. It is not concerned with the creation or transfer of any interest in real property. The question presented by the instant case relates solely to the rights and liabilities of the parties as a matter of contractual obligation. Accordingly, it is to be determined by the law governing the contract, even though the subject matter of the contract may be land in another State. . . .

In enacting section 233, the Legislature was attempting to prevent the depletion of funds deposited with the lessor. The method used was to transform the usual debtor-creditor relationship between the lessor and the lessee into one of trust relationship, by operation of law. The security deposit paid over and held in this State was the thing to be protected. The lessee, resident in this State, was the person to be protected. The need for protection is obviously no less, but rather more, when the land to which the lease relates is situated outside of this State. The Legislature did not expressly limit the statute to deposits made under a contract for the use or rental of real property situated in New York, and we do not think it should be thus limited by judicial construction. The protection afforded by section 233 should apply to funds deposited in New York as security under a contract of lease made in New York between corporations created by New York, even though the real property which is the subject matter of the contract is located elsewhere. In so holding, we are not giving extraterritorial operation to the statute, but, on the contrary, in accordance with the evident legislative intent, we are permitting it to govern the rights and liabilities of corporations created by New York, under a New York contract, with respect to a New York subject matter, viz., the security deposit. . . .

---

3. This is now N.Y. Gen. Oblig. Law §7-103. — Eds.

The judgments should be reversed and the motion to dismiss the complaint denied, with costs in all courts.

FULD, J., dissents in opinion in which DESMOND and BROMLEY, JJ., concur.

Judgments reversed, etc.

Note: Security Deposits

A frequently recurring practical problem with respect to the tenant's security deposit is the liability of the landlord after the landlord no longer owns the demised premises. Is the obligation of the landlord to return the security deposit personal, arising out of the lease contract, which continues notwithstanding the landlord's transfer of the reversion? See, e.g., Gallagher v. McMann, 199 Cal. App. 688, 7 P.2d 204 (1932). What are the liabilities of a successor landlord? Does it make any difference if the transfer was by gift or by sale? What if the transfer was involuntary — e.g., by foreclosure? See generally 3 Friedman on Leases §20.5 (1978).

Varied phraseology is employed in drafting leases to designate the fund used as security, for example, "consideration for the landlord's execution of the lease," or "as liquidated damages" for any breach of the lease, or "as advance payment of rent" for the last months of the lease. Each is an effort to give the landlord a right to retain the fund without having to show that the tenant's breach caused actual damages in that amount.

These efforts have had little success when the wording of "liquidated damages" has been used; have been recognized as effective in a minority of states when the "consideration for the execution of the lease" phraseology has been employed; and have been most effective when made in the form of "advance payments of rent."[4] Is this merely another example of form over substance?

For an example of a detailed statute relating to security deposits, see Mass. Gen. Laws ch. 186, §15B.

B. Rent Acceleration

Another frequently used device, an "acceleration of rent" clause, is inserted in leases to bludgeon a tenant into performance and also to enable the landlord to seek relief at the earliest possible sign of difficulty with the

---

4. Wilson, Lease Security Deposits, 34 Colum. L. Rev. 426 (1934).

In Harcum v. United States, 164 F. Supp. 650 (E.D. Va. 1958), a lessor was involved who had received a security deposit that was to be applied to discharge the rent for the last few months of the term, if it had not been forfeited prior to that time. The issue was when did the lessor have to report such deposit as income for federal income tax purposes. The court held the lessor did not have to report the deposit as income until it was used to discharge the rent or was forfeited.

See further in regard to the tax aspects of security deposits Rev. Rul. 77-260, 1977-2 C.B. 466.

tenant. The clause is designed to cause the rent for the entire term to become due immediately upon a default by the tenant. Rent acceleration clauses should be distinguished from clauses providing for the payment of several months' rent in advance, which is a different type of "security" device.[5]

In discussing rent acceleration clauses, the court in Ricker v. Rombough, 120 Cal. App. 2d 912, 261 P.2d 328 (1953), comments as follows:

> From the foregoing it follows that a provision in a lease of real property for rent acceleration upon breach of a covenant to pay rent is unenforceable and void as being either an agreement for liquidated damages when the damages are readily ascertainable or a penalty. This is particularly true in this case for the reason that the lease here under consideration expressly declares the rent acceleration clause to be "in addition to any other remedies which lessor may have upon such default, failure or neglect." Under this lease, upon any default of the lessee, the lessor has the right to terminate the lease and re-enter the premises and at the same time sue for all of the unpaid rent reserved for the entire term of the lease. Such a provision has no relation whatever to the actual damages which may be sustained and is the clearest kind of a penalty. The validity of a liquidated damage clause is to be determined at the time the lease is entered into. Hanlon Drydock, etc., Co. v. W. McNear, Inc., 70 Cal. App. 204, 232 P. 1002; Better Food Markets, Inc. v. American District Telegraph Co., 40 Cal. 2d 179, 253 P.2d 10; Atkinson v. Pacific Fire Extinguisher Co., *supra.*
>
> Respondent urges that rent acceleration clauses in leases are similar to acceleration clauses in promissory notes, the validity of which is, of course, unquestioned. We cannot agree that these two types of clauses are similar. In leases the tenant pays rent for the possession and use of the property leased. In promissory notes the borrower pays interest for the possession and use of the money loaned. For an acceleration clause in a note to be similar to a rent acceleration clause in a lease it would have to provide that upon default all of the interest agreed to be paid should become immediately due and payable. Note acceleration clauses provide for acceleration of the payment of the principal sum loaned not for acceleration of interest. Concerning a similar contention made in Gentry v. Recreation Inc., *supra,* 7 S.E.2d at page 65, the Court said:
>
>> The view taken by appellant is that such a clause is effective for this purpose, because among other things it is a well-established principle that if a debt is payable in installments it is perfectly legal to provide that upon failure to meet any installment, or in certain other contingencies, the entire amount of the debt shall become immediately due and payable. There is, however, quite an obvious difference between the acceleration of an ordinary debt and the acceleration of rent. In the case of an ordinary debt the debtor has already received the entire consideration, either in money or in property, while in the case of rent an acceleration would require him to pay for that which he has not yet received.
>
> [120 Cal. App. 2d at 919-920, 261 P.2d at 331-332.]

5. See Note, 45 Yale L.J. 537 (1936).

Examine the following case with the comments of the court in Ricker v. Rombough in mind.

FIFTY STATES MANAGEMENT CORP.
v. PIONEER AUTO PARTS INC.
46 N.Y.2d 573, 389 N.E.2d 113, 415 N.Y.S.2d 800 (1979)

COOKE, C.J.

The question posed on this appeal is whether equity will intervene to prevent enforcement of a provision in a 20-year lease between commercial parties providing for the acceleration of the rent due for the entire lease term upon the tenant's default in the payment of a monthly rental installment. Reasoning that enforcement of the acceleration clause would exact an unconscionable forfeiture, the Appellate Division affirmed the dismissal of the landlord's complaint by Supreme Court, Erie County.

There should be a reversal. By failing to tender payment of two monthly rental payments or even offering to cure the default, defendant tenant was in willful breach of a material term of the lease. As the tenant is entitled to possession of the demised premises upon payment of the rent reserved for the balance of the lease term (as well as continued performance of other covenants of the lease) and there is no claim of fraud or exploitive overreaching on the part of the plaintiff in compelling performance of its bargained-for right, the agreement of the parties must be enforced in accordance with its terms.

Fifty States Management Corp. (referred to variously as "Fifty States" and "landlord") and Pioneer Auto Parts, Inc. (referred to variously as "Pioneer" and the "tenant"), entered into a 20-year lease of commercial property located in Buffalo in 1972. In return for possession, Pioneer covenanted to make rental payments the first of each month throughout the term of the lease. To secure these payments, Fifty States insisted that Pioneer supply a financially responsible guarantor. It also bargained for and received a clause in the lease giving it the option of accelerating future rent due for the balance of the lease term following default in the payment of a monthly installment from which the frequent provisions requiring the landlord to give formal notice of default and granting the tenant a grace period within which to cure its default were conspicuously absent. Defendant Lyon executed and delivered to Fifty States an instrument in which he unconditionally guaranteed the payment of rent fixed and the performance by Pioneer of all terms and conditions of the lease.

No claim has been made that the acceleration clause is boilerplate, unknowingly assented to by the tenant as a result of its being compelled to enter into a contract of adhesion. Indeed, there is nothing in the record which detracts from the conclusion that the clause was anything but the result of intensive negotiations between commercial parties of equal bargaining strength.

The first three rental payments were timely made. However, the check covering the August, 1973 rent was never received by the landlord. The envelope containing the check was incorrectly addressed and was returned to the tenant while its president was on vacation. During that period, however, Pioneer was on notice that the check had not been delivered. Fifty States informed Pioneer's president that there had been no receipt of the August rental payment and the guarantor inquired of him the reason tenant failed to make payment as required by its lease. On August 20, 1973, the parties met in Buffalo to discuss the problem. When there was no tender of payment by Pioneer, its president was served with a summons and complaint seeking acceleration of the rent payments in accordance with the terms of the lease. The complaint was subsequently amended to reflect the fact that tenant also failed to pay the following month's rent.

Pioneer resists enforcement of the acceleration clause on the ground that it constitutes a penal forfeiture, long disfavored by equity. It is true that equity will often intervene to prevent a substantial forfeiture occasioned by a trivial or technical breach (see J.N.A. Realty Corp. v. Cross Bay Chelsea, 42 N.Y.2d 392, 397-398, 397 N.Y.S.2d 958, 960-961, 366 N.E.2d 1313, 1316; Noyes v. Clark, 7 Paige 179, 32 Am. Dec. 620). To permit literal enforcement of an instrument in such circumstances, it is reasoned, is to elevate the nonperformance of some collateral act into the cornerstone for the exaction of a penalty (5 Pomeroy, Equity Jurisprudence (5th ed.), §455a). Similarly, equity may relieve against the effect of a good faith mistake, promptly cured by the party in default with no prejudice to the creditor to prevent unconscionable overreaching (Graf v. Hope Bldg. Corp., 254 N.Y. 1, 13, 171 N.E. 884, 888 (Cardozo, Ch. J., dissenting); 5 Pomeroy, Equity Jurisprudence (5th ed.), §440a; cf. W.F.M. Rest. v. Austern, 35 N.Y.2d 610, 614, 364 N.Y.S.2d 500, 502, 324 N.E.2d 149, 151). And, of course, equity abhors forfeitures and courts will examine the sum reserved under an instrument as liquidated damages to insure that it is not disproportionate to the damages actually arising from the breach or designed to coerce the performance of a party (Wirth & Hamid Fair Booking v. Wirth, 265 N.Y. 214, 223, 192 N.E. 297, 301; Ward v. Hudson Riv. Bldg. Co., 125 N.Y. 230, 235, 26 N.E. 256, 257; cf. Uniform Commercial Code, §2-718, subd. (1)).

Thus, in rare cases, agreements providing for the acceleration of the entire debt upon the default of the obligor may be circumscribed or denied enforcement by utilization of equitable principles. In the vast majority of instances, however, these clauses have been enforced at law in accordance with their terms (e.g., First Nat. Stores v. Yellowstone Shopping Center, 21 N.Y.2d 630, 638, 290 N.Y.S.2d 721, 725, 237 N.E.2d 868, 871, *mot. for rearg. den.* 22 N.Y.2d 827, 292 N.Y.S.2d 919, Conditioner Leasing Corp. v. Sternmor Realty Corp., 17 N.Y.2d 1, 4, 266 N.Y.S.2d 801, 802, 213 N.E.2d 884, 885; 5 Pomeroy, Equity Jurisprudence (5th ed.), §439; Rasch, New York Landlord and Tenant (2d ed.), §376). Absent some element of fraud, exploitive overreaching or unconscionable conduct on the part of the landlord to exploit a technical breach, there is no warrant, either in law or equity, for a court to refuse enforcement of the agreement of the parties. Here, Pioneer points to no circumstances which would justify relieving it of the consequences of its bargain and subsequent default.

Generally, where a lease provides for acceleration as a result of a breach of any of its terms, however trivial or inconsequential, such a provision is likely to be considered an unconscionable penalty and will not be enforced by a court of equity. For example, a clause authorizing acceleration for failure to comply with a covenant collateral to the primary obligation of the tenant is generally held to constitute a forfeiture, for the damages reserved in the lease are disproportionate to any loss which could possibly accrue to the landlord (see Seidlitz v. Auerbach, 230 N.Y. 167, 173, 129 N.E. 461, 463, 884 West End Ave. Corp. v. Pearlman, 201 App. Div. 12, 193 N.Y.S. 670, *affd.* 234 N.Y. 589, 138 N.E. 458). A covenant to pay rent at a specified time, however, is an essential part of the bargain as it represents the consideration to be received for permitting the tenant to remain in possession of the property of the landlord. Often the landlord relies on timely payment of rent to meet its own outstanding obligations, such as a mortgage on the demised premises. Thus, an acceleration clause, so common in other commercial transactions, is merely a device in the landlord-tenant relationship intended to secure the tenant's obligation to perform a material element of the bargain and its enforcement works no forfeiture. This, of course, presumes that the sum reserved for liquidated damages is no greater than the amount the tenant would have paid had it fully performed and that the tenant would be entitled to possession upon payment (see, generally, McManus, The Enforcement of Acceleration Clauses in New York, 8 N.Y.L.F. 466; Ann., 104 A.L.R. 223, Provisions by Which Upon Breach of Contract the Entire Amount Remaining Unpaid Thereon Shall Become Immediately Due as One for Penalty or for Liquidated Damages).

There can be no claim that the sum reserved under the acceleration clause here bears no relationship to the damages sustained by landlord as a result of the breach. The clause is nothing more than a bargained-for device which seeks to insure the performance of a material element of the obligation of the tenant and fixes the damages for its breach. Upon failure to tender a rental payment, the landlord was merely afforded its contractual option to receive the rental payments reserved for the remainder of the lease term as a condition of defendant's continued occupancy. While it is true, as Pioneer maintains, that it will lose interest on the money advanced, this factor alone is no more effective in creating a penalty than the parties contracting to receive the entire rent at the beginning of the lease term (Belnord Realty Co. v. Levison, 204 App. Div. 415, 417, 198 N.Y.S. 184, 185).

It may very well be that since the initial failure to tender timely payment of the August rent was due to clerical error, equitable relief would have been available to Pioneer had its default been immediately cured upon discovery of the error in the absence of prejudice to plaintiff (see Graf v. Hope Bldg. Corp., 254 N.Y. 1, 12-14, 171 N.E. 884, 888-889 (Cardozo, Ch. J., dissenting), *supra;* 100 Eighth Ave. Corp. v. Morgenstern, 4 A.D.2d 754, 164 N.Y.S.2d 812). In such a case, the failure of the landlord to accept a cure for a trifling mistake without prejudice to himself and then seek enforcement of the acceleration clause would be at least exploitive and, perhaps, unconscionable (see Giles v. Austin, 62 N.Y. 486, 493-494; cf Jones v. Gianferante, 305 N.Y. 135, 138, 111 N.E.2d 419). But Pioneer made no attempt to cure its default after being notified by both its guarantor and the landlord that the August rent had not been received. Rather, it blithely sat by and exacerbated the effects of its willful breach by purposely failing to tender the rent due the following month. It would be a perversion of equitable principles to relieve a party of the impact of its intentional default.

In sum, the facts of this case do not justify equitable intervention. The parties freely bargained for the inclusion of a clause in their lease whereby the rent for the remainder of the lease term would be accelerated upon breach of tenant's covenant to pay rent. The landlord was not required to give formal notice of default to trigger the acceleration clause, nor was the tenant given a grace period within which to cure it. Notwithstanding the lack of ameliorative provisions in the lease, Fifty States did send Pioneer notice of its default and went so far as to arrange a meeting between the parties at which the default could have been readily cured. That honoring at least this aspect of its bargain may cause Pioneer fiscal hardship does not, standing alone, serve as a basis for construing the acceleration clause as a penalty under the guise of applying equitable principles to a routine commercial transaction.

Accordingly, the order of the Appellate Division should be reversed, with costs, and the case remitted to Supreme Court, Erie County for a determination of the amount due appellant under the lease in accordance with this opinion.

GABRIELLI, JONES, WACHTLER and FUCHSBERG, JJ., concur with COOKE, C.J.

JASEN, J., taking no part.

Order reversed, with costs, and the case remitted to Supreme Court, Erie County for further proceedings in accordance with the opinion herein.

Note: Rent Acceleration Clauses — Penalty Versus Liquidated Damage Provisions

Landlords and their counsel understandably wish to avoid the need for and the expense of multiple, successive lawsuits against defaulting tenants in order to collect the rent or additional rent due for the balance of the lease term. In a jurisdiction where a landlord is not obligated to mitigate damages (i.e., no obligation to make reasonable efforts to re-rent the demised premises after the tenant's default), is the following default clause a reasonable liquidated damage provision or an unenforceable penalty?

> In the event Tenant defaults in the performance of the obligations hereunder, after notice and failure to cure, Landlord shall be entitled to immediately collect from Tenant the "Discounted Present Value" of all future unpaid rent and additional rent for the balance of the lease term. As used herein, "Discounted Present Value" means the actuarial cash equivalent of the stipulated lost income stream (i.e., rent and additional rent provided for in the lease) reduced to present value using an 8 percent discount rate.

Alternatively, even in a jurisdiction where a landlord is obligated to mitigate damages, consider whether the following default clause is a reasonable liquidated damage provision or an unenforceable penalty:

> In the event the Tenant defaults in the performance of the obligations hereunder, after notice and failure to cure, Landlord shall be entitled to immediately collect from Tenant the "Discounted Present Value" of the difference between (x) the rent and additional rent provided for in the lease during the balance of the term and (y) the reasonable rental value of the demised premises for the balance of the lease term, determined as of the time of Tenant's default.

C. Forfeiture Clauses

JAMAICA BUILDERS SUPPLY CORP. v. BUTTELMAN

25 Misc. 2d 326, 205 N.Y.S.2d 303
(City of New York Mun. Ct., Queens County, 1960)

MARGULIES, J.

Summary proceedings to remove the tenant on the ground that he is holding over without the permission of the landlord after the expiration of the tenant's term. Civil Practice Act, §1410, subd. 1.

The tenant occupies an apartment in a multiple dwelling free from rent control under a written lease dated May 6, 1960, commencing on May 1, 1960, and expiring April 30, 1962, two paragraphs of which read as follows:

> The Tenant shall pay the said rent at the time and in the manner above provided without demand therefor.
> This lease is given and accepted upon the express understanding that in the event of the breach of any condition or covenant herein, or if the Landlord or the Landlord's Agents or assigns shall hereafter deem the tenancy an undesirable one, the Landlord or the Landlord's Agents or assigns may terminate the lease by giving to the Tenant five days written notice of an intention to terminate the same, and the term of this lease shall in that event run to, and expire upon the date therein mentioned, and any rent paid by the Tenant, in advance, for a period extending beyond the said date of termination, shall and

may be retained by the Landlord in liquidation of damages and not by way of penalty or forfeiture, but nothing herein contained shall be deemed a waiver by the Landlord of any claim for damages for injury to the property prior to the said date of termination.

Standing alone, the latter paragraph creates a conditional limitation. Burnee Corp. v. Uneeda Pure Orange Drink Co., Inc., 132 Misc. 435, 230 N.Y.S. 239; Ehret Holding Corp. v. Anderson Galleries, Inc., 138 Misc. 722, 247 N.Y.S. 235.

A lease containing a similar clause in a case tried in the Municipal Court, Second District, Queens, was found to be a conditional limitation and the landlord was entitled to recover possession of the premises demised to the tenant. Rayzel Corp. v. Meyers, aff'd App. Term Second Department, June 1937.

In the instant case the tenant failed to pay the August rent provided for in said lease on August 1, 1960, and on August 9th the landlord caused to be served upon the tenant a written notice terminating the said lease as of August 16th.

This court finds that the notice was proper and complies with the terms of the lease quoted above. If that was all to this case the answer would be simple and this court would direct a final order in favor of the landlord entitling it to possession.

However, the courts, to prevent an immediate forfeiture of a tenancy, seem ever to be on the alert to create a condition as we have come to know it rather than a limitation, to permit the tenant to escape the harsh result by reason of waiver or a technicality.

The cases finding a conditional limitation were those where the language was plain and the intent clear.

By reason of the attitude of the courts, a reading of the cases deciding the question as to whether the lease provides for a limitation or a condition finds subtle distinctions, technicalities and situations difficult to reconcile.

In an early treatise on this question McAdam on Landlord and Tenant this comment was made: "Whether a provision in a lease creates a conditional limitation or condition subsequent is frequently subtle, and the construction must depend upon each particular case presented. Conditions tending to defeat a grant are generally strictly construed, and the question must therefore be determined by this strict rule of construction."

The distinction between a condition and a conditional limitation is principally in order to terminate a lease in case of a condition, some act must be done upon the happening of the contingent event such as making an entry; while, in case of a conditional limitation, the mere happening of the event is, in itself, the limit beyond which the lease no longer exists; in such a case, no entry or other act is necessary to terminate the lease.

The above definition of condition and conditional limitation seems clear enough, but as this court indicated, the subject is replete with attempts to avoid a limitation or if one is found some excuse to avoid its effect. 3 N.Y. Law of Landlord and Tenant, Sections 971, 973. This court will attempt to review some of the cases holding to this point of view. In 98 Delancey St. Corp. v. Barocas. Sup., 82 N.Y.S.2d 802, *affirmed without opinion* 275 App. Div. 651, 86 N.Y.S.2d 659, Judge Pecora found a condition subsequent because a valuable leasehold was at stake and the default consisted of failure to make a minor repair. In Benner v. Coury, Co. Ct., 106 N.Y.S.2d 857, 859, there was no provision for termination of the lease other than the words "landlord may sue for same, or re-enter said premises, or resort to any legal remedy." In Small v. De Bruyn, 187 Misc. 1045, 65 N.Y.S.2d 591, where an occupant under a lease containing a conditional limitation became a statutory tenant, the court refused to project the condition into the statutory tenancy. There are several cases where by reason of acceptance of rent after due date constituting waiver of the requirement that rent be paid on date provided in lease.

Likewise in the instant case if the landlord sought to terminate the tenancy by reason of the conditional limitation clause because the tenant violated paragraph 1 of the lease ". . . The tenant shall not drill into, drive nails . . ." this court would find that the item complained of was inconsequential and not contemplated by the agreement as a condition which may result in a forfeiture.

In all of the leading cases it appears that the search is for the intention of the parties from the language of the entire lease and only if there is a clear intention that when an event happens the lease by its terms comes to an end. In that connection this court would like to consider the impact of paragraph 20 of the lease.

> In the event that rent shall not be paid to Landlord within five days of due date thereof provided herein, and by reason thereof, Landlord shall by attorney and counselor-at-law institute summary proceedings based upon such non-payment of rent. The Tenant hereby agrees to pay the reasonable value of such attorney's services, which is hereby fixed and stipulated to be Twenty-Five Dollars. Such charge shall be payable on demand, and upon failure of Tenant to pay same, such charge shall be added to the next month's rent thereafter to become due, and the Landlord shall be entitled to the same rights and remedies as if it were rent.

This clause was typewritten.

Clearly this paragraph gives an additional remedy to the landlord by reason of non-payment of rent on the due date. The first sentence is ineptly worded so that one is left up in the air at its conclusion, but it does contemplate a situation where rent may not be paid when due and the lease would not come to an end. Searching for the intention of the parties, the typewritten portion prevails over the printed clauses and would be the one that the tenant would be more apt to read. Mindful that forfeitures are not favored, it seems to this court that the parties did not intend a termination of the lease by reason of non-payment of rent on August 1, 1960. . . .

Perhaps in the final analysis this question should be resolved by the legislature. There should be no reason for the courts to strain to avoid forfeiture. Certainly it should be contrary to public policy that a tenant of residential property who fails to pay rent when due may be evicted without notice and an opportunity to cure default. A similar situation existed prior to 1921 where by reason of the same paragraph tenants were evicted because in the opinion of the landlord the tenant was undesirable. Manhattan Life Ins. Co. v. Gosford, 3 Misc. 509, 23 N.Y.S. 7, wherein the court held that the lease did not circumscribe the landlord's discretion to proceed from sufficient grounds and it was immaterial what reason landlord gave to terminate the lease. Now by reason of Section 1410, subd. 6,

> A proceeding seeking to recover possession of real property by reason of the termination of the term fixed in the lease pursuant to a provision contained therein giving the landlord the right to terminate the time fixed for occupancy under such agreement, if he deem the tenant objectionable, shall not be maintainable unless the landlord shall by competent evidence establish to the satisfaction of the court that the tenant is objectionable. (Section added by L. 1921 ch. 199, April 14. Code S 2231.)

It is the opinion of this court that the only summary proceedings available to the landlord is the remedy set forth in Section 1410, subd. 2 of the C.P.A. Petition dismissed and final order in favor of tenant.

Note: Summary Proceedings Versus Ejectment — Lindsey v. Normet

As the preceding case indicates, whether a landlord has the reserved power to terminate a lease upon proof of the tenant's violation of the tenant's obligations is a frequently litigated question. Leases commonly include a multitude of covenants which the tenant agrees to perform, and if the lease is silent, a violation of any one of these covenants merely gives rise to an action for breach of contract and damages. However, the lease is rarely silent, and thus the problem is one of the interpretation of the clause giving a power to terminate the lease. The choice is between a "condition" and a "conditional limitation," and the choice is procedurally important since the landlord must first regain possession by ejectment in the former but may resort to summary proceedings in the latter.[6] The distinction between

---

6. See the discussion in Niles, Conditional Limitations in Leases in New York, 11 N.Y.U.L.Q. Rev. 15 (1933).

ejectment and summary proceedings is of the greatest importance. The common-law action of ejectment, with statutory modifications, exists in every state as a method for trying the right to the possession of land; however, historically and even today it is a relatively slow, fairly complex, and substantially expensive procedure. It obviously is not well adapted to meet the needs of modern landlords who desire to oust a tenant, especially if one remembers that a landlord's expenses, e.g., insurance, debt service, taxes, etc., continue to accrue whether the tenant pays the rent or not. A new remedy was therefore devised in the nineteenth century, the so-called summary proceeding. As its title implies, it is a simple, speedy procedure in which the right to possession can be tried. Practice varies too greatly from state to state to attempt any general analysis here; you should check your own statutes for a guide.

A summary proceeding will be slowed down considerably if the tenant who has not paid the rent can raise various defenses that, if proved, will justify the non-payment of rent and if any judgment that is obtained in the summary proceeding against the tenant may be easily appealed. The Oregon statute relating to summary proceedings to recover the possession of leased property from the tenant for non-payment of rent limits triable issues in the summary proceeding to the tenant's default in the payment of rent; the statute precludes the consideration of defenses based on the landlord's breach of a duty to maintain the premises. To curtail appeals from a decision in the summary proceeding, the tenant is required to post a bond of twice the amount of rent expected to accrue pending an appellate decision. The constitutionality of the Oregon statute was at issue in Lindsey v. Normet, 405 U.S. 56, 92 S. Ct. 862 (1972), on the ground that the statute violated both the equal protection and due process clauses of the fourteenth amendment. In regard to the restriction on triable issues, the court rejected the claim of unconstitutionality:

> Nor does Oregon deny due process of law by restricting the issues in FED actions to whether the tenant has paid rent and honored the covenants he has assumed, issues that may be fairly and fully litigated under Oregon procedure. The tenant is barred from raising claims in the FED action that the landlord has failed to maintain the premises, but the landlord is also barred from claiming back rent or asserting other claims against the tenant. The tenant is not foreclosed from instituting his own action against the landlord and litigating his right to damages or other relief in that action. [405 U.S. at 65-66, 92 S. Ct. at 870.]

In regard to the tenant's posting of the bond in order to appeal an adverse decision in the summary proceeding, the *Lindsey* case held as follows:

> We do not question here reasonable procedural provisions to safeguard litigated property, cf. National Union of Marine Cooks and Stewards v. Arnold, 348 U.S. 37, 75 S. Ct. 92, 99 L. Ed. 46 (1954), or to discourage

patently insubstantial appeals, if these rules are reasonably tailored to achieve these ends and if they are uniformly and nondiscriminatorily applied. Moreover, a State has broad authority to provide for the recovery of double or treble damages in cases of illegal conduct that it regards as particularly reprehensible, even though posting an appeal bond by an appellant will be doubly or triply more difficult than it otherwise would be. In the case before us, however, the State has not sought to protect a damage award or property an appellee is rightfully entitled to because of a lower court judgment. Instead, it has automatically doubled the stakes when a tenant seeks to appeal an adverse judgment in an FED action. The discrimination against the poor, who could pay their rent pending an appeal but cannot post the double bond is particularly obvious. For them, as a practical matter, appeal is foreclosed, no matter how meritorious their case may be. The nonindigent FED appellant also is confronted by a substantial barrier to appeal faced by no other civil litigant in Oregon. The discrimination against the class of FED appellants is arbitrary and irrational, and the double-bond requirements of ORS §105.160 violates the Equal Protection Clause. [405 U.S. at 78-79, 92 S. Ct. at 877.)

See also Note: Forcible Entry and Detainer Statutes, page 600 *infra*.

D. Self-Help: Distraint and Forcible Entry and Detainer Statutes

Note: Distraint

One of the oldest as well as one of the most efficient of the common-law remedies available to a landlord for the collection of rent was called "distraint"—a term which was not derived from the distress it no doubt caused the tenant to suffer. This feudal right allowed the landlord to go to the demised premises and seize *anything* that might be found there (whether belonging to the tenant or a stranger)[7] and hold it until the rent was paid. In many jurisdictions, distraint for rent either has been expressly abolished by statute or has been deemed by the courts to be impliedly abolished by the adoption of other statutes relating to speedy remedies for the recovery of rent.[8] Because the landlord's self-help remedy requires no prior judicial approval or subsequent supervision, there is a serious question about whether such a remedy violates fundamental procedural due process rights.[9]

7. See Annot., Goods Owned by Stranger or Subject to an Encumbrance in His Favor as Subject to Distraint for Rent, 62 A.L.R. 1106 (1929).
8. See generally 49 Am. Jur. 2d Landlord and Tenant §§726 et seq. and 52 C.J.S. Landlord and Tenant §§674 et seq.
9. See, e.g., Sniadach v. Family Finance Corp., 395 U.S. 337, 89 S. Ct. 1820 (1969). In Holt v. Brown, 336 F. Supp. 2 (W.D. Ky. 1971), the court held that the Kentucky distraint statutes were unconstitutional on precisely this ground. Compare the following two cases: Luria Brothers & Co. v. Allen, 672 F.2d 347 (3d Cir. 1982), and Callen v. Sherman's Inc., 92 N.J. 114, 455 A.2d 1102 (1983).

The following case does not involve distraint but does involve retaking possession of the leased property by self-help.

JORDAN v. TALBOT
55 Cal. 2d 597, 361 P.2d 20, 12 Cal. Rptr. 488 (1961)

TRAYNOR, J.

Plaintiff was a tenant in defendant's apartment house. The lease provided that the lessor had a right of re-entry upon the breach of any condition in the lease and a lien upon all personal effects, furniture, and baggage in the tenant's apartment to secure the rents and other charges. One of the conditions was the payment of $132.50 rent on the first of each month. Plaintiff paid the rent for eight months. After she was two months in arrears in rent, defendant, without her consent and during her temporary absence, unlocked the door of her apartment, entered and removed her furniture to a warehouse, and refused to allow her to re-occupy the apartment. Thereupon plaintiff filed this action for forcible entry and detainer and for conversion of her furniture and other personal property.

The jury returned a verdict of $6,500 for forcible entry and detainer and for conversion and $3,000 punitive damages. Plaintiff appeals from an order granting defendant's motion for a new trial. . . .

The order granting the new trial specifies that it is based solely on the ground of error occurring at the trial. "In the absence of the specification of insufficiency of the evidence to support the verdict, we are precluded from considering the question whether the evidence was sufficient to sustain the verdict unless it was without conflict and insufficient as a matter of law." Adams v. American President Lines, 23 Cal. 2d 681, 683, 146 P.2d 1, 2.

Defendant contends that there is no evidence that he violated either section 1159 or 1160 of the Code of Civil Procedure and that the evidence is therefore insufficient as a matter of law to sustain a verdict for forcible entry and detainer. He bases this contention on the grounds that (1) his entry was not unlawful, since he had a right of re-entry; (2) he did not violate subdivision 1 of section 1159, since he did not use force to enter the premises; (3) he did not violate subdivision 2 of section 1159, since that subdivision applies only when a stranger to the title obtains a "scrambling" possession (a possession concurrent with that of the person having a right to possession); (4) he did not violate subdivision 1 of section 1160, since he neither unlawfully nor forcibly detained possession to the apartment; and that (5) in any case his entry was privileged by virtue of his lien on the property in the apartment.

DEFENDANT'S RIGHT OF RE-ENTRY IS NOT A DEFENSE
TO AN ACTION FOR FORCIBLE ENTRY

In defining forcible entry section 1159 of the Code of Civil Procedure refers to "every person," thereby including owners as well as strangers to the title.

Under section 1172 of the Code of Civil Procedure the plaintiff "shall only be required to show, in addition to the forcible entry or forcible detainer complained of, that he was peaceably in the actual possession at the time of the forcible entry, or was entitled to the possession at the time of the forcible detainer. The defendant may show in his defense that he or his ancestors, or those whose interest in such premises he claims, have been in the quiet possession thereof for the space of one whole year together next before the commencement of the proceedings, and that his interest therein is not ended or determined; and such showing is a bar to the proceedings." Nowhere is it stated that a right of re-entry is a defense to an action for forcible entry or detainer.

Nor can such a defense be implied from the historical background or purpose of the statute.

Both before and after the enactment of the present forcible entry and detainer statutes this court held that ownership or right of possession to the property was not a defense to an action for forcible entry. In McCauley v. Weller, 1859, 12 Cal. 500, 524 [decided before the enactment of sections 1159 through 1179a of the Code of Civil Procedure] and in Voll v. Hollis, 1882, 60 Cal. 569, 573 [decided after the enactment of the foregoing sections] it was held that evidence of defendant's ownership of the land was irrelevant to the question of liability for a forcible entry and detainer. "[T]he action of forcible entry and detainer is a summary proceeding to recover possession of premises forcibly or unlawfully detained. The inquiry in such cases is confined to the actual peaceable possession of the plaintiff and the unlawful or forcible ouster or detention by defendant — the object of the law being to prevent the disturbance of the public peace, by the forcible assertion of a private right. Questions of title or right of possession cannot arise; a forcible entry upon the actual possession of plaintiff being proven, he would be entitled to restitution, though the fee-simple title and present right of possession are shown to be in the defendant. The authorities on this point are numerous and uniform."

In Lasserot v. Gamble [114 Cal. xvi, 46 P. 917 (1896)]; Kerr v. O'Keefe [138 Cal. 415, 71 P. 447 (1903)]; California Products, Inc. v. Mitchell [52 Cal. App. 312, 198 P. 646 (1921)], and Martin v. Cassidy [149 Cal. App. 2d 106, 307 P.2d 981 (1957)], the landlord entered pursuant to a lease granting him a right of re-entry similar to defendant's right of re-entry in the present case. In each case the court held that absent a voluntary surrender of the premises by the tenant, the landlord could enforce his right of re-entry only by judicial process, not by self-help. Under section 1161 of the Code of Civil Procedure a lessor may summarily obtain possession of his real property within three days. This remedy is a complete answer to any claim that self-help is necessary.

As in the foregoing cases, the lease herein is silent as to the method of enforcing the right of re-entry. In any event a provision in the lease expressly permitting a forcible entry would be void as contrary to the public policy set forth in section 1159. Spencer v. Commercial Co., 30 Wash. 520, 71 P. 53,

55 [involving forcible entry and detainer statutes identical with section 1159]; cf. California Products, Inc. v. Mitchell, *supra,* 52 Cal. App. 312, 314-315, 198 P. 646. Regardless of who has the right to possession, orderly procedure and preservation of the peace require that the actual possession shall not be disturbed except by legal process.

DEFENDANT WAS GUILTY OF FORCIBLE ENTRY

Section 1159 Subdivision 1 prohibits an entry by means of breaking open doors or windows. Defendant violated this section when he unlocked plaintiff's apartment without her consent and entered with the storage company employees to remove her furniture, even though there was no physical damage to the premises or actual violence. . . .

In Winchester v. Becker, *supra,* 4 Cal. App. 382, 384, 88 P. 296, defendant also used a key to unlock the tenant's door in the absence of the tenant. The court held that any unauthorized opening of a closed door is a breaking open of the door within the meaning of this subdivision. The words "breaking open" in section 1159 were given the meaning they had in the common law of burglary. Likewise in McNeil v. Higgins, *supra,* 86 Cal. App. 2d 273, 725, 195 P.2d 470, 471, the court held that an entry through an open window was an entry "gained by exercise of unlawful force" and in violation of section 1159. . . .

In Illinois, under a statute similar to 5 Richard II c. 7., force has been defined as an entry against the consent of the occupant. The court there stated that an entry by force means "no more than the term 'vi et armis' means at common law; that is, 'with either actual or implied force.'" Phelps v. Randolph, 147 Ill. 335, 35 N.E. 243, 245; see also Prosser on Torts 100 (2d ed.); 1 Harper and James, The Law of Torts 262; 2 Taylor, Landlord and Tenant 414, Footnote 1 (9th ed.).

Even if we were to interpret the first subdivision of section 1159 as being inapplicable unless a door or window was physically damaged or threats of violence actually occurred, the evidence in the instant case would nevertheless support a finding of forcible entry as defined by subdivision 2 of section 1159. Under that subdivision a forcible entry is completed if, after a peaceable entry, the occupant is excluded from possession by force or threats of violence. The removal of plaintiff's furniture without her consent rendered the apartment unsuitable for residence and forced her to seek shelter elsewhere. Moreover, when plaintiff returned to her apartment at 1:30 A.M. and inquired about her belongings defendant's employee ordered her to "Get the hell out of here. You're out of this place. Don't talk to me about it. Call Mr. Talbot." The jury could reasonably conclude that plaintiff was justified in believing that any attempt on her part to reinstall her furniture would be met by force. It has long been settled that there is a forcible entry under subdivision 2 if a show of force is made that causes the occupant to refrain from re-entering. McCauley v. Weller, 12 Cal. 500, 527; Treat v. Forsyth, 40 Cal. 484, 488; Kerr v. O'Keefe, 138 Cal. 415, 421-422, 71 P. 447. . . .

In Baxley v. Western Loan & Building Co., *supra,* 135 Cal. App. 426, 429, 27 P.2d 387, on which defendant relies, the court held that subdivision 2 of section 1159 applies only to cases of "scrambling possession." No authority was cited for this proposition. It conflicts with the express holdings of this court in McCauley v. Weller, *supra;* Treat v. Forsyth, *supra,* and Kerr v. O'Keefe, *supra,* and is therefore disapproved. Potter v. Mercer, 53 Cal. 667, 674, which held that subdivision 2 of section 1159, is not applicable when the owner of the land prohibits re-entry by the occupant, likewise conflicts with the foregoing cases and is overruled.

DEFENDANT WAS GUILTY OF A FORCIBLE DETAINER

Subdivision 1 of section 1160 of the Code of Civil Procedure provides that a person is guilty of a forcible detainer if he *"[b]y force or by menaces and threats of violence unlawfully* holds and keeps the possession of any real property, whether the same was acquired peaceably or otherwise." (Italics added.) In the present case there is evidence that the apartment was withheld by force and menace and that such withholding was unlawful.

Force and menace can be implied from defendant's agent's removal of plaintiff's furniture and his admonishment to "Get the hell out of here. You're out . . ."

The detention was unlawful, for a person who obtains possession to property by a forcible entry does not have the right to retain possession. . . .

DEFENDANT WAS NOT AUTHORIZED TO ENFORCE HIS LIEN BY ENTERING PLAINTIFF'S HOME

The provision in the lease granting defendant a lien does not specify a means of enforcement. In Childs Real Estate Co. v. Shelburne Realty Co., 23 Cal. 2d 263, 268, 143 P.2d 697, 699, where the lessor had a similar lien, we stated "in the absence of provisions in the lease for enforcement, equitable action would be necessary to make the lien operative [citations]." Childs Real Estate Co. v. Shelburne Realty Co., 23 Cal. 2d 263, 268, 143 P.2d 697. Even if the lease had authorized a forcible entry it would be invalid as violating the policy of the forcible entry and detainer statutes. See California Products, Inc. v. Mitchell, 52 Cal. App. 312, 315, 198 P. 646; Spencer v. Commercial Co., 30 Wash. 520, 71 P. 53, 55. . . .

We conclude therefore that the evidence supports the verdict of forcible entry and detainer. There was evidence that defendant entered plaintiff's apartment without her consent. Such an entry violates section 1159 of the

Code of Civil Procedure. There was evidence that defendant refused to allow plaintiff to re-enter her apartment. Such conduct violates section 1160 of the Code of Civil Procedure. Since the policy of these sections is the preservation of the peace, the rights thereunder may not be contracted away; thus defendant's right of re-entry and his lien on personal property in the apartment did not justify his entry into the apartment.

DEFENDANT DID NOT CONVERT PLAINTIFF'S GOODS

Defendant stored most of the items removed from plaintiff's apartment in a warehouse in plaintiff's name. The items that the warehousemen had difficulty removing were stored in the lessor's basement and held for the plaintiff. The lessor did not use any of plaintiff's belongings or make any claim of ownership to them. In Zaslow v. Kroenert, 29 Cal. 2d 541, 551, 176 P.2d 1, we held that the removal of another's property and storing it in the owner's name without any other exercise of dominion or control is not a conversion. We there stated that "[w]here the conduct complained of does not amount to a substantial interference with the possession or the right thereto, but consists of intermeddling with or use of or damages to the personal property, the owner has a cause of action for trespass or case, and may recover only the actual damages suffered by reason of the impairment of the property or the loss of its use." Zaslow v. Kroenert, *supra,* 29 Cal. 2d at page 551, 176 P.2d at page 7; see Prosser on Torts, pp. 102-107 (2d ed.); Fleming on Torts 58.

Plaintiff is therefore entitled only to actual damages in an amount sufficient to compensate her for any impairment of the property or loss of its use. Zaslow v. Kroenert, *supra,* 29 Cal. 2d 549-552, 176 P.2d 6-8.

Furthermore, plaintiff had a duty to minimize damages. Valencia v. Shell Oil Co., 23 Cal. 2d 840, 844, 147 P.2d 558. She knew that the property was being held in storage in her name. If she had the funds, or could obtain them by a lien on the property held, she was under a duty to recover her goods as soon as possible and is entitled only to costs of storage for whatever time is reasonable to make new arrangements. Plaintiff would have had to move to new quarters under any circumstances since she was in arrears in her rent and defendant had the right to re-enter pursuant to legal process. There was testimony that additional loans could have been obtained on the furniture. On retrial, however, plaintiff may show that she was without funds or means of obtaining them to pay the storage costs. In that case she would not be under a duty to recover the furniture to minimize damages. "The duty to minimize damages does not require an injured person to do what is unreasonable or impracticable, and, consequently, when expenditures are necessary for minimization of damages, the duty does not run to a person who is financially unable to make such expenditures." Valencia v. Shell Oil Co., *supra,* 23 Cal. 2d 840, 846, 147 P.2d 558, 561.

The verdict for conversion was as a matter of law unsupported by the evidence. The new trial was therefore properly granted. . . .

GIBSON, C.J., and PETERS and DOOLING, JJ., concur.

SCHAUER, Justice (dissenting).

McCOMB and WHITE, JJ., concur.

Rehearing denied; SCHAUER, McCOMB and WHITE, JJ., dissenting.

SECTION 2.   REMEDIES AVAILABLE TO THE TENANT

As noted in Chapter 17, the basic common-law rule is that in the absence of a statute or agreement to the contrary, the landlord is not obligated to make repairs within the demised premises — either to put the premises in repair or to keep them in repair during the lease term.

An operative standard in contracts for voiding the obligations of one party is that there is a failure of consideration. Thus, in a bilateral contract, upon the failure of A to carry out A's obligations, B may rescind the contract on a failure of consideration. However, the covenants in a lease historically have been treated as independent.

Because of the so-called independence of lease covenants and limitations upon the doctrine of constructive eviction at common law (Chapter 19), the tenant's only remedy when faced with a situation in which the leased premises are not fit for their intended purpose, or any other situation in which the landlord is in default, is to terminate the lease and sue for damages. With respect to housing, it may be particularly burdensome (and in many cases, in view of the post-World War II rental housing shortage, well-nigh impossible) for the tenant to move out and find decent substitute housing. Tenants, especially those with limited resources, faced with the current housing shortage may be forced to accept housing conditions that fall short of habitability.

This section is concerned with methods the tenant may be able to employ to improve his or her bargaining position and hence the condition of the premises, thereby providing an alternative to the sometimes Pyrrhic act of terminating the lease.

As you will see from your reading of Chapter 19, Section 2, particularly part B, which deals with the breach of the implied warranty of fitness and/or habitability, many jurisdictions have abolished the doctrine of independence of lease covenants and have permitted tenants to defend rent actions by alleging the landlord's breach of this implied covenant.

Note: New York's Statutory Arsenal Used to Attack
the Tenant's Problem of Substandard Housing

New York State has at least eight major legal devices created by its legislature, each designed to eliminate substandard housing in its own way.

1. The oldest tenant remedy, the rent strike, as one possible remedy for a constructive eviction, is now made legitimate. N.Y. Real Prop. Acts. Law §775.[10]

2. Rent may be withheld by a petition of one-third of the tenants. N.Y. Real Prop. Acts. Law art. 7A, §770.[11]

3. Rent may be withheld by the welfare authorities. Soc. Serv. Law §143-b.[12]

4. Rent may be abated during the continuance of certain "rent impairing" violations. N.Y. Mult. Dwell. Law §302-a.[13]

5. The owners of such substandard housing may be criminally prosecuted. N.Y. Mult. Dwell. Law §304.[14]

6. The offending building may be ordered vacated. N.Y. Mult. Dwell. Law §309.[15]

7. Controlled rents may be involuntarily reduced. N.Y.C. Admin. Code §Y-51-5.0(h).[16]

8. The offending building may be put into receivership, so that the city can make the necessary repairs and obtain a prior lien on all rents to secure reimbursement. N.Y. Mult. Dwell. Law §309.[17]

In considering the efficacy of New York's veritable arsenal, you should not fall into the trap of thinking that these statutes only affect the indigent tenant.[18]

10. This is the first statute ever passed which legitimized the "rent strike," enacted in 1939. A section 755 proceeding originates with the withholding of rent by a tenant (or tenants, in the context of a rent strike) of a building against which violations have been recorded by a "code enforcement agency," which violations are deemed tantamount to a constructive eviction. The tenant may defend an action for rent by obtaining a court order declaring that the code violations are substantial enough to constitute a constructive eviction, which order stays the eviction proceeding. During the period of the stay, the rent is to be paid into court, and when the violations are dismissed, the withheld rent is paid to the landlord. The law has been sustained against attack. Emray Realty Corp. v. DeStefano, 5 Misc. 2d 352, 160 N.Y.S.2d 433 (Sup. Ct. 1957).

11. Effective July 1, 1965. Where one-third of the tenants in a building join in a petition alleging the existence of conditions dangerous to health or safety (not necessarily code violations), an administrator may be appointed to collect the rents and make repairs. See Stang, Tenant Initiated Repairs: New York's Article 7-A, 2 Harv. C.R.L. Rev. 201 (1967). This statute has been held constitutional in Himmel v. Chase Manhattan Bank, 47 Misc. 2d 93, 262 N.Y.S.2d 515 (N.Y. Civ. Ct. 1965).

12. Compare Trozze v. Drooney, 35 Misc. 2d 1060, 232 N.Y.S.2d 139 (Binghamton City Ct. 1962) (holding statute unconstitutional), with Schaeffer v. Montes, 37 Misc. 2d 722, 233 N.Y.S.2d 444 (City of New York Civ. Ct., Bronx County, 1962) (holding it constitutional). The latter view was upheld in Farrell v. Drew, 19 N.Y.2d 486, 227 N.E.2d 824 (1967). See also Simmons, Passion and Prudence: Rent Withholding Under New York's Spiegel Law, 15 Buffalo L. Rev. 572 (1966).

13. See Comment, Rent Withholding and the Improvement of Substandard Housing, 53 Calif. L. Rev. 304 (1965). Under this statute the rent-impairing violations must have been in

A. *Rent Abatement*

The remedy of rent abatement is not new, but until recently abatement was available only in limited situations, such as where the leased premises were partially condemned by public authorities or partially destroyed through no fault of the tenant.

The Restatement (Second) of Property (Landlord and Tenant) §§5.1-5.4 recognizes that an abatement in rent is a remedy available to the tenant in specified situations where due to the default of the landlord the leased property is unsuitable for the use contemplated by the parties. Section 11.1 of the Restatement provides as follows:

> If the Tenant is entitled to an abatement of the rent, the rent is abated to the amount of that proportion of the rent which the fair rental value after the event giving the right to abate bears to the fair rental value before the event. Abatement is allowed until the default is eliminated or the lease terminates, whichever first occurs.

TEODORI v. WERNER
490 Pa. 58, 415 A.2d 31 (1980)

ROBERTS, J.

Tenant William Werner (appellant) seeks to open both a confessed money judgment and a confessed judgment of possession entered in favor of

---

existence for six months. After that time the tenant may cease paying rent but must save the rent until an action is commenced against him or her, at which time the rent is paid into court.

14. See former Penal Law §2040. In 1965, the average fine in New York City was $13.96. N.Y. Times, Apr. 15, 1966, at 36, col. 5. See Gribetz & Grad, Housing Code Enforcement: Sanctions and Remedies, 66 Colum. L. Rev. 1254, 1275-1281 (1966), for a good discussion of the reasons for the statute's failure.

15. In recent years, very few vacate orders have been issued by the Department of Buildings; see, e.g., 1964 New York Department of Buildings Annual Report 102. Code administrators hesitate to act even when this drastic remedy is clearly justifiable because if a building is officially condemned, it would only mean more evicted tenants with no place to go. See Wald, Law and Poverty: 1965, Report to the National Conference on Law and Poverty 14 (1965).

16. The rents may be reduced to one dollar a month.

17. See Gribetz, New York City's Receivership Law, 21 J. Housing 297 (1964); Pratt, Receiverships in the Rehabilitation of Urban Housing, 2 Harv. C.R.L. Rev. 219 (1967). The statute recognized the inadequacy of economic compulsion in hard core cases and attempted to assure that needed repairs would be made by enabling the city's department of real estate to perform them in return for a lien against the building. Unfortunately, the liens were never paid, and the city administrator stated that the receivership program was to be "scuttled." N.Y. Times, Jan. 14, 1967, at 33, col. 8. Only 8 of 118 landlords had reimbursed New York City for the repair expenditures made by receivers. These stark statistics are not really surprising, for in allowing the building to be taken by a receiver instead of making the repairs, the landlord had in effect made the judgment that the condition of the building had so deteriorated that it was uneconomical to invest capital in repairs in light of the existing rent roll.

18. See Himmel v. Chase Manhattan Bank, 47 Misc. 2d 93, 262 N.Y.S.2d 515 (Civ. Ct. 1965).

landlords Carlo and Mildred Teodori (appellees). Primarily at issue on this appeal is whether landlords' breach of the lease's "non-competition" clause provides tenant a defense to the landlords' actions for sums due and in ejectment. We are persuaded by our established case law, e.g., McDanel v. Mack Realty Co., 315 Pa. 174, 172 A. 97 (1934), and modern authority, e.g., Restatement (Second) of Property, Landlord and Tenant (1977), that tenant has a valid defense.

I

Tenant leases a 1500 square foot retail storeroom in Donaldson's Crossroads Shopping Center where he operates his own retail jewelry business and gift shop. The parties' most recent written lease agreement, executed in June of 1973, provides for a five-year term of occupancy beginning August 1, 1973 and ending July 31, 1978. In the parties' "non-competition" clause, landlords agree not to "lease or operate as owner any space in the shopping center or any extension thereof primarily as a jewelry or gift shop."

In addition to a monthly base payment of $437.50, tenant annually is to pay to landlords five percent of the gross proceeds from jewelry sales and ten percent from gifts. Tenant also is to pay ten cents per square foot annually for maintenance of outside areas as well as increases in taxes owed by landlords and all charges for gas, water, sewer use, steam, electricity, light, heat or power, and telephone. Tenant is to render an annual "certified statement" showing the total gross proceeds of all business done upon the premises during the preceding year. Tenant also agrees, "on every default of payment of rent," or "on any and every breach of covenant or agreement," to "empower any attorney of any court of record" to appear for tenant and confess judgment against him. By the terms of the instrument this power of confession extends to an action for the sum due and/or an action in ejectment.

On September 2, 1977, eleven months before expiration of the stated term of the lease, landlords instituted a proceeding against tenant for entry of judgments by confession, seeking both a "specific amount due" and ejectment. Landlords based their requests for both judgments on averments that tenant owed them monthly base payments, maintenance charges and utilities, and increased taxes. Landlords additionally claimed that tenant failed to provide landlords with a timely certified statement of gross proceeds and failed to pay the percentage of proceeds owing. Acting pursuant to the warrant of attorney contained in the lease agreement, counsel appeared for tenant and confessed judgment in landlords' favor in the amount of $7,056.29.[19] Counsel also confessed judgment of possession. The prothonotary entered judgments the same day.

---

19. The confessed money judgment of $7,056.29 includes a sum of $4,812.50 reflecting future rents for the eleven months remaining in the stated term of occupancy.

On September 15, 1977, less than two weeks after entry of the confessed judgments, tenant petitioned the Court of Common Pleas of Washington County to open both of the confessed judgments. As a defense, tenant alleged that landlords violated the parties' non-competition clause by leasing shopping center space to "Pennsylvania Wholesalers" for operation of a competing jewelry and gift shop business. Tenant also alleged that he did provide a certified statement of gross receipts and did pay the appropriate percentage.[20]

The same day the chancellor issued a rule on appellees to show cause why the confessed judgments should not be opened, "all proceedings to stay meanwhile." In landlords' answer, they claimed that as to the alleged breach of the non-competition clause tenant "has no legal ground to stop paying rent in the present case." As to the certified statement clause, landlord alleged that "regardless of the statement of the defendant, he did not file a certified statement and a simple showing of evidence will prove this."[21]

Landlords did not, however, seek a rule on tenant either to take depositions on the disputed factual issue concerning compliance with the certified statement clause or to order the case for argument. See Pa. R. Civ. Proc. 209. Instead, at the time they filed their answer, landlords requested the chancellor to set the matter for hearing. The chancellor granted landlords' request and scheduled a hearing. Landlords then filed an amended answer, setting forth the same claims contained in their original answer.

The matter then proceeded to argument, as requested by landlords. After argument, the chancellor dismissed the tenant's petition to open.[22] Executions were stayed when tenant filed a bond of $7300. On tenant's appeal, the Superior Court affirmed. This Court granted allowance of appeal.

II

At the outset we agree with tenant that landlords have admitted the factual allegations of tenant's petition to open.

Because we accept as true tenant's factual allegations, the confessed judgments cannot stand on landlords' claim that tenant failed to comply with the parties' certified statements clause. Rather, the judgments can stand only if landlords are correct in their claim that, regardless of their compliance with the parties' non-competition clause, tenant owes an independent, continuing obligation throughout the term fully to pay them the stated rents. We agree, however, with the tenant that landlords' view of tenant's obligation must be rejected.

Landlords' theory is unsupportable. It is true that "[a]t old common law

---

20.   Accompanying tenant's petition to open is a petition to strike off the confessed money judgment on the ground that it improperly included the future rents. See supra note [19].

21.   In their answer, landlords admitted that inclusion of the future rents is improper in view of their simultaneously-obtained judgment of possession.

22.   The court also dismissed tenant's petition to strike off the confessed money judgment.

the promises made by a landlord in a lease were independent obligations, so that the failure of the landlord to perform them did not give the tenant any right to disregard his obligations under the lease." Restatement (Second) of Property, Landlord and Tenant, *supra,* Introductory Note to Chapter 7. See generally I Friedman on Leases §1.1 (1974). It is now clear, however, that this view of landlord-tenant relations, incorrectly resting more on notions of property law than on principles of contracts, has no place in modern jurisprudence. As long ago as 1934 this Court in McDanel v. Mack Realty Co., *supra,* recognized the error of the independence-of-obligations approach as applied to a commercial lease transaction. At issue in *McDanel* was the scope of the commercial tenant's remedies where the commercial landlord defaulted on its covenant to heat the leased premises. In addition to the options of (1) performing "at his own expense" and deducting this cost from the rent due or (2) surrendering the premises "to relieve himself from any further payment of rent," the tenant "(3) . . . can retain possession of the premises and deduct from the rent the difference between the rental value of the premises as it would have been if the lease had been fully complied with by the landlord and the rental value in the condition it actually was." *McDanel,* 315 Pa. at 178, 172 A. at 98. See Gorman v. Miller, 27 Pa. Super. 62, 68 (1905). And "[t]he emerging judicial sentiment in regard to the landlord's obligation to provide leased property that meets health and safety standards repudiates the independence-of-obligations approach in leases in that area. . . ." Restatement (Second) of Property, Landlord and Tenant, *supra.* See Pugh v. Holmes, 486 Pa. 272, 405 A.2d 897 (1979); Commonwealth v. Monumental Properties, Inc., 459 Pa. 450, 329 A.2d 812 (1974); Reitmeyer v. Sprecher, 431 Pa. 284, 243 A.2d 395 (1968). See also Albert M. Greenfield & Co. v. Kolea, 475 Pa. 351, 380 A.2d 758 (1977) (tenant relieved of rental obligation where accidental fire destroys premises).

So too the independence-of-obligations approach must be rejected where the landlord's promise to perform "is a significant inducement to the making of the lease by the tenant." Restatement (Second) of Property, Landlord and Tenant, *supra.* It is obvious that a landlord's non-competition promise is critical to a commercial lease agreement like the one here. "The mere presence in a lease of a noncompetition promise by the landlord justifies the conclusion that it is essential that the promise be observed if the tenant is to conduct his business on the leased property profitably." Id. at §7.2 Comment b, p. 254. See also Friedman, *supra,* at p. 7 (citing cases). It therefore must be concluded that absent a contrary agreement between the parties a tenant's obligations are not independent of a landlord's promise under a non-competition clause.

Here, in withholding the full prescribed payments, tenant acted well within his rights. Section 7.2 of the Restatement provides:

Except to the extent the parties to a lease validly agree otherwise, the failure of the landlord to perform a promise contained in the lease that he, or someone holding under him, will not use other property in a manner that will compete with a business of the tenant, or of someone holding under the tenant, on the leased property, makes the landlord in default under the lease, if he does not cease, or cause to cease, the competing business within a reasonable time after being requested by the tenant to do so. For that default, the tenant may: . . .

(2) continue the lease and, if the landlord's promise is valid, obtain appropriate equitable and legal relief including the various remedies prescribed in §7.1(2).

These parties have not agreed otherwise. There is no dispute that tenant seasonably requested landlords to cease their violation. Nor is there any dispute that landlords' promise is valid.[23] The various remedies "prescribed" include under section 11.1 abatement of rent. See McDanel v. Mack Realty Co., *supra*.[24] Both judgments therefore must be opened to permit tenant an opportunity to establish his defense. . . .[25]

Order of the Superior Court reversed and case remanded for proceedings consistent with this opinion.

---

23. Indeed, this promise, reasonable both in duration and scope, can serve a proper function. As Commentary to the Restatement points out, "the need for landlord's noncompetition promises is particularly significant in connection with the development of a shopping center designed to provide complete shopping services within a specific area. Using the space in the area for several businesses of the same type cuts down on the space available to provide different types of businesses, and makes it less likely that the shopping center complex will be able to attract the quality of businesses that may be essential to its financial success." Restatement (Second) of Property, Landlord and Tenant, *supra*, §7.2 at Comment d. See id. at Reporter's Note Item 2; Hoffman v. Rittenhouse, 413 Pa. 587, 198 A.2d 543 (1964); Harris Calorific Co. v. Marra, 345 Pa. 464, 29 A.2d 64 (1942); Cleaver v. Lenhart, 182 Pa. 285, 37 A. 811 (1897); Restatement (Second) of Contracts §§328-330 (Tent. Draft No. 12, 1977). "[P]arties are entitled to a degree of freedom in contracting to protect their own economic interests and . . . controlled development of a given business center may be desirable." Note, Restrictive Covenants in Shopping Center Leases, 34 N.Y.U.L. Rev. 940 (1959). See Cragmere Holding Corp. v. Socony-Mobil Oil Co., 65 N.J. Super. 322, 167 A.2d 825 (1961).

24. Section 11.1 of Restatement (Second) of Property, Landlord and Tenant, provides:

> If the tenant is entitled to an abatement of the rent, the rent is abated to the amount of that proportion of the rent which the fair rental value after the event giving the right to abate bears to the fair rental value before the event. Abatement is allowed until the default is eliminated or the lease terminates, whichever first occurs.

See also id. at §7.2(1) (termination); id. at §7.1(2)(a) (damages); id. at §7.1(2)(c) (use rent to perform landlord's promise); id. at §7.1(2)(d) (withhold rent). See generally III Friedman on Leases §§28.601-28.604 (1978). It appears that the remedy of abatement set forth in the Restatement is based at least in part on *McDanel, supra*. See Reporter's Note to §11.1, Item 2. As the Reporter's Note points out, however, the Restatement's "proportional value" rule differs from *McDanel*'s "loss of fair rental value" rule. See id.; id. at Item 4.

25. We note that landlords urge "that a commercial tenant in a shopping center cannot unilaterally make a decision that the landlord has breached the no-competition clause by leasing space to a third party." Brief for Appellees at 12. According to landlords, tenant's relief lies in equity, not in a defense to proceedings instituted by landlords. We cannot agree. As Restatement (Second) points out,

> [f]requently the rent abatement will be accomplished in a judicial proceeding brought by the landlord to evict the tenant for the failure to pay the rent. In this proceeding, if the tenant is entitled to abate the rent, he is entitled to defend against eviction by establish-

Note: The Restatement's Position on Rent Abatement

Section 11.1 of the Restatement (Second) of Property (Landlord and Tenant) adopts the self-help approach taken by the Pennsylvania courts. In other jurisdictions, only retroactive abatement of the rent during the period of the landlord's default may be available. See the *Javins* case, page 507 *infra,* and Hinson v. Delis, 26 Cal. App. 3d 62, 102 Cal. Rptr. 661 (1972).

Note: The Appropriate Measure of Abatement

L grants T a ten-year lease in L's shopping mall for $2,000 a month. The lease provides that T will be entitled to a storefront on the main concourse and also a storage area in another part of the mall. At the time of the signing of the lease, the storage area represented approximately 10 percent of the rent, or $200 a month. Two years into the lease period, L fills the storage space with Christmas decorations. Because the mall has been such a success (and the need for storage area even more important), the fair rental value of the storefront and storage space is now $5,000 a month, and of the storefront without the storage space $4,000 a month. Assuming T seeks an abatement, should the monthly abatement be

1. $1,000 (the loss in rental value);
2. $400 (the proportionate loss—i.e., 20 percent—in rental value without the storage space);
3. $0 (abatement to fair rental value); or
4. some other amount?

What if the monthly rental value of the lease is now $1,500 with the storage space and $1,350 without? See Restatement (Second) of Property (Landlord and Tenant) §11.1 and Item 4 of the accompanying Reporter's Note. What if T sued for or claimed actual partial eviction? Consider whether damages (as distinct from abatement) is in some instances a more suitable tenant remedy.

B. Rent Application

As previously noted, at common law the landlord is not responsible for maintaining the leased premises (see Chapter 17, Section 2, Part B). There is,

---

ing his right to abate the rent and paying to the landlord the amount of the abated rent as judicially determined in the proceedings.

Section 11.1 Comment b at p. 358. See also id. (recommending availability of declaratory relief); McDanel v. Mack Realty Co., *supra* (abatement). Landlords also suggest that the "Rent Withholding Act," Act of January 24, 1966, P.L. (1965) 1534, §1, as amended, 35 P.S. §1700-1 (1977), which authorizes rent withholding where a local health department certifies a dwelling as unfit for human habitation, "preempts" judicial creation of any mode of non-equitable relief. We reject this contention out of hand. See Pugh v. Holmes, *supra,* 486 Pa. at 286-287, 405 A.2d at 904-905.

however, a definite trend away from this common law rule, primarily evidenced by statutes specifically providing for the remedy of rent application. The statutes are collected in the Statutory Note to Chapter 5 of the Restatement (Second) of Property (Landlord and Tenant), Item 3. In addition, a limited number of courts have permitted rent application as a self-help remedy where there was no express promise to repair.

The Restatement (Second) of Property (Landlord and Tenant) §§5.1-5.4 recognizes the use of rent application by a tenant to eliminate an unsuitable condition in specified situations where due to the default of the landlord the leased property is unsuitable for the use contemplated by the parties. Section 11.2 of the Restatement provides as follows: "If the tenant is entitled to apply his rent to eliminate the landlord's default, the tenant, after proper notice to the landlord, may deduct from his rent reasonable costs incurred in eliminating the default."

The following case considers the right of the tenant to the remedy of rent application.

MARINI v. IRELAND
56 N.J. 130, 265 A.2d 526 (1970)

HANEMAN, J.

This matter concerns the appealability of County District Court landlord and tenant dispossess judgments; the scope of a landlord's duty to make repairs; and the right to offset the cost of such repairs against accruing rent on the failure of the landlord to make same, if found to be required.

On or about April 2, 1969, plaintiff, landlord, and defendant, tenant, entered into a one-year lease for an apartment located in a two-family duplex building at 503-B Rand Street, Camden, New Jersey. The annual rent of $1,140 was agreed to be paid in monthly installments of $95. The lease incorporated a covenant of quiet enjoyment but did not include a specific covenant for repairs.

On or about June 25, 1969, defendant alleges that she discovered that the toilet in the leased apartment was cracked and water was leaking onto the bathroom floor. She further alleges that repeated attempts to inform plaintiff of this condition were unsuccessful. On or about June 27, 1969, defendant hired one Karl T. Bittner, a registered plumber, to repair the toilet. Bittner repaired the toilet at a cost of $85.72, which the tenant paid.

On July 15, 1969, defendant mailed plaintiff a check for $9.28 together with the receipt for $85.72 in payment of the July rent. Plaintiff challenged the offsetting of the cost of the repair and demanded the outstanding $85.72.

When his demands were refused, plaintiff instituted a summary dispossess action for nonpayment of rent in the Camden County District Court pursuant to N.J.S.A. 2A:18-53(b) alleging the nonpayment of the July rent in the amount of $85.72 and August rent of $95. A hearing was had on August 15, 1969. Plaintiff argued that he was entitled to the $85.72 because he had no duty to make repairs and consequently, defendant's payment of the cost of repair could not be offset against rent.

The judge conceived the issue as entirely a legal one and determined that the facts which defendant alleged did not create a duty upon the landlord to make repairs. Thus, without trying out the issues tendered by defendant, he found a default in payment of rent of $85.72 (July) and $95 (August) plus costs and rendered a judgment for possession. Defendant appealed to the Appellate Division.

On August 29, 1969, a judge of the Appellate Division granted a temporary stay of the judgment for possession and the warrant of eviction. The Appellate Division granted a stay pending appeal on September 23, 1969 and ordered defendant to pay all the rents then due except the contested July rent. The Appellate Division also then denied plaintiff's cross-motion to dismiss the appeal. Before the Appellate Division heard argument, this Court certified the case on its own motion. R. 2:12-1.

The issues which evolve on this appeal are: Did defendant's claimed right to offset her cost of repairs against rent raise a "jurisdictional" issue. If the answer to that query is in the affirmative, did the landlord have a duty to repair and may the issue of failure to comply with such duty be raised in a dispossess action. Also involved in the latter question is the right of the tenant to make repairs upon the landlord's failure to so do and the right to offset the cost thereof against rent. . . .

We hold, therefore, that equitable as well as legal defenses asserting payment or absolution from payment in whole or part are available to a tenant in a dispossess action and must be considered by the court. Denial of a motion by defendant directed at the complaint for failure to make adequate factual allegations, or of a motion at the conclusion of the trial for failure to supply proof that the amount of rent alleged in the complaint is in default, both going to the question of jurisdiction, are each appealable.

Insofar as Peters v. Kelly, 98 N.J. Super. 441, 237 A.2d 635 (App. Div. 1968), conflicts with the foregoing it is overruled.

It becomes necessary to consider the merits of defendant's equitable defense that the failure of the landlord to repair the toilet constituted a breach of the covenant of habitability or quiet enjoyment and gave rise to defendant's entitlement to self-help, permitting her to repair the toilet and offset the cost thereof against her rent. We need not concern ourselves with the covenant of quiet enjoyment as will hereafter become apparent.

We are here concerned with the lease of premises for residential purposes. The lease provides:

> WITNESSETH, that the said party of the first part hath let, and by these presents doth grant, demise and to farm let unto the said party of the second part, all that contains 4 rooms and bath, apartment situated in the city and county of camden [*sic*], state [*sic*] of New Jersey, known and designated as 503-B Rand Street. . . . nor use or permit any part thereof to be used for any other purpose than dwelling. . . .

As the lease contains no express covenant to repair, we are obliged to determine whether there arises an implied covenant, however categorized, which would require the landlord to make repairs.

A lease was originally considered a conveyance of an interest in real estate. Thus, the duties and obligations of the parties, implied as well as express, were dealt with according to the law of property and not of the law of contracts. In Michaels v. Brookchester, Inc., 26 N.J. 379 (1958), this Court said at p. 382, 140 A.2d 199, at p. 201:

> Historically a lease was viewed as a sale of an interest in land. The concept of caveat emptor, applicable to such sales, seemed logically pertinent to leases of land. There was neither an implied covenant of fitness for the intended use nor responsibility in the landlord to maintain the leased premises. Bauer v. 141-149 Cedar Lane Holding Co., 24 N.J. 139, 145, 130 A.2d 833 (1957); Bolitho v. Mintz, 106 N.J.L. 449, 148 A. 737 (E. & A. 1930). This principle, suitable for the agrarian setting in which it was conceived, lagged behind changes in dwelling habits and economic realities. 1 American Law of Property (1952), §3.78, p. 347. Exceptions to the broad immunity inevitably developed.

The guidelines employed to construe contracts have been modernly applied to the construction of leases. 3 Thompson on Real Property 377 (1959). See also 6 Williston on Contracts, 3d ed. Jaeger, §890A, p. 592 (1962): "There is a clearly discernible tendency on the part of the courts to cast aside technicalities in the interpretation of leases and to concentrate their attention, as in the case of other contracts, on the intention of the parties. . . ." . . .

So here, the lease expressly described the leased premises as "4 rooms and bath, apartment" and restricted the use thereof for one purpose—"dwelling." Patently, "the effect which the parties, as fair and reasonable men, presumably would have agreed on," was that the premises were habitable and fit for living. The very object of the letting was to furnish the defendant with quarters suitable for living purposes. This is what the landlord at least impliedly (if not expressly) represented he had available and what the tenant was seeking. In a modern setting, the landlord should, in residential letting, be held to an implied covenant against latent defects, which is another manner of saying, habitability and livability fitness. See Hyland v. Parkside Investment Co., Inc., 10 N.J. Misc. 1148, 162 A. 521 (Sup. Ct. 1932). It is a mere matter of semantics whether we designate this covenant one "to repair" or "of habitability and livability fitness." Actually it is a covenant that at the inception of the lease, there are no latent defects in facilities vital to the use of the premises for residential purposes because of faulty original construction or deterioration from age or normal usage. And further it is a covenant that these facilities will remain in usable condition during the entire term of the lease. In performance of this covenant the landlord is required to maintain those facilities in a condition which renders the property livable.

It is eminently fair and just to charge a landlord with the duty of warranting that a building or part thereof rented for residential purposes is fit for that purpose at the inception of the term and will remain so during the entire term. Of course, ancillary to such understanding it must be implied that he has further agreed to repair damage to vital facilities caused by ordinary wear and tear during said term. Where damage has been caused maliciously or by abnormal or unusual use, the tenant is conversely liable for repair. The nature of vital facilities and the extent and type of maintenance and repair required is limited and governed by the type of property rented and the amount of rent reserved. Failure to so maintain the property would constitute a constructive eviction.

It becomes necessary to consider the respective rights and duties which accompany such an implied covenant. We must recognize that historically, the landlord's covenant to alter or repair premises and the tenant's covenant to pay rent were generally regarded as independent covenants. The landlord's failure to perform did not entitle the tenant to make the repair and offset the cost thereof against future rent. It only gave rise to a separate cause of action for breach of covenant. Duncan Development Co. v. Duncan Hardware, Inc., 34 N.J. Super. 293 at 298, 112 A.2d 274 (App. Div. 1955), *cert. denied* 19 N.J. 328, 116 A.2d 829 (1955); Stewart v. Childs Co., 86 N.J.L. 648, 92 A. 392 (E. & A. 1914). This result also eventuated from the application of the law of real estate rather than of contract. The concept of mutually dependent promises was not originally applied to the ascertainment of whether covenants in leases were dependent or independent. However, presently we recognize that covenants are dependent or independent according to the intention of the parties and the good sense of the case. Higgins v. Whiting, 102 N.J.L. 279, 131 A. 879 (Sup. Ct. 1925); 3 Thompson on Real Property, §1115 (1959 Replacement).

In Higgins v. Whiting, *supra,* the court said at pp. 280 and 281, 131 A. at p. 880 concerning the test of dependency of express covenants:

> In 24 Cyc. 918, it is said that covenants are to be construed as dependent or independent according to the intention and meaning of the parties and the good sense of the case. Technical words should give way to such intention. 7 R.C.L. 1090, §7. So, the rule is thus stated; where the acts or covenants of the parties are concurrent, and to be done or performed at the same time, the covenants are dependent, and neither party can maintain an action against the other, without averring and proving performance on his part. 13 Corpus Juris 567. . . .
>
> In the present case, the covenant to pay rent and the covenant to heat the apartment are mutual and dependent. In the modern apartment house equipped for heating from a central plant, entirely under the control of the landlord or his agent, heat is one of the things for which the tenant pays under the name "rent."

Our courts have on a case by case basis held various lease covenants and covenants to pay rent as dependent and under the guise of a constructive eviction have considered breach of the former as giving the right to the tenant to remove from the premises and terminate his obligation to pay rent. See McCurdy v. Wyckoff, 73 N.J.L. 368, 63 A. 992 (Sup. Ct. 1906); Weiler v. Pancoast, 71 N.J.L. 414, 58 A. 1084 (Sup. Ct. 1904); Higgins v. Whiting, 102 N.J.L. 279, 131 A. 879 (Sup. Ct. 1925); Stevenson Stanoyevich Fund v. Steinacher, 125 N.J.L. 326, 15 A.2d 772 (Sup. Ct. 1940).

It is of little comfort to a tenant in these days of housing shortage to accord him the right, upon a constructive eviction, to vacate the premises and end his obligation to pay rent. Rather he should be accorded the alternative remedy of terminating the cause of the constructive eviction where as here the cause is the failure to make reasonable repairs. See Reste Realty Corporation v. Cooper, *supra,* footnote 1, 53 N.J. pp. 462, 463, 251 A.2d 268. This latter course of action is accompanied by the right to offset the cost of such repairs as are reasonable in the light of the value of the leasehold against the rent. His pursuit of the latter form of relief should of course be circumscribed by the aforementioned conditions.

If, therefore, a landlord fails to make repairs and replacements of vital facilities necessary to maintain the premises in a livable condition for a period of time adequate to accomplish such repairs and replacements, the tenant may cause the same to be done and deduct the cost thereof from future rents. The tenant's recourse to such self-help must be preceded by timely and adequate notice to the landlord of the faulty condition in order to accord him the opportunity to make the necessary replacement or repair. If the tenant is unable to give such notice after a reasonable attempt, he may nonetheless proceed to repair or replace. This does not mean that the tenant is relieved from the payment of rent so long as the landlord fails to repair. The tenant has only the alternative remedies of making the repairs or removing from the premises upon such a constructive eviction.

We realize that the foregoing may increase the trials and appeals in landlord and tenant dispossess cases and thus increase the burden of the judiciary. By way of warning, however, it should be noted that the foregoing does not constitute an invitation to obstruct the recovery of possession by a landlord legitimately entitled thereto. It is therefore suggested that if the trial of the matter is delayed the defendant may be required to deposit the full amount of unpaid rent in order to protect the landlord if he prevails. Also, an application for a stay of an order of removal on appeal should be critically analyzed and not automatically granted.

In the light of the foregoing we find it unnecessary to pass on defendant's other grounds of appeal.

Reversed and remanded for trial in accordance with the above.

For reversal and remandment: Chief Justice WEINTRAUB and Justices JACOBS, FRANCIS, PROCTOR, HALL, SCHETTINO and HANEMAN — 7.

For affirmance: None.

Note: Marini v. Ireland

What if Mr. Bittner (the plumber) had not been able to repair the toilet? Should Ms. Ireland be able to apply three months' rent toward the purchase of a new toilet? Consider the California statute on rent application:

> (a) If within a reasonable time after written or oral notice to the . . . landlord or his agent, as defined in subdivision (a) of Section 1962, of dilapidations rendering the premises untenantable which . . . the landlord ought to repair, . . . the landlord neglects to do so, the . . . tenant may repair the same himself where the cost of such repairs does not require an expenditure . . . more than one month's rent of the premises and deduct the expenses of such repairs from the rent when due, or the . . . tenant may vacate the premises, in which case . . . the tenant shall be discharged from further payment of rent, or performance of other conditions as of the date of vacating the premises. This remedy shall not be available to the . . . tenant more than . . . twice in any 12-month period.
>
> (b) For the purposes of this section, if a . . . tenant acts to repair and deduct after the 30th day following notice, he is presumed to have acted after a reasonable time. The presumption established by this subdivision is a rebuttable presumption affecting the burden of producing evidence and shall not be construed to prevent a tenant from repairing and deducting after a shorter notice if all the circumstances require shorter notice.
>
> (c) The tenant's remedy under subdivision (a) shall not be available if the condition was caused by the violation of Section 1929 or 1941.2.
>
> (d) The remedy provided by this section is in addition to any other remedy provided by this chapter, the rental agreement, or other applicable statutory or common law. [Cal. Civ. Code §1942.]

If Ms. Ireland had lived in Los Angeles, would she have been able to replace her toilet? What if the cost of the toilet was the equivalent of two months' rent? See generally Annot., Tenant's Right, Where Landlord Fails to Make Repairs, to Have Them Made and Set Off Cost Against Rent, 40 A.L.R.3d 1369 (1971).

C. *Rent Withholding*

The Restatement (Second) of Property (Landlord and Tenant) §§5.1-5.4 recognizes that the tenant may withhold rent in specified situations where due to the default of the landlord the leased property is unsuitable for the use contemplated by the parties. Section 11.3 of the Restatement provides as follows:

> If the tenant is entitled to withhold the rent, the tenant, after proper notice to the landlord, may place in escrow the rent thereafter becoming due until the default is eliminated or the lease terminates, whichever first occurs. Whenever

there has been a proper abatement of the rent, only the abated rent is placed in escrow.

The following excerpt from the court's opinion in Teller v. McCoy, 253 S.E.2d 114 (W. Va. 1978), discusses rent withholding:

> In order to protect the landlord from the assertion of a frivolous implied warranty claim by a tenant in possession, to assure the landlord that any rent money adjudicated as owed to him will be available, and to encourage the landlord to make timely repairs so as to minimize a tenant's damages, several courts have held that the trial court, upon request, after determining that a fact question exists as to a breach of warranty of habitability, may, during the pendency of the action, require the tenant in possession to make future rent payments or part thereof unto the court as they become due. Javins v. First National Realty Corp., 138 U.S. App. D.C. 369, 428 F.2d 1071, *cert. denied,* 400 U.S. 925, 91 S. Ct. 186, 27 L. Ed. 2d 185 (1970); Green v. Superior Court, 10 Cal. 3d 616, 111 Cal. Rptr. 704, 517 P.2d 1168 (1974); Fritz v. Warthen, 298 Minn. 54, 213 N.W.2d 339 (1973); King v. Moorehead, 495 S.W.2d 65 (Mo. Ct. App. 1973); Restatement (Second) of Property §11.3 (1977). See Moscowitz, op. cit., *supra* at 1473-1486; Note, 28 Stan. L. Rev. 729, 769-772 (1976).
>
> The courts are sharply divided over whether these protective escrow orders should be allowed, and, where they are allowed, whether they should be the exception or the rule. We adopt the compromise approach set out in the leading case of Bell v. Tsintolas Realty Co., 139 U.S. App. D.C. 101, 430 F.2d 474 (1970). Such protective orders are not favored, but are permitted "only in limited circumstances, only on motion of the landlord, and only after notice and opportunity for a hearing on such a motion." Id. at 106, 430 F.2d at 479. According to *Bell,* the burden is on the landlord to show "an obvious need for such protection." Id. at 111, 430 F.2d at 484.
>
> When ruling upon the motion for the protective order, the trial court may consider:
>
> > . . . the amount of rent alleged to be due, the number of months the landlord has not received even a partial rent payment, the reasonableness of the rent for the premises, the amount of the landlord's monthly obligations for the premises, whether the tenant has been allowed to proceed in the forma pauperis, and whether the landlord faces a substantial threat of foreclosure.
>
> The "obvious need" of the landlord of the protective order is to be balanced against "the apparent merits of the tenant's defense." If the landlord proves his "obvious need," then the court may require the tenant in possession to make payments into the court pending disposition of the case. If the court believes that the tenant has a strong likelihood of succeeding on the merits, the court might refuse to enter a protective order. And if it both appears that the landlord has an "obvious need" and the tenant's claim some "apparent merit," the court might order that an amount less than the monthly

contract rent be paid into the escrow account. See Blanks v. Fowler, 141 U.S. App. D.C. 244, 437 F.2d 677 (1971).

The trial court, in lieu of establishing a court-administered escrow account, or the parties by mutual agreement might establish a *private* escrow arrangement that adequately protects the landlord. Fritz v. Warthen, *supra.*

This escrowed money represents rent only for the period between the filing of suit and trial. At trial, the escrowed amount should be apportioned between the parties consistent with the final judgment.

Finally, the courts have been very reluctant to allow the turnover order, that is, the pre-judgment award to the landlord of part or all of an escrow account. We agree with this position. Courts may not invade escrow accounts before final judgment without the consent of the parties. [253 S.E.2d at 129-130.]

CHAPTER 19

WHEN PARTIES ARE EXCUSED FROM PERFORMANCE

SECTION 1. ACTS BEYOND THE CONTROL OF THE PARTIES

A. *The Doctrine of Commercial Frustration in Leases*

LLOYD v. MURPHY
25 Cal. 2d 48, 153 P.2d 47 (1944)

TRAYNOR, J.

On August 4, 1941 plaintiffs leased to defendant for a five year term beginning September 15, 1941 certain premises located at the corner of Almont Drive and Wilshire Boulevard in the city of Beverly Hills, Los Angeles County, "for the sole purpose of conducting thereon the business of displaying and selling new automobiles (including the servicing and repairing thereof and of selling the petroleum products of a major oil company) and for no other purpose whatsoever without the written consent of the lessor" except "to make an occasional sale of a used automobile." Defendant agreed not to sublease or assign without plaintiffs' written consent. On January 1, 1942, the federal government ordered that the sale of new automobiles be discontinued. It modified this order on January 8, 1942, to permit sales to those engaged in military activities, and on January 20, 1942, it established a system of priorities restricting sales to persons having preferential ratings of A-1-j or higher. On March 10, 1942, defendant explained the effect of these restrictions on his business to one of the plaintiffs authorized to act for the others, who orally waived the restrictions in the lease as to use and subleasing and offered to reduce the rent if defendant should be unable to operate profitably. Nevertheless defendant

459

vacated the premises on March 15, 1942, giving oral notice of repudiation of the lease to plaintiffs, which was followed by a written notice on March 24, 1942. Plaintiffs affirmed in writing on March 26th their oral waiver and, failing to persuade defendant to perform his obligations, they rented the property to other tenants pursuant to their powers under the lease in order to mitigate damages. On May 11, 1942, plaintiffs brought this action praying for declaratory relief to determine their rights under the lease, and for judgment for unpaid rent. Following a trial on the merits, the court found that the leased premises were located on one of the main traffic arteries of Los Angeles County; that they were equipped with gasoline pumps and in general adapted for the maintenance of an automobile service station; that they contained a one-story storeroom adapted to many commercial purposes; that plaintiffs had waived the restrictions in the lease and granted defendant the right to use the premises for any legitimate purpose and to sublease to any responsible party; that defendant continues to carry on the business of selling and servicing automobiles at two other places. Defendant testified that at one of these locations he sold new automobiles exclusively and when asked if he were aware that many new automobile dealers were continuing in business replied: "Sure. It is just the location that I couldn't make a go, though, of automobiles." Although there was no finding to that effect, defendant estimated in response to inquiry by his counsel, that 90 percent of his gross volume of business was new car sales and 10 percent gasoline sales. The trial court held that war conditions had not terminated defendant's obligations under the lease and gave judgment for plaintiffs, declaring the lease as modified by plaintiffs' waiver to be in full force and effect, and ordered defendant to pay the unpaid rent with interest, less amounts received by plaintiffs from re-renting. Defendant brought this appeal, contending that the purpose for which the premises were leased was frustrated by the restrictions placed on the sale of new automobiles by the federal government, thereby terminating his duties under the lease.

Although commercial frustration was first recognized as an excuse for nonperformance of a contractual duty by the courts of England (Krell v. Henry [1903] 2 K.B. 740 [C.A.]; Blakely v. Muller, 19 T.L.R. 186 [K.B.]; see McElroy and Williams, The Coronation Cases, 4 Mod. L. Rev. 241) its soundness has been questioned by those courts (see Maritime National Fish, Ltd., v. Ocean Trawlers, Ltd. [1935] A.C. 524, 528-29, 56 L.Q. Rev. 324, arguing that Krell v. Henry, *supra,* was a misapplication of Taylor v. Caldwell, 3 B & S 826 [1863], the leading case on impossibility as an excuse for nonperformance), and they have refused to apply the doctrine to leases on the ground that an estate is conveyed to the lessee, which carries with it all risks (Swift v. McBean, 166 L.T. Rep. 87 [1942] 1 K.B. 375; Whitehall Court v. Ettlinger, 122 L.T. Rep. 540, (1920) 1 K.B. 680, [1919] 89 L.J. [K.B.] N.S. 126; 137 A.L.R. 1199, 1224; see collection and discussion on English cases in Wood v. Bartolino, 48 N.M. 175 [146 P.2d 883, 886-887]). Many courts, therefore, in the United States have held that the tenant bears all risks as owner of the estate (Cusack Co. v. Pratt, 78 Colo. 28 [239 P. 22]; Yellow Cab Co. v. Stafford-Smith Co., 320 Ill. 294 [150 N.E. 670]), but the modern cases have recognized that the defense may be available in a proper case, even in a lease. As the author declares in 6 Williston, Contracts (rev. ed. 1938), §1955, pp. 5485-87,

> The fact that lease is a conveyance and not simply a continuing contract and the numerous authorities enforcing liability to pay rent in spite of destruction of leased premises, however, have made it difficult to give relief. That the tenant has been relieved, nevertheless, in several cases indicates the gravitation of the law toward a recognition of the principle that fortuitous destruction of the value of performance wholly outside the contemplation of the parties may excuse a promisor even in a lease. . . .
> Even more clearly with respect to leases than in regard to ordinary contracts the applicability of the doctrine of frustration depends on the total or nearly total destruction of the purpose for which, in the contemplation of both parties, the transaction was entered into.

The principles of frustration have been repeatedly applied to leases by the courts of this state and the question is whether the excuse for nonperformance is applicable under the facts of the present case.

Although the doctrine of frustration is akin to the doctrine of impossibility of performance (see Civ. Code, §1511; 6 Cal. Jr. 435-450; 4 Cal. Jur. Ten-year Supp. 187-192; Taylor v. Caldwell, *supra*) since both have developed from the commercial necessity of excusing performance in cases of extreme hardship, frustration is not a form of impossibility even under the modern definition of that term, which includes not only cases of physical impossibility but also cases of extreme impracticability of performance. Performance remains possible but the expected value of performance to the party seeking to be excused has been destroyed by a fortuitous event, which supervenes to cause an actual but not literal failure of consideration.

The question in cases involving frustration is whether the equities of the case, considered in the light of sound public policy, require placing the risk of a disruption or complete destruction of the contract equilibrium on defendant or plaintiff under the circumstances of a given case (Fibrosa Spolka Akcyjina v. Fairbairn Lawson Combe Barbour, Ltd. [1942], 167 L.T.R. [H.L.] 101, 112-113; see Smith, Some Practical Aspects of the Doctrine of Impossibility, 32 Ill. L. Rev. 672, 675; Patterson, Constructive Conditions in Contracts, 42 Columb. L. Rev. 903, 949; 27 Cal. L. Rev. 461), and the answer depends on whether an unanticipated circumstance, the risk of which should not be fairly thrown on the promisor, has made performance vitally different from what was reasonably to be expected (6 Williston, op. cit. *supra,* §1963, p. 5511; Restatement, Contracts, §454). The purpose of a contract is to place the risks of performance upon the promisor, and the relation of the parties, terms of the contract, and circumstances surrounding its formation must be examined to determine whether it can be fairly inferred that the risk of the event that has supervened to cause the alleged frustration was not reasonably foreseeable. If it was foreseeable there should have been provision for it in the contract, and the absence of such a provision gives rise to the inference that the risk was assumed.

The doctrine of frustration has been limited to cases of extreme hardship so that businessmen, who must make their arrangements in advance, can rely with certainty on their contracts (Anglo-Northern Trading Co. v. Emlyn Jones and Williams, 2 K.B. 78; 137 A.L.R. 1199, 1216-1221). The courts have required a promisor seeking to excuse himself from performance of his obligations to prove that the risk of the frustrating event was not reasonably foreseeable and that the value of counterperformance is totally or nearly totally destroyed, for frustration is no defense if it was foreseeable or controllable by the promisor, or if counterperformance remains valuable.

Thus laws or other governmental acts that make performance unprofitable or more difficult or expensive do not excuse the duty to perform a contractual obligation. It is settled that if parties have contracted with reference to a state of war or have contemplated the risks arising from it, they may not invoke the doctrine of frustration to escape their obligations.

At the time the lease in the present case was executed the National Defense Act (Public Act. No. 671 of the 76th Congress [54 Stat. 601], §2A), approved June 28, 1940, authorizing the President to allocate materials and mobilize industry for national defense, had been law for more than a year. The automotive industry was in the process of conversion to supply the needs of our growing mechanized army and to meet lend-lease commitments. Iceland and Greenland had been occupied by the army. Automobile sales were soaring because the public anticipated that production would soon be restricted. These facts were commonly known and it cannot be said that the risk of war and its consequences necessitating restriction of the production and sale of automobiles was so remote a contingency that its risk could not be foreseen by defendant, an experienced automobile dealer. Indeed, the conditions prevailing at the time the lease was executed, and the absence of any provision in the lease contracting against the effect of war, gives rise to the inference that the risk was assumed. Defendant has therefore failed to prove that the possibility of war and its consequences on the production and sale of new automobiles was an unanticipated circumstance wholly outside the contemplation of the parties.

Nor has defendant sustained the burden of proving that the value of the lease has been destroyed. The sale of automobiles was not made impossible or illegal but merely restricted and if governmental regulation does not entirely prohibit the business to be carried on in the leased premises but only limits or restricts it, thereby making it less profitable and more difficult to continue, the lease is not terminated or the lessee excused from further performance. Defendant may use the premises for the purpose for which they were leased. New automobiles and gasoline continue to be sold. Indeed, defendant testified that he continued to sell new automobiles exclusively at another location in the same county.

Defendant contends that the lease is restrictive and that the government orders therefore destroyed its value and frustrated its purpose. Provisions that prohibit subleasing or other uses than those specified affect the value of a lease and are to be considered in determining whether its purpose has been frustrated or its value destroyed (see Owens, The Effect of the War Upon the Rights and Liabilities of Parties to a Contract, 19 California State Bar Journal 132, 143). It must not be forgotten, however, that "[t]he landlord has not covenanted that the tenant shall have the right to carry on the contemplated business or that the business to which the premises are by their nature or by the terms of the lease restricted shall be profitable enough to enable the tenant to pay the rent but has imposed a condition for his own benefit; and, certainly, unless and until he chooses to take advantage of it, the tenant is not deprived of the use of the premises." (6 Williston, Contracts, op. cit. *supra,* §1955, p. 5485; see, also, People v. Klopstock, 24 Cal. 2d 897, 901 [151 P.2d 641].) In the present lease plaintiffs reserved the rights that defendant should not use the premises for other purposes than those specified in the lease or sublease without plaintiffs' written consent. Far from preventing other uses or subleasing they waived these rights, enabling defendant to use the premises for any legitimate purpose and to sublease them to any responsible tenant. This waiver is significant in view of the location of the premises on a main traffic artery in Los Angeles County and their adaptability for many commercial purposes. The value of these rights is attested by the fact that the premises were rented soon after defendants vacated them. It is therefore clear that the governmental restrictions on the sale of new cars have not destroyed the value of the lease. Furthermore, plaintiffs offered to lower the rent if defendant should be unable to operate profitably, and their conduct was at all times fair and cooperative.

The consequences of applying the doctrine of frustration to a leasehold involving less than a total or nearly total destruction of the value of the leased premises would be undesirable. Confusion would result from different decisions purporting to define "substantial" frustration. Litigation would be encouraged by the repudiation of leases when lessees found their businesses less profitable because of the regulations attendant upon a national emergency. Many leases have been affected in varying degrees by the widespread governmental regulations necessitated by war conditions.

The cases that defendant relies upon are consistent with the conclusion reached herein. In [a cited case], the lease provided that the premises should not be used other than as a saloon. When national prohibition made the sale of alcoholic beverages illegal, the court excused the tenant from further performance on the theory of illegality or impossibility by a change in domestic law. The doctrine of frustration might have been applied, since the purpose for which the property was leased was totally destroyed and there was nothing to show that the value of the lease was not thereby totally destroyed. In the present case the purpose was not destroyed but only restricted, and plaintiffs proved that the lease was valuable to defendant. In [another cited case], the lease was for the purpose of conducting a "saloon and cigar store and for no other purpose" with provision for subleasing a portion of the premises for bootblack purposes. The monthly rental was $650. It was clear that prohibition destroyed the main purpose of the lease, but since the premises could be used for bootblack and cigar store purposes, the lessee was not excused from his duty to pay the rent. In the present case new automobiles and gasoline may be sold under the lease as executed and any legitimate business may be conducted or the premises may be subleased under the lease as modified by plaintiff's waiver. Colonial Operating Corp. v. Hannon Sales & Service, Inc., 34 N.Y.S.2d 116, was reversed in 265 App. Div. 411 [39 N.Y.S.2d 217], and Signal Land Corp. v. Loecher, 35 N.Y.S.2d 25; Schantz v. American Auto Supply Co., Inc., 178 Misc. 909 [36 N.Y.S.2d 747]; and Canrock Realty Corp. v. Vim Electric Co., Inc., 37 N.Y.S.2d 139, involved government orders that totally destroyed the possibility of selling the products for which the premises were leased. No case has been cited by defendant or disclosed by research in which an appellate court has excused a lessee from performance of his duty to pay rent when the purpose of the lease has not been totally destroyed or its accomplishment rendered extremely impracticable or where it has been shown that the lease remains valuable to the lessee.

The judgment is affirmed.[1]

Problems

19.1. T, a manufacturer of automobile parts, executed a lease for ten years with L for premises "to be used for manufacturing, assembling and shipping of automobile parts, and for no other purpose whatsoever." T entered into possession and began manufacturing automobile parts; after a short time T was advised by the building inspector that the manufacturing activities were in violation of the local zoning ordinance and therefore were illegal. L knew or should have known that the only use permitted under the lease was not permitted under the zoning laws, but T did not know this at the time the lease was executed. T has found a better location for manufacturing at a lower rent and would like to get out of the lease, especially since T has no use for a vacant building and the building inspector will not allow the manufacture of automobile parts. What advice would you give T? See Warshawsky v. American Automotive Products Co., 12 Ill. App. 2d 178, 138 N.E.2d 816 (1956).

19.2. L and T entered into a written lease for ten years for certain premises which were to be used for business purposes. Several months after

1. See generally Annot., Modern Status of the Rules Regarding Impossibility of Performance as Defense in Action for Breach of Contract, 84 A.L.R.2d 12 (1962); Note, "Commercial Frustration" as Applied to Leases of Real Property, 43 Mich. L. Rev. 598 (1944); American Law of Property §3.104 (Casner ed. 1952). — EDS.

the lease began, T was drafted into the military service of the United States. T abandoned the premises on the day T was drafted. Is T liable for rent coming due after the abandonment of the leased premises? Would your answer be any different if T had enlisted? See N.Y. Mil. Law §310 and the Federal Soldiers and Sailors Relief Act of 1940, 50 U.S.C.A. §534.

19.3. In Problem 19.2, assume that T's son, for whom T had leased the premises, was drafted. Assume also that it could be shown that T had signed the lease only because L would not allow T's son, a minor, to sign. L had told T's son, "Get your parents to sign." Is T liable for rent? See Erlich v. Landman, 179 Misc. 972, 40 N.Y.S.2d 516 (Sup. Ct. 1943).

Note: Bankruptcy of the Landlord or the Tenant

The effect of the bankruptcy of the landlord or the tenant on the lease and the obligations of the parties thereunder is referred to at this point because the bankruptcy of either party has a frustrating effect on carrying out the purposes of the lease. In regard to bankruptcy, see Restatement (Second) of Property (Landlord and Tenant), §21.1 on the effect of the bankruptcy of the tenant and §21.2 on the effect of the bankruptcy of the landlord.

B. Destruction of the Leased Premises

The rule was well settled at common law that the destruction of buildings on the leased premises would not relieve the tenant of the liability for rent. The general dissatisfaction with the common-law rule is evidenced by the widespread enactment of statutes such as N.Y. Real Prop. Law §227 and Wis. Stat. §234.17. Reread Suydam v. Jackson, Chapter 17 at page 401, and see Pines v. Perssion, this chapter at page 502, and the note following it for a discussion of both of these statutes. Suffice it to say at this point that the language of the statutes is not as inclusive as it initially appears to be.

In drafting a provision in a lease as to the consequences of the destruction of a building on the leased premises, there may be a tendency to construe the lease provision narrowly. See, for example, Scharbauer v. Cobean, 42 N.M. 427, 80 P.2d 785 (1938), where the lease provided as follows: "It is understood that in the event of the destruction of the premises by fire or other casualty to such an extent as to render the same untenantable, this lease shall become void and of no effect." The court held that where the damage by fire was repairable in four or five days, even though the premises were not usable for that short period, the leased premises were not "untenantable" within the meaning of that term in the lease provision.

Examine the following case against the background of the above comments.

ALBERT M. GREENFIELD & CO. v. KOLEA
475 Pa. 351, 380 A.2d 758 (1977)

MANDERINO, J.

This is an appeal from an order of the Superior Court, affirming the judgment of the Court of Common Pleas of Delaware County. Appellee (lessor) had sued appellant (lessee) for breach of two lease agreements. The trial court awarded appellee $7,200.00. Appellant's motions for judgment n.o.v., arrest of judgment, and new trial were denied. The Superior Court affirmed the trial court per curiam. Greenfield v. Kolea, 232 Pa. Super. 701, 331 A.2d 824 (1975). Appellant's petition for allowance of appeal was granted by us and this appeal followed. We reverse.

The appellee's claim in this case is based on two separate, but related, lease agreements. The first lease, executed on March 20, 1971, covered ". . . all that certain one story garage building and known as 5735-37 Wayne Avenue, extending to Keyser Street in the rear [Philadelphia] . . . to be used and occupied as storage of automobiles. . . ." This lease, executed for a term of two years beginning May 1, 1971, provided for an annual rental of $4,800.00. The second lease, covering adjoining property, was also executed on March 20, 1971. The second lease covered ". . . all those certain lots or pieces of ground known as 5721-33 Wayne Avenue . . . to be used and occupied for the sale and storage of automobiles . . ." The second lease, also executed for a two-year term beginning May 1, 1971, provided for an annual rental of $2,500.00. There was no building located on the real estate covered by the second lease. Neither lease contained a provision with respect to the tenant's obligations in the event of destruction of the building.

On May 1, 1972, after the appellant had occupied the premises for one year, fire completely destroyed the building covered by lease number one. The fire was labeled as accidental by the Fire Marshall's office. The day after the fire the remaining sections of the exterior walls were razed by the lessor, and barricades were placed around the perimeter of the premises covered by both leases. Appellant thereafter refused to pay rent under either of the leases.

The general rule has been stated that in the absence of a lease provision to the contrary, a tenant is not relieved from the obligation to pay rent despite the total destruction of the leased premises. Magaw v. Lambert, 3 Pa. 444 (1846); Hoy v. Holt, 91 Pa. 88 (1879).

The reason for the rule has been said to be that although a building may be an important element of consideration for the payment of rent, the interest in the soil remains to support the lease despite destruction of the building. It has also been said that since destruction of the building is usually by accident, it is only equitable to divide the loss; the lessor loses the property and the lessee loses the term. See generally, Sum. Pa. Jur. Landlord and Tenant, §72.

Two exceptions designed to afford relief to the tenant from the harshness of the common law principle have been created. These exceptions reflect the influence of modern contract principles as applied in the landlord-tenant relationship.

The first exception provides that where only a portion of a building is leased, total destruction of the building relieves the tenant of the obligation to pay rent. Moving Picture Co. of America v. Scottish Union & Nat'l. Ins. Co. of Edinburgh, 244 Pa. 258, 90 A. 642 (1914). See also Paxson & Comfort Co. v. Potter, 30 Pa. Super. 615 (1906). This exception recognizes that in the leasing of a part of a building there is no implication that any estate in land is granted. This Court, in other words, has recognized that in a landlord-tenant relationship with respect to an apartment, the parties have *bargained for* a part of a building and not the land beneath.

The influence of contract principles of bargained for exchange is also apparent in the second exception to the general common law rule. The second exception is based on the doctrine of *impossibility of performance,* and is stated in Greenburg v. Sun Shipbuilding Co., 277 Pa. 312, 313, 121 A. 63, 64 (1923):

> Where a contract relates to the use and possession of specific property, the existence of which is necessary to the carrying out of the purpose in view, a condition is implied by law, as though written in the agreement that the impossibility of performance arising from the destruction of the property without fault of either party, shall end all contractual obligations relating to the thing destroyed.

See also Rest. Contracts, §460, 6 Corbin on Contracts, §1337.

As was said in West v. Peoples First Nat'l. Bank & Trust Co., 378 Pa. 275, 106 A.2d 427 (1954),

> . . . where a contract relates to specific property the existence or maintenance of which is necessary to the carrying out of the purpose of the agreement, the condition is implied by law, just as though it were written into the agreement, that the impossibility of performance or the frustration of purpose arising from the destruction of the property or interference with its use, without the fault of either party, ends all contractual obligations relating to the property. Moreover, impossibility in that connection means not only strict impossibility but impracticability because of extreme and unreasonable difficulty, expense, or loss involved. [Footnote omitted.]

The Rest. Contracts §454, also applies the test of impracticability rather than strict impossibility: ". . . [I]mpossibility means not only strict impossibility but *impracticability* because of extreme and unreasonable difficulty, expense, injury, or loss involved." (Emphasis added.)

In the instant case, it is apparent that when the building was destroyed by fire it became impossible for the appellee to furnish the agreed consideration—". . . all that one story garage building . . ." Nothing in the first lease implies that any interest in the land itself was intended to be conveyed. It is also obvious that the purpose of the lease with respect to the appellant was thereby frustrated. As noted in the lease, the parties contemplated that appellant would use the building for the repair and sale of used motor vehicles. Without a building appellant could no longer carry on a used car business as contemplated by the parties at the time they entered into the lease agreement. It became extremely impracticable for the appellant to continue using the adjoining lot when his business office and repair stations were destroyed by the fire. Additionally, because of the dangerous condition created by the fire, the city required appellee to barricade the property covered by both leases, thus preventing appellant from entering the property.

In reaching our decision that the accidental destruction of the building by fire excused the parties from further performance of their obligations under the lease agreements, we are cognizant of the fact that we are allocating the risk to be assumed by the parties. Such an allocation of risk can be accomplished in one of two ways. First, the parties could specifically provide for risk assumption with respect to certain possible contingencies. In the absence of an express recognition and assumption by the parties, the court is left with the task of determining what the parties would have done had the issue arisen in the contract negotiations. See Restatement, Second, Property (Landlord and Tenant) §5.4. In reaching such a decision a court must consider many factors. As stated in 6 Corbin on Contracts §1325:

"There is no rule of law by which the issue can be deductively determined; it depends upon the practices and customs of men in like cases, upon the prevailing mores of the time."

In reaching a decision involving the landlord-tenant relationship, too often courts have relied on outdated common law property principles and presumptions and have refused to consider the factors necessary for an equitable and just conclusion. In this case, for example, if we applied the general rule and ignored the realities of the situation, we would bind the appellant to paying rent for barren ground when both parties to the lease contemplated that the building would be used for the commercial enterprise of repair and sale of used motor vehicles.

The trial court's decision to bind the lessee to the lease was simply an application of an outdated common law presumption. That presumption developed in a society very different from ours today: one where the land was always more valuable than the buildings erected on it. Buildings are critical to the functioning of modern society. When the parties bargain for the use of a building, the soil beneath is generally of little consequence. Our laws should develop to reflect these changes. As stated in Javins v. First Nat'l. Realty Corp., 138 U.S. App. D.C. 369, 372, 428 F.2d 1071, 1074, *cert. denied,* 400 U.S. 925, 91 S. Ct. 186, 27 L. Ed. 2d 185 (1970):

> Courts have a duty to reappraise old doctrines in the light of the facts and values of contemporary life — particularly old common law doctrines which the courts themselves created and developed. As we have said before, "[T]he continued vitality of the common law . . . depends upon its ability to reflect contemporary values and ethics." [Footnote omitted.]

The presumption established in *Magaw* and *Hoy, supra,* no longer has relevance to today's landlord-tenant relationships. It is no longer reasonable to *assume* that in the absence of a lease provision to the contrary the lessee should bear the risk of loss in the event of total destruction of the building. Where the parties do not expressly provide for such a catastrophe, the court should analyze the facts and the lease agreement as any other contract would be analyzed. Following such an analysis, if it is evident to the court that the parties bargained for the existence of a building, and no provision is made as to who bears the risk of loss if the building is destroyed, the court should relieve the parties of their respective obligations when the building no longer exists.

Accordingly, we reverse the order of the Superior Court, and remand to the trial court with directions to grant the appellant's motion for judgment n.o.v.

JONES, former C.J., did not participate in the decision of this case.

ROBERTS, J., filed a concurring opinion.

NIX, J., filed a concurring opinion.

POMEROY, J., concurs in the result.

ROBERTS, J., concurring.

I join in the opinion of the majority because the rule established reaches the same result as the Restatement, Second, Property (Landlord and Tenant) Section 5.4 (Unsuitable Condition Arises After Entry — Remedies Available) which states:

> Except to the extent the parties to a lease validly agree otherwise, there is a breach of the landlord's obligation if, after the tenant's entry and without fault of the tenant, a change in the condition of the leased property . . . caused suddenly by a nonmanmade force, makes the leased property unsuitable for the use contemplated by the parties and the landlord does not correct the situation within a reasonable time after being requested by the tenant to do so. For that breach, the tenant may:
>
> (1)　terminate the lease. . . .

The unexpressed intent of the parties is thus irrelevant.

NIX, J., concurring.

Insofar as the majority opinion represents the adoption in this Commonwealth of Section 5.4 of the Restatement, Second, Property, I am in complete agreement. The common law rule that an accidental fire which totally destroys a building is no defense to the claim for rent for the premises, is clearly inappropriate in our present society.

As I view our holding today, it replaces a rule of law, which may have had validity in a predominantly agrarian society but is clearly outmoded today.

C. *Condemnation*[2]

When leased property is condemned, three major questions are raised: (1) what is the effect of the taking on the lease, (2) is the tenant entitled to receive some part of the award, and (3) if so, how should the tenant's share be determined? Section 8.1 of the Restatement (Second) of Property (Landlord and Tenant) provides as follows:

> (1) If there is a taking by eminent domain of all of the leased property for all of the lease term, the lease is terminated.
> (2) Except to the extent the parties to a lease validly agree otherwise, if there is a taking by eminent domain of less than all of the leased property or for less than all of the lease term, the lease:
>   (a) is terminated if the taking significantly interferes with the use contemplated by the parties; and
>   (b) is not terminated if the taking does not significantly interfere with the use contemplated by the parties, but the tenant is entitled to an abatement of the rent to the extent prescribed in §11.1.

The determination of the amount which the tenant is entitled to receive out of the condemnation award has been the subject of much litigation. It depends, in part, upon the effect which the condemnation has upon the tenant's continued liability for rent. As the next case shows, frequently this depends upon the inclusiveness of the interest condemned.

LEONARD v. AUTOCAR SALES & SERVICE CO.
392 Ill. 182, 64 N.E.2d 477 (1945)

THOMPSON, C.J., delivered the opinion of the court.

Appellees, A. G. Leonard, F. H. Prince, and D. H. Reimers, as trustees of the Central Manufacturing District, recovered a judgment in the superior court of Cook county against the Autocar Sales and Service company, a

---

2. See generally Polasky, Condemnation of Leasehold Interests, 48 Va. L. Rev. 477 (1962); Boyer & Wilcox, An Economic Appraisal of Leasehold Valuation in Condemnation Proceedings, 17 U. Miami L. Rev. 245 (1963); Note, Compensation for Leasehold Interest Where No Provision Is Contained in the Lease, 48 Marq. L. Rev. 90 (1964); Kizer, Valuation of Leasehold Estates in Eminent Domain, 67 W. Va. L. Rev. 101 (1965).

corporation, in the sum of $9536.10. The Appellate Court affirmed the judgment, and the cause is now before us for review upon a certificate of importance granted by the Appellate Court.

On September 1, 1926, appellees and appellant entered into a written lease whereby appellees demised to appellant certain property at the intersection of Pershing road and South Hermitage avenue in the city of Chicago for a term of years from December 1, 1926, to and including November 30, 1946. Shortly prior to March 11, 1943, the Secretary of War requested the Attorney General of the United States to institute proceedings to acquire by condemnation the temporary use of the entire property for a term ending June 30, 1943, with the right to extend the term for additional yearly periods thereafter at the election of the Secretary of War. Pursuant to the request, the Attorney General, on March 11, 1943, filed in the District Court of the United States a petition for an order condemning the property for such temporary use and granting the government the right of immediate possession for military and other war purposes. On the same day, March 11, 1943, the District Court entered an order declaring the temporary use of the property condemned for a term ending June 30, 1943, with the right to extend the term for additional yearly periods thereafter at the election of the Secretary of War, and granting the United States the right of immediate possession. About March 25, 1943, appellant removed its place of business from the premises described in the lease, and thereafter refused to pay further rent under its lease of said premises. On May 1, 1943, the Secretary of War served notice of his election to extend the term of such temporary use for an additional yearly period beginning July 1, 1943, to and including June 30, 1944.

January 7, 1944, appellees brought this action to recover the stipulated rental provided in the lease for the period from April 1, 1943, to and including January 1, 1944. Defendant answered, setting up the above facts as to the appropriation of the leased premises by the Federal Government for military and war purposes, and alleging that by reason thereof it was evicted by paramount right from the entire premises and the relation of landlord and tenant terminated by law; that the premises were rendered incapable of occupation for any purpose consistent with the lease and all liability of the defendant to pay rent under the lease ceased on March 11, 1943, the date of the order of condemnation. A motion to strike the answer was sustained. Appellant stood by its answer. A hearing was had assessing appellees' damage and judgment entered for the amount asked in the complaint.

The question in this case is whether appellant is liable under the lease to pay rent during the time that the exclusive possession and temporary use of the demised premises has been taken by the government and appropriated to military and war purposes. The judges of the Appellate Court certified that in their opinion the questions of law involved in this case were of such importance that they should be passed upon by this court. These questions are (1) whether the taking and appropriation by the government, under the power of eminent domain, of the temporary and exclusive use of demised premises for an indefinite period, which may fall short of or exceed the remaining term of the lease, by operation of law terminates the lease and abrogates the relation of landlord and tenant; (2) whether the doctrine known as "frustration of purpose" or "commercial frustration" is applicable to a lease; and (3) whether such appropriation of the demised premises to public use, in the event the same should not be considered as dissolving the contract of leasing, would nevertheless operate to abate the rent pro tanto, and to discharge the lessee from liability to the lessor for rent accruing during the period of such appropriation by the government of the use of the demised premises.

Accepting for discussion the theory that in ascertaining the rights of the parties the lease should be treated solely as a contract and its aspects as a conveyance entirely disregarded, we will first refer to some general principles governing the construction and enforcement of contracts. They are well established and the general rule is that where parties, by their own contract and positive undertaking, create a duty or charge upon themselves, they must abide by the contract and make the promise good, and subsequent contingencies, not provided against in the contract, which render performance impossible, do not bring the contract to an end. This doctrine has been often announced by this court. Deibler v. Bernard Bros., Inc., 385 Ill. 610, 53 N.E.2d 450; Phelps v. School District No. 109, 302 Ill. 193, 134 N.E. 312; Summers v. Hibbard, Spencer, Bartlett & Co., 153 Ill. 102, 38 N.E. 899; Steele v. Buck, 61 Ill. 343; Bunn v. Prather, 21 Ill. 217. To this general rule there are certain exceptions. In Steele v. Buck, 61 Ill. 343, performance was not excused although rendered impossible by act of God, nevertheless we find in the earlier case of Dehler v. Held, 50 Ill. 491, the statement, recently quoted with approval in Deibler v. Bernard Bros., Inc., 385 Ill. 610, 53 N.E.2d 450, 453: "As a general rule, where a party binds himself to perform an act, he is held to its performance, except where it is rendered impossible by the act of God or the public enemy." No authority is cited or reason given for recognizing these exceptions. A further exception has been recognized that in contracts to whose performance the continued existence of a particular person or thing is necessary, a condition is always implied that the death or destruction of that person or thing shall excuse performance. Martin Emerich Outfitting Co. v. Siegel, Cooper & Co., 237 Ill. 610, 86 N.E. 1104. The reason given for this exception, which is itself a rule, is that without any express stipulation that the destruction of the person or thing shall excuse the performance, that excuse is by law implied, because from the nature of the contract it is apparent that the parties contracted on the basis of the continued existence of the particular person or thing. Ellis v. Atlantic Mutual Ins. Co., 108 U.S. 342, 2 S. Ct. 746; 12 Am. Jur. 945, sec. 372. The doctrine of frustration is an extension of this exception to cases where the cessation or nonexistence of some particular condition or state of things has rendered performance impossible and the object of the contract frustrated. It rests on the view that where from the nature of the contract and the surrounding circumstances the parties when entering into the contract must have known that it could not be performed unless some particular condition or state of things would continue to exist, the parties must be deemed, when entering into the contract, to have made their bargain on the footing that such particular condition or state of things would continue to exist, and the contract therefore must be construed as subject to an implied condition that the parties shall be excused in case performance becomes impossible from such condition or state of things ceasing to exist. Greek Catholic Congregation of Borough of Olyphant v. Plummer, 338 Pa. 373, 12 A.2d 435; 12 Am. Jur. 953, sec. 377. While not new, this doctrine of frustration or "commercial frustration," as it is so termed, first came into prominence following the first World War when contracts for the sale of specified materials or for the shipment on specific vessels or to specific ports were made impossible of performance by war restrictions, embargoes, or seizure of the vessel, and relief was sought on the theory that the parties had contracted on the footing that peace would continue to exist.

The exceptions to the rule that performance of a contract is not excused because of subsequent events rendering performance impossible grow out of the mode of construing the contract; and it is for the purpose of fulfilling the intention of those who entered into the contract that a condition excusing performance is implied. The contracting parties are, in each instance where an exception to the general rule is applicable, absolved from their obligations, not because subsequent contingencies have rendered performance impossible, but because the contract was not in reality an absolute contract, binding them to perform under such changed conditions. It may readily be conceded that one may absolutely bind himself to perform a certain act; but the question in all cases is whether it was the intention of the parties that he should be so bound. A construction that the parties to the contract did so intend must be put upon an unqualified undertaking where the event which caused the impossibility might have been anticipated or guarded against in the contract. Chicago, Milwaukee & St. Paul Railway Co. v. Hoyt, 149 U.S. 1, 13 S. Ct. 779, 784; Phelps v. School District, 302 Ill. 193, 134 N.E. 312.

It is apparent, from a reading of the decision in the Phelps case, that the defense there urged by the school district, although not designated by such nomenclature, was in reality none other than the defense urged in the case at bar as the doctrine of frustration, namely, that changed conditions, not existing when the contract was entered into, rendered performance of the contract impossible and its purpose thwarted. The contention was not sustained. A like holding was made in Deibler v. Bernard Bros. Inc., 385 Ill. 610. While the subject matter of the contract in the present case is not the same as that of the contract in the Phelps case, there is a decided analogy between the two cases. It is well settled that where a lessee has expressly covenanted to pay rent, an assignment by him of the lease does not relieve him of liability for rent subsequent to the assignment, since in such case, although the privity of estate is terminated by the assignment, the privity of contract is unaffected. 32 Am. Jur. 313, sec. 358; Barnes v. Northern Trust Co., 169 Ill. 112, 48 N.E. 31; Consolidated Coal Co. v. Peers, 166 Ill. 361, 46 N.E. 1105; Grommes v. St. Paul Trust Co., 147 Ill. 634, 35 N.E. 820. When it is remembered that every lease possesses a double aspect, being both a conveyance and a contract, a ready explanation may be found for the view that a lessee may cease to be entitled to the possession yet remain bound by his contractual obligation to pay rent.

Nor is there any place here for an application of the rules governing the construction of contracts whose subject matter had subsequently been destroyed or ceased to exist. The subject matter of the contract is the property located at the intersection of Pershing road and South Hermitage avenue in Chicago. This property, which was demised and conveyed by the lease-contract for a term of years ending November 30, 1946, is undestroyed and still in existence. The appropriation of its temporary use by the United States for a period from March 11, 1943, to June 30, 1944, merely carved out of appellant's long-term lease a short-term occupancy (United States v. General Motors Corp., 323 U.S. 373, 65 S. Ct. 357), and destroyed neither the property nor appellant's lease-hold estate therein. Nor does the provision in the order of condemnation granting to the United States the right to extend the term of its occupancy for additional yearly periods, operate to destroy appellant's lease-hold estate. It does not appear that the United States has extended its term of occupancy for additional periods covering the entire remaining term of the lease or has appropriated the whole of such remaining term; and, until it does do so, there is no basis for any claim that the leasehold estate granted to appellant has ceased to exist or has been destroyed. Whether the lease would be terminated and appellant absolved from liability thereunder in the event the government should so appropriate the whole of the remaining term of the leasehold estate, is a question not before us and upon which we express no opinion.

The next question for determination is the lease and its aspect as a conveyance of an interest in real estate and the effect of the condemnation proceedings upon the leasehold estate and the relation of the parties as landlord and tenant. The right of eminent domain is an inherent attribute of sovereignty. It is defined as the right of the Nation or State, or those to whom the power has been lawfully delegated, to condemn private property for public use, and to appropriate the ownership or possession of such property for such use, upon paying the owner just compensation, to be ascertained according to law. Sanitary District v. Manasse, 380 Ill. 27, 42 N.E.2d 543. It extends to every kind of property, including not only that which is tangible, but all rights and interests of any kind. South Park Comrs. v. Montgomery Ward & Co., 248 Ill. 299, 93 N.E. 910. The right of the citizen to own, possess and enjoy his property must necessarily give way to the right of the sovereign to appropriate it to public uses, when, in the judgment of the sovereign power, public interest will be promoted. Penn Mutual Life Ins. Co. v. Heiss, 141 Ill. 35, 31 N.E. 138. A lessee, as tenant of an estate for years, takes and holds his term in the same manner as any other owner of real property holds his title, subject to the right of the sovereign to take the whole or any part of it for public use, upon the payment to him of just compensation. Corrigan v. City of Chicago, 144 Ill. 537, 33 N.E. 746; Stubbings v. Village of Evanston, 136 Ill. 37, 26 N.E. 577. That appellant is entitled to receive from the government full compensation for so much of its leasehold estate as is appropriated to public use and thereby obtain complete indemnity for its loss is not open to question. United States v. General Motors Corp., 323 U.S. 373, 65 S. Ct. 357. Accordingly there is no hardship or injustice in holding it to the payment of the rent which is the consideration for which the term was granted. In cases where the land itself is taken, no owner would attempt to claim that his liability for payment of the purchase price to his grantor from whom he received the property would be thereby extinguished or that a mortgage upon the condemned premises would, as between the parties thereto, be invalidated. When the reversion and the leasehold unite in the same owner, the leasehold estate comes to an end by reason of its merger in the reversion; and the same result occurs when the interests of both the reversioner and the lessee are taken by some public authority under its power of eminent domain. The rule is well settled that where the complete estates of both landlord and tenant in the entire demised premises are taken by condemnation, the obligation to pay rent ceases (Corrigan v. City of Chicago, 144 Ill. 537, 33 N.E. 746); and that where the complete estates of both landlord and tenant in a part only of the premises are so taken, leaving a part susceptible of occupation under the lease, the tenant is not relieved from the payment of any part of his rent. Yellow Cab Co. v. Stafford-Smith Co., 320 Ill. 294, 150 N.E. 670; Corrigan v. City of Chicago, 144 Ill. 537, 33 N.E. 746; Stubbings v. Village of Evanston, 136 Ill. 37, 26 N.E. 577.

It is appellant's contention that the taking by the United States in this case of the temporary use of the entire leased property for a definite period of shorter duration than the remaining term of the lease, with the right to extend said temporary use for additional yearly periods, constitutes a termination of the lease by operation of law and absolves appellant from liability for further payment of rent. Appellees contend that the condemnation proceedings do not excuse appellant from its liability on the covenant to pay rent. Both cite and rely, in support of their respective contentions, on the cases of Corrigan v. City of Chicago, 144 Ill. 537, 33 N.E. 746, and Yellow Cab Co. v. Stafford-Smith Co., 320 Ill. 294, 150 N.E. 670. Appellant contends that according to these decisions the test to apply in determining whether the condemnation operated to excuse the further payment of rent is whether the taking rendered the leased premises incapable of occupation under the lease. Appellees claim the test is whether the estate of the landlord has been extinguished.

For full explanation it is necessary to make, in this respect, an extended analysis. In the Corrigan case the appellant was the owner of the north 40-feet of a lot fronting on Congress street in the city of Chicago. The north half of this parcel of land he leased to one Emma Brinkworth for a term of 26 years; and on the same day by a similar lease for the same period of time, he leased the south half to one McCarty. During the term of these leases the city of Chicago condemned the north 34-feet of the lot, thus taking the entire premises leased to Brinkworth and 14 feet of the property leased to McCarty. The purpose and effect of the condemnation proceedings were not to acquire merely the leasehold interest in the property taken, but to appropriate to public use the property itself and all interests therein. Just compensation for the property taken was found by the jury to be $102,000, and the same was awarded to the landowner, less the amounts found as the value of the leasehold estates in the land taken, which were awarded to the respective tenants. The court instructed the jury "that the taking of property held by a tenant, under a lease existing at the time of filing the petition to condemn, does not release the tenant from the payment of rent, or any part thereof." The landlord was not satisfied with the distribution of the compensation to be paid by the city for the property. He appealed to this court, challenging the correctness of this instruction. This instruction we held erroneous as to the tenant Brinkworth, whose whole tract of land was condemned, and proper as to the tenant McCarty, only a portion of whose land was condemned. We there stated that when a portion only of the land is taken, and a portion remains which is susceptible of occupation under the lease, the covenants of the lease are not abrogated, and the tenant is bound by his covenant to pay full rent according to its terms; that in such case the lessee would not be entitled to apportionment or an abatement of the rent for the part of the land taken, but was bound to pay rent for the whole of the premises demised. We further said:

> We think, that while the condemnation proceeding may not amount to a technical eviction, that where the entire tract of land, or lot, is taken, the effect is to abrogate the relation of landlord and tenant. By virtue of such proceeding, whatever title the tenant has in the land passes to the State, or corporation, in whose behalf the right of eminent domain is exercised; and precisely the same is true of the landlord's estate or interest. The effect is an absolute extinguishment of the right and title of both in, or control over, the subject of the demise. It is in effect eviction by paramount right, and has all the force of an eviction by a paramount title, coupled with a conveyance by the owners of their respective interests.

We called attention to the rule that a tenant, although not allowed to dispute his landlord's title, may always plead that his interest terminated before the alleged cause of action arose, and pointed out that in the cases from other jurisdictions where rent was sought to be collected from a lessee of demised premises taken by the public through exercise of the power of eminent domain, the discharge of the lessee from liability for rent was placed upon the ground that the landlord's title was absolutely extinguished in the leased estate and he could not, therefore, after its extinguishment, enforce the contract for the payment of rent. We said:

> It would seem, therefore, that where the title of the landlord is extinguished in the whole estate during the term, the liability of the tenant to pay rent also ceases; and that in any action brought by the landlord for the rent accrued after the termination of his estate, the tenant may plead such termination in defense.

And further:

> We are of opinion that the better rule is, that where the estate of the landlord, in the whole of the demised premises, as well as that of the tenant, is extinguished by the condemnation proceedings, the liability of the tenant to pay rent ceases upon the termination of such estates.

From what was said in the *Corrigan* case, the rule seems to be well settled that in order for a tenant to be excused from the payment of rent because of the condemnation of the demised premises, it is essential that the estate of the landlord be extinguished by the condemnation proceedings. No decision of this court can be found inconsistent with this rule; and we can see no reason for departing therefrom. We regard this rule and the reasoning upon which it is based as sound; therefore, it necessarily follows, that the taking by the United States of the temporary use, only of the premises in question does not affect the liability of appellant for the payment of rent.

We deem it unnecessary to enter upon a further discussion of the case. We are satisfied that the judgment of the Appellate Court is right, and it is affirmed.[3]

Note: Determining the Tenant's Share of the Condemnation Award

Kentucky Department of Highways v. Sherrod, 367 S.W.2d 844 (Ky. 1963), adopts the following formula to determine a tenant's share of the condemnation award:

> After thorough deliberation we have worked out what we consider to be the most reasonably fair and workable method for determining compensation in cases of condemnation of property that is under lease. Under this method the

---

3. This case is commented upon, for the most part critically, in 24 Chi.-Kent L. Rev. 275 (1946), 46 Colum. L. Rev. 653 (1946), 34 Ill. B.J. 402 (1945), and 40 Ill. L. Rev. 558 (1946). See generally American Law of Property §3.54 (Casner ed. 1952). — EDS.

proof should be directed towards showing, and the instructions should require the jury to find, only the following three values:

A.   The fair market value of the leased tract as a whole immediately before the taking, giving consideration to the fact that it has rental value but *evaluating it as if free and clear of the lease.* (This will be factor A.)

B.   The fair market value of the leased tract as a whole, immediately before the taking, *if sold subject to the existing lease.* (This will be factor B.)

C.   The fair market value of so much of the leased tract as remains immediately after the taking, giving consideration to the fact that it has rental value but evaluating it as if free and clear of the lease. (This will be factor C.) (Of course, if the entire tract is taken by the condemnation, this value will be zero and need not be found by the jury, but for the purpose of the following computations C will be considered to be zero.)

After the jury has fixed the foregoing three values the *judge* will compute and apportion the damages as follows:

(1)   Subtract C from A. The result is the total damages payable by the condemnor.

(2)   If B is the *same* as or *more* than A, *ignore* B. In this situation *all* of the damages will go to the *landowner,* because the leasehold had no value, by reason of the fact that the existence of the lease has not impaired the market value of the tract.

(3)   If B is *less* than A, subtract B from A, and then *divide* the difference by A. The result will be the *percentage of ownership interest* the *lessee* is deemed to have had in the leased tract before the condemnation.

(4)   *Multiply* the total damages, found under (1) above, by the percentage found under (3) above. The result will be the *lessee's* share of the total damages. Subtracting his share from the total damages will leave the *landowner's* share. [367 S.W.2d at 850.]

The court commented on this formula as follows:

It is proper for the foregoing computations to be made by the judge because they involve only mathematical computations and not a determination of disputed facts. It would confuse the jury to require them to make the computations.

We believe the foregoing method is fair because it fixes a market value on the lease and then gives the lessee damages in the same proportion that the entire property is damaged. As pointed out by Nichols, "The award stands in the place of the land and the owners of each interest may recover out of the award the same proportionate interest which they had in the land condemned." 4 Nichols on Eminent Domain, Sec. 12.42, p. 290. The method of course is based on the assumption that the lease value depreciates in the same ratio as the sale value of the entire property, which we feel is a legitimate assumption when it is considered that a commonly accepted method of determining property values is by capitalizing rental values. It is true that the lease value *to the particular lessee for his special purposes* might depreciate more, but the lessee can protect himself against loss from that factor by assigning the lease to someone who will rent the property for a different use.

The method is fair because if the lessee is compensated for the percentage of interest he had in the property taken, by virtue of his advantageous lease, he still retains the same percentage of interest in the remaining tract, which presumably he can realize upon by assigning his lease.

Under our view it is immaterial whether the lessee, after the condemnation, will be allowed a reduction in rent in proportion to the reduction in total value of the leased tract, or will be required to continue to pay the originally agreed rent, or will have the privilege of surrendering his lease and being relieved to rent entirely. By virtue of the condemnation, the lessee who originally had an advantage (or the equivalent of an interest in the property) by reason of a favorable rental price, will lose that advantage in the same percentage that the whole value of the leased tract is reduced, whether or not he is allowed a reduction in rent. If by operation of law or by special terms of his contract he is required to continue to pay the same rent *he loses more* (as between him and the landowner but not as between him and the condemnor), but to give him a *larger share* of the damages paid by the condemnor would be in effect to relieve him in part from his obligation to the landowner to pay full rent; therefore, it would be improper to give him a larger share. If the lessee exercises a privilege to surrender the lease and be relieved of rent entirely, the result will be that he has lost *all* of the original advantage he had from his favorable lease, instead of only a portion of such advantage, but the extra loss is due to his *election* to surrender the lease and not to the condemnation. (Presumably he could assign his lease, for a consideration, to another person who would have a use for the property in its changed condition, and thus avoid the extra loss.) The *landowner* cannot be damaged more in such a situation, because he has been freed of a lease that was *disadvantageous* to him.

Whether as a matter of law a lessee, after condemnation of *part* of the leased tract, should be allowed a proportionate reduction in rent is a matter we need not decide. However, see 32 Am. Jur., Landlord and Tenant, Sec. 492, p. 493; Annotations, 43 A.L.R. 1182, 3 A.L.R.2d 330; 1 Orgel on Valuation Under Eminent Domain, Second Ed., Sec. 121, p. 522.

We are dealing in the instant case with a short-term lease involving property the buildings on which were constructed by the landowner. However, we see no reason why the method or formula we have outlined would not work in case of a long-term (99-year) lease, or in a case where the lessee constructed a building which at the end of the lease term would revert to the landowner. (In the latter case the lessee would be paying a much lower rent than if the landowner had constructed the building, so the lessee's *advantage* would be great in applying the formula.) Special complications might arise in a case where the lessee erected structures on the land which by express provisions of the lease he was entitled to remove at the end of the term, but we believe those complications could be met by requiring such structures to be valued separately from the land. [367 S.W.2d at 850-851.]

Compare the Kentucky court's observations with those of the United States Supreme Court in Alamo Land & Cattle Co. v. Arizona, 424 U.S. 295, 96 S. Ct. 910 (1976). In this case, the Court considered the rights on condemnation of a holder of an unexpired leasehold interest in the land taken:

Ordinarily, a leasehold interest has a compensable value whenever the capitalized then fair rental value for the remaining term of the lease, plus the value of any renewal right, exceeds the capitalized value of the rental the lease specifies. . . . A number of factors, of course, could operate to eliminate the existence of compensable value in the leasehold interest. . . .

A difference between the rental specified in the lease and the fair rental value plus the renewal right could arise either because the lease rentals were set initially at less than fair rental value, or because during the term of the lease the value of the land, and consequently its fair rental value, increased.[4] [424 U.S. at 304, 96 S. Ct. at 916-917.]

SECTION 2. ACTS WITHIN THE CONTROL OF THE PARTIES

A. Abandonment of the Leased Premises by the Tenant[5]

When a tenant abandons the leased premises without any justifiable excuse, what are the possible positions the landlord may wish to take, assuming there is no contractual clause in the lease covering the situation? The following are suggested as typical:

1.   The landlord may wish to take back the leased premises and forget about the tenant as rapidly as possible. All courts agree that the landlord may do this, thereby accepting a surrender of the leased premises from the tenant and terminating the lease for all purposes. The tenant, in other words, is relieved of any liability for rent which has not yet become due.

2.   The landlord may wish to ignore the abandonment by the tenant of the leased premises and continue to hold the tenant liable under the terms of the lease as though the tenant had remained in possession thereof. Is the landlord free to do this, or must the landlord undertake to mitigate the damage?

3.   The landlord may wish to relet the leased premises and hold the tenant liable for the difference in the amount of rent reserved in the lease and the amount of rent received on the reletting. The difficulty with this

---

4.   Mass. Gen. Laws ch. 79, §§24 and 27, recognizes the right of a tenant for life, a tenant for years, remainderman or reversioner, and one having other estates or interest in the condemned land to be compensated according to their respective interests. Riedel v. Plymouth Redevelopment Authority, 345 Mass. 664, 241 N.E.2d 852 (1968), dealt with the right of one who had been in possession of the condemned land for six years under a written memorandum of terms to be included in a lease to be negotiated. The memorandum provided that the lease to be entered into would be for ten years with option to renew for ten years, and the rental was to be determined at the time of entering into the lease. The court concluded the one in possession of the land was at most a tenant at will and as such had no interest in the land that would entitle him to damage under Mass. Gen. Laws ch. 79. — EDS.

5.   See generally American Law of Property §3.99 (Casner ed. 1952).

position is that the reletting by the landlord looks like such an assumption of control over the leased premises as to amount to an acceptance of the tenant's surrender of them.

LEFRAK v. LAMBERT
89 Misc. 2d 197, 390 N.Y.S.2d 959
(New York City Civ. Ct., Queens County, 1976)

POSNER, J.

In the Book of Leviticus (Ch. 19:15) it is written, "Ye shall do no unrighteousness in judgment: Thou shalt not respect the person of the poor, nor favour the person of the mighty: but in righteousness shalt thou judge thy neighbour."

If ever there was a classic case to test the mettle of a judge's ability to live up to this time-honored precept, this is the case. We were faced with the vexing problem of balancing the common law with common justice.

This is an action for money damages in the sum of $5,462, allegedly resulting from the breach of a lease for an apartment in a multi-family dwelling. The plaintiff is well known and respected in this city as one of the largest (if not *the* largest) individual owner of residential apartment houses. The apartment in question is one of five thousand in the privately owned development known as "Lefrak City." The defendants are a young couple who were represented by the husband (Kenneth), appearing pro se; and responding to the complaint with an ingenuous answer. The answer, hand-written by Kenneth Lambert, stated:

> My wife and I, left the apartment due to the new birth of my son and the loss of my wife's income. At the time we were two months behind in rent and had received a 30 day eviction notice. I wrote a letter to the mandalay leasing company explaining our problem. Our two month security covered the two months we lived there without paying. I will pay any *fair amount decided upon* [emphasis supplied].

Besides not being represented by counsel, the defendant sat mute during the entire trial and offered no evidence whatsoever in his own behalf. Since the trial, the court has received a memorandum of law from the plaintiff. The memo bears out the fact that the common law for centuries is that a landlord is under no obligation to mitigate damages stemming from the tenant's breach of the lease agreement. The defendant has not submitted any memorandum of law.

Since the defendant offered no defense to the issue of liability, the sole issue at the trial was the question of "damages." While the plaintiff's attorney claimed before the trial began that his client had no obligation to mitigate damages, he nevertheless presented one witness and several documents in an attempt to prove that an effort was made to re-rent the apartment. The witness was an assistant manager in Lefrak City, who, while not directly involved in the rental office, exercised certain administrative duties in connection with the rental of apartments. He introduced into evidence the lease (a printed standard form) which showed a rental term of three years from 9/15/73 to 9/30/76 with rent payable in "equal monthly installments" of $258 per month. The witness testified that defendants moved out of the apartment on 11/20/74 owing rent for October and November. The landlord had at that time a security deposit of $502. The apartment was vacant for seventeen (17) months and not re-rented until 5/1/76. During this period the defendants paid $45 in September, 1975. The plaintiff claimed (in his complaint) unpaid rent of $4552 and $910 for legal fees, pursuant to a clause in the lease providing for 20% liquidated damages — resulting in a total claim of $5462. However, the court's computation of 19 months rent at $258 per month less the security deposit of $502 and the $45 payment made in September, 1975 came to $4355. There was no testimony of what the difference of $197 consisted of and the attorney's testimony of the value of his services (in justification of the 20% damage clause) only persuaded the court to the amount of $300 — resulting in a total of $4655.

As to the efforts made by the landlord to re-rent the apartment, the witness testified that the apartment went on an "availability" list 11/25/74 and remained on that list until rented. He testified that the rental office consisted of five full time employees who interview prospective tenants and show them apartments. In addition, advertisements are run daily in the major newspapers to attract tenants. Invoices totaling more than $124,000 were introduced into evidence. However, he could produce no witness nor records to show that an effort was made to rent the defendants' apartment, except for two documents (introduced into evidence) indicating that an application was received for this apartment on 7/19/76 but rejected as a poor credit risk. The witness, himself, indicated no personal knowledge of the procedure and practices of the rental office, other than the fact that he approved credit for rental applications.

Based upon all the evidence presented by the plaintiff, the court came to the conclusion that he had failed to establish that he acted in good faith to re-rent the defendants' apartment. This presupposes that by operation of law, he had a duty to mitigate his damages. The landlord had no duty to rent this apartment before he rented similar apartments that had become vacant prior to this one. However, he introduced not one shred of evidence as to what his rental policies were at the time. For all the court knows, he may have had a policy to first rent out apartments that became vacant upon expiration of lease, and to leave breach of lease apartments vacant. It is not for the court to speculate, but the burden of the plaintiff to prove he has a prima facie case. This is especially so when the facts are known only to him or employees under his control. The plaintiff's only witness testified that there were five employees working in the rental office. Not one of these employees was produced as a witness, though they obviously must know what the rental procedures were during the period in question. The law of evidence is well settled that failure to produce a witness under your control leads to an inference that the testimony of the uncalled person(s) would not support the plaintiff's version of the facts. (Noce v. Kaufman, 2 N.Y.2d 347, 161 N.Y.S.2d 1, 141 N.E.2d 529; Schwier v. N.Y.C. & H.R.R. Co., 90 N.Y. 558; Bleecker v. Johnston, 69 N.Y. 309.)

The plaintiff's evidence that he spent over $124,000 in advertising, during this period, and that he had five people working full time in the rental office, only proves that he generated a lot of prospective tenants *for* Lefrak City, *not* for this specific apartment. This court is in no position to speculate why it took the plaintiff seventeen months to re-rent this apartment with all that advertising and all those employees working in the rental office. This court finds, that as a matter of law, seventeen months is an unreasonable period of time for a middle-class apartment in a middle-class neighborhood to remain vacant, absent proof by the landlord that a good faith effort was made to re-rent.

Disposing of the factual determination was simple compared to the disposition of the legal question. As stated, heretofore, plaintiff's attorney claimed, before the trial even began, that a landlord is under no obligation to mitigate damages stemming from the tenants' breach of the lease agreement. As his authority, he cites Rasch (New York Landlord and Tenant, 2nd Ed., Sec. 875) as follows:

> Therefore, it is well established that the usual obligation in the law of contracts to reduce damages has no application to a contract of leasing, and a landlord is under no obligation or duty to his tenant to relet, or attempt to relet, abandoned premises in order to minimize his damages.
>
> A lease grants in praesenti a term which the tenant thereof agrees to pay for. It is like the sale of specific personal property. Title has passed, and all that is left is liability for the purchase money.
>
> The tenant's absolute liability, therefore, is unaffected by a landlord's refusal to relet the premises.

To support this ancient rule of law (dating back to feudal England), he cites a 1964 lower court case (Fermaglich v. Warshawiak, Rockland Cty. Ct., 42 Misc. 2d 1077, 249 N.Y.S.2d 963), a 1927 Appellate Division 1st Department case (Sancourt Realty Corp. v. Dowling, 220 App. Div. 660, 222 N.Y.S. 288), and a 1876 Court of Appeals case (Becar v. Flues, 64 N.Y. 518). However, let it not be said that a valid rule of law does not survive time and changing circumstances. The paramount question is whether this rule of law deserves to be validated or summarily abandoned. Law is justice and justice must be the foundation of the law. The Hon. Judge Irwin Shapiro in a recent article entitled, "The Law: Yesterday, Today, Tomorrow" (NYLJ 10/18/76 P. 1) wrote:

The law not only helps formulate and strengthen the beneficial institutions of our way of life but also, like those institutions, grows and alters to meet the needs of our society for a system of justice that accords with the changing patterns of morality and custom which our improved technology continually brings about in our life.

There is no longer good reason — if there ever was — why leases should be governed by rules different from those applying to contracts in general (Parkwood Realty Co. v. Marcano, 77 Misc. 2d 690, 353 N.Y.S.2d 623, 1974; Sherman Taylor Corp. v. Cohen, NYLJ, 7/10/73, Civ. Ct. N.Y. Co.; Gracie Towne House v. Weinstein, NYLJ; 3/14/73, App. Term 1st Dept.; see also Howard Stores Corp. v. Robison Rayon Co. Inc., 36 A.D.2d 911, 320 N.Y.S.2d 861.) The greatest strength of the common law is its ability to adapt to changing conditions. It is a living, growing, changing thing and nowhere is that growth and that change more evident than in the law of landlord-tenant. Courts across the nation are rejecting the conveyance theory of landlord-tenant law in favor of simple contract law (Gallet, "The Evolution of Landlord-Tenant Law," NYLJ, August 13, 1976). That trend was recently recognized by this court in Cohen v. Werner, 82 Misc. 2d 295, 368 N.Y.S.2d 1005. My colleague Judge Charles H. Cohen approached the problem head on saying:

> In recent years, however, traditional rules of law involved in the landlord-tenant relationship have been changing. In general, this has involved the recognition of a lease not as a conveyance of land but as a contract involving mutual obligations in which the principal of interdependency of covenants should be applied . . . "The assault upon the citadel" surrounding the traditional concepts of the law of landlord and tenant "is proceeding these days apace" in accordance with the adaptability of our judicial system and its resilient capacity to respond to new developments . . .

If ever there was good reason to treat leases as a conveyance, that reason no longer exists. With the possible exception of cooperative and condominium apartments where our income tax laws require some vestige of ownership, residential landlords and tenants do not consider the renting of an apartment as a conveyance. It is the owner who keeps title, takes depreciation, deducts real estate taxes and interest and maintains all of the indicia of ownership. A tenant does no more than contract for a package of goods and services to be supplied. Javins v. First National Realty Corp., 138 U.S. App. D.C. 369, 428 F.2d 1071, *cert. den.* 400 U.S. 925, 91 S. Ct. 186, 27 L. Ed. 2d 185.

The modern concept of a lease, as viewed both by the courts of this state (Goldner v. Doknovitch, Sup., App. Term, 1st Dept., 388 N.Y.S.2d 504; West, Weir & Bartel, Inc. v. Carter Paint Co., 29 A.D.2d 526, 286 N.Y.S.2d 459; 25 N.Y.2d 535, 307 N.Y.S.2d 449, 255 N.E.2d 709; Tonetti v. Penati,

48 A.D.2d 25, 367 N.Y.S.2d 804; Barasch v. Goldbetter, NYLJ 4/15/75), and the legislature (Sections 226-b, 235-b, 235-c of the Real Property Law, enacted in 1975 and 1976) is that a lease is a contract and that the contract principle of interdependency of covenants should be applied. Further, recognition has been given, that the landlord and tenant are not in equal bargaining positions. Both the courts and the legislature have applied these principles in matters dealing with (1) the right to sub-let; (2) the warranty of habitability and (3) in striking out unconscionable clauses. The only major area not yet dealt with by the appellate courts and legislature of this state is this question of "Mitigation of Damages." A number of other states have responded judicially. American Jurisprudence, Sec. 621, P. 597 states: "On the other hand, there is direct authority, as well as dicta, which takes the view, respecting the duty of the landlord in this regard, that it is the duty of a landlord on wrongful abandonment of the premises by his tenant, to make reasonable efforts to reduce the damages from the breach by reletting the premises to a new tenant." (Benson v. Iowa Bake-Rite Co., 207 Iowa 410, 221 N.W. 464; Marmont v. Axe, 135 Kan. 368, 10 P.2d 826; Weinstein v. Griffin, 241 N.C. 161, 84 S.E.2d 549; Wright v. Baumann, 239 Or. 410, 398 P.2d 119; Patton v. Milwaukee Commercial Bank, 222 Wis. 167, 268 N.W. 124.) "According to considerable authority, also, if the landlord re-enters in pursuance of a forfeiture or under a provision of the lease permitting him to do so after his tenant has abandoned the premises, he must then use diligence in seeking a new tenant in order to lessen the damages." (Int'l Trust Co. v. Weeks, 203 U.S. 364, 27 S. Ct. 69, 51 L. Ed. 224; Bradbury v. Higginson, 162 Cal. 602, 123 P. 797; Kanter v. Safran (Fla.), 68 So. 2d 553; Jordan v. Nickell (Ky.), 253 S.W.2d 237; Crow v. Kaupp (Mo.), 50 S.W.2d 995; Carey v. Hejke, 119 N.J.L. 594, 197 A. 652; John Church Co. v. Martinez (Tex. Civ. App.), 204 S.W. 486; Brown v. Hayes, 92 Wash. 300, 159 P. 89.)

If the lease is now viewed as a contract, then all the rules of law regarding contracts should apply, including the requirement that the injured party make a reasonable effort to mitigate damages. It's interesting to note, that, even though the plaintiff's attorney did not point out the clause in the lease, there is a clause, entitled, "Remedies of Landlord," which give contractually to the landlord the same rights he is claiming under the common law. The clause is so unconscionable on its face that even without the recently enacted statute (ch. 828, Laws of 1976 — effective 7/26/76 and applicable to all leases, regardless of when executed), this court would have ruled it unenforceable. Gov. Carey in his memorandum of approval, acknowledged that, "[t]he concept of unconscionability is not new to the law of this state. The Uniform Commercial Code, at the time of its enactment in 1962, codified the doctrine as it related to the law of sales. It has, however, had limited applicability in landlord and tenant disputes until recently. The doctrine is only now beginning to be judicially applied in such cases. (See, Tai on Luck Corp. v. Cirota, 35 A.D.2d 380 [316 N.Y.S.2d 438]; SKD

Enterprises v. L & M Offset, 65 Misc. 2d 612 [318 N.Y.S.2d 539]; Seabrook v. Commuter Housing Co., 72 Misc. 2d 6 [338 N.Y.S.2d 67], and Harwood v. Lincoln Square Apts., 78 Misc. 2d 1097 [359 N.Y.S.2d 387]). This bill would codify the doctrine and establish a defense of unconscionability in landlord and tenant proceedings."

A colleague of mine, in this court, in a decision dated 4/27/76 (Birchwood Ass'n v. Stern, 86 Misc. 2d 607, 383 N.Y.S.2d 175)[6] disagreed with the opinion expressed in Parkwood Realty Co. v. Marcano (See *Supra*) that a change in the law is warranted. He stated that, "Such a change, if a change is warranted should be made either by our appellate courts or the legislature." But how will the appellate courts have an opportunity to change an unjust law if a court of the first instance does not present them with a case that sharpens the issues and provides a clear opportunity for the appellate courts to deal with the merits of the rule of law? Rarely, if ever, will the tenant appeal. He who must breach a lease for lack of funds and defends himself, will hardly be able to take an appeal. As for waiting for the legislature "to make the change," are we an independent branch of government or not? Do we have to wait for another branch of government to tell us when we are wrong? Judge-made law should be changed by judges, not legislators. Though admittedly, they came very close this year when the Assembly (by a vote of 113-25) passed a bill that would have made the landlord's duty to mitigate damages a statutory one. Alas, it did not get out of committee in the Senate, perhaps to give the courts an opportunity to right their own wrong. (Assembly 278-c, 1975-1976). Judge Fuld writing for the majority in Bing v. Thunig, 2 N.Y.2d 656, 667, 163 N.Y.S.2d 3, 11, 143 N.E.2d 3, 9, in striking down a rule of law that had been in existence for over a hundred years, stated,

> The rule of non-liability is out of tune with the life about us, at variance with modern-day needs and with concepts of justice and fair dealing. It should be discarded. To the suggestion that stare decisis compels us to perpetuate it until the legislature acts, a ready answer is at hand. It was intended not to effect a petrifying rigidity, but to assure the justice that flows from certainty and stability. If, instead, adherence to precedent offers not justice but unfairness, not certainty but doubt and confusion, it loses its right to survive, and no principle constrains us to follow it. On the contrary, as this court, speaking through Judge Desmond in Woods v. Lencet, 303 N.Y. 349, 355, 102 N.E.2d 691, declared, we would be abdicating our own function in a field peculiarly non-statutory, were we to insist on legislation and "refuse to reconsider an old and unsatisfactory court-made rule." [7]

6. It is interesting to note that the Appellate Term, 2d Dept., affirmed the court in *Birchwood* because of the court's finding that the landlord made a diligent effort to re-rent. The court took notice of the new trend but stated, "We need not decide whether this rule should be adopted, because it is apparent from the papers submitted in the motion for summary judgment that plaintiff diligently attempted to relet the premises" (NYLJ 11/16/74, P. 12).

7. The great Cardozo in his treatise "The Nature of the Judicial Process," in regard to adherence to precedent, stated,

There is something basically unjust, basically unreasonable and, therefore, basically not legal about a landlord in an urban society with a housing shortage having no obligation to try to re-rent an apartment and mitigate damages. There is something unfair about permitting tenants to be in a different category than other persons entering into a contract. To be sure, a tenant should be required to pay every penny of damage actually sustained by a reasonable landlord acting to mitigate damages but to allow what is really a draconian remedy is foreign to our modern concept of justice.

Since the plaintiff has failed to establish that he acted in good faith to mitigate damages, the court finds that he was entitled only to a reasonable period of time in which to re-rent. In this case that was three (3) months. Therefore, adding the three months to the two months unpaid at the time tenants vacated and subtracting the $502 security plus $45 payment made in September, 1975, plaintiff is entitled to a judgment in the sum of $743 for unpaid rent and $148 for legal expenses (20% × $743) for a total of $891 with statutory costs.

LEFRAK v. LAMBERT
93 Misc. 2d 632, 403 N.Y.S.2d 397 (Sup. Ct. App. Term 1978)

Before Pino P.J., and Rinaldi and Buschmann, JJ.
Per Curiam.
Judgment of the court below (89 Misc. 2d 197, 390 N.Y.S.2d 959) unanimously modified by increasing the amount of plaintiff's recovery to $4,222 plus attorney's fees in the sum of $750; as so modified, affirmed without costs.

I think that when a rule, after it has been duly tested by experience, has been found to be inconsistent with the sense of justice or with the social welfare, there should be less hesitation in frank avowal and full abandonment. We have had to do this sometimes in the field of constitutional law. Perhaps we should do so oftener in fields of private law where considerations of social utility are not so aggressive and insistent. There should be greater readiness to abandon an untenable position when the rule to be discarded may not reasonably be supposed to have determined the conduct of the litigants, and particularly when in its origin it was the product of institutions or conditions which have gained a new significance or development with the progress of the years. In such circumstances, the words of Wheeler, J., in Dwy v. Connecticut Co., 89 Conn. 74, 99 [92 A. 883], express the tone and temper in which problems should be met: "That court best serves the law which recognizes that the rules of law which grew up in a remote generation may, in the fullness of experience, be found to serve another generation badly, and which discards the old rule when it finds that another rule of law represents what should be according to the established and settled judgment of society, and no considerable property rights have become vested in reliance upon the old rule. It is thus great writers upon the common law have discovered the source and method of its growth, and in its growth found its health and life. It is not and it should not be stationary. Change of this character should not be left to the legislature." If judges have woefully misinterpreted the mores of their day, or if the mores of their day are no longer those of ours, they ought not to tie, in helpless submission, the hands of their successors.
[P. 150-152]

Defendant herein vacated his apartment before the expiration of his term and plaintiff relet it some months thereafter. It is our opinion that under the circumstances herein plaintiff is entitled to prevail on his cause of action to recover rent for the period that the apartment remained vacant.

While there seems to be a trend whereby the courts have been modernizing traditional concepts of landlord and tenant law and in some instances have held that a landlord is obligated to attempt to relet premises when a tenant vacates before the expiration of his term, we need not decide whether such rule should be adopted in the case at bar. The evidence adduced at trial established that plaintiff made reasonable and diligent efforts to rerent defendant's apartment (Birchwood Associates v. Stern, 88 Misc. 2d 937, 390 N.Y.S.2d 505).

In addition, the record was sufficient to support a finding that plaintiff was entitled to the sum of $750 as reasonable attorney's fees.

Note: The Restatement's Position

The Restatement (Second) of Property (Landlord and Tenant) §12.1(3) provides as follows in regard to the abandonment of the leased premises by the tenant.

> (3)   Except to the extent the parties to the lease validly agree otherwise, if the tenant abandons the leased property, the landlord is under no duty to attempt to relet the leased property for the balance of the term of the lease to mitigate the tenant's liability under the lease, including his liability for rent, but the landlord may:
>
> (a)   accept the tenant's offer of surrender of the leased property, which offer is inherent in the abandonment, and thereby terminate the lease, leaving the tenant liable only for rent accrued before the acceptance and damage caused by the abandonment; or
>
> (b)   notify the tenant that he will undertake to relet the leased property for the tenant's account, thereby relieving the tenant of future liabilities under the lease, including liability for future rent, to the extent the same are performed as a result of a reletting on terms that are reasonable.

Problems

19.4. L and T entered into a written lease of certain premises. The lease was for a term of five years at a monthly rental of $250. During the second year of the lease, T assigned the lease to T_1, with the consent of L. T_1 remained on the leased premises for a few months and then abandoned the same. L notified T that L was going to relet the premises and hold T liable for the difference between the rent under the lease and the amount received on the reletting. L then sued T to recover such difference. T set up as a defense that the assignment of the lease to T_1 had the effect of making T a surety for the performance of the covenants in the lease and the failure of L to notify the primary obligor (T_1) of the reletting released the surety. Has T stated a defense? See DeHart v. Allen, 26 Cal. 2d 829, 161 P.2d 453 (1945). See also American Law of Property §§3.61, 3.99 (Casner ed. 1952).

19.5. L and T entered into a written lease of certain premises at a monthly rental of $50. T abandoned the premises, and L relet the same for the balance of the term of T's lease for a monthly rental of $75. Can T recover from L the excess monthly rental L obtained on such reletting? See Whitcomb v. Brant, 90 N.J.L. 245, 100 A. 175 (1917). See also American Law of Property §§3.61, 3.99 (Casner ed. 1952).

19.6. If L re-enters and takes possession of the leased premises for non-payment of rent when the lease contains a covenant permitting such action, what are L's rights against T under the following circumstances:

a. L makes no attempt to relet the premises.
b. L is unable to relet the premises except for a term longer than the unexpired term of the lease from L to T and L refuses to relet for such longer term.
c. L relets the premises at a ridiculously low rental.

See Woodbury v. Sparrell Print, 198 Mass. 1, 84 N.E. 441 (1908). See also American Law of Property §§3.97, 3.99 (Casner ed. 1952).

19.7. L and T entered into a written lease of certain premises. The lease provided: "If the lessee shall fail to make any of the payments of rent, or to fulfill any of the covenants of the lease, it shall be lawful for the lessor to re-enter and take and hold possession without such re-entry working a forfeiture of the rents to be paid by the lessee during the full term of this lease."

a. Suppose T fails to pay the rent and L re-enters and takes possession. May L recover from T the full amount of the rent reserved in the lease without making any allowance for the value of the use of the property by L?
b. Suppose T fails to pay the rent and L re-enters and takes possession and then relets the property to another. May L recover from T the full amount of the rent reserved in the L-to-T lease without making any allowance for the amounts received by L under the reletting?

See Broniewicz v. Wysocki, 306 Ill. App. 187, 28 N.E.2d 283 (1940). See also American Law of Property §§3.97, 3.99 (Casner ed. 1952).

WRIGHT v. BAUMANN
239 Or. 410, 398 P.2d 119 (1965)

O'CONNELL, J.

Plaintiffs seek to recover for breach of agreement under which plaintiffs agreed to erect an office building and defendant, a dentist, agreed to enter into a lease of one of the offices after the building was constructed. Both parties waived a jury trial. Defendant appeals from a judgment for plaintiffs.

Defendant's principal assignments of error are directed at the trial court's rejection of evidence tending to show that plaintiffs had the opportunity to mitigate damages but refused to do so. Plaintiffs' objections to defendant's questions relating to mitigation were sustained by the trial court, apparently on the ground that the instrument signed by the parties was a lease rather than a contract and that, being a lease, the lessor had no obligation to mitigate damages. Defendant contends that the rule relied upon by plaintiffs is inapplicable because the "Agreement" in question is not a lease but is a contract to make a lease, and that therefore plaintiffs are required to mitigate as in any other contract case. Finally, plaintiffs counter with the contention that the case was tried by defendant upon the theory that the "Agreement" was a lease and that he is now estopped to assert that it is a contract to enter into a lease.

Defendant's offer of proof clearly indicates that he made a reasonable effort to mitigate the damages resulting from his refusal to take possession of the part of the premises intended for his occupancy. The offer of proof showed that plaintiffs notified defendant on August 27, 1956, that the building would be ready for occupancy on September 24, 1956. On September 6, 1956, defendant notified plaintiffs that he did not desire to enter into a lease of any part of the building. It was further shown that defendant informed two doctors that the space allotted to him was available and that during September, 1956, the two doctors had offered to lease the space allotted to defendant on the terms and conditions specified in the "Agreement" in question but that plaintiffs refused to lease the office space to them, giving no reasons for the refusal to do so.

A majority of the courts, including Oregon, hold that a lessor is not required to mitigate damages when the lessee abandons the leasehold. In a few states it is incumbent upon the lessor to use reasonable means to mitigate damages. If the transaction is a contract to make a lease rather than an executed lease, it is universally recognized that the landowner has an obligation to mitigate damages upon a breach of the contract by the promisor.

The majority view, absolving the lessor from any obligation to mitigate is based upon the theory that the lessee becomes the owner of the premises for a term and therefore the lessor need not concern himself with lessee's abandonment of his own property. That view might have some validity in those cases where there is simply a lease of the land alone with no covenants except the covenant to pay rent. But a modern business lease is predominantly an exchange of promises and only incidentally a sale of a part of the lessor's interest in the land. As 2 Powell on Real Property, ¶221, p. 182 (1950) observes, the "growth in the number and detail of specific lease covenants has reintroduced into the law of estates for years a predominantly contractual ingredient" and that as a consequence "[i]n practice, the law today concerning estates for years consists chiefly of rules determining the construction and effect of lease covenants." These covenants in a modern business lease, particularly where only a part of the space in a building is leased, relate for the most part to the use of the space. The lessor's duties do not end with the execution of the lease. The case of Whitaker v. Hawley, 25 Kan. 674, 687 (1881) expresses this view as follows: ". . . a lease is in one sense a running rather than a completed contract. It is an agreement for a continuous interchange of values between landlord and tenant, rather than a purchase single and completed of a term or estate in lands."

The covenants in the instrument in the present case relate to the continuing obligations of the respective parties. The transaction is essentially a contract. There is no reason why the principle of mitigation of damages should not be applied to it. ". . . [I]t is important that the rules for awarding damages should be such as to discourage even persons against whom wrongs have been committed from passively suffering economic loss which could be averted by reasonable efforts. . . ." McCormick, Damages, p. 127 (1935).

Lessors as well as contract promisors should be made to serve this salutary policy. To borrow again from McCormick, "the realities of feudal tenure have vanished and a new system based upon a theory of contractual obligations has in general taken its place." He reminds us that in disregarding the contractual nature of modern leases we have "neglected the caution of Mr. Justice Holmes, 'that continuity with the past is only a necessity and not a duty.'" Writing in 1925, McCormick predicted that eventually "the logic, inescapable according to the standards of a 'jurisprudence of conceptions' which permits the landlord to stand idly by the vacant, abandoned premises and treat them as the property of the tenant and recover full rent, will yield to the more realistic notions of social advantage which in other fields of the law have forbidden a recovery for damages which the plaintiff by reasonable efforts could have avoided." We believe that it is time for McCormick's prediction to become a reality.

It does not seem that the burden imposed upon a lessor in mitigating damages would ordinarily be any greater than that imposed upon promisees of contracts not relating to the occupancy of land. However, if it could be said that it is unreasonable to require the lessor to seek out other tenants, plaintiffs in the present case would not be benefited by that argument because defendant presented a willing and, we may assume, suitable substitute tenant. If defendant had entered into possession and thereafter had offered the landlord a person willing to sublet the premises, plaintiffs under the terms of the "Agreement" could not have refused to accept the new tenant without reasonable grounds for doing so. The situation is essentially the same when the proposed new tenant is offered for the purpose of reducing the tenant's damages.

Even if we were to perpetuate the distinction between a lease and a contract in the application of the principle of mitigation of damages, we would reach the same result. The agreement in question is a contract to make a lease rather than a lease. At the time the agreement was entered into the office building had not been constructed, and the office which was to constitute defendant's leasehold could not then be identified. Consequently, there was nothing that could constitute the subject matter of a conveyance at that time. Conceding that one may make a present demise of a term of being in the future, it is difficult to conceive of the present transfer of the title (or a part of it in the case of a lease) when that which is to be transferred has no existence. The analogy to mortgages on after acquired property immediately suggests itself. Such mortgages do not transfer a legal estate or interest; they create only an equitable mortgage. And whether they are regarded as arising out of contract or conveyance, a court of equity should require the plaintiff seeking equity to do equity by making a reasonable effort to avoid damages.

Plaintiffs contend that defendant should not now be permitted to argue that the transaction was a contract to make a lease because the case was tried on the theory that the transaction was a lease. We have found nothing in the transcript indicating that defendant treated the instrument in question as creating a lease rather than a contract to make a lease. Neither defendant's pleadings nor his conduct in the course of trial clearly points one way or the other with respect to the character of the transaction. In his motion for a new trial defendant admitted that the question of the character of the instrument was not "squarely" presented to the court. But there was nothing to suggest that defendant was not relying upon the theory that the transaction was a contract to make a lease. On the contrary, it might be said that since all but three states have refused to require a lessor to mitigate damages defendant's offer of proof on the point of mitigation indicated that he was proceeding on the assumption that the transaction was a contract only.

The judgment is reversed and the cause is remanded for a new trial.

B.　Constructive Eviction[8]

Eviction, whether actual (when the landlord deprives the tenant of physical possession of the leased property) or constructive (when the landlord so deprives the tenant of the use of the property that the landlord's action is tantamount to depriving the tenant of physical possession), is a breach of the covenant of quiet enjoyment. You should re-examine at this point the material relating to the duty of the landlord to protect the tenant in his quiet enjoyment of the leased property, Chapter 17, at page 368.

The following excerpt from the court's opinion in Automobile Supply Co. v. Scene-in-Action Corp., 340 Ill. 196, 172 N.E. 35 (1936), is a good starting point in relation to constructive eviction:

8.　Re-examine introduction to Chapter 18, Section 2, at page 443.

The eviction of a tenant from the possession or enjoyment of the demised premises, or any part thereof, by the landlord releases the tenant from the further payment of rent. Rent is the return made to the lessor by the lessee for his use of the land, and the landlord's claim for rent therefore depends upon the tenant's enjoyment of the land for the term of his contract. It follows that if the tenant is deprived of the premises by any agency of the landlord the obligation to pay rent ceases, because such obligation has force only from the consideration of the enjoyment of the premises. The eviction which will discharge the liability of the tenant to pay rent is not necessarily an actual physical expulsion from the premises or some part of them, but any act of the landlord which renders the lease unavailing to the tenant or deprives him of the beneficial enjoyment of the premises constitutes a constructive eviction of the tenant, which exonerates him from the terms and conditions of the lease and he may abandon it.

Not every act of a landlord in violation of his covenants or of the tenant's enjoyment of the premises under the lease will amount to a constructive eviction. Some acts of interference may be mere acts of trespass to which the term "eviction" is not applicable. To constitute an eviction there must be something of a grave and permanent character done by the landlord clearly indicating the intention of the landlord to deprive the tenant of the longer beneficial enjoyment of the premises in accordance with the terms of the lease. The failure of a landlord to furnish heat for the demised premises in accordance with the terms of his covenant in the lease justifies the tenant in removing from the premises, and if he does so he is discharged from the payment of rent thereafter. Giddings v. Williams, 336 Ill. 482, 168 N.E. 514. These facts constitute a constructive eviction. There can be no constructive eviction, however, without the vacating of the premises. Where a tenant fails to surrender possession after the landlord's commission of acts justifying the abandonment of the premises the liability for rent will continue so long as possession of the premises is continued. Whether the acts of the landlord amount to a constructive eviction is ordinarily a question of fact for the decision of a jury, depending upon the circumstances of the particular case. [340 Ill. at 200-202, 172 N.E. at 37-38.]

BARASH v. PENNSYLVANIA TERMINAL REAL ESTATE CORP.

26 N.Y.2d 77, 256 N.E.2d 707 (1970)

BREITEL, J.

Defendant landlord appeals from an affirmed order denying its motion to dismiss tenant's complaint for legal insufficiency (CPLR 3211, subd. (a), par. 7). The allegations for this purpose are accepted as true (Cohn v. Lionel Corp., 21 N.Y.2d 559, 562, 289 N.Y.S.2d 404, 407, 236 N.E.2d 634, 636).

The first cause of action, alleging a partial actual eviction, is to relieve tenant from payment of rent, and, notably, is not a claim for damages. The second is for reformation of the lease to conform to alleged prior oral agreements.

With respect to the first cause of action, the question is whether landlord's allegedly wrongful failure to supply a continuous flow of fresh air on evenings and weekends to offices leased by tenant constitutes a partial actual eviction relieving tenant from the payment of rent or, at most, a constructive eviction requiring the tenant to abandon the premises before he may be relieved of the duty to pay rent. Also at issue is whether grounds for reformation are pleaded by the second cause of action.

Plaintiff, a lawyer, alleges that on September 15, 1967, while the premises known as 2 Pennsylvania Plaza in New York City were being constructed, he entered into a written lease with defendant landlord for rental of office space to be used for the practice of law. Involved is a 29-story glass-enclosed, completely air-conditioned office building. Its windows are sealed and the supply and circulation of air inside the building is under the landlord's exclusive control.

Defendant landlord, through its authorized renting agents, had represented that the building would be open 24 hours a day, 7 days each week, to enable tenants and others to occupy the offices at all times. Prior to signing the lease, plaintiff inquired as to the manner in which air would be circulated "when the air-conditioning system was not in operation." He was informed, fraudulently he alleges, "that the offices in question would be constructed with a duct system, which would always provide a natural and continuous flow of air . . . [making] the offices . . . comfortable and usable at all evening hours and also on weekends, even when the air-conditioning and heating systems were not in operation." The tenant, on the basis of these representations, known by the landlord to be false, signed the lease.

The lease provides, in pertinent part:

> As long as Tenant is not in default under any of the covenants of this lease Landlord shall furnish air cooling during the months of June, July, August and September on business days from 9 A.M. to 6 P.M. when in the judgment of the Landlord it may be required for the comfortable occupancy of the demised premises and at other times during business days and similar hours, ventilate the demised premises.

The lease also contains a general merger clause:

> Landlord or Landlord's agents have made no representations or promises with respect to said building, the land upon which it is erected or the demised premises except as herein expressly set forth and no rights, easements or licenses are acquired by Tenant by implication or otherwise except as expressly set forth herein. The taking possession of the demised premises by Tenant shall be conclusive evidence, as against Tenant, that Tenant accepts the same, "as is" and that said premises and the building of which the same

form a part were in good and satisfactory condition at the time such possession was so taken.

Plaintiff tenant took possession on May 15, 1968 and that evening at 6:00 P.M. defendant "turned off all air" in the offices. By 7:00 P.M. the offices became "hot, stuffy, and unusable and uninhabitable." Upon protest the landlord refused to provide afterhour ventilation unless paid for by the tenant at a rate of $25 per hour. The tenant refused to pay the reserved rent or the additional charge and brought the instant action. The landlord sought dispossession for the nonpayment. This was denied, but the tenant was directed to pay rent into court pending the outcome of the instant action.

The first cause of action, based on the unreformed lease, alleges a partial actual eviction. Even assuming that the leased premises became "hot, stuffy, and unusable and uninhabitable" so that no one was able to work or remain in the offices after 7:00 P.M., these allegations are insufficient, as a matter of law, to make out an actual eviction.

To be an eviction, constructive or actual, there must be a wrongful act by the landlord which deprives the tenant of the beneficial enjoyment or actual possession of the demised premises (Edgerton v. Page, 20 N.Y. 281; 1 Rasch, Landlord and Tenant, §849). Of course, the tenant must have been deprived of something to which he was entitled under or by virtue of the lease (52 C.J.S. Landlord & Tenant §477, p. 292). A right to 24-hour ventilation cannot be established, in the absence of reformation of the lease, by alleging fraudulent representations concerning ventilation when the lease itself expressly limits ventilation rights.

But even if the lease were to be read to include the allegations concerning ventilation (the gravamen of the tenant's second cause of action in reformation), the facts alleged, and accepted as true, would still fall short of, and not constitute, an actual eviction.

An actual eviction occurs only when the landlord wrongfully ousts the tenant from physical possession of the leased premises. There must be a physical expulsion or exclusion (Fifth Ave. Bldg. Co. v. Kernochan, 221 N.Y. 370, 117 N.E. 579; 2 McAdam, Landlord and Tenant (5th ed.), §329, p. 1391; 1 N.Y. Law of Landlord and Tenant (Edward Thompson Co.), §250). And where the tenant is ousted from a portion of the demised premises, the eviction is actual, even if only partial (Fifth Ave. Bldg. Co. v. Kernochan, *supra;* 524 West End Ave. v. Rawak, 125 Misc. 862, 212 N.Y.S. 287).

Thus, for example, where the landlord barred the tenant from entering the premises it has been held a partial actual eviction (Lawrence v. Edwin A. Denham Co., 58 Misc. 543, 109 N.Y.S. 752 (App. Term); 2 McAdam, op. cit., *supra,* §332, p. 1410). Similarly, where the landlord changes the lock, or padlocks the door, there is an actual eviction (see Lester v. Griffin, 57 Misc.

628, 108 N.Y.S. 580 (App. Term); Morgan v. Short, 13 Misc. 279, 34 N.Y.S. 10).

On the other hand, constructive eviction exists where, although there has been no physical expulsion or exclusion of the tenant, the landlord's wrongful acts substantially and materially deprive the tenant of the beneficial use and enjoyment of the premises (City of New York v. Pike Realty Corp., 247 N.Y. 245, 160 N.E. 359; Ann. — Nonhabitability of Leased Dwellings, 4 A.L.R. 1453, 1461-1463, supp. 29 A.L.R. 52, supp. 34 A.L.R. 711; 1 Rasch, op. cit., *supra*, §§871-875). The tenant, however, must abandon possession in order to claim that there was a constructive eviction (Boreel v. Lawton, 90 N.Y. 293, 297; Two Rector St. Corp. v. Bein, 226 App. Div. 73, 76, 234 N.Y.S. 409, 412; 1 N.Y. Law of Landlord and Tenant (Edward Thompson Co.), *supra*, §253).

Thus, where the tenant remains in possession of the demised premises there can be no constructive eviction (Edgerton v. Page, 20 N.Y. 281, 284, *supra*). It has been said to be inequitable for the tenant to claim substantial interference with the beneficial enjoyment of his property and remain in possession without payment of rent (City of New York v. Pike Realty Corp., *supra*, 247 N.Y., at p. 247, 160 N.E. 359, 360; Edgerton v. Page, *supra*).

In the case of actual eviction, even where the tenant is only partially evicted liability for all rent is suspended although the tenant remains in possession of the portion of the premises from which he was not evicted. In the leading case of Fifth Ave. Bldg. Co. v. Kernochan (221 N.Y. 370, 373, 117 N.E. 579, 580, *supra*), the court stated: "We are dealing now with an eviction which is actual and not constructive. If such an eviction, though partial only, is the act of the landlord, it suspends the entire rent because the landlord is not permitted to apportion his own wrong."

This then presents the nub of the·appeal. The tenant, who has not abandoned the premises, asserts that there has been an actual eviction, though partial only, thus permitting him to retain possession of the premises without liability for rent. To support this contention it is claimed that failure to supply fresh air constitutes actual eviction, if only, albeit, during the hours after 6:00 P.M. and on weekends.

There is no previous known reported case involving a like situation in a substantially sealed building. The resolution of this appeal turns therefore on the application of general principles to the novel complex of facts presented.

All that tenant suffered was a substantial diminution in the extent to which he could beneficially enjoy the premises. Although possibly more pronounced, tenant's situation is analogous to cases where there is a persistent offensive odor, harmful to health, arising from a noxious gas (Tallman v. Murphy, 120 N.Y. 345, 24 N.E. 716), an open sewer (Sully v. Schmitt, 147 N.Y. 248, 41 N.E. 514), or defective plumbing (Lathers v. Coates, 18 Misc. 231, 41 N.Y.S. 373 (App. Term)). The possible odor-producing causes are innumerable (see, generally, 1 Rasch, op. cit., *supra,* §891). In all such cases there has been held to be only a constructive eviction.

In the *Tallman* case *(supra),* which involved coal gas, the court stated:

> In such a building as the one under consideration there is very much that remains under the charge and control of the landlord . . . [I]f he persistently neglects them, and by reason of such neglect . . . his apartments are filled with gas or foul odors . . . and the apartments become unfit for occupancy, the tenant is deprived of the beneficial enjoyment thereof . . . and there is a constructive eviction [id. 120 N.Y. at p. 352, 24 N.E. at p. 718].

Given these well-established rules, proper characterization of the instant failure to ventilate follows easily, assuming there be such duty under the lease as written, or as reformed to conform to the representations. The tenant has neither been expelled nor excluded from the premises, nor has the landlord seized a portion of the premises for his own use or that of another. He has, by his alleged wrongful failure to provide proper ventilation, substantially reduced the beneficial use of the premises.

As long as the tenant remains in possession it matters little whether he can remedy the situation by his independent action. Nor does it matter whether the proposed 24-hour use has become practically impossible. In City of New York v. Pike Realty Corp. *(supra),* the land was leased from the city for construction of a parking garage. The city, however, thereafter refused to give tenant a building permit. The court held this refusal "was at most a . . . constructive eviction" (id. 247 N.Y. at p. 247, 160 N.E. at p. 360).

Tenant's reliance on Schulte Realty Co. v. Pulvino, 179 N.Y.S. 371 (App. Term, per Lehman, J.), which held that a tenant had suffered a partial actual eviction, is misplaced. The landlord, in that case, interfered with tenant's "easement" of light and air by allowing another to cover a large portion of an airshaft upon which tenant's windows opened. The court, relying on Adolphi v. Inglima, 130 N.Y.S. 130 (App. Term), held that the lease included a right to light and air from the shaftway, and that there was, therefore, a partial eviction. It was observed that there could be no constructive eviction because the premises had not been rendered untenantable. In the *Adolphi* case a landlord had sealed up a window on the tenant's premises, and it was said to justify a finding of a partial eviction. On the other hand, in Solomon v. Fantozzi, 43 Misc. 61, 86 N.Y.S. 754 (App. Term) the court held that blocking the ventilation of a water closet did not constitute a partial constructive eviction, let alone a partial actual eviction. The distinguishing feature of these cases, if indeed they be not anomalies, is that they deal with the destruction of an easement or appurtenance of light and air granted by the landlord (1 Rasch, op. cit., *supra,* §895). Here there is no claim to an appurtenant right to air external to the demised premises but rather the failure to provide an essential service within the demised premises, which failure traditionally constitutes a constructive eviction (Tallman v. Murphy, *supra*).

It would seem moreover, apart from or despite the cases last discussed, that interference with easements or appurtenances of light and air insofar as they diminish the tenant's beneficial enjoyment of the demised premises, constitutes a constructive and not an actual eviction. Thus in Two Rector St. Corp. v. Bein (226 App. Div. 73, 234 N.Y.S. 409, *supra*) the substantial "diminution of light, air and view" constituted at most a constructive eviction requiring a surrender by the tenant (id. at pp. 75-76, 234 N.Y.S. at p. 411). (See, generally, 52 C.J.S. Landlord & Tenant §458, p. 312.)

Since the eviction, if any, is constructive and not actual, the tenant's failure to abandon the premises makes the first cause of action insufficient in law (33 N.Y. Jur., Landlord & Tenant, §170, and cases cited). The first cause of action, therefore, should have been dismissed.

Tenant, in his second cause of action for reformation, repeats all the allegations made in support of his first cause of action. He adds, however, that the lease as signed "does not reflect the actual and total agreement of/and between the parties, and the lease was incorrectly drawn regarding the defendant's representations and warranties as to the 'continuous flow of air' and 'usability of the said offices in the evenings and weekends'." He further alleges that these fraudulent representations induced the execution of the lease.

It is argued that because of the fraud of the landlord plus the unilateral mistake of the tenant, an agreement intended to be a part of the written lease was omitted. To be sure, this constitutes the classic case for reformation (Welles v. Yates, 44 N.Y. 525, 529; see, also, Metzger v. Aetna Ins. Co., 227 N.Y. 411, 417, 125 N.E. 814, 816; 6 N.Y. Jur., Reformation of Instruments, §§47, 48). The presence of the general merger clause does not bar the introduction of the parol evidence of fraudulent representations in actions to rescind a contract (Sabo v. Delman, 3 N.Y.2d 155, 161, 164 N.Y.S.2d 714, 717, 143 N.E.2d 906, 908; Carlinger v. Carlinger, 21 A.D.2d 656, 249 N.Y.S.2d 761). So, too, a general merger clause does not bar an action to reform a contract, which by reason of fraud and mistake does not contain the agreement of the parties (Brandwein v. Provident Mut. Life Ins. Co., 3 N.Y.2d 491, 495-496, 168 N.Y.S.2d 964, 966-967, 146 N.E.2d 693, 694-695).

The rule of Fogelson v. Rackfay Constr. Co. (300 N.Y. 334, 340, 90 N.E.2d 881, 883) is inapplicable since in that case there was no allegation of fraud. Also, since the merger clause in this case is a general one, the limited exception in cases of specific merger clauses does not control (see Danann Realty Corp. v. Harris, 5 N.Y.2d 317, 320-321, 184 N.Y.S.2d 599, 601-602, 157 N.E.2d 597, 598-599).

However, the fatal defect in the second cause of action is tenant's failure to allege that there was a unilateral mistake on his part. All that is pleaded is that "the lease was incorrectly drawn." It does not appear from this ambiguous and conclusory allegation that the pleader is alleging unilateral mistake, an essential element in an action for reformation based on another's fraud. So critical a fact should be made express and clear if it indeed is present in the action. Therefore, this cause of action should be dismissed.

Although it is necessary to dismiss the complaint because neither cause of action is legally sufficient, plaintiff may wish to move for permission to replead. The record does not reveal that plaintiff sought leave to replead in the event that the motion to dismiss was granted. Consequently, plaintiff may not be granted leave to replead based on the present state of the record (see CPLR 3211, subd. (e)).

Accordingly, the order of the Appellate Division should be reversed, the question certified answered in the negative, with costs to abide the ultimate event, the complaint dismissed, but with leave to plaintiff tenant to apply at Special Term for leave to replead, if so advised.

FULD, C.J. (dissenting in part).

I agree with the court's opinion that a plaintiff, in order to state a sufficient cause of action for reformation, must allege fraud by the defendant and unilateral mistake on his own part. The plaintiff before us has, concededly, pleaded fraud and it seems to me that his allegation that "the lease was incorrectly drawn" is the equivalent of an assertion that he was under a mistake when he signed the lease. Our rules of pleading have never demanded the use of particular or magic words as long as the language employed conveys the requisite meaning. In the present case, only insistence on an excessive technicality can justify dismissal of the second cause of action. I would, therefore, affirm so much of the order appealed from as sustains that count.

BURKE, SCILEPPI, BERGAN, JASEN and GIBSON, JJ., concur with BREITEL, J.

FULD, C.J., dissents in part and votes to affirm so much of the order appealed from as sustains the second cause of action, in a memorandum.

Order reversed and the case remitted to Special Term for further proceedings in accordance with the opinion herein, with costs to abide the ultimate event. Question certified answered in the negative.

Note: The Restatement's Position as to Whether the Tenant Must Give Up Possession to Claim Constructive Eviction

Section 6.1 of the Restatement (Second) of Property (Landlord and Tenant) rejects total non-payment of rent as a remedy for partial eviction and rejects the requirement that the tenant abandon the leased property before claiming a constructive eviction. The Reporter's Note to Section 6.1 recognizes that in these respects the section is contrary to the weight of judicial authority.

Problem

19.8.   L and T entered into a written lease of store premises. The term of the lease was four years, commencing July 1. The lease provided that the premises were to be used exclusively for the conduct of a furniture business. L covenanted that during the term of the lease L would not let or permit the occupation of any other space in the store building "for the purpose of conducting therein a furniture store." In January, T held a "retirement" sale, ceased doing business on the leased property, vacated the premises, and failed to pay the rent. On April 2, L rented the adjoining store on a month-to-month basis beginning May 1 to a business which would conduct the "sale of linoleum and kindred products." In June, T sued to rescind the lease on the ground that L had breached the covenant not to rent to any competing business and that such action either constituted a constructive eviction terminating T's duty to pay rent as of May 1 or constituted an acceptance of T's surrender of the premises terminating T's duty to pay rent as of May 1. What decision? See Kulawitz v. Pacific Woodenware & Paper Co., 25 Cal. 2d 664, 155 P.2d 24 (1944). Consider the majority, concurring, and dissenting opinions and place yourself in the position of the attorney for L. What would you have advised L if L had come to you on April 2?

Note: Does the Present Doctrine of Constructive Eviction Solve the Tenant's Problem of Habitable Premises?

Two factors tend to reduce the usefulness of the defense of constructive eviction. Firstly, the common law imposes no duty to repair on the landlord, and thus it is only where the landlord by conduct, rather than by neglecting to repair, has breached the covenant of quiet enjoyment that constructive eviction is brought into play. Actually, courts have been liberal in finding breaches of the covenant of quiet enjoyment, and therefore this impediment is not as great as it first seems. The interference with the tenant's quiet enjoyment need only be of so substantial a nature that the premises are no longer fit for habitation; this probably adequately protects the tenant. Secondly, however, the tenant must evidence the substantiality of the interference by vacating the premises within a reasonable time after the condition comes into existence; otherwise, the tenant is deemed to waive all rights under this doctrine.[9] Considering the current acute shortage of low cost housing, this requirement is harsh and unrealistic, to say the least.[10]

The Massachusetts Supreme Judicial Court[11] has stated that while at law abandonment of the leased premises must occur within a reasonable time, "abandonment is not essential to one seeking equitable relief." The court found an equitable constructive eviction and awarded the tenant as damages the difference between the fair value of what the tenant would have received absent the landlord's breach and the fair value of what the tenant did receive, saying:

> Such relief [equitable] is more nearly adequate than the incomplete and hazardous remedy at law which requires that the lessee (a) determine at its peril that the circumstances amount to a constructive eviction, and (b) vacate the demised premises, possibly at some expense, while remaining subject to the risk that a court may decide that the lessor's breaches do not go to the essence of the lessor's obligation.[12]

C. Breach of Implied Warranty of Fitness/Habitability

As noted in a previous chapter,[13] the common law has held consistently that the landlord does not impliedly covenant or warrant the premises to be in a tenantable, fit, or suitable condition[14]—subject to two well-defined exceptions. The first exception is made in cases where the defects are not readily discoverable by a reasonable inspection and where the defects are known to the landlord.[15] The second exception is made in some jurisdictions in cases where there is a short-term lease of furnished premises.[16] Consider the following case in the light of these two exceptions.

---

9. See Annot., Time Within Which Tenant Must Yield or Abandon Premises after Constructive Eviction, 91 A.L.R.2d 638 (1963).

10. Simmons, Passion and Prudence: Rent Withholding Under New York's Spiegel Law, 15 Buffalo L. Rev. 572, 577 (1966). Professor Simmons concludes that there has been a regrettable lack of judicial experimentation or innovation in landlord-tenant law.

11. Charles E. Burt, Inc. v. Seven Grand Corp., 340 Mass. 124, 163 N.E.2d 4 (1959).

12. 340 Mass. at 129, 163 N.E.2d at 7. Although this case involved a detailed commercial lease which the Court found breached by the failure of the landlord to supply heat, power, and elevator service, the court's language and reasoning seem equally applicable—if not more so—to low rent housing.

13. See Chapter 17, especially Franklin v. Brown, page 363 *supra.*

14. See American Law of Property §3.45 (Casner ed. 1952).

15. See id. §3.45.

16. See, e.g., Ingalls v. Hobbs, 156 Mass. 348, 31 N.E. 286 (1892). A third exception sometimes has been made for premises within a building not yet completed when the lease was made, e.g., Young Corp. v. McClintic, 26 S.W.2d 460 (Tex. Civ. App. 1930), *rev'd,* 66 S.W.2d 676 (Tex. Commn. App. 1933).

PINES v. PERSSION
14 Wis. 2d 590, 111 N.W.2d 409 (1961)

Action by plaintiffs Burton Pines, Gary Weissman, David Klingenstein and William Eaglestein, lessees, against defendant Leon Perssion, lessor, to recover the sum of $699.99, which was deposited by plaintiffs with defendant for the fulfillment of a lease, plus the sum of $137.76 for the labor plaintiffs performed on the leased premises. After a trial to the court findings of fact and conclusions of law were filed which determined that plaintiffs could recover the lease deposit plus $62 for their labor, but less one month's rent of $175. From a judgment to this effect defendant appeals. Plaintiffs have filed a motion for review of that part of the judgment entitling defendant to withhold the sum of $175.

At the time this action was commenced the plaintiffs were students at the University of Wisconsin in Madison. Defendant was engaged in the business of real estate development and ownership. During the 1958-1959 school year plaintiffs were tenants of the defendant in a student rooming house. In May of 1959 they asked the defendant if he had a house they could rent for the 1959-1960 school year. Defendant told them he was thinking of buying a house on the east side of Madison which they might be interested in renting. This was the house involved in the lease and is located at 1144 East Johnson Street. The house had in fact been owned and lived in by the defendant since 1951, but he testified he misstated the facts because he was embarrassed about its condition.

Three of the plaintiffs looked at the house in June, 1959 and found it in a filthy condition. Pines testified the defendant stated he would clean and fix up the house, paint it, provide the necessary furnishings and have the house in suitable condition by the start of the school year in the fall. Defendant testified he told plaintiffs he would not do any work on the house until he received a signed lease and a deposit. Pines denied this.

The parties agreed that defendant would lease the house to plaintiffs commencing September 1, 1959 at a monthly rental of $175 prorated over the first nine months of the lease term, or $233.33 per month for September through May. Defendant was to have a lease drawn and mail it to plaintiffs. It was to be signed by the plaintiffs' parents as guarantors and a deposit of three months' rent was to be made.

Defendant mailed the lease to Pines in Chicago in the latter part of July. Because the plaintiffs were scattered around the country, Pines had some difficulty in securing the necessary signatures. Pines and the defendant kept in touch by letter and telephone concerning the execution of the lease, and Pines came to Madison in August to see the defendant and the house. Pines testified the house was still in terrible condition and defendant again promised him it would be ready for occupancy on September 1st. Defendant testified he said he had to receive the lease and the deposit before he would do any work on the house, but Pines could not remember him making such a statement.

On August 28th Pines mailed defendant a check for $175 as his share of the deposit and on September 1st he sent the lease and the balance due. Defendant received the signed lease and the deposit about September 3rd.

Plaintiffs began arriving at the house about September 6th. It was still in a filthy condition and there was a lack of student furnishings. Plaintiffs began to clean the house themselves, providing some cleaning materials of their own, and did some painting with paint purchased by defendant. They became discouraged with their progress and contacted an attorney with reference to their status under the lease. The attorney advised them to request the Madison building department to inspect the premises. This was done on September 9th and several building code violations were found. They included inadequate electrical wiring, kitchen sink and toilet in disrepair, furnace in disrepair, handrail on stairs in disrepair, screens on windows and doors lacking. The city inspector gave defendant until September 21st to correct the violations, and in the meantime plaintiffs were permitted to occupy the house. They vacated the premises on or about September 11th.

The pertinent parts of the lease, which was dated September 4, 1959, are as follows:

> 1. For and in consideration of the covenants and agreements of the Lessees hereinafter mentioned, Lessor does hereby devise, lease and let unto Lessees the following described premises, to-wit:
>
> The entire house located at 1144 East Johnson Street, City of Madison, Dane County, Wisconsin, including furniture to furnish said house suitable for student housing.
>
> 2. Lessees shall have and hold said demised premises for a term of one (1) year commencing on the first day of September, 1959. . . .
>
> 3. [Total annual rent was $2,100, to be paid in monthly installments in advance, prorated over the first nine months of the term, or $233.33 per month. The deposit of three months' rent of $699.99 was to be applied for March, April and May of 1960.]
>
> 4. The Lessees also agree to the following: . . . to use said premises as a private dwelling house only. . . .
>
> 7. If Lessees shall abandon the demised premises, the same may be re-let by Lessor for such reasonable rent, comparable to prevailing rental for similar premises, and upon such reasonable terms as the Lessor may see fit; and if a sufficient sum shall not be realized, after paying the expenses of re-letting, the Lessees shall pay and satisfy all deficiencies. . . .

The trial court concluded that defendant represented to the plaintiffs that the house would be in a habitable condition by September 1, 1959; it was not in such condition and could not be made so before October 1, 1959; that sec.

234.17, Stats. applied and under its provisions plaintiffs were entitled to surrender possession of the premises; that they were not liable for rent for the time subsequent to the surrender date, which was found to be September 30, 1959.

MARTIN, C.J.

We have doubt that sec. 234.17, Stats. applies under the facts of this case. In our opinion, there was an implied warranty of habitability in the lease and that warranty was breached by the appellant.

There is no express provision in the lease that the house was to be in habitable condition by September 1st. We cannot agree with respondents' contention that the provision for "including furniture to furnish said house suitable for student housing" constitutes an express covenant that the house would be in habitable condition. The phrase "suitable for student housing" refers to the "furniture" to be furnished and not to the general condition of the house.

Parol evidence is inadmissible to vary the terms of a written contract which is complete and unambiguous on its face. Hunter v. Hathaway, 1901, 108 Wis. 620, 84 N.W. 996; 32 Am Jur., Landlord and Tenant, secs. 130, 134.

The general rule is that there are no implied warranties to the effect that at the time a lease term commences the premises are in a tenantable condition or adapted to the purposes for which leased. A tenant is a purchaser of an estate in land, and is subject to the doctrine of caveat emptor. His remedy is to inspect the premises before taking them or to secure an express warranty. Thus, a tenant is not entitled to abandon the premises on the ground of uninhabitability. See I American Law of Property, sec. 3.45; 32 Am. Jur., Landlord and Tenant, sec. 247.

There is an exception to this rule, some courts holding that there is an implied warranty of habitability and fitness of the premises where the subject of the lease is a furnished house. This is based on an intention inferred from the fact that under the circumstances the lessee does not have an adequate opportunity to inspect the premises at the time he accepts the lease. See I American Law of Property, sec. 3.45; 35 N.Y. Univ. L. Rev. 1279, 1283-1287; Collins v. Hopkins (1923), 2 K.B. 617, 34 A.L.R. 703, 705. In the Collins Case the English court said:

> Not only is the implied warranty on the letting of a furnished house one which, in my own view, springs by just and necessary implication from the contract, but it is a warranty which tends in the most striking fashion to the public good and the preservation of public health. *It is a warranty to be extended rather than restricted.* [Emphasis supplied.]

See, also, Delamater v. Foreman, 1931, 184 Minn. 428, 239 N.W. 148; Ingalls v. Hobbs, 1892, 156 Mass. 348, 31 N.E. 286, 16 L.R.A. 51.

We have not previously considered this exception to the general rule.

Obviously, however, the frame of reference in which the old common law rule operated has changed.

Legislation and administrative rules, such as the safeplace statute, building codes and health regulations, all impose certain duties on a property owner with respect to the condition of his premises. Thus, the legislature has made a policy judgment — that it is socially (and politically) desirable to impose these duties on a property owner — which has rendered the old common law rule obsolete. To follow the old rule of no implied warranty of habitability in leases would, in our opinion, be inconsistent with the current legislative policy concerning housing standards. The need and social desirability of adequate housing for people in this era of rapid population increases is too important to be rebuffed by that obnoxious legal cliché, caveat emptor. Permitting landlords to rent "tumbledown" houses is at least a contributing cause of such problems as urban blight, juvenile delinquency and high property taxes for conscientious landowners.

There is no question in this case but that the house was not in a condition reasonably and decently fit for occupation when the lease term commenced. Appellant himself admitted it was "filthy," so much so that he lied about owning it in the first instance, and he testified that no cleaning or other work was done in the house before the boys moved in. The filth, of course, was seen by the respondents when they inspected the premises prior to signing the lease. They had no way of knowing, however, that the plumbing, heating and wiring systems were defective. Moreover, on the testimony of the building inspector, it was unfit for occupancy, and:

> The state law provides that if the building is not in immediate danger of collapse the owner may board it up so that people cannot enter the building. His second choice is to bring the building up to comply with the safety standards of the code. And his third choice is to tear it down.

The evidence clearly showed that the implied warranty of habitability was breached. Respondents' covenant to pay rent and appellant's covenant to provide a habitable house were mutually dependent, and thus a breach of the latter by appellant relieved respondents of any liability under the former.

Since there was a failure of consideration, respondents are absolved from any liability for rent under the lease and their only liability is for the reasonable rent value of the premises during the time of actual occupancy. That period of time was determined by the trial court in its finding No. 9, which is supported by the evidence. Granting respondents' motion for review, we direct the trial court to find what a reasonable rental for that period would be and enter judgment for the respondents in the amount of their deposit plus the amount recoverable for their labor, less the rent so determined by the court.

Cause remanded with instructions to enter judgment for the respondents consistent with this opinion. Respondents may tax double costs in this court for appellant's failure to comply with Rule 6(3), W.S.A. 251.26 as to inclusion of record or appendix page references in the statement of facts.[17]

Note: The Meaning of Pines v. Perssion

Pines v. Perssion is subject to conflicting interpretations: (1) Wisconsin merely applied the well-recognized exception noted above to a case where the defects were not discoverable by reasonable inspection and the landlord knew of these defects; (2) Wisconsin joined a few other states in departing from the mossbound doctrine of no implied covenants, at least as to short-term leases of furnished premises; (3) Wisconsin will now generally imply a covenant of habitability, at least in leases of one year or less.[18] At this point, reread the opinion and consider the arguments for each interpretation. 45 Marq. L. Rev. 630 (1962) argues for a limited interpretation of this case. However, the Wisconsin Supreme Court cited *Pines* for the third interpretation.[19] The sweeping language of the *Pines* opinion itself suggests that the implied warranty recognized by the court is not limited to either of the well-recognized exceptions.

A second point to notice in *Pines* is the summary fashion in which the Wisconsin Supreme Court treated Wis. Stat. §234.17,[20] the statutory form of constructive eviction. The trial court found for the plaintiff relying on that statute, stating:

> Section 234.17 clearly provides that where premises become untenantable and unfit for occupancy *for any cause,* the tenant may under certain conditions surrender possession of the leasehold premises without penalty. . . . It is clear therefore that Section 234.17 does apply to the case in question and we find that based on the evidence herein the plaintiffs were entitled to surrender possession of the leasehold premises and were not liable to pay to the lessor rent for the time subsequent to the surrender.

---

17. Reread the last paragraph of the decision. Do you think this might have had some bearing on the court's decision? A word to the wise: future lawyers take note! — EDs.

18. By Wis. Stat. §706.10(6), no covenants are to be implied in conveyances, and by Wis. Stat. §706.01(2), leases for one year or more are deemed conveyances. However, it is in the short-term lease that the implied covenant is most needed, so this limitation is not really significant.

19. Earl Millikin, Inc. v. Allen, 21 Wis. 2d 497, 501, 124 N.W.2d 651, 654 (1963).

20. Now §704.07(4). Section 234.17 read:

> Lessee may surrender premises, when. Where any building, which is leased or occupied, is destroyed or so injured by the elements, or any other cause as to be untenantable, and unfit for occupancy, and no express agreement to the contrary has been made in writing, the lessee or occupant may, if the destruction or injury occurred without his fault or neglect, quit and surrender possession of the leasehold premises, and of the land so leased or occupied; and he is not liable to pay to the lessor or owner, rent for the time subsequent to the surrender.

Note that this statute is identical in language with N.Y. Real Prop. Law §227.

On appeal, counsel for the plaintiffs asserted only the propriety of the trial court's application of section 234.17. The Wisconsin Supreme Court disagreed in rather summary fashion, beginning its opinion, "We have doubt that sec. 234.17 applies under the facts of this case." It is clear from the decisions in both New York[21] and Wisconsin interpreting this statute that the language "by the elements, *or any other cause* as to be untenantable, and unfit for occupancy" is not as inclusive as it would initially appear.

California has created an implied warranty of habitability by statute. Section 1941 of the California Civil Code provides: "The lessor of a building intended for the occupation of human beings must, in the absence of an agreement to the contrary, put it into a condition fit for such occupation . . ."[22] Is there any reason this statute permits an exculpatory clause absolving the landlord from the obligation imposed by the statute?[23]

Note: Breach of Implied Warranty of Habitability as a Defense to an Action on the Part of the Landlord for Past Due Rent and Possession

Following *Pines,* may a Wisconsin tenant being sued by a landlord for past due rent use as a defense the fact that the landlord has breached the implied warranty of habitability? See Posnanski v. Hood, 46 Wis. 2d 172, 174 N.W.2d 528 (1970), and consider the following case. In this connection, see the comments on Lindsey v. Normet, page 435 *supra.*

JAVINS v. FIRST NATIONAL REALTY CORP.
428 F.2d 1071 (D.C. Cir. 1970)

WRIGHT, J.: These cases present the question whether housing code violations which arise during the term of a lease have any effect upon the tenant's obligation to pay rent. The Landlord and Tenant Branch of the District of Columbia Court of General Sessions ruled proof of such violations inadmissible when proffered as a defense to an eviction action for nonpayment of rent. The District of Columbia Court of Appeals upheld this ruling. Saunders v. First National Realty Corp., 245 A.2d 836 (1968).

Because of the importance of the question presented, we granted appellants' petitions for leave to appeal. We now reverse and hold that a warranty of habitability, measured by the standards set out in the Housing Regulations for the District of Columbia, is implied by operation of law into leases

---

21. Reread Suydam v. Jackson, page 401 *supra.*
22. This statute also imposes a duty on the lessor to repair subsequent dilapidations.
23. See the discussion in Section 2.E of this chapter on onerous terms in a lease, page 538 *infra.*

of urban dwelling units covered by those Regulations and that breach of this warranty gives rise to the usual remedies for breach of contract.

I

The facts revealed by the record are simple. By separate written leases, each of the appellants rented an apartment in a three-building apartment complex in Northwest Washington known as Clifton Terrace. The landlord, First National Realty Corporation, filed separate actions in the Landlord and Tenant Branch of the Court of General Sessions on April 8, 1966, seeking possession on the ground that each of the appellants had defaulted in the payment of rent due for the month of April. The tenants, appellants here, admitted that they had not paid the landlord any rent for April. However, they alleged numerous violations of the Housing Regulations as "an equitable defense or [a] claim by way of recoupment or set-off in an amount equal to the rent claim," as provided in the rules of the Court of General Sessions. They offered to prove "[t]hat there are approximately 1500 violations of the Housing Regulations of the District of Columbia in the building at Clifton Terrace, where Defendant resides some affecting the premises of this Defendant directly, others indirectly, and all tending to establish a course of conduct of violation of the Housing Regulations to the damage of Defendants. . . ." Settled Statement of Proceedings and Evidence, p. 2 (1966). Appellants conceded at trial, however, that this offer of proof reached only violations which had arisen since the term of the lease had commenced. The Court of General Sessions refused appellants' offer of proof and entered judgment for the landlord. The District of Columbia Court of Appeals affirmed, rejecting the argument made by appellants that the landlord was under a contractual duty to maintain the premises in compliance with the Housing Regulations. Saunders v. First National Realty Corp., *supra,* 245 A.2d at 838.

II

Since, in traditional analysis, a lease was the conveyance of an interest in land, courts have usually utilized the special rules governing real property transactions to resolve controversies involving leases. However, as the Supreme Court has noted in another context, "the body of private property law . . . , more than almost any other branch of law, has been shaped by distinctions whose validity is largely historical." Courts have a duty to reappraise old doctrines in the light of the facts and values of contemporary life — particularly old common law doctrines which the courts themselves created and developed. As we have said before, "[T]he continued vitality of the common law . . . depends upon its ability to reflect contemporary community values and ethics."

The assumption of landlord-tenant law, derived from feudal property law, that a lease primarily conveyed to the tenant an interest in land may have been reasonable in a rural, agrarian society; it may continue to be reasonable in some leases involving farming or commercial land. In these cases, the value of the lease to the tenant is the land itself. But in the case of the modern apartment dweller, the value of the lease is that it gives him a place to live. The city dweller who seeks to lease an apartment on the third floor of a tenement has little interest in the land 30 or 40 feet below, or even in the bare right to possession within the four walls of his apartment. When American city dwellers, both rich and poor, seek "shelter" today, they seek a well known package of goods and services — a package which includes not merely walls and ceilings, but also adequate heat, light and ventilation, serviceable plumbing facilities, secure windows and doors, proper sanitation, and proper maintenance. . . .

Some courts have realized that certain of the old rules of property law governing leases are inappropriate for today's transactions. In order to reach results more in accord with the legitimate expectations of the parties and the standards of the community, courts have been gradually introducing more modern precepts of contract law in interpreting leases. Proceeding piecemeal has, however, led to confusion where "decisions are frequently conflicting, not because of a healthy disagreement on social policy, but because of the lingering impact of rules whose policies are long since dead."

In our judgment the trend toward treating leases as contracts is wise and well considered. Our holding in this case reflects a belief that leases of urban dwelling units should be interpreted and construed like any other contract.[24]

III

Modern contract law has recognized that the buyer of goods and services in an industrialized society must rely upon the skill and honesty of the supplier to assure that goods and services purchased are of adequate quality. In

---

24. This approach does not deny the possible importance of the fact that land is involved in a transaction. The interpretation and construction of contracts between private parties has always required courts to be sensitive and responsive to myriad different factors. We believe contract doctrines allow courts to be properly sensitive to all relevant factors in interpreting lease obligations.

We also intend no alteration of statutory or case law definitions of the term "real property" for purposes of statutes or decisions on recordation, descent, conveyancing, creditors' rights, etc. We contemplate only that contract law is to determine the rights and obligations of the parties to the lease agreement, as between themselves. The civil law has always viewed the lease as a contract, and in our judgment that perspective has proved superior to that of the common law. See 2 M. Planiol, Treatise on the Civil Law §1663 et seq. (1959); 11 La. Stat. Ann., Civil Code, Art. 2669 (1952).

interpreting most contracts, courts have sought to protect the legitimate expectations of the buyer and have steadily widened the seller's responsibility for the quality of goods and services through the implied warranties of fitness and merchantability. Thus without any special agreement a merchant will be held to warrant that his goods are fit for the ordinary purposes for which such goods are used and that they are at least of reasonably average quality. Moreover, if the supplier has been notified that goods are required for a specific purpose, he will be held to warrant that any goods sold are fit for that purpose. These implied warranties have become widely accepted and well established features of the common law, supported by the overwhelming body of case law. Today most states as well as the District of Columbia have codified and enacted these warranties into statute, as to the sale of goods, in the Uniform Commercial Code.

Implied warranties of quality have not been limited to cases involving sales. The consumer renting a chattel, paying for services, or buying a combination of goods and services must rely upon the skill and honesty of the supplier to at least the same extent as a purchaser of goods. Courts have not hesitated to find implied warranties of fitness and merchantability in such situations. In most areas product liability law has moved far beyond "mere" implied warranties running between two parties in privity with each other.

The rigid doctrines of real property law have tended to inhibit the application of implied warranties to transactions involving real estate. Now, however, courts have begun to hold sellers and developers of real property responsible for the quality of their product.[25] For example, builders of new homes have recently been held liable to purchasers for improper construction on the ground that the builders had breached an implied warranty of fitness.[26] In other cases courts have held builders of new homes liable for breach of an implied warranty that all local building regulations had been complied with.[27] And following the developments in other areas, very recent decisions[28] and commentary[29] suggest the possible extension of liability to

25. See generally Bearman, Caveat Emptor in Sale of Realty — Recent Assaults Upon the Rule, 14 Vand. L. Rev. 541 (1961); Dunham, Vendor's Obligation as to Fitness of Land for a Particular Purpose, 37 Minn. L. Rev. 108 (1953).

26. See Waggoner v. Midwestern Development, Inc., S.D., 154 N.W.2d 803 (1967); Bethlahmy v. Bechtel, 91 Idaho 55, 415 P.2d 698 (1969); Schipper v. Levitt & Sons, Inc., *supra* Note 7; Carpenter v. Donohoe, 154 Colo. 78, 388 P.2d 399 (1964); Loraso v. Custom Built Homes, Inc., La. App., 144 So. 2d 459 (1962). Other cases still continue the older limitation on the vendor's liability to homes sold before construction is complete. See, e.g., Hoye v. Century Builders, 52 Wash. 2d 830, 329 P.2d 474 (1958).

27. See Schiro v. W. E. Gould & Co., 18 Ill. 2d 538, 165 N.E.2d 286 (1960); Annot., 110 A.L.R. 1048 (1937).

28. Connor v. Great Western Savings and Loan Ass'n, 69 Cal. 2d 850, 73 Cal. Rptr. 369, 447 P.2d 609 (1968) (in bank) (Traynor, Ch. J.). Chief Justice Traynor's excellent opinion utilizes tort doctrines to extend liability beyond the immediate seller.

29. Comment, Liability of the Institutional Lender for Structural Defects in New Housing, 35 U. Chi. L. Rev. 739 (1968).

parties other than the immediate seller for improper construction of residential real estate.

Despite this trend in the sale of real estate, many courts have been unwilling to imply warranties of quality, specifically a warranty of habitability, into leases of apartments. Recent decisions have offered no convincing explanation for their refusal; rather they have relied without discussion upon the old common law rule that the lessor is not obligated to repair unless he covenants to do so in the written lease contract. However, the Supreme Courts of at least two states, in recent and well reasoned opinions, have held landlords to implied warranties of quality in housing leases. Lemle v. Breeden, S. Ct. Hawaii, 462 P.2d 470 (1969); Reste Realty Corp. v. Cooper, 53 N.J. 444, 251 A.2d 268 (1969). See also Pines v. Perssion, 14 Wis. 2d 590, 111 N.W.2d 409 (1961). In our judgment, the old no-repair rule cannot coexist with the obligations imposed on the landlord by a typical modern housing code, and must be abandoned in favor of an implied warranty of habitability. In the District of Columbia, the standards of this warranty are set out in the Housing Regulations.

IV

A. In our judgment the common law itself must recognize the landlord's obligation to keep his premises in a habitable condition. This conclusion is compelled by three separate considerations. First, we believe that the old rule was based on certain factual assumptions which are no longer true; on its own terms, it can no longer be justified. Second, we believe that the consumer protection cases discussed above require that the old rule be abandoned in order to bring residential landlord-tenant law into harmony with the principles on which those cases rest. Third, we think that the nature of today's urban housing market also dictates abandonment of the old rule.

The common law rule absolving the lessor of all obligation to repair originated in the early Middle Ages.[30] Such a rule was perhaps well suited to an agrarian economy; the land was more important[31] than whatever small living structure was included in the leasehold, and the tenant farmer was

30. The rule was "settled" by 1485. 3 W. Holdsworth, A History of English Law 122-123 (6th ed. 1934). The common law rule discussed in text originated in the even older rule prohibiting the tenant from committing waste. The writ of waste expanded as the tenant's right to possession grew stronger. Eventually, in order to protect the landowner's reversionary interest, the tenant became obligated to make repairs and liable to eviction and damages if he failed to do so. Ibid.

31. The land was so central to the original common law conception of a leasehold that rent was viewed as "issuing" from the land: "[T]he governing idea is that the land is bound to pay the rent. . . . We may almost go to the length of saying that the land pays it through [the tenant's] hand." 2 F. Pollock & F. Maitland, The History of English Law 131 (2d ed. 1923).

fully capable of making repairs himself.[32] These historical facts were the basis on which the common law constructed its rule; they also provided the necessary prerequisites for its application.[33]

Court decisions in the late 1800's began to recognize that the factual assumptions of the common law were no longer accurate in some cases. For example, the common law, since it assumed that the land was the most important part of the leasehold, required a tenant to pay rent even if any building on the land was destroyed. Faced with such a rule and the ludicrous results it produced, in 1863 the New York Court of Appeals declined to hold that an upper story tenant was obliged to continue paying rent after his apartment building burned down. The court simply pointed out that the urban tenant had no interest in the land, only in the attached building.

Another line of cases created an exception to the no-repair rule for short term leases of furnished dwellings. The Massachusetts Supreme Judicial Court, a court not known for its willingness to depart from the common law, supported this exception, pointing out:

> . . .[A] different rule should apply to one who hires a furnished room, or a furnished house, for a few days, or a few weeks or months. Its fitness for immediate use of a particular kind, as indicated by its appointments, is a far more important element entering into the contract than when there is a mere lease of real estate. One who lets for a short term a house provided with all furnishings and appointments for immediate residence may be supposed to contract in reference to a well-understood purpose of the hirer to use it as a habitation. . . . It would be unreasonable to hold, under such circumstances, that the landlord does not impliedly agree that what he is letting is a house suitable for occupation in its condition at the time. . . .[34]

These as well as other similar cases demonstrate that some courts began some time ago to question the common law's assumptions that the land was the most important feature of a leasehold and that the tenant could feasibly make any necessary repairs himself. Where those assumptions no longer reflect contemporary housing patterns, the courts have created exceptions to

32. Many later judicial opinions have added another justification of the old common law rule. They have invoked the time-worn cry of caveat emptor and argued that a lessee has the opportunity to inspect the premises. On the basis of his inspection, the tenant must then take the premises "as is," according to this reasoning. As an historical matter, the opportunity to inspect was not thought important when the rule was first devised. See Note 30 *supra*. . . .

33. Even the old common law courts responded with a different rule for a landlord-tenant relationship which did not conform to the model of the usual agrarian lease. Much more substantial obligations were placed upon the keepers of inns (the only multiple dwelling houses known to the common law). Their guests were interested solely in shelter and could not be expected to make their own repairs. "The modern apartment dweller more closely resembles the guest in an inn than he resembles an agrarian tenant, but the law has not generally recognized the similarity." J. Levi, P. Hablutzel, L. Rosenberg & J. White, Model Residential Landlord-Tenant Code 6-7 (Tent. Draft 1969).

34. Ingalls v. Hobbs, 156 Mass. 348, 31 N.E. 286 (1892).

the general rule that landlords have no duty to keep their premises in repair.

It is overdue for courts to admit that these assumptions are no longer true with regard to all urban housing. Today's urban[35] tenants, the vast majority of whom live in multiple dwelling houses, are interested, not in the land, but solely in "a house suitable for occupation." Furthermore, today's city dweller usually has a single, specialized skill unrelated to maintenance work; he is unable to make repairs like the "jack-of-all-trades" farmer who was the common law's model of the lessee. Further unlike his agrarian predecessor who often remained on one piece of land for his entire life, urban tenants today are more mobile than ever before. A tenant's tenure in a specific apartment will often not be sufficient to justify efforts at repairs. In addition, the increasing complexity of today's dwellings renders them much more difficult to repair than the structures of earlier times. In a multiple dwelling repair may require access to equipment and areas in the control of the landlord. Low and middle income tenants, even if they were interested in making repairs, would be unable to obtain any financing for major repairs since they have no long-term interest in the property.

Our approach to the common law of landlord and tenant ought to be aided by principles derived from the consumer protection cases referred to above. In a lease contract, a tenant seeks to purchase from his landlord shelter for a specified period of time. The landlord sells housing as a commercial businessman and has much greater opportunity, incentive and capacity to inspect and maintain the condition of his building. Moreover, the tenant must rely upon the skill and bona fides of his landlord at least as much as a car buyer must rely upon the car manufacturer. In dealing with major problems, such as heating, plumbing, electrical or structural defects, the tenant's position corresponds precisely with "the ordinary consumer who cannot be expected to have the knowledge or capacity or even the opportunity to make adequate inspection of mechanical instrumentalities, like automobiles, and to decide for himself whether they are reasonably fit for the designed purpose." Henningsen v. Bloomfield Motors, Inc., 32 N.J. 358, 375, 161 A.2d 69, 78 (1960).[36]

Since a lease contract specifies a particular period of time during which the tenant has a right to use his apartment for shelter, he may legitimately expect that the apartment will be fit for habitation for the time period for which it is rented. We point out that in the present cases there is no allegation that appellants' apartments were in poor condition or in violation

35. In 1968 more than two thirds of America's people lived in the 228 largest metropolitan areas. Only 5.2% lived on farms. The World Almanac 1970 at 251 (L. Long ed.). More than 98% of all housing starts in 1968 were non-farm. Id. at 313.

36. Nor should the average tenant be thought capable of "inspecting" plaster, floorboards, roofing, kitchen appliances, etc. To the extent, however, that some defects *are* obvious, the law must take note of the present housing shortage. Tenants may have no real alternative but to accept such housing with the expectation that the landlord will make necessary repairs. Where this is so, caveat emptor must of necessity be rejected.

of the housing code at the commencement of the leases.[37] Since the lessees continue to pay the same rent, they were entitled to expect that the landlord would continue to keep the premises in their beginning condition during the lease term. It is precisely such expectations that the law now recognizes as deserving of formal, legal protection.

Even beyond the rationale of traditional products liability law, the relationship of landlord and tenant suggests further compelling reasons for the law's protection of the tenants' legitimate expectations of quality. The inequality in bargaining power between landlord and tenant has been well documented. Tenants have very little leverage to enforce demands for better housing. Various impediments to competition in the rental housing market, such as racial and class discrimination and standardized form leases, mean that landlords place tenants in a take it or leave it situation. The increasingly severe shortage of adequate housing further increases the landlord's bargaining power and escalates the need for maintaining and improving the existing stock. Finally, the findings by various studies of the social impact of bad housing has led to the realization that poor housing is detrimental to the whole society, not merely to the unlucky ones who must suffer the daily indignity of living in a slum.

Thus we are led by our inspection of the relevant legal principles and precedents to the conclusion that the old common law rule imposing an obligation upon the lessee to repair during the lease term was really never intended to apply to residential urban leaseholds. Contract principles established in other areas of the law provide a more rational framework for the apportionment of landlord-tenant responsibilities; they strongly suggest that a warranty of habitability be implied into all contracts[38] for urban dwellings.

B.   We believe, in any event, that the District's housing code requires that a warranty of habitability be implied in the leases of all housing that it covers. The housing code — formally designated the Housing Regulations of the District of Columbia — was established and authorized by the Commissioners of the District of Columbia on August 11, 1955. Since that time, the code has been updated by numerous orders of the Commissioners. The 75 pages of the Regulations provide a comprehensive regulatory scheme setting forth in some detail: (a) the standards which housing in the District of Columbia must meet; (b) which party, the lessor or the lessee, must meet each standard; and (c) a system of inspections, notifications and criminal penalties. The Regulations themselves are silent on the question of private remedies.

Two previous decisions of this court, however, have held that the Hous-

37.   In Brown v. Southall Realty Co., 237 A.2d 834 (1968), the District of Columbia Court of Appeals held that unsafe and unsanitary conditions existing at the beginning of the tenancy and known to the landlord rendered any lease of those premises illegal and void.

38.   We need not consider the provisions of the written lease governing repairs since this implied warranty of the landlord could not be excluded. See Henningsen v. Bloomfield Motors, Inc., [32 N.J. 358, 161 A.2d 69 (1960)]; Kay v. Cain, 81 U.S. App. D.C. 24, 25, 154 F.2d 305, 306 (1946). . . .

ing Regulations create legal rights and duties enforceable in tort by private parties. In Whetzel v. Jess Fisher Management Co., 108 U.S. App. D.C. 385, 282 F.2d 943 (1960), we followed the leading case of Altz v. Lieberson, 233 N.Y. 16, 134 N.E. 703 (1922), in holding (1) that the housing code altered the common law rule and imposed a duty to repair upon the landlord, and (2) that a right of action accrued to a tenant injured by the landlord's breach of this duty. As Judge Cardozo wrote in *Lieberson:*

> . . . We may be sure that the framers of this statute, when regulating tenement life, had uppermost in thought the care of those who are unable to care for themselves. The Legislature must have known that unless repairs in the rooms of the poor were made by the landlord, they would not be made by any one. The duty imposed became commensurate with the need. The right to seek redress is not limited to the city or its officers. The right extends to all whom there was a purpose to protect. . . . [134 N.E. at 704.]

Recently, in Kanelos v. Kettler, 132 U.S. App. D.C. 133, 135, 406 F.2d 951, 953 (1968), we reaffirmed our position in *Whetzel,* holding that "the Housing Regulations did impose maintenance obligations upon appellee [landlord] which he was not free to ignore."[39]

The District of Columbia Court of Appeals gave further effect to the Housing Regulations in Brown v. Southall Realty Co., 237 A.2d 834 (1968). There the landlord knew at the time the lease was signed that housing code violations existed which rendered the apartment "unsafe and unsanitary." Viewing the lease as a contract, the District of Columbia Court of Appeals held that the premises were let in violation of Sections 2304 and 2501 of the Regulations and that the lease, therefore, was void as an illegal contract. In the light of *Brown,* it is clear not only that the housing code creates privately enforceable duties as held in *Whetzel,* but that the basic validity of every housing contract depends upon substantial compliance with the housing code at the beginning of the lease term. The *Brown* court relied particularly upon Section 2501 of the Regulations which provides:

> Every premises accommodating one or more habitations shall be maintained and kept in repair so as to provide decent living accommodations for the occupants. This part of this Code contemplates more than mere basic repairs and maintenance to keep out the elements; its purpose is to include repairs and maintenance designed to make a premises or neighborhood healthy and safe.

By its terms, this section applies to maintenance and repair during the lease term. Under the *Brown* holding, serious failure to comply with this

---

39. *Kanelos* and *Whetzel* have effectively overruled, on the basis of the enactment of the housing code, Bowles v. Mahoney, 91 U.S. App. D.C. 155, 202 F.2d 320 (1952) (two-to-one decision, Judge Bazelon dissenting).

section before the lease term begins renders the contract void. We think it untenable to find that this section has no effect on the contract after it has been signed. To the contrary, by signing the lease the landlord has undertaken a continuing obligation to the tenant to maintain the premises in accordance with all applicable law.

This principle of implied warranty is well established. Courts often imply relevant law into contracts to provide a remedy for any damage caused by one party's illegal conduct. In a case closely analogous to the present ones, the Illinois Supreme Court held that a builder who constructed a house in violation of the Chicago building code had breached his contract with the buyer:

> . . . [T]he law existing at the time and place of the making of the contract is deemed a part of the contract, as though expressly referred to or incorporated in it. . . .
> The rationale for this rule is that the parties to the contract would have expressed that which the law implies "had they not supposed that it was unnecessary to speak of it because the law provided for it." . . . Consequently, the courts, in construing the existing law as part of the express contract, are not reading into the contract provisions different from those expressed and intended by the parties, as defendants contend, but are merely construing the contract in accordance with the intent of the parties.[40]

We follow the Illinois court in holding that the housing code must be read into housing contracts — a holding also required by the purposes and the structure of the code itself. The duties imposed by the Housing Regulations may not be waived or shifted by agreement if the Regulations specifically place the duty upon the lessor.[41] Criminal penalties are provided if these duties are ignored. This regulatory structure was established by the Commissioners because, in their judgment, the grave conditions in the housing

---

40. Schiro v. W. E. Gould & Co., *supra* Note [27], 18 Ill. 2d at 544, 165 N.E.2d at 290. As a general proposition, it is undoubtedly true that parties to a contract intend that applicable law will be complied with by both sides. We recognize, however, that reading statutory provisions into private contracts may have little factual support in the intentions of the particular parties now before us. But, for reasons of public policy, warranties are often implied into contracts by operation of law in order to meet generally prevailing standards of honesty and fair dealing. When the public policy has been enacted into law like the housing code, that policy will usually have deep roots in the expectations and intentions of most people. See Costigan, Implied-in-Fact Contracts and Mutual Assent, 33 Harv. L. Rev. 376, 383-385 (1920).

41. Any private agreement to shift the duties would be illegal and unenforceable. The precedents dealing with industrial safety statutes are directly in point:

> . . . [T]he only question remaining is whether the courts will enforce or recognize as against a servant an agreement express or implied on his part to waive the performance of a statutory duty of the master imposed for the protection of the servant, and in the interest of the public, and enforceable by criminal prosecution. We do not think they will. To do so would be to nullify the object of the statute. . . .

Narramore v. Cleveland, C., C. & St. L. Ry. Co., 6 Cir., 96 F. 298, 302 (1899). See W. Prosser, Torts §67 at 468-469 (3d ed. 1964) and cases cited therein.

market required serious action. Yet official enforcement of the housing code has been far from uniformly effective. Innumerable studies have documented the desperate condition of rental housing in the District of Columbia and in the nation. In view of these circumstances, we think the conclusion reached by the Supreme Court of Wisconsin as to the effect of a housing code on the old common law rule cannot be avoided:

> . . . [T]he legislature has made a policy judgment — that it is socially (and politically) desirable to impose these duties on a property owner — which has rendered the old common law rule obsolete. To follow the old rule of no implied warranty of habitability in leases would, in our opinion, be inconsistent with the current legislative policy concerning housing standards. . . .[42]

We therefore hold that the Housing Regulations imply a warranty of habitability, measured by the standards which they set out, into leases of all housing that they cover.

V

In the present cases, the landlord sued for possession for nonpayment of rent. Under contract principles,[43] however, the tenant's obligation to pay rent is dependent upon the landlord's performance of his obligations, including his warranty to maintain the premises in habitable condition. In order to determine whether any rent is owed to the landlord, the tenants must be given an opportunity to prove the housing code violations alleged as breach of the landlord's warranty.[44]

At trial, the finder of fact must make two findings: (1) whether the alleged violations[45] existed during the period for which past due rent is claimed, and (2) what portion, if any or all, of the tenant's obligation to pay rent was suspended by the landlord's breach. If no part of the tenant's rental obligation is found to have been suspended, then a judgment for possession may issue forthwith. On the other hand, if the jury determines that the entire

42. Pines v. Perssion, 14 Wis. 2d 590, 596, 111 N.W.2d 409, 412-413 (1961). Accord, Buckner v. Azulai, 251 Cal. App. 2d Supp. 1013, 59 Cal. Rptr. 806 (1967).

43. In extending all contract remedies for breach to the parties to a lease, we include an action for specific performance of the landlord's implied warranty of habitability.

44. To be relevant, of course, the violations must affect the tenant's apartment or common areas which the tenant uses. Moreover, the contract principle that no one may benefit from his own wrong will allow the landlord to defend by proving the damage was caused by the tenant's wrongful action. However, violations resulting from inadequate repairs or materials which disintegrate under normal use would not be assignable to the tenant. Also we agree with the District of Columbia Court of Appeals that the tenant's private rights do not depend on official inspection or official finding of violation by the city government. Diamond Housing Corp. v. Robinson, 257 A.2d 492, 494 (1969).

45. The jury should be instructed that one or two minor violations standing alone which do not affect habitability are de minimis and would not entitle the tenant to a reduction in rent.

rental obligation has been extinguished by the landlord's total breach, then the action for possession on the ground of nonpayment must fail.[46]

The jury may find that part of the tenant's rental obligation has been suspended but that part of the unpaid back rent is indeed owed to the landlord. In these circumstances, no judgment for possession should issue if the tenant agrees to pay the partial rent found to be due. If the tenant refuses to pay the partial amount, a judgment for possession may then be entered.

The judgment of the District of Columbia Court of Appeals is reversed and the cases are remanded for further proceedings consistent with this opinion.[47]

So ordered.

ROBB, J., concurs in the result and in Parts IV-B and V of the opinion.

Note: Promise by the Tenant to Keep Leased Property in Repair

If the parties to a lease agree in exchange for a reduction in rent that the tenant, not the landlord, is responsible for putting (and thereafter for keeping) the leased property in a sufficient state of repair to comply with housing code standards, is the old common-law rule reinstated? The following is a quotation from the *Javins* case: "The duties imposed by Housing Regulations may not be waived or shifted by agreement if the Regulations specifically place the duty upon the lessor." Compare the following comments of Justice Neely, in a footnote in a dissenting opinion in *Teller v. McCoy*, 253 S.E.2d 114 (W. Va. 1979):

> Perhaps some of the most grievous examples of poor housing in West Virginia are found when the tenants are also students; however, the student-

46. As soon as the landlord made the necessary repairs rent would again become due. Our holding, of course, affects only eviction for nonpayment of rent. The landlord is free to seek eviction at the termination of the lease or on any other legal ground.

47. Appellants in the present cases offered to pay rent into the registry of the court during the present action. We think this is an excellent protective procedure. If the tenant defends against an action for possession on the basis of breach of the landlord's warranty of habitability, the trial court may require the tenant to make future rent payments into the registry of the court as they become due; such a procedure would be appropriate only while the tenant remains in possession. The escrowed money will, however, represent rent for the period between the time the landlord files suit and the time the case comes to trial. In the normal course of litigation, the only factual question at trial would be the condition of the apartment during the time the landlord alleged rent was due and not paid.

As a general rule, the escrowed money should be apportioned between the landlord and the tenant after trial on the basis of the finding of rent actually due for the period at issue in the suit. To insure fair apportionment, however, we think either party should be permitted to amend its complaint or answer at any time before trial, to allege a change in the condition of the apartment. In this event, the finder of fact should make a separate finding as to the condition of the apartment at the time at which the amendment was filed. This new finding will have no effect upon the original action; it will only affect the distribution of the escrowed rent paid after the filing of the amendment.

tenant probably also presents the best example of possible intelligent bargaining leading to low rent and a waiver of the covenant of habitability. If a group of male students prefer to spend their money on the purchase of beer, the playing of pool, and the chasing of women instead of paying rent for luxurious accommodations, then they should be permitted to do so. Students are frequently lessees of slum dwellings at rather high prices partially because very few landlords of well-maintained property are interested in renting to students. While there are many responsible students, landlords predicate their rental practices on statistical averages, and, on the average, students are less mindful of other people's property than older persons. Furthermore, while the working family devote their premises to the nurture of their children and frequently dedicate it to the pursuit of peace and quiet as a relief from the pressures of the working world, the student is as likely to dedicate it to extensive social entertaining, and may be tempted to provide accommodations to as many of his friends as wish to use it as a transient abode. When there is a recognizable class of tenants who rejoice in "tearing the place apart" that pursuit must be accommodated in both the level of the rent and the quality of the dwelling. [253 S.E.2d at 133.]

Note: The Restatement's Position in Regard to Implied Warranty of Habitability

Sections 5.1 to 5.6 of the Restatement (Second) of Property (Landlord and Tenant) recognize the implied warranty of habitability. The Reporter's Notes to these sections illustrate the swing in favor of the *Javins* case that has occurred since that case was decided in 1970.

Note: Constructive Eviction Versus Implied Warranty of Habitability

Where by an affirmative act the landlord causes a change in the condition of the property such that it is no longer suitable for its contemplated use, the landlord usually has been held in default under the doctrine of constructive eviction. May a tenant in such a situation plead breach of implied warranty of habitability as well? What are the advantages of proceeding under one or the other theory?

In relation to the question just raised, the court in Darmetko v. Boston Housing Authority, 378 Mass. 758, 393 N.E.2d 395 (1979), observed as follows:

The BHA does not challenge the judge's conclusion that its failures to repair the leaky roof and the defective floors were breaches of its implied warranty of habitability or his determination that the leaky roof interfered with the plaintiff's quiet enjoyment of the leased premises. We see no reason, however, for the plaintiff to recover cumulatively for a breach of the implied warranty of habitability and for interference with her quiet enjoyment of the premises. In the absence of any statute authorizing recovery beyond her actual loss, she may not recover for the same wrong under each theory. [378 Mass. at 761, 393 N.E.2d at 398.]

Footnote 4 to the foregoing observation is as follows:

> Damages for breach of the covenant of quiet enjoyment where the tenant remains in possession of the premises are measured by the difference between the value of what the lessee should have received and the value of what he did receive. Charles E. Burt, Inc. v. Seven Grand Corp., 340 Mass. 124, 130, 163 N.E.2d 4 (1959). Damages for breach of the implied warranty of habitability are measured by "the difference between the value of the dwelling as warranted (the rent agreed on may be evidence of this value) and the value of the dwelling as it exists in its defective condition." Boston Hous. Auth. v. Hemingway, 363 Mass. 184, 203, 293 N.E.2d 831, 845 (1973) (footnote omitted). These remedies are "quite similar."

Section 14 of Mass. Gen. Laws ch. 186 expands the measure of damages to include all "actual and consequential damages" where, as here, there has been a breach of the covenant of quiet enjoyment.

Note: *Implied Warranty of Habitability in Leases of Dwelling Units Constructed and Operated as Public Housing Projects*

Alexander v. United States Department of Housing and Urban Development, 555 F.2d 166 (7th Cir. 1977), observed as follows:

> We decline plaintiffs' invitation to follow these state court decisions implying a warranty of habitability in urban residential leases in the private sector. We decline to do so because we are not persuaded that such warranties should be implied in leases of dwelling units constructed and operated as public housing projects. In contrast to housing projects in the private sector, the construction and operation of public housing are projects established to effectuate a stated national policy "to remedy the unsafe and insanitary housing conditions and the acute shortage of decent, safe, and sanitary dwellings for families of low income." 42 U.S.C. §1401. As such, the implication of a warranty of habitability in leases pertaining to public housing units is a warranty that the stated objectives of national policy have been and are being met. We feel that the establishment of any such warranty that national policy goals have been attained or that those goals are being maintained is best left to that branch of government which established the objectives. [555 F.2d at 171.]

Note: Implied Warranty of Fitness in Commercial Leases

The Restatement (Second) of Property (Landlord and Tenant) does not take a position on whether there is an implied warranty of fitness in a commercial lease, given the fact that the present state of statutory and judicial development does not as yet warrant taking a position one way or the other. See Restatement (Second) of Property (Landlord and Tenant) §5.1. Compare Reste Realty Corp. v. Cooper, 53 N.J. 444, 251 A.2d 268 (1969), and Earl Millikin, Inc. v. Allen, 21 Wis. 2d 497, 124 N.W.2d 651 (1963), with Cameron v. Calhoun Smith Distributing Co., 442 S.W.2d 815 (Tex. Civ. App. 1969). The doctrines of commercial frustration and impossibility of performance, discussed in the previous section, are related.

Note: The Restatement's Position on Tort Liability for Breach of Implied Warranty of Habitability

§17.6 Landlord Under Legal Duty to Repair Dangerous Condition

A landlord is subject to liability for physical harm caused to the tenant and others upon the leased property with the consent of the tenant or his subtenant by a dangerous condition existing before or arising after the tenant has taken possession, if he has failed to exercise reasonable care to repair the condition and the existence of the condition is in violation of:

(1) an implied warranty of habitability; or
(2) a duty created by statute or administrative regulation.

Note: Obligation to Keep Leased Property Secure From Intruders

Does the landlord's duty to provide safe and healthy premises for tenants extend to making the common areas of a multi-unit apartment building secure against intruders? Kline v. 1500 Massachusetts Ave. Apartment Corp., 439 F.2d 477 (D.C. Cir. 1970), considered this issue in the context of a case where the plaintiff was criminally assaulted and robbed at approximately 10:15 P.M. by an intruder in the common hallway of an apartment house in which the plaintiff lived. The apartment house contained 585 individual apartment units. At the time the plaintiff moved into her apartment, the building had a 24-hour security service, but this service was not kept up. The assault on the plaintiff was not the first one in the building. The landlord had had notice of the crimes that had been committed and had been urged to take steps to secure the building. After holding that on the facts of the case the landlord was liable to the plaintiff, the court observed:

Having said this, it would be well to state what is *not* said by this decision. We do not hold that the landlord is by any means an insurer of the safety of his tenants. His duty is to take those measures of protection which are within his power and capacity to take, and which can reasonably be expected to mitigate the risk of intruders assaulting and robbing tenants. The landlord is not expected to provide protection commonly owed by a municipal police department; but as illustrated in this case, he is obligated to protect those parts of his premises which are not usually subject to periodic patrol and inspection by the municipal police. We do not say that every multiple unit apartment house in the District of Columbia should have those same measures of protection which 1500 Massachusetts Avenue enjoyed in 1959, nor do we say that 1500 Massachusetts Avenue should have precisely those same measures in effect at the present time. Alternative and more up-to-date methods may be equally or even more effective. [439 F.2d at 487-488.]

Trentacost v. Brussel, 82 N.J. 214, 412 A.2d 436 (1980), concluded that the landlord's implied warranty of habitability obliges him to furnish reasonable safeguards to protect tenants from foreseeable criminal activity on the premises. The court said:

Among the "facilities vital to the use of the premises" are the provisions for the tenant's security. Unfortunately, crime against person and property is an inescapable fact of modern life. Its presence threatens the suburban enclave as well as the inner city. Tenants universally expect some effective means of excluding intruders from multiple dwellings; without a minimum of security, their well-being is as precarious as if they had no heat or sanitation. Recognizing that a safer and more secure apartment is truly more livable, landlords frequently offer superior protective measures as an inducement for entering into premium lease agreements. Under modern living conditions, an apartment is clearly not habitable unless it provides a reasonable measure of security from the risk of criminal intrusion. [82 N.J. at 227, 412 A.2d at 443.]

D. Retaliatory Conduct

The tenant who attempts to better housing conditions either by resort to statutory remedies or by affirmative action in the courts will frequently be subjected to retaliatory action by the landlord—either by way of a rent increase or eviction. Present case law and statutes entitle the landlord to terminate a tenancy at will or at sufferance or from month to month, limited only by a thirty-day notice requirement. The tenant is usually faced with the rule that a landlord has the right to evict the tenant on termination of the tenancy for any or no reason. No inquiry into the motives of the landlord will be made, and it sometimes has been argued that any attempt to restrict the landlord's right in this respect would be unconstitutional as a deprivation of his property without due process of law. Consider the plight of Yvonne C. Edwards in the cases which follow.

HABIB v. EDWARDS
Civ. Div. No. LT75895 (D.C. Ct. Gen. Sess. 1965)

GREENE, J.[48] . . .

[A default judgment for the landlord was entered initially in the Landlord and Tenant Branch of the District of Columbia Court of General Sessions. The tenant now moves to set aside the default judgment because of excusable neglect of counsel. Part I of the opinion held that a showing of excusable neglect had been made out, and "thus, the issue is whether the defendant has set up a 'defense sufficient, if proved, to bar the claim.'"]

II

. . . The principal defense asserted is that on constitutional grounds this Court is precluded from awarding possession to the plaintiff under the facts here presented. Essentially the claim is that the defendant is being evicted and possession is being sought solely because she has given information to the District of Columbia authorities concerning violations of the statutes and regulations governing the sanitary conditions on the premises. . . .

The testimony shows that defendant informed these authorities of violations of the housing statutes and regulations with respect to the premises; that as a result of the inspections certain violations of the law were discovered; and that plaintiff has been given time within which to correct the violations or face prosecution. . . .

III

At the threshold defendant is faced with the familiar rule that in suing for possession under D.C. Code, 1961, §45-910, the landlord need not assign any reason whatever for his notice to quit and that evidence concerning his reasons for serving the notice is inadmissible. Yet, like all other statutes, section 910 is, of course, subject to and limited by the Constitution.

In Rudder v. United States, 96 U.S. App. D.C. 329, 226 F.2d 51 (1955), possession under section 910 was denied on constitutional grounds, notwithstanding the adequacy of the formal eviction papers. To be sure, in *Rudder* the plaintiff was the government, not a private party; but the principle of constitutional supremacy in possession suits recognized by that decision obviously applies to everyone. The difficulty a tenant faces in resisting eviction by a private landlord is not that he is unable to demonstrate that the Constitution must be complied with — that is obvious; his

---

48. Judge Greene's memorandum opinion is reprinted in full in Housing for the Poor: Rights and Remedies 43 (Project on Social Welfare Law Supplement No. 1, 1967). — EDS.

problem is that he must find a constitutional provision which would be violated by the grant of possession to the landlord. Since under ordinary circumstances constitutional rights are protected only against invasion by governmental authority, this is usually an impossible task.

Defendant attempts to overcome this hurdle by claiming that his rights to free speech and to petition for a redress of grievances were denied by the combined action of the landlord (in serving the notice to quit) and the government (in permitting the landlord to terminate the tenancy by such a notice and in judicially enforcing the notice).

In support of this position defendant relies primarily upon an unreported decision of the United States District Court for the Southern District of New York. Tarver v. G. & C. Construction Corp. (S.D.N.Y., November 9, 1964, MacMahon, J.). In that case, the court issued a preliminary injunction restraining a landlord from evicting his tenant upon allegations and proof that the landlord had greatly increased the rent and had served notice to terminate the tenancy after the tenant had complained to the Health Department of Westchester County concerning insanitary and unsafe conditions on the premises. This decision was based upon a holding that the activities of the landlord constituted a violation of the constitutional right of the tenant to petition for a redress of grievances.

This Court is unable to agree with the position of the defendant on this issue or with the reasoning of the court in the *Tarver* case.

The First Amendment to the Constitution of the United States provides that "*Congress* shall make no law . . . abridging the freedom of speech . . . or the right of the people . . . to petition the Government for a redress of grievances" (emphasis added). While this prohibition has been read by the courts to extend to each State by virtue of the Fourteenth Amendment, neither the First nor the Fourteenth Amendment is applicable to purely private acts of private parties. In the shorthand phrases that have been used, these constitutional prohibitions apply only to "state action" and to "action under color of law."

To be sure, as the defendant correctly points out, state action and action under color of law are not limited to that action which is taken at the express command of the State or Federal governments; it may be action of which those governments are ignorant or with which they disagree. Even action by private persons may be reached provided there is a nexus with governmental power.

Defendant argues that the required nexus is provided here by the enactment by the Congress of the statute permitting her eviction and by the judicial enforcement of the notice to quit. Her theory is that the otherwise private action of the landlord is transformed into governmental action, subject to constitutional restraints, when that private action is enforced and given effect by the court, an arm of government.

This argument proves too much. If for constitutional purposes every private right were transformed into governmental action by the mere fact of court enforcement of that right, the distinction between private and governmental action would be obliterated. A private homeowner, for example, when faced with a stranger on his premises who is there engaged in what would otherwise be regarded as protected free speech, would be unable to call upon the police or the courts for assistance in having the stranger removed. Under defendant's theory, that call for governmental assistance would transform the private rejection of the speaker into a governmental act subject to all of the restraints of the Constitution. It is obvious that such an interpretation of the concepts of "state action" and "color of law" would, for all practical purposes, destroy the concept of private action, and would make the constitutional prohibitions — at least those of the First and the Fourteenth Amendments — applicable to all private as well as to all governmental action. Such a result is neither called for by applicable court decisions nor is it desirable as a matter of public policy.

IV

This does not, however, resolve the case.

D.C. Code, 1961, §5-616 authorizes the Commissioners of the District of Columbia to examine into the sanitary conditions of all buildings in the District and to cause them to be put into sanitary condition or to be demolished. Other provisions in Title 5 of the Code implement the general power to condemn and to require repairs, and D.C. Code, 1961, §5-631 provides criminal penalties for violations of these various statutes. In addition, the Commissioners have issued extensive regulations dealing with housing and sanitary conditions in housing for the purpose of preserving and promoting the public health, safety, welfare and morals.

If the testimony of the defendant is true, she is being evicted because she gave information to her government concerning a violation of these laws and regulations. As will be developed *infra,* defendant has a constitutional right to provide such information to the government. Moreover, that right — unlike the right encompassed within the First and Fourteenth Amendments — *is protected not only against interference by the government but also against interference by private persons.*

In In re Quarles, 158 U.S. 532 (1895), the defendants were convicted of conspiring to injure, oppress, threaten and intimidate a citizen of the United States in his right and privilege to give information to the federal government concerning violations of the internal revenue laws. In its opinion denying a writ of habeas corpus to the defendant, the Supreme Court stated (158 U.S. at 536-538):

> The right of a citizen informing of a violation of law, like the right of a prisoner in custody upon a charge of such violation, to be protected against lawless violence, does not depend upon any of the amendments to the

constitution, but arises out of the creation and establishment by the constitution itself of a national government, paramount and supreme within its sphere of action. . . .

The right of the private citizen who assists in putting in motion the course of justice, and the right of the officers concerned in the administration of justice, stand upon the same ground, just as do the rights of citizens voting and of officers elected, of which Mr. Justice Miller, speaking for this court, in Ex parte Yarbrough, above cited, said: "The power in either case arises out of the circumstances that the function in which the party is engaged, or the right which he is about to exercise, is dependent on the laws of the United States. In both cases it is the duty of that government to see that he may exercise this right freely, and to protect him from violence while so doing, or on account of so doing. This duty does not arise solely from the interest of the party concerned, but from the necessity of the government itself, that its service shall be free from the adverse influence of force and fraud practiced on its agents, and that the votes by which its members of congress and its president are elected shall be the free votes of the electors, and the officers thus chosen the free and uncorrupted choice of those who have the right to take part in that choice." 110 U.S. 662, 4 Sup. Ct. 152. . . .

The crucial distinction between the rights discussed in the preceding part of this opinion and the constitutional right, recognized in *Quarles,* to be free to provide information to the government concerning law violations, is that the former are protected only against invasion by persons acting under color of law, while the latter is guaranteed against violation by anyone, private or public. The reason for this difference in treatment is that the First Amendment, the Fourteenth Amendment, and similar provisions, as their language and history indicate, were aimed exclusively at government. They were designed to protect the citizen from government and from those acting on behalf of government. But other constitutional rights — such as that under discussion here — have a different history and a different purpose, and to achieve that purpose it was necessary to protect them against all injury, from whatever source. . . .

In short, the defendant in this case has a constitutional right to inform the proper governmental authorities of violations of the law, as well as the correlative right not to be injured or punished by anyone for having availed herself of her basic right to provide such information. . . . The ultimate question in this case, then, is whether D.C. Code 1961, 45-910 compels this Court to assist the plaintiff in consummating the punishment of the defendant for having exercised her constitutional right to inform the government of a violation of law.

In the opinion of this Court, that question must be answered in the negative. Congress can hardly be presumed to have intended to impose a duty upon the Court to be a party to the deprivation of the constitutional rights of the litigant before it. Apart from the result that any construction of section 910 leading to such a result would raise serious constitutional questions and must therefore be avoided for that reason alone, there is no evidence to indicate that Congress did, in fact, intend such a construction of the statute.

Additionally, as the *Quarles* case teaches, the interest at stake here is not only that of the citizen in his freedom to provide information to the authorities but also that of the government in the free and unimpeded access to such information. Intimidation of the sources of information injures the interest of the government in the effective enforcement of the laws. Congress cannot be presumed to have intended by the enactment of section 910 (permitting the court to order ejectment), to mandate an injury both to the interest of the government in the proper enforcement of its laws[49] and to the interest of the defendant in her constitutional right to provide information.

The conclusion that the Court need not award judgment to the plaintiff under these circumstances is strengthened by the fact that the information this defendant has provided concerns housing. Whatever may be the proper rule with respect to other species of violations by the landlord, where the reprisals occur in connection with complaints of housing violations, there is special reason for not granting relief in the landlord's possessory action. The various housing codes were enacted in large measure as a means of protecting tenants against unsafe, unsanitary, and other inhuman conditions. To permit landlords to evict tenants who avail themselves of the remedies provided in these codes frustrates the public policy expressed in the statutes and seriously impairs their effective enforcement.

This court has recognized that a close relationship exists between actions for the possession of real estate, on the one hand, and violations of the housing laws and regulations, on the other, by providing that both types of actions shall be heard in the Landlord and Tenant Branch of the Court. This combination of the two functions was designed to afford the judge sitting in that Branch the opportunity to consider the problems presented by the two types of actions for what they are: twin, interrelated problems, requiring joint consideration. . . .

V

This does not mean that the landlord is bound to retain this particular tenant in perpetuity. In the *Tarver* case, *supra,* the judgment sought was an order enjoining the landlord from evicting the tenant for any cause other than the nonpayment of the rent agreed upon between the parties, and the

---

49. An eviction of defendant under the circumstances of this case would not only punish her for making the complaint; it would also stand as a warning to others not to be so bold in the future. As such, it would be bound to impair the ability of the government efficiently to enforce the laws protecting the safe and sanitary condition of housing.

court apparently enjoined the landlord from dispossessing the tenant for any cause whatever. Such an order is needlessly broad. A landlord may evict for any reason or for no reason; what he is precluded from doing, and the only thing he is precluded from doing, is to evict for the purpose of depriving the tenant of the right to inform the government of violations of the law. The landlord's purpose must, of course, be determined in each individual case by the trier of facts; and the burden will be upon the tenant in each instance to demonstrate that the landlord's purpose was unlawful.

That kind of distinction — between action which is permitted when done for a lawful purpose but prohibited when done for an unlawful or impermissible purpose — is not at all unusual. The labor laws, for example, which permit the firing of employees for legitimate reasons, preclude their discharge (and even a refusal to hire) on account of labor union activity. Similarly, the civil rights statutes prohibit the imposition of economic sanctions for the purpose of intimidation in connection with the exercise of the right to vote in federal elections, but they do not interfere with legitimate economic pursuits. In all such matters, the courts and the administrative agencies concerned have found little difficulty in distinguishing between the permissible and the impermissible. There is no reason why similar factual judgments cannot be made by courts and juries in the context of economic retaliation for providing information to the government.

The motion to set aside the default is granted, and the case is restored to the trial calendar of the Landlord and Tenant Branch.[50]

EDWARDS v. HABIB
227 A.2d 388 (D.C. 1967)

Hood, C.J.:

This appeal is by a tenant from a judgment in favor of her landlord for possession of a dwelling house which she had rented under a lease by the month (from month to month) in March of 1965. After taking possession the tenant made a number of complaints to the Housing Division of the Department of Licenses and Inspections of the District of Columbia regarding the condition of the premises. The Housing Division had the premises inspected, discovered certain violations of the Housing Code, and directed the landlord to make numerous repairs. In August 1965 the landlord gave the tenant a thirty days' notice to quit. At trial before a jury the tenant's main defense was that the landlord's purpose in giving the notice to quit and suing for possession was to retaliate for the tenant's complaints to the housing authority, and that a retaliatory eviction would violate the tenant's

---

50. At trial, however, evidence of retaliatory intent was excluded by a different judge (who did not feel bound by Judge Greene's opinion) on the theory that at common law a landlord has the right to evict a month-to-month tenant for any or no reason. Judgment for the landlord was then appealed to the District of Columbia Court of Appeals. — Eds.

Constitutional rights to freedom of speech, freedom to inform the government of violations of the law and freedom to petition the government for redress of grievances. The trial court ruled that evidence of the landlord's purpose in bringing the action was inadmissible and directed a verdict for the landlord. That ruling is the major issue on this appeal.

Our Code provides that a tenancy from month to month may be terminated by either the landlord or tenant by a thirty days' notice expiring on the day of the month from which the tenancy commenced to run. The Code does not require that either the landlord or tenant give any reason for terminating the tenancy. Accordingly, this court has held that a notice to quit by a landlord need assign no reason and that evidence as to the reason for seeking possession is inadmissible. This is in accord with decisions of other courts. In De Wolfe v. McAllister, 229 Mass. 410, 412, 118 N.E. 885, 887 (1918), where a landlord's purpose in terminating a lease was questioned, it was said that it was "unimportant whether she did it because of ill will toward him or because he had failed to pay the rent due; her motives were immaterial." In Wormood v. Alton Bay Camp Meeting Ass'n, 87 N.H. 136, 175 A. 233 (1934), it was said that the motives of a landlord in seeking to terminate a tenancy were immaterial. And in Gabriel v. Borowy, 324 Mass. 231, 234, 85 N.E.2d 435, 438 (1949), it was said: "A landlord could at common law terminate a tenancy at will for any purpose he might desire and the tenant could not question his motives or attack his reasons."

There are three distinct lines of cases wherein a landlord's right to terminate a tenancy has been limited. The first of those is where a governmental body is landlord. In Rudder v. United States, 96 U.S. App. D.C. 329, 331, 226 F.2d 51, 53 (1955), it was said that where the government is landlord it "must not act arbitrarily, for, *unlike private landlords,* it is subject to the requirements of due process of law. Arbitrary action is not due process." (Emphasis supplied.) . . .

The second line of cases deals with emergency rent control legislation restricting the contractual rights of landlords. Such legislation is justified by the exercise of the police power during emergency periods. The impact of such legislation was well stated in Calvin v. Martin, 64 Ohio Law Abst. 265, 268, 111 N.E.2d 786, 788 (Ohio App. 1952), where it was said:

> At common law, a tenant has no right of occupancy of demised premises except in accordance with the terms of his lease at the expiration of which he may be evicted by due process with or without cause and a landlord can terminate a tenancy at will, for any purpose and his motives are not subject to attack. However, the Housing and Rent Act has modified the common-law rights of the landlord to the extent of prohibiting him from bringing and maintaining eviction proceedings except in accordance with the provisions of the Act.

The third line of cases deals with actions involving the eviction of tenants in apparent retaliation for their registering or voting. See United States v.

Beaty, 288 F.2d 653 (6th Cir. 1961), and the somewhat related case of United States v. Bruce, 353 F.2d 474 (5th Cir. 1965). Also somewhat analogous to these cases are cases under the National Labor Relations Act holding that it is an unfair labor practice to deny employment to one who has filed charges against the employer. See John Hancock Mut. L. Ins. Co. v. National Labor Rel. Bd., 89 U.S. App. D.C. 261, 191 F.2d 483 (1951); National Labor Rel. Bd. v. Lamar Creamery Co., 246, F.2d 8 (5th Cir. 1957). Each of these cases concerns specific Congressional legislation. The voting statutes prohibit coercion through physical or economic intimidation in connection with the right to vote, and the labor statutes bar unfair practices connected with an employee's union activity. As with emergency rent control acts, specific legislation has been enacted to protect voting rights and labor employee rights. We feel this distinguishes those cases from the one before us.

One case, not falling within any of the above groupings, is that of Abstract Investment Co. v. Hutchinson, 204 Cal. App. 2d 242, 22 Cal. Rptr. 309 (1962), where a tenant was permitted to show as a defense that his eviction was sought solely because of his race. No claim of racial discrimination is made here.

The tenant also argues that the landlord's resort to the court to obtain possession of his property under the statute constitutes action "under color of law," and that her rights to free speech and to petition for redress of grievances would be violated if through court action she were evicted from the premises. We agree with the following statement of the motions judge who set aside the default judgment in this case: "If for constitutional purposes every private right were transformed into governmental action by the mere fact of court enforcement of that right, the distinction between private and governmental action would be obliterated." We reject the contention that the "color of law" cases have application here.

The tenant further contends that she has a Constitutional right to inform the government of law violations and to protection from reprisals by the violator in the form of eviction. She relies strongly on In re Quarles, 158 U.S. 532, 15 S. Ct. 959, 39 L. Ed. 1080 (1895), to support this proposition. There it was held that a citizen has a right to inform the authorities of a violation of internal revenue law, and that those who conspire to injure, oppress, threaten or intimidate such citizen for the exercise of such right, may be punished under a statute forbidding such conspiracy. Here, again, is a case where Congress enacted special legislation to secure certain rights.

It is evident that Congress may enact legislation to protect rights and immunities of citizens, and prescribe the penalties, criminal or otherwise, for violation of such rights and immunities. In the present situation, however, Congress gave the landlord the right to terminate the tenancy and placed no restriction on that right. We are not persuaded that the courts should attempt to limit that right and fashion a new form of tenancy. If the landlord is denied recovery in this action, how long may the tenant remain in possession? As long as she is able to convince a jury that the landlord is still seeking a retaliatory eviction? In any subsequent action would the burden be upon the landlord to show a valid reason for seeking possession? Would any tenant by complaining to the housing authority be entitled to have a jury infer that any eviction action was retaliatory in nature? Would such a defense be available when a landlord seeks possession at the expiration of a fixed term? Would the ruling sought be restricted to dwelling property or would it include commercial property?

All of these considerations lead us to the conclusion that if the rights of the landlord are to be restricted and the rights of the tenants are to be enlarged, it should be by legislation spelling out the restrictions and rights, with specific provisions as to the manner of enforcement. If, as some believe, the law relating to landlords and tenants is outdated, it should be brought up-to-date by legislation and not by court edict.

Affirmed.

EDWARDS v. HABIB

397 F.2d 687 (D.C. Cir. 1968), *cert. denied,* 393 U.S. 1016, 89 S. Ct. 618 (1969)

[In Part I of the opinion, Judge J. Skelly Wright examines the constitutional limits of "state action" under Shelley v. Kraemer[51] and New York Times Co. v. Sullivan, 376 U.S. 254, 84 S. Ct. 710 (1964). In Part II he discusses the constitutional implications of In re Quarles, 158 U.S. 532, 15 S. Ct. 959 (1895).]

III

But we need not decide whether judicial recognition of this constitutional defense is constitutionally compelled. We need not, in other words, decide whether 45 D.C. Code §910 could validly compel the court to assist the plaintiff in penalizing the defendant for exercising her constitutional right to inform the government of violations of the law; for we are confident that Congress did not intend it to entail such a result.

45 D.C. Code §910, in pertinent part, provides:

> Whenever . . . any tenancy shall be terminated by notice as aforesaid [45 D.C. Code §902, see Note 1 *supra*], and the tenant shall fail or refuse to surrender possession of the leased premises, . . . the landlord may bring an action to recover possession before the District of Columbia Court of General Sessions, as provided in sections 11-701 to 11-749.

And 16 D.C. Code §1501, in pertinent part, provides:

51. Shelley v. Kraemer is dealt with in Chapter 32, Section 1.

When a person detains possession of real property . . . after his right to possession has ceased, the District of Columbia Court of General Sessions . . . may issue a summons to the party complained of to appear and show cause why judgment should not be given against him for restitution of possession.

These provisions are simply procedural. They neither say nor imply anything about whether evidence of retaliation or other improper motive should be unavailable as a defense to a possessory action brought under them. It is true that in making his affirmative case for possession the landlord need only show that his tenant has been given the 30-day statutory notice, and he need not assign any reason for evicting a tenant who does not occupy the premises under a lease. But while the landlord may evict for any legal reason or for no reason at all, he is not, we hold, free to evict in retaliation for his tenant's report of housing code violations to the authorities. As a matter of statutory construction and for reasons of public policy, such an eviction cannot be permitted.

The housing and sanitary codes, especially in light of Congress' explicit direction for their enactment, indicate a strong and pervasive congressional concern to secure for the city's slum dwellers decent, or at least safe and sanitary, places to live. Effective implementation and enforcement of the codes obviously depend in part on private initiative in the reporting of violations. Though there is no official procedure for the filing of such complaints, the bureaucratic structure of the Department of Licenses and Inspections establishes such a procedure, and for fiscal year 1966 nearly a third of the cases handled by the Department arose from private complaints. To permit retaliatory evictions, then, would clearly frustrate the effectiveness of the housing code as a means of upgrading the quality of housing in Washington.

As judges, "we cannot shut our eyes to matters of public notoriety and general cognizance. When we take our seats on the bench we are not struck with blindness, and forbidden to know as judges what we see as men." Ho Ah Kow v. Numan, C.C.D. Cal., 12 Fed. Cas. 252, 255, (No. 6546) (1879). In trying to effect the will of Congress and as a court of equity we have the responsibility to consider the social context in which our decisions will have operational effect. In light of the appalling condition and shortage of housing in Washington,[52] the expense of moving, the inequality of bargain-

52. See Report of the National Capital Planning Commission, Problems of Housing People in Washington, D.C. . . .

Poor families are responding to Washington's housing shortage by doubling and overcrowding; by living in structurally substandard or other hazardous housing; by sharing or doing without hot water, heat, light, or kitchen or bathroom facilities; by farming out their children wherever they can; by denying their children exist to landlords and public officials; by paying rents which are high compared to incomes so they must sacrifice other living necessities; and by living without dignity or privacy. Each one of these features has been measured separately or has been observed in Washington's poverty areas. . . .

ing power between tenant and landlord,[53] and the social and economic importance of assuring at least minimum standards in housing conditions,[54] we do not hesitate to declare that retaliatory eviction cannot be tolerated. There can be no doubt that the slum dweller, even though his home be marred by housing code violations, will pause long before he complains of them if he fears eviction as a consequence. Hence an eviction under the circumstances of this case would not only punish appellant for making a complaint which she had a constitutional right to make, a result which we would not impute to the will of Congress simply on the basis of an essentially procedural enactment, but also would stand as a warning to others that they dare not be so bold, a result which, from the authorization of the housing code, we think Congress affirmatively sought to avoid.

The notion that the effectiveness of remedial legislation will be inhibited if those reporting violations of it can legally be intimidated is so fundamental that a presumption against the legality of such intimidation can be inferred as inherent in the legislation even if it is not expressed in the statute itself. Such an inference was recently drawn by the Supreme Court from the federal labor statutes to strike down under the supremacy clause a Florida statute denying unemployment insurance to workers discharged in retaliation for filing complaints of federally defined unfair labor practices. While we are not confronted with a possible conflict between federal policy and state law, we do have the task of reconciling and harmonizing two federal statutes so as to best effectuate the purposes of each.[55] The proper balance

---

53. See Kay v. Cain, 81 U.S. App. D.C. 24, 25, 154 F.2d 305, 306 (1946).

54. "Miserable and disreputable housing conditions may do more than spread disease and crime and immorality. They may also suffocate the spirit by reducing the people who live there to the status of cattle. They may indeed make living an almost insufferable burden. They may also be an ugly sore, a blight on the community which robs it of charm, which makes it a place from which men turn. The misery of housing may despoil a community as an open sewer may ruin a river." Berman v. Parker, 348 U.S. 26, 32-33 (1954). See also Frank v. Maryland, 359 U.S. 360, 371 (1959):

> The need to maintain basic, minimal standards of housing, to prevent the spread of disease and of that pervasive breakdown in the fiber of a people which is produced by slums and the absence of the barest essentials of civilized living, has mounted to a major concern of American government.

According to the Report of the Planning Commission . . . "more than 100,000 children are growing up in Washington now under one or more housing conditions which create psychological, social, and medical impairments, and make satisfactory home life difficult or a practical impossibility." . . .

55. See, e.g., United States v. Borden Co., 308 U.S. 188, 198 (1939); Rawls v. United States, 8 Cir., 331 F.2d 21, 28 (1964). When Congress enacted 45 D.C. Code §§902 and 910, it did not have in mind their possible use in effectuating retaliatory evictions. Indeed, when they were enacted there was no housing code at all. And in all probability Congress did not attend to the problem of retaliatory evictions when it directed the enactment of the housing code. Our task is to determine what Congress would have done, in light of the purpose and language of the statute, had it confronted the question now before the court. And where there is a possible conflict, the more recent enactment, the housing code, should be given full effect while leaving an area of effective operation for the earlier statute. International Union of Electrical, Radio etc. Workers v. N.L.R.B., 110 U.S. App. D.C. 91, 95, 289 F.2d 757, 761 (1960). This task, we think, our resolution of the issue accomplishes.

can only be struck by interpreting 45 D.C. Code §902 and 910 as inapplicable where the court's aid is invoked to effect an eviction in retaliation for reporting housing code violations.[56]

This is not, of course, to say that even if the tenant can prove a retaliatory purpose she is entitled to remain in possession in perpetuity. If this illegal purpose is dissipated, the landlord can, in the absence of legislation[57] or a binding contract, evict his tenants or raise their rents for economic or other legitimate reasons, or even for no reason at all.[58] The question of permissible or impermissible purpose is one of fact for the court or jury, and while such a determination is not easy, it is not significantly different from problems with which the courts must deal in a host of other contexts, such as when they must decide whether the employer who discharges a worker has committed an unfair labor practice because he has done so on account of the employee's union activities. As Judge Greene said, "There is no reason why similar factual judgments cannot be made by courts and juries in the context of economic retaliation [against tenants by landlords] for providing information to the government."

Reversed and remanded.

McGowan, J., concurring except as to Parts I and II: The considerations bearing upon statutory construction, so impressively marshalled by Judge Wright in Part III of his opinion, have made it unnecessary for me to pursue in any degree the constitutional speculations contained in Parts I and II; and it is for this reason that I do not join in them. The issue of statutory construction presented in this case has never seemed to me to be a difficult one, nor to require for its resolution the spur of avoidance of constitutional questions. A Congress which authorizes housing code promulgation and enforcement clearly cannot be taken to have excluded retaliatory eviction of the kind here alleged as a defense under a routine statutory eviction mechanism also provided by Congress.

Danaher, J., dissenting: Basically at issue between my colleagues and me is a question as to the extent to which the power of the court may here be exercised where by their edict the landlord's right to his property is being

56. In a recent important decision the DCCA has held that as a matter of public policy a landlord who has rented housing space knowing that it contained housing code violations could not collect back rent from his ex-tenant. Brown v. Southall Realty Co., DCCA, No. 4199, February 7, 1968.

57. There have been several bills introduced in Congress which deal expressly with the problem of retaliatory evictions. Hearings were held in the Senate . . . on three bills but none was reported out of committee. H.R. 257, 90th Cong., 1st Sess. (1967), is now before the House Committee on the District of Columbia. Its companion bill, S. 1910, 90th Cong., 1st Sess. (1967), has been introduced in the Senate. The bill would forbid an eviction, except for specified reasons, during the nine months following the filing of a complaint. The proposed legislation is discussed in Note, Retaliatory Evictions and the Reporting of Housing Code Violations in the District of Columbia, 36 G.W.L. Rev. 190, 196-203 (1967). . . .

58. Of course, because of his prior taint the landlord may not be able to disprove an illicit motive unless he can show a legitimate affirmative reason for eviction.

denied. They concede as they must "that in making his affirmative case for possession the landlord need only show that his tenant has been given the 30-day statutory notice, and he need not assign any reason for evicting a tenant who does not occupy the premises under a lease."

That fundamental rule of our law of property must give way, it now develops. My colleagues so rule despite the absence of a statutory prescription of discernible standards as to what may constitute "violations," or of provision for compensating[59] the landlord for the deprivation of his property. They say that the court will not "frustrate the effectiveness of the housing code as a means of upgrading the quality of housing in Washington." Since they recognize that there is an "appalling condition and shortage of housing in Washington," [60] they say the court must take account of the "social and economic importance of assuring at least minimum standards in housing conditions." So to meet such needs, the burden would now be met, not pursuant to a congressionally prescribed policy, with adequate provision for construction or acquisition costs, or for compensation to property owners, but by private landlords who will be saddled with what should have been a public charge.

Note how my colleagues achieve that result as they rule:

> But while the landlord may evict for any legal reason or for no reason at all, he is not, we hold, free to evict in retaliation for his tenant's report of housing code violations to the authorities. As a matter of statutory construction and for reasons of public policy, such an eviction cannot be permitted.

Just as do my colleagues, I deplore the effort of any landlord for a base reason to secure possession of his own property, but if his right so to recover in accordance with our law is to be denied, Congress should provide the basis. Appropriate standards as a pre-condition thus could be spelled out in legislation and just compensation thereupon be awarded if found to be due.[61]

---

59. Berman v. Parker, 348 U.S. 26 (1954), held for the first time that the government here might condemn one's property and turn it over to another private "person"—but not without due process, not without compensation.

60. It is common knowledge that following Berman v. Parker . . . the housing structures in one entire quadrant of the City of Washington were razed, driving thousands of tenants to seek whatever "appalling" accommodations they could find. In place of the destroyed housing, beautiful apartment buildings have been built, to be sure, with "co-ops" in some costing up to $100,000 per apartment, with rentals in others priced far beyond the capacity to pay of thousands of those who had been displaced. And even the affluent tenants having chosen to do so, must be presumed, at least until now, to have taken the premises in the condition in which they found them, cockroaches and all.

The Washington Post on April 1, 1968 editorialized upon the need for a renewal project after "the wholesale bulldozing of slums and massive uprooting of families with them which characterized the Southwest development."

61. As Chief Judge Hood observed, writing for a unanimous District of Columbia Court of Appeals: "If, as some believe, the law relating to landlords and tenants is outdated, it should be brought up-to-date by legislation and not by court edict." Edwards v. Habib, 227 A.2d 388, 392 (1967). . . . he quoted from Collins v. Hardyman, 341 U.S. 651, 663 (1951), "It is not for this Court to compete with Congress or attempt to replace it as the Nation's law-making body."

I am not alone in my position, I dare say, as I read the Congressional Record for March 13, 1968, page H 1883. In President Johnson's message to the Congress he said:

> One of the most abhorrent injustices committed by some landlords in the District is to evict — or threaten to evict — tenants who report building code violations to the Department of Licenses and Inspections.
> This is intimidation, pure and simple. It is an affront to the dignity of the tenant. It often makes the man who lives in a cold and leaking tenement afraid to report those conditions.
> Certainly the tenant deserves the protection of the law when he lodges a good faith complaint.
> *I recommend legislation to prevent retaliatory evictions by landlords in the District.* [Emphasis added.]

He seems to think as do I that congressional action is required. It may be doubted that the President would so have recommended legislation except upon the advice of the legal authorities upon whom he relies. Certainly he is aware of the due process protective considerations which must be accorded to a landlord, even one who might be guilty of "an affront to the dignity" of a tenant. He must know that a community burden is not to be borne alone by landlords, charged with allegedly "retaliatory" [62] evictions because of complaints of "violations," undefined and vague and lacking in standards.

That my colleagues ultimately upon reflection began to doubt the sufficiency of their position seems clear enough, for they observe: "This is not, of course, to say that *even if the tenant can prove a retaliatory purpose* she is entitled to remain in possession in perpetuity." (Emphasis added.)

"Of course" *not,* I say; *not at all* as the law has read, until now, I may add. My colleagues continue: "If this illegal purpose is dissipated, the landlord can, in the absence of legislation or a binding contract, evict his tenants or

---

62. For background and as a matter of convenient reference, let it be noted that Edwards and Habib entered into a monthly tenancy agreement as of March 24, 1965. The tenant paid one month's rent in advance, and, of course, took the premises as she found them. The agreement provided that failure thereafter to pay the rental in advance would constitute a default and that the agreement was to operate as a notice to quit and that the statutory 30 days' notice to quit was expressly waived. Repeatedly thereafter the tenant was in default of payment of the rental. As of October 11, 1965, neither the appellant nor her counsel appeared in the Landlord-Tenant Branch of the Court of General Sessions. A later motion to reopen a default judgment was granted, a two-day trial followed, and a directed verdict for the landlord was entered.

This court was asked to stay the judgment after the District of Columbia Court of Appeals refused to do so. I then dissented from this court's order for reasons set forth in Edwards v. Habib, 125 U.S. App. D.C. 49, 51 366 F.2d 628, 630 (1965), to which I now refer. In the meanwhile, time and again, further defaults occurred with resulting harassment and vexation to the landlord which this court has often overlooked. The landlord is still without possession of his property which should have been available to him for remodeling or sale, or even that the structure might be razed. Unless its condition could justify its condemnation by lawful authority, his should have been the option as to future use of the property.

It is difficult for me to understand how this court can sustain so studied a deprivation as has here occurred.

raise their rents for economic or other legitimate reasons, or even for no reason at all."

And so, it may be seen according to the majority, we need never mind the Congress, the aid of which the *President* would invoke. We may disregard, even reject, our law of such long standing. We will simply leave it to a jury to say when a landlord may regain possession of his own property, although "the determination is not easy," my colleagues concede:[63]

I leave my colleagues where they have placed themselves.[64]

Note: Tort Remedies for Retaliatory Eviction

Although this is not a book on torts, for the sake of completeness you should not overlook the possibility of "abuse of process" or "prima facie tort" as possible remedies for the tenant. The process would be the eviction action, whereas the misuse consists of the landlord using this process of eviction to suppress reports of violations to the housing authorities or other tenant assertion of rights and remedies. For a discussion of the possible application of prima facie tort to the retaliatory eviction, see Schoshinski, Remedies of the Indigent Tenant: Proposal for Change, 54 Geo. L.J. 519, 548-551 (1966).

You should not overlook the very difficult problem of proving retaliatory eviction, i.e., the landlord's motives. However, the landlord, if the landlord's motive is really to deter other tenants from asserting their rights, will probably have made statements to the other tenants that complaints to the housing authorities or the assertion of rights will mean eviction, such as "Remember Yvonne Edwards!"

Note: Defense of Retaliatory Eviction in
Commercial Setting

The Restatement (Second) of Property (Landlord and Tenant) §14.8 confines the definition of "retaliatory action" to situations involving resi-

---

63. And with the results in riot-torn Washington so painfully obvious the prospect now being opened up may seem horrendous indeed, whether the "violations" were committed by the tenants themselves or by others whose conduct created conditions with which the landlord must cope. I cannot accept the premise that Congress even remotely entertained any such "intent" as my colleagues so confidently proclaim.

64. Ill. Rev. Stat., ch. 80, §71, provides:

It is declared to be against the public policy of the State for a landlord to terminate or refuse to renew a lease or tenancy of property used as a residence on the ground that the tenant has complained to any governmental authority of a bona fide violation of any applicable building code, health ordinance, or similar regulation. Any provision in any lease, or any agreement or understanding, purporting to permit the landlord to terminate or refuse to renew a lease or tenancy for such reason is void.

See generally, Note, Landlord and Tenant—Retaliatory Evictions, 3 Harv. Civ. Rts. L. Rev. 193 (1967); Note, Retaliatory Eviction—Is California Lagging Behind? 18 Hastings L.J. 700 (1967); Schoshinski, 54 Geo. L.J. 519, 541-552 (1966).—EDS.

dential housing because almost all statutes and reported decisions are so limited. A recent case, Custom Parking Inc. v. Superior Court, 138 Cal. App. 3d 90, 187 Cal. Rptr. 674 (1982), holds that the defense of retaliatory eviction could be raised in an unlawful detainer action brought against a commercial tenant. If the tenant is evicted in retaliation for the tenant's refusal to participate in business dealings which violate the anti-trust laws, the anti-trust defense may be preferable given the fact that such a defense is better established and that a successful litigant is awarded treble damages. Compare Mobil Oil Corp. v. Rubenfeld, 48 A.D.2d 428, 370 N.Y.S.2d 943 (1975) (defense of retaliatory eviction not available to commercial tenant), with Lessig v. Tidewater Oil Co., 327 F.2d 459 (9th Cir. 1964) (case with fact situation similar to Mobil Oil Corp. v. Rubenfeld; successful defense based on anti-trust violation).

E. Unconscionability: Onerous Terms in the Lease Forced on the Tenant

A housing shortage in a large urban area gives rise to what is called a landlord's market, meaning that a tenant seeking a dwelling is in the unhappy position of accepting a tenancy on whatever terms the landlord dictates.

In the landmark case of Henningsen v. Bloomfield Motors, Inc.,[65] the New Jersey Supreme Court recognized the factors inherent in a contract of adhesion and refused to enforce a broad disclaimer of an implied warranty of merchantability found in a standard automobile purchase contract.

O'CALLAGHAN v. WALLER & BECKWITH REALTY CO.

15 Ill. 2d 436, 155 N.E.2d 545 (1958)

SCHAEFER, J.

This is an action to recover for injuries allegedly caused by the defendant's negligence in maintaining and operating a large apartment building. Mrs. Ella O'Callaghan, a tenant in the building, was injured when she fell while crossing the paved courtyard on her way from the garage to her apartment. She instituted this action to recover for her injuries, alleging that they were caused by defective pavement in the courtyard. Before the case was tried, Mrs. O'Callaghan died and her administrator was substituted as plaintiff. The jury returned a verdict for the plaintiff in the sum of $14,000, and judgment was entered on the verdict. Defendant appealed. The Appel-

---

65.   32 N.J. 358, 161 A.2d 69 (1960).

late Court held that the action was barred by an exculpatory clause in the lease that Mrs. O'Callaghan had signed, and that a verdict should have been directed for the defendant. 15 Ill. App. 2d 349, 146 N.E.2d 198. It therefore reversed the judgment and remanded the cause with directions to enter judgment for the defendant. We granted leave to appeal.

In reaching its conclusion the Appellate Court relied upon our recent decision in Jackson v. First National Bank, 415 Ill. 453, 114 N.E.2d 721. There we considered the validity of such an exculpatory clause in a lease of property for business purposes. We pointed out that contracts by which one seeks to relieve himself from the consequences of his own negligence are generally enforced "unless (1) it would be against the settled public policy of the State to do so, or (2) there is something in the social relationship of the parties militating against upholding the agreement." 415 Ill. at page 460, 114 N.E.2d at page 725. And we held that there was nothing in the public policy of the State or in the social relationship of the parties to forbid enforcement of the exculpatory clause there involved.

The exculpatory clause in the lease now before us clearly purports to relieve the lessor and its agents from any liability to the lessee for personal injuries or property damage caused by any act or neglect of the lessor or its agents. It does not appear to be amenable to the strict construction to which such clauses are frequently subjected. See 175 A.L.R. 8, 89. The plaintiff does not question its applicability, and she concedes that if it is valid it bars her recovery. She argues vigorously, however, that such a clause is contrary to public policy, and so invalid, in a lease of residential property.

Freedom of contract is basic to our law. But when that freedom expresses itself in a provision designed to absolve one of the parties from the consequences of his own negligence, there is danger that the standards of conduct which the law has developed for the protection of others may be diluted. These competing considerations have produced results that are not completely consistent. This court has refused to enforce contracts exculpating or limiting liability for negligence between common carriers and shippers of freight or paying passengers (Chicago and Northwestern Railway Co. v. Chapman, 133 Ill. 96, 24 N.E. 417, 8 L.R.A. 508), between telegraph companies and those sending messages (Tyler, Ullman & Co. v. Western Union Telegraph Co., 60 Ill. 421), and between masters and servants (Campbell v. Chicago, Rock Island and Pacific Railway Co., 243 Ill. 620, 90 N.E. 1106). The obvious public interest in these relationships, coupled with the dominant position of those seeking exculpation, were compelling considerations in these decisions, which are in accord with similar results in other jurisdictions. See 175 A.L.R. 8.

On the other hand, as pointed out in the Jackson case, the relation of lessor and lessee has been considered a matter of private concern. Clauses that exculpate the landlord from the consequences of his negligence have been sustained in residential as well as commercial leases. There are intimations in other jurisdictions that run counter to the current authority. The

New Hampshire court applies to exculpatory clauses in all leases its uniform rule that any attempt to contract against liability for negligence is contrary to public policy. Papakalos v. Shaka, 1941, 91 N.H. 265, 18 A.2d 377. But apart from the *Papakalos* case we know of no court of last resort that has held such clauses invalid in the absence of a statute so requiring.

A contract shifting the risk of liability for negligence may benefit a tenant as well as a landlord. See Cerny-Pickas & Co. v. C.R. Jahn Co., 7 Ill. 2d 393, 131 N.E.2d 100. Such an agreement transfers the risk of a possible financial burden and so lessens the impact of the sanctions that induce adherence to the required standard of care. But this consideration is applicable as well to contracts for insurance that indemnify against liability for one's own negligence. Such contracts are accepted, and even encouraged. See Ill. Rev. Stat. 1957, chap. $95\frac{1}{2}$, pars. 7-202 (1) and 7-315.

The plaintiff contends that due to a shortage of housing there is a disparity of bargaining power between lessors of residential property and their lessees that gives landlords an unconscionable advantage over tenants. And upon this ground it is said that exculpatory clauses in residential leases must be held to be contrary to public policy. No attempt was made upon the trial to show that Mrs. O'Callaghan was at all concerned about the exculpatory clause, that she tried to negotiate with the defendant about its modification or elimination, or that she made any effort to rent an apartment elsewhere. To establish the existence of a widespread housing shortage the plaintiff points to numerous statutes designed to alleviate the shortage (see Ill. Rev. Stat. 1957, chap. $67\frac{1}{2}$, passim and to the existence of rent control during the period of the lease. 65 Stat. 145 (1947), 50 U.S.C.A. Appendix, §1894.

Unquestionably there has been a housing shortage. That shortage has produced an active and varied legislative response. Since legislative attention has been so sharply focused upon housing problems in recent years, it might be assumed that the legislature has taken all of the remedial action that it thought necessary or desirable. One of the major legislative responses was the adoption of rent controls which placed ceilings upon the amount of rent that landlords could charge. But the very existence of that control made it impossible for a lessor to negotiate for an increased rental in exchange for the elimination of an exculpatory clause. We are asked to assume, however, that the legislative response to the housing shortage has been inadequate and incomplete, and to augment it judicially.

The relationship of landlord and tenant does not have the monopolistic characteristics that have characterized some other relations with respect to which exculpatory clauses have been held invalid. There are literally thousands of landlords who are in competition with one another. The rental market affords a variety of competing types of housing accommodations from simple farm house to luxurious apartment. The use of a form contract does not of itself establish disparity of bargaining power. That there is a shortage of housing at one particular time or place does not indicate that such shortages have always and everywhere existed, or that there will be shortages in the future. Judicial determinations of public policy cannot readily take account of sporadic and transitory circumstances. They should rather, we think, rest upon a durable moral basis. Other jurisdictions have dealt with this problem by legislation. McKinney's Consol Laws of N.Y. Ann., Real Property Laws, sec. 234, Vol. 49, Part I; Ann. Laws of Mass., Vol. 6, c. 186, sec. 15. In our opinion the subject is one that is appropriate for legislative rather than judicial action.

The judgment of the Appellate Court is affirmed.

Judgment affirmed.

BRISTOW, J., and DAILY, C.J. (dissenting).

We cannot accept the conclusions and analysis of the majority opinion, which in our judgment not only arbitrarily eliminates the concept of negligence in the landlord and tenant relationship, but creates anomalies in the law, and will produce grievous social consequences for hundreds of thousands of persons in this State.

According to the undisputed facts in the instant case, this form lease with its exculpatory clause, was executed in a metropolitan area in 1947, when housing shortages were so acute that "waiting lists" were the order of the day, and gratuities to landlords to procure shelter were common. (U.S. Sen. Rep. 1780, Committee on Banking & Currency, vol. II, 81st Cong., 2nd Sess. (1950), p. 2565 et seq.; Cremer v. Peoria Housing Authority, 399 Ill. 579, 589, 78 N.E.2d 276.) While plaintiff admittedly did not negotiate about the exculpatory clause, as the majority opinion notes, the record shows unequivocally that the apartment would not have been rented to her if she had quibbled about any clause in the form lease. According to the uncontroverted testimony, "If a person refused to sign a [form] lease in the form it was in, the apartment would not be rented to him."

Apparently, the majority opinion has chosen to ignore those facts and prevailing circumstances, and finds instead that there were thousands of landlords competing with each other with a variety of rental units. Not only was the element of competition purely theoretical — and judges need not be more naive than other men — but there wasn't even theoretical competition, as far as the exculpatory clauses were concerned, since these clauses were included in all form leases used by practically all landlords in urban areas. Simmons v. Columbus Venetian Stevens Building, Inc., Ill. App., 155 N.E.2d 372; 1952 Ill. Forum, 321, 328. This meant that even if a prospective tenant were to "take his business elsewhere," he would still be confronted by the same exculpatory clause in a form lease offered by another landlord.

Thus, we are *not* construing merely an isolated provision of a contract specifically bargained for by one landlord and one tenant, "a matter of private concern," as the majority opinion myopically views the issue in order to sustain its conclusion. We are construing, instead, a provision affecting thousands of tenants now bound by such provisions, which were foisted upon them at a time when it would be pure fiction to state that they had anything but a Hobson's choice in the matter. Can landlords, by that technique, immunize themselves from liability for negligence, and have the blessings of this court as they destroy the concept of negligence and standards of law painstakingly evolved in the case law? That is the issue in this case, and the majority opinion at no time realistically faces it.

In resolving this issue, it is evident that despite the assertion in the majority opinion, there is no such thing as absolute "freedom of contract" in the law. West Coast Hotel Co. v. Parrish, 300 U.S. 379, 392, 57 S. Ct. 578, 582, 81 L. Ed. 703. As Mr. Justice Holmes stated, "pretty much all law consists in forbidding men to do some things that they want to do, and contract is no more exempt from law than other acts." Dissent, Adkins v. Children's Hospital of District of Columbia, 261 U.S. 525, 568, 43 S. Ct. 394, 405, 67 L. Ed. 785. Thus, there is no freedom to contract to commit a crime; or to contract to give a reward for the commission of a crime; or to contract to violate essential morality; or to contract to accomplish an unlawful purpose, or, to contract in violation of public policy. 12 I.L.P. Contracts §§151, 154.

In the instant case we must determine whether the exculpatory clause in the lease offends the public policy of this State. We realize that there is no precise definition of "public policy" or rule to test whether a contract is contrary to public policy, so that each case must be judged according to its own peculiar circumstances. First Trust & Savings Bank of Kankakee v. Powers, 393 Ill. 97, 102, 65 N.E.2d 377. None would dispute, however, that there is a recognized policy of discouraging negligence and protecting those in need of goods or services from being overreached by those with power to drive unconscionable bargains.

Even the majority opinion recognizes this policy as a possible limitation on the concept of "freedom of contract" in its statement, "when that freedom expresses itself in a provision designed to absolve one of the parties from the consequences of his own negligence, there is danger that the standards of conduct which the law has developed for the protection of others may be diluted." Diluted? As applied in the instant case, the word is "destroyed." When landlords are no longer liable for failure to observe standards of care, or for conduct amounting to negligence by virtue of an exculpatory clause in a lease, then such standards cease to exist. They are not merely "diluted." Negligence cannot exist in abstraction. The exculpatory clause destroys the concept of negligence in the landlord-tenant relationship, and the majority opinion, in sustaining the validity of that clause, has given the concept of negligence in this relationship a "judicial burial."

This court, however, has refused to countenance such a destruction of standards of conduct and of the concept of negligence in other relationships. We have invalidated such exculpatory clauses as contrary to our public policy in contracts between common carriers and shippers or paying passengers (Checkley v. Illinois Central Railroad Co., 257 Ill. 491, 100 N.E. 942, 44

L.R.A., N.S., 1127; Chicago and Northwestern Railway Co. v. Chapman, 133 Ill. 96, 24 N.E. 417, 8 L.R.A. 508); between telegraph companies and those sending messages (Tyler, Ullman & Co. v. Western Union Telegraph Co., 60 Ill. 421), and between employers and employees (Campbell v. Chicago, Rock Island and Pacific Railway Co., 243 Ill. 620, 90 N.E. 1106; Devine v. Delano, 272 Ill. 166, 111 N.E. 742; Consolidated Coal Co. of St. Louis v. Lundak, 196 Ill. 594, 63 N.E. 1079; Himrod Coal Co. v. Clark, 197 Ill. 514, 64 N.E. 282).

By what logic and reasoning can you hold that such clauses are void and contrary to public policy in an employer-employee contract, but valid in contracts between landlords and tenants, as the majority opinion does? If the criterion for invalidating exculpatory clauses is the presence of "monopolistic characteristics" in the relationship, as the majority opinion suggests, then do employers have a greater monopoly on the labor market than landlords have on the tenant market? Is there less competition among employers for employees than among landlords for tenants? The facts defy any such reasoning. Nor are there any other cogent grounds for distinguishing between these categories.

The legal anomaly of sustaining such clauses in leases, while voiding them in other types of contracts, when the grounds on which they are held void can be matched by similar grounds in the relationship of landlord and tenant, is pointed out by the court in the aforementioned *Simmons* case, where the court made a scholarly review of the decisions in Illinois and other jurisdictions respecting exculpatory clauses in leases and other contracts. The court stated:

> Is it more important that a man should have a safe place to work than that he should have a safe place to live, and is there any more reason in the employer-employee relationship that the employer should not be allowed to avoid liability for his negligence than there is that a landlord should not be able to avoid the liability for negligence in maintaining the common area which must be used by people to attain ingress and egress when they rent a portion of the premises? Is safety while working more important than safety while living?

This patent inconsistency respecting the validity of an exculpatory clause, created by the majority opinion, is in no way required by Illinois precedents. The only Illinois authority cited — and this is done indirectly by referring to the Appellate Court's reliance on the case — is Jackson v. First National Bank of Lake Forest, 415 Ill. 453, 114 N.E.2d 721. However, even a cursory reading of that case reveals that the court, in sustaining an exculpatory clause in a business lease, inferred that a different result would have followed if there was anything in the record indicating that the parties were not on an equal footing, or that the lessee had no freedom of choice, or had to accept what was offered. That court stated at page 463 of 415 Ill., at page 726 of 114 N.E.2d:

This is a business lease. There is nothing to suggest that the parties were not dealing at arms' length and upon equal footing. No facts are brought to our attention from which it might be reasonable to infer that the lessee was forced to take the storeroom upon lessor's terms.

Compare that situation with the facts in the instant case, where it is admitted that there were waiting lists for the apartment and that if a person refused to sign the lease with the exculpatory clause in the form it was in, the apartment would not be rented to him. Only by the blind application of precedent can the Jackson case be deemed determinative herein. Nor is there any established line of authority elsewhere sustaining exculpatory clauses in leases, but only conflicting decisions, and a disposition to emasculate such exculpatory clauses by giving them a strict, if not distorted construction. 175 A.L.R. 8, 90; 15 Univ. Pitt. L. Rev. 493, 496.

Furthermore, while stare decisis has a strong social justification, it should not be used to stifle the growth of the law. When experience, which Mr. Justice Holmes has stated is the "life of the law," makes manifest that a rule is without vitality, a court cannot abdicate its responsibility of reappraisal.

The basis of voiding exculpatory clauses is that they are contrary to the public policy of discouraging negligence and protecting those in need of goods or services from being overreached by those with power to drive unconscionable bargains. Bisso v. Inland Waterways Corp., 349 U.S. 85, 91, 75 S. Ct. 629, 99 L. Ed. 911. In determining whether such clauses should be deemed void, the courts have weighed such factors as the importance which the subject has for the physical and economic well-being of the group agreeing to the release; their bargaining power; the amount of free choice actually exercised in agreeing to the exemption; and the existence of competition among the group to be exempted. (Williston, Contracts, vol. 6, p. 4968: "The Significance of Bargaining Power in the Law of Exculpation," 37 Col. L. Rev. 248; 175 A.L.R. 8, 48; 15 Univ. Pitt. L. Rev. 493.) Adjudged by such criteria, it is evident that the subject matter of the exculpatory clause herein — shelter — is indispensable for the physical well being of tenants; that they have nothing even approaching equality of bargaining power with landlords and no free choice whatever in agreeing to the exemption, since they will be confronted with the same clause in other form leases if they seek shelter elsewhere. Although the majority opinion claims that such clauses may also benefit tenants, it is hard for us to envisage a tenant on a waiting list for an apartment, insisting that the lease include a provision relieving him from liability for his negligence in the maintenance of the premises. Consequently, in our judgment, every material ground for voiding the exculpatory clause exists in the lease involved in the instant case.

Similar conclusions have been reached by other courts, after recognizing the change in the status and bargaining power in the landlord-tenant relationship that has taken place. Kuzmiak v. Brookchester, Inc., 33 N.J. Super. 575, 111 A.2d 425; Kay v. Cain, 81 U.S. App. D.C. 24, 154 F.2d 305.

Thus, the New Jersey court stated in the *Kuzmiak* case at page 432 of 111 A.2d:

> Under *present* conditions, the comparative bargaining position of landlords and tenants in housing accommodations within many areas of the state are so unequal that tenants are in no position to bargain; and an exculpatory clause which purports to immunize the landlord from all liability would be contrary to public policy. [Italics ours.]

In the same vein, the Federal court in Kay v. Cain, 154 F.2d 305, at page 306, stated:

> Moreover, it is doubtful whether a clause which did undertake to exempt a landlord from responsibility for such negligence would *now* be valid. The acute housing shortage in and near the District of Columbia gives the landlord so great a bargaining advantage over the tenant that such an exemption might well be held invalid on the grounds of public policy.

The majority opinion, however, labels such changed conditions as "sporadic" and chooses to ignore them because they may change again at some future time. It holds that judicial determinations of public policy should "rest upon a more durable moral basis." Our concept of the judicial function is not so circumscribed, nor is it elastic in one case and restrictive in another, depending upon economic predilections. It is hard for us to fathom that this same court which enunciated the liberal and scholarly approach of interpreting common-law concepts in the light of contemporary conditions and social needs in Nudd v. Matsoukas, 7 Ill. 2d 608, 619, 131 N.E.2d 525; Amann v. Faidy, 415 Ill. 422, 114 N.E.2d 412, and Brandt v. Keller, 413 Ill. 503, 109 N.E.2d 729, can now hold with academic detachment that landlords, who are in the position to dictate whatever terms they choose to those in need of shelter, have a right to immunize themselves by contract from liability for failure to make essential repairs of areas which the tenants cannot legally repair, and that such contracts do not offend the public policy of this State. Upon what "durable moral basis" does that public policy determination rest?

We prefer to consistently follow our realistic policy of interpreting common-law concepts created by the courts in the light of contemporary conditions, as pledged in Nudd v. Matsoukas and the other cases, in accordance with the traditions of the creative jurists of our time. Holmes, Southern Pacific Co. v. Jensen, 244 U.S. 205, 221, 37 S. Ct. 524, 61 L. Ed. 1086; Cardozo, "Growth of the Law."

As Mr. Justice Cardozo explained in his treatise, "Growth of the Law" (Selected Writings of Cardozo, p. 246):

> A rule which in its origin was the creation of the courts themselves and was supposed in the making to express the mores of the day, may be abrogated by

the courts when the mores have so changed that perpetuation of the rule would do violence to the social conscience. . . . This is not usurpation. It is not even innovation. It is the reservation for ourselves of the same power of creation that built up the common law through its exercise by the judges of the past.

In this connection, Mr. Chief Justice Warren more recently observed: "A . . . reason for the success of our legal system is its adaptability to changing circumstances. As Pollock said, all courts have a duty, which ours generally try to perform, 'to keep the rules of law in harmony with the enlightened common sense of the nation.'" "The Law of the Future," Mr. Chief Justice Warren, Fortune Magazine, Nov. 1955, p. 107.

The majority opinion apparently dismisses whatever misgivings it has for the resulting social consequences of its decision with the observation that the problem is "appropriate for legislative rather than judicial action," and refers to the New York and Massachusetts statutes. McKinney's Consol. Laws of N.Y. Ann., Real Prop. Laws, sec. 234, vol. 49, part I; Ann. Laws of Mass. vol. 6, chap. 186, sec. 15.

Future legislation on this subject will be of small comfort to the hundreds of persons with cases pending in our courts for injuries sustained through conduct of landlords tantamount to common-law negligence. What help can the legislature give to such persons? Their only protection lies in the inherent power of the courts to adjudicate common-law rights and their duty to strike down contracts in derogation of the public policy of the State. That duty is in no way abridged by the fact that some legislatures have declared such exculpatory clauses contrary to public policy. We cannot perceive how such legislative action elsewhere relieves this court from its duty of also recognizing the public policy in the case law, which is an equally cogent source of a State's public policy. People ex rel. Nelson v. Wiersema State Bank, 361 Ill. 75, 86, 197 N.E. 537, 101 A.L.R. 501.

Moreover, for this court, which has recently and repeatedly expressly refused to relegate to the legislature the task of reinterpreting common-law concepts necessary in the development of the law (People ex rel. Noren v. Dempsey, 10 Ill. 2d 288, 293, 139 N.E.2d 780; Nudd v. Matsoukas, 7 Ill. 2d 608, 131 N.E.2d 525), to now abdicate to the legislature, as the majority opinion has done, is not only inconsistent but an admission of failure to resolve the problem. Legislative intrusion into the field of the common law can only be justified when courts have refused to exercise their own function. (Green, "Freedom of Litigation," 38 Ill. L. Rev. 355, 378, 382.) There should be no such refusal by this court in the instant case.

In our judgment, authorizing landlords to immunize themselves from liability for negligence, as the majority opinion has done, at a time of critical housing shortages, recognized by Congress and the courts, is not only inconsistent with much law and the public policy of this State, but it is in derogation of our duty "to keep the rules of law in harmony with the enlightened common sense of the nation." Therefore, we believe it our obligation to dissent from that opinion, and to protest against the destruction of the common law rights of a significant proportion of the population of this State.

Note: Unconscionable Contract Provisions

Consider the possible application of U.C.C. §2-302, which, although only applicable to the sale of goods, has been said to be a mere codification of the inherent common-law power of every court.[66] That section provides:

> (1) If the court as a matter of law finds the contract or any clause of the contract to have been unconscionable at the time it was made the court may refuse to enforce the contract, or it may enforce the remainder of the contract without the unconscionable clause, or it may so limit the application of any unconscionable clause as to avoid any unconscionable result.
> (2) When it is claimed or appears to the court that the contract or any clause thereof may be unconscionable the parties shall be afforded a reasonable opportunity to present evidence as to its commercial setting, purpose and effect to aid the court in making the determination.[67]

It has been suggested that if a standard form lease is a contract of adhesion, the states might find the insurance contract a useful analogue and thus regulate some of the lease's more onerous terms, just as states now regulate many terms in an insurance contract. In fact, New York has drafted a whole fire insurance policy which companies must use if they wish to insure any property in New York.[68] Other states have not gone so far, merely requiring the companies to submit their forms to a state administrator who must approve the forms before they can be used. Wisconsin has taken what may be the first step. There, standard form leases must be issued or approved by the Wisconsin Real Estate Commission. In exercising its approval power, the Commission was entrusted by the legislature with the responsibility of "safeguarding the interests of the public." Wis. Stat. §136.02, 136.05(1), 136.08. In an article which examines the Wisconsin experiment,[69] the author questions whether the Commission, in approving lease forms which are drafted to heavily favor the landlord, is sufficiently carrying out its responsibility. He cites many examples of clauses found in the forms

66. Cf. Williams v. Walker-Thomas Furniture Co., 350 F.2d 445 (D.C. Cir. 1965).
67. See generally Leff, Unconscionability and the Code—The Emperor's New Clause, 115 U. Pa. L. Rev. 485 (1967) (arguing that the code is purposefully ambiguous as to whether it refers to procedural or substantive unconscionability); Note, Bargaining Power and Unconscionability; A Suggested Approach to UCC Section 2-302, 114 U. Pa. L. Rev. 998 (1966); Note, The Doctrine of Unconscionability, 19 Me. L. Rev. 81 (1967) (applauding the failure of the drafters to reduce the section to definitional certainty).—EDS.
68. N.Y. Ins. Law §168.
69. Bell, Standard Form Leases in Wisconsin, 1966 Wis. L. Rev. 583.

approved by the Commission which are clearly contrary to law or to positively formulated state policies.

Finally, you should consider whether a legislature which has taken at least the "first faltering steps" towards a solution is not demonstrating its utter naiveté whenever it enacts a statute giving the tenant certain rights and then adding the pernicious "in the absence of an agreement to the contrary"! For example, California's Civil Code §1941 requires the landlord to put every building intended to be used as a dwelling into a condition fit for such habitation "in the absence of an agreement to the contrary." Would it surprise you to learn that almost all leases used in California have an express disclaimer? "Freedom of contract," the shibboleth of both bench and bar, may be nothing but "tyranny of contract" when examined from the viewpoint of the tenant.

SWENEY GASOLINE & OIL CO. v. TOLEDO, Peoria & Western Railroad
42 Ill. 2d 265, 247 N.E.2d 603 (1969)

KLINGBIEL, J. The Sweney Gasoline & Oil Company brought an action in the circuit court of Peoria County against the Toledo, Peoria & Western Railroad to recover for damage to the plaintiff's property allegedly caused through defendant's negligence. After a non-jury trial, judgment was rendered for defendant. Plaintiff appeals directly to this court, on the theory that a constitutional question is involved.

The plaintiff oil company leased from the defendant railroad certain premises adjacent to the railroad tracks, on which plaintiff maintained a bulk oil station for the storage and distribution of gasoline, oil and other petroleum products. On January 21, 1963, a freight train operated by defendant became derailed and ran onto the leased premises, damaging the structures comprising the bulk oil station. The written lease between the parties contained an exculpatory clause providing that the "Lessee shall protect, indemnify and hold harmless Railroad, its agents, servants and employees, from and against any and all claims, demands, judgments, suits, costs, expenses and attorneys fees arising out of . . . loss or damage to property of any of the parties hereto, . . . whether caused by the negligence of Railroad or its agents, servants or employees or otherwise." In holding that the defendant was thereby exonerated from liability the trial court took note of a statute, passed in 1959, which declared void certain exculpatory clauses in leases. The statute provides:

> Every covenant, agreement or understanding in or in connection with or collateral to any lease of real property, except those business leases in which any municipal corporation, governmental unit, or corporations regulated by a State or Federal Commission or agency is lessor or lessee, exempting the lessor

from liability for damages for injuries to person or property caused by or resulting from the negligence of the lessor, his agents, servants or employees, in the operation or maintenance of the demised premises or the real property containing the demised premises shall be deemed to be void as against public policy and wholly unenforceable. [Ill. Rev. Stat. 1967, ch. 80, par. 15a.]

Claiming that the statute was the basis for the trial court's judgment, the plaintiff urges that it be held unconstitutional for making a discriminatory classification without any reasonable basis and for unlawfully granting to "regulated" corporations a special privilege and immunity. We agree with this argument and are of the opinion that the statute violates article IV section 22 of our constitution, S.H.A. We see no reasonable basis for exempting municipal corporations, governmental units or corporations regulated by a state or federal commission from the provisions of this statute. The statute in effect grants immunity to these governmental units and regulated corporations in an unconstitutional manner and is therefore void.

The relation of lessor and lessee has long been recognized as primarily a matter of private concern, and, in the absence of the above statute (which we have held unconstitutional), exculpatory agreements in residential as well as in business leases are ordinarily given effect, relieving the lessor from liability for injuries to the tenant's property due to the negligence of the landlord or his employees. (O'Callaghan v. Waller & Beckwith Realty Co., 15 Ill. 2d 436, 155 N.E.2d 545; Jackson v. First National Bank of Lake Forest, 415 Ill. 453, 114 N.E.2d 721.) This accords to the individual the dignity of being considered capable of making and standing by his own agreements.

Where there is such disparity of bargaining power between the parties that the lessee has no practical choice but to accept what is offered, enforcement will be denied on the ground that it would result in great injustice, and the plaintiff claims that such is the case here. To support the position, however, no facts are adduced. What the plaintiff relies on are simply general statements that "an entrepreneur desiring to enter a business requiring railroad service as a matter of common knowledge is required, except at excessive expense, to locate its business facility upon or adjacent to a railroad right of way" and that: "Its alternatives are to accept the terms of the railroad lease or not to have available to it that which it must have in order to carry on business; namely, the service of a railroad." Plaintiff points to nothing in this record to indicate that the parties were not dealing at arm's length and upon an equal footing. No evidence was introduced to show that to locate its facility elsewhere the plaintiff would incur "excessive expense," or that the expense thereof would be greater than others incur who are so located, or who use other kinds of transportation facilities, or that other circumstances were present forcing the oil company to take this particular location upon terms offered by the railroad.

It is also argued that the damage was inflicted as a result of a trespass by the railroad, and that the lease does not purport to exculpate from liability for trespass. By the provisions in question the lessee undertook to hold the railroad harmless from liability for damage to its property "whether caused by the negligence of Railroad or its agents, servants or employees or otherwise." There is no claim that the train was intentionally derailed and caused to run upon the premises, and regardless of whether a technical trespass occurred the cause of the accident can be attributed to nothing more on the part of defendant than its alleged negligence.

Plaintiff further contends the clause in question is phrased in confusing language, and should be strictly construed against the party benefited by it. We think the intent of the present one is visible, through its legalistic jargon. However verbose its language may be, it exempts the railroad from liability to the lessee for any damage to the latter's property caused by the negligence of the railroad and is adequate to cover the present situation.

It is lastly urged that this court re-examine its holding in O'Callaghan v. Waller & Beckwith Realty Co., 15 Ill. 2d 436, 155 N.E.2d 545, sustaining the validity of exculpatory clauses. It is pointed out that O'Callaghan concluded with a statement that the subject is one more appropriate for legislative than judicial action, and that shortly after the decision in that case the statute was enacted. We have no way of knowing whether the legislature would have enacted the statute without the fatal exceptions; however, we are still of the opinion that this is a matter for the legislature.

After carefully considering all of the plaintiff's contentions we find that as applied to the facts shown by this record the exculpatory provisions in question are not invalid, that as drawn they are sufficient to cover the present situation, and that there is nothing in the relationship of the parties to prevent enforcement. The circuit court was correct in finding for the defendant, and its judgment is affirmed.

Judgment affirmed.

SCHAEFER, J. (dissenting): In 1958, in O'Callaghan v. Waller & Beckwith Realty Co., 15 Ill. 2d 436, 155 N.E.2d 545, this court considered the validity, at common law, of exculpatory clauses in residential leases. The case was a very close one, and two members of the court joined in a strong dissent from the opinion which sustained their validity. The prevailing opinion concluded with a request for legislative action: "Other jurisdictions have dealt with this problem by legislation. In our opinion the subject is one that is appropriate for legislative rather than judicial action." (15 Ill. 2d at 441, 155 N.E.2d at 547.) The General Assembly responded promptly, and in 1959 adopted the statute which is now held unconstitutional.

I agree that the statute as written violates the constitution, for the reasons stated in the opinion of the majority. But I regard the enactment of the statute as an expression of the public policy of the State which this court should respect, even though it cannot be given complete effect according to its terms. That statute declares "void as against public policy and wholly unenforceable" every exculpatory clause in any lease, business or residential, with the narrow and irrational exception in favor of particular lessors and lessees of business property which totally defeats its major purpose. I would hold that the statute, despite its invalidity, is an expression of public policy which fully justifies this court in now holding, as a matter of common law, that exculpatory clauses in leaseholds are void.

Note: Exculpatory Provisions in Leases

Henrioule v. Marin Ventures, Inc., 20 Cal. 3d 512, 573 P.2d 465, 143 Cal. Rptr. 247 (1978), comments as follows on exculpatory clauses in leases:

> In holding that exculpatory clauses in residential leases violate public policy, this court joins an increasing number of jurisdictions. (See, e.g., Kuzmiak v. Brookchester, Inc. (1955), 33 N.J. Super. 575, 111 A.2d 425; Old Town Development Co. v. Langford (Ind. App. 1976) 349 N.E.2d 744; Weaver v. American Oil Co. (Ind. 1971) 276 N.E.2d 144 (such clauses are void in all leases); Papakalos v. Shaka (1941) 91 N.H. 265, 18 A.2d 377, 379 (such clauses are void in all contracts); Billie Knitwear, Inc. v. New York Life Ins. Co. (N.Y. Sup. 1940) 174 Misc. 978, 22 N.Y.S.2d 324, *affd.* (1942) 288 N.Y. 682, 43 N.E.2d 80 (such clauses invalidated by statute in all leases); see generally, Annot., Validity of Exculpatory Clause in Lease Exempting Lessor from Liability (1971) 49 A.L.R.3d 321.) Indeed, in 1975 the California Legislature enacted Civil Code section 1953, which declared invalid exculpatory clauses in residential leases executed on or after January 1, 1976. (Civ. Code, §1953, Stats. 1975, ch. 302, §1, p. 749.) [20 Cal. 3d at 519-520, 573 P.2d at 469-470, 143 Cal. Rptr. at 251-252.]

Note: The Restatement's Position on Unconscionable Provisions in Leases

§5.6 *Parties Agree Otherwise as to Landlord's Obligations in Regard to Condition of Leased Property*

The parties to a lease may agree to increase or decrease what would otherwise be the obligations of the landlord with respect to the condition of the leased property and may agree to expand or contract what would otherwise be the remedies available to the tenant for the breach of those obligations, and those agreements are valid and binding on the parties to the lease unless they are unenforceable in whole or in part because they are unconscionable or significantly against public policy. . . .

e. *Unconscionable agreement or agreement against public policy.* An agreement is unconscionable when it would shock the conscience if enforced. Cf. Uniform Commercial Code §2-302 and Restatement of the Law, Second,

Contracts, §234 (Tent. Draft No. 5, 1970). This is a concept not capable of precise definition. An agreement between the parties to a lease, designed to shift significantly among the parties responsibility for the condition of the premises (from what it would otherwise be in the absence of the agreement), must be tested by this somewhat vague and imprecise rule. An agreement or provision may be against public policy if it will materially and unreasonably obstruct achievement of a well defined statutory, regulatory, or common law policy.

Although, in the interest of certainty, the provisions of written lease instruments should not be disregarded lightly for insubstantial reasons, factors which may be considered in determining whether an agreement in a lease is in whole or in part unenforceable, because unconscionable or against public policy, include:

(1) Whether and to what extent the agreement will be counter to the policy underlying statutory or regulatory provisions, especially those relating to the public health and safety and those relating to the tenants of moderate income in multi-unit residential or office properties;

(2) Whether the agreement or provision appears in a lease of commercial or industrial property or of an entire building or a large portion of a building, or of a substantial residence or estate designed for single family occupancy, properties concerning which freedom of negotiation is usually permissible;

(3) Whether and to what extent the agreement or provision serves a reasonable business purpose and appears to have been the result of conscious negotiations for the distribution of risks as part of the total bargain contained in the lease;

(4) Whether the provision appears to be part of an unduly harsh and unreasonable standard, "boilerplate" lease document;

(5) Whether and to what extent the parties or either of them, habitually (or on a discriminatory basis) disregard and do not enforce the agreement or provision in actual operations under the lease or, in the case of a landlord, under similar leases;

(6) Whether and to what extent the agreement or provision (especially if it relates to low or moderate income residential property) imposes unreasonable liabilities or burdens on persons who are financially ill-equipped to assume those burdens and who may have had significant inequality of bargaining power; and

(7) Whether and to what extent the parties were each represented by counsel in the course of negotiating the lease.

CHAPTER 20

ASSIGNMENT AND SUBLETTING

In reading the cases in this chapter, always ask yourself what the rights and duties of the following parties would be if the same issues arose between them:
1. the landlord against the original tenant, and vice versa;
2. the landlord against the transferee (either assignee or subtenant), and vice versa;
3. the original tenant against the transferee (either assignee or subtenant), and vice versa.

Although frequently blurred in some transactions, you will find that there are clear and significant differences between an assignment and a sublease.[1] Ask yourself if the parties would have been better served if they had chosen one or the other form of structuring their transaction.

SECTION 1. LIABILITY OF THE TENANT AFTER ASSIGNMENT (HEREIN PRIVITY OF CONTRACT)[2]

SAMUELS v. OTTINGER
169 Cal. 209, 146 P. 638 (1915)

SLOSS, J. The plaintiff appeals from a judgment in favor of the defendant. The judgment disposed of three separate actions, which, with the consent of the parties, had been consolidated for trial. The appeal is on the judgment-roll.

---

1. See generally 1 Friedman on Leases §7.4 (1976).
2. See generally 49 Am. Jur. 2d Landlord and Tenant §437 et seq.

The actions were brought to recover installments of monthly rent accruing under a written lease of real property. The three proceedings differed only in the months for which rental was claimed.

A jury trial having been waived, the court made findings as follows: On December 20, 1906, D. Samuels Realty Company, a corporation, as lessor, leased to the defendants, as lessees, a certain lot in the city of San Francisco. A copy of the lease is set out in the answers and referred to by the findings. The term of the lease was ten years, commencing on the twentieth day of December, 1906. The rent of the premises was one hundred and fifty dollars per month, payable in advance, for the first five years of the term, and one hundred and seventy-five dollars per month, payable in advance, for the next five years. Other provisions of the lease will be mentioned in the course of the discussion to follow.

The defendants went into possession of the premises under the lease, and paid the monthly installments of rent to and including the nineteenth day of May, 1908. On that day they sold and assigned the lease to one Altschular. The lessor was at the same time, notified of the assignment. Altschular paid the rent for the month commencing May 20, 1908, and said payment was received and accepted by the lessor. The monthly installments of rent payable on the twentieth days of the successive months from June, 1908, to March, 1910, have not been paid. D. Samuels Realty Company, the original lessor, has conveyed the premises, and assigned its claim against the defendants, to the plaintiff.

The single question presented for decision is whether the defendants, the original lessees, are absolved from liability to pay rent by their assignment to Altschular, and the payment by Altschular to the lessor of one month's rent. The general rule of law governing the controversy is settled beyond the possibility of dispute. A lease has a dual character — it presents the aspect of a contract and also that of a conveyance. (Pollock on Contracts, 3d Am. ed., p. 531.) "Consequently the lease has two sets of rights and obligations — one comprising those growing out of the relation of landlord and tenant, and said to be based on the 'privity of estate,' and the other comprising those growing out of the express stipulations of the lease, and so said to be based on 'privity of contract.' " (Tiffany on Real Property, sec. 46.) An obligation to pay rent, without an express agreement to that end, arises from the mere occupancy as tenant, of the premises. A lessee who has not agreed to pay rent is, by his transfer to an assignee, with the consent of the landlord, relieved of any further obligation to pay rent. Such obligation is thereafter upon the assignee who has come into "privity of estate" with the landlord. But where the lessee has expressly agreed to pay rent, his liability under his contract remains, notwithstanding an assignment with the consent of the lessor. "The lessee cannot by assigning his lease rid himself of liability under the covenants." (Brosnon v. Kramer, 135 Cal. 36, 39, 66 P. 979, 980.) "The effect of the assignment is to make the lessee a surety to the lessor for the assignee, who, as between himself and the lessor, is the principal bound, whilst he is assignee, to pay the rent and perform the covenants." (Id.; Wood on Landlord and Tenant, 2d ed., sec. 347; Bonetti v. Treat, 91 Cal. 223, 14 L.R.A. 151, 27 P. 612; Sutliff v. Atwood, 15 Ohio St. 186; Sexton v. Chicago Storage Co., 129 Ill. 318, 16 Am. St. Rep. 274, 21 N.E. 920.)

The test of the assigning lessee's liability is, then, whether he has, in the lease, agreed to pay rent during the term. The rule of law is sometimes phrased thus: The obligation to pay rent remains on the lessee, after his assignment, when the obligation was created by his express agreement. It does not survive an assignment with the lessor's consent when the obligation is implied. By "express agreement," in this connection, is meant not merely a promise, in exact words, to pay a given sum as rental; any language necessarily importing an undertaking on the part of the lessee to pay the rent will satisfy the requirement of the rule. For the distinction to which we have referred rests on the nature of the lessee's obligation. If that obligation arises solely from the fact that he occupies the premises as tenant, if, in other words, it is based on the "privity of estate" alone, the assignee who succeeds to that privity becomes the party to whom the landlord must look. But if the obligation be one arising from the tenant's contract to pay rent, it is not ended by the assignment. Whether there be a contract to pay rent must depend on whether such contract is to be found in the words of the lease, giving such words a fair and reasonable interpretation. (Tiffany, on Landlord and Tenant, sec. 50.)

The lease in question was executed by the lessees, as well as by the lessor. It begins by stating that the lessor leases the premises to the lessees, for the term of ten years, at the monthly rental above stated, "payable in advance on the twentieth day of each and every month." By subsequent clauses the lessees agree to pay all bills for water, gas, and electricity furnished to the premises, and all taxes on improvements to be erected by said lessees. The privilege of subleasing is expressly given, as is permission to erect buildings, which, if they comply with certain conditions, are to be purchased by the lessor at the expiration of the term. The lessees agree to insure the improvements, "and said insurance shall be made payable to the lessor and the lessees jointly, for the purpose of securing the said lessor in the payment of the rents herein stipulated. . . ." By another clause it is agreed that the improvements to be erected "shall be security for the rent herein stipulated to be paid. . . ." Finally, it is agreed that if the lessees hold over beyond the term provided in the lease, such holding over shall be deemed merely a tenancy from month to month, "and at the same monthly rental that shall have been payable hereunder by said lessees immediately prior to such holding over."

If it is possible to express a contractual obligation to pay rent by any form of words other than a direct promise, in exact terms, to pay such rent, the language we have quoted from the lease before us, imposes that obligation on the lessees. The lessor agrees to lease the premises to the lessees at a given rental, "payable" at stated times. The writing is signed by the lessees as well as by the lessor. Where both parties sign an agreement whereby one agrees to sell to the other a tract of land at a certain price, and to convey a good title upon payment of that price, the writing, as has been held in this court, imposes upon the vendee the obligation to buy and pay for the land, although he has not in words agreed to buy or to pay. (Preble Abrahams, 88 Cal. 245, 22 Am. St. Rep. 301, 26 P. 99; see, also, King Keystone Oil Co. v. San Francisco Brick Co., 148 Cal. 87, 82 Pac. 839.)

But beyond this, there are various other provisions in the lease plainly indicating the intention and understanding of the parties that the lessees were bound to pay the rent. Insurance is to be taken out for the purpose of securing the lessor in the "payment of the rents herein stipulated." Improvements are to be security for the rent "herein stipulated to be paid." A holding over shall be deemed a tenancy from month to month at the same monthly rental as shall have been "payable hereunder by said lessees" prior to such holding over. We find, first, a reference to the payment of "rents herein stipulated," then a provision for security for "rent herein stipulated to be paid," and finally a clause which speaks of "rents payable hereunder by said lessees." These expressions afford a convincing showing that the parties to the lease believed and understood that the writing embodied a "stipulation" for the payment of rents, and that it made such rents payable by the lessees. The obligation to pay rent is not implied from the relation of landlord and tenant, but is expressed by the words used by the parties in their writing.

There are decisions to the effect that a lease which merely provides for a letting upon a certain rental, "payable at the expiration of each and every year of the lease" (Fanning v. Stimson, 13 Iowa 42), or which demises the premises to the tenant, he "yielding and paying" certain rents (Kimpton v. Walker, 9 Vt. 191), creates only an implied obligation, which does not survive an assignment of the leasehold interest and acceptance of rent from the assignee. On the other hand, a contrary view has been declared in cases involving the liability of a lessee to pay rent notwithstanding the destruction of the buildings by fire. The obligation to pay rent in the event of such destruction rests upon the lessee where the lease contains a covenant on his part to pay rent during the term, and the underlying principle is therefore the same as that governing the case at bar. A covenant to pay rent was held to be expressed in a lease, signed by both parties, in which the lessor let the premises to the lessee for two years, "for $300.00 per annum, payable quarter-yearly." (Linn v. Ross, 10 Ohio 412 (36 Am. Dec. 95).) So of a lease of land with a building, "at the rent of six hundred dollars per annum, until the first day of April, 1869, and thereafter, for the term of five years, at the rate of eight hundred dollars per annum, the rent to be paid monthly." (Bussman v. Ganster, 72 Pa. St. 285.)

But if it be held that mere words of demise, "at" or "subject to" a given rental, "payable" at stated times, will not import an agreement by the lessee to pay rent, the other provisions of the lease are certainly sufficient to establish such agreement. In this aspect the case is very similar to Consumers' Ice Co. v. Bixler, 84 Md. 437, 35 A. 1086, where the court reached the conclusion just expressed by us. . . .

The judgment is reversed, with directions to the court below to enter judgment in favor of the plaintiff as prayed in the three several complaints.

SHAW, J., LORIGAN, J., MELVIN, J., and ANGELLOTTI, C.J., concurred.

Problem

20.1. L and T execute a lease giving T the right to assign the lease. T assigns the lease to T_1, who later defaults in the payment of rent. L recovers a judgment against T_1 for the amount of the rent due. If that judgment is not satisfied by T_1, may L then sue T for the same default in rent? If so, on what basis? If T pays the rent due, may T sue T_1 for the amount of such payment? If so, on what basis? See American Law of Property §§3.61, 3.64 (Casner ed. 1952).

SECTION 2. LIABILITY OF THE TENANT'S ASSIGNEE (HEREIN PRIVITY OF ESTATE AND COVENANTS IN LEASES THAT RUN WITH THE LAND)[3]

REID v. WIESSNER BREWING CO.
88 Md. 234, 40 A. 877 (Md. 1898)

McSHERRY, C.J., delivered the opinion of the court.

This suit was instituted in the Superior Court of Baltimore City by the appellant against the appellee. The appellant by a deed under seal leased to one Charles Miller certain premises for the period of five years from September the fourteenth, eighteen hundred and ninety-five, at and for an annual rent of twelve hundred dollars payable in equal monthly installments. Miller covenanted to pay the rent, and he likewise covenanted that he would not assign or sub-let the premises without the written permission of the lessor. On the same day the lessee, with the written assent of the lessor given by her agent, assigned the lease, "with all its covenants, terms and conditions," to the appellee, a body corporate. On June the thirtieth, eighteen hundred and ninety-seven, the appellee assigned the lease to John W. Jones. This suit was brought on August the fourth, eighteen hundred and

---

3. See generally Chapter 16 of Restatement (Second) of Property (Landlord and Tenant).

ninety-seven, to recover from the appellee four installments of rent which fell due in April, May, June and July, eighteen hundred and ninety-seven. To the declaration three pleas were filed. The first and second need not be alluded to. The third, after confessing the assignment of the lease by Miller to the appellee, averred by way of avoidance, that after such assignment and before suit brought, the defendant, now the appellee, by a proper instrument, assigned all its rights and interest in the lease to one John W. Jones. To this plea a demurrer was interposed, but was overruled. Thereupon three replications were filed to the same plea. Upon the first there was a joinder of issue, and to the second and third the defendant demurred. This demurrer was sustained. The case then proceeded to trial. At the close of the evidence each party presented one prayer for instruction to the jury. The plaintiff's prayer was rejected; the defendant's was granted. The verdict and judgment were rendered for the defendant and the plaintiff has appealed.

The declaration presents the case of a lessor suing an assignee of a lease for the non-payment of rent covenanted to be paid by the lessee. That and that alone is the cause of action declared on.

The liability of an assignee of a term to the original lessor for rent grows out of and is founded on the privity of estate, in the absence of an independent agreement; and such liability continues, when dependent upon privity of estate alone, just so long as that privity exists. During the continuance of that privity the assignee is liable upon all covenants that run with the land, such as covenants for the payment of rent and the like, and for any breach of such covenants the lessor may sue the assignee during the continuance of the assignment. As his liability, in the absence of an independent agreement, arises wholly from his relation to the land, it results and is everywhere held, that when he severs that relation, he puts an end to his liability for any future breaches of covenants contained in the lease; and it is equally well settled in this State, though a different doctrine prevails in some other jurisdictions, that an action at law by a lessor against an assignee for a breach of a covenant running with the land, if not brought before the assignee divests himself of the estate, cannot be maintained against him at all. Hintze v. Thomas, 7 Md. 346; Donelson v. Polk, 64 Md. 504; Bixler v. Consumers Ice Co., 84 Md. 437. In the last-cited case, whilst the doctrine just announced was recognized and reaffirmed, the assignee was held liable, not as assignee, or by reason of the assignment, but solely in consequence of a distinct, independent agreement between the lessor and the assignee.

This being the extent of an assignee's liability to the original lessor where no independent agreement is relied on, and the declaration in the pending case, proceeding, as it does, wholly and exclusively upon the liability arising out of the privity of estate existing between the lessor and the assignee; the plea which confessed the assignment but set up by way of defence that the privity of estate had been terminated by the subsequent assignment to Jones before the suit had been brought, presented, if true, a complete and an insuperable bar to the action. There was obviously, then, no error in overruling the demurrer interposed to it. And this brings us to the second and third replications that were demurred to by the defendant.

The second replication avers that the brewing company did not, with the consent in writing of the plaintiff, assign all its right and interest in the lease to Jones. We are dealing now entirely with the pleadings. The declaration alleges that Miller, the lessee, covenanted that he would not assign nor sub-let the premises without the written permission of the lessor; and it further alleges that Miller did with the written consent of the lessor, assign the lease with all its covenants, terms and conditions, to the brewing company. The covenant prohibiting an assignment was, as is conceded by and alleged in the declaration, unqualifiedly waived when the assignment was made by Miller, and having been thus waived, that is, waived without the superaddition of a restriction on subsequent assignments, it was gone forever and therefore was not binding on the brewing company. This principle was announced as early as the reign of Elizabeth in Dumpor's case, 4 Coke 119. Whilst Sir James Mansfield observed that the profession had always wondered at Dumpor's case, still he held in Doe v. Bliss, 4 Taunt. 736, that the decision had "been law so many centuries that" it could not be reversed. Later decisions have carried the doctrine even farther than as applied in Dumpor's case, for it is held that whether the license to assign be general, as in Dumpor's case, or particular as "to one particular person subject to the performance of the covenants in the original lease," still the condition is gone in both instances and the assignee may assign without license. Brummel v. Macpherson, 14 Ves. 173; Taylor's Land. and Ten., sec. 410. The restriction having been waived by the lessor as to the assignment made by Miller, the lessee, the brewing company was not bound by that restrictive covenant, and consequently no assent on the part of the lessor to the assignment by the brewing company to Jones was necessary; and such assent not being necessary the assignment made without it was perfectly valid. The replication, then, in setting up the want of such assent, when no assent was requisite, was clearly bad and the demurrer to it was properly sustained.[4]

The third replication avers that by an assignment under seal dated September the fourteenth, eighteen hundred and ninety-five, and executed by Miller, the lessee, Mrs. Reid, the lessor, and the brewing company, the assignee, said lease with all its covenants, terms and conditions, was assigned and set over to the brewing company. This was demurred to. If it was designed by this replication to set up and to rely on an independent agreement between the lessor and the assignee, and thus to found a right of recovery on a distinct contractual relation between them it is bad, as a replication, because a clear departure. And it is a departure because the declaration proceeds upon the single ground of a liability arising out of the

---

4. The ancient rule of Dumpor's case, as noted above, has been criticized frequently; however, it is generally the law in many jurisdictions. Consider why this is so.—Eds.

privity of estate and not out of a privity of contract. The replication presented no issue at all if it did not mean this, for it merely repeated precisely what had been admitted in the plea and averred in the declaration. There was certainly, therefore, no error in sustaining the demurrer to it.

The prayers are brief and read as follows: Plaintiff's prayer: "That the paper dated June 30th, 1897, and offered in evidence, does not operate as an assignment of the lease, assigned to defendant, dated Sept. 14th, 1895." This was rejected. Defendant's prayer: "The jury are hereby instructed that the uncontradicted evidence in this case being that the defendant, on the 30th day of June A.D. 1897, assigned the lease offered in evidence in this case to John W. Jones, their verdict must be for the defendant." This was granted. The assignment of the lease by Miller to the brewing company is in these words: "For value received, and as security for a loan, with the consent of the landlord, I hereby assign and set over this lease with all its covenants, terms and conditions to the John F. Wiessner and Sons Brewing Company of Baltimore City, a body corporate." And the assignment by the brewing company to Jones is thus set out in the record: "For value received the John F. Weissner and Sons Brewing Company doth assign the above mortgage or security for loan[5]; and all its rights, title and interest therein, to John W. Jones," etc. It was strenuously insisted in the argument that the terms of the assignment by Miller included an express covenant on the part of the brewing company to pay the rent; and that, therefore, the case fell within the principle laid down in Bixler v. Ice Co., *supra.* To this we cannot agree. Assuming that this question is brought before us by the prayers though it obviously is not by the pleadings as we have already pointed out—the contention is wholly untenable. There is certainly no undertaking, promise or agreement in express terms, on the part of the brewing company to pay the rent which Miller specifically covenanted to pay; and unless the assignment of the lease, *"with all its covenants, terms and conditions,"* has a wider scope that a bare assignment unaccompanied by the words in italics would have had, there is no independent agreement binding the company at all. These words, "with all its covenants, terms and conditions," add nothing to the legal effect of the assignment. They certainly are not contractual words of the assignee. They embody no promise by the brewing company to the lessor. They are simply words of description and not words of contract, and they impose no greater obligation to the brewing company than would have existed had they been entirely omitted from the assignment. Wahl v. Barroll, 8 Gill 288; Walveridge v. Steward, 30 E.C.L.R. 312. In Bixler's case there was a distinct agreement on the part of the assignee to perform all the covenants of the lease which the lessee had undertaken to perform; and the

---

5.   Note that the assignment of the lease by Miller to the Wiessner Brewing Co. "as security for a loan" occurred on the very day the lease with L was signed! In determining "privity of estate" questions, is a leasehold mortgagee (i.e., the collateral assignee of a tenant's leasehold estate) liable prior to actually taking possession? As to leasehold mortgagees and the liability of the leasehold mortgagee for rent and other tenant obligations, see 1 Friedman on Leases §7.802 (1976).—Eds.

suit was brought on that agreement, and the liability was not made to rest solely and exclusively upon the privity of estate, as it is in this case.

This view of the legal effect of the assignment by Miller, and the conclusions we have reached and expressed upon the questions of pleading first discussed, cover all the issues presented by the record, and sufficiently indicate that there was no error committed in the rulings on the prayers for instructions to the jury. The judgment will, therefore, be affirmed.

Judgment affirmed with costs above and below.

Problem

20.2. The Wiessner Brewing Co. (T_1) used the premises during April, May, June, and July without paying rent. The court not only held that it did not have to pay the rent for the month following its assignment to Jones (T_2) but also decided that it did not have to pay rent for April, May, or June! Who would be liable for the rent for those months — T or T_2? If T_1 had expressly promised L that it would pay the rent, would T continue to be liable for the rent?

MASURY v. SOUTHWORTH
9 Ohio St. 340 (1859)

In error to the District Court of Cuyahoga County.

The plaintiff in error brought an action against the defendants in error, in the court of common pleas of Cuyahoga County. The petition in that action stated, that on the 25th day of February, 1854, S. A. Powers and Joseph C. Foster executed a lease, which was duly acknowledged and recorded. By this lease, a lot in the city of Cleveland, was demised by Powers to Foster, for a term beginning on the 1st day of April, 1854, and ending the 1st day of July, 1867. The petition alleged "that, by one of the covenants in said lease, the said Foster was to keep said leasehold premises fully insured for the benefit of Powers, and that, if at any time the said Foster should fail to keep the same so insured, that the said Powers might cause insurance to be placed on said premises at the expense of said Foster, and in the name and for the benefit of said Powers. And by a further stipulation in said lease, it was further agreed that, in case that said building should burn down during the continuance of said lease, that the said Foster should have the benefit of said insurance money for the purpose of rebuilding said premises, in case he should elect to rebuild the same." The petition further stated, that on the 14th of October, 1854, "Powers assigned and sold to plaintiff all his interest in said lease"; and "that the interest of Foster in said premises and lease was sold under an order of court to satisfy judgments against said Foster, and that the defendants became the purchasers of said Foster's interest in said premises at said sale." It is also stated, that the defendants went into possession of said premises; that at the time they went into possession, a policy procured by Foster was running; that when it expired the plaintiff notified the defendants to insure the premises, which they neglected and refused to do. The amount which the plaintiff claims to recover is what it had cost him to procure an insurance on the premises.

The lease is referred to as a part of the petition. It states that the lease of the lot is made "at and for the rents and conditions hereinafter specified; to have and to hold the leased and demised premises upon the terms and conditions hereinafter specified." Among the terms and conditions so specified is found the covenant to insure, stated in the body of the petition. In connection with that covenant, and preceding it, was one that the lessee "will erect upon said premises a good and substantial brick building, the height of which shall be equal to that of the building on Bank street, known," etc.; which covenant contained a description of the size and style of the building, and the use to which it was to be put — the rooms on the ground floor to be "used and kept for store-rooms, during the continuance of this lease." It is this building, by the terms of the lease, which is to be kept fully insured.

To the petition of the plaintiff, the defendants filed a demurrer, upon the ground, that it did not contain facts sufficient to constitute a cause of action.

This demurrer was sustained by the court of common pleas, and judgment entered against the plaintiff.

To reverse this judgment a petition in error was filed in the district court, where the judgment was affirmed.

To reverse the judgment of affirmance in the district court, upon leave obtained, a petition in error was filed in this court.

GHOLSON, J. In consequence of the rule of the common law, that a chose in action was not assignable, the assignee of a reversion could not maintain an action upon a covenant contained in a lease, against the lessee, though the covenant might run with the land. There was a distinction made between the assignee of the reversion, and the assignee of the lease; and while the latter might maintain, and be liable to, an action upon such a covenant, it was different as to the former. To remedy this, the statute of 32 H. 8, cap. 34, was enacted, which gave, generally, to the assignee of the reversion the same right of action that the lessor had, upon the covenants in the lease. But this statute did not extend to mere personal and collateral covenants; it embraced those only which touched and concerned the thing demised.

It has been decided by this court, that the statute of 32 H. 8, cap. 34, is not in force in this state, and that an assignee of the reversion cannot maintain an action upon the covenants in the lease. But if the covenant be assignable in equity, so that an action might have been maintained in the name of the assignor, or relief obtained by a suit in equity, our code of civil procedure operates upon the remedy, even more extensively than the statute of 32 H. 8, cap. 34. For whether the covenant be collateral, or inhere in the land, if it be assigned, the assignee not only may, but, as the party beneficially interested, must sue in his own name. For example, if there be a contract by a lessee to build a house or a wall upon the land, at any time, and whether to be used by the lessee or not, the lessor, in selling the reversion, may also assign the benefit of such a contract, and the action of the assignee for a breach would, under the code, be in his own name.

In the present action, it may be inferred from the pleadings that the lessor, Powers, has assigned to the plaintiff the covenant to keep the house insured for the benefit of the lessor and lessee. This covenant Powers might well assign; and the plaintiff, being the assignee of the reversion, and entitled also to the benefit of the covenant, might bring an action for its breach, in his own name, against the lessee of Powers. But does this right of action extend to the assignee of the lessee? It may be, that the lessee would be liable on the covenant, but not the assignee of the lessee. There is a manifest difference between assigning a right of action, and creating, by assignment, a liability to an action. The latter must, generally, assume the shape of a contract to indemnify, and could not usually affect the rights of the party holding the original claim. It would be really a new contract, and not in the nature of an assignment of another contract. In this view of the liability of an assignee of the lease to the assignee of the reversion, the principle governing the assignment of a chose in action, or the benefit of a covenant, must be thrown out of view, and the inquiry be made on other principles and considerations.

The covenant must run with the land — must be so connected with, be attached to, and inhere in the land, that the assignee of the reversion or the assignee of the lease, as the case may be, would have a right to the advantage of it, or be bound to perform it. Such is the general principle; but whether a covenant so runs with the land, must depend, in the first place, upon the nature and character of the particular covenant and of the estate demised, as connected with the respective rights of lessor and lessee in reference to the subject-matter of the covenant; and, in the next place, upon the intent of the parties in the creation of the estate, as shown by the language of the instrument creating it, construed with reference to the relative position of the parties, and to the subject-matter to which their contract and convey-ance is to be applied. The nature and character of the covenant may be such, that it may run with the land; and yet, if it be clearly the agreement of the parties that it shall not so run, it would not be annexed, in spite of the agreement so expressed. And, on the contrary, however clearly and strongly expressed may be the intent and agreement of the parties, that the covenant shall run with the land, yet, if it be of such a character that the law does not permit it to be attached, it cannot be attached by the agreement of the parties, and the assignee would take the estate clear of any such covenant.

From this view, it is obvious that, as to the first point, the nature and character of a covenant which may inhere in the land, we are to look at the reason and policy of the law; and, as to the second point, whether it does so inhere as to give a right and create an obligation in the case of assignees, we must look at the intent of the parties creating the estate. The law must say that it may inhere, and the parties must say that it shall inhere.

The first point depends upon a question of public policy. It would be mischievous and inconvenient to allow every species of covenant, which wit or caprice might devise, however collateral to the use of the land demised, to be connected with the estate. Therefore, from the earliest times, the distinction between such covenants as may run with the land, and such as are collateral and cannot, has been taken and maintained. It has been a matter of some dispute, whether a covenant to insure might run with the land. A covenant, to run with the land, must have for its subject-matter something which sustains the estate and the enjoyment of it, and is, therefore, beneficial both to lessor and lessee. A covenant to insure, which had for its object the benefit of the lessor only, as where the money paid in the event of a loss would go to him, has been regarded as collateral; but if the money is to be applied to repair or rebuild, then it is in its character like a covenant to repair, which may run with the land. Under this view, we think the covenant to insure, in the present case, was one which might run with the land.

The second point is one which, in its application to the present case, in view of the decisions and dicta in England and in this country, presents considerable difficulty. When any effect, such as to pass an estate or create an obligation, is dependent upon the intent of parties as expressed in a writing, it is an important inquiry whether the law has prescribed certain words or expressions as essential to be used to indicate that intent. If it be so, those words must be used, and none others will suffice. The word "heirs," in the case of a conveyance to create an estate in fee-simple, is an instance. But where the law has prescribed no such words, then the intent of the parties must be ascertained from the whole instrument, interpreted and construed by just and proper rules. In the latter class of cases, as a general rule, whether the intent be very clearly and plainly expressed, or be ascertained after some difficulty by the rules of construction, can make no difference. It is not a question of degree. The intent is either expressed or it is not, and the effect is the same without reference to the degree of clearness.

In determining whether a particular covenant was intended to run with the land, the fact that its particular subject-matter was not in existence at the time the estate was created, is undoubtedly very important and material, and in many instances might be regarded as a controlling consideration. In such a case, though the subject-matter be connected with the land, as a house or wall to be built upon it at a future day during the term, yet if nothing more appeared to indicate the intent, it might be regarded as a personal covenant, and not running with the land. If, however, an intent be shown that the covenant shall run with the land, by binding the "assigns" in so many words, then the covenant does run with the land, and the assignee of the lease is bound. Thus it was resolved, in the leading case upon this subject:

If the lessee had covenanted for him and his assigns that they would make a new wall upon some part of the thing demised, that forasmuch as it is to be done upon the land demised, that it should bind the assignee; for although the covenant doth extend to a thing to be newly made, yet is to be made upon the thing demised, and the assignee is to take the benefit of it, and therefore shall bind the assignee by express words. [Spencer's case, 5 Coke, 16b.]

In the first resolution of the same case it had been said:

When the covenant extends to a thing in esse, parcel of the demise, if the thing to be done by force of covenant is in any manner annexed and appurtenant to the thing demised, it shall go with the land and bind the assignee, although he be not bound by express words; but where the covenant extends to a thing which is not in being at the time of the demise made, it cannot be appurtenant or annexed to the thing which hath no being.

And it was further said as to the case at bar:

The covenant concerns a thing (a wall) which was not in esse at the time of the demise made, but to be newly built after, and therefore shall bind the covenantor, his executors and administrators, and not the assignee, for the law will not annex the covenant to a thing which hath no being.

Between the first and second resolutions in Spencer's case, there is an apparent inconsistency, and the unsatisfactory character of the second resolution has been a subject of remark and comment. In the first resolution it seems to be considered that the law will not permit such a covenant as the one under consideration — a covenant to build a wall upon the land demised — to be annexed to the estate and run with the land. And if this be so, on the ground that it is to be regarded as a collateral covenant, not proper to be annexed to the land, then the concluding part of the second resolution shows that the agreement of the parties, whether expressed by the word "assigns," or otherwise, could not make it a covenant running with the land and binding upon the assignee. Yet, in the second resolution, it is said, of a supposed case, if the lessee had covenanted for him and his assigns, it would bind the assignee by express words: and thus showing, apparently, in a case in which it had been before said, that the covenant could not be appurtenant or annexed to the land, that the parties might make it so. It is to be observed, however, that in the second resolution an element is introduced, not found in the statement of the case in the first resolution, viz.: that the building of the wall would be beneficial to the estate demised, and the assignee would have the benefit of it. The result, then, would be, that if the thing to be done upon the land, though not existing at the time of the demise, would be of a permanent nature, connected with the use and enjoyment of the land, and beneficial to the assignee, an intent that it should run with the land and bind the assignee, shown by naming him in the deed, would be effectual.

Thus understood, the two resolutions are not inconsistent, and there may have been some omission in expressing the second resolution which has led to the apparent inconsistency. The question then arises, whether an intent to bind the assignee, in the case of such a covenant, may be effectual without the word "assigns"? Whether that word is used in the technical sense, and cannot be supplied by other words. If, for example, in the case stated, instead of "for him and his assigns," it was said "for him and any other person or persons to whom the estate demised shall be conveyed," or other equivalent words.

Our conclusion, is, that the word "assigns" is not used in a technical sense and as the only word appropriate for the purpose, but that equivalent words, or any clear manifestation of intent will suffice. We think the real question must be, the covenant being one which may be annexed to the estate and run with the land, whether such was the intention of the parties, as expressed in the deed. The important consideration is, whether the covenant is annexed to the estate and runs with the land. If this be so, the rights and liabilities of those who take the estate and possess the land during the term, flow from a privity of estate, and not from any assignment of right or contract. If the covenant cannot, or does not, run with the land, no words of assignment can create a privity of estate; if a privity of estate be created, no words of assignment are necessary. The word "assigns" could only show that the covenant was intended to run with the land, for if the covenant were otherwise attached to the land and the privity of estate created, as in the ordinary case of covenant to repair, that word is shown by all the authorities not to be requisite to bind the assignee of the lease.

Upon principle and authority, "the law does not require any particular form of words to constitute such a covenant which shall run with the land." Trill v. Eastman, 3 Metcalf, 121-124. "Any words in a deed, which show an agreement to do a thing, make a covenant." Williams v. Burrell, 1 M.G. & S. 402-429, Comyns Dig. Tit. Covenant. "To charge a party with a covenant, it is not necessary that there should be express words of covenant or agreement. It is enough if the intention of the parties to create a covenant be apparent." Wolveridge v. Steward, 3 M. & S. 561 (30 E.C.L. 312); Courtenay v. Taylor, 6. M. & G. 851; Williams v. Burrell, 1 C.B. 402-430; Great N. Railway Co. v. Harrison, 12 C.B. 576-609; Savage v. Mason, 3 Cushing, 500-505.

In the present case, that the covenant to keep the building fully insured, was intended to accompany the estate in the event of any assignment, is, we think, shown as well by the immediate object in view as by the language. The land demised was a vacant lot to be rendered more productive and valuable by an improvement corresponding with those on other lots in the neighborhood. It was to be improved with a view to permanent and continuous business — the rooms were to be kept and used for stores. That the lot might lie unimproved, or the building after its erection be burned and not be rebuilt, either by lessor or lessee, was never contemplated by the parties. The language in the instrument is, that the lease was made "at and for the rents and conditions" specified; and it was to be held "upon the terms and conditions" expressed. We feel, therefore, authorized, for the reasons given and for others on which it is not necessary to enlarge, to use an expression of the American annotators on Spencer's case, and say, that the covenant to insure in this case did not relate solely to something not in esse at the time it was made, but related to the land so directly and in such manner that it may bind an assignee of the lessee. 1 Smith's Leading Cases, Am. Ed. 177.

We are aware that there are authorities which may be regarded as in conflict with the views we have taken, and there are others by which they are sustained. Among the former we have not overlooked the recent case of Doughty v. Bowman, 11 Q.B. 444; and among the latter we may name Kellogg v. Robinson, 6 Verm. 276. We do not think proper to cite, much less to review and compare, the authorities which we have examined. The most of them contain a mere repetition of the resolutions in Spencer's case. It may be noticed, however, that one of the earlier cases, Bally v. Wells, is differently stated in the reports, and that one statement would strongly favor the view we have taken, while the other might not. 3 Wilson, 25; Wilmot's Notes, 344; Allen v. Culver, 3 Denio, 296-7. . . .

Judgment reversed.[6]

Problems

20.3. L and T enter into a written lease of certain premises. The lease contains a covenant by L to keep the premises in repair. T assigns the lease to T_1. After such assignment, the leased premises need repairs, and T sues L for breach of L's covenant to keep the premises in repair. Is T entitled to maintain such a suit? Would T_1 be entitled to maintain such a suit? See American Law of Property §§9.1, 9.5 (Casner ed. 1952).

20.4. L and T enter into a written lease of certain premises. The lease contains a covenant by T to keep the premises in repair. T assigns the lease to T_1. After such assignment, the leased premises need repairs, but T_1 has not made them. T sues T_1 for the damage caused to the leased premises by virtue of the failure of T_1 to keep the premises in repair. Is T entitled to recover? Would L be entitled to sue T_1? See Farrington v. Kimball, 126 Mass. 313 (1879). See also American Law of Property §3.61 (Casner ed. 1952); id. §9.5.

---

6. The running of the benefit and the burden of covenants relating to the use of land inserted in deeds conveying the fee is dealt with in Part VIII. As to the running of the benefit and the burden of covenants in leases, see generally Bigelow, The Content of Covenants in Leases, 12 Mich. L. Rev. 639 (1914); Abbott, Covenants in a Lease Which Run With the Land, 31 Yale L.J. 127 (1921); American Law of Property §§9.1-9.7 (Casner ed. 1952).—EDS.

20.5. L and T enter into a written lease of certain premises. The lease contains a covenant as follows:

> The said lessor should purchase the improvements upon said land at the end of the term at a valuation to be agreed upon by the parties, or if they cannot so agree, at a valuation to be ascertained by three disinterested referees; or if the lessor shall prefer not to purchase said improvements, the lessees shall purchase said land.

L transfers L's interest to L_1. At the end of the term of the lease, L_1 refuses to sell the land to T and takes possession of the land; L_1 also refuses to pay for the improvements T has placed on the land. What are T's rights? See Carpenter v. Pocasset Manufacturing Co., 180 Mass. 130, 61 N.E. 816 (1901); Judkins v. Charette, 255 Mass. 76, 151 N.E. 81 (1926). See also American Law of Property §9.4 (Casner ed. 1952).

20.6. L executed a one-year lease with T, "with an option to renew said lease for a further term of five years, at the expiration of the one year, and with a further option of five years at the expiration of the first five-year option." During the initial year, T assigned the lease to T_1. T_1 wishes to exercise the option to renew. May T_1 exercise the option? Assume T_1 duly exercised the first option to renew and duly exercised the second option to renew. During the period covered by the second option, T_1 defaulted in the payment of rent and taxes (the original lease contained a covenant by T that these items would be paid) and subsequently vacated the premises. In L's action against T for the unpaid rent and taxes, T defends on the ground that T duly assigned the lease to T_1 and that when T_1 exercised the options to renew a new contract was formed between L and T_1, thus relieving T of any liability. What decision? Kornblum v. Henry E. Mangels Co., 167 So. 2d 16 (Fla. Dist. Ct. App. 1964). See also Annot., 10 A.L.R.3d 818 (1966).

SECTION 3.   LIABILITY OF THE TENANT'S SUBTENANT[7]

DAVIS v. VIDAL
105 Tex. 444, 151 S.W. 290 (1912)

Error to the Court of Civil Appeals, Fourth District, in an appeal from El Paso County.

Mrs. Davis sued Vidal, and appealed from a judgment for defendant, on affirmance of which she obtained writ of error.

---

7. As between tenant and subtenant, see generally 49 Am. Jur. 2d Landlord and Tenant §503 et seq. and as between landlord and subtenant id. §508 et seq.

DIBRELL, J., delivered the opinion of the court.

This is a suit by Antoinette W. Davis brought in the District Court of El Paso County against Lewis Vidal, to recover the sum of $1,200.00, alleged to be due her by Vidal for the use of certain premises situated in the City of El Paso, of which Vidal was in possession as the assignee of the Dallas Brewery. The sole question of law involved in the case is whether a certain instrument of writing executed by the Dallas Brewery to the defendant, Vidal, on October 1, 1907, was an assignment of its lease from the plaintiff, Antoinette W. Davis, of date April 26, 1907, or a sub-letting of the premises in question. If the instrument referred to was an assignment of the lease then plaintiff was authorized to recover of the defendant the rent due on her contract of lease with the Dallas Brewery, by virtue of the privity of estate and contract that subsists between them; but if on the other hand the instrument was a sub-letting of the premises to Vidal by the original lessee the plaintiff could not recover against defendant as a sub-tenant, since in such case there is neither privity of estate nor of contract between the original lessor and the under-tenant. Harvey v. McGrew, 44 Texas, 415; Legierse & Co. v. Green, 61 Texas, 131; Taylor's Landlord & Tenant, sec. 16.

The instrument in question was construed by the trial court and the Court of Civil Appeals to be a sub-letting of the premises by the Dallas Brewery to the defendant Vidal, and in accordance with that holding judgment was rendered for the defendant. Upon appeal of the case to the Court of Civil Appeals the judgment of the lower court was affirmed.

That the question involved and decided may be fully understood we embody the instrument executed by the Dallas Brewery to Vidal:

Know All Men by These Presents, That, whereas, on the 26th day of April, 1907, Mrs. Antoinette W. Davis, acting by her agents, A. P. Coles & Brother, did lease to the Dallas Brewery the following parcel of land with the tenements thereon in the City of El Paso, County of El Paso, State of Texas, to-wit: Being the one-story and adobe composition roof building situated on lot 1 and south 24 feet of lot 2, block 135, Campbell's addition to the City of El Paso, Texas, known as Nos. 415-419 Utah street, same being leased from the 1st day of May, 1907, for three years, to be ended and completed on the 30th of April, 1910, and in consideration of same lease the said Dallas Brewery yielding and paying therefor during said term the sum of $100.00 per month, payable in advance on the first day of each and every month; and,

Whereas, said lease provides that said premises or any part thereof may be sublet by said Dallas Brewery without the consent of said Mrs. Davis; and,

Whereas, it is desired to transfer, assign and sublet all of said above premises so leased by the said Mrs. Davis to said Dallas Brewery to Lou Vidal;

Now, therefore, in consideration of the premises and the sum of $300.00 to it in hand paid, the receipt whereof is hereby acknowledged, said, the Dallas Brewery, does hereby sublet, assign and transfer the said above premises and does assign and transfer the above said lease, to the said Lou Vidal, and in consideration therefor the said Vidal does well and truly agree and promise to pay the rents in said lease agreed to be paid, to-wit: the sum of one hundred

($100.00) dollars per month, each and every month hereafter ensuing, begin-
ning on the first day of November, 1907, in advance, on the first day of each
month so hereinafter ensuing.

And the said Vidal does agree, and bind himself and obligates himself to in
all respects indemnify, save and hold harmless said Dallas Brewery by reason
of any of the terms or conditions in said lease contained, including the
payment of rent therein provided to be paid, and should the said Dallas
Brewery elect to pay any rent therein provided, or be called upon to pay any
rent therein provided, upon same being done the said Vidal agrees to pay the
same with interest at the rate of ten per cent per annum; or if the said Vidal
neglects or fails to pay said rent promptly, as in said lease provided to be paid,
then and in such event the Dallas Brewery can and may at its option declare
this transfer null and void, and thereupon oust the said Vidal, and assume
possession thereof, and this without notice of any character or kind to the said
Vidal; and the failure to pay any rent as in said lease provided to be paid, at the
election of the said Dallas Brewery, can and may authorize it without notice to
re-enter and repossess said premises.

In construing the effect of the foregoing instrument it is not conclusive as
to its form, since it may be in form an assignment and yet be in effect a
sub-lease. The question is one of law to be determined from the estate
granted by the instrument. As a general proposition if the instrument
executed by the lessee conveys the entire term and thereby parts with all of
the reversionary estate in the property the instrument will be construed to be
an assignment, but if there remains a reversionary interest in the estate
conveyed the instrument is a sub-lease. The relation of landlord and tenant
is created alone by the existence of a reversionary interest in the landlord.
Out of this fact arises the distinction made between assignments and
sub-tenancies. To state the test slightly different from that already stated, if
the instrument is of such character by its terms and conditions that a
reversionary interest by construction remains in the grantor of the property,
he becomes the landlord and the grantee the tenant. The tenant who parts
with the entire term embraced in his lease becomes an assignor of the lease
and the instrument is an assignment, but where the tenant by the terms,
conditions or limitations in the instrument does not part with the entire
term granted him by his landlord so that there remains in him a reversionary
interest, the transaction is a subletting and not an assignment. Forrest v.
Durnell, 86 Texas 647, 26 S.W. 481; Gulf C. & S.F. Ry. Co. v. Settegast, 79
Texas 263, 15 S.W. 228; 24 Cyc., 974-975; Wood on Landlord & Tenant, 2
ed., sec. 65.

It will be observed that in stating the general rule as to what constitutes an
assignment of a lease as distinguished from a sublease, the requirement is
that the instrument must convey the whole term, leaving no interest or
reversionary interest in the grantor.

By the word, "term," as used in the statement of this principle of law is
meant something more than the mere time for which the lease is given, and

the instrument must convey not only the entire time for which the lease runs, but the entire estate or interest conveyed by the lease. Mr. Blackstone in his commentaries, book 2, page 144, in commenting on the significance of the word, "term," when used in leases, says: "Thus the word term does not merely signify the time specified in the lease, but the estate also and interest that passes by the lease; and therefore the term may expire, during the continuance of the time; as by surrender, forfeiture and the like." The meaning of the word term as defined by Blackstone above was adopted by the Supreme Court of Massachusetts in the case of Dunlop v. Bullard, 131 Mass. 162, and by a number of text writers on the subject of assignments and subleases.

Mr. Blackstone in his commentaries, book 2, page 327, defines an assignment to be and draws the distinction between an assignment and a lease of property as follows:

> An assignment is properly a transfer, or making over to another, of the right one has in any estate, but it is usually applied to an estate for life or years. And it differs from lease only in this: that by a lease one grants an interest less than his own, reserving to himself a reversion; in an assignment he parts with the whole property, and the assignee stands to all intents and purposes in the place of the assignor.

If we may accept this definition from so eminent authority upon the common law, which definition and distinction so concisely stated and drawn seems to have met the approval of this court in other cases, and apply it to the facts of the case at bar the conclusion must be reached that the instrument executed by the Dallas Brewery to Vidal was a sub-lease and not an assignment. The instrument speaks for itself. By its terms the whole estate granted to the Dallas Brewery by its lease from Mrs. Davis is not conveyed, for the reason there is reserved to the Dallas Brewery a contingent reversionary interest in the estate, to be resumed summarily upon the failure of Vidal to pay rent. More than this, and of equal significance, by the terms of the instrument the Dallas Brewery reserved the right to pay the rent to the original lessor, and thereby the right was reserved to forestall Mrs. Davis, upon the failure of Vidal to pay the rent, from exercising the right to re-enter and possess the premises. That right was reserved to the Dallas Brewery and gave it the power to control the estate in the premises upon failure by Vidal to pay it the rent.

If the instrument was an assignment of the lease the Dallas Brewery must of necessity have parted with all its estate and interest in said premises, and could therefore exercise no right in or control over the premises. If the instrument was an assignment of the lease the legal effect was to substitute Vidal in lieu of the Dallas Brewery. But this was not the case. By the terms of the instrument the Dallas Brewery retained the control of the possession of the leased premises, thereby denying the legal effect of an assignment, which would have given Mrs. Davis the right of re-entry and possession of the property upon Vidal's failure to pay the rent.

We are aware that there is great conflict of authority upon this subject, and that it would be futile to attempt to reconcile such conflict. Many of the authors of the text books on the subject of the assignment of leases and sub-letting under leases, and the decisions of a great many of the States in this Union hold that the fact that the right of re-entry is reserved in the assignment to the assignor upon failure of the assignee to pay rent does not change the instrument of assignment from such to a sub-lease. The holding of such authors and decisions is based upon the theory that the right of re-entry is not an estate or interest in land, nor the reservation of a reversion. They hold that the reservation of the right of re-entry upon failure to pay rent is neither an estate nor interest in land, but a mere chose in action, and when exercised the grantor comes into possession of the premises through the breach of the condition and not by reverter.

Those authorities which hold the contrary doctrine base their ruling upon the idea that the reservation in the instrument of the right of re-entry is a contingent reversionary interest in the premises, resulting from the conveyance of an estate upon a condition subsequent where there has been an infraction of such condition. This view of the law is strongly presented in the opinion in the case of Dunlap v. Bullard, 131 Mass. 163, as follows:

Where an estate is conveyed to be held by the grantee upon a condition subsequent, there is left in the grantor a contingent reversionary interest. It was said in Austin v. Cambridgeport Parish, 21 Pick., 215, 223, that the grantor's contingent interest in such case was an estate which was transmissible by devise and passed under a residuary devise in the will of the grantor. It was declared to be a contingent possible estate, which, united with that of the tenants, "composed only the entire fee-simple estate, as much so as the ordinary case of an estate for life to A, remainder to B." In Brattle Square Church v. Grant, 3 Gray, 142, 147, it was said, that when such an estate is created "the entire interest does not pass out of the grantor by the same instrument of conveyance. All that remains after the gift of grant takes effect, continues in the grantor, and goes to his heirs. This is the right of entry, which, from the nature of the grant, is reserved to the grantor and his heirs only, and which gives them the right to enter as of their old estate, upon the breach of the condition." These considerations are equally applicable whether the estate subject to the condition subsequent is an estate in fee, or an estate for life or years. They apply where, by the terms of an instrument which purports to be an underlease, there is left in the lessor a contingent reversionary interest, to be availed of by an entry for breach of condition which restores the sub-lessor to his former interest in the premises. The sub-lessee under such an instrument takes an inferior and different estate from that which he would acquire by an assignment of the remainder of the original term, that is to say, an interest which may be terminated by forfeiture on new and independent grounds long before the expiration of the original term. If the smallest reversionary interest is retained, the tenant takes as sub-lessee, and not as assignee.

We are not able to discern why there may not be a contingent reversionary estate as an interest in land, as well as any other contingent estate or interest. It certainly cannot be contended upon sound principle that because the right of re-entry and resumption of possession of land is contingent that it is thereby any the less an estate or interest in land. The very definition of a contingent estate as distinguished from a vested estate is that "the right to its enjoyment is to accrue on an event which is dubious and uncertain." 1 Washburn on Real Property, 38.

That the right of re-entry is an estate or interest in land seems to have been recognized by Platte in his work on Leases, volume 2, page 218: ". . . a right of re-entry, whether immediate or future, and whether vested or contingent, into or upon any tenement or hereditament in England, of any tenure, may now be disposed of by deed."

We think it deducible from respectable authority that where the tenant reserves in the instrument giving possession to his transferee the right of re-entry to the premises demised, upon failure to pay rent, he necessarily retains a part of or an interest in the demised estate which may come back to him upon the happening of a contingency.

The instrument under consideration does not convey the entire estate received by the Dallas Brewery by its lease from Mrs. Davis, but retains by the right of possible re-entry a contingent reversionary interest in the premises. That the interest retained is a contingent reversionary interest does not, it seems to us, change the rule by which an assignment may be distinguished from a sublease. If by any limitation or condition in the conveyance the entire term, which embraces the estate conveyed in the contract of lease as well as the length of time for which the tenancy is created, may by construction be said not to have passed from the original tenant, but that a contingent reversionary estate is retained in the premises the subject of the reversion, the instrument must be said to constitute a sub-letting and not an assignment.

The following test may be applied to determine whether the instrument in question is an assignment of the original lease, or a sub-letting of the premises. If it is an assignment its legal effect must be a transfer of the right of possession of the property conveyed to Vidal and the creation of a privity of estate and contract between Mrs. Davis, the original lessor, and Vidal, to whom the possession was granted by the Dallas Brewery. This would be essential to constitute the instrument an assignment, and if it was an assignment Vidal obligated himself to pay the rent to Mrs. Davis and the Dallas Brewery had no further connection with or interest in the transaction. But such a result can by no fair or reasonable construction of the language and provisions of the instrument be deduced therefrom. On the contrary the Dallas Brewery reserved the privilege of paying the rent to its lessor, and upon non-payment of rent by Vidal it reserved the right to declare the instrument forfeited and to repossess the premises without notice to or the consent of Vidal. There can be but one theory upon which the Dallas Brewery considered itself interested in seeing that the rent was promptly paid by Vidal, and that is that it desired to control the property in question and therefore intended and by the language and reservation in the instrument made it a sub-lease.

We do not think the proposition tenable that by the express terms of the agreement between the Dallas Brewery and Vidal, or by implication, Vidal obligated himself to pay the rent to Mrs. Davis. The provision of the contract relied upon to establish the fact that Vidal obligated himself to pay the rent to the lessor in the original lease is the following, "and in considera- tion therefor the said Vidal does well and truly agree and promise to pay the rents in said lease agreed to be paid, to-wit: the sum of one hundred dollars per month." Under the uniform rule of construction the latter part of the above sentence explains and qualifies the preceding part. The obligation of Vidal was to pay the rents in said lease agreed to be paid, that is, the sum of one hundred dollars per month, payable on the first day of each month in advance. There is nothing in the agreement from which it may be inferred that Vidal obligated himself to pay the rents directly to Mrs. Davis.

Having reached the conclusion that the instrument executed by the Dallas Brewery to Vidal conveying the premises in question was a sub-lease and not an assignment, by reason of the provision reserving to the Dallas Brewery the right of re-entry, which had the effect to withhold a part of the term granted by the original lease, or which retained an interest in said estate; and because by the other terms of the instrument reserving to the Dallas Brewery the discretion to pay the rents upon its own responsibility and upon the failure of Vidal to pay the same to it, the right to declare the instrument forfeited and to re-enter and take possession of the premises indicate the intention and purpose of the parties to enter into a sub-letting of the premises and not to assign the original lease, we conclude there exists no privity of estate or contract between the plaintiff, Mrs. Davis, and the defendant, Lewis Vidal, and that Mrs. Davis has no cause of action authoriz- ing her to recover judgment against Vidal.

Other questions presented in briefs of counsel are not discussed, for the reason their disposition is not essential to the decision of the case, in consequence of the view we have taken of its merits.

The court is of the opinion the judgments of the Court of Civil Appeals and of the trial court should be affirmed, and it is accordingly so ordered. Affirmed.[8]

8.   Some states have passed statutes which permit the original lessor to recover rent from a sublessee. See, for example, Ky. Rev. Stat. §383.010, paragraph (5), which provides as follows: "Rent may be recovered from the lessee or other person owing it, or his assignee or underten- ant, or the representative of either by any of the remedies given in this chapter. But, the assignee or subtenant shall be liable only for the rent accrued after his interest began."

See Ferrier, Can There Be a Sublease for the Entire Unexpired Portion of a Term? 18 Calif. L. Rev. 1 (1929); Wallace, Assignment and Sublease, 8 Ind. L.J. 359 (1933); Note, Assignment or Sublease, 1 Idaho L. Rev. 98 (1964); Jackson, Subleases as Assignments, 31 Conv. & Prop. Law. (n.s.) 159 (1967). See generally American Law of Property §3.57 (Casner ed. 1952); id. §9.6.—EDS.

Problem

20.7. The Old Colony R.R. Co., serving southern Massachusetts, made a long-term lease of all its property at a fixed annual rental to the New York, New Haven & Hartford R.R. Co. The lease was made at a time when the Old Colony was a valuable property making handsome profits; the rental was based upon the assumption that this would continue. As time went by, competition from bus lines and automobiles so reduced the income of the Old Colony that serious annual losses resulted. The New Haven floated a bond issue, the X Trust Co. serving as assignee of the New Haven's assets for the benefit of the bondholders (see page 743 *infra* as to the corporate mortgage). Among the assets assigned to the X Trust Co. was the Old Colony lease. When the rent was not paid by the New Haven to the Old Colony, the latter sued the X Trust Co. Is the X Trust Co. liable? Kirby v. Goldman, 270 Mass. 444, 170 N.E. 414 (1930); McLaughlin v. Minnesota Loan & Trust Co., 192 Minn. 203, 255 N.W. 839 (1934); American Law of Property §9.5 (Casner ed. 1952). If you had represented the New Haven in the original lease negotiations, what provision as to rent would you have insisted upon? If you had represented the X Trust Co. at the time it became trustee for the bondholders, how would you have handled the Old Colony lease? If you were representing the X Trust Co. after the Old Colony had made its claim for rent, what action would you recommend?

SECTION 4.   THE LANDLORD'S RIGHT TO WITHHOLD CONSENT TO AN ASSIGNMENT OR A SUBLETTING

GRUMAN v. INVESTORS DIVERSIFIED SERVICES, INC.
247 Minn. 502, 78 N.W.2d 377 (1956)

GALLAGHER, J.

Action to recover rent alleged to be due on a written lease. Upon motion for summary judgment, the court ordered judgment for plaintiffs in the sum of $20,656.63. This is an appeal from the judgment entered pursuant thereto. It is conceded that the amount found due on the lease is correct if plaintiffs were not under obligation to accept defendant's proposed subtenant who was ready, able, and willing to rent the premises for a part of the unexpired portion of the lease. The latter is the issue for determination here.

The facts are as follows: On June 8, 1948, plaintiffs' predecessor in title entered into the lease with defendant. Thereunder, for a term of seven years and one month from September 1, 1948, or until September 30, 1955, defendant rented a portion of the ground floor and basement of the premises known as the WCCO Building at 629 Second Avenue South, Minneapolis, at a total rental of $176,375, payable $2,075 monthly on or before the tenth day of each month. Contained in the lease was a covenant that the lessee agreed not to ". . . assign this lease nor underlet said premises, or any part thereof, without the consent of Lessor in writing." Also contained therein was the customary reentry clause providing that, in case the lessee defaulted in completing any of the terms or conditions of the lease, the lessors might reenter the leased premises and at their option annul any such termination, the lessee would indemnify the lessors against all loss of rents which might be incurred during the residue of the term of the lease.

Defendant took possession of the premises September 1, 1948, and thereafter all rentals required under the lease up to and including the rental for the month of July 1954 were paid by it. On or about July 1, 1954, it advised plaintiffs in writing that it would vacate the leased premises prior to August 1, 1954; that it would immediately commence looking for a desirable subtenant therefor; and that plaintiffs should likewise look for such a subtenant. On July 7, 1954, defendant submitted a proposed lease whereunder the premises would be rented to the postmaster general of the United States for use as a regional operations office for a period of 11 months from August 1, 1954, at a monthly rental of $1,795.50. For the purposes of the motion for summary judgment, it was agreed that the subtenant thus proposed was ready, able, and willing to assume the obligations of the lease to the extent described and was otherwise a suitable subtenant therefor.

On July 12, 1954, plaintiffs advised defendant that they would not consent to the proposed sublease and would not permit the premises to be subleased by anyone for any part of the unexpired portion of the lease but would require that defendant pay the full rental due each month thereon. As an alternative they proposed that defendant pay them $20,000 for a release covering all its obligations under the lease. This was rejected by defendant. Thereafter, in July 1954, defendant vacated the premises and subsequently each month until the lease expired tendered to plaintiffs as rental a sum equal to the difference in the amount due under the lease and the amount the postmaster general would have paid had the sublease been accepted by plaintiffs. Such tenders were rejected by plaintiffs.

Subsequently, this action was instituted. In its answer defendant claimed an offset in the amount claimed due for the unexpired term of the lease equal to the rental that would have been paid under the sublease by the postmaster general. Plaintiffs thereupon moved for summary judgment. As indicated above, it was then stipulated that the postmaster general of the United States was in all respects a highly satisfactory, desirable, and suitable subtenant, plaintiffs' sole contention being that, under the provision of the lease above quoted, they were not obligated to accept *any* subtenant *suitable* or otherwise and might arbitrarily refuse to sublease to anyone proposed by the lessee. It was also agreed for the purpose of this motion that plaintiffs had at no time consented to defendant's removal from, or surrender of, the premises and that they had at no time consented to any assignment or sublease thereof or accepted defendant's forfeiture thereof so as to terminate its liability thereon.

In computing the amount due for the unexpired portion of the lease, defendant was credited with an amount subsequently paid by a subtenant, the Reynolds Company, under a sublease with plaintiffs, it being stipulated that such sublease would in no way affect the rights of the parties in the instant litigation except by way of a reduction in the amount claimed due for the unexpired term equal to the amount paid by such subtenant during that period.

The only issue presented for determination is whether under the lease clause above quoted plaintiffs could arbitrarily refuse to accept the suitable subtenant proffered by defendant. Examination of our decisions indicates that we have had no prior case involving a similar fact situation. In foreign jurisdictions, where the question has been presented, a majority of the courts have held that in a lease such as this the lessor does not have the duty of mitigating damages; may arbitrarily refuse to accept a subtenant suitable and otherwise responsible; and may recover from the lessee the full rentals due under the lease as and when they become due. [Citations from 22 jurisdictions are omitted.]

The reasons expressed in support of this rule are that, since the lessor has exercised a personal choice in the selection of a tenant for a definite term and has expressly provided that no substitute shall be acceptable without his written consent, no obligation rests upon him to look to anyone but the lessee for his rent, . . . that a lease is a conveyance of an interest in real property and, when a lessor has delivered the premises to his lessee, the latter is bound to him by privity of estate as well as by privity of contract, . . . ; that a lessor's right to reenter the premises upon lessee's default or abandonment thereof is at the lessor's option and not the lessee's, Kulawitz v. Pacific Woodenware & Paper Co., 25 Cal. 2d 664, 155 P.2d 24; Rau v. Baker, 118 Ill. App. 150; and that a lessee's unilateral action in abandoning leased premises, *unless accepted by his lessor,* does not terminate the lease or forfeit the estate conveyed thereby, nor the lessee's right to use and possess the leased premises and, by the same token, his obligation to pay the rent due therefor. . . .

Where this court has had occasion to consider the principles involved in the present appeal, although not like fact situations. it has expressed a viewpoint which appears to be in accord with the majority rule. Thus, in Haycock v. Johnston, 81 Minn. 49, 52, 83 N.W. 494, 495 (first case), where the lease did not contain a re-entry clause, this court rejected the lessee's contention that the lessor should have made an effort to rerent the leased

property after the lessee had surrendered possession thereof, holding that:
". . . Plaintiff did not accept defendant's surrender of the property, and
had no right to re-rent it. If he had accepted it back, and re-rented it to some
other person, a rescission of the contract of lease would have been thereby
effected, and defendant wholly released from his obligation." In the second
case, Haycock v. Johnston, 97 Minn. 289, 106 N.W. 304, this court approved the above rule, citing in support thereof Buckingham Apartment
House Co. v. Dafoe, 78 Minn. 268, 80 N.W. 974; Stern v. Thayer, 56 Minn.
93, 57 N.W. 329; Bowen v. Hassell, 53 Minn. 480, 55 N.W. 629; Nelson v.
Thompson, 23 Minn. 508, but held that, because the evidence then disclosed that the lessor had accepted a surrender of the premises by lessee, the
lease thereby became canceled. In Stern v. Thayer, *supra,* where the lease
prohibited its assignment or the subletting of the leased premises and
contained a reentry clause, it was held that the lessor's actions under the
reentry clause clearly manifested this intention to continue the lease and did
not constitute an acceptance of its surrender. There we stated, 56 Minn. 98,
57 N.W. 330:

> . . . The landlord had a right to refuse to permit defendant to select a tenant.
> He had a right to devise any scheme or plan to rent the rooms should they
> become vacant, and everything that he did with Dr. James was in strict
> accordance with, and under the conditions found in, the lease.

In Nelson v. Thompson, 23 Minn. 508, 512, it was held:

> . . . That [a surrender by operation of law], as said by Parke, B., in Lyon v.
> Reed, 13 M. & W. 285, 306, can only take place "where the owner of a
> particular estate has been a party to some act, the validity of which he is by law
> afterwards estopped from disputing, and which would not be valid if his
> particular estate had continued to exist." Such would be the case of a lessor
> taking unqualified possession of demised premises, and dealing with them in a
> way wholly inconsistent with the continuance of an already existing and
> unexpired term. In such a case, as against the lessor, the law, upon the
> principle of estoppel, implies a mutual agreement between him and his lessee,
> whereby the possession of the premises has been abandoned by the latter, and
> resumed by the former, in pursuance of such agreement.

The cited cases of course are to be distinguished from those wherein a
lessor by some act or statement has indicated his acceptance of a lessee's
abandonment of leased premises and thus in effect terminated the lease. The
remedy there of course is for damages resulting from the breach with the
attendant obligation upon the lessor to use reasonable efforts to mitigate
such damages subsequent to the breach.

A number of writers have advanced the theory that a more modern and
just viewpoint should be applied in situations such as the present; that the

rule applicable in ordinary breach of contract cases, requiring efforts to mitigate damages after breach, should be applied to leases; and in further-ance of this view that a lessor should be obligated to accept a suitable subtenant offered by the lessee. See, 2 Powell, Real Property, par. 229, note 79; McCormick, Rights of Landlord Upon Abandonment, 23 Mich. L. Rev. 211, 222; 44 Harv. L. Rev. 993; 34 Harv. L. Rev. 217. Defendant also cites decisions from the Supreme Courts of Iowa, Kansas, and Wisconsin as giving support to this viewpoint. In some of the decisions from such jurisdictions, it is frankly acknowledged that the viewpoint adopted is "in conflict with the weight of authority in the United States, . . ." Lawson v. Callaway, 131 Kan. 789, 791, 293 P. 503, 504. Likewise, it appears that in some of the decisions cited, while the principles expressed lend support to defendant's contentions, the evidence therein discloses that the lessors involved had accepted the lessees' abandonment of leased premises and in consequence were under obligation to mitigate the damages.

We feel that we must adhere to the majority rule. In reaching this conclusion we are motivated by the fact that the language of the assignment provision is clear and unambiguous and that many leases now in effect covering a substantial amount of real property and creating valuable prop-erty rights were carefully prepared by competent counsel in reliance upon the majority viewpoint. It would seem clear from the language adopted in all such cases that the lessors therein are entitled to place full reliance upon the responsibility of their respective lessees for the rentals they have contracted to pay. Should a lessee desire the right to assign or sublet to a suitable tenant, a clause might readily be inserted in the lease similar to those now included in many leases to the effect that the lessor's written consent to the assign-ment or subletting of the leased premises should not be unreasonably withheld. There being no clause in the present lease to such effect, we are compelled to give its terms their full force and effect as have the courts of a majority of other jurisdictions.

The judgment is affirmed.

Affirmed.

DRESS SHIRT SALES INC. v. HOTEL MARTINIQUE ASSOCIATES
12 N.Y.2d 339, 190 N.E.2d 10 (1963)

BURKE, J.

Plaintiffs were the lessees of space in defendant's hotel under a lease prohibiting subletting without defendant lessors' written consent. The lease, executed in 1955, was for a term of 10 years with a rental of $10,000 per year for the first five and $12,000 per year for the last five. In 1959 plaintiffs vacated but continued to pay rent. Then and at all times thereafter defendants assured plaintiffs of their willingness to allow a subletting and plaintiffs displayed a "for rent" sign on the premises with defendants' consent. Three months later one Bencini approached plaintiffs with a desire to rent the premises. While defendants at first orally stated there "would be no problem," they thereafter refused to consent to the proposed sublease because the inexpensive sandwich-type restaurant contemplated by Bencini (and, for that matter, any restaurant) was not what defendants wanted in their hotel. At the same time defendants proposed a cancellation of the lease for $75,000. Defendants' representations were false in that defendants then intended to and did thereafter negotiate with Bencini to lease the same space for the same type of restaurant. Five months later plaintiffs again tried to persuade defendants to consent to the Bencini proposition and defendants again refused for the same reasons. It is alleged that, as a result of defendants' refusal and in reliance on the truthfulness of their representation that the restaurant was not wanted, plaintiffs agreed on October 31, 1959 to pay $30,000 for cancellation of the lease. Two weeks later defendants leased to Bencini, at a higher rent than plaintiffs were paying. Most of these facts are denied by defendants, but their point on this summary judgment motion is that, in any event, the law denies recovery.

Plaintiffs allege, in effect, two causes of action. One is an arbitrary refusal to consent to a sublease and a further breach of the alleged oral agreement to permit subleasing in general and to Bencini in particular. It is settled that, unless the lease provides that the lessor's consent shall not be unreasonably withheld, a provision against subleasing without the lessor's consent permits the lessor to refuse arbitrarily for any reason or no reason. (Symonds v. Hurlbut, 208 App. Div. 147, 203 N.Y.S. 223; Arlu Associates, Inc. v. Rosner, 14 A.D.2d 272, 220 N.Y.S.2d 288.) Since the lease contained a provision that no part could be changed or waived orally, the Real Property Law, Consol. Laws, c. 50 (§282, subds. 1, 3, par. (a)) clearly invalidates the fully executory oral consent to subleasing given by defendants' agent. Even if plaintiffs gave consideration by promising to do that which they would not be obligated to do anyway (act as guarantors of the proposed new tenant's performance — which is really a lesser duty than that imposed by law, i.e., remain primarily liable), the purpose of section 282 is to enable parties to protect themselves against false claims of oral change, including waiver, by providing for a writing. (See 1952 Report of N.Y. Law Rev. Comm., p. 143.) From a policy viewpoint the suggestion that defendants' permission to display a "for rent" sign is an executed waiver and advance acceptance of any new tenant has little to recommend it.

Plaintiffs' other cause of action sounds in fraud.

While defendants' actions seem to amount to a fraud on plaintiffs to the extent of $30,000, and are clearly unconscionable, we do not think plaintiffs sufficiently show how the misrepresentation concerning defendants' unwillingness to accept Bencini's restaurant resulted in damage. Misrepresentation of an existing fact (present intention to accept a restaurant) and scienter clearly appear on the record. In plaintiffs' view, the allegations could also justify a finding that reliance on the truthfulness of the representation caused plaintiffs to buy out their lease for $30,000, believing that to be the only way out of an unprofitable situation. Had it not been for the lie, plaintiffs may well have out-waited defendants who were in fact anxious to fill an unsightly vacancy.

It is doubtless true that only wrong to which plaintiffs can point, i.e., the false reason given for refusal, is of dubious independent significance over and above the real lever by which plaintiffs were induced to buy out their lease — the refusal itself. Defendants had an unqualified contractual privilege to refuse to accept Bencini and plaintiffs would have had no remedy if defendants had simply said nothing and remained adamant in refusing to accept Bencini as a sublessee until plaintiffs gave in and paid for a cancellation of the lease. Defendants' acceptance of Bencini as a new lessee immediately thereafter would be an instance of hard dealing and nothing more. Nevertheless, a fraudulent misrepresentation need not be the sole inducing cause for entering into the bargain complained of (Kley v. Healy, 127 N.Y. 555, 28 N.E. 593; Adams v. Gillig, 199 N.Y. 314, 92 N.E. 670, 32 L.R.A., N.S., 127) and plaintiffs would be entitled to a factual determination of the materiality of the representation upon which they allege reliance.

However, with respect to the final element necessary to an action for damages for fraud — damage itself — plaintiffs' action must fail. In contrast to an action for rescission, in an action for damages for fraud actual pecuniary loss must be shown. (Urtz v. New York Cent. & H.R.R. Co., 202 N.Y. 170, 95 N.E. 711.) Here, any loss must be measured by the difference between the actual value of the remainder of the term and the price plaintiffs paid for it by reason of the lessors' deceit. (Sager v. Friedman, 270 N.Y. 472, 1 N.E.2d 971; Hanlon v. Macfadden pub., 302 N.Y. 502, 99 N.E.2d 546, 24 A.L.R.2d 733.) Since defendants gave up the legal right to hold plaintiffs for six years' rent and, more to the point, since plaintiffs received a release from that amount of liability, can it be said that pecuniary loss resulted? The misrepresentation possibly influenced the bargaining in that it gave a false impression of defendants' obstinacy in insisting on holding plaintiffs to their bargain; but can an element so completely within defendants' control lessen the "true" value of the consideration received by plaintiffs? In Urtz v. New York Cent. & H.R.R. Co., 202 N.Y. 170, 95 N.E. 711, *supra,* an action for damage for fraudulently procuring a release from tort liability, we disallowed as too speculative a recovery based on the difference between the amount given for the release and the worth of plaintiff's unresolved claim as it stood when the release was given. Again, in Ritzwoller v. Lurie, 225 N.Y. 464, 122 N.E. 634, we upheld a dismissal of a cause of action for an accounting for damages for fraudulently inducing plaintiff to abandon an allegedly profitable contract of employment for one allegedly less profitable.

We think, therefore, that this case falls within the policy of our consistent refusal to allow damages for fraud based on the loss of a contractual bargain, the extent, and, indeed, in this case, the very existence of which is completely undeterminable and speculative.

Accordingly, the judgment should be affirmed, with costs.

DESMOND, C.J. (concurring).

I concur for affirmance but I cannot agree that these facts make out any of the elements of a cause of action in fraud. The terms of the lease gave the landlord a complete and perfect right to refuse consent to a sublease. Since the courts give relief against actionable wrongs only and not against improprieties or unsportsmanlike conduct, we simply have no function at all in the premises. If this lease had contained the familiar provision (see authorities cited in Ogden v. Riverview Holding Corp., 134 Misc. 149, 234 N.Y.S. 678) that "the consent to sublet will not unreasonably or arbitrarily be withheld," then plaintiffs could try out the issue as to the reasonableness of defendants' conduct. But the provision in this lease against subletting without consent was a clearly legal term of the grant and once the lease was signed the tenant was bound by it under all circumstances. Since the landlord did not have to give any reason for refusal to consent, no legal consequences flow from any false statement as to its reason for refusal. The tenant chose, for its own purposes, to move out but it remained liable for $75,000 rent for the balance of the term. When the landlord accepted $30,000 in exchange for a release of this obligation, the tenant necessarily knew that the landlord contemplated re-renting the property and the landlord's right so to re-rent it thereafter was unconditional.

DYE, FULD, VAN VOORHIS and SCILEPPI, JJ., concur with BURKE, J.

DESMOND, C.J., concurs in a separate opinion in which FOSTER, J., concurs.

Judgment affirmed.

Note: The Restatement's Position

The Restatement (Second) of Property (Landlord and Tenant) §15.2 provides:

> (2) A restraint on alienation without the consent of the landlord of the tenant's interest in the leased property is valid, but the landlord's consent to an alienation by the tenant cannot be withheld unreasonably, unless a freely negotiated provision in the lease gives the landlord an absolute right to withhold consent.

Compare the following recently enacted New York statute:

§226-b. *Right to sublease or assign.*

1. Unless a greater right to assign is conferred by the lease, a tenant renting a residence may not assign his lease without the written consent of the

owner, which consent may be unconditionally withheld without cause provided that the owner shall release the tenant from the lease upon request of the tenant upon thirty days notice if the owner unreasonably withholds consent which release shall be the sole remedy of the tenant. If the owner reasonably withholds consent, there shall be no assignment and the tenant shall not be released from the lease.

2. a.   A tenant renting a residence pursuant to an existing lease in a dwelling having four or more residential units shall have the right to sublease his premises subject to the written consent of the landlord in advance of the subletting. Such consent shall not be unreasonably withheld.

   b.   The tenant shall inform the landlord of his intent to sublease by mailing a notice of such intent by certified mail, return receipt requested. Such request shall be accompanied by the following information:

   (i)   the terms of the sublease;
   (ii)   the name of the proposed sublessee;
   (iii) the business and permanent home address of the proposed sublessee;
   (iv)   the tenant's reason for subletting;
   (v)   the tenant's address for the term of the sublease;
   (vi)   the written consent of any co-tenant or guarantor of the lease; and
   (vii) a copy of the proposed sublease, to which a copy of the tenant's lease shall be attached if available, acknowledged by the tenant and proposed subtenant as being a true copy of such sublease.

   c.   Within ten days after the mailing of such request, the landlord may ask the tenant for additional information as will enable the landlord to determine if rejection of such request shall be unreasonable. Any such request for additional information shall not be unduly burdensome. Within thirty days after the mailing of the request for consent, or of the additional information reasonably asked for by the landlord, whichever is later, the landlord shall send a notice to the tenant of his consent or, if he does not consent, his reasons therefor. Landlord's failure to send such a notice shall be deemed to be a consent to the proposed subletting. If the landlord consents, the premises may be sublet in accordance with the request, but the tenant thereunder, shall nevertheless remain liable for the performance of tenant's obligations under said lease. If the landlord reasonably withholds consent, there shall be no subletting and the tenant shall not be released from the lease. If the landlord unreasonably withholds consent, the tenant may sublet in accordance with the request and may recover the costs of the proceeding and attorneys fees if it is found that the owner acted in bad faith by withholding consent.

3. The provisions of this section shall apply to leases entered into or renewed before or after the effective date of this section, however they shall not apply to public housing and other units for which there are constitutional or statutory criteria covering admission thereto nor to a proprietary lease, viz.:

a lease to, or held by, a tenant entitled thereto by reason of ownership of stock in a corporate owner of premises which operates the same on a cooperative basis.

Problem

20.8. L has covenanted not to withhold unreasonably L's consent to a proposed assignment (or a statute exists which imposes such a duty on L). As L's attorney, what are the standards you would apply in determining the circumstances under which it might be reasonable for L to withhold consent to a proposed assignment? See Bragar v. Berkeley Associates Co., 111 Misc. 2d 333, 444 N.Y.S.2d 355 (Sup. Ct. 1981). For example, would it be reasonable for L to withhold consent because the proposed assignee did not in L's judgment make a good appearance? Or because the proposed assignee was of a religious faith of which L did not approve? Or because the proposed assignee was a member of a racial group that did not inhabit the neighborhood in which the leased property was located? See the Civil Rights Act of 1968, discussed at page 957 *infra*.

Note: Implied Covenant Not to Assign a Lease

Rowe v. Great Atlantic & Pacific Tea Co., 46 N.Y.2d 62, 385 N.E.2d 566 (1978), comments as follows in regard to the circumstances under which a covenant not to assign a lease may be implied:

> An implied covenant limiting the right to assign will often be found in those situations in which it is evident that the landlord entered into the lease in reliance upon some special skill or ability of the lessee which will have a material effect upon the fulfillment of the landlord's reasonable contractual expectations. In the typical lease in which the landlord is assured of a set monthly rent, and has not placed any unusual restrictions upon the use of the premises, there is no occasion to find an implied covenant precluding or limiting assignment. This is so because the only reasonable expectation of the landlord is that the rent will be paid and the premises not abused, and thus the identity of the tenant is not material to the landlord's expectations under the lease. If, however, the expectations of the landlord are substantially dependent upon some special skill or trait of the lessee, the lack of which might endanger the lessor's legitimate contractual expectations, then it may be appropriate to find the existence of an implied covenant limiting the right to assign, for in such circumstances no reasonable person would enter into the contract without assurance that the tenant could not be replaced by an assignee lacking the requisite skills or character traits. Even in such a case, however, the implied restrictions must of course be limited to the extent possible without destroying the landlord's legitimate interests. [46 N.Y.2d at 70, 385 N.E.2d at 570.]

Note: Arrangements Which Fall Short of Being an Assignment or a Sublease

In Presbey v. Benjamin, 169 N.Y. 377, 62 N.E. 430 (1902), a tenant of an apartment in New York City had his porter stay in his apartment during his absence from the city to look after things for him. The lease of the apartment of the tenant contained a covenant that the tenant would not assign or sublet the premises or any part thereof without the consent of the landlord under penalty of forfeiture. Since the landlord did not consent to the arrangement for the occupancy of the apartment, the question was raised as to whether the tenant had violated the covenant. The court said:

> It is first to be observed that "such covenants are restraints which courts do not favor. They are construed with the utmost jealousy, and very easy modes have always been countenanced for defeating them." Thus a covenant not to assign does not prevent an under-letting, and a covenant not to under-let the premises is not broken by a sub-lease of a part of the premises. In this case it is not at all necessary to go to the extent of the authorities cited. It is clear that even under a liberal construction of the covenant, to constitute a violation of this lease the defendant must have attempted to put in possession of the premises a new tenant, not merely a new occupant. To be a tenant a person must have some estate, be it ever so little, such as that of a tenant at will or at sufferance. A person may be in occupation of real property simply as a servant or licensee of his master. In that case the possession is not changed; it is always in the master. Therefore, if the defendant sought to place his porter in occupation of the premises as caretaker or as servant he was entirely within his rights. [169 N.Y. at 380, 62 N.E. at 431.]

See American Law of Property §3.58 (Casner ed. 1952).

CHAPTER 21

THE TENANT WHO HOLDS OVER[1]

FETTING MANUFACTURING JEWELRY CO. v. WALTZ
160 Md. 50, 152 A. 434 (1930)

Action by Ada R. Waltz and others against the A. H. Fetting Manufacturing Jewelry Company. From the judgment for plaintiffs, defendant appeals. Affirmed.

PARKE, J., delivered the opinion of the court.

The plaintiffs, Ada R. Waltz, Zora A. Klare and Bertha F. Kuhnert, are the owners of an improved lot on Liberty Street, in Baltimore City, which they demised to the A. H. Fetting Manufacturing Jewelry Company, the defendant, by a lease under seal, dated October 10th, 1922, for a term of five years that would end on November 4th, 1927. The rent reserved for the first three years of the lease increased to $7,000 during the succeeding two years, and was payable in equal installments at the beginning of every month. There are numerous covenants in the lease, whose statement is unnecessary, because the covenants of the lessee to vacate the premises at the end of the term, and to become liable to the lessors for all loss or damage which the lessors might suffer through a loss of sale or of lease or otherwise by reason of its failure to leave as agreed, are the only covenants whose effect is in controversy.

There is no material conflict in the testimony. It tended to establish that, some months before the expiration of the term, the lessee discussed with its lessors the execution of a new demise for a further period of five and ten years, but that the parties could not agree, and that the tenant wrote on August 23rd, 1927, that it was preparing to move but that, if its plans miscarried so that it would be unable to open its new place of business before

1. See generally American Law of Property §§3.32-3.36, 3.92 (Casner ed. 1952); 49 Am. Jur. 2d Landlord and Tenant §1115. See also Restatement (Second) of Property (Landlord and Tenant) §§14.1-14.7.

the expiration of the lease, the tenant would consider it a great favor if the lessors would extend the lease for a month or two, as might be necessary; and that it would meet the lessors for the purpose of making arrangements which would be fair to all parties. The lessors replied four days later by letters directing the tenant to confer with their agent, who was engaged in the real estate business in Baltimore, and who had the matter involved in his charge; and concluding with the statement that they felt sure a satisfactory arrangement could be made. This agent and the tenant met the first week of October, and their negotiations were fruitless, because the agent, who had full authority from his principals, would not agree to prolong the period of the lease for less than six months. After this futile meeting, nothing more was done during the term, and the original demise continued to fix the duration of the renting and the rights and liabilities of the parties.

Upon the expiration of the term the lessee did not surrender the premises as it had covenanted, but remained in actual possession until November 26th, 1927, and on December 1st, 1927, forwarded by mail to the lessors checks which aggregated $583.33, which was a sum equivalent to the monthly installment of the yearly rent reserved under the original lease. The lessors declined to receive the checks except as a payment of the monthly installment of rent which had accrued due by the lessee as a tenant holding over for an additional year; and the lessee insisted that a payment of rent to December 4th, 1927, was a full discharge of its liability. In the assertion of those conflicting positions, the checks and keys were repeatedly sent and returned between the disputants. Ultimately the checks for $583.33 were accepted by the lessors upon an understanding that the acceptance was without prejudice to the rights of either side, and the keys were retained by the lessors under circumstances having a similar effect. Notwithstanding the effort of the owners to secure a tenant for the benefit of the lessee, the property remained unoccupied from the time the lessee left until after the owners began an action, on January 2nd, 1929, against their former lessee for the recovery of the rents issuing from the premises for the period of one year. The judgment recovered by the plaintiffs was for $6,416.67, which sum was the yearly rental under the first demise, less the payment of $583.33, which had been accepted by the plaintiffs without prejudice to the rights of any party.

The defendant's contention on this appeal is presented by the refusal of the court at nisi prius to grant its prayer which denied a right of recovery. This demurrer prayer was not addressed to the pleading, and the theory upon which it was submitted is that the defendant was not a tenant holding over under a new renting, and that the failure of the tenant to surrender the premises at the expiration of the original period of the renting did not cause the plaintiffs any loss within the contemplation of the inclusive covenants of the lease.

The defendant was a tenant for years, and did not surrender the premises to the landlords at the expiration of the period of its tenancy, but remained for almost a month, when the tenant abandoned the premises, and then offered in full the amount of the monthly installment of the rent which had been reserved under the original lease. Under these circumstances the defendant became a trespasser in the sense of being wrongfully in possession, or a tenant from year to year at the election of the landlords. The defendant, however, had no such election. In the language of an eminent authority: "His mere continuance in possession fixes him as tenant for another year if the landlord thinks proper to insist upon it. And the right of the landlord to continue the tenancy will not be affected by the fact, that the tenant refused to renew the lease and gave notice that he had hired other premises." Taylor on Landlord and Tenant (9th ed.), sec. 22. In a later work of equal authority the prevailing rule is similarly stated in this language: "By the decided weight of authority in this country, one holding over may be held liable as a tenant for a further period without reference to his actual wishes on the subject. As is frequently expressed, the landlord has the option to treat him as a tenant for a further term or a trespasser." Tiffany's Landlord and Tenant, secs. 209, 211, 212.

This rule does not seem to have been expressly adopted in this jurisdiction. It was mentioned in the late case of Rice v. Baltimore Apartment Co., 141 Md. 507, 517, 518, 119 A. 364; but earlier instances in the reports of asserted liability on the part of a tenant holding over are referable to a new contract resulting from the express or implied consent of the parties.

The rule is sometimes stated to be based on the theory that the tenant holding over presumably intends to prolong the duration of his tenancy by another term, and that he cannot overcome this presumption by setting up, to the disadvantage of the landlord, that he is holding as a wrongdoer. See Tiffany on Landlord and Tenant, vol. 2, p. 1472. Mr. Williston finds the rule to be an illustration of the "general principle that when an act may rightfully be done with certain consequences or effect, the actor cannot assert for his own advantage to avoid that effect, that the act was done wrongfully." Williston on Contracts, vol. 3, sec. 1856, pp. 3179, 3180.

It is difficult to ascribe the liability to contract, when this liability exists notwithstanding any statement, however explicit, of a contrary intention by the tenant. Mr. Tiffany prefers, and it seems the better view, to regard the liability of the tenant wrongfully holding over as one imposed by law on the tenant, without his express or implied consent, and enforceable in an action at law as a quasi-contractual obligation in order that justice may be done between the parties. Tiffany on Landlord and Tenant, vol. 2, p. 1472; Williston on Contracts, vol. 1, sec. 3; sec. 21, no. 20, p. 24. Corbin's Anson on Contracts, p. 571 and notes. Tiffany on Real Property (2nd Ed.), vol. 1, pp. 247 et seq.

The rule imposes a penalty upon the individual tenant wrongfully holding over, but ultimately operates for the benefit of tenants as a class by its tendency to secure the agreed surrender of terms to incoming tenants who have severally yielded possession of other premises in anticipation of promptly entering into the possession of the new. This makes for confidence in leasehold transactions. Again, the terms of the leases of property which is rented for business, commercial, residential, and agricultural uses tend to begin and end at a customary date or during a particular season of the year, as determined by the nature of the use of the specific property, and as the value of any piece of property is largely dependent upon its actual or potential continuing yield in periodic rent, the social and economic importance of the landlord being able certainly to deliver, and the prospective tenant so to obtain possession on the stipulated day, is obvious.

These considerations afford a sound and rational basis for the adoption of a rule which is supported by the great weight of authority in this country and, now, probably, in England. *Supra;* Dougal v. McCarthy (1893) L.R. 1 Q.B. 736.

If the tenant had intended to hold over and the landlords had accepted the payment of the installment of rent, a tenancy from year to year would have arisen by agreement of the parties. Hall v. Myers, 43 Md. 446. Because of their close analogy the quasi-contractual obligation imposed by law should be similar to the one imposed by the tenant holding over by consent, so, the tenancy in the instant case was a tenancy from year to year. *Supra.*

The testimony is clear that, when the defendant failed to surrender the premises at the end of the original period of letting, without any basis in law or fact for such action, the landlords forthwith exercised their option and elected to treat the defendant as their tenant from year to year. This new tenancy was subject to the provisions of the original lease with reference to the rent and to the other obligations so far as they are applicable, as though the new tenancy had been created by the consent of the parties. The defendant was, therefore, bound to pay $7,000 as the stipulated rent for the year next ensuing the end of period of the first lease.

The defendant further contends that, even if there were a new tenancy from year to year, the following clause of the original lease limits the loss and damage recoverable by the plaintiffs, and that there was no legally sufficient proof that the plaintiffs had sustained any injury within the contemplation of this clause:

> The tenant agrees that it will vacate the premises on the expiration date as originally fixed herein, or upon the earlier termination of said term, in the event of a sale or contract of sale as above provided or upon any other termination of said lease in accordance with the terms hereof. In the event of a failure of the tenant to so vacate, then the tenant shall be liable to the landlords for all loss or damage which the landlords may suffer through a loss of sale or loss of lease or otherwise by reason of said failure to vacate and said liability and the rights of the landlords shall be in addition to all the rights which said landlords might be entitled under any present or future law for speedy ejectment or recovery of possession of said premises.

The election by the landlords to continue the defendant as their tenant for another year created a tenancy from year to year, that began with the termination of the original period of renting and made the defendant's possession rightful from this beginning of his new tenancy. So, by this election, the landlords waived all claim against the defendant with respect to its failure to surrender possession at the close of the first period, and the terms of the tenancy from year to year will determine the rights and liabilities of the parties. 2 Tiffany on Landlord and Tenant, sec. 212, p. 1496. If the quoted provisions be assumed to be consistent with the tenancy from year to year, and, therefore, become provisions of this tenancy, they do not affect the right of the landlord to recover the unpaid installments of the yearly rent of the new tenancy. These quoted provisions do not relate to rent, but to damages which the landlord may sustain by a failure of the tenant to surrender possession as agreed. This is made clear by the subsequent and express provision of the original lease that, if the rent be and remain in arrear for a prescribed time, the landlords may re-enter, and determine the lease, and demise the premises; and, at the option of the landlords, the tenant shall remain liable during the unexpired portion of the term for the deficit between any rent received by the landlords and the rent stipulated to be paid. Furthermore, the covenants in the lease to pay rent and to be liable for damages for a failure to surrender the premises as agreed create obligations with reference to two different undertakings.

In the instant case, the tenant did not refuse to vacate the premises during the new tenancy. On the contrary, after paying one monthly installment of the yearly rent, the tenant repudiated the tenancy, abandoned the premises, and refused to pay the rent. The testimony shows that the landlords did not resume possession to the exclusion of the tenant, but notified the tenant that it would be held for the rent unpaid. The fact that the plaintiffs made diligent effort to procure a tenant for the unexpired term did not relieve the defendant of its liability for rent but, by the implied terms of the tenancy, would have inured to the benefit of the defendant, if a tenant had been procured at any time before the expiration of the year of the defendant's tenancy. Oldewurtel v. Wiesenfeld, 97 Md. 165, 176, 54 A. 969; Tiffany on Real Property (2nd Ed.), sec. 43, p. 1586.

For the reasons stated there was no error in the court's refusal to grant the defendant's instruction for a directed verdict in its favor, and the judgment will be affirmed.

Judgment affirmed, with costs to the appellee.[2]

---

2. But see N.Y. Real Prop. Law §232-c, which provides:

> Where a tenant whose term is longer than one month holds over after the expiration of such term, such holding over shall not give to the landlord the option to hold the tenant for a new term solely by virtue of the tenant's holding over. In the case of such a holding over by the tenant, the landlord may proceed, in any manner permitted by law, to remove the tenant, or, if the landlord shall accept rent for any period subsequent to the expiration of such term, then, unless an agreement either express or implied is made providing otherwise, the tenancy created by the acceptance of such rent shall be a tenancy from month to month commencing on the first day after the expiration of such term.

As to terminating a tenancy from month to month, see N.Y. Real Prop. Law §232-a for tenancies in New York City and §232-b for tenancies outside the city of New York. See also the Massachusetts statutory material discussed at page 246, footnotes 36-38, *supra.* — EDS.

MASON v. WIERENGO'S ESTATE
113 Mich. 151, 71 N.W. 489 (1897)

Lyman G. Mason presented a claim for rent against the estate of Andrew Wierengo, deceased. The claim was disallowed by the commissioners, and claimant appealed to the circuit court. From a judgment for part of the amount claimed, on verdict directed by the court, claimant brings error. Reversed.

HOOKER, J. The plaintiff, being owner of a building, leased the same for a term of years, at an annual rental, to Wierengo, who occupied it as a store. A short time before the expiration of the lease, Wierengo rented another building, and informed the plaintiff that he should vacate the building owned by him at the expiration of the lease. Preparation for removal began September 19th, and actual removal began before September 26th. Counsel for the defendant claim that the lease expired October 1st, at midnight. On September 26th, after the removal began, Wierengo was taken sick. The work of removal was continued by his clerks, but was not finished until October 11th. Mr. Wierengo died on the 6th of October. Under these circumstances, counsel for the defense assert that the presumption of a renting for another year is rebutted. They also contend that it was made impossible for Wierengo to vacate, by the act of God.

If it is contended that the act of God excuses one from the performance of his express contract to yield possession at the expiration of his lease, we are unable to acquiesce in the contention. It is only in those contracts which the act of God renders impossible of performance — as where the subject-matter of the contract dies, or is destroyed, or where personal labor is contracted for, and the person dies or becomes incapacitated through the act of God — that a party is excused from performance. See Beach, Cont. Sec. 217, where this question is discussed, and 1 Am. & Eng. Enc. Law (2d Ed.), 588-592, where a large list of authorities confirm this doctrine. If, therefore, the sickness of Mr. Wierengo has any bearing upon the case, it is as a circumstance bearing upon the question of the rebuttal of the presumption.

Counsel urge strenuously that the presumption of an intention to renew the lease for a year arising from holding over is not conclusive, but that it may be rebutted. As a matter of fact, undoubtedly it may; but it is not so clear that it would constitute a defense against the claim of a landlord who should acquiesce, and elect to treat the holding over as a renewal of the lease for a year, rather than as a trespass. In the absence of qualifying circumstances implying consent to a holding under some new arrangement, the holding over is a legal trespass, and does not depend upon the intention of the tenant. It is a wrongful holding, whatever the cause, though perhaps not culpable in a moral sense, and the rights of the landlord are definitely fixed by the law. This question was reviewed in Campau v. Michell, 103 Mich. 617, 623, 61 N.W. 890, and the opinion of the court as there indicated was contrary to the defendant's position in this case. That case was exceptional, in that the defendant's tenant was induced to hold over by the mistake or misconduct of the plaintiff's agent, and the doctrine of estoppel was applied. See, also, Bradley v. Slater, 50 Neb. 682, 70 N.W. 258.

We think that there is uniformity in the decisions against the contention that the intention to vacate as soon as possible can affect the right of the landlord to elect to treat the holding over as a renewal of the lease for a year. It requires some express or implied consent upon his part to a holding over upon other conditions. This is wanting here. Counsel urge the hardship of the application of the rule in this case, but we cannot say that there is or is not hardship, or that we would be justified in imposing a burden upon the plaintiff to relieve the defendant from a legal obligation He appears to have tried to rent the place, and has given defendant credit for what he has been able to derive from the building. Had Wierengo lived, he might have made the same claim if asked to pay the rent for another year, but it would not have relieved him. The situation, as it is, only differs in the degree of inconvenience, intensified as it is by the death of Wierengo, and the change in his affairs naturally resulting. It is unfortunate for his representatives that the store was not vacated, but we discover no legal reason for lifting the burden of misfortune from them, and imposing it upon another, who is in no way responsible for it.

The judgment is reversed, and a new trial ordered.[3]

The other Justices concurred.

Problems

21.1. L and T entered into a written lease of residential premises. The term of the lease was one year. Prior to the end of the year T vacated all but one room of the leased premises. The one room not vacated was a bedroom in which T's mother was confined by a dangerous illness; the physician in charge had advised T that any moving or disturbing of T's mother at the time the lease expired would imperil her life. T moved the mother from the bedroom 15 days after the date on which the lease expired, at which time she had passed the dangerous phase in her illness. L has elected to hold T as a tenant for another year. Is L entitled to do so? See Herter v. Mullen, 159 N.Y. 28, 53 N.E. 700 (1899).

21.2. L and T entered into a written lease of an apartment for a term of one year. The lease contained a clause providing that if T did not relinquish possession of the leased premises at the expiration of the lease, T would be liable for double rent for the period T held over. T notified L two months before the expiration of the lease that T would vacate at the end of the term. T made arrangements with a moving company and began vacating the

---

3. See American Law of Property §3.33 (Casner ed. 1952).—Eds.

leased premises three days before the lease expired. By twelve o'clock on the night the lease expired, everything had been moved out of the apartment except the bedroom furniture and a few rugs. T and T's family and servants slept in the apartment that night and promptly moved everything out the next morning. L served T with a notice on the morning after the lease expired which stated that since the apartment was not vacated at the expiration of the lease L had "elected, and does hereby elect, to treat you as a hold-over tenant for another year." T refused to pay the rent for the succeeding months, and L brought an action to recover the same. Judgment for whom? See Commonwealth Building Corp. v. Hirschfield, 307 Ill. App. 533, 30 N.E.2d 790 (1940).

21.3. L and T entered into a written lease of certain premises for a term of one year. Shortly before the end of the year, L and T entered into negotiations for a new lease. They were still negotiating when the term expired, and T remained in possession of the leased premises. They were unable to come to an agreement on a new lease, and T moved from the leased premises as soon as negotiations broke off. Since T did not vacate the premises at the end of the term, may L hold him as a tenant for another year? See Lawson v. West Virginia Newspaper Publishing Co., 126 W. Va. 470, 29 S.E.2d 3 (1944).

21.4. At this point you should go back to Problem 17.3 and carefully reconsider the potential liability of the hold-over T_1 not only to L but also to T_2, analyzing all possible theories of recovery by each.

MARGOSIAN v. MARKARIAN
288 Mass. 197, 192 N.E. 612 (1934)

Tort. Writ in the Central District Court of Worcester dated June 7, 1933.

In the District Court, the action was heard by Wall, J. Material evidence, and findings and rulings made by him, are described in the opinion. He found for the defendant and reported the action to the Appellate Division for the Western District. The record did not disclose whether, before the giving of the notice to vacate described in the opinion, the plaintiff's husband was a tenant at will or a tenant under a lease in writing. The report was ordered dismissed. The plaintiff appealed.

CROSBY, J. This is an action of tort to recover for personal injuries received by the plaintiff on April 18, 1933, as the result of a fall on a defective stairway upon premises occupied by the plaintiff and her husband and owned by the defendant.

The trial judge found that "Upon all the evidence . . . the plaintiff was injured by reason of a defect in a stairway in a house owned and controlled by the defendant and that said injuries happened on April 18, 1933 . . . that the notice to vacate for nonpayment of rent was duly received by the plaintiff's husband on April 1, 1933 . . . [and] that on

April 14, 1933, the defendant commenced action for possession of the premises occupied by the plaintiff and the plaintiff's husband." He ruled "that the plaintiff's husband at the time of the accident was a tenant at sufferance in the premises . . . [and] that the plaintiff is in no better position in regard to the premises than her husband." He further found "that there was no wanton or wilful act committed by the defendant which caused the injuries to the plaintiff, and that the husband of the plaintiff and the plaintiff herself both stand in the position as tenants at sufferance," and he therefore found for the defendant. The plaintiff in her brief states that she "is the widow of a former tenant at will of the defendant." The trial judge found, and the plaintiff's counsel admitted, that the plaintiff's husband was in arrears for rent, that he had received a notice to quit for nonpayment of rent more than fourteen days prior to the accident, and that her husband had been served with summary process to vacate the premises at a date prior to the accident. The judge also found that the defendant introduced evidence that the writ of summary process was returnable on April 22, 1933, and that on May 31, 1933, execution was issued in that action. The plaintiff claimed a report to the Appellate Division. That court ordered the following entry to be made: "Report dismissed. No prejudicial error found."

The only question presented for decision is whether the trial judge erred in ruling that the plaintiff's husband at the time of the accident was a tenant at sufferance, that the plaintiff was in no better position than her husband, and accordingly in the absence of wanton or wilful act on the part of the defendant the plaintiff was not entitled to recover.

A tenant at sufferance has no estate nor title, but only a naked possession, without right and wrongfully, and stands in no privity to the landlord. Benton v. Williams, 202 Mass. 189, 192, 88 N.E. 843. A tenant at sufferance is not entitled to notice to quit but is a holder without right. Kelly v. Waite, 12 Metc. 300, 302. A tenant at sufferance is a bare licensee to whom the landlord owes merely the duty not wantonly nor wilfully to injure him. There was no evidence which would warrant a finding that the plaintiff's injuries were due to any wanton or wilful act committed by the defendant. In addition to the common law rule that a tenancy at sufferance comes into existence when the landlord gives notice to quit for nonpayment of rent, the same result follows under G.L. (Ter. Ed.) c. 186, Sec. 12, which provides in part as follows: ". . . in case of neglect or refusal to pay the rent due from a tenant at will, fourteen days' notice to quit, given in writing by the landlord to the tenant, shall be sufficient to determine the tenancy."

Counsel for the plaintiff has cited Osborne v. Wells, 213 Mo. App. 319, 249 S.W. 705. In that case the court denied a request for a ruling in substance to the effect that where a notice to quit for nonpayment of rent had been given the landlord was liable only for wanton and wilful conduct. The court held that "Although defendant had instituted proceedings to dispossess plaintiff, still, at any time before the order of dispossession was served on him plaintiff might have paid up the rent and continued the tenancy." The answer to this statement is that under our statute a tenant at will who has received a fourteen days' notice to quit for nonpayment of rent cannot by paying the rent in full revive the tenancy, and a fortiori, a tenant who not only has received a notice to quit for nonpayment, but upon whom summary process has already been served, cannot revive the tenancy. G.L. (Ter. Ed.) c. 186, Sec. 11, provides:

> Upon the neglect or refusal to pay the rent due under a written lease, fourteen days' notice to quit, given in writing by the landlord to the tenant, shall be sufficient to determine the lease, unless the tenant, at least four days before the return day of the writ, in an action by the landlord to recover possession of the premises, pays or tenders to the landlord or to his attorney all rent then due, with interest and costs of suit.

This is the only provision in our statutes for reviving a tenancy by paying overdue rent. However, G.L. (Ter. Ed.) c. 186, Sec. 12, which provides for the termination of a tenancy at will by fourteen days' notice to quit for nonpayment of rent, contains no provision permitting the tenant after notice to revive the tenancy. [Section 12 was amended in 1946 to allow a tenant who has not received a similar notice in the previous 12 months to retain his estate if he pays the rent within five days of receiving the notice.] The distinction between these two statutes is pointed out by Chief Justice Morton in Hodgkins v. Price, 137 Mass. 13, at page 18.

As there was no error in the rulings given and in the judge's refusals to rule, or in the decision of the Appellate Division, the entry must be

Order dismissing report affirmed.

GOWER v. WATERS
125 Me. 223, 132 A. 550 (1926)

On report. An action of trespass quare clausum alleging a breaking and entering of plaintiff's dwelling-house. The defendant, Angeletta P. Waters, owned in fee the dwelling-house described in the writ, and the plaintiff, on March 3, 1925, occupied, as tenant of Mrs. Waters, a part of the dwelling-house, the rest being reserved for her own use by Mrs. Waters. The plaintiff being in arrears in rent the defendant gave him the statutory written notice to quit, and on the expiration of the thirty days, the plaintiff continued to occupy the premises against the wishes of defendant, who with the other defendants entered and demanded possession of that part of the dwelling-house occupied by plaintiff. Defendants contended that there was no breaking and entering because the defendant, Waters, had a right to enter the premises, the plaintiff being a tenant at sufferance, and that an action of trespass quare clausum could not be maintained under such circumstances. At the close of the testimony by consent of the parties the case was reported to the Law Court for final determination, including damages to plaintiff, if he should prevail. Judgment for defendants.

The case fully appears in the opinion.

WILSON, C.J. An action of trespass quare clausum in which it is alleged that the defendants broke and entered the plaintiff's dwelling-house located on the close described in the writ.

The case is reported to this court on the evidence. From the reported evidence we find that the plaintiff prior to April 2, 1925 occupied a portion of a certain dwelling-house belonging to the defendant, Angeletta P. Waters, as a tenant at will; that on the third day of March, 1925 the owner, Mrs. Waters, caused to be served on the plaintiff a notice that his tenancy in the premises described in the writ in this action would terminate on April 2, 1925; that the plaintiff did not vacate said premises on April 2, but remained and was still occupying said premises on April 6th following; that on April 6th, the defendant with the defendant, Alfred W. Huston, a deputy sheriff, and the other two defendants who were nephews of Mrs. Waters went to the premises for the purpose of taking possession of the part occupied by the plaintiff; that the defendants first went to the back or side door leading to the part occupied by the plaintiff as a kitchen and asked to be permitted to enter and were refused admission by the plaintiff's wife, the plaintiff being away at the time; that the defendants then entered the front door of the dwelling-house and the front hall which was then and had been in the sole possession of Mrs. Waters, who also retained in her own possession several other rooms in the house; that while in the hall the plaintiff's wife notified the defendants that she forbade their entering the part occupied by the plaintiff, that while the defendant Huston was again talking with the plaintiff's wife at the side or back door, Mrs. Waters opened a door leading from the front hall into a room occupied by the plaintiff as a bedroom; which door was not locked, but was fastened on the hall side by a hook or hasp; that Mrs. Waters then entered the bedroom and thence the sitting room occupied by the plaintiff without using any more force than was necessary to open the door leading from the hall into the bedroom, and was followed by the other defendants.

After Mrs. Waters entered in the above manner, she demanded possession of the premises, and later the plaintiff returned and an agreement was entered into for the payment of rent to date, and the plaintiff was permitted to remain until he obtained another tenement.

The present action is the result of the entry above described. There appears to be no question, from the above facts, that at the time of the entry the plaintiff's tenancy at will had been terminated on April 2, and he was, on April 6th, only a tenant at sufferance, and that the defendant, Mrs. Waters, had a right to possession.

The only issues here are, whether the entry of Mrs. Waters was a peaceful entry, and if not, whether a tenant at sufferance can maintain trespass quare clausum against his landlord who, using no more force than may be necessary to effect an entrance, enters to dispossess him.

If a peaceful entry is had, it is already settled that a tenant at sufferance cannot maintain trespass quare clausum against his landlord. Sterns v. Sampson, 59 Me. 568. While there is a conflict, the great weight of authority appears to be that, unless affected by some local statute, a landlord as against a tenant at sufferance may enter to take possession, using no more force than is necessary to effect an entrance and in expelling the tenant no more than would enable him to maintain a plea of molliter manus; and by reasoning that appears unassailable, it is further held by courts of the highest standing, that regardless of the force used in entering, trespass quare clausum is not maintainable.

In Reed v. Reed, 48 Me. 388, Allen v. Bicknell, 36 Me. 436, 438, and Sterns v. Sampson, *supra,* this court appears to have recognized the same principles upon which the above authorities are based, though the facts did not require them to be carried to the same extent.

As the court said in Dunning v. Finson, 46 Me. 546, 556: "A tenant at sufferance can hardly be called a tenant at all as his holding is without right of any kind," unless, under some circumstances, he is entitled to a reasonable time for the removal of his goods. It is because of the nature of the tenancy at sufferance that the Massachusetts and other courts have held that such a "tenant could not maintain an action in the nature of trespass quare clausum, because the title and the lawful right to possession are in the landlord, and the tenant as against him has no right of occupation whatever"; hence it has been held that even if entry by the landlord was obtained by force, trespass quare clausum will not lie. Low v. Elwell, *supra;* Mentzer v. Hudson Savings Bk., *supra;* Benton v. Williams, *supra.*

The courts which hold the contrary view, Dustin v. Cowdry, 23 Vt. 631, Mason v. Hawes, 52 Conn. 12, Reader v. Purdy, 41 Ill. 280, either rest their decisions in the main upon the English cases of Hillary v. Gay, 6 C. & P. 284, a case decided at nisi prius, and Newton v. Harland, 1 M. & G. 644, which was later overruled; see Harvey v. Brydges, 14 M. & W. 437; Davis v. Burrell, 10 C.B. 821; or upon a construction of a statute substantially of the tenor of the early English statute, 5 Rich. II., C. 8: "That none from henceforth shall make any entry into lands or tenements, but in case where entry is given by law, and in such case, not with strong hand nor with multitude of people, but only in a peaceable and easy manner" and making a forcible entry an indictable offense. The Vermont Court rests its decision mainly upon the authority of the English cases, while the Illinois Court holds that a statute similar to that of Rich. II. makes a forcible entry unlawful, and if it is unlawful, it is a trespass.

These cases have been extensively reviewed and their reasoning criticized in 4 Am. Law Rev. 429. The decisions in the various courts as to the right of tenant at sufferance to maintain trespass quare clausum against his landlord may be found in 16 L.R.A. 798, Note; 42 L.R.A. (N.S.) 392, Note.

It may be noted at this point, that we have no statute similar to that of Rich. II., although forcible entry is recognized as an offense at common law, Hardings Case, 1 Maine, 22, indicating that the statute has been adopted as a part of our common law.

However, this statute did not change the nature of a tenancy at sufferance or restrict the rights of the landlord to enter except to make him liable to indictment for the use of unnecessary force. Neither the English Courts nor those in this country above cited, holding that trespass quare clausum will not lie even though the entry be forcible, regard this, or similar statutes, as having any effect upon the civil liability of the landlord. Sterling v. Warden, *supra,* Page 232. Without such a statute and with the common law in this respect unmodified, under which the landlord had the right to enter by force, if necessary, in case of a tenancy at sufferance, Taylor's Landlord & Tenant, Vol. II., Sec. 531, we see no reason why this court should not adopt the rule laid down by the English Courts and the courts of Massachusetts, Rhode Island, New Hampshire, and New York.

It is true that in Brock v. Berry, 31 Me. 293, this Court in a brief opinion without reasoning or citation of authorities, held that a landlord had no right to enter by force. It is not clear that the court in this case was stating its conclusions as applicable to a tenancy at sufferance. Although the parties had agreed the tenancy was at sufferance, the facts showed the tenancy was at will and had not been terminated, hence the mandate was correct. It is significant, however, that this case has never been cited by this court in support of the rights of a tenant at sufferance, but always in support of the rule that a landlord cannot enter and oust a tenant at will by force. Cunningham v. Holton, 55 Me. 33, 38; Kimball v. Sumner, 62 Me. 305, 309; Bryant v. Sparrow, 62 Me. 546; Marden v. Jorden, 65 Me. 9.

Moore v. Boyd, 24 Me. 242, cited by the Vermont Court in Dustin v. Cowdry as sustaining the doctrine that a landlord is liable in an action of trespass quare clausum for a forcible entry in case of a tenancy at sufferance, goes no further than to hold that a landlord may not enter by force to terminate a tenancy at will and remove the tenant's goods without first giving the tenant a reasonable opportunity to remove his own effects, and was decided before the present statute was enacted for terminating tenancies at will by notice in writing. It has no bearing on the question here at issue.

A statement of the law upon the subject may be found so full and logical, in Sterling v. Warden, 51 N.H. 217, Low v. Elwell, 121 Mass. 309, and 4 Am. L. Rev., 429, that a further discussion here would be a work of supererogation.

At common law the process known as forcible entry and detainer was criminal or quasi criminal in its nature, Eveleth v. Gill, 97 Me. 315, 54 A. 756, and was only permitted where the entry or the detainer or both were with actual force. By Chapter 268, Public Laws, 1824 this state created a civil remedy more or less summary in its nature and known by the same name, but also available only in case of a forcible entry or detainer, except in case of a terminated tenancy, when after thirty days' notice in writing following the termination thereof such process would lie, if the tenant then "unlawfully refused to quit" the premises.

However, the existence of this civil process, enlarged as it appears in Chap. 94 R.S., 1857, did not deprive a landlord of his common law right to terminate a tenancy at will without notice and enter upon such termination, Gordon v. Gilman, 48 Me. 473. It furnishes him with a convenient and speedy process to regain possession of his premises of which he may avail himself instead of resorting to an entry without legal process and with force, if necessary, and a consequent liability to indictment in case of the use of excessive force, for which no exact standard can be prescribed for his guidance; but except so far as the statute regulating the use of this process is expressly or by necessary implication in conflict with the common law, it should not be held to deprive a landlord of his common law rights.

We are, therefore, of the opinion and hold that the case of Brock v. Berry should not be regarded as authority against the right of a landlord to enter by the use of reasonable force, if necessary, to expel a tenant at sufferance; and that even in case of the use of excessive force in entering while he is subject to indictment, he is not liable in an action of trespass quare clausum. Seavey v. Cloudman, 90 Me. 536, 38 A. 540.

Entry will be:

Judgment for the defendants.[4]

Note: Forcible Entry and Detainer Statutes

Statutes commonly referred to as forcible entry and detainer statutes exist in most states. Among other things, these statutes provide summary proceedings for the recovery of land by a landlord against a tenant holding over. The historical background of these statutes is summarized in City of Chicago v. Chicago Steamship Lines, Inc., 328 Ill. 309, 159 N.E. 301 (1927), as follows:

> At common law if anyone had a right of entry he was permitted to enter with force and arms and to retain his possession by force, where his entry was lawful. (3 Bacon's Abridgment by Gwillim, p. 248.) It is also stated by this author that this right of entry by the lords created great inconvenience by their arming their tenants and in a manner encouraging those in mischief, who were always too forward in rebellions and contentions in their neighborhood; also that it gave an opportunity to powerful men, under the pretense of feigned titles, forcibly to eject their weaker neighbors. To remedy these evils several statutes were passed, purely criminal in their main features, the first being that of 5 Richard II, chapter 8 [1381], which provided:
>
>> That none from thenceforth should make any entry into any lands and tenements but in cases where entry is given by law, and in such cases not with strong hand nor with multitude of people but only in a peaceable and easy manner; and if any man from henceforth should do the contrary, and thereof be duly convict, he should be punished by imprisonment of his body and thereof ransomed at the king's will.

---

4. Reread at this point Jordan v. Talbot, page 438 *supra*. — EDS.

Said statutes, as stated in the side notes to Bacon's Abridgment (vol. 3, p. 249), gave no speedy remedy, leaving the party injured to the common course of proceeding by way of indictment and made no provision at all against forcible detainer. It was followed later by 15 Richard II, chapter 2 [1391], which provided that said statute, and all others against forcible entries, should be duly executed; "and further, that at all times that such forcible entry shall be made and complaint thereof cometh to the justices of the peace, or to any of them, that the same justices or justice take sufficient power of the county and go to the place where the force is made, and if they find any that hold such place forcibly, after such entry made, they shall be taken and put into the next gaol, there to abide, convict by the record of the same justices or justice, until they have made fine and ransom to the king." As stated by the author, this latter statute gave no remedy against those who were guilty of forcible detainer after a peaceable entry, or against those who were guilty of both a forcible entry and detainer, if they were removed before the coming of a justice of the peace, and it gave the justice of the peace no power to restore the party to his possession. Such power to restore the ousted party to his possession was later given by 8 Henry VI, chapter 9 [1429], in this language:

> That though such persons making such entries be present, or else departed before the coming of the said justices or justice, notwithstanding the same justices or justice in some good town next to the tenement so entered, or in some other convenient place, according to their discretion, shall have, and either of them shall have, authority and power to inquire by the people of the same county, as well of them that makes such forcible entries in lands and tenements, as of them which the same held with force; and if it be found before any of them that any doth contrary to this statute, then the said justices or justice shall cause to re-seize the lands and tenements so entered and holden as aforesaid, and shall put the party so put out in full possession of the same lands and tenements so entered or holden as before.

This statute also gave the party aggrieved a remedy by assize of novel disseizin or by an action of trespass to recover treble damages for being ousted by force. It appears from the authorities cited by the author in his side notes, that to said actions the defendant might plead in bar thereof that he had good title and right of entry before his unlawful entry, if in his plea he further traversed the entry by force. If the matter in bar was found for the defendant, — that is, that he had good title at law and right of entry, — he prevailed in the suit for the reason that the party ousted should not recover if he had no right to damages, but if the plaintiff prevailed then the force must be inquired of, and treble damages assessed to plaintiff in case the plaintiff succeeded on that issue. The statute of 8 Henry VI further provided: "That they who keep their possessions with force in any lands and tenements whereof they or their ancestors, or they whose estate they have in such lands and tenements, have continued their possession by three years or more, be not endamaged by force of this statute." This last provision is further enforced and explained by 31 Elizabeth, chapter 11 [1589], which provides:

> That no restitution upon any indictment of forcible entry or holding with force be made to any person if the person so indicted has had the

occupation or been in quiet possession for the space of three whole years together next before the day of such indictment so found and his estate therein not ended, which the party indicted may allege for stay of restitution, and restitution to stay till that be tried, if the other will deny or traverse the same.

For the provisions of said statutes and comments aforesaid, see 3 Bacon's Abridgment by Gwillim, pp. 249-252. [328 Ill. at 312, 159 N.E. at 302.]

The local statutes on forcible entry and detainer vary to such an extent that generalizations about them are unsafe. You are referred to your own jurisdiction for details.[5]

JONES v. TAYLOR
136 Ky. 39, 123 S.W. 326 (1909)

Opinion of the court by CARROLL, J. — Reversing.

This is the second appeal of this case. The former opinion may be found in 104 S.W. 782, 31 Ky. Law Rep. 1148. From the facts therein stated it appears that Jones under parol contracts rented and cultivated the farm of Mrs. Bedford for the year beginning March 1, 1904, and ending March 1, 1905, and for the year beginning March 1, 1905, and ending March 1, 1906 — the agreed rental each year being $500 — and that Jones, insisting that he had again rented the farm for the year beginning March 1, 1906, refused to surrender possession of the premises on March 1, 1906. Upon his refusal to surrender possession Mrs. Bedford obtained a writ of forcible detainer against him. On the trial of this writ a jury in the country found Jones not guilty, but upon a traverse in the circuit court he was found guilty of forcibly detaining the premises, and a judgment of restitution awarded Mrs. Bedford. From this judgment Jones prosecuted an appeal to this court, which affirmed the judgment of the lower court; the judgment of this court becoming final on November 27, 1907. In 1908 this action was brought against Jones and his securities in a supersedeas bond executed to stay the judgment of the circuit court, to recover $500, the reasonable rent of the premises for the year beginning March, 1, 1906, and also $500 additional, as double rent for his wrongful refusal to deliver possession of the premises for the year 1906. In his answer Jones did not dispute the right to recover rent, but resisted the attempt to make him pay double rent. He set up, in substance, that he contested the efforts of Mrs. Bedford to recover the premises because he in good faith believed that he had rented the same from her for the year beginning March 1, 1906; that pending the disposition of the appeal in the Court of Appeals, and until its judgment was entered in the circuit court, he remained in possession of the premises; that he did not prosecute the appeal or remain in the occupation of the premises with any desire to wrongfully keep Mrs. Bedford out of possession, but because he believed in good faith that the judgment of the Bourbon circuit court would be reversed upon appeal; that before March 1, 1906, he employed and advised with competent attorneys concerning the dispute between himself and Mrs. Bedford, and placed them in full possession of all the facts relating to the matter, and, after being so informed, the attorneys advised him that he could retain possession of the premises for the year beginning March 1, 1906, and, acting upon their advice, he resisted the efforts of Mrs. Bedford to evict him, and prosecuted the appeal from the judgment of the Bourbon circuit court to this court. To this answer a general demurrer was sustained, and, declining to plead further, a judgment was rendered against Jones for $500, the reasonable rent of the place for 1906, and for the further sum of $500 as double rent. Jones paid the $500 adjudged against him as rent, and all of the cost of the action, and prosecutes this appeal only from so much of the judgment as requires him to pay $500 as double rent.

The only matter for our decision is, Did the answer of Jones present a good defense to so much of the action as sought to recover double rent? In the consideration of this question we must accept as true the statements in his answer, which were admitted by the demurrer. Section 2293 of the Kentucky Statutes (section 4551, Russell's St.), under which double rent was allowed by the lower court, reads as follows:

> A tenant who, after having given notice of his intention to quit possession of the premises, fails to do so at the time specified, or a tenant whose term expires at a time certain who shall refuse to deliver possession, or a tenant who, having entered under an agreement to dispense with notice, refuses to deliver possession when the same is demanded, shall pay to the landlord double the rent he would have otherwise been bound to pay, to be computed from the time he should have surrendered possession, recoverable in same manner as original rent. If, by the contract, the term is to expire at a time certain or notice to quit is dispensed with, none need be given.

This statute is substantially a copy of an English statute passed during the reign of George II. The English statute provided that if a tenant willfully held over, he should be liable for double rent, and it was decided by the English courts in several cases that, if a tenant remained in possession under a fair, though mistaken, claim of right, he was not liable to an action for double rent, and that the question of whether his right to hold over was bona fide or mere pretense was for the jury. Wood's Landlord & Tenant, sec. 485; Woodfall's Landlord & Tenant, p. 584.

In Swinfen v. Bacon, 6 Hurlstone & Norman's English Reports, p. 845, Chief Justice Cockburn said, in a case involving the construction of the English statute:

Ever since the case of Wright v. Smith, 5 Esp. 203, 215, decided more than half a century ago, the interpretation put upon St. 4 Geo. II, c. 28, has been that when a person holds over, not contumaciously as against the person entitled to the possession, but under a bona fide belief that he has a right to do so, the statute does not apply. I think it would be very mischievous, as well as contrary to the true construction of the act, if we were to hold otherwise, for I am strongly of opinion that "willfully" holding over applies only when a tenant holds over in the absence of a bona fide belief that he is justified in doing so. In the present case the defendant, who held under the testator as tenant from year to year, accepted a fresh grant from the devisees. After that he found the heir at law disputing the will, and was in doubt whether he was tenant to the heir at law or the devisee, not knowing whether the devisee had power to grant him a fresh term or not, but bona fide believing that the grant was inoperative. It is in fact admitted that the defendant acted under a bona fide belief that Captain Swinfen had the better title, and that the devisee had no title. We do not think that this is a case to which the statute was intended to apply. It has been long held, and we think rightly, that the statute applies only to the case of a tenant who holds over though he is conscious that he has no right to retain possession.

In Aull v. Bowling Green Opera House Co., 130 Ky. 789, 114 S.W. 284, we had before us a case in which a landlord was seeking to recover double rent under the statute, and we said:

> As we construe this section, it means that if a tenant, knowingly and wrongfully, remains in the possession of property, not believing, nor having any reason to believe, that he has a right to remain in possession thereof, refuses to deliver to his landlord possession of the property, then he may be adjudged to pay double rent. The case before us is not of that character. Appellant had what he had reason to believe was a binding contract with the landlord, which permitted him to remain in possession of the property, as tenant, for a term of three years, and such a contract as courts might differ as to the effect of, and his remaining in possession of the property under such circumstances, ought not to place upon him the liability of paying double rent, and the court did not err in failing to charge him with it.

In the light of these authorities, which accord with our views of the proper construction of the statute, the answer presented a defense upon which Jones was entitled to a jury trial. If he in good faith, based upon reasonable grounds, believed that he had a valid contract with Mrs. Bedford, under which he had the right to remain in possession of the rented premises upon the payment of the rent agreed upon, and, actuated by this belief, resisted her efforts to deprive him of the property, he is not liable for double rent. The statute was enacted for the purpose of preventing a tenant, to the prejudice and loss of the landlord, from wrongfully withholding the property without having in good faith cause to believe he could rightfully do so. And so, unless it appears that in refusing to deliver the possession the tenant is acting in good faith, produced by an honest belief, based on reasonable facts and circumstances, he cannot escape the penalty for his refusal to deliver possession according to the contract or when his term expired. The tenant cannot relieve himself from the statutory penalty by the mere statement that he believed he had a right to hold the premises. He must furnish reasons sufficient to induce a jury or court hearing the case to believe that he in good faith, based upon reasonable grounds, believed he had a right to remain in possession. Whether a tenant acts in good faith is a question of fact, and it is admissible for him to show that he laid his case before a competent attorney, and was advised that he had a contract right to remain in possession of the premises. But evidence as to the advice of counsel will not be competent, unless the client placed before him all the facts in his possession relating to the case.

Wherefore, the judgment is reversed, with directions to the court below to grant a new trial in conformity with this opinion.[6]

Problem

21.5. T, the owner of a used car business, leased certain business premises from L for a ten-year term. T decided to move the business to another city and subleased the premises to T_1 for a period ending two weeks before the end of the original lease. T_1 subleased the premises to T_2, falsely informing T_2 that T_1 had the right of possession until the end of the original ten-year term. T_2 then negotiated with L for an additional ten-year term commencing at the end of the original lease. T_2 then took possession and began operating T_2's business until T reappeared and informed T_2 that T_1 only had the right of possession until two weeks before the end of the original lease and that T retained the leasehold interest for that two-week period. T_2 did not want to move for two weeks and then return, so T_2 offered to buy T's two-week term (at a reasonable price); T refused this offer. T_2 then leased larger and more convenient premises just up the block and offered these premises to T for the two-week period; T again refused, insisting on the right of possession of these particular premises for the two-week period. T gave T_1 and T_2 the requisite notice to quit the premises, which notice T_2 ignored. T sued T_2 for $20,000 (the alleged amount of profits T would have made during the two-week period T_2 wrongfully held over). Is it relevant in deciding this case that T did not mitigate T's damage? McCullagh v. Goodyear Tire & Rubber Co., 342 Mich. 244, 69 N.W.2d 731 (1955).

---

6. See N.Y. Real Prop. Law §229, which provides that a tenant is liable for double rent for the period the tenant holds over *after* the tenant gives notice of the intention to quit the premises. — EDS.

CHAPTER 22

FIXTURES[1] (INCLUDING REFERENCE TO EMBLEMENTS)

SIGROL REALTY CORP. v. VALCICH
12 A.D.2d 430, 212 N.Y.S.2d 224 (1961),
aff'd mem., 11 N.Y.2d 668, 180 N.E.2d 904 (1962)

BELDOCK, J.

In 1891, six members of the Wilmore family acquired the tract of waterfront land in Richmond County involved in this action, known as "Robinson's Beach." During the Wilmore ownership seven frame bungalows were placed on the land by various tenants who rented the land space from the landowners for that purpose. The tenants paid rent for the use of the land; they paid for the maintenance and insurance of the bungalows; and from time to time they repaired, altered and sold the bungalows without let or hindrance from the landowners. The tenants occupied the bungalows during the Summer months only.

The bungalows rested on cinder blocks which were not sunk into the ground; the bungalows were not bolted to the ground; and they had no basements. It is not disputed that, upon severance of the water and electrical connections, the bungalows were so constructed that they could be removed without injury either to them or to the land.

Some of the tenants who originally erected the bungalows sold them without requesting or obtaining permission from the Wilmores, the landowners. The seven defendants, either as the original tenants or as their assignees, assert their ownership of the bungalows.

---

1. The late Professor E. H. Warren defined a fixture as "realty with a chattel past and the fear of a chattel future." See generally Note, Fixtures in the Landlord-Tenant Relationship, 34 U. Chi. L. Rev. 617 (1967); American Law of Property §§19.1-19.14 (Casner ed. 1952). See also Restatement (Second) of Property (Landlord and Tenant) §§12.2, 12.3.

On April 9, 1959, the Wilmores, for the sum of $12,250, contracted to sell to the plaintiff the land acquired by them in 1891, with the buildings and improvements thereon, *subject to the rights of tenants, if any.* The contract contained the printed provision that fixtures and articles of personal property attached or appurtenant to the premises "are represented to be owned by the seller, free from all liens and encumbrances." This provision was amended, however, to read that the seller merely represented that all such fixtures and articles of personal property "which are owned by the seller, are free from all liens and encumbrances." On June 11, 1959, the Wilmores executed and delivered a deed in accordance with the contract.

On September 25, 1959, the plaintiff, as landlord, obtained against defendants a final order in a summary proceeding awarding plaintiff possession of the land here involved by reason of the expiration of defendants' term, with a stay to defendants for the removal of their personal property.

When defendants attempted to remove the bungalows, plaintiff, on October 6, 1959, instituted this action to declare that it has title to the bungalows and to restrain defendants from removing them. On October 30, 1959, plaintiff obtained a temporary injunction against such removal. After trial in February, 1960, the court held in favor of plaintiff and made the injunction permanent, on the theory: (1) that the bungalows on the land had the attributes of realty; (2) that the delivery of the deed by the Wilmores to plaintiff carried with it title to the bungalows on the land unless there was an agreement between the Wilmores and defendants pursuant to which defendants' ownership of the bungalows and their right to remove them were recognized; and (3) that defendants failed to prove such an agreement.

For the purpose of determining whether chattels annexed to realty remain personalty or become realty, chattels are divided into three classes: (1) some chattels, such as gas ranges, because of their character as movables, remain personalty even after their annexation, regardless of any agreement between the chattel owner and the landowner (Central Union Gas Co. v. Browning, 210 N.Y. 10); (2) other chattels, such as brick, stone and plaster placed in the walls of a building, become realty after annexation, regardless of any agreement to the contrary between the chattel owner and the landowner; such personal property does not retain its character as such if it be annexed to the realty in such manner as to become an integral part of the realty and be immovable without practically destroying the personal property, or if all or a part of it be essential to the support of the structure to which it is attached (East New York El. Co. v. Petmaland Realty Co., 243 N.Y. 477); and (3) still other chattels, after attachment, continue to be personalty or become realty, in accordance with the agreement between the chattel owner and the landowner (Madfes v. Beverly Development Corp., 251 N.Y. 12, 15).

In my opinion, these bungalows were in the third class, i.e., they were movables which continued to be personalty or became realty, depending on the agreement between the bungalow owners and the landowners, the

Wilmores. There is no contention by plaintiff that the Wilmores ever claimed ownership of the bungalows during their long ownership of the land after the bungalows were placed thereon. The bungalows were erected by defendants or by their predecessors in title without any intention of making them permanent accessions to the realty. The manner of their annexation was such as to make them easily removable without injury either to them or to the land. Defendants and their predecessors in title were tenants of land space only. They repaired, maintained, insured, altered, and sold the bungalows without the consent or interference by the Wilmores.

The fair inference to be drawn from the evidence is that the agreement between the Wilmores and the original owners and the latters' vendees, was that the bungalows were to remain personalty; that the lessees of the land space, at the expiration of the term, would have the right to remove the bungalows as their own personal property; and that the landowner would have no right to prevent them from making such removal (cf. Ombony v. Jones, 19 N.Y. 234, 239, 243). . . .

This plaintiff is not a purchaser for value without notice. It does not claim that the Wilmores ever represented to it, either orally or in writing, that they owned the seven bungalows in question. Only the fixtures and articles of personalty *owned by the Wilmores* were sold. The contract of sale expressly negatived any representation by the Wilmores that they did own the fixtures and articles of personalty. Under the contract the Wilmores sold and the plaintiff purchased the land subject to the rights of the defendants.[2]

The judgment in favor of plaintiff should, therefore, be reversed and judgment should be directed in favor of defendants.

In re ALLEN STREET AND FIRST AVENUE
256 N.Y. 236, 176 N.E. 377 (1931)

LEHMAN, J.

Pursuant to resolution of the board of estimate and apportionment, adopted May 27, 1926, the city of New York instituted proceedings to acquire title in fee to real property required for the widening of Allen street. Title to this real property became vested in the city on December 10, 1926. Greater New York Charter, L. 1901, ch. 466, §976 added by Laws 1915, c. 606 amended by Laws 1917, c. 631. Compensation or damages must be awarded and paid to the owner of the real property taken (section 970 amended by Laws 1922, c. 563); and an owner includes any "person having an estate, interest or easement in the real property to be acquired or a lien, charge or encumbrance thereon" (section 969, subd. 3).

---

2. What possible difference would it make in this action between the purchaser and the tenant if the Wilmores (the landlord) had represented that they owned the seven bungalows in question? —EDS.

At the time the proceedings were instituted, a tenant, David J. Ershowsky, occupied the premises designated on the damage map as parcels Nos. 41 and 42. He used the premises to conduct a butcher trade or business. As between the landlord and himself, he had the right to remove the fixtures at the termination of the lease. Except for the condemnation proceedings, the term of the lease would have expired on May 1, 1927, a few months after the date when title to the real property vested in the city. The lease contained a provision for its earlier termination:

> If the whole or a substantial part of the premises hereby leased shall be taken by the City, County, State or Federal authority for any public purpose, then the term of this lease shall cease from the day when possession of the whole or part so taken shall be acquired for such public purpose, and the rent shall be paid up to that day.

An award has been made to the owner for the value of the leased property, and an award has been made to the tenant as compensation for the fixtures annexed to the property.

Upon this appeal the only question presented is whether the tenant's fixtures are "real property" within the meaning of the statute. At the hearing the city stipulated that "without waiving any objection to the lessee's right to recover in this proceeding compensation for the fixtures installed in the building on Parcels Damage Nos. 41 and 42, the City agrees that if the Court should hold that the lessee is entitled to compensation for the fixtures installed therein, the amount of such compensation shall be the sum of $9,175." We are not concerned with the measure of damages. We must decide only whether the fixtures are so annexed to the land and building that they have become part of them and have been taken by the city.

No testimony was offered at the hearing which would show how these fixtures were annexed to the building, or, indeed, which describes them. It is evident that the court and both parties proceeded upon the assumption that implicit in the stipulation was a concession that the "fixtures" were so annexed to the real property that, while by agreement between landlord and tenant they remained the personal property of the tenant, they would have become part of the real property if they had been installed permanently by the owner of the fee. Our consideration of the record must proceed upon the same assumption.

It is, indeed, conceded by the city that it has become the accepted rule that an award must be made to a tenant for fixtures or structures annexed to the real property, though these are the personal property of the tenant, whenever the city in taking the real property destroys the leasehold interest of the tenant. See Matter of Willcox, 165 App. Div. 197, 151 N.Y.S. 141; Matter of City of New York, 192 N.Y. 295, 84 N.E. 1105, 18 L.R.A. (N.S.) 423, 127 Am. St. Rep. 903. The city does not now ask us to overturn that rule. It urges only that the rule does not apply in any case where, at the time of the appropriation, the term of the lease has expired, or, as in this case, where the lease provides that it shall come to an end when possession of the property is acquired by a public authority for a public purpose. In such case, it is said by the appellant, the fixtures cannot be appurtenant to the fee which is appropriated, for they are not the property of the owner of the fee; they cannot be appurtenant to any leasehold appropriated, for no leasehold survives the appropriation of the fee. From these premises the deduction is drawn that the tenant's fixtures must be personal property and are not taken by the city.

The distinction which we are asked to draw ignores the nature of what the city takes by condemnation and its consequent obligation to pay compensation. The city takes the real property condemned, as it then exists. What is so annexed as to become a part of the real property taken is acquired by the city. . . .

No leasehold can survive the appropriation of the land itself, and, where the city takes annexations to leased real property, it takes them, not because they are owned by either landlord or tenant or are appurtenant to some interest in the property, but because they are part of the real property. "The public right is exercised upon the land itself, without regard to subdivisions of interest by which the subject is affected through the various contracts of individual owners." Edmands v. City of Boston, 108 Mass. 535, 544.

In fixing awards in condemnation proceedings, the value of what has been taken must be determined, and then that value must be divided among those whose interests are extinguished by the taking. Those interests may be defined by contract of the parties interested, and in the same way the parties may determine by agreement how compensation shall be divided upon the extinguishment of those interests by the sovereign. In this case, the clause of the lease which provided for its termination upon the vesting of title to the land in the city evidences an agreement between landlord and tenant that the tenant shall receive out of the award no compensation for his leasehold interest. Even so, the tenant retains the right to compensation for his interest in any annexations to the real property which, but for the fact that the real property has been taken, he would have had the right to remove at the end of his lease. Matter of Mayor, etc., of City of New York, 168 N.Y. 254, 61 N.E. 249; Poillon v. Gerry, 179 N.Y. 14, 71 N.E. 262. Towards the sovereign exercising the power of eminent domain, the agreement of the parties could have no effect and was not intended to have effect. What the sovereign takes in the exercise of its power, it determines by its own decree. By statute the sovereign has decreed that all that constitutes real property, as defined by the statute, is appropriated by condemnation proceedings, and that all interests in the real property as so defined are extinguished by the taking. The agreement of the parties cannot change that definition. Our problem is to determine whether the tenant's fixtures constitute real property within that definition. . . .

The real property taken "includes all lands and *improvements* . . . and

every estate, interest, . . . privilege, easement and franchise . . . including terms for years and liens by way of judgment, mortgage or otherwise."
Greater New York Charter, §969, subd. 4. . . . Question as to the ownership of, or succession to, structures or fixtures annexed to the land has arisen
in many forms between landlord and tenant, vendor and vendee, heirs and
personal representatives. In each case the problem presented is the proper
division, if any, which is to be made between the owner of the real property,
his assigns, privies, or successors, who base their claim of ownership upon
the assertion that the fixtures or structures have become a part of the real
property, and other parties who base their claim of ownership upon the
assertion either that the structures or fixtures have never been so annexed to
the realty as to lose their quality of personal property or that they have been
so severed, actually or constructively, as to gain or regain the quality of
personal property. In each case the underlying question may be formulated:
Do the structures or fixtures constitute real or personal property between
rival claimants of title? Varying factors have dictated the answers given by
the courts when they were called upon to decide the question between rival
claimants of title. What may constitute personal property where the contest
is between landlord and tenant may be real property where the claimants
stand in other relation. The nature of the structure or fixture and the mode
of its annexation may be the decisive factor in some cases; not in all. Judicial
definitions of what constitutes real property or personal property must often
be limited to the problem presented in the particular case which called for
formulation of the definition. Here the contest is not between rival claimants of the property. The city has taken the real property in the condition in
which it was at the time of the appropriation. It may have been the intention
of these owners that annexations to the realty should not become part of the
real property. As between the parties the courts will, at least at times, give
effect to that intention; but, when the city takes the property, it takes the
property itself with all its "improvements" and extinguishes the title of all
who had any interest therein. That rule constitutes the foundation of the
decisions that the city must pay for fixtures annexed to the real property by a
tenant, though as between landlord and tenant the annexations remained
the personal property of the tenant, severable by him at least before the
expiration of his term. See Matter of City of New York, 118 App. Div. 865,
103 N.Y.S. 908, *Affirmed*, 189 N.Y. 508, 81 N.E. 1162; Phipps v. State of
New York, 69 Misc. Rep. 295, 127 N.Y.S. 260, both cited with approval in
Jackson v. State, *supra*; Nichols on Eminent Domain, §234.

Distinction must, of course, be made between chattels which have "such
a determinate character as movables that they remain personal property,
after their annexation to real estate, independently of any agreement between the owner of the chattels and the owner of the realty which so
provides," and the "class of movables which, after attachment, continued to
be personal property, or became real estate, accordingly as the owner of the
chattels and the owner of the real estate might have agreed." Madfes v.

Beverly Development Corp., 251 N.Y. 12, 15, 166 N.E. 787, 788. Though both are sometimes referred to as "fixtures," articles which are "in their nature, mere furniture, and, therefore, chattels, and not appurtenances to the building," cannot constitute a part of the realty. McKeage v. Hanover Fire Ins. Co., 81 N.Y. 38, 41, 37 Am. Rep. 471. The term "fixtures" as used in this opinion is confined to articles so affixed to the realty that they would have become part of the realty if they had been installed permanently by the owner of the fee. It excludes "goods affixed to realty which, in the absence of an agreement that their original character should be retained, would not have 'become part thereof.'" Madfes v. Beverly Development Corp., *supra*.

Though agreement between landlord and tenant may determine that a tenant's title to "fixtures" after they are affixed to the realty remains in the tenant and shall not become merged in the title to the real estate, the fixtures do not even as between the parties to the agreement remain in full sense personal property, for it has been held that that property in tenant's fixtures which are not removed at the expiration of the term of the lease or upon surrender of possession of the land to which they are attached vests in the landlord. Talbot v. Cruger, 151 N.Y. 117, 45 N.E. 364. "On the whole the tenor of the authorities is that, during the period within which the tenant has a right of removal, he has an actual interest in the things affixed by him or purchased by him as fixtures; an interest which is neither an interest in chattels nor an interest in land, but it is a chattel interest in things for the time being affixed to land." Tyler on Fixtures, p. 165.

The courts, recognizing that by agreement title to and property in articles affixed to the realty may at times be retained by the original owner, have sustained actions brought for interference with or deprivation of such title and property. For that purpose the courts disregard the annexation to the land, and treat the articles as chattels. For wrongful deprivation of his property in such articles, the owner may bring an action for conversion. Treating the articles, as between the parties to such actions, as chattels, the courts have at times referred to the articles as "chattels." The courts have never by the use of the word "chattel" intended to indicate that in all circumstances and as between all parties, fixtures annexed to realty, without intention that they should become a permanent part thereof, are to be treated as chattels.

"An article which remains all the time in the same position and condition may turn out to be real property as between some claimants, and as between others personal property." Reeves on Real Property, §10. An interesting example is to be found in Mott v. Palmer, 1 N.Y. 564. There the defendant conveyed a farm to the plaintiff with warranty of seizin. A fence had been erected upon the farm which would have passed to the plaintiff with the land if it belonged to the defendant. In fact, the fence had been affixed to the land by an occupant upon an agreement with the defendant that the fence might be removed by the occupant. Consequently the plaintiff, who refused to permit its removal, had been compelled to pay damages to the owner of the fence in an action for conversion. He was then permitted to recover the amount of these damages in an action against the defendant for breach of his warranty of seizin because as between grantor and grantee of the land the fence was part of the land as described in the deed. The agreement between the occupant and the owner resulted in the retention of title to the fence by the occupant though affixed to the land. Nevertheless that agreement could not affect the fact that by annexation to the land the fence became part of the land as described in the deed. So here the agreement of the landlord and tenant resulted in retention of title to the fixtures in the tenant. It cannot affect the description of real estate contained in the statute, and within that description the fixtures are part of the real estate which the city has taken. So long as they constitute "improvements" to the real estate, it is immaterial whether for other purposes the courts of this jurisdiction would regard them as chattels.

That result is in accordance with the decisions of the courts of this state, and the uniform practice in condemnation proceedings. The fixtures of the tenant were annexed to the land, and, though the personal property of the tenant as between himself and his landlord, they constitute "improvements" to the land, within the meaning of the statute, at least so long as they could be used in connection with the land. At the time of the appropriation of the land, the improvements were still annexed to the land and could be used by the tenant in connection with the land. By the force of the statute, the tenant's rights under the lease ceased when the city took title to the land; by agreement of the parties, the tenant's right to compensation for the value of the leasehold did not survive the taking. That agreement did not change the nature of the annexations or the title of the tenant to the annexations. So long as they were not severed, the annexations could be used in connection with the real property, enhanced the value of the real property and were part of the real property taken by the city. The city appropriated the real property in the condition in which it was at the time it took title, and then the fixtures were part of the real property and enhanced its value. Perhaps severance at the expiration of the tenant's term, five months after the date when the city took title to the real property, might have destroyed some of the value of the property; perhaps the parties might have chosen to preserve that value either by renewal of the lease or by transfer of title to the fixtures from the tenant to the owner of the fee. Choice lay with the tenant and landlord, and how that choice would have been exercised rests in speculation which does not concern the courts in this jurisdiction. As we have pointed out, in some jurisdictions appropriation of the real property may be qualified by excepting fixtures which the state does not desire to retain. Here no such qualification was made. The city has taken the real property together with the annexations to this property. It is immaterial that, if the property had not been taken, some of that value might have been destroyed a few months thereafter by the severance of the annexation. The taking of the property has destroyed any right to severance which the tenant might otherwise have had at the expiration of the lease. The physical condition of the property is not altered by the circumstance that title to the annexations was in the tenant while title to the land was in the landlord, nor does such division of title affect the value of the whole. The taking itself destroys all outstanding titles and renders severance impossible except by the will of the taker. The city must pay the value of what it takes. To the extent that the value of the real property as a whole is enhanced by the fixtures annexed thereto, the value of the fixtures must be included in what the city pays, and the tenant is entitled to part of the award, not because the fixtures added to the value of the leasehold, but because they belonged to him and their value enters into the value of what the city has taken.

The order should be affirmed, with costs. . . .

CARDOZO, C.J., and POUND and HUBBS, JJ., concur with LEHMAN, J.

CRANE and KELLOGG, JJ., dissent in opinions, in which O'BRIEN, J., concurs.

Order affirmed.

CAMERON v. OAKLAND COUNTY GAS & OIL CO.
277 Mich. 442, 269 N.W. 227 (1936)

POTTER, J. The contest in this case is between the landlord, the owner of leased premises, and the tenant who erected buildings thereon for the purpose of operating an oil and gas station. The lease contained no specific provision as to the ownership of the buildings at the expiration of the leasehold. The rights of the parties are governed by the applicable law.

The sole question involved is whether the tenant has a right to remove the buildings erected by him upon the leased premises, during the continuance of his lease or within a reasonable time after its expiration.

There is no claim the buildings were on the premises when leased or that the landlord contributed anything toward their building and erection. On the one hand, it is contended these buildings, having been structures more or less permanent, remain a part of the real estate and may not be removed. On the other, it is contended they were erected for the purpose of carrying on the business or trade of the tenant and may be removed by him.

In the early case of Van Ness v. Pacard, 2 Pet. (27 U.S.) 137, this question was before the Supreme Court of the United States, and in the opinion therein Mr. Justice Story reviewed the authorities. It is said, p. 143:

> The general rule of the common law certainly is, that whatever is once annexed to the freehold, becomes part of it, and cannot afterwards be removed, except by him who is entitled to the inheritance. The rule, however, never was, at least so far back as we can trace it in the books, inflexible, and without exceptions. It was construed most strictly between executor and heir,

in favor of the latter; more liberally, between tenant for life or in tail and remainder-man or reversioner, in favor of the former; and with much greater latitude, between landlord and tenant, in favor of the tenant. But an exception of a much broader cast, and whose origin may be traced almost as high as the rule itself, is of fixtures erected for the purposes of trade. Upon principles of public policy, and to encourage trade and manufactures, fixtures which were erected to carry on such business were allowed to be removed by the tenant during his term, and were deemed personalty, for many other purposes. . . .

It has been already stated, that the exception of buildings and other fixtures, for the purpose of carrying on a trade or manufacture, is of very ancient date, and was recognized almost as early as the rule itself. The very point was decided in 20 Hen. VII. 13 a and b, where it was laid down, that if a lessee for years made a furnace for his advantage, or a dyer made his vats or vessels to occupy (Carry on) his occupation, during the term, he may afterwards remove them. That doctrine was recognized by Lord Holt, in Poole's Case, 1 Salk, 368. (91 Eng. Rep. 320), in favor of a soap-boiler, who was tenant for years. He held, that the party might well remove the vats he set up in relation to trade; and that he might do it by the common law (and not by virtue of any custom), in favor of trade, and to encourage industry. In Lawton v. Lawton, 3 Atk. 13 (26 Eng. Rep. 811), the same doctrine was held, in a case of a fire-engine, set up to work a colliery by a tenant for life. Lord Hardwicke there said, that since the time of Henry VII., the general ground the courts have gone upon, of relaxing the strict construction of law is, that it is for the benefit of the public, to encourage tenants for life to do what is advantageous to the estate, during the term. He added, "one reason that weighs with me, is, its being a mixed case, between enjoying the profits of the land, and carrying on a species of trade; and, considering it in this light, it comes very near the instances in brewhouses, etc., of furnaces and coppers. The case, too, of a cider-mill, between the executor and heir . . . is extremely strong; for though cider is a part of the profits of the real estate, yet, it was held by Lord Chief Baron Comyns, a very able common lawyer, that the cider-mill was personal estate notwithstanding, and it should go to the executor. It does not differ in my opinion, whether the shed be made of brick or wood, for it is intended to cover it from the weather and other inconveniences." In Penton v. Robart, 2 East, 88 (102 Eng. Rep. 302), it was further decided, that a tenant might move his fixtures for trade, even after the expiration of his term, if he yet remained in possession; and Lord Kenyon recognized the doctrine in its most liberal extent.

It has been suggested at the bar, that this exception in favor of trade, has never been applied to cases like that before the court, where a large house has been built, and used in part as a family residence. But the question, whether removable or not, does not depend upon the form or size of the building, whether it has a brick foundation or not, or is one or two stories high, or has a brick or other chimney. The sole question is, whether it is designed for purposes of trade or not? A tenant may erect a large as well as a small messuage, or a soap-boilery of one or two stories high, and on whatever foundations he may choose. . . .

The rule thus established by the supreme court of the United States is the rule in relation to buildings of this kind. . . .

The right of the tenant to remove the erections made by him in further-ance of the purpose for which the premises were leased is one founded upon public policy and has its foundation in the interest which society has that every person shall be encouraged to make the most beneficial use of his property the circumstances will admit of. Kerr v. Kingsbury, [39 Mich. 150, 33 Am. Rep. 362]; Manwaring v. Jenison, 61 Mich. 117. Throughout all the lumbering regions of Michigan, saw mill operators erected engine and mill foundations of brick, stone and concrete, to which their machinery was attached, and this machinery was usually covered with buildings of a more or less permanent character; and no one ever contended that, though these buildings were erected upon land, the title to which was not in the saw mill builder or operator, he did not have a right to remove his mill when the timber was cut or removed from the premises.

The reason property of this kind is personal, rather than real, is based upon the rule the law implies an agreement that it shall remain personal property from the fact the lessor contributes nothing thereto and should not be enriched at the expense of his tenant when it was placed upon the real estate of the landlord with his consent. There is no unity of title between the owner of the land and the owner of the structures, and the buildings were not erected as permanent improvements to the real estate, but to aid the lessee or licensee in the use of his interest in the premises.

The decree of the trial court is reversed, with costs.

The concurring opinion of WIEST, J., and dissenting opinion of NORTH, C.J., are omitted.

OLD LINE LIFE INSURANCE CO. OF AMERICA v. HAWN
225 Wis. 627, 275 N.W. 542 (1937)

NELSON, J. On April 21, 1922, Cassius D. Hawn, the husband of the defendant, Mary E. Hawn, was the owner of a certain farm in Pierce county. On that day he borrowed from the plaintiff the sum of $6,000. To evidence such indebtedness, he made, executed, and delivered to the plaintiff his promissory note, secured by a real-estate mortgage signed by him and the defendant Mary E. Hawn. Thereafter, he conveyed all of his interest in the farm to the defendant, Mary E. Hawn, subject to the mortgage. On October 15, 1930, the defendant, Mary E. Hawn, leased the farm to the defendant, Ray Hawn, who entered into the possession thereof as tenant, and contin-ued to occupy it until shortly before the foreclosure of the plaintiff's mortgage had been fully completed on November 15, 1935. Shortly after entering into the possession of the farm as a tenant, the defendant, Ray Hawn, installed at his own expense, in the cellar or basement of the house situated upon the farm, a pipeless furnace. He also installed in the barn seventeen steel stanchions, certain drinking cups for his stock, and certain pipe equipment. He also installed in the barn a hay carrier and a manure carrier. He also brought upon the farm a brooder house. Later on he erected upon the farm a hen house, garage, tool shed, and a maple-sugar shed, which housed certain equipment used by him in manufacturing maple syrup and sugar. Shortly prior to the time that the foreclosure proceedings were completed by confirmation of the sale, the defendant, Ray Hawn, either removed from said premises, or authorized others, who had purchased some of the properties from him, to remove, all of the above-mentioned properties. The plaintiff asserted that all of said properties were common-law fixtures by virtue of their attachment to the soil, that they were subject to the lien of its mortgage, and that the removal thereof constituted waste. The defendant, Mary E. Hawn, asserted that she was in no manner responsible for the removal of said properties by the defendant, Ray Hawn. The defendant, Ray Hawn, asserted that all of said properties were brought upon the premises by him as a tenant, and that he had the right to remove them at any time before the termination of his tenancy. The court found that all of said properties, with the exception of the maple-sugar house and equipment, were common-law fixtures subject to the lien of the plaintiff's mortgage, and not removable, and that the amount of the damages sustained by the plaintiff was $700. The court further found, as to the defendant, Mary E. Hawn, that she at no time consented to the sale or removal of any of the properties mentioned.

The plaintiff contends that the court erred in finding, (1) that the maple-sugar house and equipment were properly removed; (2) that Mary E. Hawn knew little about what her son did on the farm, and that she at no time claimed or received any benefit from the removal of the fixtures; (3) that her business experience had been very limited; (4) that she was not aware at the time of the auction sale that the buildings and fixtures were sold, and that she did not consent to their sale; and (5) that she did not breach any duty to protect and preserve the premises covered by plaintiff's mortgage; and also in concluding (1) that the defendant, Mary E. Hawn, was not liable to the plaintiff for the damages found, and (2) that the plaintiff's complaint should be dismissed as to her. The motion to review assails the judgment against the defendant, Ray Hawn, which is based upon the findings and conclusions of the court that all of the properties mentioned, with the exception of the maple-sugar house and equipment, were common-law fixtures subject to the lien of the plaintiff's mortgage and therefore not removable.

In view of our conclusion that all of the properties mentioned were removable by Ray Hawn as tenant, and never became subject to the lien of the plaintiff's mortgage, we need not discuss the contentions of the plaintiff relative to the defendant, Mary E. Hawn, since obviously if Ray Hawn had the right to remove the properties mentioned before or at the termination of his lease, there could be no liability on the part of Mary E. Hawn to the plaintiff for the removal of such properties.

It is undisputed that the relationship between Mary E. Hawn and Ray Hawn was that of landlord and tenant; that all of the properties mentioned either belonged to Ray Hawn at the time he entered into the possession of the farm or were constructed by him upon it with his own funds and labor; that he had no intention of making said properties common-law fixtures, and always asserted his right to remove them from the premises at the conclusion of his term; that Mary E. Hawn had full knowledge of such intention and acquiesced therein, although expressing a doubt as to the right of Ray Hawn to remove all of the properties, especially the chicken house, should she lose the farm to the plaintiff on foreclosure, and that she consulted an attorney in reference to the matter of removing some of the properties, and was advised that Ray Hawn had such right.

It is our opinion that to such a situation the law of trade fixtures should be applied. This court has adopted a liberal rule with respect to trade fixtures brought upon, installed in, or erected upon, leased premises by tenants. . . .

In Standard Oil Co. v. La Crosse S.A. Service, [217 Wis. 237, 258 N.W. 791], the right of the plaintiff to remove gasoline pumps and tanks installed upon certain premises by it as a tenant, with the understanding with the owner that it might remove them upon the termination of its lease, was upheld as against a mortgagee whose mortgage was prior to the plaintiff's lease. It was there said, pages 244, 245:

> Trade fixtures are ordinarily installed or attached to the freehold by the tenant for his own use and for the purpose of promoting his business, and with no intention on his part or on the part of anyone that such trade fixtures shall become, as a result of mere annexation, a part of the freehold. We are of the opinion that our liberal rule with respect to trade fixtures is sound and just, is promotive of business, fosters the leasing of premises, and works no injustice to prior or existing mortgagees who are protected in situations where such fixtures may not be removed without material or substantial injury to the freehold. To hold otherwise in this case would amount to holding that our very liberal rule as to trade fixtures has no application to situations where the freehold is in fact mortgaged and no consent of the mortgagee has been obtained permitting the tenant to remove them after they are once physically annexed. If that were declared to be the law, every prospective tenant who intends to install trade fixtures in premises leased by him would have to ascertain whether the premises were mortgaged and, if so, would have to obtain from the mortgagee an agreement permitting the removal of the trade fixtures upon the termination of his lease.

The following rule applicable to such a situation was thus considerately stated:

> Where land is mortgaged and the mortgagor is not prohibited from leasing the premises, and the premises are in fact leased to one who installs therein or thereon trade fixtures for temporary purposes connected with his business or in furtherance thereof, which trade fixtures may be removed without material

injury to the freehold upon the termination of the lease, removal of such trade fixtures should be allowed as against the mortgagee. [Standard Oil Co. v. La Crosse S. A. Service, *supra,* p. 245.]

No case involving trade fixtures or fixtures in the nature of trade fixtures, put upon a farm by a tenant for the purpose of promoting agriculture, raising chickens, manufacturing maple sugar, or promoting the convenient care of a dairy herd, has been before us, but we perceive no just reason why the law as to trade fixtures should not be applied to tenants engaged in the production of milk, eggs, and poultry, maple sugar, or other farm products. Agriculture should be encouraged and fostered as much as trade and manufacture. There are, of course, cases whose holdings are to the contrary. Elwes v. Maw, 3 East (Eng.) 38; 2 Smith's Leading Cas. 189, decided in 1802. The supreme court of the United States at an early date questioned the soundness of the English rule. Van Ness v. Pacard, 2 Pet. (U.S.) 137, 144, 7 L. Ed. 374. After referring to the holding in the English case, Mr. Justice Story, speaking for the court, said:

> The distinction is certainly a nice one between fixtures for the purposes of trade, and fixtures for agricultural purposes; at least in those cases, where the sale of the produce constitutes the principal object of the tenant, and the erections are for the purpose of such a beneficial enjoyment of the estate.

In 26 C.J. p. 703, after referring to the English case cited and the holding therein, it is stated:

> There are, however, in this country quite a number of decisions where a contrary view has been expressed, based on the ground that it is a matter of public policy to encourage tenants to improve property for agricultural purposes as well as for trade purposes. Likewise an article annexed to a farm for the purpose of putting agricultural products in form or condition for the market has been regarded as removable as a trade fixture.

There is, in our opinion, no sound reason for applying one rule to tenants engaged in trade or manufacture and another to tenants engaged in agriculture. Such being our conclusion, this controversy is ruled by Standard Oil Co. v. La Crosse S.A. Service, *supra.* Any other holding would amount to a rank discrimination between tenants engaged in trade or manufacture and tenants engaged in agriculture.

The present controversy does not involve the right of a subsequent innocent purchaser or mortgagee of land without notice to claim as common-law fixtures, buildings and equipment which from all appearances are permanently attached to the freehold. See Annotation, 58 A.L.R. 1352 et seq. That question is not here.[3]

---

3.   What if the mortgage were subsequent to the tenant's annexation, instead of prior to the annexation? What other facts would you like to know? — EDS.

By the court. — The judgment of the circuit court as to Mary E. Hawn is affirmed. The judgment of the circuit court against Ray Hawn is reversed, with directions to dismiss the complaint against him.

The dissenting opinion of FOWLER, J., is omitted.

Note: Removal of Fixtures After Renewal of a Lease

It is frequently stated as the law that the tenant must remove the fixtures before the tenant leaves the premises or within a reasonable time after the termination of the tenancy or else forfeit them to the landlord. The validity of this rule to present-day circumstances is subject to considerable doubt,[4] but some courts, fascinated by their own logic, have carried this forfeiture rule to a reductio ad absurdum in the case of a lease renewal or a new lease, holding that in the absence of an express reservation of the right to remove fixtures in the new lease, the tenant loses the right the tenant had to remove the fixtures placed on the land.[5] Some states passed statutes to change this clear "trap for the unwary." Md. Real Prop. Code Ann. §8-114 provides: "The right of a tenant to remove fixtures erected by him is not lost or impaired by his acceptance of a subsequent lease of the same premises without any intermediate surrender of possession." To the same effect, see N.Y. Real Prop. Law §226-a.

Problems

22.1. L and T entered into a written lease of certain premises, which were to be used by T as a residence. There was no garage on the leased premises, so T rented a portable garage from A for an agreed amount per month and placed the same on the leased premises. L ousted T from the land for failure to pay rent. A then demanded from L the portable garage, which had been left on the leased premises by T. L refused to deliver the garage to A or to allow A to come on the land to remove it. A brings an action of trover against L for the conversion of the garage. Judgment for whom? See Hanson v. Ryan, 185 Wis. 566, 201 N.W. 749 (1925).

22.2. L leases a store to T for T to use for the purpose of selling plumbing equipment. The lease provides that the lessee shall not deface or injure the premises in any way, "whether by removal of any fixture or otherwise," and that the lessee will deliver up the premises at the end of the term "and all erections and additions made to or upon the same, clean and in good repair in all respects." The lease further provides that the lessee may make such alterations and additions as are necessary for the lessee's business and that the lessee may remove them at the end of the term, "provided the

---

4. See American Law of Property §19.11 (Casner ed. 1952).

5. See, e.g., Loughran v. Ross, 45 N.Y. 792 (1871), and Watriss v. First National Bank, 124 Mass. 571 (1878).

lessee puts the premises in as good repair as they were at the beginning of said term."

T installs six bathrooms for demonstration purposes. At the end of the term T vacates the premises but does not remove the bathrooms. L removes the bathrooms and sues T for the cost of doing so. What judgment? See Perry v. J. L. Mott Iron Works Co., 207 Mass. 501, 93 N.E. 798 (1911).

Suppose that L, instead of removing the bathrooms, had sought to hold T for rent as a hold-over tenant. (See Mason v. Wierengo's Estate, page 592 *supra*). What judgment in a jurisdiction that would hold for T in solving the question in the preceding paragraph? In a jurisdiction that would hold for L in solving such question? See Mott Pipe & Supply Corp. v. Blue Ridge Coal Corp., 208 Misc. 601, 146 N.Y.S.2d 607 (New York City Mun. Ct. 1955).

Note: *Security Interests in Fixtures*

Section 9-313 of the Uniform Commercial Code reads as follows:

§9-313.   *Priority of Security Interests in Fixtures*[6]

(1)   In this section and in the provisions of Part 4 of this Article referring to fixture filing, unless the context otherwise requires
   (a)   goods are "fixtures" when they become so related to particular real estate that an interest in them arises under real estate law;
   (b)   a "fixture filing" is the filing in the office where a mortgage on the real estate would be filed or recorded of a financing statement covering goods which are or are to become fixtures and conforming to the requirements of subsection (5) of Section 9-402;
   (c)   a mortgage is a "construction mortgage" to the extent that it secures an obligation incurred for the construction of an improvement on land including the acquisition cost of the land, if the recorded writing so indicates.

(2)   A security interest under this Article may be created in goods which are fixtures or may continue in goods which become fixtures, but no security interest exists under this Article in ordinary building materials incorporated into an improvement on land.

(3)   This Article does not prevent creation of an encumbrance upon fixtures pursuant to real estate law.

(4)   A perfected security interest in fixtures has priority over the conflicting interest of an encumbrancer or owner of the real estate where
   (a)   the security interest is a purchase money security interest, the interest of the encumbrancer or owner arises before the goods become fixtures, the security interest is perfected by a fixture filing before the goods become fixtures or within ten days thereafter, and the debtor has an interest of record in the real estate or is in possession of the real estate; or

---

6.   See generally Coogan, Security Interests in Fixtures Under the Uniform Commercial Code, 75 Harv. L. Rev. 1319 (1962); Kripke, Fixtures Under the Uniform Commercial Code, 64 Colum. L. Rev. 44 (1964). — EDS.

    (b)   the security interest is perfected by a fixture filing before the interest of the encumbrancer or owner is of record, the security interest has priority over any conflicting interest of a predecessor in title of the encumbrancer or owner, and the debtor has an interest of record in the real estate or is in possession of the real estate; or

    (c)   the fixtures are readily removable factory or office machines or readily removable replacements of domestic appliances which are consumer goods, and before the goods become fixtures the security interest is perfected by any method permitted by this Article; or

    (d)   the conflicting interest is a lien on the real estate obtained by legal or equitable proceedings after the security interest was perfected by any method permitted by this Article.

(5)   A security interest in fixtures, whether or not perfected, has priority over the conflicting interest of an encumbrancer or owner of the real estate where

    (a)   the encumbrancer or owner has consented in writing to the security interest or has disclaimed an interest in the goods as fixtures; or

    (b)   the debtor has a right to remove the goods as against the encumbrancer or owner. If the debtor's right terminates, the priority of the security interest continues for a reasonable time.

(6)   Notwithstanding paragraph (a) of subsection (4) but otherwise subject to subsections (4) and (5), a security interest in fixtures is subordinate to a construction mortgage recorded before the goods become fixtures if the goods become fixtures before the completion of the construction. To the extent that it is given to refinance a construction mortgage, a mortgage has this priority to the same extent as the construction mortgage.

(7)   In cases not within the preceding subsections, a security interest in fixtures is subordinate to the conflicting interest of an encumbrancer or owner of the related real estate who is not the debtor.

(8)   When the secured party has priority over all owners and encumbrancers of the real estate, he may, on default, subject to the provisions of Part 5, remove his collateral from the real estate but he must reimburse any encumbrancer or owner of the real estate who is not the debtor and who has not otherwise agreed for the cost of repair of any physical injury, but not for any diminution in value of the real estate caused by the absence of the goods removed or by any necessity of replacing them. A person entitled to reimbursement may refuse permission to remove until the secured party gives adequate security for the performance of this obligation.

Problems

22.3. Suppose the trade fixture annexed to the leased property by a tenant has been purchased under a conditional-sales contract and it is not removed by T when the lease expires. What are L's rights? If L sells reversion to L_1, is the right of the conditional sales vendor superior to that of L_1? Answer these questions on the following assumptions:

    a. If the conditional sales contract has been recorded?

    b. If the conditional sales contract has not been recorded?

22.4. L was the owner of certain vacant premises. L borrowed $10,000 from M and executed a mortgage of the vacant premises in favor of M as security for the loan. This mortgage was duly recorded. Thereafter L leased the mortgaged premises to T for a period of two years. T installed three underground tanks and four gasoline pumps upon a concrete base constructed for that purpose and used the premises to sell gasoline and oil. M foreclosed the mortgage as a result of L's default on the loan, bought in at the foreclosure sale, and demanded the premises from T. T surrendered possession of the premises to M but at the same time claimed the right to remove the tanks and pumps. When T came to get the tanks and pumps, M refused to surrender them. T brings an action of replevin to recover them. Judgment for whom? Why? See Standard Oil Co. v. La Crosse Super Auto Service, Inc., 217 Wis. 237, 258 N.W. 791 (1935). Would the result be any different if the case arose under U.C.C. §9-313? What if X purchased the premises at the foreclosure sale?

22.5. O devised Blackacre to O's daughter, L, for life, remainder to O's son, S, in fee. After O's death, L and T entered into a written lease of Blackacre for a term of ten years. The lease provided that all improvements and fixtures placed on the leased premises by T should remain the property of T, with T having the right of removal within a reasonable time after the termination of the lease. T placed on the leased premises two tobacco auction warehouses, erected on concrete foundations, with 100,000 feet of floor space. The buildings cost approximately $73,000.

    a. During the lifetime of L, T undertakes to remove the warehouses, and S seeks an injunction in equity to prevent such removal. Is he entitled to the injunction?

    b. L dies, and T, within a reasonable time after L's death, undertakes to remove the buildings T erected. S seeks an injunction in equity to prevent such removal. Is he entitled to the injunction?

See Haywood v. Briggs, 227 N.C. 108, 41 S.E.2d 289 (1947).

Note: Fixtures as Between the Vendor and the Purchaser, Devisee and the Legatee, the Mortgagor and the Mortgagee, Etc.

The question of whether a thing formerly a chattel has become a part of the realty can arise in several different but recurring situations: (1) vendor versus purchaser; (2) mortgagor versus mortgagee; (3) heir versus executor; (4) trespasser, under color of title or not versus landowner; (5) life tenant versus remainderman; (6) tenant versus landlord; and (7) co-tenant versus co-tenant. The first three situations generally may be called problems of successive ownership, and the last four generally may be classified as problems of concurrent ownership. Overlapping these two general classifications are the situations where the person who annexes the chattel to the realty does not own the chattel, e.g., the chattel is subject to an outstanding security interest. Questions invariably arise as to the rights in the chattel between the secured party and the landowner. Some courts, unfortunately, fail to perceive that each of these situations involves different policy considerations. The problem of vendor versus purchaser is surely different from that of tenant versus landlord, and a court would not be inconsistent if it had different rules for the two problems. Before reading any of the problems that follow, you should carefully consider each of the above situations and see if you can articulate the different policy considerations involved in each.

Problems

22.6. O, owner of Blackacre, installs a furnace and a gas range attached by a coupling to a gas service pipe in the house on Blackacre.
   a. O sells Blackacre to P, and no mention of the furnace or the gas range is made in the deed. As between O and P, who is entitled to the furnace and the gas range?
   b. O dies, leaving a will devising Blackacre to A and bequeathing all the rest of O's property to B. As between A and B, who is entitled to the furnace and the gas range?
   c. O borrows $5,000 from M and executes a mortgage on Blackacre to M to secure the loan. The mortgage is duly recorded. May O remove the furnace or the gas range over the objection of M? What if the furnace and the gas range were installed after the mortgage to M?[7]

22.7. O is the owner of Blackacre, on which is situated a house. A enters the land, innocently believing she is the owner, and installs a furnace and a gas range in the house. May A remove the furnace and the gas range over the objections of O? What if A enters the land knowing that she is not the owner?[8]

22.8. O, owner of Blackacre, buys a furnace from A under a conditional-sales contract and installs the same in a house on Blackacre. O fails to meet the payments on the furnace. May A remove the furnace from the house?[9] What if after buying the furnace O borrows $5,000 from M and executes a mortgage on Blackacre to secure the loan? This mortgage is duly recorded, and O then fails to meet payments on the furnace. May A remove

---

7. See American Law of Property §§19.5-19.7 (Casner ed. 1952).
8. See id. §19.9.
9. See id. §19.12.

the furnace from the house, over M's objection, if A recorded the conditional-sales agreement at the time of the sale? If A did not record?[10]

22.9. O, owner of Blackacre, borrows $5,000 from M and executes a mortgage on Blackacre to secure the loan. This mortgage is duly recorded. O then buys a furnace from A under a conditional-sales contract and installs the same in the house on Blackacre. O fails to meet the payments on the furnace. May A remove the furnace from the house if A recorded at the time of the sale? If A never recorded?[11]

Note: Emblements

The same parties who may become involved in a dispute over the removal of fixtures from the land may also become involved in disputes over the removal of trees, crops, and other things planted on the land. These latter disputes concern what is sometimes referred to as the right to "emblements." See American Law of Property §§19.15, 19.16 (Casner ed. 1952).

---

10. See U.C.C. §9-313, and Coogan, Security Interests in Fixtures Under the Uniform Commercial Code, 75 Harv. L. Rev. 1319, 1330-1334 (1962).
11. See U.C.C. §9-313 and Coogan, footnote 10 *supra.*

PREVIEW OF PRACTICE: NEGOTIATING AND DRAFTING A LEASE ON A PARTICULAR COMMERCIAL PROPERTY

In this chapter we set before you a segment of landlord-tenant practice that involves an affluent tenant. The cases and problems which you studied in Chapters 17 through 22 deal with certain portions of the law of leases; the case study of the present chapter should considerably broaden the field of your familiarity with this subject. It should also

1. act as review material for those subjects already treated;
2. give unity and reality to the general subject by focusing a considerable number of issues upon a single practical situation;
3. indicate the compromises with perfection that must be accepted in a negotiated transaction; and
4. teach you to read and reread a document — an art which is among the most difficult to master.

The events here presented are not hypothetical; they did occur, substantially as stated. Names, dates, figures, and locations have been changed, and negotiations have been simplified. In addition, portions of the negotiations sometimes have been put in quotation marks, though no stenographer was present. The data were provided to us by counsel for the lessee, whom we shall call Mr. Porter of Clay, Webster & Calhoun, and the narrative adopts his point of view. Doubtless the narrative which counsel for the lessors might produce would read quite differently.

Counsel Is Retained by the Lessee

On April 4, the vice president of the Security State Bank of the city of New York, a regular client of Clay, Webster & Calhoun, had a conference with

Mr. Porter, a partner in that firm. At the close of the conference, Mr. Porter dictated the following memorandum as a summary of the conference:

Security State Bank wants to establish a branch at 346 Eastern Avenue, Brooklyn. They want us to negotiate a purchase, if possible; if not, to negotiate a long-term lease. They are prepared to pay up to $400,000 for the property or $50,000/year rent for a 20-year lease. If they get a lease, they also want an option to purchase at the lowest possible figure and the earliest possible date. However, they are most anxious to establish the branch and want at least to have a look at any proposition offered, even though it is less favorable than the terms just stated.

The property is now occupied by a loan company, which holds a lease expiring May 1 of next year, at a monthly rental of $3,800. Through banking connections our client is informed that this company does not want to continue as lessee; indeed, they got out of the premises several years ago for some months and tried to sublet without success, then returned and have since continued their loan business. The availability of the premises was called to our client's attention by a broker retained by the owner. It is not known whether other potential tenants are considering these premises. However, a survey of the population of this area, their income level, and other banking facilities available to them indicates that this location is a natural for a bank, and our client suspects that other banks may be giving this location very serious thought.

The property is owned by the three children and one grandchild of Olive Olmsted, who died in 1980, leaving a will by which all her real estate was devised to her four children equally. In 1978, one of the children (Dora Olmsted Selkirk) had died, leaving an only child, George Selkirk, Jr., who took his mother's interest under Olive Olmsted's will by virtue of the Anti-Lapse Statute.[1] The ownership appears to rest in the following persons in equal one-fourth interests:

1. George Selkirk, Jr., a minor, whose general guardian is his father, George Selkirk, Sr. The Selkirks are residents of New York City
2. Harry Olmsted of Warren, Ohio
3. Ethel Olmsted Stanley of Boulder, Colorado
4. Arthur Olmsted of New York City

It is believed that Arthur Olmsted has a power of attorney for Harry and Ethel. He is represented by Fred C. Durham of 29 Nassau Street, New York City. Durham runs a one-man office, largely concerned with surrogate and trust matters.

The lease must be conditional upon the bank's receiving permission from the New York State Superintendent of Banks to open this branch.

---

1. (a) Unless the will provides otherwise:
   (1) Whenever a testamentary disposition is made to the issue or to a brother or sister of the testator, and such beneficiary dies during the lifetime of the testator leaving issue surviving such testator, such disposition does not lapse but vests in such surviving issue, per stirpes.
   (2) The provisions of subparagraph (1) apply to a disposition made to issue, brothers or sisters as a class as if the disposition were made to the

Negotiation of the Basic Agreement

Porter took up the matter with Durham and was told the following. Olive Olmsted, the mother of three of the owners and grandmother of the fourth, was a very strong-willed and competent businesswoman. She had a flair for real estate dealings and felt that her investments in the vicinity of Eastern Avenue were particularly valuable. On Eastern Avenue she owned not only the property at 346, which the bank wants to buy, but also the adjoining small medical office building at 350, and a garage which backs up to these two lots, at 348 Snelling Street. She had always urged her children never to sell these properties, and Durham doubted that they would be willing to do so. He undertook, however, to put the proposition of a sale up to the owners.

Some ten days later Durham reported that Ethel Olmsted Stanley absolutely refused to sell, that Harry Olmsted was willing to consider a proposal of sale but preferred not to sell, that Arthur Olmsted was in about the same situation, but that George Selkirk, Sr., was eager to have the property sold. However, Selkirk had always retained cordial relations with his wife's family and would probably not force a sale by commencing partition proceedings. He particularly did not wish to cause any unpleasantness with Arthur Olmsted, who is childless and who had always displayed great affection for George Selkirk, Jr.

Porter then told Durham that his client, the Security State Bank, would consider a long-term lease but that this business of consulting on all details with four people located all over the country promised to drag out any dealings to the point that the Security State Bank had better look for some other premises or give up the project entirely. He asked whether Durham could not bring it about that Arthur Olmsted would have real authority from the other owners. Durham replied that Arthur already had authority to negotiate and that his judgment would be respected by the others but that the others would have to ratify any deal made by Arthur.

Thereupon discussions commenced concerning the terms of the lease. Arthur Olmsted declared that he would recommend the following proposition to the other owners if the bank would offer it:

1. A lease for 21 years at a rental of $48,000 a year.
2. The lessee to pay any real estate taxes in excess of those being presently paid.

---

beneficiaries by their individual names, except that no benefit shall be conferred hereunder upon the surviving issue of an ancestor who died before the execution of the will in which the disposition to the class was made.

(b) As used in this section, the terms "issue," "surviving issue" and "issue surviving" include adopted children and illegitimate children; for this purpose, an illegitimate is the child of his mother and is the child of his father if he is entitled to inherit from his father under 4-1.2. [N.Y. Est. Powers & Trusts Law §3-3.3.]

3. The lessee to have an option on May 1 of the sixth year of the lease to buy all three properties—the bank building, the office building, and the garage—for $960,000 cash. (Olmsted stated that he would not be interested in selling the bank building alone but only in disposing of all of the real estate in that district. The present approximate value of the three properties, based upon a 60 percent assessed valuation, was $720,000.

4. The lessee to have "a right of first refusal" as to any offer to purchase the lessor's interest which is made up to the sixth year of the lease.

5. The property is now free and clear, but the owners are to have the right to mortgage it up to $300,000, the mortgage to be senior to the lease when and if made. Any outstanding balance due on the mortgage to be deducted from the purchase price if the lessee exercises its option.

6. The bank to have the privilege to sublet or assign only with the prior consent of the lessors.

7. The bank to have the right to cancel within 90 days of the execution of the lease, upon forfeiting $4,000, if the bank is unable to get an authorization for the branch from the state department of banks.

8. It is recognized that these represent the business aspects of the proposed arrangement and that the legal aspects will have to be worked out between counsel.

Porter put this proposition up to the bank, which, at a directors' meeting, decided that it was satisfactory. Porter then drafted a letter embodying the proposal in substantially the above-stated terms and adding thereto the following:

> The foregoing comprises a statement that this bank is willing to enter into a lease upon the foregoing terms if a lease is presented in terms satisfactory to the bank's counsel and if other legal aspects of the transaction, such as the soundness of the title of the present owners, are satisfactory to such counsel. This letter is not to be taken as an offer of a contract for a lease. No legal obligation is to be incurred by the Bank except upon execution of a definitive lease.

The letter was signed by the president of the bank and sent to Arthur Olmsted. In response to this letter Durham informed Porter by letter that the three owners and George Selkirk, Sr., approved the arrangement.

Negotiation of the Terms of the Lease

Porter telephoned Durham, stating that the bank wanted to get moving on the drafting of the lease. Durham said he would send a lease over to

Porter for approval in a couple of days. Thereupon the following conversation ensued:

Porter: I am afraid you are a little optimistic in stating that you can put together a lease on this matter in a couple of days. This is likely to prove a pretty complex affair.

Durham: I suppose that you big offices have to do something to carry your overhead. I have had experiences of this kind before. You fellows make a big complicated thing out of something that is really simple. We won't have any trouble if you fellows are willing to be reasonable.

Porter: We've had quite a bit of experience in drawing these leases for branch banks. Why don't you let us put together a draft and send it over to you, and then you tear it to pieces when we get down to discussing it?

Durham: Not a bit of it. You know as well as I do that it is customary for the owner's counsel to draw the lease. And I want to tell you right now that I don't propose to be pushed around.

Porter: I was only trying to be helpful. Naturally if you want to draft the lease in the first instance we have no objection, though we would be willing to take that burden. I wonder whether you would care to let us prepare the first draft of the option to purchase. The real estate department of our bank has its own views about options and, if we really want to expedite this deal, it might be better to offer them something they are familiar with.

Durham: I don't want to be put in the position of saying no to everything you suggest, though I still think that the entire lease is properly my concern. If you want to draft the option to purchase, go ahead; but I think I ought to warn you that I am not going to approve something just because your clients are stubborn.

Nothing happened for three and a half weeks, despite repeated telephone calls to Durham. At the end of this time Durham sent to Porter a printed law-stationer's form lease containing 25 printed clauses with 13 additional clauses included in a typewritten rider. Porter handed the lease to one of his associates for comment and criticism and received back a statement that it was a hopeless monstrosity. The associate then submitted a draft of his own to Porter and recommended that Porter seek to have it used as the basis for discussion. Durham refused to do this and insisted on treating his own draft as the basic document. Then began an arduous series of conferences in which objections were made by Porter to clause after clause of Durham's lease. Redrafts were gradually made; but, in the face of Durham's mounting annoyance at demonstrations of the inadequacies of his lease, approximations and compromises frequently had to be accepted.

Difficulties in the Execution of the Lease

Durham had expected that the lease would be signed by Arthur Olmsted under his power of attorney for the two non-New Yorkers, but Porter pointed out to him that the power of attorney dealt only with managing and leasing of the premises and gave no power to sell and that therefore it gave Arthur no power to give an option to sell. Porter insisted on signature on the lease by each owner individually. He also insisted upon each owner's acknowledging the lease before a notary public, so that the lease would be eligible for recordation and, when recorded, would constitute constructive notice to purchasers from any of the four owners.[2]

Durham did not think that it was necessary for George Selkirk, Sr., as general guardian to get authorization from the supreme court to execute this lease. Porter pointed out that if authorization were not obtained from the supreme court, the option to purchase would not be valid against the infant under the domestic relations law and the real property actions and proceedings law.[3] Durham vehemently protested that such a supreme court proceeding was not necessary to protect the bank and suggested that Porter was insisting upon it simply to complicate the case and magnify his services. Whereupon Porter stated that the bank would of course want title insurance on the lease, including the option to purchase, and that if the Lawyers Title Corporation would issue a policy without a supreme court proceeding Porter would accept the lease. The Lawyers Title Corporation was consulted and refused to insure the title unless the general guardian was authorized by court order to execute the instrument. Thereupon a proceeding was brought by Durham in the supreme court, and permission to sign the document was obtained.[4]

After the lease was finally agreed to, Durham sent it to Ethel Olmsted Stanley in Boulder, Colorado, and Harry Olmsted in Warren, Ohio, for execution. When the lease came back, Harry's signature was not notarized. Ethel's signature was notarized, but there was no certificate of a clerk of

---

2. All four parties must acknowledge to achieve this result. N.Y. Real Prop. Law §291; People ex rel. Oaklawn Corp. v. Donegan, 226 N.Y. 84, 123 N.E. 71 (1919). The recording of instruments affecting the title to land is dealt with in detail in Chapter 28.

3. N.Y. Dom. Rel. Law §83; N.Y. Real Prop. Acts. Law §§1711 et seq.; In re Title Guaranty & Trust Co., 242 A.D. 80, 273 N.Y.S. 158 (1934).

4. The proceeding involves the following steps:

a. Petition by the general guardian to the supreme court, setting forth all the facts and praying that the general guardian be authorized to execute the lease.

b. Appointment of a special guardian of the infant with reference to the petition for permission to execute the lease.

c. Appointment of a referee to inquire into the merits of the application and the soundness of the lease from the infant's point of view.

d. Hearing before the referee in which witnesses testify as to the business desirability of the lease.

e. Report by the referee to the court recommending a granting of the petition. An order of the court granting to the general guardian leave to execute the lease on behalf of the infant.

court in Colorado as to the authenticity of the signature and seal of the notary public. Hence, the lease had to be returned to Boulder for a notarial authentication certificate and to Warren for notarization plus a certificate as to the notary's authority.[5] Insistence on these formalities caused great irritation to Durham.

The Lease as Finally Agreed Upon

Here follows the lease that was finally executed by the parties. Mr. Porter comments as follows:

> This instrument is a long way from what we could have obtained if we had started out with our own draft instead of the printed form as supplemented by Durham. Durham's initial effort did not advance the work but only gave us a very difficult starting point. The final lease still shows the effect of this unfortunate procedure. There are some clauses that are almost self-contradictory; these arose where Durham refused to give up his original language even though he had agreed to accept terms which substantially contradicted his original clause. There are also some clauses which do not give the lessee bank the protection it should theoretically have; but we have to accept slight risks in view of Durham's stubbornness and the chance that some other lessee would come along with equally favorable terms which Durham would induce his clients to accept. This last risk was a real one, as may be seen from the fact that negotiations started on April 4 and the lease did not become fully effective until December 11, despite constant pressure by us to expedite the matter.

In reading this lease, we suggest that you adopt the following procedure:
1. Read a paragraph.
2. Underscore its key operative words.
3. Ask yourself what situation this clause is intended to meet, what problems can arise, and how effectively the clause meets the problems.
4. Finally, look at the footnotes to the clause. These contain our comments on the significance of the particular clauses and, in some instances, Mr. Porter's remarks on the same subject.[6]

---

5. If the notary public is an official of the local state (New York, in this instance), his signature and notarial seal on the certificate of acknowledgment are sufficient. However, if acknowledgment is made before a notary public in another state, it is necessary to add to the notary's certificate of acknowledgment a certificate by some official of that other state to the effect that the person purporting to be a notary public is in fact a notary public and that his signature is genuine. The procedure in this matter is governed by N.Y. Real Prop. Law §§299-299a, which provides that authentication of a notary's authority may be provided by several types of officials, including the clerk of a court of record. The seal of the court must appear upon the certificate.

6. In 1976 California Continuing Legal Education published an excellent volume entitled Commercial Real Property Lease Practice, which not only explains how and why a commercial lease transaction is (and should be) drafted but also reprints in annotated form a detailed shopping center lease with commentary on every clause appearing therein (at 39-267).

THIS AGREEMENT, dated this 18th day of July, [*insert year*], between ARTHUR OLMSTED residing at 241 East Ninetieth Street, New York City, N.Y., ETHEL OLMSTED STANLEY, residing at 814 Twelfth Street, Boulder, Colorado, HARRY OLMSTED, residing at 345 Maple Road, Warren, Ohio, and GEORGE SELKIRK, JR., an infant, by GEORGE SELKIRK, his General Guardian, both residing at 12 Beekman Place, New York City, N.Y. (hereinafter collectively referred to as the "Lessor"), and SECURITY STATE BANK OF THE CITY OF NEW YORK, a New York banking corporation, having its principal office at 160 Broadway, New York City, N.Y. (hereinafter referred to as the "Lessee").[7]

WITNESSETH: The Lessor hereby leases to Lessee, and Lessee hereby hires from Lessor, the parcel, with the buildings thereon, known as 346 Eastern Avenue, in the Borough of Brooklyn, County of Kings, State of New York, bounded and described as follows:

> Beginning at a point on the easterly side of Eastern Avenue distant 140 feet southerly from the corner formed by the intersection of the easterly side of Eastern Avenue with the southerly side of Appleton Boulevard; running thence Easterly, at right angles to the easterly side of Eastern Avenue, 70 feet; thence Northerly, parallel with the easterly side of Eastern Avenue, 6 feet $1\frac{1}{2}$ inches; thence Easterly, at right angles to the easterly side of Eastern Avenue, 47.67 feet; thence Southerly, parallel with the easterly side of Eastern Avenue, 46 feet $1\frac{1}{2}$ inches; thence Westerly, at right angles to the easterly side of Eastern Avenue, 117.67 feet to the easterly side of Eastern Avenue; thence Northerly, along the easterly side of Eastern Avenue, 40 feet to the point or place of Beginning.

(hereinafter referred to as the "demised premises"), reserving, however, therefrom the right in the Lessor to the use of all water, gas, electric pipes, meters, and all plumbing and sewers in the basement of the aforesaid premises which are connected with or which supply service to the tenants of premises known as No. 350 Eastern Avenue, Brooklyn, New York,[8] for a

---

7. This first paragraph describes the parties to the lease. It raises two issues.

1. Does this lease bind the dower rights of wives of lessors? In New York, dower is abolished unless both the marriage and the spouse's acquisition of title occurred prior to September 1, 1930. Hence, in this case, since all lessors acquired their title upon the death of Olive Olmsted in 1980, no rights in spouses can arise and no release of such rights is called for.

2. Since the lessee is a corporation, it is necessary that the board of directors pass a vote authorizing the execution of this lease. You will find at the end of this lease a certificate of the officer executing the lease that such a vote has been passed. However, many counsel representing this lessor would require that the terms and date of the vote be set forth, for he or she may wish to satisfy himself or herself that these terms are sufficient authorization.

8. Since this lease covers only part of the real estate owned by the lessor at this general location, it is quite probable that there are various service pipes and wires in 346 which relate to 350. Hence the exception of these from the lease is important. Should not the lessor also have provided for access to these service pipes? See paragraphs 6 and 7, which may not be sufficient for this purpose.

term of twenty-one (21) years commencing on the first day of May, one thousand, nine hundred and [*insert year*], and terminating on the thirtieth day of April, two thousand and [*insert year*], to be used and occupied by Security State Bank of the City of New York only for the conduct of Lessee's banking business upon the covenants and conditions following:

RENTAL

1.   Lessee shall pay to the Lessor for the demised premises an annual rental of forty-eight thousand dollars ($48,000), which shall be payable in equal monthly installments in advance on the first day of each month throughout the term; the aforesaid payments of rental to be made without demand at 241 East 90th Street, New York City, or such other place as Lessor may designate by notice in writing to Lessee and by checks drawn to the order of Arthur Olmsted,[9] without any offset or deduction whatsoever. At or prior to the execution and delivery of this Agreement, Lessee has paid to Lessor the sum of $4,000, the receipt of which is hereby acknowledged by Lessor, to be applied to the payment of the rent first coming due hereunder, except as hereinafter provided in paragraph numbered 33.

OCCUPANCY

2.   Lessor does not warrant that actual occupancy shall be available to Lessee at the date fixed for the commencement of the term of this lease since the demised premises are presently rented to another tenant. In the event that such tenant shall not have removed from the demised premises on or before the said May 1, then Lessee shall be entitled to a pro-rating of rent and other charges with respect to such period as it shall not be in occupancy of the said premises following the said May 1. Lessor agrees however, in the event that the present tenant vacates the said premises at any time on or before the said May 1, to deliver possession of the said premises to Lessee hereunder immediately thereafter in which event Lessor shall be entitled to, and Lessee shall pay rent and other charges on a pro rata basis for the period beginning on the date of such delivery and ending on the following April 30. The term of this lease, in any event, shall terminate on April 30, [*insert year*].[10]

9.   Where there are several lessors, obviously it is important for the tenant to have one person to whom the tenant can pay the rent, give notices, and the like. See paragraph 32. Query: where consent of the lessors is required under this lease, must all four jointly consent? What if one or more refuse? Must court approval be obtained each time the consent of George Selkirk is required? Does this lease adequately deal with this situation?

10.   Where the commencement date is uncertain, either because of construction or the possibility of an existing tenant holding over, it is nevertheless important to designate a precise expiration date.

ORDINANCES

3. Lessee shall promptly execute and comply with all statutes, ordinances, rules, orders, regulations, and requirements of the Federal, State, and City government and of any and all of their Departments and Bureaus applicable to the demised premises and for the correction, prevention, and abatement of nuisances or other grievances, in, upon, or connected with the demised premises during said term; it shall promptly comply with and execute all rules, orders, and regulations of the New York Board of Fire Underwriters for the prevention of fires at Lessee's own cost and expense.[11]

REPAIRS

4. Lessee shall take good care of the demised premises and of the fixtures, and of all alterations, additions, and improvements in the demised premises throughout the term hereof and shall promptly make all repairs, alterations, and changes, ordinary and extraordinary, in, to, and about the said premises necessary to preserve them in good order and condition, which shall be in quality and class equal to the original work, and Lessee shall promptly pay the expense of such repair, suffer no waste or injury, and at the end of the term, deliver up the demised premises in good order and condition in all respects, damage attributable to acts of God or the elements excepted. If the Lessor shall deem that the Lessee has not duly and promptly made the necessary repairs, alterations, and changes in this paragraph referred to, and the Lessor shall give to the Lessee written notification of the requirement so to do during the term of the within lease, the Lessee shall have a reasonable time following the giving of said notice in which to comply therewith.[12]

11. Various regulatory bodies may impose requirements with regard to structural safety, fire hazards, and health. Some of these are easy to comply with, e.g., not storing gasoline or providing fire extinguishers. Others may be very expensive and involve structural change, e.g., providing exterior fire escapes or interior automatic sprinklers. A clause such as paragraph 3 usually is not construed to require the tenant to make structural changes.

12. In dealing with repairs and the condition of the premises, the following matters are relevant:

a. What obligations does the landlord undertake as to the condition of the premises at the time the lease period begins? (In leases of dwelling houses or apartments this obviously is an important factor. It may also be important in leases of business properties because, among other things, a previous tenant may remove fixtures in such a way as to do substantial damage.)

b. Who has the obligation to repair during the term of the lease? (There are various types of "repairs," all the way from routine correction of wear and tear to serious and expensive structural work made necessary by fire. Frequently a distinction is drawn between outside repairs and inside repairs or between structural repairs and others. It should be made clear whether the obligation is one to repair only when notice is given of the necessity therefor or to maintain an inspection of the premises and keep them in good shape without notice.)

c. What are the tenant's obligations as to condition of the premises on redelivery to the landlord? (Provision should be made for restoration of alterations, removal of additions, structural condition, and cleanliness.)

Paragraph 4 of this lease should be evaluated in the light of what has been said above.

ASSIGNMENT, SUBLETTING

5.   Lessee, its successors or assigns, shall not assign this agreement or sublet or underlet the demised premises or any part thereof without prior consent of landlord which shall not be unreasonably withheld. In the event of any such assignment, subletting, or underletting, Lessee shall remain liable to Lessor for the payment of rent and the performance of all other obligations of the Lessee hereunder.[13]

INSPECTION

6.   Lessor shall have the right from time to time to designate a representative to inspect the demised premises or any part thereof, at reasonable times and without interference with the conduct of Lessee's business.[14]

The material in Chapter 17 should be reconsidered at this point. Mr. Porter says:

The printed form of lease carried a stock provision that the tenant would take care of the premises and surrender the same at the expiration of the term in good order or condition, damages by the elements excepted. This raised the question with us as to the possible liability on the part of the tenant for possible damage by earthquake or lightning which did not result in fire. We therefore revised the provisions to include "damage attributable to acts of God or the elements excepted." This provoked a controversy with Durham over the terms which he finally accepted. To avoid a possible default by the tenant under this repair provision, we inserted a provision that if the landlord deemed that the tenant had not duly and promptly made the necessary repairs, the landlord was required to give the tenant written notice of the same during the term of the lease and that the tenant should have a reasonable time thereafter to comply with the notice.

See American Law of Property §3.79 (Casner ed. 1952).

13.   A tenant may assign his lease (i.e., transfer his entire interest) or sublet (i.e., create a new landlord-tenant relationship between himself and a subtenant) unless the lease provides to the contrary. (Indeed, under the rules as to restraints on alienation, the tenant may assign or sublet no matter what the lease says; but these rules permit the lease to give the landlord a right of reentry if the tenant assigns or sublets. Compare the "spendthrift trusts" in which A creates a trust to pay the income to B during B's life and provides that B's interest shall be inalienable. This equitable interest *is* inalienable. If B attempts to assign it to C, C has nothing and the trustee must still make payment to B.)

Paragraph 5 shows the scars of disagreement and amendment. The clause against unreasonable withholding of the landlord's assent makes a substantial nullity of the clause prohibiting assignment and sublease. It was very important for the bank to have the right to assign or sublet in the event that the branch bank should prove unprofitable as a result of a change in the character of the neighborhood or increased competition.

It is usually provided that "assent to any assignment or sublease shall not release the prohibition as to assignment and sublease or constitute an assent to any other assignment or sublease."

The last sentence in paragraph 5 is unnecessary. If the lessee assigns or sublets, even with the lessor's assent, the lessee still remains liable on the lease.

The material in Chapter 20 should be reconsidered at this point. See also American Law of Property §§3.56-3.58, 3.61, 3.62 (Casner ed. 1952).

14.   Bear in mind that "the lessor" in this case is four different people. For this reason the usual clause permitting the lessor to inspect might involve some inconvenience. It is for this reason that the lessor is given the right only to designate *a* representative to inspect.

OFFERING PREMISES FOR SALE OR LEASE

7.   Lessor or its agents shall be entitled to show the premises at reasonable times to persons wishing to purchase the same; and Lessee further agrees that on or after the November 1 which precedes the April 30 on which the lease term ends Lessor or its agents shall have the right to show the premises for rental purposes and to place reasonable notices on the front of said premises or any part thereof, offering the premises "To Let" or "For Sale," and Lessee hereby agrees to permit the same to remain thereon without hindrance or molestation; provided, however, that such notices shall not interfere with Lessee's signs or the conduct of Lessee's business.

RIGHTS UPON DEFAULT

8.   If default be made in the payment of the said rent or any part thereof, or if default be made in the performance of any of the covenants herein contained, except those referred to in paragraph numbered 14(b) herein, Lessor or its representatives may re-enter the premises by force, summary proceedings, or otherwise and remove all persons therefrom, without being liable to prosecution therefor, and Lessee hereby expressly waives the service of any notice in writing of intention to re-enter.[15] In the event of re-entry by reason of such default or by the removal of Lessee by summary proceedings or otherwise, Lessee shall pay at the same time as the rent becomes payable under the term hereof the sum equivalent to the rent reserved herein, and Lessor may rent the premises on behalf of Lessee, reserving the right to rent the premises for a longer period of time than fixed in the original lease without releasing Lessee from any liability, applying any moneys collected first to the expense of resuming or obtaining possession, second to restoring the premises to rentable condition, and then to the payment of the rent and all other charges due and to grow due to Lessor, any surplus to be paid to Lessee, who shall remain liable for any deficiency.[16] Lessee hereby expressly waives the service of any notice in writing of intention to re-enter, as provided by any law of the State of New York.

---

15.   This clause is a pretty rough proposition if it means what it says. It gives the landlord the right to terminate the lease upon *any* default in any of the numerous covenants made by the tenant. There may be some equitable relief against forfeiture for trifling breaches, but many leases protect the tenant by providing that the landlord shall have no right to forfeit until a breach by the tenant has been called to the tenant's attention and has not been cured within 30 days. See American Law of Property §§3.94-3.96 (Casner ed. 1952).

16.   What is the status of the landlord when he re-enters under this paragraph? Does the tenant's interest continue, or is it terminated? The clause providing that "Lessor may rent the premises on behalf of Lessee" seems to indicate that the lessee's interest still exists. However, the clause providing that "in the event of re-entry . . . Lessee shall pay at the same time as the rent becomes payable under the terms hereof *the sum equivalent to the rent reserved herein*" (italics added) seems to indicate that the rent is no longer due and, by inference, that the lessee's estate has terminated. The ambiguity may cause trouble. It is more usual to provide that the landlord may re-enter and thereby terminate the lease; after such termination, the tenant will be liable for any amount by which the rent received from another tenant is less than the rent

DAMAGE TO PREMISES

9.   In case of any damage or injury occurring to the glass in the demised premises, Lessee shall promptly replace the same at its own expense. In case of damage and injury to the demised premises, of any kind whatsoever (except damage and injury attributable to acts of God which demolish the demised structure), whether or not said damage or injury is caused by carelessness, negligence, or improper conduct on the part of Lessee or its agents or employees, Lessee shall cause the said damage or injury to be repaired as speedily as possible at Lessee's own cost and expense.[17]

OBSTRUCTIONS

10.   Lessee shall neither encumber nor obstruct the sidewalk in front of, entrance to, or halls and stairs of said premises nor allow the same to be obstructed or encumbered in any manner.[18]

SIGNS

11.   Lessee shall not place or cause or allow to be placed any exterior sign or signs at, in, or about the entrance to said premises or any other part of the same except in or at such places as may be indicated by Lessor and consented to by Lessor in writing, which consent, however, shall not be unreasonably withheld. Notwithstanding the foregoing, Lessee shall have the right to erect a sign on the roof of the demised premises with respect to its

---

reserved in the lease. In New York there are procedural reasons it is desirable to have the tenant's estate terminate automatically upon notice by the landlord rather than upon the landlord's re-entry; the former method provides a more expeditious remedy. Observe that paragraph 14(a) deals with the same subject matter, i.e., rights of the lessor upon default by the lessee. It is there clearly provided that notice by the lessor terminates the lease, but note well that it is nowhere provided in paragraph 14(a) that the lessee has any liabilities after such termination. It is at least strongly arguable that if the lessor terminates by giving a notice under paragraph 14(a), as distinguished from making an entry under paragraph 8, the lessee is relieved of all liability.

To protect a lessor's right to rent, the lessor should have at least three things:
1.   A covenant by the lessee to pay the rent.
2.   A right to terminate the lease if the rent is not paid.
3.   A right to hold the tenant to his rent obligation, minus rents later received from others, even though the lease is terminated.

All three of the above must be provided for the lessor's protection in any well-drawn instrument. Even these three, however, will not protect the lessor against insolvency on the part of the lessee (see Chapter 18, Section 1, for a reference to the security devices which may be employed to protect the lessor against the lessee's insolvency) or against inflation (how can the lessor protect himself against inflation?).

The material in Chapter 18, Section 2.A, and Chapter 21 should be reconsidered at this point. See also American Law of Property §3.97 (Casner ed. 1952).

17.   It would seem clear that paragraph 9 deals with the same subject matter as paragraph 4 and thus should have been coordinated with and incorporated in it.

18.   This clause is a relic of the printed form which was the starting point of negotiations. It is useful where a portion of a building is being rented and there are stairways, hallways, and sidewalks used in common by the lessee and other tenants of the building. It is meaningless where an entire building is being leased.

own banking and insurance business and to place other signs relating to its banking and insurance business on the exterior of the said premises; the said signs to be erected and maintained in strict accordance with the rules, regulations, and requirements of any and all departments, municipal or otherwise, having jurisdiction thereof. Lessee shall also have the right to erect, install, and maintain any signs in the interior of the demised premises relating to its banking activities.[19]

EXEMPTION OF LESSOR FROM LIABILITY

12.   Lessor shall be exempt from any and all liability for any damage or injury to person or property caused by or resulting from steam, electricity, gas, water, rain, ice or snow, or any leak or flow from or into any part of said building or from any damage or injury resulting or arising from any other cause or happening whatsoever unless said damage or injury be caused by or be due to the negligence of Lessor.[20]

SUBORDINATION TO MORTGAGES

13.   This instrument shall not be a lien against the demised premises in respect of any mortgages which are now on or which hereafter may be placed against said premises to the limit of the principal sum of three hundred thousand dollars ($300,000), and the recording of any such mortgage or mortgages not in excess of such principal amount shall have preference and precedence and be superior and prior in lien to this lease, irrespective of the date of recording, and Lessee agrees to execute any such instrument without cost which may be deemed necessary or desirable to further effect the subordination of this lease to any such mortgage or mortgages, and a refusal to execute such instrument shall entitle Lessor, or its successors and assigns, to the option of cancelling this lease without incurring any expense or damage, and the term hereby granted is expressly limited accordingly.[21]

---

19.   This clause is a masterpiece of self-contradiction. In substance, it says: "The Lessee shall not erect any signs except the signs the Lessee wants to erect." This is a classic example of starting with a bad draft and trying to "amend" the draft.

20.   As to any clause which purports to create an exemption from tort liability, it is relevant to ask:
  1.   Who is bound by the exemption? (In this case, it is Security State Bank of the city of New York, a corporation which is quite unlikely to break its leg on a defective stairway.)
  2.   What types of liabilities, otherwise existing, are eliminated? (Nearly all tort liabilities of a lessor are founded upon the lessor's negligence—and damage by the lessor's negligence is excepted from this exemption.)
  Is this a covenant of indemnity?

21.   Suppose the lessor wants to raise $300,000 on the property; the mortgagee is dissatisfied with the protection given him in paragraph 13 and requires that the lessee join in the mortgage; the lessee refuses to join in the mortgage; and the lessor cancels the lease under paragraph 13. Does the lessee thereafter have any liability to the lessor? This clause provides none, and the fact that a specific remedy for this particular breach of covenant is given in paragraph 13 would, arguably, prevent the lessor from proceeding under paragraph 8, which does give him a right to future payments from the lessee.

FURTHER RIGHTS OF LESSOR

14. (a) If Lessee shall default in the payment of rent or any part thereof, or if the default be made in the performance of any of the covenants herein contained, or if Lessee shall file a petition in bankruptcy or be adjudicated a bankrupt, or make an assignment for the benefit of creditors, or take advantage of any Insolvency Act, apart from any other rights, privileges, or action available to the Lessor hereunder or at law, the Lessor may at its election at any time thereafter terminate this lease and the term hereof, promptly upon the giving of written notice of Lessor's intention so to do; and this lease and the term thereof shall expire and come to an end upon the giving of such notice, as if the said date were the date originally fixed in this lease for the expiration thereof.[22]

(b) If Lessee shall fail to comply with any of the Statutes, Ordinances, Rules, Orders, Regulations, and Requirements of the Federal, State, and City governments or of any and all of their Departments and Bureaus applicable to said premises or hereafter established, as herein provided, then the Lessor may at its election at any time thereafter terminate this lease and the term thereof, by giving Lessee ten (10) days notice in writing of Lessor's intention so to do, and this lease and the term thereof shall expire and come to an end on the date fixed in such notice, as if said date were the date originally fixed in this lease for the expiration hereof; providing, however, that Lessee shall have the benefit of any additional time permitted by such governmental Department, Bureau or Agency to correct the noncompliance with such Statute, Ordinance, Rule, Regulation, or Requirement.[23]

WATER CHARGES

15. Lessee shall pay to Lessor the rent or charge which may, during the demised term, be assessed or imposed for the water used or consumed in or on the said premises, whether determined by meter or otherwise, as soon as and when the same may be assessed or imposed and will also pay the expense for the setting of a water meter on the said premises should the latter be required. If such rent or charge or expenses are not so paid, the same shall be added to the next month's rent, thereafter to become due.[24]

---

22. This deals with the same subject matter as paragraph 8. See footnotes 15 and 16 for comment. Paragraphs 13 and 14(b) also deal with the lessor's remedy for a particular type of default. All the questions as to the lessor's remedies upon default should be treated in a single paragraph and on a uniform basis unless there are substantial reasons for nonuniformity.

23. This paragraph deals redundantly with a matter already treated in paragraph 3. It gives the lessor a particular remedy for default, and in this it deals with the same subject matter as paragraphs 8, 13, and 14(a) — all of which should have been treated together. In the event that the lessor terminates the lease for this breach, this paragraph does not provide for any further liability of the lessee.

24. Water charges are an expense the lessee should bear. The clause which permits adding these to the rent is helpful; in many states particularly effective remedies are available for collecting "rent."

FIRE INSURANCE RATES

16.   Lessee will not, nor will it permit its undertenants or other persons to do anything in said premises, or bring anything into said premises, or permit anything to be brought into said premises or to be kept therein, which will in any way increase the rate of fire insurance on said demised premises, nor use the demised premises or any part thereof, nor suffer or permit their use for any business or purpose which would cause an increase in the rate of fire insurance on said building, and Lessee agrees to pay on demand any such increase as well as any increase in fire rates caused by the occupancy of Lessee, apart from its conduct therein.[25]

NO WAIVER OF RIGHTS

17.   The failure of either party to insist upon a strict performance of any of the terms, covenants, and conditions herein shall not be deemed a waiver of any rights or remedies of either such party and shall not be deemed a waiver of any subsequent breach or default in any of the terms, conditions, and covenants herein contained. This instrument may not be changed, modified, or discharged orally.[26]

CONDEMNATION

18.   If all or substantially all of the demised premises shall be taken by condemnation, the lease hereby created shall terminate upon such taking by the acquiring authority and the rent and other charges shall be apportioned accordingly. No part of any award, however, shall belong to the tenant. If less than all or substantially all of the demised premises shall be so taken, the

25.   Conduct of the lessee on the premises may cause the fire insurance premium to be increased. If this occurs, all the lessor is properly interested in is having the lessee bear the increased cost. There is no justification for requiring a covenant of the lessee not to cause such an increase, for remember that, for breach of such a covenant, the lessor can terminate the lease under paragraphs 8 and 14(a).

Conduct of the lessee may be such as to give the insurance company a defense to an action on the policy if a fire occurs. What the lessor needs is a covenant by the lessee that he will engage in no such conduct and will pay any loss by fire to whatever extent his conduct precludes liability on the insurance policies.

Fire insurance is also dealt with in the first part of paragraph 27; these matters ought to be treated together.

26.   There is some law to the effect that failure to insist upon performance of a covenant is a waiver of later breaches, so this paragraph performs a function.

The last sentence has no effect. If the instrument would be capable of oral amendment or cancellation apart from this clause and if the parties want to amend or cancel it orally, they simply begin by canceling out the last sentence of paragraph 17 and then proceed to do anything else with the instrument they want to. But see N.Y. Gen. Oblig. Law §§1-203, 15-301, relating to when a written instrument cannot be changed, discharged, or terminated by an oral *executory* agreement. The statute has been held inapplicable to an *executed* oral waiver. Alcon v. Kinton Realty, Inc., 2 A.D.2d 454, 156 N.Y.S.2d 439 (1956). See American Law of Property §3.95 (Casner ed. 1952).

rent for the remaining premises shall thereupon be proportionately apportioned.[27]

REMOVAL OF FIXTURES

19. If after default in payment of rent or violation of any other provision of this lease, or upon the expiration of this lease, Lessee moves out or is dispossessed and fails to remove any trade fixtures or other property within five days following such default, removal, expiration of lease, or issuance of the final order or execution of the warrant, then and in that event the said fixtures and property shall be deemed abandoned by the said Lessee and shall become the property of the Lessor.[28]

WAIVER OF STATUTORY REDEMPTION

20. Lessee waives all rights to redeem under Section 761 of the Real Property Actions and Proceedings Law.[29]

27. Mr. Porter says:

The condemnation clause [paragraph 18] is not as we should like to have it. We should like to have a right to a portion of the award which would represent the damages to the leasehold. We should also like to have the right to surrender the lease if part of the premises were taken and that remaining was no longer suitable for our use. We should also like to have had a provision for using part of the award to reconstruct the remaining part of the property. However, it was not possible to obtain the kind of clause that we wanted. Our suggestions were strenuously resisted by the landlord's counsel. There is no reason to expect any condemnation in this neighborhood; hence we decided to take the clause as it now stands.

You should reconsider at this point Chapter 19, Section 1.C. See American Law of Property §3.54 (Casner ed. 1952).

28. A "fixture" is a chattel which has been incorporated into the real estate but which the tenant may have the privilege of removing and taking with him. There are some fixtures so firmly incorporated into the real estate that the tenant is not privileged to remove them; these are commonly called "landlord's fixtures." Tenants frequently find it not worthwhile to remove those fixtures which they are privileged to remove, i.e., "tenant's fixtures"; such chattels are frequently peculiarly adapted to the particular building, would have no use elsewhere, and have no junk value. The law as to when the tenant must remove tenant's fixtures or forfeit them is unsatisfactory, and it is well to specify a removal period in the lease.

Observe a joker in paragraph 19. If the tenant commits a breach of covenant and is dispossessed by force, this paragraph seems to say that he forfeits all fixtures which have not been removed "within five days following such default"—and the default may have taken place many days before the dispossession.

The material in Chapter 22 should be reconsidered at this point. See American Law of Property §19.11 (Casner ed. 1952).

29. N.Y. Real Prop. Acts. Law §761 provides that where summary proceedings (an expeditious remedy for recovery of the possession of land, prescribed in article 7 of N.Y. Real Prop. Acts. Law §701) are brought to evict a lessee who has defaulted in rent and at least five years of the lease term are unexpired, the lessee may recover the premises and reinstate the lease by paying all rent due with interest plus the lessor's costs and charges, if this is done within one year after the execution of the warrant in the summary proceedings. Section 761 expressly authorizes waiver of the rights created therein. Section 765 gives some protection to a new tenant to whom the lessor has given a lease before redemption.

This waiver relates to the landlord's remedies upon default and should have been included in a single paragraph with the clauses which now appear in paragraphs 8, 13, 14(a), and 14(b).

DUTY OF LESSEE DURING ALTERATION

21.   In the event that Lessee, in the making of any authorized alterations, requires the relocation of water, gas, electric pipes and meters, or plumbing and sewers in the basement of the demised premises, Lessee shall not in any manner render untenantable the premises known as 350 Eastern Avenue, adjoining the demised premises nor unreasonably interfere with or deprive the tenants of the said adjoining premises of the use and enjoyment thereof and the service thereto.[30]

BOILER LIABILITY INSURANCE

22.   Throughout the term hereof, Lessee shall procure and maintain boiler insurance and public liability insurance indemnifying Lessor in the sum of $50,000 for injury or death to one person and $100,000 for injury or death to persons or damage to property in any one occurrence covering the demised premises, including the sidewalk adjacent thereto. In the event Lessee shall fail to procure and maintain such insurance in force throughout the term hereof, Lessor may, at its election, procure issuance of such coverage, at the expense of Lessee, and the sums paid by Lessor therefor shall be considered as rent and added to the rental due for the month immediately following the procurement of said insurance coverage and shall be payable as rent, together with the rent otherwise reserved or any other sums to become due and constitute rent as in this Agreement provided.[31]

SNOW REMOVAL

23.   Lessee shall, at its own cost and expense, keep the sidewalks and curbs directly in front of the premises free from snow and ice and also keep clean the entrance leading into the demised premises.[32]

HEAT, HOT WATER

24.   No heat or hot water is to be furnished by Lessor, and Lessee, at its own cost and expense, shall make and furnish all heat for the demised premises (and hot water if it so desires) during the term hereof, but Lessee shall have no obligation to furnish heat, hot water, or any other service,

---

30.   This clause is a sensible precaution in view of the fact that service pipes for No. 350 are in the basement of No. 346.

31.   Such insurance clauses for the protection of the lessor usually require that the insurance be in companies acceptable to the lessor, that the policies be delivered to the lessor, and that renewal policies be delivered at least 30 days before the expiration of existing policies. Otherwise how does the lessor know that he has adequate coverage? In determining what liability insurance coverage the landlord should have, reexamine Chapter 17, Section 1.D.

32.   Ordinances frequently impose upon owners the obligation to remove snow and ice from the sidewalks. The lessee of the building should assume this obligation.

supply, or utility to any other person or persons or to any other building or buildings.[33]

ALTERATIONS

25. In the event Lessee desires to make any alterations and changes in the demised premises, it is understood and agreed that the same shall not be made without the prior consent of the Lessor, which shall not be unreasonably withheld. All alterations, decorations, additions, and improvements, including paneling, partitions, railings, galleries, and the like, except movable trade or banking fixtures, shall become the property of Lessor upon installation. It is understood and agreed that upon the expiration or prior termination of the term of this lease Lessor may require Lessee, at the election of Lessor and at the expense of Lessee, to restore the demised premises to the character and condition which prevailed before any said alterations or changes were made by Lessee.[34]

TAXES

26. Throughout the term hereof, in addition to the rental and other charges agreed to be paid by Lessee, Lessee shall also pay the amount of real estate taxes which shall be levied and assessed against the demised premises in excess of the amount of taxes levied and assessed against said premises for the tax year commencing July 1 of the year this lease is dated. In the event Lessee shall fail to duly pay the aforesaid amount, Lessor may pay same, and the said amount or amounts, together with interest thereon, shall be added to any rent then due or thereafter falling due and shall be deemed rent due hereunder; and Lessor shall have the right to take such action as may be

---

33. You should expect that this clause was a relic of the printed form since it is clearly inapplicable to the lease of an entire building which has its own heating plant to which the landlord could not have access except by committing a trespass. But this is not the case; the clause, for some unexplained reason, was added to the printed form by Durham. Porter had no objection to it.

34. If the lessee in this case were less responsible, this clause would not give adequate protection to the lessor. When tenants undertake to make alterations, several unfortunate things may happen:

1. The alterations may be commenced and then left uncompleted.
2. The tenant may fail to pay his contractors and subcontractors, with the result that mechanics' liens may attach to the premises.
3. The tenant may install equipment which is subject to chattel mortgages or bought on conditional sale.

Hence it is usually desirable for the lessor to require a provision that no alterations shall be made unless the lessee provides to the lessor a surety company bond guaranteeing completion of the work, free and clear of mechanics' liens, chattel mortgages, and conditional sales. Possibly the lessor could protect himself by demanding such a bond as a condition of assenting to an alteration, and this would not be considered an unreasonable withholding of assent. Observe that the first sentence of paragraph 25 deals with "alterations and changes," whereas the second deals with "alterations, decorations, additions, and improvements." What is the effect of this variation of terminology? See Problem 23.1, which appears at the end of this lease.

permissible hereunder for the collection thereof as in the case of default in the payment of fixed rent.[35]

Lessee shall, however, have the right to contest by legal proceedings, conducted at its own expense, in the name of the Lessor or Lessee, any and all such taxes assessed or imposed against or upon the demised premises, and in case any such taxes, as a result of any such legal proceedings, be reduced, Lessee shall be entitled to refunds to the extent that such reduction shall relate to taxes theretofore paid by Lessee, together with any interest received thereon.[36]

Lessor shall pay all taxes and assessments levied against the demised premises and all interest and principal payments on any mortgage on the demised premises before default shall occur thereon. In default of such payments by Lessor, Lessee may pay said amounts, and such payments, with interest thereon, shall be deducted from the rent due hereunder, and any excess shall be paid with interest by Lessor to Lessee on demand.[37]

FIRE

27.   Lessor agrees during the term of the lease hereby created to keep the demised premises insured against loss by fire in the amount of $50,000. Before the commencement of the term of the lease hereby created Lessor and Lessee shall each appoint a representative to consult and agree upon an amount of additional fire insurance to be provided by the Lessee which shall be sufficient to bring the total of fire insurance coverage on the demised premises up to 80 percent of the full insurable value of said demised premises. All policies of fire insurance on the demised premises are to contain the usual 80 percent co-insurance clause contained in standard fire insurance policies. In the event of failure of said representatives to agree upon the amount of such additional fire insurance, said representatives shall choose a third party to decide the issue. Upon the determination of the

---

35.   In any long-term lease, the parties must consider (1) real estate taxes, and (2) betterment assessments levied against the property. In the absence of a provision in the lease, the taxes are paid by the lessor; betterment assessments are paid by the lessor, but there is frequently a statutory provision as to addition of a percentage of the betterment assessment to any tenant's rent. For example, see Mass. Gen. Laws Ann. ch. 80, §11. No such provision exists in New York. Therefore, if special assessments (for street paving, sewers, street widening, etc.) are levied upon this property during the term of the lease, the landlord pays them; and a covenant by the lessee to pay "taxes," as in the present lease, does not include special assessments. McVickar Gaillard Realty Co. v. Garth, 111 A.D. 924, 97 N.Y.S. 640 (1906). If such assessment is made, this may cut into the net rent seriously.

36.   Property owners can seek relief from real estate taxes by petitions seeking to have the assessed value of their properties reduced. In this case, since the lessee is bound to pay any increase in the taxes, he should have the right to seek reductions in assessed valuations.

You recall that the lessor also owns the office building on the adjoining lot, No. 350 Eastern Avenue. There is a danger that these two parcels belonging to the same owner are assessed as one lot. If this is true, application must be made to the assessors to make separate assessments.

37.   Since taxes, betterment assessments, and mortgages have seniority to the lease, the tenant must have the right to pay off these liens and thus prevent their foreclosure and the consequent destruction of the tenant's interest. Do you find that the sentence to which this footnote is appended is consistent with the rest of the lease?

amount of such additional fire insurance, Lessee shall provide the same, payable, in case of loss, to Lessor and Lessee jointly, it being intended that said funds are to be used to repair or rebuild the demised premises and not for distribution in any part to Lessee.[38]

In the event of total destruction of the demised premises by fire, Lessee shall have the right, at its option, by notice in writing given as provided in Article 32 hereof to Lessor within ten days after the said total destruction to terminate the lease hereby created. If the lease is so terminated Lessee shall, within ten days from such termination, execute any documents necessary to turn over to Lessor the proceeds of such fire insurance policy. If the lease shall not be so terminated, Lessor covenants to proceed promptly to repair, rebuild, and restore the demised premises to its previous design and construction, or as near thereto as possible, the standard of workmanship and materials to be not less than that used in the present structure, and the proceeds of said fire insurance coverage shall be promptly made available to the Lessor therefor as the work of rebuilding the demised premises progresses. Upon the issuance of a certificate of occupancy for the demised premises by the proper authorities, Lessee shall promptly turn over to Lessor the balance of the proceeds not theretofore used in said rebuilding. The rent and other charges for the demised premises shall be abated proportionately for any period during which the premises are untenantable.[39]

The fire insurance to be provided by Lessee shall be for a five-year term.

---

38. The "usual 80 percent co-insurance clause" provides that if the property is not insured up to 80 percent of its full insurable value, the owner is a co-insurer as to the difference between the amount of insurance and such 80 percent. This can best be explained by an example. O owns a building worth $100,000. He insures it for $60,000 under a policy containing the usual 80 percent clause. He thus becomes a co-insurer with the company as to $20,000. If a fire occurs, he and the insurance company will bear the loss in the proportion of 20 to 60. Thus if he has a $10,000 fire loss, he can recover from the company only $7,500.

The provision for arbitration of the amount of insurance (or any other matter that has to be agreed to during the course of the term) is a common and useful clause.

39. As to the provisions concerning rebuilding and the like, Mr. Porter says:

We provided that in the event of loss the insurance money would be payable to the landlord and tenant jointly, to the end that the funds would be used to repair or rebuild the demised premises. We had considerable difficulty with Durham on this provision. We were faced with the possibility that these lessors or one or more of them might get their hands on the fire insurance money and refuse to rebuild, in which event we could only have recourse to the law. But, since several of the co-owners are non-residents, we could be faced with a problem of getting jurisdiction over them. It took considerable battling to get this provision, and Durham insisted upon circumscribing it with provisions which would pin us down to rebuilding. That resulted in the drafting of a formula which he finally agreed to. The substance of the provision is that in the event of total destruction the tenant has the option to give notice within a specified time of its election to terminate the lease and, if the lease is so terminated, to release the fire insurance fund to the landlord. In the event the tenant does not so elect, the landlord covenants to repair, rebuild, and restore the demised premises. This latter course raised the question of whether the restoration would be acceptable to the building authorities for occupancy, so we had to provide that the proceeds of the fire insurance policies would be made available as the work of rebuilding progressed and, upon the issuance of a certificate of occupancy for the premises, to turn over to the lessor the balance of the proceeds not theretofore used in rebuilding. We also provided for the proportionate abatement of the rent during the period in which the premises were untenantable.

Sixty days before the expiration of each five-year term Lessor and Lessee shall each appoint a representative to consult and determine as hereinbefore set forth, upon the amount of fire insurance to be provided by Lessee during the ensuing five-year period.

OFFICIAL CERTIFICATE

28.   In any suit or proceeding of any kind or nature, arising or growing out of the failure of Lessee to pay any moneys hereunder, the certificate or receipt of the department or official charged with its collection, showing that such charge is due and payable or has been paid, or the receipt of such firm or concern to whom payment shall be made hereunder, shall be prima facie evidence that such charge or payment was due and payable, as a lien or charge against the demised premises or for work or obligations due or to be made or paid hereunder and has been paid as such by Lessor.[40]

LEASES TO OTHER BANKS

29.   So long as the demised premises are occupied hereunder by a bank or other financial or lending institution, the Lessor shall not permit any other bank or financial or lending institution to occupy any part of the adjoining premises known as No. 350 Eastern Avenue.[41]

COVENANT OF QUIET ENJOYMENT

29a.   On paying the said rent and in performing the covenants aforesaid, Lessee shall and may peaceably and quietly have, hold, and enjoy the said demised premises for the term aforesaid.[42]

---

40.   The tenant is bound to pay certain additional taxes (paragraph 26), water charges (paragraph 15), and additional fire insurance premiums (paragraphs 16 and 22). If the lessor should have to bring suit against the lessee to obtain such payment, he would have to establish (1) that the charge was a proper one, and (2) that the lessor had paid it. The purpose of paragraph 28 is to simplify the problem of proof on these issues. Its net effect is to throw upon the lessee the burden of establishing that payments made by the lessor are not justified, and this is a sensible provision.

41.   Covenants against leases to competing businesses are very common where the lessor controls a significant amount of space which could potentially be used by a competitor. For example, if L owns a large block of stores and T leases one store for the sale of haberdashery, it is important to T that there be a covenant against another haberdashery store in the same block. However, in the present instance, a covenant against another banking or financial institution in the lessor's one adjoining building gives rather slight protection. It is clear that the New York State Commissioner of Banks would not authorize such competition by a state bank, and a federally controlled banking institution would be as unlikely to relish being next door to the Security State Bank as the latter would relish having the federal institution move in. Still, the covenant can do no harm. See American Law of Property §3.42 (Casner ed. 1952).

42.   This covenant is of no effect since a covenant of quiet enjoyment is implied even if it is not expressed. Note that (1) if O sells Blackacre to P, no covenant of quiet enjoyment is implied, but (2) if L leases Blackacre to T, a covenant of quiet enjoyment is implied. In the lease a situation of tenurial relationship exists, and from feudal times, we inherit the principle that it is the obligation of the lord to protect the tenant in his tenancy against those who assert a title paramount to that of the lord. See American Law of Property §3.47 (Casner ed. 1952).

PROPERTY OWNED BY THE LESSOR[43]

30.   Lessor represents and warrants that Lessor has unencumbered good and marketable title in fee simple absolute to the following described real property:

[Here appears a courses-and-distances description of Parcels A, B, and C, being respectively the bank building, the medical office building at 350 Eastern Avenue, and the garage at 348 Snelling Street immediately behind the bank building and the office building. The descriptions are in the general form of the description of the bank building, which appears in the early part of this lease.][44]

In consideration of the execution of this lease by Lessee, Lessor hereby grants to Lessee (a) a right of first refusal applicable to all or any part of the above described premises (including improvements), and (b) an option to purchase all of such premises (including improvements) which, at the time of the exercise of such option, shall not have been sold by Lessor in the manner permitted herein. Such right and option shall be irrevocable, and such option shall be exercisable only at the expiration of eight years after the effective date of the lease hereby created and on the terms and conditions hereinafter set forth. Lessor covenants that, except to the extent that Lessor shall convey all or a part of such premises in the manner permitted in this Article 30, Lessor will continue to own such premises throughout said eight-year period and until the August 1 following such eighth year.

RIGHTS OF FIRST REFUSAL

30a.   *Right of first refusal.* Whenever, within said period of eight years from the effective date of this Lease, Lessor receives a written offer from a

---

43.   Paragraphs 30 to 34 inclusive were born into the world without the handicaps of parenthood which stunted and warped most of the earlier paragraphs. Even so, these five paragraphs were the product of negotiation and compromise; they represented no one party's entire wish or sole draftsmanship, but they did start from a sound first draft. You will observe a notable contrast with the earlier portions of the lease.

The options given in paragraph 30 might have been in an entirely separate document. Since the lease relates only to the bank building and the option relates to the bank, the office building, and the garage, the option must necessarily begin with a description of all three parcels. Moreover, the warranty of quiet enjoyment which would be implied as to the leasehold interest of the bank building does not apply with reference to the option to purchase (since no tenurial relationship will exist if the option is exercised); therefore the option must also begin with the warranty of title which is customary in New York transactions involving the sale of a fee simple. The various covenants for title which are customary in connection with conveyances in fee simple are dealt with in Chapter 27.

44.   Counsel for the bank had to worry about the question of whether his client, as a state bank, had power under the New York banking laws to purchase the office building and the garage. A New York state bank, unlike insurance companies, has no power to invest in the ownership of real estate. It can, of course, acquire real estate on foreclosure of a mortgage and hold it temporarily, pending disposal; it also can purchase property for its own bank premises. Mr. Porter says:

> Someone can raise a captious point perhaps that the bank cannot purchase a medical office building which it does not intend to use for banking purposes, even though it intends to sell it right away. However, I think there will be no difficulty since it is necessary to buy it in order to obtain banking premises.

responsible person or persons to purchase all or any part of the above-described premises, Lessor shall deliver to Lessee, in the manner provided in Article 32 hereof, a duplicate original thereof, together with such other instruments as may be required to show the bona fides of the offer. Lessee may elect to purchase the premises to which said offer relates on terms and conditions not less favorable to Lessor than those contained in said offer by giving to Lessor, in the manner provided in Article 32 hereof, written notice of such election within thirty (30) days after delivery to Lessee of said offer. If Lessee does not elect to meet such offer within said thirty-day period, Lessor may accept the offer and the premises to which it relates shall be deemed released, for a period of six months from the date of said offer, from this right of first refusal, but only for the purpose of accepting said offer and completing the conveyance contemplated therein in accordance with the terms thereof. Any such conveyance of all or any part of the demised premises shall be subject to all the provisions of the lease hereby created.[45]

OPTION TO PURCHASE

30b.   *Option to purchase.* Between the dates of May 1 at the end of such eighth year and the August following the end of such eighth year Lessee shall have an option to purchase all of the above-described premises which have not theretofore been sold by Lessor to Lessee or others in the manner provided in subparagraph (a) above for the sum of nine hundred and sixty thousand dollars ($960,000), less the sale price of any part of the above-described premises which theretofore has been sold. For the purpose of the preceding sentence, any part of the premises which, at the time of the exercise of this option, is under contract of sale made pursuant to the provisions of subparagraph (a) shall be treated as if sold and paid for at the contract price, although the conveyance is not yet completed. This option shall be exercised by notice to Lessor, given by Lessee during the period May 1 to August 1, in the manner provided in Article 32 hereof, of its election so to do. Failure duly to give such notice shall be deemed to constitute rejection and abandonment of the option by Lessee.

45.   Mr. Porter says:

A "right of first refusal" may have any number of different forms and degrees of enforceability. They may be very general, without specific dates and methods for notification and exercise, and they may be without any provisions to assure that there is a bona fide offer. If there is no bona fide offer, the optionee may have a pistol put at his head and be compelled to decide whether to buy the property when there is no real occasion. If he refuses to buy the property, his right of first refusal may be simply lost, regardless of whether the owner sells the property to his alleged offeree. Such a right of first refusal is, obviously, of no great value. On the other hand, the clause may be so tight that the owner can, as a practical matter, hardly ever get an offer from an outsider. For instance, there may be requirements of substantial deposit of cash by the outside offeror to guarantee its bona fides, which may be burdensome, particularly if the offeror knows that his offer can be met. We tried to make this right of first refusal effective without making it actually offensive and impossible of acceptance by the landlord.

30c. *Closings.* In the event Lessee shall exercise either the right of first refusal provided for in subparagraph (a) above, or the option provided for in subparagraph (b) above, the closing and settlement of the transaction shall be held forty-five (45) days following the giving by Lessee of notice of the exercise thereof, unless such date shall be a Sunday or a holiday, in which event the closing shall be held on the next succeeding business day. The closing shall be held at the principal office of Lessee in the City of New York, State of New York. At the closing, the Lessor shall deliver to Lessee a bargain and sale deed to the premises with respect to which such right or option is exercised, with required Revenue stamps attached, sufficient to convey good, marketable, and unencumbered title in fee simple absolute, with contiguity of the demised premises with the premises known as 350 Eastern Avenue, insurable by a Title Insurance Company of recognized standing in the City of New York. At the closing, all moneys shall be paid and all instruments signed, executed, and delivered in accordance with the provisions of this Article 30 and the usual apportionments of rents, taxes, insurance, and other items shall be made in accordance with the practice prevailing at the time in respect to sales and conveyances of real property situated in Kings County, New York.[46]

EFFECTIVE DATE

31. The effective date of this Agreement shall be the date on which a counterpart original signed by or on behalf of all of the parties hereto shall be delivered to Security State Bank of the City of New York.[47]

NOTICES

32. All notices and other instruments required or authorized to be given or delivered pursuant to any provision of this Agreement shall be effectively given or delivered if personally delivered or deposited in the United States Mail, postpaid and registered, addressed, in the case of Lessor, to Arthur Olmsted, 241 East 90th Street, New York City, New York, and in the case

46. Mr. Porter says:

With respect to both the option of first refusal and the option of purchase, it is necessary to be very definite about the dates and methods of exercise of the options and the method of closing, so that when the notice of exercise has been mailed or delivered, a contract for the sale of real estate will arise which is so definite as to apportionments and other details that it can be specifically enforced even though no other instrument is signed.

47. Observe that the date of the instrument, as given in the first sentence thereof, is July 18. However, this is only for identification purposes. In view of the fact that numerous people must sign the instrument and that there must be court authorization for binding the interest of the minor, it is desirable to provide for a date upon which the instrument shall take effect. An instrument takes effect upon delivery, but there can be much dispute as to what constitutes delivery. It is desirable to resolve these difficulties by specifying an event which will bring the instrument into effect.

of Lessee, to Security State Bank of the City of New York, 160 Broadway, New York City, New York, or to such other addresses as the parties hereto may respectively designate by notice in writing given as provided in this Article 32.

TITLE INSURANCE

33.   Lessee represents that it has applied to Lawyers Title Corporation of New York for title insurance on the leasehold hereby created. In the event that such insurance, with any exceptions to be satisfactory to counsel for Lessee, is not issued by said Title Corporation within thirty days from the effective date hereof, Lessee shall have the right at its option, by notice in writing given to Lessor within thirty days after the expiration of such thirty-day period, as provided in Article 32 hereof, to terminate this Agreement; whereupon the sum of $4,000 paid on account of the rent first coming due hereunder shall promptly be refunded by Lessor to Lessee. However, if valid objection to title is made and is such as may be corrected or cleared up by action or petition by Lessor, the Lessor shall have sixty days after the date of the making of such objection in which so to do before Lessee shall have the right to give the notice of termination of agreement referred to in this paragraph, and in the event that such objection shall not have been so cured within such sixty-day period, Lessee shall have thirty days after the expiration of such sixty-day period in which to give said notice.[48]

PERMITS FOR BRANCH

34.   Lessee shall promptly apply to the Superintendent of Banks of the State of New York for permission to open and occupy a branch of its Bank in the demised premises. In the event that such permission is not granted

---

48.   It is routine procedure for a title insurance company, after examining the title, to specify certain defects in the title which have not been cleared up and to declare that in issuing a policy it will except these defects from the insured risk. One of the defects in this case was that the estate of Olive Olmstead (from whom all lessors derived title) had not been closed, and there was no evidence that New York and federal estate taxes had been paid thereon; therefore these taxes were a potential lien against the property. The title insurance company notified Porter of this difficulty, and Porter notified Durham. It was Durham's job to clear up the matter by obtaining an acknowledgment of full payment of taxes from New York and federal authorities.

The demands of the title insurance company as to clearing the title were a great boon to Mr. Porter in this matter, because the title insurance company took off Porter's shoulders the onus of insisting on steps which Durham considered the requirements of a quibbling perfectionist. In any negotiation it is always a good thing to have a client, partner, or other third person upon whom the burden of non-acquiescence can be placed. In David Copperfield, you will remember, Mr. Spenlow contrived to get his way by attributing stubborn qualities to his partner, Jorkins, a mild and complacent man whom Spenlow kept securely out of sight in a back room.

Suppose the Title Insurance Company declares its willingness to insure the lease for 21 years but not the option to purchase. What are the bank's rights?

Title insurance is considered in Chapter 31.

within ninety days from the effective date of this Agreement, then Lessee shall have the right at its option, by notice in writing given to Lessor within ten days after the expiration of such ninety-day period, as provided in Article 32 hereof, to terminate this Agreement. In the event that this Agreement is terminated under the provisions of this Article 34 rather than under the provisions of Article 33 hereof, Lessee shall not be entitled to refund of said sum of $4,000 paid on account of rent hereunder, but the same shall be retained by Lessor for services, expenses, and damages incurred in connection herewith.[49]

IN WITNESS WHEREOF, the parties hereto have duly executed this agreement.

> *Arthur Olmsted*
> *Ethel Olmsted Stanley*
> *Harry Olmsted*
> George Selkirk, Jr.,
> By *George Selkirk,*
> His general guardian.
> SECURITY STATE BANK OF THE
> CITY OF NEW YORK
> By *George F. Wentworth,*
> President.

State of New York ⎱
County of New York ⎰ ss.:

On the 11th day of July [*insert year*], before me personally came Arthur Olmsted, to me known, and known to me to be the individual described in and who executed the foregoing instrument, and he duly acknowledged to me that he executed the same.

> *Joseph Novick,*
> Notary Public in the State of New York,

[Here appears Mr. Novick's Notarial Seal.] residing in New York County, N.Y. Co. Clk. No. 31, Reg. No. 48-N-9. Commission expires March 30, [*insert year*]

---

49. Mr. Porter faced a time problem with regard to obtaining authorization for the branch bank from the superintendent of banks. He did not want to wait until the petition of the guardian of George Selkirk, Jr., for leave to execute the lease had ambled its patient way through the supreme court. On the other hand, he did not wish to present a petition to the superintendent of banks which was purely hypothetical. He was helped out in this matter by the fact that Durham did not believe a guardian's petition would be necessary and hence had advised George Selkirk, Sr., that he could sign as general guardian. Therefore, Porter could declare to the superintendent of banks that Selkirk had signed, that confirmation of his petition to sign was being sought, and that there was every reason to expect that such confirmation would be granted. This was accepted by the superintendent of banks as sufficient basis for granting permission for the branch bank.

State of Ohio $\Big\}$ ss.:
County of Trumbull

On the 9th day of July, [*insert year*], before me personally came Harry Olmsted, to me known, and known to me to be the individual described in and who executed the foregoing instrument, and he duly acknowledged to me that he executed the same.

Joseph P. Rossi
Notary Public

My commission expires Oct. 26, [*insert year*]

THE STATE OF OHIO $\Big\}$ ss.:   CERTIFICATION OF NOTARY
TRUMBULL COUNTY

I, Violet J. Campana, Clerk of the Court of Common Pleas of the County of Trumbull, State of Ohio, and also Clerk of the Appellate Court of said County, the same being Courts of Record, having a seal, do here certify that Joseph P. Rossi whose name is subscribed to the certificate of the proof, acknowledgment, or affidavit, of the annexed instrument, and thereon written, is a resident of said County, and at the time of taking such proof of acknowledgment, or affidavit, he was a Notary Public, in and for said County duly commissioned and sworn, and authorized by the laws of said State to take proofs of acknowledgments, and administer oaths, and also to take acknowledgments and proofs of deeds of conveyances of land, and mortgages, and other instruments of writing.

I further certify that I am acquainted with the handwriting of such officer and verily believe that the signature on the annexed instrument purporting to be his, is genuine, and the said instrument is executed and acknowledged in conformity with the Laws of said State.

In TESTIMONY WHEREOF, I have hereunto set my hand and affixed the seal of the said Court and County at Warren, Ohio, this 24th day of July, [*insert year*].

[Here appears the Seal   *Violet J. Campana,* Clerk.
of the Court of Common
Pleas for Trumbull
County, Ohio.]

[Here follows a similar acknowledgment by Ethel Olmsted Stanley before a notary public in Colorado and a similar "certification of notary" by the clerk of the appropriate Colorado court of record.]

State of New York $\Big\}$ ss.:
County of New York

On the 15th day of July, [*insert year*] before me personally came George F. Wentworth, to me known, who, being by me duly sworn, did depose and say that he is President of SECURITY STATE BANK OF THE CITY OF NEW YORK, the corporation described in and which executed the foregoing instrument; that he knows the seal of said Corporation; that the Seal affixed to said instrument is such corporate seal; that it was so affixed by order of the Board of Directors of said corporation, and that he signed his name thereto by like order.

> *Gilbert Corwin,*
> Notary Public, State of New York, residing in New York County, N.Y. Co. Clk's No. 500, Reg. No. 888-C-8, Commission expires Mar. 30, [*insert year*]

Problems

The following problems concern the construction of a written instrument — the foregoing lease. Each problem raises a difficult question which may involve consideration of clauses other than the obvious ones. For example, any answer to Problem 23.1 must discuss at least four paragraphs of the lease, and it is up to you to find out which four. There is only one way: Read the lease with this issue in mind. Your other reading without this issue in mind merely gives you a good background to start from. By way of warm-up, have you answered the questions posed in footnotes 37 and 48?

23.1.   Suppose you are a junior associate in Mr. Porter's office. He hands you a letter from the Security State Bank, which reads as follows:

> After further thought concerning the Eastern Avenue Branch we have come to the conclusion that major architectural changes must be made. These will principally involve constructing an additional story on the back half of the building for additional offices and turning some of the second floor offices into additional space for customers. Our architects have given us a figure of $230,000 as the probable cost. The expected volume of business at this branch will probably enable us to write off this additional expense in the first 15 years of operation. We should like your assistance in telling us whether we are within our rights in this matter and in taking any steps that may be desirable to put us in the most favorable legal position.

Mr. Porter asks you to look into this matter and give him a memorandum as to the bank's legal situation with reference to this project and what action you would recommend. Write such a memorandum.

23.2.   Five years after the beginning date of the lease, the spouses of the three lessors who are of full age and the second wife of George Selkirk, Sr., form a corporation, Opportunity Realty, Inc. They contribute $1,600,000 in cash as capital and take 25 percent of the corporate stock each. Opportunity Realty, Inc., offers in writing to buy the three parcels (bank, stores, and apartment house) for $1,600,000, making a deposit of $400,000 cash with the four owners. George Selkirk, Sr., readily gets the permission of the supreme court to sell the interest of George Selkirk, Jr., for $400,000. The lessors notify the bank that this offer has been made, enclose a duplicate original of the offer, and state that Opportunity Realty, Inc., has the balance of $1,200,000 cash in the bank and that its books and bank account are available for inspection. They give the bank 30 days in which to meet the offer, under paragraph 30(a).

The bank consults you as to what it should do, stating that it has invested heavily in improvements in the property; that business is excellent; that it wants to purchase at the $960,000 figure when its option is available; and that the property is now worth $1,200,000. Advise the bank.

23.3. Suppose the lease continues without change until shortly before the option to purchase becomes exercisable. At that time the four lessors execute a note for $300,000 payable to M, a brother-in-law of one of the lessors, in 25 years at the maximum rate allowed by law. The note is secured by a mortgage on the bank building at 346 Eastern Avenue. The bank decides that it wants to exercise its option when it becomes exercisable — and indeed this was a foregone conclusion in view of the rise in realty values, the brisk business being done by the bank, and the substantial and expensive improvements the bank had made in the building. The bank asks you to handle the transaction of exercising the option. You discover the mortgage. You are well aware that the going rate of interest on a first mortgage of this character is at least 3 percent lower than that provided in the note to M. Upon inquiry you discover that M is not interested in having the principal paid; he likes the investment. Advise the bank as to its position with reference to the mortgage. (By way of a variant on this, suppose that the title to the property has been transferred to a corporation and that the corporation has borrowed from the four original owners $300,000 for 100 years at 20 percent interest and has given a mortgage on the bank building to secure the same.)

23.4. Suppose the bank fails to make the Eastern Avenue branch pay and decides to sublet. You represent Ralph P. Grayson, Inc., realtors, who desire to sublet the first floor. You negotiate satisfactory terms with the bank. Arthur Olmsted says that the lessors have no objection. Draft the letter which you desire your client to receive from the lessors indicating their approval of the sublease. How many signatures will you want on this letter? What, if any, formalities will you require?

23.5. In what manner would you revise the lease for the purpose of causing it to be adequate to forestall embarrassment to the bank in the cases above?

Note: *Fixing the Rent in a Commercial Lease (Also a Problem in Some Noncommercial Leases)*

The rental clause in a commercial lease normally provides for rent to be paid in any one of the following ways:

1. *An initial single lump-sum payment with no further payments called for.* This type of clause is rarely used except in short-term leases (less than five years) where lessor is doubtful about the lessee's continued solvency. If the premises would normally rent for $200 a month for 36 months, this $7,200 must be "discounted" at some appropriate rate, to equal the present cash value of the right to receive $200 a month for 36 months.

2. *Periodic payments with a provision that on the completion of the term, the lessee will become the owner of the leased premises (sometimes called an "amortized lease").* This type of lease is frequently used in the leasing of commercial and industrial equipment. See Note, A Lease by Any Other Name: Or When is a Lease a Conditional Sale? 44 B.U.L. Rev. 103 (1964).

3. *A flat-rate periodic rental to continue throughout the term.* This type of lease is very poorly adapted to meet changing economic conditions. See Denz, Lease Provisions Designed to Meet Changing Economic Conditions, 1952 U. Ill. L.F. 344, 347-348. A variation of the flat-rate rental lease is the "net-lease," which provides that in addition to a fixed-base rental, the lessee is obligated to pay some or all of the leasehold expenses, e.g., taxes, repairs, maintenance, and insurance. See Van Doren, Some Suggestions for the Drafting of Long Term Net and Percentage Leases. 51 Colum. L. Rev. 186 (1951).

4. *A series of graded step-ups at stated intervals through the term of the lease.* A step-up lease is usually predicated on the assumption that inflation will never cease and that the utility of the leased premises must inevitably rise. There is one good reason for using the step-up lease: It makes it possible to keep the rent relatively low at the outset when the lessee must begin a new business, perhaps with large capital expenditures for improvements, and allows the lessee to make up for this after the property and the lessee have reached their full productivity.

5. *Reappraisals at stated intervals, with an accompanying recalculation of the rent on the basis of such appraisals.* The reappraisal lease, depending upon the skill of the appraiser, is an excellent solution to the problem of meeting changing economic conditions — especially local conditions. Lefcoe, Land Development Law 1068 (1966), reports that Irvine Ranch, California, is leasing home sites for 75-year terms, with periodic reappraisals of the land to determine the rent — 6 percent of the appraised value of the land at the end of the twentieth, fortieth, and fifty-fifth years. A modern variation of the reappraisal lease is a type of lease which directly meets the problem raised by the fluctuating value of the dollar. This type of lease provides that the dollar rental shall be adjusted, usually annually, on the basis of the cost-of-living index published by the United States Bureau of Labor Statistics. See Denz, Lease Provisions Designed to Meet Changing Economic Conditions, 1952 U. Ill. L.F. 344, 357-358.

6. *A flat-rate periodic rental coupled with a percentage clause based upon the quantity of business done by the lessee on the leased premises.* You will no doubt recognize that the predecessor of the modern percentage lease was the English feudal lease, under which L, the lord, agreed to permit T, the

tenant, to occupy land for a stated time in return for some share of the crops grown on the land. The percentage rates of almost every business in each area of the United States have been established by past bargaining. Tables are published at frequent intervals by the National Institute of Real Estate Brokers. In order to insure the success of a percentage leasing arrangement, numerous covenants peculiar to such leases must be included. A comprehensive treatise on this subject is McMichael & O'Keefe, Leases: Percentage, Short and Long Term (5th ed. 1959). See also Note, The Percentage Lease — Its Functions and Drafting Problems, 61 Harv. L. Rev. 317 (1948); Van Doren, Some Suggestions for the Drafting of Long Term Net and Percentage Leases, 51 Colum. L. Rev. 186 (1951); Denz, Lease Provisions Designed to Meet Changing Economic Conditions, 1952 U. Ill. L.F. 344 (1952); Note, Resolving Disputes Under Percentage Leases, 51 Minn. L. Rev. 1139 (1967). The principal purpose of a percentage lease is to divide the risk of productivity or utility between the lessor and the lessee and to cause both to share in the benefits or hardships of inflation or deflation.

Note: The Sale and Leaseback of Commercial Property

As the term implies, a "sale and leaseback" transaction consists of a sale by the owner of commercial property, followed by the execution of a lease back to the seller as lessee. This same basic device is available to a prospective purchaser or even to a lessee; the latter merely sells his leasehold interest and takes back a sublease. Thus it may be seen that a sale and leaseback transaction is basically an alternative to raising capital via the mortgage route. There are, of course, other reasons[50] for engaging in such a transaction. The leaseback will usually be a long-term net lease with the rental set to provide for complete amortization of the purchase price plus a net return to the investor of some appropriate percentage.

Sale and leaseback transactions leave the seller (lessee) in basically the same position as the owner of the property with a mortgage, the main difference being that instead of a mortgage, which requires monthly payments of interest and amortization, there is now a lease, which requires monthly rental payments. However, the financial and tax pictures can undergo dramatic changes. A party seeking financing can obtain, in effect, 100 percent mortgage financing by means of sale and leaseback. A company already mortgaged to the hilt, unable to borrow further funds, finds a sale and leaseback arrangement peculiarly attractive. From an accounting standpoint, future installments of rent are not considered as liabilities to be

50. See generally Agar, Sales and Leasebacks, 1965 A.B.A. Sec. Real Prop., Prob. & Tr. L. Proc. 61; Wison, Sale and Leaseback, 16 S. Cal. Tax Inst. 149 (1964); Bernard & Perlstadt, Sale and Leaseback Transactions, 1955 U. Ill. L.F. 635 (1955); Burke, Why Some Sale and Leaseback Arrangements Succeed While Others Fail, 26 J. Taxn. 130 (1967).

reflected on the company's balance sheet, as a mortgage most certainly would. Finally there are the hoped-for tax advantages. These include a loss on the sale of the asset as a charge against ordinary income, or a capital gain on the sale of the asset at a profit;[51] and the deductibility of the full rental payment as an ordinary and necessary business expense,[52] as compared with the frequently smaller allowance for depreciation and mortgage interest. The purchaser (lessor) has the benefit of a long-term tenant, which in case of default can frequently be treated more summarily than a mortgagor. You probably have realized that to the extent that the seller-lessee receives a tax advantage in rent deductions, the investor-lessor should have a corresponding tax detriment, i.e., rent is fully taxable,[53] whereas only the interest received by an investor in a mortgage loan would be taxable, not the repayment of principal. You would be right if the investor-lessor was a taxable organization, but frequently tax-exempt organizations, or insurance companies which are quasi-exempt organizations, become the investor-lessor in sale and leaseback financing. Since sale and leaseback is usually motivated largely by tax factors, it is essential to insure that any anticipated tax benefits will be recognized by the Internal Revenue Service.[54]

Tax Note: Commercial Leases

A lawyer engaged in the negotiation and drafting of a lease must consider problems which may arise in connection with the federal income tax. In some instances, careful negotiation and drafting will take care of problems in advance. When this is not possible, the lawyer should at least be able to tell the client what the probable consequences of any contemplated action would be.

1. If a lease is of business property, as is the Security State Bank lease, page 634 *supra,* the lessee may deduct the rent the lessee pays to the lessor under section 162(a)(3) of the Internal Revenue Code of 1954. Suppose, however, the Security State Bank lease had provided in paragraph 30(b) that, if the option to purchase were exercised, the last eight years' rent would be a credit against the purchase price. If the lease were cast in this form, the Treasury would argue that the "rent" was nothing more than an advance payment of the purchase price and therefore would not be deductible all at once by the lessee, any more than would a lump-sum payment for a new building pursuant to an ordinary contract for the sale of land. Section 263 of the Code provides: "No deduction shall be allowed for (1) any amount paid

51. I.R.C. §1231.
52. I.R.C. §162(a)(3).
53. I.R.C. §61(a)(5).
54. Scott, How to Analyze the Tax Cost of Owning vs. Leasing Business Realty, 22 J. Taxn. 194, 195-196 (1965). For an analysis of the tax aspects of leasing personal property, see Katcher, Lease vs. Purchase: Interplay of Code Provisions Creates Hidden Tax Traps, 22 J. Taxn. 263 (1965).

out for new buildings or for permanent improvements or betterments made to increase the value of any property or estate." The principle that you may not deduct a "capital expenditure" is of much wider scope than section 263 of the Code would indicate. You may, however, take a depreciation deduction, as is pointed out in paragraph 2 below.

The lessor, on the other hand, would like to establish that the "rent" received was really an advance payment for the sale of the building to the lessee, for then the lessor would have to report as income only the excess of what was received for it over the lessor's basis (usually cost) as a capital gain, taxable at much lower rates than ordinary income, which rent ordinarily is.

Thus, aside from a complex and currently unsettled question of tax law, insofar as the lessor and the lessee have directly opposed interests in the matter, there is a problem of negotiation. Whether the "rent" is in about the same amount as if there were no option, and whether the option price is in about the same amount as if there were no lease, will have important bearing on the result. The wording and the form of the instrument may be very important, as well as what a court may surmise is the intention of the parties. Thus there is a drafting problem. See Benton v. Commissioner, 197 F.2d 745 (5th Cir. 1952). Consider the controlling section of the Code, section 162(a)(3), which provides:

> There shall be allowed as a deduction all the ordinary and necessary expenses paid or incurred during the taxable year in carrying on any trade or business, including . . . (3) rentals or other payments required to be made as a condition to the continued use or possession, for purposes of the trade or business, of property to which the taxpayer has not taken or is not taking title or in which he has no equity.

See Note, Tax Treatment of "Lessors" and "Lessees" under Lease-Purchase Agreements, 62 Yale L.J. 273 (1953).

Thus whether there will be large tax savings or larger tax payments initially is up to the negotiating and drafting lawyer.

2.   In paragraph 26, the Security State Bank lease makes provision for alteration by the lessee. Suppose Security State Bank, with the consent of the lessor, makes extensive interior improvements. These are "capital expenditures" under section 263 of the Code, quoted above, and therefore are not deductible all at once in the year in which they are made. Section 167 of the Code, however, provides: "There shall be allowed as a depreciation deduction a reasonable allowance for the exhaustion, wear and tear . . . (1) of property used in the trade or business." Regulations under this section provide that the lessee may deduct the expenses borne by him over the useful life of the property or over the term of the lease, whichever period is shorter. Premature termination, renewal provisions, and options to purchase obviously will make what started out to be a simple proposition not so simple, however.

3.   The improvements made by Security State Bank may still be of some

value at the expiration of the lease, and they belong to the lessor if the lessor wants them, under paragraph 25. Why should not the value of the improvements be included in the income of the lessor? A logical answer might well be that they should be, and so the Supreme Court held in Helvering v. Bruun, 309 U.S. 461 (1940). But supposed hardship on the part of lessors led Congress to enact sections 109 and 1019 of the Code, which together provide that the value of the improvements are not income to the lessor on the expiration of the lease but that they do not affect the "basis" of the property, so that when and if the lessor sells the property as improved for a greater amount than if it were not improved, the lessor will have a larger gain or smaller loss (sale price minus "basis") to report. The regulations under section 109 make it clear, however, that if the circumstances are such that the value of the improvements left behind really take the place of money rent, they are taxable to the lessor as ordinary rent.

4. Suppose the lessor wants the lessee to leave before the expiration of the lease. The lessor may have to make a substantial payment to the lessee to cancel the lease. Section 1241 of the Code provides that the payment is to be considered a payment in exchange for the lease, and thus the payment may qualify for the lower rates imposed on capital gains. The lessee essentially is selling property to the lessor.

But suppose the lessee is the one who wants to buy out of the lease. Is a payment to the lessor on this account a payment in exchange for the lease, thus qualifying for capital gains treatment, or is it ordinary income? The answer was given in Hort v. Commissioner, 313 U.S. 28 (1941), wherein it was held that such a payment was essentially a payment in lieu of rent and thus ordinary income; whether the lessor might be considered as selling "property" or not, the Court stated, should make no difference.

5. If the lessee covenants to deliver up the premises at the end of the term in as good a condition as they were at the beginning (reasonable wear and tear *not* excepted), it has been held that the lessor can take no depreciation deduction under section 167 of the Code, which is quoted above. Commissioner v. Terre Haute Electric Co., 67 F.2d 697 (7th Cir.), *cert. denied,* 292 U.S. 624 (1933). Consider paragraphs 4 and 9 of the Security State Bank lease. Can the lessor take a depreciation deduction? Do you think this could have been made more clear in the instrument?[55]

---

55. See generally Young, Tax Aspects of Real Estate Leases, 1952 U. Ill. L.F. 601; American Law of Property §§3.105-3.115 (Casner ed. 1952).

PART VII

THE MODERN LAND TRANSACTION

Note: The Processes by Which the Legal Profession Seeks to Provide Security of Land Titles

As a profession we are charged with assuring to members of the public the security of the titles to land for which they lay out good money either as purchasers or as lenders. Title security for the public requires two things:
1. a workable system, and
2. lawyers professionally trained to operate the system with skill.

If a workable system does not exist, or if the present one can be improved, it is our job to see that the legislatures take necessary corrective action. It is the task of the law schools to train lawyers to operate the existing system and, if necessary, improve upon it.

The present part of this casebook offers a group of chapters designed to lead you through a present-day transaction in the sale of land, including its financing aspects. We here consider
1. the dealings, if any, with a broker;
2. the contract of sale — its terms and their interpretation and the rather unexpected problems it may create;
3. the mortgage and its operation;
4. the deed, in its two functions of conveying the grantor's title and giving promissory guarantees to the grantee;
5. the recording system as a means of facilitating professional evaluation of a title;
6. title registration as a means of providing judicial protection for a title;
7. title insurance as a means of providing private indemnification for defective titles; and
8. the "closing" transaction, where the actual conveyance takes place (see Note: The Closing, Chapter 25, Section 1).

We study each phase of the transaction and each instrumentality as we come to it. Of course, the treatment is not, and should not be, uniform. In considering the contract of sale we treat only those peculiarities of land contracts which are especially significant to the office lawyer, realizing that you will learn of the general principles of contracts and of their enforcement in other courses. In the chapter on mortgages we give you a general survey which will have its uses whether or not you take a full-scale course on the subject. We lean heavily on the recording system, since that is the heart of the American system of title security (even where title registration and title insurance are used), and you will not get any considerable treatment of this subject elsewhere.

Land law is local; so also are the customs of the conveyancing bar and those who make a business out of dealings in real estate. There is no interstate commerce in land and no serious requirement of uniformity. In constructing this casebook we considered whether to

1. provide a scattering of contract and deed forms covering several states,
2. provide contract and deed forms from one state, with notations as to local peculiarities which would probably not be found elsewhere, or
3. construct a fictitious state — e.g., Indihoma — and fictitious forms designed to be typical.

We chose the second course of action, and since our combined experience has centered in Massachusetts more than elsewhere, we have chosen Massachusetts as the pilot state. This does not signify by any means that you are getting a course in Massachusetts law as such. It does signify that in your study of general doctrine you are getting an example of the specific application of general doctrine in one state, which happens to be Massachusetts.

The house you live in was acquired through the processes we here discuss. Some lawyer advised the purchase, and some buyer risked money on the advice. The probability is that you will buy a house at some time, and if so, it will be through these processes. Certainly this is true as to many of your future clients. Some of your classmates — possibly you — will spend professional lives operating this system. In a word, these things are present realities which affect almost everyone, whether he or she realizes it or not. Your study will be more effective and vivid if you visualize these problems as applied to real people — yourself, your friends, and your future clients.

In order to give you an overall view of the lawyer's role in the residential real estate transaction, we set forth at this point a report of a special committee on residential real estate transactions of the American Bar Association, as approved for distribution by the ABA House of Delegates on August 9, 1978 (copyright © 1978 American Bar Association; reproduced with permission).

RESIDENTIAL REAL ESTATE TRANSACTIONS: THE LAWYER'S PROPER ROLE-SERVICES-COMPENSATION

14 Real Prop., Prob. & Tr. J. 581, 581-607 (1979)

INTRODUCTION

Throughout modern history the methods used in transferring land have been under attack by both laymen and some segments of the bar. In England an official investigation was carried out as early as 1829. After a century marked by further inquiries, debate and legislative tinkering, Parliament enacted the Real Property Acts of 1925, designed to put an end to the controversy. However, the Property Acts resulted in only a brief respite, and alleged deficiencies in conveyancing[1] practice are currently the occasion for lively skirmishing in the public press, in Parliament and among lawyers.

In this country the assault upon conventional procedures began in the closing decades of the nineteenth century and has continued unabated to the present. It has resulted in an enormous volume of legal literature and a considerable body of legislation but no significant amelioration in the basic problems of which there has been great complaint. In other words, the issues raised are neither new nor do they lend themselves to easy solution.

During recent years the debate over the conveyancing problem has become increasingly vocal. Certain members of the United States Congress and others have vigorously attacked the pattern of "settlement" or "closing" costs paid by home buyers at the time they make their purchases. These attacks reflect in part long-standing generalized discontent with the land transfer process and the more recent concern with consumerism. However, the immediate trigger for the Congressional concern was press reports of abuses in the Washington, D.C. area, followed by a report on nationwide title costs submitted by the Department of Housing and Urban Development and the Veterans Administration.

Closing procedures vary greatly across the country. Complete and representative information has been difficult to obtain. Much of the investigation has been directed toward effects rather than fundamental causes; attention has been centered on high costs without considering their relation to essential services, and various types of charges having no connection have been compounded in a single figure. In some cases the bar has been blamed, either directly or by implication, for abuses for which it has no responsibility.

---

1. The term "conveyancing" is used more in England that in this country. It embraces all of the legal work performed by lawyers supervising land transfers. A "conveyancer" is simply a lawyer engaged in conveyancing. The "conveyancing problem" embraces all objections, real or imagined, to the system in use. This terminology is employed in this Paper because it has the advantages of brevity and comprehensiveness.

LIMITATIONS ON THE SCOPE OF THIS PAPER

The bar, as a professional body intimately connected with the conveyancing process, has a special responsibility to make clear the causes for existing abuses and to suggest methods by which services to the public can be increased at the same time costs are minimized. In undertaking to discharge this responsibility it places two limitations upon what it can say.

In the first place, where costs are under consideration, lawyers are specially qualified to speak only about charges for legal work. In most transactions legal fees are a relatively minor part of the total amount paid in closing costs. Brokers' commissions, financing charges, governmental exactions (such as various taxes and recording fees) and escrow requirements at the closing (such as real estate taxes), are generally major items and they frequently exceed what is paid to lawyers. These other costs and requirements are matters outside the special expertise of lawyers, and the bar will leave to others the task of determining whether they are both proper and reasonable.

The second limitation placed on this Paper is that it deals only with procedures used in buying and selling homes. Similar procedures may be used in consummating other land transactions. However, such transactions generally raise specialized problems and are not currently the subject of inquiry. In any event, the purchase and sale of homes constitute the bulk of all land transfers and furnish the starting point for the current dispute over issues of policy and practice.

SCOPE OF THIS PAPER

The concerns of the organized bar considered in this Paper are:
1. whether the parties to the home-buying transaction receive adequate legal services;
2. whether they pay more for these services than they should; and,
3. whether, in any event, existing procedures can be modified in such a fashion as to afford the parties necessary services at a reasonable cost.

A HYPOTHETICAL HOME PURCHASE TRANSACTION

Before the concerns mentioned above can be addressed it is important to inquire what steps are needed to consummate a routine purchase and sale of a home financed by a mortgage given by an institutional lender. In the description which follows, this Paper consciously resorts to what may seem to be overgeneralization. It does so because differences in practice and nomenclature lead many otherwise knowledgeable conveyancers and laymen, at one extreme, to look upon procedures used in their communities as unique, and at the other, as universal. In fact, while there is diversity in the details of practice, there is fundamental unity in the underlying problems facing conveyancers everywhere.

A.   THE BROKERAGE CONTRACT

Initially a seller will enter into a brokerage contract with a real estate agent. In many jurisdictions this contract is not required to be in writing with all of the usual dangers of unwritten contracts. A special peril faced by sellers who have not had the advantage of legal counsel is that they may employ more than one broker and, in the absence of a clear understanding concerning the conditions under which the brokerage fee is earned, the seller may become liable to pay more than one fee.

In practice, a high percentage of brokerge contracts are in writing. A common assumption is that the contract is simple and standardized. In fact, a properly drawn contract will anticipate a number of legal problems of some complexity, such as the right of the seller to negotiate on the seller's own behalf, the effect of multiple listings, the disposition of earnest money if the buyer defaults, the rights of the broker if the seller is unable to proffer a marketable title, the duration of any exclusive listing and, as already brought out, the point at which the brokerage fee is earned. Most of the terms are negotiable and, in theory, a new contract should be drawn each time a broker is employed.

Standardized forms, where carefully drawn, have certain advantages. There are no objections to form contracts per se, as used by either brokers or other participants in the land transfer transaction. The objections to form contracts are that they may be inappropriate to the particular transaction, badly drawn initially or incorrectly filled in.

Any seller signing such a contract should have it approved by the seller's lawyer before signing. The seller should have the lawyer explain its meaning and be on hand to see that it is properly executed. (It is presumed that if the seller consults a lawyer, the lawyer will advise against entering into any oral agreement.) In other words, the seller needs the traditional legal services embraced in the expression "advice, representation and drafting." The broker needs similar services at one time or another and receives them from the broker's own lawyer as needed. In routine transactions the broker is sufficiently familiar with the details to be able to handle the matter without resort to professional assistance.

B.   THE PRELIMINARY NEGOTIATIONS

When the broker has found a potential buyer, negotiations between the buyer and the seller will begin, with the broker acting in the role of intermediary. In some cases the seller will leave to the broker all the work of negotiation and will merely ratify the agreement reached with the buyer.

It is generally thought that neither the buyer nor the seller needs a lawyer in the course of the negotiations. In theory this assumption is correct because neither party is bound until a written sales contract is signed. In fact, a great deal of trouble can be avoided if both the buyer and the seller consult their own lawyers during the course of the negotiations. If they are to make a proper bargain, they must know what to bargain about.

Aside from the question of price, which seems paramount in the minds of both parties, they should consider such problems as the mode of paying the purchase price and the tax consequences resulting therefrom, the status of various articles as fixtures or personal property, the time set for occupancy and the effect of loss by casualty pending the closing.

They can make whatever agreement they want, but they should anticipate all important questions and be certain a complete understanding has been reached. Failure to do so in the preliminary negotiations may mean, at the time for signing a contract, that they will have to start negotiations all over again. Worse, they may enter into a contract highly disadvantageous to one or the other, so uncertain as to require litigation to determine its meaning, or so ambiguous as to be void for indefiniteness.

C. THE COMMITMENT FOR FINANCING

Before entering into a sales contract, it would be desirable for the buyer to obtain as much of a commitment as possible for necessary financing.

Many lenders, however, refuse to make the necessary inspections, appraisals and credit investigations to make such a commitment until the buyer can exhibit a signed purchase and sale agreement, and many buyers are reluctant to risk losing the property to a higher offer by deferring the execution of the purchase and sale agreement. All of this leads to the common practice of including in the agreement a "subject to financing" clause which should be examined by the lawyers for the parties before the contract is signed.

Finding a willing lender is not part of a lawyer's professional duties. In practice a lawyer, being a person of affairs, may be able to render this service. Legal expertise is exercised when the lawyer advises the buyer about problems the buyer should anticipate in coming to terms with the lender. By way of illustration, the buyer will seldom have any understanding of the potential effect of an acceleration clause. The buyer should know what the legal and practical consequences of such a clause will be. The buyer should also obtain an estimate of the closing costs that will have to be paid and should obtain legal advice as to all items found in the estimate.

The commitment contract between the lender and buyer will normally be prepared by the lender's lawyer. Before it is accepted, the buyer's lawyer should ascertain that it properly anticipates all important contingencies, comports with the oral agreement previously reached and binds the lender.

Normally the lender has much greater financial expertise than the buyer. This advantage may not have been of as much importance formerly as it is today, because the financing of homes has in many instances become extremely complex. For this reason, when dealing with the lender the buyer is in need of legal assistance.

D. THE CONTRACT OF SALE

Once an informal agreement has been reached, the buyer and the seller will enter into a formal contract of sale. The importance of this document cannot be overemphasized. Once it is signed, the rights and obligations of the parties are fixed. Each transaction is unique and, in theory, a contract should be specially drafted for each.

The interested parties are the broker, the buyer and the seller. The contract should contain an appropriate provision with regard to the broker's commission. The buyer and the seller want assurance that the writing reflects their understanding. If they have not received legal advice during the preliminary negotiations, they will need to know what questions should have been anticipated and whether firm and advantageous provisions are found in the document. When the instrument is executed, their lawyers should be present to assure that the proper formalities are observed to make it binding. Here again the parties need legal services in the form of drafting, advice, and representation.

This need is not avoided by the use of forms. Even if the form is properly drawn, the printed portion may not adequately express the particular agreement made between the parties, or the words used in filling in blanks may distort its effectiveness. As a matter of practice standardized forms are widely used, and it is recognized that this practice likely will continue. It is recommended that local bar associations draft standard forms of sales agreements, and that joint seminars with real estate brokers and others regarding residential real estate transactions be held regularly. Whenever forms are used, any insertion should be carefully checked by the buyer's and seller's lawyers, and the appropriateness of the form for the particular transaction should be determined by the buyer's and seller's lawyers. The buyer and the seller are often unaware of what the contract means, what they should anticipate, and what steps are needed to make the instrument binding. They should be advised by their own legal counsel.

Prior to the time the contract is signed, the buyer and the seller should have detailed advice about many legal aspects of the transaction. For example, they may not be aware of the need to anticipate the question of who bears the loss or damage to, or destruction of, buildings on the premises between the time the contract is signed and the time of closing. They also may be unaware of the existence of such problems as whether the contract so changes the interest of the seller as to affect insurance policies; whether either the buyer or seller, or both, should execute new wills; whether federal and state gift and death tax matters are involved; whether joint tenancies or tenancies by the entireties will be affected; and the like.

E.   DETERMINING THE STATUS OF THE TITLE

After the contract of sale is executed, the state of the seller's title must be determined to the satisfaction of both the buyer and the lender. This is generally the most important legal work connected with the transaction. The initial examination will be made by the lawyer for the buyer, the seller, the lender, or the title insurer, relying upon the official land title records or an abstract thereof, or a title plant maintained by a title insurance company. Where a lawyer's certificate is relied upon, either the lender or the buyer, or both, may desire additional protection in the form of a title insurance policy.

Whoever makes the title examination, the buyer's lawyer should inform the buyer of the limitations, if any, which impair the title. The buyer should also receive formal protection by a written opinion from the lawyer, an owner's title insurance policy, or both. If the buyer applies for title insurance, the buyer's lawyer should negotiate the provisions to be included or excluded from the policy. The lawyer should also make clear to the buyer what the policy means. In particular, the exceptions to coverage contained in the policy should be explained.

The use of standardized exceptions is common to title insurance. They are complex and restrictive and are frequently not understood by the layman.

Each title insurance policy is unique in that it may contain exceptions peculiar to that individual title. The buyer must first be made aware of the existence of these exceptions and must then be made to understand them. If the exception is to a $10,000 mortgage and the buyer sees the provision, the buyer will probably not mistake its meaning. But if the exception is to "all of the conditions and restrictions found in deed of X to Y, recorded in the office of the clerk of the court of Z County, in Deed Book 309 at page 873," the buyer will not, in the first place, realize that the exception is important, or, if the buyer does, will not understand its meaning without assistance from the lawyer.

F.   THE SURVEY

Survey problems arise in many transactions, and the lawyers for all parties should inform their clients of such problems. At some time prior to the approval of title the buyer, the lender, or the title insurance company may demand a survey. The primary purpose of the survey will be to find whether the legal description of the land conforms to the lines laid down on the ground. An additional purpose may be to determine whether structures on the premises violate restrictive covenants or zoning ordinances or constitute an encroachment. When the survey has been completed, the parties should have their lawyers advise them about any legal implications of the surveyor's findings and the scope and extent of the surveyor's certification.

G.   CURATIVE ACTION

In some cases curative action is needed to make titles marketable. Any such curative action should be carried out by a lawyer for the seller, the buyer, or the lender. If the curative action is carried out by the lawyer for the seller, it should be checked for sufficiency by the lawyers for the buyer and lender; if by the lawyer for the buyer, by the lawyer for the lender; and if by the lawyer for the lender, by the lawyer for the buyer.

H.   TERMITE INSPECTION

In jurisdictions where a termite inspection must be made and a certificate given to the buyer, showing that the premises are free of infestation or damage by termites, the certificate may be ordered by the broker, lender or the lawyer for any of the parties.

In jurisdictions where such certificates are not required, a provision should be added to the contract requiring the seller to provide a current termite certificate by a licensed pest control agency. If there is infestation or damage, the cost of treatment and the cost of necessary repairs of termite-caused damage usually are borne by the seller. The contract should spell out the seller's obligation. A termite clause should be included in all standard form contracts.

I.   DRAFTING INSTRUMENTS

Before closing, a lawyer should draft the deed, mortgage and the bond or note secured by the mortgage. As a matter of convenience these papers are commonly drafted by the mortgagee's attorney, although the representative of either of the other parties is equally qualified. Whoever does the work, the product should be examined by lawyers for each of the other two parties and the title insurance company, and they should be advised whether the instruments are effective and create the interests intended.

The drafting of these instruments is sometimes considered merely routine work. This is not true. For example, the description of the parties must be so phrased as to prevent confusion, and the description of the land must be complete and accurate. The importance of the form of warranties is often overlooked. By way of illustration, if the title is encumbered by equitable covenants or utility easements, either or both may be acceptable to the buyer and lender, but they should be excepted from the warranty.

How title is to be taken should have been provided in the initial contract between the buyer and the seller, and the buyer should be advised as to the tax and other effects of the manner in which title is taken.

Of equal importance are other special agreements reached earlier in the transaction. The controlling law may provide that the deed supersedes prior understandings so that if they are not embraced in the deed they are nullified. Each deed must therefore be examined to determine whether it carries out what has been agreed upon.

J.   INCIDENTAL PAPER WORK

The Real Estate Settlement Procedures Act requires the preparation of a settlement statement in virtually all residential real estate transactions. In addition, the Truth-In-Lending form must be filled in and executed. If the mortgage loan is to be insured by FHA, VA or by a private mortgage insurance company, more paper work is required. The required documents are standardized and can be completed without resort to legal expertise. They are part of the financing, rather than the legal aspects of the sale and mortgage. Nevertheless, lawyers are frequently called upon to do this work. With a few exceptions, the government has taken the position that whoever performs these services shall receive no compensation therefor.

K.   OBTAINING TITLE INSURANCE

Where a title insurance policy for the buyer is based on the certificate of a lawyer not employed by a title insurance company, the lawyer may make an application for the initial binder and, after closing, send in a final certificate and procure a policy. This is work for which the lawyer normally, and properly, should be paid by the client to the extent the lawyer is not paid for these services as the agent of the title company. The lawyer should not accept compensation from a title insurance company solely for referring business to that company. This is, of course, clearly improper and contrary to the recorded position of the American Bar Association. The Real Estate Settlement Procedures Act specifically prohibits the acceptance of any "kickbacks" from the title insurance company.

L.   CLOSING

A closing statement is generally prepared prior to final closing. The statement may take various forms and is designed to indicate the allocation of debits and credits to the various parties. In some cases it is prepared by a layman, in others by a lawyer. The buyer's and seller's lawyers should make certain their clients understand the nature and amount of all closing costs. The American Bar Association supported the adoption of legislation requiring a uniform closing statement in all government-related mortgage transactions. In addition it is recommended that local bar associations draft uniform closing statement forms for use in all other real estate transactions. Even a standard closing form in itself is not sufficient, unless the parties are assured by their own lawyers of the appropriateness of each item.

Unless there is an escrow closing, a further check of title should be made immediately prior to closing. If this check is not made, it is possible that the parties will be unaware that the title has been impaired between the time of the original examination and the closing date. This further check will generally be carried out by the lawyer, abstracter or title insurance company certifying or insuring title.

The closing is the proceeding at which the parties exchange executed instruments, make required payments, and conclude the formal aspects of the transaction. At this point the buyer, the seller, and the lender should be represented by their own lawyers. They require advice and may need representation if a disagreement arises. They should be assured that the legal documents they exchange create the interests intended, that they receive the protection to which they are entitled and that correct payments have been made to those entitled to receive them.

As a part of the closing, arrangements must be made for insurance, taxes, and other incidents of ownership. Instruments must be recorded and a final check of title made. Disbursements must be made and documents distributed to the parties entitled to receive them. Title insurance policies, where called for, must be procured. If a lawyer handles the closing, the lawyer will attend to all or virtually all of these details.

THE CONFLICTS OF INTEREST

At every step set out above it has been said that buyers and sellers should have representation, advice and draftmanship. This is to say, each needs separate legal representation and should not rely on services rendered by a lawyer for some other party. Why, it will be asked, is so much legal service needed to consummate a routine, uncontested transaction? No two transactions are identical, and none is simple. Because of the complexity of property law a "minor" slip may cause great expense and inconvenience. To the buyer, at least, the purchase of a house may be the most important legal and financial transaction of a lifetime.

All of the parties have conflicting interests. Some of them have wide experience with land transfers. To others the transaction may be a once-in-a-lifetime event. Houses are bought and sold by the inexperienced as well as by the sophisticated. The buyer and seller, without representation, will usually not have as much knowledge of conveyancing as the other parties. Only their own attorneys will be motivated to explain fully the transaction.

It is sometimes said the parties require disinterested advice. This misstates the case. Instead of disinterested advice, each requires the assistance of someone dedicated to that person's interest and equipped with sufficient skill to protect that person. The escrow company used in some sections of the country is theoretically disinterested. Actually its primary loyalty usually is to the institutions which are the sources of its business.

A.   BROKER AND SELLER

As has been seen, the initial step in selling a house will probably be the signing of a brokerage contract. Upon the signing of the contract the broker becomes the seller's agent. The broker and seller will have a common interest in obtaining a maximum price from the buyer. So, of course, will the lawyer for the seller. The lawyer has an interest in seeing to it that all other terms of the sale are as favorable to the seller as possible. An apprehension that the signing of the sales contract may be jeopardized by an overmeticulous attention to the other terms sometimes makes the broker reluctant to submit a proposed contract of sale to the seller's lawyer. On the other hand, many brokers realize that the seller's lawyer can help to prepare a contract that is specifically enforceable by the seller. This relieves the broker of the risk that the broker's commission will be nullified by the collapse before the closing of a contract improperly drawn. This may happen when qualifications on the seller's title have not been properly expressed.

It has been indicated that a fear of delay or disruption of the transaction often makes the broker somewhat less than enthusiastic about advising the buyer to submit a proposed contract to a lawyer. The lawyer who lets the contract of sale gather dust does much to foster this feeling. The lawyer should not surrender the client's vital interests, but should remember that the client wants the house, and should not unnecessarily impede the closing. Lawyers are trained in the art of finding fair and reasonable solutions to what might otherwise be deadlocks.

Attention is called to the statement of principles applicable to relations between lawyers and real estate brokers which has been approved by the American Bar Association and the National Association of Realtors, formerly the National Association of Real Estate Boards. (Such principles have been promulgated by the National Conference of Lawyers and Realtors.)

B. BUYER AND SELLER

The interests of the buyer and the seller conflict in the sense that one wants a minimum and the other a maximum price. They do not need lawyers to advise them on this point. What they do not realize is that the contract of sale does or should contain a multitude of provisions relative to the mode of payment and to other important terms of the sale. These provisions are freely negotiable. If future dispute and possibly litigation are to be avoided the parties must be made aware of the need for true negotiation before a contract is signed. They must also be made aware that the drafting of a contract clearly expressing their agreement is a complex undertaking. In particular, they should not sign "standard form" contracts without the advice of their own lawyers.

C. BROKER AND LENDER

Except in unusual circumstances there will be no conflict between the interests of the broker and the lender. The real danger is that their common interest will conflict with that of the buyer. If the buyer, as frequently happens, leaves financing to the broker, the broker may resort to a lending institution with which the broker normally does business. The arrangement between these two may be highly beneficial to them but disadvantageous to the buyer, who, if properly counseled, may shop around for better terms. Many sellers of homes do not rely on brokers or, even if they do, have their own sources of credit to which they direct buyers. In these cases similar conflicts of interest arise.

D. BUYER AND LENDER

The buyer wants to obtain money from the lender at as low an interest rate as possible. It is frequently assumed that, once the interest rate and the amount of monthly payments are agreed upon, the buyer and the lender have only common concerns. This is not true. In the first place, the terms of the financing agreement can be framed in such a way as to be beneficial to one at the expense of the other. For example, an acceleration clause wanted by the lender may be onerous to the buyer. By contrast, an anticipation clause beneficial to the buyer may be objectionable to the lender.

In the second place, the title requirements of the lender and buyer are dissimilar. The buyer wants assurance of maximum enjoyment of the property and freedom from post-settlement claims from third parties. The lender wants assurance that title is not impaired to the point where its value will be reduced below the amount of an outstanding indebtedness. A restrictive covenant or zoning ordinance increasing the value of the property may also prevent an intended use by the buyer. The lender would not object to the restriction; the buyer would find it unacceptable.

In another type of case, where the examiner makes a mistake, either by overlooking a partial impairment of title or by making an incorrect legal judgment about marketability, the error, in theory, adversely affects both the buyer and the lender. In practice, if the error relates to a matter which does not impair the value of the land to the point where the value is less than the amount of the mortgage indebtedness, the lender will suffer no loss. If the lawyer represents only the lender, the loss will therefore fall on the buyer. The lender's lawyer is not the buyer's lawyer and owes allegiance only to the lender. [See Page v. Frazier, 388 Mass. 55, 445 N.E.2d 148 (1983).]

The buyer's and the lender's interests may also conflict at the time of closing. The buyer wants to keep costs to a minimum because the buyer generally pays the major portion. The lender conventionally pays none of the closing costs and has little or no concern in reducing them other than as a business expedient.

E.   THE TITLE INSURER AND BUYER OR LENDER

It is sometimes assumed there is no conflict between the interests of the title insurer, on the one hand, and the buyer and lender on the other. Any such assumption is false. The insurer wants minimum risk; the other parties maximum protection. In no event is the insurer liable for any loss exempted by the terms of the policy. (In most policies, exemptions are listed under the heading "Schedule B.") Where there is no exemption, its liability is confined to situations where there has been loss to the policyholder.

If the policy runs to the mortgagee alone, even an unexpected impairment of title may result in no loss to the mortgagee. In such a case the insurer incurs no liability and the buyer without coverage must pay the cost.

The fact that the lender and the insurance company deal at arm's length is well understood by both. What is not understood by the buyer is that, by the nature of the contract, the buyer's interests are in conflict with those of the insurer. The two can enter into a binding agreement giving protection spelled out and limited by the terms of the contract. The inherent conflict, however, between the interests of the parties stands in the way of the insurer either advising or representing the insured. Although the insurer has no fiduciary relation to the lender, it looks upon the lender as a primary source of business and may render special services for purely economic reasons. However, dealings with buyers are usually one-time transactions and insurers have no inducement to offer concessions.

An individual lawyer has the same need to be protected by exceptions in the lawyer's title opinion. The lawyer must advise the buyer as to the significance of such exceptions — whether they can be accepted, if the buyer really wants the property, without undue risk of dispossession or financial loss. The lawyer can explain the difference between a good record title, a marketable title, and a merchantable title. If there is title insurance, the lawyer can negotiate for assurance that, notwithstanding a record defect that goes to marketability, the buyer's possession will not be disturbed. There is no duty on the title insurance company to explain the exceptions to its customer.

How the System Works in Practice

What has gone before is a largely theoretical explanation of the steps taken in completing a residential real estate transaction, the conflicts of interest engendered in the process and the need for the legal services created by these conflicts. To what extent does this explanation comport with what actually takes place?

A great variety of practices are employed throughout the country and generalizations should be expressed with caution. However, it is probably safe to say that in a high percentage of cases the seller is unrepresented and signs the contracts of brokerage and sale on the basis of faith in the broker. The buyer does not employ a lawyer. The contract of sale is signed without reading it and, once financing has been obtained, the details of title search and closing are left to the lender or broker. In many closings no lawyer will appear.

Does the System Work Well or Badly?

Because of the large volume of legal services needed by the various parties to the home-buying transaction, any adequate system will necessarily generate substantial legal costs. Costs and services are therefore properly correlative. We have only limited information about patterns of costs and services throughout the country. What little is available leads to the tentative conclusion that in some sections charges may be excessive, in the sense that they are disproportionate to the services received. On the other hand, in other areas they may be so low as to discourage the rendering of needed legal assistance.

What should be apparent is that the system we employ prima facie encourages inequities. The broker, the lender, the escrow company, and the title insurance company are well aware of their legal needs. They require and receive protection. The buyer and seller, who directly or indirectly pay all legal charges, often receive only residual protection and none of the other legal services which they need. They lack both the expertise and the organization to either understand their needs or to make their demands heard. It is therefore the duty of the bar to spell out what services are needed and how these services can be supplied at a reasonable price.

Where the supplying of certain services generates unnecessary expense, the bar should suggest that appropriate measures be adopted to reduce cost. Likewise, where parties to the transaction need services they are not getting, they should be so informed, particularly when they pay for the services.

In the past the bar has not met its responsibility in this respect. The result has been widespread criticism. This criticism has been frequently ill-informed and destructive, but is a warning that unless the bar institutes needed reform it can anticipate political action from those lacking proper skill to do what is needed.

Aside from the question of services and costs, the present system raises ethical problems which lawyers cannot ignore. Although the seller and the buyer are frequently not receiving adequate legal services, they think they are. They have no comprehension of the conflicts of interests between the parties nor of their own need for legal services. They rely upon established institutions and the lawyers of such institutions. They are sometimes advised that they do not need independent representation. The bar is aware of existing practices and has a special responsibility to see that substantial changes are made.

OBJECTIVES

Merely to complain against the present system is not enough. Adequate reform will await a clear understanding of our objectives, the means of obtaining them and the obstacles in the way of success. A primary goal is to simplify present procedures and make them less expensive.

Less well understood is the need to increase the legal services afforded the parties. At first blush these two objectives appear in conflict. However, the thrust of this Position Paper is that, assuming the adoption of adequate reforms, both can be achieved. Many nonlegal costs, such as brokerage fees and real estate transfer taxes, which constitute a large part of closing expenses, are outside the designated scope of this Paper. However, the largest single *legal* expense when homes are bought and sold is created by the need to establish title. If this expense can be reduced, more adequate legal services can be provided without increasing the total cost.

To make this assertion is not to underestimate the difficulties involved. No one measure will be sufficient. An adequate "package" will embrace not merely legislation but alterations in conventional institutional practices. Action will be needed at the national, state and local levels. In some instances there are no obstacles to implementing reforms almost immediately, but some fundamental measures can become fully effective only over protracted periods.

THE REDUCTION IN COST

A. TITLE EXAMINATION COSTS

Title examination often is expensive because of the excessive labor input under the present system. This high labor input is the result of the following major causes: (1) Condition of public land title records; (2) Lack of marketable title legislation; and (3) Lack of title curative legislation.

1. Condition of Public Land Title Records

Our system of public land title records was designed to fit the needs of a rural community. It was invented by the Massachusetts colonists and has not been essentially changed in the interim. The records often are so scattered in different offices, so voluminous, or so badly indexed, as to make the task of separating the relevant from the irrelevant long and arduous. Where lawyers must resort to direct examination of these records, the cost, in terms of their time, is clearly apparent.

Less apparent is the high cost arising out of the use of private title plants, whether these plants are the property of individuals, abstract companies or title insurance companies. These plants duplicate the public records except that all relevant material is consolidated and efficiently indexed. They should not be needed. They are expensive to create and maintain, and until they are superseded by adequate public records we cannot realistically expect to reduce the cost of title proof.

The creation and maintenance of a title plant in a major city is extremely expensive. Unless something is done to check this expense, title and abstract companies may price themselves out of the market while there is still no practical substitute for the services they perform. The economic repercussions of such an eventuality cannot be assessed but would undoubtedly be serious. These repercussions must be avoided by the creation of adequate public records at government expense.

In some of our largest cities, title companies have ceased to maintain full plants; in others consolidation of facilities has been resorted to, and everywhere efforts are being made to keep costs within manageable limits. Excessive expense entailed in the daily takeoff has led some title insurance executives to become proponents of adequate public records. In 1968 the then treasurer of the American Land Title Association took this position and stigmatized the waste involved in private title plants as "immoral," "unconscionable" and "reprehensible."

At this point it should be made clear there is no criticism of the individuals and corporations who have created title plants in an effort to meet an immediate public demand. However, if the public records were adequate, title plants would not be necessary. It would be unwise to assume we will continue to use them indefinitely; it would be unrealistic to assume we can dispense with them immediately.

It is universally assumed that we can eliminate the need for private title plants and reduce the high cost of title examination only by the creation of an efficient system of public land records. Agreement about the details of any new system is lacking. Currently most investigation is directed toward the creation of computerized land data banks. Computerization offers a fruitful field for investigation and should be the object of further study. At the same time the field of investigation should be expanded to non-computerized systems. Such less sophisticated systems, which can be installed in the near future and at limited expense, are urgently needed. Such systems can undoubtedly be created. Block indexing in New York City, Baltimore and Mississippi, and the official and unofficial tract indexes found in courthouses in Mississippi, Oklahoma and some other states are prototypes upon which highly efficient systems might be developed. Alabama has adopted a self-indexing system along novel lines. None of these approaches is specifically endorsed. Other systems may be practicable. As many systems as possible should be investigated and it should be kept in mind that a system satisfactory for installation in one part of the country may not be suitable elsewhere. National uniformity is not necessary and may not be desirable.

There are reports now nearing completion under the sponsorship of the federal Department of Housing and Urban Development into ways to improve the efficiency of public records and to lower costs for title searching and examination.

2. Lack of Marketable Title Legislation

A second means of reducing title costs can be achieved by shortening the period of search. While the invention of the recording system was a great improvement over the then existing English system, or non-system, it would have been a greater improvement if a limit had been placed on the duration of the notice created by recording.

While the various statutes of limitations can be relied upon to bar many ancient claims, there are other interests as to which the applicable statute does not begin to run until the interest has been violated. A purchaser needs, of course, to know about these. As a consequence, in theory, it is necessary to trace every title back to its origin in the state. To do so is already impractical in much of our country and will ultimately become so elsewhere. As a consequence, conveyancers conventionally limit search to an arbitrary number of years. Aside from the fact that this practice is resorted to at the risk of the lawyer's client, the periods set, ranging up to sixty or more years, result in an enormous and unnecessary input of labor.

What is needed is a theory of title which will permit the examining lawyer to trace the title back for only a relatively short number of years with complete confidence that his client will be protected from all adverse claims antedating a record root of title. This reform should be accompanied by limitations on the period during which title claims, including those of record and those not of record, remain viable. Much legislation is developing piecemeal, in a number of states, some based on shortening the applicable statutes of limitations, others based on a periodic rerecording requirement for certain specific interests, and others based on marketable title acts. All these approaches can be improved and extended. Special attention is directed to the need to amend the existing marketable title acts.

The Uniform Simplification of Land Transfers Act, recently adopted by the National Conference of Commissioners on Uniform State Laws and approved by the American Bar Association, sets forth a uniform marketable title act, and deserves serious consideration by the organized bar and state legislatures.

A prerequisite to completely effective marketable title acts is the adoption of federal legislation permitting the application of these acts to federal lands and federal claims. Unlike statutes of limitation, marketable title acts can be made to apply to federal lands without serious adverse effects even in areas where the government owns large tracts of unimproved and unpoliced property. All that is necessary is to require, as a prerequisite to marketability, the assessment of land for taxes for a given period of time. This provision must be coupled with a requirement that local tax assessors notify the attorney general when public land is assessed to private individuals. This system results in the government being given reasonable warning of any effort to acquire marketable title to its holdings. When so notified the government can, at little or no expense, take necessary steps to prevent loss of title. If adverse possession were to operate against the federal government, the government could lose land without being made aware of the fact. No such result would follow the enactment of properly drafted marketable title legislation.

3. Lack of Title Curative Legislation

Many titles may be unmarketable because of formal defects in the record. These defects are cost-generating because they must be removed by time-consuming investigation and curative action. While adequate marketable title legislation will wipe out the effect of older defects, many recent defects, not barred by marketable title acts, are the result of highly artificial rules of law or unintentional blunders by the parties. Any such impediments to marketability should be cured in a much shorter time than that set by even the most liberal marketable title act. To achieve this result, a large volume of title curative legislation is required. Some such legislation will be needed because of law peculiar to a particular locality. However, a number of problems are universal. They can be cured by title curative legislation in virtually every state. Adequate models to assist legislatures in their task of systematic reform are required.

B. OTHER CONVEYANCING COSTS

Other areas of the conveyancing process are ripe for efforts to increase efficiency and to reduce costs. Some inefficiencies are the result of outside forces; others arise from the practice of lawyers themselves. An example of the former is the large and increasing amount of paper work demanded by governmental organizations. The effect of the adoption of the Real Estate Settlement Procedures Act, the effect of the Truth-In-Lending Act and FHA and VA demands for "uncompensated" work has already been alluded to. Increasing federal demands for paper work are incompatible with the efforts to reduce closing costs and it is unrealistic to believe that services demanded by the government will not result in higher closing costs.

Internal inefficiencies may result from improper procedures and allocations of personnel within a given law office. These inefficiencies have been under study by the American Bar Association and many state bar associations for many years and are being eliminated as rapidly as possible. Other internal inefficiencies result in title practice, as in other fields of the law, from an outdated legal structure which compels elaborate and time-consuming procedures to accomplish routine ends.

THE INCREASE OF SERVICES

The lender and broker insist upon and receive adequate legal services. On the other hand, the seller, and particularly the buyer, who pay all the legal costs and need a broad spectrum of legal services, frequently receive none at all. This system is prima facie inequitable. Although high costs of title proof can be reduced by properly designed legislation, a realistic effort to increase legal services must come about primarily through education and persuasion. You can compel a public official to use a stipulated system of recording. Likewise you can say to the holder of an ancient claim against land that the claim must be rerecorded or be barred. But it is not practicable to force legal services on unwilling recipients or to compel lenders to follow procedures so distasteful as to discourage them from entering the mortgage market. You can bring home to buyers and sellers knowledge of their legitimate needs for legal services and can make clear to lenders that these needs can be met without impairing the protection the lenders require. When this process of education has been brought to a certain point, the law of the marketplace will take command and all parties will come to expect and demand the services they need.

Any program of education must begin with an attack upon two beliefs widely held in this country. The first is that only one lawyer is needed to complete a title transaction. The second is that, if a lawyer is employed, the lawyer is needed only late in the transaction. The first is probably the harder to attack. "Why," asks a seller or buyer, "do I need a lawyer when the lender or title insurance company will do all that is necessary? Aren't banks, title insurance companies and escrow companies competent and can't I rely upon them to represent my interest?" In answer to this question the public must be made to understand that competence and conflict of interest are entirely different matters; that the parties are engaged in an arm's length proceeding; and from the nature of the transaction the lawyer for one cannot properly represent the other.

Once the buyer and seller are induced to employ their own lawyers they must be made to see why they need representation as early as possible. Early representation provides the attorney the opportunity to explain fully all aspects of the real estate transaction, including the components of closing costs, to the client. In some sections of this country all parties are represented by lawyers from the beginning and the system works well. In England, in modern times, this has been the universal practice and this system provides greater services at less cost than in America.

The conclusion to be drawn from the previous discussion is that it is desirable for all parties in the residential real estate transaction, the seller, the buyer and the lender, to be represented by counsel. The most glaring defect in the system that now generally prevails is the lack of representation of the buyer. A significant step in the direction of curing this defect would be made if the lawyer paid to examine the title, whether the buyer's lawyer or the lender's lawyer, was required to give an opinion for which the lawyer would be responsible to both the buyer and the lender. The rendition of such an opinion as to the state of the title does not place the lawyer in a conflict of interest position as to either the buyer or the lender. In other words efforts should be made to promote a more universal acceptance of a single opinion of the state of the title for all parties.

A step in the same direction would be made if the protection under a title insurance policy were to run to both the buyer and the lender. The present trend is in that direction.

The place of title insurance in residential real estate transactions should be understood by all parties involved. A lawyer's title certificate or title opinion does not protect the buyer or lender from fraud, mistakes and other defects, dehors the record and for which the lawyer is not responsible. The client, buyer or lender, should be advised by the lawyer as to these risks and the availability of additional protection through title insurance, if the client so desires.

Title practice is highly technical in many aspects, requiring considerable expertise on the part of the lawyer. A fatal title defect may not be apparent except to the experienced and knowledgeable examiner. Other apparent defects may not, for one reason or another, affect marketability of the title, and may be "certified over" under accepted standards of title. While every member of the bar is qualified in the legal sense to examine and render an opinion of title, not every lawyer is necessarily prepared to do so if that lawyer's legal training and practice have not been in this area.

State and local bar associations have recognized this fact, and in order to help the public and the bar identify those lawyers who, by training and choice, have developed special expertise in title practice, some bar associations have adopted programs of certification. The general subject of specialization is presently under study by a committee of the American Bar Association, and certification in the area of real property law and practice has been studied and reported on by a committee of the Real Property, Probate and Trust Law Section of the Association.

If and when a workable program of certification in real property title law has been adopted by a state or local bar association, a possible solution for one of the vexing problems of title practice may be at hand. Lawyers have been under attack because of the repeated reexamination, either in time or concurrently, of the same title. The cautious title lawyer is presently not willing to advise the client that a previous examination and opinion of the title may be relied upon if the skill and judgment of the previous examiner are not known to the lawyer. The lawyer must accept the risks inherent in basing the certification in part on the previous opinion, or fully advise the client of those risks, allowing the client to choose between a full reexamination or a "bring down" opinion, perhaps at a lower cost.

This decision, whether made by the lawyer or the client, would be facilitated if the previous examiner were, by reason of certification, identifiable as a skilled title lawyer. Local standards of title might even provide that the examining lawyer may "build" the opinion on the former opinion of a certified title lawyer. This should result in a substantial decrease in the cost to the lawyer, and thus to the buyer, of the title search or examination and certification.

The acceptance of a single opinion of the state of the title for all parties involves a significant part of the problem of the representation of the buyer, but not all of the problem. The balance of the representation the buyer needs cannot appropriately be given to the buyer by the lender's lawyer because of the inherent conflicts of interest that are involved. Thus the lawyer who provides the certification of title for both the buyer and the lender can thereafter represent one or the other, but not both parties. If, however, a lawyer who has not made the title examination can rely on the title examination that has been made, that lawyer can adequately advise the client without the necessity of repetitious title examination. The cost of representation is thereby kept within reasonable bounds.

An important side effect of adequate representation for the buyer would be to curtail the need for far reaching consumer protection legislation. If the buyer were properly advised by the buyer's own lawyer, statutory safeguards would be of less urgency.

IMPLEMENTATION OF AN EFFECTIVE PROGRAM

The basic premise of this Paper is that legal costs in home buying transactions can be reduced at the same time services to the public are enlarged. A number of remedial measures have been suggested. They are not self-implementing. Precisely what is needed to put them into effect?

Top priority should be given to a three-pronged program designed to create a useable system of public land records, to shorten the period of title search, and to quickly purge the records of technical defects. Any study of the recording system should include a consideration of how all public records affecting land titles can be consolidated in a single office and how matters arising out of federal law can be better incorporated in the local recording system. Such a program can be implemented fully only by state legislatures, acting in some instances with federal assistance. If they are to be induced to act, it will be necessary to think in both technical and political terms. The first task will be to furnish workable model statutes. Drafting should be done initially at the national level to insure the best possible product and, at the same time, to avoid costly duplication. These national models can later be modified or enlarged to meet particular local conditions.

Several efforts to frame model statutes have been made by different groups. The most notable, of course, is the Uniform Simplification of Land Transfer Act mentioned above. The Department of Housing and Urban Development is moving to implement the requirements of Section 13 of the Real Estate Settlement Procedures Act to provide demonstration public recording projects.

The modernization of public recording offices should be encouraged. Additional model acts are required. Drafting teams composed of lawyers, office system experts and representatives of all interested parties should be provided. This work can probably best be carried out by a private or semipublic organization such as a university or a law school. Substantial funding will be required. The American Bar Association, and state and local bar associations, can encourage such a venture by providing needed funds.

With the availability of adequate model acts, state legislatures must be induced to pass them. It can be assumed that legislatures will act only if there is substantial demand. Presently this demand is latent and will require mobilization. There is great dissatisfaction with the existing system. The home-buying public feels it is being overreached. Vocal elements have made this feeling known to the Congress but there is little evidence that state legislators have been informed. In addition to the home-buying public, groups such as real estate brokers, mortgage lenders and home builders have cried out against the difficulty and expense of proving title. Finally, an increasing number of lawyers are coming to realize not only that the present system is inequitable but that, unless reforms are implemented, radical changes inimical to both the public and the bar are inevitable.

Given a workable and properly publicized program, these several groups can be brought together and can provide the demand necessary to induce legislative action. State bars will bear primary responsibility for mobilizing political support and for explaining to legislators the technical reasons why given measures are needed and can work effectively. Local bar associations, title groups, conveyancers' associations and other concerned organizations can play a particularly significant role in this process because of their special expertise in real estate transactions.

The American Bar Association can carry out a national educational program to inform the public and the bar what is needed and what can be done. A special task force to plan and implement education on a nationwide basis is needed.

State and local bar associations should also form special committees to draft the uniform sales agreements and other instruments alluded to earlier in this Paper and should work with other interested groups to promote their use.

The Congress can make at least three contributions toward the reduction of costs. The first is an investigation into how government paper work required in financing homes can be reduced to a minimum. The second would be for Congress to pass legislation which will require government agencies to simplify and standardize their loan procedures. Thirdly, Congress should pass enabling legislation to extend the application of marketable title acts to federal lands and claims.

Perhaps the quickest ways by which legal services can be expanded without any significant increase in cost are to limit successive examinations of the title to the period between the last title opinion and the current date, and to encourage the acceptance of a single title opinion by all parties to the transaction.

Successive and repetitive examinations of the same title may be eliminated where a state or local bar association elects to adopt a plan of certification of title lawyers. Such certification would not only assist the public in recognizing lawyers who have particular competence in title matters, but might also provide the foundation for a system of incorporating former title opinions of certified title lawyers into current title opinions without the necessity of reexamination of the base title.

Recognition of a lawyer's expertise in the area of title practice through certification also may facilitate acceptance by all parties to the transaction of a single opinion of title, thus eliminating the cost of duplicate title examinations for the buyer and the lender.

A joint conference should be established by the American Bar Association and other interested organizations for the purpose of formulating a statement of principles governing acceptance by all parties of a single opinion of title.

The American Bar Association, through its committees, has appeared before the Congress to testify, regarding consumer legislation, that if proper representation can be obtained for the buyer, such legislation will be of less importance. However, this consumer legislation does contain one important provision. Ideally title insurance should provide protection for both the buyer and the lender. This practice is employed by the Florida Lawyer's Title Guaranty Fund. Serious study should be given to whether this practice can be made universal. In the interim a major fault in the present system of title insurance is not so much that the buyer is not covered by a mortgagee policy but that he does not know he is not covered. The Real Estate Settlement Procedures Act provides that the closing statement in federally related mortgage loans must indicate whether the buyer, the mortgagee, or both are protected. The Special Committee on Residential Real Estate Transactions of the American Bar Association has drafted a Model Home Buyer's Title Protection Notice Act which requires notice to the home buyer of the fact that the buyer is not protected by a mortgagee's title certificate, opinion or policy. The Special Committee has recommended that the American Bar Association approve the Act and that it be adopted by the state legislatures.

COMPENSATION OF LAWYERS

The belief has been expressed that lawyers receive excessive fees for handling residential real estate transactions and that the system of pricing is inequitable. However, the general feeling of the profession is that title work is relatively poorly rewarded and that the great danger is not that the lawyers will make too much money but that they will cease to render needed but unprofitable services. As has been indicated, in many instances present charges can be reduced. But, except in limited areas where clear abuses exist, any such reduction can come only after basic reforms have been put into operation.

Complaints against the pricing system have generally been directed against fees based on a percentage of the amount of the sales price or the mortgage debt. It is often asserted that charging on the basis of work performed will produce more equitable results. A third formula, whereby fees are computed by making specific charges for each item of work, is little used. It tends to inflate cost unduly and is justifiably unpopular.

Justification for the percentage system can be based on the fact that the risk assumed by the lawyer and the lawyer's malpractice insurer is greater or less in proportion to the value of the property. Since the examination of title to an inexpensive home may be as arduous as that for a mansion, if a percentage formula is used, the lawyer can "average out" and can render service to the small buyer at a price that otherwise would not be possible. On the other hand, pricing on the basis of the amount of work done appeals to the ordinary man's sense of justice. Although no one formula is entirely equitable, fees should be based at least on work performed and responsibility assumed.

TITLE INSURANCE

In some sections of the country the use of title insurance has eliminated the lawyer from conveyancing or drastically reduced the lawyer's role. For this reason any statement of the proper role of the lawyer in the residential real estate transaction which ignores the relationship between the title insurers and the bar is unrealistic.

The value of some form of title insurance is recognized. Also, there is no immediate prospect of fundamental change in the traditional system of recording evidence of title. So long as this present system of recording evidence of title is used, national mortgage lenders may insist upon title insurance in addition to the certificate or opinion conventionally furnished by an examining lawyer. Although the national mortgage market is the primary source of demand for title insurance, a lesser but increasing demand comes from local lenders and from home buyers who want owner coverage. The insurance can be provided by commercial companies or by bar-related title insurers.

The objection to private title plants already has been stated. It is to be noted that reliance on private title plants results in absorbing the fee paid for title examination, which frustrates efforts to increase needed legal services to the home buyer.

A legitimate question is whether the public can be better served by commercial title companies or the bar. It has been pointed out that the interests of the insurer and the insured are in conflict and that the insurer cannot, from the nature of the enterprise, furnish needed legal services. The role of the title company should be confined to title insurance. Conveyancing should be left to independent lawyers. The independent lawyer in private practice will protect the client's interests at each stage of the transaction and provide the necessary counseling when any difficulties arise. The objective is to provide needed legal services to the buyer and seller by their own lawyers at reasonable cost.

Attention is called to the statement of principles with respect to the mutual roles of the lawyer and the title insurer in real estate transactions which have been promulgated by the National Conference of Lawyers, Title Insurance Companies and Abstracters and approved by the American Bar Association and the American Land Title Association.

CONCLUSIONS AND RECOMMENDATIONS

The lawyer should play a primary role in the residential real estate transaction because no one else is in a position to furnish needed legal services. At the present and for years past, the lawyer's role has steadily declined and in some places the lawyer plays no role at all. This trend should be reversed. At the same time the cost to the home buyer should be reduced. Both these objectives are practicable but can be achieved only by a systematic, long-range program of reform. The major measures required, and the part to be played by various groups if success is to be anticipated, have been set out in this Paper.

The specific measures to be adopted and the bodies having primary responsibility for their implementation can be summarized as follows:

1. The American Bar Association should:
   (a) Continue, with the assistance of state and local bar associations, to support model or uniform legislation for submission to state legislatures covering the fields of the recording acts, marketable title acts and curative acts; and
   (b) Set up a joint conference with mortgage lenders for the purpose of encouraging the acceptance of a single title certificate or opinion of the state of the title for all parties; and
   (c) In cooperation with state and local bar associations, embark upon a long-term educational project designed to make buyers and sellers of houses aware of their need for legal services and the desirability of employing lawyers before binding commitments have been entered into; and
   (d) Encourage state and local bar associations to consider whether a plan for the certification of land title specialists should be adopted; and
   (e) Encourage the use, under the supervision and responsibility of a lawyer, of paraprofessionals in land title transactions as one method of improving efficiency within law offices.

2. State and local bar associations should:
   (a) Pursue, with the assistance of the American Bar Association, a program of supporting model or uniform legislation for submission to state legislatures covering the fields of the recording acts, marketable title acts and curative acts; and
   (b) Attempt to mobilize support for the state legislative program outlined above; and
   (c) Attempt in every way possible to induce all parties to accept a single certification of title; and
   (d) Consider whether some program for the certification of title specialists should be adopted, and if adopted, provide for the abandonment by specialists of repeated reexamination of the same title; and

    (e)   Create at the local level panels of qualified title specialists, and publicize their availability to represent the buyers of homes, if a plan for certification of title specialists is adopted; and

    (f)   Create special committees, wherever they do not already exist, to give continuing study to means for improving title practice and for increasing services rendered buyers of homes; and

    (g)   Cooperate with the American Bar Association in the educational program set out above; and

    (h)   Create committees to draft uniform sales contracts and other instruments to be used when individualized documents are impracticable.

3.   The Congress should:

    (a)   Encourage and assist the drafting of model legislation for submission to state legislatures, covering the fields of the recording acts, marketable title acts and curative acts; and

    (b)   Enact legislation making marketable title acts and title registration acts conforming to certain standards applicable to federal land and claims; and

    (c)   Require all federal agencies dealing in, or insuring home mortgages to submit programs for the reduction of paper work required in a residential real estate transaction; and

    (d)   Pass legislation which will provide for simplified and standardized procedures for loans from federal agencies, federally related lenders, or both, and encourage the use of legal counsel by home buyers.

4.   State legislatures should, after study and consideration:

    (a)   Adopt programs of legislation designed to make title proof simple and economical. (A minimum program will include a reorganization of the recording system, the adoption of an effective marketable title act and the enactment of a large body of curative legislation); and

    (b)   Require, by adoption of the Model Home Buyer's Title Protection Notice Act, title insurers issuing mortgage policies and lawyers writing mortgagee title certificates or opinions, to notify the home buyers that they are not covered.

5.   Lawyers should:

    (a)   Establish an understanding as to their fees at the time they are employed and base such fees on a work-done-plus-responsibility formula; and

    (b)   Constantly improve their skills as conveyancers in all ways possible, including participation in continuing legal education programs.

Admittedly much else needs to be done to improve title practice. Whether or not such additional measures are adopted will have no effect upon the basic role played by the lawyer. No attempt has been made to discuss all desirable reforms. Actions which tend to gloss over basic deficiencies or temporarily alleviate them should be avoided while full attention should be directed to the major problems of conveyancing.

> Respectfully submitted,
> AMERICAN BAR ASSOCIATION
> SPECIAL COMMITTEE ON
>   RESIDENTIAL REAL ESTATE
>   TRANSACTIONS
> H. HENLEY BLAIR
> L. STEWART BOHAN
> WILLIAM P. DICKSON, JR.
> THOMAS R. DYER
> LOUIS L. RAMSAY, JR.
> PATRICK W. RICHARDSON
> A. JAMES CASNER, *Chairman*

This Committee was created in February 1972. Former members are:

MITCHELL E. PANZER, *Chairman* — 1972[2]
WM. B. SPANN, JR., *Chairman* — 1972-73
J. FOY GUIN, JR. — 1972-73
J. STANLEY MULLIN — 1972-73
BEN J. WEAVER — 1972-74
CHARLES L. EDSON — 1972-77
RICHARD B. JOHNSON — 1972-77
IRVING KAGAN — 1974-75[3]
WILLIAM P. DICKSON, JR., *Board Liaison through August 1972*
JAMES H. HIGGINS, *Board Liaison August 1972-February 1975*
HONORABLE WILLIAM R. GOLDBERG, *Board Liaison February 1975-August 1975*
EARL Q. GRAY, *Board Liaison August 1975-August 1976*
JOHN A. KLUWIN, *Board Liaison August 1976-August 1977*
S. SHEPHERD TATE, *Board Liaison August 1977-*

Committee Staff Director: FREDERICK R. FRANKLIN (1972-78)

Note: Uniform Acts

Two Uniform Acts recently approved and recommended for enactment in all the states are the Uniform Land Transactions Act and the Uniform Simplification of Land Transfers Act. The provisions of these two new Uniform Acts should be examined in relation to modern land transactions.

2. Mr. Panzer was not on the Committee during the time of the preparation of this Position Paper.
3. Mr. Kagan was unable to participate in the deliberations of the Committee or in the preparation of this Position Paper.

CHAPTER 24

THE STATUTE OF FRAUDS

In this chapter we shall first deal with the two provisions of the English Statute of Frauds which are immediately relevant to the modern land transaction; then give you the historical background of the statute; and finally sketch its principal provisions, some relating to real estate and some not.

Conveyances Under the Statute

It has already been pointed out that originally the feudal law required that conveyances take place by feoffment, i.e., a ceremonial physical transfer with both parties on the land; no instrument in writing was required, and none could render the ceremony unnecessary. Then came the Statute of Uses (1536), under which a conveyor could transfer title to a conveyee by a document (the bargain and sale or covenant to stand seised), creating an equitable estate which the statute transformed into a legal estate. Thus documentary transfer, not accompanied by any physical delivery, became permissible.

The Statute of Frauds (1677), among many other things, declared that no freehold estate could be created or transferred except by an instrument in writing signed by the grantor. It thus made documentary transfer compulsory and established the basis for a workable system of title security.

Contracts for Sale of Land Under the Statute[1]

Section 4(4) of the English Statute of Frauds, which generally has been copied almost word for word, provides:

---

1. See generally American Law of Property §§11.2-11.12 (Casner ed. 1952).

> No action shall be brought . . . upon any contract or sale of lands, tenements or hereditaments, of any interest in or concerning them . . . unless the agreement upon which such action shall be brought, or some memorandum or note thereof, shall be in writing, and signed by the party to be charged therewith, or some other person thereunto by him lawfully authorized.

The fact that real estate prices are the product of individual bargaining very frequently brings this section of the statute into play. O_1, owning Blackacre, dickers with P_1 for a week or two and finally makes a deal for a sale at $11,500—possibly over the phone. O_1 and P_1, honorable persons who know each other casually, don't bother with a written contract. Characteristically, O_1 figures he ought to have gotten a better price and P_1 thinks she could have traded O_1 down if she had held off a few days. Ten days later P_2, who likes the location, offers O_1 \$13,000 for the land—or O_2, pressed for cash, offers P_1 a better buy for \$10,000. It is at this point that the limitations of honorable persons are likely to become noticeable. So our colleagues in the trial department do a rather flourishing business in asserting this section of the statute or seeking to circumvent it.

The doctrine of part performance.[2] Out of the blue—i.e., with no justification in the words of the statute—the courts have ruled that a party to an oral agreement who has made part performance of such type as to indicate the existence and general content of the agreement may secure specific performance. This doctrine was developed in equity as part of the body of law relating to specific performance, but in some jurisdictions it is now extended to actions at law for damages.[3]

Historical Background

Having now noted the clauses of the Statute of Frauds which have continual importance in the modern land transaction, let us now glance briefly at the history and content of the statute. It and its American counterparts are basic materials in many fields of the law.

The early legislation that you have studied thus far has affected the land law profoundly, but these effects have been incidental consequences of measures primarily motivated by avarice, class advancement, and political designs. De Donis was straightforward class legislation aimed at perpetuating a class of great landowners and protecting their lands from the debts which they had incurred and which the Statute of Merchants (1283) had made collectible out of their real estate. Quia Emptores formed a part of the

2. See American Law of Property §§11.7-11.12 (Casner ed. 1952).
3. There are a large number of cases on what types of part performance take the case out of the statute. No accurate simple statement is possible. See American Law of Property §11.11 (Casner ed. 1952).

program of Edward I for strengthening the central authority of the Crown.[4] The Statute of Uses had the purpose of bailing Henry VIII out of his fiscal difficulties and providing additional business for the common-law lawyers.

Against this background it is refreshing to discover that the Statute of Frauds was a true measure of law reform. Enacted in the reign of Charles II, whose mind was on other matters, it was drafted and sponsored by the finest lawyer of his day, Heneage Finch, later Lord Nottingham.[5] It sought to make ordinary people more secure in their property holdings and in their contracts and to protect them against trumped-up claims.

Two aspects of seventeenth century procedural law made the need for the Statute of Frauds acute: (1) juries could still decide cases upon their own "knowledge," regardless of the evidence, and it was therefore desirable to require written evidence for the proof of certain types of transactions, thereby placing some limitation on the whims of the jury; (2) both parties to a transaction were disqualified as witnesses, and it was therefore desirable to have a written document as the basis of proof of the transaction.

Real Property Provisions of the Statute

The Statute of Frauds dealt with a wide variety of matters. As far as the law of real property is concerned, the most important provisions were the following:

1. No estate in land could be created or transferred except by an instrument in writing signed by the grantor. Any other attempted conveyance created an estate at will only. An exception was made for

---

4. Incidentally, do not commit the error of thinking of Edward I as just another king with one of the common English names and a number. He was one of the great vital forces of law development of all time, as well as being a personality of color and power. For good reading on the subject, see the chapter on Edward Plantagenet in Seagle, Men of Law From Hammurabi to Holmes (1947).

5. Here also is a personality you should become acquainted with. Nottingham is known as the father of equity. In property law his fame rests on the Duke of Norfolk's Case, 3 Ch. Cas. 1 (1682), in which he established the basis of the rule against perpetuities, rejecting unanimous opinions to the contrary of the three chief justices of the common-law courts. In this case he gave the classic answer to the contention that a particular course of action must not be permitted because it would be impossible to draw the line between it and other courses of action obviously undesirable:

Where will you stop if you do not stop here? I will tell you where I will stop:
I will stop wherever any visible inconvenience doth appear. . . .

For an abridgment of the Duke of Norfolk's Case, see Leach & Logan, Cases and Text on Future Interests and Estate Planning 672 (1961). For the authorship and background of the Statute of Frauds, see 6 Holdsworth's History of English Law 380 et seq. (2d ed. 1937); Plucknett, Concise History of the Common Law 55 (5th ed. 1956).

leases not exceeding three years, if there was a rent reserved equal to at least two-thirds of the rental value of the property (sections 1 to 3).

2. Leases could not be surrendered except in writing "or by act and operation of law" (section 3).

3. "No action shall be brought whereby to charge any person upon any contract or sale of lands or any interest in or concerning them unless the agreement or some memorandum thereof shall be in writing and signed by the party to be charged therewith" (section 4 (some words omitted)).

4. Wills of land had to be in writing, signed by the testator, and attested and subscribed by three witnesses in the testator's presence (section 5), and such wills could be revoked only by prescribed formalities (section 6).

5. Declarations or assignments of trusts of land had to be in writing and signed (sections 7 and 8), but this requirement did not apply to trusts which "may arise or result by the implication or construction of Law" (section 8).

The statute also dealt with other minor property matters, but the foregoing are the ones which have had lasting importance and which form the basis of legislation presently existing in the United States. In this course, the statute is frequently in the background of various problems, but special treatment of it is given only occasionally.[6] The making and revocation of wills is treated in the course you will have in estate planning[7] or wills. Courses in contracts and specific performance deal with the provisions of section 4 as to contracts for the sale of land.[8]

Other Provisions

In addition to the property matters above set forth, the Statute of Frauds, in section 4, required certain other types of contracts to be evidenced by a note or memorandum in writing. These types of contracts include:

1. promises to answer for the debt or default of another, i.e., contracts of suretyship;

2. agreements in consideration of marriage (but not including promises to marry);

3. agreements not to be performed within a year.

---

6. In Part VI, page 480 *supra,* surrender of a lease by operation of law is considered, and in Part VIII, page 1024, footnote 81, the enforceability of an oral agreement to restrict the use of land is referred to.

7. See Casner, Estate Planning ch. 3 (4th ed.).

8. In the consideration of the contract for the sale of land in Chapter 25 and of the deed in Chapter 27, compliance with a statute of frauds generally is assumed.

Section 17 of the statute required that contracts for the sale of goods in substantial amount (the original statute placed the amount at ten pounds, but the figure has since been raised substantially in various jurisdictions) be evidenced by (1) the buyer receiving part of the goods, (2) the buyer giving something in earnest to bind the bargain or in part payment, or (3) a signed memorandum.[9]

9. On these provisions of the statute, see Restatement (Second) of Contracts.

CHAPTER 25

THE CONTRACT FOR THE SALE OF LAND (HEREIN THE LAW OF VENDOR AND PURCHASER)

Note: ***The Real Estate Broker and the Broker's Commission***

It is usually with a light heart that one with property to sell goes to a realtor and seeks help in the selling. Not always does the lightness of heart persist through the process of paying the commission, for the broker's compensation can run into serious money. The broker is well aware of the uncertainties of his or her business, the effort fruitlessly expended on one property after another. To the customer these things are likely to seem fairly unimportant; the customer's thought is directed at the slight effort that may have been involved in selling the particular property he or she owned. Thus it is not surprising that actions for brokers' commissions are among the most common on the dockets of our trial courts.

This is no place for detailed treatment of the contractual relationships between broker and customer. Still, it is appropriate to call attention to those aspects of the subject which will help you to guide the actions of your vendor clients.

Doing without a broker. If you have 1,000 shares of General Electric stock to sell, you probably will have to sell it through a broker with stock exchange connections. But the same is not true of real estate. Certainly, the attorney for an owner who wishes to sell should place before the client the advantages and disadvantages of trying to effect a sale without a broker. If the seller succeeds, there is no commission, and the gross is the net. Still, prospective buyers do go to brokers and thus enable brokers to provide a wider market; the broker takes a lot of trouble off the shoulders of the owner; the broker pays for newspaper advertisements, whether or not successful; and an experienced broker has developed a sales technique which perhaps can convince a buyer who would otherwise look and pass on. For better or worse, however, the owner seldom consults a lawyer until a buyer has been found and a contract is about to be drawn.

The rates of commissions for brokers. In the absence of express agreement, the broker is entitled to "reasonable" compensation. However, this is not determined by the effort expended in the particular case; the broker has an all-or-nothing business — all if a customer is produced, nothing if a customer is not produced. Real estate boards — which are brokers' organizations — fix standard rates for particular localities, and these are generally accepted as criteria of reasonable compensation.

When the broker earns the commission. When the broker earns the commission is a matter which is not generally understood. In the absence of express agreement, the broker earns the commission if the broker is the effective cause of producing a customer willing and able to buy on terms acceptable to the owner. The following two situations are not uncommon:

1. O places property in the hands of B for sale. B shows the property to P, whom B has found. P looks at the property but tells B no sale. P later goes to O and says, "Why should I buy through your broker? You sell to me direct, and we'll adjust the price by splitting the commission you would otherwise have to pay B." This seems a splendid idea to O. May B collect a commission? Yes.

2. O places property in the hands of B for sale. B produces P. O and P sign a contract. Then it proves that P cannot raise the money — either because P never had it and merely had hoped to borrow it or because P suffered losses between the date of the contract and the stipulated date for conveyance. May B collect a commission? Generally, yes.

From the foregoing, it is obvious that a vendor may be stuck for two or more commissions for the same sale. For example:

3. O places property in the hands of B_1, B_2, and B_3 for sale at $10,000. B_1 produces a customer at $10,000. Before a contract is signed, B_2 produces a customer at $11,000, so O refuses to sign with B_1's customer and instead signs with B_2's customer. B_2's customer suffers losses and cannot go through with the sale. Thereupon B_3 shows up with a customer at $9500, and O, disgusted with the whole affair, signs with B_3's customer and goes through with the deal. O has to pay three commissions.

Of course, the contract with the broker can specify that the commission will not be earned unless the transaction is consummated. Conversely, it can — and, believe it or not, sometimes does — provide that a commission will be payable to a particular broker even if the customer is produced by another broker or even by the owner.[1]

---

1. See Currier, Finding the Broker's Place in the Typical Residential Real Estate Transaction, 33 U. Fla. L. Rev. 655 (1981).

Who can be a broker. In some states, real estate brokers have to be licensed, in others, not. Where licensing is not required, there are grave risks in an owner indicating a willingness to accept the friendly help of anyone in selling property. What the owner considers as the acceptance of friendly help may be considered as the creation of an owner-broker relationship by the other person. Too often, after a customer has been produced, the owner sends around a bottle of Scotch with an appreciative note and the friend returns it with a bill for a commission. This situation produces its fair share of lawsuits.

Restrictions on the brokerage contract. In some states the contract with the broker must be in writing, and certain statutes also require that the commission rates be specified. These provisions have a salutary and sobering effect.

TRISTRAM'S LANDING, INC. v. WAIT
367 Mass. 622, 327 N.E.2d 727 (1975)

TAURO, C.J. This is an action in contract seeking to recover a brokerage commission alleged to be due to the plaintiffs from the defendant. The case was heard by a judge, sitting without a jury, on a stipulation of facts. The judge found for the plaintiffs in the full amount of the commission. The defendant filed exceptions to that finding and appealed.

The facts briefly are these: The plaintiffs are real estate brokers doing business in Nantucket. The defendant owned real estate on the island which she desired to sell. In the past, the plaintiffs acted as brokers for the defendant when she rented the same premises.

The plaintiffs heard that the defendant's property was for sale, and in the spring of 1972 the plaintiff Van der Wolk telephoned the defendant and asked for authority to show it. The defendant agreed that the plaintiffs could act as brokers, although not as exclusive brokers, and told them that the price for the property was $110,000. During this conversation there was no mention of a commission. The defendant knew that the normal brokerage commission in Nantucket was five per cent of the sale price.

In the early months of 1973, Van der Wolk located a prospective buyer, Louise L. Cashman (Cashman), who indicated that she was interested in purchasing the defendant's property. Her written offer of $100,000, dated April 29, was conveyed to the defendant. Shortly thereafter, the defendant's husband and attorney wrote to the plaintiffs that "a counter-offer of $105,000 with an October 1st closing" should be made to Cashman. Within a few weeks, the counter offer was orally accepted, and a purchase and sale agreement was drawn up by Van der Wolk.

The agreement was executed by Cashman and was returned to the plaintiffs with a check for $10,500, representing a ten per cent down payment. The agreement was then presented by the plaintiffs to the defendant, who signed it after reviewing it with her attorney. The down payment check was thereafter turned over to the defendant.

The purchase and sale agreement signed by the parties called for an October 1, 1973, closing date. On September 22, the defendant signed a fifteen day extension of the closing date, which was communicated to Cashman by the plaintiffs. Cashman did not sign the extension. On October 1, 1973, the defendant appeared at the registry of deeds with a deed to the property. Cashman did not appear for the closing and thereafter refused to go through with the purchase. No formal action has been taken by the defendant to enforce the agreement or to recover damages for its breach, although the defendant has retained the down payment.

Van der Wolk presented the defendant with a bill for commission in the amount of $5,250, five percent of the agreed sales price. The defendant, through her attorney, refused to pay, stating that "[t]here has been no sale and consequently the 5% commission has not been earned." The plaintiffs then brought this action to recover the commission.

In the course of dealings between the plaintiffs and the defendant there was no mention of commission. The only reference to commission is found in the purchase and sale agreement signed by Cashman and the defendant, which reads as follows: "It is understood that a broker's commission of five (5) percent on the said sale is to be paid to . . . [the broker] by the said seller." The plaintiffs contend that, having produced a buyer who was ready, willing and able to purchase the property, and who was in fact accepted by the seller, they are entitled to their full commission. The defendant argues that no commission was earned because the sale was not consummated. We agree with the defendant, and reverse the finding by the judge below.

1.   The general rule regarding whether a broker is entitled to a commission from one attempting to sell real estate is that, absent special circumstances, the broker "is entitled to a commission if he produces a customer ready, able, and willing to buy upon the terms and for the price given the broker by the owner." Gaynor v. Laverdure, 291 N.E.2d 617 (1973), quoting Henderson & Beal, Inc. v. Glen, 329 Mass. 748, 751, 110 N.E.2d 373 (1953). In the past, this rule has been construed to mean that once a customer is produced by the broker and accepted by the seller, the commission is earned, whether or not the sale is actually consummated. Fitzpatrick v. Gilson, 176 Mass. 477, 57 N.E. 1000 (1900). Ripley v. Taft, 253 Mass. 490, 149 N.E. 311 (1925). Spence v. Lawrence, 337 Mass. 355, 149 N.E.2d 606 (1958). Talanian v. Phippen, 357 Mass. 765, 256 N.E.2d 445 (1970). Furthermore, execution of a purchase and sale agreement is usually seen as conclusive evidence of the seller's acceptance of the buyer. Roche v. Smith, 176 Mass. 595, 58 N.E. 152 (1900). Johnson v. Holland, 211 Mass. 363, 97 N.E. 755 (1912). Stone v. Melbourne, 326 Mass. 372, 94 N.E.2d 783 (1950). Richards v. Gilbert, 336 Mass. 617, 146 N.E.2d 921 (1958).

Despite these well established and often cited rules, we have held that "[t]he owner is not helpless" to protect himself from these consequences. "He may, by appropriate language in his dealings with the broker, limit his liability for payment of a commission to the situation where not only is the broker obligated to find a customer ready, willing and able to purchase on the owner's terms and for his price, but also it is provided that no commission is to become due until the customer actually takes a conveyance and pays therefor." Gaynor v. Laverdure, *supra,* 291 N.E.2d at 622.

In the application of these rules to the instant case, we believe that the broker here is not entitled to a commission. We cannot construe the purchase and sale agreement as an unconditional acceptance by the seller of the buyer, as the agreement itself contained conditional language. The purchase and sale agreement provided that the commission was to be paid "on the said sale," and we construe this language as requiring that the said sale be consummated before the commission is earned.

While we recognize that there is a considerable line of cases indicating that language providing for payment of a commission when the agreement is "carried into effect" or "when title is passed" does not create a condition precedent, but merely sets a time for payment to be made, Alvord v. Cook, 174 Mass. 120, 121, 54 N.E. 499 (1899); Rosenthal v. Schwartz, 214 Mass. 371, 372, 101 N.E. 1070 (1913); Lord v. Williams, 259 Mass. 278, 156 N.E. 421 (1927); Canton v. Thomas, 264 Mass. 457, 162 N.E. 769 (1928), we do not think the course of events and the choice of language in this case fall within the *Alvord* case and its progeny. This is not a case, like Canton v. Thomas, where a separate agreement was made between the seller and the broker wherein the broker would receive a commission " 'in consideration of . . . procuring a purchaser.' " 264 Mass. at 458, 162 N.E. at 769 (1928). Similarly, Rosenthal v. Schwartz, *supra,* is distinguishable on its facts, as there the seller himself defaulted, thus depriving the broker of a commission by his own acts. Maher v. Haycock, 301 Mass. 594, 18 N.E.2d 348 (1938), cited by the defendant here and by the court in the *Gaynor* case, is not necessarily to the contrary, as there the words "if . . . sold" were construed to require other than the consummation of the sale in order to avoid the prohibition against Sunday contracts, and not merely to determine whether the broker was entitled to a commission.

To the extent that there are cases (such as those collected in the *Gaynor* case), unique on their facts, which may appear inconsistent with this holding and seem to indicate a contrary result, we choose not to follow them.

In light of what we have said, we construe the language "on the said sale" as providing for a "special agreement," Gaynor v. Laverdure, *supra,* . . . 291 N.E.2d 617, or as creating "special circumstances," Henderson & Beal, Inc. v. Glen, 329 Mass. 748, 751, 110 N.E.2d 373 (1953), wherein consummation of the sale became a condition precedent for the broker to earn his commission. Cf. McCarthy v. Daggett, 344 Mass. 577,

579, 183 N.E.2d 502 (1962). Accordingly, since the sale was not consummated, the plaintiffs were not entitled to recover the amount specified in the purchase and sale agreement.

2. Although what we have said to this point is determinative of the rights of the parties, we note that the relationship and obligations of real estate owners and brokers inter se has been the "subject of frequent litigation," Henderson & Beal, Inc. v. Glen, *supra,* 329 Mass. at 751, 110 N.E.2d 373. See Note, 23 Rutgers L. Rev. 83, 85 (1968). In two of the more recent cases where we were faced with this issue, we declined to follow the developing trends in this area, holding that the cases presented were inappropriate for that purpose. See LeDonne v. Slade, 355 Mass. 490, 492, 245 N.E.2d 434 (1969); Gaynor v. Laverdure, 291 N.E.2d 617. We believe, however, that it is both appropriate and necessary at this time to clarify the law, and we now join the growing minority of States who have adopted the rule of Ellsworth Dobbs, Inc. v. Johnson, 50 N.J. 528, 236 A.2d 843 (1967).[2]

In the *Ellsworth* case, the New Jersey court faced the task of clarifying the law regarding the legal relationships between sellers and brokers in real estate transactions. In order to formulate a just and proper rule, the court examined the realities of such transactions. The court noted that "ordinarily when an owner of property lists it with a broker for sale, his expectation is that the money for the payment of commission will come out of the proceeds of the sale." Id. at 547, 236 A.2d at 852. It quoted with approval from the opinion of Lord Justice Denning, in Dennis Reed, Ltd. v. Goody, [1950] 2 K.B. 277, 284-285, where he stated: "When a house owner puts his house into the hands of an estate agent, the ordinary understanding is that the agent is only to receive a commission if he succeeds in effecting a sale. . . . The common understanding of men is . . . that the agent's commission is payable out of the purchase price. . . . The house-owner wants to find a man who will actually buy his house and pay for it. He does not want a man who will only make an offer or sign a contract. He wants a purchaser 'able to purchase and able to complete as well.'" Id. at 549, 236 A.2d at 853.

The court went on to say that the principle binding "the seller to pay commission if he signs a contract of sale with the broker's customer, regardless of the customer's financial ability, puts the burden on the wrong shoulders. Since the broker's duty to the owner is to produce a prospective

___

2. Both Kansas and Oregon have adopted the *Ellsworth* rule in its entirety. See Winkelman v. Allen, 214 Kansas 22, 519 P.2d 1377 (1974); Brown v. Grimm, 258 Or. 55, 59-61, 481 P.2d 63 (1971). Additionally, Vermont, Connecticut and Idaho have cited the case with approval. See also Potter v. Ridge Realty Corp., 28 Conn. Supp. 304, 311, 259 A.2d 758 (1969); Rogers v. Hendrix, 92 Idaho 141, 438 P.2d 653 (1968); Staab v. Messier, 128 Vt. 380, 384, 264 A.2d 790 (1970). Other States and the District of Columbia also have similar, but more limited rules which were adopted prior to the *Ellsworth* case. See generally Gaynor v. Laverdure, — Mass. — n.2, 291 N.E.2d 617 (1973).

buyer who is financially able to pay the purchase price and take title, a right in the owner to assume such capacity when the broker presents his purchaser ought to be recognized." Id. at 548, 236 A 2d at 853. Reason and justice dictate that it should be the broker who bears the burden of producing a purchaser who is not only ready, willing and able at the time of the negotiations, but who also consummates the sale at the time of closing.

Thus, we adopt the following rules:

> When a broker is engaged by an owner of property to find a purchaser for it, the broker earns his commission when (a) he produces a purchaser ready, willing and able to buy on the terms fixed by the owner, (b) the purchaser enters into a binding contract with the owner to do so, and (c) the purchaser completes the transaction by closing the title in accordance with the provisions of the contract. If the contract is not consummated because of lack of financial ability of the buyer to perform or because of any other default of his . . . there is no right to commission against the seller. On the other hand, if the failure of completion of the contract results from the wrongful act or interference of the seller, the broker's claim is valid and must be paid.

Id. at 551, 236 A.2d at 855.

Accordingly, we hold that a real estate broker, under a brokerage agreement hereafter made, is entitled to a commission from the seller only if the requirements stated above are met. This rule provides necessary protection for the seller and places the burden with the broker, where it belongs. In view of the waiver of the counts in quantum meruit, we do not now consider the extent to which the broker may be entitled to share in a forfeited deposit or other benefit received by the seller as a result of the broker's efforts.

We recognize that this rule could be easily circumvented by language to the contrary in purchase and sale agreements or in agreements between sellers and brokers. In many States a signed writing is required for an agreement to pay a commission to a real estate broker. See Restatement 2d: Contracts, 418, 420 (Tent. drafts Nos. 1-7, 1973). Such a requirement may be worthy of legislative consideration, but we do not think we should establish such a requirement by judicial decision. Informal agreements fairly made between people of equal skill and understanding serve a useful purpose. But many sellers, unlike brokers, are involved in real estate transactions infrequently, perhaps only once in a lifetime, and are thus unfamiliar with their legal rights. In such cases agreements by the seller to pay a commission even though the purchaser defaults are to be scrutinized carefully. If not fairly made, such agreements may be unconscionable or against public policy.

Exceptions sustained.

Judgment for the defendant.

SECTION 1. SAMPLE CONTRACT FOR THE SALE OF LAND[3]

This *fifteenth* day of *August, [insert year], A. B. of Boston in the Commonwealth of Massachusetts* hereinafter called the SELLER, agrees to SELL and *C. D. of Worcester in said Commonwealth* hereinafter called the BUYER or PURCHASER, agrees to BUY, upon the terms hereinafter set forth, the following described premises, viz.: *a certain parcel of land situated on W. street in said Boston, and bounded as follows: — East on said street, thirty feet; — South on land now or late of L. M., fifty feet; — West on land of N. O., thirty feet; — and North on the same, fifty feet and seven inches; — and being the same parcel that was conveyed to the SELLER by R. S. by deed dated 7th Dec., 1970, and recorded in Suffolk Registry of Deeds, book 4790, page 638.*[4]

Included in the sale as a part of said premises are the buildings, structures, and improvements now thereon, and the fixtures belonging to the SELLER and used in connection therewith including, if any, all venetian blinds, window shades, screens, screen doors, storm windows and doors, awnings, shutters, furnaces, heaters, heating equipment, stoves, ranges, oil and gas burners and fixtures appurtenant thereto, hot water heaters, plumbing and bathroom fixtures, electric and other lighting fixtures, mantels, outside television antennas, fences, gates, trees, shrubs, plants, and, if built in, air conditioning equipment, ventilators, garbage disposers, dishwashers, washing machines and driers, and *[any other item which should be specifically mentioned]* but excluding *[exclude here any items which should be specifically excluded]*

Said premises are to be conveyed by a good and sufficient warranty[5] deed running to the BUYER, or to the nominee designated by the BUYER by

---

3. This *sample* contract was prepared by counsel for the Boston Real Estate Board (copyright © 1978); it is reproduced here with permission. The contract is under continuous study by such counsel with a view to making improvements. The use of this contract on the advice of non-lawyers who may not fully understand the legal problems involved raises serious issues as to unauthorized practice of the law. See People ex rel. Illinois State Bar Association v. Schafer, 404 Ill. 45, 87 N.E.2d 773 (1949) (real estate broker who followed the practice of preparing deeds, mortgages, and contracts in connection with real estate sales was held guilty of unauthorized practice of the law and adjudged to be in contempt of court).

4. Section 3 of Chapter 27 is devoted to a consideration of the problems which may arise in connection with the description of land.

5. The financial obligations assumed by the seller when he or she gives a warranty deed are considered in Section 4 of Chapter 27. If you represent the seller, you should advise the seller whether to give a warranty deed or one that imposes on him or her lesser guarantees as to the title. In Massachusetts a grantor usually gives only a quitclaim deed with so-called "quitclaim covenants." This type of deed is described in Section 1 of Chapter 27. If the grantor is a fiduciary (such as an executor or a trustee), the fiduciary normally will not give any guarantees as to title in the deed.

written notice to the SELLER at least seven days before the deed is to be delivered as herein provided, and said deed shall convey a good and clear record and marketable title thereto,[6] free from encumbrances, except

(a) Provisions of existing building and zoning laws;
(b) Existing rights and obligations in party walls which are not the subject of written agreement;
(c) Such taxes for the then current year as are not due and payable on the date of the delivery of such deed;
(d) Any liens for municipal betterments assessed after the date of this agreement;
(e) [*Include here by specific reference any restrictions, easements, rights and obligations in party walls not included in (b), leases, municipal and other liens, other encumbrances, and make provision to protect SELLER against BUYER'S breach of SELLER'S covenants in leases, where necessary.*]

If said deed refers to a plan necessary to be recorded therewith the SELLER shall deliver such plan with the deed in form adequate for recording or registration.

In addition to the foregoing, if the title to said premises is registered, said deed shall be in form sufficient to entitle the BUYER to a Certificate of Title of said premises, and the SELLER shall deliver with said deed all instruments, if any, necessary to enable the BUYER to obtain such Certificate of Title.[7]

The agreed purchase price for said premises is *one hundred and fifty thousand* ($150,000) dollars, of which

$ 15,000 have been paid as a deposit this day and
$135,000 are to be paid at the time of delivery of the deed in cash or by certified, cashier's, treasurer's, or bank check.
$150,000 TOTAL[8]

Such deed is to be delivered at ten o'clock A.M. on the fourth day of September, [*insert year*], at the Suffolk County Registry of Deeds, unless otherwise agreed upon in writing. It is agreed that time is of the essence of this agreement.[9]

---

6. The meaning of "good and clear record and marketable title" is discussed in Section 2 of this chapter.

7. Title registration is dealt with in Chapter 30. This provision of the contract, of course, has no significance unless registered land is involved.

8. Normally, the purchaser will not have the full purchase price available and will have to raise part of it by means of a loan from a bank, which loan will be secured by a mortgage on the property the purchaser is buying. Chapter 26 deals with the real estate mortgage; you will find described in that chapter other methods of financing the purchase of land.

9. In the absence of a contrary provision in a contract for the sale of land, time is not of the essence. This simply means that the date specified in the contract for the closing is not vital, and each party is given a reasonable time after such date to perform the obligations under the

Full possession of said premises free of all tenants and occupants, except as herein provided, is to be delivered at the time of the delivery of the deed, said premises to be then (a) in the same condition as they now are, reasonable use and wear thereof excepted,[10] and (b) not in violation of said building and zoning laws, and (c) in compliance with the provisions of any instrument referred to in clause 4 hereof.[11] The buyer shall be entitled to an inspection of said premises prior to the delivery of the deed in order to determine whether the condition thereof complies with the terms of this clause.

If the SELLER shall be unable to give title or to make conveyance, or to deliver possession of the premises, all as herein stipulated, or if at the time of the delivery of the deed the premises do not conform with the provisions hereof, then any payments made under this agreement shall be refunded and all other obligations of the parties hereto shall cease and this agreement shall be void and without recourse to the parties hereto, unless the SELLER elects to use reasonable efforts to remove any defects in title, or to deliver possession as provided herein, or to make the said premises conform to the provisions hereof, as the case may be, in which event the SELLER shall give written notice thereof to the BUYER at or before the time for performance hereunder, and thereupon the time for performance hereof shall be extended for a period of thirty days.[12]

If at the expiration of the extended time the SELLER shall have failed so to remove any defects in title, deliver possession, or make the premises conform, as the case may be, all as herein agreed, or if at any time during the period of this agreement or any extension thereof, the holder of a mortgage on said premises shall refuse to permit the insurance proceeds, if any, to be used for such purposes, then, at the BUYER'S option, any payments made under this agreement shall be forthwith refunded and all other obligations of all parties hereto shall cease and this agreement shall be void without recourse to the parties hereto.[13]

---

contract. Thus if the vendor is not ready to perform on the date specified, the purchaser is not relieved of the purchaser's obligations under the contract, and vice versa.

Time can be made of the essence from the beginning by a provision to that effect in the contract. If such a provision is inserted in the contract, the purchaser is relieved of the purchaser's obligations if the vendor is not ready and willing to perform on the critical date, and vice versa. It is customary to insert in contracts for the sale of land a provision making time of the essence.

10. You should re-examine this clause carefully after considering the material on the risk of loss in Section 3 of this chapter.

11. Clause 4 is the one above in the agreement that describes the kind of deed to be delivered.

12. What does this provision do to the clause above in the agreement that states that time is of the essence? See footnote 9.

13. The reference in this clause to insurance should be read with the subsequent clauses in this agreement that refer to insurance on the described premises between the dates of the execution of the agreement and its performance. Section 3 of this chapter considers various insurance problems.

The BUYER shall have the election, at either the original or any extended time for performance, to accept such title as the SELLER can deliver to the said premises in their then condition and to pay therefor the purchase price without deduction, in which case the SELLER shall convey such title, except that in the event of such conveyance in accord with the provisions of this clause, if the said premises shall have been damaged by fire or casualty insured against, then the SELLER shall, unless the SELLER has previously restored the premises to their former condition, either

(a) pay over or assign to the BUYER, on delivery of the deed, all amounts recovered or recoverable on account of such insurance, less any amounts reasonably expended by the SELLER for any partial restoration, or

(b) if a holder of a mortgage on said premises shall not permit the insurance proceeds or a part thereof to be used to restore the said premises to their former condition or to be so paid over or assigned, give to the BUYER a credit against the purchase price, on delivery of the deed, equal to said amounts so recovered or recoverable and retained by the holder of the said mortgage less any amounts reasonably expended by the SELLER for any partial restoration.

The acceptance of a deed by the BUYER or his nominee as the case may be, shall be deemed to be a full performance and discharge of every agreement and obligation herein contained or expressed, except such as are, by the terms hereof, to be performed after the delivery of said deed.

To enable the SELLER to make conveyence as herein provided, the SELLER may, at the time of delivery of the deed, use the purchase money or any portion thereof to clear the title of any or all encumbrances or interests, provided that all instruments so procured are recorded simultaneously with the delivery of said deed.[14]

Until the delivery of the deed, the SELLER shall maintain insurance on said premises as follows:

	Type of Insurance	*Amount of Coverage*
(a)	Fire	$120,000
(b)	Extended coverage	
(c)	[*list any additional type of insurance and amounts as agreed*]	

14. In Greenberg v. Lannigan, 263 Mass. 594, 161 N.E. 882 (1928), the court held that the seller had defaulted when he did not have money of his own sufficient to discharge a mortgage on the land in question, even though he had in his possession a discharge of the mortgage which he was authorized to record as soon as he received the purchase price. In view of this decision, the need for a provision allowing the seller to use the purchase money to discharge encumbrances is obvious if the seller is to be protected. See American Law of Property §11.49 (Casner ed. 1952).

Unless otherwise notified in writing by the BUYER at least seven days before the time for delivery of the deed, and unless prevented from doing so by the refusal of the insurance company(s) involved to issue the same, the SELLER shall assign such insurance and deliver binders therefor in proper form to the BUYER at the time for performance of this agreement. In the event of refusal by the insurance company(s) to issue the same, the SELLER shall give notice thereof to the BUYER at least two business days before the time for performance of this agreement.[15]

Collected rents, mortgage interest, prepaid premiums on insurance if assigned as herein provided, water and sewer use charges, operating expenses (if any) according to the schedule attached hereto or set forth below, and taxes for the then current year, shall be apportioned and fuel value shall be adjusted, as of the day of performance of this agreement and the net amount thereof shall be added to or deducted from, as the case may be, the purchase price payable by the BUYER at the time of delivery of the deed. Uncollected rents for the current rental period shall be apportioned if and when collected by either party.[16]

If the amount of said taxes is not known at the time of the delivery of the deed, they shall be apportioned on the basis of the taxes assessed for the preceding year, with a reapportionment as soon as the new tax rate and valuation can be ascertained; and, if the taxes which are to be apportioned shall thereafter be reduced by abatement, the amount of such abatement, less the reasonable cost of obtaining the same, shall be apportioned between the parties, provided that neither party shall be obligated to institute or prosecute proceedings for an abatement unless herein otherwise agreed.

A broker's fee for professional services of [*insert amount of fee*] is due from the SELLER to [*insert name of broker*], the Broker(s) herein, but if the SELLER pursuant to the terms of clause 22[17] hereof retains the deposits made hereunder by the BUYER, said Broker(s) shall be entitled to receive from the SELLER an amount equal to one-half the amount so retained or an amount equal to the broker's fee for professional services, according to this contract, whichever is the lesser.

The Broker(s) named herein [*insert name of broker*] warrant(s) that he (they) is (are) duly licensed as such by the Commonwealth of Massachusetts.

---

15.   Do you see the possible advantage to the buyer of getting an assignment of the existing policies of the seller rather than procuring new policies?

16.   So much of this provision as deals with the collection of rents is not relevant unless the land involved is leased. If it is leased, however, Section 3 of this chapter brings out the necessity of an adequate provision concerning the apportionment of rent.

17.   Clause 22 is the subsequent clause in the agreement that deals with the rights of the seller in the event of the buyer's default.

All deposits made hereunder shall be held by the broker(s) [*insert name of broker*] as agent for the SELLER, subject to the terms of this agreement and shall be duly accounted for at the time for performance of this agreement.

If the BUYER shall fail to fulfill the BUYER'S agreements herein, all deposits made hereunder by the BUYER shall be retained by the SELLER as liquidated damages unless within thirty days after the time for performance of this agreement or any extension hereof, the SELLER otherwise notifies the BUYER in writing.

The BUYER agrees to buy from the SELLER the articles of personal property enumerated on the attached list for the price of [insert amount of price] and the SELLER agrees to deliver to the BUYER upon delivery of the deed hereunder, a warranty bill of sale therefor on payment of said price. The provisions of this clause shall constitute an agreement separate and apart from the provisions herein contained with respect to the real estate, and any breach of the terms and conditions of this clause shall have no effect on the provisions of this agreement with respect to the real estate.[18]

The SELLER'S spouse hereby agrees to join in said deed and to release and convey all statutory and other rights and interests in said premises.[19]

The broker(s) named herein, join(s) in this agreement and become(s) a party hereto, in so far as any provisions of this agreement expressly apply to him (them), and to any amendments or modifications of such provisions to which he (they) agree(s) in writing.

If the SELLER or BUYER executes this agreement in a representative or fiduciary capacity, only the principal or the estate represented shall be bound, and neither the SELLER or BUYER so executing, nor any shareholder or beneficiary of any trust, shall be personally liable for any obligation, express or implied, hereunder.[20]

The buyer acknowledges that the buyer has not been influenced to enter into this transaction nor has he relied upon any warranties or representations not set forth or incorporated in this agreement or previously made in writing, except the following additional warranties and representations, if any, made by either the seller or the brokers:[21]

---

18. It is important that the amount of the purchase price for personal property that is sold with the house be separately negotiated. The basis to the buyer for income tax purposes of the purchased real property will be the amount paid for the real property, and the gain to the seller for the sale of the real property will be determined by the amount paid for the real property.

19. If dower has been abolished or limited to property owned by the deceased spouse at the time the deceased spouse dies, there may be nothing for the seller's spouse to release.

20. This clause protects a fiduciary from personal liability.

21. This clause would protect the seller from any implied warranty, such as an implied warranty of habitability.

This instrument, executed in triplicate [*or in any other number which may be required*] is to be construed as a Massachusetts contract, is to take effect as a sealed instrument, sets forth the entire contract between the parties, is binding upon and enures to the benefit of the parties hereto and their respective heirs, devisees, executors, administrators, successors and assigns, and may be cancelled, modified or amended only by a written instrument executed by both the SELLER and the BUYER. If two or more persons are named herein as BUYER their obligations hereunder shall be joint and several. The captions and marginal notes are used only as a matter of convenience and are not to be considered a part of this agreement or to be used in determining the intent of the parties to it.[22]

The initialed riders, if any, attached hereto, are incorporated herein by reference.

S. B.	*A. B.*
Husband or Wife of Seller	Seller
Husband or Wife of Buyer	Buyer
	[23]
Broker	

Note: The Closing

General Instructions

(These instructions are suggestions only.)

1. Prepare agreement in quadruplicate if buyer intends to apply for VA-guaranteed or FHA-insured loan; otherwise in triplicate.
2. Any lists or schedules to be attached should be properly incorporated by reference and initialed by all parties concerned.
3. The agreement, in its printed form, may not be suitable for use by trustees or other fiduciaries unless amended.
4. Each party should bring that party's agreement with him or her when passing title.

---

22.   The captions and marginal notes of the sample contract have not been reproduced.

23.   If the contract of sale is not recorded, a bona fide purchaser of the land will cut off the buyer's interest in the land. The buyer will have to be content with his remedy against the seller for breach of the contract. Why should the seller normally be unwilling to have the contract recorded? In answering this question, consider Mass. Gen. Laws Ann. ch. 184, §17A, which provides in part as follows:

Instructions to the Seller

After the agreement has been executed by all parties, arrange at once for drawing the deed and assigning insurance and obtaining binders if insurance is to be transferred.

Bring at the appointed time to the place designated for completing the transaction:

1. The deed signed by you and your spouse, properly acknowledged before a notary and, if registered land, the owner's certificate of title.
2. A list of tenants and lessees, with a statement of amount of rents and the dates to which the rents are paid.
3. All leases on the premises and tenancy-at-will agreements; also, all permits you have for the use of the premises.
4. If buyer has agreed to purchase insurance, all insurance policies (some or all of the policies may be in the custody of the holder of the mortgage on said premises; if so, obtain certificates of such policies from your insurance agent in advance); receipted insurance bills or a statement from the insurance agent that premiums are paid in full; and assignments of seller's insurance to buyer and binders from your insurance agent in favor of the buyer.
5. Receipted bills for taxes for the last two years and all bills for taxes for the current year, whether receipted or not.
6. Water bills for the period of one year next preceding the time of performance.
7. Receipt for your last payment of interest on the mortgage, the mortgage passbook and, if any reduction has been made in the principal of the mortgage, a statement from the holder thereof showing how much is due.
8. If an existing mortgage on said premises is to be discharged, be sure to have the mortgage note available for cancellation in addition to the discharge.
9. Guarantees for roof, sidewalls, plumbing, heating, or other fixtures.
10. Documentary stamps (federal and state). (*No federal stamps have been required since January 1, 1968.*)

. . . No agreement for the purchase and sale of real estate which is recorded shall have any effect as against persons other than the parties thereto after the expiration of a period of ninety days from the date provided for the delivery of the deed by such agreement, or by such agreement as extended, as the case may be, unless prior to the expiration of such period an action or suit shall have been commenced to enforce such agreement.

You will notice that there is no acknowledgment to the contract. Mass. Gen. Laws Ann. ch. 184, §17A, provides in part as follows: "No agreement for the purchase and sale of real estate or any extension thereof shall be received for record in any registry of deeds unless such agreement or extension thereof is acknowledged by the parties agreeing to sell such real estate or one of them."

Instructions to the Buyer

If you are giving a mortgage, your spouse must join in signing it and so should be present at time of passing title. Bring at the appointed time to the place designated for completing the transaction:

1. A certified or bank's check (if acceptable to the seller) drawn payable to your order and $100 in cash, the total amount to equal the amount of payment to be made at time of passing title.
2. Sufficient additional cash to pay for apportionment of rents, taxes, water rates, insurance premiums, and other adjustments, attorney's bill, plot plans, and recording fees.

It is customary for the buyer to pay for drawing any mortgage given by the buyer and fees for recording the buyer's deed and purchase money mortgage. The buyer also pays for examination of title and for tax collector's report showing whether there are any municipal liens or unpaid taxes.

SECHREST v. SAFIOL

— Mass. — , 419 N.E.2d 1384 (1981)

HENNESSEY, C.J.

In this contract action, Robert C. Sechrest seeks to retain a $3,800 deposit made by George E. Safiol as the buyer under a purchase and sale agreement. A District Court judge ordered that the deposit be returned to Safiol. Sechrest requested a report to the Appellate Division of the District Courts, which dismissed the report, and he now appeals to this court pursuant to G.L. c. 231, §109.

The District Court judge made the following findings of fact. On September 20, 1977, the parties signed a purchase and sale agreement under which Safiol agreed to buy from Sechrest a vacant lot in Wellesley, upon which Safiol planned to build a single-family dwelling. Safiol made a deposit of $3,800. At Safiol's request, the date for performance was extended three times, from October 21, 1977, to December 9, 1977; Safiol was told no further extensions would be allowed. On December 9, 1977, Safiol notified Sechrest that he was terminating the agreement in accordance with the provisions of paragraph thirty-one of the purchase and sale agreement. That paragraph provides that [t]he BUYER'S obligations under this agreement are conditioned upon BUYER obtaining from the proper public authorities all permits and other approvals reasonably necessary, in the judgment of BUYER'S attorneys, for construction of a single family residence, similar to those in the neighborhood, on the land being purchased under this agreement. If the BUYER has not obtained all such permits and approvals, with appeal periods, if any, having expired, on or before October 14, 1977 [extended, by agreement, to December 9, 1977], then at the BUYER'S option all payments made hereunder by the BUYER shall be refunded forthwith and all other obligations of the parties hereto shall cease and this agreement shall be void and without recourse to the parties hereto.

Safiol never submitted any building plans or any application for a building permit to the town of Wellesley; nor did he seek any other town approval necessary for the construction of a single-family dwelling. He did have an architect prepare preliminary drawings, which he submitted for a price estimate to the builder he had chosen. In November, 1977, the builder informed Safiol that he would not be available for the construction. Safiol obtained estimates from other builders but did not select a builder and never completed the final plans.

The judge allowed Sechrest's request for ruling that "[w]here conditions relate to a Buyer's performance under a real estate Purchase & Sale Agreement, Buyer is obliged to use good faith and to take steps to attempt to fulfill such conditions and cannot seize upon his own inaction as the basis for terminating on the ground of nonfulfillment." The judge found that Safiol had acted in good faith, had made all reasonable efforts to obtain final plans, and had taken reasonable steps to comply with the terms of the agreement. He therefore ordered that the deposit be returned to Safiol. The Appellate Division considered the question whether reasonable effort was employed to be a question of fact and concluded that the judge's findings were not plainly wrong.

At issue here is the import of the contractual provision conditioning the buyer's performance on his "obtaining from the proper public authorities all [necessary] permits and other approvals." Sechrest contends that this provision requires the buyer to take steps reasonably calculated to obtain the necessary approval. Such steps should include some interaction with the public authorities, argues Sechrest, and as Safiol never even attempted to secure the necessary permits and approval, the judge erred in concluding that Safiol had taken reasonable steps to comply with the agreement.

Safiol urges us to abide by the language of the contractual provision, which does not expressly require the buyer to try to obtain any permit or approval. We reject such a literal interpretation. The apparent purpose of the provision in the purchase and sale agreement was to give the buyer the power to terminate the agreement in the event he was unable to obtain the necessary approval from the town. The provision cannot be viewed as creating a mere option in the buyer to purchase without any requirement of affirmative action on his part. Necessarily implied in the provision is an obligation to use reasonable efforts to obtain town approval. See Stabile v. McCarthy, 336 Mass. 399, 402-403, 145 N.E.2d 821 (1957). *Stabile* involved a purchase and sale provision conditioning the buyer's performance on his ability to secure the approval of the town planning board for his proposed subdivision. We there observed that "[i]t must have been contemplated that [the buyer] would prepare a plan conforming . . . to the basic applicable zoning laws and planning board regulations, and that he would try reasonably to obtain planning board approval . . . prior to the date set for the conveyance. Under the circumstances, the special provision implied that the [buyer] must do *at least this much,* before the condition precedent . . . to cancellation would be satisfied" (emphasis added). Id. at 403, 145 N.E.2d 821. The quantum of effort required on the part of the buyer was said to be "activity reasonably calculated to obtain the approval by action or expenditure not disproportionate in the circumstances." Id. at 404, 145 N.E.2d 821.

In *Stabile,* the buyer had prepared a working plan of the proposed subdivision and had spoken with various public officials, but had made no formal application to the planning board for approval of the plan. Characterizing the buyer's efforts as "at most preliminary and indecisive," we concluded that "[t]he evidence falls short of showing that filing and prosecution of an application and plan prepared with reasonable ingenuity would not have resulted in eventual approval, and would have been an empty gesture." Id. at 406, 145 N.E.2d 821. The facts found by the judge here compel us to reach the same conclusion.

As the evidence was insufficient to warrant a finding that Safiol had made reasonable efforts to obtain approval, the contractual condition allowing the buyer to terminate the agreement was not satisfied, and Sechrest had the right to retain the deposit. See Berger v. Siegel, 329 Mass. 74, 78, 106 N.E.2d 429 (1952); King v. Milliken, 248 Mass. 460, 463, 143 N.E. 511 (1924). The order of the Appellate Division dismissing the report is reversed, the finding for Safiol is vacated, and judgment is to be entered for Sechrest.

So ordered.

SECTION 2.   MARKETABLE TITLE[24]

Note: Implied Warranties

In this introduction, we distinguish between implied warranties in (1) a conveyance and (2) in a contract to convey.

Conveyance. If V executes and delivers a deed conveying Blackacre to P, normally there is no warranty of title except as such a warranty is expressed in the deed. Therefore, in any conveyancing transaction, one question always is: What warranties, if any, are to appear in the deed? Also, precisely what do they warrant against? This subject is dealt with in Chapter 27, Section 4, Covenants for Title. (Note a contrast. If V sells an automobile to P, there is an implied warranty that V owns the automobile. Thus, in this

---

24. See generally American Law of Property §§11.47-11.52 (Casner ed. 1952). See also the comments regarding marketable title legislation at pages 680-681, *supra* and at page 840, footnote 20, *infra.*

respect, there is a very real difference between transactions in real estate and transactions in personalty.)

Contract to convey. If V contracts to convey Blackacre to P and nothing is said about what title V must have in order to comply with the contract, it is held that V must have a "marketable" title. Many contracts specify that the vendor must have a marketable title, but in this they merely express what would otherwise be implied. There is an immense body of law on what constitutes marketability. Plainly, the word means that V must have something more than a title which will stand up if litigated, for, as the expression goes, the purchaser "does not want to buy a lawsuit." The problems in this section undertake to apply the test of marketability to various common situations.

Problems

25.1. V contracts to sell Blackacre to P. Two weeks later V executes and delivers a conveyance, and P pays the purchase price. The deed contains no warranties of title. V's title was defective; consequently, P is ejected by O, the true owner.

    a. Has P any redress against V?

    b. Suppose the contract had called upon V to convey "a sound and marketable title." Would P have any redress?

See American Law of Property §12.124 (Casner ed. 1952).

25.2. In Messer-Johnson Realty Co. v. Security Savings & Loan Co., 208 Ala. 541, 94 So. 734 (1922), the court recognized that a title acquired by adverse possession could be a "good and merchantable title," but, to establish a marketable title by adverse possession, the burden of proof is on the vendor, not only to show adverse possession but to make it clear that the purchaser will have the means at hand at all times to establish title, if it should be attacked by a third person. How can the vendor meet this test?

25.3. What significance, if any, should be attached to a willingness on the part of the vendor to indemnify the purchaser against loss due to the defects which the purchaser alleges make the title unmarketable?

25.4. V contracts to sell Blackacre to P. P discovers a mortgage on Blackacre executed by X, a previous owner, in favor of M. This mortgage has not been released of record. The mortgagee, however, is dead, and the mortgagee's estate finally settled. Though no definite proof can be presented, all indications point to the fact that the mortgage has been satisfied. P refuses to go through with the contract because P claims the title is not marketable. V brings a suit for specific performance against P, offering to leave in the hands of the purchaser, until the alleged cloud can be removed, an amount of the purchase money sufficient to indemnify P against any claim that might be made under the mortgage. Should the court decree specific performance? See Rifle v. Lybarger, 49 Ohio St. 422, 31 N.E. 768 (1892). See also American Law of Property §§11.49, 11.69 (Casner ed. 1952).

Note: Language in the Contract Which May Call for More or Less Than a "Marketable" Title

In the form of contract for the sale of land which appears in Section 1, the seller undertakes to convey "a good and clear record and marketable title." Plainly, this is a more stringent requirement than is contained in the word "marketable" alone. The evidences of title must be found in the registry of deeds and its attendant facilities, such as the registry of probate. (Of course, the offices which perform these functions are given different names in various states.) The principal difference made by the additional requirement of a "record" title is that the vendor cannot present a title dependent in any way upon adverse possession unless litigation has established the effectiveness of the adverse possession.[25]

In negotiating the lease which appears in Chapter 23, counsel for the lessee insisted upon a title upon which a particular insurance company would issue title insurance. This, too, is a common provision. And there are some others. Examine the following problems with a view to determining how much more or less than a "marketable" title each contract calls for.

Problems

25.5. V contracts to sell Blackacre to P. The contract contains no specific provision requiring the vendor to supply a marketable title. The contract, however, does provide that V is to convey the land by a quitclaim deed (one in which the grantor does not covenant against defects in the title but only conveys whatever right, title, and interest the grantor has). P refuses to perform, and V sues for specific performance. Is the defense that the title is not marketable available to P? See McManus v. Blackmarr, 47 Minn. 331, 50 N.W. 230 (1891); Wallach v. Riverside Bank, 206 N.Y. 434, 100 N.E. 50 (1912).

25.6. V contracts to sell Blackacre to P. The contract provides that the purchaser is to receive a title insured by a title company and free from all encumbrances. The title company refuses to commit itself as to the marketability of the title but nevertheless is willing to issue an insurance policy for the purchase price. It is established that there are private easements in a public street abutting the property which affect the marketability of the title.

---

25. "It is quite as true that, if the contract calls for something more or other than a 'marketable' title, the courts cannot substitute a different contract therefor. Page v. Greeley, 75 Ill. loc. cit. 405, 406. The great weight of authority supports the rule that an abstract is an epitome of the record evidence of title; that a contract calling 'for an abstract showing good title' calls for record evidence; that nothing less will 'satisfy the condition no matter what the vendor's real title might be'; that 'it is not sufficient that the title is good in fact—that is, capable of being made good by the production of affidavits or other oral testimony; it must be good of record'; that in such case title by adverse possession will not suffice" (Danzer v. Moerschel, 214 S.W. 849, 849 (Mo. 1919)).

P refuses to perform the contract. V sues for specific performance. P sets up as a defense that the title is not marketable. V claims that the contract only requires that V furnish a title which a title company will insure. Should the court decree specific performance? See New York Investors, Inc., v. Manhattan Beach Bathing Parks Corp., 229 A.D. 593, 243 N.Y.S. 548 (1930).

25.7. V contracts to sell Blackacre to P. The contract provides that the vendor is to furnish a title satisfactory to the purchaser's attorney. Should this provision be construed to mean anything different than that the vendor is to furnish a marketable title? See Church v. Shanklin, 95 Cal. 626, 30 P. 789 (1892); Singleton v. Cuttino, 105 S.C. 44, 89 S.E. 385 (1916).

Note: *Judicial Decision That Title Is Marketable and Protection Such Decision Gives the Purchaser*

If the purchaser under a contract for the sale of land refuses to perform the contract on the ground that the title is not marketable, the purchaser is contending that a third person has rights in the land which would prevent the transfer by the vendor of a clear title. If the vendor succeeds in an action for specific performance of the contract, the court is deciding that the title is marketable without the third person being a party to the lawsuit. Is the third person bound by such lawsuit?

If the issue that determines whether the third person has any rights in the land raises a question of law, the decision on the question of law by the court in the specific performance action becomes a precedent on that legal issue, and the third person would have to get the court to overrule such prededent in order to establish a claim that turned on a different conclusion as to such legal issue.

If the issue that determines whether the third person has any rights in the land turns on a question of fact, the third person is entitled to a day in court to present evidence regarding the factual issue. The conclusion reached in the specific performance action that the title is marketable is a decision on the factual issue against the third person. Should the purchaser be required to go forward when the third person may assert a claim and convince a court that the factual issue should be decided differently than in the specific performance action to which the third person was not a party? If the purchaser in the specific performance action can prevent the enforcement of the contract by merely raising a factual issue on which a third person's claim could be based, the contract of sale is not worth the paper it is written on. Yet the purchaser should not be forced to buy a lawsuit.

Even if a right in a third person is recognized, it may be so insignificant in relation to the land involved that a willing purchaser would not be deterred in going forward with the contract. In this situation, should the marketable title requirement be deemed to be satisfied?

Consider the following problems in the light of the comments in this Note.

Problems

25.8. In Lynbrook Gardens, Inc. v. Ullman, 291 N.Y. 472, 53 N.E.2d 353 (1943), the vendor obtained title to the land in question in a proceeding to foreclose a tax lien on the land. The purchaser, under the contract of sale with the vendor, refused to accept title on the ground that the tax law which authorized proceedings in rem for the enforcement of the tax lien was unconstitutional because it did not provide for personal service; hence the law deprived the owner of the owner's property without due process of law, in violation of the constitutions of the state of New York and of the United States. If the New York court decides the issue of constitutionality in favor of the vendor's title, is there any risk to the purchaser as far as the constitutional issue is concerned in going forward with the contract?

25.9. V contracts to sell Blackacre to P. The contract provides that V is to convey a good and clear title. P refuses to perform the contract, giving as the reason that V's grantor advised P not to proceed with the purchase because V had acquired the title by fraud. You are the attorney for V. V claims that the title was not acquired fraudulently. What is your advice to V? See First African Methodist Episcopal Society v. Brown, 147 Mass. 296, 17 N.E. 549 (1888). See also American Law of Property §§11.68, 11.69 (Casner ed. 1952); id. §18.7.

25.10. V contracts to sell Blackacre to P. The contract provides that V is to convey a good and marketable title. P's investigation of the title discloses that in the year 1834 a deed to Blackacre was executed, which deed provided that if at any time "the grantee, his heirs or assigns, should permit upon the premises a cemetery, slaughterhouse, manufactory of gun powder, glue, varnish, vitriol, turpentine, a tannery, blacksmith shop, forge, or furnace, then said premises and every part thereof shall revert to the grantor and his heirs." Blackacre never has been used in violation of the terms of the 1834 deed. Blackacre is now located in a residential area of a city. P refuses to go through with the contract, claiming that V's title is not marketable. V sues for specific performance. Decree for whom and why? See Van Vliet & Place, Inc. v. Gaines, 249 N.Y. 106, 162 N.E. 600 (1928). See also American Law of Property §11.49 (Casner ed. 1952).

25.11. V contracts to sell Blackacre to P for $150,000. P makes a deposit of $1,000. The contract provides that V is to convey a good and marketable title and that P is to report any defects in the title within seven days. Within the time specified, P gives notice of rescission and demands the return of his $1,000, claiming that the building on Blackacre encroached upon the public street in front of the land and that the title was consequently defective. It is agreed that the building does encroach upon the public street to the extent of two inches. V refuses to return P's $1,000, and P brings an action to rescind the contract and obtain the return of the initial payment. The court concludes that the encroachment of the building would give the city no right to have it removed and that the owner could not be required to pay more than nominal damages. Having come to this conclusion, should the court refuse to give P the requested relief? See Mertens v. Berendsen, 213 Cal. 111, 1 P.2d 440 (1931). See also American Law of Property §§11.48, 11.49, 11.70, 11.78 (Casner ed. 1952); id. §18.7.

Note: The Vendor's Title in an Installment Land Contract

In some jurisdictions, the contract of sale is used as an instrumentality for the long-range financing of the purchase of land. When so used, we refer to the arrangement as an *installment land contract.* Under such a contract, the purchaser goes into possession immediately and is obligated to pay specified installments of the purchase price from time to time, the deed from the vendor to be delivered upon the completion of such payments. The vendor's security comes from the right to retake the land on the failure of the purchaser to meet the installment payments. This means that the purchaser's default subjects the purchaser to rather harsh treatment because the purchaser loses not only the land but the payments already made. The harshness of this treatment has caused legislation to be passed in some states designed to soften the blow to the purchaser as a result of default.[26] It should be obvious to you that the installment land contract is similar to the conditional sale of personal property, previously considered.[27] In Chapter 26, we consider the mortgage, which is the more common method of financing the purchase of land, and you should compare that method with the installment land contract.

When the installment land contract is used, considerable time may elapse between the execution of the contract and final performance by the vendor. Should the purchaser be under obligation to continue payments under the contract if the purchaser can show that the vendor does not have a marketable title? Here the purchaser may suffer serious loss if he or she is obligated to continue the payments and the vendor is unable to perform when the payments are completed. The following case deals with this problem.

---

26. See Note, Installment Land Contracts: Legislative Protection of Defaulting Purchasers, 52 Harv. L. Rev. 129 (1938). See also American Law of Property §11.78 (Casner ed. 1952); id. §16.20.

27. See page 147 *supra.*

LUETTE v. BANK OF ITALY NATIONAL TRUST & SAVINGS ASSOCIATION

42 F.2d 9 (9th Cir. 1930)

KERRIGAN, J.

This is an appeal from an order dismissing a third amended and supplemental bill of complaint and from the decree of dismissal entered thereon.

The complaint alleges that the plaintiffs entered into a contract in June, 1926, with the predecessor in interest of the defendant for the purchase of a certain parcel of real property. The purchase price was $6,500, $1,625 of which was paid at the time of the execution of the contract. The balance was to be paid in monthly installments, which plaintiffs paid to July, 1928; the complaint showing that such payments would continue to May, 1933, under the contract. Plaintiffs allege in effect, construing all of the allegations as to defendant's title together, that defendant has record title to the property in question, and that an adverse claim has been asserted through the filing of homestead claims upon the theory that title to the land is in the United States, the outcome of which claims is uncertain; the matter being now before the Department of the Interior on appeal. It may be fairly concluded from the description of the present state of these homestead proceedings that the decision in the first instance in the Land Office was unfavorable to the homestead right, and that the appeal is that of the claimants; in other words, that the Land Office has held that the land in question is not part of the public domain.

Plaintiffs allege that, on discovery of the existence of the homestead claims, they demanded of defendant that it exhibit its title, and offered, if and when defendant should do so, to pay the amount due under the contract, but that defendant has refused to exhibit its title and, on demand, has refused to repay to plaintiffs the sums already paid upon the contract. The prayer of the complaint is that defendant be enjoined from canceling the contract of plaintiffs and forfeiting plaintiffs' rights thereunder, and that plaintiffs be relieved from paying further installments pending the outcome of the proceedings before the Department of the Interior. Plaintiffs further pray that, in the event the court is unable to grant the relief prayed for, the contract between plaintiffs and defendant be rescinded, and that plaintiffs have judgment for the moneys already paid under the contract. In seeking to rescind, plaintiffs allege that the only thing of value received by them is the contract of sale itself, which they tender.

In considering whether this complaint states a cause of action, its aspect as a bill for an injunction must be disregarded, as plaintiffs state no ground for the intervention of equity to preserve all of their rights under the contract pending the determination of defendant's title, while at the same time relieving them from the duty of performing their part of the bargain. There is no allegation that defendant is, or is likely to become, insolvent, nor any pleading of other equities to justify such relief. The question therefore is whether the complaint states grounds for rescission of the contract.

The vendees under an executory contract here seek to rescind on account of an uncertainty as to the state of the vendor's title, at a time long prior to the date when the vendor will be required to convey title under the installment contract. The complaint shows that the plaintiffs attempted to put the vendor in default by demanding that the title be exhibited and tendering the balance due. The rule has long been settled in California that there can be no rescission by a vendee of an executory contract of sale merely because of lack of title in the vendor prior to the date when performance is due. Joyce v. Shafer, 97 Cal. 335, 32 P. 320; Shively v. Semi-Tropic Land & Water Co., 99 Cal. 259, 33 P. 848; Brimmer v. Salisbury, 167 Cal. 522, 140 P. 30. And the vendee cannot place the vendor in default by tendering payment and demanding a deed in advance of the time and under circumstances not contemplated by the contract. Garberino v. Roberts, 109 Cal. 126, 41 P. 857; Hanson v. Fox, 155 Cal. 106, 99 P. 489, 20 L.R.A. (N.S.) 338, 132 Am. St. Rep. 72. In the present case the pleading does not show the vendor to be in default, as under the contract, assuming a defect to exist, the time within which title must be perfected does not expire until May, 1933.

In this connection an attempt is made to strengthen plaintiffs' positions by averring that, in the event that the homestead claims are allowed and the whole tract in which plaintiffs' lot is situated is declared to be part of the public domain, defendant will be financially unable to procure title to the whole tract, and hence can never perform its obligation to convey title to plaintiffs. The whole tract contains over 16,000 acres. Plaintiffs' lot comprises about one-fourth of an acre. The complaint does not show that defendant would be unable, for financial or other reasons, to procure title to the one-fourth acre which it has contracted to convey to plaintiffs and with which alone plaintiffs are concerned.

There remains to be considered the question as to whether certain allegations of fraud bring this case within the rule that, even though the vendor is not in default, the vendee may rescind an executory contract for material fraudulent misrepresentations of the vendor as to a matter of title upon which the vendee was justified in relying. Crane v. Ferrier-Brock Development Co., 164 Cal. 676, 130 P. 429; Brimmer v. Salisbury, 167 Cal. 522, 530, 140 P. 30. Plaintiffs allege that they are inexperienced in business and relied upon the defendant for fair treatment, being accustomed to put complete trust in and rely upon banks and bankers. The latter allegation is insufficient to establish a fiduciary relationship between plaintiffs and defendant, as there is no suggestion that defendant voluntarily assumed a relation of personal confidence with plaintiffs. Ruhl v. Mott, 120 Cal. 668, 53 P. 304. The parties to the contract must therefore be regarded as having dealt at arm's length. Viewing the pleading in this light and looking to the averments as to the state of the title referred to above, it appears that plaintiffs have not charged defendant with material misrepresentations, unequivocally averred to be false, upon which plaintiffs relied to their injury.

The orders appealed from are affirmed.[28]

Problem

25.12. V contracts to sell Blackacre to P for $5,000. The contract provides that P is to pay $1,000 at the date the contract is executed and $1,000 a year until the balance of the purchase price is paid, at which time V is to deliver a deed to P. Two years after the contract is executed, V mortgages Blackacre to M to secure an indebtedness in the amount of $4,000, which is due in five years. M acquires the mortgage in good faith and without notice of P's rights under the contract, and under these circumstances in the local jurisdiction, M's mortgage prevails over P. P, as soon as P learns of the mortgage to M, comes to you and asks whether the contract can be rescinded and the money already paid returned. What would be your advice if the local jurisdiction follows Luette v. Bank of Italy National Trust & Savings Association? See Miswald-Wilde Co. v. Armory Realty Co., 210 Wis. 53, 243 N.W. 492 (1933).

SECTION 3. STATUS OF THE VENDOR AND THE PURCHASER (HEREIN EQUITABLE CONVERSION)[29]

Note: The Consequences of Specific Enforceability of a Contract for the Sale of Land

When V contracts to convey Blackacre to P at a named future date, upon the payment of a named price, the contract is specifically enforceable in a court applying equitable principles. This results in

a. P having a present equitable title, and

b. an "equitable conversion" of V's land ownership into personalty and of P's contract right into realty.

This introduction undertakes to explain how these phenomena occur and how they affect the rights of various persons.

---

28. Cf. Bishop v. McIntosh, 282 Ill. App. 639 (1935) (abstract decision), commented on in 2 John Marshall L.Q. 99 (1936). See also American Law of Property §§11.49, 11.70 (Casner ed. 1952).—Eds.

29. See generally American Law of Property §§11.22-11.35 (Casner ed. 1952).

Specific enforceability. Where V contracts with P to convey land at a certain price and either party defaults, the other party can maintain an action for damages. However, courts of equity have recognized for centuries that money damages do not provide an adequate remedy to a purchaser if the vendor refuses to convey. Land, it is said, is unique, and there is no assurance that the wronged purchaser can obtain equally satisfactory land with the money collected as damages. Hence, on the traditional ground that the remedy at law is inadequate, equity steps in and requires V to convey upon payment of the stipulated price. Similarly, if P refuses to go through with the contract, equity will require P to do so; the thought is that what V may at some time get on a resale of the land, plus a jury's guess as to the difference between its value and the agreed price, is not an adequate remedy.

The equitable title of the purchaser as against the vendor. "Equity looks upon that as done, which ought to be done," goes the old maxim. Whether or not for this reason, courts applying equitable principles do treat P as owner of the land for many purposes as soon as the contract is made. There are two common types of cases where this may be important: (a) where P injures the land, i.e., commits "waste," and (b) where buildings on the land are damaged by fire or other casualty.

Equitable conversion by contract. A corollary of P's equitable title as against V is that, after the contract is made, P is considered to be an owner of real estate and V is not. This can affect the legal relationships between P and a third person, e.g., taxing authorities; or it can alter the rights of other persons inter sese, e.g., claimants of P's property on death. V's position, after the contract is made, is close to that of a mortgagee; V has a claim against P for the agreed price, secured by V's legal title, which V is not obliged to convey without receiving payment. The case and problems immediately following this Note deal with these matters.

Note that we here speak of equitable conversion *by contract.* This is because there are other situations in which an equitable conversion takes place. For example, if O devises Blackacre to a trustee with a direction to sell the land and distribute the proceeds to A and B, even before the land is sold A and B are considered to have equitable interests in personalty, not in realty. "Equity looks upon that as done, which ought to be done."

CLAPP v. TOWER
11 N.D. 556, 93 N.W. 862 (1903)

YOUNG, J. This is an action to quiet title to a section of land situated in Cass county, which was conveyed to the plaintiff by the executors of the last will and testament of Charlemange Tower, deceased. The complaint alleges that the plaintiff is the owner of said real estate, and that the defendants claim an interest therein adverse to the plaintiff, and prays that they be required to set forth their claims, to the end that their validity may be determined, and that title be quieted in the plaintiff. Defendants, in their answer, allege that they are the next of kin and all of the heirs at law of said Charlemange Tower, deceased, and all the surviving legatees under his will; that said Charlemange Tower died in, and a resident of, the city of Philadelphia, Pa., and that his will was probated there; that the land in question was sold by said deceased to one Hadley upon a contract which provided for the execution and delivery of a deed to him upon the making of certain deferred payments specified in said contract; that subsequent to the death of Charlemange Tower the executors of his will foreclosed said contract by reason of the default of said Hadley in making payments according to its terms, and that said land became a part of the estate of said deceased; that thereafter the executors, acting upon the theory that said land was subject to the principle and rule of equitable conversion, and was for the purposes of administration to be treated as personal property, sold and conveyed the same to the plaintiff, who has ever since been in possession of the same, claiming the ownership and possession thereof by virtue of said deed from said executors; that the defendants are the owners of said real estate by virtue of their heirship, and ask that the title be quieted in them. The plaintiff demurred to the answer upon the ground that it does not state facts sufficient to constitute a defense or counterclaim. The trial court sustained the demurrer, and the defendants appeal from the order sustaining the same.

The will of Charlemange Tower was before this court in the case of Penfield v. Tower, 1 N.D. 216, 46 N.W. Rep. 413. This court held that, so far as its provisions related to real estate situated in this state, it was inoperative and void, and that the real estate of said deceased in this state must be distributed according to the law of succession of this state, and that the personal property should be distributed according to the terms of the will. The only question involved upon the issue raised by the demurrer is whether the land in question should, under the facts pleaded in the answer, be treated as real estate or as personal property. If, for the purposes of administration, it retains the character of real estate, the will not being operative, it descended directly to the heirs, the defendants in this action. This is conceded. If, on the other hand, it is to be considered as personal property, it then went to the executors for the purposes of distribution, and they had full right and authority to sell and convey the same in the manner and form pursued, and to account for the proceeds to the orphans' court of the state of Pennsylvania, from which they received their appointment. It is very properly conceded by both parties that under the rule and doctrine of equitable conversion land may be treated as money and money as land, whenever, in equity, it is proper to invoke and apply the principle of that doctrine. "Equitable conversion is defined as a constructive alteration in the nature of property by which, in equity real estate is regarded as personalty or personal estate as realty." 7 Amer. & Eng. Enc. of Law (2d Ed.) p. 464. And the doctrine has its origin in the maxim of equity that that is regarded as done which should be done. Penfield v. Tower, *supra.* There is no room for doubt that upon the facts pleaded in the defendants' answer the rule of equitable conversion is applicable, and that the execution and delivery of the contract of sale of the real estate in question by Charlemange Tower during his lifetime — and the same was valid and enforceable at the time of his death — worked a conversion of the land into personalty. His interest, after the execution of the contract and at the time of his death, was the money contracted to be paid by the purchaser, and the purchaser's interest was the land contracted to be conveyed. . . .

The real estate in question, having assumed the character of personalty went to the executors, and it continued as personalty for the purposes of administration, so that the executors could, after the cancellation of the contract, sell and convey the same to the plaintiff in the manner and form pursued.

The demurrer to the answer was, therefore, properly sustained, and the order will be affirmed.[30]

Problems

25.13. V contracts to sell Blackacre to P for $10,000. The contract provides that P is to pay $2,000 at the date the contract is executed and $1,000 a year until the balance of the purchase price is paid, at which time V is to deliver a deed to P. Two years after the contract is executed, V marries; one year later, V dies. P to date has performed all of P's obligations under the contract. Is V's spouse entitled to dower in Blackacre? See Newberry Co. v. Shannon, 268 Mass. 116, 167 N.E. 292 (1929).

25.14. V contracts to sell Blackacre to P for $10,000. P is married. P dies. P's executor pays V the $10,000 and receives a deed to Blackacre. The local statute provides that a spouse is entitled to dower in all the lands of which the deceased spouse was seized of an estate of inheritance at any time during marriage. Is P's spouse entitled to dower in Blackacre? See Reed v. Whitney, 73 Mass. 533 (1856); In re Kelleher, 133 Misc. 581, 232 N.Y.S. 680 (Sur. Ct. 1929).[31]

25.15. V, a resident of the state of New Jersey, contracts to sell Blackacre, which is located in the state of Washington, to P, who is also a resident of New Jersey. V dies. The state of Washington claims an inheritance tax on Blackacre under the following statute:

All property within the jurisdiction of this state, and any interest therein, whether belonging to the inhabitants of this state or not, whether tangible or intangible which shall pass by will or by statutes of inheritances of this or any other state . . . shall, for the use of the state, be subject to a tax. . . .

---

30. See the following: Stone, Equitable Conversion by Contract, 13 Colum. L. Rev. 369 (1913); Simpson, Legislative Changes in the Law of Equitable Conversion, 44 Yale L.J. 559, 754 (1935). — Eds.

31. By statute, some states have provided specifically that a spouse is entitled to dower in land which the deceased spouse contracted to buy before the deceased spouse's death.

What argument would you advance against the claim of the state of Washington to an inheritance tax on Blackacre under the above-quoted statute? See In re Eilermann's Estate, 179 Wash. 15, 35 P.2d 763 (1934).

25.16. V enters into an agreement with P with respect to Blackacre under which agreement P is given "the exclusive right or option to purchase Blackacre at any time within 60 days from the date hereof." Within the 60-day period, V dies. V's will provides that all real property shall go to A and all personal property to B. After V's death, but within the 60-day period, P elects to exercise the option. As between A and B, who is entitled to the money received from the sale of Blackacre to P? See Eddington v. Turner, 27 Del. Ch. 411, 38 A.2d 738 (1944).

MOSES BROTHERS v. JOHNSON
88 Ala. 517, 7 So. 146 (1890)

The bill in this case was filed on the 26th August, 1889, by Moses Brothers, suing as partners, against Berry Johnson; and prayed an injunction, to restrain the defendant from cutting timber on a tract of land which the complainants had sold to him, except for repairs, fences, and other necessary purposes. An injunction was granted on the filing of the bill; and after answer filed, the defendant submitted a motion to dissolve it, both for want of equity in the bill, and on the denials of the answer. The court sustained the motion, and dissolved the injunction; and its decree is here assigned as error.

STONE, C.J. — The appellants, who were the complainants, sold one hundred and sixty acres of land to the defendant, at the agreed price of fourteen hundred and forty dollars — nine dollars per acre. Only five dollars of the purchase-money was paid. The balance, including interest, was agreed to be paid in annual installments, running through about five years from the date of the purchase, January 5, 1889. Complainants retained the title, giving Johnson, the purchaser, their obligation to make him title on payment by him of the purchase-money, and accruing taxes. The agreement stipulated further, that if Johnson failed "to pay any of said installments when due," then Moses Brothers "have the right to annul this agreement, and take possession of the premises, and to retain out of the moneys paid under this agreement (by Johnson) sixty dollars per annum as rent of the premises, said amount being hereby agreed and declared by said parties to be the annual rental value of the premises; returning the surplus, if any, to" Johnson.

What we have copied contains every stipulation in the agreement, which sheds any light on Johnson's rights acquired under the purchase. Nothing is said about felling timber, or clearing lands, or of Johnson's right to take and hold possession, farther than is implied in the language copied above. Johnson did take possession immediately after the agreement was executed, and was in possession when this bill was filed, August 26, 1889. No part of the debt for the purchase-money had then matured, and there then remained unpaid about fourteen hundred dollars.

Under our interpretation of the agreement, Johnson had the clear right to enter into possession of the land, and to remain in possession until he made default in the payment of some installment of the purchase-money. On such default, Moses Brothers had the option, secured by the contract, to put an end to the agreement, so far as it evidenced a sale, to convert Johnson's holding into a tenancy ab initio, and to retake possession of the land. This is a right of election reserved for their benefit, and they alone can exercise it. Collins v. Whigham, 58 Ala. 438; Wilkinson v. Roper, 74 Ala. 140.

When a vendor of real estate enters into an executory agreement to convey title on the payment of the purchase-money, he sustains, in substance, the same relation to the vendee, as a mortgagee does to a mortgagor. Each has a legal title, which, in the absence of stipulations for possession, will maintain an action of ejectment. Each can retain his legal title against the other party, until the purchase-money, or mortgage debt, is paid, unless he permits the other to remain in undisturbed possession for twenty years. And yet each is at last but a trustee of the legal title for the mortgagor or vendee, if the purchase-money, or mortgage debt, as the case may be, is paid, or seasonably tendered. The same mutual rights and remedies, legal and equitable, and the same limitation to the right of recovery, obtain in one relation and in the other. — Relfe v. Relfe, 34 Ala. 500; Bizzell v. Nix, 60 Ala. 281; Chapman v. Lee, 64 Ala. 483; Sweeney v. Bixler, 69 Ala. 539.

We have found but a single case precisely like the present one in its facts. In Scott v. Wharton, 2 Hen. & Munf. 25, a sale of land had been made on a credit, and title retained by the vendor. The vendee went into possession, and a bill was filed by the vendor, charging him with committing waste by cutting timber, and praying for an injunction. The court treated the case precisely as if it had been a bill by mortgagee against mortgagor, to restrain him from lessening the security by felling and removing the timber. — Fairbank v. Cudworth, 33 Wis. 358.

We feel safe in holding, that a vendor who sells on credit, retaining the title as security for the purchase-money, sustains the same relation to the vendee, so far as the question of security is concerned, as does the mortgagee to the mortgagor.

In King v. Smith, 2 Hare, 239 — 24 Eng. Ch. Rep. — it was said to be an established rule, "that if the security of the mortgagee is insufficient, and the court is satisfied of that fact, the mortgagor will not be allowed to do that which would directly impair the security — cut timber upon the mortgaged premises. . . . The cases decide, that a mortgagee out of possession is not, of course, entitled to an injunction to restrain the mortgagor from cutting timber on the mortgaged property. If the security is sufficient, the court will not grant an injunction merely because the mortgagor cuts, or threatens to cut timber. There must be a special case made out before the court will interfere. The difficulty is in determining what is meant by a 'sufficient security.' Suppose the mortgage debt, with all the expenses, to be £1,000, and the property to be worth £1,000, that is, in one sense, a sufficient security; but no mortgagee, who is well advised, would lend his money, unless the mortgaged property was worth one-third more than the amount lent at the time of the mortgage." This was considered the rule, and the only safe rule, under English values. In that country, land values were, in a measure, stationary. In this, they are fluctuating. To be a "sufficient security," with us, there should be a much broader margin between the amount of the debt and the estimated value of the property mortgaged for its security, than is considered sufficient in that older country.

This court is fully committed to the same doctrine. In Coker v. Whitlock, 64 Ala. 180, this court ruled, that when the mortgagor is committing waste which impairs the security, or renders it insufficient, chancery, at the suit of the mortgagee, will restrain him by injunction.

The bill charges, and the answer admits, that the land, which is the subject of this suit, is in value not exceeding the sum of the purchase-money that remains unpaid. The bill also charges that the defendant is insolvent. To this charge the answer interposes a general denial, but accompanies it with a statement, as follows:

> This defendant denies that he is insolvent, and avers that he is solvent; that, except the debt he owes for this land, his liabilities are small, and that he owns real estate in his own name, not subject to exemption as a homestead, in Montgomery county, Alabama, that is worth much more than any liabilities or debts he owes, excepting his debt for this land.

We understand this language to mean, that defendant's other property will pay his other debts; but we can not interpret it as affirming that it will pay any certain sum above his other debts. This leaves the land in controversy as the sole security for its promised purchase-money. The bill also charges, that the land lies near the city of Montgomery, where firewood is in demand, and commands ready sale; and that to denude the land of its timber, would greatly diminish its value as a security. The answer admits the truth of each of these averments, except the last, which it denies. It sets up that the land is fertile, and would be made more valuable, if cleared of its timber, and brought under cultivation. This last averment must be treated as affirmative, defensive matter, the proof of which rests with defendant. Such averment, until proved, furnishes no ground for dissolving the injunction. 1 Brick. Dig. 678, Secs. 567-8.

It may be, as contended, that the right to clear the land, sell the timber, and put the land in cultivation, were inducements—controlling inducements—to enter into the purchase. They were not expressed as terms of the contract, and defendant failed to stipulate for any such privilege. Considering the proximity of the land to a market for the firewood — an averment not denied, but admitted — we feel forced to presume, as charged in the bill, that the land is more valuable with the timber on it, than if cleared and put in cultivation. Hence, we hold, that the averment to the effect that the value of the land would be enhanced by clearing it, is affirmative matter, the burden of proving which is on the defendant. We may state here, that injunction is the only relief prayed, and is the only proper relief in a case like the present one.

However it may be made to appear by proof, the pleadings do not make a case for a dissolution of the injunction; and the decretal order dissolving the injunction must be reversed, and the injunction reinstated.

Reversed and rendered.[32]

Problems

25.17. V contracts to sell Blackacre to P for $10,000. The contract provides that P is to pay $2,000 at the date the contract is executed and $1,000 a year until the balance of the purchase price is paid, at which time V is to deliver a deed to P. The contract contains no provision concerning the removal of timber or fixtures. P enters into possession.

a. Two years after the execution of the contract, P begins the systematic removal of timber. V, on the basis of Moses Brothers v. Johnson, obtains an injunction. Prior to the injunction, however, P had removed timber worth $500. Under what circumstances, if any, is V entitled to recover from P the value of the timber removed?

b. One year after the execution of the contract, P builds a garage on Blackacre. Two years later P decides to remove the garage. V learns of P's intentions and brings a bill in equity to enjoin P from so doing. Under what circumstances, if any, should the injunction be issued? See American Law of Property §§11.32, 11.34 (Casner ed. 1952).

25.18. V leased Blackacre to T for five years at a quarterly rental of $675, payable in advance on April 1, July 1, October 1, and January 1 of each year. On March twenty-second of the fourth year of the lease, V contracted to sell Blackacre to P on or before April twenty-second of that year, subject to all the terms of the lease. By agreement between V and P, the deed was actually delivered on May 1 and the purchase money paid. On April 1, T paid to V the quarter's rent then due. P now sues V to recover the quarter's rent paid on April 1. Judgment for whom and why? See Singer v.

---

32. For a consideration of the liability for waste of a vendor who remains in possession, see Note, The Vendor's Liability for Permissive Waste, 48 Harv. L. Rev. 821 (1935).—EDS.

Soloman, 8 Pa. D. 402 (Allegheny County Dist. Ct. 1899). See also American Law of Property §11.25 (Casner ed. 1952).[33]

25.19. V contracts to sell Blackacre to P for $3,000. The contract recites that P is to make a payment of $50 at the time of the contract and to give notes for different sums which equal the balance of the purchase price, the last of these notes to mature in seven years. Upon the payment of the last of these notes, V is to make and deliver to P "a good and sufficient deed, clear of all encumbrances." P is to have possession of the land two years after the date on which the contract is executed. P pays all the notes as they fall due, taking possession of the land at the end of the second year. After the payment of the last note, P ascertains that the taxes on the land have not been paid since the date of the contract. P requests V to pay these back taxes. V refuses to do so. P then comes to you for advice. What advice would you give P? See Miller v. Corey, 15 Iowa 166 (1863). See also American Law of Property §11.35 (Casner ed. 1952).

Note: Controlling the Status of the Vendor and the Purchaser by the Terms of the Contract

A contract for the sale of land may expressly or impliedly solve possible disputes between the vendor and the purchaser. Thus in Moses Brothers v. Johnson, the contract could have been drafted so as to give to the purchaser the right to remove timber. Fixtures placed on the land by the purchaser clearly may be removed if the terms of the contract so provide. If the land involved is leased at the time the contract is executed, the contract may provide that all the rent shall go to the vendor, that all the rent shall go to the purchaser, or that the rent shall be apportioned between them in some designated manner. The burden of paying the real estate taxes which accrue between the date the contract is executed and the delivery of the deed can be placed on either party by the terms of the contract. In other words, in drafting the contract of sale you should attempt to anticipate possible disputes and provide expressly in the contract for their settlement.

You should not assume that the terms of the contract do not settle a particular dispute merely because you do not find a specific provision covering the point involved. A reading of the contract in its entirety may give a basis for implying an understanding between the parties which a court

---

33. It is well settled at common law that rent is not apportionable as to time. This simply means that the one who is the owner of the reversionary interest in the land on the day a rent payment becomes due is entitled to the entire amount of such payment even though he or she has not owned, or does not continue to own, the reversionary interest for all of the period covered by such payment. A typical illustration is as follows: L leases Blackacre to T at a monthly rental, payable in advance. L then transfers to A a life interest. A dies in the middle of a month. L is not entitled to any of the rent for the month in which A dies. The doctrine that rent is not apportionable as to time is followed generally today in the absence of a contrary statute. See American Law of Property §9.44 (Casner ed. 1952).

may recognize as settling the issue. Good drafting, however, does not leave important matters to implication.

Another dispute which may arise between the vendor and the purchaser is, pending the delivery of the deed pursuant to the terms of the contract, which one stands to lose if the property is damaged through no fault of either? This matter, generally referred to as the risk-of-loss problem, can also be controlled by the express terms of the contract. In the absence of a provision in the contract of sale of land regarding the risk of loss, there is a split of authority. Ross v. Bumstead, 65 Ariz. 61, 173 P.2d 765 (1946), is an example of a case that adopts the so-called majority rule that the risk of loss is on the purchaser. Capital Savings & Loan Association v. Convey, 175 Wash. 224, 27 P.2d 136 (1933), espouses the minority view that the risk of loss is on the vendor.[34] It may be that when the risk of loss is on the vendor, the vendor may be able to compel the purchaser to go forward with the contract with an abatement in the purchase price to compensate for the loss. In such case, it may be that the purchaser may enforce the contract with an abatement in the purchase price.

Problems

25.20.   V contracts to sell Blackacre to P for $10,000. The purchase price is to be paid within 90 days. The contract specifically provides that V shall deliver the premises on the payment of the purchase price "in as good a condition as they now are." During the 90-day period the building on Blackacre is destroyed by fire through no fault of either V or P.

   a.   At the end of the 90-day period, V demands $10,000 from P, and P refuses to pay such sum. V brings a suit for specific performance against P. Decree for whom in a jurisdiction which follows Ross v. Bumstead? See Brownell v. Board of Education of the Inside Tax District, 239 N.Y. 369, 146 N.E. 630 (1925).

---

34.   The Uniform Vendor and Purchaser Risk Act provides as follows:

Sec. 1. Risk of Loss.— Any contract hereafter made in this State for the purchase and sale of realty shall be interpreted as including an agreement that the parties shall have the following rights and duties, unless the contract expressly provides otherwise:

   (a)   If, when neither the legal title nor the possession of the subject matter of the contract has been transferred, all or a material part thereof is destroyed without fault of the purchaser or is taken by eminent domain, the vendor cannot enforce the contract, and the purchaser is entitled to recover any portion of the price that he has paid;

   (b)   If, when either the legal title or the possession of the subject matter of the contract has been transferred, all or any part thereof is destroyed without fault of the vendor or is taken by eminent domain, the purchaser is not thereby relieved from a duty to pay the price, nor is he entitled to recover any portion thereof that he has paid.

This act has been adopted in various states without substantial change. For comments on this act, see 51 Harv. L. Rev. 1276 (1938); 5 U. Chi. L. Rev. 260 (1938); 36 Calif. L. Rev. 476 (1948).

b. At the end of the 90-day period, P offers V $10,000 and demands a
deed. V refuses to give P a deed, claiming the contract has been
terminated by virtue of the destruction of the building on the land. It
so happens that V has an opportunity to sell the land in its present
condition at a price higher than the price P agreed to pay for the land
and the building. P brings a suit for specific performance against V.
Decree for whom in a jurisdiction which follows Capital Savings &
Loan Association v. Convey? See Hallett v. Parker, 68 N.H. 598, 39
A. 433 (1896).

25.21.   V contracts to sell Blackacre to P for $10,000. The contract
provides that P is to pay $1,000 at the time the contract is executed and
$1,000 a year until the balance of the purchase price is paid. P takes
possession of Blackacre pursuant to the terms of the contract. A trespasses
on Blackacre while it is in P's possession and removes timber worth $1,000.
P brings an action of trespass against A. Assume you are in a jurisdiction
which follows Capital Savings & Loan Association v. Convey. How much
should P recover? See Lawson v. Helmich, 20 Wash. 2d 167, 146 P.2d 537
(1944).[35]

25.22.   V contracts to sell Blackacre to P. The contract provides that P is
to pay $1,000 at the time the contract is executed and that the balance of the
purchase price is to be paid in 16 annual installments of $660 each and a
final payment of $440. P takes possession of the land pursuant to the terms
of the contract. Prior to the execution of the contract of sale, V had
constructed a pass under the public road which ran through Blackacre. This
underpass was used to take cattle from one part of Blackacre to the other
part. A, an adjoining landowner, destroys this underpass, causing damage
estimated at $250. V sues A for $250. Is V entitled to a judgment for such
sum in a jurisdiction which follows Ross v. Bumstead? In a jurisdiction
which follows Capital Savings & Loan Association v. Convey? See Adams v.
Boone Fiscal Court, 271 Ky. 729, 113 S.W.2d 1 (1937). See also American
Law of Property §11.33 (Casner ed. 1952).

Note: Insurance to Protect Against Loss Between Contract and Conveyance[36]

The vendor and the purchaser must be insurance-minded because it is
through insurance that both can obtain adequate protection against damage
to the buildings in the interval of time between the execution of the contract
and the delivery of the deed.

The vendor's need for insurance coverage is obvious if the local jurisdiction, or a provision of the contract, places on the vendor the risk of loss.

---

35. You should re-examine in connection with this problem the material in Chapter 4.
36. See American Law of Property §11.31 (Casner ed. 1952).

Even if the risk of loss is on the purchaser, the vendor may need insurance protection because the purchaser may not be financially able to go through with the contract, particularly if a substantial part of the premises is destroyed.

The purchaser, of course, needs insurance protection if the risk of loss is on the purchaser. Even if the risk of loss is placed on the vendor, the purchaser may desire to be in a position to choose either to rescind the contract or proceed with the contract by waiving any right to rescind and paying the full purchase price. The purchaser could not very well afford to waive any right to rescind and pay the full purchase price unless he or she had adequate insurance coverage.

Usually the vendor is insured against certain losses at the time the contract is executed. If the vendor has been carrying insurance, does he or she need to worry about insurance protection after the signing of the contract? The answer clearly is yes. The reason for this answer is that most insurance policies provide that the policy shall be void "if the interest of the insured be other than unconditional and sole ownership, or if any change, other than by death of the insured, takes place in the interest, title or possession of the subject of the insurance." As soon as the vendor has signed the contract of sale, is not the policy of insurance void if it contains such terms? As might be expected, the courts have not answered this question uniformly; but the majority have given the answer which is set forth in the following quotation:

> While it may be true in some instances that a vendor, under executory articles of agreement for the sale of property, does not lose the protection of his insurance under such a provision in the policy as is now before us, this is not so where he puts the vendee in possession. Mere executory contracts unaccompanied by any transfer of possession do not constitute such a change as would render the policy void. Where, as here, however, the contract is partially executed, part of the consideration paid and possession delivered to the vendee, the "interest" of the vendor is changed and he can no longer be considered "the sole and unconditional owner" within the intendment of the policy. Unless this status is consented to by the insurer, the insured forfeits his rights under the policy. [Glessner v. Neshannock Mutual Fire Insurance Co., 331 Pa. 439, 443, 1 A.2d 233, 234 (1938).]

Thus the vendor should make proper arrangements with the insurance company before executing the contract of sale, particularly if the purchaser is to take possession of the land.

Suppose the purchaser knows that the vendor has taken proper steps to keep the vendor's insurance in force. May the purchaser safely take no steps to insure? There is authority that, by paying the purchase price in full after damage to the land and reimbursing the vendor for the insurance premiums the vendor has paid, the purchaser may obtain from the vendor any money the latter has collected on an insurance policy. See William Skinner & Sons

Shipbuilding & Drydock Co. v. Houghton, 92 Md. 68, 48 A. 85 (1900). There is also authority the other way. See Comment, Vendor and Purchaser — Risk of Loss — Right to Proceeds of Insurance Policy, 4 Mo. L. Rev. 290 (1939). It is certainly not recommended that the purchaser rely on the vendor's insurance for protection.

In a jurisdiction which does not give the purchaser any right to insurance money collected by the vendor, there is unjust enrichment if the vendor is allowed to obtain the full purchase price and also to retain the insurance money. To avoid this result, after the vendor has received the full purchase price for the land, such jurisdictions allow the insurance company to obtain reimbursement from the vendor. See Castellain v. Preston, 11 Q.B.D. 380 (1883).

One piece of practical advice, however, can be given here. Most of these questions can be effectively disposed of anywhere if, immediately after the contract to sell has been executed, all insurance policies are endorsed to protect both the vendor and the purchaser "as their interests may appear." If the purchaser is a person of good credit in the community, there will seldom be any difficulty in getting the policies so endorsed by the underwriter's local agent almost at once.

Problems

25.23. You are the attorney for P. P is interested in purchasing a tract of land on which is situated a building. P plans to convert the building into a factory. Detailed architects' drawings have been prepared, on the basis of which it is estimated that the renovation of the building will cost $100,000. The cost of tearing down the old building and erecting a new building is estimated at $200,000, $25,000 of which would go to the wrecking of the old building. You know that V has been attempting to sell the land and building for about a year and has had no offer. V is now willing to sell for $50,000. There is no other equally suitable area available for the building of the factory. If V contracts to sell the land, there cannot be delivery of possession for approximately six months because it will take that time for V's business to relocate.

Draft the provision you would attempt to get inserted in the contract of sale with V, covering risk of loss and insurance prior to the time possession is delivered to your client.

25.24. V contracts to sell Blackacre to P. P agrees to pay the purchase price in installments over ten years. P goes into possession. Blackacre is located in a state which has a criminal statute that makes the person "on whose property narcotics are sold" guilty of a crime. P sells narcotics on Blackacre. V is indicted under this statute. What would be your defense? See First State Bank v. United States, 92 F.2d 132 (9th Cir. 1937); 36 Mich. L. Rev. 680 (1938).

Note: Implied Warranty of Habitability in a Contract for the Sale of Land

The development of the implied warranty of habitability in the landlord-tenant area is presented in Chapter 19, Section 2.C, *infra.* Is there any reason a vendor under a contract of sale of residential real estate should not be subject to an implied warranty of habitability with respect to such real estate offered for sale? Should this implied warranty, if it exists, survive the deed conveying the property pursuant to the contract? In regard to the development of such an implied warranty, see Peterson v. Hubschman, 76 Ill. 2d 31, 389 N.E.2d 1154 (1979).

CHAPTER 26

THE MORTGAGE

The four basic documents of commercial transactions in land are the contract of sale, the deed, the lease, and the mortgage. In this casebook the contract (Chapter 25), the deed (Chapter 27), and the lease (Chapter 23) are the subject matter of systematic and consecutive treatment. Mortgages are dealt with at many points in a secondary or incidental manner. So in this chapter we give you a summary statement to assist you in understanding the mortgage aspects of the very numerous cases in which mortgages appear. You will, of course, understand that this is a sketch, not a picture.[1]

SECTION 1. GLOSSARY AND CAST OF CHARACTERS

Let us take a simple transaction.

The owner of land worth $10,000 wants to borrow $6,000; the lender wants security. So the owner — whom we shall call MR for mortgagor — executes a promissory note to ME, the mortgagee, by which MR promises to pay $6,000 to ME, three years from date, with 12 percent interest, payable semiannually.[2] At the same time MR gives to ME a mortgage on the land to

---

1. See generally American Law of Property §§16.1-16.212 (Casner ed. 1952).

2. Of course, if you are borrowing from a bank (or anyone else) you will be presented with a printed form of mortgage, making it easy for you to get your money merely by signing on the dotted line. But wait! Although the bank is big and powerful and you small and weak, nothing says that you have to do as you are told. You want certain types of clauses which may prove distasteful to that smiling officer at "your friendly bank." Examples:

a. A provision that you may pay the principal and discharge the mortgage without penalty after some period, say two years. (Of course what this means is that if interest rates go down you can re-finance with some other bank at a lower interest rate; and this in turn means that your own friendly bank will lower the interest rate to save you the trouble.)

b. Since disaster of some kind may strike (illness, business loss, etc.) it would be well to have a clause providing that after you have lived up to the terms of the mortgage for some

secure the obligations of the note. The mortgage is a document, varying in form according to local law and custom, which gives to ME a claim against the land for repayment of the loan. The mortgage will be recorded in the appropriate registry of deeds. The note will not be recorded since it does not create any interest in land; it is not a document of title but merely a promise. Thus the first point to master is this: the usual modern mortgage transaction involves two documents, (1) the note, a document which establishes an obligation from MR to ME, and (2) the mortgage, a document by which MR gives to ME a security interest in the land to assure performance of the obligation.

At this stage MR is said to hold the "equity" in the land, whereas before giving the mortgage MR held "title." "Equity" is a shortened form of "equity of redemption" and means simply title-subject-to-a-mortgage. We shall later examine the question whether it is accurate to call MR's interest an equity; but there is no question that it is standard terminology.

Transfer of the equity. MR, holding the equity, may want to sell it. If the value of the land is sound, the equity is worth $4,000. MR finds a buyer, whom we shall call PE, for purchaser of equity, and upon payment of $4,000 gives to PE a deed of the land which recites that the land is "subject to a mortgage of $6,000 to ME." Is PE liable on the note for $6,000? Certainly not; PE has made no promise to pay anything to anybody. Only MR is liable. However, ME can enforce ME's security interest in the land — which means in substance that after default ME can compel a sale of the land and take the first $6,000 of the proceeds of sale; and this possibility, as a practical matter, compels PE to pay the $6,000 when it falls due to protect the equity in the land. But suppose ME chooses to collect the note from MR, ignoring ME's rights against the land since MR is perfectly solvent; doesn't this cause a net loss to MR and give a windfall profit to PE? It would, were it not for the doctrine of subrogation which we shall later discuss.

Since the three-party situation involving MR, ME, and PE causes difficulties by separating the obligation on the note and the ownership of the equity, MR usually tries to have PE assume the personal obligation of the note at the time PE buys the equity — i.e., MR tries to get PE to promise to pay the note and to save MR harmless. Better still MR tries to arrange a novation by which MR is released from the obligation on the note and PE becomes sole obligor. Thus, to summarize, where MR sells the equity to PE the transaction usually takes one of three forms:

---

period, say two years, you will be given a period of grace of, say six months, if you should default on interest and tax payments.

c. You may want to make additions to the house, shift from oil to electric heating, or refurnish the house. It would be nice if you could convince your bank to put in a clause that it will lend money for these purposes at the same interest rate up to, say, 60 percent of your expenditure.

You may or may not be able to induce the bank to insert such clauses. There is no harm in trying.

1. sale of the equity subject to the mortgage — MR being still liable on the note and PE not being personally liable.
2. sale of the equity subject to the mortgage which the purchaser promises to pay — both MR and PE being liable on the note to ME, but PE being obligated to indemnify MR.
3. sale of the equity with the mortgagor being discharged from liability on the note and the purchaser becoming the sole obligor.[3]

Assignment of the mortgage. ME, holding a note of MR for $6,000 secured by mortgage on the land, may want to get this money out; and ME may find someone willing to take over the investment. If so, ME endorses the note and assigns the mortgage to A-ME, assignee of the mortgage. Thereafter all obligations of MR run to A-ME, and the latter holds the security interest in the land; the assignment should be recorded in the registry of deeds.

Second mortgages. After MR has given a $6,000 mortgage to ME, MR may want to borrow more money on the land. MR has an equity worth $4,000 and can possibly find someone who will lend $2,000 upon a second mortgage — i.e., a mortgage on the equity, or a mortgage subject to the first mortgage. In that case MR gives to ME-2 a note for $2,000, usually at a higher rate of interest to compensate for the increased risk, and also gives ME-2 a mortgage on the land which recites that it is "subject to a first mortgage to ME." Third, fourth, and later mortgages can be given in the same way.

Reduction of the mortgage. As payments of interest or principal are made, the practice is for ME to endorse payments on the back of the note. No corresponding entry is made in the registry of deeds; therefore, if the registry shows an outstanding mortgage of $6,000, this may represent a lien on the land of $6,000 plus a lot of accrued interest, or it may represent a lien for a very small sum because of large amounts of principal having been paid.

When the note is paid in full, ME surrenders the note to MR and executes a *discharge* of the mortgage, which is recorded.

SECTION 2. FUNCTION OF A MORTGAGE

To the mortgagor, the mortgage represents financing; to the mortgagee, it represents security for an investment. If MR wants to buy a house for

---

3. MR may also sell to PE with a covenant against encumbrances, thus undertaking to meet the mortgage note when it falls due. In such a case PE pays the full value of the land, not merely the land value less the amount of the mortgage, and relies upon MR's promise to remove the encumbrance when the mortgage falls due. But it is plain that there are objections to this procedure from PE's point of view unless MR is of unquestioned financial standing or the covenant against encumbrances is secured.

$100,000, MR rarely has the full price at the time of purchase; the mortgage enables MR to purchase upon a down payment and then to pay off the balance by partial payments on the principal of the mortgage which ME takes.[4] In this type of transaction, ME is often a savings bank which is seeking investments that will (1) produce the yield required to meet interest requirements of savings deposits, and (2) involve relatively low risk of loss of the principal invested.

When MR buys a piece of real estate, it may be that the vendor will take back a *purchase money mortgage* to secure unpaid installments of the agreed purchase price.

Where MR has land and wants to build on it, the *construction loan mortgage* provides a convenient method. Assume that MR has land worth $30,000 on which MR wants to put a $120,000 house; MR has only $20,000 toward the cost of building. MR gives to ME a mortgage covering the land and the building to be erected. The total amount to be advanced by ME is $100,000; but this will be turned over to MR in stated installments only as the house progresses to various stages, e.g., when foundations are complete, when roof is on, when exterior finish is complete and plumbing installed, when house is complete except for grading. Thus, as the building "feeds the mortgage," the amount of the mortgage is stepped up. In this situation ME has to be careful that, as ME advances installments of the loan, statutory liens of contractors and laborers for work on the property (known as mechanics' liens) are discharged, for these liens may be senior to the

---

4. *Various methods of financing land purchases.* If O owns Blackacre and P wishes to acquire it but lacks the purchase price of a fee simple, a number of methods exist for financing the project. All, or nearly all, are available everywhere; but local custom tends to make some of them popular in one state, others in another. Here are a number of the common devices:

a. *The bank mortgage.* This is described in the text.

b. *The purchase money mortgage.* Here the mortgagee is the vendor rather than a bank.

c. *The installment land contract.* This is described in an author's Note in Chapter 25, Section 2. The vendor keeps title until the full purchase price is paid; but the purchaser takes possession upon paying the first installment. The analogy to the conditional sale of personalty is obvious.

d. *The escrow agreement.* The vendor delivers a deed to a third person under irrevocable instructions to (a) deliver the deed to the purchaser if the latter pays the price in accordance with the contract, or (b) to redeliver the deed to the vendor if the purchaser defaults. This is simply a deferred payment or installment contract, the purchaser having additional protection against the vendor's failure to convey.

e. *The long-term lease.* Instead of buying a fee simple from O, P takes a 100-year lease, renewable forever; P makes a lump-sum payment comparable in amount to what P would pay out of P's own funds if P was financing the purchase under a mortgage, and the rent is fixed at an amount that will give to O an appropriate return off of the unpaid purchase price. Of course the parties provide for a "net lease" under which P pays taxes, insurance, repairs, and all other expense. From P's point of view this arrangement has great advantages: not only is the initial outlay minimal but there will never be a time in the future when P will be faced with the necessity of raising a large principal sum.

What if O conveys to P before the price is paid? In some states, but not in all, O has an equitable lien on the land for the unpaid amount. See American Law of Property §16.41 (Casner ed., 1952). Since the lien is equitable, a bona fide purchase cuts it off. This vendor's lien might be described as another type of financing arrangement, but only rarely is it consciously used as such.

mortgage, and the builder, working on a shoestring, may not be trusted to pay off these claims.

The *corporate mortgage* supporting a bond issue is outside the scope of the present elementary survey. Its corporate finance aspect dominates its property ingredient. One peculiarity is noteworthy; nearly every general corporate mortgage is an "open end" mortgage, permitting property to be withdrawn from the mortgage and new property substituted therefor in the ordinary course of business. Out of the corporate mortgage an expanded usage of the word "equity" has grown up. Most companies are financed in part by bond issues secured by mortgage; therefore common stock in these companies represents part ownership in an equity of redemption. So common stock generally gets to be known as an equity investment or equity ownership, whether or not there is a bond issue and mortgage. Preferred stock normally has a fixed rate of return as in the case of a bond; so Wall Street parlance does not consider preferred stock an "equity" investment even though, of course, preferred stockholders do have an ownership interest in an equity of redemption where the corporation has given a mortgage to secure a bond issue.

SECTION 3. SECURITY INTERESTS OTHER THAN REAL ESTATE MORTGAGES

To put the real estate mortgage in its setting it is worth while to mention other members of the family to which it belongs.

Other security interest in real estate include:

1. *Attachments.* At the commencement of a legal proceeding the plaintiff, sometimes and in some states, attaches real estate of the defendant as security for payment of such judgment as may be obtained.

2 *Judgment liens.* In some states the rendition or docketing of a judgment against A constitutes a lien on A's real estate even though there has been no attachment.

3. *Municipal taxes and assessments.* These constitute liens upon the real estate with reference to which they are levied, and such liens are usually senior to all others.

4. *Mechanics liens.* These have already been mentioned with reference to construction loan mortgages. It is usually provided by statute that contractors, materialmen, and laborers who perform construction services on real estate have liens to secure payment, provided that they give public notice as prescribed. This notice usually consists of giving written notice in the city hall as to, first, the contract covering the transaction and, later, the amount due thereunder; time limitations for such notice are prescribed.

5. *Various trust arrangements.* In some states a deed to a trustee

performs the task of the mortgage; MR conveys the land to the trustee in trust to reconvey if the note is paid or, if not, to sell the land and satisfy ME out of the proceeds. Almost invariably this is the practice as to corporate mortgages to secure bond issues. Again, in property settlements upon a divorce, it is common practice to require the spouse to convey real estate to a trustee as security for alimony payments.

Closely related to security transactions are those in which the personal obligation of the principal debtor is buttressed by the personal obligation of a surety. For example, S endorses A's promissory note to B, or S guarantees that A will complete a construction contract with B. The principles governing the relationship between the creditor, the principal obligor, and the surety comprise the law of *suretyship,* which is related to but still apart from the law of security transactions with which we are here concerned.

SECTION 4.   THE REAL ESTATE MORTGAGE AS IT WAS DEVELOPED IN THE COURTS

Now back to our principal object of concern. It will be useful to indicate how the mortgage and its incidents grew up in the courts; then to point out the principal types of statutory variations which bring it about that mortgage practice differs substantially from state to state in this country. Let us designate as the classic mortgage the institution that grew up in the courts.

The classic mortgage was a deed from MR to ME in the usual form of a straight conveyance, plus a defeasance clause which provided that if the obligations of the note were performed (i.e., if the interest were paid periodically, the taxes on the property paid, the property kept insured for the benefit of ME in an appropriate amount, and the principal paid at maturity) the deed should thereupon become void and of no effect. In other words, the mortgage was a conveyance to the mortgagee subject to a condition subsequent. The note or mortgage usually contained an acceleration clause, declaring that if the minor obligations of MR (interests, taxes, insurance) should not be performed, the principal would thereupon become due at the option of ME. The mortgage usually contained a provision that until default MR should remain in possession.[5] If MR paid up on time, the property automatically reverted to MR under the defeasance clause. But it was customary for ME to give MR a written discharge as evidence of performance of the obligations and (in the United States) to record in the registry of deeds so that MR would thenceforth have a clear record title.

Redemption. Suppose MR did not pay the note at maturity — i.e., at the

---

5. It is recommended that you examine the forms which are used in your own state.

"law day" provided in the mortgage? At law MR's rights in the property were ended, for ME held a deed subject to a condition subsequent which could no longer happen. However, if MR later offered to pay the principal, plus interest, plus expenses to which ME may have been put as a result of MR's default, the courts of equity required ME to accept payment and reconvey the property. A usual basis for invoking equity jurisdiction has always been relief against forfeiture; and, since the value of the property often exceeded by a substantial margin the obligation secured, retention of the property by ME often constituted a windfall profit to ME at the expense of MR. So MR would bring a "bill to redeem," alleging the facts, stating a willingness to pay principal, interest, and expenses, depositing the money in court, and praying that ME be directed to reconvey the property on payment. The equity court entered a decree to that effect as a matter of course. ME was thereby made whole by recovering the amount of the debt, interest, and expenses; and MR got the property back.

Foreclosure. The possibility of redemption made things difficult for ME when MR had defaulted. ME had title to the land to be sure, but if the land should rise in value or if MR should come into money there was always a chance that MR would redeem in equity. This made the land unsalable and thereby defeated the security function of the mortgage. The equity courts provided the antidote in the "bill to foreclose." ME would bring a bill in equity against MR, alleging the facts and praying that MR be enjoined from bringing a bill to redeem. One form of decree was that MR should be so enjoined unless MR should pay up within a specified period, say three months; this was called strict foreclosure, in that it cut off all rights of MR and made ME the outright owner of the property. However, if there was reason to believe that the propery was worth more than the amount due to ME, the court would direct that the property be sold by an officer of the court and the proceeds of the sale devoted to paying expenses of the sale, satisfying ME's claims, and paying the balance to MR; this was called foreclosure by sale. ME and MR could protect their respective interests by bidding at the sale; and, indeed, in the normal course of events ME was the principal, perhaps sole, bidder. For reasons which will shortly appear, foreclosure by sale became the standard method even when the property was clearly worth less than the amount due.

Two questions as to common terminology:

1. How about the propriety of calling MR's interest an "equity"? After default, yes; before default, no. Before default the legal rights of MR under the defeasance clause of the mortgage are fully adequate to protect MR if MR meets the obligations of the note; MR has a legal future interest in the property. However, the practice is universal to call MR's interest an "equity" at all times.

2. How about the propriety of the expression "foreclosing a mortgage"? Obviously meaningless. "Foreclose" means "shut out" or "debar." The thing that is foreclosed is the mortgagor's right to redeem, not the mortgage.

Foreclosure matures or enlarges the mortgagee's security interest into an absolute title. Yet the accepted practice is to talk of foreclosing a mortgage, and of course we shall adhere to it.

Deficiency judgment. To whatever extent foreclosure puts value into ME's hands, the debt of MR to ME is discharged; but as to any deficiency ME still holds an unsecured personal claim against MR. The best way to establish the amount of deficiency, if any, is by sale of the property at which both ME and MR are free to bid or produce bidders; and it is for this reason that foreclosure by sale is customarily used where the property is insufficient in value to pay the debt and MR is of sufficient financial worth to make a judgment against MR worth having. Theoretically, after a strict foreclosure, a deficiency judgment can be obtained in an action at law on the basis of testimony as to the value of the property, but this is not done as a matter of practice. Deficiency judgments can be ruinous; a sudden break in the stock market, such as occurred in 1929 and 1930, can force lenders to call their real estate loans (many mortgages are allowed to run as "open" mortgages — not to be confused with "open end" mortgages — long after they are due) and, by causing numerous forced sales of land at a time when buyers are nonexistent, thereby depress salable values to a small fraction of the face amount of what was considered a sound mortgage.

SECTION 5.   THE MORTGAGEE'S SECURITY INTEREST: TITLE THEORY, LIEN THEORY

The classic mortgage gave to ME title to the property, subject to a condition subsequent. Yet this was always recognised in equity, and often at law, as a security interest only. For example:

1. If ME took possession either before or after default but before foreclosure, ME had to apply the net rents to the claims against MR.
2. If ME died, the property went to ME's executor or administrator with the obligation secured, not to ME's heir or devisee.
3. MR's spouse had dower, but ME's spouse had no dower rights.
4. If ME assigned the debt to A-ME but did not assign the mortgage, equity treated the mortgage as nevertheless assigned. "The mortgage follows the debt."
5. If MR had made covenants which would ordinarily "run with the land" and be binding upon a grantee from MR — e.g., a covenant to maintain a road over the land in repair, or a covenant not to use the premises for industrial purposes — ME was not liable upon these covenants, at least in the usual case where ME did not take possession.

Moreover, courts of equity developed a series of rules designed to prevent

ME from imposing on MR by realizing more than ME's security interest in the land. For example,

6. No matter how clearly it was stated in the mortgage that MR should have no right to redeem unless MR paid, MR could still redeem.

7. If ME took a straight deed with no defeasance clause but the purpose was to assure future payment of a debt (as distinguished from the property being taken in satisfaction of the debt), this created an "equitable mortgage" and MR was allowed to redeem. Human nature being what it is, allegations that outright deeds were intended as mortgages are quite frequent in times of rising real estate prices.

So, in most substantive respects, the mortgagee's interest was *treated* as a lien though it was *called* title. The "title theory," however, must always be adjusted to the idea that the mortgagee has a security interest only.

It is for this reason that the difference between "title-theory states" and "lien-theory states" is a good deal less important in the practice of the profession than it has been in academic discussion. Indeed, in a general discussion such as this the distinction merits only summary treatment.

Some states have by judicial decision on specific points so eliminated any trace of the mortgagee's "title" that they consider themselves lien theory states. Other states have enacted statutory reforms on the same specific points or expressly declare that the mortgagee's interest is a lien only.

SECTION 6.   FORECLOSURE IN
MODERN PRACTICE

The most common method of foreclosure in the various states is by judicial sale. Usually the procedure is minutely regulated by statute and is cut and dried, eliminating any discretion on the part of the court or its functionaries. Sale is made by a special master (federal courts), referee (New York), or sheriff (New Jersey). The requirements as to notice to various parties, advertisement, time and place of sale, etc. are strict, and a failure to comply with them subjects the foreclosure to attack.[6]

In other states (e.g., Massachusetts), the practice is to include in the mortgage a paragraph declaring that upon default ME may sell the property, satisfy himself or herself out of the proceeds, and pay the balance, if any, to MR. Some states prescribe this method by statute; others permit it if a power of sale is included in the mortgage; a few forbid it by requiring foreclosure by judicial sale. All who permit it regulate the procedure of conducting the sale and jealously protect the mortgagor against violation of rules designed for

6. On foreclosure by judicial sale, see American Law of Property §§16.184-16.195 (Casner ed. 1952).

the mortgagor's benefit.[7] Most permit the mortgagee to purchase at his or her own sale; a few do not.

In a few of the New England states a strict foreclosure can be made by entry by the mortgagee plus the passage of some considerable period of time without redemption—e.g., three years in Massachusetts. As a practical matter this method is used as a safeguard in addition to the foreclosure by mortgagee's sale; this additional foreclosure brings it about that after three years the purchaser at foreclosure sale has a title which is no longer subject to the peculiar infirmities of foreclosure by mortgagee's sale.[8]

SECTION 7.   TWO CHARACTERISTIC DOCTRINES OF MORTGAGE LAW

This brief survey is no place for extended discussion of the complexities which may arise out of multipartite mortgage situations; but there are two doctrines of general application which operate in the mortgage context with some frequency, and these may profitably be considered.

A.   Subrogation

Suppose MR gives to ME a note for $6,000, secured by a mortgage on Blackacre. MR later offers Blackacre for sale, and PE (purchaser of the equity) buys for $4,000, "subject to a mortgage to ME in the amount of $6,000." As we have already pointed out, this transaction does not make PE liable on the note; it does, of course, leave ME in the same situation as previously, that is with a personal claim against MR on the note secured by a mortgage on Blackacre. Now suppose that at the maturity of the note ME demands payment from MR. MR must pay up. But this leaves MR with a net loss of $6,000 since, in selling Blackacre to PE, MR accepted a $6,000 reduction in the purchase price in view of the mortgage lien that was on the land. To rectify this situation we say that MR's payment of the note causes MR to be "subrogated" to ME's rights against the land; the discharge of the mortgage by payment operates as an assignment of the mortgage to MR. To generalize: Where (1) A has a claim against B and also a claim against C (or against property in the hands of C), and where (2) as between B and C the latter (or the property) should ultimately bear the burden, and where (3) A enforces the claim against B, then B is subrogated to A's rights against C (or the property). You will discover other cases of subrogation in numerous

7. On foreclosure by exercise of power of sale, see American Law of Property §§16.204-16.212 (Casner ed. 1952).

8. See American Law of Property §§16.181 (Casner ed. 1952).

fields of the law—insurance, for example—and at the same time you will find that the generalized statement above has to be somewhat enlarged. But this will do for a starter.

B. Marshaling

Suppose MR owns Blackacre (worth $12,000) and Whiteacre (worth $6,000). MR gives to ME-1 a note for $12,000 secured by mortgage on the two lots. Then MR gives to ME-2 a note for $7,000 secured on Blackacre alone. (To assume a constant worth is of course unrealistic, but we are offering a simplified case to illustrate the legal principles.) Thus the situation is this:

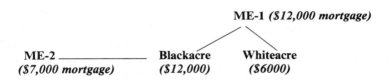

ME-1 *($12,000 mortgage)*

ME-2 _____ **Blackacre**   **Whiteacre**
($7,000 mortgage)   *($12,000)*   *($6000)*

Let us also assume that all instruments are recorded and that each mortgagee has actual notice of the other. Several things may happen:

1. MR defaults on both mortgages. ME-1 decides to foreclosure on Blackacre without bothering to foreclose on Whiteacre. As against MR, ME is entitled to do this. But when there is a junior encumbrancer in the picture, the senior encumbrancer can be compelled in equity so to enforce his or her mortgage that the junior encumbrancer is given maximum protection; the assets will be "marshaled" for the benefit of ME-2. Thus ME-1 will be required to satisfy himself or herself out of Whiteacre first and to take only the balance out of Blackacre. By this method ME-2 will get $6,000. (These situations can get pretty complex. A first stage complexity for you to toy with is the one in which , before or after the second mortgage of Blackacre to ME-2, MR sells the equity in Whiteacre to PE.)

2. ME-1 releases the mortgage on Whiteacre on payment by MR of $2,000. Were it not for ME-2, ME-1 could then foreclose on Blackacre for $10,000. But with ME-2 in the picture ME-1 is subject to ME-2's equity of marshaling, and ME-2 is entitled to participate in the proceeds of the mortgage sale of Blackacre as if ME-1 had first been satisfied out of Whiteacre. That is, out of these proceeds ME-1 takes the first $6,000 and ME-2 takes the rest. ME-1 is left with an unsecured claim for $4,000 against MR (the original claim of $12,000 less the $2,000 ME-1 got for the release of the mortgage on Whiteacre less the $6,000 ME-1 got out of Blackacre).

To generalize: When a senior encumbrancer has a claim against two funds and a junior encumbrancer against one only, the former must so enforce his or her claim as to give maximum protection to the latter.

However, rights of fourth parties (other than the debtor and the two encumbrancers) may drastically alter the application of the principle.[9]

Marshaling situations are particularly common where there has been a multiple-lot mortgage covering a land development. As lots are sold to individual buyers they may or may not be released from the blanket mortgage; the buyers may or may not put second mortgages on them; and some parties may not have notice of the claims of others. A veritable snake's nest of legal problems can result.

SECTION 8.   THREE HEADACHES FROM THE GREAT DEPRESSION

Guaranteed mortgages. During the lush days of the 1920s when everybody was going to make a million dollars, every stock on the board was going up and up, and real estate values were on a continually ascending Jacob's ladder, a number of New York title insurance companies went into the business of guaranteeing mortgages. Whereas their usual business was insuring the validity of record titles, they undertook to guarantee to mortgagees that they would get paid—which is quite a different matter. (The normal fee was one-half of 1 percent annually.) So the guaranteed mortgagee had a triple recourse against the mortgagor, the property, and the title insurance company. By 1932-1933 the successive hammerblows of the Great Depression brought the downfall of the companies that had gone into this guarantee business. Mortgagees wanted their money at a time when buyers simply were not to be found. The companies went to the wall and many of them were in the process of liquidation or reorganization for many years. On the whole the salvage has been pretty good.[10]

Mortgage participations. Where there is a big mortgage to be floated—say on a new office building—one way to do it is to float a bond issue and have the mortgage held by a trustee for the benefit of the bondholders. Another way is for the mortgage and note to be given to X and have X issue "participation certificates" assigning to each holder a fractional interest in the debt and security; X is normally given an "irrevocable agency" to handle the mortgage for the benefit of the certificate holders. In New York real estate financing of the 1920's, mortgage participations were tied in with mortgage guarantees.[11] A major problem concerning mortgage participa-

---

9. For an analogous situation, see Low v. Bankers Trust Co., 270 N.Y. 143, 200 N.E. 674 (1936); Leach & Logan, Cases and Text on Future Interests and Estate Planning 644 (1961).

10. For a discussion of this episode and its legal complications see Note, Present Problems in New York Guaranteed Mortgages, 34 Colum. L. Rev. 663 (1934). To indicate the explosive character of the situation which the guarantee business had created: As of January 1, 1933, 52 New York companies had combined assets of $234 million and combined mortgage guarantees of $3 billion. In other words, an overall 10 percent loss would wipe them out.

11. For this story, see Note, 34 Colum. L. Rev. 675 (1934).

tions was whether they were proper trustee investments, particularly where the trustee was the mortgagee and "irrevocable agent."[12] This issue became acute when all investments went down and beneficiaries of trusts began looking around for someone else to bear the losses.

Moratory legislation. Another product of the Depression was the moratorium statute designed to forestall the creation of a large class of landless people with enormous deficiency judgments hanging over their heads as the result of a global economic upheaval. These laws differed among the states. Some extended the time for redemption; others forbade foreclosure as long as the debtor paid interest and taxes; others permitted foreclosure but limited or abolished deficiency judgments. In the main the statutes purported to be temporary; but it proved to be politically unattractive to terminate them. Obvious constitutional issues are involved.

SECTION 9.   SAMPLE MORTGAGE

Set out below is a sample form of a mortgage used in Massachusetts.

A. B.

of *Boston, Suffolk* County, Massachusetts for consideration paid, grants to *C. D.*

of said *Boston*

with mortgage covenants[13] to secure the payment of *Ten Thousand (10,000.00)* Dollars in *five* years with 12 percent interest, per annum payable

---

12.   See 2 Scott, Trusts §179.4 (3d ed. 1967).

13.   A deed in substance following the form entitled "Mortgage Deed" shall when duly executed have the force and effect of a mortgage deed to the use of the mortgagee and his heirs and assigns with mortgage covenants and upon the statutory condition and with the statutory power of sale, as defined in the three following sections, to secure the payment of the money or the performance of any obligation therein specified. The parties may insert in such mortgage any other lawful agreement or condition. (Mass. Gen. Laws ch. 183, §18.)

In a conveyance of real estate, the words "mortgage covenants" shall have the full force, meaning and effect of the following words, and shall be applied and construed accordingly:

The mortgagor, for himself, his heirs, executors, administrators and successors, covenants with the mortgagee and his heirs, successors and assigns, that he is lawfully seized in fee simple of the granted premises; that they are free from all encumbrances; that the mortgagor has good right to sell and convey the same; and that he will, and his heirs, executors, administrators and successors shall, warrant and defend the same to the mortgagee and his heirs, successors and assigns forever against the lawful claims and demands of all persons; and that the mortgagor and his heirs, successors or assigns, in case a sale shall be made under the power of sale, will, upon request, execute, acknowledge and deliver to the purchaser or purchasers a deed or deeds of release confirming such sale; and that the mortgagee and his heirs, executors, administrators, successors and assigns are appointed and constituted the attorney or attorneys irrevocable of the said mortgagor to execute and deliver to the said purchaser a full transfer of all policies of insurance on the buildings upon the land covered by the mortgage at the time of such sale. [Mass. Gen. Laws ch. 183, §19.]

quarterly as provided in *promissory* note of even date,[14] the land in said Boston situated on W. street in said Boston and bounded as follows — East on said street, thirty feet; — South on land now or late of L.M., fifty feet; — West on land of N.O., thirty feet; — and north on the same, fifty feet and seven inches; — and being the same parcel that was conveyed to A. B. by R. S. by deed dated 7th Dec. 1945, and recorded in Suffolk Registry of Deeds, book 4790, page 638.

This mortgage is upon the statutory condition,[15]

for any breach of which the mortgagee shall have the statutory power of sale.[16]

S. B., wife of said mortgagor, releases to the mortgagee all rights of dower and homestead and other interests in the mortgaged premises.

Witness *our* hands and seals this 4th day of September [*insert year*]

———————————————————— *A. B.*
———————————————————— *S. B.*

The Commonwealth of Massachusetts
Suffolk   ss.   *September 4,* [*insert year*]
Then personally appeared the above named *A. B. and S. B.*
and acknowledged the foregoing to be *their* free act and deed, before me
                          X. Y.
                          Notary Public
                          My commission expires *December 31,* [*insert year*]

14.   A fixed interest mortgage that is to last for a specified period of time in a period of fluctuating interest rates may turn out to give the borrower a benefit if interest rates go up with corresponding detriment to the lender who could get more return off of the loan if the lender could collect on the loan and loan out the money to someone else. The reverse is true if interest rates go down as the borrower would be better off if the loan could be paid off and a new loan obtained at the lower interest rate.

This situation has led to the insertion in mortgages of what is termed a due-on-sale clause. This clause gives the lender the option to require the payment of the loan if the borrower sells the mortgaged land. This prevents the buyer of mortgaged land from gaining the benefit of a low-interest mortgage loan because on sale by the mortgagor, the lender will call the loan and thereby require the purchaser from the mortgagor to refinance at current interest rates. The due-on-sale clause is discussed in Dunham v. Ware Savings Bank, — Mass. —, 423 N.E.2d 998 (1981).

The lender does not want the borrower to be able to prepay the mortgage if interest rates go down and thus the lender may insist on a penalty payment on prepayment of the mortgage debt. Mass. Gen. Laws ch. 183, §56, allows certain borrowers to prepay a first mortgage without penalty at any time after three years from the date of the note, and penalties for earlier prepayment are substantially limited.

Variable rate mortgages have come into the picture. See Mass. Gen. Laws, ch. 167, §70. Variable rate mortgages, although different in detail, share some general restrictions with fixed rate mortgages containing prepayment and due-on-sale clauses, in that variable rate mortgages are limited in the amount and frequency of interest rate changes. Variable rate mortgages are but one legislative response to the problems encountered in an unpredictable economy. See footnote 11 in *Dunham* case, referred to above in this footnote.

15.   Mass. Gen. Laws ch. 183, §20:

The following "condition" shall be known as the *Statutory Condition,* and may be incorporated in any mortgage by reference:

SECTION 10. SOME PROBLEMS

On the basis of the foregoing brief survey, you should be able to see what issue of mortgage law is involved in the following situations and in most of them you should get the right result.

26.1. MR insures MR's house against fire with the I Company. The policy contains a clause as follows: "This policy shall be void if the property insured shall be alienated without the assent of the Company." MR then gives to ME a note for $5,000 secured by a mortgage on the house. A fire occurs. Is the policy void? Judge v. Connecticut Fire Insurance Co., 132 Mass. 521 (1882).

26.2. MR gives to ME a note for $5,000 secured by a mortgage on Blackacre. C is a creditor of ME. Can C attach Blackacre in an action against ME? Is there any way in which C can reach Blackacre to satisfy C's claim? See American Law of Property §16.108 (Casner ed. 1952).

(Condition)

Provided, nevertheless, except as otherwise specifically stated in the mortgage, that if the mortgagor, or his heirs, executors, administrators, successors, or assigns shall pay unto the mortgagee or his executors, administrators or assigns the principal and interest secured by the mortgage, and shall perform any obligation secured at the time provided in the note, mortgage or other instrument or any extension thereof, and shall perform the condition of any prior mortgage, and until such payment and performance shall pay when due and payable all taxes, charges and assessments to whomsoever and whenever laid or assessed, whether on the mortgaged premises or on any interest therein, or on the debt or obligation secured thereby; shall keep the buildings on said premises insured against fire in a sum not less than the amount secured by the mortgage or as otherwise provided therein for insurance for the benefit of the mortgagee and his executors, administrators and assigns, in such form and at such insurance offices as they shall approve, and, at least two days before the expiration of any policy on said premises, shall deliver to him or them a new and sufficient policy to take the place of the one so expiring, and shall not commit or suffer any strip or waste of the mortgaged premises or any breach of any covenant contained in the mortgage or in any prior mortgage, then the mortgage deed, as also the mortgage note or notes, shall be void.

16.   Mass. Gen. Laws ch. 183, §21:
The following "power" shall be known as the *Statutory Power of Sale,* and may be incorporated in any mortgage by reference:

(Power)

But upon any default in the performance or observance of the foregoing or other condition, the mortgagee or his executors, administrators, successors or assigns may sell the mortgaged premises or such portion thereof as may remain subject to the mortgage in case of any partial release thereof, either as a whole or in parcels, together with all improvements that may be thereon, by public auction on or near the premises then subject to the mortgage, or, if more than one parcel is then subject thereto, on or near one of said parcels, or at such place as may be designated for that purpose in the mortgage, first complying with the terms of the mortgage and with the statutes relating to the foreclosure of mortgages by the exercise of a power of sale, and may convey the same by proper deed or deeds to the purchaser or purchasers absolutely and in fee-simple; and such sale shall forever bar the mortgagor and all persons claiming under him from all right and interest in the mortgaged premises, whether at law or in equity.

26.3. MR gives to ME a note for $5,000 dated January 2, 1984, payable in one year, secured by mortgage on Blackacre. The note is not under seal; the mortgage is. In the jurisdiction the statute of limitations provides that "No action shall be brought of the following types beyond the following periods after the right of action accrued":

a. "Actions upon contracts under seal, 8 years."

b. "Actions upon contracts not under seal, 4 years."

c. "Actions to recover the possession of land, 12 years."

The note is not paid. What are ME's rights as to foreclosure and obtaining a deficiency judgment (i) in 1990, (ii) in 1994, and (iii) in 1997? See American Law of Property §16.163 (Casner ed. 1952).

26.4. MR gives to ME a note secured by mortgage on Blackacre. MR then leases Blackacre to T for five years. One year later MR defaults on the mortgage and ME forecloses. ME purchases at the foreclosure sale and orders T to get out. What are T's rights? If you had been T's counsel at the time T took the lease, what would you have advised T to do? See American Law of Property §§16.91-16.93 (Casner ed. 1952).

26.5. MR gives to ME a note for $5,000 secured by mortgage on Blackacre. ME borrows $3,000 from the B Bank and endorses MR's note over to the bank as security for the loan; there is no assignment of the mortgage. What are the relationships of the parties? See American Law of Property §16.108 (Casner ed. 1952).

26.6. ME is your client. ME is about to make a loan of $25,000 for five years to MR secured by a mortgage on Blackacre. ME asks you to check over the papers. The mortgage contains the following clause: "The whole of said principal sum shall become due after default in the payment of any tax, water rate or assessment for 30 days after notice and demand." Advise ME as to the wisdom of this clause. Compare Albertina Realty Co. v. Rosbro Realty Corp., 258 N.Y. 472, 180 N.E. 176 (1932). See American Law of Property §16.193 (Casner ed. 1952).

26.7. In 1984 MR gives to ME-1 a note for $5,000, payable in 1989 and secured by mortgage on Blackacre. In 1985, MR gives to ME-2 a demand note for $3,000 secured by a mortgage on Blackacre. Both mortgages are duly recorded when given. In 1986 ME-2 demands payment. MR does not pay. ME-2 forecloses by sale. How much of the proceeds of the sale go to ME-1?

CHAPTER 27

THE DEED[1]

Note: Different Types of Deeds

Deeds are classified as follows according to the degree of promissory protection which the grantor gives to the grantee:

1. A *general warranty deed* is one in which the grantor warrants the title against defects arising before and during the time the grantor was connected with the land.

2. A *special warranty deed* is one in which the grantor warrants the title against defects arising during the grantor's association with the land but not against defects arising before that time.[2] To illustrate: suppose A purchases land in 1984 and conveys to B in 1987. B conveys to C in 1992 by deed of special warranty. If it later appears that the title is defective due to a mortgage given by B in 1989 or an attachment levied against B's property in 1990, the warranty has been broken; but if the defect is due to a mortgage given by A in 1984 or an attachment levied against A's property in 1985, there is no breach. Of course a general warranty deed would cover all these defects. (In Massachusetts, by a local peculiarity of terminology, a special warranty deed is called a "quitclaim deed" or "deed with quitclaim covenants.")

3. A *quitclaim deed* is one in which the grantor warrants nothing; the grantor merely transfers what title the grantor has, if any. (In Massachusetts this is called a "deed without covenants." Since this is the type of deed given by trustees, executors, and other fiduciaries, it is also known as a "fiduciary deed.")

Nineteenth century deeds were prolix, lengthy documents. Conveyancers were disinclined to take the risks of shortening them; they knew the standard forms worked and felt they could not be equally sure of any other. To

1. See generally American Law of Property §§12.1-12.134 (Casner ed. 1952).
2. Observe the possibilities of confusion. To the layman, if the grantor "warrants specially" the title, it sounds like more than the usual warranty; but the technical meaning of this term severely limits the coverage of the warranty. For a case where both a layman and a lawyer appear to have been deceived by this, see Kendall v. Rogers, 181 Md. 606, 31 A.2d 312 (1943).

individual grantors and grantees this made little difference; but it caused registries of deeds in heavily populated areas to be unnecessarily bulky. For this reason short-form statutes were passed in many states. They provide statutory forms of deeds and declare that certain short expressions therein — e.g., "warranty covenants"— shall have the effect of whole paragraphs of long-form language. (For an example, see the deed in Section 1.B of this chapter. Footnote 6 quotes the statutory language on the meaning of "warranty covenants.") In many states (including Massachusetts) the short form is habitually used, but in others force of habit or other reason has caused the old long form to persist.

Section 1 of this chapter provides samples of the three types of deeds — general warranty, special warranty, and quitclaim — with short forms of two of these. Section 4 considers what the various warranties mean in terms of protection to the grantee — and this adds up to surprisingly little.

Section 2 deals with the requirement of "delivery," particularly with reference to the escrow agreement.

Section 3 considers the problems of construction and drafting involved in so describing the land as to fix accurate boundaries.

SECTION 1. SAMPLE DEEDS

A. GENERAL WARRANTY DEED

KNOW ALL MEN BY THESE PRESENTS that I, A. B., of Boston in the Commonwealth of Massachusetts, in consideration of one thousand dollars to me paid by C. D., of Worcester in said Commonwealth, the receipt whereof is hereby acknowledged, hereby give, grant, bargain, sell, and convey unto the said C. D. a certain parcel of land situated on W. street in said Boston, and bounded as follows: — East on said street, thirty feet; — South on land now or late of L. M., fifty feet; — West on land of N. O., thirty feet; — and North on the same fifty feet and seven inches; — and being the same parcel that was conveyed to me by R. S. by deed dated 7th Dec. 1964, and recorded in Suffolk Registry of Deeds, book 4790, page 638.

TO HAVE AND TO HOLD the granted premises, with all the privileges and appurtenances thereto belonging, to the said C. D., and his [or her] heirs and assigns, to their own use and behoof forever.

And I hereby, for myself and my heirs, executors, and administrators, COVENANT with the grantee and his [or her] heirs and assigns that I am lawfully seized in fee simple of the granted premises; that they are free from all incumbrances; that I have good right to sell and convey the same as aforesaid; and that I will, and my heirs, executors, and administrators shall, WARRANT AND DEFEND the same to the grantee and his [or her] heirs and assigns forever against the lawful claims and demands of all persons.

AND for the consideration aforesaid, I, S. B., wife [or husband] of the said A. B., hereby release unto the grantee and his [or her] heirs and assigns all right of and to both DOWER and HOMESTEAD in the granted premises.[3]

IN WITNESS WHEREOF we, the said A. B. and S. B., hereunto set our hands and seals this third day of January in the year one thousand nine hundred and eighty-four.

Signed and sealed in presence of

| E. F. to A. B. | A. B. | Seal |
| G. H. to S. B. | S. B. | Seal |

COMMONWEALTH OF MASSACHUSETTS

Suffolk ss.   January 3, 1984

Then personally appeared the above named A. B. and S. B and acknowledged the foregoing instrument to be their free act and deed, before me,

K. L.
Notary Public
(Notary's Seal)[4]

B. Statutory Form of General Warranty Deed[5]

I, A. B., of Boston in the Commonwealth of Massachusetts, County of Suffolk, for consideration paid, grant to C. D., of Worcester in said Commonwealth, with warranty covenants[6] the land situated on W. street in said Boston, and bounded as follows: — East on said street, thirty feet; — South on land now or late of L. M., fifty feet; — West on land of N. O., thirty

---

3. The spouse's signature on the deed to relinquish dower is no longer necessary in Massachusetts because dower is now restricted to the land the deceased spouse was seised of at his or her death.

4. This general warranty deed is taken from Crocker's Notes on Common Forms §22 (Swain 7th ed. 1955).

5. The various statutory form deeds in Massachusetts are set forth in Mass. Gen. Laws ch. 183, §§8-28A.

6. Mass. Gen. Laws ch. 183, §10, provides as follows:

A deed in substance following the form entitled "Warranty Deed" shall when duly executed have the force and effect of a deed in fee simple to the grantee, his heirs and assigns, to his and their own use, with covenants on the part of the grantor, for himself, his heirs, executors, administrators and successors, with the grantee, his heirs, successors and assigns, that, at the time of the delivery of such deed, (1) he was lawfully seized in fee simple of the granted premises, (2) that the granted premises were free from all encumbrances, (3) that he had good right to sell and convey the same to the grantee and his heirs and assigns, and (4) that he will, and his heirs, executors and administrators shall, warrant and defend the same to the grantee and his heirs and assigns against the lawful claims and demands of all persons.

feet; — and North on the same, fifty feet and seven inches; — and being the same parcel that was conveyed to me by R. S. by deed dated 7th Dec. 1964, and recorded in Suffolk Registry of Deeds, book 4790, page 638. I, S. B., wife [or husband] of said A. B., release to said C. D. all rights of DOWER and HOMESTEAD and other interests therein.[7]

WITNESS our hand and seal this third day of January, 1984.

Signed and sealed in presence of

E. F. to A. B.	A. B.	Seal
G. H. to S. B.	S. B.	Seal

COMMONWEALTH OF MASSACHUSETTS

Suffolk ss.   January 3, 1984

Then personally appeared the above named A. B. and S. B. and acknowledged the foregoing instrument to be their free act and deed, before me,

M. N.
Notary Public
(Notary's Seal)

C. Special Warranty Deed[8]

KNOWN ALL MEN BY THESE PRESENTS that I, A. B., of Boston in the Commonwealth of Massachusetts, in consideration of ten thousand dollars to me paid by C. D., of Worcester in said Commonwealth, the receipt whereof is hereby acknowledged, do hereby remise, release, and forever QUITCLAIM unto the said C. D. a certain parcel of land, situated on W. street in said Boston, and bounded as follows: — East on said street, thirty feet; — South on land now or late of L. M., fifty feet; — West on land of N. O., thirty feet; — and North on the same fifty feet and seven inches; — and being the same parcel that was conveyed to me by R. S. by deed dated 7th Dec. 1964 and recorded in Suffolk Registry of Deeds, book 4790, page 638.

TO HAVE AND TO HOLD the above-released premises, with the privileges and appurtenances thereto belonging, to the said C. D. and his [or her] heirs and assigns to their own use and behoof forever.

AND I hereby, for myself and my heirs, executors, and administrators, COVENANT with the said C. D., and his [or her] heirs and assigns, that the released premises are free from all incumbrances made or suffered by me, and that I will, and my heirs, executors, and administrators shall, warrant

---

7. See footnote 3.

8. In Massachusetts, by local peculiarity, this deed is called a quitclaim deed even though it contains a covenant of special warranty. See Note: Different Types of Deeds, this chapter *supra.*

and defend the same to the said C. D. and his [or her] heirs and assigns against the lawful claims and demands of all persons claiming by, through, or under me, but against none other.

And for the consideration aforesaid I, S. B., wife [or husband] of the said A. B., hereby release unto the said C. D. and his [or her] heirs and assigns all right of and to both DOWER and HOMESTEAD in the said premises.[9]

IN WITNESS WHEREOF we, the said A. B. and S. B., hereunto set our hands and seals this third day of January in the year one thousand nine hundred and eighty-four.

Signed and sealed in presence of

| E. F. to A. B. | A. B. | Seal |
| G. H. to S. B. | S. B. | Seal |

COMMONWEALTH OF MASSACHUSETTS

Suffolk ss.   January 3, 1984

Then personally appeared the above named A. B. and S. B. and acknowledged the foregoing instrument to be their free act and deed, before me,

K. L.
Notary Public
(Notary's Seal)[10]

D.   STATUTORY FORM OF SPECIAL WARRANTY DEED

I, A. B., of Boston in the Commonwealth of Massachusetts, County of Suffolk, for consideration paid, grant to C. D., of Worcester in said Commonwealth, with quitclaim covenants[11] the land situated on W. street in said Boston, and bounded as follows: — East on said street, thirty feet; — South on land now or late of L. M., fifty feet; — West on land of N. O., thirty feet; — and North on the same, fifty feet and seven inches; — and being the same parcel that was conveyed to me by R. S. by deed dated 7th Dec. 1964, and recorded in Suffolk Registry of Deeds, book 4790, page 638. I, S. B., wife

---

9. See footnote 3.

10. This special warranty deed (quitclaim deed) is taken from Crocker's Notes on Common Forms §318 (Swain 7th ed. 1955).

11. Mass. Gen. Laws ch. 183, §11, provides as follows:

A deed in substance following the form entitled "Quitclaim Deed" shall when duly executed have the force and effect of a deed in fee simple to the grantee, his heirs and assigns, to his and their own use, with covenants on the part of the grantor, for himself, his heirs, executors, administrators and successors, with the grantee, his heirs, successors and assigns, that at the time of the delivery of such deed the premises were free from all encumbrances made by him, and that he will, and his heirs, executors and administrators shall, warrant and defend the same to the grantee and his heirs and assigns forever against the lawful claims and demands of all persons claiming by, through or under the grantor, but against none other.

[or husband] of said A. B., release to said C. D. all rights of DOWER and HOMESTEAD and other interests therein.[12]

WITNESS our hand and seal this third day of January, 1984.

Signed and sealed in presence of

E. F. to A. B.	A. B.	Seal
G. H. to S. B.	S. B.	Seal

COMMONWEALTH OF MASSACHUSETTS

January 3, 1984

Then personally appeared the above named A. B. and S. B. and acknowledged the foregoing instrument to be their free act and deed, before me,

M. N.
Notary Public
(Notary's Seal)

E. QUITCLAIM DEED

KNOW ALL MEN BY THESE PRESENTS that I, A. B., of Boston in the Commonwealth of Massachusetts, in consideration of one hundred dollars to me paid by C. D., of Worcester in said Commonwealth, the receipt whereof is hereby acknowledged, do hereby remise, release, and forever QUIT-CLAIM unto the said C. D. a certain parcel of land, situated on W. street in said Boston, and bounded as follows: — East on said street, thirty feet; — South on land now or late of L. M., fifty feet; — West on land of N. O., thirty feet; — and North on the same fifty feet and seven inches; — and being the same parcel that was conveyed to me by R. S. by deed dated 7th Dec. 1964, and recorded in Suffolk Registry of Deeds, book 4790, page 638.

TO HAVE AND TO HOLD the above-released premises, with the privileges and appurtenances thereto belonging, to the said C. D. and his [or her] heirs and assigns to their own use and behoof forever.

AND for the consideration aforesaid I, S. B., wife [or husband] of the said A. B., hereby release unto the said C. D. and his [or her] heirs and assigns all right of and to both DOWER and HOMESTEAD in the said premises.[13]

IN WITNESS WHEREOF we, the said A. B. and S. B., hereunto set our hands and seals this third day of January in the year one thousand nine hundred and eighty-four.

E. F. to A. B.	A. B.	Seal
G. H. to S. B.	S. B.	Seal

12. See footnote 3.
13. See footnote 3.

COMMONWEALTH OF MASSACHUSETTS

Suffolk ss. January 3, 1984

· Then personally appeared the above named A. B. and acknowledged the foregoing instrument to be his free act and deed, before me,

M. N.
Notary Public
(Notary's Seal)

F.   FIDUCIARY'S DEED

I, X. Y., Executor under the will of A. B., by power conferred by the will of the said A. B., which will is filed in the probate court of Suffolk County, Commonwealth of Massachusetts, Docket No. 412,531, and every other power, for ten thousand dollars paid grant to C. D. of Worcester in said Commonwealth, the land situated on W. Street in said Boston, and bounded as follows: — East on said street, thirty feet; South on land now or late of L. M., fifty feet; — West on land of N. O., thirty feet; — and North on the same, fifty feet and seven inches; and being the same parcel that was conveyed to the said A. B. by R. S. by deed dated 7th Dec. 1964 and recorded in Suffolk Registry of Deeds book 4790, page 638.

WITNESS my hand and seal this third day of January, 1984.

E. F. to A. B. A. B. Seal

COMMONWEALTH OF MASSACHUSETTS

Suffolk ss. January 3, 1984

Then personally appeared the above named X. Y. and acknowledged the foregoing instrument to be his free act and deed, before me,

M. N.
(Notary's Seal)
(Notary's Seal)

SECTION 2.   REQUIREMENT OF DELIVERY OF DEED (HEREIN DELIVERY IN ESCROW)

Note: *Significance of the Grantor's Intention*

A deed of land must be delivered by the grantor in order to give it legal effectiveness.[14] Does this mean that there must be a manual transfer of the deed from the grantor to the grantee? The answer to this question is given in the language of Phenneger v. Kendrick, 301 Ill. 163, 133 N.E. 637 (1922):

> Delivery is essential to make a deed operative, but no particular ceremony is necessary. It may be by acts without words or words without acts, or both. No particular form or ceremony is necessary to constitute a delivery, and anything which clearly manifests the intention of the grantor that the deed shall presently become operative and effectual and that the grantor loses all control over it constitutes a sufficient delivery. Intention is the controlling element which determines whether a deed has been delivered, and the question depends in great measure upon the particular circumstances of each case.[15] [301 Ill. at 167, 133 N.E. at 638.]

From the quotation above, it is apparent that the requirement of delivery may be met if the grantor has manifested an intention that the deed become completely and immediately operative even though the grantor retains physical possession of the deed, or places the deed in the hands of a third person. On the other hand, if the grantor's manifested intention is that the deed is to have no legal effectiveness, there has been no delivery of it even though the grantor places it in the hands of the grantee or a third person. As might be expected, the determination of the grantor's intention has been the subject of much litigation where the deed has been carelessly handled.

We shall direct our attention in this section to a consideration of the problems which arise when the grantor's intention is to withhold from the grantee some of the incidents of complete ownership until the performance of some condition or the happening of some event. When such is the grantor's intention, we shall find the courts describe the result as a condi-

---

14. Closely associated with the requirement of delivery is the requirement that a deed of land must be accepted by the grantee. In commercial land transactions the acceptance of the deed by the grantee is normally a foregone conclusion because the previous negotiations between the parties will have removed any doubts as to acceptance by the grantee. In gift transactions relating to land, it is normally safe to assume that the grantee will accept the benefit conferred. For a consideration of the problems which may arise if there is any interval of time between the delivery of the deed by the grantor and its acceptance by the grantee or where the grantee refuses to accept the deed, see American Law of Property §§12.64, 12.70, 12.97 (Casner ed. 1952).

15. You should compare the requirement of delivery in relation to deeds of land with the requirement of delivery in the making of a gift of personal property (Chapter 5).

tional delivery or a delivery in escrow. To orient your thinking in this field, consider the following typical situations:

1. O, owner of Blackacre, enters into a contract for the sale thereof to P. The purchase price is $10,000. P is allowed 90 days in which to raise the purchase price. P wants to be certain that a deed satisfactory to P will be forthcoming if P raises the purchase price in the required time. O, therefore, executes a deed of Blackacre that is satisfactory to P and places it with the X Bank, with instructions to turn over the deed to P if P, within 90 days, deposits in the X Bank to O's credit the sum of $10,000.

2. O, owner of Blackacre, executes a deed thereof in favor of a son. O places the deed with the X Bank and instructs the bank to turn over the deed to the son on O's death.

You will notice that the first situation described above relates to a commercial transaction in land and is basically designed to assure P of a satisfactory deed when P provides the purchase money. You should ask yourself what other arrangements O and P could have made that would have been equally satisfactory to both parties. You will notice that the second situation described above is a gift transaction and is designed to accomplish by a deed something quite close to what is normally accomplished by a will. You should ask yourself in connection with this arrangement what are the differences between it and a will and is there any other way in which O's desires might be accomplished.

SWEENEY, ADMINISTRATRIX v. SWEENEY
126 Conn. 391, 11 A.2d 806 (1940)

JENNINGS, J. Maurice Sweeney, plaintiff's intestate, hereinafter called Maurice, deeded his farm to his brother John M. Sweeney, hereinafter called John, and the deed was recorded. John deeded the property back to Maurice. This deed is unrecorded and was accidentally burned. The question to be decided is whether the second deed was delivered and if so, whether or not a condition claimed to be attached to the delivery is operative. This must be determined on the finding. The following statement includes such changes therein as are required by the evidence:

The plaintiff is the widow and administratrix of Maurice but had not lived with him for the twenty years preceding his death in September, 1938, at an age of seventy-three years. Maurice lived on a tract of land of some hundred and thirty-five acres which he owned in East Hampton, where he ran a tavern. John assisted him in running the tavern to some extent. On February 2, 1937, Maurice and John went to the town clerk's office in East Hampton pursuant to an appointment made the preceding day. Maurice requested the town clerk to draw a deed of his East Hampton property to John and this was done. At the same time he requested that a deed be prepared from John to himself so that he, Maurice would be protected if John predeceased him. Both deeds were duly executed. The first was left for recording and the second was taken away by Maurice and never recorded. A week or two later Maurice took to John the recorded deed and a week or two after that took the unrecorded deed to John's house. John kept both deeds and gave the second deed to his attorney after the institution of this action. It was destroyed when the latter's office was burned. After the execution of the deeds, Maurice continued to occupy the property, paid the fixed charges, received the rents and exercised full dominion over it until his death. In April, 1937, Maurice made a written lease to Ernest Myers of a portion of the premises and on June 18, 1938, a written lease to Frank and Esther Fricke for twenty years. The first lease is lost but the second was recorded. The defendant never collected any money from tenants or paid any fixed charges or repairs prior to the death of Maurice. On these facts the trial court concluded that there was no intention to make present delivery of John's deed to Maurice, that there was no delivery or acceptance thereof, that it was not intended to operate until John's death and rendered judgment for the defendant.

This deed was, in effect, manually delivered. Maurice continued to occupy the property and exercised full dominion over it without interference by John. It follows that all the essentials of a good delivery were present unless there is something in the contentions of John which defeats this result. He claims that there was no intention on his part to make present delivery.

It is, of course, true that physical possession of a duly executed deed is not conclusive proof that it was legally delivered. McDermott v. McDermott, 97 Conn. 31, 34, 115 Atl. 638. This is so under some circumstances even where there has been a manual delivery. Hotaling v. Hotaling, 193 Cal. 368, 381, 224 Pac. 455, 56 A.L.R. 734, and note p. 746. Delivery must be made with the intent to pass title if it is to be effective. Porter v. Woodhouse, 59 Conn. 568, 575, 22 Atl. 299; McDermott v. McDermott, *supra.*

The deed having been in effect actually delivered to Maurice, the execution of the attestation clause was prima facie proof that the deed was delivered. New Haven Trust Co. v. Camp, 81 Conn. 539, 542, 71 Atl. 788. There is a rebuttable presumption that the grantee assented since the deed was beneficial to him. Moore v. Giles, 49 Conn. 570, 573. No fact is found which militates against this presumption. Where deeds are formally executed and delivered, these presumptions can be overcome only by evidence that no delivery was in fact intended. Loughran v. Kummer, 297 Pa. St. 179, 183, 146 Atl. 534; Cragin's Estate, 274 Pa. St. 1, 5, 117 Atl. 445; Stewart v. Silva, 192 Cal. 405, 409, 221 Pac. 191. The only purpose in making the deed expressed by either party was the statement by Maurice that it was to protect him in case John predeceased him. Since this purpose would have been defeated had there been no delivery with intent to pass title, this conclusively establishes the fact that there was a legal delivery.

The defendant next claims that if there was a delivery, it was on condition and that the condition (the death of John before that of Maurice) was not and cannot be fulfilled. This claim is not good because the delivery was to the grantee. "A conditional delivery is and can only be made by placing the deed in the hands of a third person to be kept by him until the happening of the event upon the happening of which the deed is to be delivered over by the third person to the grantee." Porter v. Woodhouse, *supra,* 574; Raymond v. Smith, 5 Conn. 555, 559. Conditional delivery to a grantee vests absolute title in the latter. Loughran v. Kummer, *supra,* 185; McCarthy v. Security Trust & Savings Bank, 188 Cal. 229, 234, 204 Pac. 818 (grantor retained possession of the premises and gave a mortgage of it); Stewart v. Silva, *supra,* 410; City National Bank v. Anderson, 189 Ky. 487, 225 S.W. 361 (deed surrendered to grantor); 16 Am. Jur. 506; 21 C.J. 874. As is pointed out in the *Loughran* case, *supra,* this is one of the instances where a positive rule of law may defeat the actual intention of the parties. The safety of real estate titles is considered more important than the unfortunate results which may follow the application of the rule in a few individual instances. To relax it would open the door wide to fraud and the fabrication of evidence. Although the doctrine has been criticized (2 Tiffany, Real Property (2d Ed.) p. 1764; 5 Wigmore, Evidence (2d Ed.) §§2405, 2408) no material change has been noted in the attitude of the courts in this country.

The finding does not support the conclusion. The finding shows a delivery and, even if a conditional delivery is assumed, the condition is not good for the reasons stated. Since a new trial is necessary, the one ruling on evidence made a ground of appeal is noticed. The town clerk was permitted to testify to certain statements made by Maurice when the deed was drafted. Parol evidence is not admissible to vary the terms of the deed but may be received to show the use that was to be made of it. Fisk's Appeal, 81 Conn. 433, 437, 71 Atl. 559. The ruling was correct as showing the circumstances surrounding delivery.

There is error and a new trial is ordered.[16]

Problems

27.1. O, owner of Blackacre, entered into negotiations with P regarding the sale of Blackacre. O prepared a deed of the land, which O signed, sealed,

---

16. Lerner Shops of North Carolina, Inc. v. Rosenthal, 225 N.C. 316, 34 S.E.2d 206 (1945), adopts the view that a conditional delivery may be made by the grantor to the grantee. After referring to the well-recognized rule that the grantor can establish that a deed in the possession of the grantee was not intended to have any legal effectiveness, the court said:

A delivery upon condition that the instrument should never become effective according to its terms is, in principle, as much a conditional delivery as one made upon condition that the deed should become effective only upon the happening of a specific event. [225 N.C. at 320, 34 S.E.2d at 209.]

—Eds.

and acknowledged and had attested by the proper number of witnesses, but O left the name of the grantee blank. In this condition the deed was handed to P, so that he might show it to his attorney. P inserted his own name as grantee and refused to return the deed to O when the parties could not agree on the terms of the sale. O brings a bill in equity to have the deed declared null and void. In a jurisdiction following Sweeney v. Sweeney, who would prevail? See Westlake v. Dunn, 184 Mass. 260 (1903).

27.2. O owner of Blackacre, contracts in writing to sell Blackacre to P. The purchase price is $10,000. O draws a deed which on its face transfers Blackacre to P in fee simple, and O signs, seals, and acknowledges this deed and has it attested by the proper number of witness. O then hands the deed to P on the oral condition that the deed is to be ineffective if P does not pay the $10,000 within 90 days. P does not pay the $10,000 within the 90 days. What courses of action are available to O in a jurisdiction following Sweeney v. Sweeney? See Burnett v. Rhudy, 137 Va. 67, 119 S.E. 97 (1923).

27.3. O, owner of Blackacre, draws a deed which on its face transfers Blackacre to A in fee simple, and O signs, seals, and acknowledges this deed and has it attested by the proper number of witnesses. O then hands the deed to A's attorney with instructions to record it on O's death. A's attorney records the deed immediately and A brings an action of ejectment against O. A's attorney cites Sweeney v. Sweeney as the basis of ignoring the oral instructions of O. As O's attorney, how would you distinguish that case from this one? See American Law of Property §12.66, 12.67 (Casner ed. 1952).

JOHNSON v. JOHNSON
24 R.I. 571, 54 A. 378 (1903)

TILLINGHAST, J. The only question presented for our decision by the bill, answer, and proof in this case is whether the deed under which the respondent claims title to the real estate described in the bill was so deposited or left with the witness Charles P. Moies by the grantor, during her lifetime, as to constitute an absolute delivery thereof for the use and benefit of the grantee.

The material facts in the case are these: On May 9, 1899, Mary Johnson made and executed a quitclaim deed of the premises referred to, to the respondent, Mary A. Johnson, and left it with said Charles P. Moies, with direction that in case anything happened to her (she meaning thereby, as Moies understood it, that in case she should die), he should then deliver the deed to her daughter, said Mary A. Johnson. He did not understand, however, from the instructions given him, that the grantor intended by said acts to place the deed beyond her control, but, on the contrary, he understood that she retained the right to recall the deed at any time, and also that she retained the right to sell and dispose of the property thereafterwards if she saw fit. In short, the substance of Moies' understanding, from the instructions given him, was that the deed was left with him subject to the control of the grantor during her life, and that in case of her death, without having disposed of the property, he was to deliver the deed to the grantee named therein.

The grantor continued to exercise dominion over said real estate up to the time of her death, which occurred on the 13th day of November, 1901. She advertised it for sale, and in other ways attempted to effect a sale thereof; she paid the taxes, collected the rents, and paid the interest on the mortgage thereon, and generally treated the estate as her absolute property. After her death said deed was delivered to the grantee by Moies, and by her caused to be recorded in the registry of deeds in Pawtucket. And the complainants now seek by this bill to have said deed set aside and declared void and of no effect, on the ground that no delivery thereof was ever effected by the grantor.

In view of the facts aforesaid, we are of the opinion that said deed was ineffectual to pass any title to the estate.

In order to convey title to real estate, it is necessary that the deed thereof shall be delivered to the grantee or to some one for his use. And the ordinary test of delivery is: Did the grantor by his acts or words, or both, intend to divest himself of the title to the estate described in the deed? If so, the deed is delivered. But if not, there is no delivery; and hence no title passes. See Am. & Eng. Ency. Law, vol. 9, 2nd ed. 154-8; Brown v. Brown, 66 Me. 316. In order to constitute a delivery, the grantor must absolutely part with the possession and control of the instrument. Younge v. Guilbeau, 3 Wall. 636; Hawkes v. Pike, 105 Mass. 562.

That a deed may be effectual to convey title, although delivered to a third person to hold until the grantor's death, and then to deliver it to the grantee, there can be no doubt. But in order to make such a delivery valid, the deed must be left with the depositary without any reservation on the part of the grantor, either express or implied, of the right to recall it or otherwise to control its use. Walter v. Way, 170 Ill. 96; Foster v. Mansfield, 3 Met. 412. In other words, in order to make a delivery of a deed valid when it is made to a third person for the benefit of the grantee, such delivery must be an absolute one on the part of the grantor; that is, he must divest himself of any right of future control thereof. And if such control is retained by the grantor, no estate passes. . . .

In the case at bar the evidence shows that while there was a parting with the manual possession of the deed by the grantor, she did not part with the control thereof; and hence a very essential element of delivery was lacking.

Her intended disposition of the property was evidently of a testamentary character. "In case she died," as Moies testifies, "she wanted the property to go that way." But an instrument which is intended to operate as a will, without being executed in accordance with the provisions of the statute relating thereto (Gen. Laws R.I. Chap. 203), cannot be allowed to have the effect of a will. See Providence Institution for Savings v. Carpenter, 18 R.I. 287, and Coulter v. Shelmadine, 53 At. Rep. 638.

For the reasons above given, the deed in question must be set aside and declared null and void and of no effect.

Decree accordingly.

STONE v. DUVALL
77 Ill. 475 (1875)

WALKER, J., delivered the opinion of the court:

The evidence shows that defendants in error had each been previously married, Washington having a daughter by that former marriage, who was married to William Stone; Mary (Duvall) had a son by her previous marriage, named Allen Agnew. They each owned a small amount of real estate when married, and discord afterwards having arisen between them, it was agreed that they should respectively relinquish or convey their claim to each other's property, so that the survivor would have no interest in the real estate of the other — to cut off the claim of dower by the wife in the property of the husband, and the right of curtesy of the husband in the property of the wife, and to prevent their stepchildren from claiming any interest in the property of their stepparents.[17]

In consummating this arrangement, defendants in error went to a justice of the peace, who, under their directions, prepared deeds which they executed and acknowledged. By one of these deeds the land owned by the husband was conveyed in fee to his daughter, Mrs. Mary Stone. By the other, the wife's real estate was conveyed to Allen Agnew. The justice was directed to have the deeds recorded, and to hold them until the death of the parties, and then deliver them to the respective grantees. Subsequently Mrs. Stone died, leaving her husband, and the other defendants, her minor children, surviving her. The deeds were recorded,[18] as required, by the justice of the peace, and held until after Mrs. Stone's death, when Duvall called and took the deed executed to her from the justice. It appears that Stone, with his wife, was in possession of the property conveyed to his wife when the deeds were made, and he so continued in possession until after the suit was brought.

Complainants claim that the deed to Mrs. Stone was not made in pursuance of their intentions, and contrary to their directions; that the deed was never delivered to the grantee, or to any one for her, and they asked to have it set aside and cancelled, and the property restored to Duvall, as it was before the deed was made. On a hearing, the court below granted the relief

17. On what basis could stepchildren claim an interest in the property of their stepparents? — EDS.

18. What risk did the grantor run by allowing the deed to be recorded before the occurrence of the event on which the deed was to be turned over to the grantee? See Mays v. Shields, page 772 *infra.* — EDS.

sought, and defendants bring the record to this court on error, and ask a reversal.

The evidence of the justice of the peace seems to be rather indefinite as to what the expressed purpose of the parties was when he drew the deeds. He is, however, positive that he was directed to prepare deeds to convey the land. He proposed to fix the matter by agreement, will or otherwise, but Duvall declined, saying his wife desired deeds. He, when asked the direct question whether the purpose was not to convey Duvall's interest in his wife's property to her son, and any interest she held in Duvall's property to Mrs. Stone, and whether Duvall did not so inform him, says he believes that was the meaning, but that he could not swear to the exact words. He also says that he was afterwards so informed by Mrs. Duvall. He nowhere says that it was understood or intimated that the parties intended or said they desired to retain any interest in the property. By a conveyance in fee, they undeniably would accomplish the purpose of preventing such claims as effectually as by any other mode; and it is strange, if such was the intention, that they did not say that was their only purpose.

Duvall told Stone that he intended to convey the property to his wife, as Stone states in his sworn answer. The deed having been subsequently made in accordance with this declaration, and in pursuance to the advice received from the attorney, a different purpose from that expressed in the deed should be clearly proved, before a court of chancery would interfere to set it aside. The deed itself, in proper form and duly executed, is strong evidence of the grantor's intention, and to overcome it, the evidence should be clear and convincing.

Here we find a man largely advanced in life, the father of a woman having a family of children, and of limited means, and, as it seems, fearful that his wife would, at his death, hold dower in his property, determined to secure the property to his daughter, and it is not out of the usual course of human action for him to make a conveyance to her. He inquired if he could; he said he would, and finally did so convey it. Duvall, himself, testified, and he does not state the purpose of the conveyance, nor the instructions he gave to the justice of the peace. He does not say that the deed did not carry out his purpose when it was made. He is silent as to the execution of the deed, or what he said to the justice. He does not say there was a mistake, or that the justice did not do precisely what he desired. . . .

It is manifest that complainants intended to convey some interest in, and title to these premises to Mrs. Stone, but what interest is not shown by the evidence. Whether it was to be a fee subject to a life estate in the grantor, or some other estate, does not appear. Nor do counsel suggest what estate it was. To cancel the deed would be to permit Duvall to change his mind, and to defeat his act deliberately done after consultation and advice taken, and done in accordance with his previously expressed purpose to convey to Mrs. Stone. It would be clearly wrong to abrogate the deed, unless it clearly appeared that an estate less than a fee, and such an estate as terminated with her life, or previous thereto, was intended to be conveyed, but was not by reason of a mistake.

It is urged that the deed was never delivered. It was not, to Mrs. Stone, as she was probably not aware of its existence for a considerable time afterwards, if it ever came to her knowledge. Was the delivery to the justice of the peace, with directions to record and hold it until the death of Duvall, a delivery? It was manifestly not an absolute delivery. The fact that he was directed to hold the deed, and not deliver it till the death of Duvall, renders it absolutely certain that the grantor did not intend that the deed should take effect until that time. This removes all doubt on that question. The deed did not, therefore operate to give Mrs. Stone any immediate rights or interest in the premises. If she acquired any right, it was that the title should only vest in her at her father's death.

Was this, then, a delivery as an escrow? KENT, Ch. J., in the case of Jackson v. Catlin, 2 Johns, R. 248, says: "A deed is delivered as an escrow when the delivery is conditional, that is, when it is delivered to a third person to keep until something be done by the grantee; and it is of no force until the condition be fulfilled." Sheppard, in his Touchstone, p. 58, gives substantially the same definition, except he does not limit the performance of the act to the grantee, which seems to us to be the more accurate rule. Now this deed was to be delivered on the death of Duvall. That was the express condition upon which it was placed in the hands of the justice, and, according to the authority of the case of Jackson v. Catlin, *supra,* it was delivered as an escrow, and could not take full effect until the thing happened that was conditional to its delivery; and Duvall not having died, the deed has not yet vested the title in full, and can not until that event shall occur.

Sheppard lays it down as the law, that the delivery is good, for it is said, in this case, that if either of the parties to the deed die before the conditions be performed, and the conditions be after performed, that the deed is good; for there was traditio inchoata in the lifetime of the parties; and postea consummata existens, by the performance of the conditions, it taketh its effect by the first delivery, without any new or second delivery; and the second delivery is but the execution and consummation of the first delivery. But in such a case, the delivery only relates back to the first delivery so as to carry out the intention of the grantor, and to vest the title. It would not give the grantee a right to intervening rents and profits. So in this case, the deed is an escrow, that will not take effect until Duvall's death, when it may be delivered to the heirs of the grantee, and it will be held to have taken effect so as to have vested such a title in the mother as to pass the fee to them. Until that time, Duvall will be entitled to the use of the property as though he had a life estate, and the children of Mrs. Stone the remainder.

It, then, follows that the court below erred in rendering the decree, and it is reversed.

Decree reversed.

Problems

27.4. When an oral condition is attached to a delivery of a deed to a third person that the deed is to be held by such third person and delivered to the grantee on the death of the grantor, what is the answer to the contention that the oral condition cannot be shown because of the statute of frauds? O orally contracts with P to sell Blackacre to P for $10,000. O executes a deed of Blackacre naming P as grantee and delivers the deed to X with oral instructions to deliver the deed to P if P pays X $10,000 within 90 days. P tenders the $10,000 within 90 days and X, on instructions from O, refuses to deliver the deed to P. X returns the deed to O. P sues O for specific performance. O raises the statute of frauds as a defense. Should this case be decided in the same way as the one involving a deed to be delivered to the grantee on the death of the grantor? See Campbell v. Thomas, 42 Wis. 437 (1877); Bigelow, Conditional Deliveries of Deeds of Land, 26 Harv. L. Rev. 565 (1913); Aigler, Is a Contract Necessary to Create an Effective Escrow? 16 Mich. L. Rev. 569 (1918); Gavit, The Conditional Delivery of Deeds, 30 Colum. L. Rev. 1145 (1930).

27.5. O, owner of Blackacre, draws a deed which on its face transfers Blackacre to A in fee simple, and O signs, seals, and acknowledges this deed and has it attested by the proper number of witnesses. O then hands the deed to X with instructions to deliver it to A on O's death.[19]

a. O was unmarried at the time O handed the deed to X. O marries. O dies. Is O's spouse entitled to dower in Blackacre? Smiley v. Smiley, 114 Ind. 258, 16 N.E. 585 (1888); cf. Ladd v. Ladd, 14 Vt. 185 (1842).

b. O dies leaving insufficient assets to pay all of O's debts. Can O's creditors reach Blackacre? Rathmell v. Shirey, 60 Ohio St. 187, 53 N.E. 1098 (1899).

c. O dies leaving a will which specifically devises Blackacre to B. In a dispute between A and B over Blackacre, who prevails?

d. O removes timber from Blackacre, contrary to the principles of good husbandry. A brings an action against O to recover damages for waste. Judgment for whom?

27.6. O, owner of Blackacre, draws a deed which on its face transfers Blackacre "to A and her heirs from and after the death of O," and O signs, seals, and acknowledges this deed and has it attested by the proper number of witnesses. O then hands the deed to A. Compare the situations of O and A under this arrangement with their situations under the arrangement adopted in Problem 27.5.

---

19. In a transaction of this type, the deed normally is not recorded until after the death of the grantor. Thus, so far as the land records are concerned, O appears to be the owner of the land and this appearance is bolstered by the fact that O remains in possession of the land. We shall see when we consider Chapter 28 that O has the power to defeat the rights of the grantee based on an unrecorded deed by a sale of the land to a bona fide purchaser.

27.7. O, owner of Blackacre, transfers Blackacre to X in fee simple, and X immediately executes a deed conveying Blackacre "to O for life, remainder to A and her heirs." X delivers this deed to O. Compare the situations of O and A under this arrangement with their situations under the arrangements adopted in Problems 27.5 and 27.6.

27.8. O, owner of Blackacre, contracts in writing to sell Blackacre to P. The agreed purchase price is $10,000 and is to be paid in 90 days. O draws a deed which on its face transfers Blackacre to P in fee simple, and O signs, seals, and acknowledges this deed and has it attested by the proper number of witnesses. O then hands the deed to X with instructions to deliver it to P when P pays $10,000 to X.[20]

a. In the absence of any governing provision in the contract of sale, as between O and P, who is responsible for the payment of real estate taxes falling due in the 90-day period? See Mohr v. Joslin, 162 Iowa 34, 142 N.W. 981 (1913); McMurtrey v. Bridges, 41 Okla. 264, 137 P. 721 (1913). Cf. Miller & Lux, Inc. v. Sparkman, 128 Cal. App. 449, 17 P.2d 772 (1932).

b. The fire insurance policy taken out by O before the deed was handed to X contains a clause that the policy will be void "if the insured is less than sole and unconditional owner." The house on Blackacre is destroyed by fire before the 90-day period has expired. Is the insurance company liable on the policy? See Etheredge v. Aetna Insurance Co., 102 S.C. 313, 86 S.E. 687 (1915).

c. Would you answer questions a through d under Problem 27.5 differently if they arose in connection with this deed?

MAYS v. SHIELDS
117 Ga. 814, 45 S.E. 68 (1903)

LAMAR, J. Shields, the grantor and plaintiff in fi. fa. [fieri facias], claims that he signed the deed and left it with Thompson to be delivered to Flynt, the grantee therein named, when he paid the balance of the purchase-money. The deed was recorded the same day. Sometime thereafter Flynt sold to Sanders, and he to Mays, who is the claimant here. Shields admits that he knew that the paper was recorded, but says that Sanders and Mays both had notice that it had been improperly delivered before they bought. This they deny, Mays claiming to be an innocent purchaser for value,

20. In a transaction of this type, the deed normally is not recorded until after P pays the purchase price. The contract of sale, however, may be a recordable document, and if it is recorded, notice will be given to everyone of P's rights in Blackacre. Even if the contract of sale is not recorded, the contract may provide that P is to take possession of Blackacre pending the payment of the purchase price, and in such case, P's possession of the land may give notice to others of P's rights in the land. If, however, the contract of sale is not recorded and P is not in possession of the land, O can defeat P's rights by a sale to a bona fide purchaser (Chapter 28).

without knowledge that there had been any escrow, or that the instrument had been improperly delivered and recorded. In Dixon v. Bristol Bank, 102 Ga. 461, it was ruled that where an escrow was obtained from the depositary by a fraud practiced upon him by the grantee, who had not performed the conditions upon which the delivery was to be made, no title passed, and a bona fide purchaser from the grantee would acquire no rights as against the grantor. This decision is fully supported by the great weight of authority; most of the courts holding that the improper delivery by the depositary and the subsequent purchase from the grantee is not such a case as calls for the application of the rule that, where one of two innocent parties must suffer, he should bear the loss who put it in the power of a third person to inflict the injury. Civil Code, Sec. 3940. Other courts protect the grantor on the theory that a lawful delivery is as essential to the validity of a deed as a genuine or authorized signature, and that the unlawful delivery is to have the same effect as if the deed had been forged, in which case, of course, a subsequent grantee would not acquire any rights, no matter how honest his mistake, or how great the price paid. It is a hardship on the grantor to lose his land, and an equal hardship on an innocent grantee to lose his money. The equities are equal; and where that is true, the law must prevail. But where they differ, the superior equity must prevail. Civil Code, Sec. 3927.

The case at bar differs in several points from that of *Dixon, supra.* There the entry by the grantee was under the fraudulently obtained deed; his possession was unlawful, and partook of the nature of the deed itself. Here Flynt had been rightfully in possession of the land for a year or more, under a bond for title and contract of purchase. There the purchase by the subsequent vendee was not made on the faith of the registry of the deed. In this case Shields admits that he knew that his deed had been recorded, but testified that he had a conversation with Mays in which the latter recognized his title and the invalidity of the deed to Flynt, and desired to know how much would be needed to satisfy Shields' interest in the land. This was denied by Mays; and the court charged that "if the deed was delivered to Thompson in escrow, and not to be delivered to Flynt until the purchase-money was paid, and passed from Thompson to Flynt without such payment and without the consent of Shields, no title passed to Flynt, who could not convey title to Sanders, nor could Sanders convey to Mays; and this would be true whether Sanders or Mays, or either of them, had notice of the way in which the deed was held by Thompson." There was no instruction that if Shields subsequently ratified the delivery the deed would become valid, nor was the jury told that if with knowledge that the deed was on record Shields took no steps to have the record expunged, he would be estopped from denying the title of an innocent purchaser buying on the faith of the record. Where a grantor delivers a deed in escrow, and learns that it has been improperly delivered to the grantee or that it has been recorded, he must at once take steps to prevent innocent third persons from acting to their injury. Such knowledge would bring the case within the rule as to which of two innocent persons must suffer. Civil Code, Secs. 3937, 3940.

Besides this, Flynt was in possession of the land before the execution of the deed alleged to have been delivered in escrow. Possession of itself is a high evidence of title, and in ancient times was the only method of conveying land. When one is both in possession of the property, and of muniments of title duly recorded, he is clothed with double evidence of ownership; and even in States recognizing the same rule as that laid down in the *Dixon* case, it has been distinctly ruled, that, if the grantee named in the escrow already had possession of the land, the doctrine there announced will not apply as against a grantee who purchases for value and without notice of the unlawful delivery. Quick v. Milligan, 108 Ind. 49, 58 Am. Rep. 49. The ruling which protects the grantor as against an innocent purchaser is a harsh one, and will not be extended beyond its letter, as against the rights of innocent purchasers who (Civil Code, Sec. 3540) as a class are favored in law and are to be protected. Of course, if Saunders or Mays knew of the improper delivery and record, they cannot claim the benefit of this principle. But if the jury should find that they did not have notice and bought on the faith of Flynt's possession under a recorded deed, of which Shields himself had notice, they will be protected in their purchase. Possession prior to the deed, knowledge by the grantor that the deed has been surrendered and recorded, inaction on his part thereafter, ratification of the delivery, or any act constituting an estoppel may all be used by an innocent purchaser to defend the title to land for which in good faith and without notice he has paid. While denied by Shields, there was evidence that the deed had been delivered by him to Flynt. If so, the title vested in spite of any agreement to the contrary; for if the grantor delivers the deed to the grantee, the law will not allow the solemn recitals therein of conveyance and delivery to be so modified as to show that it was held by the grantee in escrow, or for some other purpose than that of conveying title: Jordan v. Pollock, 14 Ga. 145 (2); Civil Code, Sec. 3603. Certainly is this so as against third persons. This was so material a point that it would have controlled the verdict if the jury had believed the claimant's evidence; and required a charge, even without a request. There must be a new trial, and it is therefore unnecessary to consider the other questions raised.[21]

Judgment reversed. All the Justices concur.

Problem

27.9. O, owner of Blackacre, draws a deed which on its face transfers Blackacre to A in fee simple, and O signs, seals, and acknowledges this deed and has it attested by the proper number of witnesses. O then hands the deed to X with instructions to deliver it to A on O's death.

---

21. See Roberts, Wrongful Delivery of Deed in Escrow, 17 Ky. L.J. 31 (1928).—Eds.

a. A takes the deed from X by force, records the deed, and im.
    sells Blackacre to a bona fide purchaser. If you representec
    fide purchaser in a dispute with O over Blackacre, would yc
    Mays v. Shields?
b. A fraudulently induces X to let A have the deed, records tl
    and immediately sells Blackacre to a bona fide purchaser. ıı you
    represented the bona fide purchaser in a dispute with O over Black-
    acre, would you rely on Mays v. Shields?
c. X hands the deed to A saying X does not want to hold it any longer. A
    records the deed. O learns of the situation and does nothing. Later A
    sells Blackacre to a bona fide purchaser. If you represented the bona
    fide purchaser in a dispute with O over Blackacre, would you rely on
    Mays v. Shields?

Spu bruck

SECTION 3.   THE DESCRIPTION OF THE LAND[22]

Note: Drafting the Description of Land

A deed is not effective to pass an interest in land because of the statute of
frauds unless it adequately describes the land conveyed. How detailed must
the description be in order for the deed to be valid? The test seems to be
whether the land can be located by referring to the deed and admissible
extrinsic evidence. The evidence that may be introduced to support the
description in the deed must show that from the circumstances, the words
could refer to only one piece of land. Thus, if the deed conveys "my farm,"
the land records will give meaning to the description if the grantor owns only
one farm. If the grantor owns two farms, however, the deed furnishes no
basis for identifying the land and is ineffective even though there is evidence
as to which farm the grantor intended to convey.

In commercial land transactions, the deeds tend to be very detailed in
describing the land because the purchaser's attorney will not be satisfied
with anything less than a full and complete description of the land. In a
donative transaction, however, the donee normally is not given an opportunity to examine the deed and make suggestions, and thus the descriptions
tend to be less exact. In wills, devises of real estate are often phrased in such
terms as "all the real property I may own at my death." The description of
the real property devised is in these general terms because the will does not
become legally operative until the transferor dies and he or she cannot know
for certain now what land will be owned at that time.

In undertaking a detailed description of land, the drafter may have

22.   See generally American Law of Property §§12.98-12.123 (Casner ed. 1952).

several different methods available. One is referring to the survey of public land made by the federal government. In the eighteenth century the United States government began surveying the public lands.[23] This survey divided the public lands into rectangular tracts located with reference to a base line running east and west on a true parallel of latitude, and a principal meridian running along a longitude. At every six miles along both the base line and the meridian, perpendicular lines are run. These lines intersect to form townships which are tracts six miles square and contain about 23,040 acres. A line of townships running north and south is called a range, and the ranges are numbered east and west from the meridian. Each township in a range also is numbered north and south from the base line. Each township is divided into 36 sections, each one mile square. The sections are numbered consecutively beginning in the northeast corner of the township and proceeding west to the range line, and in the next row proceeding west to east. This is continued, alternately proceeding west and east, until reaching section 36, which is in the southeast corner of the township. The sections in turn are divided into half sections and quarter sections; the quarter sections into quarter-quarter sections. A given quarter-quarter section (consisting of about 40 acres) may be identified as the NW quarter of the NE quarter of section 13 of township 2N, range 3W, principal meridian. Draw a diagram and see if you can plot this tract.[24]

The rectangular system developed by the government for the public lands is very commonly used to describe agricultural land. It is not adaptable to describing small city lots.

Another method is to describe the land by metes and bounds. This means that the land is described with reference to identifiable and permanent objects or locations which either are part of the boundary or are terminal points of lines which are the boundary. Normally, a description by metes and bounds makes use of monuments—i.e., tangible, permanent landmarks. A house, a street, a river, or stake lines run by surveyors are some of the things that may be used as monuments.

Related to the description of land by metes and bounds is a description by courses and distances. This is done by giving a starting place and the direction and length of the lines to be run.

The owner of a tract of land may divide it into lots and make a map showing the boundaries of each lot. Each lot is given a number on the map. This map usually is called a plat and in most states can be recorded.[25]

23. For an historical account of the government land survey, see Fegtly, Historical Development of Land Surveys, 38 Ill. L.R. 270 (1944).

24. Many modifications to this general scheme are necessary owing to such factors as the curvature of the earth, distance, mountains, and rivers. For a good short discussion of the government survey, see Warvelle, Abstracts of Title §§160-165 (4th ed. 1921). For an outline of the procedure followed in such surveys, see Zabriwskie, Land Laws of the United States 508 (1870). On surveying and boundary problems generally, see Clark, Surveying and Boundaries (2d ed. 1939).

25. For a discussion of the formalities in making and recording a plat, see Warvelle, Abstracts of Title §§166-171 (4th ed. 1921).

Thereafter, a lot may be described by referring to the plat and number of the lot.[26] Other types of maps may also be utilized in describing land. Many cities have made official surveys and the maps and field notes are available. Sometimes private maps are used.

Sometimes the person drafting the instrument of transfer uses a combination of descriptions. This creates no difficulty unless the descriptions used are in conflict. To resolve such conflicts when they exist, courts have developed various rules of construction. These rules are designed to give effect to what the parties most likely intended. Thus a boundary based on paper calculations is normally controlled by a boundary based on physical conditions. Accordingly, monuments referred to prevail over anything else on the theory that the premises were bought in reliance on what could be seen. The accepted order seems to be: natural monuments, artificial monuments, maps, courses and distances, and area. You must keep in mind that these are rules of construction, not of law, and you may be able to overcome them in particular cases. Thus the title examiner in checking the various deeds in the chain of title cannot rely too heavily on these rules of construction if any of the back deeds contain conflicting descriptions.

When the land is described by reference to monuments having width, such as a street or stream, and the grantor owns part or all of the street subject to the right of way in the public or owns part or all of the bed of the stream, the question may arise whether the description includes any part of the monument itself. Litigation has been very extensive on this point and usually does not come up until many years after the deed when the public street is abandoned or the stream changes its course and it becomes important for the first time to decide who owns the street or bed of the stream. Some rules of construction have been adopted to aid in resolving these disputes. Thus if the grantor owned to the center of the street, as is usual, and owned no land on the other side of the street, it will be presumed that the grantor intended to convey to the grantee title in the street which was referred to as a monument in describing the land.[27] A good drafter who uses monuments having width to describe the boundaries of land makes it unequivocally clear what the grantee is to receive. A title examiner must notice carefully references to monuments in past deeds because it may be important to the purchaser to know the status of his or her rights with respect to streets, the bed of a stream, and the like.

26. It is well settled that the owner of land may declare that the property is to be devoted to a public use. Recognized public uses include streets, parks, schools, cemeteries, and similar community benefits. Frequently, recorded plats show certain strips reserved for streets. When lots are sold by reference to a plat (and sometimes, by statute, when the plat is recorded), it is usually held that there is a dedication of the marked areas for use as streets. Thus, it is frequent that boundary disputes concern the city's right to construct roads. Depending on where the street is finally placed, land owners all over the plat are likely to find their boundaries affected. This poses a different problem from disputes involving adjoining private landowners, since the right of the public cannot readily be bought out. On dedication generally, see American Law of Property §12.112 (Casner ed. 1952).

27. Although the general rule that a conveyance in which a street or other natural monument having some width is named as a boundary passes to the grantee title to the

As an attorney, you will be concerned with descriptions of land in the following situations:

1. as the attorney for one of the parties in a dispute over boundaries, in which case you will be contending that some past description should be construed in the light most favorable to your client;
2. as the attorney for the seller of land, in which case you must make certain that the description employed does not refer to something not owned by your client, or the client may be liable on the covenants for title;
3. as attorney for the purchaser of land, in which case you must make certain that the deed offered to your client contains a clear and unambiguous description of the land your client desires to buy, and you must check carefully the descriptions in earlier deeds in the chain of title to make certain they are clear and unambiguous.

SMITH v. HADAD
366 Mass. 106, 314 N.E.2d 435 (1974)

HENNESSEY, J. This case, which is before us on the allowance of an application for leave to obtain further appellate review, presents the issue whether, in the absence of expressed intent by the parties to the transaction, a measurement given in a deed as commencing on a public way is to be presumed to begin at the center or at the side line of that way. The Land Court and the Appeals Court, Smith v. Hadad, — Mass. App. —., 305 N.E.2d 515 (1973), both rendered decisions in favor of the respondents' position that the presumed starting point is the side of the way. We affirm.

The basic facts of the case, as agreed by the parties, are as follows.

The land now owned by all the parties was at some time owned by one Raymond E. Nichols, who in 1949 conveyed a portion of it to the petitioners' predecessor in title, reserving a portion for himself. The deed of which Nichols was grantee described the northern and eastern boundaries as

---

centerline of the monument is well settled, the question is one of construction and intricate distinctions are sometimes drawn. As the court said in MacCorkle v. Charleston, 105 W. Va. 395, 142 S.E. 841 (1928):

> Quite a number of courts have seen fit to draw nice distinctions in the implication of certain words of calls, in determining whether the conveyance stops at a line of a street, or extends to the center of the street. For example, where a description calls for a *highway* or uses such expressions as "bounded by," "on," "upon," or "along" a highway, it has been held to extend the conveyance to the center of the highway; while on the other hand, if the description merely calls for *"a line"* of the highway or to run *"with the line,"* or "by the side" of the highway, some courts have held that the grantee's title stops with the line. [105 W. Va. at 401, 142 S.E. at 843.]

Is the problem any different if the directions are to measure a certain distance from a road? See Dodd v. Witt, 139 Mass. 63, 29 N.E. 475 (1885).

"following the old course of said river to Main Street; thence the line runs Southerly by said Main Street, now a state highway, to said Short Street." Nichols's grant to the petitioners' predecessor gave the same description up to Main Street but then read as follows: "[T]hence turning and running Southerly by Main Street to a point on Main Street distant eight hundred (800) feet North of the junction of Main and Short Streets; thence turning at a right angle to said Main Street and running Westerly one hundred seventy-five (175) feet; thence turning and running Southerly and parallel to Main Street and distant one hundred seventy-five (175) feet therefrom, eight hundred (800) feet more or less to said Short Street." Nichols thus reserved a 175 foot wide parcel fronting on Main Street to the east, which was later conveyed to the respondents' common predecessor in title. Left ambiguous in the deed was whether the 175 foot measurement begins at the western edge or in the center of Main Street. Since the street is sixty-six feet wide, the answer affects a 33 foot wide strip at the boundary between the petitioners' and the respondents' land. It is the dispute over ownership of this strip which has brought the issue to this court.

In our consideration of this case we examine, first, the issue of the ownership of the fee under a public way, the rights to which were taken by the Commonwealth by an easement, after a transfer of title to land of which the way is a boundary where the deed either clearly made the side line the boundary rather than the center, or left the issue ambiguous.

While it is true that after the taking of an easement for a public way the fee to the underlying land remains in the adjoining private owners, we have noted that this property right is effectively useless unless the public way is abandoned. Smith v. Slocomb, 9 Gray 36, 37 (1857); Boston v. Richardson, 13 Allen 146, 153 (1866). Nevertheless, cases have arisen where the parties neglected explicitly to settle the question in the deed, and it later became a matter of dispute. In such cases the law fathoms the unexpressed (and possibly nonexistent) intention of the parties with the aid of a presumption.

The presumption has long been that, even where the specified boundary line is clearly at the side of the way (as where it runs between two stakes, each of necessity at the side rather than in the center), the deed was intended to transfer the abbreviated rights to the fee of the way as well. See e.g., Peck v. Denniston, 121 Mass. 17 (1876); Brassard v. Flynn, 352 Mass. 185, 188-189, 224 N.E.2d 221 (1967), and cases cited. See also G.L. c. 183, §58, inserted by St. 1971, c. 684, §1. The rationale of such decisions is apparently that the grantor is unlikely to want to reserve title to the fee of the way; if he does, he may avoid the effect of the presumption by contraindicating.

The ultimate issue here is the distinct question of the starting point for a measurement, which was dealt with in Dodd v. Witt, 139 Mass. 63, 65-66, 29 N.E. 475, 476 (1885):

A majority of the court is of opinion, that it is a common method of measurement in the country, where the boundary is a stream or way, to measure from the bank of the stream or the side of the way; and that there is a reasonable presumption that the measurements were made in this way, unless something appears affirmatively in the deed to show that they began at the centre line of the stream or way.

We believe this is dispositive of the instant case. That a grantor probably had no intention to retain the fee under the adjoining way does not make it at all likely that he would therefore make a measurement from the center of the way affecting the placement of the boundary at the opposite end of the property. We note that the *Dodd* case was decided after Peck v. Denniston, *supra,* and expressly confirmed the *Peck* rule of construction. 139 Mass. at 65, 29 N.E. 475 (1885). There is nothing inconsistent between the two presumptions; rather, they both accord with common experience, good sense, and long tradition.

The petitioner argues that the holding of Dodd v. Witt, *supra,* was not that this presumption shall be made as matter of law but that evidence may be offered to demonstrate that the parties evidenced a contrary intent by erecting monuments at the boundaries. While the petitioners accurately state the holding, there is no showing of evidence in this case to rebut the presumption. The *Dodd* case clearly implies that the presumption shall be operative in the absence of such evidence. It is significant that the *Dodd* case recognized that such a presumption was widely made. It has been ever since. To change it now would create chaos in land titles, defeat the reasonable expectations of conveyancers, and cause substantial financial hardship to many innocent landowners.

Accordingly, we hold that, in the absence of a clear showing of a contrary intent, a measurement given from a stream or public or private way shall be presumed to begin at the side line of that stream or way.

Exceptions overruled.

Decision affirmed.

Problems

27.10. O owned a large tract of land: O conveyed part of this tract to A. A immediately recorded the deed. In the deed to A the land conveyed was described by courses and distances. Subsequently, O conveyed the balance of the tract to B. In the deed to B the land conveyed was described by courses and distances. P has contracted to buy B's land. You are attorney for P. Is there any reason for you to examine the description of the land conveyed in the deed from O to A?

27.11. O executes and delivers a deed to A. The deed contained the following description of land: "one tract of 700 acres in the district of Middleport near the town of West Huttonsville, being a part of a tract of 1,000 acres devised to the said O by O's father." Evidence is available to establish that the tract devised to O was 1,400 acres, not 1,000; that no other land besides this tract had been devised to O; that O had, prior to the deed to A, sold a smaller tract of the land included in the devise; that the deed of the smaller tract described the land conveyed by metes and bounds, the area being stated as 300 acres; that the area of the smaller tract was actually 400 acres, so that O owned approximately 1,000 acres when O executed the deed to A. How much, if any, of the tract devised to O is still owned by O? See Davis Colliery Co. v. Westfall, 78 W. Va. 735, 90 S.E. 328 (1916); Harris v. Woodard, 130 N.C. 580, 41 S.E. 790 (1902).

27.12. O owned a tract of land. O had a surveyor divide the land into lots, placing cornerstones at the corner boundaries of each lot. The surveyor then provided O with a description of each lot by courses and distances that made no reference to the various cornerstones. O sold the lots to various purchasers and in each deed the lot sold was described by the courses-and-distances description supplied by the surveyor. P_1 ascertained that the cornerstones relating to P_1's lot included ground not included in the courses-and-distances description. Is P_1 entitled to such additional ground? See Whitehead v. Ragan, 106 Mo. 231, 17 S.W. 307 (1891); Whitehead v. Atchison, 136 Mo. 485, 37 S.W. 928 (1896); Note, Parol Evidence and the Bona Fide Purchaser, 5 U. Chi. L. Rev. 656 (1938). In considering this problem, the following statement in Cities Service Oil Co. v. Dunlap, 115 F.2d 720 (5th Cir. 1941), is relevant: "An innocent purchaser is protected from reformation in equity, but not from construction at law of the deed as written. If the muniments of title he holds are beset with ambiguity, a court of law will resolve that ambiguity according to its own methods" (115 F.2d at 722).

SECTION 4.   COVENANTS FOR TITLE[28]

Note: Methods Available to Protect the Purchaser Against Defects in the Title

The purchaser of land naturally desires as much protection as possible against loss due to defects in the title of the land he or she is buying. This section considers the extent to which the purchaser is protected by guarantees as to the title made by the purchaser's grantor or made by prior grantors in the chain of title. Such guarantees are referred to as covenants for title. Whatever protection these covenants give to the purchaser depends, of course, on the continued solvency of the grantor giving the guarantee.

---

28.   See generally American Law of Property §§12.124-12.131 (Casner ed. 1952).

The significance of covenants for title so far as the purchaser is concerned may be better understood by examining briefly other protective devices which may be available.

1. *The opinion of the purchaser's attorney regarding the state of the title.* The attorney's opinion as to the state of the title is formulated principally on the basis of an examination of the land records where the various documents affecting the title are set forth in full. We shall see in Chapter 28 that many possible defects in the title will not be disclosed by even the most careful examination of the land records. If the attorney's examination is extended to matters which may affect the title that are outside the land records, the attorney still cannot eliminate the possibility of the existence of any defect in the title. An experienced title examiner, of course, comes to reasonably reliable judgments as to the state of the title, but the fact remains that he or she can never be absolutely certain that the conclusions are correct. This does not mean that the attorney's opinion is useless. The possible defects in the title which cannot be located are unusual, so that the attorney's opinion does give, in most cases, a reliable basis of proceeding with the purchase of the land.

From what has been said above, it is obvious that the attorney does not guarantee the title, but merely expresses an opinion as to it. If the attorney has not been negligent in the formulation of an opinion, the attorney is not liable to the purchaser if a defect in the title should turn up. In other words, securing an attorney's opinion offers no protection to the purchaser against financial loss if a defect in the title is present but not ascertainable by the investigation expected of the attorney.

2. *Title registration.* Our system of land conveyancing would bog down hopelessly if every purchaser of land insisted on a bill to quiet title being instituted in the appropriate court so that he or she would have the protection of a judicial decree as to the state of the title. If, however, a system could be devised which would result in the title being judicially determined once and thereafter being kept up to date in some manner, the maximum security for the purchaser of land might be obtained. The so-called Torrens system of title registration is thought by many to attain this goal. This system exists in some states, but not in all. We examine its advantages and disadvantages in Chapter 30. We shall see that even under this system there may be defects in the title which will cause trouble for the purchaser.

3. *Title insurance.* In some states title insurance has become the standard method of protecting a purchaser of land against defects in the title. The extent of the protection the purchaser receives, of course, depends on the terms of the policy of insurance. If the policy excepts from its operation various possible defects, the protection may be little more than is received from the opinion of a responsible attorney. The little more is that the title company gives a guarantee in the area in which the policy is to operate, whereas the attorney offers financial reimbursement only if you can prove the attorney was negligent. Bear in mind though that the purchaser of land

may need advice as to whether to proceed with the purchase in the light of all the circumstances rather than just protection against pecuniary loss if he or she proceeds and a defect in the title is present. The attorney can give such advice. Is the title company able to give such advice or can it only insure? The subject of title insurance is dealt with in Chapter 31.

The purchaser of land may stand to lose more than the initial financial investment if the title is defective. The purchaser may be subjected to attorneys' fees and other costs in defending suits, may lose the profit of the transaction if there has been an increase in land values, may have lost the opportunity to buy other land, may have placed valuable buildings on the property, etc. In comparing one protective device available to the purchaser of land with another protective device, the extent to which these items of damage, if present, are recoverable is relevant.

The covenants for title in common usage are classified either as present covenants or future covenants. A present covenant for title is one which guarantees that a described situation exists at the time the covenant is made; that situation either exists or it doesn't, so the covenant is broken when it is made or it is never broken. The standard present covenants for title are the following:

1. *Covenant for seisin (seizin)*. If the grantor covenants that he or she is lawfully seised of the land, this is normally construed to mean that the grantor guarantees that he or she owns the estate he or she is purporting to convey. The fact that the land conveyed is subject to a mortgage or is subject to some restriction as to its use does not cause a breach of this covenant.

2. *Covenant of the right to convey*. If the grantor covenants that he or she has the right to convey the land involved, the grantor has guaranteed practically the same thing as when giving a covenant for seisin. There is, however, one difference. The grantor may have the right to convey and not be the owner of the estate he or she is purporting to convey, as when he or she is conveying the land under a power.

3. *Covenant against encumbrances*. If the grantor covenants against encumbrances, he or she is guaranteeing that there are no mortgages, tax liens, judgment liens, easements, covenants restricting the use of the land, etc., outstanding against the land conveyed.

The standard future covenants for title are the following:

1. *Covenant of quiet enjoyment and covenant of general warranty.* These two covenants are for all practical purposes the same and mean that the grantor guarantees that the purchaser will not be disturbed in the future by the grantor or by some paramount claim existing at the date of the conveyance. In other words, these covenants are not broken until there has been a disturbance. The disturbance may be the result of an ouster from possession by one having a paramount title, by the foreclosure of a mortgage, by the enforcement of a covenant restricting the use of the land, etc. If

the purchaser pays off an outstanding mortgage on the land, this may be a disturbance even though the purchaser is not in fact ousted from possession.

2. *Covenant for further assurances.* This covenant simply guarantees that the grantor will do such further acts as are within the grantor's power to make the purchaser's title good.

The grantor may specifically narrow the scope of liability under any of the present and future covenants described above. For example, the grantor may except from the covenant against incumbrances certain liens on the land or may except from the covenant of general warranty disturbances from certain causes. One way of narrowing the liability under the covenant is for the grantor to guarantee only that *he or she* has done nothing that will make the title defective. Such a covenant for title on the grantor's part is said to be a special covenant for title, as distinguished from a general covenant for title where the guarantee is that no one has done anything to cause a defect in the title. Thus a covenant of special warranty is one in which the grantor guarantees that the purchaser will not be disturbed by the grantor or by any paramount claim created by the grantor.[29]

The extent to which a purchaser of land is able to obtain guarantees from the grantor as to the state of the title depends on various factors. In some states the matter is largely controlled by the prevailing practice. Thus if the local practice is to give only a quitclaim deed, a purchaser who insists on covenants for title is in a difficult position. Whether the market is a buyer's market or a seller's market at the time of the purchase is also significant. If it is a buyer's market, the purchaser's bargaining position may be such that he or she can demand any kind of a conveyance, and if it is a seller's market, just the reverse may be true.

Normally covenants for title are not implied but must be expressed in the deed. A short form of expressing these covenants in the deed, however, has been recognized in connection with statutory short form deeds.[30]

The cases and problems set forth below in this section develop a number of incidental points in regard to covenants for title but are mainly concerned with the following matters:

1. What is the measure of damages on breach of a covenant for title?

2. Is a prior grantor who has given a covenant for title liable for its breach to a remote grantee (generally phrased — does a covenant for title run with the land)?

HILLIKER v. RUEGER
228 N.Y. 11, 126 N.E. 266 (1920)

McLAUGHLIN, J. On the 1st of May, 1905, the defendants, Rueger's testator and his wife, conveyed to the plaintiff and his wife (now deceased),

---

29. See the general warranty deed, page 756 *supra,* and compare with it the special warranty deed, page 758 *supra.*

30. See statutory short-form deed, page 757 *supra.*

as tenants by the entirety, certain real property situated in the city of New York. The consideration was $7,000, of which $500 was paid down and the balance secured by a purchase-money mortgage. The grantors in the deed of conveyance covenanted that they were "seized of the said premises in fee simple and have good right to convey the same." Subsequent to the conveyance the grantees entered into a contract with one Schaefer to convey the premises to him for $8,500, of which $500 was paid on the execution of the contract and the balance agreed to be paid or secured when the title passed. Schaefer thereafter refused to complete the contract, on the ground that the title tendered was unmarketable and he demanded that the $500 paid be returned to him. The demand not being complied with, he brought an action to recover the same. It was finally determined in that action that the grantees did not have a marketable title to a part of the premises conveyed (Schaefer v. Hilliker, 140 App. Div. 173, 124 N.Y.S. 1014, *affirmed,* 206 N.Y. 708, 99 N.E. 1117), for which reason plaintiff was entitled to recover the amount paid at the time the contract was executed, with interest, expenses, etc. The defendants in the present action had notice of that action and were afforded an opportunity to defend it, which they neglected and refused to do. After Hilliker had paid the judgment recovered by Schaefer he brought this action to recover the damages alleged to have been sustained by reason of the breach of the covenant of seizin, to which reference has been made.[31] He had a judgment for a substantial amount, which was modified, and as modified affirmed (Hilliker v. Rueger, 165 App. Div. 189, 151 N.Y.S. 234), but on appeal to this court it was reversed and a new trial ordered (219

---

31. You will observe that in this case the grantors in the deed to the plaintiffs were a decedent and his wife. It is not known why the decedent's wife was a co-grantor. She may have been joining in the deed just to release her dower rights or she may have been a joint owner with her husband of the property conveyed. Whether she was personally bound by the covenant of seisin in the deed does not appear. If she was personally bound, of course, her own assets from whatever source would be available to satisfy her liability under the covenant. In any event this suit is against the wife of the decedent and another as executrices of the decedent's estate and as individuals. Other defendants were the residuary legatees under the decedent's will.

All states have statutes designed to require prompt presentation and adjudication of claims against a decedent's estate. These local statutes normally fix a time limit within which the claim must be presented to the personal representative of the decedent and fix a short statute of limitations within which actions on the claim must be commenced. Contingent claims in some states must be presented the same as other claims, together with a petition that the personal representative be required to retain assets out of the estate sufficient to pay the claim or, alternatively, to take a bond from the distributees obliging them to pay the creditor if the claim becomes absolute. In other states the contingent creditor is not required to take action but is allowed to assert a claim against distributees when the claim becomes absolute. The covenant of seisin, being a present covenant, is not a contingent claim. A future covenant, such as a covenant of warranty, which is not broken until there is a disturbance is a contingent claim if there has been no disturbance at the time the covenantor dies.

In New York at the time Rueger died, the statute (Code of Civil Procedure §2718) authorized the executor to insert a notice once each week for six months in such newspaper or newspapers printed in the county as the surrogate directs, requiring all persons having claims against the decedent to present them at a certain time, which had to be at least six months from the day the notice was first published. "If a suit be brought on a claim which is not presented to the executor or administrator within six months from the first publication of such notice, the executor or administrator shall not be chargeable for any assets or money that he may have paid

N.Y. 334, 114 N.E. 391)[32] The second trial also resulted in a judgment for the plaintiff. The trial court found there was a breach of the covenant of seizin in that the defendants' testator did not have title to a part of the premises conveyed, and by reason thereof plaintiff had sustained damage to the amount of $1,200, being the difference between $7,000, the consideration paid, and $5,800, the proportionate value of the part of the premises of which the grantors had title at the time of the conveyance, with interest on the $1,200 for six years immediately prior to the commencement of the action,[33] also for $1,500, the amount expended by the plaintiff for counsel and attorneys' fees in defending the action brought by Schaefer against him, with interest, and an extra allowance of five per cent as costs on the amount recovered. Judgment was entered to this effect, which was unanimously affirmed by the Appellate Division, second department, and defendant appeals to this court.

If a covenant of seizin be broken at all, it is at the time of the delivery of the conveyance. It is not essential in an action to recover damages for the breach of such a covenant that the grantee should be evicted. Veit v. McCauslan, 157 App. Div. 335, 142 N.Y.S. 281, *affirmed* 213 N.Y. 678, 107 N.E. 1087; Mygatt v. Coe, 124 N.Y. 212, 218, 26 N.E. 611. It is claimed, however, by the appellants that unless there be an eviction, only nominal damages can be recovered. This is not the law. Veit v. McCauslan, *supra;*

---

in satisfaction of any lawful claims, or of any legacies, or in making distribution to the next of kin before such suit was commenced." The statutes then in force in New York further provided (Code of Civil Procedure §1822) that if an executor or administrator rejects a claim presented "the claimant must commence an action for the recovery thereof against the executor or administrator, within six months after the dispute or rejection, or, if no part of the debt is then due, within six months after a part thereof becomes due; in default whereof he, and all the persons claiming under him, are forever barred from maintaining such an action thereupon, and from every other remedy to enforce payment thereof out of the decedent's property."

In this case, it is likely that no claim had been presented against the decedent's estate for the breach of the covenant of seisin so that the defendants as executrices of his estate would not be liable unless they still retained undistributed assets sufficient in amount to pay the judgment. They may have been, however, distributees of his estate and liable for a breach of the covenant to the extent of assets of his which they received as distributees.—EDS.

32.   The case was reversed on the previous appeal because the only evidence offered by the plaintiff that the covenant of seisin was broken was the record of the judgment against him in the suit brought by Schaefer which record only established he did not have a marketable title and did not establish he had no title. Why is this so? Simply because to establish that a title is not marketable requires you only to establish that there is sufficient controversy about the title so that it should not be forced on an unwilling purchaser. This can be done without proving complete failure of title. Thus the court on the previous appeal decided the plaintiff had not established a violation of the covenant of seisin by the evidence he offered.—EDS.

33.   Why interest for only six years back? This is due to the fact that the plaintiff has had the use of the land and is liable to account to the owner for mesne profits for only the last six years. Thus he has, in effect, had interest on his money to the extent that he can keep the profits from the land. See Staats v. Ten Eyck, 3 Cai. R. 111 (N.Y. Sup. Ct. 1805); Caulkins v. Harris, 9 Johns. 324 (N.Y. Sup. Ct. 1812). But the owner of the land may never demand the mesne profits for even the last six years so that the plaintiff may get interest on his money and keep the mesne profits too! Should not the court have refused interest without a showing that the owner had been paid the mesne profits for the last six years or have given interest only on the basis of the plaintiff's being required to account to the defendants for the mesne profits for the last six years if the owner does not claim them? See Annot., 61 A.L.R. 10, 176 (1929).—EDS.

Pollard v. Dwight, 4 Cranch (U.S.), 421, 430; Kent v. Welch, 7 Johns. 258; Tone v. Wilson, 81 Ill. 529; Parker v. Brown, 15 N.H. 176; Brandt v. Foster, 5 Iowa 287. Possession does not satisfy a covenant of seizin. Such covenant means that the grantor, at the time of the conveyance, was lawfully seized of a good, absolute and indefeasible estate of inheritance in fee simple and had power to convey the same. Real Property Law (Cons. Laws, ch. 50), §253. If the covenant be broken by the failure of title then an action can at once be maintained to recover the damages sustained as the direct result of the breach.

The trial court found, as indicated, that the grantors in the deed to the plaintiff did not have title to a part of the land conveyed. That finding has been unanimously affirmed. There was, therefore, a breach of the covenant of seizin which entitled plaintiff to whatever damages he had sustained by reason of it. The trial court also found that he had sustained damages to the extent of $1,200. I am of the opinion, however, that the judgment is erroneous in so far as it permitted the plaintiff to recover the $1,500, attorneys' and counsel fees paid in defending the action brought against him by Schaefer. The rule seems well established that costs and expenses, including counsel fees, can only be allowed when a direct attack is made upon the title. The grantee, when sued, of course can defend his title and possession, or take such steps as may be necessary to obtain possession. Whatever it costs him to do this, if the title fail — not exceeding the consideration paid for the part or portion of the premises involved, together with the necessary costs and disbursements — may be recovered of the grantor. Olmstead v. Rawson, 188 N.Y. 517, 81 N.E. 456; Dale v. Shively, 8 Kan. 276; Jewett v. Fisher, 9 Kan. App. 630, 58 P. 1023; Myers v. Munson, 65 Iowa 423, 21 N.W. 759; Harding v. Larkin, 41 Ill. 413. See also, Oelrichs v. Spain, 15 Wall. 211; Henry v. Davis, 123 Mass. 345. . . .

The judgment appealed from, therefore, should be modified by striking out the item of $1,500 and interest thereon, and the extra allowance of costs is reduced proportionately, and as thus modified affirmed, without costs to either party.

Judgment accordingly.[34]

Problems

27.13. In Hilliker v. Rueger, the plaintiff evidently desired to retain that portion of the land which was in fact owned by his grantors and recover only the portion of the purchase price which was properly attributable to that

---

34. Notice that as far as we can tell the plaintiff will continue to occupy the portion of the land not owned and have its benefits at least until the owner puts forth a claim. Is it fair to the defendants to compel them to return to the plaintiff what the plaintiff paid for the part not owned and allow the plaintiff to keep possession also? See Annot., 61 A.L.R. 10, 48 (1929). — Eds.

portion of the land conveyed which was not owned by them. Suppose, however, that the plaintiff had desired to get back the entire purchase price and return all the land to the grantors because the portion which was in fact owned by the grantors was not adequate for the plaintiff's purposes. In other words, the plaintiff desired in effect to rescind the transaction because of the partial failure as to the title. Should the plaintiff be entitled to such relief? See Roake v. Sullivan, 69 Misc. 429, 125 N.Y.S. 835 (Sup. Ct. 1910).

27.14. In Hilliker v. Rueger, the recovery of substantial damages for breach of the covenant of seisin was allowed though the paramount claim had not been asserted. In McGuckin v. Milbank, 152 N.Y. 297, 46 N.E. 490 (1897), the court decided that only nominal damages could be recovered for breach of a covenant against encumbrances, if the encumbrance is a mortgage and the covenantee has not been disturbed in possession or has not paid the mortgage.[35] In view of the fact that present covenants were involved in both cases, which covenants are broken when they are made if they are ever broken, can you justify the difference in result?

27.15. O conveys Blackacre to A. The deed contains a covenant that "the said premises are free from encumbrances." At the time of the conveyance, Blackacre is subject to a restrictive covenant which prevents the property from being used for other than residential purposes. It is established by proof that Blackacre is worth $1,000 less by virtue of being so restricted. A sues O for breach of the covenant against encumbrances. O proves that A has not been subjected to any action for breach of the restrictive covenant and cites McGuckin v. Milbank as authority for limiting A's recovery to nominal damages. Is McGuckin v. Milbank controlling? See Feigin v. Russek, 131 Misc. 30, 226 N.Y.S. 258 (New York City Mun. Ct. 1927).

27.16. O conveys Blackacre to A for $5,000. The deed contains a covenant of seisin. In the deed from O to A, A expressly assumes a mortgage in the amount of $3,500 in favor of M which had been placed on the land by O. In view of the fact that A assumed the mortgage, A paid O only $1,500 in

---

35. At the time McGuckin v. Milbank was decided, section 381 of the Code of Civil Procedure in New York provided that where an action is brought for breach of a covenant of seisin or a covenant against encumbrances, the cause of action for the purpose of determining when the statute of limitations begins to run (statute of limitations for an action upon a sealed instrument at that time was 20 years) shall be deemed to have accrued upon an eviction, and not before. Under such statute the covenantee will not lose the right to sue by the running of the statute of limitations before he or she can recover substantial damages. At present in New York section 213 of the Civil Practice Law and Rules requires that an action upon a sealed instrument must be commenced within six years after the cause of action has accrued, and this section omits the provision that the cause of action on a covenant of seisin or a covenant against encumbrances shall not be deemed to accrue for purposes of the statute of limitations until an eviction. Thus it would seem that a covenantee in a situation like that in McGuckin v. Milbank, whose cause of action accrues when the covenant is made, though he or she can recover only nominal damages prior to an eviction, might be barred from suing for breach of the covenant against encumbrances before he or she could recover substantial damages. The covenantee could avoid this result, of course, by paying off the encumbrance within the six years and thereby be able to prove substantial damages.

cash. A fails to pay the mortgage when it is due, and M forecloses. At the foreclosure sale, Blackacre brings an amount equal to the mortgage indebtedness. Thereafter, A learns for the first time that O did not own Blackacre. A brings an action against O for breach of the covenant of seisin. Should O recover and, if so, how much? See Bingham v. Weiderwax, 1 N.Y. 509 (1848).

27.17. If a grantor covenants "to pay all encumbrances" and there is a mortgage on the premises conveyed which the grantor does not pay when it falls due, is McGuckin v. Milbank authority for the proposition that the grantee must pay off the mortgage or wait until the mortgagee forecloses before the grantee can recover more than nominal damages? See Welch v. United States, 108 F.2d 722 (10th Cir. 1939).

Note: *Covenantor Requested to Defend in Suit Against Covenantee*

You will recall that in Hilliker v. Rueger the defendants had notice of the action brought by Schaefer against Hilliker and were afforded an opportunity to defend that suit. They refused, however, to enter a defense. Even so, the judgment against Hilliker in the Schaefer suit did not establish a breach of the covenant of seisin. Suppose, however, a suit is instituted against the covenantee of a covenant of seisin by one claiming a paramount title and the covenantor is given notice of the suit and requested to defend it. If the covenantor refuses to do so and judgment goes against the covenantee, should not that judgment be conclusive that the covenant has been broken? McCormick v. Marcy, 165 Cal. 386, 132 P. 449 (1913), answers that question as follows:

> Where a covenantee in . . . a deed . . . is sued for possession by a person claiming a paramount title, such defendant may give notice of the suit to any previous covenantor under whom he derives title and request him to come in and defend the title he warranted. . . . And whether he appears or not, he is bound by the judgment rendered in the action. It is conclusive upon the . . . [covenantor] . . . with respect to the superiority of the adverse title asserted by the plaintiff in the action. [165 Cal. at 392, 132 P. at 451]

SCHOFIELD v. IOWA HOMESTEAD CO.
32 Iowa 317 (1871)

Action upon the covenants of a deed for lands. Trial to the court without a jury, and judgment for plaintiff. Defendant appeals.

BECK, J.   I. The counsel of the respective parties agree that the action is based upon the covenant of seizin, which is sufficiently expressed in the deed. As a defense, the answer alleges that, prior to the commencement of the action, plaintiff, for value, sold and conveyed a part of the lands to another, and that the covenant declared on passed with the land, so far as the contract covered the same, to the purchaser from the plaintiff, and that recovery in this action for the land so conveyed is barred. To this defense a demurrer was sustained. The question thus presented for our determination is this: Does the covenant of seizin run with the land?

We are fully aware of the discord of authorities upon this question, and that a great majority of the American cases hold the covenant to be in praesenti, and that it is broken, if at all, when the deed is delivered, and that the claim for damages thereby becomes personal in its nature to the grantee, and is not transferred by a conveyance to a subsequent grantee. But in England the rule prevails that the covenant runs with the land, and recovery for a breach thereof may be had by the assignee of the grantee in the deed. Kingdon v. Nottle, 1 Maule & Selw. 355, 4 Maule & Selw. 53; King v. Jones, 5 Taunt. 418; 4 Maule & Selw. 186; 1 Smith's Lead. Cases, Am. notes to Spencer's case, p. 150; 4 Kent's Com. 472; I Washburne on Real Prop. 649.

The English doctrine has been adopted, and the rule in Kingdon v. Nottle, followed by the supreme courts of Ohio and Indiana, with the modification, however, in Ohio, that when the grantor has neither title nor possession, and is therefore unable to transfer either by his deed, the covenant is broken as soon as made, and becomes a mere right of action which is not transferred by a subsequent conveyance of the land. Backus, Adm'r, v. McCay, 3 Ohio 211; Foot v. Burnett, 10 Ohio 317; Divose v. Sunderlin, 17 Ohio 52; Martin v. Baker, 5 Blackf. 232.

A similar rule, applicable to covenants against incumbrances, formerly prevailed in Massachusetts, but has been abandoned. Wyman v. Ballard, 12 Mass. 304; Sprague v. Baker, 17 Mass. 586.

A like doctrine is recognized in South Carolina. McCready's Ex'r v. Brisbane, 1 Nott & McCord 104.

The English rule is commended to us by reason and justice, and Chancellor Kent, while condemning the reasons upon which it is supported in Kingdon v. Nottle, admits that the American doctrine is supported upon a "technical scruple," and assigns the most conclusive reasons in support of the opposite English rule. 4 Kent, 472.

The object of all covenants in conveyances of lands, relating to their title or their enjoyment, is to secure indemnity to the party entitled to the premises in case he is deprived of them. The subsequent vendee, in the language of Kent, "is the most interested and the most fit person to claim the indemnity secured by them (the covenants), for the compensation belongs to him as the last purchaser and first sufferer."

The American rule will operate oppressively in all cases where the land has been subsequently conveyed by the grantee, either toward the grantor or subsequent purchaser. If the purchaser is evicted he ought to receive the indemnity secured by the covenant, for he is not only, as is said by Kent, the first sufferer, but the only sufferer in every instance, except when he has not paid for the land. When the grantee, under the deed containing the covenant, has sold and received pay for the land, it would be gross injustice to permit him to recover, for he would not in that case sustain damages. But under the rule, to which we are now objecting, the grantee may recover on the covenant of seizin and, if there be a covenant of warranty in the deed, the subsequent grantee may also recover upon that contract against the first grantor. But if there be no covenant of warranty, we would have the equally strange case of a party, the first grantee, recovering damages when he is entitled to none, and the party really injured unable to recover. Other instances of unjust and unreasonable results could be mentioned.

The "technical scruple," as it is called by Kent, upon which the American doctrine is based, is this: The covenant is broken the instant the conveyance is delivered; it then becomes a chose in action held by the grantor [grantee] in the deed. Brady v. Spuck, 27 Ill. 478; King v. Adm'x of Gilson, 32 Ill. 348. But how can this be a reason in support of the doctrine under laws of this State which permit the assignment of all choses in action? What legal principle would be violated by holding that the deed from the first grantee operates as an assignment of this chose in action?

Deeds under the laws of this State have been reduced to forms of great simplicity. Intricate technicalities have been pruned away, and they are now as brief and simple in form as a promissory note. All choses in action, as I have just remarked, may be assigned and transferred. The covenant of seizin (if it be held that such a covenant exists in a deed of the form authorized by the laws of this State), as we have seen, is intended to secure indemnity for the deprivation of the title and enjoyment of the lands conveyed. Why not brush away the "technical scruples" gathered about the covenant of seizin, as we have the like technical and cumbrous forms of the instrument itself, and enforce it for the benefit of the party who is really injured by its breach, even though, in so doing, we find it necessary to hold that a chose in action is assigned and transferred by the operation of the deed?

To my mind, the position reached by this course of argument is impregnable, and I cannot be driven from it by the great weight of authorities in support of the contrary doctrine.

We conclude that plaintiff was not entitled to recover for the land conveyed by him, and that the court erred in rendering judgment for the full amount of the consideration paid, as shown by the deed.

II. The plaintiff's counsel argues that, admitting the covenant runs with the land, being entire, a conveyance of a portion of the premises vests no right of action in the grantee. But this position is in conflict with the authorities. It is held that covenants running with the land are susceptible of division, so that if the land be conveyed in parcels to several persons, each may maintain an action upon the covenant to recover for the land in which he has an interest. Kane v. Sanger, 14 Johns. 89; Dickinson v. Hoomes, 8 Grat. 353.

This rule is based upon sound reason, and accords with the analogies of the law. . . .

On account of the error in holding that the covenant sued upon does not run with the land, the judgment of the circuit court is

Reversed.

Problems

27.18. A conveys Blackacre to B for $5,000. The deed contains a covenant of seisin. B conveys Blackacre to C for $4,000. C is ousted from possession by O, who has a paramount title which O acquired prior to the conveyance by A to B. In answering the following questions, assume you are in a jurisdiction which holds that the covenant of seisin does not run with the land.

    a.   The deed from B to C is a quitclaim deed. Is B entitled to recover from A for breach of the covenant of seisin, and, if so, how much is B entitled to recover?

    b.   The deed from B to C contains a covenant of seisin. C has not brought any suit against B for breach of the covenant of seisin, nor has B made any settlement with C regarding such breach. Is B entitled to recover from A for breach of the covenant of seisin, and, if so, how much is B entitled to recover?

    c.   The deed from B to C contains a covenant of seisin. C sues B for breach of the covenant of seisin and recovers $4,000 plus interest. Is B entitled to recover from A for breach of the covenant of seisin, and, if so, how much is B entitled to recover? See McCormick v. Marcy, 165 Cal. 386, 132 P. 449 (1913); Clement v. Bank of Rutland, 61 Vt. 298, 17 A. 717 (1889).

27.19. Assume you are in a jurisdiction that follows Schofield v. Iowa Homestead Co. What would be your answers to the questions raised in Problem 27.18? See Withy v. Mumford, 5 Cow. 137 (N.Y. Sup. Ct. 1825).

SOLBERG v. ROBINSON
34 S.D. 55, 147 N.W. 87 (1914)

POLLEY, J. On the 27th day of January, 1906, one C. C. Robinson and wife executed and delivered to W. J. and J. L. Smith a certain warranty deed, purporting to convey to said Smiths, with other property, a quarter section of land in Hughes County. On the 9th day of January, 1907, said Smiths executed and delivered to plaintiffs a warranty deed, purporting to convey said land to plaintiffs, but neither the Robinsons nor the Smiths were ever in the actual possession of the land. Thereafter, one Vesey commenced an action against plaintiffs for the purpose of quieting title to said premises and to enjoin plaintiffs in this action from asserting further claim thereto. Said action was defended by plaintiffs but, on the trial, it developed that, from a time long prior to the attempted conveyance from the Robinsons to the Smiths and down to the time of the trial, said Vesey was the absolute owner in fee of the land in question; that, while Robinson's title appeared to come through Vesey, the deed which purported to divest him of his title proved to be a forgery and he had judgment as prayed for. Upon appeal to this court, said judgment was affirmed: Vesey v. Solberg, 27 S.D. 618, 132 N.W. 254. In the deed from Robinson to the Smiths, Robinson and wife covenanted with the Smiths:

> Their heirs and assigns that they are well seized in fee of the lands and premises aforesaid and have good right to sell and convey the same in manner and form aforesaid, [and that] the above bargained and granted lands and premises in quiet and peaceable possession of the said parties of the second part, their heirs and assigns, and against all persons lawfully claiming or to claim the whole or any part thereof the said parties of the first part will warrant and forever defend.

The deed from the Smiths to plaintiffs contained covenants of similar import.

After the affirmance of the judgment quieting title to the said premises in Vesey, plaintiffs commenced this action against the defendant as administrator of the estate of the said C. C. Robinson, who had died in the meantime, for the purpose of recovering on the above quoted covenants in the Robinson deed of January 27, 1906. During all of this time, the land in question was vacant and unoccupied. The Smiths were named as defendants in the summons, but only one of them was ever served, and as to him, the action was dismissed. Plaintiff seeks to recover the amount Robinson had received for the land with interest, together with the expenses necessarily incurred in defending the *Vesey* case in the circuit court, upon appeal to this court and upon motion for rehearing, including attorney's fees for conducting all of these proceedings. Plaintiffs had judgment in the circuit court for $1183.98. From this judgment and the order denying a new trial, defendant appeals.

(1) It is contended by appellant that, as Robinson had neither possession nor right of possession at the time he executed the deed to the Smiths, the covenants sued upon were broken as soon as made and, therefore, did not run with the land nor inure to the benefit of his remote grantees. As to the covenant of seizin, this contention is undoubtedly correct. Our statute, Sec. 1139 Civ. Code, enumerates certain covenants as those which run with the land, but no mention is made of the covenant of seizin, and this covenant does not run with the land: Gale v. Frazier, 4 Dak. 196, 30 N.W. 138.

Under a statute like ours it would appear that it is only the immediate grantee of the covenantor who can recover on this covenant. Plaintiffs could have recovered from the Smiths upon the breach of this covenant, and they, in turn, could have recovered from defendant, provided they brought their action within the period of the statute of limitations: 3 Wash. Real Property, 5th Ed. 504. But there was no such privity of contract between plaintiffs and defendant's intestate as would entitle them to recover against defendant.

(2)   The other covenant set out in plaintiff's complaint (that of quiet enjoyment) presents a different proposition. By express statute, this covenant does run with the land: Civ. Code Sec. 1139. This covenant is made for the benefit of remote as well as immediate grantees, and, unless there is something in the facts connected with this case to relieve appellant from liability on the covenant, the plaintiff is entitled to recover, and the judgment should be affirmed. This is conceded by appellant, but, to avoid liability, he contends that, because his intestate had no estate whatever in the premises at the time of making the covenant, and because his intestate's grantee did not go into possession of the land, there was nothing to which the covenant could attach to carry it to the covenantor's remote grantees. He also contends that, the covenantor having neither possession nor right of possession at the time he made the covenant, a constructive eviction took place at once and that the covenant immediately ripened into a cause of action in favor of his covenantee that neither ran with the land nor passed to his covenantee's grantee, and that, in any event, more than six years had elapsed since the breach of the covenant and plaintiffs' action is barred by the six years statute of limitations. In other words, that, in this particular case, the effect of both covenants is exactly the same, and plaintiffs are not entitled to recover on either. If appellant's position is correct, the covenant for quiet enjoyment contained in the Robinson deed could never, under the facts in this case, become the basis for a recovery by anyone except his immediate grantee. Although the deed purporting to divest Vesey of his title was a forgery and conveyed no title in fact, it appeared upon its face to be a valid conveyance and the apparent chain of title from Vesey to plaintiffs was perfect. For ought plaintiffs knew, or could know until Vesey asserted his title, they were the absolute owners of the fee and could have gone into the physical possession of the land at any time. Supposing plaintiffs had taken possession and afterward had learned the facts relative to the title to the land, and, before they had been disturbed by Vesey, had brought this suit against defendant for breach of the covenant for quiet enjoyment, he could have said:

> You have not been disturbed in your rightful possession of the land and and you may never be disturbed. While your deed may not be good, it is yet color of title, and if you are not disturbed by Vesey within the time for bringing an action for that purpose, your present title, although defective, will ripen into a title that can never be disturbed by anyone. In other words, you have no cause of action until you have been actually ousted by a decree of court.

This would be a complete defense to plaintiff's demand, or the most they could recover would be nominal damages only.

That the proposition that covenants found in deeds purporting to convey title to land do not run with the land unless the covenantor was possessed of some estate in the land to which the covenant could attach is supported by many, if not the great weight of, judicial decisions is not questioned. Notable among the more recent decisions to this effect is Bull v. Beiseker, 16 N.D. 290, 113 N.W. 870, and reported with an extended note, in 14 L.R.A., N.S., 514; Mygatt v. Coe, 147 N.Y. 456, 42 N.E. 17, a New York case; and Wallace v. Pereles, 109 Wis. 316, 85 N.W. 371, 53 L.R.A. 644, 83 Am. St. Rep. 898. . . .

The covenants usually found in deeds of conveyance of real property are the subject of legislative enactment in many of the states. Our statute, Sec. 1138 Rev. Civ. Code, reads as follows: "Every covenant contained in a grant of an estate in real property, which is made for the direct benefit of the property, or some part of it then in existence runs with the land."

Sec. 1139. "The last section includes covenants of warranty, for quiet enjoyment, or for further assurance on the part of a grantor. . . ."

But these statutes do not seem to have changed the rule that, in order that the covenant will run with the land so as to inure to the benefit of a remote grantee, the covenantee must have received some estate in the land to which the covenant could attach.

It seems to be generally held that, where the covenantor delivers the possession of the land to his grantee and he, in turn, puts his grantee in possession, this constitutes a privity of estate sufficient to carry the covenant with the land. And it may be taken as true that the reason for the rule originated at a time when physical possession of land was the chief muniment of title thereto. But this reason no longer exists. A person who has a grant of land from the owner of the fee becomes the absolute owner thereof and is entitled to all the benefits that can be derived therefrom, even though neither of them was ever in the actual possession thereof. This being the case, why should it be necessary that actual, as distinguished from constructive, possession should be delivered in order to carry a covenant with the land when the covenantor was without title? It is for the purpose of protecting the covenantee and his grantees in their right of possession of the land, and to protect them against defective title thereto that the covenant is made. The right of quiet enjoyment of a piece of land is its most valuable attribute, and a covenant from a grantor that his grantee shall be protected in the quiet enjoyment thereof adds materially to the value of the land itself, and a material portion of the consideration paid for the grant may be, and as a rule is, paid because of the covenantee's expectation of the right of quiet enjoyment of the demised premises. If a perfect title is passed to the grantee then he need never avail himself of the covenant in his deed, while, on the other hand, if it should develop that the covenantor had no estate whatever in the premises attempted to be conveyed, the grantee could not, except as against his immediate covenantor, avail himself of the covenant. This, at least, is the logical conclusion to be drawn from the decisions holding that a remote grantee cannot recover upon a covenant unless the covenantor had some estate in the land when the covenant was made. Some cases, notably Kimball v. Bryant, 25 Minn. 496, and Iowa Loan & Trust Co. v. Fullen, 141 Mo. App. 633, 91 S.W. 58, hold that, although a covenantor must have some estate in land at the time of making the grant to which covenants can attach in order to enable a remote grantee to recover on a breach of the covenant, yet, nevertheless, such grantee, however remote, who is holding under said grant at the time of the assertion of, and eviction under, the paramount title, may recover the damages occasioned by the lack of title. This is upon the ground that the covenant was broken as soon as made and at once ripened into a chose in action in favor of the covenantee, and that the transfer of the land by successive warranty deeds passed this cause of action along through the successive grantees until such time as an actual eviction by paramount title took place, when the party who suffered damage by reason thereof might enforce the cause of action that accrued in favor of the first grantee against the original covenantor. Against this doctrine, this court is already committed: Hills v. City, 145 N.W. 570. We believe plaintiffs should recover; but we think they should recover as upon the covenant itself, rather than upon successive assignments of a cause of action that had accrued in favor of some prior grantee. Under the theory adopted by the Missouri and Minnesota courts, unless the eviction take place and the action be commenced within the period prescribed by the statute of limitations for bringing such action, then the right to recover will be barred by the statute, and the party who is holding under the grant at the time of the eviction and the one who suffers the real damage cannot reach the covenantor at all: Iowa L. & T. Co. v. Fullen, *supra.*

(3)   But, again, since it is held that a delivery of the possession of the disputed premises is necessary in order that the covenant of a grantor without title may inure to the benefit of his remote grantees, then the constructive possession of the grantee ought to be sufficient to carry the covenant. In this case, while the Smiths acquired no title to the land by virtue of their deed from the Robinsons, still they had the apparent title even as against Vesey himself. The county record showed that they had a perfect chain of title, and, therefore, the Smiths and their grantees (plaintiffs in this action), as against the defendant should be held to have had constructive possession of the granted premises, and that plaintiffs are entitled to recover against the defendant because of the eviction by Vesey. This, of course, involves the doctrine of estoppel by deed; and we believe this to be a proper case for the application of this doctrine.

True, no case has been called to our attention where a covenantor has been held to be estopped by his deed from claiming that he had no estate in the land, attempted to be conveyed, at the time he made the covenant, and thereby escape liability to a remote grantee who had been evicted; but neither has any reason been suggested why this should not be done; and we hold that the defendant is estopped by the covenants in his intestate's deed from denying that his intestate possessed any estate in the land in question at the time the deed was made; and that respondent is entitled to recover upon the broken covenant.

(4)   The trial court awarded respondent the amount paid for the Robinson deed, with interest thereon for a period of six years. This is urged as error. Sec. 2296 Rev. Civ. Code fixes the measure of damages for breach of the covenant involved at the price paid to the grantor, with interest thereon during the time the grantee derived no benefit from the property, not exceeding six years. Appellant bases his contention upon the ground that there is no evidence in the record to show that the respondents derived no benefit from the land involved; that they were entitled to possession of the land until they were evicted and, therefore, are presumed to have derived benefit therefrom. In this contention appellant is right in part only. Having already held that the appellant is estopped from denying that respondent was in the constructive possession of the land and allowed respondent to recover on the covenant upon the theory that respondents and their immediate grantors, believing themselves to be the absolute owners of the land, were in the constructive possession thereof, it would be inconsistent and illogical to allow respondent to recover interest on the purchase price upon the ground that they were not in possession of the land, and, therefore, derived no benefit therefrom. As against appellant, respondent's constructive possession continued so long as they believed themselves to be entitled to the actual possession. When they received notice of Vesey's title, their constructive possession terminated, and it is from the date of receiving such notice that interest on the purchase price should be computed. So far as appears from this record, respondents were first notified of Vesey's ownership by the commencement of his action against them, and interest should be allowed from that date only.

(5)   The trial court also awarded respondents' costs and expenses, including witness fees, incurred by them in defending their supposed title in the circuit court and the supreme court, and attorney's fees paid by them in that action. The allowance of these two items is assigned as error. By the provisions of Sec. 2296 Rev. Civ. Code, the respondents are entitled to recover not only the consideration paid for the land and interest thereon, but any expenses properly incurred by them in defending their possession. The objection to the allowance of these items is based upon the fact that appellant was not notified of the commencement of the suit by Vesey and required to come in and defend in that action. These expenses were properly incurred by respondents in defending their possession and are within the meaning of Sec. 2296, and, unless a condition is read into that section that was not placed there by its authors, respondents are entitled to recover these expenses. It is true that some courts have held that a covenantee cannot

recover from the covenantor the expenses of defending his title unless the covenantor was notified and required to come in and defend the action in which the expenses were incurred. . . .

This is without reference to either statute or notice, and our attention has been called to no case that has been decided under a statute like ours. In the case at bar, the expenses of defending the title attempted to be conveyed were clearly within the contemplation of appellant's intestate when he made the covenant. He knew that, if the title were not such as he covenanted it to be, his grantees would, in all probability, be called upon to defend as against the rightful owner. He knew that, if such suit were commenced, his grantee must necessarily incur expenses and pay counsel fees. The statute fixed his liability, and this liability is not conditioned upon receiving notice from his grantees of the commencement of a suit by the owner of the paramount title; and it does not now lie in defendant's mouth to say that, had he received such notice, he might have complied with his covenant by admitting his liability and paying to his grantees the damages to which they were entitled, and thus prevent the incurring of the items of expense involved herein, for even now he is resisting the payment of such damages with the same vigor that he is resisting the payment of the costs and attorney's fees. No complaint is made that any of the expenses that were allowed by the trial court were improperly incurred, or that the defense was not properly conducted, or that the amount paid for counsel fees was exorbitant or unnecessary; and it is our opinion that the items in dispute were properly allowed.

The judgment should be modified in regard to the amount of interest allowed respondents as herein indicated, and as so modified it is affirmed.

Problems

27.20. A conveys Blackacre to B for $10,000. At the time of the deed form A to B, Blackacre is owned by O. The deed from A to B contains both a covenant of seisin and a covenant of general warranty.

 a. Several years later A buys Blackacre from O for $8,000. B then learns that A did not own Blackacre at the time of the deed from A to B. B sues A for breach of the covenant of seisin. You are attorney for A. What is your defense? See Meyer v. Thompson, 183 N.C. 543, 112 S.E. 328 (1922).

 b. Several years later O ousts B from the possession of the land. A then buys Blackacre from O for $8,000. B sues A for breach of the covenant of general warranty. You are attorney for A. Would you use the same defense you adopted in a, above? See Resser v. Carney, 52 Minn. 397, 54 N.W. 89 (1893); Southern Plantations Co. v. Kennedy Heading Co., 104 Miss. 131, 61 So. 166 (1913).

27.21. A conveys Blackacre to B for $10,000. A's deed to B contains a covenant of general warranty. B conveys Blackacre to C for $8,000 by a quitclaim deed. C conveys Blackacre to D for $12,000, and this deed contains a covenant of general warranty. O, who has a paramount title that antedates A's deed to B, ousts D from the land, and at the time of the ouster Blackacre is worth $14,000. How much can D recover from C? How much can D recover from A? If D recovers from C, can C recover from A? If so, on what theory, and how much can C recover from A? See Taylor v. Wallace, 20 Colo. 211, 37 P. 963 (1894). If the increase in value from $8,000 to $12,000 was due to improvements placed on the land by C, will this affect the amount that C or D can recover from A? See the special Massachusetts rule of damages described in Crocker's Notes on Common Form §146 (7th ed. 1955). Will O be required to reimburse D for the improvements placed on the land by C? See Mass. Gen. Laws ch. 237, §17.

CHAPTER 28

RECORDING[1] *(Herein Bona Fide Purchaser of Real Property)*

Note: *The Grantor-Grantee Index and the Tract Index*

In Chapter 9 you examined the body of law which has developed in the field of bona fide purchasers of personal property. That body of law is the basis of deciding between conflicting claims to personal property, and you saw that it developed largely unaided by any system of recording. The only instances where recording plays a significant part in the field of personal property are in connection with chattel mortgages and with conditional sales agreements. Almost the entire story of determining priorities between claims to real property, however, must be developed in the light of the recording acts which have been adopted in the various states. As background to a consideration of the recording system, you should have some picture of the guiding principles which are the basis of deciding between conflicting claims to real property in the absence of an applicable recording act. These guiding principles are as follows:

1. As between conflicting claims to legal interests in land, the first in time prevails unless the claimant who is prior in time is estopped, by virtue of his or her actions, to assert a claim.
2. As between conflicting equitable claims to land, the first in time prevails unless the claimant who is prior in time is estopped, by virtue of his or her actions, to assert a claim, or unless the claimant who is subsequent in time acquires the legal title in good faith (that is, without notice of the prior equity) and for a valuable consideration.
3. As between a claimant of a legal interest and a claimant of an equitable interest, the former always prevails if that claim is the

---

1. See generally American Law of Property §§17.4-17.36 (Casner ed. 1952); Johnson, Purpose and Scope of Recording Statutes, 47 Iowa L. Rev. 231 (1962); Cross, Weaknesses of the Present Recording System, 47 Iowa L. Rev. 245 (1962); Cook (assisted by Lombardi), American Land Law Reform: Modernization of Recording Statutes, 13 Case W. Res. L. Rev. 639 (1962).

earlier in time, and also prevails if the claim is subsequent in time, provided he or she acquired the legal title in good faith and for a valuable consideration.

The determination of the extent to which these guiding principles have been eliminated by the recording acts as the basis of deciding conflicting claims to land, and the development of an understanding of the new guiding principles established by the recording acts, are the principal purposes of this chapter.

It is essential to an understanding of the system of recording documents affecting the title to land that you have some knowledge of what may be called the "mechanics" of title examinations. This is, you must know how you locate on the public records the recorded documents which must be evaluated in order to determine the state of the record title. To put it another way, a purchaser of land ought not to be compelled to take subject to claims against the land set forth on the public records unless a reasonable search of the records will reveal such claims. You cannot determine what a purchaser of land may reasonably be expected to find on the public records without knowing something about the mechanical job of locating recorded documents.

When you take a document of title to the recorder's office, that document is copied in full (in some localities a photostatic copy may be made), and the copy is placed in a bound volume.[2] That bound volume contains many other copies of instruments affecting land in the county. When one volume is filled with copies of instruments, another volume is started. If you are looking for a particular document, you might take months to locate it if you had to turn the pages of all the volumes in which the documents are copied in full. It should be obvious to you that some kind of index must be kept which will enable you to obtain a reference to the volume and page in which the document you are interested in is copied. But what kind of index will do the job?

Grantor-grantee index. The recorder's office keeps what is called a grantor-grantee index. This simply means that every recorded document is indexed both by the name of the grantor in the document and by the name of the grantee. The names of the grantors and the grantees are arranged in the index in alphabetical order. Thus if you are buying land from Adams, you can go to the recorder's office of the county in which the land is located and, by starting with the latest index book containing the names of grantees whose names begin with A (you start with the grantee book because Adams, from whom you are buying, was a grantee in the deed that conveyed the property to Adams), you can trace back until you find indexed a conveyance to Adams. When you find an index reference of such conveyance, you will

---

2. The bound volumes referred to in the text take up a great amount of space. To solve the space problem, documents are being recorded on microfilm in some states. A print may be made from the microfilm when needed. See Cook (assisted by Lombardi), American Land Law Reform: Modernization of Recording Statutes, 13 Case W. Res. L. Rev. 639, 664 (1962).

find opposite the name of Adams the volume and page at which the deed to Adams is copied in full. The index also gives a brief description of the property conveyed to Adams and the name of Adams's grantor. You can then repeat this process in the appropriate grantee index that applies to the name of the grantor of Adams and find the deed by which Adams's grantor obtained title, and so on.

The grantor index is used to ascertain whether a particular owner of property made any conveyances that will prevail over the conveyance under which you will be claiming if you buy. Thus, when you are buying from Adams, you use the grantee index to ascertain where Adams got the property; but you use the grantor index to ascertain whether Adams has made conveyances that will prevail over you if you buy the property.

Tract index. Some states have authorized the establishment of another type of index, which is called a "tract" or "block" index.[3] Such index is keyed to the description of the land conveyed rather than to the names of the parties involved in a conveyance.

In order for a tract index to be established, the area covered by the index (the area normally is a county, but may be a city if the index is established only on a city-wide basis) is divided into small segments, usually referred to as blocks, and each block is given a number. These blocks are not necessarily all of the same size. Each block then is divided into smaller segments, usually called lots. Each lot is bounded so as to include within it an area under single ownership (or possibly concurrent ownership) at the time the index is established. The lots thus marked off are given numbers.

A map of the county, or city, showing the boundaries and number of each block and the boundaries and number of each lot within a block, is located in the recorder's office. An index is established for each block, and a separate page in that index is devoted exclusively to conveyances of each lot within the block. Thus when you are examining the title to a particular tract of land, you go to the recorder's office and look at the map of the county, or city; determine the number of the block in which your land is located; ascertain the number of your lot within the block; go to the index volume for conveyances of land in your block; turn to the page containing references of conveyances of your numbered lot; and on that one page you find a list of the conveyances of your lot from the date the index was established. Opposite each listed conveyance is a reference to the volume and page where the document concerning that conveyance is copied in full.

The description of the tract index given above is that of an ideal one. You must examine the local situation to determine to what extent the tract index as established falls short of this ideal.

Combination tract and grantor-grantee index. A combination tract and

3. Cook (assisted by Lombardi), American Land Law Reform: Modernization of Recording Statutes, 13 Case W. Res. L. Rev. 639, 649 (1962), lists in a footnote the following states as requiring the keeping of a tract index: Nebraska, North Dakota, Oklahoma, South Dakota, Utah, Washington, and Wyoming.

grantor-grantee index may be established. Under such a combination index, the county is divided into numbered blocks as in the tract index, and you locate first the numbered block in which your particular land is located. The conveyances of land in that block, however, are indexed by the names of the parties, so that you locate your references by the grantor-grantee index method. This combination speeds up the use of the grantor-grantee index because the area covered by each such index is not county-wide as in most localities. This naturally tends to cut down on the number of grantors and grantees with names similar to the ones you are running in the index.

Descent or devise of land. Neither the grantor-grantee index nor the tract index, as they now exist, make any provision for indexing the passage of title to land by descent or devise. Thus under either index system, if your indexed chain of ownership contains a gap, it is probably due to the fact that title has passed at some time by descent or devise. We refer you to Chapter 29 for the job of the title examiner in trying to locate in the probate records the necessary evidence that title passed to a certain person.

Determining land owned by particular person. It may be important, for some purposes, just to go to the land records and locate all the real property owned of record by an individual in a particular county. You can do this under a grantor-grantee index system very easily. It would be an almost impossible task under a tract index. Do you see why?

Statutory construction. You have had occasion from time to time, in considering the previous material in this book, to examine the influence of statutes on particular problems. This should have given you some experience in statutory construction. In this chapter statutory construction predominates. The recording system is based on statutes, and practically every case you consider turns on the meaning to be given to a statute. Get into the habit of reading with extreme care the exact wording of the statute involved in each case. You should attempt to become an expert in the handling of statutory material.

Note: Retrieval of Land Title Information

The present cumbersome, expensive, time-consuming method of retrieval of land title information is under examination with a view to the introduction of computerization of land title records. The most difficult problem is the development of land parcel identifiers for information systems. In this regard, see a book published in 1973 by the American Bar Foundation (in cooperation with many other interested organizations) entitled Land Parcel Identifiers for Information Systems. The introduction in that book states as follows:

> The goal of the conference on "Compatible Land Identifiers — The Problems, Prospects, and Payoffs (CLIPPP)" was to recommend a single, compati-

ble land parcel and point identifier system that would facilitate the collection, storage, manipulation, and retrieval of all land-related data-information about ownership, use, zoning and other public or private land-use restrictions, tax records, natural resources, resource pollution, resource production and extraction, ecology, demography, transportation, public health and safety, etc. Such a system, primarily, should facilitate automatic data processing for high-volume use and, secondarily, should be appropriate for manual filing and retrieval in counties with a low volume of transactions. The user should be able to gain access to the system by using any one of a number of common identifiers, such as street address or rural route box number. To help verify the identification and to identify parcels for which no mailing address exists, the user should be aided by an area map showing parcel boundaries and identifier numbers. [Land Parcel Identifiers for Information Systems, at 1-2.]

Note: *Alabama Statute on Self-Indexing*

Alabama Laws 1973, Act No. 656, is designed to provide for a system of self-indexing of all land transfer instruments recorded in probate offices in counties having a population of not less than 115,000 nor more than 150,000 persons according to the last or any subsequent federal decennial census.

SECTION 1. SIGNIFICANCE OF FAILURE TO RECORD

Note: *Effect if No Purchaser Is Involved*

If O executes a deed purporting to convey Blackacre to A, and A does not record the deed, is the legally operative situation the same in all respects as though A did record as long as no subsequent purchaser from O is involved? The answer to this question depends on the terms of the controlling recording statute. But in construing a recording statute, even though the language is very explicit, keep in mind the purposes to be accomplished that led to the enactment of the statute, because it may not be appropriate to give the statute an effect that has no relation to the accomplishment of such purposes.

Suppose the controlling recording statute reads as follows: "No deed of real property shall be valid for the purpose of passing title unless acknowledged and recorded as herein directed." See Md. Ann. Code art. 21, §12. Contrast the wording of such statute with the following: "No deed, mortgage or other instrument in writing, not recorded in accordance with section

71-2-1, shall affect the title or rights to, in any real estate, of any purchaser, mortgagee in good faith, or judgment lien creditor, without knowledge of the existence of such unrecorded instruments." See N.M. Stat. Ann. §71-2-3. Can you visualize any case not involving a purchaser of the land referred to in the unrecorded deed that would be solved differently under these two statutes? In this regard, consider the following problems.

Problems

28.1. O executes a deed purporting to convey Blackacre to A. A does not record the deed but goes into possession of Blackacre. O brings an action of ejectment against A. Judgment for whom under the Maryland statute? Judgment for whom under the New Mexico statute?

28.2. O executes a deed purporting to convey Blackacre to A. A does not record the deed. B is an adverse possessor on Blackacre but has not been in adverse possession for a sufficient length of time to acquire title as against O. A brings an action of ejectment against B. Judgment for whom under the Maryland statute? Judgment for whom under the New Mexico statute. See West v. Pusey, 113 Md. 569, 77 A. 973 (1910).

28.3. O executes a deed purporting to convey Blackacre to A. A does not record. O intends to make a gift of Blackacre to A. Later O executes another deed purporting to convey Blackacre to B, B paying O no consideration for the deed of Blackacre. B does not record. B goes into possession of Blackacre. A brings an action of ejectment against B. Judgment for whom under the Maryland statute? Judgment for whom under the New Mexico statute? See Kohn v. Burke, 294 Pa. 282, 144 A. 75 (1928).

28.4. O executes a deed purporting to convey Blackacre to A. A does not record. O then executes a deed for a valuable consideration which recites that O conveys "all the land that I now own in X county" to B. Blackacre is located in X County. In determining whether Blackacre is included in the description in B's deed of "all the land that I now own in X County," is the wording of the Maryland or New Mexico statute a relevant consideration in any dispute between A and B? See Ames v. Robert, 17 N.M. 609, 131 P. 994 (1913). Should the answer change any if O, instead of executing a deed to B of "all the land that I now own in X County," had executed a will in which O gave S "all the land that I now own in X County," and then O died, and then S for a valuable consideration had executed a deed to B of "all the land that I now own in X County"?

EARLE v. FISKE
103 Mass. 491 (1870)

Writ of entry against Elizabeth L. Fiske, (wife of Benjamin Fiske) and Mary E. Fiske, to recover land in Malden. Writ dated April 14, 1868. Plea, nul disseisin.

At the trial in the superior court, before Putnam, J., these facts appeared: Nancy A. Fiske, being owner of the demanded premises, conveyed them to Benjamin and Elizabeth for their lives, and, subject to their life estate, to Mary E. Fiske, by deeds dated April 22, 1864, but not recorded till 1867, and died in 1865, leaving said Benjamin, her son, as her sole heir, and he in 1866 executed and delivered to the demandant a deed of the premises, which was recorded in the same year. Upon these facts, the judge ruled that Nancy A. Fiske "had no seisin, at her death, which would descend to Benjamin Fiske, so as to enable him to convey a good title" to the demandant. Upon this ruling, the demandant, who made no claim to any estate less than a fee simple, submitted to a verdict for the tenants, and alleged exceptions.

AMES, J. The formalities which shall be deemed indispensable to the valid conveyance of land are prescribed and regulated by statute. A deed duly signed, sealed and delivered is sufficient, as between the original parties to it, to transfer the whole title of the grantor to the grantee, though the instrument of conveyance may not have been acknowledged or recorded. The title passes by the deed, and not by the registration. No seisin remains in the grantor, and he has literally nothing in the premises which he can claim for himself, transmit to his heir at law, or convey to any other person. But when the effect of the deed upon the rights of third persons, such as creditors or bona fide purchasers, is to be considered, the law requires something more, namely, either actual notice, or the further formality of registration, which is constructive notice. It may not be very logical to say that, after a man has literally parted with all his right and estate in a lot of land, there still remains in his hands an attachable and transferable interest in it, of exactly the same extent and value as if he had made no conveyance whatever. But, for the protection of bona fide creditors and purchasers, the rule has been established that although an unrecorded deed is binding upon the grantor, his heirs and devisees, and also upon all persons having actual notice of it, it is not valid and effectual as against any other persons. As to all such other persons, the unrecorded deed is a mere nullity. So far as they are concerned, it is no conveyance or transfer which the statute recognizes as binding on them, or as having any capacity adversely to affect their rights, as purchasers or attaching creditors. As to them, the person who appears of record to be the owner is to be taken as the true and actual owner, and his apparent seisin is not divested or affected by any unknown and unrecorded deed that he may have made. Gen. Sts. c. 89, Sec. 3.[4]

It is argued, however, that, as the unrecorded deed from Nancy A. Fiske was valid and binding upon herself and her heirs at law, nothing descended from her to her son Benjamin, and he had no seisin or title which he could

---

4. "No bargain and sale or other like conveyance of an estate in fee simple, fee tail, or for life, and no lease for more that [than] seven years from the making thereof, shall be valid and effectual against any person other than the grantor, and his heirs and devisees, and persons having actual notice thereof, unless it is made by a deed recorded as aforesaid."

The corresponding statute now in force in Massachusetts is Mass. Gen. Laws Ann. ch. 183, §4, which is set out in full on page 813 *infra.* — Eds.

convey to the plaintiff. A case is cited (Hill v. Meeker, 24 Conn. 211) in which the supreme court of Connecticut (Hinman and Storrs, JJ.) in 1855 decided that a deed of land, not recorded until after the death of the grantor, is valid against a purchaser from his heir at law, although such purchaser has no knowledge of the existence of the deed. From this decision the chief justice (Waite) dissented, saying,

> So far as my researches have extended, this is the first case in the whole history of our jurisprudence, in which it has ever been holden that an unrecorded deed shall defeat the title of a bona fide purchaser or mortgagee, having no knowledge of the existence of any such deed, unless it were recorded within a reasonable time.

The cases cited from the decisions of the supreme court of Kentucky are to the effect also that the protection afforded by their registration laws against an unrecorded deed only extend to purchasers from the grantor himself, and not to purchasers from his heirs or devisees. Ralls v. Graham, 4 T.B. Monr. 120. Hancock v. Beverly, 6 B. Monr. 531. That court however in a more recent case, decided in 1857, say that, if it were a new question, "and had not been heretofore decided," they should be strongly inclined to give to the statute a liberal construction, and make it operate as a remedy for the whole evil which it was intended to guard against. They add, however, that as the previous decision had become a settled rule of property, it is better that the law should remain permanent, "although settled originally upon doubtful principles." Harlan v. Seaton, 18 B. Monr. 312.

We do not, under the circumstances, incline to yield to the authority of these cases in the construction of a local statute of this Commonwealth. It appears to us that the plain meaning of our system of registration is, that a purchaser of land has a right to rely upon the information furnished him by the registry of deeds, and in the absence of notice to the contrary he is justified in taking that information as true, and acting upon it accordingly. It is impossible to see why the unrecorded deed of Nancy A. Fiske should have any greater weight or force after her decease than it had immediately after it was first delivered. It could not be any more or less binding on her heir at law than it was upon herself; he was as much the apparent owner of the land as she had been during her lifetime. The manifest purpose of our statute is, that the apparent owner of record shall be considered as the true owner, (so far as subsequent purchasers without notice to the contrary are concerned,) not-withstanding any unrecorded and unknown previous alienation. As against the claim of this plaintiff, the unrecorded deed of Nancy A. Fiske had no binding force or effect, and the objection of the defendants, that in conse-quence of her having given that deed nothing descended to her son Benja-min from her, is one of which they cannot avail themselves. As a purchaser without notice, the plaintiff is in a position to say that the unrecorded deed had no local force or effect; that she died seised; that the property descended to Benjamin, her son and sole heir at law. Upon that assumption, his deed would take precedence over the unrecorded deed of his mother, in exactly the same manner as a deed from his mother in her lifetime would have been over any unrecorded or unknown previous deed from herself. The ruling at the trial was therefore erroneous, and the plaintiff's Exceptions are sustained.

Note: The Penumbra of Earle v. Fiske

Benjamin Fiske is not an attractive character. He and his wife were life tenants under the 1864 unrecorded deed from his mother, Nancy A. Fiske; so there could be no question about Benjamin's knowledge that that deed existed. Then, when his mother died leaving him as sole heir, he gave a deed in fee simple to Nicholas H. Earle, said to be a bona fide purchaser, which thus cuts out the interest of Mary E. Fiske, who was Benjamin's own daughter, as a remainderman under the 1864 deed.

As you consider this sequence of events don't you wonder whether this is the whole story? Don't answer now, until we have placed before you some elements of Massachusetts probate practice:

When a person dies intestate (as did Benjamin's mother, Nancy A. Fiske) a petition is filed in the probate court praying that an administrator be appointed to handle the estate. Normally the administrator is the sole heir, if there is one. This would be Benjamin Fiske. Upon appointment he must qualify by giving a bond with sureties to guarantee that he will perform his fiduciary duties properly. His first duty is to file an inventory of all real and personal property owned by the decedent. Then he must pay debts, distribute the net estate to those entitled, and render accounts.

Reading over the previous paragraph, are you not curious to examine some document in the estate of Nancy A. Fiske? Right — the inventory. Did Benjamin Fiske really have the nerve to include the Malden real estate in this inventory when he had already received a life estate under the 1864 deed? If the real estate is not in the inventory, isn't Earle's position as a bona fide purchaser somewhat shaky?

So let us examine the Nancy A. Fiske estate papers in the probate court of Middlesex County, Massachusetts. As expected, Benjamin Fiske petitioned for administration and was named administrator. First surprise: One of the two sureties on Benjamin's bond, which among other things requires him to file a true inventory, is Nicholas H. Earle. Second surprise: *No inventory has been filed to this day.*

Thus it appears that in 1865 Nicholas H. Earle was so personally close to Benjamin Fiske that he would go surety for him on a bond; also that Earle took title from Fiske when the chain of record title was incomplete due to Benjamin's failure to file an inventory — a failure which was a breach of the condition of the bond upon which Earle himself was surety. How easy it would have been for Earle to request Benjamin to file the inventory and thus complete the record chain. This would have put it up to Benjamin, knowing full well of the 1864 deed, whether he would risk being held in contempt of court for knowingly filing a false inventory. Was it not a matter of common prudence for Earle to require the inventory before paying out his money? Can he stand cross-examination on why he failed to do this? If not, how can he pose as a bona fide purchaser entitled to cut out the prior interest of Mary E. Fiske? Besides, were not Earle's connections with the Fiske family such as to give him knowledge or reason to know of the 1864 deed?

Now what document would you like to examine? We choose the brief for the tenants (the defendants) in the Supreme Judicial Court. We want to know whether Earle's status as a bona fide purchaser was attacked and what capital was made out of the evidence available in the probate records.

The files of the court yield a brief which will not go down in history as one of the great classics of advocacy. Including the heading, the brief covers one and one-quarter printed pages. It does not cite Hill v. Meeker, 24 Conn. 211 (1855), decided fifteen years previously and squarely in favor of the defendant's position. As to the probate inventory it has this to say:

> In this case the record title was not in Benjamin, but, on the contrary, if inventory of Nancy's estate was filed by the administrator in accordance with his bond, as is to be presumed (omnia rite actu praesumuntur), the probate records must have shown that the estate in question did not belong to Nancy at her death and consequently did not descend to Benjamin.

In other words this noble practitioner of the lawyer's art had not even taken the trouble to look into the probate records upon which his opponent's title might well depend.

The lawyer's performance is so bad that the cynic might suspect collusion between Benjamin Fiske and Nicholas H. Earle to destroy the remainder interest of Mary E. Fiske. But other facts gleaned from the records make this improbable and suggest that there must have been a full-scale bust-up between Earle and the Fiskes sometime before this suit was begun. In addition to the writ of entry brought against the Fiskes (the starting point of Earle v. Fiske) Earle brought another action against Benjamin to establish at least his right to present occupancy. There was no question about Earle's right to an estate for the life of Benjamin, even assuming the full effectiveness of the April 22, 1864 deed, for under that deed Benjamin and his wife Elizabeth had life estates by the entirety, a situation which would have permitted Benjamin to transfer to Earle full rights of occupation during Benjamin's life. Earle was successful in this second case, got a writ of execution, and had the sheriff eject both Benjamin and his wife Elizabeth from the property. Elizabeth then sued the sheriff, named Chamberlin, on the ground that the writ did not run against her and hence a tort had been committed in ejecting her. Fiske v. Chamberlin, appearing in the Massachusetts Reports immediately after Earle v. Fiske, holds that the sheriff was justified. It is thus apparent that the Fiskes have a batting average of .000.

The history of this title from the time it came into the Fiske family is not without interest. Here it is:

April 14, 1864: One Waite conveyed to Benjamin Fiske. The deed was not then recorded.

April 21, 1864: Benjamin Fiske conveyed to his mother, Nancy A. Fiske. The deed was promptly recorded.

April 22, 1864: Nancy A. Fiske conveyed to Benjamin and Elizabeth for their lives, remainder to Mary E. Fiske. (This is the deed in Earle v. Fiske.) It was not then recorded.

July 19, 1865: The deed from Waite to Benjamin was recorded.[5]

Sept. 1865: Nancy A. Fiske died.

Feb. 7, 1866: Benjamin conveyed to Earle. Recorded promptly.

Feb. 13, 1867: The 1864 deed to Benjamin, Elizabeth, and Mary E. Fiske was recorded.

This series of transactions justifies two comments:

1. Benjamin Fiske was probably in financial trouble and certainly is shown by the record to be a slippery and secretive character. He did not record the deed by which he received the property in 1864, and he promptly got the property out of his hands by a conveyance to his mother, taking back a deed which gives creditors little to levy execution upon. The deed out to his mother is recorded; the deed back is not. It is clear that Benjamin knows about the recording system and is manipulating it to his supposed advantage. Furthermore, on the issue of Earle's bona fides, Benjamin's failure to record the April 14, 1864, deed for more than a year is apparent in the registry of deeds and suggests the desirability of caution.

2. The deed of April 21, 1864, from Benjamin to his mother was placed on the record. But was it "recorded" within the meaning of the Massachusetts recording act? Suppose that in August, 1864, Waite should give another deed to a bona fide purchaser. How would the purchaser's conveyancer locate the April 21, 1864, deed? Who would prevail between the August bona fide purchaser and Nancy A. Fiske?

Acknowledgment: Most of the research above indicated was provided, on their own initiative, by Messrs. Samuel A. Chaitowitz, Stephen Charnas, James P. Kehoe, John B. Winston, Wilton S. Sogg, and Jerome S. Sowalsky, all of the Harvard Law School Class of 1959.

---

5. Why did Benjamin record his deed at this date? Because on the same date Earle took a $2,000 mortgage on the land from Nancy A. Fiske and apparently wanted the chain of title perfected (Middlesex Deeds, South, book 951, p. 298). Thus it is apparent that Earle knew the necessity of having a chain of title back of instruments he took — which makes it the more surprising that he did not require an inventory in the Estate of Nancy A. Fiske. This mortgage was still undischarged when Earle took his conveyance of February 7, 1866.

Note: The Hill v. Meeker View

In Hill v. Meeker, 24 Conn. 211 (1855), the Connecticut court had before it a case similar to the case of Earle v. Fiske and decided in favor of the original purchaser under the unrecorded deed rather than in favor of the subsequent purchaser from the heir of the original grantor. Judge Hinman in his opinion for the court quoted the Connecticut statute which is as follows: "No deed shall be accounted good and effectual to hold such houses and lands against any other person or persons, but the grantor or grantors, and their heirs, unless recorded as aforesaid." [6] Then he stated as follows:

> Now, as it is by force of the statute alone, that deeds for any purpose are required to be recorded, it follows that they are as effectual without recording, as they were at common law, except so far as the statute has made them ineffectual. But, by the statute, they shall not be accounted good against any person but the grantor, or grantors, and their heirs. Of course, they remain good against the grantor and his heirs. Would the language have been any clearer, if it had expressly said that unrecorded deeds shall be good and effectual against the grantor and his heirs, but void against all others? We cannot think it would. Jonathan's deed, then, was good against him, he being the grantor; and it was good against Arza, his only heir, by force of the statute. But as it was good against Jonathan, he at his death, had no title to transmit to his heir; and Arza, taking nothing by inheritance, had nothing that he could mortgage to Hill. [24 Conn. at 213.]

Note: Protection of Creditors Under Recording Acts

The language of the recording acts vary considerably in regard to the protection given creditors against unrecorded instruments. Sometimes the statutes mention creditors specifically as persons entitled to prevail over unrecorded instruments. The following are examples "creditors," "all creditors," "any creditor," "judgment lien creditors," and the like. Sometimes the statutory language is quite vague, as for example when the statute says "any person" prevails over unrecorded instruments. Sometimes the statutory language excludes creditors as when the only persons protected are

---

6.   The statute quoted is the statute that was in force in Connecticut in 1849 (see Conn. Stat. Rev. tit. 29, §13 (1849)). The subsequent purchaser, however, came into the picture in 1840. The statute then in force in Connecticut (Conn. Comp. Stat., tit. 58, §9 (1835)) was exactly like the statute quoted, except that the word "only" appears after the word "heirs." This difference does not appear to be material, but it serves to emphasize the importance, in dealing with a recording problem, of ascertaining the exact wording of the statute in force at the controlling date.

The corresponding language in the statute now in force in Connecticut, Conn. Gen. Stat. Ann. §47-10, is as follows: "No conveyance shall be effectual to hold any land against any other person but the grantor and his heirs, unless recorded on the records of the town in which the land lies. . . ."

described as "subsequent purchasers in good faith and for a valuable consideration." The local statute must be carefully examined whenever the dispute is between a grantee under an unrecorded deed and a creditor. See American Law of Property §§17.9, 17.29 (Casner ed. 1952).

Note: Classification of Recording Acts

The extent to which a subsequent purchaser is protected against a prior unrecorded deed depends on the type of statute in the local jurisdiction. There are four distinct types of statutes.

1. *Notice* statutes which place no premium on the race to the recorder's office, and protect the bona fide purchaser whether he or she records first or not.
2. *Race-notice* statutes, which place a premium on the race to the recorder's office, and protect the bona fide purchaser only if he or she records first.
3. *Period-of-grace* statutes, which give the prior grantee a period of grace in which to record, and protect the bona fide purchaser only if the prior grantee does not record in the time allowed by the statute.
4. *Race* statutes, which place a premium on the race to the recorder's office and protect the purchaser, whether the purchaser has notice or not, if he or she records first.

The following are illustrations of each of the four types of statutes mentioned above.

Notice

Mass. Gen. Laws Ann. ch. 183, §4:

A conveyance of an estate in fee simple, fee tail or for life, or a lease for seven years, or an assignment of rents or profits from an estate or lease, shall not be valid as against any person, except the grantor or lessor, his heirs and devisees and persons having actual notice of it, unless it, or an office copy as provided in section thirteen of chapter thirty-six, or, with respect to such a lease or an assignment of rents or profits, a notice of lease or a notice of assignment of rents or profits, as hereinafter defined, is recorded in the registry of deeds for the county or district in which the land to which it relates lies. A "notice of lease," as used in this section, shall mean an instrument in writing executed by all persons who are parties to the lease of which notice is given and shall contain the following information with reference to such lease: — the date of execution thereof and a description, in the form contained in such lease, of the premises demised, and the term of such lease, with the date of commencement of such term and all rights of extension or renewal.

Race-Notice

Mich. Comp. Laws §565.29:

Every conveyance of real estate within the state hereafter made, which shall not be recorded as provided in this chapter, shall be void as against any subsequent purchaser in good faith and for a valuable consideration, of the same real estate or any portion thereof, whose conveyance shall be first duly recorded. . . .

Period of Grace

Del. Code Ann. tit. 25, §153:

If a deed concerning lands or tenements is not recorded in the proper office within 15 days after the day of the sealing and delivery thereof, the deed shall not avail against a subsequent fair creditor, mortgagee or purchaser for a valuable consideration unless it appears that such creditor when giving the credit, or such mortgagee or purchaser, when advancing the consideration, had notice of such deed. This provision shall not extend to a lease under a fair rent for a term not exceeding twenty-one years, when the possession accompanies the lease, or the lessee is to come into possession within one year after the making of it.

This statute was repealed by 56 Del. Laws ch. 318 (1968). See American Law of Property §17.32 (Casner ed. 1952).

Race

N.C. Gen. Stat. §47-18:

No conveyance of land, or contract to convey, or option to convey, or lease of land for more than three years shall be valid to pass any property as against lien creditors or purchasers for a valuable consideration from the donor, bargainor or lessor, but from the time of registration thereof within the county where the land lies . . .

Problems

28.5. If you are representing the purchaser in a notice jurisdiction, what should you do before paying the purchase price to the grantor to assure that your client will prevail over prior deeds or other instruments executed by the grantor and which have not been recorded? What should you do in a race-notice jurisdiction? In a period-of-grace jurisdiction? In a race jurisdiction?

28.6. O executes and delivers to A a deed conveying to A certain land O owns. A does not record. O then executes and delivers to B a deed of the same land, and B purchases in good faith and for a valuable consideration. B does not record. A then records and, after recording A executes and delivers a deed to C of the same land, and C purchases in good faith and for a valuable consideration. As between B and C, who prevails in a jurisdiction having a notice statute? In a jurisdiction having a race-notice statute? In a jurisdiction having a period-of-grace statute, if A's recording is after the period of grace has expired? In a jurisdiction having a race statute?

28.7. O executes and delivers to A a deed conveying to A certain land O owns. A does not record. O then executes and delivers to B a deed of the same land, and B purchases with knowledge of A's prior unrecorded deed. B records and then executes and delivers to C a deed of the land, and C purchases the same without knowledge of A's prior unrecorded deed. A then records. C then records. As between A and C, who prevails in a jurisdiction having a notice statute? In a jurisdiction having a race-notice statute? In a jurisdiction having a period-of-grace statute, if A records after the period of grace? In a jurisdiction having a race statute? See Bowman v. Holland, 116 Va. 805, 83 S.E. 393 (1914). Suppose that B repurchases the land from C. Will the answer to the various questions change if the dispute is between B and A? See Clark v. McNeal, 114 N.Y. 287, 21 N.E. 405 (1889).

28.8. O owns a tract of land valued at $20,000. O borrows $5,000 from A and executes and delivers to A a mortgage on the land to secure the loan. A does not record this mortgage. O then borrows $7,000 from B and executes and delivers to B a mortgage on the land to secure the loan. B had actual knowledge of the prior unrecorded mortgage in favor of A. B records the mortgage on the day it is delivered. O then borrows $3,000 from C and executes and delivers to C a mortgage on the land to secure the loan. C had no knowledge of A's prior unrecorded mortgage but was aware of B's prior recorded mortgage. C recorded the mortgage on the day it was delivered. O's land is sold pursuant to foreclosure proceedings, and the sum of $10,000 is realized from the sale. How should the $10,000 be distributed among A, B, and C? See Day v. Munson, 14 Ohio St. 488 (1863).[7] Cf. Hoag v. Sayre, 33 N.J. Eq. 552 (1881).[8]

28.9. O owned Blackacre in 1965 in a state where the statute of limitations is in the following form: "An action for the recovery of land shall be

---

7. The transactions in Day v. Munson involved chattel mortgages rather than real estate mortgages. In establishing priority between successive chattel mortgages, the controlling statute in force in Ohio at the date that was critical in Day v. Munson was a notice statute.

8. The transactions in Hoag v. Sayre also involved chattel mortgages. In establishing priority between successive chattel mortgages, the controlling statute in force in New Jersey at the date that was critical in Hoag v. Sayre was a notice statute.

commenced only within twenty years after the right of action first accrued."
A is an adverse possessor who entered on Blackacre in 1965 under a title
which A now concedes to be defective and remained there, claiming title,
until 1987, at which time there was a fire on the place, the house burned
down, and A moved elsewhere. B entered on the land in 1988 and, when A
challenged B, exhibited a deed from O dated 1988. B having refused to get
out, A brought ejectment.

At the trial B's counsel asked A's counsel to stipulate that O had title in
1965 and that the only deed from O in the registry of deeds is the deed to B.
A's counsel said that the stipulation would be agreed upon if B would
stipulate that A had been in continuous, open possession of the land from
1965 to 1987 under claim of right. B's counsel surprisingly agreed; so all
these facts were stipulated. B took the stand, produced in evidence the deed
from O to B, and testified that in 1988 he had no knowledge of A's claim or
that A had ever been on the land. B's counsel called O to the stand; O
testified that in 1980 O had given A a deed to Blackacre and produced a copy
of it. A's counsel said, "I have no objection to this deed going in, though I
know nothing about it. The more titles my opponent can prove that my
client has, the better I like it."

At the close of the evidence, counsel for B moved for a directed verdict.
Rule on the motion in a jurisdiction having a notice statute. Would the
ruling be any different under one of the other types of statutes? See Winters
v. Powell, 180 Ala. 425, 61 So. 96 (1912).

SECTION 2.   RECORD NOTICE

Note: Recorded Instrument in the "Chain of Title"

If a deed is properly recorded, a subsequent purchaser will take with
notice of the contents of the deed. This is referred to as "record notice" (or
"constructive notice," see page 49 *supra* in regard to constructive notice).
Unless the deed is discoverable by a search of the records that it is reasonable
to expect a purchaser's attorney to make, that is, unless the deed is in the
"chain of title," the purchaser should not be deemed to have "record
notice." The wording of the controlling recording act will determine what
deeds placed on the record are in the "chain of title" so that they will be
regarded as discoverable by the purchaser's attorney, and hence give "record
notice" to the purchaser. The following cases are concerned with the
differing views the courts have reached in construing statutes that are not
unequivocally clear on this matter. A deed may not be in the "chain of title"
under a grantor-grantee index that would be in the "chain of title" under a
tract index. Do you see why this is true? If you do not see why this is true
now, you should after examining the cases which follow.

Note: Deed Not Indexed

If a deed is placed on the record but is not indexed, it will not be discoverable by the title examiner unless he or she examines the books in which the deeds are copied in full, turning each page and examining the deeds to see if the land described in each deed is the land the title examiner is interested in. One such title search might be a lifetime job. Jones v. Folks, 149 Va. 140, 140 S.E. 126 (1927), contended that the statute before it did not make indexing a part of recording.

Whether this act upon the part of the law making body was wise or not, it cannot be questioned that the legislature had the power to enact the statute in its present form and eliminate therefrom the requirement that a deed should also be indexed, as well as admitted to record.[9] [149 Va. at 145-146, 140 S.E. at 128.]

Note: Deed Indexed Under Wrong Name or Wrong Initial

If a deed is indexed but under the wrong name, an examination of each entry in the index would disclose the deeds in which the title searcher is interested. This would be only the normal burden under a tract index but would be an enormous task under a grantor-grantee index.

The indexer may make only a slight mistake in the name, such as a mistake in the middle initial. The title searcher would not have a very burdensome task under a grantor-grantee index if he checked all last names in his chain of title, regardless of whether the initials with such last names would indicate a different person was involved, unless the last named involved was Smith or Jones or some other widely prevalent name. In Prouty v. Marshall, 225 Pa. 570, 74 A. 550 (1909), the relevant name to the title searcher was "L. J. Marshall," but both in the index and on the record the name appeared as "S. J. Marshall." The instrument involved was a mortgage that L. J. Marshall had given to a mortgagee and the issue was whether such mortgage was on the record in such manner as to give "record notice" to a subsequent purchaser from L. J. Marshall. The court said:

In the case at bar, the duty was upon the mortgagee to give notice that L. J. Marshall had executed to her a mortgage upon the premises in question. If from any cause she fell short of giving legal notice, the consequence must fall upon her. She cannot hide behind the mistake of the recorder. It is an easy matter for a mortgagee, or a grantee in each particular instance, either in person, or by a representative, to look at the record, and see that the instrument has been properly entered. The instrument itself is at hand. The names

---

9. In regard to indexing as a part of recording see Cross, The Record "Chain of Title" Hypocrisy, 57 Colum. L. Rev. 787 (1957). — Eds.

of the parties are known, and comparisons are easily made. How would it be possible for a subsequent purchaser to know anything about the facts? The duty thus imposed upon the mortgagee in this respect, involves no more, and no less, than is required of a mortgagee, for his own protection, when before the money is paid out upon the loan, an inspection of the judgment indexes is necessary to see whether or not a judgment has been entered against the mortgagor upon the same day on which the mortgage is recorded. Some care must be exercised in every such transaction. There is every reason why it should be made the duty of the mortgagee to see that his instrument is properly recorded. This will not in any way interfere with the principle that when the instrument is certified as recorded, it shall import notice of the contents from the time of filing. But that must be understood as in connection with an instrument properly recorded. As said above, the record is notice of just what it contains, no more and no less. The obligation of seeing that the record of an instrument is correct, must properly rest upon its holder. If he fails to protect himself, the consequence cannot justly be shifted upon an innocent purchaser. [225 Pa. at 576-577, 74 A. at 552.]

Before you accept without question the view of the court in the *Prouty* case, consider carefully how much of a job it is for the purchaser (or the purchaser's attorney) to go back to the recorder's office and check to see whether the recorded document has been indexed properly. In this connection, keep in mind that the initial indexing is not the final indexing. See Chapter 29.

Problem

28.10. O owned Blackacre in 1965. He conveyed to Elsa Smith in that year, and she recorded the deed to her at that time. In 1976 Elsa Smith married one Arthur B. Taylor. In 1977 she mortgaged the land to A to secure a note for $5,000. She signed the mortgage as "Elsa S. Taylor"; the mortgage was duly recorded. In 1980 Elsa S. Taylor obtained a decree of divorce from her husband, in which decree she was permitted to resume her maiden name. In 1984 she conveyed Blackacre for consideration to B, who had no knowledge of the mortgage to A or of Elsa's marital history; in this deed she signed herself "Elsa Smith." The recording act provides, "a conveyance shall not be valid as against any person except the grantor, his heirs and devisees and persons having actual notice of it unless it is recorded as provided in this Chapter." The recording act further provides that all recorded deeds shall be indexed in a grantor-grantee index.

a.   Is A's mortgage valid as against B?

b.   If, in the course of the dealings between Elsa and B, Elsa had said, "I hate to sell this place, but since my divorce I'm pretty hard up," would this have affected the result?

c.   If there were a tract index instead of a grantor-grantee index, would this have affected the result?

Note: Recorded and Indexed Deed Not Discoverable

If O, the owner of land, conveys it to A and A does not record, and then A conveys the same land to B and B records, a conveyance at this stage by O to C should result in C's prevailing over B if a grantor-grantee index is involved. B's deed is not discoverable by the title examiner for C, even though it is recorded, because the record shows no conveyance out of O to A. See Board of Education v. Hughes, 118 Minn. 404, 136 N.W. 1095 (1912), which held that C should prevail over B's recorded deed, even in a race notice jurisdiction. If a tract index is involved, however, C's title examiner would see the A to B deed, and C should not prevail even though the O to A deed is not recorded.

Problem

28.11.   O conveys Blackacre to A on July 1, 1984. A records on December 1, 1984. O conveys Blackacre to B on September 1, 1984, and B records on February 1, 1985. B conveys Blackacre to C on November 1, 1984, and C records immediately. B and C did not have actual notice of the deed to A. The attorney for A cites Board of Education v. Hughes as establishing that A prevails over C. You are C's attorney. Would you agree that the case cited is controlling?

Note: Deed of Grantor Recorded Prior to Time
Grantor Acquired Property

O purports to transfer property by deed to A prior to the time O acquires the property described in the deed. A records. O, after acquiring the property, offers to sell the property to B. The title examiner for B will not discover on the record the O to A deed, unless the title examiner runs the grantor index under O's name for a period of time prior to the date the record shows that O acquired the property. The following case considers whether the recording of the O to A deed will give record notice to B of its existence.

AYER v. PHILADELPHIA & BOSTON
FACE BRICK CO.
159 Mass. 84, 34 N.E. 177 (1893)

[This case appeared before the Supreme Judicial Court twice. Each time the opinion was written by Holmes, J. In neither is the statement of facts wholly satisfactory. The following data are drawn from the original record:

The land in question was waterfront property on Medford Street, Charlestown, including buildings and wharf structures. Anthony Waterman acquired title to the land on October 1, 1866, by a deed duly recorded.

On March 1, 1872, Waterman gave a mortgage to Boston Five Cents Savings Bank to secure payment of $40,000 three years from date. It was promptly recorded.

On February 21, 1874, Waterman gave a mortgage (which later came into the hands of Frederick F. Ayer by assignment) to secure the payment of $40,000 three years from date. It was promptly recorded. This second mortgage, in the granting clause, described the land as subject to a certain right of drainage, a certain easement, "and the mortgage hereinafter named." It also contained a covenant by the mortgagor "that I am lawfully seized in fee simple of the aforementioned premises; that they are free from all encumbrances, except a certain mortgage given by me to the Boston Five Cents Savings Bank, dated March 1, 1872, to secure the sum of forty thousand dollars, the right of drainage and the easement aforesaid; and that I will, and my heirs, executors and administrators shall, warrant and defend the same to the said grantees and their heirs and assigns forever, against the lawful claims and demands of all persons, except the right of drainage and the easement aforesaid."

On July 6, 1876, the savings bank entered to foreclose its mortgage and a certificate of entry was duly recorded. On August 19, 1876, the savings bank exercised the power of sale given in the mortgage; Barstow was purchaser at the foreclosure sale. The deed to Barstow and the affidavit of sale were duly recorded. (For general information on this double type of foreclosure, see page 747 *supra* and Crocker, Notes on Common Forms 301 (Swaim 7th ed. 1955). The certificate of entry is not required to state the names of present holders of the equity or of junior mortgagees. See Crocker at 301. Notice of the foreclosure sale must be published in a newspaper in the manner prescribed by the statute, but no other notice need be given to the owner of the equity or to junior mortgagees. Crocker at 319. A third form of foreclosure in Massachusetts is by writ of entry; this form is being used in the case printed below; it was not used by the savings bank in foreclosing the first mortgage.)

(Prior to October 26, 1877, Waterman was discharged in bankruptcy; but this fact was not included in the agreed statement of facts before the court in the earlier case (157 Mass. 57). The later case, which is the one here printed, arises out of the attempt to add this fact to the agreed statement of facts.)

On October 26, 1877, Waterman purchased the land, through a mesne conveyance, from Barstow, purchaser at the foreclosure sale.[10] This deed was duly recorded.

10. The actual transaction was as follows. Barstow, an officer of the savings bank, purchased at the foreclosure sale. On the same day he conveyed to Denio, also an officer of the bank; and Denio executed a deed of trust declaring that he held the premises for the benefit of the savings bank and would convey at its request. When Denio conveyed to Waterman on

On June 1, 1888, Anthony Waterman conveyed to William L. Waterman; William L. Waterman executed a mortgage to Anthony Waterman; and William L. Waterman conveyed to the Philadelphia & Boston Face Brick Co., subject to the last-named mortgage. The agreed statement of facts is silent as to whether the brick company knew of the 1874 mortgage, which came into the hands of Ayer.[11]

After the conveyance to the brick company, Ayer as demandant (i.e. plaintiff) brought a writ of entry against the Brick Company as tenant (i.e. defendant) to foreclose the 1874 second mortgage. When this case first came before the Supreme Judicial Court in 1892 (157 Mass. 57) the only question passed on by the Court was whether Waterman's covenant in the second mortgage could be construed to obligate him to warrant and defend against the first mortgage. Holmes, J., speaking for a divided court, concluded that the failure to exclude the mortgage from the operation of the "warrant and defend" clause when it had been excluded in the covenant against encumbrances, justified the inference that Waterman was warranting that he would protect the second mortgage from the first mortgage. Thus it was ruled that, when Waterman reacquired the title, the doctrine of estoppel by deed applied, and Waterman's new title inured to the benefit of the second mortgagee.

Only after losing the first case on the issue of construction of the covenant did the brick company's counsel raise issues based upon (1) Waterman's discharge in bankruptcy, and (2) the brick company's position as a bona fide purchaser.]

HOLMES, J. When this case was before us the first time, 157 Mass. 57, it was assumed by the tenant [Waterman's grantee] that the only question was whether the covenant of warranty in the second mortgage should be construed as warranting against the first mortgage. No attempt was made to

---

October 26, 1877, the deed stated that this was in accordance with the deed of trust and that Waterman had been designated as grantee by the savings bank. All deeds were promptly recorded.

If Waterman's attorney had foreseen the trouble he could get into by reacquiring the land, could he have avoided the difficulty by taking title in the name of a straw man (such as Denio) and following the procedure Denio followed?

11. On whom is the burden of proof as to whether an alleged bona fide purchaser had notice of an "unrecorded" instrument? No Massachusetts case on this point has been found. The matter is discussed on an analytical basis in American Law of Property §17.35 (Casner ed. 1952), where it is suggested that the matter may turn on the form of statute—as to which, compare the Massachusetts and Michigan statutes quoted at pages 813 and 814 *supra*. The cases are in conflict, but without differentiation based on differences in the form of statute. The authors of American Law of Property suggest that, as a practical matter, it would be sound to place the burden on the alleged bona fide purchaser since the matter is peculiarly within his or her knowledge.

Incidentally, what do you think of the competence of counsel for the brick company in omitting from the statement of facts (a) Waterman's discharge in bankruptcy, and (b) the issue of the brick company's knowledge of the 1874 mortgage? This was no trifling litigation. The land was obviously valuable, since it supported a $40,000 savings bank mortgage; and Ayer's writ of entry sought to foreclose another $40,000 mortgage.

deny that, if it was so construed, the title afterwards acquired by the mortgagor would inure to the benefit of the second mortgagee under the established American doctrine. The tenant now desires to reopen the agreed facts for the purpose of showing that after a breach of the covenant in the second mortgage, and before he repurchased the land, the mortgagor went into bankruptcy and got his discharge. The judge below ruled that the discharge was immaterial, and for that reason alone declined to reopen the agreed statement, and the case comes before us upon an exception to that ruling.

The tenant's counsel frankly avow their own opinion that the discharge in bankruptcy makes no difference. But they say that the inuring of an after acquired title by virtue of a covenant of warranty must be due either to a representation or to a promise contained in the covenant, and that if it is due to the former, which they deem the correct doctrine, then they are entitled to judgment on the agreed statement of facts as it stands, on the ground that there can be no estoppel by an instrument when the truth appears on the face of it, and that in this case the deed showed that the grantor was conveying land subject to a mortgage. If, however, contrary to their opinion, the title inures by reason of the promise in the covenant, or to prevent circuity of action, then they say the provision is discharged by the discharge in bankruptcy.

However anomalous what we have called the American doctrine may be, as argued by Mr. Rawle and others (Rawle on Covenants, (5th ed.) Secs. 247 et seq.), it is settled in this State as well as elsewhere. It is settled also that a discharge in bankruptcy has no effect on this operation of the covenant of warranty in an ordinary deed where the warranty is coextensive with the grant. It would be to introduce further technicality into an artificial doctrine if a different rule should be applied where the conveyance is of land subject to a mortgage against which the grantor covenants to warrant and defend. No reason has been offered for such a distinction, nor do we perceive any.

But it is said that the operation of the covenant must be rested on some general principle, and cannot be left to stand simply as an unjustified peculiarity of a particular transaction without analogies elsewhere in the law, and that this general principle can be found only in the doctrine of estoppel by representation, if it is held, as the cases cited and many others show, that the estoppel does not depend on personal liability for damages. Rawle on Covenants, (5th ed.) Sec. 251.

If the American rule is an anomaly, it gains no strength by being referred to a principle which does not justify it in fact and by sound reasoning. The title may be said to inure by way of estoppel when explaining the reason why a discharge in bankruptcy does not affect this operation of the warranty; but if so, the existence of the estoppel does not rest on the prevention of fraud or on the fact of a representation actually believed to be true. It is a technical effect of a technical representation, the extent of which is determined by the scope of the words devoted to making it. A subsequent title would inure to the grantee when the grant was of an unencumbered fee although the parties agreed by parol that there was a mortgage outstanding; (Chamberlain v. Meeder, 16 N.H. 381, 384; see Jenkins v. Collard, 145 U.S. 546, 560, 12 S. Ct. 868); and this shows that the estoppel is determined by the scope of the conventional assertion, not by any question of fraud or of actual belief. But the scope of the conventional assertion is determined by the scope of the warranty which contains it. Usually the warranty is of what is granted, and therefore the scope of it is determined by the scope of the description. But this is not necessarily so; and when the warranty says that the grantor is to be taken as assuring you that he owns and will defend you in the unencumbered fee, it does not matter that by the same deed he avows the assertion not to be the fact. The warranty is intended to fix the extent of responsibility assumed, and by that the grantor makes himself answerable for the fact being true. In short, if a man by a deed says, I hereby estop myself to deny a fact, it does not matter that he recites as a preliminary that the fact is not true. The difference between a warranty and an ordinary statement in a deed is, that the operation and effect of the latter depends on the whole context of the deed, whereas the warranty is put in for the express purpose of estopping the grantor to the extent of its words. The reason "why the estoppel should operate, is, that such was the obvious intention of the parties." Blake v. Tucker, 12 Vt. 39, 45.

If a general covenant of warranty following a conveyance of only the grantor's right, title, and interest were made in such a form that it was construed as more extensive than the conveyance, there would be an estoppel coextensive with the covenant. See Blanchard v. Brooks, 12 Pick. 47, 66, 67; Bigelow, Estoppel, (5th ed.) 403. So in the case of a deed by an heir presumptive of his expectancy with a covenant of warranty. In this case, of course, there is no pretence that the grantor has a title coextensive with his warranty. Trull v. Eastman, 3 Met. 121, 124. In Lincoln v. Emerson, 108 Mass. 87, a first mortgage was mentioned in the covenant against encumbrances in a second mortgage, but was not excepted from the covenant of warranty. The title of the mortgagor under a foreclosure of the first mortgage was held to inure to an assignee of the second mortgage. Here the deed disclosed the truth, and for the purposes of the tenant's argument it cannot matter what part of the deed discloses the truth, unless it should be suggested that a covenant of warranty cannot be made more extensive than the grant, which was held not to be the law in our former decision. See also Calvert v. Sebright, 15 Beav. 156, 160.

The question remains whether the tenant stands better as a purchaser without actual notice, assuming that he had not actual notice of the second mortgage.

"It has been the settled law of this Commonwealth for nearly forty years, that, under a deed with covenants of warranty from one capable of executing it, a title afterwards acquired by the grantor inures by way of estoppel to the grantee, not only as against the grantor, but also as against one holding by descent or grant from him after acquiring the new title. Somes v. Skinner, 3 Pick. 52. White v. Patten, 24 Pick. 324. Russ v. Alpaugh, 118 Mass. 369, 376. We are aware that this rule, especially as applied to subsequent grantees, while followed in some States has been criticised in others. See Rawle on Covenants, (4th ed.) 427 et seq. But it has been too long established and acted on in Massachusetts to be changed, except by legislation." Knight v. Thayer, 125 Mass. 25, 27." See Powers v. Patten, 71 Me. 583, 587, 589; McCusker v. McEvey, 9 R.I. 528; Tefft v. Munson, 57 N.Y. 97.

It is urged for the tenant that this rule should not be extended. But if it is a bad rule, that is no reason for making a bad exception to it. As the title would have inured as against a subsequent purchaser from the mortgagor had his deed made no mention of the mortgage, and as by our decision his covenant of warranty operates by way of estoppel notwithstanding the mention of the mortgage, no intelligible reason can be stated why the estoppel should bind a purchaser without actual notice in the former case, and not bind him in the latter.

Upon the whole case, we are of opinion that the demandant is entitled to judgment. Our conclusion is in accord with the decision in a very similar case in Minnesota. Sandwich Manuf. Co. v. Zellmer, 48 Minn. 408.

Exceptions overruled.[12]

Problems

28.12. A conveys Blackacre to B by a warranty deed on July 1, 1957, and B records immediately. At the date of A's deed to B Blackacre was owned by O. O conveys Blackacre to A June 1, 1984, and A records immediately. A conveys Blackacre to C on September 1, 1984, and C records immediately. If you are the attorney for a prospective purchaser of Blackacre from C, for what years should you run A's name in the grantor index in order for your client to be protected against the possibility of loss due to a conveyance made by A before A acquired title in 1984,

    a.   If Blackacre is situated in Connecticut?

    b.   If Blackacre is situated in Massachusetts?

28.13. If you were to draft a statute designed to deal with the problem presented in Wheeler v. Young and Ayer v. Philadelphia & Boston Face Brick Company, what would your statute provide? Idaho Code Ann. §55-811, provides in part as follows:

> Every conveyance of real property acknowledged or proved, and certified, and recorded as prescribed by law, and which is executed by one who thereafter acquires an interest in said real property by a conveyance which is construc-

---

12. Massachusetts at the time of this case was and at present is a notice jurisdiction. See Mass. Gen. Laws Ann. ch. 183, §4, at page 813 *supra*. Massachusetts has no tract index.

The Connecticut case of Wheeler v. Young, 76 Conn. 44, 55 A. 670 (1903), is contra to the *Ayer* case. — EDS.

tive notice as aforesaid, is, from the time such latter conveyance is filed with the recorder for record, constructive notice of the contents thereof to subsequent purchasers and mortgagees.

See American Law of Property §§17.19, 17.20 (Casner ed. 1952).

Note: Deed of Grantor Recorded After Grantor Disposed of Property.

O transfers property to A by deed and A does not record until after O purports to transfer the same property to B by a deed which is recorded prior to the recording of the O to A deed. B offers to sell the property to C. The title examiner for C will not discover on the record the O to A deed, unless the title examiner runs the grantor index under O's name for a period of time after the record shows that O conveyed the property to B. The following case considers whether the recording of the O to A deed will give record notice to C of its existence.

MORSE v. CURTIS
140 Mass. 112, 2 N.E. 929 (1885)

MORTON, C.J. This is a writ of entry. Both parties derive their title from one Hall. On August 8, 1872, Hall mortgaged the land to the demandant. On September 7, 1875, Hall mortgaged the land to one Clark, who had notice of the earlier mortgage. The mortgage to Clark was recorded on January 31, 1876. The mortgage to the demandant was recorded on September 8, 1876. On October 4, 1881, Clark assigned his mortgage to the tenant, who had no actual notice of the mortgage to the demandant. The question is which of these titles has priority.

The same question was directly raised and adjudicated in the two cases of Connecticut v. Bradish, 14 Mass. 296, and Trull v. Bigelow, 16 Mass. 406. These adjudications establish a rule of property which ought not to be unsettled, except for the strongest reasons.

It is true, that, in the later case of Flynt v. Arnold, 2 Met. 619, Chief Justice Shaw expresses his individual opinion against the soundness of these decisions; but in that case the judgment of the court was distinctly put upon another ground, and his remarks can only be considered in the light of dicta, and not as overruling the earlier adjudications.

Upon careful consideration, the reasons upon which the earlier cases were decided seem to us the more satisfactory, because they best follow the spirit of our registry laws and the practice of the profession under them.[13]

---

13. Why wasn't the court equally concerned in the *Ayer* case, decided eight years later, to "follow the spirit of our registry laws and the practice of the profession under them"? — EDS.

The earliest registry laws provided that no conveyance of land shall be good and effectual in law "against any other person or persons but the grantor or grantors, and their heirs only, unless the deed or deeds thereof be acknowledged and recorded in manner aforesaid." St. 1783, c. 37, Sec. 4.

Under this statute, the court, at an early period, held that the recording was designed to take the place of the notorious act of livery of seisin; and that, though by the first deed the title passed out of the grantor, as against himself, yet he could, if such deed was not recorded, convey a good title to an innocent purchaser who received and recorded his deed. But the court also held that a prior unrecorded deed would be valid against a second purchaser who took his deed with a knowledge of the prior deed, thus engrafting an exception upon the statute. Reading of Judge Trowbridge, 3 Mass. 575. Marshall v. Fisk, 6 Mass. 24.

This exception was adopted on the ground that it was a fraud in the second grantee to take a deed, if he had knowledge of the prior deed. As Chief Justice Shaw forcibly says, in Lawrence v. Stratton, 6 Cush. 163, the rule is "put upon the ground, that a party with such notice could not take a deed without fraud, the objection was not to the nature of the conveyance, but to the honesty of the taker; and, therefore, if the estate had passed through such taker to a bona fide purchaser, without fraud, the conveyance was held valid."

This exception by judicial exposition was afterwards engrafted upon the statutes, and somewhat extended, by the Legislature. Rev. Sts. c. 59, Sec. 28. Gen. Sts. c. 89, Sec. 3. Pub. Sts. c. 120, Sec. 4. It is to be observed that, in each of these revisions, it is provided that an unrecorded prior deed is not valid against any persons except the grantor, his heirs and devisees, "and persons having actual notice" of it. The reasons why the statute requires actual notice to a second purchaser, in order to defeat his title, is apparent: its purpose is that his title shall not prevail against the prior deed, if he has been guilty of a fraud upon the first grantee; and he could not be guilty of such fraud, unless he had actual notice of the first deed.

Now, in the case before us, it is found as a fact that the tenant had no actual knowledge of the prior mortgage to the demandant at the time he took his assignment from Clark; but it is contended that he had constructive notice, because the demandant's mortgage was recorded before such assignment.

It was held in Connecticut v. Bradish, *ubi supra,* that such record was evidence of actual notice, but was not of itself enough to show actual notice, and to charge the assignee of the second deed with a fraud upon the holder of the first unrecorded deed. This seems to us to accord with the spirit of our registry laws, and with the uniform understanding of and practice under them by the profession.

These laws not only provide that deeds must be recorded, but they also prescribe the method in which the records shall be kept and indexes prepared for public inspection and examination. Pub. Sts. c. 24, Secs. 14-26.

There are indexes of grantors and grantees, so that, in searching a title, the examiner is obliged to run down the list of grantors, or run backward through the list of grantees. If he can start with an owner who is known to have a good title, as, in the case at bar, he could start with Hall, he is obliged to run through the index of grantors until he finds a conveyance by the owner of the land in question. After such conveyance, the former owner becomes a stranger to the title, and the examiner must follow down the name of the new owner to see if he has conveyed the land, and so on. It would be a hardship to require an examiner to follow in the indexes of grantors the names of every person who, at any time, through perhaps a long chain of title, was the owner of the land.

We do not think this is the practical construction which lawyers and conveyancers have given to our registry laws. The inconveniences of such a construction would be much greater than would be the inconvenience of requiring a person, who has neglected to record his prior deed for a time, to record it, and to bring a bill in equity to set aside the subsequent deed, if it was taken in fraud of his rights.

The better rule, and the one least likely to create confusion of titles, seems to us to be, that, if a purchaser, upon examining the registry, finds a conveyance from the owner of the land to his grantor, which gives him a perfect record title completed by what the law, at the time it is recorded, regards as equivalent to a livery of seisin, he is entitled to rely upon such record title, and is not obliged to search the records afterwards, in order to see if there has been any prior unrecorded deed of the original owner.

This rule of property, established by the early case of Connecticut v. Bradish, ought not to be departed from, unless conclusive reasons therefor be shown.

We are therefore of opinion, that, in the case at bar, the tenant has the better title; and, according to the terms of the report, the verdict ordered for the demandant must be set aside, and a

New trial granted.[14]

Problems

28.14. O conveys Blackacre to A on July 1, 1965, and A records on July 1, 1980. O conveys Blackacre to B on February 1, 1966, and B has notice of the prior unrecorded deed. B records immediately. If you are now the attorney for a prospective purchaser of Blackacre from B, for what years should you run O's name in the grantor index in order for your client to be protected against the possibility of loss due to a conveyance made by O prior

---

14. If Massachusetts had a race-notice statute or had a tract index should the result be different in this case? For a case which reaches an opposite result to that of Morse v. Aldrich, see Woods v. Garnett, 72 Miss. 78, 16 So. 390 (1894). — EDS.

to O's conveyance to B, which prior conveyance B took subject to because B had notice of it.

    a.   If Blackacre is situated in Massachusetts?

    b.   If Blackacre is situated in a jurisdiction that does not follow Morse v. Curtis?

28.15. O conveys Blackacre to A on August 1, 1980, and A records on June 1, 1982. O conveys Blackacre to B on September 1, 1981, and B has notice of the prior unrecorded deed. B records immediately. A now learns of O's deed to B. What steps should A take in a state like Massachusetts in order to prevent B from defeating A's rights in Blackacre by a conveyance to a bona fide purchaser? See American Law of Property §17.11 (Casner ed. 1952).

28.16. O executes and delivers to A a deed of certain land O owns. A does not record. O then executes and delivers to B a deed of the same land, and B purchases in good faith and for a valuable consideration. A then records. B then records. A then executes and delivers to C a deed of the same land, and C purchases in good faith and for a valuable consideration. Who prevails, B or C, in a notice jurisdiction? In a race-notice jurisdiction? See White v. McGregor, 92 Tex. 556, 50 S.W. 564 (1899).[15] See American Law of Property §17.21 (Casner ed. 1952).

Note: *Recordable Documents*

Only recordable documents will give "record notice" when placed on the land records, but a non-recordable document that is placed on the record in the chain of title may be seen by one examining the title so that the purchaser will take with knowledge of it. Priorities with respect to non-recordable documents which affect the title to land are unaffected by the recording acts. See the discussion of common-law priority rules at page 801 *supra.*

The controlling local statute must be examined to ascertain what documents are recordable. The principal exclusion from the requirement of recording is a short-term lease.

An instrument that purports to be a deed but which has not been executed with the formalities required by law, such as a deed that has not been acknowledged, may not be a recordable document, so that placing it on the record will not provide "record notice" to anyone in regard to it (see Graves v. Graves, 72 Mass. (6 Gray) 391 (1856)). Curative acts are passed from time to time in some states which are designed to cure formal defects in instruments, so that from and after the date of the curative act all purchasers will be deemed to have "record notice" of the former formally defective document if it has been recorded.

---

15.   Texas at the time of White v. McGregor was and at present is a notice jurisdiction. See Tex. Rev. Civ. Stat. Ann. art. 6627.

Note: Multiple Deeds out of a Common Grantor

We now turn to examine the recording problem that typically arises in relation to a land development which contemplates multiple transfers out of a common grantor, with various types of restrictive covenants inserted in the deeds out that are designed to restrict not only the land conveyed but also the land retained by the common grantor. The many other aspects of restrictive covenants are considered in Part VIII. In regard to the deeds-out recording problem, see Ryckman, Notice and The "Deeds Out" Problem, 64 Mich. L. Rev. 421 (1966).

BUFFALO ACADEMY OF THE
SACRED HEART v. BOEHM BROTHERS
267 N.Y. 242, 196 N.E. 42 (1935)

Appeal, by permission, from a judgment of the Appellate Division of the Supreme Court in the fourth judicial department, entered July 16, 1934, in favor of defendant, upon the submission of a controversy pursuant to sections 546-548 of the Civil Practice Act.

FINCH, J. This controversy, submitted pursuant to the provisions of the Civil Practice Act (Secs. 546-548), presents for determination the question whether title to certain real estate is marketable. The plaintiff agreed to discharge an indebtedness to the defendant by conveying to it good and marketable title to certain realty, the contract further providing that if title should prove unmarketable the plaintiff would pay the defendant $60,000 in cash. The plaintiff has tendered defendant a deed to the property in question and the defendant has refused to accept, on the ground that title is unmarketable.

It bases its refusal on the following grounds:

1. That the subdivision "University Terrace," in which the lots are situated, is subject to a uniform building plan which restricts the use of each and every lot in said subdivision to the erection of buildings for residential purposes only.

2. That a deed conveying four lots in said subdivision to the Kendall Refining Company prohibited the erection and operation of gasoline filling stations and the sale of motor oil and fuel on any of the lots in the subdivision other than the four so conveyed to the Kendall Refining Company.

The Appellate Division decided against the defendant on the first point, finding that there was no uniform building plan, but granted judgment for the defendant on the ground that the property was subject to a restrictive covenant prohibiting the erection or operation of gasoline filling stations. Defendant, therefore, had judgment in the sum of $60,000.

Taking up the question of a uniform building plan, it is clear that the

Appellate Division was correct in deciding that the property was not subject to the restriction of a plan limiting the use of the property to residential purposes. The plaintiff's grantor set up two adjoining subdivisions. They were called "University Terrace, Part One" and "University Terrace, Part Two." Surveys were made, streets and lots laid out, maps prepared and filed in the County Clerk's office. No plan or declaration of a purpose to restrict any particular portion of the sub-divisions or lots thereon to residential or other specific purposes was included or indicated in the maps filed, nor do any of the deeds contain covenants on the part of the grantor that the remainder of the tract should be subject to restriction. The plaintiff's grantor in selling the lots did not follow a uniform policy of development pursuant to which restrictions either for or against the grantees in the various deeds were established. Some lots were restricted to the erection of two-family houses; others to one-family houses. Stores were permitted on some lots, provided no gasoline or oil business should be conducted. In a great number of deeds a "saving clause" was inserted, providing that the grantee obtained no rights in other lots of the subdivision by reason of the restrictive provisions of the deeds. Many deeds contained no restrictions. It is apparent that restrictions were made whenever the grantor thought them necessary or advisable to bring about and maintain the desirability and salability of the property. Clearly he was not following a fixed plan of restricting the use of the lots sold and did not intend to bind himself or his remaining lots by the covenants contained in the deeds which he gave. The defendant emphasizes the "saving clause" found in many of the deeds and seeks to deduce from this that the earlier deeds were in accordance with a plan which restricted the plaintiff's grantor and that, therefore, the clause was inserted to prevent later deeds from carrying the benefit of the covenants already made. The argument cuts both ways. It is equally potent as showing that no general plan to restrict all lots ever was contemplated. If the grantor had in fact restricted all his property in the subdivisions, of what use was the denial of the benefits under the covenants to the later purchasers, when sixty-two prior purchasers already possessed the power to enforce such restrictions? Thus we are brought to the conclusion that no uniform building plan ever came into being.[16]

16. In the brief of the defendant the following points were brought out in support of the contention that a uniform building plan existed. There were 538 lots in the subdivision and 427 had been sold. Three hundred and eighty-seven of the 427 lots sold were conveyed subject to uniform restrictive covenants limiting the property so conveyed to residential purposes. The maps of the subdivision which were filed in the office of the clerk of the county in which the subdivision was located showed that the lots were all approximately equal in size and suitable for the erection of residences.

The defendants were contending on the basis of these facts that it was proper to imply a right in the purchaser of each lot, expressly restricted, to enforce like restrictions on the other lots in the subdivision. The implication of such reciprocal rights where a uniform building plan exists has been recognized by a court applying equitable principles in order to carry out what is believed to be the basic understanding of all the parties. The court, however, will only enforce such implied reciprocal rights against purchasers with actual or constructive notice of their

The defendant next urges that the deed given by the plaintiff's predecessor to the Kendall Refining Company prohibited the erection and operation of a gas filling station upon all the other lots in the subdivision; that, although no mention of such restriction is made in the deed or chain of title to the plaintiff, it is binding on the property deeded to him; and that, therefore, the title offered to the defendant is not marketable.

The clause in the deed to the Kendall Company reads as follows:

> This conveyance is made and accepted subject to the following restrictions, which shall be covenants running with the land:
>
> First: So long as the said premises shall be used as a gasoline or motor fuel distributing station, the party of the second part or its assigns or successors agree: (a) That any grease pit or pits must and shall be level with the ground. (b) That there shall not be more than 8 pump housings for the distribution of motor oils and fuels. (c) That there shall not be more than one building for the sale or distribution of motor fuels.
>
> Second: That at no time will the said premises be used for what is known as industrial or factory purposes. And the party of the first part covenants that he will not sell, or cause or permit to be sold, gasoline or lubricating oils, or motor fuels, nor erect, or cause to be erected, or permit to be erected, any other gasoline, lubricating oils or motor fuels distributing or sale station or stations upon the entire tracts of land known as University Terrace Number (or Part) I and University Terrace Number (or Part) 2; and that in the event that the party of the first part acquires the tract of land adjoining the said University Terrace tracts on the east, or any interest therein, the foregoing restrictive covenants to apply thereto to equal force and effect.

Upon the face of the foregoing deed, the only covenants which expressly are made to run with the land are those imposing obligations upon the Kendall Company, namely, pits must be level with the ground, the number of pump housings and buildings limited and the premises never used for industrial or factory purposes. When the grantor comes to covenanting on his part he starts covenanting anew and omits, apparently purposely, to provide that such covenant shall run with the land, although having so provided expressly with reference to the covenant on the part of the grantee, less than a dozen lines back in the same instrument. That the covenant on the part of the grantor only purports to be a personal undertaking is strengthened by the fact that the grantor binds himself alone and does not,

---

existence. Thus, even if the court had agreed with the defendant's contention as to the existence of a uniform building plan, the court would have had to find that the plaintiff purchased with notice of its existence. Since the plaintiff did not have actual notice, notice would have to be established by determining that the plaintiff was under a duty to examine the deeds out of the plaintiff's grantor, which deeds would have disclosed restrictions on other lots from which the plaintiff should have inferred a uniform building plan on the basis of which reciprocal rights would be implied. Cf. Sprague v. Kimball, page 1024 *infra,* on the statute of frauds as an obstacle to implying a reciprocal right even though a uniform building plan exists. See also Sanborn v. McLean, page 837 *infra.* — EDS.

either expressly or by legal implication, attempt to bind his heirs, grantees or assigns. The grantor's covenant was that he would not sell gasoline and oil or erect filling stations on his remaining lots, but he avoided sedulously any covenant that his grantee would not do these things. Taking the restrictions in the order in which they appear in the deed, we find that those expressly intended to run with the land are the restrictions upon the use of the land conveyed, which are applicable only to it, namely, those limiting the extent and nature of the structures upon the land. The remainder of the covenant is nothing more than an agreement prohibiting the grantor personally from becoming a competitor of the grantee in the filling station business. Nowhere do we find any provision extending such prohibition to the assigns of the grantor.

Thus, the covenant is personal to the grantor and cannot by implication be impressed upon future owners of other premises. The grantor could have made his covenant an obligation upon the lots of the plaintiff by inserting a covenant in the deed prohibiting a gasoline station upon such lots, but the grantor did not do so but gave a deed to the plaintiffs free of any such covenant. Therefore, his obligation under this covenant stopped at himself and never attached to the lots later transferred to the plaintiff. Clark v. Devoe, 124 N.Y. 120, 26 N.E. 275.

In Clark v. Devoe the court said:

> In construing the covenant, it is to be observed that the grantor, . . . confined the restriction to himself alone, by agreeing that he, the grantor, would neither erect or cause to be erected any building that should be regarded as a nuisance. According to the literal, and hence natural, interpretation of this language, the parties meant that the grantor should not personally do or cause to be done any of the inhibited acts. No doubt could arise as to the correctness of this construction, if the parties had not agreed in behalf of themselves and their assigns. The substance of the covenant, however, is limited to the covenantor, and purports to restrict his action only. While the capacity in which he assumes to contract is in behalf of himself and others, the actual contract, or the thing agreed not to be done, is limited to his own acts. [124 N.Y., p. 124, 26 N.E. 276.]

And again:

> He did not agree that his . . . assigns should not build but only that he would not build. He used no words that connected anyone except himself with the restriction against building, or that imposed an obligation in that regard upon any other person. It was not a general covenant "not to erect," (as in Phoenix Ins. Co. v. Continental Ins. Co., 87 N.Y. 400), but a special covenant that the grantor would not erect, showing an intention to contract against the acts of one person only. [124 N.Y., p. 125, 26 N.E. 276.]

Moreover, in construing conveyances containing covenants running with the land, the authorities uniformly hold that restrictive covenants must always be construed strictly against those seeking to enforce them; that they must be construed as they read and not be given a construction extending beyond the literal meaning of their terms. Reformed Protestant Dutch Church v. Madison Ave. Building Co., 214 N.Y. 268, 108 N.E. 444; Shoonmaker v. Heckscher, 171 App. Div. 148, 157 N.Y.S. 75, *affirmed* 218 N.Y. 722, 113 N.E. 1066.

Assuming, however, that the deed embodies a restrictive covenant running with the land, intended to bind not only the grantor but in addition all the property in the subdivision owned by the grantor, for the defendant to succeed it is necessary also to find that this will bind land in the subdivision subsequently sold by deeds which make no mention of the covenant and which transfer property to grantees who are unaware of the existence of the covenant. The defendant claims that the mere fact that this one deed contains a restrictive covenant furnished constructive notice to all subsequent purchasers of property from the same grantor. To so claim goes contrary to the well-settled principle that a purchaser takes with notice from the record only of incumbrances in his direct chain of title. In the absence of actual notice before or at the time of his purchase or of other exceptional circumstances, an owner of land is only bound by restrictions if they appear in some deed of record in the conveyance to himself or his direct predecessors in title. Clark on Real Covenants and Other Interests which "Run with the Land," p. 162. This rule would seem to be implicit in the acts providing for the recording of conveyances. Recording constitutes notice only of instruments in the chain of title of the parcel granted. To have to search each chain of title from a common grantor lest notice be imputed would seem to negative the beneficent purposes of the recording acts. Schermerhorn v. Bedell, 163 App. Div. 445, 148 N.Y.S. 896, *affirmed* 221 N.Y. 536, 116 N.E. 1074.

In several States it has been held that a purchaser of a lot which formed part of a larger tract is not charged with notice of restrictive covenants contained in a prior deed from the same grantor to any other lot or parcel of the same general tract, although the deed is recorded and by its terms applies to all other lots. Hancock v. Gumm, 151 Ga. 667, 107 S.E. 872; Glorieux v. Lighthipe, 88 N.J.L. 199, 96 A. 94; Wichita Valley Ry. Co. v. Marshall, 37 S.W.2d (Tex. Civ. App.) 756; Yates v. Chandler, 162 Tenn. 388, 38 S.W.2d 70.

It is true that in some other States it has been held that the recording of such a deed by a common grantor affords notice to all his subsequent grantees. Lowes v. Carter, 124 Md. 678, 93 A. 216; Finley v. Glenn, 303 Pa. 131, 154 A. 299. In New York no authorities in the Court of Appeals have been brought to our attention which prescribe the principle to be followed. In the Appellate Division there is an instance where a covenant in one deed has been held to affect property subsequently deeded by the common grantor free from the covenant. In that case, however, the covenant in the prior deed sought to establish a front line for adjacent houses. From the facts and circumstances it was held that the defendant had notice of the restrictive covenant in the earlier deed. Any one building in a residential section who projects his house farther into the street line than the adjacent house might be said to be put on notice as to whether he is restricted from so doing, either by a general plan of building or by some right or easement which his adjacent neighbor may have acquired. Holt v. Fleischman, 75 App. Div. 593, 78 N.Y.S. 647.[17]

In the absence of exceptional circumstances, the consideration of which we may well leave until they arise, New York should follow the general well-settled principle that a purchaser takes with notice from the record only of incumbrances in his direct chain of title.

The judgment should be reversed and judgment directed in accordance with this opinion, with costs.

Judgment accordingly.[18]

Problem

28.17. Assume that the defendant in Buffalo Academy of the Sacred Heart v. Boehm Brothers, after acquiring the land in dispute in that case, undertakes to build on it a gasoline filling station. The Kendall Refining Company institutes a suit to enjoin the use of the defendant's land for such a purpose. Will the defendant be protected by the decision in the Buffalo Academy of the Sacred Heart v. Boehm Brothers? See Jeffries v. Jeffries, 117 Mass. 184 (1874); Hill v. Levine, 252 Mass. 513, 147 N.E. 837 (1925).

GUILLETTE v. DALY DRY WALL, INC.
367 Mass. 355, 325 N.E.2d 572 (1975)

BRAUCHER, J. A recorded deed of a lot in a subdivision refers to a recorded plan, contains restrictions "imposed solely for the benefit of the other lots shown on said plan," and provides that "the same restrictions are hereby imposed on each of said lots now owned by the seller." A later deed of another lot from the same grantor refers to the same plan but not to the restrictions. The plan does not mention the restrictions, and the later grantee took without knowledge of them. We reject the later grantee's

---

17. Assume that you are the attorney for the purchaser of the first lot being sold in a land development in New York. What steps will you insist be taken in order to make certain that the purchasers of the other lots in the development will take subject to the same restrictions as those inserted in the deed to your client? — EDS.

18. New York at the time of this case was and at present is a race-notice jurisdiction. See N.Y. Real Prop. Acts. Law §291. Should the result in this case be different merely because a notice jurisdiction is involved?

Should the result in this case be different if a tract index is involved? — EDS.

contention that it was not bound by the restrictions because they were not contained in a deed in its chain of title, and affirm a decree enforcing the restrictions.

The plaintiffs, owners of three lots in the subdivision, brought suit in the Superior Court to enjoin the defendant, owner of a lot in the same subdivision, from constructing a multifamily apartment building on its lot. The case was referred to a master, and his report was confirmed. A final decree was entered enjoining the defendant from "constructing any structures designed, intended, or suited for any purpose other than a dwelling for one family and which . . . [do] not conform to the restrictions contained in a deed from Wallace L. Gilmore to Pauline A. Guillette and Kenneth E. Guillette." The defendant appealed, and the case was transferred from the Appeals Court to this court under G.L. c. 211A, §10(A). The evidence is not reported.

We summarize the master's findings. Gilmore sold lots in a subdivision called Cedar Hills Section I in Easton to the plaintiffs, the defendant, and others. Two of the plaintiffs, the Walcotts, purchased a lot in August, 1967, by a deed referring to a plan dated in July, 1967. The plaintiff Guillette and her husband, now deceased, purchased a lot in May, 1968, by a deed referring to a plan dated in March, 1968. The 1967 and 1968 plans are the same for all practical purposes; neither mentions restrictions. The plaintiffs Paraskivas purchased a lot in June, 1968, by a deed referring to the 1968 plan. Each of these deeds and five other deeds to lots in the subdivision either set out the restrictions or incorporated them by reference. Only the Guillette deed and one other contained a provision restricting lots retained by the seller. It was the intention of the grantor and the plaintiffs to maintain the subdivision as a residential subdivision to include only dwellings for one family.

The master further found that the defendant Daly Dry Wall, Inc. (Daly), purchased its lot from Gilmore in April, 1972, and that the deed to Daly contained no reference to any restrictions but did refer to the 1968 plan. Daly made no inquiry concerning restrictions and did not know of any development pattern. It had a title examination made. It learned of the restrictions in August, 1972. Subsequently it obtained a building permit for thirty-six apartment-type units.

In similar circumstances, where the common grantor has not bound his remaining land by writing, we have held that the statute of frauds prevents enforcement of restrictions against the grantor or a subsequent purchaser of a lot not expressly restricted. G.L. c. 183, §3. Houghton v. Rizzo, — Mass. —, 281 N.E.2d 577 (1972), and cases cited. Gulf Oil Corp. v. Fall River Housing Authy., — Mass. —, 306 N.E.2d 257 (1974). Where, as here, however, the grantor binds his remaining land by writing, reciprocity of restriction between the grantor and grantee can be enforced. See Snow v. Van Dam, 291 Mass. 477, 482, 197 N.E. 224 (1935), and cases cited. In such cases a subsequent purchaser from the common grantor acquires title subject to the restrictions in the deed to the earlier purchaser. Beekman v. Schirmer, 239 Mass. 265, 270, 132 N.E. 45 (1921). See Am. Law of Property, §9.31 (1952); Tiffany, Real Property, §§858, 861 (3d ed. 1939); Restatement: Property, §539, comment i (1944). Each of the several grantees, if within the scope of the common scheme, is an intended beneficiary of the restrictions and may enforce them against the others. Hano v. Bigelow, 155 Mass. 341, 343, 29 N.E. 628 (1892). Gulf Oil Corp. v. Fall River Housing Authy., — Mass. —, 306 N.E.2d 257 (1974). Cf. Boston & Maine R.R. v. Construction Mach. Corp., 346 Mass. 513, 521, n.5, 194 N.E.2d 395 (1963); Merrill v. Kirkland Constr. Co., Inc., — Mass. —, 310 N.E.2d 106 (1974). No question is presented as to compliance with G.L. c. 184, §27(a), as amended by St. 1969, c. 666, §4, or §30, inserted by St. 1961, c. 448, §1.

The sole issue raised by the defendant is whether it is bound by a restriction contained in deeds to its neighbors from a common grantor, when it took without knowledge of the restrictions and under a deed which did not mention them. It has, it says, only the duty to ascertain whether there were any restrictions in former deeds in its chain of title. See Stewart v. Alpert, 262 Mass. 34, 37-38, 159 N.E. 503 (1928). But the deed from Gilmore to the Guillettes conveyed not only the described lot but also an interest in the remaining land then owned by Gilmore. That deed was properly recorded under G.L. c. 36, §12, and cannot be treated as an unrecorded conveyance under G.L. c. 183, §4. As a purchaser of part of the restricted land, the defendant therefore took subject to the restrictions. See Houghton v. Rizzo, — Mass. —, 281 N.E.2d 577 (1972); Am. Law of Property, §17.24 (1952); Tiffany, Real Property, §1266 (3d ed. 1939); Restatement: Property, §§533, 539, comment m (1944); Philbrick, Limits of Record Search and Therefore of Notice (Part I), 93 U. of Pa. L. Rev. 125, 172-175 (1944); annos. 16 A.L.R. 1013 (1922), 4 A.L.R.2d 1364, 1372 (1949).

The defendant argues that to charge it with notice of any restriction put in a deed by a common grantor is to "put every title examiner to the almost impossible task of searching carefully each and every deed which a grantor deeds out of a common subdivision." But our statutes provide for indexing the names of grantors and grantees, not lot numbers or tracts. G.L. c. 36, §§25, 26. Lot numbers or other descriptive information, even though included in an index, do not change what is recorded. Cf. Gillespie v. Rogers, 146 Mass. 610, 612, 16 N.E. 711 (1888), and cases cited. In such a system the purchaser cannot be safe if the title examiner ignores any deed given by a grantor in the chain of title during the time he owned the premises in question. In the present case the defendant's deed referred to a recorded subdivision plan, and the deed to the Guillettes referred to the same plan. A search for such deeds is a task which is not at all impossible. Cf. Roak v. Davis, 194 Mass. 481, 485, 80 N.E. 690 (1907).

Decree affirmed with costs of appeal.

SANBORN v. McLEAN
233 Mich. 227, 206 N.W. 496 (1925)

WIEST, J. Defendant Christina McLean owns the west 35 feet of lot 86 of Green Lawn subdivision, at the northeast corner of Collingwood avenue and Second boulevard, in the city of Detroit, upon which there is a dwelling house, occupied by herself and her husband, defendant John A. McLean. The house fronts Collingwood avenue. At the rear of the lot is an alley. Mrs. McLean derived title from her husband and, in the course of the opinion, we will speak of both as defendants. Mr. and Mrs. McLean started to erect a gasoline filling station at the rear end of their lot, and they and their contractor, William S. Weir, were enjoined by decree from doing so and bring the issues before us by appeal. Mr. Weir will not be further mentioned in the opinion.

Collingwood avenue is a high-grade residence street between Woodward avenue and Hamilton boulevard, with single, double and apartment houses, and plaintiffs who are owners of land adjoining, and in the vicinity of defendants' land, and who trace title, as do defendants, to the proprietors of the subdivision, claim that the proposed gasoline station will be a nuisance per se, is in violation of the general plan fixed for use of all lots on the street for residence purposes only, as evidenced by restrictions upon 53 of the 91 lots fronting on Collingwood avenue, and that defendants' lot is subject to a reciprocal negative easement barring a use so detrimental to the enjoyment and value of its neighbors. Defendants insist that no restrictions appear in their chain of title and they purchased without notice of any reciprocal negative easement, and deny that a gasoline station is a nuisance per se. We find no occasion to pass upon the question of nuisance, as the case can be decided under the rule of reciprocal negative easement.

This subdivision was planned strictly for residence purposes, except lots fronting Woodward avenue and Hamilton boulevard. The 91 lots on Collingwood avenue were platted in 1891, designed for and each one sold solely for residence purposes, and residences have been erected upon all of the lots. Is defendants' lot subject to a reciprocal negative easement? If the owner of two or more lots, so situated as to bear the relation, sells one with restrictions of benefit to the land retained, the servitude becomes mutual, and, during the period of restraint, the owner of the lot or lots retained can do nothing forbidden to the owner of the lot sold. For want of a better descriptive term this is styled a reciprocal negative easement. It runs with the land sold by virtue of express fastening and abides with the land retained until loosened by expiration of its period of service or by events working its destruction. It is not personal to owners but operative upon use of the land by any owner having actual or constructive notice thereof. It is an easement passing its benefits and carrying its obligations to all purchasers of land subject to its affirmative or negative mandates. It originates for mutual benefit and exists with vigor sufficient to work its ends. It must start with a common owner. Reciprocal negative easements are never retroactive; the very nature of their origin forbids. They arise, if at all, out of a benefit accorded land retained, by restrictions upon neighboring land sold by a common owner. Such a scheme of restrictions must start with a common owner; it cannot arise and fasten upon one lot by reason of other lot owners conforming to a general plan. If a reciprocal negative easement attached to defendants' lot it was fastened thereto while in the hands of the common owner of it and neighboring lots by way of sale of other lots with restrictions beneficial at that time to it. This leads to inquiry as to what lots, if any, were sold with restrictions by the common owner before the sale of defendants' lot. While the proofs cover another avenue we need consider sales only on Collingwood.

December 28, 1892, Robert J. and Joseph R. McLaughlin, who were then evidently owners of the lots on Collingwood avenue, deeded lots 37 to 41 and 58 to 62, inclusive, with the following restrictions:

"No residence shall be erected upon said premises, which shall cost less than $2,500 and nothing but residences shall be erected upon said premises. Said residences shall front on Helene (now Collingwood) avenue and be placed no nearer than 20 feet from the front street line."

July 24, 1893, the McLaughlins conveyed lots 17 to 21 and 78 to 82, both inclusive, and lot 98 with the same restrictions. Such restrictions were imposed for the benefit of the lands held by the grantors to carry out the scheme of a residential district, and a restrictive negative easement attached to the lots retained, and title to lot 86 was then in the McLaughlins. Defendants' title, through mesne conveyances, runs back to a deed by the McLaughlins dated September 7, 1893, without restrictions mentioned therein. Subsequent deeds to other lots were executed by the McLaughlins, some with restrictions and some without. Previous to September 7, 1893, a reciprocal negative easement had attached to lot 86 by acts of the owners, as before mentioned, and such easement is still attached and may now be enforced by plaintiffs, provided defendants, at the time of their purchase, had knowledge, actual or constructive, thereof. The plaintiffs run back with their title, as do defendants, to a common owner. This common owner, as before stated, by restrictions upon lots sold, had burdened all the lots retained with reciprocal restrictions. Defendants' lot and plaintiff Sanborn's lot, next thereto, were held by such common owner, burdened with a reciprocal negative easement and, when later sold to separate parties, remained burdened therewith and right to demand observance thereof passed to each purchaser with notice of the easement. The restrictions were upon defendants' lot while it was in the hands of the common owners, and abstract of title to defendants' lot showed the common owners and the record showed deeds of lots in the plat restricted to perfect and carry out the general plan and resulting in a reciprocal negative easement upon defendants' lot and all lots within its scope, and defendants and their predecessors in title were bound by constructive notice under our recording acts. The original plan was repeatedly declared in subsequent sales of lots by restrictions in the deeds, and while some lots sold were not so restricted the purchasers thereof, in every instance, observed the general plan and purpose of the restrictions in building residences. For upward of 30 years the united efforts of all persons interested have carried out the common purpose of making and keeping all the lots strictly for residences, and defendants are the first to depart therefrom.

When Mr. McLean purchased on contract in 1910 or 1911, there was a partly built dwelling house on lot 86, which he completed and now occupies. He had an abstract of title which he examined and claims he was told by the grantor that the lot was unrestricted. Considering the character of use made of all the lots open to a view of Mr. McLean when he purchased, we think he was put thereby to inquiry, beyond asking his grantor whether there were restrictions. He had an abstract showing the subdivision and that lot 86 had 97 companions; he could not avoid noticing the strictly uniform residence character given the lots by the expensive dwellings thereon, and the least inquiry would have quickly developed the fact that lot 86 was subjected to a reciprocal negative easement, and he could finish his house and, like the others, enjoy the benefits of the easement. We do not say Mr. McLean should have asked his neighbors about restrictions, but we do say that with the notice he had from a view of the premises on the street, clearly indicating the residences were built and the lots occupied in strict accordance with a general plan, he was put to inquiry, and had he inquired he would have found of record the reason for such general conformation, and the benefits thereof serving the owners of lot 86 and the obligations running with such service and available to adjacent lot owners to prevent a departure from the general plan by an owner of lot 86.

While no case appears to be on all fours with the one at bar the principles we have stated, and the conclusions announced, are supported by Allen v. City of Detroit, 167 Mich. 464, 133 N.W. 317, 36 L.R.A., N.S., 890; McQuade v. Wilcox, 215 Mich. 302, 183 N.W. 771, 16 A.L.R. 997;[19] French v. White Star Refining Co., 229 Mich. 474, 201 N.W. 444; Silberman v. Uhrlaub, 116 App. Div. 869, 102 N.Y.S. 299; Boyden v. Roberts, 131 Wis. 659, 111 N.W. 701; Howland v. Andrus, 80 N.J. Eq. 276, 83 A. 982.

We notice the decree in the circuit directed that the work done on the

---

19. In McQuade v. Wilcox, Wilcox was the owner of a large tract of land and divided it into lots for a residential subdivision. Various lots were conveyed subject to the express restriction that they were to be used only for residential purposes, and in the deeds conveying these lots was the following language: "These conditions are for the benefit of all present and future owners of property in this subdivision. . . . " The last lot in the subdivision was sold without any such restriction in the deed. It was purchased without actual notice of the restrictions that had been placed on the other lots. The court held that the recording of the deeds of the other lots gave notice to the purchaser of the last lot that the restriction applied to the lot he or she was purchasing. Why didn't the court in Sanborn v. McLean hold that McQuade v. Wilcox was controlling and thus dispense with the problem of inquiry notice? —EDS.

building be torn down. If the portion of the building constructed can be utilized for any purpose within the restrictions it need not be destroyed.

With this modification the decree in the circuit is affirmed, with costs to plaintiffs.[20]

Problem

28.18. O was the owner of a tract of land, and on the westerly part of this tract of land O built a house with a driveway leading from the street to the garage in back of the house. This driveway was built along the easterly side of the house. O then executed and delivered to A a deed of that portion of O's land on which the house was situated. A recorded the deed promptly. The description of the land in the deed to A was by metes and bounds, and such description did not actually include part of the land on which the driveway was built. Nevertheless A used the entire driveway to reach the garage in back of the house A had purchased without any objection from O. Two years later O executed and delivered to B a deed conveying that portion of the tract of land which had not been previously conveyed to A. The deed to B did not refer to the previous deed to A but described the land conveyed to B by metes and bounds, which description actually included the land on which a portion of the driveway was situated. B promptly recorded the deed. B had no actual notice that part of the driveway leading to A's garage was located on the land B was buying. Does A have the right to use that portion of the driveway located on the land B purchased? See Gorton-Pew Fisheries Co. v. Tolman, 210 Mass. 402, 97 N.E. 54 (1912); Backhausen v. Mayer, 204 Wis. 286, 234 N.W. 904 (1931). See also American Law of Property §17.24 (Casner ed. 1952); Easements by Implication, 57 Mich. L. Rev. 724 (1959); and the discussion of easements by implication beginning at page 1060 *infra*.

Note: Period of Time Covered by Title Examination — So-Called Marketable Title Statutes

In the examination of the land records there is no point at which the examiner can stop and be able to say with complete certainty that nothing might appear on the land records earlier than the date at which the examiner stops that will affect the title. This imposes a tremendous burden on the examiner if the examiner does a complete job in searching for possible

---

20. Michigan, at the time of this case and at present, protects a subsequent purchaser "in good faith and for a valuable consideration." See Mich. Comp. Laws Ann. §565.29. — Eds.

defects in the title. In some states an attempt has been made by statute to make it safe to stop short of a complete examination of the land records. See Mich. Comp. Laws §§565.101-565.109, part of which is as follows:

565.101. *Marketable Record Title.*

§1. Any person, having the legal capacity to own land in this state, who has an unbroken chain of title of record to any interest in land for 40 years, shall at the end of such period be deemed to have a marketable record title to such interest, subject only to such claims thereto and defects of title as are not extinguished or barred by application of the provisions of succeeding sections of this act and subject also to such interests and defects as are inherent in the provisions and limitations contained in the muniments of which such chain of record title is formed and which have been recorded during said 40 year period: *Provided, however,* That no one shall be deemed to have such a marketable record title by reason of the terms of this act, if the land in which such interest exists is in the hostile possession of another.

565.102. *Same; Who Deemed to Have.*

§2. A person shall be deemed to have the unbroken chain of title to an interest in land as such terms are used in the preceding section when the official public records disclose:

(a) A conveyance or other title transaction not less than 40 years in the past, which said conveyance or other title transaction purports to create such interest in such person, with nothing appearing of record purporting to divest such person of such purported interest; or,

(b) A conveyance or other title transaction not less than 40 years in the past, which said conveyance or other title transaction purports to create such interest in some other person and other conveyances or title transactions of record by which such purported interest has become vested in the person first referred to in this section, with nothing appearing of record purporting to divest the person first referred to in this section of such purported interest.

565.103. *Same; By Whom Held; Successors in Interest;*
Notices of Claims; Filing for Record.

§3. Such marketable title shall be held by such person and shall be taken by his successors in interest free and clear of any and all interests, claims, and charges whatsoever the existence of which depends in whole or in part upon any act, transaction, event or omission that occurred prior to such 40 year period, and all such interest, claims, and charges are hereby declared to be null and void and of no effect whatever at law or in equity: *Provided, however,* That any such interest, claim, or charge may be preserved and kept effective by filing for record during such 40 year period, a notice in writing, duly verified by oath, setting forth the nature of the claims. No disability or lack of knowledge of any kind on the part of anyone shall suspend the running of said 40 year period. For the purpose of recording notices of claim for homestead interests and the date from which the 40 year period shall run shall be the date or recording of the instrument, non-joinder in which is the basis for such claim. Such notice may be filed for record by the claimant or by any other person acting on behalf of any claimant who is:

    (a)   Under a disability,

    (b)   Unable to assert a claim on his own behalf,

    (c)   One of a class but whose identity cannot be established or is uncertain at the time of filing such notice of claim for record.

565.104.   *Same; Failure to File Notice Not to Bar Right to Possession.*

§4.   This act shall not be applied to bar any lessor or his successor as reversioner of his right to possession on the expiration of any lease or any lessee or his successor of his rights in and to any lease; or to bar any interest of a mortgagor or a mortgagee or interest in the nature of that of a mortgagor or mortgagee until after such instrument under which such interests are claimed shall have become due and payable, except where such instrument has no due date expressed, where such instrument has been executed by a railroad, railroad bridge, tunnel or union depot company, or any public utility or public service company; or to bar or extinguish any easement or interest in the nature of an easement, the existence of which is clearly observable by physical evidences of its use; or to bar or extinguish any easement or interest in the nature of an easement, or any rights appurtenant thereto granted, excepted or reserved by a recorded instrument creating such easement or interest, including any rights for future use, if the existence of such easement or interest is evidenced by the location beneath, upon or above any part of the land described in such instrument of any pipe, valve, road, wire, cable, conduit, duct, sewer, track, pole, tower, or other physical facility and whether or not the existence of such facility is observable, by reason of failure to file the notice herein required. Nor shall this act be deemed to affect any right, title or interest in land owned by the United States, nor any right, title or interest in any land owned by the State of Michigan, or by any department, commission or political subdivision thereof.[21]

Massachusetts General Laws ch. 260, §31A, which was enacted in 1956, provides that if a possibility of reverter or right of entry is one created prior to January 2, 1955, no remedy will be available to enforce it after January 1, 1964, unless the owner of the interest makes a prescribed current recording of it. Massachusetts General Laws ch. 184, §§26-30, enacted in 1961, is designed to give fairly current notoriety to outstanding covenants which impose restrictions on the use of land by requiring prescribed recording of the covenants. It should be noted, however, that a statute somewhat like the

---

21.   For a discussion of the Michigan statute, see Aigler, Clearance of Land Title—A Statutory Step, 44 Mich. L. Rev. 45 (1945); Basye, Streamlining Conveyancing Procedure, 47 Mich. L. Rev. 1097 (1949); Aigler, Constitutionality of Marketable Title Acts, 50 Mich. L. Rev. 185 (1951); Jossman, Forty Year Marketable Title Act: A Reappraisal, 37 U. Det. L.J. 422 (1960).

Massachusetts one on possibilities of reverter and rights of entry ran into constitutional difficulties in New York in Board of Education v. Miles, 15 N.Y.2d 364, 207 N.E.2d 181 (1965), but survived a constitutional attack in Illinois in Trustees of Schools of Township No. 1 v. Batdorf, 6 Ill. 2d 486, 130 N.E.2d 111 (1955).

Another type of statute which places a limit on the duration of possibilities of reverter and rights of entry has a bearing on the backward search into the land records which the title examiner may have to make to discover these interests that may affect the title to the land he is concerned with. For examples, see Illinois Revised Statutes ch. 30, §37e (duration of 40 years); Kentucky Revised Statutes Annotated §§381.218 and 381.219 (duration 30 years); Massachusetts General Laws ch. 184A, §3 (duration 30 years); Nebraska Revised Statutes §76-2,102 (duration 30 years).

If a state limits common-law dower to property owned by a deceased spouse at death, the title examiner need not check to see whether a prior grantee in the claim of title was married. In Massachusetts inchoate dower was abolished and the court held that such abolition, even as to outstanding rights of inchoate dower was constitutional. See Opinion of the Justices, 337 Mass. 786, 151 N.E.2d 475 (1958).

See further in regard to so-called marketable title statutes, the comments at page 1053 *infra*.

SECTION 3. INQUIRY NOTICE

Note: Investigation Outside the Record

The language of the recording act may be significant in determining the extent to which a purchaser of land is required to make inquiries outside the record to attempt to locate unrecorded rights. A few states have statutes similar to the Massachusetts statute (Mass. Gen. Laws Ann. ch. 183, §4) which says that an unrecorded instrument is effective against "persons having *actual notice* of it." Can a person ever have "actual notice" if all that can be said is that the individual would have learned of the existence of an unrecorded instrument if some inquiry had been made? In contrast to the Massachusetts statute, the Michigan statute (Mich. Comp. Laws §565.29) simply says that an unrecorded instrument is void against a subsequent purchaser "in good faith and for a valuable consideration." Will it be easier to find that a person who would have learned of an unrecorded right if some inquiry had been made is not a purchaser in "good faith" than to find such person is a purchaser with "actual notice"?

You must keep in mind that even though it is held that a purchaser is under no duty to make any investigation outside the record to ascertain the existence of outstanding rights represented by recordable instruments, that does not mean that the purchaser will prevail over outstanding rights which are not represented by recordable documents (short-term leases, rights acquired by adverse possession).

You must also keep in mind that an unrecorded recordable document may be referred to in some instrument that is recorded. If so, you may be deemed to have notice of that unrecorded document. This illustrates that you should read the documents in your claim of title to see if they refer to unrecorded recordable documents. In this regard, see Guerin v. Sunburst Oil & Gas Co., 68 Mont. 365, 218 P. 949 (1923).

Note: *Purchasers Under Quitclaim Deeds as Bona Fide Purchasers Who Prevail Over Unrecorded Recordable Documents*

The court in Moelle v. Sherwood, 148 U.S. 21, 13 S. Ct. 426 (1893), discussed whether a taker under a quitclaim deed could be a bona fide purchaser, using the following language:

> The doctrine expressed in many cases that the grantee in a quitclaim deed cannot be treated as a bona fide purchaser does not seem to rest upon any sound principle. It is asserted upon the assumption that the form of the instrument, that the grantor merely releases to the grantee his claim, whatever it may be, without any warranty of its value, or only passes whatever interest he may have at the time, indicates that there may be other and outstanding claims or interests which may possibly affect the title of the property, and, therefore, it is said that the grantee, in accepting a conveyance of that kind, cannot be a bona fide purchaser and entitled to protection as such; and that he is in fact thus notified by his grantor that there may be some defect in his title and he must take it at his risk. This assumption we do not think justified by the language of such deeds or the general opinion of conveyancers. There may be many reasons why the holder of property may refuse to accompany his conveyance of it with an express warranty of the soundness of its title or its freedom from the claims of others, or to execute a conveyance in such form as to imply a warranty of any kind even when the title is known to be perfect. He may hold the property only as a trustee or in a corporate or official character, and be unwilling for that reason to assume any personal responsibility as to its title or freedom from liens, or he may be unwilling to do so from notions peculiar to himself; and the purchaser may be unable to secure a conveyance of the property desired in any other form than one of quitclaim or of a simple transfer of the grantor's interest. It would be unreasonable to hold that, for his inability to secure any other form of conveyance, he should be denied the position and character of a bona fide purchaser, however free, in fact, his conduct in the purchase may have been from any imputation of the want of good faith. In many parts of the country a quitclaim or a simple conveyance of

the grantor's interest is the common form in which the transfer of real estate is made. A deed in that form is, in such cases, as effectual to divest and transfer a complete title as any other form of conveyance. There is in this country no difference in their efficacy and operative force between conveyances in the form of release and quitclaim and those in the form of grant, bargain and sale. If the grantor in either case at the time of the execution of his deed possesses any claim to or interest in the property, it passes to the grantee. In the one case, that of bargain and sale, he impliedly asserts the possession of a claim to or interest in the property, for it is the property itself which he sells and undertakes to convey. In the other case, that of quitclaim, the grantor affirms nothing as to the ownership, and undertakes only a release of any claim to or interest in the premises which he may possess without asserting the ownership of either. If in either case the grantee takes the deed with notice of an outstanding conveyance of the premises from the grantor, or of the execution by him of obligations to make such conveyance of the premises, or to create a lien thereon, he takes the property subject to the operation of such outstanding conveyance and obligation, and cannot claim protection against them as a bona fide purchaser. But in either case if the grantee takes the deed without notice of such outstanding conveyance or obligation respecting the property, or notice of facts which, if followed up, would lead to a knowledge of such outstanding conveyance or equity, he is entitled to protection as a bona fide purchaser, upon showing that the consideration stipulated has been paid and that such consideration was a fair price for the claim or interest designated. The mere fact that in either case the conveyance is unaccompanied by any warranty of title, and against incumbrances or liens, does not raise a presumption of the want of bona fides on the part of the purchaser in the transaction. Covenants of warranty do not constitute any operative part of the instrument in transferring the title. That passes independently of them. They are separate contracts, intended only as guaranties against future contingencies. The character of bona fide purchaser must depend upon attending circumstances or proof as to the transaction, and does not arise, as often, though, we think, inadvertently, said, either from the form of the conveyance or the presence or the absence of any accompanying warranty. Whether the grantee is to be treated as taking a mere speculative chance in the property, or a clear title, must depend upon the character of the title of the grantor when he made the conveyance: and the opportunities afforded the grantee of ascertaining this fact and the diligence with which he has prosecuted them, will, besides the payment of a reasonable consideration, determine the bona fide nature of the transaction on his part. [148 U.S. at 28-30, 13 S. Ct. at 428-429.]

The following is quoted from Johnson v. Williams, 37 Kan. 179, 14 P. 537 (1887):

We would think that in all cases, however, where a purchaser takes a quitclaim deed he must be presumed to take it with notice of all outstanding equities and interests of which he could by the exercise of any reasonable diligence obtain notice from an examination of all the records affecting the title to the property, and from all inquiries which he might make of persons in the possession of the property, or of persons paying taxes thereon, or of any person who might, from any record or from any knowledge which the purchaser might have, seemingly have some interest in the property. In nearly all cases between individuals where land is sold or conveyed, and where there is no doubt about the title, a general warranty deed is given; and it is only in cases where there is a doubt concerning the title that only a quitclaim deed is given or received; hence, when a party takes quitclaim deed, he knows he is taking a doubtful title and is put upon inquiry as to the title. [37 Kan. at 182, 14 P. at 539.]

In 1931, New Jersey passed the following statute:

Any conveyance or instrument executed and delivered after July fourth, one thousand nine hundred and thirty-one, which shall purport to remise, release or quitclaim to the grantee therein any claim to or estate or interest in the lands described therein, there being nothing in such conveyance or instrument which indicates an intent on the part of the grantor therein to reserve to himself any part of his claim to or estate or interest therein, shall be effectual to pass all the estate which the grantor could lawfully convey by deed of bargain and sale, and the grantee in such conveyance or instrument shall be presumed to be a bona fide purchaser to the same extent as would be the grantee in a deed of bargain and sale. [N.J. Rev. Stat. §46:5-3; see also §§46:5-4 to 46:5-9.]

The following quotation is from Houston Oil Company of Texas v. Niles, 255 S.W. 604 at 610 (Tex. Com. App. 1923):

[T]he holder of a title in which there appears, however remote, a quitclaim deed is prevented from asserting the defense of innocent purchaser as against an outstanding title or secret trust or equity existing at the time the quitclaim deed was executed.

Mich. Comp. Laws Ann. §565.29 contains the following provision:

The fact that such first recorded conveyance is in the form or contains the terms of a deed of quit-claim and release shall not affect the question of good faith of such subsequent purchaser, or be of itself notice to him of any unrecorded conveyance of the same real estate or any part thereof.[22]

Note: Inquiry of Person in Possession

If the person in possession of the land is not the seller, an inquiry of such person as to the basis of his or her right to possess the land may reveal the name of a person who claims under an unrecorded recordable deed. Is the purchaser required to make such inquiry or else be deemed to take with

---

22. See Bohannan, Quitclaim Deeds Under the Recording Acts, 32 Va. L. Rev. 190 (1945); American Law of Property §17.16 (Casner ed. 1952).

notice of an unrecorded recordable deed that such an inquiry would reveal? Such an inquiry is necessary to ascertain the existence of rights in others, such as rights based on adverse possession, that are not represented by recordable documents. But the insistence on such inquiry to discover unrecorded recordable documents undermines the reliability of the record title in situations where conceivably the record title ought to be reliable. The following cases consider the issue of inquiry of the person in possession.

GALLEY v. WARD
60 N.H. 331 (1880)

Bill in equity, to set aside the levy of an execution. Facts found by a referee. May 13, 1871, Jane Smith, wife of Robert Smith, being seized in her own right of a tract of land called the "Little lot," sold it to the plaintiff for $800, and intended and believed that she did then convey it in fee simple to him. But the deed, by mistake of the scrivener, was executed by her husband, in which she merely released dower and homestead. This was not recorded till November 12, 1875. September 18, 1878, Jane and Robert executed and delivered to the plaintiff a deed of the lot, for the purpose of ratifying and confirming the latter's title, and of fulfilling all that they supposed they did do by their former deed. The plaintiff entered into possession of the lot upon receiving the first deed, and has remained in the open, visible, exclusive, and notorious possession of it ever since, cultivating the land, cutting the grass, pasturing his cattle therein, cutting off the wood, rebuilding the walls and fences, and tearing down the buildings, which were old and dilapidated, and from the best of the timber erecting a coopers' shop.

The defendant Ward, in 1876, without any consideration, assigned to the defendant Morris a claim against Jane Smith; Morris, in April, 1876, brought suit on this claim, and obtained an execution, which was levied on the "Little lot." Before bringing the suit, Morris made inquiries at the registry of deeds to ascertain if Jane Smith had conveyed this lot, and was informed that she had not. The deed of May 13, 1871, was indexed "Smith Robert to Galley William." Before the attachment, Morris had no knowledge or suspicion that Jane had sold the lot, and it did not appear when he first learned of it. Ward and Morris both live in Boston, Mass.

FOSTER, J. At the time of Morris's attachment and levy, the plaintiff held the equitable title to the "Little lot" by virtue of the agreement made with Jane Smith in 1871, under which he had paid the full consideration for the property, and had entered into its occupation. He was entitled to a decree for a specific performance of this agreement, and to such a conveyance as he received September 18, 1878.

It is not claimed that Morris had any actual knowledge of the plaintiff's title. He merely knew as a fact that the legal title appeared by the record to be in Jane Smith. And if the plaintiff's title is to prevail in this suit, it must be on the ground of constructive notice. It is substantially admitted in the brief for Morris, and is undoubtedly the law in this state, that a purchaser of land, knowing that a third person is in the open, visible, and notorious occupation of it, — an occupation inconsistent with the idea that he is a tenant, — is chargeable with notice of such facts in reference to the latter's title, whether legal or equitable, as he would have learned upon reasonable inquiry. And the nature of the plaintiff's possession in this case was sufficient to put a purchaser having knowledge of the facts on inquiry as to the plaintiff's title.

But it is contended that Morris did not know of the plaintiff's possession of the land, and that therefore the doctrine of constructive notice cannot be applied to him. If he had known it, on the authorities above cited he could have gained no title against the plaintiff by his attachment and levy. Is his ignorance sufficient excuse? When a grantee records his deed, a subsequent purchaser is chargeable with constructive notice of its contents. It is wholly immaterial whether he has seen the deed, or has any knowledge of its existence. It is, as sometimes expressed, a conclusive presumption of law that he had notice of the grantee's deed. Malone Real Prop. Trials 427; Morrison v. Kelly, 22 Ill. 610. On the same ground it is at least a prima facie presumption, that when there is such a possession by a third party as would charge a purchaser who knew of that possession with knowledge of an adverse title, a purchaser ignorant of that possession without excuse would be equally chargeable. And this doctrine, in both cases, rests on the ground of fraud or culpable negligence. As it is a part of a purchaser's duty to examine the record, to inform himself as to the legal title he expects to acquire, a failure to attend to that duty would amount to negligence on his part, and would be a fraud on a previous purchaser under a recorded deed, if he could, by proving his ignorance, acquire a title. By the same mode of reasoning, if he is wilfully ignorant of such facts of notorious occupation by a stranger as would put a purchaser cognizant of those facts on his guard against some unrecorded deed or equitable claim, his want of knowledge is due to his own laches and failure to attend to an apparent duty. In Hughes v. U.S., 4 Wall. 232, Field, J., says that if a purchaser neglects to make an inquiry as to the possession, "he is not entitled to any greater consideration than if he had made it and ascertained the actual facts of the case." Nor is there any distinction in this respect between a purchaser and a creditor. A creditor is bound by constructive notice of the contents of a recorded deed, as well as a purchaser, and there seems to be no reason why they should not both stand on the same ground with reference to an equitable title in a third party, in a case like the present.

The defendant Morris had no knowledge that the plaintiff was in possession of the land in question, but, so far as the plaintiff or anybody else was concerned, he was at liberty to examine the apparent condition of the premises. He was not deceived by any misrepresentations or concealments of the plaintiff. He relied on his own judgment, and neglected an apparent duty. Like a purchaser having knowledge of facts sufficient to put him on his guard, he must be held chargeable with what he would have learned upon reasonable inquiry as to the plaintiff's right of possession. And it appears from the case that he would have learned of the plaintiff's equitable title. His title therefore cannot prevail in this suit.

It is unnecessary, in the view we have taken of the case, to consider the further question, whether the want of consideration for the assignment of the claim to Morris by Ward would prevent the former from acquiring a title against the plaintiff.

Decree according to the prayer of the bill.[23]

TOUPIN v. PEABODY
162 Mass. 473, 39 N.E. 280 (1895)

Bill in equity, filed in the Superior Court on September 5, 1893, for specific performance of a covenant for renewal contained in a lease of certain premises in Haverhill. The case was submitted upon agreed facts, in substance as follows.

Hannah Driscoll, being the owner in fee of certain land in Haverhill, upon which was a building, the lower story of which was used for shops and the upper stories for dwelling purposes, and occupied by several different tenants, executed and delivered, on August 20, 1888, a lease of the lower story thereof to the plaintiff, containing, after the habendum, (which was for the term of five years from September 1, 1888,) the following clause: "And said lessee is to have the privilege of renewing this lease upon the same terms for the further term of five years."

The plaintiff entered under his lease, and continued to occupy the demised premises down to the filing of this bill, paying Driscoll the rent reserved in the lease as long as she continued to be the owner of the reversion. The land, with the building thereon, was conveyed by Driscoll to the defendant and William H. Floyd, by deed dated December 9, 1891, for a valuable consideration. The deed was duly recorded, and contained full covenants against all encumbrances, except certain mortgages not material to be stated. At the times of the negotiation for the purchase and of the conveyance to them, the defendant and Floyd knew that the plaintiff was in possession of the demised premises, and was occupying them as a tenant of Driscoll for the purposes of a drug store, but they were informed by Driscoll, and believed, that the plaintiff and the other tenants had no written leases.

---

23. N.H. Rev. Stat. Ann. §477:7 is as follows:

No deed of bargain and sale, mortgage nor other conveyance of real estate, nor any lease for more than seven years from the making thereof, shall be valid to hold the same against any person but the grantor and his heirs only, unless such deed or lease be attested, acknowledged and recorded, according to the provisions of this chapter.

The statute in force at the time of Galley v. Ward was substantially the same. — EDS.

The plaintiff did not inform the defendant or Floyd of his lease, and neither the defendant nor Floyd made any inquiry of the plaintiff as to the terms of his tenancy. Before the conveyance was made, the defendant procured a search of the title to be made by a competent conveyancer, who pronounced the title to be good.

Two months after the conveyance by Driscoll to them, the defendant and Floyd learned for the first time that the plaintiff had a written lease of the premises occupied by him, and were informed of the terms thereof. The plaintiff continued until the expiration of the lease to pay to the defendant and Floyd the amount of rent reserved in the lease at the times therein appointed for its payment, claiming to pay the same under and by virtue of the terms of the lease. The defendant and Floyd accepted the amount of the rent paid by the plaintiff, protesting, however, that it was not received under the provisions of the lease, and that by receiving the same they did not intend in any way to confirm or recognize the lease. It is admitted that they have not ratified the lease, nor admitted it to be valid against them.

Prior to the bringing of this bill, Floyd conveyed to the defendant his interest in the property so conveyed to them by Driscoll, and the defendant is now the sole owner of the fee. The plaintiff duly gave written notice to the defendant of his intention to avail himself of the privilege of renewal contained in the lease, and demanded a lease for the additional term of five years. The defendant has refused to renew the lease, has given the plaintiff notice to quit the premises, and has begun proceedings at law to recover the premises and to eject the plaintiff therefrom.

The plaintiff, upon a complaint charging him with maintaining a nuisance by using the premises demised in the lease for the illegal sale and keeping of intoxicating liquor, between April 17, 1890, and June 1, 1890, was duly found guilty and sentenced at the October term, 1890, of the Superior Court. Driscoll, after judgment upon the complaint, continued to receive the rent from the plaintiff at the times appointed in the lease for its payment, and never took any proceedings to avoid the lease. Neither the defendant nor Floyd has taken any proceedings to avoid the lease by reason of such conviction, except by an allegation in respect thereto in the answer in this cause.

The lease was never recorded in the registry of deeds.

The case was reserved by Dunbar, J., upon the pleadings and agreed facts, for the consideration of this court.

BARKER, J. Assuming that the instrument of August 20, 1888, is not a demise for two successive terms of five years each, we are nevertheless of the opinion that it is "a lease for more than seven years from the making thereof," within the meaning of Pub. Sts. c. 120, Sec. 4, which enacts that "[a] conveyance of an estate in fee simple, fee tail, or for life, or a lease for more than seven years from the making thereof, shall not be valid as against any person other than the grantor or lessor and his heirs and devisees, and persons having actual notice of it, unless it is recorded in the registry of deeds for the county or district in which the real estate to which it relates is situated." [24] The statute is part of our system of registration of titles to land, and the general purpose for which it was established was to enable a purchaser of land to rely upon the information furnished him by the registry of deeds, if he has no actual notice of some different state of facts as to the title. See Dole v. Thurlow, 12 Met. 157; Earle v. Fiske, 103 Mass. 491.

The intention of the particular clause in question is that a bona fide purchaser without actual notice may rely with certainty upon the fact that no instrument which does not appear of record, and of which he does not have actual notice, can give a tenant for years the right to any longer term than for seven years from the making of the instrument. The statute is a remedial one, and upon the principles of construction applicable to such statutes its general intention and purpose are to be given due effect, and cases which are clearly within its general intention are to be governed by it.

The general intention of the section in which the clause is found is, that no instrument operating to create an interest in land greater than an estate for seven years shall, unless duly recorded, be valid as against any person other than the one who makes it or his heirs or devisees, unless such person has actual notice of the instrument. In expressing this intention, conveyances in fee simple, fee tail, and for life are first specified, and the enumeration closes with the words, "or a lease for more than seven years from the making thereof." In respect of estates for years, the term during which the land which a purchaser had bought could be kept from his possession by the holder of an unrecorded lease was the important matter to be fixed by the statute, as by his conveyance the purchaser acquired the right to rent and the other rights of the lessor. In fixing upon seven years from the making of the lease as the length of a term which might be valid as against a bona fide purchaser without actual notice, the Legislature intended that to be the utmost which a lessee for years under an unrecorded instrument could claim as against such a purchaser, whether the instrument demised directly a longer term, or provided for its indirect creation by an agreement for renewal at the lessee's option. A lease for five years, with the right to have a renewal for five more, is as much within the mischief which the statute seeks to remedy as a lease for a term of ten years, and the reasons for requiring the latter to be recorded apply equally to the other, so far as the renewal term is concerned.

We do not decide whether an instrument which makes a present demise for a term of seven years or less, and which provides for a further term which with the present demise will exceed seven years from the making of the instrument, either by way of a new lease to be made by the lessor or by the effect of the lessee's mere continuance in possession after the expiration of the first term, if not recorded, is wholly void as to a bona fide purchaser

---

24. The present statute also contains the words "actual notice." See Mass. Gen. Laws Ann. ch. 183, §4, quoted at page 813 *supra.* —EDS.

without actual notice, or whether it may be good for the first term of seven years or less.

It is enough for the purposes of this case to hold that as to any extension, or second term, or agreement for renewal, which will carry the possession of the lessee to more than seven years from the making of the instrument, every instrument which confers an estate for years is within the meaning of the statute. The instrument on which the plaintiff relies was of this nature, and so far as it purported to give him the right to a second term of five years it was invalid as against a purchaser without actual notice.

The plaintiff contends that it may well be claimed that the defendant had actual notice of the lease. But while it appears from the agreed facts that the defendant knew that the plaintiff was in possession of the drug store as a tenant, it also appears that the defendant was informed and believed that the plaintiff had no written lease, and that it was not until two months after the purchase that the defendant first learned that the plaintiff had a written lease, and was informed of its terms. It is well settled that facts sufficient to put a purchaser upon inquiry are not sufficient to affect him with actual notice of an unrecorded instrument within the meaning of the language of the statute. Upon this branch of the case the only legitimate inference from the agreed facts is that the defendant did not have actual notice of the lease.

Nor can the plaintiff rely upon the case of Cunningham v. Pattee, 99 Mass. 248, in which it was held that, in equity, one who purchases an estate knowing it to be in possession of a tenant is bound to inquire into the nature of the tenant's interest, and is affected with notice of its extent, and, if the tenant has a written lease, with notice of that fact and of the contents of the lease, including a covenant to renew. The clear distinction between that case and the present is, that in Cunningham v. Pattee the original term and the extension were together for less than seven years, and the statute now under consideration had no application. As the statute applies here, we must give it the same force in equity as at law, with the result that, as the defendant had no actual notice of the lease, it is not valid against him either in equity or law.

Our view of the effect of the statute makes it unnecessary to consider the question whether the plaintiff's conviction of the offence of maintaining a common nuisance in the drug store during a portion of the first term of his tenancy ought to preclude him from maintaining a bill in equity for specific performance of the agreement for renewal.

The case was reserved upon the pleadings and the agreed facts for the consideration of this court in banc. Let the bill be dismissed, with costs.[25]

So ordered.

---

25. S.C. Code Ann. §60-109 provides:

No possession of real property described in any instrument of writing required by law to be recorded shall operate as notice of such instrument. Actual notice shall be deemed and held sufficient to supply the place of registration only when such notice is of the instrument itself or of its nature and purport.

— EDS.

BRINKMAN v. JONES
44 Wis. 498 (1878)

[This is an action of ejectment against Alonzo D. Jones to recover the possession of land situated in Manitowoc County. On August 27, 1870, Benjamin Jones was the owner in fee of the lands in dispute. On that day he and his wife executed and delivered to Theodore C. Shove a warranty deed of the premises, for a consideration, as expressed therein, of $2,300, which deed was on the same day duly recorded in the office of the register of deeds of Manitowoc County. At the time of the grant of the land to him, T. C. Shove executed and delivered to Benjamin Jones a contract in which he agreed to reconvey the land to Jones, his heirs or assigns if Jones paid or caused to be paid a stipulated sum within a certain time (the court held that the effect of the deed and contract together created the relationship of mortgagor and mortgagee between Jones and Shove). The contract to reconvey, however, was never recorded.

T. C. Shove and wife executed and delivered a warranty deed of the land to the plaintiff on October 12, 1876, in consideration of $6,000 and this deed was recorded on the same day.

Benjamin Jones had occupied the lands continuously, by tenants or in person, from 1857 to January 8, 1877, when he conveyed the lands by quitclaim deed to his son, Alonzo D. Jones, the defendant who was in possession when this action was commenced, in March, 1877.

By direction of the court, a verdict was rendered for the plaintiff; and from a judgment thereon defendant appealed.]

TAYLOR, J. . . .

It is further argued, with great ability and zeal, by the counsel for the respondent, that, admitting that the relation of mortgagor and mortgagee existed between Jones and Shove at the date of the deed to the plaintiff, the plaintiff is a bona fide purchaser without notice of the title or interest of Jones, and therefore is entitled to recover in this action.

This argument is based mainly upon the provisions of sec. 32, ch. 86, R.S. 1858.[26] And it is insisted that the evidence does not tend to show that the plaintiff had "actual notice," within the meaning of said section, of the rights of Jones as mortgagor, at the time of his purchase.

It is sought to give force to this argument by the claim that this provision of our statute was taken verbatim from the laws of Massachusetts, and that we are therefore to be controlled in its construction by the decisions of the highest court of that state, made before our adoption of the law here. It is

---

26. "When a deed purports to be an absolute conveyance in terms, but is made or intended to be made defeasible by force of a deed of defeasance or other instrument for that purpose, the original conveyance shall not be thereby defeated or affected as against any person other than the maker of the defeasance or his heirs or devisees or persons having actual notice thereof, unless the instrument of defeasance shall have been recorded in the office of the register of deeds of the county where the lands lie." This statute has been continuously in effect in Wisconsin. The present form of the statute is Wis. Stat. Ann. §706.08(5). — EDS.

true that the section above quoted is found as an existing law in the statute of Massachusetts at the time of its enactment here. It is also true that the same provision is found in the R.S. of Michigan of 1846; and from an examination of our ch. 59, R.S. 1849, and ch. 65, R.S. of Michigan of 1846, it will be found that our law is in most of its provisions a more exact copy of the law of Michigan than it is of that of Massachusetts.[27] Our law declaring the effect of the want of registry of a deed as to subsequent purchasers is entirely different from the law of Massachusetts, and is exactly the same as the law of Michigan, and so in many other particulars.[28] We may, therefore, come to the conclusion that, so far as our registry law is adopted from the law of any other state, it was adopted from Michigan directly, and not from Massachusetts. The decisions of the supreme court of Massachusetts construing this law are not, therefore, entitled to more weight than those of any other court of equal learning and ability, which may have construed the same or like provisions of statute law.

That the purchaser had notice of the mortgagor's rights in this action must be found, if found at all, upon proof of the following facts:

> That the mortgagor remained in the actual and exclusive possession of the lands in controversy from the date of the deed, August 27, 1870, down to the date of the plaintiff's deed, 1876; that the plaintiff knew of this possession at the time he took his deed; that he knew the land was called the Jones farm; that, only a few weeks before he took his deed from Shove, he went to the son of Jones, the defendant in this action, and offered to buy the south twenty acres, and to pay $3,000 for it; that he had spoken with Benjamin Jones about buying it; that he had always known it as the Jones farm, but did not know who was the owner of it, whether it was Benjamin Jones, *Alonzo D. Jones,* or Mr. Shove; that when he made the offer to buy the twenty acres, he thought the property belonged to Mr. Jones, and that he did not know that it belonged to Shove; that when he was spoken to by Shove to buy the land, he went to the register's office to have the title examined, and the register told him it was all

---

27.   Both Massachusetts and Michigan have statutes, which have been continuously in effect, that are substantially identical with the Wisconsin statute quoted in the preceding footnote. The present form of the Massachusetts statute is Mass. Gen. Laws Ann. ch. 183, §53. The present form of the Michigan statute is Mich. Comp. Laws Ann. §565.29. — Eds.

28.   The present Wisconsin statute on the effect of the failure to record a deed as against a subsequent purchaser, which statute has been continuously in effect in Wisconsin in substantially the same form, is as follows:

> Every conveyance (except patents issued by the United States or this state, or by the proper officers of either) which is not recorded as provided by law shall be void as against any subsequent purchaser in good faith and for a valuable consideration of the same real estate or any portion thereof whose conveyance shall first be duly recorded.

Wis. Stat. Ann. §706.08(1). The corresponding Michigan statute which also has been continuously in effect in Michigan provides, like the Wisconsin statute, that the subsequent purchaser "in good faith and for a valuable consideration" is protected. See Mich. Comp. Laws Ann. §565.29. In Massachusetts, however, the corresponding statute now protects, and from the beginning has protected, the subsequent purchaser unless he or she had "actual notice." See Mass. Gen. Laws Ann. ch. 183, §4, quoted at page 813 *supra.* — Eds.

right, that Mr. Shove would give him a warranty deed, and that Shove owned the land; that he knew nothing about the contracts between Shove and Jones; that he believed Shove's word and Franz's (the register's) word.

The defendant testified that when the plaintiff came to buy the twenty acres, "I told him I could not sell for that price, and plaintiff said he was talking with Shove, and I stated to him I had a claim to the property, and until that was settled he had better let it alone or he would get himself in trouble." The evidence also shows that the defendant is the son of Benjamin Jones, and was looking after his business generally.

The learned counsel for the plaintiff insists that this evidence was insufficient to justify a jury in finding that the plaintiff had actual notice of the rights of Jones, within the meaning of the statute, and therefore the court was right in refusing to submit that question to the jury. We do not agree with the learned counsel, and are of opinion that the learned circuit judge erred in refusing to submit this question to the jury. The actual notice required by the statute is not synonymous with actual knowledge. None of the cases, not even those cited from Massachusetts, hold that, in order to charge the purchaser with actual notice, it must be shown that he had actual knowledge of the precise claim of the person holding the unrecorded defeasance. We think the true rule is, that notice must be held to be actual when the subsequent purchaser has actual knowledge of such facts as would "put a prudent man upon inquiry, which, if prosecuted with ordinary diligence, would lead to actual notice of the right or title in conflict with that which he is about to purchase." Where the subsequent purchaser has knowledge of such facts, it becomes his duty to make inquiry, and he is guilty of bad faith if he neglects to do so, and consequently he will be charged with the actual notice he would have received if he had made the inquiry. . . .

We recognize the obligation to give some effect to the term "actual notice," as distinguished from mere "notice," and must therefore hold that no constructive knowledge shall be imputed to the purchaser as a ground of notice. For example, this court has held that actual, open and visible occupation, whether known to the purchaser or not, shall be deemed sufficient notice to the purchaser of the rights and equities of such occupant. This rule could not be applied to a case like the one at bar, unless such actual occupation was known to the purchaser. . . .

It is insisted that the possession of Jones after the execution and recording of his deed, though known to the plaintiff, was no notice that he had or claimed any title to the land in hostility to his deed.

The authorities cited by counsel for the respondent would seem to countenance the proposition stated; but the statement made by the courts in the cases cited, that the possession of a grantor cannot be considered hostile to the rights of his grantee, are very broad and general, and are not supported by argument. We are of the opinion that the rule as stated in these cases must be qualified by at least two considerations: first, that such occupation is not inconsistent with the rights of the grantee; and second, that the length of time that the occupancy has continued ought to be considered. . . .

The fact that the evidence shows that it was A. D. Jones, the son of the grantor, who had the conversation about selling the land to the plaintiff, and that, in warning him not to buy of Shove, he said he had a claim on the land, and did not state that his father had any claim, and the fact that on the trial it appeared that at that time A. D. Jones had no interest in the land, do not destroy the effect of the evidence so as to justify the court in entirely disregarding the same. The evidence showed that A. D. Jones was son of the grantor of Shove, and was looking after the affairs of his father; and it was for the jury to say whether, in speaking of his interest, he was not speaking of the interest of his father, and whether it was not so understood by the plaintiff at the time.

The objection that the defense was insufficiently pleaded is without force in this state. This court held in Kent v. Agard, *supra,* that when the proof in an action of ejectment shows that the plaintiff's title is in fact a mortgage, his suit must fail. The fact that his interest in the premises sought to be recorded is only a mortgage interest, is fatal to the action.

By the court. — The judgment of the circuit court is reversed, and a new trial awarded.[29]

TOLAND v. COREY
6 Utah 392, 24 P. 190 (1890)

Appeal from a judgment of the district court of the first district and from an order refusing a new trial. The opinion states the facts.

BLACKBURN, J.   This action is brought by the appellant for the cancellation of a deed to the respondents to a part of a lot in Ogden City, Utah, on the ground of fraud and inadequacy of consideration. It appears by the complaint and answer that the appellant owned a life estate in the premises, and her son, Isaac A. Crowford, owned the remainder; that he conveyed his interest to William Toland, the husband of the appellant, and he conveyed the same to her, but these deeds were not put upon record until the mortgages hereinafter mentioned were given and recorded, but they were made and delivered prior to the giving of these mortgages. It further appears that the said Crowford and appellant had given a mortgage on these premises to one Doon for $350; and after that, without the knowledge of appellant, and after she acquired the fee in the premises, Crowford, without her knowledge or consent, gave two other mortgages on the premises to said Doon to secure, separately, $150 and $117.75; and after that, Crowford, without appellant's knowledge, gave two other mortgages on the premises to

29.   See American Law of Property §§17.11, 17.12 (Casner ed. 1952). — EDS.

the respondents, to secure debts due them from him. All these mortgages were duly recorded, and prior to the record of the deeds conveying the fee in the premises to the appellant. On the tenth day of August, 1885, Doon brought suit to foreclose his three mortgages against the appellant, and made the respondents parties; and, before judgment, appellant, to pay off the mortgages, and for no additional consideration, made the deed this action seeks to have set aside. The whole amount called for by the mortgages was $1,236.60. The allegations of the complaint, which are denied by the answer, are to the effect that the mortgages given to Doon, except the one for $350, were given with notice of appellant's full ownership of the premises, and Crowford had no interest whatever to incumber, and that the mortgages to respondents were taken with like notice; that the deed to respondents this action seeks to set aside was obtained by misrepresentation and other improper conduct by the respondents, and others associated with them in the transaction; that appellant was poor, in bad health, and without friendly advice, and thus was forced to sign the deed against her will; that the consideration was grossly inadequate; and that the deed was not voluntarily acknowledged, and not delivered on her authority, or by her.

The first question is, did Doon and the respondents have actual notice of the deed of Crowford to Toland, and Toland to appellant, at the time of making these mortgages by Crowford, these deeds being unrecorded? The appellant was in the possession of the premises, occupying them as a home, and this fact was well known to respondents and the agent of Doon, and it is not pretended that Doon or the respondents had ever heard of the deeds by which appellant claimed title; but the contention of counsel is that appellant's exclusive and notorious possession of the premises was actual notice to Doon and the respondents of her title. Our statute requires actual notice, and constructive notice is not sufficient. The statute is as follows:

> That every conveyance of real estate and every instrument of writing, setting forth an agreement to convey any real estate, or whereby any real estate may be affected, proved, acknowledged and certified in the manner prescribed by this act to operate as notice to third persons, shall be recorded in the office of the recorder of the county in which such real estate is situated, but shall be valid and binding between the parties thereto without such record, and to all other persons who have had *actual* notice.

Sec. 2611, 2 Comp. Laws 1888, p. 99.[30]

The demands of the statute are answered if a party dealing with the land has information of a fact or facts that would put a prudent man upon inquiry, and which would, if pursued, lead to actual knowledge of the state

---

30. The statute now in force in Utah does not contain the words "actual notice" but protects the subsequent purchaser "in good faith and for a valuable consideration." See Utah Code Ann. §57.3-3. Does this mean that this case would be decided differently in Utah today? — Eds.

of the title; and this is actual notice. 2 Pom. Eq. Jur., Secs. 597, 598, et seq. The appellant was in the actual occupancy of the premises, and actual occupancy is enough to put parties dealing with the premises upon inquiry. Id. Sec. 616, note 3, and Sec. 617. But the contention of the respondents is that the possession of the appellant was consistent with the title shown by the record, and therefore the mortgagees were under no obligation to look beyond the record, and were authorized to consider her possession as under her life-estate only. On this question the authorities are both ways. Id. Sec. 616, note 3, and Sec. 617. We think the better doctrine is that an occupant's possession is actual notice of his title, and all persons with notice of such possession must at their peril take notice of his full title in the premises, no difference what the record shows. Until the recording statutes were enacted, possession was notice of ownership, and a conveyance made by a party out of possession was void. The purpose of these statutes was not to change the rule that possession was evidence of title and notice to all the world of ownership, but to afford the means of preserving the chain of title, and give notice of the ownership of unoccupied lands. It would be an unwarranted application of the recording acts to say that they destroy the effect of occupancy as notice and evidence of ownership. We think, therefore, that a person at his peril deals with or purchases real estate of one, in the possession of another, although said possession may be consistent with the record title. It is easy to find out the real situation by inquiry of the party in possession, and it is his duty to do so. The conclusion, therefore, is that none of these mortgages, except the one for $350, were liens upon the premises of appellant. . . .

The $350 is a lien upon the land, and the decree ought to be that the deed be canceled; that the appellant pay this mortgage and interest by a day to be named by the court, and in default of payment the premises be sold on the time and terms property is sold on the foreclosure of mortgages by the provisions of the statute, and out of the proceeds this mortgage and interest be paid, and the remainder be paid to appellant. This cause is reversed and remanded, with direction to the district court to have entered a decree in accordance with this opinion, and that the respondents pay the costs of this court and the costs of the court below up to date.

Problems

28.19. O was the owner of a certain tract of land which was in the possession of T, O's tenant. T, pursuant to instructions from O, paid the rent to A, who was O's attorney and agent. O executed and delivered to B a deed of the land, and thereafter A was instructed by B to continue to collect the rent from the land and turn over the same to B. The deed from O to B was not recorded. O then executed and delivered to C a deed of the land, and C, prior to paying the purchase price, inquired of T as to whom T paid the rent. T informed C that the rent was paid to A. C knew A was acting as attorney and agent for O in money matters, and, therefore, C paid O the purchase price for the land. Who prevails, B or C? See Penrose v. Cooper, 88 Kan. 210, 128 P. 362 (1912).

28.20. O owned a tenement building containing 43 apartments and occupied by 23 different families as tenants. Three of these apartments were occupied by T, a tenant, and T kept a liquor store in one of these apartments. O executed and delivered to T a deed of the entire building, and thereafter T continued to occupy the same space in the building and collected the rent from the other tenants. T did not record. O then executed and delivered to M a mortgage on the building and land to secure a loan from M. M had no actual knowledge of any title in T in the premises. Who prevails, T or M? See Phelan v. Brady, 119 N.Y. 587, 23 N.E. 1109 (1890).

SECTION 4.   WHEN A PERSON IS A PURCHASER[31]

STRONG v. WHYBARK
204 Mo. 341, 102 S.W. 968 (1907)

WOODSON, J.   This is a bill in equity, instituted in the circuit court of Butler county, wherein plaintiff seeks to have her title quieted to five hundred and twenty acres of land. John R. Boyden was one of the several defendants named in the bill. He filed an answer claiming an interest in and to one hundred and sixty acres of said land, and also denied generally the allegations of the bill. No point is made against the pleadings, and he is the only defendant whose interest is involved in this appeal.

The facts in the case are undisputed and are as follows:

Seth D. Hayden was the common source of title, and on March 6, 1861, by his warranty deed, for a recited consideration in the deed of six hundred and forty dollars, conveyed said land to William A. Moore, and on August 26, 1863, said Hayden, by his quit-claim deed, for a recited consideration of "natural love and affection and five dollars," conveyed the same land to Josephine Hayden. The deed to Hayden was recorded April 11, 1868, and the one to Moore was recorded December 14, 1874.

The plaintiff's title is derived through mesne conveyances from Josephine Hayden, while defendant's title is derived through similar conveyances from William A. Moore. It was admitted that the land was wild and unoccupied. This was all the evidence in the case.

The court found for defendant and rendered judgment for him. The plaintiff in due time filed his motion for a new trial, which was overruled by

---

31. The problems considered in this section are like some of the problems considered in Chapter 10.

the court, and to the action of the court in overruling said motion the plaintiff duly excepted, and has appealed the cause to this court.

The sole question involved in this case is, did the subsequently executed quitclaim deed of Seth D. Hayden to Josephine Hayden, dated August 26, 1863, by virtue of its prior recordation, have the force and effect of conveying to her the title to the land in controversy by force and operation of the registry act, and thereby render invalid and inoperative the prior warranty deed made by him to William A. Moore, dated March 6, 1861, but not filed for record until December 14, 1874?

There is no evidence whatever in this record tending to show that Josephine Hayden had any notice or knowledge of the execution of the prior unrecorded warranty deed from Seth D. Hayden to said Moore, at the time he made the quitclaim deed to her, nor is there any evidence of fraud or collusion between Seth D. Hayden and Josephine Hayden. Both William A. Moore and Josephine Hayden neglected for years to file their deed for record, as provided for by section 923, Revised Statutes 1899, yet the latter filed her deed about six years prior to the time when he filed his.

The statute provides that "no such instrument in writing shall be valid, except as between the parties thereto, and such as have actual notice thereof, until the same shall be deposited with the recorder for record." R.S. 1899, sec. 925.

According to the provisions of this section, the deed from Hayden to Moore was invalid and conveyed no title to the land in controversy in so far as Josephine Hayden was concerned, because she had no notice of its execution at the time she filed her deed for record. If the exception mentioned in the section just quoted was the only exception or limitation to that statute, then there would be no question as to the title of Josephine Hayden and those claiming under her, but the courts upon principles of equity and justice have repeatedly held that if the subsequent purchaser either had notice of the prior unrecorded deed, or if he was a purchaser without having paid a good and valuable consideration for the land, then he would take nothing by his purchase and deed. Maupin v. Emmons, 47 Mo. 304; Aubuchon v. Bender, 44 Mo. 560. The question now presenting itself is, was Josephine Hayden a purchaser of the land in question for a good and valuable consideration? The deed recites that the conveyance was made for and in "consideration of natural love and affection and five dollars to him in hand paid by the party of the second part, the receipt of which is hereby acknowledged."

A valuable consideration is defined to be money or something that is worth money. 2 Washburn on Real Prop. (4 Ed.), p. 394; 1 Chitty on Contracts (11 Am. Ed.), 27. It is not necessary that the consideration should be adequate in point of value. Although small or even nominal, in the absence of fraud, it is enough to support a contract entered into upon the faith of it. It seems to us that it would be a useless waste of time and energy to cite authorities in support of the proposition that five dollars or any other stated sum of money in excess of one cent, or dime, or one dollar, which are the technical words used to express nominal considerations, is a valuable consideration within the meaning of the law of conveyancing.

It has been suggested that a quitclaim deed is notice of pre-existing equities, and that those who claim under Josephine Hayden had notice that her title to this land was questionable, and that neither she nor they could defend upon the ground that they were bona fide purchasers for a valuable consideration without notice of the title of the true owner. Stivers v. Horne, 62 Mo. 473; Mann v. Best, 62 Mo. 491; Ridgeway v. Holliday, 59 Mo. 444.

But the rule last suggested has no application to a case where the grantee under a subsequent quitclaim deed from the same grantor acquired the title for value and without notice of the former unrecorded deed. Fox v. Hall, 74 Mo. 315. "A purchaser for value by quitclaim deed is as much within the protection of the registry act as one who becomes a purchaser by a warranty deed." Munson v. Ensor, 94 Mo. 504, 1. c. 509, 7 S.W. 108; Campbell v. Gas Co., 84 Mo. 352; Brown v. Coal Co., 97 Ill. 214; Elliott v. Buffington, 149 Mo. 663, 1. c. 676, 51 S.W. 408; Ebersole v. Rankin, 102 Mo. 488, 15 S.W. 422.

Where the controversy is between the vendee of a duly recorded deed and the vendee of a prior unrecorded deed from the same vendor, the settled rule of law in this State seems to be that the consideration in the latter must be such as the law denominates a valuable consideration as distinguished from a good consideration. We know of no case which has gone farther and holds that the purchaser under the recorded deed must have paid a full and adequate consideration for the land.

If fraud is made an issue in the case, then the inadequacy of the consideration paid may be taken into consideration with all the other facts and circumstances in the case for the purpose of establishing fraud; but in the absence of fraud, a want of consideration cannot be shown against a recital of a consideration for the purpose of defeating the operative words of a deed.

In the case at bar, however, there was no evidence introduced tending to prove the recited consideration of five dollars was not in fact paid.

Counsel for defendant, in both his oral and written arguments, contends that Josephine Hayden procured her deed from Seth D. Hayden by fraud. It is a sufficient answer to that to say that no such issue is made by the pleadings in the case, nor was there a word of evidence introduced at the trial tending to establish that fact.

If defendant wished to rely upon fraud as a defense, he should have alleged and proved it. The burden of proving such an issue is upon the defendant. Jackson v. Wood, 88 Mo. 76; Nauman v. Overle, 90 Mo. 666, 3 S.W. 380; Taylor v. Crockett, 123 Mo. 300, 27 S.W. 620.

It follows from what has been said that the judgment of the circuit court must be reversed, and the cause remanded for a new trial.[32]

All concur.

---

32. American Law of Property §§17.10, 17.16 (Casner ed. 1952). — EDS.

DURST v. DAUGHERTY
81 Tex. 650, 17 S.W. 388 (1891)

[The plaintiff brought this suit against the defendants for the recovery of a tract of land. At the September term, 1888, of the District Court of Haskell County, judgment was rendered in favor of the plaintiff for the entire tract of land. It is agreed that the plaintiff purchased the land without notice of the claims of the defendants, and that he paid one-half of the purchase money for the land before he had any knowledge of any adverse claims, and that he has not paid the other one-half of the purchase money.]

FISHER, J. . . .

Appellants insist that the court erred in rendering judgment in favor of appellee for the entire tract of land, because it appears by the agreement that appellee purchased the land without notice of appellants' title, and only paid one-half of the purchase money before he obtained knowledge of the claim of Monroe Edwards and of defendants, and that the other half of the purchase money has not been paid. We believe in this respect the judgment is erroneous, and for this reason solely we reverse it. The pro tanto protection accorded an innocent purchaser is so well recognized by American courts that we deem it unnecessary to cite authority in support of the right. The difficulty lies in the application of the rule, and how the relief should be administered. Some of the courts adopt that rule that allows the innocent purchaser to retain of the land purchased the proportion paid for. Some admit a lien in favor of the innocent purchaser upon the land for the amount of the purchase money paid. Other courts give to the innocent purchaser all the land, with a right in the real owner to recover from him the purchase money unpaid at the time of notice. 2 Pom. Eq., sec. 750; 16 Am. and Eng. Encyc. of Law, p. 835.

In determining which of these rules should be applied in any case it is necessary to ascertain the equities, if any, of the respective parties. For in the application of these rules the adjustment of the equities of each given case is the primary object to be accomplished. The rule that should be applied in one case may be inequitable if applied to another. Consequently it is not proper that a court select one rule to the exclusion of the others as a rule that should govern alike in all cases. In ascertaining what the equities of the parties are it is permissible to inquire into the price paid for the land by the innocent purchaser, and if or not he had placed upon the land permanent and valuable improvements, and if or not the land, situated as it is at the time, is in a condition to be partitioned or divided so that it would not effect or destroy its usefulness and render it of little or no value to either party, or if a partition could be had without injury to the innocent purchaser. And it is further proper to show the conduct of the parties with reference to their acts of diligence, laches, or negligence, if any, in order to ascertain what party, if any, is in fault, so that the court can determine who is the more entitled to its equitable relief, and if the land by reason of the improvements, if any, placed thereon by the innocent purchaser has increased in value since its purchase.

An investigation of the case may develop other facts that it may be important to consider, but those mentioned suggest the importance of the inquiry and why the application of either of the rules should depend upon the facts of each case. A few illustrations are not improper to show the importance of an inquiry into the equities of the respective parties. Take the case of an innocent purchaser buying the land for much less than its true value. In such a case it may be inequitable to compel the true owner to accept the amount of the purchase money unpaid in satisfaction of his demand, and the proper remedy may be the application of the rule that permits the true owner to recover the proportion of the land unpaid for; or the proper remedy may be the rule that permits the owner to recover the entire tract upon reimbursing the innocent purchaser the amount by him paid, with the value of the improvements, if any, erected prior to the time he obtained notice of the true title. On the other hand, if the innocent purchaser has paid full value for the land and has erected improvements on it, and the land is so situated that it could not without injury to the rights of the innocent purchaser be divided, the proper rule to be applied in such case may be that which awards to the innocent purchaser the entire tract charged in favor of the true owner with the purchase money unpaid before notice. The record before us is silent as to the status of the land, and does not inform us of the equities of the parties. Therefore this court cannot with propriety say what rule should govern in this case. This can be ascertained by a trial in the court below upon a full hearing of the facts.

We report the case for reversal.

Reversed and remanded.

Problem

28.21. O executed and delivered to A a deed of certain land O owned. A did not record. O then executed and delivered to T a lease of the land for five years. Five-year leases were not recordable documents. Under the terms of the lease, T agreed to pay an annual rent of $2,400, the rent for each year to be paid at the beginning of the year. T paid the first year's rent to O and went into possession of the land. During the first year, T learned of the prior unrecorded deed to A. What would you advise T to do? See Waskey v. Chambers, 224 U.S. 564, 32 S. Ct. 597 (1912). Cf. Topping v. Parish, 96 Wis. 378, 71 N.W. 367 (1897).

McDONALD & CO. v. JOHNS
62 Wash. 521, 114 P. 175 (1911)

Appeal from a judgment of the superior court for Douglas county, Steiner, J., entered March 7, 1910, upon findings in favor of the defendants, after a trial on the merits before the court without a jury, in an action to foreclose a mortgage. Affirmed.

DUNBAR, C.J.   Incorporated in the record in this case is a very lucid and forceful opinion rendered by the trial judge, and a very succinct statement of the facts, which we will adopt, there being no question raised as to the facts found by the court. Johns and wife, whom we will hereafter refer to as Johns, were indebted to appellant in the principal sum of $2,210, evidenced by three promissory notes, all executed and delivered at times prior to May 5, 1908. On May 5, 1908, Johns executed and delivered to appellant a mortgage on certain lands specified. Johns was also at the time indebted to Bechtol, one of the respondents, in the sum of $662.16, evidenced by a promissory note executed and delivered at a time prior to May 4, 1908. On May 4, 1908, Johns executed and delivered to Bechtol a mortgage on the same lands which had been mortgaged to appellant, and above described. Both mortgages were given to secure the payment of a preexisting indebtedness, and no new or additional consideration or extension of time of payment was given as an inducement to the execution of either of said mortgages. The Bechtol mortgage was executed and delivered first. The McDonald mortgage was recorded first. Quoting from the opinion of the court:

> Upon these facts the ultimate question is: which of these mortgages has the prior lien on the land in said sections 25 and 30? McDonald claims to be a "bona fide purchaser" (incumbrancer) without notice of the Bechtol mortgage prior to the execution and delivery of his own. I will assume (without finding or deciding at this time) that he had no notice. The law upon which his claim to priority must rest is found at Sec. 4441, Pierce's Code (Ren. & Bal. Code, Sec. 8781) and reads: "All deeds, mortgages and assignments of mortgages shall be recorded in the office of the county auditor of the county where the land is situated, and shall be valid as against bona fide purchasers from the date of their filing for record in said office; and when so filed shall be notice to all the world." Of course, the term "bona fide purchaser" means bona fide mortgagee or incumbrancer, as well; else the statute would have no application to mortgages at all. Hence, the statutory phrase will be used in that sense herein. This statute is for the protection of those who become bona fide purchasers *subsequent* to a given conveyance or mortgage, and has nothing to do with those who become such *prior* thereto. In other words, the recording act reaches forward with its benefits, and not backward. It imposes upon any given mortgagee the duty of making a public record of his mortgage for the information, guidance and protection of those who at a *subsequent* time may have occasion to deal concerning the land, failing in the discharge of which duty he shall lose the priority otherwise to be accorded to him. But a mortgagee owes no such duty to those who *precede* him, and as against them he neither gains nor loses anything by recording his mortgage (except in those states where the statutes expressly provide otherwise).

In the opinion of the learned judge there are collated and distinguished the principal cases on this subject, and the court concluded, as indicated, that the priority should be accorded to the party having received the first mortgage, and judgment was entered accordingly.

A review of the authorities convinces us that the judgment in this case should be affirmed. The doctrine of mortgages was originally, of course, purely equitable, and is yet as between the mortgagor and the mortgagee; and as between them it makes no difference whether the mortgage is recorded or not. The recording statutes were for the purpose, as is universally understood now, of giving constructive notice to innocent purchasers and incumbrancers, and the practical question in all these cases is, who are innocent purchasers and incumbrancers. Pomeroy, in the second volume of his Equity Jurisprudence (3d ed.), Sec. 749, says:

"A conveyance of real or personal property as security for an antecedent debt does not, upon principle, render the transferee a bona fide purchaser, since the creditor parts with no value, surrenders no right, and places himself in no worse legal position than before. The rule has been settled, therefore, in very many of the states, that such a transfer is not made upon a valuable consideration, within the meaning of the doctrine of bona fide purchase"; citing cases from Alabama, Arkansas, New York, Vermont, Massachusetts, New Jersey, Pennsylvania, Kentucky, Illinois, Mississippi, Tennessee, Texas, and Indiana, to sustain the text. It is also stated by the author that the doctrine is not universal, but that the weight of authority is in accordance with the text announced. It is also said, in discussing the question, at Sec. 747:

> What constitutes a valuable consideration within the meaning of the doctrine which gives protection to a bona fide purchaser? No person who has acquired title as a mere volunteer, whether by gift, devise, inheritance, post-nuptial settlement on wife or child, or otherwise, can thereby be a bona fide purchaser. Valuable consideration means, and necessarily requires under every form and kind of purchase, something of actual value, capable, in estimation of the laws, of pecuniary measurement,—parting with money or money's worth, or an actual change of the purchaser's legal position for the worse.

And ordinary examples are given, as a contemporaneous advance or loan of money, or a sale, transfer, or exchange of property, made at the time of the purchase or execution of the instrument; the surrender or relinquishment of an existing legal right, or the assumption of a new legal obligation which is in its nature irrevocable. Jones, on Mortgages, vol. 1 (6th ed.), p. 433, also states that the weight of authority is to the effect that the equitable mortgage, the mortgage first given, will prevail over the subsequent mortgage recorded prior to it. In People's Sav. Bank v. Bates, 120 U.S. 556, 7 S. Ct. 679, a case which cannot be distinguished in principle from the case at bar, it was held that the doctrine that the bona fide holder for value of negotiable paper, transferred as security for an antecedent debt merely, and without other circumstances, is unaffected by equities or defenses between prior parties of which he had no notice, does not apply to instruments conveying real or personal property as security in consideration only of preexisting indebtedness; the court quoting from 2 American Leading Cases (5th Am. ed.), p. 233, where it is said:

"Whatever the rule may be in the case of negotiable instruments, it is well settled that the conveyance of lands or chattels as security for an antecedent debt will not operate as a purchase for value, or defeat existing equities."

"A creditor who takes a mortgage on realty merely as security for the payment of a debt or demand already due to him, and without giving any new consideration or being induced to change his condition in any manner, is not entitled to the protection accorded to a bona fide purchaser for value, as against prior liens or equities." 27 Cyc. 1191.

See, also, 24 Am. & Eng. Ency. Law (2d ed.), 139.

Outside of general authority, this view of the law has been distinctly sustained by this court in Hicks v. National Surety Co., 50 Wash. 16, 96 Pac. 515. That was where a surety company took a bill of sale as security for a preexisting debt upon a breached contractor's bond where a prior unrecorded bill of sale had been given, and it was held that the surety company was not an incumbrancer for value in good faith, and that its lien was inferior to that of a prior bill of sale valid as between the parties, although not executed so as to be valid as to creditors of the vendor or subsequent incumbrances in good faith. The court concluded its announcement in that case by saying:

> The instrument under which the appellant claims was taken as security for a preexisting debt or preexisting contingent liability. Under such circumstances does it come within the definition of an incumbrancer for value and in good faith, as that term is defined in law? Under the great weight of authority it does not.

And the first case cited was People's Sav. Bank v. Bates, *supra*.

The judgment is affirmed.

Problem

28.22. Suppose a creditor extends the time for the payment of the indebtedness at the time the debtor executes and delivers to the creditor a mortgage to secure the preexisting debt. Should the mortgagee be deemed a purchaser for a valuable consideration? See Gilchrist v. Gough, 63 Ind. 576 (1878).

Note: Cancellation of Preexisting Debt

In McDonald & Co. v. Johns, the preexisting debt was not canceled, but in Cammack v. Soran, 71 Va. (30 Gratt.) 292 (1878), it was. Should that make any difference? The Virginia court stated as follows:

> The party receiving property in payment of a debt has paid value for it as fully as if he had advanced so much money at the time. He has surrendered not merely the right to proceed to judgment and execution, but the debt itself is extinguished. How is it possible for the court to say that he might not or could not have obtained payment in some other way, or provided himself with some other security? . . . In this case the appellee is a bona fide purchaser of the property, and for a valuable consideration; she is therefore within the very letter of the statute, and this court can defeat her title only by a judicial repeal of the law. [71 Va. at 297-298.]

CHAPTER 29

TITLE EXAMINATION IN MASSACHUSETTS
By Richard B. Johnson[1]

1. Introduction

The mechanics of searching the public records to locate the various things which may affect the title to real estate will vary from state to state, and even, to a lesser degree, from county to county within one state. With due allowance, however, for such differences, an examination of the recording system in one state and the mechanics of title search there should give us a sufficiently representative picture.

The discussion here is confined to the system of recording prevailing in the commonwealth of Massachusetts and is written from the point of view of the practicing conveyancer.[2] Keep in mind that the practicing conveyancer is a very cautious person, not because he or she likes to be stuffy, but because the conveyancer wants the title to be so clear that no other conveyancer will object to it when the land comes up for sale again. It is not just a question of insuring that the client gets a title good enough to stand up in later litigation. The title may be secure against adverse claimants, or it may be good enough to entitle the client to enforce a contract if the client later sells it; but, whereas purchase and sale agreements are usually entered

---

1. Prior to his death in 1977, Mr. Johnson practiced law in Boston, Massachusetts, with the law firm of Ropes & Gray and specialized in title examination and conveyancing. His development of Title Examination in Massachusetts has been reproduced in substantially expanded form in the seventh edition of Crocker's Notes on Common Forms (1955), the standard Massachusetts text on conveyancing. It is printed here in essentially the same form, but with several editorial changes and additions and with updating to October, 1983, by the Ropes & Gray Real Estate Department. The aforementioned seventh edition was prepared by Roger D. Swaim, Esq., of the Boston bar and published by Little, Brown & Company. See generally American Law of Property §§18.1-18.100 (Casner ed. 1952) in regard to the subject of title examination.

2. Massachusetts also has a system of registration of title to land (Mass. Gen. Laws ch. 185). This statement is concerned only with examination of title to unregistered land.

into prior to examination of title by the buyer's attorney, banks and insurance companies and other mortgagees — in Massachusetts, at least — seldom commit themselves to lend money on a mortgage until *after* their attorneys have examined the title. Hence it is not enough to get your client a title that could be sustained by a diligent study of the law or by evidence dehors the record. Regardless of the fine points of the law, the title must be good enough to satisfy a mortgagee's attorney *without* lengthy citation of cases, or elaborate investigation of outside facts. Therefore, unlike water, all conveyancers seek the highest level.[3]

This highest level is not always logical or consistent when carefully scrutinized in the light of the cases and statutes. Sometimes it is above, and sometimes below, the standard that the cases and statutes, particularly the statutes, would seem to indicate. Examples of this variance from practice by the book will be considered herein. It is almost more important to know what conveyancers think the law is than to know what it actually is.

2. The Contents of a Registry of Deeds

a. *Grantor and grantee indexes.* In the office of the register of deeds of a typical Massachusetts county (or of the district into which large counties are divided for recording purposes) a visitor will find two principal types of volumes: the volumes in which the documents[4] are copied in full, and the volumes containing the index which enables him or her to locate documents copied in the first-mentioned volumes. The former volumes are numbered consecutively, and there may be several thousand of them. The index volumes are divided into two kinds: the grantor index and the grantee index.

3. Of course, if your client has already signed a purchase agreement, you will have the problem of deciding whether a title defect is serious enough to enable the client to avoid the contract. See Marketable Title, Chapter 25, Section 2, *supra.* Mass. Gen. Laws ch. 93, §70, now requires that the mortgagee's attorney certify title to the mortgagor.

4. Deeds, mortgages, and discharges of mortgages are by far the most numerous documents found on the record.

Contracts of sale are very seldom recorded because the seller normally insists on a provision in the contract of sale that if the contract is recorded, it shall be void. (The standard printed forms in Massachusetts used to contain such a provision.) The reason the seller desires that the contract should not be recorded is that if the sale is not completed, the seller does not want the public records to reveal the price at which the seller was willing to sell the land. The recording of the contract of sale does not create any serious cloud on the title if the sale is not completed because the recorded contract is not effective against persons other than the parties thereto after ninety days from the date provided in the contract for the delivery of the deed except under limited circumstances. Mass. Gen. Laws ch. 184, §17A (added by chapter 270 of the Acts of 1939).

Leases, when required to be recorded, are not normally copied in full in the record. This is due to the fact that the recording of what is called "notice of lease" is sufficient to satisfy the requirement that a lease be recorded. Mass. Gen. Laws ch. 183, §4 (added by chapter 85 of the Acts of 1941). The "notice of lease" is an instrument in writing executed by all persons who are parties to the lease and must set forth the date of execution of the lease, a description of the leased premises, and the term of the lease, with the date of commencement of such term and all rights of extension or renewal. In a "notice of lease" many important terms of the lease do not have to be revealed to the general public.

Of the two, the grantor index is by far the more significant in making the title search, as will appear later.

As documents are received for record, they are stamped with a serial number, in the order of their reception. The number may be one of the series beginning each day, each month, or each year. They also are stamped with the date and the hour and minute they are received.

A document received for record is entered next on a "daily sheet," which lists, in the order of reception, each document, giving its number, the name of the grantor, the name of the grantee, and the nature of the document (deed, mortgage, etc.).

As rapidly as possible,[5] each document is entered in the grantor index for the current year. In some registries this is a collection of large volumes, often compiled alphabetically in groups, in which each document is entered alphabetically according to the grantor's last name. Where several documents are listed under one surname, they are entered in order of reception under that name, so that in checking a common name toward the end of the year, there may be quite a list which must be read from beginning to end. In other registries they have installed various types of card indexes. These can be and are completely alphabetized, thus saving the examiner's time.

The current index contains more information than the daily sheet. This index is required to contain six columns,[6] headed as follows: date of reception, grantors, grantees, book (volume where instrument copied), leaf or page (page of volume where instrument copied), and town where the land lies. In addition, it usually lists the nature of the document and a brief identification of the land, taken from the deed, by a reference to the streets abutting or a plan, etc. If the document is an assignment or a discharge of a mortgage in the usual statutory form,[7] it will not recite the town where the land lies; so the register will list only the book and page where the mortgage affected is recorded.[8]

In setting up the current index the clerks take the names from the prior current index and space them through each volume; but to avoid crowding, in the event that one name may be more active than it was the year before, and in the event that some new names may appear, they space them liberally. Sometimes they underestimate the space needed for a certain name, and it becomes necessary to call the examiner's attention, by a reference in the appropriate place, to an appendix at the end, where they have a reserve of space to fall back on.

The document is also entered in the grantee index for the current year, which is just like the grantor index, except that the columns containing the names of the grantor and grantee are transposed and arranged alphabetically according to the grantee's surname.

---

5. Mass. Gen. Laws ch. 36, §26, requires this to be done within twenty-four hours, but few registries achieve this perfection.
6. Mass. Gen. Laws ch. 36, §25.
7. See Mass. Gen. Laws ch. 183, §55, and following.
8. Mass. Gen. Laws ch. 36, §21.

Date of Reception	GRANTORS[9]	GRANTEES	Town where Land lies
	SWASEY & c. (cont.)		
1936 July 31	Reuben A.	(Affidavit of sale)	Saugus &)
			Revere)
1939 Sept. 30	Samuel E.	Marblehead Sav. Bk.	Marblehead
1936 Apr. 3	Sinclair et al (& 3 Plans)		"
" " "	Sylvia E. et al (& 3 Plans)		"
1937 May 21	Thomas Est.	Lillian Swasey	"
" " "	" "	" "	"
" " "	" "	Jennie G. Brown	"
" " "	" R. Est.	Lillian Swasey	"
	SWASKI also SEWASKY SVIRSKAS		
1936 July 24	Joseph P.	Mary Sewasky	Haverhill
1939 July 18	Nellie (ux Peter)	Pentucket Sav. Bk.	"
" " "	Peter et ux	" " "	"
	SWEATT see SWEET		
	SWEDA also SZWED		
1936 Nov. 18	Michael et al	(Affidavit of low value)	Middleton
	SWEENEY also SWEENY		
1936 Dec. 16	Alice et al	Mary Sweeney	Salem
1938 Sept. 16	" F.	Francis D. Sweeney	"
1937 Dec. 21	Anna M. et al	Salem Sav. Bk.	
1938 " 20	" " "	" " "	
" " 31	" " "	(Statement as to water rates)	Salem
1939 Apr. 25	" " "	Salem Sav. Bk.	
" " "	" " (ux John H.) by) Atty. & c.)	" " "	Salem
" " "	" " (" " ") —	(Affidavit of sale)	"
" May 22	" " et al	(Dis. of statements as to) water rates))	
1940 Sept. 14	" " (or Annie M.)	Frances Sweeney	Nahant
1938 July 15	Annie (ux Harold L.)	Progressive Workmen's) Credit Union)	Saugus
1936 May 14	" M. et al	(Not. of contract)	Nahant
" June 3	" " "	(Dis. of not. of contract)	
1937 Jan. 5	" " "	Thomas F. Reddy	Nahant
1940 Sept. 14	" " (or Anna M.)	Frances Sweeney	"
1937 Nov. 12	Arthur et al Trs.	George W. Rowell	
1939 May 31	" " "	William W. Tuxbury	
1938 Sept. 29	" J. by Gdn.	Cleophas Martin	Salem
1937 June 16	Catherine (or Catherine E.) (ux Denis)	Lynn Co-op. Bk.	Lynn
1940 Sept. 27	" —	City of Lynn	"
1936 Aug. 28	" E.	" " "	"
" " "	" " "	" " "	"

9.   The affidavits of sale indexed under Reuben A. Swasey and Anna M. Sweeney are those required by Mass. Gen. Laws ch. 244, §15, which makes them, if recorded within thirty days, evidence that the power of sale in a mortgage was duly executed.

The takings indexed under Sinclair Swasey et al. and Sylvia E. Swasey et al. were eminent domain proceedings recorded pursuant to Mass. Gen. Laws ch. 79, §3. The recording that this requires does not give you 100 percent protection, however.

Book	Page	Instrument	DESCRIPTION
3079	445		Mtge. B. 2846 P. 394
3194	536	Mtge.	Merritt St. (fmly. "Okum Boy")
3069	249	Taking & c.	Village St. from Railroad Bridge to Knight Av.
"	249	" "	" " " " " " " "
3109	507	Deed	Lincoln Av. (fmly. Pitman St.) Lot 5 & Part of
			Lot 6 Pl. Pac. 861–88 $\frac{1}{3}$ of $\frac{2}{3}$ undiv., $\frac{1}{4}$ of $\frac{1}{3}$ undiv.)
"	509	"	Lincoln Av. (fmly. Pitman St.) Lot 5 & part Lot 6
"	510	"	" " (" " ") " " " " " "
"	507	"	" " (" " ") " " " " " ")
			Pl. Rec. 861–88 $\frac{1}{3}$ of $\frac{2}{3}$ undiv., $\frac{1}{4}$ of $\frac{1}{3}$ undiv.
3079	536	Deed	Rose Av.
3187	249	Mtge.	Washington St.
"	"	"	" "
3092	39		
3095	438	Deed	Tremont St.
3157	377	"	Barr St.
3133	310	Tax Recpt.	
3169	593	" "	
3170	101		
3179	66	Possn.	Mtge. B. 3029 P. 256
"	67	D. Un. Pow.	Clifton & Summit Ave. Part lot 1 Pl. Rec. 1198–600
"	"		Mtge. B. 3029 P. 256
3181	234		See B. 3134 P. 101, B. 3170 P. 101
3229	459	Deed	1st Willow Rd. 2d Willow & Valley Rds.
3151	130	Mtge.	(Broad View) Lake Av. Lot 67 Pl. B. 47 Pl. 41B
3072	397		Valley Rd.
3074	289		See B. 3072 P. 397
3098	151	Mtge.	4 parcels
3229	459	Deed	1st Willow Rd. 2d Willow & Valley Rds.
3130	225	Discharge	Mtge. B. 2469 P. 233
3181	448	"	" " 2304 " 226
3159	321	Deed	Harbor St. $\frac{1}{4}$ int.
3111	357	Mtge.	Summer St. & a Ct.
3233	357	Tax Taking	" " —
3086	109	" "	Echo Place Lot 6 Pl. 43 A.O.
"	110	" "	Summer St. Pl. 43 A.O.

The affidavits of low value indexed under Michael Sweda is furnished by the commissioner of corporations and taxation, and, upon its recording, the collector of taxes is authorized by Mass. Gen. Laws ch. 60, §79, to sell the parcels listed in the affidavit at public auction without the expense of formal foreclosure of the right of redemption.

The tax receipts indexed under Anna M. Sweeney are recorded pursuant to Mass. Gen.

The next step begins on January 1 of each year when new current indexes are opened and the current index for the preceding year is transcribed into

---

Laws ch. 60, which requires the collector of taxes to give a certificate of payment to a person other than the owner of the fee who rightfully pays the taxes assessed on the land. Such certificate being recorded within thirty days from its date is notice of such payment and of the lien therefor. The Salem Savings Bank was a mortgagee and therefore entitled, under Mass. Gen. Laws ch. 60, §58, to pay the tax and add it to the mortgage debt, but it seems to be a general practice among careful mortgagees, to be doubly sure by taking a certificate of the collector. You must be careful not to fall into the trap of assuming that the lien for the tax created by recording the certificate is merged with the mortgage debt. It remains a separate debt and is not transferred by an assignment of the mortgage. (Dillon v. Lange, 280 Mass. 427, 182 N.E. 917 (1932).) Presumably, therefore, it is not discharged by a discharge of the mortgage, either.

The statement as to water rates indexed under Anna M. Sweeney is filed by the city under Mass. Gen. Laws ch. 40, §42A, to preserve for two more years its lien for water rates, which otherwise would expire eighteen months after the water was supplied.

The possn. indexed under Anna M. Sweeney is the certificate signed by two witnesses, of entry by the mortgagee for breach of condition, which, under Mass. Gen. Laws ch. 244, §2, must be recorded within thirty days of the entry to make it effective. Possession so obtained, if continued peaceably for three years, forever forecloses the right of redemption.

The d. un. pow. indexed under Anna M. Sweeney is the mortgagee's deed under the power of sale contained in the same mortgage, and the affidavit of sale shows that the sale was valid. The Salem Savings Bank, like all other careful mortgagees, has foreclosed by *two* statutory methods: by public sale and by entry. The latter, after three years, will cure any possible defect in the conduct of the sale (except, since 1942, the lack of a court order required by the Soldiers' and Sailors' Civil Relief Act). See American Law of Property §18.56 (Casner ed. 1952).

The dis. of statements as to water rates indexed under Anna M. Sweeney is necessary because of the previous statement recorded. Ordinarily, although the water bill is a lien, it is not necessary to record a discharge if the paid bill is exhibited. But once the city has recorded a statement, the record for the next two years can be cleared only by recording a discharge. Note that the reference under "Description" is to *two* former recordings: at book 3134, page 101, and book 3170, page 101, and that nothing at book 3134, page 101, is indexed under Anna M. Sweeney. How did this happen? Simply because the city engineer, in making up his lists of unpaid water bills, charged the 1937 water to "John Henry Sweeney et ux." and the 1937 lien is indexed under John Henry Sweeney on the next page. In 1938, however, he charged it to John Henry and Anna Marie Sweeney, and the 1938 lien is indexed under Anna's name as well as John's. This shows that particular attention must be paid to first names, especially where you are running a married woman's schedule.

The not. of contract was a notice of a written contract between Annie M. Sweeney and Thor Roofing Company for the erection, alteration, repair, or removal of a building, recorded to secure for the contractor a lien on the building and the land for payment for all labor and material thereafter furnished by virtue of the contract. The notice states the date on or before which the contract is to be completed. Mass. Gen. Laws ch. 254, §2. This lien would have been dissolved, under section 8 of ch. 254, unless the contractor had filed, within thirty days after the date on which the contract was to be performed, a sworn statement of the amount due. Apparently Annie M. Sweeney paid the contractor promptly and desired to clear the record affirmatively by a notice of dissolution, under section 10 of ch. 254, rather than by mere lapse of time.

The tax takings indexed under Catherine (or Catherine E.) Sweeney were recorded pursuant to Mass. Gen. Laws ch. 60, §§53-54, and, being recorded within sixty days, are prima facie evidence of all facts essential to the validity of the titles so taken, which thereupon vest in the town, subject to the right of redemption. The right of redemption continues until foreclosed in the land court after two years, under sections 64 through 79 of chapter 60, unless as above the commissioner certifies the land to be of insufficient value to meet the taxes, interest, and charges, in which case no right of redemption exists after the sale. Mass. Gen. Laws ch. 60, §§79-80B.

more permanent form. In the process of transcription, the entries are rearranged, if necessary, under each surname in alphabetical order according to first names, so that the bother of reading the whole list under any given surname (as was necessary in the current index if it were entered in a book and not on cards) is eliminated. Nevertheless, the fact that careless scriveners may err in inserting middle initials must be kept in mind, and a man who calls himself J. Raymond Jones in one instrument may sign his name John R. Jones in another one. Furthermore, taxes on land owned by a married woman in her own right may be assessed to her husband,[10] a fact which must be borne in mind when running a married woman's schedule, because Alice Jones may have lost the land under a tax taking indexed under John R. Jones alone. Some protection against the error of misspelling names is afforded by the practice of listing together like-sounding names. Thus, under "Roland" might appear the reference: "See Rowland," and at "Rowland" would appear "Rowland — Roland."

So far the practice is uniform. Every registry will have daily sheets, a current index, and an index for each recent year. Obviously, however, the physical effort involved in taking down and putting back a heavy volume for each year would eventually turn the conveyancers into the nation's champion weightlifters or kill them, unless some consolidation were made from time to time. At periods varying in each registry from five to ten years, the annual indexes are consolidated, so that by pulling down one volume the examiner can check several years. Sometimes the five- or ten-year indexes are reconsolidated. Generally, the indexes prior to 1800 are entirely consolidated, and in Suffolk County (Boston) the indexes for 1800 through 1899 are likewise consolidated, so that an examiner need pull down but two volumes to check one name from 1639 to 1899. A sample of a page of the grantor-grantee index, when consolidated, is set forth on page 872 *supra.*

The process of transcription and consolidation outlined above applies to the grantee index also.

Many registries are now computerized in their compilation of the grantor and grantee indexes, supplying the examiner with computer printouts even on the daily sheets; the examiner must now be concerned with computer error, as well as with documents recorded but not entered or transcribed.

Problem

29.1. If you represent the purchaser of land in Massachusetts, what is the last index you will examine before you release control of your client's funds in exchange for the deed?

---

10. Southworth v. Edmands, 152 Mass. 203, 25 N.E. 106 (1890).

b. *Miscellaneous records.* There are certain types of instruments affecting real estate titles which may, according to the local practice in each registry, be indexed in either the regular daily sheet and grantor index or in a separate sheet and index. These are attachments, bankruptcies,[11] mechanics' liens, tax liens, and water rates. The trend is toward incorporating these in the regular grantor index, which is helpful to the conveyancer in that it reduces his labor and risk of error,[12] but the only safe thing to do in a strange registry is to consult the clerk at the desk. Where a separate index is kept for one of these, it takes up relatively little space and does not often affect a title, but it must be checked just as carefully as the grantor index. These separate indexes usually fill up so slowly that a current index may cover four or five years, and it is usually not considered necessary to transcribe an old index when a new current index is opened.

A new index — for federal tax liens — has been made necessary by the decision in Glass City Bank v. United States, 326 U.S. 265, 65 S. Ct. 1184 (1945), to the effect that such liens attach to after-acquired property.[13] To save searching the grantor index for a period prior to acquisition, federal tax liens are now card-indexed separately.

c. *Atlases and plans.* Another group of volumes to which you will refer in the registry consists of the atlases and plan books. These books are particularly helpful in aiding you to obtain a picture of the boundaries and other characteristics of the land with which you are concerned. Nothing clarifies one's thinking about the land like a trip to the locus, to scramble through the bushes and find on the ground the monuments referred to in the deeds to fix the boundaries of the locus. Such an expedition is not always feasible in the limits imposed by the necessity of keeping your charges reasonable. In any

11. Until 1938, the commencement of bankruptcy proceedings in the federal district court was notice to all the world. For the convenience of examiners, the Suffolk County registry sent a clerk down to the federal district court to copy off the bankruptcy docket. The clerk then copied the list into the Suffolk registry's bankruptcy index and mailed copies to the other registries, where they were indexed. The federal bankruptcy act (11 U.S.C.A. §44 (g)) now provides that bona fide purchasers of real estate are not bound by notice of the commencement of bankruptcy proceedings by or against the seller, unless the trustee in bankruptcy records a notice thereof in the registry where the land lies. However, this does not apply to the county where the records of the bankruptcy proceedings are kept. Consequently, in Suffolk County (Boston) where the federal district court has its seat, there is no requirement of recording the notice as a protection against a bona fide purchaser. Nevertheless, the Suffolk County registry has continued its practice of sending a clerk to the district court each day to copy the entries in bankruptcy. Most conveyancers take this index as entirely adequate, even though it is 24 hours behind and theoretically exposes them to the risk of an error by the clerk. Careful conveyancers, in important cases, have been known to go outside the Commonwealth to check the records in other federal districts against a possible bankruptcy prior to 1938 if a nonresident or a foreign corporation appeared in the chain of title before that year. The Reform Act of 1978, which replaced the Bankruptcy Act of 1978, deleted the requirement that bankruptcy notice be filed with the registry, effective August, 1983. Nearly all registries, however, continue to adhere to tradition and require bankruptcy notice fiing.

12. In examining abstracts from other states, I am occasionally appalled at the variety of indexes involved.

13. See Mass. Gen. Laws ch. 36, §1971, as amended by chapter 278 of the Laws of 1983.

event, a conveyancer will consult every available atlas and plan which refers to the land, and the modern conveyancer will order photostats of the pertinent maps of the land for permanent incorporation in the abstract. Every registry still carries a supply of tracing paper, however, and the ancient custom of laboriously tracing out a plan of the land has by no means died, especially in the small country registries which have not yet acquired photostatic machinery. Where no atlas or recorded plan referring to the land is available, the conveyancer must create his or her own working sketch of the land from whatever references are in the recorded deeds to monuments, courses, and distances. A simple protractor and scale ruler are useful tools. Sometimes, of course, it is necessary to call upon a professional surveyor for assistance, or even an architect where party walls are involved.

Atlases and assessors' maps, where they exist, are kept in separate volumes on a separate shelf or table. No index is necessary. Plans recorded with deeds may be kept in separate volumes or, if the plan is small enough or lends itself to reproduction on a smaller scale,[14] it may be bound right in with the deed in the deed volumes. A plan index is usually kept, but in the grantor-grantee system, this index is only a convenience and not an essential part of the title search.[15]

Problem

29.2. If you represent the purchaser of land, and the deed to the seller describes the land as "the land familiarly known as Green Tree Stables, containing 200 acres more or less," how would you go about establishing the boundaries of the land?

3. Public Records Outside the Registry of Deeds

a. *Probate records.* The most important records outside the registry of deeds affecting land titles are probate records of the devise and descent of land. The registry of probate and the registry of deeds for each county or district are almost always in the same building. Unfortunately, the probate court of another county may have exercised jurisdiction over the locus, so it is not always a matter of stepping across the hall to find the necessary information. Estates are indexed under the name of the decedent. This is

14. Watch out for changes in the scale of blueprints and photostats of plans. Some registries thoughtfully stamp a warning on such plans. It is best to measure a line, the length of which is known, and compare it with the stated representative fraction.

15. So far as I know, no one has ever attempted to record a *photograph,* aerial or otherwise, of a piece of real estate. There seems to be no logical reason why, with modern equipment, this should not be feasible. Conceivably it might be useful; for example, to show the condition of an abandoned right of way.

obviously the only practical way to do it, but this causes a difficulty which will be elaborated later.

b. *Other court records.* The superior court, sitting in any county, the supreme judicial court, the land court, and the federal courts (all of which usually sit in Boston) may also have matters on their records which must be investigated, as will be discussed later. Their records are usually indexed under all the parties.

c. *Town or city records.* The assessors and the collector of taxes have records directly affecting the locus. It is not always easy to determine in whose name these records are kept, but street or block references can eventually be ascertained. The town or city clerk may have pertinent vital statistics, and the city engineer can often advise you as to streets and utilities.

d. *County records.* In early days, it was the practice to file highway and railroad locations with the county commissioners. It is not necessary to investigate these records in normal cases, but only where there are special reasons for so doing. The occasion for such a check is usually fairly apparent from the start.

e. *State records.* The commissioner of corporations and taxation and the secretary of the commonwealth will have corporate and tax records and vital statistics which it may be helpful or necessary to check.

f. *Federal records.* Congress has thoughtfully provided in almost every case (except for estate and gift taxes, eminent domain, and perhaps judicial proceedings) for local recording as an element in the establishment of private or governmental rights affecting real estate under federal law.

4. *Compiling the History of the Title*

The preceding paragraphs describe the sources in which the history of the title is buried. Now how do you set about extracting all the essential information and assembling it into an abstract and brief chronicle on which you, or perhaps a senior lawyer, may base a conclusion as to the present state of the title?

a. *What limit shall you set to your search?* In logical analysis, this is the first decision you should make, based on a number of factors, including, among others, the nature, location, and value of the property, your client's wishes (and willingness to pay), and, perhaps, the practice prevailing in the district. Actually, you will formulate this judgment (or hunch) as you learn more about the title in your progress through the steps described in the succeeding paragraphs. For example, a series of warranty deeds clearly describing the property and mortgages to banks known to employ competent counsel will give you great comfort. A series of deeds " of all my right, title and interest, if any" will send you digging back and back into history.

Sometimes people who have heard of a statute of limitations ask: Why do you have to go back more than twenty years? Twenty years is not necessarily safe because many factors may suspend the operation of the statute of limitations. A person with a record interest adverse to the grantor may have been a minor, or insane, or a remainderman, against whom the statute of limitations may not even have begun to run.[16] There may be an ancient mortgage outstanding, on which payments have been made within twenty years. Important restrictions or conditions which are still effective may have been placed on the land by a deed recorded more than twenty years ago. And, of course, the mere existence of a record title for twenty years does not mean that twenty years of open, notorious, and continuous adverse possession can be established.

On the other hand, it is usually impracticable to examine the records all the way back to the book of possessions.[17] The cost to the client for such a search might exceed the value of the land. Some reliance may be placed on the fact that reputable persons recite, in their deeds, restrictions and conditions known to them to exist. Thus, if no deed within fifty or sixty years mentions a restriction or condition, the risk that someone may dig one up in an earlier deed and enforce it becomes relatively slight. By the same token, life estates created in earlier deeds and wills will probably have ended, and minors will have reached their majority.[18] An old rough rule used to be quoted: "sixty years to a warranty deed." Recent legislation, designed to reduce the labor and expense of title examination, has encouraged many careful conveyancers to shorten this to fifty years, and the unfashionableness of warranty deeds in the twentieth century often makes it necessary to start with a quitclaim deed.[19] Disabilities cannot extend the statute of limitations beyond twenty-five years[20]; restrictions must be brought forward on the record every twenty or thirty years[21]; ancient rights of entry and possibilities of reverter were largely wiped out by a re-recording requirement[22] and new ones are limited to thirty years[23]; some long leases turn into freehold estates by a requirement that the reversioner record his claim[24]; and

16. Daley v. Daley, 300 Mass. 17, 14 N.E.2d 113 (1938); Daley v. Daley, 308 Mass. 293, 32 N.E.2d 286 (1941).

17. Ordered by the general court in 1634, complied with in Boston about 1640, and reprinted by the city in 1877. See the introduction to the 1880 reprint of Volume I of the records in the Suffolk registry of deeds. See also Haskins, The Beginning of the Recording System in Massachusetts, 21 B.U.L. Rev. 281, 287 (1941).

18. For dramatic examples of title defects emerging from the distant past and ancient claims not barred by lapse of time, see The History of a Title, A Conveyancer's Romance, by Uriel H. Crocker, Esq., of the Suffolk bar, 10 Am. L. Rev. 60 (1875).

19. In Massachusetts, this means a deed with covenants against encumbrances made by the grantor. Mass. Gen. Laws ch. 183, §§11, 17.

20. Laws 1959, ch. 269, §§1, 2, amending Mass. Gen. Laws ch. 260, §§25, 26.

21. Mass. Gen. Laws ch. 184, §§26-30.

22. Mass. Gen. Laws ch. 184, §19, ch. 260, §31A.

23. Mass. Gen. Laws ch. 184A, §§3, 4 (drafted and sponsored by the authors of this casebook).

24. Mass. Gen. Laws ch. 184, §19.

mortgages cannot be foreclosed after fifty years unless brought forward on the record.[25] All such new recordings must be indexed under the name of the current owner.

In the final analysis your judgment must guide you as to the time in the past at which you feel safe in stopping your search. If considerations require a briefer search than you deem sufficient, then in your opinion to the client you should disclose the extent of your search and give the client your estimate of the risk involved in *not* making the search more extensive, and of the cost of extending it.

5.   Title Standards

The Massachusetts Conveyancers Association has promulgated title standards which set forth certain accepted practices of the conveyancing bar in Massachusetts.

Problem

29.3. If you represent the purchaser of land and you find that the largest bank in the community accepted a mortgage on the land two years earlier to secure a loan equal to 75 percent of the value of the land at that time, what reasons will you give your client for putting him or her to the expense of searching the records for more than the last two years?

b. *Finding the starting point.* Let us assume that you have decided that you want to start your search with a deed, circa 1918. How in the world do you know where to look for it? How will you find out who owned the property then?

First you will want to see the purchase and sale agreement, which, if carefully drawn, will describe with accuracy the real estate to be conveyed. If the contract does not describe the property by metes and bounds, or by reference to a plan, but *does,* nevertheless, describe it accurately enough to be valid, you must consult your client to make sure just what and where the "locus" is. Then you will ask the seller to give you a reference by volume and page number to the place where the deed under which the seller claims title is recorded. You will look up the deed on record under which the land was conveyed to the seller, and if that deed has been drawn properly, it will contain in it a reference to the instrument on record which gave title to the person who conveyed to the present seller. By working back in this way, the complete chain of owners frequently may be built up quickly.

25.   Mass. Gen. Laws ch. 260, §§33, 34.

If at any point in your backward progress you encounter a deed which omits its grantor's title reference (the cardinal sin of conveyancing),[26] you must pick up the thread, if you can, by examining the grantee index under the name of the grantor in the earliest deed you have found to see if you can find an entry therein of the deed to such person, in which deed, of course, such person will appear as grantee.

If the grantee index does not disclose from whom the grantor in the earliest deed you have found obtained such grantor's title (which will become apparent to you after you have run such grantor's name in the grantee index backward from the date of such grantor's deed for a period corresponding to what can be said to be the maximum span of such grantor's life), the only other way such grantor could have obtained a record title is by descent or by devise, and to obtain a record of the passage of the title in either of these ways you must pay a visit to the registry of probate.

In the registry of probate you will find an alphabetical index by years (example A-K, 1910-1920) of all decedents whose estates have passed through that probate court, which index will disclose the town in which each listed decedent resided and the year when the petition to settle such decedent's estate was filed, and will also give you a docket number, under which a folder is kept in the files, containing all documents entered in the estate. You are seeking to find the decedent from whom your last grantor obtained title to the locus by descent or devise. Unfortunately the only thing you know when you go to the registry of probate is the name of your last grantor and the locus, and there is no index in that registry based on the location of land or the names of heirs or devisees. Thus your only hope is to find, by a shrewd guess or a hunch, in the alphabetical index of decedents' estates, a decedent who might be an ancestor of your last grantor and by the examination of the file of documents in the estate to ascertain that your last grantor was in fact such decedent's heir or devisee. If the surname is a common one in your town or city, such as "Johnson," you may have such a tremendous task before you to find the decedent to whom your last grantor is related that it will be more expeditious to try to pick up the thread in some other way. Even if you should be fortunate enough to find an estate listing your last grantor as an heir or devisee, you still must determine whether the locus was involved in that estate. Even if there is a will in that estate, it probably will not describe any real estate by metes and bounds, and it may be an intestate estate. If an inventory of the assets of the decedent has been filed as required by law, however, this inventory will disclose the decedent's real property located in Massachusetts; but such real property will be described in very general terms. Usually it will show enough to tell you whether you are on the right track. If you think you are on the right track,

---

26. The usual reference is to the deed from the grantor's immediate predecessor in title. Logically there is no reason why reference should not be made to an earlier deed, and such a reference would assist later examiners even more, but the average scrivener is either reluctant to make things too easy for other lawyers or fears the possibility of inaccuracy.

you must then go back to the registry of deeds and run the grantee index under the name of the decedent and see if you can find a deed to the decedent covering the locus. If you can, you have picked up the thread. If not, you can go back to the registry of probate and try again.

It may be, however, that you can get no lead in the registry of probate. Such would be true if your last grantor received the land by devise from a friend, or if the estate of the decedent who owned it was probated in another county. Without knowing the name of the friend or without knowing the other county, there is no way to get started in the alphabetical index in the probate court. In such a situation you must extend your fishing expedition to other sources which may give you the lead you need to pick up the missing link in the probate court, such as an old atlas, the assessors, a local history, other conveyancers, or old inhabitants in the neighborhood of your land. If you get completely baffled, you may be able to unravel the mystery by running the title to adjoining land because thereby you may pick up references to the ownership of your land. For example, a deed to the lot adjoining on the north may describe that lot as "bounded southerly by land of Zaccheus Burnham."

The more experience a title examiner has, the more instinct is developed for ferreting out leads to pick up the thread of a title in the backward search.

The foregoing are some of the obstacles which face you as you go back through the records to the point at which you deem it safe to turn around and commence running down the title in the grantor index to see what conveyances were made by the various owners during the time each owned the land.

Problem

29.4. Assume you have traced a title back to a deed from B to C, dated July 14, 1886, which deed contains no reference as to the source of B's title; that you have run the grantee index under B's name back to 1800 without finding any reference of a deed to B; that you have caused every probate index in Massachusetts to be examined for possible ancestors of B and have found no references to possible ancestors in such indexes; that you did find in the 1860 atlas a plan of the locus marked "A's homestead;" that you have run the grantor index and the probate index under A's name from 1860 to 1890 without finding any reference to the locus.

    a.   Does it necessarily follow that B was not the owner of the locus in 1886? Why?

    b.   What further examination of the record would you make? Why?

c. *The grantor schedules.* Suppose we assume you have found a deed, good on its face, covering the locus and recorded, say, in 1915, and in the light of all the circumstances it appears reasonably safe to stop at this point in your backward search. You then begin to run the grantor index. This is the important part of your work. An oversight in checking the grantee index on your way back merely means more work for yourself in picking up the thread. An oversight in checking the grantor index means that the title you have certified to your client may fail, you may find yourself explaining "a little hitch,"[27] and you may have to make good the loss.[28]

Accordingly, you go to the shelf containing the consolidated grantor index for a period including 1915 (it may be 1910 to 1920, for example), and you note carefully everything appearing therein under the name of the grantee in the 1915 deed which has been recorded since the date of the 1915 deed, or the date of acknowledgment, whichever is earlier. The date of the deed may precede the date of recording by several days or months, especially in the old days when it was more of a chore than it is now to travel to the registry.[29] Actually the date of acknowledgment may be more significant than the date of the deed, which is often arbitrary. Since the deed is effective from the date of delivery, as between the parties and those with notice, you must take the earliest date shown on the records.

You must watch carefully for everything listed in the grantor index under the name of the grantee in the 1915 deed, but, at the same time, you must begin to exercise considerable judgment. Most indexes will refer to the town or towns in which the deeds recite that the land is located.[30] By rights, this should entitle you to disregard any document indexed as concerning land in another town, and most conveyancers doubtless do. Nevertheless, it has been held that if the land can be identified from the particular description, an error in the name of the town will be disregarded and the deed will be effective.[31] The court seems to have overlooked the fact that the erroneous recital will be the part of the description most likely to appear in the index, to the misleading of conveyancers. This would appear to be a case where the law departs from sound practice.

Urban or suburban land may be described with sufficient accuracy by the brief description in the index so that you can be certain whether the instrument referred to in the grantor index deals with property in the neighborhood of the locus. If you have the slightest doubt, you must consult the instrument itself before checking it off as not affecting the locus, and it may be necessary to compare the description therein with the description of the locus and perhaps consult a plan or atlas to make sure. One trap for the unwary is the fact that one and the same parcel may bound on two or more streets. You cannot assume that a deed of land on Elm Street will not affect

27. See Hodgins, Mr. Blandings Builds His Dream House 150 (1946).
28. Dorr v. Massachusetts Title Insurance Co., 238 Mass. 490, 131 N.E. 191 (1921).
29. Bear in mind that a mortgage recorded more than four months after its date is not valid against an assignee of the estate of the mortgagor if insolvency proceedings are begun within one year from the recording. Mass. Gen. Laws ch. 216, §37.
30. Perry v. Clark, 157 Mass. 330, 32 N.E. 226 (1892).
31. Ibid.

the locus on Maple Street unless you keep in mind the names of all the streets surrounding the block in which the locus lies. Furthermore, the names of streets often change, and if the old atlases show such a change in name or location of a street, you must keep this in mind as you examine the index. Today the law requires that the address of the property be recited in the deed. Mass. Gen. Laws ch. 183, §6B.

Most abstracters tend to rely on a recital in the index that the land described in the indexed instrument lies "north of the old county road," and to disregard that instrument if the locus lies south of the old county road. This practice ought to be sustained by the law, but it is not, because the instrument may affect the locus notwithstanding such an error.[32]

The locus may have been at one time a part of a larger tract, other parts of which may have been conveyed away before your land. If such is the case, then, as you come across the references to these "deeds out," whether they are "north" or "south" of the old county road, you must examine them to ascertain whether thereby the grantor or the local planning board subjected his remaining land, all or part of which you are interested in, to any easements or restrictions. Fortunately for the examiner, the statute of frauds forbids an oral or implied agreement to subject the grantor's remaining land to restrictions.[33] It must be done by appropriate language in the deeds, or on any plans referred to therein. Watch out, therefore, for building lines on the plans. However, for some obscure reason, the statute of frauds does not forbid the grant of an easement by implication,[34] and easements may exist over tidal lands or lands adjoining great ponds, from early colonial ordinances.[35] The existence of such an easement may be apparent from the record, or it may be discovered only by a view of the locus.[36]

You must also check the measurements with care, to make sure that the grantor had as much land left after a deed out, as the locus is supposed to contain.

Problem

29.5. Assume you represent the purchaser, and your client is buying a house and lot located in a suburban development. In tracing the title back, you eventually come to the X Development Company which at one time owned all the land in the development. As you run the name of the X Development Company in the grantor index, you see the various conveyances of the other lots, not your lot, in the suburban development. By actual

32. Cook v. Cook, 293 Mass. 29, 199 N.E. 333 (1935).
33. Sprague v. Kimball, 213 Mass. 380, 100 N.E. 622 (1913).
34. Jasper v. Worcester Spinning & Finishing Co., 318 Mass. 752, 64 N.E.2d 89 (1945).
35. Massachusetts Colonial Ordinances, 1641-1647.
36. Mount Holyoke Realty Corp. v. Holyoke Realty Corp., 284 Mass. 100, 187 N.E. 227 (1933). See also American Law of Property §§17.24, 18.87 (Casner ed. 1952).

count there are 120 such deeds out of the X Development Company of other lots in the suburban development. Are you going to read each of the 120 deeds of the other lots before giving your client an opinion as to the state of the title of the lot your client is buying?

d. *Need the links in the chain overlap? (herein of estoppel by deed and deeds recorded late)*[37] In your search, both back through the grantee index and forward again through the grantor index, should you disregard the grantor index as to each successive owner prior to the date when each acquired title? This would appear to be the natural and logical thing to do, were it not for a series of cases applying the doctrine of estoppel by deed to the dismay of subsequent bona fide purchasers and in complete disregard of the realities of the registry system.[38] This rule has been criticized,[39] and other states have refused to follow it.[40] Nevertheless, Judge Gray ruled in 1878 that it had been too long established in Massachusetts to be changed, except by legislation.[41] The legislature has never seen fit to change it. However, even though this is the law in Massachusetts, it is not the practice to examine the grantor index as to an owner prior to the date such owner acquired title. Thus we have an example of a variance between law and practice in which the conveyancers are clearly right and the law is clearly wrong. The logical result of the law is that all title examiners, to be safe, would have to search the records before the date when any individual in the chain acquired title, to see if such individual, or an ancestor of such individual ever gave a warranty deed. It would not even be safe, in theory, to stop when the individual grantor must have been unborn. Thanks to the doctrine of lineal warranty, the heir may be estopped by an ancestor's warranty,[42] or that of his

---

37. See Chapter 28, Section 2.

38. Suppose that A gives B a warranty deed of Blackacre on July 1, 1950, but A does not own Blackacre at that time. B nevertheless accepts the deed and records it on that date. On August 1, 1968, Blackacre is conveyed to A by O by a deed which is immediately recorded. The doctrine of estoppel by deed causes the title acquired by A in 1968 to pass automatically to B pursuant to the terms of the 1950 deed. In other words, A is estopped to deny the effectiveness of the 1950 deed to pass Blackacre to B. The question we now have under consideration is whether a purchaser of Blackacre from A in 1969 can claim that the deed from A to B in 1950 is not properly recorded because A had no record title then and no one would search the grantor index under A's name before 1968 so that no reference to the 1950 deed from A to B will be found. If the purchaser from A can sustain such claim, the purchaser may be a bona fide purchaser that will cut off B's rights because B's rights are not properly recorded. The Supreme Judicial Court in Massachusetts has held that the 1950 deed from A to B is properly recorded so that a purchaser from A in 1969 takes subject to it. See White v. Patten, 41 Mass. (24 Pick.) 324 (1837); Knight v. Thayer, 125 Mass. 25 (1878); Ayer v. Philadelphia & Boston Face Brick Co., 159 Mass. 84, 34 N.E. 177 (1893).

39. See Ayer v. Philadelphia & Boston Face Brick Co., footnote 38, *supra,* and Philbrick, Limits of Record Search and Therefore of Notice, 93 U. Pa. L. Rev. 125, 176-187 (1944).

40. See Wheeler v. Young, 76 Conn. 44, 55 A. 670 (1903).

41. Knight v. Thayer, footnote 38 *supra.*

42. Russ v. Alpaugh, 118 Mass. 369 (1875).

or her spouse's ancestor![43] The wretched examiner would have to search the index under each name in the chain of title clear back to the opening of the registry in 1639, and he or she would probably never then find a deed by an ancestor with a different name.

To extend the title search to protect against the operation of the doctrine of estoppel by deed would probably cause the cost of each examination to exceed the value of the land. The title examiners may take some comfort in the thought that full warranty deeds have become obsolete in urban Massachusetts, and the supreme judicial court might decline to extend this pernicious doctrine to the deed containing only limited or quitclaim covenants. Mortgages, however, are as common as ever, and the statutory mortgage covenants are capable of feeding an estoppel,[44] but most mortgages are discharged, and a combination of estoppel by deed and a foreclosed mortgage is one that this conveyancer is not going to lose any sleep over. However, there is always the danger of reviving junior mortgages after the same have been cut off by the foreclosure of a senior mortgage if the original mortgagor obtains title subsequent to the foreclosure. See Ayer v. Philadelphia & Boston Face Brick Co., 157 Mass. 57, 31 N.E. 177 (1892), *affirmed on other grounds,* 159 Mass. 84, 34 N.E. 177 (1893).

Now let us suppose you come to a deed covering the locus, executed by the grantee in the 1915 deed and recorded in 1937. Should you check the grantor index under such grantee's name for any period of time subsequent to 1937? The answer is yes. You should check the grantor index for three more years under the name of the grantee in the 1915 deed because such grantee may have failed to pay real estate taxes, and the city or town may have foreclosed its tax lien on the locus by proceedings against such grantee during such three-year period. Can you safely stop after you have examined the grantor index for three more years? It is not impossible for a deed later recorded to bear a date prior to 1937 and, under some circumstances, it may prevail over the 1937 deed if it is deemed properly recorded so as to give notice to subsequent purchasers. In some states the earlier, though later-recorded, deed is deemed a part of the record.[45] In this situation the Massachusetts court[46] has applied the reasoning it refused to apply, though strongly urged, in the converse case of estoppel by deed and ruled that one need not examine the index under each owner from the time such owner acquired title to date, but may safely ignore each owner after such owner has given a good deed, except, of course, for the three-year tax period.

Now suppose that during that three-year period you actually see another deed out indexed. The index will recite the date of recording (not the date of the deed or the date of delivery). Is it safe, following Morse v. Curtis, to

---

43.   Bates v. Norcross, 34 Mass. (17 Pick.) 14 (1835).
44.   Mount Washington Cooperative Bank v. Bernard, 289 Mass. 498, 194 N.E. 839 (1935).
45.   Woods v. Garnett, 72 Miss. 78, 16 So. 390 (1894).
46.   Morse v. Curtis, 140 Mass. 112, 2 N.E. 929 (1885).

ignore it, having seen the index reference? Toupin v. Peabody[47] indicates that you will not be affected by mere inquiry notice. Nevertheless, there is danger that a jury would find that you had seen it and reported it to your client.[48]

e. *Completing the search of the grantor index.* You will recall that we assumed a situation where you started your search of the grantor index in 1915 and you found a deed in 1937 out of the grantee in the 1915 deed. You are now ready to transfer your attention to the grantor index for the year 1937 under the name of the new record owner to see what conveyances were made by that person during the time he or she owned the land. This process is repeated until you have traced the title through the names of all the persons in the chain of title or until you come to one who has made no deed which is of record. You will know, if you have made a complete backward search, whether any of the persons in your chain of title transferred an interest by descent or devise. Such knowledge you will have gained in picking up the thread in your backward search when your last grantor did not appear in the grantee index. Even if you were given a very early title reference and thus spared the necessity of a backward search, as you come down in the grantor index and you find no deed therein from the last grantee, your search in the registry of probate is very much simpler than on a backward search because you know the name of the decedent. Even though you know when you start your search in the grantor index that the particular person devised the land by will, you must run that person's name in the grantor index as fully as all others to make sure that person did not do something with it before that person died (not forgetting the three-year carry-over after death for a tax deed).

Problem

29.6. Assume the record contains the following instruments:
a. Deed from A to B, dated July 1, 1915, acknowledged September 15, 1916 and recorded December 1, 1931.
b. Deed from B to C, dated June 1, 1950, acknowledged on the same date and recorded two days later.

Your client is buying from C. What names will you run in the grantor index and for what period of time?

5. *Sundry Matters*

a. *Mortgages.*[49] In the course of your search, you may find that the land has been mortgaged from time to time. Mortgages are indexed in the grantor

---

47. 162 Mass. 473, 39 N.E. 280 (1895).
48. Hughes v. Williams, 218 Mass. 448, 105 N.E. 1056 (1914).
49. American Law of Property §18.89 (Casner ed. 1952).

index in the same manner as deeds. If a mortgage is assigned or discharged, the instrument by which this is accomplished will refer to the volume and page where the mortgage is recorded, and, upon receipt for record, it is the duty of the register to make an appropriate reference in the margin of the page where the mortgage is recorded.[50] As a general rule, therefore, old mortgages that are discharged of record will so appear at a glance, and it will only be necessary to examine the discharge to see that it is in proper form and effective, and not necessary to run the grantor index under the name of the mortgagee, even though Massachusetts is a "title-theory" state. It is unlikely that the mortgagor would have paid and taken a discharge from anyone but the record holder of the mortgage who at the same time would be required to deliver up the note. Of course, if the mortgage is outstanding, you will not let your client deal with anyone who cannot produce the note which is secured by the mortgage. It seems to be assumed that mortgagees don't have troubles with creditors of their own who might attach the mortgagee's interest in equity, or with bankruptcy. Furthermore, it is possible that taxes now in arrears might have been assessed on the locus in the name of the mortgagee, but all conveyancers rely on the fact that in practice this is never done. Here, again, practice and theory diverge.

You may find that your title derives from a mortgagee under a foreclosed mortgage. If so, you will note and abstract carefully the steps in foreclosure to make sure of its validity. The essential elements will be recorded in the registry of deeds, so that resort to outside records will not be necessary. In Massachusetts, a mortgage may be foreclosed in three ways:[51] by entry,[52] by action,[53] or by exercise of the power of sale[54] contained in the usual statutory form of mortgage. Foreclosure by action is relatively rare, but most mortgagees foreclose both by entry and sale. Thus, if they slip up on the technicalities of the sale, the entry and possession thereunder will ripen into good title in three years. For the entry to be effective, a certificate thereof must be recorded within thirty days thereafter. An effective sale must comply with the terms of the power in the mortgage and the requirements of the statute.[55] The statute[56] requires the person selling to record, within thirty days, a copy of the notice and an affidavit as to the circumstances of the sale. This must be examined to make sure that the requirements of the power of sale and of the statute have in all respects been complied with.[57]

Since World War II, mortgagees have had to comply with the federal Soldiers' and Sailors' Civil Relief Act[58] by obtaining from the superior court

50. This duty is imposed by Mass. Gen. Laws ch. 36, §21.
51. All set forth in Mass. Gen. Laws ch. 244.
52. §§1, 2.
53. §§1, 3-13.
54. §§11-16.
55. §14.
56. §15.
57. Tamburello v. Monahan, 321 Mass. 445, 73 N.E.2d 734, (1947).
58. 50 U.S.C.A. §532; 54 Stat. 1182, as amended; 56 Stat. 771, 772.

or the land court an order authorizing foreclosure. A statute[59] provides that a recorded copy of such an order shall be conclusive evidence of such compliance.

b. *Tax titles.*[60] Sometimes, in running the title back through the grantee index you will find a tax deed or taking in your chain of title.[61] If this tax title has not been foreclosed, you will report the title as bad without going further because, under the statute,[62] any person having an interest in the land, at any time prior to foreclosure, may redeem it by paying the amount stated in the tax deed with interest at $16\frac{1}{2}$ percent, plus a small fee for examination of title and a deed of release.

However, you may find that the right of redemption has been foreclosed by a decree of the land court.[63] If all parties in interest received notice of the proceedings, the holder of the tax title will have good and clear title to the property involved. Ryder v. Garden Estate, Inc., 329 Mass. 10, 105 N.E.2d 852 (1952).

If you find a tax deed outstanding against your chain of title which is redeemable, then it will be necessary to obtain from the record holder a release of all the items in the tax account secured by the tax deed. If the record holder is still the town or city, this will include taxes accruing since the year for which the tax deed was made.[64]

c. *Trusts.* You will often find that the title has passed through trusts of various sorts: testamentary or inter vivos. Among the latter are the very common Massachusetts business trusts and the so-called nominee trust, which are especially popular for investments in real estate. In the case of a testamentary trust, you will want to make sure that the trustees properly qualified in the probate court, and you will examine carefully the terms of the will to make sure that the trustees had adequate power to sell and convey, if they sold before the trust terminated. If the trust terminated before the property was sold, you will examine the language by which the testator disposed of the remainder to see whether the trustees or the remaindermen were the proper parties to make conveyance. Probably you will find that someone has required all of them to join, out of abundance of caution.

If it is an inter vivos trust, you will make the same study of the deed or declaration of trust. The latter may or may not be recorded in the same county, being a lengthy and expensive instrument to record, as a rule.

Until 1959, the worst thing you could find in a title examination was a deed describing the grantee as a "trustee" and nothing more. This "undisclosed trust" has been held to be a defect warranting rejection of the title, and there seems to be no way to cure it, short of proceedings in the land

---

59. Mass. Gen. Laws ch. 244, §14.
60. American Law of Property §18.67 (Casner ed. 1952).
61. Under Mass. Gen. Laws ch. 60, §§45, 54.
62. Mass. Gen. Laws ch. 60, §62.
63. Sections 64 through 73 and section 75 of chapter 60. Section 75 provides for recording and indexing the decree in the registry of deeds.
64. Mass. Gen. Laws ch. 60, §61.

court, because everyone is on notice that someone has a beneficial interest, but no one knows who can release it. Affidavits and confirmatory deeds by the grantor won't do it, because the grantor has become a stranger, and, a fortiori, releases from strangers claiming to be beneficiaries will not do it.[65] This unhappy state of affairs has been cured by Mass. Gen. Laws ch. 184, §25, cl. 3, which relieves purchasers, otherwise bona fide, of the burden of inquiring into the trust.

The absence of stamps, denoting that no consideration was furnished by the grantee, might be considered to put everyone on notice of a resulting trust for the grantor, but a statute provides protection for later purchasers in good faith.[66]

d. *Corporations.* A corporation may hold title to land. Where the title has derived from a corporation, you will want a certificate by the clerk recorded, showing a proper vote by the directors (or by the stockholders if the property sold or mortgaged is all the property of the corporation) authorizing the conveyance and the execution, sealing, acknowledgment, and delivery of the deed by the person who actually appears to have done all these things. This authority may appear from recorded extracts from the bylaws, plus a certificate of the officer's due election to his or her position. It is not necessary to demand a copy of all the bylaws, if all the foregoing appear, because any inconsistent limitation of authority has been held to be a secret limitation on the agent's apparent authority and not binding on a bona fide purchaser.[67] Mass. Gen. Laws ch. 155, §8, provides that the deed may be executed by the president and the treasurer of the corporation, in which event a corporate vote is not necessary.

It is customary, nevertheless, to insist on the corporate seal being actually affixed, notwithstanding the statute[68] which provides that the recital of a seal is sufficient. The reason commonly given is that the bylaws may specially require it. This seems inconsistent with the rule against secret limitations, but you will find it a lot easier to put the seal on than to argue with the diehards.

The same principles apply to foreign corporations, with special attention to the laws of its home state where there is any question of authority. Logically, foreign corporations ought to be required to comply with the statutes[69] relating to qualification in Massachusetts, but this does not seem to be insisted upon very often.

Charitable, municipal, and public service corporations are sui generis. Fortunately they do not engage in a great deal of real estate activity. When they do, their acts require special study. For ordinary business corporations

---

65. Cleval v. Sullivan, 258 Mass. 348, 154 N.E. 920 (1927).
66. Mass. Gen. Laws ch. 203, §3.
67. Boston Food Products Co. v. Wilson & Co., 245 Mass. 550, 139 N.E. 637 (1923).
68. Mass. Gen. Laws ch. 4, §9A.
69. Mass. Gen. Laws ch. 181, §§3, 5.

the acquisition and conveyance of real estate can be assumed to be intra vires.

If a corporation sells or transfers all or substantially all of its assets situated in the commonwealth, it must, at least five days in advance,[70] notify the commissioner of corporations and taxation, file all necessary tax returns, and pay all corporate taxes due from it. Otherwise the commonwealth has a lien on all the corporation's assets in the commonwealth. This lien can be, and usually is, waived and it terminates three years after the sale or transfer, unless enforced.

e. *Liens of various kinds.* Some encumbrances will appear, recorded in the grantor index under the name of the person assessed as owner, because the statutes authorizing the creation of these encumbrances require recording.[71] Other encumbrances, such as unpaid taxes and water rates, may appear of record if foreclosure has begun, because the statutes providing for collection by foreclosure on the land require recording of a notice.[72] If such a notice has been recorded, the encumbrance can be removed only by a discharge in proper form, executed by the collector of taxes for the town or city and likewise recorded. However, unpaid taxes, municipal electric charges, and water rates are a lien on the property even before such a notice is recorded,[73] and to guard against such unrecorded liens it is necessary to apply to the collector of taxes for a "certificate of municipal liens," the fee for which is fixed by statute.[74]

Unfortunately, this certificate is not binding on the town or city unless recorded, and even then, not as to taxes, rates, and charges accruing within three years immediately preceding the date of the certificate; and if the collector has made an error, the certificate will not prevent the town from enforcing its lien.[75] However, it will protect you from a charge of negligence. Since a recording of a municipal lien certificate in some circumstances may operate to discharge the lien for any taxes, assessments, or portions thereof which do not appear on the certificate, the conveyancing bar now records municipal lien certificates in all instances where available at the time of the conveyance. Since a recorded alienation of the property will cut off all liens for taxes after two years, there is little point in recording the certificate when a conveyance is contemplated. Theoretically, the certificate should be recorded when only a mortgage is contemplated, but few conveyancers bother to do so.

---

70. Mass. Gen. Laws ch. 63, §76.
71. For examples, see Mass. Gen. Laws ch. 254, §§1 and 2 (mechanics' and contractors' liens); §§25, 26 (the police chief's lien for the expense of removing obstructions in gaming houses); I.R.C. §§6321-6326 (1954) (federal tax liens generally).
72. Mass. Gen. Laws ch. 40, §42B (water rates); ch. 60, §37 (taxes).
73. Mass. Gen. Laws ch. 60, §37 (taxes) and ch. 40, §42A (water rates).
74. Mass. Gen. Laws ch. 60, §23.
75. Graton v. Cambridge, 250 Mass. 317, 145 N.E. 453 (1924).

Debts of the estate, unpaid pecuniary legacies,[76] and federal[77] and state[78] death taxes are also liens on real estate passing by devise or descent. The existence of these is suggested by the probate records, and can be cleared from the title only by receipts or waivers duly filed. It is true that section 6324(a) (2) of the Internal Revenue Code of 1954 provides that the locus shall be divested of the lien for federal estate taxes upon sale to a bona fide purchaser for an adequate consideration, but no conveyancer will rely on this. Why this should be is not clear, unless each suspects his client of not being a bona fide purchaser. Of course, every deed lacking revenue stamps may be a gift in contemplation of death, or subject to a gift tax, but no one tries to do anything about that. Also, you must bear in mind that property passing to the survivor in the case of a joint tenancy or a tenancy by the entireties may be subject to a lien for federal and Massachusetts estate taxes. In this regard, keep in mind that the decedent may have had life insurance, so that the probate inventory may be a very unreliable indication of the inventory for tax purposes.

Certain state environmental laws may affect title. For example, if hazardous waste has been disposed on land, no interest in that land can be conveyed or leased until notice of that fact has been recorded in the registry. Mass. Gen. Laws ch. 21(c), §7. Additionally, the state "Superfund" law, Mass. Gen. Laws ch. 21(e), empowers the state department of environmental quality engineering (DEQE) to arrange for response actions in the event of a release or threat of release of oil or hazardous materials and provides that if any liability to the commonwealth arises by virtue of the statute the commonwealth may place a lien on the property of the responsible parties. Such a lien takes priority over all other liens and, in the case of real property, must be filed in and recorded in the appropriate registry. Coastal and inland wetlands may also be subject to restrictive orders imposed by state or local conservation commissions. Such orders, along with the plan of the affected land and the list of the assessed owners, must be recorded in the registry of deeds or the office of the assistant Recorder for the district where the land lies. Mass. Gen. Laws ch. 131, §40 et seq.

f. *Eminent domain.* A notice of eminent domain proceedings under the authority of the commonwealth[79] must be recorded; but it is possible, under the eminent domain statutes, that a person's land may be taken without

---

76.   Mahoney v. Nollman, 309 Mass. 522, 35 N.E.2d 265 (1941) (on residuary real estate).

77.   I.R.C. §6324 (1954). The requirement that federal tax liens generally must be recorded does not apply to federal estate tax liens, see Detroit Bank v. U.S., 317 U.S. 329, 63 S. Ct. 297 (1943).

78.   Mass. Gen. Laws ch. 65, §9. This section was completely reworded in Acts of 1957, ch. 502. If the land is sold by someone entitled to sell it pursuant to a decree of the probate court, the lien is discharged on the land and attaches to the proceeds in the case of resident decedents, and upon certain conditions of notice to the commissioner of corporations and taxation in the case of nonresident decedents. Elaborate limitations are placed on the time that the lien may run against the property, ranging from about ten to twenty-five years under different conditions.

79.   Mass. Gen. Laws chs. 79, 80A.

notice to him or her, and, a fortiori, without any indication of it in the grantor schedule under his or her name. The town or city is expected to use good faith and reasonable intelligence toward notifying the owner, but lack of notice does not invalidate the taking.[80] One method of protection against such an unindexed taking is to examine the plans recorded in the registry, which are indexed by streets. An order for taking, under the statute,[81] or of intention to take under the statute,[82] unlike an order for betterment assessments,[83] is not required to refer to a plan; but, as a practical matter today, all takings are by plan and such plans are usually recorded, and if you look at the plan index and perhaps consult the city engineers, you have done all that can reasonably be expected. Certainly you cannot run the grantee schedule for fifty years under the town, the county, the commonwealth, and all the public and private corporations that may have the power of eminent domain. However, strange as it may seem, this risk of being burned by a taking without notice is as great after your client has paid money and taken a deed or mortgage and, not unreasonably, thinks it unnecessary to return to the registry again and again to check up on the state of the title.[84]

From 1888 to 1951, Congress provided that federal eminent domain proceedings should conform to state practice, "as near as may be."[85] It has never been decided whether this includes a requirement of recording. The question has never arisen, because it has been the custom of United States Attorneys to record the petition or the judgment, or both, as a matter of courtesy to the bar. In 1951, with the adoption of rule 71A of the Federal Rules of Civil Procedure, conformity to state practice was replaced by uniformity of federal practice, and no provision at all is made for recording. Fortunately, the United States Attorney for Massachusetts still adheres to the custom of recording as a courtesy. The conveyancing bar should realize, however, that we depend entirely upon his or her good nature for any recorded warning of a federal taking.

g. *Access to land.* You will also be concerned with means of access to your land. The office of the city engineer or a reliable atlas will show you whether a way leading to or by the locus is a public way. If it is not, you must ascertain, and report whether or not the seller is able to grant good and sufficient rights of record in the way.

h. *Partition.* Sometimes, in running the title back, you may find a deed from commissioners appointed by the probate court to make partition.[86] If the partition is by sale, the order of court should be examined in the probate records, to see that it was fully complied with. If the partition is by division, a

---

80. Barnes v. Peck, 283 Mass. 618, 187 N.E. 176 (1933); Grove Hall Savings Bank v. Dedham, 284 Mass. 92, 187 N.E. 182 (1933).
81. Mass. Gen. Laws ch. 79.
82. Mass. Gen. Laws ch. 80A.
83. Mass. Gen. Laws ch. 80.
84. Grove Hall Savings Bank v. Dedham, footnote 80 *supra.*
85. See former section 258 of title 40, United States Code.
86. Mass. Gen. Laws ch. 241.

copy of the decree, certified by the register of probate will be recorded in the registry of deeds, and will bind all the co-tenants. Unlike the foreclosure of a tax title in the land court, the decree of the probate court in partition proceedings is not binding upon a person who has not appeared and who has a title paramount to all the co-tenants. The statute[87] expressly gives such a person a right to maintain an action for the land against any or all of the parties, or persons holding under them. Consequently, it is necessary to carry the title examination on beyond the partition. However, the statute[88] also authorizes the court to direct an examination of the title if it seems useful or desirable. If this has been done, the probate file may contain material of great assistance to you in working your way back through the title.

i. *Litigation affecting locus.*[89] Occasionally you will find in the superior court records or even in Massachusetts Reports that a question of fact or law relating to your locus has been adjudicated. There is no systematic way of finding this, however. A statute[90] provides that the recording of certified copies of decrees of the supreme judicial or superior court shall have the same effect as the recording of deeds, and another statute[91] provides that a judgment or decree rendered after June 8, 1892, affecting title to land, binds only the parties, their heirs and devisees and persons having notice, unless a certified copy has been recorded. This takes care of writs of entry and bills in equity to quiet title to the locus, but questions of law or fact may be raised by your abstract to which the answer may be furnished, by the principle of res adjudicata, by a decision in a case outside the scope of section 17. For example, in Amory v. Amherst College,[92] it was adjudicated that a trust, subject to which land had been conveyed in 1844, had been eliminated by repudiation in 1879 and subsequent lapse of time. From all that appeared of record, the land was still subject to the trust in 1946, and examiners in that year properly declined to pass the title until we called their attention to this case.

Pending litigation in state or federal courts may affect the title to land directly or indirectly, notice of which is often recorded by means of a lis pendens. Mass. Gen. Laws ch. 184, §15. In the courts of the commonwealth, land may be directly affected by actions at law,[93] by suits in equity,[94] by

---

87. Mass. Gen. Laws ch. 241, §21.
88. Mass. Gen. Laws ch. 241, §17.
89. American Law of Property §§18.84 (Casner ed. 1952).
90. Mass. Gen. Laws ch. 183, §44.
91. Mass. Gen. Laws ch. 184, §17.
92. 229 Mass. 374, 118 N.E. 933 (1918).
93. Writs of entry, Mass. Gen. Laws ch. 237; writs of dower, Mass. Gen. Laws ch. 238; summary process for possession, Mass. Gen. Laws ch. 239; Sheehan Construction Co. v. Dudley, 299 Mass. 51, 12 N.E.2d 182 (1937); foreclosure by action, Mass. Gen. Laws, ch. 244, §§3-10.
94. To quiet title, Mass. Gen. Laws ch. 240, §§6-10; to reach and apply property fraudulently conveyed, Mass. Gen. Laws ch. 214, §3(d); to interpret written instruments, Mass. Gen. Laws, ch. 213, §3 (10A); or under general equity jurisdiction, to establish trusts, to compel

petitions to the land court,[95] or by proceedings in the probate courts.[96] At common law, pendency of the litigation is constructive notice to all persons.[97] However, it is provided by statute that writ of entry or other proceeding, either at law or in equity, which affects the title to real property or the use and occupation thereof or the buildings thereon, shall not bind bona fide purchasers until a memorandum is recorded.[98] This does not apply to proceedings other than proceedings in equity in the probate courts. Nevertheless, either inherently or by special provision, you are reasonably safe from the probate courts. If the owner of land lived to make a deed, you can disregard the risk of probate jurisdiction arising from administration of decedents' estates. If the owner has become insane or a spendthrift and a guardian or conservator has been appointed, provision has been made for recording notice thereof, which makes void the ward's deed thereafter.[99] Recording this notice does not seem to be a prerequisite to the validity of the guardian's deed, but the guardian has got to get a license, on such notice as the court may order,[100] which may include recording, and it is unlikely that anyone who took a deed from a guardian which did not recite the guardian's capacity and the name of the ward, could avoid a strong imputation of fraud. Of course, if the ward's name is recited in the deed, it will be indexed under the ward's name. Furthermore, an honest and careful grantee would

---

specific performance of contracts, to set aside deeds procured by fraud, to enjoin continuing trespasses, or to compel re-execution and delivery of lost or wrongfully withheld deeds, Mass. Gen. Laws ch. 214, §1.

95. For registration, Mass. Gen. Laws ch. 185; to require action to try title, Mass. Gen. Laws ch. 240, §§1-5; to determine the validity of encumbrances, Mass. Gen. Laws ch. 240, §§11-14; to obtain a discharge of mortgages, Mass. Gen. Laws ch. 240, §15; to determine the boundaries of flats, Mass. Gen. Laws ch. 240, §§19-26; to determine the existence and extent of a power to sell, Mass. Gen. Laws ch. 240, §§27-28; to register a right of way for public access to a great pond, Mass. Gen. Laws, ch. 91, §18A; or to foreclose tax titles, Mass. Gen. Laws ch. 60, §§64-75.

96. The Probate Courts have jurisdiction in general of probate of wills, of administration of estates; of guardians and conservators; of adoption; of change of name; and of divorce; Mass. Gen. Laws ch. 215, §3. They also have had, since 1964, general equity jurisdiction, except for labor disputes; Mass. Gen. Laws ch. 215, §6. They have jurisdiction to enforce specific performance of decedents' contracts for land, to compel reconveyance of decedents' land improperly held, to cancel decedents' deeds, Mass. Gen. Laws ch. 204, §1; to authorize the sale of land dependent on the consent of deceased persons, Mass. Gen. Laws ch. 204, §2, or subject to future interests or annuities, Mass. Gen. Laws ch. 183, §§49-52; to sell land of a deceased person or a ward to pay his debts, Mass. Gen. Laws ch. 202, §§1, 2, 5, and 21, or free of dower or curtesy, Mass. Gen. Laws ch. 202, §3; to marshal assets, Mass. Gen. Laws ch. 202, §9; to recover land fraudulently conveyed by a deceased person, Mass. Gen. Laws ch. 202, §18; to sell land of a deceased person for distribution, Mass. Gen. Laws ch. 202, §19; or assign dower or curtesy, Mass. Gen. Laws ch. 189 §§1, 10-15; to partition land, Mass. Gen. Laws ch. 241; to assign homestead rights, Mass. Gen. Laws ch. 188, §3; to release dower or curtesy of an insane person, Mass. Gen. Laws ch. 209, §18; and to enforce a lien for legacy and succession taxes due the commonwealth, Mass. Gen. Laws ch. 65, §§21, 31.

97. Haven v. Adams, 90 Mass. (8 Allen) 363 (1864); Steele v. Estabrook, 236 Mass. 252, 128 N.E. 23, (1920).

98. Mass. Gen. Laws ch. 184, §15.

99. Mass. Gen. Laws ch. 201, §10.

100. Mass. Gen. Laws ch. 202, §11.

insist on obtaining and recording an affidavit of notice of the sale.[101] By the same token, if the owner should change his or her name,[102] an honest grantee would insist on a recital of the grantee's former name. So, also, if a single woman marries. Adoption creates an expectancy at most, cut off by sale. Special provision is made in divorce for attachment as at law[103] and enforcement of decrees as in equity.[104] If the probate court assigns to the wife rights in her husband's homestead, the judgment must be recorded.[105] If your landowner disappears or absconds, the probate court may appoint a receiver, but the receiver's title depends upon a recorded notice.[106] Trusts must be recorded.[107] Notice of partition must be recorded "forthwith." [108]

Under Mass. Gen. Laws ch. 216, now repealed, there was no protection against an assignment in insolvency, except examinations of the records of the register of insolvency (same person as the register of probate), in the county where your landowner resided or had a usual place of business for three months. The assignee is supposed to record the assignment,[109] but this requirement has been held to be merely directory and not essential to the vesting of title in the assignee.[110] Fortunately the operation of the state insolvency law has been suspended since 1898 by the federal bankruptcy act,[111] and there is a six-year limitation on actions by assignees.[112]

The federal courts may also acquire jurisdiction over the locus, by diversity of citizenship or otherwise. Fortunately, it has been held in the Fifth Circuit, and strongly intimated in the Supreme Court, that a state statute requiring recording of notice to bind bona fide purchasers pendente lite is a rule of property and applies to litigation in the federal courts also.[113]

Litigation affecting the locus may have gone to judgment. At common law, this judgment would bind the parties and their privies. Even bona fide purchasers would be privies and thus bound. But since 1892, it has been provided by statute that judgments and decrees affecting land must be recorded to bind bona fide purchasers.[114] Presumably this, too, is a rule of property and applies to federal judgments.

---

101.   Mass. Gen. Laws ch. 202, §16. This affidavit, however, may be recorded twenty-four years later, when it would escape most examiners. Thomas v. LeBaron, 43 Mass. (8 Met.) 355 (1844).
102.   Mass. Gen. Laws ch. 210, §§12-14.
103.   Mass. Gen. Laws ch. 208, §§12-14.
104.   Mass. Gen. Laws ch. 208, §35.
105.   Mass. Gen. Laws ch. 188, §3.
106.   Mass. Gen. Laws ch. 200, §2.
107.   Mass. Gen. Laws ch. 203, §2, ch. 184, §25.
108.   Mass. Gen. Laws ch. 241, §7.
109.   Mass. Gen. Laws ch. 216, §52.
110.   Colby v. Shute, 219 Mass. 211, 106 N.E. 1006 (1914).
111.   Deitrick v. Siegel, 313 Mass. 612, 48 N.E.2d 698 (1943); Rogers v. Boston Club, 205 Mass. 261, 91 N.E. 321 (1910); Parmenter Manufacturing Co. v. Hamilton, 172 Mass. 178, 51 N.E. 529 (1898).
112.   Mass. Gen. Laws ch. 216, §60; Colby v. Shute, footnote 110 *supra.*
113.   United States v. Calcasieu Timber Co., 236 F. 196 (5th Cir. 1916). See Romeu v. Todd, 206 U.S. 358, 26 S. Ct. 724 (1907). Contra King v. Davis, 137 F. 198 (W.D. Va. 1903); Stewart v. Wheeling & L.E. Ry., 53 Ohio St. 151, 41 N.E. 247 (1895).
114.   Mass. Gen. Laws ch. 184, §17.

In some states, a judgment affects not only land which is the subject of the controversy, but it is also an automatic lien on all real estate of the judgment debtor in the county where the court was sitting, or even throughout the state. This is not so in Massachusetts. Creditors are enabled to secure their claims by attachment[115] and execution of judgment,[116] both of which must be recorded to be effective. The Federal Rules of Civil Procedure adopt the state practice as to attachments and executions.[117] In addition, a federal statute provides that judgments and decrees rendered in federal courts shall be liens on property throughout the state in the same manner as judgments and decrees of state courts.[118] This was evidently designed for federal courts sitting in states where judgments are automatic liens.

But what of a judgment in a writ of entry, or a decree in a bill in equity directly adjudicating title to the locus? Perhaps the word "lien" in the federal statute can be stretched to cover a judgment for the plaintiff, but by what stretch of the imagination could a judgment for defendant be construed to be a "lien"? Yet a judgment for the defendant in an action brought by the record owner would demolish a record title.

Perhaps the federal courts would follow the reasoning of the *Calcasieu* case (note 113) and hold the Massachusetts statute to be a rule of property and require federal judgments and decrees to be recorded. Until the question has been determined by a federal court, it would seem prudent to examine the federal district court records.[119] But this is rarely done.

j. *Registration as it affects a title chain.* I have already pointed out that this statement is limited to the examination of unregistered land. You may ask, "How shall I know that the land is unregistered?" The statute[120] requires a petitioner for registration to file in the registry of deeds a memorandum stating that the petition has been filed, and a copy of the description, in the petition of the land. Thus, it is impossible for a dishonest person, after registering his title and selling it to A, to sell it again, as unregistered land, to B. Many people are of the opinion that the memorandum should also be indexed under the names of the adjoining owners. The petitioner is required to file in the registration proceedings an affidavit of the assessors as to the abutters according to their records. Without an exhaustive search for mortgagees and other people interested in the abutting parcels, an indexing under the names of the abutting taxpayers would afford, as a practical matter, sufficient assurance that notice of the fixing of the boundary would somehow come to the attention of examiners of the adjoining titles. However, the land court has never seen fit to require this. The petitioner may seek to confirm title in his name, which decree of confirmation will be

115. Mass. Gen. Laws ch. 223, §§63-66.
116. Mass. Gen. Laws ch. 236.
117. Rules 64 and 69.
118. Act of August 1, 1888, ch. 729, §1, 25 Stat. 357, as amended June 25, 1948, ch. 646, 62 Stat. 958, 28 U.S.C.A. §1962.
119. Kooman, Necessity for Searching Federal Court Records in Examining Florida Real Estate Titles, 19 Fla. L.J. 135 (1945); Patton, Titles §654 (2d ed. 1957).
120. Mass. Gen. Laws ch. 185, §27.

recorded, and the title to the premises followed through the registry as unregistered land thereafter.

k. *The state of the law which controls.* Of course, each instrument must be examined in the light of the law as it stood at the time it was executed. This may involve ascertaining both what the supreme judicial court has said the law was, and what conveyancers generally thought the law was. The latter is not conclusive, but it may have some bearing on the intent of the parties to the deed.[121]

l. *The abstract of title.* When your examination of the grantor index is completed, your notes, taken as you proceeded, with a separate sheet for each instrument affecting the title, are arranged in order for incorporation in the abstract of title. The completeness of the abstract will depend on various factors. An abstract which is being prepared for the examination of a senior lawyer must show that all the relevant records were examined, and must present the essential elements of every instrument affecting the locus. It may be prepared on form sheets with different colors for each class of instrument, or it may be prepared on blank sheets. The latter method requires more thought on the part of the abstracter and seems preferable to the former, which may lull the abstracter into doing no more than filling the blanks.

The top sheet of the abstract will contain your conclusion as to the state of the title, listing encumbrances, easements, restrictions, conditions, liens, taxes, legacies, etc., and questions of law which the record raises in your mind. It also gives the date when your examination ends.

The abstract will include tracings, sketches, or photostats of plans and atlas maps of the neighborhood, with courses and distances where they are given, date and north arrow, with the locus outlined in red or green, and with the parcels conveyed by "deeds out" also indicated.

If the land is composed of parcels with separate histories, a note of explanation should appear. A brief summary of the chain of title, with dates, is also customarily set forth.

The abstract will contain the "grantor schedule" of each person, which will show the period during which each name was looked up in the grantor index and will list every instrument found thereunder which might affect the title. A trustworthy abstracter should exercise some independent judgment here and reduce this to manageable proportions. It should be unnecessary to list instruments which the index itself shows as lying in another town. A safe rule is to list in the abstract every instrument affecting land in the same town, together with the brief description set forth in the index. If that does not make it readily apparent that the land affected lies at a distance from your land, it will be necessary to go to the instrument itself and take down enough of the description to make this apparent. If your land is part of a development, the grantor's schedule in the abstract should bear a note as to

---

121. Compare Brown v. Peabody, 228 Mass. 52, 116 N.E. 958 (1917), with Erickson v. Ames, 264 Mass. 436, 163 N.E. 70 (1928).

the absence of restrictions and easements affecting your land imposed thereon by covenants in prior deeds of other land in the development.

Finally, the abstract will contain, on separate sheets, the essential elements of each instrument affecting the title, although many examiners will provide duplicated copies of instruments.

For the conveyancer reading an abstract prepared by someone else, there are many of the elements of a detective story, in that the conveyancer must consider every character who passes through the history of the title as a potential villain and scrutinize every word for clues to villainy (or carelessness, anyway); but there is one important difference, in that the conveyancer cannot tell how the story will come out by looking at the last page.

m. *Title defects not on the record.* One observation should be made. The discussion above concentrates on the finding of things which are a matter of public record and which may affect the land your client is buying. Do not lose sight of the fact that there are things which may affect your client's title which are not required to be made a matter of public record, such as short-term leases and interests acquired by adverse possession.[122] It may be advisable to emphasize to your client the fact that your search is limited to the records, so that non-record inquiries may be made if the client so desires.

n. *Title insurance and survey matters.* With the sale of mortgage notes to the secondary mortgage market, it has become the practice of lending institutions to require a plot plan of property certifying its dimensional accord with the local zoning bylaw, together with information as to its inclusion in a floodplain district, and further to request title insurance insuring against both matters of record and certain matters, such as fraud, which are not revealed by the records.

---

122. For a catalogue of matters which may affect a title which appears on the records to be perfect, see Chaplin, Record Title to Land, 6 Harv. L. Rev. 302 (1893), and Chaplin, The Element of Chance in Land Title, 12 Harv. L. Rev. 24 (1898).

C H A P T E R   3 0

TITLE REGISTRATION[1]

Note: *Sir Richard Torrens and the Growth and Variation of His System*

The recording acts, as we have seen, provide for the recording of instruments of conveyance, and it is up to the purchaser through the purchaser's attorney to examine the instruments on the record and formulate conclusions as to their effect on the title. Title registration, as its name might indicate, is designed to provide a public record of the state of the title itself, so that the purchaser of land is not called upon to formulate conclusions in this regard.

The difference between the recording acts and title registration was expressed by Chief Justice Start of Minnesota in State ex rel. Douglas v. Westfall, 85 Minn. 437, 89 N.W. 175 (1902), as follows:

> The basic principle of this system is the registration of the title of land, instead of registering, as the old system requires, the evidence of such title. In the one case only the ultimate fact or conclusion that a certain named party has title to a particular tract of land is registered, and a certificate thereof delivered to him. In the other the entire evidence, from which proposed purchasers must, at their peril, draw such conclusion, is registered. [85 Minn. at 438, 89 N.W. at 175.]

The use of the system of title registration by the English-speaking countries was started by Sir Richard Torrens in Australia, and the title registration acts are sometimes called the Torrens acts because of this origin. Torrens had been in the office concerned with the registration of the title of ships, and when his interests were transferred to land titles, he evidently conceived the idea of registering the title to land in the same manner as the title to a ship was registered.

---

1. See Goldner, The Torrens System of Title Registration: A New Proposal for Effective Implementation, 29 U.C.L.A.L. Rev. 661 (1982). See generally American Law of Property §§17.37-17.48 (Casner ed. 1952).

Only a limited number of states have enacted statutes providing for the registration of title to land. Such statutes exist in Colorado, Georgia, Hawaii, Illinois, Massachusetts, Minnesota, Nebraska, New York, North Carolina, Ohio, South Dakota, Tennessee, Utah, Virginia, and Washington.[2] In these states, the old recording system is not replaced because the registration of a title is not compulsory. In fact the voluntary registration of titles by landowners has proceeded at a very slow pace, so that in these states the old system continues to predominate in connection with conveyances of land.

You may ask why this is so. You may or may not get an answer to this question that will satisfy you. The controversy between those who would adhere to the old system and those who would abolish it in favor of the new system has been quite heated at times. See, for example, Powell, Registration of the Title to Land in the State of New York (1938), in favor of the old system, and a review of Professor Powell's book by McDougal and Brabner-Smith in 48 Yale L.J. 1125 (1939) entitled Land Title Transfer: A Regression, condemning Professor Powell's conclusions.[3]

The language of the local statute which permits the registration of the title to land must be carefully examined to ascertain the method of obtaining a registered title, the effect it has on possible claimants of an interest in the land, and the steps to be taken to transfer a title once it is registered.

When the necessary steps have been taken to register the title to land, a certificate of title is issued. The original is kept on file, and a duplicate is issued to the owner. All future transactions with respect to the registered land will be noted on the certificate of title. When a transfer is made of the registered land, the transferor's certificate of title is canceled and a new certificate of title is issued to the transferee. The case that follows considers what may happen if the certificate of title gets into the hands of someone other than the owner.

ELIASON v. WILBORN
281 U.S. 457, 50 S. Ct. 382 (1930)

Appeal from a judgment of the Supreme Court of Illinois affirming the dismissal of a petition under the state Torrens Act for the cancellation of certain deeds and certificates of title, and for other relief.

2. California repealed its Torrens act in 1955, effective April 30, 1955.
3. See also on the Torrens system of title registration McCall, The Torrens System, After Thirty-Five Years, 10 N.C.L. Rev. 329 (1932); Patton, The Torrens System of Land Title Registration, 19 Minn. L. Rev. 519 (1935); Fairchild & Springer, A Criticism of Prof. Richard R. Powell's book entitled Registration of Title to Land in the State of New York, 24 Cornell L.Q. 557 (1939); Bordwell, The Resurrection of Registration of Title, 7 U. Chi. L. Rev. 470 (1940); McDougal, Title Registration and Land Law Reform; a Reply, 8 U. Chi. L. Rev. 63 (1940); Johnson, Rights Arising Under Federal Law Versus the Torrens Systems, 9 Miami L.Q. 258 (1955); Maher, Registered Land—Revisited, 8 Case W. Res. L. Rev. 162 (1957); Head, Torrens System in Alberta; A Dream in Operation, 35 Can. B. Rev. 1 (1957); Davies, "New Look" for the Torrens System in New South Wales, 34 Austl. L.J. 257 (1961); Fiflis, Land Transfer Improvement: The Basic Facts and Two Hypotheses for Reform, 38 U. Colo. L. Rev. 431 (1966).

Mr. Justice HOLMES delivered the opinion of the court.

The appellants had been holders of a certificate of title under the Torrens Act of Illinois. As a result of negotiations they entrusted this certificate to one Napletone, who is alleged to have presented it together with a forged conveyance to himself to the Registrar and by those means to have obtained from the Registrar a new certificate of title in Napletone, on May 19, 1926. Napletone a few days later sold and conveyed to the Wilborns, appellees, whose good faith is not questioned. After the Wilborns had bought but before a new certificate was issued to them, they had notice of the appellant's claim and the appellants notified the Registrar of the forgery and demanded a cancellation of the deeds and certificates to Napletone and the Wilborns and the issue of a certificate to themselves. The Registrar refused and this petition is brought to compel him to do what the appellants demand. It was dismissed on demurrer by the Circuit Court of the State, and the judgment was affirmed by the Supreme Court. 335 Ill. 352. The Supreme Court construed the statutes as giving title to the Wilborns, who purchased in reliance upon the certificate held by Napletone. Whether we are bound to or not we accept that construction and its result. The petitioners appealed to this Court on the ground that the statute, construed as it was construed below, deprived the appellants of their property without due process of law contrary to the Constitution of the United States, by making the certificate of title issued by the Registrar upon a forged deed without notice to them conclusive against them.

The sections objected to are appended. They are as in the original Act of 1897, except §40, amended by the Laws 1925, p. 250.[4]

The appellants seem to claim a constitutional right to buy land that has been brought under the Torrens Act free from the restrictions that that Act

---

4. §40:

The registered owner of any estate or interest in land brought under this Act shall, except in cases of fraud to which he is a party, or of the person through whom he claims without valuable consideration paid in good faith, hold the same subject to the charges hereinabove set forth and also only to such estate, mortgages, liens, charges and interests as may be noted in the last certificate of title in the registrar's office and free from all others except:

(1) Any subsisting lease or agreement for a lease for a period not exceeding five years, where there is actual occupation of the land under the lease. The term lease shall include a verbal letting. [Eliminated in 1929.]

(2) General taxes for the calendar year in which the certificate of title is issued, and special taxes or assessments which have not been confirmed.

(3) Such right of appeal, writ of error, right to appear and contest the application, and action to make counterclaim as is allowed by this Act.

§42:

Except in case of fraud, and except as herein otherwise provided, no person taking a transfer of registered land, or any estate or interest therein, or of any charge upon the same, from the registered owner shall be held to inquire into the circumstances under which or the consideration for which such owner or any previous registered owner was registered, or be affected with notice, actual or constructive, of any unregistered trust, lien, claim, demand or interest; and the knowledge that an unregistered trust, lien, claim, demand or interest is in existence shall not of itself be imputed as fraud.

imposes. But they have no right of any kind to buy it unless the present owner assents, and if, as in this case, the owner from whom the appellants bought, offered and sold nothing except a Torrens title we do not perceive how they can complain that that is all that they got. Even if the restrictions were of a kind that was open to constitutional objection, the appellants bought knowing them and got what they paid for, and knew that they were liable to lose their title without having parted with it and without being heard. Even if they had been the original holders under the Torrens Act and had attempted to save their supposed rights by protest the answer would be that they were under no compulsion when they came into the system, that an elaborate plan was offered of which the provisions objected to were an

---

§46:

The bringing of land under this act shall imply an agreement which shall run with the land that the same shall be subject to the terms of the act and all amendments and alterations thereof. And all dealings with land or any estate or interest therein, after the same has been brought under this act, and all liens, incumbrances and charges upon the same, subsequent to the first registration thereof, shall be deemed to be subject to the terms of this act.

§47:

A registered owner of land desiring to transfer his whole estate or interest therein, or some distinct part or parcel thereof, or some undivided interest therein, or to grant out of his estate an estate for life or for a term of not less than ten years, may execute to the intended transferee a deed or instrument of conveyance in any form authorized by law for that purpose. And upon filing such deed or other instrument in the registrar's office and surrendering to the registrar the duplicate certificate of title, and upon its being made to appear to the registrar that the transferee [*sic*] has the title or interest proposed to be transferred and is entitled to make the conveyance, and that the transferee has the right to have such estate or interest transferred to him, he shall make out and register as hereinbefore provided a new certificate and also an owner's duplicate certifying the title to the estate or interest in the land desired to be conveyed to be in the transferee, and shall note upon the original and duplicate certificate the date of the transfer, the name of the transferee and the volume and folium in which the new certificate is registered, and shall stamp across the original and surrendered duplicate certificate the word "canceled."

§54:

A deed, mortgage lease or other instrument purporting to convey, transfer, mortgage, lease, charge or otherwise deal with registered land, or any estate or interest therein, or charge upon the same, other than a will or a lease not exceeding five years where the land is in actual possession of the lessee or his assigns, shall take effect only by way of contract between the parties thereto, and as authority to the registrar to register the transfer, mortgage, lease, charge or other dealing upon compliance with the terms of this act. On the completion of such registration, the land, estate, interest or charge shall become transferred, mortgaged, leased, charged or dealt with according to the purport and terms of the deed, mortgage, lease or other instrument.

§58 (omitting immaterial parts):

In the event of a duplicate certificate of title being lost, mislaid or destroyed, the owner . . . may make affidavit . . . and the registrar, if satisfied, as to the truth of such affidavit and the bona fides of the transaction, shall issue to the owner a certified copy of the original certificate . . . and such certified copy shall stand in the place of and have like effect as the missing duplicate certificate.

important part, and that they could take it as it was or let it alone. There are plenty of cases in which a man may lose his title when he does not mean to. If he entrusts a check indorsed in blank to a servant or friend he takes his chance. So when he entrusts goods to a bailee under some factors' acts that are well known. So, more analogous to the present case, a man may be deprived of a title by one who has none; as when an owner who has conveyed his property by a deed not yet recorded executes a second deed to another person who takes and records the later deed without notice of the former. There are few constitutional rights that may not be waived.

But there is a narrower ground on which the appellants must be denied their demand. The statute requires the production of the outstanding certificate, as a condition to the issue of a new one. The appellants saw fit to entrust it to Napletone and they took the risk. They say that according to the construction of the act adopted the Registrar's certificate would have had the same effect even if the old certificate had not been produced. But that, if correct, is no answer. Presumably the Registrar will do his duty, and if he does he will require the old certificate to be handed in. It does not justify the omission of a precaution that probably would be sufficient, to point out that a dishonest official could get around it. There is not the slightest reason to suppose that Napletone would have got a certificate on which the Wilborns could rely without the delivery of the old one by the appellants. As between two innocent persons one of whom must suffer the consequence of a breach of trust the one who made it possible by his act of confidence must bear the loss.

Decree affirmed.[5]

Problems

30.1. If a state attempted to make title registration compulsory, does Eliason v. Wilborn indicate that such state action would be unconstitutional?[6]

30.2. The following statute was in force in Illinois at the time of Eliason v. Wilborn:

Any person sustaining loss or damage through any omission, mistake or misfeasance of the registrar, or of any examiner of titles, or of any deputy or clerk of the registrar in the performance of their respective duties under the provisions of this act, and any persons wrongfully deprived of any land or any interest therein, through the bringing of the same under the provisions of this

---

5. See Annot., 42 A.L.R.2d 1387 (1955), entitled Transferees Entitled to Protection Under Torrens Act Certificate of Title. — Eds.

6. See Fairchild & Gluck, Various Aspects of Compulsory Land Title Registration, 15 N.Y.U.L.Q. Rev. 545 (1938); Moore, Compulsory Conversion to Torrens Title — An Admission of Failure? 40 Austl. L.J. 190 (1966).

act, or by the registration of any other person as owner of such land, or by any mistake, omission or misdescription in any certificate, or in any entry or memorandum in the register book, or by any cancellation, and who by the provisions of this act is barred or in any way precluded from bringing an action for the recovery of such land or interest therein, or claim upon the same, shall have a right of action for the damages thus sustained against the county in which such land shall be registered, and may file a claim with the county board, or bring an action at law against the county in which said land is situated for the recovery of such damages. [Ill. Rev. Stat. ch. 30, §138.]

Could the appellants in Eliason v. Wilborn have recovered for the loss they sustained under the terms of this statute?

Note: *Reliance on Certificate of Title*

If a purchaser can rely on the certificate of title held by the seller, the purchaser receives much greater protection than when unregistered land is the subject of the sale. To the extent that interests in others that are not noted on the certificate of title can be asserted against the purchaser, an examination of some kind must be made outside the certificate of title in order for the purchaser to know the real state of the title.

In this regard, the following sections of chapter 185 of the Massachusetts General Laws are relevant:

§46. *Encumbrances affecting certificates of title.* Every plaintiff receiving a certificate of title in pursuance of a judgment of registration, and every subsequent purchaser of registered land taking a certificate of title for value and in good faith, shall hold the same free from all encumbrances except those noted on the certificate, and any of the following encumbrances which may be existing:

First, Liens, claims or rights arising or existing under the laws or constitution of the United States or the statutes of this commonwealth which are not by law required to appear of record in the registry of deeds in order to be valid against subsequent purchasers or encumbrances of record.

Second, Taxes, within two years after they have been committed to the collector.

Third, Any highway, town way, or any private way laid out under section twenty-one of chapter eighty-two, if the certificate of title does not state that the boundary of such way has been determined.

Fourth, Any lease for a term not exceeding seven years.

Fifth, Any liability to assessment for betterments or other statutory liability, except for taxes payable to the commonwealth, which attaches to land in the commonwealth as a lien; but if there are easements or other rights appurtenant to a parcel of registered land which for any reason have failed to be registered, such easements or rights shall remain so appurtenant notwithstanding such failure, and shall be held to pass with the land until cut off or extinguished by the registration of the servient estate, or in any other manner.

Sixth, liens in favor of the United States for unpaid taxes arising or existing under the Internal Revenue Code of 1954 as amended from time to time.

§53. *Prescription, adverse possession or right of way by necessity.* No title to registered land, or easement or other right therein, in derogation of the title of the registered owner, shall be acquired by prescription or adverse possession. Nor shall a right of way by necessity be implied under a conveyance of registered land.

The following cases raise issues about the reliability of the certificate of title from the standpoint of the purchaser of registered land.

ABRAHAMSON v. SUNDMAN
174 Minn. 22, 218 N.W. 246 (1928)

Plaintiffs appealed from a judgment of the district court for Hennepin county, Reed, J. decreeing defendant to be the owner of a certain lot in said county. Affirmed.

HOLT, J. Plaintiffs appeal from a judgment decreeing defendant to be the owner in fee of a certain lot in Hennepin county.

The title to the lot was registered under the Torrens act and a certificate of title issued to Tuxedo Park Company, a Minnesota corporation, January 16, 1914. Several years later, but prior to August, 1923, Tuxedo Park Company conveyed the lot by warranty deed to Swan J. Johnson, who erected a house thereon and then conveyed to plaintiffs who went into possession August 31, 1923, and have ever since remained in possession; but neither of said deeds was ever filed in the registrar's office, and no memorial in respect to said lot was ever noted on the registration certificate until September 14, 1923, when the Glass-Melone Lumber Company filed a mechanic's lien statement for lumber furnished Swan J. Johnson for building the house upon the lot. On June 1, 1924, notice of lis pendens was duly filed with the registrar to foreclose said lien, in which action Swan J. Johnson and wife and Tuxedo Park Company were made defendants, judgment was duly entered and the lot sold, the sale confirmed by the court, and after the time for redemption expired, there being no redemption, on application to the court, the certificate of the Tuxedo Park Company to the lot was canceled February 10, 1926, and a new certificate of title duly issued to the Glass-Melone Lumber Company and in turn canceled, that company having conveyed to defendant, to whom a new certificate of title was issued. Although plaintiffs were in possession of the lot, they were not made parties to the lien foreclosure proceeding nor served with notice of the application made to the court, after the expiration of the time for redemption, to cancel the registered title held by the Tuxedo Park Company and for the issue of a new certificate in lieu thereof to defendant, the vendee of the Glass-Melone Lumber Company.

We have then this situation: Since 1914 Tuxedo Park Company has been the owner in fee of the lot by a title established under the Torrens act. In the registrar's records that title has now passed to defendant. No flaw is found in the proceedings under the Torrens act by which the Glass-Melone Lumber Company established and enforced its mechanic's lien, and which eventually resulted in the extinguishment of the record ownership of Tuxedo Park Company and the succession thereto of defendant, unless the lien claimant was required to take notice of plaintiffs' possession and make them parties to the lien foreclosure. A title is created by the decree and certificate of registration. Henry v. White, 123 Minn. 182, 143 N.W. 324, L.R.A. 1916 D, 4, and cases therein cited. There is here no question but that, when the title to the lot was originally registered under the Torrens act, all parties were served so that the decree entered created an indefeasable title in fee in Tuxedo Park Company. When the Glass-Melone Lumber Company filed and foreclosed its mechanic's lien, could it safely rely on the fact that no memorial or notation had been entered on the registration certificate nor any document filed with the registrar affecting the lot? In other words, was it necessary to ascertain who was in possession and make him a party to the foreclosure? No one acquires rights in registered land by going into possession. The law provides:

"No title to registered land in derogation of that of the registered owner shall be acquired by prescription or by adverse possession." G.S. 1923, §8248.

Section 8271 provides:

> Every person receiving a certificate of title pursuant to a decree of registration, and every subsequent purchaser of registered land who receives a certificate of title in good faith and for a valuable consideration, shall hold the same free from all incumbrances, and adverse claims, excepting only such estates, mortgages, liens, charges and interests as may be noted in the last certificate of title in the office of the registrar, and also excepting any of the following rights or incumbrances subsisting against the same, if any, namely: . . .
>
> 3. Any lease for a period not exceeding three years when there is actual occupation of the premises thereunder. . . .

Hence the only right or title that the occupation and possession by one other than the registered owner indicates or gives notice of is a leasehold interest of not more than three years' duration. No contract or deed concerning registered land can take effect as a conveyance or bind or affect the land except as authority to registrar to make registration. "The act of registration shall be the operative act to convey or affect the land." §8293. A Torrens title being created by a decree of court and protected by statute so that no one may thereafter acquire any right, lien or interest therein by or through possession or occupation, no reason is apparent for making the occupant, who by no memorial or notation upon the certificate of registration is connected with the title, a party defendant in any action foreclosing a mortgage or mechanic's lien duly registered.

We have found but two cases on the question which directly hold that possession of real estate taken after the title thereto has been duly registered is not notice of any rights therein to one who is a good faith purchaser for value. One is Bjornberg v. Myers, 212 Ill. App. 257. It is true, the Illinois Torrens act has a section, not found in our act, which reads:

> Except in case of fraud, and except as herein otherwise provided, no person taking a transfer of registered land, or any estate or interest therein, or of any charge upon the same, from the registered owner shall be held to inquire into the circumstances under which or the consideration for which such owner or any previous registered owner was registered, or be affected with notice, actual or constructive, of any unregistered trust, lien, claim, demand or interest; and the knowledge that an unregistered trust, lien, claim, demand or interest is in existence shall not of itself be imputed as fraud. [Smith-Hurd Rev. St. 1923, c. 30, §86.]

In that case the registered owner gave a written contract for deed to one who at once went into possession, but did not file his contract with the registrar; the registered owner duly mortgaged the land to one who had actual knowledge both of the possession and the contract, and it was held that the mortgage took precedence over the rights of the occupant.

Colorado's Torrens act is virtually the same as ours concerning the provisions herein pertinent, and it was held, three justices dissenting, in Sterling Nat. Bank v. Fischer, 75 Colo. 371, 226 P. 146, that one who takes a certificate of registered land for value and in good faith is a purchaser in good faith, though the land is in possession of another.

There can be no question but that one who by virtue of a mechanic's lien acquires title to registered land is a purchaser in good faith for value. The only question here is whether in the foreclosure of such a lien he can terminate all rights and interests to the property by making those only parties to the suit who appear from the certificate or some memorial or notation thereon to have some right, title, or interest in the land. We think he can, except the rights only of one in possession under a lease for a term of not more than three years.

Plaintiffs rely on Follette v. Pacific L. & P. Corp., 189 Cal. 193, 208 P. 295, 23 A.L.R. 965, and Riley v. Pearson, 120 Minn. 210, 139 N.W. 361, L.R.A. 1916 D, 7; but it is to be noted that both cases relate to occupants who, at the time the original registration was decreed, were not made parties thereto, and hence could attack the decree. To such authorities may be added Gil v. Frances Inv. Co. (C.C.A.) 19 F.2d 880. But that is quite another question from the one here presented, where a conceded valid decree as to all the world has registered the title to land in a certain party. From thence on that land and the title thereto can be affected, transferred or encumbered only under the provisions of the Torrens act. All persons attempting to deal with the land and the title thereto have to take notice of the fact that the land is registered. Therefore one who takes possession without any notation or memorial of his right upon the registration certificate must be charged with knowledge that his possession is not notice of any interest in him, and that such possession will never ripen into a right adverse to the registered owner.

In the instant case, the registered owner from 1914 was Tuxedo Park Company; its certificate contained no notation or memorial of a claim of lien, interest, or estate of any other person until the mechanic's lien of Glass-Melone Lumber Company was properly filed and noted thereon. This lien was subsequently adjudicated and the title of Tuxedo Park Company transferred through the judicial sale under a decree which bound and cut off the right of redemption of all who had any interest in the title as disclosed by the original certificate or by any memorial or notation thereon. This transfer of the title to defendant is without flaw as to everyone who under the Torrens act had or could have any interest in the lot. None other can question the indefeasible title defendant obtained, except an occupant under a lease of a term not exceeding three years. Plaintiffs claim no leasehold interest.

Plaintiffs rely on a decree in an action between them and Swan J. Johnson wherein the conveyance from the latter to plaintiffs was rescinded for fraud, and damages in the sum of $1,500 were awarded plaintiffs and they decreed possession until such damages were paid. Neither defendant nor her predecessor in interest was made a party defendant, nor was notice of lis pendens filed with the registrar, nor any memorial or certified copy of the judgment or any notation of plaintiffs' right in virtue of that judgment filed with the registrar. It is clear that that judgment has no effect on defendant's Torrens title.

The judgment is affirmed.

KILLAM v. MARCH
316 Mass. 646, 55 N.E.2d 945 (1944)

SPALDING, J. The plaintiffs, who are owners of a parcel of registered land, bring this bill in equity in the Land Court to remove a cloud from their title. See G.L. (Ter. Ed.) c. 185, Sec. 1(k), as amended by St. 1934, c. 67, Sec. 1. The case was heard by a judge of the Land Court who made findings of fact and an order for a decree, and pursuant thereto a decree was entered dismissing the bill, from which the plaintiffs appealed.

The judge found the following facts. On October 14, 1941, the plaintiffs, husband and wife, purchased a parcel of registered land in Melrose and became the holders of a certificate of title issued by the South Registry District of Middlesex County. It was noted on the certificate that the land was subject to a mortgage held by a bank and to sewer assessments; no other encumbrances appear.

The defendants own land lying easterly of and abutting on the premises of the plaintiffs. On the plaintiffs' land is a driveway leading to a garage; the defendants have been using both the driveway and the garage ever since the plaintiffs acquired their title. They claim the right to do so by virtue of a lease dated August 8, 1938, given to them by Alphonsus G. and Katherine A. MacDonald, the plaintiffs' predecessors in title. This instrument, which was acknowledged and under seal, purported to give to the defendants, for a period of twenty-five years, a demise of that part of the plaintiffs' premises on which the garage and driveway were situated. It was recorded with a plan on September 23, 1941, in the Middlesex South District Registry of Deeds but was not registered in the land registration division thereof.

The judge found that prior to October 14, 1941 (the date when the land in question was acquired from the MacDonalds), the "plaintiffs had actual notice of the lease held by the defendants on part of the premises . . . and that the plaintiffs . . . [were] not holders for value without notice thereof." Since the evidence is not before us, we can consider only whether the specific facts found are as a matter of law inconsistent with this conclusion. McCarthy v. Lane, 301 Mass. 125, 127, 16 N.E.2d 683. We find no such inconsistency and this finding must stand.

The question presented for decision is this: Does one purchasing registered land take subject to an unregistered lease for more than seven years if he has actual notice of it? The trial judge held that he does and we think he was right. It appears that this question has never been decided in this Commonwealth although similar questions in the case of unregistered land have been passed on many times.

In considering this question we place no reliance on the fact that the lease was recorded in that section of the registry of deeds that had to do with unregistered land. Such a recording could not affect registered land in view of G.L. (Ter. Ed.) c. 185, Sec. 71, which provides that "Leases of registered land for a term of seven years or more shall be registered in lieu of recording." See also G.L. (Ter. Ed.) c. 185, Secs. 57 and 59. The trial judge did not deal with the case as one where there was constructive notice but treated it as one where there was actual notice, and we shall deal with it on that basis.

General Laws (Ter. Ed.) c. 185 (originally enacted as St. 1898, c. 562), providing a system for the registration of land titles, contains provisions relative to the original registration of land (Secs. 26-45) and also provisions relative to transfers or dealings with land subsequent to the original registration thereof. The instant case does not require us to consider the conclusiveness of an original decree of registration obtained by an owner with actual notice of an outstanding interest in another where such interest has not been included in the owner's certificate of registration. We are concerned here only with the conclusiveness of a certificate of registration acquired by purchase subsequent to original registration where the purchaser at the time he acquired his title had actual notice of a prior unregistered interest.

The provisions of the act that bear most directly on this issue are Secs. 46 and 57, the material portions of which are as follows: "Section 46. Every petitioner receiving a certificate of title in pursuance of a decree of registration, and every subsequent purchaser of registered land taking a certificate of title for value and in good faith, shall hold the same free from all encumbrances except those noted on the certificate" and certain stated encumbrances not herein material.

> Section 57. An owner of registered land may convey, mortgage, lease, charge or otherwise deal with it as fully as if it had not been registered. . . . But no deed, mortgage or other voluntary instrument, except a will and a lease for a term not exceeding seven years, purporting to convey or affect registered land, shall take effect as a conveyance or bind the land, but shall operate only as a contract between the parties, and as evidence of authority to the recorder or assistant recorder to make registration. The act of registration only shall be the operative act to convey or affect the land.

It should be noted that Sec. 46 provides that, in order for a subsequent purchaser to "hold . . . free from all encumbrances except those noted on the certificate" he must take the "certificate of title for value and in good faith." Section 57, however, speaks of the "act of registration only" as "the operative act to . . . affect the land" and considered with Sec. 71, requiring the registration of all leases for more than seven years, seems to point to a conclusion that in no event can a party claim a leasehold interest for more than seven years in registered land where the lease has not been registered. This view finds some support in a statement by Holmes, C.J., in Tyler v. Judges of the Court of Registration, 175 Mass. 71, at page 81, 55 N.E. 812, at page 816, where it was said in speaking of transfers or dealings subsequent to the original registration, "It must be remembered that at all later stages no one can have a claim which does not appear on the face of the registry. The only rights are registered rights." In Malaguti v. Rosen, 262 Mass. 555, at page 568, 160 N.E. 532, at page 538, it was said, "Persons dealing with the land in the future (after original registration) may rely on the files at the registry and the interests of no one require changes in the records. G.L. c. 185, Secs. 58, 114." But in neither the *Tyler* nor the *Malaguti* case was the question now under consideration before the court, and therefore we do not consider them as binding authorities in this respect. See Vigeant v. Postal Telegraph Cable Co., 260 Mass. 335, 343, 157 N.E. 651.

In construing the sections of c. 185 under consideration certain well settled principles of statutory construction should be kept in mind. Where several sections of a statute are under consideration they "must, if reasonably possible, be interpreted so as to be harmonious and not contradictory, and all the words of each given some practical effect." Moloney v. Selectmen of Milford, 253 Mass. 400, 402, 149 N.E. 317, 318; Commissioner of Banks v. McKnight, 281 Mass. 467, 472, 183 N.E. 720. "The legislative intention in enacting the statute must be ascertained, 'not alone from the literal meaning of its words, but from a view of the whole system of which it is but a part, and in the light of the common law and previous statutes on the same subject.' Armburg v. Boston & Maine Railroad, 276 Mass. 418, 426, 177

N.E. 665, 670." Boston v. Quincy Market Cold Storage & Warehouse Co., 312 Mass. 638, 644, 45 N.E.2d 959, 964.

An inquiry into the origin and development of the recording acts in this Commonwealth, prior to the enactment of St. 1898, c. 562 (not G.L. (Ter. Ed.) c. 185), the land registration act, discloses a uniform course of decisions to the effect that one acquiring title as the plaintiffs did with actual notice of the defendants' lease would take subject to it. The earliest recording act after the provincial period was St. 1783, c. 37, Sec. 4. This provided that no conveyance of land should be good and effectual in law "against any other person or persons but the grantor or grantors, and their heirs only, unless the deed or deeds thereof be acknowledged and recorded." This statute from its passage was held to mean that although an unrecorded deed passed title as between the grantor and the grantee it would not prevail as against a subsequent deed which was recorded. But if the second purchaser had notice of the prior unrecorded deed he took subject to that interest. Thus an exception was engrafted upon the statute. Norcross v. Widgery, 2 Mass. 506, 508; Farnsworth v. Childs, 4 Mass. 637, 639; Priest v. Rice, 1 Pick. 164; M' Mechan v. Griffling, 3 Pick. 149; Adams v. Cuddy, 13 Pick. 460, 464; Lawrence v. Stratton, 6 Cush. 163, 167.

It was said by Shaw, C.J., in the *Lawrence* case, at page 167, that this exception was "put upon the ground, that a party with such notice could not take a deed without fraud; the objection was not to the nature of the conveyance, but to the honesty of the taker; and, therefore, if the estate had passed through such taker to a bona fide purchaser, without fraud, the conveyance was held valid." See also Morse v. Curtis, 140 Mass. 112, 2 N.E. 929; Wenz v. Pastene, 209 Mass. 359, 362, 95 N.E. 793.

When the Revised Statutes were compiled in 1836, St. 1783, c. 37, Sec. 4, was substantially unchanged, and where they provided that no conveyance or lease for more than seven years should be valid "against any person other than the grantor and his heirs and devisees" unless it was recorded, there was added the clause "and persons having actual notice thereof." Rev. Sts. c. 59, Sec. 28. This provision has been retained in all the subsequent revisions and now appears in G.L. (Ter. Ed.) c. 183, Sec. 4, as amended. In Wenz v. Pastene, 209 Mass. 359, at page 362, 95 N.E. 793, it was said "The additional words, 'and persons having actual notice thereof,' incorporated in the Rev. Sts. c. 59, Sec. 28, did not change the law, but merely put in statutory form what already had been declared by judicial exposition. Lawrence v. Stratton, 6 Cush. 163, 166. Morse v. Curtis, 140 Mass. 112, 113, 2 N.E. 929."

We are of the opinion that the provisions of G.L. (Ter. Ed.) c. 185 relating to transfers or dealings with land subsequent to registration, construed according to the language used and in the light of the foregoing historical background, compel the conclusion that the Legislature did not intend to give certificate holders such as the plaintiffs an indefeasible title as against interests of which they had actual notice. Any other construction would ignore the wording of Sec. 46 which provides that one acquires registered land free from unregistered encumbrances if he is a purchaser for value and in "good faith." Although there are many differences between the two systems it is inconceivable that circumstances that would amount to bad faith with respect to unregistered land, namely, acquiring title with notice of an unrecorded interest, would constitute good faith in the case of registered land. Section 71, requiring leases of more than seven years to be registered and Sec. 57 to the effect that the "act of registration only shall be the operative act to convey or affect the land" must be construed together with Sec. 46.

There is no merit in the plaintiffs' exception to the admission of the purchase and sale agreement between the plaintiffs and their predecessors in title. There was inserted in this agreement a reference to the lease with the defendants. This was clearly admissible on the issue of notice.

The final decree dismissing the bill is affirmed with costs.

So ordered.

STATE STREET BANK & TRUST CO. v. BEALE
353 Mass. 103, 227 N.E.2d 924 (1967)

SPALDING, J.

The objective of this bill in equity, brought in the Land Court, is to impose a constructive trust in favor of the plaintiffs on a parcel of land in Rockland (the locus) which, it is alleged, the defendant fraudulently caused to be registered in his name.

The averments of the bill may be summarized as follows: The plaintiffs were the owners of the locus, a twenty-five acre parcel of woodland. The defendant, knowing of their ownership, or claim of ownership, petitioned the Land Court for a decree of registration, and fraudulently represented that he did not know of any other persons having an estate or interest in the locus. Consequently, the plaintiffs did not receive the notice by registered mail afforded a party in interest in a registration proceeding. The only notice given was one by newspaper publication of which the plaintiffs had no knowledge. The title examiner appointed by the court reported that the defendant did not have a record title proper for registration. The defendant thereupon filed two false affidavits in support of a claim that he and predecessors in interest had acquired title by adverse possession. One affidavit, by the chief assessor of Rockland, asserted that the defendant predecessors in interest had been assessed for the locus (twenty-five acres) for many years, although the assessors' records show that for most of that time the defendant's predecessors had been assessed for five acres. The affiant, who was familiar with the actual facts, made the affidavit either with intent to defraud the Land Court or with such wilful disregard of the facts as to be tantamount to fraud. The other affidavit recited certain information concerning the ownership, and use of the locus, of which the affiant, in fact, either had no knowledge or knew to be false. The defendant knew of the falsity of this affidavit and filed it with the intention of deceiving the court. In reliance on these affidavits, the Land Court, on October 31, 1960, entered a decree registering the locus in the defendant's name.

The present bill was brought on March 20, 1962. The defendant demurred. The basis of the demurrer was that the bill was not brought within one year of the decree of registration in accordance with the provisions of G.L. c. 185, §45. The provisions of §45 relied on are those which provide that a decree of confirmation and registration "shall be conclusive upon and against all persons . . . [and] shall not be opened by reason of the absence, infancy or other disability of any person affected thereby, nor by any proceeding at law or in equity for reversing judgments or decrees; subject, however, to the right of any person deprived of land or of any estate or interest therein, by a decree of registration obtained by fraud to file a petition for review within one year after the entry of the decree, provided no innocent purchaser for value has acquired an interest."

The judge rendered a decision in which he ruled that the plaintiffs' bill was "in the nature of a petition for review under c. 185, §45, and that the plaintiffs have not complied with the statutory provision that a petition for review be filed within one year after the entry of the decree of registration." The judge further ruled "that the Land Court has no jurisdiction [in equity] to award damages for fraud in procuring the decree." An interlocutory decree sustaining the defendant's demurrer and a final decree dismissing the plaintiffs' bill were entered. The plaintiffs appealed.

It is well settled that a traditional remedy for a person who has been deprived of land through fraud is specific restitution. "A person who has tortiously acquired or retained a title to land . . . is under a duty of restitution to the person entitled thereto." Restatement: Restitution, §130. The duty to make such restitution is often enforced by imposing a constructive trust. In Barry v. Covich, 332 Mass. 338, at p. 342, 124 N.E.2d 921, at p. 924, we said,

> A constructive trust may be said to be a device employed in equity, in the absence of any intention of the parties to create a trust, in order to avoid the unjust enrichment of one party at the expense of the other where the legal title to the property was obtained by fraud. . . .

See Restatement: Restitution, §160.

The bill prays that the defendant "be ordered to convey . . . [the locus] to [the] Plaintiffs . . . by a good and sufficient deed such as to entitle the Grantees to a certificate of title . . . [and for] such other . . . relief as shall . . . seem meet and proper." The bill does not directly challenge the registration decree; the plaintiffs do not ask that the decree be declared void and the locus removed from the registration system. Rather they acknowledge that the legal title is now vested in the defendant and claim title by means of a constructive trust. The question, then, is whether a bill to impose a constructive trust on registered land may properly be treated as a "petition for review" of the registration decree, and thus, pursuant to G.L. c. 185, §45, must be brought within one year of that decree. We are of opinion that it may not be so treated.

Several other provisions of G.L. c. 185 (the land registration statute) are relevant. Section 45, upon part of which the defendant's demurrer was based, also provides in part that "any person aggrieved by such decree [of registration] in any case may pursue his remedy in tort against the petitioner or against any other person for fraud in procuring the decree." Section 62, which deals with the presentation of the owner's duplicate certificate upon the transfer of registered land, provides in part: "In all cases of registration procured by fraud, the owner may pursue all his legal and equitable remedies against the parties to such fraud. . . ." And §75 explicitly recognizes that registered land may be held subject to a constructive trust. Thus in three sections of the land registration statute, including the very section upon which the defendant relies, it appears that the remedies of a person deprived of land by fraud are preserved. Nor is there any indication that the remedy of restitution is excluded. As noted, §75 specifically refers to constructive trusts. Section 62 refers to "legal and equitable remedies."

If "petition for review," as used in §45, were so broadly construed as to conclude a bill for the imposition of a constructive trust, the above enumerated provisions which appear to preserve that remedy would be severely weakened. Unless the defrauded person discovered the fraud and filed his bill within a year, a valuable — and often the most valuable — remedy would be unavailable.

We do not think that the purpose of G.L. c. 185 was to reduce the availability of the traditional remedy of restitution. The purpose of land registration is to provide a means by which title to land may be readily and reliably ascertained. See Malaguti v. Rosen, 262 Mass. 555, 567-568, 160 N.E. 532; Deacy v. Berberian, 344 Mass. 321, 328, 182 N.E.2d 514. But these benefits of the registration system are intended primarily for those who act in good faith. It is not a purpose of the system to afford those who deal with registered land in bad faith any greater protection than they would have in similar dealings with unregistered land. See Killam v. March, 316 Mass. 646, 650-651, 55 N.E.2d 945.

We hold that a "petition for review," as used in §45, does not include a proceeding which seeks to impose a constructive trust, as distinct from one brought to alter or set aside a registration decree. The distinction between an attack upon a decree and a suit in equity to avoid the consequences thereof has been recognized. Currier v. Esty, 110 Mass. 536, 544. See Morris v. Small, 160 F. 142 (D. Mass.); Restatement: Judgments, §112f and §114a. Since the remedy of restitution operates only against the person who has committed the fraud, our holding does not run counter to the land registration act's purpose of furnishing good faith purchasers with a ready and reliable means of ascertaining title to land.

Interlocutory decree reversed.

Final decree reversed with costs of appeal.

CHAPTER 31

TITLE INSURANCE

*Note: **Commercial Title Insurance Companies and
Lawyers' Title Guaranty Funds***

In recent years, in several states lawyers' title guaranty funds have come into being to provide title insurance. Appendix C of Pamphlet No. 1 entitled Bar-Related Title Assuring Organizations, issued in 1963 by the Special Committee on Lawyers' Title Guaranty Funds of the American Bar Association, describes the various state plans. The Florida plan is explained as follows.

1) The Florida Plan

Florida's Lawyers' Title Guaranty Fund is a Massachusetts or business trust administered by trustees elected from Florida's 16 Judicial Circuits by the members in the respective circuits. Members make an original capital contribution of $200.00 and with each later exposure a set amount which is roughly about 18 per cent of the premium charged by commercial companies. Each member has an account in which his contributions are listed. At the end of each year, expenses are pro-rated to each account, on the basis of their respective contributions, and each account is given a net credit balance for that year. At the discretion of the trustees, and subject to reserve requirements, members may withdraw the net credit balances at the expiration of seven years. The Fund's 1962 assets exceed two and a half million dollars. [Bar-Related Title Assuring Organizations, at 16-17.]

See Carter, New Role for Lawyers: The Florida Lawyers Title Guaranty Fund, 45 A.B.A.J. 803 (1959).

Formal Opinion 304 of the Standing Committee on Professional Ethics of the American Bar Association, reproduced below, relates to a lawyer's participation in a lawyers' title guaranty fund.

AMERICAN BAR ASSOCIATION, STANDING COMMITTEE ON PROFESSIONAL ETHICS, FORMAL OPINION 304 (1962)

A number of questions have been asked the Committee on the ethical problems arising out of the relationship between lawyers and title insurance companies and title guaranty funds. The questions stem primarily from bar association funds and companies but the problems posed are much larger and must be considered in broader context. Since the protection of clients' titles has been historically the business of lawyers through the issuance of title opinions, and since title companies and title guaranty funds have, in a number of states, been created by private industry as well as by bar associations, and since in many of these states the very lawyers who are engaged by clients to examine titles and who are expected by clients to protect them, are intimately involved in the operation of the company and the funds and have financial interest in these funds, this opinion is needed.

Several plans are in operation and are proposed. The essential details of two broad categories are:

A.   Lawyers initially fund a trust or corporation which issues title guaranty certificates on the opinion of a member lawyer issued to the client. From the fee charged the client, the lawyer remits to the fund or corporation a dollar sum per $1,000 of insurance requested. The insurance covers not only the negligence of the lawyer but also all defects not specifically excluded in the opinion and all undiscoverable defects such as forgeries, etc. A record of each lawyer's experience is kept by the fund or corporation and the unused portion of his premiums, after deducting the operational costs of the program as well as the losses of others beyond their premiums, are ultimately returned to him or kept in a fund for charitable and educational purposes.

B.   A title company, either privately operated or operated by an association of lawyers, is authorized by the state to write title insurance. A lawyer consulted by a client for a title opinion, without giving an opinion on the title or in addition to giving an opinion to the client and charging him a fee for this service, may recommend title insurance. If the policy is issued, sometimes based on the lawyer's opinion and sometimes requiring additional examination by company's lawyers, the company remits to the original lawyer a commission on the cost of the insurance. This commission may sometimes be paid on the issuance of the policy or it may be delayed for a year or more. Sometimes the company employs the client's lawyer to give it a title opinion on which the policy is issued and pays the lawyer for this opinion.

In both situations the title company or guaranty fund sometimes advertise the value of their service to the public generally.

The ultimate aim of the lawyer is to provide the fullest protection to his client, the purchaser or the lender, as the case may be. This normally is accomplished by a careful examination of the title, the giving of an opinion, and at times clearing the title. There are times, however, when the purchase of title insurance may be in the best interest of the client. In fact, in every instance, the client's security is furthered in some degree by the addition of some kind of insurance to protect against the lawyer's negligence and against defects the lawyer could not know about.

One ethical question in these situations arises from the obligation of the lawyer not to have any conflicting interests as stated in Canon 6, but even more succinctly stated, as it relates to the problem at hand, in Canon 38:

> Canon 38. Compensation, Commissions, and Rebates.
> A lawyer should accept no compensation, commissions, rebates or other advantages from others without the knowledge and consent of his client after full disclosure.

The possible conflict of interest question in category A arises from the fact that the lawyer may have an interest in the funds paid to the fund or corporation, which in reality the client pays through his fee. In category B it stems from the commission paid to the lawyer for recommending the title insurance to the client or from the fee paid the client's lawyer by the company or fund for the title opinion on which the policy is issued.

In each instance it is argued that the amounts that may come back to the lawyer may warp his judgment on the need for such insurance. It is argued that the situation is like that condemned by the New York County Opinion 203 and the New York City Opinion 876 quoted in Drinker, Legal Ethics, at pp. 95-96, as follows:

> New York County 203. He should not advise a client to employ an investment company in which he is interested, without informing him of this. [p. 95]
> New York City 876. If he invests the client's money in buying mortgages from his wife, he must so advise the client. [p. 96]

Important to the decision of this matter is our Opinion 196, the headnote of which states:

> It is improper for a lawyer to retain, pursuant to arrangement with an abstract company, one-fourth the charge for an abstract, made by it for his client, as commission for bringing it the business, unless such retention is with the knowledge and consent of the client after full disclosure.

On the other hand, the difficulty must be balanced against the security afforded the client in these situations.

It is our opinion that

1.   A lawyer who receives a commission (whether delayed or not) from a

title insurance company or guaranty fund for recommending or selling the insurance to his client, or for work done for the client or the company, without either fully disclosing to the client his financial interest in the transaction, or crediting the client's bill with the amount thus received, is guilty of unethical conduct. Such conduct would be a direct violation of Canon 38. On the other hand, there is nothing unethical in recommending title insurance per se.

2. A lawyer who merely provides a greater security for his client through the use of a type of insurance or guaranty fund to buttress his opinion or to provide for contingencies beyond his knowledge is not guilty of unethical conduct.

This is true although the charges made by the company or fund may or may not be based on the amounts of insurance or guaranty provided each client and even though some portion of this amount may be returned to the lawyer based on the experience of the lawyer or the bar generally, or may be kept by the fund and used for charitable or educational purposes. The financial interest in such a transaction is so remote as not to be a violation of the Canons of Ethics. . . .

> WALTER P. ARMSTRONG, JR., *Chairman*
> A. JAMES CASNER
> HERBERT JOHNSON
> CHARLES W. JOINER
> HALE MCCOWN
> CHARLES W. PETTENGILL
> JAS. L. SHEPHERD, JR.
> E. B. SMITH

Note: The Title Insurance Policy

The policy of title insurance describes the extent of the protection given to the purchaser of the land. That protection is substantial or slight depending on the scope of the scheduled exceptions and conditions of the policy. Sometimes, of course, the terms of the policy are not conclusive on the point at issue, and litigation may be necessary to determine whether the particular loss is within the protection given by the policy.[1]

1. See generally on the subject of title insurance the following: Haymond, Title Insurance Risks of Which the Public Records Give No Notice, 2 S. Cal. L. Rev. 139 (1928); Young, MacGregor & Solether, Report of the Special Committee of the Hennepin County Bar Association Appointed to Study Title Insurance, 19 Minn. L. Rev. 354 (1935); Cushman, Torrens Titles and Title Insurance, 76 U. Pa. L. Rev. 589 (1937); Rhodes, Contract of Title Insurance, 16 Title News 24 (1937); Clayton, Standardization of Exceptions in Title Policies, 17 Title News 5 (1937); Rhodes, Treatment of Restrictions in Title Underwriting, 20 Title News 13 (1940); Randel, Title Insurance, 26 Title News 19 (1947); Goth, Title Insurance in California, 39 Calif. L. Rev. 235 (1951); Payne, The Crisis in Conveyancing, 19 Mo. L. Rev. 214 (1954); Johnstone, Title Insurance, 66 Yale L.J. 492 (1957); Payne, In Search of Title, 14 Ala. L. Rev. 11, 278 (1962).

If the only defects insured against are those easily discoverable by a search of the records, the policy does not provide any greater protection to the buyer than an attorney's opinion, except for the possible greater financial resources of the insurance company to satisfy claims as compared with the financial resources of an attorney to meet the liability for the attorney's negligence. The following cases illustrate the exceptions from coverage that may be in a title insurance policy.

BOTHIN v. CALIFORNIA TITLE INSURANCE & TRUST CO.
153 Cal. 718, 96 P. 500 (1908)

Appeal from a judgment of the Superior Court of the City and County of San Francisco and from an order denying a new trial. John Hunt, Judge.

The facts are stated in the opinion of the court.

LORIGAN, J. This action was brought to recover damages for breach of a covenant in a title insurance policy. The facts either admitted or proven, are as follows: On March 1, 1900, the plaintiff H. E. Bothin having entered into a contract for the purchase from the Sharon Estate Company of City Slip lots 71 and 72 in the city and county of San Francisco, applied to the defendant, a corporation engaged in issuing title insurance policies, for a policy insuring the title to said lots.

On December 13, 1900, the defendant duly issued its policy of insurance on said lots, guaranteeing the title to the same to be in plaintiff, who at the same time took a conveyance thereof from the Sharon Estate Company.

Among other things, the policy provided that the defendant, The California Title Insurance and Trust Company, covenanted to indemnify and insure said plaintiff "from all loss or damage, not exceeding $10,000 which the said assured shall sustain by reason of defects in the title of the assured to the estate or interest described in Schedule A, or by reason of liens or encumbrances affecting the same on the 13th day of December, 1900 . . . excepting only such as are specified in Schedule B; subject to the conditions and stipulations on the third page hereof, which with the schedules aforesaid are a part of this policy."

Schedule B referred to provides, in part, as follows:

> Schedule B—defects of or objections to the title, and liens, charges and encumbrances thereon against which the company does not insure; 1. Tenure of the present occupants . . . ; 4. Instruments, liens, encumbrances, judicial proceedings and pending suits not shown by any public record thereof in the city and county of San Francisco; and secret trusts known to the assured and not disclosed to the company.

It appears that when this policy was issued there was, and for some time prior thereto had been, on record in the recorder's office of the city and county of San Francisco a deed of trust by which one P. M. Partridge conveyed to the trustees of the San Francisco Savings Union about fourteen feet of the westerly portion of said lot 71. Subsequent to the issuance of the policy to plaintiff it was discovered that the adjoining owners of property to the west of lots 71 and 72 described in the policy had encroached about fourteen feet thereon with their building, and that the buildings of plaintiff encroached to a like extent upon the owners of City Slip lots 73 and 74 on the east. In fact, it appeared that neither the owners of property to the west of the lots purchased by plaintiff nor the predecessors in title of plaintiff had erected their buildings on the true line, but respectively about fourteen feet easterly thereof. One of said encroaching owners was said P. M. Partridge, whose trust-deed above referred to was on record when the policy was issued. The description in that deed did not refer to lot 71 by name, and that it embraced any portion thereof could only be determined by a survey according to the calls of the trust-deed. Some question arising subsequent to the issuance of the policy as to the lines between them, Partridge brought an action against plaintiff to quiet his title to the fourteen feet of the westerly portion of lot 71 which was in his actual occupancy and which was embraced in his trust-deed, and one John A. Schmidt, adjoining him on the north, brought a similar suit against plaintiff to quiet title to about the same number of feet on the westerly portion of lot 72 which was in his possession and occupied by his buildings. Judgment in these actions went in favor of the plaintiffs to the portions of lots 71 and 72 and their title quieted thereto. Plaintiff here likewise brought actions against parties claiming under the record title to about fourteen feet of the property to the east of said lots and beyond the easterly line thereof, but of which he was actually in the occupancy with his buildings, and obtained judgments quieting his title thereto.

It further appears from the findings that plaintiff here, while not obtaining possession of the entire property embraced within lots 71 and 72, obtained the identical property that he had looked at and had in mind when he obtained his deed from the Sharon Estate Company, and substantially of the same dimensions as there called for.

There is no claim that P. M. Partridge had any title of record to any portion of lot 71, or that the trust-deed executed by him embraced in its description any of the improvements of plaintiff which were supposed to cover the entire lot. Neither is there any claim that lot 72 was embraced within the calls of any instruments in writing, save those constituting the chain of title of plaintiff, and it is conceded that the plaintiff had the record title to both these lots.

The claim of plaintiff was that he had sustained damages embracing an amount which he had paid for attorney's fees and expenses in defending the actions brought by Partridge and Schmidt, as also damages for alleged depreciation in value of the property described in the policy, occasioned through the irregular shape in which the judgments in these suits left the remainder of the lots.

The court awarded judgment in favor of defendant, and from said judgment and the order denying his motion for a new trial, the plaintiff appeals.

The main point on this appeal is relative to the title of Partridge to the portion of lot 71 which was included in his deed of trust, it being insisted by appellant that there was a breach of the covenants contained in the policy by reason of this trust-deed being upon the record. Taking, however, into consideration the covenants of the policy, this claim is not tenable. It is quite clear from the conditions of that instrument that what was insured by the respondent was that the record title to the lot was in appellant. It is not insisted, nor could it be, that Partridge had a record title to any portion of the lot in question. The evidence shows that he had not. In fact, it was admitted that the record title to the lot was in the appellant, and it is evident from the policy that this was all that the respondent insured. The only title which Partridge had was a title to a portion of the lot acquired by adverse possession, but this, the respondent not only did not insure, but expressly declared it did not in that provision of Schedule B wherein it is stated that, among other defects of or objections to the title not insured against, was the "tenure of the present occupants." "Tenure" is a term of extensive signification. While it means the mode by which one holds an estate in land, it imports any kind of holding from mere possession to the owning of the inheritance. Bouvier Law Dic.; Anderson's Law Dic.: Term "Tenure."

Now, the only title that Partridge held to the lot was the title acquired by adverse possession. His tenure of the property was exclusively that of an adverse occupant. He had no title of record and against his title acquired by reason of his adverse occupancy the policy expressly declared it did not insure when it provided it did not insure against the "tenure of the present occupant." As far as the record title to the lot is concerned, the respondent did insure it to be in appellant, but as against any title or right to the property asserted by one who might be in possession thereof, holding adversely to the record title, insurance was expressly denied. It was left to the appellant to determine by an inspection and examination of the property whether there was adverse occupancy or not; to determine for himself by actual measurement, survey, or examination of the premises whether he was getting what he contracted to purchase, or whether there was an adverse claim of title of any character by the occupants of the whole or any portion of the premises. Necessarily the record title is all that a title insurance company can safely or judiciously insure. While the title to real property may be disclosed by the record to be in one person, it may, in fact, be in another through adverse possession or in one in occupation of the property under an unrecorded conveyance. It is the possibility of the existence of these conditions as to the title which an insurance company provides against by insuring the record title, and none other. In the case at bar the policy only insured the record title and as that is conceded to have been in appellant and the title of Partridge to the portion of the lot in question resting solely upon adverse possession against which respondent did not insure, there was no breach of the policy of insurance.

But it is claimed by counsel for appellant that the provision in Schedule B of the policy that the insurance company did not insure against "the tenure of the present occupants" is not controlling as to the responsibility of the respondent under the evidence in the case, but it is insisted that there was a breach of the policy as to the Partridge title under the fourth subdivision of Schedule B which provides that the company does not insure instruments, liens, or encumbrances not shown by any public record. The claim is that under this subdivision appellant was insured against any "defect" in the title disclosed by public records of the city and county of San Francisco, and that the deed of trust from Partridge to the San Francisco Savings Union was a "defect" in the title as that term is used in the policy of insurance. Undoubtedly, the policy does insure against any defect in the record title, but the trust-deed of Partridge was not a defect in such title. There was no title appearing of record in Partridge to any portion of the lot in question. There was no instrument of any kind or character of record which purported to convey any interest in this lot to him. He was not connected with the chain of title in any respect. That chain produced from the records showed the title to be in appellant. This being true, the deed of trust from Partridge created no defect in the record title. As far as the record title was concerned, Partridge was a mere interloper. One who is not connected by any conveyance whatever with the record title to a piece of property and makes a conveyance thereof, does not thereby create any defect in the record title of another when such title is deducible by intermediate effective conveyances from the original owners to that other. This we think so clear that it is idle to attempt to elaborate it. Such a deed would not even be constructive notice. Our code provides that every conveyance of real property, acknowledged and recorded, is from the date of recordation constructive notice of its contents to subsequent purchasers and mortgagees. Civ. Code, sec. 1213. This language is very general, applying in terms to every conveyance, but it is held that this only contemplates conveyances, by one having legal title to the property conveyed and is applied where there are conflicting conveyances made by persons claiming under the same common grantor. It does not apply to a deed by a stranger; one who is not connected in any manner with the title of record. No notice whatever is conveyed by such a deed. Long v. Dollarhide, 24 Cal. 218; Garber v. Gianella, 98 Cal. 529, 33 P. 458; Sharon v. Minock, 6 Nev. 377; Rankin v. Miller, 43 Iowa 19; Edwards v. McKernan, 55 Mich. 520, 526, 22 N.W. 20.

It may be suggested, too, in this connection, that the loss to appellant of a portion of his lot 71 did not arise out of the alleged defect in the record title of appellant created by the trust-deed from Partridge, but for a cause entirely independent of it. It arose from the fact that Partridge had acquired title by adverse possession of the land; not from any defect in appellant's record title. This title by adverse possession respondent did not insure against, but expressly provided that it did not.

While there is involved in the appeal a claim of breach of the covenants as to that portion of lot 72 to which Schmidt had title by adverse possession, little need be said on the subject. What we have said relative to the Partridge title applies equally to the Schmidt title. As to this lot 72 there were no instruments of any character on record embracing any portion of it, except such instruments as made out the record title of appellant. Schmidt's tenure of the portion of lot 72 at the time of the issuance of the policy was solely that of an adverse occupant or claimant. He had no title of record and his title by adverse possession was not insured against, because, as we have seen, it was expressly provided in the policy that the respondent did not insure against "the tenure of the present occupants."

The judgment and order denying the motion for a new trial are affirmed.

METROPOLITAN LIFE INSURANCE CO.
v. UNION TRUST CO.
283 N.Y. 33, 27 N.E.2d 225 (1940)

Appeal from Supreme Court, Appellate Division, Fourth Department.

Action by the Metropolitan Life Insurance Company against the Union Trust Company of Rochester and the Abstract Title & Mortgage Corporation for breach of provisions in title insurance policies issued by defendants. From a judgment of the Appellate Division, 257 App. Div. 906, 12 N.Y.S.2d 1010, affirming a judgment for defendant title company, 168 Misc. 657, 6 N.Y.S.2d 410, on an order of the Special Term granting such defendant's motion to dismiss the complaint as to it on the merits, plaintiff appeals by permission after denial of appeal in the Appellate Division, 257 App. Div. 1044, 14 N.Y.S.2d 492.

Affirmed.

CONWAY, J. Plaintiff sues for a breach of provision in each of a number of policies of title insurance issued in September, 1929. After service of answer, defendant title company had summary judgment dismissing the complaint under rule 113 of the Rules of Civil Practice.

Taking the text of the policies in provision most favorable to plaintiff, they insured against "defects in, incumbrances upon or liens or charges against the title of the mortgagors or grantors to premises described in the mortgage or trust deed" existing at or prior to the date of the policy "and not excepted under Schedule 'B.' " This form of policy was suggested by plaintiff and the assessments hereafter referred to were not excepted. It is not claimed that these assessments were statutory liens at the time of the issuance of the policies but it is contended that they were charges and incumbrances within the meaning of those terms as used in the policies. The typical complaint alleges in paragraph Twelfth that the certificate and policy of insurance of defendant title company "did not state or mention that future assessments would be made against the said real estate on account of improvements already made which when made would become prior liens" to the mortgage purchased by plaintiff and that it was defendant's duty under its contract to do so.

The assessments came into being because of local improvements such as sewers, pavements and sidewalks, which had been constructed, under applicable statutes, in suburban property in certain towns in Monroe county outside the city of Rochester. The improvements had been completed one or two years prior to the issuance of the policies and paid for through bond issues of the several towns. The bonds were to be paid by annual assessments to be levied upon the individual properties benefited. The parties in their briefs have selected chapter 549 of the Laws of 1926 as the statute principally involved. The other statutes are substantially similar.

Taking as an example the town of Brighton, the minutes of the Town Board showed that on June 9, 1928, there was considered the question of the apportionment of the cost of certain street improvements which had theretofore been made; that a proposed assessment roll, apportioning the expenses of the improvements upon the property benefited, having been prepared and submitted, was approved, and a date for the hearing of objections to the said roll was set and the Town Clerk ordered to give the notices required by law; that on June 25, 1928, the Board met for the purpose of hearing objections to said roll, and none having been made the roll and the apportionment therein made on the several lots was finally approved and adopted and the tax therein provided assessed.

Under chapter 549 of the Laws of 1926 the only power to levy assessments is found in section 11. It reads:

> The town board shall thereafter in each year, and before the annual meeting for that year of the board of supervisors of the county in which such town is situated, report to said board of supervisors, the amount of such bonds, which will mature within the ensuing year; and the amount of interest payable within said ensuing year; and a statement of the lots or parcels of land liable to pay the same, and the amount chargeable to each. The board of supervisors shall levy such amounts against the property liable, and shall state the amount of the assessment in a separate column, in the annual tax roll, under the name "street improvement"; and such assessment when collected shall be paid to the supervisor, and be by him applied in payment of the principal and interest of said bonds. The amount annually apportioned by the town board, as provided in this section, on any lot or parcel, and included in the annual tax roll by said board of supervisors, shall be a lien prior and superior to any lien or claim except the lien of an existing tax or local assessment.

The power of apportionment and assessment was conferred on the Town Board by section 9 of chapter 549 and permission granted a property owner to pay in full based upon such assessment, but there could be no levy and no lien until there was annual report by the Town Board of the amount of bonds maturing during the ensuing year, with the amount of interest payable for the same period, followed by annual apportionment by the

Town Board upon the lots and parcels liable therefor and inclusion in the annual tax roll by the Board of Supervisors of the county.

It is clear that there was no lien at the time of the issuance of the policies. The question remains, Was there a charge or incumbrance? If we consider the insurance contract as analogous to a covenant against incumbrances, it is evident that in this State the word charges is used synonymously with liens and incumbrances. It has no larger meaning. In the Real Property Law (Consol. Laws, ch. 50 §253) it is provided:

> 3. Freedom from incumbrances — A covenant "that the said premises are free from incumbrances," must be construed as meaning that such premises are free, clear, discharged and unincumbered of and from all former and other gifts, grants, titles, charges, estates, judgments, taxes, assessments, liens and incumbrances, of what nature or kind soever.

In Doonan v. Killilea, 222 N.Y. 399, 401, 118 N.E. 851, 852, it was said that section 253 of the Real Property Law had reference "not to inchoate assessments or other charges, but to legal liens fully matured. The covenant against incumbrances operates in praesenti and is broken the instant it is made, if an incumbrance exists; but, unless the assessment is then an actual lien, the covenant is not broken."

The case of Mayers v. Van Schaick, 268 N.Y. 320, 197 N.E. 296, is controlling here. It is stronger against plaintiff than is the instant case, since the word used there was "requirements." There Judge Loughran said:

> Title insurance operates to protect a purchaser or a mortgagee against defects in or incumbrances on a title existing at the date of such insurance. It is not prospective in its operation and has no relation to liens or requirements arising thereafter. Trenton Potteries Co. v. Title Guarantee & Trust Co., 176 N.Y. 65, 72, 68 N.E. 132. . . . It follows, we think, that Lawyers Title & Guarantee Company no more agreed with plaintiff to protect him against liability for the unpaid assessment in question than it undertook to indemnify him for taxes to be levied against the premises after delivery of its certificate of title insurance.

268 N.Y. at pages 323, 324, 197 N.E. at page 297. . . .

The judgment should be affirmed with costs.

Problems

31.1. A policy of title insurance specifically excepted "Restrictive covenants in instrument recorded in Liber 211 of Conveyances at page 13 in the office of the Register of the County of New York." The instrument mentioned in the exception provides that in the event of a breach of the covenant, "then this deed shall become void and all the estate, right, title and interest, of said party of the second part, his heirs and assigns in and to the premises hereinbefore described shall cease, determine and become vested in said parties of the first part, their heirs and assigns." The insured in order to obtain a loan on the insured land had to pay $5,000 to obtain releases from the people who might claim the land if the aforementioned covenants were broken. Can the insured collect the $5,000 so paid from the title insurance company? See Holly Hotel Co. v. Title Guarantee & Trust Co., 147 Misc. 861, 264 N.Y.S. 3 (1932), *affirmed*, 239 A.D. 773, 264 N.Y.S. 7 (1933).

31.2. A policy of title insurance was issued to the insured. Schedule B did not specifically except the matter hereafter considered. About a year after the policy was issued, the city in which the insured land was located undertook to grade the street adjacent to the insured premises. As a result of the grading operations, the level of the street was raised about seven feet. As a consequence, the insured was required to raise his house and fill in the land to conform to the new level of the street. At the time the policy of title insurance was issued, there was in existence, on file in the topographical bureau of the borough of Queens, a map of the street system for the area in which the insured's property was located, and this map indicated that the change in grade of the street adjacent to the insured's property had been proposed. Is the title insurance company liable for the expenses incurred by the insured in raising the house and filling in the land to conform to the new level of the street? See Sperling v. Title Guarantee & Trust Co., 227 A.D. 5, 236 N.Y.S. 553 (1929), *affirmed*, 252 N.Y. 613, 170 N.E. 163 (1930).

31.3. A mortgagee obtained a policy of title insurance on the mortgaged land in which policy the mortgagee was insured against any loss or damage by reason "of any defect in the title of the insured to the estate or interest described." The mortgage, shortly thereafter, was declared invalid under the bankruptcy law as a preference. This particular result was not specifically excepted in the policy of title insurance. Does the policy of title insurance protect the mortgagee against such risk? See First National Bank & Trust Co. v. New York Title Ins. Co., 171 Misc. 854, 12 N.Y.S.2d 703 (1939).

31.4. A policy of title insurance specifically provided that the policy would be of no effect if the insured "was not a purchaser for value." The insured was a purchaser for value, but she had actual knowledge of the defect in the title. Is the insured protected by the policy of title insurance in such a case? See Alabama Title & Trust Co. v. Millsap, 71 F.2d 518 (5th Cir. 1934).

Note: Extent to Which Title Insurance Gives the Buyer an Opinion as to the State of the Title

A title insurance policy describes the extent to which defects in the title are insured against. Indirectly, by noting the exceptions to coverage under the policy, one may draw some conclusion as to the state of the title. A lawyer's opinion should directly inform the client of the state of the title. If the buyer is planning to build a million dollar hotel on the land, the buyer wants to have a reliable opinion as to the state of the title, not just an insurance policy that will enable the buyer to recover the price of the land in the event the title is defective. If the title insurance company gives the insured an opinion as to the state of the title, will the insurance company take on a liability in excess of that described in the insurance policy? Consider the following case in answering this question.

GLYN v. TITLE GUARANTEE & TRUST CO.
132 A.D. 859, 117 N.Y.S. 424 (1909)

Appeal by the plaintiff, Mary R. H. Glyn, from a judgment of the Supreme Court in favor of the defendant, entered in the office of the clerk of the county of New York on the 21st day of December, 1908, upon the dismissal of the complaint by direction of the court at the opening on a trial at the New York Trial Term.

SCOTT, J. The complaint was dismissed at the trial before any evidence was introduced. This amounted practically to sustaining a demurrer to the complaint, for insufficiency, and was erroneous if, in any aspect, upon the facts stated in the complaint, the plaintiff was entitled to any recovery. Abbott v. Easton, 195 N.Y. 372, 88 N.E. 572. From the judgment entered upon the dismissal the plaintiff appeals. The complaint attempts to state two causes of action. It sets forth that in November, 1904, plaintiff contracted to buy from one Weed the premises known as No. 47 East Sixty-fifth street in the city of New York, and from one Goodkind the premises known as No. 49 East Sixty-fifth street, and "retained and employed the defendant herein to search the titles to said premises"; that thereafter the defendant certified to plaintiff the title to premises No. 47 East Sixty-fifth street, and said premises were conveyed to plaintiff on or about December 1, 1904; that on December 23, 1904, defendant wrote to plaintiff's husband that it had completed the examination of the title to No. 49 East Sixty-fifth street, and that the letter contained the following statement: "The survey shows variations between the locations of the fences, stoops and record lines. We can guarantee, however, that the stoop of the building may remain undisturbed so long as the same stands. Policy will state no title can be insured to any land lying west of the centre of the westerly part of the party wall and the line in continuation thereof, nor east of a line parallel with Park Avenue and distant 134 feet westerly. As there are party walls on both sides and the lines run through the walls, these cannot affect the marketability of your title. The lines on which we will insure only differ very slightly from the deed dimensions. There are no other incumbrances and objections to title, except as above stated"; that depending and relying upon said report plaintiff took title to said premises No. 49 East Sixty-fifth street; that a long time after she had taken title to said premises, plaintiff discovered that the stoop, the door cap and the pilaster of No. 51 East Sixty-fifth street encroached nine inches or more on the said premises of No. 49 East Sixty-fifth street, and that the newel post of said stoop of No. 51 East Sixty-fifth street encroached one foot and nine inches on said premises No. 49 East Sixty-fifth street, and that said encroachment had existed for over twenty years, and that such encroachments rendered the title to No. 49 East Sixty-fifth street unmarketable; that in engaging defendant to act for her in searching the titles to said premises, plaintiff did not engage the services of a lawyer, but relied entirely upon the defendant, as said defendant well knew; that defendant was careless and negligent and misled plaintiff to her damage.

The second cause of action is based upon a policy of title insurance issued to plaintiff, wherein defendant insured plaintiff's title to said premises No. 49 East Sixty-fifth street, excepting, however, from its contract of insurance "variations between the location of the fences and stoops and the record lines, but the stoop of the building on the premises described in Schedule A may remain undisturbed so long as same stands." The breach of the policy, as alleged, consists of the same encroachments of the door cap, pilaster, stoop and newel post of No. 51 East Sixty-fifth street, described in the first cause of action.

It will be observed that defendant undertook to act for plaintiff in two capacities — as a conveyancer, who examined the title and undertook to advise her whether it was good and marketable, and as an insurer, who undertook to insure that she had a good and marketable title. In the former capacity, the defendant assumed the same responsibilities and owed to the plaintiff the same duty as if it had been an individual attorney or conveyancer. This involved upon its part the exercise of due care and skill in investigating the title, and the utmost frankness toward the plaintiff in disclosing to her the result of its investigations, and in advising her as to what course she should take in view of the facts which had been discovered respecting the title. It has assumed toward the plaintiff the relation of attorney, and thereby assumed all the obligations of an attorney to his client. Ehmer v. Title Guarantee & Trust Co., 156 N.Y. 10, 50 N.E. 420. The encroachments upon the property, which were patent upon inspection, and of which the defendant is chargeable with knowledge, consisted apparently of the overlapping upon plaintiff's premises of the ornamental and nonessential portions of the stoop and portico of the adjoining house, apparently not of a character to found upon it a claim of title to any part of the fee of plaintiff's premises, but perhaps sufficient for the foundation of a claim to the right of support. Whether such encroachments would in point of fact render plaintiff's title unmarketable is perhaps a question (Van Horn v. Stuyvesant, 50 Misc. 432, 100 N.Y.S. 547), but it is apparent that they might to some degree interfere with the free development and improvement of the property, and to that extent might affect its market value. At all events, it was due to the plaintiff that she should be advised of the exact character and nature of the encroachments, to the end that she might be able intelligently to determine whether or not she would accept title to the property incumbered by these encroachments. The only advice or information upon the subject, so far as appears, which the defendant communicated was that contained in the letter above quoted. Clearly, that letter was not calculated to convey to the lay mind the true facts of the case. It is true that the letter states that the survey shows variations between the locations of the fences, stoops and record lines. It does not state what these variations are, and what follows in the letter was calculated and no doubt intended to lead plaintiff to believe that whatever variations were found were of slight importance, or of none at all, and did not affect the marketability of the title. This letter falls far short of informing plaintiff of or even suggesting to her the true state of the encroachments upon the property. Upon the complaint as it stands, the first count, as we think, sufficiently alleges negligence and a failure of duty upon the part of defendant.

The second count seeks to charge defendant upon its contract liability as insurer, and involves many of the same considerations which apply to the first cause of action. The policy insures plaintiff against "any defect or defects of title affecting said premises or affecting the interest of the assured therein, or by reason of unmarketability of the title or by reason of liens or incumbrances at the date of the policy, excepting as the policy might save or exempt." The encroachments described in the complaint, with the right of continued support so long as they might stand, undoubtedly constituted an incumbrance upon the property referred to in the policy, for they were matters which might interfere with or prevent the free use and improvement of the property by the owner, and which the owner could not at will remove, and they are not in our opinion exempted from the operation of the policy by the words contained in the exemption clause, "variations between the location of the fences and stoops and the record lines," for this clause makes no reference to the door cap and pilaster, which also overlap and encroach. It is objected that the complaint does not sufficiently allege damage. It contains as to each cause of action the general allegation that by reason of the premises the plaintiff has suffered damage in the sum of $12,608, with interest. It is true that the plaintiff does not allege in her complaint any facts upon which the amount of her damage can be estimated. It is not necessary that she should do so, for her general allegation of damage is sufficient to permit proof of such damage as is the naturally and legally presumable consequence of the injury done her. Laraway v. Perkins, 10 N.Y. 371. She is entitled to recover the difference between the value of the property when purchased, as it was with the encroachments, and its value as it would have been if there had been no such encroachments. Kidd v. McCormick, 83 N.Y. 391. Whether or not there was any such difference is, of course, a matter of proof; but if it should be established that there was a difference, the allegations of the complaint are sufficient to permit its recovery.

The judgment appealed from must be reversed and a new trial granted, with costs to appellant to abide the event.

McLaughlin, Clarke and Houghton, JJ., concurred.

INGRAHAM, J. (concurring). I do not think that the letter of December 23, 1904, can be treated as giving to the plaintiff an independent cause of action. It was simply a letter that the title had been examined; that a policy would be issued which should insure the plaintiff's title to the property with certain exceptions; and the plaintiff's subsequent acceptance of the policy of insurance issued by the company was an acceptance by the plaintiff of the obligation of the defendant which it assumed by its letter. I think, therefore, the liability of the defendant must depend upon the terms of the policy subsequently issued and accepted by the plaintiff, and that a recovery upon the first cause of action could not be sustained.

Upon the second cause of action I am inclined to agree with Mr. Justice SCOTT that a cause of action was stated, and that it was error to dismiss the complaint. I also agree with his statement as to the measure of damages. I, therefore, concur in the reversal of the judgment.

Judgment and order reversed, new trial ordered, costs to appellant to abide event.

Note: Amount Recoverable Under Title Insurance Policy for Defect in Title Covered by Policy

The title insurance policy will set a maximum amount that is recoverable under the policy if a defect insured against comes to the surface. The following case considers the measure of damages recoverable under a policy.

BEAULLIEU v. ATLANTA TITLE & TRUST CO.
60 Ga. App. 400, 4 S.E.2d 78 (1939)

Action for damages; from Fulton superior court — Judge Humphries. October 19, 1938.

STEPHENS, P.J. C. B. Beaullieu brought suit against Atlanta Title & Trust Company for an alleged breach of a contract of title insurance, to the plaintiff's damage. In the petition plaintiff alleges that he bought from B. P. Hancock a certain described parcel of real estate in the County of Fulton, State of Georgia, and contracted to pay therefor $8,000; that the defendant, on March 18, 1937, for a consideration of $60 paid to it, issued to the plaintiff its title guaranty policy by which it insured the plaintiff against all loss or damage, not exceeding $7,000, which the plaintiff should sustain by reason of any defect or defects of title affecting the property which the plaintiff had contracted to purchase; that the plaintiff entered into possession of the land, and, after proceeding to build thereon a house early in the month of March, 1937, he ascertained that Mrs. Hal Padgett had an easement in and over the property; that plaintiff notified the defendant of this fact; that the defendant admitted the validity of the easement and requested the plaintiff to allow it to bring suit in the plaintiff's name against

Hancock in order to minimize the damage which the plaintiff had sustained; that the plaintiff agreed to this; that on the date of the issuance of the policy the true market value of the property, if unencumbered by the easement, was $15,000; that on this date the true market value of the property encumbered by the easement was $5,000, and that in order to extinguish the easement the plaintiff would be obliged to purchase the land to which the easement is appurtenant at a cost of $50,000. The plaintiff alleges that the defendant has, on demand of the plaintiff, failed and refused to pay the loss which the plaintiff sustained by the easement upon the property, to the plaintiff's damage of $7,000, for which the plaintiff prays.

The defendant filed no general demurrer to the petition, but specially demurred thereto on the ground, among others, that the allegation as to the market value of the property was irrelevant and immaterial, and that the plaintiff in alleging his damage to be the difference between the market value of the property, namely $15,000, without the easement or encroachment thereon, and the value with the easement or encroachment thereon, namely $5,000, alleged the wrong measure of damage by reason of the defendant's breach of its contract of title insurance, and that the correct measure of the plaintiff's damage is the difference between the purchase-money of the property, namely $8,000, and the market value of the property with the easement or encroachment thereon. The defendant also specially demurred to the allegations in the petition that before the purchase of the land the plaintiff had been engaged in the business of selling building supplies; that the land purchased was adapted to the plaintiff's business, and what land of this character would cost. The court in an order dated Oct. 19, 1938, sustained all these demurrers and gave the plaintiff twenty days in which to amend by alleging damages "in reduction of the price paid according to the relative value of the interests lost," . . . . Plaintiff did not amend the petition, but . . . tendered and had certified a bill of exceptions, excepting to the judgment sustaining the special demurrers.

The court properly sustained the special demurrers except the two which are first above referred to. The sole question for determination is what is the plaintiff's measure of damage for the defendant's breach of its contract of title insurance. The plaintiff contends that the measure is the difference between the true market value of the land, as it would be without the easement upon it, and the true market value of the land encumbered with the easement. The defendant contends that the true measure of damage is the difference between the purchase-price of the land and the market value of the land with the easement upon it. The suit is against the title insurer and not against the vendor for breach of warranty.

In respect to a breach of covenant in a deed to land by the covenantor or vendor it is stated in 14 Am. Jur. 604, §186, as follows:

Where an encumbrance is a servitude or easement which can not be removed at the option of either the grantor or grantee, damages will be awarded for the injury proximately caused by the existence and continuance of the encumbrance, the measure of which is deemed to be the difference between the value of the land as it would be without the easement and its value as it is with the easement. This is the rule applicable where the covenant against encumbrances is broken by the existence, at the time of the execution of the deed, of a continuing right of way over the land granted, in favor of a third person, which materially affects the value of the land.

The plaintiff alleges the existence of a servitude or easement upon his property which can not be removed either at his option or at the option of the grantor or the defendant. It can be removed only by agreement with the owner of the dominant tenement. . . .

As stated by the Supreme Court of this State in Mobley v. Lott, *supra,* "The law aims to place the injured party, so far as money can do it, in the position he would have occupied if the contract had been fulfilled. Such is the rule as recognized in this State." In City of New York v. New York & South Brooklyn etc. Co., 231 N.Y. 18 (16 A.L.R. 1059), the defect in the title was a servitude on the land, and the court held that the measure of damages for a breach of warranty was the difference between the value of the land without the servitude and the value of the land with the servitude, or the money reasonably expended by the owner in freeing the land by extinguishing the burden. The decrease in the market value of the land may usually be taken as a proper criterion by which to measure the damages caused by the existence of an easement. Notes 3 L.R.A. 790; 61 A.L.R. 72, 73, 75; 100 A.L.R. 1199; Bronson v. Coffin, 108 Mass. 175.

A contract of title insurance is an agreement whereby the insurer, for a valuable consideration, agrees to indemnify the assured in a specified amount against loss through defects of title to real estate, wherein the latter has an interest, either as purchaser or otherwise; a contract to indemnify against loss through defects in the title to real estate or liens or encumbrances thereon. 62 C.J. 1053, §1. Whatever may be the rule as to the measure of damages in a suit by a vendee against the vendor of land with reference to a breach of warranty of title, and by the Code, §29-202,[2] which refers to the measure of damages against the vendor of realty where the vendee loses a part of the land from a defect in the title warranted, the measure of damage for a breach by an insurer under a policy insuring the title against encumbrances or encroachments is the difference between the value of the property when purchased with the encumbrance or encroachment thereon, and the value of the property as it would have been if there had been no such encumbrance or encroachment. . . . The court erred in sustaining the demurrers directed to the allegations as to the measure of damage.

Judgment reversed.[3] SUTTON, J., concurs. FELTON, J., dissents.

2. "If the purchaser loses part of the land from defect of title, he may claim either a rescission of the entire contract, or a reduction of the price according to the relative value of the land so lost." — EDS.
3. Annot., Measure, Extent or Amount of Recovery on Policy of Title Insurance, 60 A.L.R.2d 972 (1958). — EDS.

PART VIII

LAND USE PLANNING AND DEVELOPMENT[1]

1. Donald S. Snider, Esq., whose contribution and assistance in relation to Part VI is described in the footnote at page 353, assisted in the preparation of Part VIII in the second edition. Because of the rigors and time constraints of an active private law firm practice, Mr. Snider was unable to participate in the revision of this material in the third edition, but his contributions to the second edition have had a carryover effect in revising this material for the third edition.

937

C H A P T E R 3 2

PRIVATE LAW DEVICES

Note: The Common-Interest Residential Community

Land use planning and development in relation to residential property frequently involves imposing mutual restrictions on the use of property in a defined area for the benefit of all the property owners in the area, in combination with some of the area being set aside for the common use of all residents. In order to be specific in considering various matters, the layout and design of the proposed development with which we will be concerned, Lakeville, appears on page 941.

The plans for Lakeville may be developed by the application of common-law rules relating to—

1. covenants that run with the land;
2. conditions that result in the creation of determinable fee simple estates or fee simple estates subject to a right of entry;
3. easements, appurtenant or in gross; and
4. licenses that are revocable or irrevocable.

These various common-law concepts will be the subject of separate study as the foundational background of property law as it operates in the development of the common-interest residential community.

The organizational framework of the common-interest residential community may take several different forms. The following are the principal examples:

1. *The homeowners' association.* Homesites can be purchased in fee with the common areas and facilities owned by a home owners association. Membership in the association is normally an automatic incident of ownership of the homesite. The association would levy assessments on its members for taxes, operating expenses and general community improvements. It would also be charged with the duty of enforcing all "restrictions" for the benefit of the development. The Uniform Planned Community Act (UPCA) is designed to codify the law of homeowners' associations promulgated by the Commissioners on Uniform State Laws.

2. *The condominium.* Homesites can be purchased in fee with the

common areas and facilities owned by all those who own units in the development as tenants in common. Although the condominium (or the cooperative, discussed in the paragraph following) is usually utilized to create property interests in "vertical" estates, i.e., high-rise apartment buildings, the principles applicable to either can usefully be applied to "horizontal" estates. The Commissioners on the Uniform State Laws have also promulgated a Uniform Condominium Act (UCA).

3. *The cooperative.* Shares can be purchased in a corporation which owns the land and the common area and facilities. Each "cooperator," besides owning shares of stock in the corporation, has a long-term, renewable "proprietary lease" giving him or her the right to the exclusive possession of a homesite. The relationship of the homeowners to the cooperative corporation is therefore twofold: they are tenants of the corporation with respect to their homes and they are owners of the corporation by virtue of their shares of stock in it. The Commissioners on Uniform State Laws have adopted a Model Real Estate Cooperative Act (MRECA) which codifies the law of cooperatives.[2] See also the consolidation of the UCA and the UPCA and MRECA into the Uniform Common Interest Ownership Act (UCIOA). This act is discussed in Geis, Beyond the Condominium: The Uniform Common Interest Ownership Act, 17 Real Prop., Prob. & Tr. J. 757 (1982).

4. *The lease.* Persons may rent their homesite under a long-term lease, with periodic reappraisals of the land value to redetermine the rent—the developer, not wanting to "cash-out," retains title to the whole development as lessor. In considering any of the problems which follow, you should ask yourself whether a change in legal form would increase the chances of accomplishment of a desired objective, e.g., the selection of one's neighbors.

These private law devices for controlling the use of land must be contrasted with controls established by some governmental agency. The public law devices for controlling the use of land are considered in Chapter 33.

---

2. It has not been the practice of lenders to finance the purchase of residential leaseholds, and the cooperative, therefore, does not rely on individual financing of each unit but rather relies on a "blanket mortgage" covering all of its properties. Each cooperator takes subject to this blanket mortgage and agrees in the lease to contribute a pro rata share of its interest and amortization. However, each cooperator is jointly and severally liable on this blanket mortgage, which creates unique problems of interdependence. The primary advantage found in the condominium form of ownership, as compared to the cooperative, is that it supplies a form of ownership which permits individual financing of the purchase and resale of each unit. When all the units have been sold, no portion of the site is subject to a blanket mortgage on which all the owners are jointly and severally liable. In other words, the condominium form of ownership is designed to get away from the interdependence characteristic of the cooperative form of ownership. You will of course notice that this advantage of the condominium over the cooperative is irrelevant when comparing the condominium to the homeowners' association since the latter presents no problem of separate financing. See generally Rohan & Reskin, Cooperative Housing Law and Practice (1967); Organization and Management of Cooperative and Mutual Housing Associations (Bureau of Labor Statistics Bulletin No. 858 1946). The MRECA undertakes to provide a statutory mechanism to make cooperative apartment units mortgageable interests in real estate.

LAYOUT AND DESIGN OF PROPOSED DEVELOPMENT

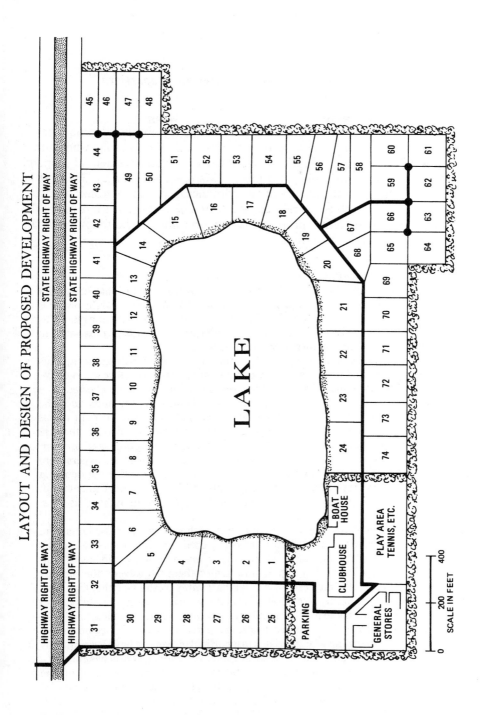

Note: Restricting Conversion of Rental Property to Condominiums

The conversion of rental property to condominiums in some areas is depleting the stock of rental property so severely that persons who cannot afford to buy a condominium have difficulty in finding residential property to rent. Flynn v. City of Cambridge, — Mass. —, 418 N.E.2d 335 (1981), discusses the constitutionality of an ordinance designed to protect an occupant of housing subject to rent control from being evicted as a result of the conversion of the rental property to condominiums. The following is the language of the court's opinion:

II. *The Constitutionality of the Ordinance.*
The plaintiffs contend that the ordinance is unconstitutional because it eliminates an owner's right to possess his condominium unit, and the owner is not compensated for this deprivation. Such a deprivation, claim the plaintiffs, is unduly oppressive and arbitrary in its allocation of rights of possession to persons other than the owner. We do not agree.

The ordinance does deny a condominium owner the right to occupy his unit if it was used for rental housing on and not converted before the effective date of the ordinance. There are two classes of owners who are affected. The first class, those owners who purchase their condominium units after the effective date of the ordinance, are on notice that they have no right to use their property as owner-occupied housing. They are fairly warned that they are purchasing property which may be used for rental housing only, and presumably the purchase price reflects this use restriction. Since these owners were notified that they had no right to occupy their unit, they were not denied a right to which they had a legitimate expectation. Clearly the government is not required to compensate an individual for denying him the right to use that which he has never owned.

The second class of owners is comprised of those owners whose units were purchased prior to, and which were being used for rental housing on, the effective date of the ordinance. These owners, under prior law, did have a right to occupy their unit. That right is now denied them. However, "the submission that [plaintiffs] may establish a 'taking' simply by showing that they have been denied the ability to exploit a property interest that they heretofore had believed was available for development is quite simply untenable. . . . 'Taking' jurisprudence does not divide a single parcel into discrete segments and attempt to determine whether rights in a particular segment have been entirely abrogated. In deciding whether a particular governmental action has effected a taking, [the focus is] rather both on the character of the action and on the nature and extent of the interference with rights *in the parcel as a whole*" (emphasis added). Penn Central Transp. Co. v. New York City, 438 U.S. 104, 130-131, 98 S. Ct. 2646, 2662-63, 57 L. Ed. 2d 631 (1978). In *Penn Central* two factors persuaded the Court that no taking had occurred: the governmental action did not interfere with the owner's primary expectation concerning the use of the property, and the owner was still able to obtain a reasonable return on its investment. Id. at 136, 98 S. Ct. at 2665. The presence of these two factors in this case likewise convinces us that no taking has occurred. By definition, any owner in the second class of owners was using his unit for rental housing on the effective date of the ordinance, so his primary expectation has not been frustrated. While the use restrictions subsequently enacted undeniably diminish the value of the property, this alone does not establish a taking. See Euclid v. Ambler Realty Co., 272 U.S. 365, 47 S. Ct. 114, 71 L. Ed. 303 (1926); Hadacheck v. Sebastian, 239 U.S. 394, 36 S. Ct. 143, 60 L. Ed. 348 (1915). "Government hardly could go on if to some extent values incident to property could not be diminished without paying for every such change in the general law." Pennsylvania Coal Co. v. Mahon, 260 U.S. 393, 413, 43 S. Ct. 158, 159, 67 L. Ed. 322 (1922). In addition, the owner of a controlled rental unit is assured by §7(a) of c. 36, of the right to receive a fair net operating income for his unit. It is not disputed that the ordinance serves a legitimate public purpose. We conclude that there has been no taking. In similar cases, analysis of the factors that we have considered herein has lead to identical conclusions. See, e.g., Agins v. Tiburon, 447 U.S. 255, 261, 100 S. Ct. 2138, 2142, 65 L. Ed. 2d 106 (1980); Andrus v. Allard, 444 U.S. 51, 64-68, 100 S. Ct. 318, 326-328, 62 L. Ed. 2d 210 (1979); Penn Central Transp. Co. v. New York City, 438 U.S. 104, 136, 98 S. Ct. 2643, 2665, 57 L. Ed. 2d 631 (1978). [—Mass at —, 418 N.E.2d at 339.]

Note: *Promotion of Owner Occupancy of Condominiums*

It is believed that widespread occupancy of condominium units by renters tends to cause a deterioration in the enjoyment of condominium ownership. The renter occupancy increases as the condominium ownership is in persons primarily interested in an investment rather than a place to live. To meet this problem, the bylaws of a condominium were amended by the trustees to restrict to two the number of condominium units which could be owned by any one person or entity. This amendment was challenged in Franklin v. Spadafora, 388 Mass. 764, 447 N.E.2d 1244 (1983), on the ground that it was an illegal restraint on alienation. The accepted declared purpose of the amendment was to encourage maximum occupancy by resident owners. The court held that the amendment was a reasonable restraint on alienation and could be enforced. A constitutional challenge was made to the enforcement of the bylaw on the ground that it deprived the plaintiffs of their right to due process and equal protection. The court in rejecting the constitutional attack held that the bylaw served a legitimate purpose and that the means adopted were rationally related to the achievement of that purpose, and thus its enforcement is not unconstitutional.

Tax Note

It is difficult to move in relation to any land transaction without producing some tax consequence. The thoughtful attorney always exposes the tax consequences that will be produced by proposed action. As an illustration of this in relation to the development of a residential area, we consider Rev. Rul. 478, 1968-2 C.B. 330.

The taxpayer in the case considered by Rev. Rul. 478 acquired a large tract of land to be developed as a real estate subdivision. As part of the plan, the taxpayer conveyed to a nonprofit country club part of the land and the improvements thereon, including a golf course, lake, dam, and related recreational facilities, in order to enhance the value of the remaining property and make more saleable the lots being developed for sale. In addition to the allocable cost of the land so conveyed, the taxpayer incurred costs in constructing the golf course, dam, lake, and related recreational facilities. The taxpayer retained no ownership in the land conveyed to the nonprofit country club. Under the local nonprofit corporation law, upon dissolution of the country club entity all its assets will be distributed to a similar corporation or corporations qualifying under state law as nonprofit corporations.

The tax question is, may the developer add the cost of the land transfers and the cost of the improvements on the land made by the developer to the cost basis of the lots retained for sale? If so, the developer's taxable income on the sale of the lots will be reduced. The following is quoted from the ruling in regard to this question:

> If a person engaged in the business of developing and exploiting a real estate subdivision constructs a facility thereon for the basic purposes of inducing people to buy lots therein, the cost of such construction is properly a part of the cost basis of the lots, even though the subdivider retains tenuous rights, without practical value, to the facility constructed (such as contingent reversion). However, if the subdivider retains ownership and control of the facility and has not parted with the property then the cost of such facility is not properly a part of the cost basis of the lots.
>
> The basic purpose of the expenditures, in the instant case, was to make more saleable the lots in the remaining property. Accordingly, the cost of each lot, for the purpose of determining gain or loss, includes a pro rata portion of the cost of the land transferred plus a pro rata portion of the payments made for construction of the golf course, the dam, the lake, and related recreational facilities. [1968-2 C.B. at 331.]

The cooperative would be a highly undesirable form of residential ownership if the interest on any mortgage indebtedness and the real estate taxes payable could not be passed through to the tenant-stockholders as an income tax deduction. Section 216 of the Internal Revenue Code makes these deductions available to the tenant-stockholders.

The assessment payable by each property owner in the development will provide funds to do many of the things a political subdivision does with the money it raises by taxation. The real estate taxes paid to a political subdivision by a property owner are deductible for federal income tax purposes. See section 164 of the Internal Revenue Code. A gift to or for the use of a political subdivision of a state is deductible for federal income tax purposes, subject to certain limitations, under section 170(c) (1) of the Internal Revenue Code. Will the assessments paid by property owners to maintain the development be treated as real estate taxes or as a gift to a political subdivision for federal income tax purposes? If a deduction is allowed for the assessments paid, the federal government will be underwriting to some significant extent the cost of the maintenance of the exclusive residential area contemplated in the development.

Revenue Ruling 485, 1968-2 C.B. 107, denied any deductions under section 170. The ruling stated:

> The organization has as its objective the maintenance of a private residential community of an exclusive nature and its activities are directed toward that purpose. However, such activities, within the context of a private community in which access to and use of the facilities in question are restricted essentially to residents of that community, serve largely to enhance or preserve private property interests and are not for public or charitable purposes within the meaning of the term 'charitable' of §170(c) (2) of the Code. [1968-2 C.B. at 108.]

Revenue Ruling 95, 1976-2 C.B. 43, provides as follows:

> Advice has been requested whether annual assessments paid to a home-owners association by its members are deductible as real property taxes under section 164(a) of the Internal Revenue Code of 1954.
>
> The homeowners association is a corporation organized to maintain and care for the common property of a residential housing project. Each person who owns a lot within the confines of the housing project is a member of the association. Membership is appurtenant to and may not be separated from ownership of a lot, and ownership of a lot is the sole qualification for membership in the association. The association imposes an annual assessment on the owner of each lot to be used exclusively to promote the recreation, health, safety, and welfare of the residents of the project and to maintain the common areas of the project. Under the association's by-laws each member is required to pay the annual assessment. An unpaid assessment is a charge on the land and is a continuing lien on the property against which the assessment is made.
>
> Section 164(a) of the Code allows as a deduction state and local, and foreign, real property taxes paid or accrued within the taxable year.
>
> Section 164(b)(3) of the Code provides that a state or local tax includes only a tax imposed by a state, a possession of the United States, or a political subdivision of any of the foregoing, or by the District of Columbia.

In this case, the annual assessments are imposed by the association and not by the state or political subdivision in which the housing project is located.

Accordingly, in the instant case, the annual assessments paid to the association by its members are not state or local real property taxes and, therefore, are not deductible as real property taxes under section 164(a) of the Code.

Though contributions to a central organization responsible for maintaining the common areas of the development are not deductible, the organization may be tax-exempt if it is not organized for profit. Section 528 of the Internal Revenue Code provides as follows:

(a) *General Rule.*—A homeowners association (as defined in subsection (c)) shall be subject to taxation under this subtitle only to the extent provided in this section. A homeowners association shall be considered an organization exempt from income taxes for the purpose of any law which refers to organizations exempt from income taxes.

(b) *Tax Imposed.*—A tax is hereby imposed for each taxable year on the homeowners association taxable income of every homeowners association. Such tax shall be equal to 30 percent of the homeowners association taxable income.

(c) *Homeowners Association Defined.*—For purposes of this section—

(1) *Homeowners Association.*—The term "homeowners association" means an organization which is a condominium management association or a residential real estate management association if—

    (A)   such organization is organized and operated to provide for the acquisition, construction, management, maintenance, and care of association property,

    (B)   60 percent or more of the gross income of such organization for the taxable year consists solely of amounts received as membership dues, fees, or assessments from—

        (i)   owners of residential units in the case of a condominium management association, or

        (ii)   owners of residences or residential lots in the case of a residential real estate management association.

    (C)   90 percent or more of the expenditures of the organization for the taxable year are expenditures for the acquisition, construction, management, maintenance, and care of association property,

    (D)   no part of the net earnings of such organization inures (other than by acquiring, constructing, or providing management, maintenance, and care of association property, and other than by a rebate of excess membership dues, fees, or assessments) to the benefit of any private shareholder or individual, and

    (E)   such organization elects (at such time and in such manner as the Secretary by regulations prescribes) to have this section apply for the taxable year.

(2) *Condominium management association.*—The term "condominium management association" means any organization meeting the requirement

of subparagraph (A) of paragraph (1) with respect to a condominium project substantially all of the units of which are used by individuals for residences.

(3) *Residential real estate management association.* — The term "residential real estate management association" means any organization meeting the requirements of subparagraph (A) of paragraph (1) with respect to a subdivision, development, or similar area substantially all the lots or buildings of which may only be used by individuals for residences.

(4) *Association property.* — The term "association property" means —

    (A)   property held by the organization,

    (B)   property commonly held by the members of the organization,

    (C)   property within the organization privately held by the members of the organization, and

    (D)   property owned by a governmental unit and used for the benefit of residents of such unit.

(d) *Homeowners Association Taxable Income Defined.* —

(1) *Taxable income defined.* — For purposes of this section, the homeowners association taxable income of any organization for any taxable year is an amount equal to the excess (if any) of—

    (A)   the gross income for the taxable year (excluding any exempt function income), over

    (B)   the deductions allowed by this chapter which are directly connected with the production of the gross income (excluding exempt function income), computed with the modifications provided in paragraph (2).

(2) *Modifications.* — For purposes of this subsection —

    (A)   there shall be allowed a specific deduction of $100,

    (B)   no net operating loss deduction shall be allowed under section 172, and

    (C)   no deduction shall be allowed under part VIII of subchapter B (relating to special deductions for corporations).

(3) *Exempt function income.* — For purposes of this subsection, the term "exempt function income" means any amount received as membership dues, fees, or assessments from —

    (A)   owners of condominium housing units in the case of a condominium management association, or

    (B)   owners of real property in the case of a residential real estate management association.

See also in regard to tax exemption on grounds other than section 528 the following: Rev. Rul. 99, 1974-1 C.B. 131; Rev. Rul. 494, 1975-2 C.B. 214; Rev. Rul. 63, 1980-1 C.B. 116. In regard to whether payments to a nonexempt homeowners' association is income or a contribution to capital, see Rev. Rul. 563, 1974-2 C.B. 38; Rev. Rul. 370, 1975-2 C.B. 25; Rev. Rul. 371, 1975-2 C.B. 52.

SECTION 1. THE SELECTION OF NEIGHBORS

Note: The Developer's Desire

In almost every development or community, whether from a desire to live among neighbors with similar social or economic backgrounds — caused either by prejudice or snobbishness — or from a desire to maintain property values, etc., people frequently seek a legal means to select their neighbors and exclude therefrom those they consider social "undesirables."[3] When reading the material in this section, you should consider the problem posed by the following memorandum written by a senior partner of your law firm:

> A client of ours owns some valuable lake-front property in a residential area. The client proposes to develop this tract of land into various homesites and plans to retain one homesite. For the sake of persons who might be willing to pay a substantial price to live in an exclusive residential colony, the client wants to retain some control over transfers of ownership or possession so that the "colony" can guard against the transfer of ownership or possession to persons they consider undesirable. How can such an arrangement be legally established?
>
> I am only vaguely familiar with the various legal forms available to develop a tract of land. The possibility of a home owners association, a condominium set up, a cooperative housing corporation or long-term leasing immediately come to mind, and I would appreciate your comments as to whether the legal form our client selects will determine whether the objective may lawfully be attained, and if so, which form you suggest.

SHELLEY v. KRAEMER
334 U.S. 1, 68 S. Ct. 836 (1948)

On Writ of Certiorari to the Supreme Court of the State of Missouri.

On Writ of Certiorari to the Supreme Court of the State of Michigan.

Suit by Louis Kraemer and wife against J. D. Shelley and wife to enforce restrictive covenants against occupancy or ownership of property by people of the Negro race. A judgment for defendants was reversed by the Supreme Court of Missouri, 355 Mo. 814, 198 S.W.3d 679, and the defendants bring certiorari.

Reversed.

Suit by Benjamin J. Sipes and others against Orsel McGhee and wife to

---

3. The term "undesirables" has been carefully selected so as to avoid any editorial prejudgment of values and to permit the fullest possible discussion of its possible content, leaving to those wiser than we the task of suitable definition.

enforce a covenant that property should not be used or occupied by any person except those of the Caucasian race. A judgment for plaintiffs was affirmed by the Supreme Court of Michigan, 316 Mich. 614, 25 N.W.2d 638, and the defendants bring certiorari.

Reversed.

Mr. Chief Justice VINSON delivered the opinion of the court.

These cases present for our consideration questions relating to the validity of court enforcement of private agreements, generally described as restrictive covenants, which have as their purpose the exclusion of persons of designated race or color from the ownership or occupancy of real property. Basic constitutional issues of obvious importance have been raised. . . .

Whether the equal protection clause of the Fourteenth Amendment inhibits judicial enforcement by state courts of restrictive covenants based on race or color is a question which this Court has not heretofore been called upon to consider. . . .

It is well, at the outset, to scrutinize the terms of the restrictive agreements involved in these cases. In the Missouri case, the covenant declares that no part of the affected property shall be [355 Mo. 814, 198 S.W.2d 681] "occupied by any person not of the Caucasian race, it being intended hereby to restrict the use of said property . . . against the occupancy as owners or tenants of any portion of said property for resident or other purpose by people of the Negro or Mongolian Race." Not only does the restriction seek to proscribe use and occupancy of the affected properties by members of the excluded class, but as construed by the Missouri courts, the agreement requires that title of any person who uses his property in violation of the restriction shall be divested. The restriction of the covenant in the Michigan case seeks to bar occupancy by persons of the excluded class. It provides that [316 Mich. 614, 25 N.W.2d 642] "This property shall not be used or occupied by any person or persons except those of the Caucasian race." . . .

It is . . . clear that restrictions on the right of occupancy of the sort sought to be created by the private agreements in these cases could not be squared with the requirements of the Fourteenth Amendment if imposed by state statute or local ordinance. We do not understand respondents to urge the contrary. In the case of Buchanan v. Warley, [245 U.S. 60, 38 S. Ct. 16, 62 L. Ed. 149 (1917)] a unanimous Court declared unconstitutional the provisions of a city ordinance which denied to colored persons the right to occupy houses in blocks in which the greater number of houses were occupied by white persons, and imposed similar restrictions on white persons with respect to blocks in which the greater number of houses were occupied by colored persons. During the course of the opinion in that case, this Court stated: "The Fourteenth Amendment and these statutes enacted in furtherance of its purpose operate to qualify and entitle a colored man to acquire property without state legislation discriminating against him solely because of color."

In Harmon v. Tyler, 1927, 273 U.S. 668, 47 S. Ct. 471, 71 L. Ed. 831, a unanimous court, on the authority of Buchanan v. Warley, *supra,* declared invalid an ordinance which forbade any Negro to establish a home on any property in a white community or any white person to establish a home in a Negro community, "except on the written consent of a majority of the persons of the opposite race inhabiting such community or portion of the City to be affected."

The precise question before this Court in both the Buchanan and Harmon cases, involved the rights of white sellers to dispose of their properties free from restrictions as to potential purchasers based on considerations of race or color. But that such legislation is also offensive to the rights of those desiring to acquire and occupy property and barred on grounds of race or color, is clear, not only from the language of the opinion in Buchanan v. Warley, *supra,* but from this Court's disposition of the case of City of Richmond v. Deans, 1930, 281 U.S. 704, 50 S. Ct. 407, 74 L. Ed. 1128. There, a Negro, barred from the occupancy of certain property by the terms of an ordinance similar to that in the *Buchanan* case, sought injunctive relief in the federal courts to enjoin the enforcement of the ordinance on the grounds that its provisions violated the terms of the Fourteenth Amendment. Such relief was granted, and this Court affirmed, finding the citation of Buchanan v. Warley, *supra,* and Harmon v. Tyler, *supra,* sufficient to support its judgment.

But the present cases, unlike those just discussed, do not involve action by state legislatures or city councils. Here the particular patterns of discrimination and the areas in which the restrictions are to operate, are determined, in the first instance, by the terms of agreements among private individuals. Participation of the State consists in the enforcement of the restrictions so defined. The crucial issue with which we are here confronted is whether this distinction removes these cases from the operation of the prohibitory provisions of the Fourteenth Amendment.

Since the decision of this Court in the Civil Rights Cases, 1883, 109 U.S. 3, 2 S. Ct. 18, 27 L. Ed. 835, the principle has become firmly embedded in our constitutional law that the action inhibited by the first section of the Fourteenth Amendment is only such action as may fairly be said to be that of the States. That Amendment erects no shield against merely private conduct, however discriminatory or wrongful.

We conclude, therefore, that the restrictive agreements standing alone cannot be regarded as a violation of any rights guaranteed to petitioners by the Fourteenth Amendment. So long as the purposes of those agreements are effectuated by voluntary adherence to their terms, it would appear clear that there has been no action by the State and the provisions of the Amendment have not been violated. Cf. Corrigan v. Buckley [271 U.S. 323, 46 S. Ct. 521, 70 L. Ed. 969 (1926)].

But here there was more. These are cases in which the purposes of the agreements were secured only by judicial enforcement by state courts of the restrictive terms of the agreements. . . .

We have no doubt that there has been state action in these cases in the full and complete sense of the phrase. The undisputed facts disclose that petitioners were willing purchasers of properties upon which they desired to establish homes. The owners of the properties were willing sellers; and contracts of sale were accordingly consummated. It is clear that but for the active intervention of the state courts, supported by the full panoply of state power, petitioners would have been free to occupy the properties in question without restraint.

These are not cases, as has been suggested, in which the States have merely abstained from action, leaving private individuals free to impose such discriminations as they see fit. Rather, these are cases in which the States have made available to such individuals the full coercive power of government to deny to petitioners, on the grounds of race or color, the enjoyment of property rights in premises which petitioners are willing and financially able to acquire and which the grantors are willing to sell. The difference between judicial enforcement and non-enforcement of the restrictive covenants is the difference to petitioners between being denied rights of property available to other members of the community and being accorded full enjoyment of those rights on an equal footing. . . .

We hold that in granting judicial enforcement of the restrictive agreements in these cases, the States have denied petitioners the equal protection of the laws and that, therefore, the action of the state courts cannot stand. We have noted that freedom from discrimination by the States in the enjoyment of property rights was among the basic objectives sought to be effectuated by the framers of the Fourteenth Amendment. That such discrimination has occurred in these cases is clear. Because of the race or color of these petitioners they have been denied rights of ownership or occupancy enjoyed as a matter of course by other citizens of different race or color. . . .

Respondents urge, however, that since the state courts stand ready to enforce restrictive covenants excluding white persons from the ownership or occupancy of property covered by such agreements, enforcement of covenants excluding colored persons may not be deemed a denial of equal protection of the laws to the colored persons who are thereby affected. This contention does not bear scrutiny. The parties have directed our attention to no case in which a court, state or federal, has been called upon to enforce a covenant excluding members of the white majority from ownership or occupancy of real property on grounds of race or color. But there are more fundamental considerations. The rights created by the first section of the Fourteenth Amendment are, by its terms, guaranteed to the individual. The rights established are personal rights. It is, therefore, no answer to these petitioners to say that the courts may also be induced to deny white persons rights of ownership and occupancy on grounds of race or color. Equal protection of the laws is not achieved through indiscriminate imposition of inequalities.

Nor do we find merit in the suggestion that property owners who are parties to these agreements are denied equal protection of the laws if denied access to the courts to enforce the terms of restrictive covenants and to assert property rights which the state courts have held to be created by such agreements. The Constitution confers upon no individual the right to demand action by the State which results in the denial of equal protection of the laws to other individuals. And it would appear beyond question that the power of the State to create and enforce property interests must be exercised within the boundaries defined by the Fourteenth Amendment. Cf. Marsh v. Alabama, 1946, 326 U.S. 501, 66 S. Ct. 276, 90 L. Ed. 265. . . .

For the reasons stated, the judgment of the Supreme Court of Missouri and the judgment of the Supreme Court of Michigan must be reversed.

Reversed.

Mr. Justice REED, Mr. Justice JACKSON, and Mr. Justice RUTLEDGE took no part in the consideration or decision of these cases.

BARROWS v. JACKSON
346 U.S. 249, 73 S. Ct. 1031 (1953)

Mr. Justice MINTON delivered the opinion of the Court.

This Court held in Shelley v. Kraemer, 334 U.S. 1, 92 L. Ed. 1161, 68 S. Ct. 836, 3 A.L.R.2d 441, that racial restrictive covenants could not be enforced in equity against Negro purchasers because such enforcement would constitute state action denying equal protection of the laws to the Negroes, in violation of the Fourteenth Amendment to the Federal Constitution. The question we now have is: Can such a restrictive covenant be enforced at law by a suit for damages against a co-covenantor who allegedly broke the covenant?

Petitioners sued respondent at law for damages for breach of a restrictive covenant the parties entered into as owners of residential real estate in the same neighborhood in Los Angeles, California. The petitioners' complaint alleged in part:

> That by the terms of said Agreement each of the signers promised and agreed in writing and bound himself, his heirs, executors, administrators, successors, and assigns, by a continuing covenant that no part of his said real property, described therein, should ever at any time be used or occupied by any person or persons not wholly of the white or Caucasian race, and also agreed and promised in writing that this restriction should be incorporated in all papers and transfers of lots or parcels of land hereinabove referred to; provided, however, that said restrictions should not prevent the employment by the owners or tenants of said real property of domestic servants or other employees who are not wholly of the white or Caucasian race; provided, further, however, that such employees shall be permitted to occupy said real property only when actively engaged in such employment. That said Agreement was agreed to be a covenant running with the land. That each provision in said Agreement was for the benefit for all the lots therein described.

The complaint further alleged that respondent broke the covenant in two respects: (1) by conveying her real estate without incorporating in the deed the restriction contained in the covenant; and (2) by permitting non-Caucasians to move in and occupy the premises. The trial court sustained a demurrer to the complaint, the District Court of Appeals for the Second Appellate District affirmed, 112 Cal. App. 2d 534, 247 P.2d 99, and the Supreme Court of California denied hearing. We granted certiorari, 345 U.S. 902, *supra,* 1339, 73 S. Ct. 644, because of the importance of the constitutional question involved and to consider the conflict which has arisen in the decisions of the state courts since our ruling in the *Shelley* Case (U.S.) *supra.* . . .

The trial court in the case here held that a party to a covenant restricting use and occupancy of real estate to Caucasians could not maintain a suit at law against a co-covenantor for breach of the covenant because of our ruling in *Shelley, supra.* In *Shelley,* this Court held that the action of the lower courts in granting equitable relief in the enforcement of such covenants constituted state action denying to Negroes, against whom the covenant was sought to be enforced, equal protection of the laws in violation of the Fourteenth Amendment. This Court said:

> We conclude, therefore, that the restrictive agreements standing alone cannot be regarded as violative of any rights guaranteed to petitioners by the Fourteenth Amendment. So long as the purposes of those agreements are effectuated by voluntary adherence to their terms, it would appear clear that there has been no action by the State and the provisions of the Amendment have not been violated. . . ." [334 U.S. 1, 13, 92 L. Ed. 1161, 1180, 68 S. Ct. 836, 3 A.L.R.2d 441.]

That is to say, the law applicable in that case did not make the covenant itself invalid, no one would be punished for making it, and no one's constitutional rights were violated by the covenantor's voluntary adherence thereto. Such voluntary adherence would constitute individual action only. When, however, the parties cease to rely upon voluntary action to carry out the covenant and the State is asked to step in and give its sanction to the enforcement of the covenant, the first question that arises is whether a court's awarding damages constitutes state action under the Fourteenth Amendment. To compel respondent to respond in damages would be for the State to punish her for her failure to perform her covenant to continue to discriminate against non-Caucasians in the use of her property. The result of that sanction by the State would be to encourage the use of restrictive covenants. To that extent, the State would act to put its sanction behind the covenants. If the State may thus punish respondent for her failure to carry out her covenant, she is coerced to continue to use her property in a discriminatory manner, which in essence is the purpose of the covenant. Thus, it becomes not respondent's voluntary choice but the State's choice that she observe her covenant or suffer damages. The action of a state court at law to sanction the validity of the restrictive covenant here involved would constitute state action as surely as it was state action to enforce such covenants in equity, as in *Shelley, supra.*

The next question to emerge is whether the state action in allowing damages deprives anyone of rights protected by the Constitution. If a state court awards damages for breach of a restrictive covenant, a prospective seller of restricted land will either refuse to sell to non-Caucasians or else will require non-Caucasians to pay a higher price to meet the damages which the seller may incur. Solely because of their race, non-Caucasians will be unable to purchase, own, and enjoy property on the same terms as Caucasians. Denial of this right by state action deprives such non-Caucasians, unidentified but identifiable, of equal protection of the laws in violation of the Fourteenth Amendment. See *Shelley, supra.*

But unlike *Shelley, supra,* no non-Caucasian is before the Court claiming to have been denied his constitutional rights. May respondent, whom petitioners seek to coerce by an action to pay damages for her failure to honor her restrictive covenant, rely on the invasion of the rights of others in her defense to this action?

Ordinarily, one may not claim standing in this Court to vindicate the constitutional rights of some third party. . . .

There is such a close relationship between the restrictive covenant here and the sanction of a state court which would punish respondents for not going forward with her covenant, and the purpose of the covenant itself, that relaxation of the rule is called for here. It sufficiently appears that mulcting in damages of respondent will be solely for the purpose of giving vitality to the restrictive covenant, that is to say, to punish respondent for not continuing to discriminate against non-Caucasians in the use of her property. This Court will not permit or require California to coerce respondent to respond in damages for failure to observe a restrictive covenant that this Court would deny California the right to enforce in equity, *Shelley, supra;* or that this Court would deny California the right to incorporate in a statute, Buchanan v. Warley, 245 U.S. 60, 62 L. Ed. 149, 38 S. Ct. 16, L.R.A.1918C 210, Ann. Cas. 1918A 1201; or that could not be enforced in a federal jurisdiction because such a covenant would be contrary to public policy. . . .

Consistency in the application of the rules of practice in this Court does not require us in this unique set of circumstances to put the State in such an equivocal position simply because the person against whom the injury is directed is not before the Court to speak for himself. The law will permit respondent to resist any effort to compel her to observe such a covenant, so widely condemned by the courts, since she is the one in whose charge and keeping reposes the power to continue to use her property to discriminate or to discontinue such use. The relation between the coercion exerted on respondent and her possible pecuniary loss thereby is so close to the purpose of the restrictive covenant, to violate the constitutional rights of those discriminated against, that respondent is the only effective adversary of the unworthy covenant in its last stand. She will be permitted to protect herself and, by so doing, close the gap to the use of this covenant, so universally condemned by the courts. . . .

It is contended by petitioners that for California courts to refuse to enforce this covenant is to impair the obligation of their contracts. Article I, §10, of the Federal Constitution provides: "No State shall . . . pass any . . . Law impairing the Obligation of Contracts. . . . " The short answer to this contention is that this provision, as its terms indicate, is directed against legislative action only.

"It has been settled by a long line of decisions, that the provision of §10, Article I, of the Federal Constitution, protecting the obligation of contracts against state action, is directed only against impairment by legislation and not by judgments of courts. . . . " Tidal Oil Co. v. Flanagan, 263 U.S. 444, 451, 68 L. Ed. 382, 385, 44 S. Ct. 197.

It is finally contended that petitioners are denied due process and equal protection of the laws by the failure to enforce the covenant. The answer to that proposition is stated by the Court in *Shelley, supra,* in these words:

"The Constitution confers upon no individual the right to demand action by the State which results in the denial of equal protection of the laws to other individuals. . . . " 334 U.S. 1, 22, 92 L. Ed. 1161, 1185, 68 S. Ct. 836, 3 A.L.R.2d 441.

The judgment is affirmed.

[The dissenting opinion of VINSON, C.J., is omitted.]

Problem

32.1. A fee simple determinable is an estate that ends automatically when the terminating event occurs and the person who held the possibility of reverter automatically becomes the owner in fee simple of the property. If the person who owned the fee simple determinable does not leave the property after the occurrence of the terminating event, such person can be removed by an action of ejectment. O, the developer of Lakeville, sells Lot 1 "to A and his [or her] heirs as long as the title to Lot 1 and the possession of Lot 1 are in a Caucasian." A sells Lot 1 to B, a non-Caucasian, who takes possession thereof. O brings an action of ejectment against B. If the state court allows O to prevail in the action of ejectment, is this state action prohibited by the fourteenth amendment? See Charlotte Park & Recreation Commission v. Barringer, 242 N.C. 311, 88 S.E.2d 114 (1955), *cert. denied,* 350 U.S. 983 (1956). See also Evans v. Abney, 396 U.S. 435, 90 S. Ct. 628 (1970). See also Sams, Application of the Doctrine of Shelley v. Kraemer to the Determinable Fee, 33 Miss. L.J. 200 (1962); Goldstein, Rights of Entry and Possibilities of Reverter as Devices to Restrict the Use of Land, 54 Harv. L. Rev. 248 (1940).

Note: The Civil Rights Act of 1866

The Civil Rights Act of 1866[4] provides: "All citizens of the United States shall have the same right, in every state and Territory, as is enjoyed by the white citizens thereof to inherit, purchase, lease, sell, hold, and convey real and personal property." Prior to 1968, this was believed by many to protect blacks only against "state action," and the battle was fought over what constituted state action. In Jones v. Alfred H. Mayer Co., 392 U.S. 409, 88 S. Ct. 2186 (1968), the United States Supreme Court held that this statute "means exactly what it says":

> So long as a Negro citizen who wants to buy or rent a home can be turned away simply because he is not white, he cannot be said to enjoy "the *same* right . . . as is enjoyed by white citizens . . . to . . . purchase [and] lease . . . real and personal property." 42 U.S.C. §1982 (Emphasis added.)
> On its face, therefore, §1982 appears to prohibit *all* discrimination against Negroes in the sale or rental of property—discrimination by private as well as discrimination by public authorities. Indeed, even the respondents seem to concede that, if §1982 "means what it says"—to use the words of the respondents' brief—then it must encompass every racially motivated refusal to sell or rent and cannot be confined to officially sanctioned segregation in housing. Stressing what they consider to be the revolutionary implications of so literal a reading of §1982, the respondents argue that Congress cannot possibly have intended any such result. Our examination of the relevant history, however, persuades us that Congress meant exactly what it said. [392 U.S. at 421–422, 88 S. Ct. at 2193–2194.[5]]

The Supreme Court concluded that section 1982 "bars *all* racial discrimination, private as well as public, in the sale or rental of property, and that the statute, thus construed, is a valid exercise of the power of Congress to enforce the Thirteenth Amendment."

Problem

32.2. In light of the *Jones* case, how would you advise a developer who comes to you and asks your advice as to the possible use of a fee simple determinable to assure the exclusion of blacks from an exclusive residential suburb?

---

4. 14 Stat. 27, 42 U.S.C. §1982.
5. See Kinoy, Constitutional Right of Negro Freedom Revisited: Some First Thoughts on Jones v. Alfred H. Mayer Company, 22 Rutgers L. Rev. 537 (1968); Note: Discrimination in Employment and in Housing: Private Enforcement Provisions of the Civil Rights Acts of 1964 and 1968, 82 Harv. L. Rev. §834 (1969).

Note: *The Civil Rights Act of 1968*

You should also consider, in this area, the impact of Title VIII of the Civil Rights Act of 1968, discussed in Jones v. Alfred H. Mayer Co., *supra,* as follows:

Whatever else it may be, 42 U.S.C. §1982 is not a comprehensive open housing law. In sharp contrast to the Fair Housing Title (Title VIII) of the Civil Rights Act of 1968, Pub. L. 90-284, 82 Stat. 73, the statute in this case deals only with racial discrimination and does not address itself to discrimination on grounds of religion or national origin.[6] It does not deal specifically with discrimination in the provision of services or facilities in connection with the sale or rental of a dwelling.[7] It does not prohibit advertising or other representations that indicate discriminatory preferences.[8] It does not refer explicitly to discrimination in financing arrangements[9] or in the provision of brokerage services.[10] It does not empower a federal administrative agency to

6. Contrast the Civil Rights Act of 1968, §804(a). [This section provides that ". . . it shall be unlawful — (a) To refuse to sell or rent after the making of a bona fide offer, or to refuse to negotiate for the sale or rental of, or otherwise make unavailable or deny, a dwelling to any person because of race, color, religion, or national origin." In 1974, this wording was expanded to include "sex."]

7. Contrast §804(b). [This section provides that it should be unlawful "(b) To discriminate against any person in the terms, conditions, or privileges of sale or rental of a dwelling, or in the provision of services or facilities in connection therewith, because of race, color, religion, or national origin." In 1974, this wording was expanded to include "sex."]

8. Contrast §804(c),(d),(e). [These sections provide that it shall be unlawful "(c) To make, print, or publish, or cause to be made, printed, or published any notice, statement, or advertisement, with respect to the sale or rental of a dwelling that indicates any preference, limitation, or discrimination based on race, color, religion, or national origin, or an intention to make any such preference, limitation, or discrimination. [In 1974, this wording was expanded to include "sex."] (d) To represent to any person because of race, color, religion, or national origin that any dwelling is not available for inspection, sale or rental when such dwelling is in fact so available. [In 1974, this wording was expanded to include "sex."] (e) For profit, to induce or attempt to induce any person to sell or rent any dwelling by representations regarding the entry or provective entry into the neighborhood of a person or persons of a particular race, color, religion, or national origin. [In 1974, this wording was expanded to include "sex."]."]

9. Contrast §805. [This section provides: "After December 31, 1968, it shall be unlawful for any (financial institution), to deny a loan or other financial assistance to a person applying therefor for the purpose of purchasing, constructing, improving, repairing, or maintaining a dwelling or to discriminate against him in the fixing of the amount, interest rate, duration, or other terms or conditions of such loan or other financial assistance, because of the race, color, religion, or national origin of such person or of any person associated with him in connection with such loan or other financial assistance or the purchase of such loan or other financial assistance, or of the present or prospective owners, lessees, tenants, or occupants of the dwelling or dwellings in relation to which such loan or other financial assistance is to be made or given: . . ."]

10. Contrast §806. . . . [This section provides: "After December 31, 1968, it shall be unlawful to deny any person access to or membership or participation in any multiple-listing service, real estate brokers' organization or other service, organization, or facility relating to the business of selling or renting dwellings, or to discriminate against him in the terms or conditions of such access, membership or participation, on account of race, color, religion, or national origin."]

assist aggrieved parties.[11] It makes no provision for intervention by the Attorney General.[12] And, although it can be enforced by injunction, it contains no provision expressly authorizing a federal court to order the payment of damages.[13]

Thus, although §1982 contains none of the exemptions that Congress included in the Civil Rights Act of 1968,[14] it would be a serious mistake to

11.   Contrast the Civil Rights Act of 1968, §808-811.
12.   Contrast §813(a).
13.   Contrast the Civil Rights Act of 1968 §812 (c). . . .
14.   The discrimination in the sale or rental of housing prohibited by §804 is subject to the exemptions provided in §803(b) and in §807. These exemptions are as follows:

Sec. 803.   (b) Nothing in section 804 (other than subsection (c)) shall apply to—

(1)   any single-family house sold or rented by an owner: *Provided,* That such private individual owner does not own more than three such single-family houses at any one time: *Provided further,* That in the case of the sale of any such single-family house by private individual owner not residing in such house at the time of such sale or who was not the most recent resident of such house prior to such sale, the exemption granted by this subsection shall apply only with respect to one such sale within any twenty-four month period: *Provided further,* That such bona fide private individual owner does not own any interest in, nor is there owned or reserved on his behalf, under any express or voluntary agreement, title to or any right to all or a portion of the proceeds from the sale or rental of, more than three such single-family houses at any one time: *Provided further,* That after December 31, 1969, the sale or rental of any such single-family house shall be excepted from the application of this title only if such house is sold or rented (A) without the use in any manner of the sales or rental facilities or the sales or rental services of any real estate broker, agent, or salesman, or of such facilities or services of any person in the business of selling or renting dwellings, or of any employee or agent of any such broker, agent, salesman, or person and (B) without the publication, posting or mailing, after notice, of any advertisement or written notice in violation of section 804(c) of this title; but nothing in this proviso shall prohibit the use of attorneys, escrow agents, abstractors, title companies, and other such professional assistance as necessary to perfect or transfer the title, or
(2)   rooms or units in dwellings containing living quarters occupied or intended to be occupied by no more than four families living independently of each other, if the owner actually maintains and occupies one of such living quarters as his residence.

(c)   For the purposes of subsection (b), a person shall be deemed to be in the business of selling or renting dwellings if—

(1)   he has, within the preceding twelve months, participated as principal in three or more transactions involving the sale or rental of any dwelling or any interest therein, or
(2)   he has, within the preceding twelve months, participated as agent, other than in the sale of his own personal residence in providing sales or rental facilities or sales or rental services in two or more transactions involving the sale or rental of any dwelling or any interest therein, or
(3)   he is the owner of any dwelling designed or intended for occupancy by, or occupied by, five or more families.

Sec. 807.   Nothing in this title shall prohibit a religious organization, association, or society, or any nonprofit institution or organization operated, supervised or controlled by or in conjunction with a religious organization, association, or society, from limiting the sale, rental or occupancy of dwellings which it owns or operates for other than a commercial purpose to persons of the same religion, or from giving preference to such

suppose that §1982 in any way diminishes the significance of the law recently enacted by Congress. [392 U.S. at 413–415, 88 S. Ct. at 2189–2190.]

persons, unless membership in such religion is restricted on account of race, color, or national origin. Nor shall anything in this title prohibit a private club not in fact open to the public, which as an incident to its primary purpose or purposes provides lodgings which it owns or operates for other than a commercial purpose, from limiting the rental or occupancy of such lodgings to its members or giving preference to its members.

[Sec. 810. (a) Any person who claims to have been injured by a discriminatory housing practice or who believes that he will be irrevocably injured by a discriminatory housing practice that is about to occur (hereafter "person aggrieved") may file a complaint with the Secretary. Complaints shall be in writing and shall contain such information and be in such form as the Secretary requires. Upon receipt of such a complaint the Secretary shall furnish a copy of the same to the person or persons who allegedly committed or are about to commit the alleged discriminatory housing practice. Within thirty days after receiving a complaint, or within thirty days after the expiration of any period of reference under subsection *(c)*, the Secretary shall investigate the complaint and give notice in writing to the person aggrieved whether he intends to resolve it. If the Secretary decides to resolve the complaint, he shall proceed to try to eliminate or correct the alleged discriminatory housing practice by informal methods of conference, conciliation, and persuasion. Nothing said or done in the course of such informal endeavors may be made public or used as evidence in a subsequent proceeding under this title without the written consent of the persons concerned. Any employee of the Secretary who shall make public any information in violation of this provision shall be deemed guilty of a misdemeanor and upon conviction thereof shall be fined not more than $1,000 or imprisoned not more than one year.

(b) A complaint under subsection (a) shall be filed within one hundred and eighty days after the alleged discriminatory housing practice occurred. Complaints shall be in writing and shall state the facts upon which the allegations of a discriminatory housing practice are based. Complaints may be reasonably and fairly amended at any time. A respondent may file an answer to the complaint against him and with the leave of the Secretary, which shall be granted whenever it would be reasonable and fair to do so, may amend his answer at any time. Both complaints and answers shall be verified.

(c) Wherever a State or local fair housing law provides rights and remedies for alleged discriminatory housing practices which are substantially equivalent to the rights and remedies provided in this title, the Secretary shall notify the appropriate State or local agency of any complaint filed under this title which appears to constitute a violation of such State or local fair housing law, and the Secretary shall take no further action with respect to such complaint if the appropriate State or local law enforcement official has, within thirty days from the date the alleged offense has been brought to his attention, commenced proceedings in the matter, or, having done so, carries forward such proceedings with reasonable promptness. In no event shall the Secretary take further action unless he certifies that in his judgment, under the circumstances of the particular case, the protection of the rights of the parties or the interests of justice require such action.

(d) If within thirty days after a complaint is filed with the Secretary or within thirty days after expiration of any period of reference under subsection (c), the Secretary has been unable to obtain voluntary compliance with this title, the person aggrieved may, within thirty days thereafter, commence a civil action in any appropriate United States district court, against the respondent named in the complaint, to enforce the rights granted or protected by this title, insofar as such rights relate to the subject of the complaint: *Provided,* That no such civil action may be brought in any United States district court if the person aggrieved has a judicial remedy under a State or local fair housing law which provides rights and remedies for alleged discriminatory housing practices which are substantially equivalent to the rights and remedies provided in this title. Such actions may be brought without regard to the amount in controversy in any United States district court for the district in which the discriminatory housing practice

Problems

32.3. The plan for the development of Lakeville contemplates a recreational area for the common use of the residents of Lakeville. Would it be a violation of the Civil Rights Act of 1866 to restrict the use of the recreational area to white residents only? See Sullivan v. Little Hunting Park, 396 U.S. 229, 90 S. Ct. 400 (1969). Tillman v. Wheaton-Haven Recreation Associa-

---

is alleged to have occurred or be about to occur or in which the respondent resides or transacts business. If the court finds that a discriminatory housing practice has occurred or is about to occur, the court may, subject to the provisions of section 812, enjoin the respondent from engaging in such practice or order such affirmative action as may be appropriate.

(e) In any proceeding brought pursuant to this section, the burden of proof shall be on the complainant.

(f) Whenever an action filed by an individual, in either Federal or State court, pursuant to this section or section 812, shall come to trial the Secretary shall immediately terminate all efforts to obtain voluntary compliance.]

[Sec. 811. (a) In conducting an investigation the Secretary shall have access at all reasonable times to premises, records, documents, individuals, and other evidence or possible sources of evidence and may examine, record, and copy such materials and take and record the testimony or statements of such persons as are reasonably necessary for the furtherance of the investigation: *Provided, however,* That the Secretary first complies with the provisions of the Fourth Amendment relating to unreasonable searches and seizures. The Secretary may issue subpenas to compel his access to or the production of such materials, or the appearance of such persons, and may issue interrogatories to a respondent, to the same extent and subject to the same limitations as would apply if the subpenas or interrogatories were issued or served in aid of a civil action in the United States district court for the district in which the investigation is taking place. The Secretary may administer oaths.

(b) Upon written application to the Secretary, a respondent shall be entitled to the issuance of a reasonable number of subpenas by and in the name of the Secretary to the same extent and subject to the same limitations as subpenas issued by the Secretary himself. Subpenas issued at the request of a respondent shall show on their face the name and address of such respondent and shall state that they were issued at his request.

(c) Witnesses summoned by subpena of the Secretary shall be entitled to the same witness and mileage fees as are witnesses in proceedings in United States district courts. Fees payable to a witness summoned by a subpena issued at the request of a respondent shall be paid by him.

(d) Within five days after service of a subpena upon any person, such person may petition the Secretary to revoke or modify the subpena. The Secretary shall grant the petition if he finds that the subpena requires appearance or attendance at an unreasonable time or place, that it requires production of evidence which does not relate to any matter under investigation, that it does not describe with sufficient particularity the evidence to be produced, that compliance would be unduly onerous, or for other good reason.

(e) In case of contumacy or refusal to obey a subpena, the Secretary or other person at whose request it was issued may petition for its enforcement in the United States district court for the district in which the person to whom the subpena was addressed resides, was served, or transacts business.

(f) Any person who willfully fails or neglects to attend and testify or to answer any lawful inquiry or to produce records, documents, or other evidence, if in his power to do so, in obedience to the subpena or lawful order of the Secretary, shall be fined not more than $1,000 or imprisoned not more than one year, or both. Any person who, with intent thereby to mislead the Secretary, shall make or cause to be made any false entry or statement of fact in any report, account, record, or other document submitted to the

tion, Inc., 410 U.S. 431, 93 S. Ct. 1090 (1973). Would such restriction violate the Civil Rights Act of 1968? See section 804(b) and section 803(b), quoted in footnote 14.[15]

32.4. Elderly people may prefer to live in an area that is quiet and peaceful. If it is decided to develop Lakeville as a community for elderly citizens by providing that no property in Lakeville shall be owned or occupied by persons under the age of 65, will such restriction encounter any constitutional difficulty or be in violation of either the Civil Rights Act of 1866 or the Civil Rights Act of 1968? See Doyle, Retirement Communities: The Nature and Enforceability of Residential Segregation by Age, 76 Mich. L. Rev. 64 (1977).

Secretary pursuant to his subpena or other order, or shall willfully neglect or fail to make or cause to be made full, true, and correct entries in such reports, accounts, records, or other documents, or shall willfully mutilate, alter, or by any other means falsify any documentary evidence, shall be fined not more than $1,000 or imprisoned not more than one year, or both.

(g) The Attorney General shall conduct all litigation in which the Secretary participates as a party or as amicus pursuant to this Act.]

[Sec. 812. (a) The rights granted by sections 803, 804, 805, and 806 may be enforced by civil actions in appropriate United States district courts without regard to the amount in controversy and in appropriate State or local courts of general jurisdiction. A civil action shall be commenced within one hundred and eighty days after the alleged discriminatory housing practice occurred: *Provided, however,* That the court shall continue such civil case brought pursuant to this section or section 810(d) from time to time before bringing it to trial if the court believes that the conciliation efforts of the Secretary or a State or local agency are likely to result in satisfactory settlement of the discriminatory housing practice complained of in the complaint made to the Secretary or to the local or State agency and which practice forms the basis for the action in court: *And provided, however,* That any sale, encumbrance, or rental consummated prior to the issuance of any court order issued under the authority of this Act, and involving a bona fide purchaser, encumbrancer, or tenant without actual notice of the existence of the filing of a complaint or civil action under the provisions of this Act shall not be affected.

(b) Upon application by the plaintiff and in such circumstances as the court may deem just, a court of the United States in which a civil action under this section has been brought may appoint an attorney for the plaintiff and may authorize the commencement of a civil action upon proper showing without the payment of fees, costs, or security. A court of a State or subdivision thereof may do likewise to the extent not inconsistent with the law or procedures of the State or subdivision.

(c) The court may grant as relief, as it deems appropriate, any permanent or temporary injunction, temporary restraining order, or other order, and may award to the plaintiff actual damages and not more than $1,000 punitive damages, together with court costs and reasonable attorney fees in the case of a prevailing plaintiff: *Provided,* That the said plaintiff in the opinion of the court is not financially able to assume said attorney's fees.]

15. For additional cases relating to the scope and reach of the Civil Rights Act of 1866, see the following: Clark v. Universal Builders, Inc., 501 F.2d 324 (7th Cir. 1974); City of Memphis v. Greene, 450 U.S. 100, 101 S. Ct. 1584 (1981). For cases relating to the Civil Rights Act of 1968, see the following: Trafficante v. Metropolitan Life Insurance Co., 409 U.S. 205, 93 S. Ct. 364 (1972); Curtis v. Loether, 415 U.S. 189, 94 S. Ct. 1005 (1974); Gladstone Realtors v. Village of Bellwood, 441 U.S. 91, 99 S. Ct. 1601 (1979); Havens Realty Corp. v. Coleman, 455 U.S. 363, 102 S. Ct. 1114 (1982).

Note: The Developer Who Has No Desire to Discriminate on the Ground of Race, Color, Religion, Sex, or National Origin

Assume that after reading the preceding cases, you reported the conclusions of your preliminary research to your senior partner and received the following confirmatory memorandum.

> After explaining the constitutional and statutory limitations to our client, I am confident that the client has absolutely no desire to discriminate on the basis of race, color, religion, sex, or national origin. The client simply believes the homesites will command a higher price on the market if prospective purchasers can be assured that they will have the ability to select their neighbors and to exclude the truly undesirable from the residential development.

Now examine the material that follows against this background.

PENTHOUSE PROPERTIES, INC. v. 1158 FIFTH AVENUE, INC.
256 A.D. 685, 11 N.Y.S.2d 417 (1939)

UNTERMEYER, J. This submitted controversy concerns the validity of certain restrictions upon the right to transfer stock and upon the assignment of a proprietary lease in a co-operative apartment house. . . .

About March 17, 1938, Mrs. Harriss wrote to the defendant corporation stating that she intended to dispose of her stock and leases, but that before making any other disposition she would sell to the corporate defendant at a substantial sacrifice. That offer was refused. About a week thereafter Mr. Harriss formed the plaintiff. Its entire capital stock was issued to him and is still owned by him. Mrs. Harriss then sold to the plaintiff her 777 shares of stock and all rights in the three proprietary leases. On March 28, 1938, she wrote to the corporate defendant to that effect. On the following day, the plaintiff demanded the transfer to it of the 777 shares of stock upon the corporate books and execution of three new proprietary leases in place of those previously held by Mrs. Harriss. The plaintiff also tendered to the defendant corporation the three certificates of stock in the name of Mrs. Harriss, duly endorsed for transfer with the necessary documentary stamps attached, and demanded that new certificates be issued in its name.

The defendant corporation notified the plaintiff of its refusal to recognize the transfer of the stock on account of non-compliance by the holder of the lease and stock with Articles X and XVII(d) of the proprietary lease under which the apartment was rented and the stock held. The defendant corporation also refused to accept checks tendered by the plaintiff in payment of monthly assessments and other charges for operating expenses, the bills for which had been sent to Mrs. Harriss. The monthly assessments for April to November, 1938, inclusive, amount to $5,184.27, for which the corporate defendant claims, among other things, to be entitled to judgment against Mrs. Harriss. . . .

It has been stipulated that the plaintiff was organized for the purpose of acquiring 777 shares of stock from Mrs. Harriss and to procure from the defendant corporation in connection therewith proprietary leases to the apartments. The plaintiff's certificate of incorporation provides that said apartments are to be used for private residential purposes only and by an individual or individuals approved by its board of directors.

It is conceded that the stock was acquired by Mrs. Harriss, as well as by the plaintiff from her, with full knowledge of the provisions contained in the leases and on the stock certificate, with respect to the transfer of the stock and leases.

These provisions are as follows:

> X.   That Lessee shall not cause or permit any of his stock and/or this lease, or any right of Lessee arising therefrom, to be assigned or subjected to any lien or encumbrance, except as in Article XVII, subdivision (d), hereof, specifically provided; and shall not sublet the demised premises or any part thereof without the prior written consent of Lessor. . . .
>
> XVII.   That this lease shall be terminated, otherwise than by expiration, as follows: . . .
>
> (d)   By and upon a sale, assignment or transfer of the stock owned by Lessee, together with Lessee's right to a lease of the demised premises for the remainder of the term hereof, with the consent of Lessor in writing, and the assumption, in writing, by the assignee, of obligations identical with those of Lessee under this lease, for the remainder of the term hereof, either upon acceptance by the assignee of an assignment of this lease or of a new lease; the consent of Lessor to be by authority of the Board of Directors or, upon refusal thereof by said Board, by authority of the holders of two-thirds of the capital stock; provided, that the failure of the Board of Directors to authorize such consent within thirty days after application therefor shall be equivalent to a refusal thereof and that the vote of the members of the Board of Directors and of stockholders on such authorization may be expressed in writing or by telegram without a formal meeting. When this lease has been so terminated and Lessee has discharged all accrued obligations under this lease, he shall have no further liability hereunder and Lessor shall execute, acknowledge and deliver to Lessee a written release of Lessee from all further liability under this lease.

These are the provisions referred to in the endorsement on the stock certificate, with which, it is asserted, Mrs. Harriss failed to comply in undertaking to assign the stock and leases. It is these provisions which the plaintiff and Mrs. Harriss contend are invalid and unenforceable as in restraint of alienation.

Accordingly the plaintiff requests judgment, as does also Mrs. Harriss, that the following relief be granted: That the defendant corporation be required to recognize as valid the sale by Mrs. Harriss to the plaintiff of 777 shares of stock of the defendant corporation, and that the plaintiff be accorded all the rights of a stockholder therein, including the right to new certificates and new proprietary leases of the apartments allocated thereto.

In addition to a money judgment against Mrs. Harriss for $5,184.27 with interest, the defendant corporation demands a declaratory judgment that Mrs. Harriss is not entitled to assign her leases and stock without written consent of the Board of Directors of the corporate defendant or two-thirds of the stockholders, that her assignment to the plaintiff be declared ineffective, and for judgment dismissing the plaintiff's claim for transfer of the stock and the execution of new leases.

The question now presented, apparently never decided in this State, is the validity of the restrictive plan under which co-operative apartment houses have been constructed and the stock sold. The validity of such a plan is challenged by the plaintiff and by Mrs. Harriss on the ground that restraints against the alienation of the corporate stock imposed by the limitations contained in the lease, prohibiting any sale without the consent of the directors or two-thirds of the stockholders, are against public policy and therefore unenforceable.

The general rule that ownership of property cannot exist in one person and the right of alienation in another has in this State been frequently applied to shares of corporate stock and cognizance has been taken of the principle that "the right of transfer is a right of property, and if another has the arbitrary power to forbid a transfer of property by the owner, that amounts to an annihilation of property." The same rule has been applied in other States. But restrictions against the sale of shares of stock, unless other stockholders or the corportion have first been accorded an opportunity to buy, are not repugnant to that principle. The weight of authority elsewhere is to the same effect. Likewise, restrictions against the assignment by the tenant of a leasehold, or against subletting, without the consent of the landlord first obtained, have frequently been sustained.

We are now required to decide within which of these divergent principles the co-operative apartment house restrictive plan is to be classified. In the consideration of that question the residential nature of the enterprise, the privilege of selecting neighbors and the needs of the community are not to be ignored. The tenant stockholders in a co-operative apartment building are concerned in the purchase of a home. Necessarily, therefore, the permanency of the individual occupants as tenant owners is an essential element in the general plan and their financial responsibility an inducement to the corporation in accepting them as stockholders. Under the "Plan of Organization" each stockholder is entitled to vote upon the choice of neighbors and their financial responsibility. The latter consideration becomes important when it is remembered that the failure of any tenant to pay his proportion of operating expenses increases the liability of other tenant stockholders. Thus, in a very real sense the tenant stockholders enter into a relation not unlike a partnership, though expressed in corporate form. Holmes, C.J., in Barrett v. King, 181 Mass. 476, 63 N.E. 934, 935, said of this:

> Furthermore, looking at the stock merely as property, it might be said that, so far as appears and probably in fact, it was called into existence with this restriction inherent in it, by the consent of all concerned . . . there seems to be no greater objection, to retaining the right of choosing one's associates in a corporation than in a firm.

Although it is true that the corporation which holds title to the real estate is not organized in co-operative form, it is manifest from the conceded facts that it was organized as a vehicle for the establishment of a community of homes rather than for the purpose of pecuniary profit to the stockholders. The primary interest of every stockholder was in the long term proprietary lease alienation of which the corporation had the power to restrain. See authorities above cited. The stock was incidental to that purpose and afforded the practical means of combining an ownership interest with a method for sharing proportionately the assessments for maintenance and taxes.

From all these considerations it follows that if restraint on alienation of the stock may be said to be imposed at all, it is a restraint which in every respect is reasonable and appropriate to the lawful purposes to be attained. We are unwilling to declare that arrangement to be illegal and unenforceable, particularly since such a declaration would invalidate a form of enterprise to which the Legislature has accorded implied recognition. Civil Practice Act, Section 1410, Subdivision 1-a. We conclude, therefore, that the special nature of the ownership of co-operative apartment houses by tenant owners requires that they be not included in the general rule against restraint on the sale of stock in corporations organized for profit.

It is proper to add that we have not considered nor do we decide whether the consent of the directors or stockholders may be, or has been, arbitrarily withheld. Justification for refusing to consent to a transfer, if justification is required, ordinarily presents an issue of fact which is not presented by the agreed statement of facts nor argued in the briefs.

Judgment should accordingly be granted in favor of the defendant corporation, as prayed for in the submission, against the plaintiff, and in favor of the defendant corporation against the co-defendant Belle C. Harriss for the sum of $5,184.27 with interest, but without costs.

Judgment unanimously granted in favor of the defendant corporation, as prayed for in the submission, against the plaintiff, and in favor of the defendant corporation against the co-defendant Belle C. Harriss for the sum of $5,184.27 with interest, but without costs. Settle order on notice. All concur.

WEISNER v. 791 PARK AVENUE CORP.
6 N.Y.2d 426, 160 N.E.2d 720 (1959)

BURKE, J.

Plaintiff instituted this action for specific performance of a written contract negotiated by a real estate broker and entered into between plaintiff and defendant Gilbert, providing for the sale of 330 shares of stock of the defendant 791 Park Avenue Corporation, and for the assignment to plaintiff of a proprietary lease of an apartment at 791 Park Avenue, New York City. By an order to show cause served with the complaint, plaintiff moved for an injunction pendente lite restraining the assignment of the lease and the sale of the corporate stock to others. The answer of defendant Gilbert alleges the defense of impossibility of performance of the contract of sale and sets forth as a second separate and partial defense facts alleging prospective damages including maintenance charges on the apartment, interest, counsel fees and other expenditures which defendant Gilbert will sustain if an injunction pendente lite is granted. Special Term denied the injunction, but on appeal the Appellate Division granted it. The order of reversal of the Appellate Division directs that undertakings theretofore given by the plaintiff shall continue as security for any damage, including interest, which defendant Gilbert might sustain by reason of the injunction granted by that court.

These appeals are here by permission of the Appellate Division which certified the following question for review by this court. "Did the Appellate Division err in reversing the order of Special Term denying plaintiff's motion for an injunction pendente lite and in granting said motion?"

We believe the question should be answered in the affirmative. No cause of action against either of the defendants is stated whether the complaint be considered alone or with all the other papers before the courts below. The order granting plaintiff an injunction pendente lite cannot be upheld in the absence of facts which establish either rights of the plaintiff or duties of the defendant Gilbert which would constitute a cause of action on behalf of the plaintiff against defendants.

The appellant corporation, formed in 1947 pursuant to a plan of co-perative organization, is the owner of an apartment house at Park Avenue and East 74th Street in New York City. The building is occupied by 31 tenants, each of whom has a proprietary lease, identical in form, for his apartment, and stock in 791 Park Avenue Corporation. Defendant Gilbert's lease contains the following provisions:

> The Lessee shall not assign this lease, or any interest therein, and no such assignment shall take effect as against the Lessor for any purpose, unless and until all of the following requirements have been complied with and satisfied: . . .
>
> 4. A written consent to such assignment, authorized by a resolution of the board of directors, or signed by a majority of the directors or by lessees owning

of record at least two-thirds of the capital stock of the Lessor accompanying proprietary leases then in force, must be delivered to the Lessor.

And it is further provided:

No executor, administrator, personal representative or successor of the Lessee, or trustee, or anyone to whom the interest of the Lessee hereunder shall pass by law, shall be entitled to assign this lease, or to sublet the apartment, or any part thereof, except upon compliance with the requirements of this paragraph Sixth. The character of and restriction upon the occupancy of the apartment, and upon assignment of this lease, as hereinbefore expressed, restricted and limited, are an especial consideration and inducement for the granting of this lease by the Lessor to the Lessee.

There are similar provisions in the by-laws of the corporation.

Gilbert contracted with the plaintiff, a member of the Bar of this State, to transfer her stock in the 791 Park Avenue Corporation and the lease for her apartment in the building. The following clause was made a condition of the agreement:

This sale is subject to the approval of 791 Park Avenue Corporation in the manner required under the Certificate of Incorporation, by-laws and proprietary lease. If the said approval is not obtained, this contract shall become null and void and neither party hereto shall be under any liability to the other by reason thereof, and all sums paid on account of this contract shall be returned, without interest, by the Seller to the Purchaser.

During the period intervening between the execution of the contract by the plaintiff on May 7, 1958 and its delivery to the plaintiff on May 16, 1958, several conversations took place between the plaintiff and defendant Gilbert's attorney, who was in charge of the pending negotiation.

On May 12th plaintiff spoke to Gilbert's attorney and requested him to withhold submission of the contract to the 791 Park Avenue Corporation for a few days to enable plaintiff to assemble and submit his references.

Pursuant to plaintiff's request the managing agent for defendant 791 Park Avenue Corporation was not formally notified of the proposed sale until May 16, 1958 when a copy of the contract was sent by certified mail to the agent. On the same day the duplicate original of the contract was delivered to plaintiff, together with a letter which reminded plaintiff that: "your application to purchase the cooperative apartment must be approved by a majority of the Board of Directors under Article Sixth of the lease. Accordingly, I would suggest that you submit several reference letters."

Before the contract was delivered to the corporation, plaintiff was informed that there would be difficulties in procuring the requisite consent. Plaintiff could have withdrawn from the contract before it was delivered, instead he preferred to proceed. He was then given forms to supply information to the board which he did not utilize. During the period of 12 days between the delivery of the contract and the directors' meeting, plaintiff endeavored to persuade individual directors to accept him as a fellow tenant.

Plaintiff concedes that he consulted with the managing agent. On May 28, 1958 the agent notified the attorney for Gilbert that a meeting of the board of directors of 791 Park Avenue Corporation had been held and that the board did not approve of the proposed transfer by Gilbert of her apartment to plaintiff. The attorney immediately informed plaintiff of the board action and sent him a copy of the notice.

On June 2, 1958 Gilbert's attorney telephoned and then personally called upon a Mr. Gustave Ross who was the treasurer and a director of defendant 791 Park Avenue Corporation. On both occasions he requested a reconsideration and resubmission to the board of the plaintiff's application to purchase Gilbert's apartment. The request was refused.

While the case was sub judice in the Appellate Division, Gilbert, at the suggestion of a Justice of the Appellate Division, solicited the consent of the stockholders. Eighteen of the 31 who received her request returned it with the notation that they did not consent to the transfer; only 1, the defendant Gilbert, voted to the contrary.

It is properly asserted by the respondent that the order granting the injunction may be reversed only if as a matter of law the plaintiff has no standing to sue or the directors of 791 Park Avenue Corporation have an absolute right to restrain the transfer of stockholders' interests in the corporation.

Respondent assumes that the defendant Gilbert had a contract obligation to persuade the directors and/or stockholders to look with favor on his references. No such duty is imposed on Gilbert either by law or the terms of the agreement. Indeed, plaintiff gave a practical construction to the agreement when he acknowledged his obligation to convince the board members or the stockholders of his worth as a fellow tenant and co-owner by requesting time to gather the necessary references. Further recognition that the exercise of diligence and persuasion rested on his shoulders is found in his activity in arranging personal interviews with the treasurer of the corporation and two of the director-tenants. At no time prior to the notice of rejection did he indicate a belief that Gilbert was under a duty to plead his cause.

In this case the condition inserted in the contract, in terms, rebuts any presumption that Gilbert was willing to agree to procure the approval of the corporation. Words of condition were carefully chosen to avoid the imposition on Gilbert of any burden relative to procuring the required consent. By express condition her obligation is merely made "subject" to the favorable action by 791 Park Avenue Corporation. Since the consent of the corporation was not obtained, the plaintiff is not entitled to specific performance (see e.g. Connor v. Rockwood, 320 Mass. 360, 69 N.E.2d 454).

Plaintiff, having agreed that the leasestock transfer had to be ratified by the corporation in accordance with the conditions of the lease and in the manner provided by the by-laws, is bound insofar as Gilbert is concerned, by his failure to secure approval of the transaction.

The statute which prohibits discrimination in co-operatives because of race, color, religion, national origin or ancestry is not involved in this case. Absent the application of these statutory standards, and under the terms of the agreement between plaintiff and Gilbert, there is no reason why the owners of the co-operative apartment house could not decide for themselves with whom they wish to share their elevators, their common halls and facilities, their stockholders' meetings, their management problems and responsibilities and their homes.

The distinction between clauses importing an obligation to seek and obtain approval as a condition precedent to the exercise of a right to terminate and clauses making the vendor's obligation to convey merely "subject" to the granting of an approval is aptly stated in the case of Stabile v. McCarthy, 336 Mass. 399, 403, 145 N.E.2d 821: "If the parties had intended no obligation on the plaintiff to take action they could have used a clause in the special provision importing no suggestion of obligation, inability or impossibility, or could have made the vendor's obligation to convey and the vendee's obligation to purchase 'subject to' the granting of approval (compare Connor v. Rockwood, 320 Mass. 360, 69 N.E.2d 454; Livoli v. Stoneman, 332 Mass. 473, 475-476, 125 N.E.2d 785), instead of making inability to obtain planning board approval a condition precedent to the exercise of a right to cancel."

Since the complaint does not state a meritorious cause of action against either of the defendants, the issuance of the injunction pendente lite is unwarranted.

Accordingly, the order of the Appellate Division should be reversed, the injunction pendente lite should be dissolved, with costs, and the matter remitted to the Special Term. The certified question is answered in the affirmative.

CONWAY, C.J., and DESMOND, DYE, FULD and FROESSEL, JJ., concur.

VAN VOORHIS, J., dissents and votes to affirm.

Order reversed, with costs in this court and in the Appellate Division, and the matter remitted to Special Term for further proceedings in accordance with the opinion herein. Question certified answered in the affirmative.[16]

---

16. Compare Northwest Real Estate Co. v. Serio, 156 Md. 229, 144 A. 245 (1929), where the challenged covenant read:

And for the purpose of maintaining the property hereby conveyed and the surrounding property as a desirable high class residential section for themselves, their successors, heirs, executors, administrators and assigns that until January 1, 1932, no owner of the land hereby conveyed shall have the right to sell or rent the same without the written consent of the grantor herein which shall have the right to pass upon the character,

Problem

32.5. L, a developer, instead of selling the building lots decides to lease them. L provides in the lease that no tenant may assign or sublet without receiving L's written consent. T acquires a building lot under a long-term 99-year renewable lease with L. T builds an expensive house on the lot and subsequently decides to move. T advertises and finds T₁, a willing buyer, but L considers T₁ to be an "undesirable" tenant and refuses to consent to an assignment or sublease to T₁. T brings suit for declaratory judgment arguing that the clause in the lease is an unlawful restraint on alienation, citing cases like Northwest Real Estate Co. v. Serio, and maintaining that a long-term renewable residential lease should be treated the same as a fee simple ownership — which is the actual understanding of all the parties. L cites cases like Gruman v. Investors Diversified Services, Inc., page 575 *supra,* and Penthouse Properties, Inc. v. 1158 Fifth Ave, Inc. What result?

Does Title VIII of the Civil Rights Act of 1968 now require L to come forward and state L's reasons for not consenting to an assignment or subletting, if discrimination is alleged? Who has the burden of proof if discrimination is alleged?

LAUDERBAUGH v. WILLIAMS
409 Pa. 351, 186 A.2d 39 (1962)

O'Brien, J.

These appeals are from decrees entered in an action to Quiet Title and an Equity Action to set aside a deed of conveyance of land. The cases involve the same questions and were tried together. In 1940, Mildred B. Lauderbaugh and her husband, Dayton S. Lauderbaugh, became the owners by purchase of land in Wayne and Monroe Counties which included a lake known as Watawga. The Lauderbaughs laid out some lots in a plan on the westerly shore and began the sale of lots in 1949. In June, 1951 the purchasers of the lots and the Lauderbaughs entered into an agreement whereby, as a condition precedent, future purchasers of land along the shore of the lake were required to be members of the Lake Watawga Association. The Association was formed to control the development along the shore of the lake. Many attractive homes representing a substantial investment had

---

desirability and other qualification of the proposed purchaser or occupant of the property. . . .

The majority held this restraint void, holding that the owner could sell or lease to anyone without receiving the written consent of the grantor. Ink v. Plott, 175 N.E.2d 94 (Ohio App. 1960), held valid a restrictive covenant used in a residential development which purported to prohibit resale of the land without the written consent of the adjoining lot owners on each side of the property.— Eds.

been erected. After the formation of the Association and Agreement other lots were sold to those who became members of the Association and homes were built. Mrs. Lauderbaugh instituted an action to quiet title in March, 1958, her husband being deceased, to remove a cloud on her title by seeking to have the agreement restricting the sale of property to members of the Association declared void. In February, 1960, Mrs. Lauderbaugh, together with Asher Seip, Jr., and Jacob Seip were named defendants in a complaint in Equity to set aside a deed of December 3, 1959, for land along the lake shore from Mrs. Lauderbaugh to Asher Seip, Jr.,—Jacob Seip being the partner of Asher Seip, Jr., grantee in the deed—as a violation of the agreement of June 1951, and to enjoin Mrs. Lauderbaugh from conveying land along the lake shore except to persons approved for membership in the Lake Watawga Association. The plaintiffs in the Equity case were mostly the persons named as defendants in Action to Quiet Title. The trial court entered a decree upholding the validity of the agreement but restricted its application to the westerly shore of the lake and entered a decree setting aside the deed from Mrs. Lauderbaugh to Asher Seip, Jr., and enjoining her from conveying land on the western shore of the lake except in accordance with the agreement of June, 1951, and in accordance with the rules, regulations and by-laws of the Lake Watawga Association. Both sides filed exceptions, which exceptions were dismissed, thereby giving rise to the instant appeals.

The agreement of June, 1951 provides that:

The First Parties [the Lauderbaughs], for themselves, their heirs and assigns, agree that membership in the Lake Watawga Association shall be a condition precedent for future purchasers of land along the shore of Lake Watawga; that in the event such prospective purchasers qualify as members as aforesaid, the First Parties will, upon payment of purchase price, execute and deliver to them deeds. . . .

The pertinent portions of the By-Laws of the Lake Watawga Association provide as follows:

Article V
Membership
Section 1. No person shall be eligible to membership in the Association who does not meet the requirements hereinafter specified. Such person shall be either the owner or a prospective owner of property along the shore of Lake Watawga, but such ownership or prospective ownership shall not in itself entitle such person or persons to become a member of this Association. This by-law can be amended only by a vote of three-fourths of the total membership of the Association.
Section 4. Application for membership shall be made to the Secretary, and by him referred to the Board of Directors, who shall act upon the same at their earliest convenience. Notice of the application for membership shall be given to every member at least 10 days prior to the time when such application

shall be acted upon. The Board of Directors shall carefully consider any objections made to applicants. An Investigation Committee composed of three members of the Board of Directors shall be appointed by the President of the Board, which Committee shall report its findings to the Board of Directors before the application is acted upon. If written objections are filed by one member of the Association, when the membership is less than ten, the applicant shall be rejected. If written objections are filed by three or more members, when the membership of the Association is more than ten, the applicant shall be rejected. If written objections are filed by less than three members, when the membership is more than ten, the applicant may be elected by a two-thirds vote of the Directors present when such application is considered.

Essentially the question is the legality of the agreement restricting alienation of lake shore property to members of the Association only. This precise question has never before been decided by this court. However, while we do not have prior cases presenting similar factual conditions we are amply supplied with firmly established legal principles. Every restraint on alienation of real property is not necessarily void. True, such restraints are not favored in the law. Further, an absolute restraint is against public policy and, therefore, of no legal effect. However, a limited and reasonable restraint on the power of alienation may be valid. See, Restatement of Property, §406, and 26 C.J.S. Deeds §145.

Whether the agreement of June, 1951 is construed to create a condition precedent, a covenant not to convey or anything else, it is clear that its effect, when read in conjunction with the requirements of membership in the Association, is to limit unreasonably the free alienation of land bordering Lake Watawga, since conveyances may be made only to members of the Association. Control over the membership of the Association lies not with the grantor, but with others, the consent of all but two of whom must be obtained in order for any prospective alienee to be eligible for membership.

We do not seek to impugn the motives of the members of the Association and, for the purposes of deciding the issues presented, assume that their motives are of the purest, their sole concerns being the orderly development of the area and, quite properly, the protection of their investments. Be that as it may however, the fact remains that no standards for admission to the Association are set out in its by-laws and it is possible that three members by whim, caprice or for any reason, good or bad, or for no reason, could deny membership to any prospective alienee, thereby depriving Mrs. Lauderbaugh of her right to alienate her land. It must be further noted that the restriction is not limited in time and purports to be a perpetual one, a fact which militates strongly against its enforcement.

The decree of the court below, entered at No. 73 January Term, 1958, which is appealed from at Nos. 202 and 235, is reversed insofar as it declares the agreement of June, 1951 to be valid and binding with respect to certain lots on the Westerly shore of Lake Watawga, and affirmed in all other particulars.

The decree of the court below, entered at No. 1 January Term, 1960, which forms the basis of the appeals at Nos. 203 and 234, is reversed. Each party to bear own costs.

Note: *Restraints on Alienation*

The policy against restraints on aliention is said to be based on the belief that restraints remove property from commerce, concentrate wealth, prejudice creditors, and discourage property improvements.[17] Clauses restraining alienation can be phrased in a variety of ways, and have been divided into three major types: disabling, forfeiture, and promissory.[18] Disabling restraints purport to withhold the power to convey from the grantee. Forfeiture restraints purport to create a reversion or gift over to a third person if alienation is attempted, i.e., purport to divest the grantee of title if alienation is attempted. Promissory restraints are covenants not to convey, which if valid, are specifically enforceable. Each of these types may be further subdivided into restraints which are unlimited as to time or permissible class of grantees, or restraints which are limited, i.e., which purport to restrain alienation only for a limited time or to a limited class.

Restraints in the form of a right of first refusal—frequently called a preemptive right—are usually more acceptable to the courts than an absolute right to disapprove of prospective transferees. This device also has the merit of retaining effective control over unwanted transferees, yet avoiding the pitfalls of unwittingly locking yourself in if in the future you desire to sell.[19]

GALE v. YORK CENTER COMMUNITY COOPERATIVE, INC.

21 Ill. 2d 86, 171 N.E.2d 30 (1960)

HOUSE, J.

The principal question presented by this appeal is whether a co-operative housing association may partially restrain the alienability of its members' property interests in order to maintain its existence as a co-operative enterprise. The circuit court of Du Page County held such restraints and all other portions of the written agreements between York Center Community Cooperative, Inc., a co-operative housing association, and the seven plaintiff families, members of the association, to be valid, and directed five of the plaintiff families to reconvey the properties they occupy to the association.

---

17. Schnebly, Restraints upon the Alienation of Legal Interests, 44 Yale L.J. 1186 (1935).
18. See Restatement (Second) of Property (Donative Transfers) §§3.1-3.3.
19. See Restatement (Second) of Property (Donative Transfers) §4.4.

Five of the plaintiff families have appealed from the decree. A freehold is involved.

York Center is a subdivision located just south of Lombard. There are 72 families living in the subdivision, each of whom is a member of the defendant association, a not-for-profit corporation organized for the purpose of establishing and maintaining a co-operative housing community. Legal title to all real estate in the subdivision is held by the association and the members each own a membership entitling them to the perpetual use and occupancy of their respective dwellings.

The rights and duties of membership are set out in uniform written agreements between each member and all other members, in which the association acts as the contracting party for the other members. The membership contract, certificate of membership, and bylaws of the association constitute the agreement. Membership is open to all persons, regardless of race, color or creed, who are in agreement with the aims and purposes of the association and who, in the judgment of the board of directors, can comply with the bylaws of the association. Each member holds only one membership, which is equal in value to the appraised value of his home and lot plus his interest in the association. The membership entitles the member to one vote in the conduct of affairs of the association.

The association, by action and participation open to all of its members, acts to develop and maintain the subdivision as a carefully planned, nonspeculative, attractive community. To this end it may use surplus savings to provide or replace community facilities; levy assessments for taxes, operating expenses, and general community improvements; redeem membership upon a member's notice of withdrawal; pass on requests for approval of membership transfers; pass on redemption of membership or approval of heirs or legatees in case of a member's death; pass on the admission of new members; decide on the expulsion of members guilty of seriously detrimental conduct and redeem their memberships; pass on all building and roadside planting plots and plans; adopt occupancy standards; correct nuisances; terminate undesirable nonresidential uses; and require repairs to dwellings. In all other respects each member enjoys all the incidents of individual ownership with respect to the dwelling he occupies. Thus, the members have built their own homes, have done their own financing, make their own mortgage payments, arrange and pay for the insurance on their homes and otherwise conduct themselves in many respects as the owners of the dwellings they occupy.

The plaintiffs argue that restrictions on their right to transfer their memberships violate the rule against restraints on alienation of property and are therefore void. The agreement provides that when a member wishes to withdraw, he shall give written notice of his intent to the board of directors. The association then has a twelve-month period in which to purchase the membership at any of the following prices, as determined by the association: (1) at the selling price fixed in the notice; or (2) at whatever price the member and the association agree on; or (3) at the price determined by impartial appraisal. If the association does not exercise its option within twelve months, the membership may be sold on the open market. If the purchaser is not acceptable to the association, it may redeem the membership within 90 days. If this redemption is not exercised in 90 days, the purchaser then acquires the membership upon request. It is provided, nevertheless, that membership may be transferred subject to the written approval of the board.

The agreement further provides that upon written request the association will give to a member a deed for the purpose of obtaining a loan secured by a mortgage on the premises he occupies. The member is to reconvey the premises after he obtains his loan. The mortgagee is not required to inquire as to compliance with the agreement as long as the member has a deed from the association, and he may treat the member as the fee-simple owner of the mortgaged premises.

The agreement also provides that when a member dies and his membership passes by will or by statute of descent to a single family household headed by a son, daughter, spouse, or parent of the deceased member, such family shall, upon application and execution of the membership agreement, become a member without further inquiry by the association. If the membership passes to several individuals who are not members of the same family household, they are to decide which family household is to receive the membership rights; and if the family so chosen is headed by a child, spouse or parent of the deceased member, he shall, upon application and execution of the membership agreement, become a member without further inquiry from the board. If the membership passes to an individual or group not wishing to become a member, the association may redeem the membership within twelve months. If the membership passes to an individual or group not including a child, spouse, or parent of the deceased member and the individual applies for membership, his application is to be given first consideration; and if he is not approved, the association may redeem within twelve months. If the membership passes to a group of individuals who cannot agree within twelve months as to the disposition to make of the membership, the association is to have a second twelve-month period in which to redeem the membership.

It seems to us the agreements show a studied effort on the part of the association to retain some voice in the selection of new members and at the same time to give its members as much freedom as possible in alienating their interests. Experience shows this to be the only way to keep co-operative housing co-operative. ("Organization and Management of Co-operative and Mutual Housing Associations," Bureau of Labor Statistics Bulletin 858 (1946); "Mutual Housing," National Housing Agency (1946).) As necessary as these restrictions may be to co-operative housing, it must be determined whether they violate the rule against restraints on alienation.

It should be noted at the outset, that the rule has not had a logical and consistent development. (For an extended treatment of this subject see Gray, Restraints on Alienation of Property, 2d ed., and Schnebly, Restraints Upon the Alienation of Legal Interests, 44 Yale L.J. 961, 1186, 1380.) This seems to be due to the fact that such restraints vary greatly in form, and the application of the rule has turned largely on such considerations as the kind of property involved, the quality of the interest, and the form of the restraint. It has been stated that "probably nowhere in the law does one find more resort to dogma than here." Carey and Schuyler, Illinois Law of Future Interests, p. 542.

While other reasons are sometimes given for the rule, it seems to call for no other than that of sound public policy. Davis v. Hutchinson, 282 Ill. 523, 118 N.E. 721; Gray, Restraints on the Alienation of Property, 2d ed., sec. 21; Carey and Schuyler, Illinois Law of Future Interests, sec. 421; Tiffany, The Law of Real Property, 2d ed., sec. 592. Restraints on alienation keep property out of commerce, they tend to concentrate wealth, they may prevent the owner consuming the property except as to the income from it, they may deter the improvement of the property and they may prevent creditors from satisfying their claims. Against these and other social and economic disadvantages to the public, the only benefit that would often accrue from such restraints is the satisfaction of the capricious whims of the conveyor. Thus, as a general rule, restraints on alienation are void even though they are limited in time (McFadden v. McFadden, 302 Ill. 504, 135 N.E. 31), or as to mode (Noth v. Noth, 292 Ill. 536, 127 N.E. 113), or as to persons (Jenne v. Jenne, 271 Ill. 526, 111 N.E. 540) or whether the restraint is upon the alienation of a fee (McNamara v. McNamara, 293 Ill. 54, 127 N.E. 130), or of a life estate (Randolph v. Wilkinson, 294 Ill. 508, 128 N.E. 525), or of a vested future interest (Tolley v. Wilson, 371 Ill. 124, 20 N.E.2d 68), or of personal property. State Street Furniture Co. v. Armour & Co., 345 Ill. 160, 177 N.E. 702, 76 A.L.R. 1298. Such a restraint may be sustained, however, when it is reasonably designed to attain or encourage accepted social or economic ends. Thus, in Swannell v. Wilson, 400 Ill. 138, 79 N.E.2d 26, a restraint on alienation of property contained in a divorce decree was sustained for the protection of the divorced wife and to maintain the stability of the property settlement agreement; and in Dickenson v. City of Anna, 310 Ill. 222, 141 N.E. 754, 30 A.L.R. 587, a restraint upon alienation of property given to charity was upheld.

From the authorities here mentioned and many others examined, it would appear that the crucial inquiry should be directed at the utility of the restraint as compared with the injurious consequences that will flow from its enforcement. If accepted social and economic considerations dictate that a partial restraint is reasonably necessary for their fulfillment, such a restraint should be sustained. No restraint should be sustained simply because it is limited in time, or the class of persons excluded is not total, or all modes of alienation are not prohibited. These qualifications lessen the degree to which restraints violate general public policy against restraining alienation of property and should be considered to that extent; but they are not, in themselves, sufficient to overcome it. In short, the law of property, like other areas of the law, is not a mathematical science but takes shape at the direction of social and economic forces in an ever changing society, and decisions should be made to turn on these considerations.

We are of the opinion that the utility of the restraints in this agreement outweigh the injurious consequences to the public, if any. The legislature has given its approval to ownership of residential property on a co-operative basis by providing that not-for-profit corporations may be organized for this purpose. Ill. Rev. Stat. 1957, chap. 32, par. 163a3. The restrictions on transfer of a membership are reasonably necessary to the continued existence of the co-operative association. This demonstrates the social utility of the partial restraints and might of itself be a basis for sustaining them. In addition, however, enforcement of the restraints in question would not appear to produce injurious consequences to the public. They would not tend to keep the property in the same family and concentrate wealth, but would seem to some extent to prevent retention by one family. The member is not prevented from liquidating his interest and therefore consuming the property. Creditors are not prevented from satisfying their claims. Members are encouraged to improve their homes and the value of any improvement will be realized when they liquidate their interest. Co-operative ownership of residential property in this country seems to be increasing in popularity, and the extent to which these partial restraints would keep property out of commerce is entirely problematical.

Plaintiffs also argue that the agreements between them and the association are ambiguous, conflicting, vague and indefinite. They have set forth a number of hypothetical situations and allege that the agreements do not spell out the respective rights and duties of the parties in those situations.

In order for a contract to be binding, it must be definite and certain in all of its terms. Morey v. Hoffman, 12 Ill. 2d 125, 145 N.E.2d 644. It is sufficiently definite and certain, however, if the court is able from the terms and provisions thereof, under proper rules of construction and applicable rules of equity, to ascertain what the parties have agreed to do. Bonde v. Weber, 6 Ill. 2d 365, 128 N.E.2d 883; Ruddock v. American Medical Association, 415 Ill. 63, 112 N.E.2d 107; Welsh v. Jakstas, 401 Ill. 288, 82 N.E.2d 53. We are of the opinion that the agreement in question meets this test. It is not necessary or proper for us to construe in abstraction the terms of the agreement the plaintiffs assail. We are satisfied that when situations arise which call for their application, the courts will have no difficulty in ascertaining what the parties have agreed to do.

It is finally argued that the association is not entitled to deeds of reconveyance from the plaintiffs as decreed by the trial court. The association gave deeds to some of the plaintiffs for the purpose of obtaining mortgage financing pursuant to the membership agreement. Although the agreement provides that deeds of reconveyance are to be executed after the financing is complete and the plaintiffs have completed their financing, they have refused to execute deeds. Specific performance was properly decreed. The fact that the association permitted the plaintiffs to make their mortgage payments directly to the mortgagees, rather than through the association as is provided in the agreement, does not preclude the association's right to reconveyance.

We find no error in the decree of the circuit court of Du Page County, and it is accordingly affirmed.

Decree affirmed.[20]

Note: Preemptive Rights

Should the decision on whether a "preemptive right" is a restraint on alienation depend upon a consideration of how disproportionate the price required to be paid to exercise the right may be in relation to the current market value — the problem of fixed-price formulae? See, e.g., Doss v. Yinglin, 95 Ind. App. 494, 172 N.E. 801 (1930), upholding a book value formula; Boston Safe Deposit & Trust Co. v. North Attleborough Chapter of the American Red Cross, 330 Mass. 114, 111 N.E.2d 447 (1953), upholding a par value formula; Allen v. Biltmore Tissue Corp., 2 N.Y.2d 534, 141 N.E.2d 812 (1957), upholding an original issue price formula.

See Restatement (Second) of Property (Donative Transfers) §4.4 and the Statutory Note and the Reporter's Note to that section for consideration of preemptive provisions.

Problem

32.6. O sold a lot to P, retaining an adjoining 50-foot lot. The deposit receipt included the following clause: "If seller decides to sell the other 50-foot lot the seller will give buyer the first chance to purchase it at $10,000.000." Six years later O sold the 50-foot lot for $22,000. P sues O for breach of contract, and the trial court awards P $12,000. O appeals. What result? Mercer v. Lemmens, 230 Cal. App. 167, 40 Cal. Rptr. 803 (1964).[21]

---

20. Restatement (Second) of Property (Donative Transfers), Chapter 4, considers the validity of restraints on alienation in donative transfers. In commercial transactions the restraint that is used will be either a disabling one, a promissory one, or a preemptive provision. The Statutory Note to section 4.1 and the Reporter's Note to that section discuss these restraints in commercial transactions.—EDS.

21. Before you condemn the inequity of a fixed price formula for a right of first refusal, consider what a right of first refusal at current market value determined by a bona fide offer entails. Would you be excited about bidding on land burdened by such a restriction? If you bid too high, i.e., make a bad bargain, the right will probably not be exercised. If you bid too low, i.e., make a good bargain, the right will probably be exercised. Also, the sale is held up while the holder of the right of first refusal decides whether to exercise it. If the decision is not to exercise it, you must worry whether that judgment or your judgment was wrong. If the decision is to exercise it, you have wasted your time and energy. In considering rights of first refusal, recall Problem 23.2 in Chapter 23, Negotiating and Drafting a Lease.

Note: Elimination of an Undesirable Owner

In connection with the problem of excluding undesirable newcomers, you should consider the possibility that in spite of careful screening and interviewing, a person who moves into the development may become noisy and generally obnoxious to the community. Could a developer who leases building lots instead of selling them evict a resident-tenant who violates the rules and regulations of the lease? Could a homeowners' association "evict" a resident-owner who violates the rules and regulations of the association? Could a board of directors in a cooperative "evict" a resident-stockholder-tenant who violates the rules and regulations of the lease? The material which follows relates to these questions.

JUSTICE COURT MUTUAL HOUSING COOPERATIVE, INC. v. SANDOW

50 Misc. 2d 541, 270 N.Y.S.2d 829 (Queens County Sup. Ct. 1966)

SHAPIRO, J.

This is an action for a declaratory judgment and a permanent injunction.

The plaintiff is a cooperative housing corporation which operates and maintains a cooperative apartment building located in this County. The defendants are shareholder-tenants of the plaintiff who, together with their two daughters, reside in a three bedroom apartment in the plaintiff's building.

At issue is the right and power of the board of directors of the plaintiff to adopt the following rule and regulation:

> Be it Resolved, that the playing of musical instruments shall be prohibited except during the following hours:
>
> (a) Between the hours of 10:00 A.M. to 8:00 P.M. during weekdays.
>
> (b) Between the hours of 11:00 A.M. to 8:00 P.M. during Saturdays, Sundays and Legal Holidays.
>
> Be It Resolved that the playing of musical instruments in excess of an hour and one-half per day by any one person is prohibited unless special approval is requested and received in writing by the Board of Directors.

In its first cause of action the plaintiff seeks a judgment declaring that the plaintiff corporation, by its directors, has the power to enact and enforce the aforesaid rule and regulation and that the defendants must adhere to and abide by the provisions of the said rule and regulation. In the second cause of action, the plaintiff prays that the defendants be perpetually enjoined and restrained from causing and allowing musical instruments to be played in their apartment in violation of the rule and regulation set forth herein.

The facts are not in dispute. The defendants' two daughters are musical artists. One plays the violin and the other the flute. In furtherance of their training, these girls are required to practice their respective instruments at least three and one-half hours a day. The defendants moved into this building in 1959 after being assured by the plaintiff's sponsor that their daughters would be permitted to practice their art. Until April 29, 1965, the girls were allowed to practice their art. Until April 29, 1965, the girls were allowed to practice without interference. On that date, following complaints by the tenants of adjoining apartment units, the rule and regulation set forth above was adopted, the plaintiff's Board of Directors apparently agreeing with Keats that "heard melodies are sweet but those unheard are sweeter."

The neighbors particularly complained about the flute which, by its nature, makes a loud piercing sound. The defendants refused to comply with the rule and regulation. The plaintiff then commenced a summary proceeding in the Civil Court of the City of New York, County of Queens, which ultimately was dismissed without prejudice.

The defendants herein are doubly related to the plaintiff. They are both stockholders as well as tenants of the plaintiff's building. Article 5 of the corporate by-laws gives the Board of Directors the power to promulgate such rules and regulations pertaining to the use and occupancy of the premises as may be deemed proper. The proprietary lease provides, in part:

Article 5.   Premises to be Used for Residential Purposes Only.

The Member shall occupy the dwelling unit covered by this agreement as a private dwelling for himself and his immediate family, and for no other purpose, and may enjoy the use, in common with the other members of the Corporation, of all community property and facilities of the project, so long as he continues to own common stock of the Corporation, occupies his dwelling unit, and abides by the terms of this agreement.

The member shall not permit or suffer anything to be done or kept upon said premises . . . which will obstruct or interfere with the rights of other occupants, or annoy them by unreasonable noises or otherwise, nor will he commit or permit any nuisance on the premises . . .

Article 6.   Member's Right to Peacable Possession.

In return for the Member's continued fulfillment of the terms and conditions of this agreement the Corporation covenants that the Member may at all times while this agreement remains in effect, have and enjoy for his sole use and benefit the property hereinabove described, after obtaining occupancy . . .

Article 14.   Member to Comply with all Corporate Regulations.

The Member covenants that he will preserve and promote the cooperative ownership principles on which *(sic)* the Corporation has been founded, abide by the Charter, By-Laws, rules and regulations of the Corporation and any amendments thereto, and by his acts of cooperation with its other members bring about for himself and his co-members a high standard in home and community conditions.

In an early case (Thousand Island Park Association v. Tucker, 173 N.Y. 203), the Court of Appeals, in discussing a somewhat similar lease which provided that the tenant should keep and perform all such conditions or rules and regulations as the landlord should from time to time impose, had occasion to compare the right of a landlord under such a provision to that of a corporation to modify or repeal by-laws. At page 212 of that case the court stated:

> The lease contained the further condition that the tenant should keep and perform all such conditions or rules and regulations as the landlord should from time to time impose. Thus there was reserved to the landlord the power to subsequently make new regulations. Such power, however, though general in form, is not absolute or unqualified. A new regulation established under this reservation, to be valid, must be reasonable. In this respect the case is entirely analogous to that of a member of a corporation where power is reserved to the corporation either by the statute or by its constitution to modify or repeal by-laws and to enact new ones. "If, then, the power is reserved to alter, amend or repeal, and that reservation enters in a contract, the power reserved is to pass reasonable by-laws, agreeable to law. But a by-law that will disturb a vested right is not such."

The plaintiff cites a number of cases involving the right of cooperative housing corporations to enact binding regulations, but none of these stands for the proposition that such regulations may be unreasonable or arbitrary. (cf. Opoliner v. Joint Queensview Housing Enterprise, 11 A.D. 2d 1076; 11 N.Y. Jurisprudence, p. 62).

The issue then is whether the instant rule and regulation is reasonable. The court has been unable to find any decision, reported or otherwise, in which the right of a cooperative housing corporation to enact a regulation prohibiting or restricting the playing of musical instruments has been decided. The defendants cite an analogous case (Twin Elm Management Corpn. v. Banks, 181 Misc. 96) which was a summary proceeding by a landlord to recover possession of an apartment on the ground that the tenants' daughter played the piano continuously each day for a twelve hour period. The case was decided by Mr. Justice Crawford who was then sitting in the Municipal Court. The court held that the playing of the piano was not so unreasonable as to constitute a nuisance and that mere annoyance to other tenants in and of itself did not create a nuisance or make the tenancy of the occupant undesirable.

All the cases cited by the plaintiff are distinguishable since they involved the right of a cooperative housing corporation to ban or restrict dogs or other animals (Knolls Cooperative Section II, Inc., v. Cashman, 19 A.D. 2d 789, aff'd 14 N.Y.2d 579), or to outlaw the use of washing machines (Vernon Manor Co-op Apartments, Section I, Inc., v. Salatino, 15 Misc. 2d 491; Hilltop Village Cooperative No. 4, Inc. v. Wolman, 13 Misc. 2d 753), or food freezers. The presence of dogs or other animals may create problems of safety or sanitation. Mechanical devices, such as washing machines or food freezers, may adversely affect the plumbing or electrical components of the building or even endanger the structure itself. Regulations dealing with animals or mechanical devices which are attached to the property are essentially regulations pertaining to the use of the land. The instant regulation is basically different since it attempts to regulate the mode of living of the occupants of the building (cf. Thousand Island Park Association v. Tucker, *supra*).

Spinoza once said that "one and the same thing can at the same time be good, bad or indifferent." That applies here with full force. To their neighbors the emanations from the defendants' apartment may sound like discordant ululations, while the defendants may well feel with Nietzsche that "without music life would be a mistake." But whether "music is the most sublime noise that has ever penetrated into the ear of man" is not a matter for judicial determination. It suffices for present purposes to hold that a regulation which would mandate a ban upon the exercise of the musical art, or the enjoyment of music, clearly would be arbitrary and unreasonable. If the plaintiff's regulation restricting the playing of musical instruments to one and one-half hours per day were strictly enforced, it is doubtful that any of its tenants could ever acquire or maintain expertise as a musician for even those who are fortunate enough to be born with an aptitude for music, must, in order to maintain the necessary proficiency therein, engage in extensive training and practice.

The one and a half hour provision of the regulation bears internal evidence of its arbitrary character. Take as an example the very defendants in this case and their two daughters. Together they constitute four occupants of the apartment. If each one of them individually availed himself or herself of the right to play a musical instrument for one and a half hours a day, the total playing time thus consumed would be six hours. That would not be prohibited because the regulation provides only that "the playing of musical instruments in excess of an hour and a half per day *by one person* is prohibited." It is obvious that the plaintiff's other tenants would not be less disturbed if the musical playing over a period of six hours were accomplished by four people instead of by two or by one. Under the circumstances, the limitation to one and one-half hours bears no reasonable relationship to the alleged mischief sought to be met. The court therefore finds the hour and a half regulation to be arbitrary and unreasonable.

The other portion of the regulation prohibits the playing of "musical instruments" after 8:00 P.M. It is just about that hour that most city dwellers, after having returned from work or school, finish their dinner and have an opportunity for the first time during the day to engage in avocational pursuits. Under the circumstances, to ban the playing of a musical instrument after 8 P.M. is in effect tantamount to banning its use completely. To uphold the 8 P.M. regulation would mean that no tenant could have a party or social gathering accompanied by piano playing and singing in the evening. So, too, under the broad category of "musical instruments" the playing of stereophonic equipment might well be banned. And if this "musical instrument" regulation were to be held valid, it would necessarily follow that a similar regulation prohibiting the playing of a television set or a radio after 8 P.M. would be valid.

While sympathizing with the desire of the plaintiff to secure peace and quiet for its tenants, and recognizing that the daily continuous playing even of a Van Cliburn can be too much of a good thing, the court is constrained to conclude that neighbors and noise are one of the penalties of a modern civilization. The 8 P.M. regulation is therefore held void as being arbitrary and unreasonable.

The court expresses the hope that the defendants will not so avail themselves of the rights here accorded them as to conclude with Longfellow that "the night shall be filled with music."

Accordingly, the court determines that the plaintiff has no right to enforce the rules and regulations adopted by it on April 29, 1965, with respect to the playing of musical instruments, since such rules and regulations, under the circumstances here present, are arbitrary and unreasonable. It follows that the plaintiff is not entitled to an injunction.

Ordinarily, defeat of a plaintiff results in a dismissal of its complaint, but where, as here, the plaintiff seeks a declaratory judgment and is unsuccessful in its quest, the court is required to declare the rights of the parties and not merely to deny the plaintiff the relief it seeks (Wunderlin v. Lutheran Cemetery, 49 Misc. 2d 836, 268 N.Y.S.2d 514). Therefore, the plaintiff's complaint in so far as it seeks a permanent injunction is dismissed and a judgment is rendered declaring the rules and regulations adopted by the plaintiff's board of directors to be of no force and affect. No costs. Proceed accordingly.

GREEN v. GREENBELT HOMES, INC.
232 Md. 496, 194 A.2d 273 (1963)

HORNEY, J.

In an action for declaratory relief, the Circuit Court for Prince George's County, ordered and decreed that the mutual ownership contract between Greenbelt Homes, Inc., a cooperative housing development, and Carolyn E. F. Green, a member of the corporation, had been lawfully terminated. The member appealed, claiming that the terms of the contract permitting termination were legally inconsistent with the nature of the estate she acquired under the contract.

In pertinent part, the mutual ownership contract provided that:

2. Sale and Purchase of Perpetual Use: Subject to all the provisions of this Contract and for the Purchase Price hereinafter set forth, the Corporation hereby agrees to sell to the Member, and the Member hereby agrees to purchase from the Corporation, a right of Perpetual use and enjoyment . . . of the following dwelling unit and the lot on which situated, the boundaries of which shall be determined by the Corporation, located at the Greenbelt Housing Project, Greenbelt, Maryland. . . .

6 B Plateau Place Unit #2639 Type G2M

Balance due on this contract is $1,727.41 in 232 monthly payments with four percent interest on the unpaid balance. This makes a total interest and amortization payment due each month of $10.71. This payment is quite apart from necessary payments of taxes and operating expenses.

13. Termination of Contract by Corporation for Default or for Cause: In the event of default by the Member . . . of any payments or charges required under this Contract, or violation of any of the provisions hereof, the Corporation may terminate this contract upon ten (10) days written notice to the Member. The Corporation may terminate this Contract upon thirty (30) days written notice of its board of directors subject to and in accordance with provisions of the By-Laws of the Corporation, shall determine that the Member, for sufficient cause is undesirable as a resident in Greenbelt because of objectionable conduct on the part of the Member or of a person living in his dwelling unit. To violate or disregard the rules and regulations provided for in paragraph 7(b) hereof, after due warning, shall be deemed to be objectionable conduct.

The member had occupied the premises for about two years, when, as a result of complaints by other occupants of the housing development, and after a hearing thereon at her request, the board of directors of the corporation duly notified her of the termination of the mutual ownership contract, and at the same time advised her of the right to appeal the decision of the board to the membership of the corporation.

In the notice of termination, the member was informed that the board of directors had found, on the basis of evidence presented at the hearing, that she had "persistently and grossly" violated the contract in that an adult man who was not related by blood or marriage was living with her; that she had failed to provide sanitary care for the pets she maintained on the premises; that as a result of her failure to maintain adequate housekeeping standards she had created offensive odors and had infested her home and the homes of others with vermin; and that she had permitted her teen-age daughter to give noisy, unchaperoned parties during the day and at night which disturbed the peace and quiet of the neighborhood.

The member having appealed pursuant to the by-laws, a membership meeting of the corporation was held to consider the matter. At the meeting, after hearing and discussing the charges, the action of the board of directors in terminating the contract was approved and ratified by a majority vote of the membership.

The corporation promptly notified the member of the result of the appeal and requested her to vacate the premises forthwith. At the same time she was advised that she could sell her "perpetual use right" on the open market, or if she preferred, the corporation was ready to offer her $1750 for it. But the member refused to vacate, and this action followed. The proceedings were submitted to the lower court on bill and answer and the exhibits filed therewith.

Since the parties concede that no factual questions are involved, and further concede that the corporation followed the prescribed procedures in terminating the mutual ownership contract, the only question confronting the court is whether the provisions of the contract relating to termination were valid. It is the contention of the member that the financial terms and the wording of the contract — to the effect that the corporation agreed to "sell" and the member agreed to "purchase" the right of "perpetual use and enjoyment" of the dwelling unit and the lot on which it was situated — was sufficient indicia of ownership to classify her as an owner of real property rather than a holder of a leasehold interest. She bases her claim primarily on the decision in Tudor Arms Apts. v. Shaffer, 191 Md. 342, 62 A.2d 346 (1948), involving a proprietary lease which was substantially the same as the mutual ownership contract in this case. That case, however, instead of supporting the appellant's contention that she was an owner and not a lessee, clearly indicates that in a case such as this — where the issue concerns the right of a member to occupy a dwelling unit after proof of her miscon-duct — the member of the cooperative corporation would be held to be a lessee rather than an owner. It is true that in Tudor Arms, where this Court was construing the effect of a rent control act, it was held that a purchaser-lessee of a cooperative apartment unit was an owner within the meaning of the Federal Housing and Rent Act of 1947 and came within the exception to that act which permitted a landlord or owner to maintain a possessory action against a tenant who refused to yield possession of an apartment. Nevertheless, it is important to note that this Court in referring to the cooperative plan stated (62 A.2d at p. 348) that "the essence of the transac-tion is that in exchange for a capital investment, a prospective purchaser will obtain a right, under the proprietary lease, to occupy a particular unit for an indefinite period, *during good behavior.*" (Emphasis added.) It is also true that many courts, in considering the purposes of rent control acts and other statutes, have found it justifiable to disregard the corporate entity and to hold that members or shareholders of a cooperative apartment or housing project were the owners. See Abbot v. Bralove, 81 F. Supp. 532 (D.D.C. 1948); Hicks v. Bigelow, 55 A.2d 924 (D.C. Mun. App. 1947). See also In re Pitts' Estate, 218 Cal. 184, 22 P.2d 694 (Cal. 1933), involving a statute affording a right to offset a lien claim against the purchase price of real property. But such cases, including Tudor Arms, must be considered in light of the particular statute involved, and certainly cannot be interpreted to mean that the right of the purchaser-lessee in the cooperative apartment was equivalent to a fee simple interest.

In 1 American Law of Property (Casner ed. 1952), §3.10, it is said (at p. 198) that:

> From the standpoint of legal structure the so-called cooperative apartment housing may take one of three general forms. . . . The third form involves the use of a corporation which holds legal title to the property. Shares of stock or, if a non-stock corporation, memberships are sold to persons who will occupy the housing units, the number of shares or the cost of the membership required depending on the value of the particular apartment or unit.

When shares of stock are sold, proprietary leases are made by the corporation to the shareholders, in which there are, among other things, the provisions concerning the term of the lease and the payment of rent, which is based on estimates of operational costs and capital indebtedness. Other provisions include covenants against assignment without the consent of the corporation, that the tenant will make inside repairs but no structural changes, and that the corporation may forfeit the lease for a breach of the covenants or violation of the rules of conduct. But when memberships are sold in a non-stock corporation, as was the case here, the sale is evidenced by a contract made between the corporation and a member who purchases a membership, in which, among other things, there are provisions for payment of taxes and operating expenses. Other provisions pertain to the occupancy of the dwelling unit by the member, the rules and regulations relating to occupancy, and the termination of the contract for default or for cause arising out of a violation of the rules and regulations or other misconduct on the part of a member.

It is further stated at p. 200 (of Casner's edition of 1 American Law of Property) that:

> [I]n legal theory the corporation is distinct from its shareholders [or members], no one of whom has a right to receive legal title to any specific property of the corporation under the better-drawn plans, and it is necessary that this distinction be observed in order to carry out the purposes of the cooperative. The courts have recognized that the relation is that of landlord and tenant in allowing the corporation the usual remedies of a landlord against a tenant.

An important factor in the maintenance of a cooperative housing project is the control of the activities of the cooperative members living within the project. In a recent article, Restrictions on the use of Cooperative Apartment Property, by Arthur E. Wallace, 13 Hastings Law Journal, 357, 363, it is said:

> The economic and social interdependence of the tenant-owners demands cooperation on all levels of cooperative life if a tolerable living situation is to be maintained. Each tenant-owner is required to give up some of the freedoms he would otherwise enjoy if he were living in a private dwelling and likewise is

privileged to demand the same sacrifices of his cotenant-owners with respect to his rights.

By analogy, the cooperative agreement is really a community within a community, governed, like our municipalities, by rules and regulations for the benefit of the whole. Whereas the use of lands within a city is controlled by zoning ordinances, the use of apartments within the cooperative project is controlled by restrictive covenants. The use of the common facilities in the project is controlled on the same theory that the use of city streets and parks is regulated. In both situations compliance with the regulations is the price to be paid to live in and enjoy the benefits of the particular organization.

To determine the intent of the parties and the status created, it is necessary to look to "the writings between the parties, to the circumstances under which they were made, and to the matters with which they deal." 1915 16th St. Co-op. Assn. v. Pinkett, 85 A.2d 58 (D.C. Mun. App. 1951). We think it is clear from the mutual ownership contract that the restrictions on the use of the cooperative dwelling unit were covenants between the member and the corporation, the breach of which gave the corporation the right to terminate the contract. We see no practical difference between this contract and a lease which provides that it can be terminated by the lessor when its provisions as to the use to be made of the premises by the lessee are breached. For a case upholding the validity of such a lease, see Baltimore Butchers Abattoir & Live Stock Co. v. Union Rendering Co., 179 Md. 117, 17 A.2d 130 (1941). See also 1 American Law of Property §3.10, at p. 198. In her tenant status, the member was given the right of occupancy so long as she did not make "[u]se of the dwelling unit or any part thereof for any purpose contrary to the interests of the Corporation or its members." It is apparent, we think, that the objectionable conduct of the member was a sufficient breach of covenant to warrant the corporation exercising its right to terminate the interest of the member in the dwelling unit.

Since we find no error in the ruling of the lower court, the decree must be affirmed.

Decree affirmed; the appellant to pay the costs.[22]

SECTION 2. COVENANTS RUNNING WITH THE LAND

It is contemplated that the purchasers of lots in Lakeville will covenant to do or not do various things. We are now interested in examining who it is that

---

22. In regard to the constitutional requirements of procedural due process when a state agency is involved in terminating a tenant's interest on ground of nondesirability of the tenant, see Escalera v. New York City Housing Authority, 425 F.2d 853 (2d Cir.), cert. denied, 400 U.S. 853, 91 S. Ct. 54 (1970). See also Note, Public Landlords and Private Tenants: The Evictions of "Undesirables" from Public Housing Projects, 77 Yale L.J. 988, 1003 (1968).—EDS.

will enforce these covenants, the extent to which these covenants will be enforceable against successors to the original purchasers of lots, and whether the enforcement will be by way of a claim for damages, or by specific enforcement or injunction in equity. We will be examining these questions primarily on the basis of common-law rules, keeping in mind that there may be statutory provisions that are applicable depending on whether we have a homeowners' association, a cooperative, a condominium, or some other framework adopted for Lakeville.

A. Covenants Enforceable at Law

Note: Various Technical Requirements[23]

In this section you face the problem of determining when the benefit and the burden of covenants between owners in fee[24] "run with the land"[25] at law. In other words, to what extent will persons who succeed to the land benefited by the covenant be entitled to enforce it at law, and to what extent will persons who succeed to the land burdened by the covenant be liable at law if they do not live up to its terms?[26]

The essentials of a real covenant are: (1) observance of certain formalities; (2) an intention of the parties that the covenant "run with the land"; (3) a promise of such kind that it may be said "to touch or concern the land"; and (4) "privity of estate."[27]

The first two essentials need not concern us except to note certain problems which may arise, and in drafting the covenants, to make sure they do not arise. According to the strict or technical rule of the common law, the covenant must be (1) in writing, (2) signed, and (3) sealed by the covenantor.

---

23. This introduction is substantially a paraphrase of a portion of the late Judge Clark's classic work Real Covenants and Other Interests Which Run With the Land (2d ed. 1947) (hereinafter in this chapter cited as Clark). The editors gratefully acknowledge their debt to Judge Clark, the accepted authority in what he called "this narrow corner of the law." Although "there may be real doubt of the worth of devoting more good white paper to so narrow a corner of the law" (Clark, Appendix I, at 208), for obvious reasons, this caveat must be ignored.

24. The idea of the benefit or burden of a covenant "running with the land" should not be new to you. You observed this in connection with covenants in a lease sought to be enforced either by an assignee of the landlord or an assignee of the tenant. (See Chapter 20, especially Masury v. Southworth, page 561 supra.)

25. Strictly speaking, it is inaccurate to say that a covenant "runs with the land." It runs not with the land but with the estate of a party to the covenant. Clark, at 111-115. But see Bordwell, Disseisin and Adverse Possession, 33 Yale L.J. 285, 290-293 (1924), suggesting that covenants should run with the land rather than with the estate.

26. It should be noted that we are not here concerned with the enforcement of covenants between the original covenanting parties—they are in "privity of contract." Whether they are enforceable as between the original covenanting parties is left to the contracts course, and for our purposes, it is assumed that the covenant would be enforceable as between the original covenanting parties.

27. Clark, at 94.

The sealing of instruments has long been regarded as a useless formality, and in most jurisdictions distinctions between instruments under seal and those not under seal have been abolished by statute.[28] If the instrument creating the covenant must be signed by the covenantor, how can the acceptance of a deed poll — a deed which is executed only by the grantor — have the effect of binding the grantee as covenantor? It could not under the strict rule of the common law, but the deed poll is now the accepted and generally used form of conveyance, and as you might expect, the majority of jurisdictions now recognize the act of acceptance of the deed poll by the grantee containing covenants to be performed by the grantee, as effectively binding the grantee to the performance of these covenants as would be the signing and sealing an indenture deed.[29] The requirement of having the covenant respecting the use of land in writing is still significant in those jurisdictions which hold that a covenant is unenforceable if it fails to satisfy the statute of frauds.[30] In ascertaining the intent of the parties, the question arises whether the covenantor must agree not only for himself or herself, but also expressly "for his [or her] assigns"?[31] The great majority of courts have held that as between owners in fee, as compared to covenants found in a lease, "whether a covenant runs is to be determined from the intention of the parties as disclosed by the entire instrument and not by the presence or absence of the technical word 'assigns.'"[32]

The requirement that the covenant be of such kind that it may be said to "touch or concern" the land operates to limit the covenants permissible as encumbrances on title.[33] It is designed to establish some degree of connection between the covenant and the land. It is impossible to state any absolute, litmus paper test to determine what covenants touch and concern

28. See, e.g., Atlanta, K. & N. Ry. v. McKinney, 124 Ga. 929, 53 S.E. 701 (1906). At some time you should check the law in your own jurisdiction on this point. In jurisdictions where the significance of the seal has not been eliminated, the requirement of a seal, a fortiori, must be met. See generally American Law of Property §9.9 (Casner ed. 1952).

29. See, e.g., Ga. Code Ann. §29-102, applied in Lawson v. Lewis, 205 Ga. 227, 52 S.E.2d 859 (1949).

30. In a majority of states, the provisions of the statute of frauds as to interests in land do not apply. Sims, The Law of Real Covenants: Exceptions to the Restatement of the Subject by the American Law Institute, 30 Cornell L.Q. 1, 26-30 (1944). Compare Sprague v. Kimball, 213 Mass. 380, 100 N.E. 622 (1913), discussed at page 1024 *infra*, with Johnson v. Mount Baker Park Presbyterian Church, 113 Wash. 458, 194 P. 536 (1920).

31. One of the resolutions laid down in Spencer's Case, 5 Co. 16a, 77 Eng. Rep. 72 (K.B. 1583), was that a covenant relating to something not in esse would not bind the assignees of a party, i.e., run with the land, unless the assigns were expressly mentioned, but if a covenant related to something in esse, then it would bind the assignees without express words. The case involved covenants between landlord and tenant, and the doctrine still has some vitality in covenants found in leases, although it is clearly on the wane. See American Law of Property §9.4 (Casner ed. 1952).

32. American Law of Property §9.10 (Casner ed. 1952).

33. The more important and basic resolution laid down by Spencer's Case, footnote 31 *supra*, was the requirement that a covenant in a lease could not run "if the thing to be done be merely collateral to the land, and doth not touch or concern the thing demised in any sort." This same requirement has been repeatedly applied by the courts to covenants as between owners in fee. American Law of Property §9.13 (Casner ed. 1952).

the land and what covenants do not, and most courts have adopted a practical, realistic approach[34]—first suggested by Professor Harry A. Bigelow.[35] The method he suggests is to measure the legal relations of the parties with and without the covenant. If the covenantor's legal relations, i.e., legal rights, powers or privileges, in connection with the land in question, and not merely as a member of the community in general, are lessened or rendered less valuable, then the *burden* of the covenant "touches or concerns" the land. If the covenantee's legal relations in respect to the land in question are increased, or rendered more valuable, then the *benefit* of the covenant "touches or concerns" the land. As Clark succinctly put it: "where the parties, as laymen and not as lawyers, would naturally regard the covenant as intimately bound up with the land, aiding the promisee as landowner or hampering the promisor in similar capacity, the requirement should be held fulfilled." [36] Ordinarily, if the burden of a covenant "touches or concerns" the land, the benefit will also, and vice versa, but it is important that the running of the benefit and the running of the burden be approached as separate and distinct questions, for such is not always the case.[37] Hence we should test each end of the covenant separately, to ascertain both if the parties intended it to run and if it may legally be permitted to run.

The requirement of "privity of estate" has caused even greater difficulty, mainly because this elusive concept is used by different courts in three distinct senses:[38] (1) succession to the estate of one of the original covenanting parties, (sometimes called vertical or successive privity); (2) in addition to the first, succession of estate between covenantor and covenantee at the time of the making of the covenant (sometimes called horizontal or simultaneous privity); and (3) mutual and simultaneous interests of both parties to the covenant in the same land, (sometimes called the Massachusetts doctrine of "substituted privity" or tenurial privity). It isn't really as complicated as it sounds and perhaps an example will serve to illustrate the differences.[39] If CE_1 wishes to enforce against CR_1 a covenant originally entered into between CE and CR, their respective predecessors in title, there is sufficient privity of estate under the first definition by the mere succession of interest between CE_1 and CE; under the second, there must also have been a conveyance between CE and CR at the time the covenant was entered into; and under the third, CE and CR at the time the covenant was entered into

34. See, e.g., Neponsit Property Owners' Association, Inc. v. Emigrant Industrial Savings Bank, 278 N.Y. 248, 15 N.E.2d 793 (1938), set out at page 994 *infra*.
35. Bigelow, The Content of Covenants in Leases, 12 Mich. L. Rev. 639 (1914).
36. Clark, at 99.
37. Clark, at 111. If the burden and the benefit are not to be tested separately, no covenants with fees which are in gross can run, but there are certain covenants in gross which have been held to run—noteworthy examples are the covenants restricting competition. These are discussed at page 1003 *infra*.
38. Clark, at 111.
39. The illustration is basically Clark's (see Clark, at 146), but the lettering has been changed so as to conform with the system we have used throughout this chapter.

must each have had a recognizable legal interest in the same land, e.g., landlord and tenant or holder of an easement and owner of the servient tenement.[40] In a jurisdiction which has adopted the second definition as the required "privity of estate," how could two adjoining landowners, strangers to the title of each other, enter into running covenants? Clark forcefully argues that the requirement of a conveyance between CR and CE at the time of entering into the covenant "amounts to a barren formality akin to that formerly required for the transfer from husband to wife through the instrumentality of a third person. Let CE transfer to CR and the CR transfer back to CE while giving the covenant, and the formality is supplied. No policy, such as preventing encumbrances on title is affected in the least. Under our recording system notice of a covenant is as easily acquired as notice of a conveyance."[41] Notwithstanding the soundness of this argument, the great majority of American jurisdictions have stated the requirement of "privity of estate" as succession of estate between CR and CE.[42] The Massachusetts doctrine began in 1837[43] when the court held that a covenant running with the land at law could be created in a deed conveying a fee if the deed either granted or reserved an easement—"the covenant in aid of an easement." How can this type of privity always be achieved, if the parties are aware of the problem? No jurisdiction outside of Massachusetts has adopted this added requirement, but can you articulate "the understandable policy behind this rule"?[44] Even if the first is adopted as a complete statement of the requirement of "privity of estate," as Clark suggests, the concept would still

---

40. Since the law of real covenants had its origin in Spencer's Case, footnote 31, *supra,* involving covenants between landlord and tenant, which of the three types of privity would you suppose the English law courts initially favored?

41. Clark, at 117. According to the Restatement of Property, the proper privity test depends on whether the burden or the benefit is to run. Section 547 provides that privity between CR and CE (the second) is not essential to the running of the *benefit.* Section 534, however, provides that privity between CR and CE is essential to the running of the *burden.* The position of the Restatement has been severely criticized by the late Judge Clark, and the Restatement's position has been vigorously defended by the late Oliver S. Rundell, Reporter for Volume 5 of the Restatement. For that verbal battle and an interesting behind the scenes look at how a Restatement of the Law is arrived at, see Clark, The American Law Institute's Law of Real Covenants, 52 Yale L.J. 699 (1943); Rundell, Judge Clark on the American Law Institute's Law of Real Covenants: A Comment, 53 Yale L.J. 312 (1944); Clark, A Note on Professor Rundell's Comment, 53 Yale L.J. 327 (1944); Clark, More About the Law of Real Covenants and Its Restatement, 30 Cornell L.Q. 378 (1944). See also Sims, The Law of Real Covenants: Exceptions to the Restatement of the Subject by the American Law Institute, 30 Cornell L.Q. 1 (1944); Walsh, Covenants Running With the Land, 21 N.Y.U.L.Q. Rev. 28 (1946).

42. See, e.g., Wheeler v. Schad, 7 Nev. 204 (1871), where the parties neglected to insert the covenant in their deed of conveyance and drew it up six days later after discovering their oversight. The court held that it was unenforceable because at the time of making the covenant, there was no "privity of estate" between CR and CE. See generally American Law of Property §9.11 (Casner ed. 1952).

43. Morse v. Aldrich, 36 Mass. (19 Pick.) 449 (1837).

44. Clark, at 128-129. After explaining what he felt that policy was, he says; "if the policy . . . is justifiable, it deserves to be isolated and independently stated, not applied under cover of a doctrine which has an importance of its own."

have its problems.[45] The following problems are concerned with the simple requirement of privity between CR and CR$_1$ and CE and CE$_1$.

Problems

32.7.   CE sold a portion of her land to CR, and in the deed to CR was a covenant that the land so conveyed would be used only for residential purposes. The deed from CE to CR was recorded. AP ousted CR from possession and remained in open, notorious, continuous, and hostile possession of the land for 20 years. AP then used the land for other than residential purposes. Is CE entitled to maintain an action at law against AP for damages? What if AP ousted CE from possession of her remaining land and continued in open, notorious, continuous, and hostile possession of the land for 20 years? CR then used his land for other than residential purposes. Is AP entitled to maintain an action at law against CR for damages? See Bordwell, Disseisin and Adverse Possession, 33 Yale L.J. 285, 290-293 (1924); American Law of Property §§9.15, 9.20 (Casner ed. 1952).

32.8.   CE conveyed a portion of her land to CR, and the deed to CR contained a covenant that the land was to be used only for residential purposes. CE died and by her will devised the land retained by her to C for life, remainder to D in fee simple. CR died and by his will devised the land conveyed to him to E for life, remainder to F in fee simple. E has placed a building on the land and is using it for business purposes. C sues E to recover damages for the breach of the covenant in the deed from CE to CR. E contends that the burden of the covenant made by CR does not bind her because she has not succeeded to the entire interest of CR in the burdened land. She also contends that C should not be entitled to the benefit of the covenant because C has not succeeded to CE's entire interest in the benefited land. Are either of these contentions sound? American Law of Property §§9.15, 9.20 (Casner ed. 1952).

32.9.   CE conveyed a portion of her land to CR. The deed to CR contained a covenant that CR or his heirs and assigns would maintain a fence between the land retained by CE and the land conveyed to CR. CE contracts to sell the land retained by her to CE$_1$, payment to be made in installments over five years, at which time CE is to give CE$_1$ a deed. CE$_1$ goes into possession of the land pursuant to the terms of the contract. Two years later, CE$_1$ having performed all obligations to date under the contract, CR refuses to repair the boundary fence. CE$_1$ repairs it and sues CR for the cost of the repairs. You are the attorney for CR. What defense would you offer? See Haynes v. Buffalo, N.Y. & P.R.R., 38 Hun 17 (N.Y. Sup. Ct. 1885).

45.   Clark, at 147.

Note: Remedy at Law Compared With Equitable Relief

You should remember that the requirements we have been discussing up to this point are the essentials of a covenant running *at law,* and you will see in the next section the extent to which a court applying equitable principles will give relief where the technical requirements for the running of the benefit and/or the burden at law have not been met.

As you read the material which follows, you should ask yourself: (1) What is the nature of the promise involved? Is it (a) affirmative, i.e., does it obligate CR (or CR₁) to build or maintain a structure or pay money? or (b) negative (frequently called restrictive or protective), i.e., does it obligate CR (or CR₁) not to use the land in some way or not to build on the land nearer than so many feet from the property line? (2) What is the nature of the remedy being sought? Is CE (or CE₁) seeking (a) a legal remedy, e.g., money damages? or (b) an equitable remedy, e.g., specific performance or injunction? Finally, as a future practitioner in "this narrow corner of the law," ask yourself what promises you would desire a legal remedy for and what promises you would desire an equitable remedy for, and whether the existing law places any insuperable hurdle in your way.

Note: Going Forward With Lakeville

With the preceding introduction in mind, assume you have received the following memorandum from the senior member of your law firm:

> Since my last memorandum to you, much has happened. Our client had a market survey made of the area surrounding the lake. The report was quite favorable, and the client decided to develop the entire lake area as a year-round housing community. The client was able to purchase the remaining land around the lake at a very reasonable price, and took options on additional parcels of land in the area in case the development proves successful.[46]
>
> Our client has asked our firm to do the legal work necessary to carry out the plans for the proposed development. As you know, a final subdivision plat of the development has been prepared[47] and is ready for recording. We are now in the midst of preparing the declaration of covenants and restrictions we will

---

46. The firm has already handled the title checking, contracting, and conveyancing problems incident to these purchases. Recall Chapters 28, 25, and 27, respectively. We are considering the possibility of registering the land in order to avoid possible future disputes over adverse possession. What do you think? Recall Chapter 30.

47. In most jurisdictions, the use of a plat in the subdivision of land and the sale of any land by reference thereto, is illegal unless the subdivision plat has been presented to and approved by an appropriate local public authority. The statutes are collected in Yokley, The Law of Subdivision ch. 14 (1963).

make applicable to the platted area[48] and your assistance is desired with respect to this task.

We have carefully considered the possible legal forms available to develop the lake area and have decided tentatively on the homeowners' association, mainly because it is the simplest to understand and therefore the easiest to market. We of course want the homeowners' association to be able to enforce all the covenants and restrictions and to maintain the common properties and facilities. The association will collect an annual assessment in order to conduct its activities. We want each and every owner of land, initial and subsequent, to be bound to pay this annual charge. Are there any problems involved in drafting such an affirmative legal covenant? Examine *Neponsit Property Owners' Association, Inc.* with this question in mind.

NEPONSIT PROPERTY OWNERS' ASSOCIATION, INC. v. EMIGRANT INDUSTRIAL SAVINGS BANK
278 N.Y. 248, 15 N.E.2d 793 (1938)

LEHMAN, J.   The plaintiff, as assignee of Neponsit Realty Company, has brought this action to foreclose a lien upon land which the defendant owns. The lien, it is alleged, arises from a covenant, condition or charge contained in a deed of conveyance of the land from Neponsit Realty Company to a predecessor in title of the defendant. The defendant purchased the land at a judicial sale. The referee's deed to the defendant and every deed in the defendant's chain of title since the conveyance of the land by Neponsit Realty Company purports to convey the property subject to the covenant, condition or charge contained in the original deed. . . .

It appears that in January, 1911, Neponsit Realty Company, as owner of a tract of land in Queens county, caused to be filed in the office of the clerk of the county a map of the land. The tract was developed for a strictly residential community, and Neponsit Realty Company conveyed lots in the tract to purchasers, describing such lots by reference to the filed map and to roads and streets shown thereon. In 1917, Neponsit Realty Company conveyed the land now owned by the defendant to Robert Oldner Deyer and his wife by deed which contained the covenant upon which the plaintiff's cause of action is based.

That covenant provides:

And the party of the second part for the party of the second part and the heirs, successors and assigns of the party of the second part further covenants that the property conveyed by this deed shall be subject to an annual charge in such an amount as will be fixed by the party of the first part, its successors and assigns, not, however exceeding in any year the sum of four ($4.00) Dollars per

---

48.   The importance of recording the plat and the declaration of covenants and restrictions in order to show a "general plan" or scheme of development was discussed in Chapter 28, especially in Sanborn v. McLean, page 837 *supra.*

lot 20 × 100 feet. The assigns of the party of the first part may include a Property Owners' Association which may hereafter be organized for the purposes referred to in this paragraph, and in case such association is organized the sums in this paragraph provided for shall be payable to such association. The party of the second part for the party of the second part and the heirs, successors and assigns of the party of the second part covenants that they will pay this charge to the party of the first part, its successors and assigns on the first day of May in each and every year, and further covenants that said charge shall on said date in each year become a lien on the land and shall continue to be such lien until fully paid. Such charge shall be payable to the party of the first part or its successors or assigns, and shall be devoted to the maintenance of the roads, paths, parks, beach, sewers and such other public purposes as shall from time to time be determined by the party of the first part, its successors or assigns. And the party of the second part by the acceptance of this deed hereby expressly vests in the party of the first part, its successors and assigns, the right and power to bring all actions against the owner of the premises hereby conveyed or any part thereof for the collection of such charge and to enforce the aforesaid lien therefor.

These covenants shall run with the land and shall be construed as real covenants running with the land until January 31st, 1940, when they shall cease and determine.

Every subsequent deed of conveyance of the property in the defendant's chain of title, including the deed from the referee to the defendant, contained, as we have said, a provision that they were made subject to covenants and restrictions of former deeds of record.

There can be no doubt that Neponsit Realty Company intended that the covenant should run with the land and should be enforceable by a property owners' association against every owner of property in the residential tract which the realty company was then developing. The language of the covenant admits of no other construction. Regardless of the intention of the parties, a covenant will run with the land and will be enforceable against a subsequent purchaser of the land at the suit of one who claims the benefit of the covenant, only if the covenant complies with certain legal requirements. These requirements rest upon ancient rules and precedents. The age-old essentials of a real covenant, aside from the form of the covenant, may be summarily formulated as follows: (1) it must appear that grantor and grantee intended that the covenant should run with the land, (2) it must appear that the covenant is one "touching" or "concerning" the land with which it runs; (3) it must appear that there is "privity of estate" between the promisee or party claiming the benefit of the covenant and the right to enforce it, and the promisor or party who rests under the burden of the covenant. (Clark on Covenants and Interests Running with Land, p. 74.) Although the deeds of Neponsit Realty Company conveying lots in the tract it developed "contained a provision to the effect that the covenants ran with the land, such provision in the absence of the other legal requirements is insufficient to accomplish such a purpose." (Morgan Lake Co. v. N.Y., N.H.

& H.R.R. Co., 262 N.Y. 234, 238, 186 N.E. 685.) In his opinion in that case, Judge Crane posed but found it unnecessary to decide many of the questions which the court must consider in this case.

The covenant in this case is intended to create a charge or obligation to pay a fixed sum of money to be "devoted to the maintenance of the roads, paths, parks, beach, sewers and such other public purposes as shall from time to time be determined by the party of the first part (the grantor), its successors as assigns." It is an affirmative covenant to pay money for use in connection with, but not upon, the land which it is said is subject to the burden of the covenant. Does such a covenant "touch" or "concern" the land? These terms are not part of a statutory definition, a limitation placed by the State upon the power of the courts to enforce covenants intended to run with the land by the parties who entered into the covenants. Rather they are words used by courts in England in old cases to describe a limitation which the courts themselves created or to formulate a test which the courts have devised and which the courts voluntarily apply. (Cf. Spencer's Case, Coke, vol. 3, part. 5, p. 16; Mayor of Congleton v. Pattison, 10 East, 316.) In truth the test so formulated is too vague to be of much assistance and judges and academic scholars alike have struggled, not with entire success, to formulate a test at once more satisfactory and more accurate. "It has been found impossible to state any absolute tests to determine what covenants touch and concern land and what do not. The question is one for the court to determine in the exercise of its best judgment upon the facts of each case." (Clark, op. cit. p. 76.)

Even though that be true, a determination by a court in one case upon particular facts will often serve to point the way to a correct decision in other cases upon analogous facts. Such guideposts may not be disregarded. It has been often said that a covenant to pay a sum of money is a personal affirmative covenant which usually does not concern or touch the land. Such statements are based upon English decisions which hold in effect that only covenants, which compel the covenanter to submit to some restriction on the use of his property, touch or concern the land, and that the burden of a covenant which requires the covenanter to do an affirmative act, even on his own land, for the benefit of the owner of a "dominant" estate, does not run with his land. (Miller v. Clary, 210 N.Y. 127, 103 N.E. 1114.) In that case the court pointed out that in many jurisdictions of this country the narrow English rule has been criticized and a more liberal and flexible rule has been substituted. In this State the courts have not gone so far. We have not abandoned the historic distinction drawn by the English courts. So this court has recently said: "Subject to a few exceptions not important at this time, there is now in this state a settled rule of law that a covenant to do an affirmative act, as distinguished from a covenant merely negative in effect, does not run with the land so as to charge the burden of performance on a subsequent grantee (citing cases). This is so though the burden of such a covenant is laid upon the very parcel which is the subject-matter of the conveyance." (Guaranty Trust Co. v. New York & Queens County Ry. Co., 253 N.Y. 190, 204, 170 N.E. 887, opinion by Cardozo, Ch. J.)

Both in that case and in the case of Miller v. Clary (*supra*) the court pointed out that there were some exceptions or limitations in the application of the general rule. Some promises to pay money have been enforced, as covenants running with the land, against subsequent holders of the land who took with notice of the covenant. (Cf. Greenfarb v. R.S.K. Realty Corp., 256 N.Y. 130, 175 N.E. 649; Morgan Lake Co. v. N.Y., N.H. & H.R.R. Co., *supra*.) It may be difficult to classify these exceptions or to formulate a test of whether a particular covenant to pay money or to perform some other act falls within the general rule that ordinarily an affirmative covenant is a personal and not a real covenant, or falls outside the limitations placed upon the general rule. At least it must "touch" or "concern" the land in a substantial degree, and though it may be inexpedient and perhaps impossible to formulate a rigid test or definition which will be entirely satisfactory or which can be applied mechanically in all cases, we should at least be able to state the problem and find a reasonable method of approach to it. It has been suggested that a covenant which runs with the land must affect the legal relations — the advantages and the burdens — of the parties to the covenant, as owners of particular parcels of land and not merely as members of the community in general, such as taxpayers or owners of other land. (Clark, op. cit. p. 76. Cf. Professor Bigelow's article on The Contents of Covenants in Leases, 12 Mich. L. Rev. 639; 30 Law Quarterly Review, 319.) That method of approach has the merit of realism. The test is based on the effect of the covenant rather than on technical distinctions. Does the covenant impose, on the one hand, a burden upon an interest in land, which on the other hand increases the value of a different interest in the same or related land?

Even though we accept that approach and test, it still remains true that whether a particular covenant is sufficiently connected with the use of land to run with the land, must be in many cases a question of degree. A promise to pay for something to be done in connection with the promisor's land does not differ essentially from a promise by the promisor to do the thing himself, and both promises constitute, in a substantial sense, a restriction upon the owner's right to use the land, and a burden upon the legal interest of the owner. On the other hand, a covenant to perform or pay for the performance of an affirmative act disconnected with the use of the land cannot ordinarily touch or concern the land in any substantial degree. Thus, unless we exalt technical form over substance, the distinction between covenants which run with land and covenants which are personal, must depend upon the effect of the covenant on the legal rights which otherwise would flow from ownership of land and which are connected with the land. The problem then is: Does the covenant in purpose and effect substantially alter these rights?

The opinion in Morgan Lake Co. v. N.Y., N.H. & H.R.R. Co. *(supra)* foreshadowed a classification based upon substance rather than upon form. It was not the first case, however, in which this court has based its decision on the substantial effect of a covenant upon legal relations of the parties as owners of land. Perhaps the most illuminating illustration of such an approach to the problem may be drawn from the "party wall" cases in this State which are reviewed in the opinion of the court in Sebald v. Mulholland, 155 N.Y. 455, 50 N.E. 260. The court there pointed out that in cases, cited in the opinion, where by covenant between owners of adjoining parcels of land, "a designated party was authorized to build a party wall, the other agreeing to pay a portion of its value when it should be used by him," the court was constrained to hold that "the agreement was a present one, the party who was to build and the one who was to pay were expressly designated, and the covenant to pay was clearly a personal one" (p. 464, 50 N.E. page 263). At the same time, the court also pointed out that such covenants must be distinguished from the covenants (passed upon by the court in the earlier case of Mott v. Oppenheimer, 135 N.Y. 312, 31 N.E. 1097), "by which the parties conferred, each upon the other, the authority to erect such (party) wall, and dedicated to that use a portion of each of their lots, with an agreement that if either should build the other might have the right to use it by paying his share of the expense" (p. 463, 50 N.E. page 262). In such a case, it was said by the court, "It was not and could not then be known who would build, or who was to pay when the wall was used. The agreement was wholly prospective, and its purpose was to impose upon the land of each, and not upon either personally, the burden of a future party wall, and to secure to the land and, thus, to its subsequent owners, a corresponding right to the use of the wall by paying one-half of its value. . . . In that case the character of the agreement, its obvious purpose, its prospective provisions, and the situation of the lands when the agreement was made, all concurred in showing an intent that its covenants should run with land, and clearly justified the court in so holding" (pp. 463-464, 50 N.E. page 262).[49]

Looking at the problem presented in this case from the same point of view and stressing the intent and substantial effect of the covenant rather than its form, it seems clear that the covenant may properly be said to touch and concern the land of the defendant and its burden should run with the land. True, it calls for payment of a sum of money to be expended for "public purposes" upon land other than the land conveyed by Neponsit Realty Company to plaintiff's predecessor in title. By that conveyance the grantee, however, obtained not only title to particular lots, but an easement or right of common enjoyment with other property owners in roads, beaches, public parks or spaces and improvements in the same tract. For full enjoyment in common by the defendant and other property owners of these easements or rights, the roads and public places must be maintained. In

---

49. See generally on party wall covenants Aigler, The Running With the Land of Agreements to Pay for a Portion of the Cost of Party Walls, 10 Mich. L. Rev. 187 (1912); Clark, footnote 23, *supra,* ch. 5, at 144 et seq.; American Law of Property §9.21 (Casner ed. 1952).—Eds.

order that the burden of maintaining public improvements should rest upon the land benefited by the improvements, the grantor exacted from the grantee of the land with its appurtenant easement or right of enjoyment a covenant that the burden of paying the cost should be inseparably attached to the land which enjoys the benefit. It is plain that any distinction or definition which would exclude such a covenant from the classification of covenants which "touch" or "concern" the land would be based on form and not on substance.

Another difficulty remains. Though between the grantor and the grantee there was privity of estate, the covenant provides that its benefit shall run to the assigns of the grantor who "may include a Property Owners' Association which may hereafter be organized for the purposes referred to in this paragraph." The plaintiff has been organized to receive the sums payable by the property owners and to expend them for the benefit of such owners. Various definitions have been formulated of "privity of estate" in connection with covenants that run with the land, but none of such definitions seems to cover the relationship between the plaintiff and the defendant in this case. The plaintiff has not succeeded to the ownership of any property of the grantor. It does not appear that it ever had title to the streets or public places upon which charges which are payable to it must be expended. It does not appear that it owns any other property in the residential tract to which any easement or right of enjoyment in such property is appurtenant. It is created solely to act as the assignee of the benefit of the covenant, and it has no interest of its own in the enforcement of the covenant.

The arguments that under such circumstances the plaintiff has no right of action to enforce a covenant running with the land are all based upon a distinction between the corporate property owners' association and the property owners for whose benefit the association has been formed. If that distinction may be ignored, then the basis of the arguments is destroyed. How far privity of estate in technical form is necessary to enforce in equity a restrictive covenant upon the use of land, presents an interesting question. Enforcement of such covenants rests upon equitable principles (Tulk v. Moxhay, 2 Phillips, 774; Trustees of Columbia College v. Lynch, 70 N.Y. 440; Korn v. Campbell, 192 N.Y. 490, 185 N.E. 687), and at times, at least, the violation "of the restrictive covenant may be restrained at the suit of one who owns property, or for whose benefit the restriction was established, irrespective of whether there were privity either of estate or of contract between the parties, or whether an action at law were maintainable." (Cheseboro v. Moers, 233 N.Y. 75, 80, 134 N.E. 842, 843). The covenant in this case does not fall exactly within any classification of "restrictive" covenants, which have been enforced in this State (Cf. Korn v. Campbell, 192 N.Y. 490, 85 N.E. 687), and no right to enforce even a restrictive covenant has been sustained in this State where the plaintiff did not own property which would benefit by such enforcement so that some of the elements of an equitable servitude are present. In some jurisdictions it has been held that no action may be maintained without such elements. (But cf. Van Sant v. Rose, 260 Ill. 401, 103 N.E. 194). We do not attempt to decide now how far the rule of Trustees of Columbia College v. Lynch (*supra*) will be carried, or to formulate a definite rule as to when, or even whether, covenants in a deed will be enforced, upon equitable principles, against subsequent purchasers with notice, at the suit of a party without privity of contract or estate. (Cf. "Equitable Rights and Liabilities of Strangers to a Contract," by Harlan F. Stone, 18 Columbia Law Review, 291.) There is no need to resort to such a rule if the courts may look behind the corporate form of the plaintiff.

The corporate plaintiff has been formed as a convenient instrument by which the property owners may advance their common interests. We do not ignore the corporate form when we recognize that the Neponsit Property Owners' Association, Inc., is acting as the agent or representative of the Neponsit property owners. As we have said in another case: when Neponsit Property Owners' Association, Inc., "was formed, the property owners were expected to, and have looked to that organization as the medium through which enjoyment of their common right might be preserved equally for all." (Matter of New York (Public Beach), 269 N.Y. 64, 75, 199 N.E. 5, 9). Under the conditions thus presented we said: "it may be difficult, or even impossible, to classify into recognized categories the nature of the interest of the membership corporation and its members in the land. The corporate entity cannot be disregarded, nor can the separate interests of the members of the corporation" (p. 73, 199 N.E. page 8). Only blind adherence to an ancient formula devised to meet entirely different conditions could constrain the court to hold that a corporation formed as a medium for the enjoyment of common rights of property owners owns no property which would benefit by enforcement of common rights and has no cause of action in equity to enforce the covenant upon which such common rights depend. Every reason which in other circumstances may justify the ancient formula may be urged in support of the conclusion that the formula should not be applied in this case. In substance if not in form the covenant is a restrictive covenant which touches and concerns the defendant's land, and in substance, if not in form, there is privity of estate between the plaintiff and the defendant.[50] . . .

[Order which denied a motion by the defendant for judgment on the pleadings affirmed.]

---

50. In Nassau County v. Kensington Association, 21 N.Y.S.2d 208 (1940), a covenant binding lot owners in a subdivision to pay an annual assessment to a property owners' association was held to be an affirmative covenant to pay money which could not be permitted to run with the land, distinguishing *Neponsit* by pointing out at 21 N.Y.S.2d at 215 that here the association "is not committed by its terms to use the funds collected for any particular purpose or in fact to spend the money at all," even though it was shown that the association did in fact maintain a park, collected garbage and performed other services for its members.— EDS.

Note: More on the Affirmative Covenant

Haywood v. Brunswick Permanent Benefit Building Society, 8 Q.B.D. 403 (C.A. 1881) held that the burden of an affirmative covenant does not run with the land so as to bind an assignee of the covenantor. Cotton, L.J., made the oft-quoted statement: "The covenant to repair can only be enforced by making the owner put his hand in his pocket, and there is nothing which would justify us in going that length."[51] New Jersey is an example of an American jurisdiction which has consistently followed the English rule of not permitting the burden of covenants to run with the land.[52] As the principal case illustrates, in Miller v. Clary, 210 N.Y. 127, 103 N.E. 1114 (1913), New York originally adopted this rule as to affirmative covenants, but the extent to which it still exists in New York is subject to considerable question.[53] In other jurisdictions:

> It is the general rule in the American courts that covenants which otherwise satisfy the requirements of necessary intention, privity, and "touch and concern" do run, both at law and in equity, both as to benefit and burden. . . . In reaching this result, the courts have apparently regarded the question whether the burden of the covenant was affirmative or negative as immaterial, seldom referring to this point at all, and occasionally stating affirmatively that the positive nature of the covenant was immaterial. [Annot., Affirmative Covenants as Running With the Land, 68 A.L.R.2d 1022, 1027 (1959).[54]]

In *Neponsit,* the plaintiff brought the action "to foreclose a lien" upon the land which the defendant succeeded to. Was this a legal or equitable remedy?[55] Should a suit to foreclose a lien be treated differently than an action on the debt which creates the lien? The former is enforceable against the land, whereas the latter is enforceable against the landowner. The late Professor Rundell, the Reporter for Volume 5 of the Restatement of Property, argued:

51. 8 Q.B.D. at 409. It should be noted that in England the *benefit* of both affirmative and negative covenants will run with the land, both at law and in equity, and it is only the *burden* of covenants which will not run. Note, Affirmative Duties Running With the Land, 35 N.Y.U.L. Rev. 1344, 1347 (1960), criticizing this as a historic anomaly. The appendix to this student note examines the law in 35 jurisdictions.

52. Furness v. Sinquett, 60 N.J. Super. 410, 159 A.2d 455 (1960). This case involves a covenant to construct and maintain a sidewalk in a new housing development.

53. Consider Nicholson v. 300 Broadway Realty Corp., 7 N.Y.2d 240, 164 N.E.2d 832 (1959), and Note, Affirmative Covenants in New York After *Nicholson,* 16 N.Y.U. Intra. L. Rev. 266 (1961).

54. See generally American Law of Property §9.16, 9.36 (Casner ed. 1952).

55. See University Gardens Property Owners Association, Inc. v. Steinberg, 40 Misc. 2d 816, 244 N.Y.S.2d 208 (Nassau County Dist. Ct. 1963), where the plaintiff association sued to recover an annual assessment. The court said that in *Neponsit* the association had sued in equity to foreclose a lien and inasmuch as this court had no equity jurisdiction, it had to dismiss the complaint.

A mortgagor of land may promise earnestly that his successor will pay the mortgage. No matter how solemnly or earnestly such promises were made, the successors do not have to perform the promise. Hence the successor to the title to land knows that, while he may conceivably lose the land unless he pays either a possible unpaid balance of a purchase price or a mortgage agreed to be paid by his predecessor, he cannot be held personally responsible for any predecessor's unwise bargains or foolish borrowings.[56]

In discussing a covenant enforceable by a lien, the late Judge Clark said:

One wonders, in view of the drastic nature of this remedy [i.e., enforcement by judicial sale of the property] and the interdiction put upon the parties desires by other parts of this Restatement, how it came to be treated with such exceptional favor. . . . For in character and extent it seems much more drastic than the money judgment.[57]

In addition it might be asked where does the lien come from? The Restatement of Property (Running of Burdens—Liability to Lien) §540 provides:

When a promise respecting the use of land of the promisor creates or is secured by a lien upon the land respecting the use of which the promise was made, the lien is enforceable against the successors in title or possession of the promisor to the extent it was enforceable against him except in so far as they are entitled to the protection of the doctrine of bona fide purchaser or of the recording acts.

The late Judge Clark was especially critical of this section:

That section seems to the author to be of the subterfuge nature which to him is so distasteful a feature of this Restatement. On the surface it seems to accord a simple and effective remedy for the enforcement of covenants (by lien on the land) so as to make the remedy of a money judgment seem unnecessarily harsh to the parties. If the remedy by lien were freely available, it might be argued that the money judgment was unnecessary, though hardly that it was by nature harsher than the lien. But, of course, it is rarely available, except as a step in enforcing a judgment; that is, the money judgment is, by history and by practice, a necessary condition precedent, save in the rare cases where a statute may have specially accorded the remedy or the parties may have contracted for it. The fact is that, generally speaking, this is not a separate remedy, but only a step in the enforcement of judgments.[58]

As a practical matter, which is more likely to cause financial ruin—a

---

56.   Rundell, Judge Clark on the American Law Institute's Law of Real Covenants: A Comment, 53 Yale L.J. 312, 314 (1944).
57.   Clark, footnote 23, *supra*; Appendix I, at 224-225.
58.   Clark, Appendix I, at 224.

judgment of money damages for failure to pay an annual assessment or one to foreclose a lien, enforceable by judicial sale of the property?[59]

Note: The Covenant Not to Compete

Assume you have just received the following additional memorandum from a senior partner:

> As you can see by the layout and design of Lakeville, our client hopes to create a small shopping plaza for the benefit of the residents in the common areas.
>
> The client discussed the idea with a broker friend, who said that it would be easier to market space in the plaza if the broker were able to assure each business that no other business in the plaza would compete with it. The client has not decided whether to sell or lease the space. How should the client proceed?

The following material relates to this question.

DICK v. SEARS-ROEBUCK & CO.
115 Conn. 122, 160 A. 432 (1932)

MALTBIE, C.J.

The plaintiff owned certain premises in Danbury upon which was a building built especially for and peculiarly adapted to the conduct of a retail business. For several years subsequent to 1900 he conducted such a business in the building as an individual, but thereafter it was conducted by a partnership which consisted of himself, his wife, and his son, but in which he held the greatest interest. While it was so being conducted he conveyed a lot of land across the street to certain grantees by a deed in which was inserted the following covenant: "The grantees herein by the acceptance hereof covenant and agree on behalf of themselves, their heirs and assigns, that they will not rent the premises hereby conveyed for the purpose of conducting thereon a retail or wholesale furniture business and that they will not permit the said premises to be so used for a period of fifteen years from and after the date hereof and said covenants and agreements are hereby declared to be made the joint and several covenants and agreements of the grantees."

Thereafter the business was incorporated, but the plaintiff continued to manage it and to have the largest financial interest in it. The grantees of the lot across the street conveyed it to a corporation and in the deed to it a covenant similar to that quoted was inserted. The corporation constructed a building upon the lot and leased it for a period of ten years from May 1,

59. Id. at 210.

1929, to the defendant, to be used for the sale and storage of merchandise. The lease contained no reference to the covenants in the deeds. The defendant conducts on the premises a general retail department store and since April, 1931, has had in it a department for the sale at retail of articles of household furniture of all descriptions. It has conspicuously advertised the department and has sold furniture in it to a substantial amount. This has been done in direct competition with the business conducted by the plaintiff, to the substantial injury of that business and the plaintiff's property. The complaint sought and the trial court granted an injunction restraining the defendant from engaging in the retail or wholesale furniture business upon the premises occupied by it.

There can be no question that when the plaintiff conveyed the premises on which is the defendant's store both he and his grantees intended that the covenant should be binding not only upon them but upon subsequent grantees of the property. This is indicated by the use of terms in the covenant which bound not only the grantees but also their heirs and assigns; as far as the plaintiff was concerned, its obvious purpose was to protect the furniture business he was conducting across the street from competition, a purpose which would be easily defeated if the grantees might at any time convey the land free of the restriction; and as far as the grantees are concerned, their intent that the covenant should be binding upon their successors in title is shown by the insertion of an identical covenant in the deed by which they conveyed the premises. The language of the covenant and the surrounding circumstances mark it as one the burden of which was intended to run with the land and this intent is an important element in determining its nature. Bradford Realty Corp. v. Beetz, 108 Conn. 26, 30, 142 A. 395. A covenant in a deed which restrains the use to which the land may be put in the future as well as in the present, and which might very likely affect its value, touches and concerns the land. Davis v. Lyman, 6 Conn. 249, 255; Bigelow, The Content of Covenants in Leases, 12 Michigan Law Review, 639, 640.

The intent of the parties and the nature and form of the covenant established that it was a covenant real. Clark, Covenants & Interests Running with the Land, p. 74. Such a restriction as is contained in it is not invalid; a restriction upon the conduct of a certain business upon a particular piece of land for a reasonable purpose and covering a reasonable period does not violate public policy. The covenant is not against the establishment of a furniture store in competition with that conducted by the plaintiff but against the conduct of a rival furniture business. Considering its purpose it is evident that it would be just as much violated by the conduct of a furniture department of a general retail store as it would be by the establishment of a store devoted exclusively to the sale of furniture, where the result was, as it was found to be in this case, to afford substantial and harmful competition. The maintenance of the furniture department by the defendant falls within the fair intent of the restriction in the covenant. The deeds being of record, the defendant was bound with notice of the covenants contained in them though its lease did not refer to them.

If the plaintiff still owned the business upon his property there would be no question of his right to enforce the covenant against the defendant. That business, since the making of the covenant, has been incorporated, and were the corporation seeking to enforce it we might be confronted with the difficult question of the assignability of the benefits of such a covenant. Clark, Op. Cit., p. 80 and following. It is the covenantee who is seeking to enforce it, and the question is: Has he now such an interest as equity ought to protect by the injunction? Conduct contrary to the provision of the covenant would be a breach of it and of itself give him a right at least to nominal damages. But the situation as found by the trial court goes much beyond that. The plaintiff has, in the words of the finding, the largest financial interest in the corporation, and clearly anything that seriously affects its business must affect his interest in it and the income he will receive from it. The substantial damage to the business which the trial court has found to have been caused by the defendant's breach of the covenant gave to the plaintiff such an interest in requiring obedience to it as justified the trial court in granting the injunction, in the exercise of its reasonable discretion.

There is no error.

The other Judges concurred.

Note: More About Covenants Not to Compete

The *Dick* case merely involved the question of whether the *burden* of a covenant not to compete runs with the land so as to bind a tenant of the covenantor. "[W]ere the corporation seeking to enforce it, we might be confronted with the difficult question of the assignability of the benefits of such a covenant." See generally Bialkin & Bohannan, Covenants Not to Establish a Competing Business — Does the Benefit Pass? 41 Va. L. Rev. 675 (1955). In our client's shopping plaza situation, which would you imagine we would be more concerned with, the running of the burden or the running of the benefit? To what extent does the fact that most of the land in the development we are considering will be restricted to residential purposes eliminate the necessity of covenant not to compete? The Restatement of Property has taken the position that the benefit of this type of covenant will run with the covenantee's land,[60] but that the burden is personal to the covenantor.[61]

Note also the summary fashion the court treated the problem of whether a covenant not to compete "touches and concerns" the land: "A covenant in

---

60. Restatement of Property §543(2)(b) comment e (1944).
61. Id. §537 comment f, set out in the next paragraph.

a deed . . . which might very likely affect its value touches and concerns the land." If only the law were so clear! The Restatement of Property §537 comment f provides:

> f. *Physical use or enjoyment.* For a promise to run with the land of the promisor it is not enough that the performance of the promise operates to benefit either the promisor or the beneficiary of the promise in the use of his land but it must operate to benefit him in the physical use of his land. It must in some way make the use or enjoyment more satisfactory to his physical senses. It is not enough that the income from it is increased by virtue of it. Thus a promise that land of the promisor will not be so used as to compete with a business carried on upon the land of the promisee does not so affect the land of the promisor that it can be made to run with it. Though the benefit to the promisee in being free from competition may be clear, the risk of social harm involved in a possible monopoly of business uses of land in an extended area is sufficient to induce the refusal to extend the "running of promises" to such cases.

Is this persuasive? Consider the following case from a jurisdiction which rivals the Restatement of Property in its grudging enforcement of covenants.

SHELL OIL CO. v. HENRY OUELLETTE & SONS CO.
352 Mass. 725, 227 N.E.2d 509 (1967)

CUTTER, J.

The principal plaintiff (Shell) seeks to enforce a restriction in a 1962 deed from Henry Ouellette & Sons Co., Inc. (Ouellette) to Gordon F. Bloom and others (the trustees) which purports to restrict the uses to which Ouellette and its successors in title may put its remaining land adjacent to the land so conveyed. Stafac Inc. (Stafac), present owner of part of the land conveyed to the trustees by Ouellette in 1962, was allowed to intervene. Socony Mobil Oil Company (Mobil), the holder of an option to purchase a part of Ouellette's remaining land, is also named as a defendant.

The case was heard in the Superior Court upon the pleadings and a statement of agreed facts amounting to a case stated. The trial judge ruled that the alleged restriction in the 1962 deed "was personal, did not create a covenant running with the land, and does not inure to the benefit of remote or successive grantees." See Norcross v. James, 140 Mass. 188, 2 N.E. 946; Shade v. M. O'Keefe, Inc., 260 Mass. 180, 156 N.E. 867. He then reported the case for our decision.[62]

---

62. Because (1) the case involves important conveyancing questions and (2) Shell asks that we overrule the *Norcross* and *Shade* cases, we have afforded opportunity to The Abstract Club and Massachusetts Conveyancers Association to file a brief as amici curiae. They have done so by a useful joint brief, which on grounds of general conveyancing policy supports the

Ouellette owned about 100 acres of land in Methuen. By the 1962 deed, Ouellette conveyed about twenty acres of this land to the trustees. The deed contained the provision set out in the margin.[63]

By recorded deed dated April 30, 1963, the trustees conveyed to Shell a part of the land acquired by them under the 1962 deed. [Footnote omitted.] On March 30, 1964, Shell conveyed to Stafac the land which it had received from the trustees. Stafac leased the premises back to Shell.

Shell then with "knowledge of and taking into consideration the language in . . . the [1962] deed from Ouellette to the [t]rustees . . . at a cost . . . of more than $100,000, constructed an automobile service station." This was completed on November 1, 1964, and has been in operation since that date.

On February 8, 1965, Ouellette granted to Mobil an option to buy part of Ouellette's remaining land for the construction of a gasoline service station. Mobil has received from the town of Methuen a license for the storage and sale of gasoline products. Shell on March 23, 1965, wrote to Mobil inviting its attention to the 1962 restrictions (fn. [63]) and claiming the benefit for Shell of that restriction as preventing the establishment of a competing service station on Ouellette's land subject to the Mobil option.

The question is thus presented whether the benefit of the 1962 restrictions (fn. [63]) accrues to Shell as lessee of a transferee from the trustees of a portion of the land conveyed to them by that 1962 deed. Shell now attempts to enforce the restriction and to impose its burden upon Ouellette, the original grantor, and upon Mobil, a proposed transferee from Ouellette (with notice of the restriction) of a part of the land now subject to the 1962 restriction.

The defendants contend that this case is controlled by Norcross v. James, 140 Mass. 188, 2 N.E. 946, in which in 1885, Mr. Justice Holmes spoke for

---

rule in Norcross v. James. Professor W. Barton Leach has also filed a helpful brief as amicus curiae in which he urges this court at some time to overrule Norcross v. James.

63.   The provision (emphasis supplied) reads in part,

Grantor [Ouellette] for itself, *its successors and assigns* covenants . . . that the grantor's adjacent property . . . for a period of two years after the recording hereof will not be used . . . [then follow restrictions against certain retail use, not here relevant] or for a period of fifty years after the recording hereof will not be permitted to be used in whole or in part for the construction or in connection with the operation of a super market; or *for a period of fifteen years after such recording will not be subject in whole or in part to any use or occupation which at the time such use or occupation is commenced is competitive with any of the following uses of the premises hereby conveyed:* (a) *A use then being made, or a use which shall have been made, within the six months next prior thereto.* (b) An intended use under a then existing contract, provided that the then owner of record of said adjacent land had actual notice of such contract. The term "use" as used in this paragraph (b) means a general use for a class of store. The grantor agrees that there shall be included in any deed by him or his representative of all or any part of said adjacent property similar restrictions on the uses of any part of said adjacent property, which restrictions shall be in effect for the then remainders of the respective durations of the restrictions above set forth.

this court. One Kibbe had conveyed to one Flynt a quarry of six acres in Longmeadow bounded by other land of Kibbe. The deed contained a covenant by Kibbe, "I . . . for myself, my heirs, executors, and administrators, covenant with . . . Flynt, his heirs and assigns . . . that I will not open or work, or allow any person or persons to open or work, any quarry or quarries on my farm or premises in . . . Long Meadow." Norcross and another acquired Flynt's quarry. James and another became the owners of Kibbe's surrounding land and began to quarry stone on that land. Norcross sought to enjoin this activity. The bill was dismissed.

The question of current importance in the *Norcross* opinion (pp. 191-192, 2 N.E. pp. 948-949), is whether, if it be assumed "that the covenant [against opening a quarry on Kibbe's remaining farm] was valid as a contract between the parties, it is of a kind which the law permits to be attached to land in such a sense as to restrict the use of one parcel in all hands for the benefit of whoever may hold the other." The opinion goes on to say, "[E]quity will no more enforce every restriction that can be devised than the common law will recognize as creating an easement every grant purporting to limit the use of land in favor of other land. The principle of policy applied to affirmative covenants, applies also to negative ones. They must 'touch or concern,' or 'extend to the support of the thing' conveyed. . . . They must be 'for the benefit of the estate.' . . . Or, as it is said more broadly, new and unusual incidents cannot be attached to land by way either of benefit or of burden. . . . [This] covenant . . . falls outside the limits of this rule, even in the narrower form."[64] The opinion thus holds principally (1) that a restriction of the use of land for the competitive benefit of adjacent land does not directly concern the use of the dominant parcel and operate to its advantage; and (2) that the benefit of the restriction will not so pass by a deed of the dominant parcel to a successor in title of the original grantee of the dominant parcel as to permit that grantee, even in equity, to enforce the restriction at least against a successor in title of the owner of the servient parcel who imposed the original restriction.

Norcross v. James was followed in Shade v. M. O'Keefe, Inc., 260 Mass. 180, 183, 156 N.E. 867, 868 (holding that the "implied promise of . . . [a] grantee not to carry on a grocery business" on the granted premises "does

---

64. The opinion continues (at p. 192, 2 N.E. at p. 949),

It [the covenant] does not make the use or occupation of . . . [the plaintiffs' quarry] more convenient. It does not in any way affect the use or occupation; it simply tends indirectly to increase its value, by excluding a competitor from the market for its products. . . . [W]hether a difference of degree or of kind, the distinction is plain between a . . . covenant that looks to direct physical advantage in the occupation of the dominant estates, such as light and air, and one which only concerns it in the indirect way . . . mentioned. The scope of the covenant and the circumstances show that it is not directed to the quiet enjoyment of the dominant land. . . . If it is of a nature to be attached to land, as . . . [Norcross] contends, it creates an easement of monopoly, — an easement not to be competed with, — and in that interest alone a right to prohibit an owner from exercising the usual incidents of property.

not make the use . . . of the land more convenient" but "simply tends to increase" the value of the dominant land "by excluding a competition"). The doctrine has been the subject of substantial adverse comment by authorities, some of which are mentioned in Boston & Maine R.R. v. Construction Mach. Corp., 346 Mass. 513, 519, fn. 4, 194 N.E.2d 395. See Clark, Real Covenants and Other Interests Which "Run with Land" (2d ed.) pp. 105, 113-115, 128-131, 170-172, 206-207, 252-253; Walsh, Conditional Estates and Covenants Running with the Land, 14 N.Y.U.L.Q. Rev. 163, 170-172; Walsh, Covenants Running with the Land, 21 N.Y.U.L.Q. Rev. 28, 46-50.[65] These authorities (and the decisions therein cited) indicate that, outside of Massachusetts, there is strong disinclination to be bound (a) by technical rules for the creation and enforcement of the type of equitable servitude discussed in Tulk v. Moxhay, 2 Phil. Ch. 774, 777-779 (see e.g. Neponsit Property Owners' Assn. Inc. v. Emigrant Ind. Sav. Bank, 278 N.Y. 248, 255-262, 15 N.E.2d 793, 118 A.L.R. 973; see also 165 Broadway Bldg. Inc. v. City Investing Co., 120 F.2d 813, 815-820 [2d Cir.]); and (b) by any such narrow view of what constitutes a covenant or restriction "touching" the land as that laid down in Norcross v. James. Certainly, no such restrictive view has been adopted with respect to leasehold estates even in Massachusetts. See Sheff v. Candy Box Inc., 274 Mass. 402, 406-407, 174 N.E. 466.

There is much to be said for the position advanced by one of the amici curiae[66] that it is not "unreasonable to approve covenants . . . which protect . . . [business] investments — very large in most instances — against competition close by," where the protection will be very limited geographically and will not constitute, in the particular circumstances, an unreasonable restraint of trade. If we were without precedent, we might (in 1967 conditions) reach a conclusion different from that of our predecessors upon the facts which appeared in Norcross v. James, and in Shade v. M. O'Keefe, Inc. We recognize that there may be substantial reasons for permitting those, having privity of estate with a covenantee of a reasonable covenant restricting competition, to enforce such a covenant in equity against a person having (a) actual or constructive notice of the covenant, and (b) privity of estate with the covenantor.

It is pressed upon us, however, by the other amici curiae that the Massachusetts cases just cited are "widely recognized and relied upon by our

---

65. Other authorities include Reno, Enforcement of Equitable Servitudes in Land, 28 Va. L. Rev. 951, 970, 1070-1071, and Bialkin and Bohannan, Covenants Not to Establish a Competing Business — Does the Benefit Pass? 41 Va. L. Rev. 675, 676-678. See Am. Law of Property, §9.13, pp. 376-380. Cf. Restatement: Property, §§537, 543(2)(b); Proceedings, Am. Law Inst. vol. 20 (1943) pp. 130-140; vol. 21 (1944) pp. 335-343. Cf. also Covenants in the Future, 111 Sol. J. 143.

66. He points out the significance, in planning large retail sales building and land investments, of market surveys to establish the extent of prospective competition for the available patronage. This, he suggests, tends to establish the importance of reasonable equitable restrictions against competition.

bar," although these amici curiae concede that there is a demand for covenants restricting competition "particularly for shopping centers and service stations." The fact of bar reliance in the past, however, must be given weight where a rule affecting real estate is involved. Less persuasive to us are their arguments that prohibiting the "running" with the land (apparently even in equity against persons with notice) of covenants restricting competition serves "practical purposes in supporting free marketability of title" and makes it unnecessary that references to the restrictions "be included in [conveyancers'] abstracts" of title.

It seems to us that in this case, as in probably numerous other past transactions, there may reasonably have been reliance upon Norcross v. James and Shade v. M. O'Keefe, Inc. Our decisions have not heretofore expressed any uncertainty about the soundness of those cases under modern conditions. We follow them in this case although, apart from their authority as precedents, we might have permitted Shell and Stafac to enforce in equity the 1962 restrictions against Ouellette and such of its successors in title as may have had actual or constructive notice of the restrictions.[67]

A final decree is to be entered in the Superior Court dismissing the bill. So ordered.

Note: Still More About Covenants Not to Compete

According to the Restatement, since the benefit of the covenant not to compete runs[68] but the burden does not,[69] Shell should have been permitted to enforce the covenant as against Ouellette, but not as against Mobil. Does this make any sense? Reread footnote 67. What is its significance? What kind of "bar reliance" is the court protecting? Would it be fair to characterize it something like this? "Relying on this court's past decisions, lawyers might have advised their clients, 'If the buyer is insisting on such a covenant and you can't make the sale without it, go ahead and sign. The idiot obviously doesn't know it is unenforceable in this jurisdiction.'"[70]

---

67. We need not now decide what result should be reached in the case of a reasonably limited covenant (of similar import) hereafter made, which shows clearly the parties' intention that the burden and benefit of the covenant are to run to successors in title of the covenantor and the covenantee. We do not now overrule Norcross v. James and Shade v. M. O'Keefe, Inc. prospectively or otherwise. See United States ex rel. Angelet v. Fay, 333 F.2d 12, 16-17 (2d Cir.), *affd.* 381 U.S. 654, 85 S. Ct. 1750, 14 L. Ed. 2d 623; Leach, Property Law Indicted, pp. 14-31. See also Cardozo, Nature of the Judicial Process, 142-156, and Growth of the Law, 117-126. We can consider whether to do so when there is before us a case arising upon a covenant made in the future. In the meantime, application of the pertinent legal principles may have been affected by legislation.

68. See footnote 60, *supra.*

69. See footnote 61, *supra.*

70. If you say that this is wrong since it is at least enforceable as against the original covenanting parties, consider what happens when X, the seller, desires to violate the covenant and conveys the burdened land to X, Inc. To be fair to the court, it is probable that it was concerned about reliance on the part of Mobil's attorneys rather than on the part of Ouellette.

Note: More About the Ouellette *Case*

In Gulf Oil Corp. v. Fall River Housing Authority, 364 Mass. 492, 306 N.E.2d 257 (1974), the Supreme Judicial Court of Massachusetts again considered a covenant against competition:

> This brings us to the requirement that the covenant "touch and concern" the land, and the defendants' argument that this requirement is not met here because the covenant is against competition and thus only personal under our holdings in Norcross v. James, 140 Mass. 188, 2 N.E. 946 (1885), Shade v. M. O'Keefe, Inc., 260 Mass. 180, 156 N.E. 867 (1927), and Shell Oil Co. v. Henry Ouellette & Sons Co. Inc., 352 Mass. 725, 227 N.E.2d 509 (1967).The plaintiffs argue inter alia that if this court determines that these cases are applicable to the current controversy we should consider overruling them. We do not reach this question because we believe the covenant here is distinguishable and is not a covenant against competition in the sense intended in the cited cases. Surely not every restrictive covenant which has some anticompetitive effect is denied enforcement. See Jenney v. Hynes, 282 Mass. 182, 195, 184 N.E. 444 (1933). Whether the covenant is primarily against competition and thus fails to "touch and concern" the land must largely be a question of intention. In Norcross v. James, *supra,* the grantor covenanted that he would not operate a stone quarry on his remaining and adjacent land in competition with that on land conveyed. Justice Holmes stated that "[t]he scope of the covenant and the circumstances show that it is not directed to the quiet enjoyment of the dominant land." Id. 140 Mass. at 192, 2 N.E. at 949. In Shade v. M. O'Keefe, Inc., *supra,* the grantee of land adjacent to the grantor's grocery store covenanted not to compete with it for ninety-nine years. The court found this restriction "simply tends to increase . . . [the benefitted land's] value by excluding a competition." Id. 260 Mass. at 183, 156 N.E. at 868. In Shell Oil Co. v. Henry Ouellette & Sons Co. Inc., *supra,* the grantor explicitly covenanted not to use his adjacent remaining land for any purpose competitive with the uses of the conveyed land. In each case the plain and practically exclusive reason for the covenant was to eliminate possible competition for the promisee. The case before us is quite different. The restriction was inserted not by an adjacent landowner but by the authority as required by statute. It was not intended to enrich any particular landowner by granting him a monopoly but to assure the orderly and mutually beneficial development of the entire area.[71] We think this is evident from the fact that the plan places no limit on the number of service stations in the project, only upon their location. Other service stations are permitted in General Commercial A. The restrictions favor the development of service stations in this area by forbidding such use in General Commercial B once a station has been established in the other sector, and the drafters of the plan no doubt believed this

---

71. It may be that an intermediate purpose of the restriction was to grant businessmen in the area a limited freedom from competition in order to assist the prosperity of the development. Since, however, there appears to have been no limit on further service stations within General Commercial A, this seems highly unlikely. Furthermore, it is obvious that the overriding intention of the restriction was the promotion of the public welfare rather than the business success of individual landowners.

would foster the general betterment of the area. Such a development might contribute to the aesthetics of the Project Area, confine the adverse effects of the gas stations upon the environment or improve the traffic flow. There is no question that Gulf will reap private gain from the elimination of competition by the defendants. But a landowner's motive does not affect his right to enforce a restriction. Hamlen v. Sorkin, 251 Mass. 143, 153, 146 N.E. 265 (1925). In any event, there is no likely competitive benefit to the credit union from a restraint of the defendants' use. We believe the restriction is primarily directed at planning goals which directly affect the actual physical enjoyment of the plaintiff's property and therefore "touches and concerns" the land and is enforceable. [364 Mass. at 499-500, 306 N.E.2d at 262-263.]

The Supreme Judicial Court of Massachusetts finally unshackled itself from the past in Whitinsville Plaza, Inc. v. Kotseas, 378 Mass. 85, 390 N.E.2d 243 (1979), with the following words:

In short, our decisions support what we hereby state to be the law: reasonable covenants against competition *may* be considered to run with the land when they serve a purpose of facilitating orderly and harmonious development for commercial use. To the extent they are inconsistent with this statement, *Norcross, Shade,* and *Ouellette* are hereby expressly overruled.

We recognized in our decision in *Ouellette* that "[t]he fact of bar reliance in the past, however, must be given weight where a rule affecting real estate is involved." 352 Mass. at 730, 227 N.E.2d at 512. The fact of such reliance is a persuasive reason for excluding all covenants executed before June 13, 1967, the date of the *Ouellette* decision, from the operation and effect of the new rule which we have declared in the preceding paragraph of the present opinion. We believe that parties who, after the date of the *Ouellette* decision, executed restrictive covenants of the kind involved in this case could reasonably have relied on the expectation that on the next appropriate occasion thereafter this court would overrule the *Shade* and *Norcross* decisions, as we have done by our present decision. We believe further that parties who executed such covenants after *Ouellette* could not reasonably expect that the covenants would continue to be unenforceable under the rule of the *Shade* and *Norcross* decisions. We therefore hold that our overruling of the rule of the *Shade* and *Norcross* decisions shall apply to all such covenants executed after the *Ouellette* decision. What we have said should not be construed as an invitation to legal draftsmen to insert unlimited, "boilerplate"-type covenants against competition in real estate documents. As we have said, an enforceable covenant will be one which is consistent with a reasonable overall purpose to develop real estate for commercial use. In addition, the ordinary requirements for creation and enforcement of real covenants must be met. We have summarized many of these requirements earlier in this opinion. Others are found in G.L. c. 184, §§27, 30, which regulate enforcement of land-use restrictions generally. Within these limits, however, commercial developers may control the course of development by reasonable restrictive covenants free from resort to devious subterfuges in their attempts to avoid the doubts created by the *Norcross* rule and our efforts to apply or reconcile it in later cases. [378 Mass. at 97-99, 390 N.E.2d at 250.]

Tax Note

If some portion of the purchase price is attributable to the covenant not to compete made by the seller, the seller may have made a costly arrangement from a tax standpoint and the buyer may have made an advantageous deal. The tax effects in such a situation are as follows: The seller is required to report as ordinary income the portion of the purchase price allocated to the covenant not to compete, and the buyer is entitled to depreciate the cost of the covenant not to compete.

B. *Equitable Servitudes*[72]

TULK v. MOXHAY
2 Phil. 774, 41 Eng. Rep. 1143 (Ch. 1848)

In the year 1808 the Plaintiff, being then the owner in fee of the vacant piece of ground in Leicester Square, as well as of several of the houses forming the Square, sold the piece of ground by the description of "Leicester Square Garden or Pleasure Ground, with the equestrian statue then standing in the centre thereof, and the iron railing and stone work round the same," to one Elms in fee: and the deed of conveyance contained a covenant by Elms, for himself, his heirs, and assigns, with the Plaintiff, his heirs, executors, and administrators, "that Elms, his heirs, and assigns should, and would from time to time, and at all times thereafter at his and their own costs and charges, keep and maintain the said piece of ground and Square Garden, and the iron railing round the same in its then form, and in sufficient and proper repair as a Square Garden and Pleasure Ground, in an open state, uncovered with any buildings, in neat and ornamental order; and that it should be lawful for the inhabitants, of Leicester Square, tenants of the Plaintiff, on payment of a reasonable rent for the same, to have keys at

---

72. See generally American Law of Property §§9.24-9.40 (Casner ed. 1952); Clark, footnote 23, *supra,* ch. 6; Reno, The Enforcement of Equitable Servitudes in Land, 28 Va. L. Rev. 951 (1942); Jones, Equitable Restrictions on the Use of Real Property and Their Relation to Covenants Running With the Land, 13 Chi.-Kent L. Rev. 33 (1934); Paulus, Use of Equitable Servitudes in Land Planning, 2 Willamette L.J. 399 (1963).

There are two competing theories which run through the law of equitable servitudes. The first theory treats them as contracts concerning land to be specifically enforced in equity but which do not create "an interest in the land." See Ames, Specific Performance for and Against Strangers to the Contract, 17 Harv. L. Rev. 174 (1904); Stone, The Equitable Rights and Liabilities of Strangers to a Contract, 18 Colum. L. Rev. 291 (1918). The second theory treats them as creating interests in the land itself, to be enforced substantially like an easement. See Pound, The Progress of the Law, 33 Harv. L. Rev. 813 (1920); Clark, at 174. For a discussion of both views, see Reno, 28 Va. L. Rev. 951, 1067 (1942). The latter is accepted by a clear majority of courts. What difference does it make which theory is adopted? Compare Sprague v. Kimball, discussed at page 1024, footnote 81, *infra,* with Johnson v. Mount Baker Park Presbyterian Church, 113 Wash. 458, 194 P. 536 (1920).

their own expense and the privilege of admission therewith at any time or times into the said Square Garden and Pleasure Ground."

The piece of land so conveyed passed by divers mesne conveyances into the hands of the Defendant, whose purchase deed contained no similar covenant with his vendor: but he admitted that he had purchased with notice of the covenant in the deed of 1808.

The Defendant having manifested an intention to alter the character of the Square Garden, and asserted a right, if he thought fit, to build upon it, the Plaintiff, who still remained owner of several houses in the Square, filed this bill for an injunction; and an injunction was granted by the Master of the Rolls, to restrain the Defendant from converting or using the piece of ground and Square Garden, and the iron railing round the same, to or for any other purpose than as a Square Garden and Pleasure Ground in an open state, and uncovered with buildings.

The LORD CHANCELLOR.

That this Court has jurisdiction to enforce a contract between the owner of land and his neighbour purchasing a part of it, that the latter shall either use or abstain from using the land purchased in a particular way, is what I never knew disputed. Here there is no question about the contract: the owner of certain houses in the Square sells the land adjoining, with a covenant from the purchaser not to use it for any other purpose than as a Square Garden. And it is now contended, not that the vendee could violate that contract, but that he might sell the piece of land, and that the purchaser from him may violate it without this Court having any power to interfere. If that were so, it would be impossible for an owner of land to sell part of it without incurring the risk of rendering what he retains worthless. It is said that, the covenant being one which does not run with the land, this Court cannot enforce it; but the question is, not whether the covenant runs with the land, but whether a party shall be permitted to use the land in a manner inconsistent with the contract entered into by his vendor, and with notice of which he purchased. Of course, the price would be affected by the covenant, and nothing could be more inequitable than that the original purchaser should be able to sell the property the next day for a greater price, in consideration of the assignee being allowed to escape from the liability which he had himself undertaken.

That the question does not depend upon whether the covenant runs with the land,[73] is evident from this, that if there was a mere agreement and no covenant, this Court would enforce it against a party purchasing with notice of it; for if an equity is attached to the property by the owner, no one purchasing with notice of that equity can stand in a different situation from the party from whom he purchased. . . .

With respect to the observations of Lord Brougham in Keppell v. Bailey

---

73. In England it became established at an early date that the burden of covenants between owners in fee would not run at law. See Austerberry v. Oldham, 29 Ch. D. 750 (1885).—EDS.

he never could have meant to lay down, that this Court would not enforce an equity attached to land by the owner, unless under such circumstances as would maintain an action at law. If that be the result of his observations, I can only say that I cannot coincide with it.

I think the cases cited before the Vice-Chancellor and this decision of the Master of the Rolls perfectly right, and, therefore, that this motion must be refused with costs.[74]

Note: The Notice Requirement and Nomenclature

The rule that a person who succeeds to real property with notice of a restriction upon it will not in equity and good conscience be permitted to violate the terms of such restriction is often referred to as the doctrine of Tulk v. Moxhay. To enforce restrictions in equity, it is generally agreed that "privity of estate" (whichever definition of that elusive concept has been adopted) has no significance.[75] Notice is obviously the key to this doctrine.[76] If either CE or CE_1 wish to enforce a restriction in equity against CR_1, he or she must show that CR_1 had actual, record, or inquiry notice of the restriction. What constitutes actual notice is self-explanatory. As to what constitutes record notice, reread Buffalo Academy of the Sacred Heart v. Boehm Brothers, page 829 *supra,* and the case which follows it to see whether a purchaser has record notice of restrictions not in the purchaser's "direct chain of title." As to what constitutes inquiry notice, reread Sanborn v. McLean, page 837 *supra.*

You should be warned that the semantic jungle is particularly thick here, for "equitable servitudes" have been variously called "negative easements," "covenants which run at equity," and "equitable easements." As stated in Springer v. Gaddy, 172 Va. 533, 2 S.E.2d 355 (1939):

It is often referred to, from the English case that is its foundation, as the *doctrine of Tulk v. Moxhay.* It is also called the *doctrine of restrictive covenants in equity,* and the rights and obligations established by it are known as *equitable easements* and *equitable servitudes.* The doctrine is, in brief, that when, on a transfer of land, there is a covenant or even an informal contract or understanding that certain restrictions in the use of the land conveyed shall be

---

74. In 1881, the English courts decided that the doctrine of Tulk v. Moxhay should be confined to negative (or restrictive) covenants and that it ought not to be extended to affirmative covenants. Haywood v. Brunswick Permanent Benefit Building Society, 8 Q.B.D. 403 (C.A. 1881) (covenant to repair). See page 994 *supra* for a discussion of affirmative covenants. See also American Law of Property §9.36 (Casner ed. 1952).— Eds.

75. Restatement of Property §539 comment i (1944).

76. However, even without notice, persons who are not "purchasers for value" take subject to these restrictions. Thus, it is clear that a donee is subject to them even without actual, record, or inquiry notice. Since an adverse possessor (AP) of the burdened land is not a "purchaser for value," AP should be bound even though AP has no notice. Restatement of Property §539 comment i (1944). But see Sims, The Law of Real Covenants: Exceptions to the Restatement of the Subject by the American Law Institute, 30 Cornell L.Q. 1, 35 (1944), objecting to this result.

observed, the restrictions will be enforced by equity, at the suit of the party or parties intended to be benefited thereby, against any subsequent owner of the land except a purchaser for value without notice of the agreement. [172 Va. at 540, 2 S.E.2d at 358.]

WERNER v. GRAHAM
181 Cal. 174, 183 P. 945 (1919)

Appeal from a judgment of the Superior Court of Los Angeles County. Chas. Wellborn, Judge. Reserved.

The facts are stated in the opinion of the court.

OLNEY, J.— This is an action to quiet title to real property, the purpose being to obtain a judicial determination that the land of the plaintiff is free of certain restrictions as to its use contained in a deed to a previous owner through whom the plaintiff claims. The land consists of one of the lots of a considerable tract and the defendants are other lot owners within the same tract. The judgment of the lower court was that the plaintiff's title was as to all the defendants, subject to the restrictions in question, and from this judgment the plaintiff appeals.

It appears that one Marshall was, in 1902, the owner of the whole tract, which was at that time unimproved and in that year he subdivided it into blocks and lots and filed of record a map of the tract as so subdivided. This map showed no building lines or anything else to indicate any purpose of restricting in any way the manner in which the different lots might be built upon or otherwise improved or the uses to which they might be put. Immediately following the recording of the map Marshall began to sell and convey the lots. There were 132 lots in all and by October 21, 1905, he had sold and conveyed 116 of them, including the lot now owned by the plaintiff. In all of the deeds from Marshall appear restrictive provisions, which, while differing slightly in some instances, dependent upon the location of the particular lot, as, for instance, upon its facing east or west, are yet so uniform and consistent in character as to indicate unmistakably that Marshall had in mind a general and common plan which he was following. The restrictions in the deed by Marshall conveying the plaintiff's lot are typical and read:

> Provided, however, that this conveyance is made upon and shall be subject to the following express conditions. [The wording of the restrictions on use, location, and cost of buildings is omitted.] If the said party of the second part, his heirs, assigns or successors in estate, shall in any way fail to keep or perform the conditions above specified, or any one of them, in any respect whatsoever, then any and all right, title, interest and estate hereby granted or conveyed shall revert to and become vested in the said parties of the first part, their heirs or assigns.
>
> The said party of the second part accepts this deed and conveyance upon and subject to each and all of the said conditions herein set forth. It is further

understood and agreed that each and all of said conditions and covenants shall run with said premises and shall be binding upon the heirs, assigns and all successors in estate of the said party of the second part.

Some of the conveyances so made by Marshall were prior to his conveyance of the plaintiff's lot and some of the defendants are now the owners of lots so previously conveyed. The larger number of conveyances were made subsequent to the deed through which the plaintiff claims title, and others of the defendants are now the owners of lots so subsequently conveyed.

On October 21, 1905, when, as we have said, Marshall had sold 116 out of a total of 132 lots in the tract, Marshall quitclaimed to the then owner of the plaintiff's lot any interest in it. The effect of this deed was, of course, to release the restrictive provisions as to the plaintiff's lot so far as it was in the power of Marshall to release them.

After the giving of this quitclaim deed Marshall continued to sell lots until he had disposed of them all. The deeds for these lots likewise contain the restrictive provisions. It does not appear clearly whether or not any of the defendants are the present owners of lots conveyed by Marshall subsequent to his quitclaim deed, but we assume some of them are.

It also appears in evidence that in selling the lots Marshall represented to the respective purchasers, that he was exacting the same restrictive provisions from all purchasers. Residences were built upon the tract from time to time by purchasers of lots, and the tract became, and has remained, an exclusively residential district of the better sort.

It should also be mentioned that the immediate deed by which the plaintiff acquired title contained no restrictions. It is claimed by the defendants that he nevertheless had actual notice that all of the lots in the tract were subject to uniform restrictions according to a general and common plan. This the plaintiff denies, but in view of the conclusion we have reached it is of no importance whether he had such notice or not.

It should also be noted that the restrictions are cast in the form of conditions and not of covenants, that is, the conveyance by its terms is made upon the condition that so and so shall not be done, and if it is done the property conveyed shall revert. In the last paragraph of the restrictive provisions they are referred to as "conditions and covenants," but this single expression is the only language of obligation, as distinguished from that of condition, and essentially the form is one of conditions and not covenants, the defendants are not entitled to enforce them against the plaintiff, for the reversion clause runs in favor of Marshall, his heirs and assigns, and does not include the defendants, since by assigns must be meant in this state assignees of the reversion or right of re-entry. (Civ. Code, secs. 768, 1046; Johnson v. Los Angeles, 176 Cal. 479, 485, 168 Pac. 1047.[77])

---

77. See also Finchum v. Vogel, 194 So. 2d 49 (Fla. Dist. Ct. App. 1966), where the deeds from the common grantor contained many "restrictions" but concluded with a paragraph that any breach of the "conditions" shall cause the property to revert to the seller with right of entry

Assuming, however, for the purpose of discussion, that the restrictive provisions in the deed amount to covenants, as well as conditions, there is yet no privity of contract between the plaintiff and the defendants. Neither the plaintiff nor any of the defendants were original parties to the covenants, nor has the plaintiff contractually assumed their obligations, nor have the defendants acquired by assignment from Marshall his rights as covenantee. Marshall has in fact surrendered those rights.

Likewise there is no privity of estate between the plaintiff and the defendants, at least in the usual sense of the word. The plaintiff does not hold under or through any of the defendants, nor any of them under or through him. It follows that the covenants are not covenants recognized by the common law as running with the land, such as covenants between lessor and lessee, or between grantor and grantee for the benefit of the estate conveyed, as, for instance, warranties of title, for all of which a privity of estate is required. Furthermore, the covenants here involved are manifestly not for the benefit of the estate conveyed, but to its detriment.

If, then, these covenants are to be given force, as between the plaintiff and the defendants, it clearly must be because: (a) The burden imposed by them was one upon the land conveyed and incident to its ownership, so that the plaintiff, when he acquired his lot, acquired it subject to such burden; and (b) the benefit of the covenants was an incident of the ownership of the other lots in the tract, so that when Marshall parted with them the benefit of the covenants passed with them as an incident of their ownership and the defendants are now entitled to such benefit as the present owners of the lots. In other words, in order that the covenants have force, not merely as between the original parties, but as between the plaintiff and the defendants, it must appear that their insertion in the deed by Marshall was, in effect, the creation of what amounts to a servitude, to the burden of which the plaintiff's lot was subjected as the servient tenement, and to the benefit of which the remainder of the tract was entitled as the dominant tenement. . . .

Viewing the facts of the present case in the light of what has just been said, and leaving out of consideration for the time being the element of a general and uniform plan of restriction, it is quickly evident that as to those lots

---

and possession. "This reverter provision changes the entire character of the 'restrictions' so that in fact each of the grantees received title as an estate on condition subsequent. . . . It therefore necessarily follows that these so-called 'restrictions' may not be construed as covenants for the benefit of all grantees from the common grantor, and no grantee has any rights against any other grantee by way of enforcement which they would have in the absence of . . . a provision for reverter having the effect of a condition subsequent" (194 So. 2d at 52). But see Arrowhead Mutual Service Co. v. Faust, 260 Cal. App. 2d 567, 67 Cal. Rptr. 325 (1968), where the court granted injunctive relief even though the "restrictions" were worded as conditions subsequent and permitted other lot owners to enforce these "restrictions." See generally Goldstein, Rights of Entry and Possibilities of Reverter as Devices to Restrict the Use of Land, 54 Harv. L. Rev. 248 (1940); Dunham, Possibility of Reverter and Powers of Termination—Fraternal or Identical Twins? 20 U. Chi. L. Rev. 215 (1953).—EDS.

which Marshall had parted with prior to his conveyance of the plaintiff's lot, there is no equitable servitude. Marshall was no longer interested in those lots and by no possibility can it be said that the covenants in the deed to the plaintiff's lot were exacted by him for the benefit of lots which he did not own.

In like fashion it is plain that there is no servitude over the plaintiff's lot in favor of those lots which Marshall still retained when he gave the quitclaim deed of 1905 and with which he parted subsequently. If a servitude had previously existed in favor of those lots, he, as their owner, had the right to surrender it and undoubtedly did so by his quitclaim deed.

The remaining question is as to the existence of a servitude in favor of those lots which Marshall still owned when he sold the plaintiff's lot and with which he parted before he gave his quitclaim deed. This is purely a question of the construction and consequent effect of the deed by Marshall parting with the plaintiff's lot. The situation in this respect is that one, the owner of a tract of land, sells a portion of it, exacting of the grantee restrictive provisions as to its use, but without a word indicating that the land conveyed is part of a larger tract, the balance of which the grantor still retains, or that the restrictions are intended for the benefit of other lands, or that their benefit is to inure to or pass with other lands, and without any description or designation of what is an essential element of any such servitude as is claimed, namely, the land which is to be the dominant tenement. Servitudes running with the land in favor of one parcel and against another cannot be created in any such uncertain and indefinite fashion. It is true, the nature of the restrictions is such that, when considered in connection with the fact that Marshall still retained the greater portion of the tract, it is not improbable that he exacted them for the benefit of the portion so retained. But the grantee's intent in this respect is necessary, as well as the grantor's, and the deed, which constitutes the final and exclusive memorial of their joint intent, has not a word to that effect, nor anything whatever which can be seized upon and given construction as an expression of such intent. If such was their intent, it has not been expressed. Omitting, as we must, any consideration of what the understanding was between Marshall and his grantees, except as shown by the instruments between them, and construing the deed in the light of the fact that Marshall was at the time the owner of a large number of other lots in the tract, it may yet well be that the grantee intended to obligate himself only to Marshall, his heirs and assigns. Certainly, that is all that is said. It is also difficult to see how there can be any valid creation of what is practically a servitude without some designation or description of what is an essential factor, namely, the dominant tenement. The fact also that the only expression in the deed as to who may act in case of a breach of the restrictions is that in such case the land shall revert to Marshall, his heirs or assigns, is strongly indicative of the fact that it was intended that Marshall, his heirs or assigns, should alone have the right to act. It is not possible, in view of these considerations and the rule of strict construction very properly applicable, reasonably to construe the restrictions as covenants which run, not to Marshall, his heirs or assigns, but to Marshall as the owner of certain land not designated or described and to his various successors in interest in such land. . . .

So far the case has been considered without reference to the fact that Marshall in all his deeds exacted similar restrictions and clearly had in mind a uniform plan of restrictions which he intended to impose, and actually did impose, upon all the lots in the tract as he sold them. Does the addition of this element make any difference?

It is undoubted that when the owner of a subdivided tract conveys the various parcels in the tract by deeds containing appropriate language imposing restrictions on each parcel as part of a general plan of restrictions common to all the parcels and designed for their mutual benefit, mutual equitable servitudes are thereby created in favor of each parcel as against all the others. The agreement between the grantor and each grantee in such a case as expressed in the instruments between them is both that the parcel conveyed shall be subject to restrictions in accordance with the plan for the benefit of all the other parcels and also that all other parcels shall be subject to such restrictions for its benefit. In such a case the mutual servitudes spring into existence as between the first parcel conveyed and the balance of the parcels at the time of the first conveyance. As each conveyance follows, the burden and the benefit of the mutual restrictions imposed by preceding conveyances as between the particular parcel conveyed and those previously conveyed pass as an incident of the ownership of the parcel, and similar restrictions are created by the conveyance as between the lot conveyed and the lots still retained by the original owner. Of this character is Alderson v. Cutting, 163 Cal. 504, [Ann. Cas. 1914A, 1, 126 P. 157].

The difference between such a case and the one at bar is that here there is no language in the instruments between the parties, that is, the deeds, which refers to a common plan of restrictions or which expresses or in any way indicates any agreement between grantor and grantee that the lot conveyed is taken subject to any such plan. Is this difference material? This is the crux of the present case. It has been held that this difference is not material. There are decisions to the effect that when it appears that the owner of a subdivided tract has sold various lots in it from time to time and in each conveyance has exacted restrictive covenants which, it is evident, when all the deeds are considered together, were exacted in accord with a common plan, it is enough, and that mutual equitable servitudes have been created, although in any single deed taken by itself there is nothing to indicate any intent to create such reciprocal rights.

There is likewise authority to the contrary.

An analysis of such a case, however, leaves, we believe, no reasonable doubt as to which line of authorities is correct. The intent of the common grantor — the original owner — is clear enough. He had a general plan of restrictions in mind. But it is not his intent that governs. It is the joint intent of himself and his grantees, and as between him and each of his grantees the instrument or instruments between them, in this case the deed, constitute the final and exclusive memorial of such intent. It is also apparent that each deed must be construed as of the time it is given. It cannot be construed as of a later date, and in particular, its construction and effect cannot be varied because of deeds which the grantor may subsequently give to other parties. Yet that is exactly what is done in the decisions holding that mutual servitudes exist in cases where all the deeds taken together evidence a common plan of restrictions, although no single deed by itself evidences anything more than an intent to put particular restrictions on a particular lot. As a concrete instance, take the first deed given by Marshall. At that time there was nothing to evidence any general plan of restrictions, and if the question as to the effect of the deed had arisen, then it must necessarily have been construed as if no such general plan existed. If it must have been so construed at that time it must be so construed now. Whatever rights were created by the deed were created and vested then, and the fact that it later appears that Marshall was pursuing a general plan common to all the lots in the tract cannot vary those rights. The same is true of each deed as it was given. Nor does it make any difference that, as claimed by the defendants, Marshall gave each grantee to understand, and each grantee did understand, that the restrictions were exacted as part of a general scheme. Such understanding was not incorporated in the deeds, and as we have said, the deeds in this case constitute the final and exclusive memorials of the understandings between the parties. Any understanding not incorporated in them is wholly immaterial in the absence of a reformation.[78] This whole discussion may in fact be summed up in the simple statement that if the parties desire to create mutual rights in real property of the character of those claimed here they must say so, and must say it in the only place where it can be given legal effect, namely, in the written instruments exchanged between them which constitute the final expression of their understanding.

It follows that the additional element mentioned — that Marshall exacted similar restrictive covenants from all the grantees of lots in the tract — does not affect the matter and cannot change the conclusion reached without it. That conclusion, as before expressed, is that the restrictions in the deed by Marshall to the plaintiff's predecessor in interest ran personally to Marshall and not to the other lots in the tract, and that the defendants, who claim wholly as lot owners, did not acquire the right to insist upon those restrictions.

The point is made that a suit to quiet title, as this is, is a suit in equity, and that the action of the plaintiff in seeking to escape from the restrictions in question is inequitable and, therefore, relief in equity should be denied him.

---

78. Werner v. Graham, to the extent that it requires an intent to benefit the dominant tenement to be proved without the use of parol evidence, is apparently not the law in any other jurisdiction. In the other jurisdictions, although an intent that the burden run for the benefit of adjacent land is essential, the courts will admit parol evidence to prove the intent.— EDS.

This is no justification of the present judgment which goes further than denying the plaintiff relief and affirmatively makes his title subject to the restrictions. It would also do the defendants little good to secure now a dismissal of the plaintiff's action in view of what we have said as to the nonexistence of the restrictions as to the defendants. The plaintiff would be at liberty to use his lots without regard to the restrictions and the defendants could not prevent him.

But however this may be, the rule relied upon by the defendants has no application here. It may be very unneighborly and unfriendly for the plaintiff to put his lot to uses which will impair the residential character of the tract, but that is a very different thing from his seeking to clear his title of restrictions which are asserted against it, but which do not in fact exist, and which, so far as the defendants are concerned, never did exist, and that is all the plaintiff is seeking to do in this action.

The lower court found the substantial facts in the case. Upon those facts as found judgment should have been given for the plaintiff. The judgment is, therefore, reversed, with directions to the lower court to enter judgment for the plaintiff quieting his title as against the defendants.

SHAW, J., and LAWLOR, J., concurred.

Note: The Prior Purchasers and Subsequent Covenantors Problem

In the *Werner* case, the court was primarily concerned with the problem of whether *subsequent* purchasers — the defendants — from a common grantor — Marshall — might enforce an agreement previously made between their common grantor and a prior purchaser — the plaintiff.[79] A different and more difficult problem is whether *prior* purchasers from a common grantor may enforce an agreement subsequently made between their common grantor and a subsequent purchaser.[80] Before considering the next case, which discusses this problem, notice the summary manner in which Werner v. Graham handles the problem:

> [L]eaving out of consideration for the time being the element of a general and uniform plan of restriction, it is quickly evident that as to those lots, which Marshall had parted with prior to his conveyance of the plaintiff's lot, there is no equitable servitude. Marshall was no longer interested in those lots and by no possibility can it be said that the covenants in the deed to the plaintiff's lot were exacted by him for the benefit of lots which he did not own. [181 Cal. at 181, 183 P. at 948.]

---

79. See generally American Law of Property §9.29 (Casner ed. 1952).
80. See generally id. §9.30.

SNOW v. VAN DAM
291 Mass. 477, 197 N.E. 224 (1935)

[This suit related to a tract of land located on the seashore at Brier Neck in Gloucester, in Essex County. Shackelford owned the entire tract in 1907. At that time, he subdivided into lots the portion of the tract lying south of Thatcher Road, a public highway running through the tract from east to west. The portion of the tract lying north of Thatcher Road was not subdivided into lots at the same time because it was deemed unsuitable for building purposes. Between 1907 and 1923, the various lots to the south of Thatcher Road were sold, the last lot being sold on June 15, 1923. The plaintiffs in this case are purchasers of these lots.

The deeds to the lots south of Thatcher Road, with negligible exceptions, contained uniform restrictions of which the material one is that "only one dwelling house shall be erected or maintained thereon at a given time which building shall cost not less than $2,500 and no outbuilding containing a privy shall be erected or maintained on said parcel without the consent in writing of the grantor or their [*sic*] heirs."

The land north of Thatcher Road was first divided in 1919 into three parcels: C, D, and E. These three parcels were sold by Shackelford to Clark on January 23, 1923 (five months before the sale of the last of the lots south of Thatcher Road), and were sold subject to the following restrictions:

> Only one dwelling house may be maintained on each of said parcels of land at any given time, which dwelling house shall cost not less than Twenty-five Hundred Dollars ($2500) unless plans and specifications for a dwelling house of less cost shall be approved in writing by the grantor of said parcels of land, and no outbuilding containing a privy shall be maintained on either of said parcels of land without the consent in writing of the grantor. . . .

Lot D is the lot of which the larger part is now owned by the defendant Van Dam, having been conveyed to him by Robert C. Clark on February 18, 1933, subject to the restrictions contained in the deed to him "insofar as the same may be now in force and applicable." The defendants have erected on lot D a large building to be used for the sale of ice cream and dairy products and the conducting of the business of a common victualler. The plaintiffs bring this suit for an injunction, claiming a violation of the restrictions.

By order of Walsh, J., a final decree was entered "permanently" enjoining the defendants "from erecting, using or maintaining any building" "for other than dwelling house purposes" on the land of the defendant Van Dam. The defendants appealed from the final decree.]

LUMMUS, J. . . .

Prior to the conveyance from Shackelford to Robert C. Clark on January 23, 1923, there could not have been under the law of this Commonwealth, any enforceable restriction upon lot D. Sprague v. Kimball, 213 Mass. 380,

100 N.E. 622.[81] If any now exists in favor of the lands of the plaintiffs, it must have been created by that deed.

A restriction, to be attached to land by way of benefit, must not only tend to benefit that land itself but must also be intended to be appurtenant to that land. Clapp v. Wilder, 176 Mass. 332, 339, 57 N.E. 692. If not intended to benefit an ascertainable dominant estate, the restriction will not burden the supposed servient estate, but will be a mere personal contract on both sides.

In the absence of express statement, an intention that a restriction upon one lot shall be appurtenant to a neighboring lot is sometimes inferred from the relation of the lots to each other. But in many cases there has been a scheme or plan for restricting the lots in a tract undergoing development to obtain substantial uniformity in building and use. The existence of such a building scheme has often been relied on to show an intention that the restrictions imposed upon the several lots shall be appurtenant to every other lot in the tract included in the scheme. In some cases the absence of such a scheme has made it impossible to show that the burden of the restriction was intended to be appurtenant to neighboring land. In the present case, unless the lots of the plaintiffs and the defendant Van Dam were included in one scheme of restrictions, there is nothing to show that the restrictions upon the lot of the defendant Van Dam were intended to be appurtenant to the lots of the plaintiffs.

What is meant by a "scheme" of this sort? In England, where the idea has been most fully developed, it is established that the area covered by the scheme and the restrictions imposed within that area must be apparent to the several purchasers when the sales begin. The purchasers must know the extent of their reciprocal rights and obligations, or, in other words, the "local law" imposed by the vendor upon a definite tract. Reid v. Bickerstaff, (1909) 2 Ch. 305. Kelly v. Barrett, (1924) 2 Ch. 379, 399, et seq. Where such a scheme exists, it appears to be the law of England and some American

---

81. Sprague v. Kimball was a suit in equity brought by owners of certain lots in a development against their common grantor to enjoin him from conveying lot 5 without imposing thereon restrictions similar to the restrictions imposed in their deeds. The deeds to the owners contained no express covenant or promise on the part of the common grantor that in future sales similar restrictions were to be imposed, although it was clear that he had so orally promised. The court said, in part:

It is settled by our decisions, that under the [Massachusetts statute of frauds], an equitable as well as a legal interest in land must be evidenced by some sufficient instrument in writing or it is unenforceable.

If the front building line, with any language indicating the nature of the restrictions, had appeared on the plan, the defendant would have been estopped to deny an implied grant with covenants coextensive with the scope of the plan, or, if by any appropriate wording of the deeds it appeared that the remaining lots as they were sold should be subject to the restrictions, the statute would have been satisfied. . . . The judge, however, has found, and the evidence warranted the finding, that the agreement to restrict lot 5 rested wholly in parol. . . . The suit cannot be maintained, and the bill must be dismissed. [213 Mass. at 383-384, 100 N.E. at 624.]

—Eds.

jurisdictions that a grantee subject to restrictions acquires by implication an enforceable right to have the remaining land of the vendor, within the limits of the scheme, bound by similar restrictions. But it was settled in this Commonwealth by Sprague v. Kimball, 213 Mass. 380, 100 N.E. 622, that the statute of frauds prevents the enforcement against the vendor, or any purchaser from him of a lot not expressly restricted, of any implied or oral agreement that the vendor's remaining land shall be bound by restrictions similar to those imposed upon lots conveyed. Only where, the vendor binds his remaining land by writing, can reciprocity of restriction between the vendor and the vendee be enforced.

Nevertheless, the existence of a "scheme" continues to be important in Massachusetts for the purpose of determining the land to which the restrictions are appurtenant. Sometimes the scheme has been established by preliminary statements of intention to restrict the tract, particularly in documents of a public nature. More often it is shown by the substantial uniformity of the restrictions upon the lots included in the tract. In some jurisdictions the logic of the English rule, that the extent and character of the scheme must be apparent when the sale of the lots begins, has led to rulings that the restrictions imposed in later deeds are not evidence of the existence or nature of the scheme. Werner v. Graham, 181 Cal. 174, 183-186, 183 P. 945. Sailer v. Podolski, 12 Buch. 459, 464. See also Nashua Hospital Association v. Gage, 85 N.H. 335, 340, 341, 159 A. 137. In the present case there is no evidence of a scheme except a list of conveyances of different lots from 1907 to 1923 with substantially uniform restrictions. Although the point has not been discussed by this court, the original papers show, more clearly than the reports, that subsequent deeds were relied on to show a scheme existing at the time of the earlier conveyances to the parties or their predecessors in title, in [prior Massachusetts cases]. Apparently in Massachusetts a "scheme" has legal effect if definitely settled by the common vendor when the sale of lots begins, even though at that time evidence of such settlement is lacking and a series of subsequent conveyances is needed to supply it. In Bacon v. Sandberg, 179 Mass. 396, 398, 60 N.E. 936, it was said, "the criterion in this class of cases is the intent of the grantor in imposing the restrictions."

Neither the restricting of every lot within the area covered, nor absolute identity of restrictions upon different lots, is essential to the existence of a scheme. But extensive omissions or variations tend to show that no scheme exists, and that the restrictions are only personal contracts.

The existence of a "scheme" is important in the law of restrictions for another purpose, namely, to enable the restrictions to be made appurtenant to a lot within the scheme which has been earlier conveyed by the common vendor. In the present case the lots of some of the plaintiffs were sold before, and the lots of others after, the conveyance from Shackelford to Robert C. Clark on January 23, 1923, which first imposed restriction upon the lot now owned by the defendant Van Dam. The plaintiffs whose lots were sold before January 23, 1923, cannot claim succession to any rights of Shackelford or of land then retained by him. In general, an equitable easement or restriction cannot be created in favor of land owned by a stranger. Hazen v. Mathews, 184 Mass. 388, 68 N.E. 838. Compare Vogeler v. Alwyn Improvement Corp., 247 N.Y. 131, 159 N.E. 886; Lister v. Vogel, 110 N.J. Eq. 35, 158 A. 534. Nevertheless an earlier purchaser in a land development has long been allowed to enforce against a later purchaser the restrictions imposed upon the latter by the deed to him in pursuance of a scheme of restrictions. Earlier as well as later purchasers of lots within the area covered by the scheme acquire such an interest in the restrictions that the common vendor cannot release them.[82]

The rationale of the rule allowing an earlier purchaser to enforce restrictions in a deed to a later one pursuant to a building scheme, is not easy to find. DeGray v. Monmouth Beach Club House Co., 5 Dick. (50 N.J. Eq.) 329, 335-341, 24 A. 388. The simple explanation that the deed to the earlier purchaser, subject to restrictions, implied an enforceable agreement on the part of the vendor to restrict in like manner all the remaining land included in the scheme (Dean Stone, now Mr. Justice Stone, in 19 Colum. L. Rev. 177, 187), cannot be accepted in Massachusetts without conflict with Sprague v. Kimball, 213 Mass. 380, 100 N.E. 622. In Bristol v. Woodward, 251 N.Y. 275, 288, 167 N.E. 441, Cardozo, C.J., said, "If we regard the restriction from the point of view of contract, there is trouble in understanding how the purchaser of lot A can gain a right to enforce the restriction against the later purchaser of lot B without an extraordinary extension of Lawrence v. Fox (20 N.Y. 268). . . . Perhaps it is enough to say that the extension of the doctrine, even if illogical, has been made too often and too consistently to permit withdrawal or retreat."

It follows from what has been said, that if there was a scheme of restrictions, existing when the sale of lots began in 1907, which scheme included the lands of the plaintiffs and of the defendant Van Dam, and if the restrictions imposed upon the land of the defendant Van Dam in 1923 were imposed in pursuance of that scheme, then all the plaintiffs are entitled to relief, unless some special defense is shown. The burden is upon the plaintiffs to show the existence of such a scheme. In our opinion they have done so. Unquestionably there was a scheme which included all the land south of Thatcher Road. The real question is, whether in its origin it included the land north of that road, where is situated the lot of the defendant Van Dam. That lot lies at the gateway of the whole development. One must pass it to visit any part of Brier Neck. The use made of that lot

---

82. Compare Werner v. Graham, where the court said:

[I]t is plain that there is no servitude over the plaintiff's lot in favor of those lots which Marshall still retained when he gave the quitclaim deed of 1905 and with which he parted subsequently. If a servitude had previously existed in favor of these lots, he, as their owner, had the right to surrender it, and undoubtedly did so by his quitclaim deed. [181 Cal. at 181, 183 P. at 948.]

—Eds.

tends strongly to fix the character of the entire tract. It is true, that the land north of Thatcher Road was not divided into lots until 1919, but it was shown on all the plans from the beginning. The failure to divide it sooner was apparently due to a belief that it could not be sold, not to an intent to reserve it for other than residential purposes. We think that the scheme from the beginning contemplated that no part of the Brier Neck tract should be used for commercial purposes. When the lot of the defendant Van Dam was restricted in 1923, the restriction was in pursuance of the original scheme and gave rights to earlier as well as to later purchasers. . . .

Ordered accordingly.[83]

Note: The Common Scheme of Snow v. Van Dam

Gulf Oil Corp. v. Fall River Housing Authority, 364 Mass. 492, 306 N.E.2d 257 (1974), comments as follows on the common scheme of Snow v. Van Dam:

> While it is true that the legal theory behind the rule related to a common scheme "is not easy to find," Snow v. Van Dam, *supra,* 291 Mass. 485, 197 N.E. 224; Am. Law of Property, §9.30 (1952), we think the policy justifications are evident. Every property owner entering on such a planned development has voluntarily joined a system dependent on respect for mutual benefits and obligations which maintain the quality and character of the area in a manner thoroughly understood by prospective and active purchasers. See Gilbert v. Repertory, Inc., 302 Mass. 105, 107, 18 N.E.2d 437 (1939). To make this system operate, a means of private enforcement is necessary. Since all other landowners in the scheme are injured by a violation, it is sensible and just that each should have the right to demand that the restrictions be complied with. Every property owner, regardless of the order of purchase, has a real and important stake in the maintenance of the plan. See Allen v. Massachusetts Bonding & Ins. Co., 248 Mass. 378, 383, 143 N.E. 499 (1924). This is so even if the physical restrictions sought to be enforced are not uniform. It has never been held that a common scheme of this type must provide precisely the same uses and building limits on every lot in one planned area. Bacon v. Sandberg, 179 Mass. 396, 398, 60 N.E. 936 (1901). Sargent v. Leonardi, 223 Mass. 556, 112 N.E. 633 (1916). It is sufficient that each property owner understands the nature of the whole plan before purchase and that the plan envisions an orderly and harmonious development for the entire area. The trend of modern planning is to mix various uses and types of building within the same area. See generally the Symposium on Planned Unit Development, 114 U. of Pa. L. Rev. 3 (1965). This does not make the scheme any the less a common scheme, the success of which is dependent on the adherence to it by each property owner. We find such a scheme here, and hold that the plaintiffs, as prior purchasers under restrictions to abide by the plan,

---

83. In 1961, Massachusetts enacted statutory provisions relating to the enforcement of restrictive covenants. The effect of these provisions on the positions taken in Snow v. Van Dam should be noted. See Mass. Gen. Laws ch. 184, §§26-30.—Eds.

have a right to enforce it against other landowners similarly restricted. [364 Mass. at 497-498, 306 N.E.2d at 261.]

Note on Mass. Gen. Laws ch. 184, §30

Blakeley v. Gorin, 365 Mass. 590, 313 N.E.2d 903 (1974), considered the constitutionality of Mass. Gen. Laws ch. 184, §30, in providing that no restriction shall be enforced or declared to be enforceable, unless it is determined that the restriction is, at the time of the proceeding, of actual and substantial benefit to a person claiming rights of enforcement, and in providing that the restriction shall not be enforced except by award of money damages if any of several enumerated conditions are found to exist. In upholding the constitutionality of the statute, though two justices dissented, the court stated:

> The statute in question here was clearly passed to promote the "reasonable use of land for purposes for which it is most suitable," c. 184, §30(4), as well as to increase the marketability of real estate which may be impaired by obsolete restrictions. These are proper purposes, of great benefit and utility to the public, which justify the taking of property interests of the kind at issue here. [365 Mass. at 599, 313 N.E.2d at 909.]

Problem

32.10. O owns two adjoining tracts of land. O sells one tract to A, and the deed to A contains no covenants. O then sells the other tract to B, and the deed to B contains a covenant that no building above 50 feet in height shall be erected on the conveyed land unless the owner of the adjoining tract (the one conveyed previously to A) consents. B threatens to violate the covenant, and A seeks to enjoin B from so doing. B contends that the restriction was not part of a general development scheme and that therefore A may not enforce it. Is this contention sound? See Vogeler v. Alwyn Improvement Corp., 247 N.Y. 131, 159 N.E. 886 (1928).

Note: Theories Which Permit the Prior Purchaser to Enforce Restriction in Subsequent Deed

The material below, excerpted from the American Law of Property (Casner ed. 1952), explores some theories which permit the prior purchaser to enforce restrictions in a subsequent deed.[84]

---

84. In this excerpt, most footnotes have been omitted, but some have been retained and renumbered.

AMERICAN LAW OF PROPERTY
§9.30, at 424-427 (Casner ed. 1952)

[T]o justify a right of enforcement in a prior purchaser, three theories have been raised by the courts and discussed by text writers. In an early English case the court took the position that in the case of prior purchasers the common grantor holds the benefit as a trustee for their use, and as such must be joined in any action for enforcement by prior purchasers.[85] This theory seems to have gained no support from later cases, and would seem to be impliedly repudiated by the numerous decisions that the common grantor has no right to enforce the servitude after he has parted with title to all of the land intended to be benefited by the agreement.

The second theory advanced . . . is that prior purchasers enforce this contract not as assignees of the promisee but as third-party beneficiaries. This doctrine has received some judicial support, and if carried to its logical conclusion would permit the enforcement of the benefit by any neighboring landowner for whose benefit the equitable servitude was created, irrespective of whether or not he had acquired his land from the promisee. Such a conclusion would be contrary to the commonly accepted principle that the enforcement of an equitable servitude is limited to those landowners who can trace title to the promisee either prior to or subsequent to the date of the agreement. It should be noticed that if this theory is accepted there is no reason for requiring the prior purchaser to prove that he purchased from the common grantor in expectation of being able to enforce subsequently created equitable servitudes, for a third-party beneficiary is entitled to enforce a contract irrespective of whether he had any knowledge of the contract at the time of its execution or previously. The American Law Institute has seen fit to adopt this third-party beneficiary theory as the basis for permitting prior purchasers from the common grantor to enforce subsequently created equitable servitudes.[86]

The third doctrine, which has gained considerable support from text writers as well as acceptance by the courts, is that when the prior purchaser acquires his land in expectation that he will be entitled to the benefit of subsequently created servitudes, there immediately arises an implied reciprocal servitude against the common grantor's remaining land. If so, then he is enforcing, not the express agreements made by the common grantor when he subsequently sells his remaining land, but this implied reciprocal servitude created by implication at the time of the conveyance to the prior purchaser. This theory is of particular importance where the common grantor, contrary to his understanding with the prior purchaser, fails to insert express restrictions in later sales of the remaining lands.[87] . . . This

---

85. Eastwood v. Lever, 4 DeG. J. & S. 114, 46 Eng. Rep. 859 (Ch. 1863).

86. Restatement of Property §541, Comments c and f (1944).

87. This was the situation in Sanborn v. McLean [set out in the text at page 837 *supra*], where the court enforced an implied reciprocal servitude against subsequent purchasers.

explanation of the basis for permitting prior purchasers to enforce equitable servitudes justifies the requirement that the prior purchaser must have purchased in reliance and expectation of being able to enforce subsequently created equitable servitudes, for without such an understanding between himself and the common grantor there would be no basis upon which a reciprocal servitude could be implied. Likewise, it explains why the prior purchaser is limited to enforcing the type of restrictions contemplated by the building scheme at the time of his purchase. Clearly the scope of any implied reciprocal servitude must be limited to the provisions of the building scheme as they existed at that date. However, the objection to this explanation lies in the fact that the courts, in adjudicating the right of a prior purchaser to enforce restrictions under a common plan, base this right in terms not upon the implication of a reciprocal servitude against the common grantor, but upon the express agreements entered into by subsequent purchasers. Possibly the best solution is to recognize the rights of prior purchasers as being sui generis, and not based upon any established legal theory.[88]

Problem

32.11. If part of a parcel of servient land (the burdened land) is taken under eminent domain and you were representing the owner of the dominant land (the benefited land), what theory would you advance in regard to equitable servitudes that would give your client the best chance of being entitled to part of the condemnation award? See Burma Hills Development Co. v. Marr, 285 Ala. 141, 229 So. 2d 776 (1969).

SECTION 3. EQUITABLE SERVITUDES IN GROSS

Consider the status of the real estate developer of Lakeville, who, having sold *all* of the lots in the subdivision, desires nonetheless to enforce a covenant against an assignee of the covenantor — perhaps in the interest of maintaining a good business reputation, realizing that his or her next development's purchasers will be interested in seeing his or her existing developments. The developer desires to have a benefit in gross.

---

88. [Citing Snow v. Van Dam, page 1023 *supra.*]

MERRIONETTE MANOR HOMES
IMPROVEMENT ASSOCIATION v. HEDA
11 Ill. App. 2d 186, 136 N.E.2d 556 (1956)

SCHWARTZ, J.

The question before this court is whether or not the plaintiff, an association of home owners organized as a nonprofit corporation, whose membership consists of the owners of real property within an area subjected to planned and uniform restrictive covenants, has sufficient interest to bring suit to enjoin alleged violations. The association has no legal title to any property in the area, but the prospect of the formation of such an association for the purpose of requiring conformance was set forth in the declaration establishing the restrictive covenants. On motion of defendants the trial court dismissed the suit, and plaintiff appealed. Defendants filed no brief in this court and we must therefore decide the case on the brief of appellant and our own research.

The original subdivider of the property was the Merrionette Manor Corporation which on December 29, 1948, recorded its declaration of covenants designed to preserve the plan of the subdivision, the character of the homes and the arrangement for land usage. The covenant involved in the instant case reads as follows:

> A vestibule, no more than one story in height, may be erected by any owner of any residential units which shall not extend beyond the confines of the present front stoop, and may only be erected when the owner of the attached adjacent dwelling unit shall simultaneously erect a similar vestibule of the same design and construction to conform to the entire residential unit.

Other covenants prohibited the construction of trailers, tents, shacks, barns, noxious or offensive trades or activities, signs, advertisements, billboards, and other uses considered objectionable. It was further stated that in the event of the formation of a property owners association whose purpose "shall specifically include the control of all properties in the area with respect to conformance," the declarant could at its option assign the control therein set up to the property owners association.

Following this declaration of covenants, the declarant caused to be incorporated the Merrionette Manor Homes Improvement Association, plaintiff in this case, including in the purposes of the corporation the encouraging of enforcement, preservation and maintenance of protective covenants; safeguarding the owners of residences against improper use of surrounding building sites and generally to promote and encourage pride of ownership and harmonious maintenance of properties among the various owners resident in the subdivision. The plaintiff association is the assignee of the declarant as to the right to bring an action to enforce the covenants.

Defendants purchased the property in question, which was half of a duplex house, in June 1952. The deed to the property provided that title was taken subject to the restrictive covenants referred to. Despite the covenants and the warning that such action would result in plaintiff's seeking legal and equitable relief, defendants constructed a vestibule without the joint and simultaneous construction of a like vestibule by the owner of the adjacent dwelling unit and without having plans therefor approved by the declarant or the plaintiff or any agent of the declarant or the plaintiff. Thereupon this suit was instituted.

The question is one of first impression in Illinois. Home owners associations such as the plaintiff appear to be a relatively modern device, a natural outgrowth of the development of housing projects on a large scale, particularly in urban communities where the general good of all within the community requires adherence to some common standards. Everybody's business is no one's business. Hence, the enforcement of such standards had to be centralized and home owners associations came into being. While the general question of who may enforce restrictive covenants has been discussed in many cases, the particular question here presented has been considered in but one case, that of Neponsit Property Owners' Association v. Emigrant Industrial Savings Bank, 278 N.Y. 248, 15 N.E.2d 793, 118 A.L.R. 982. The case is squarely in point. There, as in the instant case, the plaintiff had not succeeded to the ownership of any property in the area nor did the plaintiff own any other property in the residential tract to which any easement or right of enjoyment was appurtenant. The plaintiff association was created solely to act as the assignee of the benefit of the covenant. The court considered the argument that such covenants cannot be enforced when there is no privity of estate between the parties, and pointed out that the enforcement of such covenants rests upon equitable principles, citing Tulk v. Moxhay, 2 Phillips 774; Trustees of Columbia College v. Lynch, 70 N.Y. 440, 26 Am. Rep. 615; Korn v. Campbell, 192 N.Y. 490, 85 N.E. 687, 37 L.R.A., N.S., 1, 127 Am. St. Rep. 925. The court said that no right to enforce a restrictive covenant where the plaintiff did not own property which would benefit by such enforcement had been sustained in New York, but as illustrating that this is not true in some jurisdictions, cited Van Sant v. Rose, 260 Ill. 401, 103 N.E. 194, 49 L.R.A., N.S., 186, which we will later discuss. The court concluded (278 N.Y. 248, 15 N.E.2d 798) that it is not necessary to lay down any definite rule as to "when, or even whether, covenants in a deed will be enforced, upon equitable principles, against subsequent purchasers with notice, at the suit of a party without privity of contract or estate." The court there considered that the solution was to look at the real character of the association, not to ignore the corporate form nor to draw aside the veil, but to recognize that the association was acting as the agent or representative of the property owners, and that the property owners were expected to and did look to that organization as the medium through which enjoyment of their common rights might be preserved equally for all. The court concluded its opinion with the following:

Only blind adherence to an ancient formula devised to meet entirely different conditions could constrain the court to hold that a corporation formed as a medium for the enjoyment of common rights of property owners owns no property which would benefit by enforcement of common rights and has no cause of action in equity to enforce the covenant upon which such common rights depend. In substance if not in form there is privity of estate between the plaintiff and the defendant.

This is a strong and well-reasoned precedent of the highest court in the largest state of the union. Unless Illinois decisions are to the contrary, it is one which we should follow. To that end we will examine the pertinent Illinois cases.

In Van Sant v. Rose, 260 Ill. 401, 103 N.E. 194, 49 L.R.A., N.S., 186, cited in the *Neponsit* case, the defendants contended that in order to entitle a complainant to relief against the violation of a restrictive covenant prohibiting the erection of a flat building, such complainant must show some right of beneficial interest in the land affected by the covenant or in adjoining lands which would be injured as a result of failure to keep the covenant. The court held that while a bill to enjoin a breach of restrictive covenants cannot be maintained by one having no connection with or interest in their enforcement, the fact that the plaintiffs owned no property in the vicinity that would be affected by a breach of the covenants or that they would in any other manner sustain damages did not deprive them of their interest and right to sue. The plaintiffs in that case were the original grantors and covenantees, but the opinion makes it clear that the law of Illinois with respect to covenants is not so strictly defined as to require in all cases that the one seeking enforcement must show some right or beneficial interest in the land affected by the covenant or in the adjoining lands. . . .

Nothing in the Illinois cases we have examined indicates a policy or trend opposed to what we think are the sound conclusions of the *Neponsit* case. The primary purpose of the plaintiff association is to enforce the covenants on behalf of and for the good of all 541 property owners who constitute its membership. The enforcement of such covenants as those here involved is based on sound equitable principles. It will, in a proper case, extend to requiring a defendant to repair an injury already done or to remove a structure already erected, but it is not every case which will call for such relief. Each case must be decided on its own circumstances.

The trial court should overrule the motion to dismiss and require the defendants to answer. . . .

[Order reversed and cause remanded with directions.]

Note: *Benefit in Gross — Effect on the Running of the Burden*

In London County Council v. Allen, [1914] 3 K.B. 642, the city of London sought to enforce a negative covenant against the wife of the original covenantor, she being considered a subsequent purchaser with notice. The question presented was "whether it is essential to the doctrine of Tulk v. Moxhay (2 Ph. 774) that the covenantee should have at the time of the creation of the covenant and, afterwards, land for the benefit of which the covenant is created, in order that the burden of the covenant may bind assigns of the land to which it relates" ([1914] 3 K.B. at 664). Scrutton, J., concluded:

> . . . I regard it as very regrettable that a public body should be prevented from enforcing a restriction on the use of property imposed for the public benefit against persons who bought the property knowing of the restriction, by the apparently immaterial circumstance that the public body does not own any land in the immediate neighbourhood. But, after a careful consideration of the authorities, I am forced to the view that the later decisions of this Court compel me so to hold. [[1914] 3 K.B. at 673.]

Parliament agreed. Housing Act, 1925, 15 Geo. 5, ch. 14, §110.

What effect, if any, do you suppose the defendant's failure to file a brief had on the outcome in *Merrionette?* How hard do you suppose the court researched the case on behalf of the defendant? In answering these questions, consider the following:

> As a general rule a covenant by the grantee of land not to place structures thereon without the consent of the grantor will not be enforced at the suit of the grantor against a grantee of the former if the plaintiff has no present interest in any land for the benefit of which the restriction was imposed. This appears to be so even though the covenant purported to bind the covenantor's heirs and assigns, and his grantee took with notice of the covenant.[89]

Note: Covenant With Respect to Use of a Chattel

Assume that the senior partner has sent you the following memo:

> Our client is considering entering into an agreement with a washing machine company to install in a building to be built in the common area a number of coin-operated washing machines and driers. The agreement with the washing machine company would provide that the company would maintain the washing machines and driers and collect the coins deposited for their use; in return, it would be agreed by our client that the premises on which the washing machines and driers would be installed would be devoted exclusively to the purposes for which such equipment is used, with access to the building being restricted to residents of Lakeville. The agreement would be for a term of ten years. It is contemplated that our client would sell the land and building to the homeowners' association at some future date. I want your opinion as to whether the homeowners' association would be required to

---

89. Annot., 19 A.L.R.2d 1274, 1276 (1951).

honor the agreement our client makes with the washing machine company after it acquires the building from our client. The following case has been brought to my attention in regard to this matter.

PRATTE v. BALATSOS
99 N.H. 430, 113 A.2d 492 (1955)

Bill in Equity, seeking "a decree permanently enjoining the defendant from breaching [an] agreement" between the plaintiff and Albert Larochelle, former proprietor of a business now conducted by the defendant in Manchester, which related to the use and operation of the plaintiff's coin-operated record player and related equipment in the place of business. The bill also sought a temporary order restraining the defendant from removing the record player from the premises.

A temporary injunction was issued. Thereafter, following a hearing on the merits before Grant, J. the injunction was dissolved and the bill dismissed. The Court found that the plaintiff and Larochelle "made an agreement on the 19th day of September, 1952, having to do with the installation of a juke box on the premises of Larochelle"; and that the contract was to remain in force for fourteen and one-half years and recited that it should be binding on the "heirs, successors and assigns" of the parties. The Court further found that when he purchased the business, the defendant "had knowledge of the existence of the contract between Larochelle and [the plaintiff]." The Court ruled that the defendant "was not bound by the terms of the contract . . . and that [the plaintiff's] remedy lies against Larochelle."

To this ruling the plaintiff duly excepted. . . .

DUNCAN, J.

The terms of the contract between the plaintiff and Larochelle are not in dispute. It provided that in return for payment of forty per cent of the income from the record player, the plaintiff might install it in "a permanent and convenient part of [Larochelle's] place of business" and that "said machine shall be operated during the term of this Agreement [fourteen years and six months] and that no similar equipment nor any other kind of coin-operated machine will be installed or operated on said premises by anyone else." Thus it was intended by the parties to the agreement that the plaintiff should have exclusive rights to operate such a record player at the location in question in connection with the conduct of Larochelle's business there.

Neither the bill of sale from Larochelle to the defendant under date of November 2, 1953, nor the contract of purchase and sale which preceded it, referred to the record player or the contract with Larochelle of September 19, 1952, relating to it. The bill of sale purported to convey "an assignment of the lease [of the premises] dated April 1, 1947." No attempt was made to assign the Larochelle contract to the defendant nor did the defendant expressly assume Larochelle's obligations under it.

On the other hand, the defendant conceded at the trial that he knew that the record player was under contract with the plaintiff and that he took it into account as a source of income in evaluating the business. He testified that some fifteen days after the sale he learned for the first time that the plaintiff would allow him only forty percent of the income. Under date of November 20, 1953, he notified the plaintiff to remove the machine within seven days, and a like notice was given by his attorneys on February 3, 1954.

The plaintiff takes the position that because of the finding that the defendant had notice of the existence of a contract with the former owner when he bought the business, the defendant is bound by the agreement. . . .

The extent to which the defendant may be charged with obligations arising out of the contract made by his predecessor in the business depends upon the nature of the rights created by the contract. No claim is made that the contract constituted a lease to the plaintiff. He hired no specific space within the premises leased to Larochelle, and no intention to create the relationship of landlord and tenant is suggested by the language of the document. Neither can it be said that the parties intended a revocable license, for the obvious purpose was to confer rights to operate the machine for a specified term. If as a matter of law the plaintiff acquired only a revocable license, specific performance would be futile and the plaintiff was properly remitted to his action for damages for breach of contract.

"The alternative antithesis of 'licenses' and 'leases' tends to cause a court to feel bound to label the transaction before it one or the other of the two, rather than to realize it has three choices, namely, lease, license or easement." 3 Powell on Real Property, 430.

In Baseball Publishing Co. v. Bruton, 302 Mass. 54, 18 N.E.2d 362, 364, 119 A.L.R. 1518, the plaintiff sought to enforce a written contract, giving him "'the exclusive right and privilege'" to maintain an advertising sign on the wall of the defendant's building. The court concluded that the writing was neither a lease, nor a license which could be revoked subject to the payment of damages, and stated: "So far as the law permits, it should be so construed as to vest in the plaintiff the right which it purports to give. . . . That right is in the nature of an easement in gross." Since the writing, like the one in the case before us, was not under seal the court held that it created an easement in equity and that the plaintiff was entitled to specific performance of the agreement. . . .

By reason of the agreement with Larochelle, the plaintiff may be considered to have acquired a right that he specifically perform. The question is presented whether that right which is in the nature of an equitable servitude is enforceable against the defendant as successor to Larochelle's interest with notice of the existence of the contract. Equitable restrictions are recognized in this jurisdiction and held to be binding upon a purchaser of the servient tenement with notice. No decisions of this court involving restrictions in gross, and personal to the covenantee have come or been called to our attention. The defendant contends that the contract in question cannot be enforced as a restrictive covenant because it plainly does not run with the land and is essentially affirmative rather than negative in its undertaking. The plaintiff contends that it is in the nature of a covenant running with the business and should be binding on that account, even though the contract was never assigned to the defendant. The situation is analogous to that presented by the early English cases involving "tied" houses, and holding that covenants for the purchase of beverages exclusively from one brewer were "for the benefit of the business" and enforceable against an underlessee with notice. It has been pointed out that these decisions would not be followed in England today in view of the decision in London County Council v. Allen, [1914] 3 K.B. 642. See II American Law of Property, 428, s. 9.32. However this result has been criticized as "illogical," and the enforcement in this country of equitable servitudes in gross is "commended" by the author of the cited text. Id., 430. See also, Clark, Covenants and Interests Running with Land (2nd ed.) 104, note 36, 181, 182. . . . In Pomeroy, Equity Jurisprudence, s. 1295, it is said that the doctrine that a purchaser with notice of a covenant with respect to the use of land takes subject to the covenant may be explained "by regarding the covenant as creating an equitable easement." The doctrine extends to affirmative covenants (Id., pp. 851, 852), and restrictive covenants creating equitable easements may be "specifically enforced in equity by means of an injunction, not only between the immediate parties, but also against subsequent purchasers with notice, even when the covenants are not of the kind which technically run with the land." Id., s. 1342.

The general rule received recognition in the early case of Burbank v. Pillsbury, 48 N.H. 475, 482, where the opinion was expressed that a stipulation in a deed providing for maintenance of a fence would be enforceable against a subsequent purchaser with notice. Relying upon the leading case of Tulk v. Moxhay, 2 Phillips Ch. 774 (see Clark, op. cit. *supra,* 170), the court said: "If [the obligation] is enforceable in equity, though not at law, the result, so far as this case is concerned, is the same. Upon the authorities we think it is enforceable in equity . . . even if it be not regarded as an agreement running with the land upon which an action at law could be maintained." . . .

Whether the defendant has such notice as to put him upon inquiry as to the terms of the contract, and what such inquiry would probably have disclosed, must be determined before the defendant's responsibility with respect to the contract can be fixed. If the Court intended by its decree to imply a finding that the notice was insufficient to subject the defendant to the plaintiff's rights, the decree may stand. If not, the facts should be found;

and if the defendant is bound by the agreement, an injunction may issue in the Court's discretion.

Remanded.

Note: The Public Policy Argument Against the Running of the Burden

The late Professor Chafee was dismayed by *Pratte*'s complete failure to consider whether it was desirable, on grounds of public policy, to enforce such an agreement. He argued:

> The real issue is whether there are strong reasons for requiring the occupant of a restaurant or similar place of business to keep a juke box there for fourteen and a half years if he does not want it. Would it not be a good idea for judges to get away for a time from old learning about easements or servitudes and instead imagine that they are listening to a juke box? Suppose that it is in a restaurant conveniently close to the courthouse where the judges like to lunch because of the good food. Will they have to go on listening to popular music for years and years when the proprietor would be delighted to get rid of the juke box and give the judges and other diners a chance to talk with each other? If for fourteen and a half years, why stop there? Does the Rule Against Perpetuities apply? Why not a hundred years? Let us assume that a man starts a restaurant on a small scale and puts in a juke box for the enjoyment of patrons of such establishments. He sells out. The new owner does better and better. He wants to redecorate and have his place the best restaurant in town. A juke box is a fatal obstacle to his ambition. So long as it stays there many of the kind of people whom he wants will stay away. Now that the United States Supreme Court holds that we are obliged to listen to music we dislike in trolley cars and busses, can't we at least enjoy the luxury of a peaceful meal? I confess that I see no strong public policy in permitting the manufacturer of these raucous devices to prevent an enterprising American citizen from creating the kind of restaurant which he wants and which a good many consumers of food would be delighted to have.
>
> Or suppose instead that the proprietor does want to have a juke box on the premises, but not this one. Perhaps all the plaintiff's competitors are dividing fifty-fifty. Or after a year or two, a rival model has a much superior tone. Is it desirable to lose the advantages of competition and let Larochelle deprive Balatsos of his freedom to choose in the market for nearly half a generation regardless of improved designs?[90]

On remand, the trial court found that the defendant should have been on inquiry notice as to the terms of the original contract and therefore rendered judgment for the plaintiff. In the meantime, the defendant's counsel must

90. Chafee, The Music Goes Round and Round: Equitable Servitudes and Chattels, 69 Harv. L. Rev. 1250, 1262–1263 (1956) (copyright © 1956 by the Harvard Law Review Association).

have read Chafee's article, for on the second appeal (101 N.H. 48, 132 A.2d 142 (1957)), the New Hampshire Supreme Court said:

> The defendant urged in effect that we overrule our previous opinion and in so doing he relies mainly on an article on "Equitable Servitudes and Chattels" by Zachariah Chafee, Jr., 69 Harv. L. Rev. 1240, discussing the *Pratte* case. Reexamination of the decision in the light of the article convinces us there is no reason to do so. In an earlier article by the same author on the same subject he said: . . .[91] [101 N.H. at 49, 132 A.2d at 143.]

SECTION 4. ARCHITECTURAL CONTROL

Assume you have received the following memorandum from the senior partner:

> I have been doing a little research on my own and have come to the conclusion that it will be a well-nigh impossible task to provide for a well-planned, first-rate residential development by way of tightly drawn, specific restrictive covenants, especially in light of the grudging attitude of the courts in interpreting the written word. No boilerplate language seems capable of assuring to our client that the development, when completed, will be anything like what our client planned. Each property is unfortunately different in size, grading, location, etc. What if we inserted the following clause in the declaration of covenants and restrictions applicable to the whole development, and of course in each and every deed:
>
>> No building, fence, wall or other structure shall be commenced, erected, or maintained, nor shall any addition to, or change or alteration therein be made, until the plans and specifications, showing the nature, kind, shape, height, materials, locations and approximate cost of such structure and the grading plan of the lot to be built upon, shall have been submitted to and approved in writing by [our client or an architectural control committee]. [Our client or an architectural control committee] shall have the right to refuse to approve any such plans or specifications or grading plan, which are not suitable or desirable, in its opinion, for aesthetic or other reasons; and in so passing upon such plans, specifications, and grading plans it shall have the right to take into consideration the use and suitability of the proposed building or structure and of the materials of which it is to be built, the site upon which it is proposed to erect the same, the harmony thereof with the surroundings, and the

---

91. Aspirants to the law reviews and others take note: beware of the prolific pen! A lawyer never knows on what side of an issue he may argue next, and as both of the editors of this casebook can testify, nothing is more embarrassing to an advocate than in the midst of argument to be cited against yourself.— EDS.

effect of the building or other structure as planned on the outlook from the adjacent neighboring property.

You should formulate your reply to this memorandum after examining the following material.

JONES v. NORTHWEST REAL ESTATE CO.
149 Md. 271, 131 A. 446 (1925)

WALSH, J. The Northwest Real Estate Company, the complainant below, filed a bill in equity against James Clawson Jones and Anita S. Jones, his wife, the defendants below, alleging that the erection of a hip-roof second-story porch on the home of the defendant was a violation of certain restrictions binding on the land on which the house was built, and, from a decree of the lower court sustaining this contention and directing that the porch be removed, the defendants have appealed.

The testimony shows that in 1920 the appellee purchased a tract of about 170 acres of land in Baltimore city, at a cost of between $460,000 and $470,000; that this tract was subsequently laid off in lots; that streets, roads, and other improvements costing approximately $500,000 were made in it, and the whole development placed on the market under the name of Ashburton. It also appeared that the completion of the improvements throughout the whole tract would cost an additional $100,000; that 400 of the 600 lots in the development had been sold; that about 225 houses had been built on the lots thus sold; and that the deeds for all lots sold contained a number of uniform restrictive covenants. The avowed purpose of these covenants was to provide a general plan or scheme of development for the whole tract, and to insure its being and continuing to be a high-class residential district.

In June, 1923, the appellee conveyed to Elias H. Read and wife a lot of ground in Ashburton lying at the northeast corner of Egerton place and Dennison road, and on May 23, 1924, the appellants acquired title to this lot from the widow of Read. Both of the deeds by which these two conveyances were made contained the restrictive covenants found in all deeds for lots in Ashburton, and it conceded that the appellants knew of the restrictions, and considered themselves bound by them. Prior to purchasing the lot, the appellants had secured plans for the erection of a two-family dwelling, and these plans called for what is known as a hip-roof second-story porch. Mr. Jones, one of the appellants, testified that, when looking at the lot with a view to purchasing it, he asked the salesman, Mr. Donovan, a representative of the George R. Morris Organization, of which Mr. George R. Morris, president of the appellee, was also president, whether or not second-story porches were permitted, and was told by him that they were, and his attention was called to several houses in the vicinity which had second-story porches, but it does not appear that the appellant Jones at that time exhibited his plans to Donovan, or advised him of the character or kind of second-story porch he proposed to erect.

Several days after he acquired title to the lot, the appellant Jones, in compliance with the ninth covenant in his deed, submitted his plans to George R. Morris for approval, and, while waiting in the office of the appellee, which was also the office of the George R. Morris Organization, Donovan, whom he found there, looked over his plans and told him "they looked mighty fine," and he did not think he would have any trouble with them. However, when the plans were shown to Mr. Morris he made several objections to them, and particularly objected to any second-story porch, Mr. Jones agreed to modify the plans to meet all of Mr. Morris' objections except as to the second-story porch, and on this point he told him of Donovan's statements to him prior to the time he bought the lot, and also stated that some of the houses already built in Ashburton had second-story porches. Mr. Donovan was then called in and confirmed the statements of Mr. Jones, and after the plans of the six or seven houses in the addition which have second-story porches had been examined, Mr. Morris stated that he would approve a second-story porch similar in design to any of those already existing, but he would not approve the sort of second-story porch shown on the appellant's plans. Mr. Jones then left, and several days later he and Mr. Tase, a builder, called on Mr. Morris and again tried to secure his approval of the plans. Mr. Morris still refused to approve them, and after Mr. Tase had said, "If I were building the house, I would build it the way shown on the plans; of course, my advice to Mr. Jones would be the same thing," both Mr. Tase and Mr. Jones left. The plans were retained by Mr. Morris, and, when a young man from Mr. Jones' office called for them a few days later, they were given him with the porch scratched off and the plans marked, "Approved, subject to changes noted." This young man signed Mr. Jones' name to the plans, per his own, purporting to accept them as modified, and subsequently Mr. Jones began the erection of the house, but did not employ Mr. Tase to build it. On October 3, 1924, an inspector for the appellee noticed that the appellants were erecting the porch called for in the original plans, and, being unable to get in personal touch with Mr. Jones, a letter was sent to him by the George R. Morris Organization, calling his attention to the second-story porch being erected, and advising him that unless the porch was changed to conform to the approved plans steps would be taken to stop the work. This letter was not answered, and on October 10, 1924, the bill of complaint in this case was filed, and the ensuing suit resulted as above set forth.

It was charged in the bill that the work on this porch was rushed for the purpose of getting it built before the appellee could interfere, but this allegation cannot be sustained, because, according to the testimony, it was practically completed before the defendants received the letter above mentioned. Nor do we find any support for the allegation in the defendants' answer that the appellee did not act in good faith in refusing to approve the plans originally presented. This disposes of the charges of improper conduct by the respective parties, and brings us to a consideration of the real question in the case, which is the validity and meaning of the ninth covenant in the defendants' deed, and the legality and effect of the conduct of the parties thereunder. This covenant reads as follows:

> (9) No building, fence, wall or other structure shall be commenced, erected, or maintained on, or shall any addition to, or change or alteration therein, be made, until the plans and specifications, showing the nature, kind, shape, height, materials, location, and approximate cost of such structure and the grading plan of the plot to be built upon, shall have been submitted to and approved in writing by the party of the first part. The party of the first part shall have the right to refuse to approve any such plans or specifications or grading plan, which are not suitable or desirable, in its opinion, for aesthetic or other reasons; and in so passing upon such plans, specifications, and grading plans it shall have the right to take into consideration the use and suitability of the proposed building or structure and of the materials which it is to be built, to the site upon which it is proposed to erect the same, the harmony thereof, with the surroundings, and the effect of the building or other structure as planned on the outlook from the adjacent neighboring property.

The appellants contend that this covenant did not authorize the appellee to enforce the attempted alteration of their building plans; that, even if it did, the appellee was estopped from enforcing it as to the second-floor porch because of the statement of Donovan made prior to the purchase of this lot by the appellants; and, finally, that the difference between the porch wanted by the appellants and that which Morris indicated he would approve was so slight as to render the action of the appellee in changing appellants' plan unreasonable and arbitrary, and hence unenforceable.

We do not think the appellants made out a case of estoppel. . . . This brings us to a consideration of the appellants' contentions regarding the covenant itself and the appellee's interpretation and application of it in this case, and these matters we will consider together.

The appellants do not seriously challenge the validity of the ninth covenant as a whole, nor do we think they could successfully challenge it. The language of the covenant is quite broad and comprehensive in its terms, and gives the appellee rather drastic control over the character of buildings to be erected, but we perceive nothing so contrary to public policy in its provisions as to warrant our striking it down. There is a constantly increasing demand on the part of the public for homes in restricted residential districts, and the restrictions desired are growing both in number and scope. Many people seem to want to live in neighborhoods in which all the houses are to be a certain distance back from the street, are to cost not less than a certain sum of money, are to be occupied by not more than a certain number of families, are to conform in size and appearance with the surrounding houses, are not to have structures other than a residence on the lot, and so on. Whether this tendency is wise, or unwise, it is not our province to determine; we are confined entirely to a consideration of the legality of the restrictions themselves and of the covenants or other means by which they are imposed. In this case we are dealing with a covenant, and we do not think that the restrictions to which the parties have voluntarily agreed interfere with the fee of the land to such an extent as to render them void. . . .

The general rule deducible from the authorities seems to be that, where the intention of the parties is clear, and the restrictions within reasonable bounds, they will be upheld. In our opinion the covenant involved in this case meets these tests. There can be no question as to the intention of the parties, the present suit shows the attitude of the appellee, and as the appellants voluntarily submitted their plans for approval and actually adopted some of the changes suggested by Morris, it can hardly be contended that they did not understand that it was the intention and purpose of the covenant that the appellee's approval of all plans should be obtained. Nor do we find the provision requiring the submission of these plans unreasonable.

The next question is whether or not the provisions set up in the covenant to guide the appellee in approving or disapproving the plans submitted are reasonable. We have no doubt as to the validity of the provisions authorizing the appellee to withhold its approval, if the use, shape, height, materials, location, and approximate cost of the structure and the grading plan of the lot did not reasonably conform to the general plan of development, and to refuse to approve the plans for buildings which would be out of harmony in any of the particulars mentioned with other structures in the addition, or which would interfere unreasonably with the outlook from other structures in the vicinity.

Whether the provision that "the party of the first part shall have the right to refuse to approve any such plans or specifications or grading plans, which are not suitable or desirable, in its opinion, for aesthetic or other reasons," is valid in its entirety is more difficult to determine. We have already seen that the appellee could validly pass upon the suitability and harmony of any proposed structure, considered in connection with the other buildings and the general surroundings in the development, but we think that any reason, assigned by the appellee for refusing to approve plans submitted to it, would have to bear some relation to the other buildings or general plan of development. Whether the appellee could decline to approve plans for "aesthetic reasons" may be open to question because of the difficulty of establishing any standard by which aesthetic values could be determined, but we do not consider it necessary to decide whether the provision in the covenant in the present case relating to aesthetic reasons is valid or not. Morris declined to approve the appellants' plans because he claimed the second-story porch shown on those plans would give the house the appearance of a two-family dwelling, and thus render it out of keeping with the surrounding structures and with the general appearance of buildings in Ashburton, and we think this reason a sustainable one under the covenant, without regard to any purely aesthetic consideration. And of course the valid provisions of the covenant can be sustained, even though the part referring to "aesthetic" reasons be invalid. The appellants, however, insist that, even though the reason assigned by Morris is good under the covenant, there is not sufficient difference between the porch shown on their plans, and the porches which Morris was willing to authorize, to justify Morris in rejecting the former.

The testimony given on this point by Morris, himself a graduate architect, is largely supported by the evidence of Mr. Palmer, consulting architect for the Roland Park Company, and by the witnesses Ellis and Johnson, both of whom were expert real estate and building men. It is true that on cross-examination both Palmer and Ellis expressed doubt as to the ability of a layman to identify a house as a two-family dwelling simply because of the character of the second-story porch on it, and the appellant Jones and two of his witnesses, one a builder and the other an architect, testified that the appellants' house was in full harmony and keeping with the surrounding properties, but we are of the opinion that the testimony in support of Morris' contention was sufficient, under the circumstances of this case, to relieve him of the charge of arbitrariness or unreasonableness in making his decision. It must be remembered that the appellants agreed to submit the size, shape, materials, etc., of their house to the approval of the appellee, and in pursuance of that agreement they actually did submit these matters. The appellee, acting through its president, Mr. Morris, declined to approve the shape of the second-story porch wanted by the appellants, on the ground that it was not in harmony with the neighboring houses, and in our opinion the evidence in the record does not justify the conclusion that this action of Mr. Morris was unreasonable. There is some discussion in the brief of the appellants as to whether the provision in the tenth covenant, giving the appellee the right to waive many, if not all, of the restrictions in any particular case, does not destroy the theory of a general plan of development, and render the covenants unenforceable on the ground of lack of mutuality. We would have to consider this in a suit brought by one lot owner against another, but we do not consider it necessary to pass upon it in this suit because we are here dealing with an original grantor, who still owns a considerable part of the land, and the assignees of an original purchaser, and, as the deed specifically states that the covenants are to bind "the grantees, their heirs and assigns," there would seem to be no question under the authorities of the grantor's right to enforce the covenants, if they are otherwise valid.

Finding no error in the case, the decree appealed from will be affirmed. Decree affirmed, with costs to the appellee.[92]

---

92. For a case which held that the person who had the power to approve plans had not acted objectively, honestly, and reasonably in refusing to approve a plan, see Donoghue v. Prynnwood Corp., 356 Mass. 703, 255 N.E.2d 326 (1970).—Eds.

Problem

32.12. The architectural control committee, acting under a covenant the same as that set out in the Jones case, brings an action against a lot owner seeking an injunction to prohibit construction of a 64-foot tower to be used for ham radio transmitting, characterizing the tower as "unsightly" and not in conformity with their general plan for the development. The lot owner defends on the grounds that (a) the proposed tower is not a "structure" within the terms of the restrictive covenant; (b) the restrictive covenant is so vague and indefinite that the same is void and unenforceable; (c) the proposed tower will be used in important civil defense work necessary to the national defense; and (d) the zoning laws permit such a tower. What decision? LaVielle v. Seay, 412 S.W.2d 587 (Ky. 1966).

SECTION 5. RETAINING FLEXIBILITY IN THE DEVELOPMENT

Assume you have received the following memorandum from your senior partner:

> My experience in drafting long-term trusts and corporate charters has taught me that we can but dimly perceive what future contingencies may someday arise. How much power and authority can we reserve to our client (or the homeowners' association) so as to accommodate the obvious need for flexibility? I would appreciate your comments on the following clause: "It is understood by and between the parties that special unforeseen conditions may require exceptions in certain cases, which may be permitted by the written consent of [our client or the homeowners' association] providing the spirit and intent of these covenants and restrictions are adhered to."

Your reply to this memorandum should be based on the material that follows.

RICK v. WEST
34 Misc. 2d 1002, 228 N.Y.S.2d 195 (Sup. Ct. 1962)

HOYT, J.

Plaintiffs, the owners of some 62 acres of vacant land in the Town of Cortland, Westchester County, New York, bring this action against the defendant, the owner of a one family house situated on a $\frac{1}{2}$ acre parcel conveyed to her by plaintiffs' predecessor in title, for a declaratory judgment to permit the sale of 15 acres from the tract for a community hospital in spite of restrictive covenants limiting the land to residential use.

Plaintiffs' predecessor in title, Chester Rick, in 1946 purchased the tract which at the time was free of restrictions and covenants and subject to no zoning ordinances. Mr. Rick in 1947 filed in the Westchester County Clerk's office a "Declaration of Covenants, Restrictions, Reservations and Agreements" which voluntarily imposed upon the 62 acres covenants restricting them to exclusive residential use with single family dwellings and provided for elaborate restrictions as to the location of houses, preservation of views, planting and road layout to conform to a community plan, whose purpose and intent was described in the Declaration . . . "to establish a community of good character and appeal to people of culture and discriminating taste at a minimum cost. . . ." In October of 1955 defendant contracted to purchase from Rick a half acre lot for the sum of $2,000.00 and in September of 1956 Rick delivered his deed to the defendant conveying said premises and about a year later defendant built her house upon this lot where she now resides.

In the period between the contract with and the conveyance to the defendant, Rick filed a revision of the Declaration of Covenants, Restrictions and Agreements which repeated the original Declaration purposes, intent, exclusive residential use, minimum size plot, etc. but deleted a declaration for the construction of bathing and play sites and certain roads and deleted provision for the formation of a Community Association for plot owners to control such areas. The revision thus indicates that some of the development features originally envisioned were abandoned, but the Declaration as revised still clearly restricted the whole tract to residential use with no more than one detached single family dwelling unit not exceeding $1\frac{1}{2}$ stories in height on each lot. These restrictions were in effect when the defendant acquired title and they were referred to in her deed and the proof shows that she discussed these restrictions with Rick when purchasing and relied upon them and was influenced by them in deciding to buy the lot and erect and make her home thereon.

A few days prior to Rick's conveyance to the defendant he contracted for the sale of 45 acres of the parcel to an industrialist, the sale being conditioned upon a rezoning of the parcel (the parcel had been zoned residential in 1957) and a release of the restrictive covenants. A few days after the conveyance to the defendant, Rick made application to the Planning Board for the zoning change and the Planning Board was not advised of the restrictive covenants affecting the premises and the defendant was not notified of the application for a hearing thereon. The Town Board on the recommendations of the Planning Board amended the Zoning Ordinance to rezone the 45 acres to light industrial use. The defendant did not release the covenants in her favor affecting the 45 acres and the sale was not consummated.

In 1959 Rick conveyed to plaintiffs the 62 acre parcel, being all the original tract less the plot sold to the defendant and a few other plots sold by him.

In May of 1961 the plaintiffs contracted to sell to the Peekskill Hospital 15 acres from the plot and defendant's refusal to consent to the same is the basis of this litigation.

The original Declaration and the Revision thereof each contained the identical Paragraph Eighth.

> EIGHTH: — These covenants and conditions are prepared to clearly indicate the character of the Community to be established, but it is understood that special unforeseen conditions may require exceptions in certain cases, which may be permitted by the written consent of the seller providing the spirit and intent of these covenants and restrictions are adhered to.

The plaintiffs contend that the proposed sale to the Peekskill Hospital is a "special unforeseen condition" requiring an exception and the plaintiffs' grantor and the plaintiffs have executed a consent and exception pursuant to said Paragraph Eighth to permit the erection of the hospital.

The plaintiffs further claim that since Rick's acquisition of the property in 1947 the neighborhood and area has changed, the zoning is now in effect where none existed, that a gas transmission line making portions unusable for residential purposes has bisected the property and that a lumber yard, manufacturing and commercial establishments have come into being adjacent to the property and that because of the changed conditions the Declaration and Amended Declaration imposing these restrictions are no longer enforceable and that the restrictions are of no actual or substantial benefit to the defendant.

A declaratory judgment is sought to permit the sale of the 15 acres for the hospital, to declare the restrictions no longer enforceable or of actual or substantial benefit and to declare the defendant be limited to pecuniary damages, if any, for any violations of the restrictions.

The plaintiffs called two witnesses to testify as to the pecuniary damages, if any, that might be sustained by defendant were the proposed hospital to be erected. One witness indicated there would be no depreciation in value and the other indicated a $5,000.00 depreciation. In view of the Court's ruling, this testimony is not of any significance.

Defendant contends and alleges as an affirmative defense that the plaintiffs' claim should be defeated because of the bad faith shown by Chester Rick. The claim of bad faith is based upon Rick's petitioning to rezone the 45 acres adjacent to defendant's home without defendant's knowledge and without notice to the Planning Board of the existence of the covenants. The Court need not consider this to determine that plaintiffs are not entitled to the relief they seek since other grounds more substantial and determinative exist.

Plaintiffs' contention that the written contract of the sellers, herein given, permit exceptions to the covenants and conditions when required by special unforeseen circumstances is untenable. The exception here sought would permit the erection of a hospital on a 15 acre plot on an elevation close to defendant's property toward which elevation the front of defendant's property faces. To sustain this contention would mean that all the covenants and conditions would be subject to repeal by the simple written consent of the sellers. The character and use of the entire 62 acre parcel could thus be changed by the sellers.

The revised declaration, although omitting the original elaborate plans for bathing and play areas and a Community Association, repeated the original restrictions that "all plots in the tract of land . . . shall be used exclusively for residential purposes and no structure shall be rented, allowed, placed or permitted to remain upon any plot other than one detached single family dwelling. . . ."

This Paragraph Eighth, which plaintiffs would treat as an escape clause, by its very terms shows the unsoundness of that position since it states ". . . these covenants and conditions are prepared to clearly indicate the character of the community to be established. . . ."

Many provisions in the restrictions could be modified without changing "the character of the Community to be established," such as minimum lot size, angle of lots or plantings. The written consent of the sellers could waive or modify these provisions. It can not, however, unencumber a 15 acre tract in the parcel from the residential restrictions.

Plaintiffs contend that substantial changes have occurred in the neighborhood since the filing of the covenants. This, they say, warrants the Court in declaring the covenants unenforceable. This contention is equally untenable. The only changes to be considered are those occurring after January 31, 1956 when the revised restrictions and covenants were filed. The gas transmission line and certain commercial establishments which it is claimed changed the neighborhood came into being before the filing of the revised restrictions.

The only changes since the refiling were two commercial establishments not visible from defendant's property and on the far side of a highway not abutting defendant's lot and not even abutting plaintiffs' tract.

There is no evidence of any substantial change in the general neighborhood since the last affirmation of the restrictions and there is no change at all within the parcel owned by the plaintiffs. . . .

The rezoning of a large part of the 62 acre parcel to an industrial use, including the area upon which it is desired to build the hospital, and omitting any consideration of the time and manner in which the rezoning was accomplished, can not be considered as affecting the restrictive covenants (Lefferts Manor Association, Inc. et al v. Fass and Brocton Associates, Inc., 28 Misc. 2d 1005, 211 N.Y.S.2d 18).

The parcel in question would doubtless by its topography and proximity to fast growing suburban areas make a desirable location for the hospital.

The hospital authorities would like to acquire it and the plaintiffs would like to sell it and it may be asked why should defendant owning a most respectable, but modest, home be permitted to prevent the sale or in any event why should the covenants be not determined nonenforceable and the defendant relegated to pecuniary damages.

Plaintiffs' predecessor owned the tract free and clear of all restrictions. He could do with the parcel as he saw best. He elected to promote a residential development and in the furtherance of his plan and as an inducement to purchasers he imposed the residential restrictions. The defendant relied upon them and has a right to continue to rely thereon. It is not a question of balancing equities or equating the advantages of a hospital on this site with the effect it would have on defendant's property. Nor does the fact that defendant is the only one of the few purchasers from plaintiffs' predecessor in title who has refused to release the covenants make defendant's insistence upon the enforcement of the covenants no less deserving of the Court's protection and safeguarding of her rights.

The opinion of Judge Cardozo in Evangelical Lutheran Church of the Ascension of Snyder v. Sahlem, 254 N.Y. 161, 166, 168, 172 N.E. 455, 457, is quoted at length since the questions therein presented are so similar to those in the case at bar.

> By the settled doctrine of equity, restrictive covenants in respect of land will be enforced by preventive remedies while the violation is still in prospect, unless the attitude of the complaining owner in standing on his covenant is unconscionable or oppressive. Relief is not withheld because the money damage is unsubstantial or even none at all. [Citations omitted.]
>
> Here, in the case at hand, no process of balancing the equities can make the plaintiff's the greater when compared with the defendant's, or even place the two in equipoise. The defendant, the owner, has done nothing but insist upon adherence to a covenant which is now as valid and binding as at the hour of its making. His neighbors are willing to modify the restriction and forego a portion of their rights. He refuses to go with them. Rightly or wrongly he believes that the comfort of his dwelling will be imperiled by the change, and so he chooses to abide by the covenant as framed. The choice is for him only. Neither at law nor in equity is it written that a license has been granted to religious corporations, by reason of the high purpose of their being, to set covenants at naught. Indeed, if in such matters there can be degrees of obligation, one would suppose that a more sensitive adherence to the demands of plighted faith might be expected of them than would be looked for of the world at large. Other owners may consent. One owner, the defendant, satisfied with the existing state of things, refuses to disturb it. He will be protected in his refusal by all the power of the law.

For the reasons stated in the above quoted portion of Judge Cardozo's opinion, and since Section 346 of the Real Property Law[93] provides no basis

---

93. This section is now section 1951 of the Real Property Actions and Proceedings Law, which is referred to at page 1055 *infra.*—EDS.

for awarding pecuniary damages when the restriction is not outmoded and when it affords real benefit to the person seeking its enforcement, no consideration can or should be given to any award of pecuniary damages to the defendant in lieu of the enforcement of the restrictions. The plaintiffs, thus, have not established their proof under either cause of action and are not entitled to the declaratory judgment they seek.

Note: *Retention by the Developer of a Right to Modify Restrictions*

The retention by a developer of a right to modify the restrictions as to any properties in the development has generally been held to negate the idea of development according to a uniform plan or scheme. (What is the significance of a finding of no uniform plan or scheme?) In fact, in many cases, the mere retention of such right, even though unexercised, has been fatal to the rights of other lot owners to enforce the covenants inter se:

> As a general rule a reservation by the common grantor of a general power to dispense with restrictions precludes one owner from enforcing restrictions as against another owner where all the property is encumbered with the same restrictions even though the dispensing power of the grantor has not been exercised. The theory is that in such an event the reservation of the power to modify negates a finding of a uniform plan of development from which the mutuality of right of enforcement among grantees might otherwise arise.[94]

Is this sound? It is one thing if the developer, pursuant to this power, actually releases or modifies the restrictions on so many of the lots so as to destroy the "general plan," but it is quite another thing if no modification or release has occurred or if the changes or modifications are slight and do not destroy the "general plan." It would seem that this should be a fact question;[95] however, given the present state of authority, it may be unwise to plan for retention by a developer of an unlimited right to alter or amend the restrictions.[96]

Note: *Provision for Periodic Review of Restrictions*

Another method used by developers to provide flexibility is periodic review by the owners, provided for in the declaration of covenants and

94. Finchum v. Vogel, 194 So. 2d 49, 52 (Fla. Dist. Ct. App. 1966). See also Maples v. Horton, 239 N.C. 394, 80 S.E.2d 38 (1954); Mauro v. Tomasullo, 28 Misc. 2d 666, 212 N.Y.S.2d 148 (Sup. Ct. 1961); Suttle v. Bailey, 68 N.M. 283, 361 P.2d 325 (1961).

95. Kreppel v. Tucker, 220 N.Y.S.2d 15 (Sup. Ct. 1961), accepts this view, but it is in conflict with a long line of other New York cases. Notice that the principal case does not mention this problem, perhaps because Rick did not retain a general "unlimited" power.

96. Retention of an unlimited power is unacceptable to the FHA. See The Homes Association Handbook §12.22(c), at 199 (Urban Land Institute, Technical Bulletin No. 50, 1966). Why is this important?

restrictions. A provision which would terminate the covenants after a stated period of time unless renewed by a majority or two-thirds vote is considered undesirable.[97] The better approach may be to provide that, after a stated initial period, the covenants shall continue automatically for periods of ten years each, unless the owners alter or terminate them by recording an instrument signed by a majority or two-thirds of the then-existing owners. A question which frequently arises is: can this power to alter or amend the covenants by a vote of less than all of the then-existing owners create a greater burden on the properties than that provided for in the original covenants?

In Van Deusen v. Ruth, 343 Mo. 1096, 125 S.W.2d 1 (1938), the agreement providing for the covenants and restrictions said:

> All or any of the foregoing provisions or restrictions may be modified, amended, released, or extinguished at any time after ten (10) years by written instrument executed, acknowledged and recorded as required by law for instruments affecting real estate, by the owners of seventy-five percent (75%) of the total number of front feet embraced in this indenture.

More than ten years after this agreement was recorded, 75 percent of the owners duly agreed to modify the agreement and prohibit the erection of an apartment house or any building to be used for commercial purposes, although such a building was permitted under the original agreement. The court held that this attempt to exclude apartment houses was ineffective and not permitted by the terms of the original agreement.[98]

If an amendment which has the effect of *increasing* the burden on the nonconsenting owners generally is not permitted,[99] what should be done to provide for increases in the annual assessments, which are frequently needed to offset inflation? One possible approach to this question would be to have an automatic increase in the amount of assessments occur whenever the dollar value decreases. This could be done by gearing the assessment rate to the consumer price index, as suggested in the Note on Fixing the Rent in a Commercial Lease, page 656 *supra*. Other methods are suggested in The Homes Association Handbook §12.36 (Urban Land Institute, Technical Bulletin No. 50, 1966).

97. The Homes Association Handbook, footnote 96, *supra*, §12.8, at 212, n.99, says that although most homeowners would probably rather see the restrictions continue, a majority or two-thirds vote to reinstate them might be difficult to marshal. Further, a legal problem might arise if the covenants were reattached by a vote of less than all of the owners. Can you see what this problem would be?

98. See also Huntington Palisades Property Owners Corp. v. Metropolitan Finance Corp., 180 F.2d 132 (9th Cir.), *cert. denied,* 339 U.S. 980, 70 S. Ct. 1027 (1950).

99. But where the modification is one which does not increase the burden on the properties, the courts uniformly have held such power effective against the nonconsenting minority — even if such amendment or modification effectively destroys the restricted nature of the whole development. See, e.g., Sharp v. Quinn, 214 Cal. 194, 4 P.2d 942 (1931); Loving v. Clem, 30 S.W.2d 590 (Tex. Civ. App. 1930).

SECTION 6.   TERMINATION OF RESTRICTIONS

A.   By the Courts

Note: Changed Conditions in the Neighborhood[100]

How much weight should a court give to changes which have occurred outside the development? In answering this question, consider the following quotation from Downs v. Kroeger, 200 Cal. 743, 254 P. 1101 (1927):

> The authorities unquestionably support the conclusion of the trial court in holding that where there has been a change in the uses to which the property in the neighborhood is being put, so that such property is no longer residence property, it would be unjust, oppressive, and inequitable to give effect to such restrictions, if such change has resulted from causes other than their breach. [200 Cal. at 747, 254 P. at 1102.]

At the same time, the following quotation must be noted:

> On this point it may be observed that there must of necessity be a dividing line somewhere. . . . It is inevitable that all lots on the fringe of a residential district may, with the changes of the surrounding neighborhood, become a buffer between the residential area and a business or commercial area. It is one of the factors inherent in considering the nature and value of such property. To lift the restriction under consideration here on the lots in question would only cut down this desirable residential area and create another buffer area. To permit the dividing line to be moved in the case at bar thereby creating another buffer district, now composed of both residences and vacant property, does not present sufficiently strong equitable considerations.[101]

If the dividing line were moved in and another buffer zone were created, how long do you think it would be before the owners in the new buffer zone appeared in court asking for the removal of their restrictions? This problem will be re-examined in the zoning context.

A court applying equitable principles, although not declaring the restriction terminated, may still refuse to enforce the covenant by way of injunction on any of the following grounds: (1) estoppel; (2) "dirty hands"; (3) acquiescence; (4) waiver; (5) laches; (6) relative hardship.[102]

---

100.   See generally American Law of Property §9.39 (Casner ed. 1952).
101.   Redfern Lawns Civic Association v. Currie Pontiac Co., 328 Mich. 463, 470, 44 N.W.2d 8, 11-12 (1950).
102.   See Restatement of Property §§560-563 (1944); American Law of Property §9.38 (Casner ed. 1952).

B. By Governmental Action (Herein the Problem of Tax Sales, Zoning, and Condemnation)

Does a purchaser at a tax sale take subject to validly recorded restrictions imposed on the land? Local tax statutes must be checked. Some merely impose a liability on the owner, not on the land—in personam statutes. If the owner does not pay, the owner's interest in the land is sold at a tax sale and the purchaser gets a "derivative" title, i.e., a title as encumbered as that of the delinquent owner. However, in a majority of states, the statutes are in rem, i.e., the land is liable for the tax and a purchaser at this tax sale gets a "new" title, theoretically free of all encumbrances; but even these statutes vary too much for generalization.[103]

Zoning ordinances normally are permissive in character, and restrictions imposed on the use of land normally are restrictive in nature. Hence there is not normally a direct conflict between the two. For example, a zoning ordinance may permit apartment houses, whereas a restrictive covenant may limit the use of land to single-family dwelling houses. The general rule is that "a valid restriction on the use of realty is neither nullified nor superseded by the adoption of a zoning ordinance, nor is the validity of the restrictions thereby affected."[104]

It is universally agreed that the state may condemn property by eminent domain and not be bound by any use restrictions imposed upon the land. The real problem arises in deciding how much compensation the state must pay to other lot owners for eliminating the restrictive covenant.[105]

C. By Legislative Action

There is a dilemma which runs through the history of property law and which is as old as the concept of liberty itself. The owner of property insists on the "freedom" to dispose of his or her property to whomever he or she

---

103. Some statutes expressly save "easements" existing at the time of the sale, whereas others expressly provide that restrictions imposed by valid covenants running with the land survive the tax sale. Engel v. Catucci, 197 F.2d 597 (D.C. Cir. 1952), involving an easement, reviews the authorities. See also American Law of Property §9.40 (Casner ed. 1952); Restatement of Property §567 (1944).

104. Hirsch v. Hancock, 173 Cal. App. 2d 745, 343 P.2d 959 (1959). See generally Berger, Conflicts Between Zoning Ordinances and Restrictive Covenants: A Problem in Land Use Policy, 43 Neb. L. Rev. 449 (1964); Comment, Restrictive Covenants and Zoning Regulations, 31 Tenn. L. Rev. 353 (1964); Note, The Conflict Between Restrictive Covenants and Zoning Laws, 13 N.Y.U. Intra. L. Rev. 68 (1957).

105. See Arkansas State Highway Commission v. McNeill, 238 Ark. 244, 381 S.W.2d 425 (1964), especially the dissenting opinion of Judge McFaddin, which reviews the law in all other jurisdictions. See generally Brickman, The Compensability of Restrictive Covenants in Eminent Domain, 13 U. Fla. L. Rev. 147 (1960); Comment, Real Property—Compensation for Abrogation of a Restrictive Covenant by Public Authority, 53 Mich. L. Rev. 451 (1955); Note, Eminent Domain, Condemnation of Land Encumbered by a Restrictive Covenant, 1957 U. Ill. L.F. 133.

pleases and with whatever restrictions he or she chooses to place thereon. However, such freedom necessarily results in imposing restrictions on the freedom of succeeding owners, who in turn insist on the same freedom. The rule against perpetuities, referred to at page 335 *supra,* is one attempt at resolution of this age-old dilemma. However, the common-law rule is not applicable to possibilities of reverter and rights of entry; nor is it generally thought applicable to covenants restricting land use.[106] The common assumption that covenants restricting the use of land are usually limited to 25, 50, or 99 years is not justified as a matter of case law.

Several states have enacted statutes which attempt to impose limitations on the unbridled freedom of an owner to impose perpetual conditions or restrictions on the property which he or she owns. Some of these statutes are prospective only, i.e., reaching conditions and restrictions created *after* their effective date and declaring them void after a stated period of time.[107] However, it is the "ancient" conditions and restrictions which have proved the most troublesome, and a statute having only prospective effect is only a partial solution. Therefore, some statutes declared that all possibilities of reverter and rights of entry — including those already in existence — shall be of limited duration.[108] Some provide that restrictions cease to have any effect after a stated number of years from the date of recordation — including those already in existence — unless its holder records an intention to

---

106.   Harris v. Pease, 135 Conn. 535, 66 A.2d 590 (1949).

107.   See, e.g., Mass. Gen. Laws ch. 184, §23, which provides:

> Conditions or restrictions, unlimited as to time, by which the title or use of real property is affected, shall be limited to the term of thirty years after the date of the deed or other instrument or the date of the probate of the will creating them, except in cases of gifts or devises for public, charitable or religious purposes. This section shall not apply to conditions or restrictions existing on July sixteenth, eighteen hundred and eighty-seven, to those contained in a deed, gift or grant of the commonwealth, or to those having the benefit of section thirty-five [relating to conservation, preservation, and agricultural restrictions].

Mass. Gen. Laws ch. 184A, §3, eliminates possibilities of reverter and rights of entry after 30 years. See also R.I. Gen. Laws Ann. §34-4-19 (20 years for possibilities of reverter or rights of entry created after May 11,1953); R.I. Gen. Laws Ann. §34-4-21 (30 years for covenants or restrictions created after May 11, 1953, if otherwise unlimited in time). If the conditions or restrictions are not "unlimited as to time," e.g., they are stated to last 100 years, then neither statute applies to cut down the duration of the conditions or restrictions to a term of 30 years. See also the marketable title statutes at page 840 *supra.*

108.   Compare Fla. Stat. Ann. §689.18, which canceled all reverter provisions in plats or deeds which had been in effect for more than 21 years and was held unconstitutional as impairing the obligations of contract as to deeds executed prior to the effective date of the statute, notwithstanding a savings clause giving the holder of the reverter one year from the date of the act to institute suit to enforce his right (Biltmore Village, Inc. v. Royal, 71 So. 2d 727 (Fla. 1954)) with Ill. Rev. Stat. ch. 30, §37e, which provided that neither possibilities of reverter nor rights of entry, whether created before or after the act, shall be valid for longer than 50 years (now 40 years) from the date of creation, with a similar savings clause; held constitutional in Trustees of Schools v. Batdorf, 6 Ill. 2d 486, 130 N.E.2d 111 (1955). Does the fact that possibilities of reverter were freely alienable in Florida and not in Illinois make any difference? See also marketable title statute at page 840 *supra.*

preserve them for an additional term. These are generally called marketable title acts,[109] and their general intent is to bar interests of ancient origin and to render titles more readily marketable by fixing a definite date beyond which it is unnecessary to make a title search.[110] The Supreme Court of Minnesota, in holding its marketable title act[111] constitutional, said:

> It is apparent from the recordation provisions of the 40-year statute which we are considering that the legislature did not intend to arbitrarily wipe out old claims and interests without affording a means of preserving them and giving a reasonable period of time within which to take the necessary steps to accomplish that purpose. The recordation provisions of the act provide for a simple and easy method by which the owner of an existing old interest may preserve it. If he fails to take the step of filing the notice as provided, he has only himself to blame if his interest is extinguished.[112]

Some statutes declare that conditions or restrictions shall cease to be valid whenever they become merely nominal and of no substantial benefit to the party in whose favor they run.[113] The Supreme Court of Minnesota, in the same opinion, carefully distinguished its marketable title act from the type of statute now under discussion:

> §500.20(1) merely applies to conditions that have become nominal. Subd. 2 limits the duration of conditions "hereafter created" to 30 years. Neither subdivision applies to bar substantial interests which were created long before the enactment of §500.20(1) and which now fetter the marketability of title. The policy of §541.023 is to require such interests to be recorded again by filing notice. Section 541.023 also assists the operation of §500.20 by requiring notice filed thereunder to state affirmatively why such conditions have not become nominal. (If nominal, the condition is barred by §500.20, even if it is filed under §541.023.)[114] [250 Minn. at 118, 83 N.W.2d at 823.]

109. A complete discussion of marketable title acts enacted in Illinois, Indiana, Iowa, Michigan, Minnesota, Nebraska, North Dakota, South Dakota, and Wisconsin is found in Bayse, Clearing Land Titles §§171-180 (1953).

110. Note the similar aims of title registration, discussed in Chapter 30.

111. Minn. Stat. Ann. §541.023.

112. Wichelman v. Messner, 250 Minn. 88, 108-109, 83 N.W.2d 800, 817 (1957). But see Board of Education v. Miles, 15 N.Y.2d 364, 207 N.E.2d 181 (1965), holding N.Y. Real Prop. Law §345 unconstitutional, as applied to possibilities of reverter and rights of entry already in existence.

113. See, e.g., Minn. Stat. Ann. §500.20, subdiv. 1, which provides:

> When any covenants, conditions, restrictions or extensions thereof annexed to a grant, devise or conveyance of land are, or shall become, merely nominal, and of no actual and substantial benefit to the party or parties to whom or in whose favor they are to be performed, they may be wholly disregarded; and a failure to perform the same shall in no case operate as a basis of forfeiture of the lands subject thereto.

See also N.Y. Real Prop. Acts. Law §1951, applying the same doctrine to all "restrictions", and Wis. Stat. Ann. §700.15.

114. See footnote 111 *supra*.

SECTION 7. EASEMENTS

Note: *Easements and Profits Distinguished and Classified*

An easement is a non-possessory interest in land.[115] The possession of the land in which the easement exists is always in another. In other words, the owner of an easement has a right to use the land of another for a specified purpose, as distinguished from a right to possess that land.

Typical easements are illustrated by the following transactions:

1. O, owner of Blackacre, grants to E, owner of Whiteacre, a right of way over a specified portion of Blackacre for passage to and from Whiteacre. The right of way thus created in E gives E an easement in O's land.

2. O, owner of Blackacre, grants to E, owner of Whiteacre, the right to free light and air over a specified portion of Blackacre, to give E an unobstructed view of the ocean. The right of view thus created in E gives E an easement in O's land.

Easements are normally classified as easements appurtenant[116] or easements in gross.[117] An easement appurtenant exists when the easement is created in order to benefit land possessed by the owner of the easement. The two typical cases given above are both illustrations of easements appurtenant. In those cases, E has an easement appurtenant to Whiteacre (the benefited land possessed by E) and Whiteacre is referred to as the dominant tenement. Blackacre, the land subject to the easement, is designated as the servient tenement.[118] An easement in gross exists whenever the easement is not created for the purpose of benefiting other land possessed by the owner of the easement. Thus, if O has a spring located on O's land and grants to E an irrevocable right to come on O's land at any time and drink from the spring, E has an easement in gross.

---

115. Restatement of Property §450:

An easement is an interest in land in the possession of another which

  (a) entitles the owner of such interest to a limited use of enjoyment of the land in which the interest exists;

  (b) entitles him to protection as against third persons from interference in such use or enjoyment;

  (c) is not subject to the will of the possessor of the land;

  (d) is not a normal incident of the possession of any land possessed by the owner of the interest, and

  (e) is capable of creation by conveyance.

116. Id. §§453-454; American Law of Property §§8.6-8.10 (Casner ed. 1952).

117. See footnote 116 *supra*.

118. Restatement of Property §455; American Law of Property §8.14 (Casner ed. 1952).

Easements may also be classified as either affirmative or negative.[119] Most are affirmative, i.e., they entitle the holder to do acts upon the servient tenement. Less common are negative easements. These entitle the holder to prevent the owner of the servient tenement from making certain uses of the servient land. Example 1 above is an affirmative easement, whereas example 2 is negative since the effect of it is to restrict the servient owner from erecting any structure on that portion of the servient land. Can you distinguish this type of negative easement from an equitable servitude?

Another non-possessory interest in land that is very similar to an easement is the profit à prendre, usually called simply a profit. The profit involves the right to go onto the land of another and sever some part of it, thereby acquiring a possessory right in the severed thing. A typical example: O, owner of Blackacre, grants to E the right to come onto Blackacre and remove coal.[120] You will notice that there is no separate treatment of profits in this book. Profits are not separately developed because we agree with the conclusion of the Restatement of Property that in the United States the rules generally applicable to easements are also applicable to profits.[121]

One may have the privilege of going onto the land of another and doing things comparable to the things done by the owner of an easement, or by the owner of a profit, but have no privilege of continuing such acts after the owner of the land has told him or her to stop. In such case, we speak of the privilege as a mere license. Difficulties naturally arise when parties intend to create the more permanent rights of an easement or profit but have not met the formalities required by law for the creation of such an interest in land. The question then is presented as to whether a mere license exists or whether, under some circumstances, the privilege becomes irrevocable, so that an interest in the land in the nature of an easement or profit, sometimes referred to as an irrevocable license, is created. In Section 8 we consider the so-called irrevocable license, but in this section the license will come into our deliberations to some extent.

119. Restatement of Property §§451-452.
120. In view of the fact that O could grant to E an estate in the coal in place, thus giving E a possessory interest in the subsurface, a question may be presented whether that is the intention of the parties or whether the intention is to grant only a profit, which gives no possessory right to E until the coal is severed.
121. Restatement of Property §450 special note:

> Interests of the sort here discussed under the title "Easements" have traditionally been discussed under the separate titles of "Easements" and "Profits." In phrasing the rules applicable to each of these interests it has been found, however, that in no case was there a rule applicable to one of these interests which was not also applicable to the other. This is not true with respect to English law. Under that law the interest designated as an easement can exist only as an appurtenance of a dominant tenement, while a profit may exist independently of such a tenement, or, as it is commonly expressed, in gross. . . . This difference does not exist in this country. Here we have "easements in gross" as well as "profits in gross."

Note: *The Senior Partner Gets In Touch With You Again*

The senior partner calls your attention to the layout and design of Lakeville, pointing out the roadways and the common area. The nature of the rights of purchasers of lots in Lakeville to make use of the roadways and the common areas must be carefully defined. Your suggestions are invited after you examine the following material.

A.   *Express Creation of an Easement*[122]

If you desire to create an easement in your land, whether an easement appurtenant or an easement in gross, it should be done by a deed which complies with all the formalities for the transfer of an interest in land, and the deed should be recorded.[123] The deed, of course, should be drafted with extreme care so as to spell out fully the understanding of the parties involved with respect to the location and use of the easement. An examination of the cases in this section will indicate to you some of the matters which should be anticipated and provided for in the terms of the deed.

The easement may be expressly created by you in a deed granting a possessory interest of a portion of your land. The easement thus created may be in the land retained by you or may be reserved to you in the land granted. If the easement is in the land retained by you, your purchaser must worry about whether the recording of the deed of the possessory interest to the purchaser will give notice of the easement to anyone who later purchases the servient land from you.[124]

MARANATHA SETTLEMENT ASSOCIATION v. EVANS
385 Pa. 208, 122 A.2d 679 (1956)

STERN, C.J.

The sole question involved in this appeal is whether a bathing right, granted in deeds to the purchasers of certain lots, constituted a license, an

---

122.   See Kratovil, Easement Draftmanship and Conveyancing, 38 Calif. L. Rev. 426 (1950); American Law of Property §§8.17-8.30, 8.64-8.67 (Casner ed. 1952).

123.   See 5 Restatement of Property ch. 38, topic B, and ch. 39, topic B; Conard, The Requirement of a Sealed Instrument for Conveying Easements, 26 Iowa L. Rev. 41 (1940); Conard, Words Which Will Create an Easement, 6 Mo. L. Rev. 245 (1941); Conard, Easements, Licenses and the Statute of Frauds, 15 Temple L.Q. 222 (1941).

124.   See The Buffalo Academy of the Sacred Heart v. Boehm Brothers, Inc. in Chapter 28, Section 2.

easement in gross, or an easement appurtenant. We are of opinion that the court below correctly decided that it was an easement appurtenant.

Evans-Yale Realty Corporation, being the owner of farm land in Lehigh County, prepared and placed on record a plan showing a division of the tract into building lots. It entered into agreements for the sale of these lots and executed deeds to the purchasers; one of the defendants holds title to a lot as an original purchaser, but all the other defendants are grantees of prior owners.

The corporation, having constructed a swimming pool on the tract, inserted in all its deeds to purchasers of the lots a provision that "The Grantee and his immediate family only, shall enjoy the free use of the swimming pool." However, plaintiff, Maranatha Settlement Association, Incorporated, which, several years later, received title to the tract from Evans-Yale Realty Corporation less the lots which had theretofore been conveyed, forbade defendants, the then owners of some of the lots, from enjoying the use of the pool, claiming that the privilege was limited to the immediate grantees from Evans-Yale Realty Corporation or from plaintiff on the ground that it was merely a license or easement in gross and did not pass to the assignees of the original purchasers. Defendants, on the other hand, interpreted the grant of the privilege as extending to them, their heirs and assigns, claiming that it attached to the estates and not merely to the persons of the owners of the lots, in short, that it was an easement appurtenant.

The court below entered a decree holding that defendants and their families were entitled to the use of the pool, but subject to the reasonable rules and regulations adopted by plaintiff with reference thereto, and that they could not dispose of their rights to anyone other than purchasers of their respective properties. Plaintiff appeals from that decree.

The extent of the grant that was made in the deeds from Evans-Yale Realty Corporation of the privilege of bathing in the pool depends entirely upon the intent of the parties as determined by a fair interpretation of the language employed and consideration of all the attendant circumstances. So viewing the question it seems utterly impossible to believe that the intention was to give the privilege of bathing in the pool only to the original purchasers of the lots as a mere easement in gross, much less a revocable license. It may well be asked why should the right have been given to the original purchasers as individuals wholly apart from their status as owners of the neighboring lots in view of the fact that such a purchaser might remain the owner merely for a very short time and then deed the title to an assignee, in which case, if plaintiff's position were correct, he would still have the right to bathe in the pool as possessing an easement in gross, but on the other hand the new owner of the property and all subsequent owners and occupants would have no right to the bathing privilege at all. It is argued that in the phrase: "The Grantee and his immediate family only, shall enjoy the free use of the swimming pool," the word "only" limits the privilege to the original grantee and his family, but a more rational interpretation is that "only" restricts the use to "immediate family" but does not qualify the word "Grantee." It is true that the words "heirs and assigns" are not included after the word "Grantee," but a subsequent provision imposes upon "The Grantee, *his heirs and assigns*" the duty of complying with any rules and regulations that the grantor might make,— a provision recognized by the court in its decree which limited defendants accordingly; from this there can be no conclusion other than that the privilege granted was not a personal one to the original grantee, which is further borne out by the fact that other provisions forbid the grantee — without adding the words "heirs and assigns"— from using his lot for commercial purposes and from constructing any cesspool thereon except by permission of the grantor; plaintiff would scarcely contend that because of the absence of the words "heirs and assigns" these restrictions were meant to apply only to the original purchasers. Moreover, whatever may have been the legal effect prior to the Act of April 1, 1909, P.L. 91, §1, as amended by the Act of April 30, 1925, P.L. 404, §1, 21 P.S. §2, of the omission of those words, that act abolished the need of words of inheritance or of perpetuity in the deed in order to convey a fee simple title, and by any reasonable interpretation of the act it must be held applicable to the grant of an easement as well as to the conveyance of the title; see American Law of Property, vol. II, p. 245, §8.23; Rest. Property, §468. . . .

Decree affirmed at appellant's cost.

Problems

32.13. Draft the clause or clauses you think desirable to grant an easement of enjoyment in and to the common properties in our client's development of Lakeville. See the Homes Association Handbook, Appendix F, Model Form: Declaration of Covenants and Restrictions, article IV.

32.14. What if after recording the plat of Lakeville and selling a few interior lots, i.e., lots not on the lake, our client realizes that the value of the land designated as common properties is grossly underestimated. The client wants to subdivide the common area into additional lots for sale and in the meantime rent the common properties as a public shore resort and nightclub. What remedies do the purchasers of the interior lots have? Williams Realty Co. v. Robey, 175 Md. 532, 2 A.2d 683 (1938). What if the client merely wants to reduce the common properties in size? What if the client wants to give up the whole scheme after a few sales, realizing it is an unprofitable venture?

B. *Creation of an Easement by Implication*

In any case, where a problem of the creation of an easement by implication is involved, it is due to the fact that in some land transactions a thorough job has not been done for the parties involved.

VAN SANDT v. ROYSTER
148 Kan. 495, 83 P.2d 698 (1938)

The opinion of the court was delivered by ALLEN, J.: The action was brought to enjoin defendants from using and maintaining an underground lateral sewer drain through and across plaintiff's land. The case was tried by the court, judgment was rendered in favor of defendants, and plaintiff appeals.

In the city of Chanute, Highland avenue, running north and south, intersects Tenth street running east and west. In the early part of 1904 Laura A. J. Bailey was the owner of a plot of ground lying east of Highland avenue and south of Tenth street. Running east from Highland avenue and facing north on Tenth street the lots are numbered respectively, 19, 20 and 4. In 1904 the residence of Mrs. Bailey was on lot 4 on the east part of her land.

In the latter part of 1903 or the early part of 1904, the city of Chanute constructed a public sewer in Highland avenue, west of lot 19. About the same time a private lateral drain was constructed from the Bailey residence on lot 4 running in a westerly direction through and across lots 20 and 19 to the public sewer.

On January 15, 1904, Laura A. J. Bailey conveyed lot 19 to John J. Jones, by general warranty deed with usual covenants against encumbrances, and containing no exceptions or reservations. Jones erected a dwelling on the north part of the lot. In 1920 Jones conveyed the north 156 feet of lot 19 to Carl D. Reynolds; in 1924 Reynolds conveyed to the plaintiff, who has owned and occupied the premises since that time.

In 1904 Laura A. J. Bailey conveyed lot 20 to one Murphy, who built a house thereon, and by mesne conveyances the title passed to the defendant, Louise H. Royster. The deed to Murphy was a general warranty deed without exceptions or reservations. The defendant Gray has succeeded to the title to lot 4 upon which the old Bailey home stood at the time Laura A. J. Bailey sold lots 19 and 20.

In March, 1936, plaintiff discovered his basement flooded with sewage and filth to a depth of six or eight inches, and upon investigation he found for the first time that there existed on and across his property a sewer drain extending in an easterly direction across the property of Royster to the property of Gray. The refusal of defendants to cease draining and discharging their sewage across plaintiff's land resulted in this lawsuit. . . .[125]

The drain pipe in the lateral sewer was several feet under the surface of the ground. There was nothing visible on the ground in the rear of the houses to indicate the existence of the drain or the connection of the drain with the houses.

As the conclusion of the law the court found that "an appurtenant

---

125. The trial court made 11 separate findings of fact. The opinion of the court at this point quoted in full each of these findings, but since they are adequately summarized in the opinion whenever relevant, we have not set forth the part of the opinion quoting them.—EDS.

easement existed in the said lateral sewer as to all three of the properties involved in the controversy here." Plaintiff's prayer for relief was denied and it was decreed that plaintiff be restrained from interfering in any way with the lateral drain or sewer.

Plaintiff contends that the evidence fails to show that an easement was ever created in his land, and, assuming there was an easement created as alleged, that he took the premises free from the burden of the easement for the reason that he was a bona fide purchaser, without notice, actual or constructive.

Defendants contend: (1) That an easement was created by implied reservation on the severance of the servient from the dominant estate by the deed from Mrs. Bailey to Jones; (2) there is a valid easement by prescription.

In finding No. 11, the court found that the lateral sewer "was an appurtenance to the properties belonging to plaintiff and Louise Royster, and the same is necessary to the reasonable use and enjoyment of the said properties of the parties."

As an easement is an interest which a person has in land in the possession of another, it necessarily follows that an owner cannot have an easement in his own land. (Johnston v. City of Kingman, 141 Kan. 131, 39 P.2d 924; Ferguson v. Ferguson, 106 Kan. 823, 189 P. 925.)

However, an owner may make use of one part of his land for the benefit of another part, and this is very frequently spoken of as a quasi easement.

> When one thus utilizes part of his land for the benefit of another part, it is frequently said that a quasi easement exists, the part of the land which is benefited being referred to as the "quasi dominant tenement" and the part which is utilized for the benefit of the other part being referred to as the "quasi servient tenement." The so-called quasi easement is evidently not a legal relation in any sense, but the expression is a convenient one to describe the particular mode in which the owner utilizes one part of the land for the benefit of the other. . . .
>
> If the owner of land, one part of which is subject to a quasi easement in favor of another part, conveys the quasi dominant tenement, an easement corresponding to such quasi easement is ordinarily regarded as thereby vested in the grantee of the land, provided, it is said, the quasi easement is of an apparent continuous and necessary character. [2 Tiffany on Real Property, 2d ed., 1272, 1273.]

Following the famous case of Pyer v. Carter, 1 Hurl & N. 916, some of the English cases and many early American cases held that upon the transfer of the quasi-servient tenement there was an implied reservation of an easement in favor of the conveyor. Under the doctrine of Pyer v. Carter, no distinction was made between an implied reservation and an implied grant.

The case, however, was overthrown in England by Suffield v. Brown, 4 De G. J. & S. 185, and Wheeldon v. Burrows, L.R. 12 Ch. D. 31. In the former case the court said:

It seems to me more reasonable and just to hold that if the grantor intends to reserve any right over the property granted, it is his duty to reserve it expressly in the grant, rather than to limit and cut down the operation of a plain grant (which is not pretended to be otherwise than in conformity with the contract between the parties), by the fiction of an implied reservation. If this plain rule be adhered to, men will know what they have to trust, and will place confidence in the language of their contracts and assurances. . . . But I cannot agree that the grantor can derogate from his own absolute grant so as to claim rights over the thing granted, even if they were at the time of the grant continuous and apparent easements enjoyed by an adjoining tenement which remains the property of him the grantor [pp. 190, 194.]

Many American courts of high standing assert that the rule regarding implied grants and implied reservations is reciprocal and that the rule applies with equal force and in like circumstances to both grants and reservations. (Washburn on Easements, 4th ed. 75; Miller v. Skaggs, 79 W. Va. 645, 91 S.E. 536.)

On the other hand, perhaps a majority of the cases hold that in order to establish an easement by implied reservation in favor of the grantor the easement must be one of strict necessity, even when there was an existing drain or sewer at the time of the severance.

Thus in Howley v. Chaffee et al., 88 Vt. 468, 474, 93 A. 120, the court said:

With the character and extent of implied grants, we now have nothing to do. We are here only concerned with determining the circumstances which will give rise to an implied reservation. On this precise question the authorities are in conflict. Courts of high standing assert that the rule regarding implied grants and implied reservation of "visible servitudes" is reciprocal, and that it applies with equal force and in like circumstances to both grants and reservations. But upon a careful consideration of the whole subject, studied in the light of the many cases in which it is discussed, we are convinced that there is a clear distinction between implied grants and implied reservations, and that this distinction is well founded in principle and supported by authority. It is apparent that no question of public policy is here involved, as we have seen is the case where a way of necessity is involved. To say that a grantor reserves to himself something out of the property granted, wholly by implication, not only offends the rule that one shall not derogate from his own grant, but conflicts with the grantor's language in the conveyance, which, by the rule, is to be taken against him, and is wholly inconsistent with the theory on which our registry laws are based. If such an illogical result is to follow an absolute grant, it must be by virtue of some legal rule of compelling force. The correct rule is, we think, that where, as here, one grants a parcel of land by metes and bounds, by a deed containing full covenants of warranty and without any express reservation, there can be no reservation by implication, unless the easement claimed is one of strict necessity, within the meaning of that term as explained in Dee v. King, 73 Vt. 375, 50 A. 1109.

See, also, Brown v. Fuller, 165 Mich. 162, 130 N.W. 621. The cases are collected in 58 A.L.R. 837.

We are inclined to the view that the circumstance that the claimant of the easement is the grantor instead of the grantee, is but one of many factors to be considered in determining whether an easement will arise by implication. An easement created by implication arises as an inference of the intentions of the parties to a conveyance of land. The inference is drawn from the circumstances under which the conveyance was made rather than from the language of the conveyance. The easement may arise in favor of the conveyor or the conveyee. In the Restatement of Property, tentative draft No. 8, section 28,[126] the factors determining the implication of an easement are stated:

> Sec. 28. Factors Determining Implication of Easements or Profits.[127] In determining whether the circumstances under which a conveyance of land is made imply an easement or a profit, the following factors are important: (a) whether the claimant is the conveyor or the conveyee, (b) the terms of the conveyance, (c) the consideration given for it, (d) whether the claim is made against a simultaneous conveyee, (e) the extent of necessity of the easement or the profit to the claimant, (f) whether reciprocal benefits result to the conveyor and the conveyee, (g) the manner in which the land was used prior to its conveyance, and (h) the extent to which the manner of prior use was or might have been known to the parties.

Comment (j), under the same section, reads:

> The extent to which the manner of prior use was or might have been known to the parties. The effect of the prior use as a circumstance in implying, upon a severance of possession by conveyance, an easement or a profit results from an inference as to the intention of the parties. To draw such an inference, the prior use must have been known to the parties at the time of the conveyance, or, at least, have been within the possibility of their knowledge at the time. Each party to a conveyance is bound not merely to what he intended, but also to what he might reasonably have foreseen the other party to the conveyance expected. Parties to a conveyance may, therefore, be assumed to intend the continuance of uses known to them which are in a considerable degree necessary to the continued usefulness of the land. Also they will be assumed to know and to contemplate the continuance of reasonably necessary uses which have so altered the premises as to make them apparent upon reasonably prudent investigation. The degree of necessity required to imply an easement in favor of the conveyor is greater than that required in the case of the conveyee (see comment b). Yet, even in the case of the conveyor, the implica-

---

126.   The reference in the final publication is 5 Restatement of Property §476 (1944).
127.   The use of the word *profits* in the title of this section and in the language of the section is eliminated in the final publication because easements are defined broadly enough to include profits.

tion from necessity will be aided by a previous use made apparent by the physical adaptation of the premises to it.

Illustrations:

9. A is the owner of two adjacent tracts of land, Blackacre and Whiteacre. Blackacre has on it a dwelling house. Whiteacre is unimproved. Drainage from the house to a public sewer is across Whiteacre. This fact is unknown to A, who purchased the two tracts with the house already built. By reasonable effort, A might discover the manner of drainage and the location of the drain. A sells Blackacre to B, who has been informed as to the manner of drainage, and the location of the drain and assumes that A is aware of it. There is created by implication an easement of drainage in favor of B across Whiteacre.

10. Same facts as in illustration 9, except that both A and B are unaware of the manner of drainage and the location of the drain. However, each had reasonable opportunity to learn of such facts. A holding that there is created by implication an easement of drainage in favor of B across Whiteacre is proper.

At the time John J. Jones purchased lot 19 he was aware of the lateral sewer, and knew that it was installed for the benefit of the lots owned by Mrs. Bailey, the common owner. The easement was necessary to the comfortable enjoyment of the grantor's property. If land may be used without an easement, but cannot be used without disproportionate effort and expense, an easement may still be implied in favor of either the grantor or grantee on the basis of necessity alone. This is the situation as found by the trial court.

Neither can it be claimed that plaintiff purchased without notice. At the time plaintiff purchased the property he and his wife made a careful and thorough inspection of the property. They knew the house was equipped with modern plumbing and that the plumbing had to drain into a sewer. Under the facts as found by the court, we think the purchaser was charged with notice of the lateral sewer. It was an apparent easement as that term is used in the books. (Wiesel v. Smira, 49 R.I. 246, 142 A. 148, 19 C.J. 868.)

The author of the annotation on Easements by Implication in 58 A.L.R. 832, states the rule as follows:

While there is some conflict of authority as to whether existing drains, pipes, and sewers may be properly characterized as apparent, within the rule as to apparent or visible easements, the majority of the cases which have considered the question have taken the view that appearance and visibility are not synonymous, and that the fact that the pipe, sewer, or drain may be hidden underground does not negative its character as an apparent condition; at least, where the appliances connected with and leading to it are obvious.

As we are clear that an easement by implication was created under the facts as found by the trial court, it is unnecessary to discuss the question of prescription.

The judgment is affirmed.

Problems

32.15. How do you reconcile the creation of easements by implied grants or implied reservations with the requirement that interests in land must be created by an instrument in writing? The statute of frauds? See American Law of Property §8.36 (Casner ed. 1952).

32.16. Does the plaintiff in the principal case have any right of action over against the plaintiff's grantor, Reynolds, because of this decision? See the discussion on covenants for title, page 781 *supra.*

32.17. The plat of Lakeville shows areas for common recreational use. Will easements be created in the purchasers of lots in the recreational property merely by the recording of the plat? See Drye v. Eagle Rock Ranch Inc., 364 S.W.2d 196 (Tex. 1962).

MAIORIELLO v. ARLOTTA
364 Pa. 557, 73 A.2d 374 (1950)

STEARNE, J.

Plaintiff and defendant are adjoining property owners. 902 South 8th Street, Philadelphia, is owned by plaintiff, while the adjoining premises, 900 South 8th Street, are owned by defendant. Defendant's premises are L-shaped, with the rear lot or yard abutting plaintiff's premises. The west brick wall of plaintiff's kitchen is built on the rear property line. The wall has windows overlooking defendant's lot. Plaintiff's building, occupying the entire lot, consists of two rooms on the first floor. The front room is used as a barber shop. The rear room, with its windows overlooking defendant's yard, constitutes the kitchen. Defendant erected a ten foot high concrete wall, *entirely upon her own land,* three inches from the party line and defendant's kitchen. The effect is to obstruct and block off plaintiff's kitchen windows and prevent the free passage of light and air into same. Plaintiff instituted the present action in equity to restrain defendant from obstructing such light and air. The learned Chancellor decreed that the height of the wall be reduced from ten feet to six feet. This appeal followed.

The facts of the present case are closely analogous to those in Cohen et ux. v. Perrino et ux., 355 Pa. 455, 50 A.2d 348, wherein this Court decided that an owner has the privilege of building, upon his own land, a structure which obstructs the light, air and view of an adjoining owner, even though such structure serves no useful purpose and is erected solely to annoy the adjoining owner and interfere with the use and enjoyment of his land. It was decided that when a wall is on the property line, windows in the wall give no easement of light and air.

The learned court below decided that because title to *both* premises had become vested in the same individual in 1916, and subsequently such owner conveyed the two properties separately, the grantor thereby created an easement of light and air, *by implication because of necessity*. Great reliance was placed upon a decision of this Court in Rennyson's Appeal, 94 Pa. 147, 30 Am. Rep. 777.

In Pennsylvania an easement to light and air cannot be acquired by *prescription:* The doctrine of ancient lights is not part of the law of this Commonwealth.[128] But an easement of light and air may be acquired, as with any other easement, by express grant: Rennyson's Appeal, *supra*.

This court early stated that an easement to light and air may be implied because of necessity: Rennyson's Appeal, *supra*. However, no case has been cited, and our research has revealed none, wherein such an implied easement has been decreed. Chief Justice Lowrie, in Haverstick v. Sipe, supra, said, 33 Pa. at page 371: "We do not say that there can be no possible case in which such an implication can arise. . . ."

But even if an easement of light and air would be *implied* in circumstances which reveal an *absolute necessity*, the finding of the learned Chancellor was that while a small amount of light and air was admitted into the kitchen, it was insufficient for the reasonable comfort, enjoyment and health of the plaintiff. This would constitute but a *partial* obstruction of light and air. But it was testified that a skylight can be placed in the ceiling of the kitchen, which would supply an ample amount of light and air. As it clearly appears that there exists no *absolute necessity*, no implied easement of light and air can be decreed.

Decree reversed and bill dismissed. Each party to pay her own costs.

Note: Spite Fences

In the principal case, the defendant had erected a ten-foot concrete wall three inches from the party line and the defendant's kitchen window. Several states have enacted statutes dealing with the problem of spite fences. For example, Mass. Gen. Laws Ann. ch. 49, §21 provides:

> A fence or other structure in the nature of a fence which unnecessarily exceeds six feet in height and is maliciously erected or maintained for the purpose of annoying the owners or occupants of adjoining property shall be deemed a private nuisance. Any such owner or occupant injured in the comfort or enjoyment of his estate thereby may have an action of tort for damages under chapter two hundred and forty-three.

In the majority of other jurisdictions, even in the absence of statutory authority, equity will enjoin a spite fence (or other structure) as a private

---

128. See Parker & Edgarton v. Foote, page 1069 *infra.*—EDS.

nuisance if it serves no useful purpose. But see Cohen v. Perrino, 355 Pa. 455, 50 A.2d 348 (1947), noted in the principal case, which is a well-researched opinion which adopts the English position in refusing to enjoin a spite fence.

Problems

32.18. Is there anything the title examiner could find on the land records which should suggest the possibility of the creation of an easement by implied grant or implied reservation?

32.19. O contracted to sell to E part of a tract of land O owned. E was permitted to go into possession under the contract of sale. The land O contracted to sell to E had a house and a garage on it. E moved the garage, so that it was located near the boundary of the land retained by O. As there was not enough space for a driveway between the house on the land E was buying and the boundary line of the land retained by O, E used approximately four feet of O's retained land in creating a driveway which would enable E to reach the garage in its new location. O also used the driveway so established by E. O then executed a deed conveying to E the land described in the contract of sale. Can O stop E from using the four feet of the driveway that is on O's land? Can E stop O from using the portion of the driveway that is on E's land? See Hubbard v. Grandquist, 191 Wash. 442, 71 P.2d 410 (1937).

32.20. O is the owner of a tract of land which borders on a public highway on the north. A strip of land 100 feet wide along the northern boundary of O's land is desired by the state for a forestry preserve, and eminent domain proceedings are being contemplated to obtain the land. If such land is taken by the state, O will have no outlet to the public highway. O asks you the following questions:

(a) If the state takes the land under its power of eminent domain, can the state be required to pay the full value of all the land owned by O at the place in question because the balance of the land will be worthless since there will be no access to it from the public highway?

(b) If an easement of way is to be granted to O over the land taken from him in order to prevent the remaining land from becoming worthless, can the state be required to pay for the building of such easement of way?

See State v. Orcutt, 211 Ind. 523, 199 N.E. 595 (1936).[129]

---

129. See generally concerning easements by implied grant and implied reservation Simonton, Ways by Necessity, 25 Colum. L. Rev. 571 (1925), and American Law of Property §§8.31-8.43 (Casner ed. 1952).

C. Creation by Prescription[130]

PARKER & EDGARTON v. FOOTE
19 Wend. 309 (N.Y. Sup. Ct. 1838)

This was an action on the case for stopping lights in a dwelling house, tried at the Oneida circuit in April, 1836, before the Hon. Hiram Denio, then one of the circuit judges.

In 1808 the defendant being the owner of two village lots situated in the village of Clinton, adjoining each other, sold one of them to Joseph Stebbins, who in the same year erected a dwelling house thereon on the line adjoining the other lot with windows in it overlooking the other lot. The defendant also in the same year built an addition to a house which stood on the lot which he retained, leaving a space of about sixteen feet between the house erected by Stebbins and the addition put up by himself. This space was subsequently occupied by the defendant as an alley leading to buildings situate on the rear of his lot, and was so used by him until the year 1832, when (twenty four years after the erection of the house by Stebbins,) he erected a store on the alley, filling up the whole space between the two houses, and consequently stopping the lights in the house erected by Stebbins. At the time of the erection of the store, the plaintiffs were the owners of the lot originally conveyed to Stebbins, by the title derived from him, and were in the actual possession thereof, and brought this action from the stopping of the lights. Stebbins (the original purchaser from the defendant), was a witness for the plaintiffs, and on his cross-examination, testified that he never had any written agreement, deed or writing granting permission to have his windows overlook the defendant's lot, and that nothing was ever said upon the subject. The village of Clinton is built upon a square called Clinton Green, the sides of the square being laid out into village lots, and contained at the time of the trial about 1000 inhabitants. On motion for a nonsuit, the defendant's counsel insisted that there was no evidence of a user authorizing the presumption of a grant as to the windows; that the user in this case was merely permissive, which explained and rebutted all presumption of a grant. That if the user, in the absence of other evidence, authorized the presumption of a grant, still that here the presumption was rebutted by the proof, that in fact there never had been a grant. The circuit judge expressed a doubt whether the modern English doctrine in regard to stopping lights, was applicable to the growing villages of this country, but said he would rule in favor of the plaintiffs, and leave the question to the determination of this court. He also decided that the fact, whether there was or was not

---

130. See generally American Law of Property §§8.44-8.63, 8.68-8.70 (Casner ed. 1952); Restatement of Property ch. 38, topic A (1944). If registered land is involved, the controlling statute may prevent an easement by prescription from being acquired; see Chapter 30.

a grant in writing as to the windows, was not for the jury to determine; that the law presumed it from the user, and it could not be rebutted by proving that none had in truth been executed. After the evidence was closed, the judge declined leaving to the jury the question of presumption of right, and instructed them that the plaintiffs were entitled to their verdict. The jury accordingly found a verdict for the plaintiffs, with $225 damages. The defendant having excepted to the decisions of the judge, now moved for a new trial.

By the Court, BRONSON, J.   The modern doctrine of presuming a right, by grant or otherwise, to easements and incorporeal hereditaments after twenty years of uninterrupted adverse enjoyment, exerts a much wider influence in quieting possession, than the old doctrine of title by prescription, which depended on immemorial usage. The period of 20 years has been adopted by the courts in analogy to the statute limiting an entry into lands; but as the statute does not apply to incorporeal rights, the adverse user is not regarded as a legal bar, but only as a ground for presuming a right, either by grant or in some other form. . . .

To authorize the presumption, the enjoyment of the easement must not only be uninterrupted for the period of 20 years, but it must be adverse, not by leave or favor, but under a claim or assertion of right; and it must be with the knowledge and acquiescence of the owner. . . .[131]

The presumption we are considering is a mixed one of law and fact. The inference that the right is in him who has the enjoyment, so long as nothing appears to the contrary, is a natural one — it is a presumption of fact. But adverse enjoyment, when left to exert only its natural force as mere presumptive evidence, can never conclude the true owner. No length of possession could work such a consequence. Hence the necessity of fixing on some definite period of enjoyment, and making that operate as a presumptive bar to the rightful owner. This part of the rule is wholly artificial; it is a presumption of mere law. In general, questions depending upon mixed presumptions of this description must be submitted to the jury, under proper instructions from the court. . . .

Some of the cases speak of the presumption as conclusive. Bealey v. Shaw, 6 East, 208. Tyler v. Wilkinson, 4 Mason, 397. This can only mean that the presumption is conclusive, where there is no dispute about the facts upon which it depends. It has never been doubted that the inference arising from 20 years enjoyment of incorporeal rights, might be explained and repelled: nor so far as I have observed, has it ever been denied that questions of this description belong to the jury. The presumption we are considering has often been likened to the inference which is indulged that a bond or mortgage has been paid, when no interest has been demanded within 20

---

131.   If the use must not be by the "leave or favor" of the servient owner, how can it be with his or her "acquiescence"? See Dartnell v. Bidwell, page 1074 *infra.*—EDS.

years. Such questions must be submitted to the jury to draw the proper conclusion from all the circumstances of each particular case. . . .

In a plain case, where there is no evidence to repel the presumption arising from 20 years uninterrupted adverse use of an incorporeal right, the judge may very properly instruct the injury that it is their duty to find in favor of the party who has had the enjoyment; but still it is a question for the jury. The judge erred in this case in wholly withdrawing that question from the consideration of the jury. On this ground, if no other, the verdict must be set aside.

The bill of exceptions presents another question which may probably arise on a second trial, and it seems proper therefore to give it some examination.

As neither light, air nor prospect can be the subject of a grant, the proper presumption, if any, to be made in this case, is, that there was some covenant or agreement not to obstruct the light. Cross v. Lewis, 2 Barn. & Cress. 686, per Bayley, J. Moore v. Rawson, 3 Barn. & Cress. 332, per Littledale, J. But this is a matter of little moment. Where it is proper to indulge any presumption for the purpose of quieting possession, the jury may be instructed to make such an one as the nature of the case requires. Eldridge v. Knott, Cowp. 214.

Most of the cases on the subject we have been considering, relate to ways, commons, markets, water-courses, and the like, where the user or enjoyment, if not rightful, has been an immediate and continuing injury to the person against whom the presumption is made. His property has either been invaded, or his beneficial interest in it has been rendered less valuable. The injury has been of such a character that he might have immediate redress by action. But in the case of windows overlooking the land of another, the injury, if any, is merely ideal or imaginary. The light and air which they admit are not the subjects of property beyond the moment of actual occupancy; and for overlooking one's privacy no action can be maintained. The party has no remedy but to build on the adjoining land opposite the offensive window.[132] Chandler v. Thompson, 3 Campb. 80. Cross v. Lewis, 1 Barn. & Cress, 686, per Bayley, J. Upon what principle the courts in England have applied the same rule of presumption to two classes of cases so essentially different in character, I have been unable to discover. If one commits a daily trespass on the land of another, under a claim of right to pass over, or feed his cattle upon it; or divert the water from his mill, or throw it back upon his land or machinery; in these and the like cases, long continued acquiescence affords strong presumptive evidence of right. But in the case of lights, there is no adverse user, nor indeed any use whatever of

132. Does this explain why England will not enjoin spite fences? Arguing for this explanation, see Rumble, Limitations on the Use of Property by Its Owner, 5 Va. L. Rev. 297, 306 (1918).—Eds.

another's property; and no foundation is laid for indulging any presumption against the rightful owner.

Although I am not prepared to adopt the suggestion of Gould, J. in Ingraham v. Hutchinson, 2 Conn. R. 597, that the lights which are protected may be such as project over the land of the adjoining proprietor; yet it is not impossible that there are some considerations connected with the subject which do not distinctly appear in the reported cases. See Knight v. Halsey, 2 Bos. & Pull. 206, per Rooke, J. 1 Phil. Ev. 125.

The learned judges who have laid down this doctrine have not told us upon what principle or analogy in the law it can be maintained. They tell us that a man may build at the extremity of his own land, and that he may lawfully have windows looking out upon the lands of his neighbor. 2 Barn. & Cress. 686. 3 id. 332. The reason why he may lawfully have such windows, must be, because he does his neighbor no wrong; and indeed, so it is adjudged as we have already seen; and yet somehow or other, by the exercise of a lawful right in his own land for 20 years, he acquires a beneficial interest in the land of his neighbor. The original proprietor is still seized of the fee, with the privilege of paying taxes and assessments: but the right to build on the land, without which city and village lots are of little or no value, has been destroyed by a lawful window. How much land can thus be rendered useless to the owner, remains yet to be settled. 2 Barn. & Cress 686. 2 Carr & Payne, 465. I id. 438. Now what is the acquiescence which concludes the owner? No one has trespassed upon his land, or done him a legal injury of any kind. He has submitted to nothing but the exercise of a lawful right on the part of his neighbor. How then has he forfeited the beneficial interest in his property? He has neglected to incur the expense of building a wall 20 or 50 feet high, as the case may be — not for his own benefit, but for the sole purpose of annoying his neighbor. That was his only remedy. A wanton act of this kind, although done in one's own land, is calculated to render a man odious. Indeed, an attempt has been made to sustain an action for erecting such a wall. Mahan v. Brown, 13 Wendell, 261.

There is, I think, no principle upon which the modern English doctrine on the subject of lights can be supported. It is an anomaly in the law. It may do well enough in England; and I see that it has recently been sanctioned with some qualification, by an act of parliament. Stat. 2 & 3, Will. 4, c. 71, Sec. 3. But it cannot be applied in the growing cities and villages of this country, without working the most mischievous consequences. It has never, I think, been deemed a part of our law. 3 Kent's Comm. 466, note (a). Nor do I find that it has been adopted in any of the states. The case of Story v. Odin, 12 Mass. 157, proceeds on an entirely different principle. It cannot be necessary to cite cases to prove that those portions of the common law of England which are hostile to the spirit of our institutions, or which are not adapted to the existing state of things in this country, form no part of our law. And besides, it would be difficult to prove that the rule in question was known to the common law previous to the 19th of April, 1775. Const. N.Y., art. 7, Sec. 13. There were two nisi prius decisions at an earlier day, (Lewis v. Price in 1761, and Dongal v. Wilson in 1763,) but the doctrine was not sanctioned in Westminster Hall until 1786, when the case of Darwin v. Upton was decided by the K.B. 2 Saund. 175, note (2). This was clearly a departure from the old law. Bury v. Pope, Cro. Eliz. 118.

There is one peculiar feature in the case at bar. It appears affirmatively that there never was any grant, writing or agreement about the use of the lights. A grant may under certain circumstances be presumed, although, as Lord Mansfield once said, the court does not really think a grant has been made. Eldridge v. Knott, Cowp. 214. But it remains to be decided that a right by grant or otherwise can be presumed when it plainly appears that it never existed. If this had been the case of a way, common, or the like, and there had actually been an uninterrupted adverse user for 20 years under a claim of right, to which the defendant had submitted, I do not intend to say that proof that no grant was in fact made would have overturned the action. It will be time enough to decide that question when it shall be presented. But in this case the evidence of Stebbins, who built the house, in connection with the other facts which appeared on the trial, proved most satisfactorily that the windows were never enjoyed under a claim of right, but only as a matter of favor. If there was any thing to leave to the jury, they could not have hesitated a moment about their verdict. But I think the plaintiffs should have been nonsuited.

The Chief Justice concurred on both points.

Cowen, J., only concurred in the opinion that the question of presumption of a grant should have been submitted to the jury.

New trial granted.

Note: The Fictional Lost Grant[133]

As the principal case shows, historically the claim of an easement by prescription rested upon the fiction of a lost grant. Is this true of a claim of title by adverse possession? Consider the following:

> Florida has aligned herself with the more contemporary authorities whose trend is to abandon the theory that prescriptive rights are based on the presumption of a prior grant and to treat the acquisition of such prescriptive rights as having been acquired by methods substantially similar to those by which title is acquired by adverse possession. Downing v. Bird, Fla. 1958, 100 So. 2d 57.
>
> In order to establish an easement by prescription, a claimant must prove actual, continuous, uninterrupted use for a period of twenty years. In acquisi-

133. See Simonton, Fictional Lost Grant in Prescription, 35 W. Va. L.Q. 46 (1928); Cook, Legal Analysis in the Law of Prescriptive Easements, 15 S. Cal. L. Rev. 44 (1941); American Law of Property §§8.44-8.52 (Casner ed. 1952).

tion of such an easement the use must be adverse under claim of right and must either be with the knowledge of the owner or by a use so open, notorious, visible, and uninterrupted that knowledge of the use by an adverse claimant is imputed to the owner. Moreover, the use must be inconsistent with the owner's use and enjoyment of his lands and also must not be a permissive use; for the use is required to be such that the owner has a right to a legal remedy to stop it. Downing v. Bird, *supra,* and J. C. Vereen & Sons, Inc. v. Houser, 123 Fla. 641, 167 So. 45 (1936).

There is a distinction between acquiring of title by adverse possession and the acquiring of a prescriptive right. In the former, title must be through possession. In the latter, a prescriptive right is through the use of the privilege without actual possession. In acquisition of the title by adverse possession, the possession must be exclusive, while in acquisition of a prescriptive right, the use may be in common with the owner or the public. Downing v. Bird, *supra.*

In either prescription or adverse possession, the use or possession is presumed to be in subordination to the title and thus is presumed to be permissive. However, the presumption of permissive use of possession is not conclusive and is ineffectual in the face of facts which cause its dissipation.[134]

DARTNELL v. BIDWELL
115 Me. 227, 98 A. 743 (1916)

SAVAGE, C.J. Trespass quare clausum. In defense, it was contended that the defendant had a right of way over the plaintiff's premises, and that the acts complained of, or some of them, at least, were done in making necessary and reasonable repairs of the way. A portion of the way was acquired by grant. The remainder was claimed by prescription. Whether she had such a prescriptive right was contested. The verdict was for the defendant. The plaintiff brings the case here on exceptions to refusals to give requested instructions, and on a motion for a new trial.

One of the issues in the case, and perhaps one decisive of the case, is whether the prescriptive easement claimed by the defendant was interrupted by the plaintiff while it was yet inchoate. The presiding justice was requested to instruct the jury that:

> The defendant must not only prove the use of the way claimed by prescription, for 20 years, but that it was continued, uninterrupted, and adverse; that is, under a claim of right, with the knowledge and acquiescense of the owner, and not as a matter of favor or courtesy on his part.

This language seems to have been taken from the opinion in Sargent v. Ballard, 9 Pick. (Mass.) 251. The presiding justice declined to give this instruction. In declining to do so he said:

"It is true that the use must be for 20 years, that it must be continued,

134.   Hunt Land Holding Co. v. Schramm, 121 So. 2d 697, 700 (Fla. 1960).

uninterrupted, and adverse, under a claim of right, but it need not be under an acquiescence of the owner."

The plaintiff excepted. While the easement was still inchoate as claimed by the plaintiff, the plaintiff wrote a letter to the defendant, in which she said:

> You are hereby notified that that portion of my land . . . which you have recently plowed and made into a road is across my private property. . . . No person has or ever had any right to pass in or over this field, and you are liable to me in damages for trespass. . . . I hereby notify you to at once go back to the original location and the original cartroad width as given in deed to Hussey to Myers in 1856. . . . I hereby forbid you or any one in your behalf to pass in or travel over any portion of my land whatsoever and especially that portion which you have unlawfully and without any right made into a road, and you are notified to hereafter travel only in the single cartroad. . . .

This letter related to the prescriptive way in question. The plaintiff at the trial contended that this letter was in interruption of the defendant's inchoate easement, and requested an instruction to that effect. A third request differently phrased was to the same effect. These requests were refused, and the plaintiff excepted. All the exceptions so far may be considered together.

A prescriptive easement is created only by a continuous use for at least 20 years under a claim of right adverse to the owner, with his knowledge and acquiescence, or by a use so open, notorious, visible, and uninterrupted that knowledge and acquiescence will be presumed. Each of the elements is essential and each is open to contradiction. The existence of all the elements for the requisite period creates a right conclusive against attack. Rollins v. Blackden, 112 Me. 459, 92 Atl. 521, and cases cited. The present controversy concerns the element of acquiescence, and the question is whether the plaintiff's acquiescence was interrupted in law by the letter from which we have quoted. It is not claimed that the defendant's use was interrupted by it.

Acquiescence is used in its ordinary sense. It does not mean license or permission in the active sense. It means passive assent, or submission. It means quiescence. It is consent by silence. Pierce's Adm'r v. Pierce, 66 Vt. 369, 29 Atl. 364; Cass County Commissioners v. Plotner, 149 Ind. 116, 48 N.E. 635; Scott v. Jackson, 89 Cal. 258, 26 Pac. 898. See Webster's Dictionary, tit. "Acquiescence." Proof of acquiescence by the owner is held essential by all authorities. It raises the presumption of a grant. Rollins v. Blackden, *supra.* Where the adverse use has continued for 20 years without interruption or denial on the part of the owner, and with his knowledge, his acquiescence is conclusively presumed. It was error then to rule that proof of acquiescence was unnecessary.

The distinction between the creation of an easement by adverse use and the gaining of a title to land by adverse possession is not always borne in mind. We said in Rollins v. Blackden, *supra,* that:

In the matter of acquiescence, the creation of a prescriptive easement logically differs from the acquiescence of a title to real estate by adverse possession. In the former the possession continues in the owner of the servient estate, and the prescriptive right arises out of adverse use. In the latter, the owner is ousted from possession, and the right or title arises out of adverse possession; and nothing short of making entry, or legal action, will break the continuity of possession.

See Workman v. Curran, 89 Pa. 226.

If the case at bar had been one of claimed adverse possession, the request would have been erroneous, and the ruling would have been right.

Anything which disproves acquiescence rebuts the presumption of a grant. Smith v. Miller, 11 Gray (Mass.) 145. It interrupts the inchoate easement. So far there is no dispute. The question now is: In what manner may acquiescence be disproved? And upon the question the authorities are divided. Upon one side is the leading case of Powell v. Bagg, 8 Gray (Mass.) 441, 69 Am. Dec. 262, in which it was said that if the owner of the land before the lapse of 20 years, "by a verbal act upon the premises in which the easement is claimed, resists the exercise, . . . and denies its existence, . . . his acquiescence . . . is disproved, and the essential elements of a title . . . by adverse use are shown not to exist." In C. & N.W. Ry. Co. v. Hoag, 90 Ill. 339, which was a case where the owner orally remonstrated against the use, the court approved the doctrine of Powell v. Bagg, and went further, and held that it was not material where the remonstrance was made, whether on or off the land. The doctrine that denials and remonstrances, on or off the land are sufficient to rebut acquiescence, and work an interruption is supported by Workman v. Curran, *supra.* . . .

On the other hand, there are courts which hold that mere denials of the right, complaints, remonstrances, or prohibitions of user, unaccompanied by physical interference to some degree, will not prevent the acquisition of a right by prescription. The leading case, perhaps, on this side is Lehigh Valley R.R. Co. v. McFarlan, 43 N.J. Law, 605. See other cases referred to in Rollins v. Blackden, supra. In the New Jersey case, the court seemed to follow by analogy the doctrine of adverse possession, and did not mark the distinction, which we have pointed out, between creating an easement and acquiring title by adverse possession.

When we consider what acquiescence means, and that nonacquiescence defeats an easement, but alone does not defeat title by adverse possession, we are persuaded that the doctrine in the former class of cases is founded upon the better reason. If acquiescence is consent by silence, to break the silence by denials and remonstrances ought to afford evidence of nonacquiescence, rebutting the presumption of a grant. In Rollins v. Blackden, *supra,* we held that the grant of an easement to A. effectually interrupted the inchoate easement to B. because it was an act of the strongest potency to rebut the presumption of acquiescence. In that aspect, there was no physical interruption nor disturbance. In the case at bar, we think that the letter of the plaintiff to the defendant expressly denying the latter's right, protesting its present, and forbidding its future, exercise, ought, in reason, to be held sufficient evidence of the plaintiff's nonacquiescence, and of an interruption of the defendant's inchoate easement. And we do hold it to be such. In fact, the statute (R.S. c.107, §12) provides expressly that an easement may be interrupted by a notice in writing served and recorded. That the notice should be served or delivered is necessary to bring knowledge of the interruption home to the claimant. Otherwise it is not notice to him. The provision for recording is to perpetuate the evidence of the interruption and give notice to third parties. But we think the statutory method is not exclusive. A notice in writing, served or delivered, but not recorded, is sufficient if proved. The plaintiff's requested instructions should have been given. . . .

ROMANS v. NADLER
217 Minn. 174, 14 N.W.2d 482 (1944)

Action in the district court for Ramsey county for the establishment of a boundary line between plaintiffs' and defendants' lots and for certain other relief. From a judgment for plaintiffs entered pursuant to findings, Albin S. Pearson, Judge, defendants appealed. Reversed with directions.

PETERSON, J. The parties are the record owners of adjoining residential properties in the city of St. Paul. Plaintiffs' lot is number 2 and defendants', which lies westerly thereof, is number 3 in a certain block. Defendants appeal from the judgment (1) adjudging plaintiffs the owners "by prescription" of three portions of lot 3 presently to be mentioned and of an easement to go upon lot 3 or so much thereof as is reasonably necessary and at such times as may be reasonably necessary for the purpose of placing ladders and other equipment thereon in connection with the putting on and taking off of screens and storm windows and of cleaning, painting, and repairing on the west side of plaintiffs' house; (2) enjoining defendants from erecting any fence or structure interfering with plaintiff's rights as established by the judgment; (3) directing defendants to remove a wire fence erected by them on lot 3 along the eastern boundary thereof under the eaves of plaintiffs' house; and (4) fixing and establishing the boundary line between the two properties.

Plaintiff Edgar D. Romans' father became the owner of lot 2 in 1898, and ever since that date plaintiffs and their predecessors in title have occupied and used the premises. Nathan Nadler became the owner of lot 3 in 1921, and ever since that time he and defendants as his successors in title have occupied and used the premises. Plaintiffs' house is close to the west line of lot 2. Their garage encroaches on lot 3. Defendants' house is a considerable distance from the line between the lots.

The first portion of lot 3 adjudged to belong to plaintiffs "by prescription" is a strip underneath the eaves of the house on lot 2. It is 49 feet long and .75 feet wide on the north and 0.9 feet wide on the south side. The evidence shows that ever since 1898 the eaves and gutters of plaintiffs' house have extended over the strip in question. According to plaintiffs' evidence, the gutters are of ample size to take care of water draining from the roof and do not drip "except under a very severe cloudburst or something of that sort which any gutter would drip over"; and that, if they get wet on the outside, they drip. There was no evidence that the gutters could or did become wet on the outside or that there was any dripping, except that since 1939, according to the testimony of one of the defendants, the gutters at times have discharged water on the wire fence. During all the time in question defendants have been in actual physical possession of the strip in question.

The second strip extends from the south side of the house to a point 1.85 feet west of the west line of lot 2 and 13 feet north on the alley in the rear. It is 1.85 feet wide on the north and 2.10 feet wide on the south. The evidence shows that it was fenced and occupied and has been used as part of lot 2 ever since 1924, if not prior to that time. The eaves and gutters of the garage project 2.20 feet over the south 6.8 feet of this strip.

The third strip is 13 feet long and 2.20 feet wide on the north and 2.43 feet on the south and extends from the alley to the southerly end of the fence. All of it lies underneath the eaves and gutters of the garage. The gutters have dripped on the entire area underneath during a period in excess of 15 years.

The evidence with respect to the easement is rather sketchy. It tends to show that plaintiff Edgar D. Romans and his father used lot 3 while putting on and taking off screens and storm windows once every six months. During the period from 1898 to 1941, the time of trial, the house was painted six times — about once in every six or seven years — and each time ladders used by the painters were set up on lot 3. The evidence shows that no express permission was given by defendants or their grantors for such entries. Plaintiff Edgar D. Romans testified that he did not think any permission was necessary, because most of the time he thought he was on his own property (lot 2) and he took for granted that he did not need permission to enter on lot 3 for the purposes mentioned, because it never occurred to him that anybody would be foolish enough to object — his words were that "anybody would object to such a foolish thing"; and because, since he never had any trouble with anybody, he would not think of asking defendants any more than he would his neighbors on the east side, some people by the name of Hartman.

The trial court established the line between lots 2 and 3 so as to include as belonging to plaintiffs all areas under the eaves and gutters of the house and the garage and the area fenced and occupied as part of lot 2. It held in effect that the projection of plaintiffs' eaves and gutters and the dripping therefrom constituted adverse possession of the parts of lot 3 underneath, which ripened into title because of its continuance for over 15 years. It also held that the uses of lot 3 for which it adjudged an easement in favor of plaintiffs had all the essentials necessary to give rise to prescriptive rights. On this appeal, the correctness of the decision below in the respects mentioned is challenged.

1. "Prescription" is the term usually applied to incorporeal hereditaments; "adverse possession" to lands. Because of the close connection between them, the terms are often used interchangeably. We construe the word prescription, where the findings and judgment refer to title by prescription, to mean adverse possession.

Adverse possession of real property ripens into title in the adverse possessor or disseizor where it continues for the period allowed for the recovery of real estate, which is 15 years, under Minn. St. 1941, Sec. 541.02 (Mason St. 1927, Sec. 9187). There are five essentials of adverse possession. It must be hostile and under a claim of right, actual, open, continuous, and exclusive. It must appear from the nature and circumstances of the possession that it is hostile and with intention to claim adversely, in order that the owner may be informed of it and that he may determine whether the acts consist of mere trespass or assertion of adverse title, lest he be misled into acquiescence in what he might reasonably suppose to be a mere trespass, when he would not acquiesce in the assertion of rights adverse to his title. It must be continuous, because, upon any cessation or interruption, the possession, in contemplation of law, is again in the holder of the legal title. The disseizor must not only claim adversely, but must make that fact known; or, as it is sometimes said, he must keep his flag flying.

Occasional and sporadic trespasses for temporary purposes, because they do not indicate permanent occupation and appropriation of land, do not satisfy the requirements of hostility and continuity, and do not constitute adverse possession, even where they continue throughout the statutory period. This is especially true where, as here, there is nothing about each separate trespass to indicate that it is anything but a trespass, much less an assertion of adverse right likely to be persisted in.

By the application of these rules to the facts of the case, plaintiffs acquired title by adverse possession to those parts of defendants' lot which they enclosed with the fence and occupied, and which they occupied and possessed by the encroachment of the garage. As to these, the possession was hostile and under claim of right, actual, open, continuous, and exclusive. But, they did not acquire any title to the parts under the eaves and gutters of the house and the garage from the end of the fence to the alley, because those parts were in the actual possession of defendants. Where property is in the actual possession of the owner, use by an adjoining owner for projection of the eaves of his building and for dripping is no basis for a claim of title by adverse possession. The entries on the part under the eaves of the house to put on and take off storm windows and screens twice a year and to paint about once in six years were occasional and sporadic only, and no title by adverse possession could be based thereon.

2. Statutes of limitation do not by their terms apply to actions involving incorporeal hereditaments such as easements. An easement by prescription rests upon the fiction of a lost grant. By analogy to title by adverse possession, an adverse user of an easement for the statutory period is held to be evidence of the prescriptive right. Subject only to such differences as are necessarily inherent in the application of the rules in such cases, the same rules of adverse user apply in cases of easements by prescription as in those of title by adverse possession. Because of such inherent differences, the same continuity of user is not required in cases of prescriptive easements as in those of title by adverse possession. In cases of easements, the requirement of continuity depends upon the nature and character of the right claimed. It is sometimes said that there must be such continuity of user as the right claimed permits. This statement of the rule, like the one governing cases of title by adverse possession, does not mean that the right can be acquired by occasional and sporadic acts for temporary purposes. If the rules of adverse user are to be maintained, there must be limits upon the extent to which the requirement of continuity of user can be relaxed. Otherwise, the rules for all practical purposes would be done. That limit is reached where, as here, the use is only occasional and sporadic. "On the other hand, an occasional user for a particular purpose has been held not sufficient to sustain the right." 17 Am. Jur., Easements, Sec. 60. The rule is supported by numerous authorities.

The projection of the eaves and gutters of the house and of the garage and the dripping (such as it was) were of such a character as to satisfy the rules of adverse user, and consequently as to those portions plaintiffs acquired by prescription an easement in defendants' land to have the eaves and gutters project and to have the gutters drip.

The periodical entries for putting on and taking off storm windows and screens and painting were occasional trespasses for the purposes mentioned, and consequently could not give rise to any prescriptive rights. . . . After all, cases of this kind should be viewed with common sense. True, an owner may sue for any trivial trespass, but not every owner wants to stand guard over his neighbors and quarrel about trivialities. It is a well-known fact that many thousands of homeowners have no boundary fences and that adjoining owners occasionally trespass on their neighbors' lands in cutting grass, trimming hedges, and the like. Such harmless trespasses are committed upon the well-founded assumption that ordinarily a neighbor will acquiesce in and consent to them. Such forbearances are expected of neighbors. They make for good relations between them. As said of the acts referred to in the *Bolton* case, such trespasses are not done with any intention of acquiring adverse rights and are acquiesced in by the owner without intending that such rights should be established. If such treapasses should be held to constitute a basis for prescriptive rights, every adjoining landowner in the case mentioned would acquire, after 15 years, an easement in his neighbors' lands to the extent of such trespasses. This shows the absurdity of allowing an easement in such cases. Under such circumstances, something more than such occasional uses of land should be required to give rise to prescriptive rights. The trespasser should be required to show by some additional acts that the entry is hostile and under claim of right, and thus run up his flag of hostile claim, so as to warn the owner that, if he acquiesces, adverse rights will be established against him. The case of Dunbar v. O'Brien, 117 Neb. 245, 220 N.W. 278, is cited contra. In that case the use was continuous, for the court found that the plaintiff there "continuously" trespassed on defendant's land for the purpose of painting the former's house, washing windows, and making necessary repairs. Here, there was no continuity of use; the trespasses were sporadic and occasional. Insofar as the cited case announces a different rule than here announced, we refuse to follow it. . . .

Our conclusion is that the judgment is correct insofar as it holds that plaintiffs acquired title by adverse possession to the parts of defendants' lot enclosed by the fence and upon which the garage encroaches, and that it is erroneous insofar as it holds that plaintiffs acquired title to any other part of defendants' land and an easement therein for the purpose of entering with ladders and other equipment for the purpose of putting on and removing storm windows and screens and painting the plaintiffs' house. Plaintiffs are entitled, however, to easements in defendants' land to have the eaves and gutters of the house and garage project and to drip. The line between the two lots should be run so as to give plaintiffs only those parts of defendants' lot to which we hold they have acquired title by adverse possession. Apparently the distances given in the judgment do not correspond with those in the findings. Discrepancies, if any, can be corrected upon the going down of the remittitur. It was error to direct defendants to remove the fence, which they erected. The judgment should be amended in accordance with the views expressed in the opinion.

Reversed with directions to amend the judgment in accordance with the views expressed in the opinion.

GALLAGHER, J. (dissenting).

Problems

32.21. If you are the attorney for a purchaser of land, how can you determine whether the land your client is buying is subject to any easements created by prescription?

32.22. O brought suit seeking to enjoin E, an upper riparian owner, in the operation of a canning plant, from placing tomato peelings, rotten tomatoes, and other debris into a non-navigable stream which flowed through O's property. O also sought damages, alleging that the refuse materials accumulated along the banks of the stream, causing obnoxious odors and stenches and making the stream unfit for human use. E admits all of the above but alleges that E has continuously been doing this for more than twenty years during the canning season (from June 1 to November 1) and thus E has acquired a prescriptive right to do all of the above-mentioned acts. O purchased the land in December, when the canning plant was not in operation. What decision? Anneberg v. Kurtz, 197 Ga. 188, 28 S.E.2d 769 (1944).

32.23.   A and B were the owners of adjoining tracts of land. In 1940 they caused a cinder driveway to be laid out between their two properties, and each built a garage which could be reached by this driveway. In 1941 A and B agreed to pave the driveway, and each paid for one-half of the cost. In 1945, A sold A's land to C and B sold B's land to D. C and D continued to use the driveway in common. D spent considerable money in landscaping, which would have to be materially altered at considerable expense if a driveway had to be built by D entirely on D's land. In 1984, C and D form a dislike for each other and C builds another driveway to C's garage and builds a fence down the middle of the original driveway, which fence is located exactly on the boundary line of C's property. Assume that the local statute of limitations requires 20 years to gain a prescriptive right to an easement. D seeks an injunction to compel the removal of the fence so that D can go on using the driveway to reach D's garage. Is D entitled to the injunction? See Lang v. Dupuis, 382 Ill. 101, 46 N.E.2d 21 (1943). See also American Law of Property §§8.57-8.59 (Casner ed. 1952).

32.24.   A and B were the owners of adjoining tracts of land. A sidewalk extended the length of A's lot on the side adjacent to B's lot. This sidewalk was located entirely on A's land. B used the sidewalk for 10 years as a means of ingress and egress. B then sold B's land to C, no mention being made of the sidewalk. C used the sidewalk for 15 years in the manner B had used it. Assuming that the local statute of limitations requires 20 years to gain a prescriptive right to an easement and assuming the use of the sidewalk by both B and C was adverse to A, has C a prescriptive right to an easement of way over the sidewalk? See Stewart v. Hunt, 303 Mich. 161, 5 N.W.2d 737 (1942). See also American Law of Property §§8.57-8.59 (Casner ed. 1952).

32.25.   A in 1947 was the owner in fee simple of Blackacre. In that year A died, and under the terms of A's will, Blackacre was devised to "B for life, remainder to C in fee simple." In 1958, D, the owner of the land adjoining Blackacre, laid a sewer pipe from D's house to the main sewer, and in so doing laid part of the pipe across a corner of Blackacre. In 1965, C died and C's remainder interest in Blackacre descended to C's son, S, who was then 15 years of age. B died in 1966. In 1984, S discovers for the first time that the sewer pipe from D's house is laid across a corner of Blackacre and seeks an injunction to compel the removal of the pipe. Assume the local statute of limitations requires 20 years to gain a prescriptive right to an easement. Is S entitled to the injunction? If S had made his discovery in 1987, would the result be any different? See Reimer v. Stuber, 20 Pa. 458 (1853). See also American Law of Property §§8.60-8.61 (Casner ed. 1952).

32.26.   The Orienta Beach Club prohibited the inhabitants of Orienta

Point from using a parcel of land belonging to the beach club for access to Long Island South for swimming and boating purposes. An action is brought by some inhabitants of Orienta Point to enjoin the beach club from interfering with such use of the land by the two inhabitants. It is alleged that for 50 years it has been the custom of the town inhabitants to use the land in question for swimming and boating and that therefore a customary right in the nature of an easement exists. Should the injunction issue? See Gillies v. Orienta Beach Club, 159 Misc. 675, 289 N.Y.S. 733 (1935). See also American Law of Property §9.57 (Casner ed. 1952).

D. Change in Character or Amount of Use

CRIMMINS v. GOULD
149 Cal. App. 2d 383, 308 P.2d 786 (1957)

BRAY, J.

Plaintiff sued in declaratory and injunctive primarily to determine that defendants have no rights in a certain roadway. Defendants cross-complained for like relief primarily to establish their rights in said roadway. From a judgment in favor of plaintiff and against defendants and cross-complainants, the latter appeal.

Questions Presented.

1. Did "McCormick Lane" become a public way?
2. Was the easement in said lane extinguished by misuse?
3. Should lesser relief have been granted plaintiff?
. 4. Amendment of complaint to conform to the proof.
5. Was the court's determination unconstitutional?

Evidence.

In 1929 McCormick owned a tract of land in Atherton. It was bounded on the north by Watkins Avenue and on the south by Fair Oaks Lane. That year McCormick built McCormick Lane to give access to Fair Oaks Lane. The lane runs northerly from Fair Oaks Lane to the junction of the southerly lines of parcels 1 and 2. Adjoining parcel 1 on the west is parcel 2. Only the southeasterly point of parcel 2 touches McCormick Lane. At the time the lane was first constructed parcel 1 as well as the land through which the lane ran was owned by McCormick. Parcel 2 never was. The McCormick land other than parcel 1 has been subdivided and is now owned by Hecker, Hans, Crimmins, Gould and Baxter. Express rights of way over McCormick Lane were deeded to all of these owners except Baxter who was given an oral right of way. In 1931 McCormick deeded the lane to Crimmins in fee. Crimmins later deeded the Crimmins property and the lane to plaintiff, his wife.

The map shows McCormick Lane as originally maintained, and the extension thereof and Burns Avenue as constructed by defendants.

The lane is paved, with a red rock fill entrance to parcels 1 and 2. Both parcels 1 and 2 now belong to defendants Walton and Emelia Gould. In 1926 McCormick conveyed parcel 1 to a predecessor of the Goulds together with "an easement of Right of Way for ingress and egress," such easement to commence five years thereafter.

At the time of trial, the Goulds, of record, appeared to own two portions of the McCormick property—the former Gibbs place with its easement over McCormick Lane, and parcel 1, which had an easement of ingress and egress to and from McCormick Lane. In addition they now own parcel 2. In 1954 they subdivided parcels 1 and 2 into 29 residential lots. Six of these are wholly within parcel 1 and two other lots lie substantially within it. By a roadway dedicated to the public and accepted by the town, defendants extended McCormick Lane northerly across parcel 1 to its junction with Watkins Avenue. They also constructed "Burns Avenue," a public road, across parcel 2 connecting it to the extension of McCormick Lane on parcel 1.

At the entrance to McCormick Lane on Fair Oaks Avenue there has been continuously posted a sign reading "McCormick Lane." At one time a sign stated "Not a Through Street" or "Dead End Street." No other signs have been posted there. About 1925, parcels 1 and 2 were planted with pear and walnut trees. During the early years the orchard and the lane were separated by a wire fence which the orchardist removed in 1941. There has been no obstruction since. From 1931 through 1954 the orchard was operated by

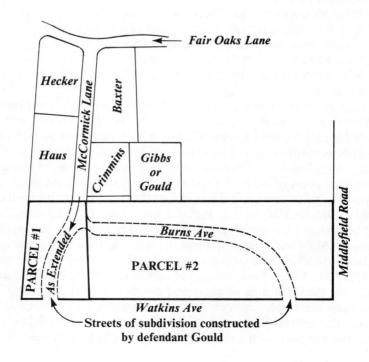

tenants who used the lane as a means of ingress and egress in their orchard operations. The peak of the use was in harvesting season when for about three and a half days fruit pickers and trucks hauling fruit used the lane. Otherwise the use by the orchardists was an average of at least once a week. Some fruit went out over Watkins Avenue.

Sometime between 1940 and 1942 Crimmins quarreled with an orchardist and put cardboard signs at the orchard end of the lane and at a place about midpoint on the lane, saying that it was a private road, permission to pass revocable. The signs were directed at the orchardist and were torn down and thrown away. None have been posted since, nor has there ever been any barricade at the Fair Oaks Lane entrance. Prior to 1948 no taxes were assessed against the lane. Since 1948 taxes for plaintiff's residence and the lane have been assessed together to plaintiff.

In 1935 Mr. Crimmins offered to deed the lane to Atherton but the offer was refused unless the road was rebuilt to specifications. Instead Crimmins resurfaced the road, the cost being borne by then property owners, McCormick, Gibbs' predecessor, Baxter and Crimmins. The other property owners including the owner of parcel 1 refused to pay. Thereafter the road was maintained solely at the expense of the four above mentioned property owners.

The lane was used by others not connected with the properties surrounding the lane. The Atherton police patrolled it occasionally. Sightseers and those who thought the lane was a public street would drive in and out. Groups would drive to the orchard end for a picnic or to park. "Necking" couples drove in. A few cars were abandoned on the road. Public utilities were granted rights of way in the lane. In 1952 sanitary district inspectors and workers used it in connection with the installation of a sewer outfall system across the parcels. About twenty years ago at its junction with Fair Oaks Lane Atherton installed guard rails on each side of the lane, and has maintained them since. At Mr. Crimmins' request in 1935, the town installed an electric street light at midpoint in the lane. Ever since the town has supplied the current and upkeep of the light. Chuckholes in the lane were repaired from time to time by the town just as any other street would be repaired. In 1946 Mr. Crimmins in a letter to defendants' predecessor claimed ownership of the lane and objected to the manner in which the tenant farmer was using the lane and several discussions were had between them in which Crimmins disputed the use of the lane. Crimmins notified defendants' predecessors that he was opposed to the proposed subdivision extending McCormick Lane into it. On learning of the new subdivision Crimmins notified defendants that the lane was not to be connected to the subdivision. Since the connection was made in 1954 the use of the lane and the wear and tear thereon has greatly increased.

On this evidence, the court found that the lane had never become a public way; that the lane was subject to an easement "as a private means of ingress and egress for Parcel 1"; that no easement or right of way in or over the lane ever existed as to parcel 2; that by defendants' acts in subdividing parcel 2 and in laying out public roads on parcels 1 and 2 connecting McCormick Lane with Watkins Avenue the burden on the lane has been substantially increased by the public and by occupants of parcel 2 and their invitees, causing substantial damage to plaintiff. The burden of maintenance on McCormick Lane was slight as compared to what it will be; that the acts of defendants are incompatible with the nature and exercise of the servitude appurtenant to parcel 1 granted in 1926 over the lane; it is impossible to use the easement granted in 1926 as it was intended to be used or to segregate the use of the lane by the owners of parcel 1 or 2, from its use by the general public; that because of defendants' acts they no longer have any right to use, occupy or pass over the lane. The court concluded that defendants had not acquired as appurtenant to parcel 2 any easement or right of way; that the easement appurtenant to parcel 1 has been extinguished and thereupon enjoined defendants from using it.

    1.   Public Way.

The foregoing recital shows that the lane never became a public way. Such use of it as was made by the public was permissive only. The small amount of improvement and repair made by the town did not constitute an adverse use or an acceptance by the town of the lane as a public way. The only offer of it as such was rejected by the town. There are only two methods by which private property may become a public way other than by purchase: (1) By an offer of dedication by the owner and a formal acceptance by a public authority or long continued use by the public itself. This did not exist here. (2) Where no express offer of dedication is made by the owner, by long continued adverse use by the public. In such event offer of dedication by the owner is presumed. The evidence showed no such situation here. See Union Transp. Co. v. Sacramento County, 42 Cal. 2d 235, 240, 267 P.2d 10, for discussion of these two methods.

Defendants contend that the use by the public of McCormick Lane was such as to give rise to the presumption mentioned in Walter G. Brix, Inc. v. Brown, 145 Cal. App. 2d—, 302 P.2d 74, 75: ". . . there is a general presumption that a use by other than the owner is adverse and not permissive . . ." The sporadic use by the public of McCormick Lane is not the type of use required. . . . In our case, if the presumption applies, it was overcome by the positive showing that the comparatively little use made of the lane by the public was a permissive one. . . .

    2.   Extinguishment of Easement.

The evidence clearly shows that parcel 2 neither by grant nor prescription acquired any right to use McCormick Lane. The small use of it made by the owners or occupants of parcel 2 over the years until recently was not an adverse one. The most serious question in the case is whether the easement of ingress and egress to and from the lane appurtenant to parcel 1 was lost by the attempted change in use. Plaintiff concedes that the change from orchard to residential estates did not extinguish the easement. It is the acts of defendants in extending McCormick Lane to Watkins Avenue dedicating it as a public street, and in allowing the owners of parcel 2 to connect with McCormick Lane as extended, a public street, which runs across parcel 2 and connects with Watkins Avenue, which plaintiff claims extinguished the easement of parcel 1. Defendants thereby attempted to use the easement appurtenant to parcel 1 for the benefit of all owners in parcel 2 and the public generally. This caused the court to declare the easement abandoned by misuse.

Civil Code, §811, subdivision 3, provides that a servitude is extinguished by "the performance of any act upon either tenement, by the owner of the servitude, or with his assent, which is incompatible with its nature or exercise; . . ." Lux v. Haggan, 1886, 69 Cal. 255, 4 P. 919, 10 P. 674, said the section was a statutory declaration of the well settled rule "that if the owner of a dominant estate does acts thereon which permanently prevent his enjoying an easement, the same is extinguished, if he authorizes the owner of the servient estate to do upon the same that which prevents the dominant estate from any longer enjoying the easement, the effect will be to extinguish it." 69 Cal. at pages 292-293 . . .

In cases involving extraordinary or excessive use, all parties in the instant case agree that the servient owner is entitled to an injunction. See De la Cuesta v. Bazzi, 1941, 47 Cal. App. 2d 661, 118 P.2d 909; Watson v. Heger, 1941, 48 Cal. App. 2d 417, 120 P.2d 153.

However, here the question is not the propriety of an injunction but rather the propriety of an extinguishment. There do not seem to be any California cases on extinguishment for excessive use by non-dominant property where the right given to the dominent estate was by grant. But there are a number of out-of-state cases. The general rule is that misuse or excessive use is not sufficient for abandonment or forfeiture, but an injunction is the proper remedy. (16 A.L.R.2d 610.) But where the burden of the servient estate is increased through changes in the dominant estate which increase the use and subject it to use of non-dominant property, a forfeiture will be justified if the unauthorized use may not be severed and prohibited. (16 A.L.R.2d 613.) See also Penn Bowling Recreation Center v. Hot Shoppes, 1949, 86 U.S. App. D.C. 58, 179, 16 A.L.R.2d [, 179] 602 F.2d 64.

The situation here is different than that in Tarpey v. Lynch, 155 Cal. 407, 101 P. 10. There a water ditch easement appurtenant to 80 acres of land under single ownership was held to accrue to each portion thereof divided among plural ownerships. Thus in our case the easement of ingress and egress appurtenant to parcel 1, although acquired at a time of single ownership of that parcel, would be extended to the subdivided portions of that parcel. But not content with that, defendants here attempted to extend it to all parts of parcel 2 which had no easement therein and also attempted to extend it to two public streets. It is not a question of merely "some increase in burden" upon a servient tenement by permitting an easement appurtenant to attach to each of the parts into which a dominant tenement may be subdivided, which comment (b) to section 488, Restatement of Property, and a number of cases cited by defendants, state is permissible. Rather it is one of the performance of acts by the owner of the servitude "which is incompatible with its nature or exercise." Civ. Code, §811, subd. 3.

The California cases holding that injunctive relief is a proper remedy of the servient owner for authorized excessive uses of an easement do not hold that it is the exclusive remedy. As hereafter pointed out an injunction could not grant plaintiff real relief where defendants have attempted to tie two public streets into their easement.

The fact that the cases which to date have interpreted section 811, subdivision 3, were ones not of misuse or overuse of an easement but were ones where a change in conditions of either the dominant or servient estates made the easement impossible of use, does not mean that the application of the section is limited to such situations. Certainly here the situation which defendants deliberately brought about is "incompatible with" the "nature or exercise" of the easement. Defendants quote 28 C.J.S., Easements, §62, p. 729:

> The right to an easement is not lost by using it in an unauthorized manner or to an unauthorized extent, *unless it is impossible to sever the increased burden so as to preserve to the owner of the dominant tenement that to which he is entitled, and yet impose on the servient tenement only that burden which was originally imposed on it without the obligation attempted to be imposed on it by alterations.* The rule is especially applicable where the servitude is not materially increased. Such a misuser does not authorize the owner of the servient estate to prevent any further use of the easement by erecting obstructions, or by restraining the owner of the easement by force or violence, the proper remedy being an action for damages, or for an injunction if the remedy at law is inadequate. [Emphasis added.]

The situation here meets the one covered by the exception described by the underlined portion of the above quotation.

3. Lesser Relief.

Defendants' contention that lesser relief than a declaration that defendants no longer had any right to use McCormick Lane is without merit. A sign as suggested by defendants to the effect that the lane was restricted to the use of residents of McCormick Lane alone would not protect plaintiff's rights. Nor would an injunction attempting to restrain all persons from using McCormick Lane other than owners or residents fronting on the lane or their invitees be practicable or enforceable. Defendants have extended the lane in a sort of an inverted "Y." The northerly ends of each section of the Y join Watkins Avenue, so that what is equal to two through streets run into McCormick Lane. Such a sign and injunction would not prevent all or any of the residents of parcel 2 as well as the general public from using McCormick Lane. The only practical way of preventing this is to close McCormick

Lane at its junction with parcels 1 and 2.[135] This compels the extinguishment of defendants' easement therein. By causing McCormick Lane as extended by defendants and Burns Avenue as joined to it to become dedicated public streets, defendants have made it impossible for the portion of McCormick Lane belonging to plaintiff to be used in a limited way. Unless a fence is built across McCormick Lane at its intersection with the southerly line of parcel 1, there is no feasible way of keeping the general public as well as the residents of parcel 2 out of McCormick Lane. . . .

While of course defendants' easement appurtenant to parcel 1 was a valuable right, the fact that the court held that by their misuse of it they had abandoned that right, is not taking defendants' property without due process. It is not taking their property at all. It is merely determining that their own acts were such as the law determines constitutes an extinguishment of the easement. By their own acts they have made it impossible for either themselves or plaintiff to confine the use of the easement to the owners of lots in parcel 1 only.

The judgment is affirmed.[136]

Note: Increased Burden on Servient Estate

The plaintiff in Crimmins v. Gould conceded that "the change from orchard to residential estates did not *extinguish* the easement" (emphasis added). Would that change have been sufficient grounds for an injunction? Comment (b) to §488, Restatement of Property (1944), referred to in the principal case, provides:

> b. *Subdivision of dominant tenement.* The burden upon a servient tenement frequently will not be greatly increased by permitting an easement appurtenant to attach to each of the parts into which the dominant tenement may be subdivided. Though some increase in burden may result from the fact that the number of users is increased by the subdivision, the extent of the use is still measured by the needs of the land which constituted the original dominant tenement. Moreover, dominant tenements are ordinarily divisible and their division is so common that it is assumed that the possibility of their division is contemplated in their creation. Hence, unless forbidden by the manner or terms of its creation, the benefit of an easement appurtenant accrues upon a subdivision of a dominant tenement to the benefit of each of the parts into which it is subdivided.

135. It should be pointed out that in doing this defendants and the owners of lots in parcels 1 and 2 are not deprived in any way of access to Watkins Avenue. Actually they continue to have two ways of reaching it from their lots. They are only deprived of direct access to Fair Oaks Lane, which they can reach by going around the block.

136. See generally Annot., Abandonment, Waiver, or Forfeiture of Easement on Ground of Misuse, 16 A.L.R.2d 609 (1951).—EDS.

Is this really the common assumption of the parties? Consider the following case.

BANG v. FORMAN
244 Mich. 571, 222 N.W. 96 (1928)

McDONALD, J. The purpose of this suit was to restrain the defendants from resubdividing into smaller lots a portion of what is known as Shady Shore plat, a recorded plat bordering on the shore of Lake Huron; from selling the smaller lots with an easement in the beach; and from constructing and using a certain roadway through the lots.

Shady Shore plat is divided into 27 lots of which 25 have a 50-foot front on the beach, and extended back to a public highway, a distance of five or six hundred feet. Two of the lots are narrower, and do not front on the beach. The land comprising the plat is described as "the most beautiful of all Port Huron's beautiful beaches." It is covered with a magnificent growth of virgin timber. It borders on an excellent bathing and boating beach, and is in every sense suitable for high-class summer homes. It was intended by the platters for such use. There is no roadway through the plat by which the public can gain access to the beach. It was the intention that the beach should be exclusively for the use and quiet enjoyment of the lot owners. The beach front is about 80 feet in width, and was dedicated to the use of lot owners in language as follows:

"The street, as shown on said plat, is hereby dedicated to the use of the public and the walks and beach front to the sole and only use of the lot owners."

All of the deeds to lot owners contained the following restriction:

"The said lot to be used for dwelling purposes only and no dwelling or obstruction shall be erected on said lots closer than seventy-five feet from the east line thereof and any dwelling house erected thereon shall not be of less value than fifteen hundred dollars."

The plaintiffs are owners of several of the lots which they have improved and beautified by landscaping, and on which they have built expensive homes.

The defendants acquired title to lots 4, 5, and 6 of the plat, and proceeded to resubdivide them into 26 small lots. Their plat, which they called "Shady Court Subdivision," shows a 14-foot cement roadway extending from the beach to the main highway on the west. Some of the lots of this subdivision have been sold on contract with "beach privileges to all owners." Regardless of objections from the plaintiffs, the defendants continued with their plan until restrained by injunction of the court.

The theory of the bill is that the plan of the Shady Court Subdivision violates the restrictions contained in the several deeds in that it provides for the building of more than one residence on each of the original lots, and provides for a roadway through the property; that the dedication of the use of the beach front to the lot owners of Shady Shore plat limits the use of the easement thereby created to such lot owners, and that persons owning a part of a lot are not entitled to the benefit of the easement; and that, by their plan in multiplying the number of lot owners who are to use the beach front, the defendants are placing an additional and extra burden on the beach easement, against the objections of other owners of the dominant estate.

The controlling question involved in this issue is whether the acts complained of increase the burden on the servient estate beyond that contemplated at the time the easement was created. This is a question of fact. 9 R.C.L. 790; Harvey v. Crane, 85 Mich. 316, 48 N.W. 582, 12 L.R.A. 601.

The rule of law governing the relative rights of the parties is correctly stated in Henrie v. Johnson, 28 W. Va. 190, as follows:

> The law seems to be well settled, that where land is granted with a right of way over other lands, the right is appurtenant to every part of land so granted, and the grantee of any part, no matter how small, is entitled to it, provided no additional burden is thereby created upon the servient estate. And this right will pass to a grantee of the dominant estate, or any subdivision thereof, as appurtenant to it, although the easement is not mentioned in the grant, and it is not really necessary to the enjoyment of the estate by the grantee.

See, also 19 C.J. 948, and 9 R.C.L. 790.

In Brossart v. Corlett, 27 Iowa, 288, it is said:

> The rule, we grant, is that an easement appurtenant to an estate is so to every part thereof, whatever the subdivision at the time or subsequently. But it is just as true that the servient estate is not to be burdened to a greater extent than was contemplated at the time of the creation of the easement.

In the instant case, that portion of the dominant estate which is now owned by the defendants has been changed since the easement was created. The change has resulted in imposing upon the easement the burden of serving a larger number of people. By subdividing three lots of the original plat into 26 small lots, and granting beach privileges to each, the defendants have materially increased the burden upon the servient estate. They have provided for 26 families with the privilege of using the easement, where originally there were but three. They have built a 14-foot cement driveway from the main highway to the beach, and at the gateway leading from the highway have placed a sign which says, "Welcome, drive in." The manner in which the public responded is described by plaintiff Bang, who testified:

> At various times, late in the evening, we can hear the shrieking and hollering of bathers, especially in the fall of the year; I have noticed a number of cottages there are rented out on short periods of a few days to a week, and so on, and they bring out crowds that are very undesirable. Within the last week I

have noticed what has been going on nights in Shady Court Plat; last evening, about eleven o'clock, I woke up and heard a woman squawking and hollering, "let go my toes; let go my toes!" we found cars in there a number of times; we would find they would drive in there in the evening, couples, in the dark, and later on they would turn on their lights when they would turn to go out and throw the lights over to our place, which is very annoying, and it is surely not the class of people we would like around there anyway.

With this and other like testimony before him, the trial court found that the acts complained of resulted in an unreasonable use of the easement in question. In his opinion he said:

> I find that the Shady Court plan will of necessity increase the burden upon this easement and cast an additional and extra burden upon it. This Shady Court plan, if carried out, will decrease the value of every other lot in Shady Shore plat for the purpose for which the lot was sold. It will decrease the value and desirability of the fine properties of plaintiffs Bang and Bishop. Property does not consist merely in the right to the soil but in the right as well to its beneficial enjoyment. Horton v. Williams, 99 Mich. 423, 58 N.W. 369; Scott v. Moore, 98 Va. 668, 37 S.E. 342, 81 Am. St. Rep. 749; Talbert v. Mason, 136 Iowa 373, 113 N.W. 918, 14 L.R.A. (N.S.) 878, 125 Am. St. Rep. 259. Shady Court Subdivision, if the plan is completed, will tend to deprive plaintiffs and other lot owners in Shady Shore Plat of this right. It is subversive of rights in Shady Shore Plat particularly of the rights of those who have made expensive improvements on their property.

The extent to which the use of the easement had been increased was a question of fact for the court. Our examination of the record convinces us that he reached a correct conclusion in finding that there had been a substantial increase.

The additional burden imposed upon the servient estate was not contemplated by the owner when he created the easement. It was not what the grantor intended. He had a purpose in dividing the plat into large lots. He worked from a general plan, and this plan did not contemplate a subdivision of the large lots into smaller ones. He advertised the fact that the lots were large, each with 50 feet front on the beach and extending back from 500 to 600 feet to the main highway. He advertised that each deed would contain a provision dedicating the beach front to the "common use of all lot owners," and that the beach was "neither too wide nor too narrow but just right." The language of the grant, considered in connection with statements in these circulars and the physical facts and circumstances existing at the time, clearly shows that the grantor did not intend such use of the easement as is proposed by the defendants.

It is not necessary to discuss other questions. As a basis for his decree, the circuit judge filed an opinion in which he carefully considered all of the issues and correctly disposed of them.

The decree entered is affirmed, with costs to the plaintiffs.

Problems

32.27. O conveyed a parcel of land to E along with a right of way of definite location, 18 feet in width, over O's retained land. O now wishes to develop this retained land by erecting a building over the land, subject to E's easement, and offers (a) to leave an opening eight feet high in the proposed building at the place where it crosses the way, and (b) lay out an additional way over level ground around the proposed building, reaching the same point as the old way, to provide access for vehicles whose height would prevent them from using the old way. E rejects these offers, insisting on retaining the original way, at a height adequate for E's present needs. Sakansky v. Wein, 86 N.H. 337, 169 A. 1 (1933).[137]

32.28. O granted to the Illinois Central Railroad Company an easement in a 100-foot strip of O's land "for the purpose of constructing, maintaining and operating thereon a single or double track railway, with all the necessary appurtenances." The railroad company leased to the Illinois Independent Oil Company a portion of the 100-foot strip to be used exclusively as a site for a combination bulk oil and service station. The lease specified a rental of $50 per year and was for a period of five years. The lease was approved by the Illinois Commerce Commission. O was operating a retail service station on O's adjoining property, and O seeks an injunction to restrain the Illinois Independent Oil Company from selling oil, gasoline, and other drive-in service station commodities at retail on the railroad right-of-way. Discuss the relevance of the following evidence in determining whether the injunction should issue:

   a. Petroleum ranks second in importance, both in tonnage and in revenue, as freight on the Illinois Central Railroad.
   b. The Illinois Independent Oil Company operates 11 bulk and 19 retail gasoline stations in central Illinois.
   c. The Illinois Independent Oil Company will use approximately twelve 8,000-gallon tank cars of gasoline annually.
   d. It is common practice for railroads to lease part of rights-of-way to shippers of petroleum so as to effect economy in making deliveries.

See Mitchell v. Illinois Central Railroad, 384 Ill. 258, 51 N.E.2d 271 (1943).

CITY OF PASADENA v. CALIFORNIA-MICHIGAN LAND & WATER CO.
17 Cal. 2d 576, 110 P.2d 983 (1941)

GIBSON, C.J. This is an action for injunction and damages based on the defendant's alleged past and threatened future invasion of certain easements

---

137. See generally Annot., Extent and Reasonableness of Use of Private Way in Exercise of Easement Granted in General Terms, 3 A.L.R.3d 1256 (1965).

owned by the plaintiff. The case was tried by the court sitting without a jury, and from a judgment entered for the defendant the plaintiff prosecutes this appeal.

The parties are competing vendors of water service in an unincorporated area situated between the cities of Arcadia and Pasadena. The defendant, under claim of right and with the admitted permission of the servient owners, installed water mains and service connections in certain five-foot easements theretofore granted to the plaintiff and partly occupied by its water mains and connections. This action was commenced by the plaintiff on the theory that the owners of the servient tenements had no power to grant easements similar to plaintiff's in the same five-foot strip of land to the defendant company, a competing distributor of water service. Plaintiff's contention was that it had a right to occupy the five-foot strip completely if the necessity arose, and that the defendant's installation substantially interfered both with plaintiff's present partial occupation of the land and with its possible future use of the land for its pipes and connections. The trial court found against the plaintiff and for the defendant upon conflicting evidence. In this appeal plaintiff contends primarily that the easement granted to the defendant was an unreasonable interference with its prior easement as a matter of law. It is asserted that there was no need to resort to evidence of the surrounding facts and circumstances, and that the court should have found for the plaintiff upon the ground that the defendant's mains interfere in law with the easement previously granted to the city, entirely apart from the question of physical interference upon which the trial court found against plaintiff. There is also a contention that the findings of the trial court are not supported by the evidence. We find ample evidence, however, to sustain the findings. We shall confine our opinion, therefore, to a consideration of the appellant's primary contention, that the easements granted to the defendant interfered with its prior easements as a matter of law.

The easements involved in the present case are described as follows in the instrument creating them: "Easements for the purpose of installing and maintaining water mains and connections thereto . . . all of said easements being five feet in width, to-wit: a. In lots 1 to 12, both inclusive, along the south line thereof . . ." This language eliminates at once the suggestion that appellant's easement was a so-called "exclusive easement." Under section 806 of the Civil Code "the extent of a servitude is determined by the terms of the grant . . . ," and there is no language in this grant which indicates any intention to make the easement held by the City of Pasadena an exclusive one. Indeed, appellant does not make a serious claim that there was an intention to make this an exclusive easement; and any such intention would seem clearly contrary to the admitted facts, since prior easements in the same land were in effect at the time when appellant's easements were granted. Furthermore, an "exclusive easement" is an unusual interest in land; it has been said to amount almost to a conveyance of the fee. (2 Thompson, Real Property (1939), sec. 578; Jones, Easements, sec. 378,

p. 302.) No intention to convey such a complete interest can be imputed to the owner of the servient tenement in the absence of a clear indication of such an intention. (See Reiver v. Voshell, 18 Del. Ch. 260, 264, 158 A. 366; Jones, *supra,* sec. 379, p. 303.)

The determination of this appeal turns upon the rights which the owner of the servient tenement retains in the land over which he has granted an easement for the laying of water pipes. It is established that the right to lay underground pipes over the land of another is an easement and is governed generally by the rules of law which govern ordinary easements of way. Where the easement is founded upon a grant, as here, only those interests expressed in the grant and those necessarily incident thereto pass from the owner of the fee. The general rule is clearly established that, despite the granting of an easement, the owner of the servient tenement may make any use of the land that does not interfere unreasonably with the easement. It is not necessary for him to make any reservation to protect his interests in the land, for what he does not convey, he still retains. (Jones, Easements, sec. 391 et seq., p. 313.) Furthermore, since he retains the right to use the land reasonably himself, he retains also the power to transfer these rights to third persons. Thus, in the instant case, the right of the defendant to use the particular land in controversy is derived from the owner of the servient tenements, and whether it is a permissible use is to be determined by whether the owner of the servient tenements could have used the land in that manner.

Whether a particular use of the land by the servient owner, or by someone acting with his authorization, is an unreasonable interference is a question of fact for the jury. In the present case, the trial court found that there was no such unreasonable interference, and this finding based upon conflicting evidence would ordinarily be conclusive.

Appellant urges the application of a different rule to the instant case upon the following grounds: That these easements are created by grant, and the language of the grant is so clear and definite that a court as a matter of law can define the relative rights of the parties from the instrument alone, without resorting to an examination of the surrounding facts and circumstances. This is said to be so because this is an easement of defined width and location, the theory being that where the easement has a defined width, the easement holder has the right to occupy it to the full width if it ever desires to do so. Therefore, it is asserted, any use of the strip of land for laying other water pipes should be held to be unreasonable interference as a matter of law.

Appellant relies upon cases which hold that a surface right of way of defined width gives the easement holder the absolute right to occupy the surface to that width whenever he chooses. These cases depend upon the theory that the easement granted is completely and clearly defined because the width and location of the right of way are specified in the grant. They do not necessarily require a similar conclusion where the easement is for the limited purpose of laying underground water pipes to serve the surrounding property with water for domestic purposes. There is a clear distinction in purpose between a right of way over the surface of the land to be used by moving vehicles and an easement for the laying of water mains in a relatively fixed and permanent position. In the case of an easement for laying underground water pipes there are important factors to be considered in addition to the width and location of the easement. These include, for example, the number and size of the pipes, the right to shift the pipes around at will, and the depth at which the pipes are to be laid. To state the point more generally, with such an easement the extent of the burden which the parties intend to impose upon the servient tenement is not definitely fixed merely by a specification of width and location. Indeed, even with the surface rights of way, a specification of width and location does not always determine the extent of the burden imposed upon the servient land.

Appellant's position does not take into consideration the difference between the burden which the easement imposes upon the servient land and the location at which the burden is to be imposed. In Winslow v. Vallejo [148 Cal. 723, 84 P. 191], a case which is strongly relied upon by appellant, the court holds that where the grant is indefinite the court may consider additional factors in determining the extent of the burden intended to be imposed upon the land. At page 725 the court says: "But the conveyance is general in its terms and affords no basis for determining the number of the pipes, their size, or their exact location." It is here recognized that there are factors other than mere location to be considered, and that the extent of the burden is not determined merely by fixing the location of such an easement. It is, of course, possible to draft an instrument which would fully define both the location and the burden of the easement, or which would make the easement exclusive. But the very general language used in the instrument under consideration here cannot be given any such effect. Considering the fact that these easements were granted for the limited purpose of securing domestic water service for the individual owners in this real estate subdivision and that no indication appears that the parties intended to protect the city against competition, we are unable to find any intent, either expressed or implied, that the owners were never to grant similar easements to anyone else. Hence, the mere granting of the second easement to the defendant did not interfere with appellant's prior easement as a matter of law. Whether the particular use under a second easement amounts to an unreasonable interference is, as we have heretofore pointed out, a question of fact, and the finding, made upon conflicting evidence, that defendant's use of its easement was not such an unreasonable interference is conclusive upon the question so far as this appeal is concerned.

We do not wish to be understood, however, as limiting the rights granted to the City of Pasadena under its easements which were properly found to be prior and paramount to those of the defendant. The rule is established that the grant of an unrestricted easement, not specifically defined as to the burden imposed upon the servient land, entitles the easement holder to a use limited only by the requirement that it be reasonably necessary and consistent with the purposes for which the easement was granted. The language of the easements here involved does not sufficiently define the burden intended to be imposed so that defendant's easement can be termed an unreasonable interference as a matter of law, but neither does it restrict the right granted to the City of Pasadena to make the fullest necessary use of the five foot strip.

It is possible that the city may, at some future time, be faced with the necessity of expanding or changing its present system, and on its behalf it is asserted that the presence of defendant's pipes may seriously hamper the reasonable use of the city's prior easement under such circumstances. But if, in the reasonable use of its prior easement, the city requires the space occupied by the pipes of the defendant, its paramount right must prevail. . . . Until a point of unreconcilable conflict is reached, however, such a concurrent use of the land for similar purposes as is illustrated here should be governed by principles permitting an equitable adjustment of the conflicting interests. The respective rights of the two parties are not absolute, but must be construed to permit a due and reasonable enjoyment of both interests so long as that is possible.

In Murphy Chair Co. v. Radiator Co. [172 Mich. 14, 137 N.W. 791], successive rights of way in the same land were involved and the court held that both easements could be used simultaneously under the existing facts, but indicated that the subsequent grant must be considered subordinate if it should ever interfere with the reasonable use of the prior easement. . . .

Under the present facts no basis is shown for the relief sought. Whether a different conclusion may be required by changed circumstances in the future cannot now be determined with certainty, and need not therefore be decided.

The judgment is affirmed.

TRAYNOR, J., CURTIS, J., and EDMONDS, J., concurred.

SHENK, J., dissenting.

Problem

32.29. O owned land bordering on a lake. She placed a 12-inch pipe five feet below the level of the lake and for over twenty years has drawn water from the lake for use on her land. The yearly average of water drawn from the lake has been 12,000 gallons. The level of the lake has now fallen, so that the 12-inch pipe is above the level of the lake. O now proposes to replace the pipe so that it will be below the new level of the lake and plans to continue to draw from the lake the same amount of water she has withdrawn in the past. A, who also owns property on the lake, seeks an injunction to prevent O from replacing the 12-inch pipe. Assume that the withdrawal of water by O over the last twenty years has been in excess of her rights as an owner of property on the lake. Is A entitled to his injunction? See Kennedy v. Niles Water Supply Co., 173 Mich. 474, 139 N.W. 241 (1913). See also American Law of Property §§8.69, 8.70 (Casner ed. 1952).

E. Transferability of Easements in Gross

GEFFINE v. THOMPSON
76 Ohio App. 64, 62 N.E.2d 590 (1945)

MORGAN, J. The plaintiff, appellee herein, brought this action to eject the defendant, appellant herein, maintaining and operating on her land in the village of Westlake in this county, a pipe line for the transportation of gas. The defendant filed his cross-petition seeking to quite his title and right to such pipe line against the claims of plaintiff, as contained in the petition. The case was tried on an agreed statement of facts and additional evidence. The trial court gave judgment to the plaintiff on her petition and also on the defendant's cross-petition. From this judgment the defendant appeals.

Plaintiff's predecessor in title, for a valuable consideration, granted in 1918 to The East Ohio Gas Company, its successors and assigns, "the right of way to lay, maintain, operate and remove a pipe line for the transportation of gas" over the land described in plaintiff's petition. In addition, the grantee agreed to pay any damages which might be caused to crops and fences on the land "from the laying, maintaining, operating and removing said pipe line."

The pipe line on plaintiff's property, about 2,000 feet in length, was constructed along the northerly boundary of the land as a part of a longer pipe line to pipe gas from gas wells constructed in the neighborhood. Later The East Ohio Gas Company found that no surplus gas was being produced beyond the demands of local consumers and the company in 1928 sold and assigned the pipe line on plaintiff's premises and an additional 4,000 feet of pipe line on other lands to J. C. Arthurs & Company, which company in turn in 1935 sold and assigned its pipe line to the defendant.

As gas wells became dry and were abandoned, other producing wells were attached to the line. At the present time the defendant is the owner of two nearby gas wells whose product is piped into the line for the use of 27 local customers, nearby property owners, who use the gas for cooking and heating. The total income to the defendant is less than $2 per day.

The plaintiff purchased the land described in the petition in 1925 and she objected to the maintenance and operation of the pipe line on her land for the first time in 1942. The part of the land where the pipe line is laid is not being farmed or used by the plaintiff.

The lower court by its judgment approved plaintiff's contention that the easement granted to The East Ohio Gas Company in 1918 by plaintiff's predecessor in title was not appurtenant to any land owned by The East Ohio Gas Company and accordingly was an easement in gross and therefore not assignable.

That ruling is clearly contrary to the intention of the parties who executed the written easement which, as stated, ran "to The East Ohio Gas Company, its successors and assigns." The record contains nothing to support a claim that the intention of the parties should not be given effect on any ground of public policy.

In the case of Junction R. Co. v. Ruggles, 7 Ohio St. 1, the Supreme Court held that a railroad right of way is assignable. The court in its decision said:

> We return then, to the question: Was this easement capable of transfer? The question seems to be one of first impression. At all events, no case is cited, and we can find none, in which the point has been adjudicated. . . . A right of way appendant to a farm, is granted or reserved as being necessary or convenient for the occupancy and use of the farm, and is therefore transferable with the farm. A railroad is an entire thing; and the entire right of way for a railroad is made up of a union of many rights derived from many individual owners; some by contracts, involving various duties and obligations, and others by appropriation, under a delegated right of eminent domain. Any one of them is appurtenant to all the remainder—necessary to the enjoyment of all the remainder—and therefore from analogy to rights of way appendant to real estate, alienable, we think, with the thing to which it is appurtenant.

It is not our understanding that the Supreme Court in that case meant to hold that the assignability of a part of a railroad right of way is dependent on a sale and transfer of the entire right of way. If there is in the case any ambiguity on this point it was cleared up and resolved in the case of Garlick v. Pittsburgh & Western Ry. Co., 67 Ohio St. 223, 65 N.E. 896, when the Supreme Court held in the second paragraph of the syllabus:

> A railroad company organized under the laws of Ohio, may acquire title to lands within the state for railroad purposes . . . and when the right of way is thus acquired, and the company has constructed its railroad thereon . . . said company may sell and convey to another corporation for like railroad purposes all, or a part of the premises so acquired. . . .

In Boatman v. Lasley, 23 Ohio St. 614, the court held that a grant to one L, his heirs and assigns, of a right of way over the grantor's land, was not assignable or inheritable. The court said (page 618):

> A mere naked right to pass and repass over the land of another, a use which excludes all participation in the profits of the land, is not, in any proper sense, an interest or estate in the land itself. Such a right is in its nature personal; it attaches itself to the person of him to whom it is granted, and must die with the person.

The decision in Junction Rd. Co. v. Ruggles, *supra,* was not referred to in Boatman v. Lasley, *supra,* and it cannot be considered to have been overruled by the later decision. In fact the court in the former case recognized the existence of the general rule as later set forth in the latter case but said further:

> The subject matter of the question—a right of way for a railroad—is itself new; and the principles, long ago established, in regards to rights of way, personal or in gross, and rights of way appurtenant to real estate, have no direct application to this new class of rights of way. It, we apprehend, is sui generis, and must be governed by reasons peculiar to itself, and the lights which may be derived from the analogies it may bear to the old classes of easements of this kind, whose incidents have been already fixed and determined.

Is this case we are now considering, involving a pipe-line easement for the transportation of gas, controlled by the decision in Junction Rd. Co. v. Ruggles, *supra,* or by the holding in Boatman v. Lasley, *supra?* In our view there can be no doubt as to the correct answer to this question. The right to construct a pipe line on land to transport gas is analogous to the right to construct a railroad track to transport passengers and freight and is not analogous to a right granted to an individual to pass and repass over the land.

In our view, therefore, the present case cannot be distinguished on principle from the case of Junction Rd. Co. v. Ruggles, *supra,* and is controlled by it.

The exact question in the present case was considered and passed on in the case of Standard Oil Co. v. Buchi, 72 N.J. Eq. 492, 66 A. 427. The New Jersey court decided in favor of the assignability of pipe-line easements.

There is an excellent article in 22 Michigan Law Review, 521, on "the assignability of easements in gross in American law" by Lewis M. Simes, now a professor of law in the University of Michigan.[138] Professor Simes takes the position that there is no good reason why easements in gross should not be held to be assignable and the fact that the contrary view has been taken in many American cases is due to a misunderstanding of certain statements of Blackstone and Kent. Grants for profits à prendre in gross are generally held to be assignable and no satisfactory reason has ever been given why a different rule should be applid to easements in gross. Professor Simes concludes his article with the following statement:

> Can we not say that, since any supposed rule making easements in gross inalienable is without adequate foundation in logic or history, its application should be strictly limited to private ways; and that in jurisdictions where the question is still an open one, these interests should be freely assignable

---

138.   See also Clark, footnote 23; *supra,* ch. 3.—Eds.

wherever it appears that the grantor did not restrict them to a designated person.

The writer of this opinion is in accord with the views expressed in the above article by Professor Simes. However, as already stated, we prefer to rest our reversal of the judgment of the trial court in this case, on the authority of Junction Rd. Co. v. Ruggles, *supra.*

The judgment of the Common Pleas Court is reversed and the cause is remanded for further proceedings according to law.

Judgment reversed.[139]

SKEEL, P.J., and LIEGHLEY, J., concur.

F. Extinguishment — Abandonment, Destruction of Premises, License to Interrupt

HOPKINS THE FLORIST, INC. v. FLEMING
112 Vt. 389, 26 A.2d 96 (1942)

Bill in chancery seeking a declaratory judgment concerning . . . an easement of view. Heard on pleadings and evidence at the April Term, 1941, Windham County, Adams, Chancellor. Findings of fact were made and decree entered in favor of plaintiff. The opinion states the case.

Decree affirmed.

BUTTLES, J. The plaintiff and the defendants Fleming are owners of adjoining parcels of real estate situated on the easterly side of Main Street in Brattleboro, title to which was derived, through mesne conveyances, from a common grantor. The deed from the common grantor to the plaintiff's predecessor in title in 1862 contains the following:

It is also agreed by the said Thompson (grantee) . . . that no building nor obstacle shall be placed or allowed to remain on the space between the east line of Main Street and a line 32 feet east of said street line which shall in any manner obstruct the southerly view of Main Street from the windows of said Todd's (grantor's) house in which he now resides.

Seven days after the delivery of this deed another instrument was executed, sealed and acknowledged by the parties to said deed whereby the grantee released to said Todd, his heirs, executors, administrators and assigns all right to obstruct the southern view of Main Street from the windows of said Todd's present dwelling, across the 32 foot strip referred to in said deed, and

---

139. Restatement of Property ch. 40, topic B, divides easements in gross into two types: commercial and noncommercial. Section 489 declares: "Easements in gross, if of a commercial character, are alienable property interests." It is commercial in character "when the use authorized by it results primarily in economic benefit rather than personal satisfaction" (§489 comment c). As to noncommercial easements, see Restatement, §§491-492. As you might expect, Clark disagreed with the Restatement. Clark, footnote 138, *supra,* at 79-83. See generally American Law of Property §§8.71-8.86 (Casner ed. 1952).—EDS.

covenanted with the said Todd, his heirs and assigns that such view should not be so obstructed.

The sufficiency of the mesne conveyances to vest in these defendants the right reserved in the deed from Todd to Thompson is not questioned. Both parties have briefed and argued the case on the basis that the right so acquired was an easement and for the purpose of this opinion we treat it as such.

In this suit in chancery the plaintiff seeks declaratory relief and asks the court to find that the defendants have no enforceable easement of view over premises owned by the plaintiff. . . . The defendants Fleming, hereinafter termed the defendants, answered; hearing was had before the chancellor, findings of fact were made and it was thereafter decreed that the easement reserved in the deed from Todd to Thompson in 1862 is lost and is no longer in force. . . .

From the chancellor's findings it appears that the defendants Fleming acquired their property in 1938 from the First Baptist Church who, prior to that time, had used the house as a parsonage. Prior to that it had been occupied by a doctor. Soon after acquiring the property, the defendants moved the house to the rear of the lot and turned it about and permanently located it so that the front which formerly faced west on Main Street now faces north on Walnut Street. In 1939 that part of the lot on which the house formerly stood was leased for three years to the defendant Fisher who erected thereon a diner or removable restaurant which he intends to remove upon the expiration of his lease or when he shall vacate the property. After moving the house to its present location the defendants did some remodelling and made it into a two family tenement. . . .

The question is raised by defendant's appeal whether the decree that the easement of view claimed by the defendants is lost and no longer in force is supported by the findings. . . .

The easement in the present case is narrowly limited. It does not include a right to light and air, except such as may be incidental to the right of view. There is reserved merely a right of view of Main Street, in a southerly direction only, from the windows of Todd's house in which he resided at the time he executed the deed to Thompson, or from the windows of his then present residence, as stated in the supplemental agreement. It seems clear that the parties intended by the language used to create an easement appurtenant only to the house then standing on the Todd property, and that when that house was permanently removed to a location where, it is found, there is no southerly view of Main Street from any of its windows, the easement was extinguished.

The conclusion which we reach makes it unnecessary to consider the other grounds upon which the easement is claimed to have been lost, or the other exceptions briefed by the respective parties.

Decree affirmed.[140]

---

140. See Annot., Loss of Private Easement by Nonuser or Adverse Possession, 25 A.L.R.2d 1265 (1952).—EDS.

UNION NATIONAL BANK v. NESMITH
238 Mass. 247, 130 N.E. 251 (1921)

JENNEY, J. The exceptions arise in proceedings for registration of title to land. In or about the year 1852, John and Thomas Nesmith, then owning adjoining lots on Merrimack Street in Lowell, simultaneously erected buildings on their respective lots with a common entrance from the street, and common stairways and landing places leading therefrom to the upper stories of the buildings.

The common entrance, stairways and landings constitute the only means of entrance and exit from the street to the upper stories of the respondents' building and to and from the third floor of the petitioner's building. The buildings remained unchanged, and the entrance, landing and stairways, half of each being on each side of the property line, have been used in common by the occupants of both buildings. The width of the entrance from the street is a little over four feet and that of the stairways a little under six feet.

The petitioner, who is successor in title to Thomas Nesmith, proposes to tear down its building and erect a new one without providing a common entrance, stairways and landing places; it offers to provide support for the portion of the respondents' building within the space now so occupied, and to take a decree of registration subject to such right. The respondents claim an easement of protection and support and also of way through the petitioner's building until such time as said building is destroyed or removed without the fault or voluntary act of its owner. The exceptions do not present any question of the right to protection or support, or of rights in the partition wall. . . .

Where there is an easement of way through a building as distinguished from such right upon and over land without reference to a structure thereon, the incorporeal hereditament is measured and limited by the existence of the structure in which it only can exist and be exercised; and the person owning the easement by the evident intent of the parties has no easement in the servient estate apart from the building. If the structure ceases to exist, the right ends as there is nothing upon which it can be exercised. This is because the owner of the servient estate is not obliged to replace the building when it ceases to exist by reason of decay, earthquake, tornado, fire, or its destruction otherwise caused without the fault or act of the owner. Shirley v. Crabb, 138 Ind. 200, 37 N.E. 130. Bonney v. Greenwood, 96 Me. 335, 52 A. 786. See Stockwell v. Hunter, 11 Met. (Mass.) 448; Ainsworth v. Mount Moriah Lodge, 172 Mass. 257, 52 N.E. 81. The same result follows where the building on the dominant tenement is destroyed by voluntary or involuntary act, or is substantially changed. The right is not one appurtenant to the estate as a whole, but is limited by intendment to the building in connection with which it is used. Cotting v. Boston, 201 Mass. 97, 87 N.E. 205. Allan v. Gomme, 11 Ad. & El. 759.

In the opinion of a majority of the court, the easement is also lost when the building is destroyed by the intentional act of the owner of the servient estate. The person entitled to such right has no interest in the land as such. This is settled by the principles already stated. He cannot compel the servient owner to maintain thereon a building, and restrain him in the use of his land by preventing a change in the manner of its enjoyment, and thereby impose what is in principle and effect a restriction upon the use of the land. The parties did not intend to and did not create a right of any greater permanency in the use of the petitioner's building than was assured by the character of the structure and the likelihood that the owner would not for a considerable time change the manner of the use of his premises. This is the reasonable construction of their rights. Compare Hubbell v. Warren, 8 Allen, 173. In Cotting v. Boston, *supra,* 201 Mass. at pages 101, 102, 87 N.E. 206, it is said:

> It has frequently been decided that a right of way through a building, in the absence of plain words to the contrary, incumbers the servient estate only so long as the building exists described in the instrument creating the right of way. We can think of no sound principle of law which prevents the extinction of a right of way with the destruction of the building upon the dominant estate, when it seems reasonable that such was the intention of the parties. . . .[141]

Problems

32.30. In a jurisdiction which will not permit the owner of the servient estate to extinguish an easement by destroying the building, will the courts require such owner to take affirmative steps to keep it in good repair?

32.31. In determining whether the servient owner may destroy a building in which an easement exists and thereby extinguish the easement, should it make any difference whether the easement was created by express grant or by prescription?

32.32. O, owner of Blackacre, borrows $5,000 from M and executes a mortgage on Blackacre to secure the loan. This mortgage is duly recorded. O then grants to E an easement of way over Blackacre, which easement is to be appurtenant to E's adjoining land. The deed granting the easement is

---

141. But see Rothschild v. Wolf, 20 Cal. 2d 17, 123 P.2d 483 (1942), examining the law in other jurisdictions and finding Massachusetts alone in holding the easement lost when the servient building is destroyed by the *intentional* act of the owner of the servient land. The court said all other jurisdictions require the building to be destroyed "without the fault of the owner of the servient estate." The court said California would adopt that rule but added:

> [W]e do not wish to be understood as intimating that depreciation or obsolescence of a building may not in the course of time so far progress as to impair property rights in the further maintenance thereof even though not to the extent of being equivalent of destruction of such building. 20 Cal. 2d at 20, 123 P.2d at 484.]

—EDS.

properly recorded. O fails to meet the payments on the indebtedness to M, and M forecloses the mortgage. Does the purchaser at the foreclosure sale take subject to the easement of way over Blackacre granted by O to E?

32.33. O and E were owners of adjoining tracts of land. O granted to E an easement of way over his (O's) land, and the deed granting the same was properly recorded. O became delinquent in the taxes assessed against the land, and the land was sold at a tax sale. A purchased the land at the tax sale. A placed a barrier across the easement of way which O had granted to E, thereby preventing E from using the easement. E seeks an injunction to compel the removal of the barrier. Is E entitled to the injunction? See Northwestern Improvement Co. v. Lowry, 104 Mont. 289, 66 P.2d 792 (1937); Engel v. Catucci, 197 F.2d 597 (D.C. Cir. 1952); American Law of Property §8.104 (Casner ed. 1952).

32.34. In 1937, O was the owner of a tract of land which was bounded on the east by the Susquehanna River. In that year, O conveyed to E, who owned the adjoining tract of land, "the right at any time and at all times hereafter to cause the water of the Susquehanna River to flow back upon, and overflow, or be withdrawn from the land of O located as follows:" (then followed a description of the part of O's land which could be flooded). This instrument of conveyance was properly recorded. In 1945, O conveyed her land to A, making no mention in the deed of conveyance of the right outstanding to flood part of the land. In 1984, E desires to build a dam on the Susquehanna River, whereby the land now owned by A will be flooded to the extent permitted by the instrument of conveyance executed in 1937. Advise E as to his rights under each of the following suppositions:

  a. The part of A's land over which flood rights were granted in 1937, is in the same condition it was in 1937, and E has refrained from building the dam in the past because he did not need it. See American Law of Property §8.97 (Casner ed. 1952).

  b. E orally told A in 1950 that he would never exercise the flood rights, but A's land over which the flood rights were granted in 1937 is in the same condition it was in 1937. Id. §§8.95, 8.97.

  c. A built a house in 1979 on the land over which the flood rights were granted in 1937; which house would be ruined by E's exercise of the flood rights.

  d. E orally told A in 1975 that he would never exercise the flood rights, and A then built a house on the land over which the flood rights were granted in 1937; which house would be ruined by E's exercise of the flood rights. Id. §§8.99, 8.100.

See Graham v. Safe Harbor Water Power Corp., 315 Pa. 572, 173 A. 311 (1934).[142]

---

142. See generally Simonton, Abandonment of Interests in Land, 25 Ill. L. Rev. 261 (1930); Restatement of Property §§504-505 (1944); American Law of Property §§8.87-8.104 (Casner ed. 1952).

SECTION 8.   LICENSES—REVOCABLE AND IRREVOCABLE

Note: *"License" Defined*

If even after examining the following you still find it well-nigh impossible to distinguish a license from a lease or easement, you will have plenty of company.[143] Consider the definition of "license" given in the Restatement of Property §512:

The term "license" as used in this chapter, denotes an interest in land in the possession of another which
(a) entitles the owner of the interest to use of the land, and
(b) arises from the consent of the one whose interest in the land used is affected thereby, and
(c) is not incident to an estate in the land, and
(d) is not an easement.

Does this distinguish a "license" from an "easement"?[144]

Note also the summary treatment the court in South Center Department Store Inc. v. South Parkway Building Corp., 19 Del. App. 2d 61, 153 N.E.2d 241 (1958), gives the question of the revocability of the license: "It is well determined that a license is a mere personal and revocable privilege to do an act or series of acts upon the land of another without possessing any interest or estate in the land and that it can be revoked at will." Clark suggests that the courts are confusing acts and the legal relations which result therefrom, "and the battle begun over words terminates in a result shaped by those words."[145] When one asks, "Why is a mere license revocable?" the answer invariably comes back, "Because it is"—although usually accompanied by a long list of authorities. "The continued insistence of the courts upon revocability as a necessary legal characteristic of a license is akin to the argument that there can be no irrevocable offer to make a contract."[146]

---

143. Hohfeld, Faulty Analysis in Easement and License Cases, 27 Yale L.J. 66, 92 (1917). See generally Conard, An Analysis of Licenses In Land, 42 Colum. L. Rev. 809 (1942); Clark, footnote 23, *supra,* ch. 2.

144. Below is the view of Professor Clark:

At first glance the black-letter definition of the Restatement appears imposing with its four clauses. But a comparison of it with the corresponding definition of an easement [see section 450, set out at page 1056 *supra*] will show that the first three clauses might well apply to the latter interest. . . . Only clause (d) is important—that the interest "is not an easement." This purely negative definition—which is never improved upon—results in, and doubtless requires, further black-letter statements as to the important details of assignability, revocation, and protection against third persons, so broad and so subject to exceptions as to be meaningless. [Clark, at 20-21.]

145. Clark, at 13-14. The distinction between license as an "operative fact" and license as a "legal relation" is discussed at 15-20.

146. Clark, at 18.

Regardless of the merits of this debate, it must be accepted that a *mere* license is revocable; but this implies that there are licenses which are not *mere* licenses. It is to these interests which we now turn.

STONER v. ZUCKER
148 Cal. 516, 83 P. 808 (1906)

HENSHAW, J. Plaintiff pleaded that defendants had entered upon his land in 1899, under license, and had constructed thereon and thereover a ditch for the carrying of water; that he never conveyed or agreed to convey to the defendants any right of way, easement, or interest in the land for the purpose, and their right to construct and maintain the ditch rested wholly upon this license; that in 1900 he served notice upon them that the license to construct and operate the ditch had been revoked and abrogated by him. Notwithstanding this notice of revocation and abrogation, the defendants, disregarding it, have continuously entered upon plaintiff's land, making repairs upon the ditch and restoring the same where it was broken and washed away, and defendants threaten to continue this trespass upon the lands of the plaintiff. Plaintiff therefore prayed that the defendants be adjudged treapassers and be enjoined from the use of the ditch or from in any manner entering upon the lands of the plaintiff to repair or otherwise maintain it. The evidence established, without controversy, that defendants constructed the ditch for the purpose of carrying water for irrigation to their own and other lands, and had expended upon the ditch the sum of seven thousand and more dollars. The court found that "a right of way for the construction and maintenance of the ditch for the purpose of taking water from Santa Ana river for use in connection with and upon defendants' lands was given and granted by the plaintiff to the defendants, and that the defendants are the owners of a right of way for said ditch for the purpose aforesaid." The court further found that there was a consideration for the "granting of said right of way, in that defendants contracted and agreed with the plaintiff to deliver to and for the use of the plaintiff on his land lying under said canal sufficient water to irrigate the land, and the defendants have at all times delivered said water so agreed to be delivered." This last finding derives no support from the evidence, and the first finding, to the effect that the plaintiff "granted" a right of way, can be supported only upon the standing that the court by "grant" meant that "permission" was given to defendants for the construction and maintenance of the ditch. So construing the findings, the question is squarely presented as to the revocability or nonrevocability of an executed parol license, whose execution has involved the expenditure of money, and where, from the very nature of the license given, it was to be continuous in use.

Appellant contends that a parol license to do an act upon the land of the licensor, while it justifies anything done by the licensee before revocation, is revocable at the option of the licensor, so that no further acts may be justified under it, and this, although the intention was to confer a continuing right, and money has been expended by the licensor upon the faith of the license, and that such a license cannot be changed into an equitable right on the ground of equitable estoppel. To the support of this proposition is offered authority of great weight and of the highest respectability. The argument in brief is that a license in its very nature is a revocable permission, that whoever accepts that permission does it with knowledge that the permission may be revoked at any time; that the rule cannot be changed, therefore, because the licensee has foolishly or improvidently expended money in the hope of a continuance of a license, upon the permanent continuance of which he has no right in law or in equity to rely; that to convert such a parol license into a grant or easement under the doctrine of estoppel is destructive of the statute of frauds, which was meant to lay down an inflexible rule; and, finally, that there is no room or play for the operation of the doctrine of estoppel, since the licensor has in no way deceived the licensee by revocation, has put no fraud upon him, and has merely asserted a right which had been absolutely reserved to him by the very terms of his permission. No one has stated this argument more clearly and cogently than Judge Cooley, who, holding to this construction of the law, has expressed it in his work on Torts. Cooley, Torts (2d Ed.) 364. But that the same eminent jurist recognized the injustice and the hardship which followed such a conclusion is plainly to be seen from his opinion in Maxwell v. Bay City Bridge Co., 41 Mich. 453, 2 N.W. 639, where, discussing this subject, he says:

> But the injustice of a revocation after the licensee, in reliance upon the license, has made large and expensive improvements, is so serious that it seems a reproach to the law that it should fail to provide some adequate protection against it. Some of the courts have been disposed to enforce the license as a parol contract which has been performed on one side.

Indeed, the learned jurist, with equal accuracy, might have stated that the majority of courts have so decided, in accordance with the leading case of Rerick v. Kern, 14 Serg. & R. 267, 16 Am. Dec. 497. That case was carefully considered, and it was held that it would be to countenance a fraud upon the part of the licensor if he were allowed, after expenditure of money by the licensees upon the faith of the license, to cut short by revocation the natural term of its continuance and existence, and that under the doctrine of estoppel, the licensor would not be allowed to do this. The decision was that the licensor would be held to have conveyed an easement commensurate in its extent and duration with the right to be enjoyed. In that case there was a parol license without consideration to use the waters of a stream for a sawmill, and it was held it could not be revoked at the grantor's pleasure, where the grantee, in consequence of the license, had erected a mill. The court in that case says, after discussion: "It is to be considered as if there had been a formal conveyance of the right, and nothing remains but to determine its duration and extent. A right under a license, when not specifically restricted, is commensurate with the thing of which the license is an accessory." And the court said further:

> Having in view an unlimited enjoyment of the privilege, the grantee has purchased by the expenditure of money, a right indefinite in point of duration, which cannot be forfeited by a nonuser unless for a period sufficient to raise the presumption of a release. The right to rebuild in case of destruction or dilapidation and to continue the business on its original footing may have been in fact as necessary to his safety, and may have been an inducement of the particular investment in the first instance.

It will not be necessary to multiply citations of authority upon this point. It is sufficient to refer to the very instructive comment of Prof. Freeman to the case of Rerick v. Kern, reported in 16 Am. Dec., at page 497. The learned author of the note concludes his review by saying, as he shows, that "it will be seen that the doctrine of the principal case, though not recognized in some of our state courts, is, nevertheless, expressive of the law as administered by the majority of them, and that the preponderance of recent judicial opinions is in harmony with the views of Judge Gibson." This court in the case of Flickinger v. Shaw, 87 Cal. 126, 25 Pac. 268, 11 L.R.A. 134, 22 Am. St. Rep. 234, discussed and approved the case of Rerick v. Kern, *supra.* It was not called upon there to pass upon the precise question here presented, because in that case defendant had entered and expended money upon a parol agreement to convey a right of way, and the court was called upon merely to decide in consonance with undisputed equitable principles that that parol agreement was enforceable, but in Smith v. Green, 109 Cal. 234, 41 Pac. 1024, the exact principle here announced is distinctly recognized, and it is said:

> The general rule, no doubt, is that one who rests his claim to an easement on a verbal contract alone, unexecuted and unaccompanied by any other facts, has no rights thereto which he can enforce. But there are many cases where a mere parol license which has been executed, and where investments have been made upon the faith of it, has been held irrevocable. Gould on Waters, §§232, 324.

The recognized principle, therefore, is that where a licensee has entered under a parol license and has expended money, or its equivalent in labor, in the execution of the license, the license becomes irrevocable, the licensee will have a right of entry upon the lands of the licensor for the purpose of maintaining his structures or, in general, his rights under his license, and the license will continue for so long a time as the nature of it calls for. Thus, for example, where the license was to erect a lumber mill, the license came to an end when the timber available for use at the mill had been worked up into lumber. The same has been held as to a milldam, the right to maintain the dam continuing so long as there was use for the mill, and the right being lost by abandonment and disuse only when the non-user had continued for a period sufficient to raise the presumption of release. In the case of irrigating ditches, drains, and the like, the license becomes, in all essentials, an easement, continuing for such length of time, under the indicated conditions, as the use itself may continue.

For these reasons the judgment and order appealed from are affirmed.

Note: Is an Irrevocable License an Easement?

What kind of interest did the court in Stoner v. Zucker conclude the defendant had — an easement or a license?

> [W]e should observe that the term "executed license" or irrevocable license is a misnomer. What we are dealing with is an easement, for that is what the licensee gets under the rule in Rerick v. Kern. . . . We should realize that we are in effect recognizing the creation of an easement even if by estoppel.[147]

The usual argument proceeds upon the theory that some "fraud or misleading" by the licensor has occurred. However, Clark doubts that any "fraud or misleading" actually occurs in most cases:

> [A] very real question is whether there has been any fraud. The answer to this question is likely to turn more on one's emotions than upon logic. Either we see fraud here or we do not. To the author it seems difficult to see fraud in the ordinary case where the licensor has not yet set a definite period of duration on his permission. Many courts think that he thereby implies that the permission is to continue indefinitely. But as an implication of fact this is doubtful, for one does not usually expect to relinquish or to acquire an extensive property interest without money or its equivalent; and as an implication of law it is lifting oneself by one's own bootstraps, for any implication of definite duration depends on our decision of the question at issue. If we decide one way, there is no definite duration; if we decide the other way, there is. In either case the parties are conclusively presumed to know the law and govern themselves accordingly. Instead of the picture of a licensor prevented by the courts from taking advantage of his own fraud, it is suggested that a truer picture is that of the kind, neighborly individual who finds himself outwitted, under this rule of law, by a clever landgrabber. It is a rule of good sense, sound morality, and hence good law that one ought not to expect something for nothing. It is to be noticed that here the ungracious neighbor who refuses to yield to the blandishments of anyone is the one who best protects his property. Surely the law ought not to penalize one for acts of neighborliness.

147. Clark, at 59-60.

Again it may be asked just when the licensor's fraud takes place. It cannot be when the permission is given, for it it well-settled that it may be taken back unless the licensee has made expenditures. The fraud seems to be in standing by while the expenditures were made. Yet it is for just this that the permission — an act itself unpenalized — was given; and this is what was planned by the parties from the beginning. When is it that this expected act of standing by becomes fraudulent and misleading? And also how much expenditure must be made by the licensee in order to obtain this immunity from revocation?[148]

Clark goes on to add that neither can the doctrine find a basis in some theory of "unjust enrichment" of the licensor, for the licensor "has no incentive to revoke simply because of the expenditures, for, as we have seen, the licensee will than have a reasonable time to remove his property."[149]

The position of the Restatement of Property §519(4) (1944) is that a licensee "who has made expenditures of capital or labor in the exercise of his license in reasonable reliance upon representations by the licensor as to the duration of the license, is privileged to continue the use permitted by the license to the extent reasonably necessary to realize upon his expenditures."

Note that the licensee may expend either capital or *labor*. Does Clark's argument that the licensee is privileged to remove his property do justice to the argument of unjust enrichment?

CROSDALE v. LANIGAN
129 N.Y. 604, 29 N.E. 824 (1892)

ANDREWS, J. This case presents a question of importance from the principle involved, although the particular interest affected by the decision is not large.

This action was brought to obtain equitable relief by injunction to restrain the defendant from tearing down a stone wall erected on the defendant's land by the plaintiff, under an alleged parol license from the defendant, and in the erection of which the plaintiff expended in labor and materials a sum exceeding one hundred dollars. The parties are the owners of adjoining lots fronting upon a public street. The plaintiff's lot is west of the lot of the defendant. The land in its natural state descended toward the east. In 1886 the plaintiff graded his lot, and in so doing, raised an embankment several feet high along the eastern line, adjacent to the lot of the defendant, and erected a house on his lot. In 1887 the defendant graded his lot and excavated the earth up to his west line, adjacent to the embankment on the plaintiff's lot, to the depth of four or more feet, thereby removing the

---

148. Clark, at 61-62.
149. Clark, at 62, citing King v. Morris, 74 N.J.L. 810, 68 A. 162 (1907), which held that a factory placed upon the land of the licensor was removable by the licensee after revocation of the license by the licensor. Accord Restatement of Property §519(2) (1944).

natural support to the lot of the plaintiff as it was in its original state. Before the defendant had completed his excavation, the parties had an interview and the question of the support of the plaintiff's embankment arose. The plaintiff claimed that the defendant was bound to build a wall where his excavation was. The defendant denied his obligation to do so and referred to the fact that the plaintiff had raised his land several feet higher than it was in its natural state. The plaintiff wanted the defendant to sell him two feet of his land to build a wall upon, which the defendant declined to do.

Both parties agree that the wall was spoken of. The plaintiff testified that nothing was said between them as to what kind of a wall the plaintiff would build, nor as to its height, dimensions or quality. The defendant on the other hand testified that the plaintiff stated he would build a wall laid up in mortar, pointed on the side facing the defendant's (proposed) house, and cement it on the top with Portland cement. Some days after the interview and on the 13th day of April, 1887, the defendant addressed a letter to the plaintiff, in which, after referring to their previous interview, he said:

> While perfectly satisfied that I am justified in grading my lot as far as I have done, and that if at any time your embankment should topple over on my land, that I could claim damages, yet, perhaps, I was a little hasty and somewhat unreasonable with you the other night, and although I came away fully determined to stand on my rights and keep every inch of ground that belonged to me, since then I have thought the matter over seriously, put myself in your place, so to speak, and decided to give you two feet asked for to build your wall on.

The plaintiff on the same day replied in writing, saying:

> I will be glad to accept your offer in the spirit in which it was given, and thus end a disagreement, etc. I expect to go to work immediately to build the wall, and will go as far into my bank as is consistent with its safety. I will also modify as much as I can the grade of the bank along the side of the front.

The plaintiff thereupon proceeded to build a wall on the defendant's land, the building of which occupied four or five days. He first made a contract with a mason to build a mortared wall, and lime and sand were drawn upon the place to be used therefor. But for some reason he changed his mind, and he built the wall of "flat, ordinary building stone, not hewn into shape and not packed into regular courses, nor dressed at all," and without mortar or cement. The wall was ninety feet in length, two feet or less in width, and four to six feet high. It does not appear that the defendant saw the wall during the course of its construction, except that he was upon the lot on one occasion when the foundation was being laid, nor does it appear that he knew that the wall was to be laid up loose, or at any time consented to the erection of such a wall as was constructed. Within two weeks after the wall was completed he notified the attorney for the plaintiff, who, at the request of his client, had written him, demanding a deed of the two feet, that he had not agreed to give a deed, and that the wall was not built according to the understanding, and that he intended to tear it down.

This case was tried and decided upon the theory that the plaintiff had a license from the defendant to build the wall on his land, which, when executed, became in equity irrevocable. It was not claimed on the trial, nor is it now claimed, that there was any contract on the part of the defendant to sell the land occupied by the wall to the plaintiff, which, by reason of part performance, equity will enforce. The claim and the finding is that the license to enter upon the defendant's land, when acted upon by the plaintiff, conferred upon him a right in equity, in the nature of an easement, to maintain the wall on the defendant's lot. If this claim is well founded, there has been created, without deed and in violation of the Statute of Frauds, an interest in the plaintiff and his assigns in the land of the defendant, impairing the absolute title which he theretofore enjoyed, and subjecting his land to a servitude in favor of the adjacent property. It is quite immaterial in result that this interest claim, if it exists, is equitable and not legal. An incumbrance has been created upon the defendant's lot, and his ownership, to the extent of such interest, has been divested.

We are of opinion that this judgment is opposed to the rule of law established in this state. There has been much contrariety of decision in the courts of different states and jurisdictions. But the courts in this state have upheld with great steadiness the general rule that a parol license to do an act on the land of the licensor, while it justifies anything done by the licensee before revocation, is, nevertheless, revocable at the option of the licensor, and this, although the intention was to confer a continuing right and money had been expended by the licensee upon the faith of the license. This is plainly the rule of the statute. It is also, we believe, the rule required by public policy. It prevents the burdening of lands with restrictions founded upon oral agreements, easily misunderstood. It gives security and certainty to titles, which are most important to be preserved against defects and qualifications not founded upon solemn instruments. The jurisdiction of courts to enforce oral contracts for the sale of land, is clearly defined and well understood, and is indisputable; but to change what commenced in a license into an irrevocable right, on the ground of equitable estoppel, is another and quite different matter. It is far better, we think, that the law requiring interests in land to be evidenced by deed, should be observed, than to leave it to the chancellor to construe an executed license as a grant, depending upon what, in his view, may be equity in the special case. There are several circumstances in the present case which render the enforcement of such a jurisdiction a dangerous precedent. The only license claimed is contained in the letter of April thirteenth. The language is: "I have decided to give you the two feet you asked for to build your wall on." How far the wall was to extend, its character, or how it was to be built, is not stated. Referring to the previous interview to which the letter alludes, the evidence of the plaintiff of what was said at the interview leaves the whole matter indefinite and uncertain. He testifies that neither the description, dimensions nor character of the proposed wall were spoken of. The testimony of the defendant is to the contrary, but perhaps it is to be assumed that the trial judge adopted the testimony of the plaintiff.

Upon the case made by the plaintiff upon the letter and the prior conversations, if it was a case of contract, it is difficult to see how it could be enforced in equity. The cases are decisive that equity will only enforce a parol contract for an interest in land when the contract is definite and certain in all its parts. The extent of the injury which will be suffered unless equity intervenes is also an element to be considered when its extraordinary jurisdiction is invoked. Here the amount expended by the plaintiff in reliance upon the license was comparatively small. The most reasonable inference is that the plaintiff confided in the good faith of the defendant as his security that the wall would be permitted to remain. It does not appear that anything was said as to the time it should be maintained. It is claimed that the wall was built for the benefit of both parties. This is founded on the assumption that the defendant's excavation removed the natural support of the plaintiff's land, and subjected him to liability. But this would not take the case out of the statute nor authorize the interference of equity to enforce the license as a grant in equity. . . .

The trial judge refused to find the facts as to the effect which would have followed from the defendant's excavation in case the plaintiff's land had continued in its natural state. He tried and decided the case on the theory that the license when executed became irrevocable. In this we think he erred. . . .

Judgment reversed.

Problem

32.35. A buys a ticket for a reserved seat to a stage performance of a play in a New York City theater. A appears at the theater on the night specified on the ticket. A is denied access to the reserved seat. Is A entitled to use self-help to get to and occupy the reserved seat? See Marrone v. Washington Jockey Club, 227 U.S. 633, 33 S. Ct. 401 (1913). See also Stern, Licenses and Self-Help — the Ticket Cases Revisited, 32 Conv. & Prop. Law. (n.s.) 49 (1968).

CHAPTER 33

PUBLIC LAW DEVICES

Note: *Eminent Domain Versus Police Power*

Underlying all legal questions in the area of governmental control of land use is a choice between full compensation to the injured landowners (under eminent domain) and no compensation to the injured landowners (under the police power). The point at which the government must employ its power of eminent domain to accomplish its objective is unfortunately not capable of precise definition. Justice Holmes expressed the test as follows:

> Government hardly could go on if to some extent values incident to property could not be diminished without paying for every such change in the general law. As long recognized, some values are enjoyed under an implied limitation and must yield to the police power. But obviously the implied limitation must have its limits, or the contract and due process clauses are gone. One fact for consideration in determining such limits is the extent of the diminution. When it reaches a certain magnitude, in most if not in all cases there must be an exercise of eminent domain and compensation to sustain the act. So the question depends upon the particular facts. The greatest weight is given to the judgment of the legislature, but it always is open to interested parties to contend that the legislature has gone beyond its constitutional power. . . .
>
> The general rule at least is, that while property may be regulated to a certain extent, if regulation goes too far it will be recognized as a taking. . . . We are in danger of forgetting that a strong public desire to improve the public condition is not enough to warrant achieving the desire by a shorter cut than the constitutional way of paying for the change. As we have already said, this is a question of degree.[1]

As you read the cases which follow in this chapter, ask yourself whether you can more precisely draw the line and whether there is any viable alternative.

---

1. Pennsylvania Coal Co. v. Mahon, 260 U.S. 393, 413-416, 43 S. Ct. 158, 159-160 (1922). See the thorough analysis of this matter in Michelman, Property, Utility, and Fairness: Comments on the Ethical Foundations of "Just Compensation" Law, 80 Harv. L. Rev. 1165 (1967). See also Sax, Takings and the Police Power, 74 Yale L.J. 36 (1964).—Eds.

SECTION 1.   ZONING (HEREIN
             GOVERNMENTAL DESIGNATION
             OF PERMITTED USES AND THE
             PROBLEM OF THE EXISTING
             NONCONFORMING USE)

Note: *Going Forward With Lakeville*

We have been examining the development of Lakeville from the stand-point of controlling the use of land by covenants, easements, and licenses. We now turn our attention to the use of governmental authority to control the use of land. We will want to explain to our client to what extent we can attain desired controls as to the use of land by zoning that we cannot attain by the private devices we have heretofore considered, and vice versa.

The subdivision plan for Lakeville may have to be approved by the zoning board. The case of William H. Eggert, 36 T.C.M. (CCH) 1071 (1977) is relevant. The issue in the *Eggert* case was whether the transfer by the petitioners of 3.64 acres of land to the Land Conservation Trust of the Town of Madison, Connecticut, as a requirement for zoning approval of the petitioners' subdivision plan entitled the petitioners to a deduction under section 162(a) of the Internal Revenue Code in the amount of their basis in the transferred property as a business expense. The Tax Court stated: "Case law clearly treats conveyances of land to governmental entities in order to secure zoning or other types of approval for proposed business endeavors as capital expenditures." The court recognized that the petitioners should be entitled to an adjustment in basis of their remaining land as a result of such capital expenditure. In a footnote, the court pointed out that the petitioners had not claimed that the value of the land was a charitable contribution deductible under section 170 of the Internal Revenue Code.

VILLAGE OF EUCLID v. AMBLER REALTY CO.
272 U.S. 365, 47 S. Ct. 114 (1926)

Appeal from a decree of the District Court enjoining the Village and its Building Inspector from enforcing a zoning ordinance. The suit was brought by an owner of unimproved land within the corporate limits of the village, who sought the relief upon the ground that, because of the building restrictions imposed, the ordinance operated to reduce the normal value of his property, and to deprive him of liberty and property without due process of law.

Mr. Justice SUTHERLAND delivered the opinion of the court.

The Village of Euclid is an Ohio municipal corporation. It adjoins and practically is a suburb of the City of Cleveland. Its estimated population is between 5,000 and 10,000, and its area from twelve to fourteen square miles, the greater part of which is farm lands or unimproved acreage. It lies, roughly, in the form of a parallelogram measuring approximately three and one-half miles each way. East and west it is traversed by three principal highways: Euclid Avenue, through the southerly border, St. Clair Avenue, through the central portion, and Lake Shore Boulevard, through the northerly border in close proximity to the shore of Lake Erie. The Nickel Plate railroad lies from 1,500 to 1,800 feet north of Euclid Avenue, and the Lake Shore railroad 1,600 feet farther to the north. The three highways and the two railroads are substantially parallel.

Appellee is the owner of a tract of land containing 68 acres, situated in the westerly end of the village, abutting on Euclid Avenue to the south and the Nickel Plate railroad to the north. Adjoining this tract, both on the east and on the west, there have been laid out restricted residential plats upon which residences have been erected.

On November 13, 1922, an ordinance was adopted by the Village council, establishing a comprehensive zoning plan for regulating and restricting the location of trades, industries, apartment houses, two-family houses, single family houses, etc., the lot area to be built upon, the size and height of buildings, etc.

The entire area of the village is divided by the ordinance into six classes of use districts, denominated U-1 to U-6, inclusive; three classes of height districts, denominated H-1 to H-3, inclusive; and four classes of area districts, denominated A-1 to A-4, inclusive. The use districts are classified in respect of the buildings which may be erected within their respective limits, as follows: U-1 is restricted to single family dwellings, public parks, water towers and reservoirs, suburban and interurban electric railway passenger stations and rights of way, and farming, non-commercial greenhouse nurseries and truck gardening; U-2 is extended to include two-family dwellings; U-3 is further extended to include apartment houses, hotels, churches, schools, public libraries, museums, private clubs, community center buildings, hospitals, sanitariums, public playgrounds and recreation buildings, and a city hall and courthouse; U-4 is further extended to include banks, offices, studios, telephone exchanges, fire and police stations, restaurants, theatres and moving picture shows, retail stores and shops, sales offices, sample rooms, wholesale stores for hardware, drugs and groceries, stations for gasoline and oil (not exceeding 1,000 gallons storage) and for ice delivery, skating rinks and dance halls, electric substations, job and newspaper printing, public garages for motor vehicles, stables and wagon sheds (not exceeding five horses, wagons or motor trucks) and distributing stations for central store and commercial enterprises; U-5 is further extended to include billboards and advertising signs (if permitted), warehouses, ice and ice cream manufacturing and cold storage plants, bottling works, milk bottling and central distribution stations, laundries, carpet cleaning, dry cleaning and dyeing establishments, blacksmith, horseshoeing, wagon and motor vehicle repair shops, freight stations, street car barns, stables and wagon sheds (for more than five horses, wagons or motor trucks), and wholesale produce markets and salesrooms; U-6 is further extended to include plants for sewage disposal and for producing gas, garbage and refuse incineration, scrap iron, junk, scrap paper and rag storage, aviation fields, cemeteries, crematories, penal and correctional institutions, insane and feeble minded institutions, storage of oil and gasoline (not to exceed 25,000 gallons), and manufacturing and industrial operations of any kind other than, and any public utility not included in, a class U-1, U-2, U-3, U-4 or U-5 use. There is a seventh class of uses which is prohibited altogether.

Class U-1 is the only district in which buildings are restricted to those enumerated. In the other classes the uses are cumulative; that is to say, uses in class U-2 include those enumerated in the preceding class, U-1; class U-3 includes uses enumerated in the preceding classes, U-2 and U-1; and so on. In addition to the enumerated uses, the ordinance provides for accessory uses, that is, for uses customarily incident to the principal use, such as private garages. Many regulations are provided in respect of such accessory uses.

The height districts are classified as follows: In class H-1, buildings are limited to a height of two and one-half stories or thirty-five feet; in class H-2, to four stories or fifty feet; in class H-3, to eighty feet. To all of these, certain exceptions are made, as in the case of church spires, water tanks, etc.

The classification of area districts is: In A-1 districts, dwellings or apartment houses to accommodate more than one family must have at least 5,000 square feet for interior lots and at least 4,000 square feet for corner lots; in A-2 districts, the area must be at least 2,500 square feet for interior lots, and 2,000 square feet for corner lots; in A-3 districts, the limits are 1,250 and 1,000 square feet, respectively; in A-4 districts, the limits are 900 and 700 square feet, respectively. The ordinance contains, in great variety and detail, provisions in respect of width of lots, front, side and rear yards, and other matters, including restrictions and regulations as to the use of bill boards, sign boards and advertising signs.

A single family dwelling consists of a basement and not less than three rooms and a bathroom. A two-family dwelling consists of a basement and not less than four living rooms and a bathroom for each family; and is further described as a detached dwelling for the occupation of two families, one having its principal living rooms on the first floor and the other on the second floor.

Appellee's tract of land comes under U-2, U-3 and U-6. The first strip of 620 feet immediately north of Euclid Avenue falls in class U-2, the next 130 feet to the north, in U-3, and the remainder in U-6. The uses of the first 620 feet, therefore, do not include apartment houses, hotels, churches, schools, or other public and semi-public buildings, or other uses enumerated in respect of U-3 to U-6, inclusive. The uses of the next 130 feet include all of these, but exclude industries, theatres, banks, shops, and the various other uses set forth in respect of U-4 to U-6, inclusive.

Annexed to the ordinance, and made a part of it, is a zone map, showing the location and limits of the various use, height and area districts, from which it appears that the three classes overlap one another; that is to say, for example, both U-5 and U-6 use districts are in A-4 area districts, but the former is in H-2 and the latter in H-3 height districts. The plan is a complicated one and can be better understood by an inspection of the map, though it does not seem necessary to reproduce it for present purposes.

The lands lying between the two railroads for the entire length of the village area and extending some distance on either side to the north and south, having an average width of about 1,600 feet, are left open, with slight exceptions, for industrial and all other uses. This includes the larger part of appellee's tract. Approximately one-sixth of the area of the entire village is included in U-5 and U-6 use districts. That part of the village lying south of Euclid Avenue is principally in U-1 districts. The lands lying north of Euclid Avenue and bordering on the long strip just described are included in U-1, U-2, U-3 and U-4 districts, principally in U-2.

The enforcement of the ordinance is entrusted to the inspector of buildings, under rules and regulations of the board of zoning appeals. Meetings of the board are public, and minutes of its proceeding are kept. It is authorized to adopt rules and regulations to carry into effect provisions of the ordinance. Decisions of the inspector of buildings may be appealed to the board by any person claiming to be adversely affected by any such decision. The board is given power in specific cases of practical difficulty or unnecessary hardship to interpret the ordinance in harmony with its general purpose and intent, so that the public health, safety and general welfare may be secure and substantial justice done. Penalties are prescribed for violations, and it is provided that the various provisions are to be regarded as independent and the holding of any provision to be unconstitutional, void or ineffective shall not affect any of the others.

The ordinance is assailed on the grounds that it is in derogation of Sec. 1 of the Fourteenth Amendment to the Federal Constitution in that it deprives appellee of liberty and property without due process of law and denies it the equal protection of the law, and that it offends against certain provisions of the Constitution of the State of Ohio. The prayer of the bill is for an injunction restraining the enforcement of the ordinance and all attempts to impose or maintain as to appellee's property any of the restrictions, limitations or conditions. The court below held the ordinance to be unconstitutional and void, and enjoined its enforcement. 297 F. 307.

Before proceeding to a consideration of the case, it is necessary to determine the scope of the inquiry. The bill alleges that the tract of land in question is vacant and has been held for years for the purpose of selling and developing it for industrial uses, for which it is especially adapted, being immediately in the path of progressive industrial development; that for such uses it has a market value of about $10,000 per acre, but if the use be limited to residential purposes the market value is not in excess of $2,500 per acre; that the first 200 feet of the parcel back from Euclid Avenue, if unrestricted in respect of use, has a value of $150 per front foot, but if limited to residential uses, and ordinary mercantile business be excluded therefrom, its value is not in excess of $50 per front foot.

It is specifically averred that the ordinance attempts to restrict and control the lawful uses of appellee's land so as to confiscate and destroy a great part of its value; that it is being enforced in accordance with its terms; that prospective buyers of land for industrial, commercial and residential uses in the metropolitan district of Cleveland are deterred from buying any part of this land because of the existence of the ordinance and the necessity thereby entailed of conducting burdensome and expensive litigation in order to vindicate the right to use the land for lawful and legitimate purposes; that the ordinance constitutes a cloud upon the land, reduces and destroys its value, and has the effect of diverting the normal industrial, commercial and residential development thereof to other and less favorable locations.

The record goes no farther than to show, as the lower court found, that the normal, and reasonably to be expected, use and development of that part of appellee's land adjoining Euclid Avenue is for general trade and commercial purposes, particularly retail stores and like establishments, and that the normal, and reasonably to be expected, use and development of the residue of the land is for industrial and trade purposes. Whatever injury is inflicted by the mere existence and threatened enforcement of the ordinance is due to restrictions in respect of these and similar uses; to which perhaps should be added — if not included in the foregoing — restrictions in respect of apartment houses. Specifically, there is nothing in the record to suggest that any damage results from the presence in the ordinance of those restrictions relating to churches, schools, libraries and other public and semi-public buildings. It is neither alleged nor proved that there is, or may be, a demand for any part of appellee's land for any of the last named uses; and we cannot assume the existence of facts which would justify and injunction upon this record in respect of this class of restrictions. For present purposes the provisions of the ordinance in respect of these uses, may, therefore, be put aside as unnecessary to be considered. It is also unnecessary to consider the effect of the restrictions in respect of U-1 districts, since none of appellee's land falls within that class.

We proceed, then, to a consideration of those provisions of the ordinance to which the case as it is made relates, first disposing of a preliminary matter.

A motion was made in the court below to dismiss the bill on the ground that, because complainant (appellee) had made no effort to obtain a building permit or apply to the zoning board of appeals for relief as it might have done under the terms of the ordinance, the suit was premature. The motion was properly overruled. The effect of the allegations of the bill is that the ordinance of its own force operates greatly to reduce the value of appellee's lands and destroy their marketability for industrial, commercial and residential uses; and the attack is directed, not against any specific provision or provisions, but against the ordinance as an entirety. Assuming the premises, the existence and maintenance of the ordinance, in effect, constitutes a present invasion of appellee's property rights and a threat to continue it. Under these circumstances, the equitable jurisdiction is clear. See Terrace v. Thompson, 263 U.S. 197, 215, 44 S. Ct. 15; Pierce v. Society of Sisters, 268 U.S. 510, 535, 45 S. Ct. 571.

It is not necessary to set forth the provisions of the Ohio Constitution which are thought to be infringed. The question is the same under both Constitutions, namely, as stated by appellee: Is the ordinance invalid in that it violates the constitutional protection "to the right of property in the appellee by attempted regulations under the guise of the police power, which are unreasonable and confiscatory?"

Building zone laws are of modern origin. They began in this country about twenty-five years ago. Until recent years, urban life was comparatively simple; but with the great increase and concentration of population, problems have developed, and constantly are developing, which require, and will continue to require, additional restrictions in respect of the use and occupation of private lands in urban communities. Regulations, the wisdom, necessity and validity of which, as applied to existing conditions, are so apparent that they are now uniformly sustained, a century ago, or even half a century ago, probably would have been rejected as arbitrary and oppressive. Such regulations are sustained, under the complex conditions of our day, for reasons analogous to those which justify traffic regulations, which, before the advent of automobiles and rapid transit street railways, would have been condemned as fatally arbitrary and unreasonable. And in this there is no inconsistency, for while the meaning of constitutional guaranties never varies, the scope of their application must expand or contract to meet the new and different conditions which are constantly coming within the field of their operation. In a changing world, it is impossible that it should be otherwise. But although a degree of elasticity is thus imparted, not to the meaning, but to the application of constitutional principles, statutes and ordinances, which, after giving due weight to the new conditions, are found clearly not to conform to the Constitution of course, must fall.

The ordinance now under review, and all similar laws and regulations, must find their justification in some aspect of the police power, asserted for the public welfare. The line which in this field separates the legitimate from the illegitimate assumption of power is not capable of precise delimitation. It varies with circumstances and conditions. A regulatory zoning ordinance, which would be clearly valid as applied to the great cities, might be clearly invalid as applied to rural communities. In solving doubts, the maxim sic utere tuo ut alienum non laedas, which lies at the foundation of so much of the common law of nuisances, ordinarily will furnish a fairly helpful clue.

And the law of nuisances, likewise, may be consulted, not for the purpose of controlling, but for the helpful aid of its analogies in the process of ascertaining the scope of, the power. Thus the question whether the power exists to forbid the erection of a building of a particular kind or for a particular use, like the question whether a particular thing is a nuisance, is to be determined, not by an abstract consideration of the building or of the thing considered apart, but by considering it in connection with the circumstances and the locality. Sturgis v. Bridgeman, L. R. 11 Ch. 852, 865. A nuisance may be merely a right thing in the wrong place,—like a pig in the parlor instead of the barnyard. If the validity of the legislative classification for zoning purposes be fairly debatable, the legislative judgment must be allowed to control. Radice v. New York, 264 U.S. 292, 294, 44 S. Ct. 325.

There is no serious difference of opinion in respect of the validity of laws and regulations fixing the height of buildings within reasonable limits, the character of materials and methods of construction, and the adjoining area which must be left open, in order to minimized the danger of fire or collapse, the evils of over-crowding, and the like, and excluding from residential sections offensive trades, industries and structures likely to create nuisances. See Welch v. Swasey, 214 U.S. 91, 29 S. Ct. 567; Hadacheck v. Sebastian, 239 U.S. 394, 36 S. Ct. 143; Reinman v. Little Rock, 237 U.S. 171, 35 S. Ct. 511; Cusack Co. v. City of Chicago, 242 U.S. 526, 529-530, 37 S. Ct. 190.

Here, however, the exclusion is in general terms of all industrial establishments, and it may thereby happen that not only offensive or dangerous industries will be excluded, but those which are neither offensive nor dangerous will share the same fate. But this is no more than happens in respect of many practice-forbidding laws which this Court has upheld although drawn in general terms so as to include individual cases that may turn out to be innocuous in themselves. Hebe Co. v. Shaw, 248 U.S. 297, 303, 39 S. Ct. 125; Pierce Oil Corp. v. City of Hope, 248 U.S. 498, 500, 39 S. Ct. 172. The inclusion of a reasonable margin to insure effective enforcement, will not put upon a law, otherwise valid, the stamp of invalidity. Such laws may also find their justification in the fact that, in some fields, the bad fades into the good by such insensible degrees that the two are not capable of being readily distinguished and separated in terms of legislation. In the light of these considerations, we are not prepared to say that the end in view was not sufficient to justify the general rule of the ordinance, although some industries of an innocent character might fall within the proscribed class. It can not be said that the ordinance in this respect "passes the bounds of reason and assumes the character of a merely arbitrary fiat." Purity Extract Co. v. Lynch, 226 U.S. 192, 204, 33 S. Ct. 44. Moreover, the restrictive provisions of the ordinance in this particular may be sustained upon the principles applicable to the broader exclusion from residential districts of all business and trade structures, presently to be discussed.

It is said that the Village of Euclid is a mere suburb of the City of Cleveland; that the industrial development of that city has now reached and in some degree extended into the village and, in the obvious course of things, will soon absorb the entire area for industrial enterprises; that the effect of the ordinance is to divert this natural development elsewhere with the consequent loss of increased values to the owners of the lands within the village borders. But the village, though physically a suburb of Cleveland, is politically a separate municipality, with powers of its own and authority to govern itself as it sees fit within the limits of the organic law of its creation and the State and Federal Constitutions. Its governing authorities, presumably representing a majority of its inhabitants and voicing their will, have determined, not that industrial development shall cease at its boundaries, but that the course of such development shall proceed within definitely fixed lines. If it be a proper exercise of the police power to relegate industrial establishments to localities separated from residential sections, it is not easy to find a sufficient reason for denying the power because the effect of its exercise is to divert an industrial flow from the course which it would follow, to the injury of the residential public if left alone, to another course where such injury will be obviated. It is not meant by this, however, to exclude the possibility of cases where the general public interest would so far outweigh the interest of the municipality that the municipality would not be allowed to stand in the way.

We find no difficulty in sustaining restrictions of the kind thus far reviewed. The serious question in the case arises over the provisions of the ordinance excluding from residential districts, apartment houses, business houses, retail stores and shops, and other like establishments. This question involves the validity of what is really the crux of the more recent zoning legislation, namely, the creation and maintenance of residential districts, from which business and trade of every sort, including hotels and apartment houses, are excluded. Upon that question this Court has not thus far spoken. The decisions of the state courts are numerous and conflicting; but those which broadly sustain the power greatly outnumber those which deny altogether or narrowly limit it; and it is very apparent that there is a constantly increasing tendency in the direction of the broader view. . . .

The matter of zoning has received much attention at the hands of commissions and experts, and the results of their investigations have been set forth in comprehensive reports. These reports, which bear every evidence of painstaking consideration, concur in the view that the segregation of residential, business, and industrial buildings will make it easier to provide fire apparatus suitable for the character and intensity of the development in each section; that it will increase the safety and security of home life; greatly tend to prevent street accidents, especially to children, by reducing the traffic and resulting confusion in residential sections; decrease noise and other conditions which produce or intensify nervous disorders; preserve a more favorable environment in which to rear children, etc. With particular reference to apartment houses, it is pointed out that the development of detached house sections is greatly retarded by the coming of apartment houses, which has sometimes resulted in destroying the entire section for private house purposes; that in such sections very often the apartment house is a mere parasite, constructed in order to take advantage of the open spaces and attractive surroundings created by the residential character of the district. Moreover, the coming of one apartment house is followed by others, interfering by their height and bulk with the free circulation of air and monopolizing the rays of the sun which otherwise would fall upon the smaller homes, and bringing, as their necessary accompaniments, the disturbing noises incident to increased traffic and business, and the occupation, by means of moving and parked automobiles, of large portions of the streets, thus detracting from their safety and depriving children of the privilege of quiet and open spaces for play, enjoyed by those in more favored localities, — until, finally, the residential character of the neighborhood and its desirability as a place of detached residences are utterly destroyed. Under these circumstances apartment houses, which in a different environment would not only be entirely unobjectionable but highly desirable, come very near to being nuisances.

If these reasons, thus summarized, do not demonstrate the wisdom or sound policy in all respects of those restrictions which we have indicated as pertinent to the inquiry, at least, the reasons are sufficiently cogent to preclude us from saying, as it must be said before the ordinance can be declared unconstitutional, that such provisions are clearly arbitrary and unreasonable, having no substantial relation to the public health, safety, morals, or general welfare. Cusack Co. v. City of Chicago, *supra,* pp. 530-531 (37 S. Ct. 190); Jacobson v. Massachusetts, 197 U.S. 11, 30-31, 25 S. Ct. 358.

It is true that when, if ever, the provisions set forth in the ordinance in tedious and minute detail, come to be concretely applied to particular premises, including those of the appellee, or to particular conditions, or to be considered in connection with specific complaints, some of them, or even many of them, may be found to be clearly arbitrary and unreasonable. But where the equitable remedy of injunction is sought, as it is here, not upon the ground of a present infringement or denial of a specific right, or of a particular injury in process of actual execution, but upon the broad ground that the mere existence and threatened enforcement of the ordinance, by materially and adversely affecting values and curtailing the opportunities of the market, constitute a present and irreparable injury, the court will not scrutinize its provisions, sentence by sentence, to ascertain by a process of piecemeal dissection whether there may be, here and there, provisions of a minor character, or relating to matters of administration, or not shown to contribute to the injury complained of, which, if attacked separately, might not withstand the test of constitutionality. In respect of such provisions, of which specific complaint is not made, it cannot be said that the land owner has suffered or is threatened with an injury which entitles him to challenge their constitutionality. Turpin v. Lemon, 187 U.S. 51, 60, 23 S. Ct. 20. In Railroad Commission Cases, 116 U.S. 307, 335-337, 6 S. Ct. 334, 388, this Court dealt with an analogous situation. There an act of the Mississippi Legislature, regulating freight and passenger rates on intrastate railroads and creating a supervisory commission, was attacked as unconstitutional. The suit was brought to enjoin the commission from enforcing against the plaintiff railroad company any of its provisions. In an opinion delivered by Chief Justice Waite, this Court held that the chief purpose of the statute was to fix a maximum of charges and to regulate in some matters of a police nature the use of railroads in the state. After sustaining the constitutionality of the statute "in its general scope" this Court said: "Whether in some of its details the statute may be defective or invalid we do not deem it necessary to inquire, for this suit is brought to prevent the commissioners from giving it any effect whatever as against this company." Quoting with approval from the opinion of the Supreme Court of Mississippi it was further said: "Many questions may arise under it not necessary to be disposed of now, and we leave them for consideration when presented." And finally: "When the commission has acted and proceedings are had to enforce what it has done, questions may arise as to the validity of some of the various provisions which will be worthy of consideration, but we are unable to say that, as a whole, the statute is invalid."

The relief sought here is of the same character, namely, an injunction against the enforcement of any of the restrictions, limitations or conditions of the ordinance. And the gravamen of the complaint is that a portion of the land of the appellee cannot be sold for certain enumerated uses because of the general and broad restraints of the ordinance. What would be the effect of a restraint imposed by one or more of the innumerable provisions of the ordinance, considered apart, upon the value of marketability of the lands is neither disclosed by the bill nor by the evidence, and we are afforded no basis, apart from mere speculation, upon which to rest a conclusion that it or they would have any appreciable effect upon those matters. Under these circumstances, therefore, it is enough for us to determine, as we do, that the ordinance in its general scope and dominant features, so far as its provisions are here involved, is a valid exercise of authority, leaving other provisions to be dealt with as cases arise directly involving them.

And this is in accordance with the traditional policy of this Court. In the realm of constitutional law, especially, this Court has perceived the embarrassment which is likely to result from an attempt to formulate rules or decide questions beyond the necessities of the immediate issue. It has preferred to follow the method of a gradual approach to the general by a systematically guarded application and extension of constitutional principles to particular cases as they arise, rather than by out of hand attempts to establish general rules to which future cases must be fitted. This process applies with peculiar force to the solution of questions arising under the due process clause of the Constitution as applied to the exercise of the flexible powers of police, with which we are here concerned.

Decree reversed.

Mr. Justice VAN DEVANTER, Mr. Justice McREYNOLDS and Mr. Justice BUTLER dissent.

Note: Euclidean Zoning

Consider what the district court thought of this zoning ordinance:

> The plain truth is that the true object of the ordinance in question is to place all the property in an undeveloped area of 16 square miles in a strait-jacket. The purpose to be accomplished is really to regulate the mode of living of persons who may hereafter inhabit it. In the last analysis, the result to be accomplished is to classify the population and segregate them according to their income or situation in life. The true reason why some persons live in a mansion and others in a shack, why some live in a single-family dwelling and others in a double-family dwelling, why some live in a two-family dwelling and others in an apartment, or why some live in a well-kept apartment and others in a tenement, is primarily economic. It is a matter of income and wealth, plus the labor and difficulty of procuring adequate domestic service. Aside from contributing to these results and furthering such class tendencies, the ordinance has also an esthetic purpose; that is to say, to make this village develop into a city along lines now conceived by the village council to be attractive and beautiful. The assertion that this ordinance may tend to prevent congestion, and thereby contribute to the health and safety, would be more substantial if provision had been or could be made for adequate east and west and north and south street highways. Whether these purposes and objects would justify the taking of plaintiff's property as and for a public use need not be considered. It is sufficient to say that, in our opinion, and as applied to plaintiff's property, it may not be done without compensation under the guise of exercising the police power.[2]

Following the *Euclid* decision, the pattern of zoning ordinances throughout the country has been to regulate land use, building height, and lot area by dividing the "zoned area" into districts with fixed boundaries—each district having a defined use, etc. This type of zoning is usually called Euclidean zoning. The basic policy assumption behind Euclidean zoning—that homogeneity of uses is desirable—frequently has been questioned. It

---

2. Ambler Realty Co. v. Village of Euclid, 297 F. 307, 316 (N.D. Ohio 1924). For an interesting discussion of the present development of the village of Euclid, see Haar, Land-Use Planning 166 (1959), noting that the Ambler Realty Company property is today zoned for industry and the property is now owned by General Motors.—EDS.

has been pointed out that frequently it is a guise behind which to hide undemocratic economic and social segregation.[3]

Note that in *Euclid* the Supreme Court promises to review specific applications of zoning ordinances with care: "[W]hen, if ever, the provisions set forth in the ordinance . . . come to be concretely applied to particular premises . . . some of them, or even many of them, may be found to be clearly arbitrary and unreasonable."[4] The opportunity to follow up on this promise came two years later, in the *Nectow* case, which follows.

NECTOW v. CITY OF CAMBRIDGE
277 U.S. 183, 48 S. Ct. 447 (1928)

Error to a judgment of the Supreme Judicial Court of Massachusetts which dismissed a bill brought in that court by Nectow for a mandatory injunction directing the city and its building inspector to pass upon an application to erect any lawful buildings upon his land without regard to an ordinance including it within a restricted residential district.

Mr. Justice SUTHERLAND delivered the opinion of the court.

A zoning ordinance of the City of Cambridge divides the city into three kinds of districts: residential, business and unrestricted. Each of these districts is sub-classified in respect of the kind of buildings which may be erected. The ordinance is an elaborate one, and of the same general character as that considered by this Court in Euclid v. Ambler Co., 272 U.S. 365, 47 S. Ct. 114. In its general scope it is conceded to be constitutional within that decision. The land of plaintiff in error was put in district R-3, in which are permitted only dwellings, hotels, clubs, churches, schools, philanthropic institutions, greenhouses and gardening, with customary incidental accessories. The attack upon the ordinance is that, as specifically applied to plaintiff in error, it deprived him of his property without due process of law in contravention of the Fourteenth Amendment.

The suit was for a mandatory injunction directing the city and its inspector of buildings to pass upon an application of the plaintiff in error for a permit to erect any lawful buildings upon a tract of land without regard to the provisions of the ordinance including such tract within a residential district. The case was referred to a master to make and report findings of fact. After a view of the premises and the surrounding territory, and a hearing, the master made and reported his findings. The case came on to be heard by a justice of the court, who, after confirming the master's report,

---

3. See, e.g., Haar, Zoning for Minimum Standards: The *Wayne Township* Case, 66 Harv. L. Rev. 1051 (1953); Williams, Planning Law and Democratic Living, 20 Law & Contemp. Probs. 317 (1955).
4. 272 U.S. 365, 395, 47 S. Ct. 114, 121 (1926).

reported the case for the determination of the full court. Upon consideration, that court sustained the ordinance as applied to plaintiff in error, and dismissed the bill. 260 Mass. 441, 157 N.E. 618.

A condensed statement of facts, taken from the master's report, is all that is necessary. When the zoning ordinance was enacted, plaintiff in error was and still is the owner of a tract of land containing 140,000 square feet, of which the locus here in question is a part. The locus contains about 29,000 square feet, with a frontage on Brookline street, lying west, of 304.75 feet, on Henry street, lying north, of 100 feet, on the other land of the plaintiff in error, lying east, of 264 feet, and on land of the Ford Motor Company, lying southerly, of 75 feet. The territory lying east and south is unrestricted. The lands beyond Henry street to the north and beyond Brookline street to the west are within a restricted residential district. The effect of the zoning is to separate from the west end of plaintiff in error's tract a strip 100 feet in width. The Ford Motor Company has a large auto assembling factory south of the locus; and a soap factory and the tracks of the Boston & Albany Railroad lie near. Opposite the locus, on Brookline street, and included in the same district, there are some residences; and opposite the locus, on Henry street, and in the same district, are other residences. The locus is now vacant, although it was once occupied by a mansion house. Before the passage of the ordinance in question, plaintiff in error had outstanding a contract for the sale of the greater part of his entire tract of land for the sum of $63,000. Because of the zoning restrictions, the purchaser refused to comply with the contract. Under the ordinance, business and industry of all sorts are excluded from the locus, while the remainder of the tract is unrestricted. It further appears that provision has been made for widening Brookline street, the effect of which, if carried out, will be to reduce the depth of the locus to 65 feet. After a statement at length of further facts, the master finds "that no practical use can be made of the land in question for residential purposes, because among other reasons herein related, there would not be adequate return on the amount of any investment for the development of the property." The last finding of the master is:

> I am satisfied that the districting of the plaintiff's land in a residence district would not promote the health, safety, convenience and general welfare of the inhabitants of that part of the defendant City, taking into account the natural development thereof and the character of the district and the resulting benefit to accrue to the whole City and I so find.

It is made pretty clear that because of the industrial and railroad purposes to which the immediately adjoining lands to the south and east have been devoted and for which they are zoned, the locus is of comparatively little value for the limited uses permitted by the ordinance.

We quite agree with the opinion expressed below that a court should not set aside the determination of public officers in such a matter unless it is clear that their action "has no foundation in reason and is a mere arbitrary or irrational exercise of power having no substantial relation to the public health, the public morals, the public safety or the public welfare in its proper sense." Euclid v. Ambler Co., *supra,* 272 U.S. p. 395, 47 S. Ct. 114.

An inspection of a plat of the city upon which the zoning districts are outlined, taken in connection with the master's findings, shows with reasonable certainty that the inclusion of the locus in question is not indispensable to the general plan. The boundary line of the residential district before reaching the locus runs for some distance along the streets, and to exclude the locus from the residential district requires only that such line shall be continued 100 feet further along Henry street and thence south along Brookline street. There does not appear to be any reason why this should not be done. Nevertheless, if that were all, we should not be warranted in substituting our judgment for that of the zoning authorities primarily charged with the duty and responsibility of determining the question. Zahn v. Board of Public Works, 274 U.S. 325, 328, 47 S. Ct. 594, and cases cited. But that is not all. The governmental power to interfere by zoning regulations with the general rights of the landowner by restricting the character of his use, is not unlimited, and other questions aside, such restriction cannot be imposed if it does not bear a substantial relation to the public health, safety, morals, or general welfare. Euclid v. Ambler Co., *supra,* 272 U.S. p. 395, 47 S. Ct. 114. Here, the express finding of the master, already quoted, confirmed by the court below, is that the health, safety, convenience and general welfare of the inhabitants of the part of the city affected will not be promoted by the disposition made by the ordinance of the locus in question. This finding of the master, after a hearing and an inspection of the entire area affected, supported, as we think it is, by other findings of fact, is determinative of the case. That the invasion of the property of plaintiff in error was serious and highly injurious is clearly established; and, since a necessary basis for the support of that invasion is wanting, the action of the zoning authorities comes within the ban of the Fourteenth Amendment and cannot be sustained.

Judgment reversed.

Note: The Nectow *Test: Unconstitutional as Applied to the Locus*

Consider what the Supreme Judicial Court of Massachusetts said of the dividing line in *Nectow:*

> It is manifest from the facts reported by the master and from the accompanying maps that the locus is near the border line between land most available for residential uses and land best adapted for commercial or manufacturing enterprises. It has not been urged that the land directly across Brookline street

or that across Henry street from the locus has not been properly zoned in a residential district. Confessedly those lands are parts of large residential areas, stamped as such by established use. The locus, so far as it ever has been improved, has been devoted exclusively to residential purposes. If there is to be zoning at all, the dividing line must be drawn somewhere. There cannot be a twilight zone. If residence districts are to exist, they must be bounded. In the nature of things, the location of the precise limits of the several districts demands the exercise of judgment and sagacity. There can be no standard susceptible of mathematical exactness in its application. Opinions of the wise and good well may differ as to the place to put the separation between different districts. Seemingly there would be great difficulty in pronouncing a scheme for zoning unreasonable and capricious because it embraced land on both sides of the same street in one district instead of making the center of the street the dividing line. . . .

Courts cannot set aside the decision of public officers in such a matter unless compelled to the conclusion that it has no foundation in reason and is a mere arbitrary or irrational exercise of power having no substantial relation to the public health, the public morals, the public safety, or the public welfare in its proper sense. These considerations cannot be weighed with exactness. That they demand the placing of the boundary of a zone one hundred feet one way or the other in land having similar material features would be hard to say as matter of law. . . .

The case at bar is close to the line. But we do not feel justified in holding that the zoning line established is whimsical, without foundation in reason. In our opinion it is not violative of the rights secured to the plaintiff by the Constitution, either of this commonwealth or by the Fourteenth Amendment to the Constitution of the United States.[5]

The Supreme Court, whether right or wrong, seemed to undertake what had been foreshadowed in *Euclid*—a close supervision of this recently validated zoning power. Having established the constitutionality of zoning, the Supreme Court, however, has left it to the various states to apply the constitutional principle of reasonableness to individual cases as they arise. As a result of this abdication, there are wide differences both in emphasis and in doctrine from state to state. It should also be noted that there has been a gradual abdication of the review function in state courts of last resort, preferring to yield to "legislative judgment."[6]

Aside from the requirement of "reasonableness," are there other constitutional roadblocks in the way of a state's justifiable interest in regulating and controlling the use of land? As previously noted, the power to regulate

5. Nectow v. City of Cambridge, 260 Mass. 441, 447, 448, 157 N.E. 618, 620 (1927). —EDS.

6. Compare the majority opinion in Vickers v. Township Committee, 37 N.J. 232, 181 A.2d 129 (1962), *appeal dismissed,* 371 U.S. 233, 83 S. Ct. 326 (1963), with Justice Hall's dissent, 37 N.J. at 252-270, 181 A.2d at 140-150. The opinions carefully consider the role of the judiciary in the review of a validly enacted zoning ordinance. The decision is discussed in Note, 61 Mich. L. Rev. 1010 (1963), and Note, 17 Rutgers L. Rev. 659 (1963).

without compensation must be derived from the police power, which is usually defined so as to embrace the preservation of public health, safety, morals, and welfare. May the police power be used to maintain some values not so clearly embraced within the traditional four purposes, e.g., economic, social, or aesthetic values? Are any one of these latter values a sufficient predicate, in and of itself, to justify the use of the police power? It is to these questions that we now turn.

We should first take a look at Village of Belle Terre v. Boraas, 416 U.S. 1, 94 S. Ct. 1536 (1974), where the issue was the constitutionality of an ordinance that restricted land use to one-family dwellings, excluding lodging houses, boardinghouses, fraternity houses, and multiple-family houses. The word "family" as used in the ordinance means "one or more persons related by blood, adoption, or marriage, living and cooking together as a single housekeeping unit, exclusive of household servants. A number of persons but not exceeding two (2) living and cooking together as a single housekeeping unit though not related by blood, adoption, or marriage shall be deemed to constitute a family." The Supreme Court remarked that this case brought to the Court "a different phase of local zoning regulations" than it had previously reviewed. In upholding the ordinance, the court observed: "The police power is not confined to elimination of filth, stench and unhealthy places. It is ample to lay out zones where family values, youth values and blessings of quiet seclusion and clean air make the area a sanctuary for people." In his dissent, Justice Marshall stressed that the freedom of association is entwined with the constitutionally guaranteed right of privacy, remarking: "By limiting unrelated households to two persons while placing no limitation on households of related individuals, the village has embarked upon its commendable course in a constitutionally faulty vessel."

Note: Zoning Laws Which Hamper the Construction of Low and Moderate Income Housing

Village of Arlington Heights v. Metropolitan Housing Development Corp., 434 U.S. 1025, 97 S. Ct. 555 (1977), upheld the validity of the action of the village of Arlington Heights in refusing to rezone a 15-acre parcel from a single-family to a multiple-family classification to enable the building of 190 clustered townhouse units for low and moderate income tenants. The Court of Appeals for the Seventh Circuit had held that the "ultimate effect" of the denial was racially discriminatory and that the refusal to rezone therefore violated the fourteenth amendment (see 517 F.2d 409 (1975)). The Supreme Court concluded that proof of a racially discriminatory intent or purpose is required to show a violation of the equal protection clause; official action will not be held unconstitutional solely because it has a disproportionate impact on a certain racial group. The Supreme Court held that the respondents simply failed to carry their burden of proving that discriminatory purpose was a motivating factor in the village's decision.

Hunter v. Erickson, 393 U.S. 384, 89 S. Ct. 557 (1969), held unconstitutional as a denial of equal protection of the laws an amendment to the city charter of Akron, Ohio, which provided that any ordinance enacted by the council of the city regulating the sale and so forth of real property "on the basis of race, color, religion, national origin or ancestry must first be approved by a majority of the electors voting on the question at a regular or general election before said ordinance shall be effective." Compare with this case James v. Valtierra, 402 U.S. 137, 91 S. Ct. 1331 (1971), which dealt with an amendment to the California state constitution which provided that no low rent housing project should be developed, constructed, or acquired in any manner by a state public body until the project was approved by a majority of those voting at a community election. The court observed that the record here would not support any claim that a law seemingly neutral on its face is in fact aimed at a racial minority and upheld the amendment to the state constitution against the attack that it denied the plaintiffs, who were persons eligible for low cost public housing, the equal protection of the laws. Justice Marshall, in his dissent, stated: "It is far too late in the day to contend that the Fourteenth Amendment prohibits only racial discrimination; and to me singling out the poor to bear a burden not placed on any other class of citizens tramples the values that the Fourteenth Amendment was designed to protect."

For a case which recognized that there was a violation of the fifth amendment by a federal agency in connection with the selection of sites for public housing in the city of Chicago to avoid the placement of black families in white neighborhoods, see Hills v. Gautreaux, 425 U.S. 284, 96 S. Ct. 1538 (1976).

See Mass. Gen. Laws ch. 40B, §20-23, enacted in 1969, and Board of Appeals v. Housing Appeals Commission in the Department of Community Affairs, 363 Mass. 399, 294 N.E.2d 393 (1973), which examines this legislation. The following is a quotation from this case (the reference to ch. 774 is the chapter in the 1969 Massachusetts laws that brought into existence ch. 40B, §§20-23):

> In conclusion, c. 774 represents the Legislature's attempt to satisfy the regional need for housing without stripping municipalities of their power to zone. By creating a "consistent with local needs" criterion which expends the scope of relevant local needs considered by the local boards to include the regional need for low and moderate income housing, the Legislature has given the boards the power to override the local exclusionary zoning practices in order to encourage the construction of such housing in the suburbs. By fixing a ceiling on the extent to which a board must override local zoning regulations, the Legislature has clearly delineated that point where local interest must yield to the general public need for housing. This ceiling establishes the minimum share of responsibility that each community must shoulder in order to allevi-

ate the housing crisis that confronts the Commonwealth. [363 Mass. at 383, 294 N.E.2d at 422-423.]

See Southern Burlington County NAACP v. Township of Mount Laurel, 67 N.J. 151, 336 A.2d 713 (1975), where the system of land use regulation by the township of Mount Laurel was attacked on the ground that low and moderate income families were excluded from the municipality. The New Jersey court commented as follows:

The legal question before us, as earlier indicated, is whether a developing municipality like Mount Laurel may validly, by a system of land use regulation, make it physically and economically impossible to provide low and moderate income housing in the municipality for the various categories of persons who need and want it and thereby, as Mount Laurel has, exclude such people from living within its confines because of the limited extent of their income and resources. Necessarily implicated are the broader questions of the right of such municipalities to limit the kinds of available housing and of any obligation to make possible a variety and choice of types of living accommodations.

We conclude that every such municipality must, by its land use regulations, presumptively make realistically possible an appropriate variety and choice of housing. More specifically, presumptively it cannot foreclose the opportunity of the classes of people mentioned for low and moderate income housing and in its regulations must affirmatively afford that opportunity, at least to the extent of the municipality's fair share of the present and prospective regional need therefor. These obligations must be met unless the particular municipality can sustain the heavy burden of demonstrating peculiar circumstances which dictate that it should not be required so to do. [67 N.J. at 173-174, 336 A.2d at 724-725.]

After discussing various aspects of exclusionary zoning which prevented housing for low and moderate income families, the court summarized the situation as follows:

By way of summary, what we have said comes down to this. As a developing municipality, Mount Laurel must, by its land use regulations, make realistically possible the opportunity for an appropriate variety and choice of housing for all categories of people who may desire to live there, of course including those of low and moderate income. It must permit multi-family housing, without bedroom or similar restrictions, as well as small dwellings on very small lots, low cost housing of other types and, in general, high density zoning, without artificial and unjustifiable minimum requirements as to lot size, building size and the like, to meet the full panoply of these needs. Certainly when a municipality zones for industry and commerce for local tax benefit purposes, it without question must zone to permit adequate housing within the means of the employees involved in such uses. (If planned unit developments are authorized, one would assume that each must include a reasonable amount of low and moderate income housing in its residential "mix," unless opportunity for such housing has already been realistically provided for elsewhere in the municipality.) The amount of land removed from residential use by allocation to industrial and commercial purposes must be reasonably related to the present and future potential for such purposes. In other words, such municipalities must zone primarily for the living welfare of people and not for the benefit of the local tax rate. [67 N.J. at 187-188, 336 A.2d at 731-732.]

In regard to the remedy for the situation considered by the court, the New Jersey court used the following language:

We are not at all sure what the trial judge had in mind as ultimate action with reference to the approval of a plan for affirmative public action concerning the satisfaction of indicated housing needs and the entry of a final order requiring implementation thereof. Courts do not build housing nor do municipalities. That function is performed by private builders, various kinds of associations, or, for public housing, by special agencies created for that purpose at various levels of government. The municipal function is initially to provide the opportunity through appropriate land use regulations and we have spelled out what Mount Laurel must do in that regard. It is not appropriate at this time, particularly in view of the advanced view of zoning law as applied to housing laid down by this opinion, to deal with the matter of the further extent of judicial power in the field or to exercise any such power. See, however, Pascack Association v. Mayor and Council of Township of Washington, 131 N.J. Super. 195, 329 A.2d 89 (Law Div. 1974), and cases therein cited, for a discussion of this question. The municipality should first have full opportunity to itself act without judicial supervision. We trust it will do so in the spirit we have suggested, both by appropriate zoning ordinance amendments and whatever additional action encouraging the fulfillment of its fair share of the regional need for low and moderate income housing may be indicated as necessary and advisable. (We have in mind that there is at least a moral obligation in a municipality to establish a local housing agency pursuant to state law to provide housing for its resident poor now living in dilapidated, unhealthy quarters.) The portion of the trial court's judgment ordering the preparation and submission of the aforesaid study, report and plan to it for further action is therefore vacated as at least premature. Should Mount Laurel not perform as we expect, further judicial action may be sought by supplemental pleading in this cause. [67 N.J. at 192, 336 A.2d at 734.]

Note: Minimum Size for Dwellings in Zoned Residential Area

Lionshead Lake Inc. v. Wayne Township, 10 N.J. 165, 89 A.2d 693 (1952), *appeal dismissed,* 344 U.S. 919, 73 S. Ct. 386 (1953), considered the following ordinance pertaining to "Residence A" districts:

(d) Minimum Size of Dwellings:
Every dwelling hereafter erected or placed in a Residence A District shall have a living-floor space, as herein defined

of not less than 765 feet for one story dwelling;

of not less than 1000 square feet for a two-story dwelling having an attached garage;

of not less than 1200 square feet for a two story dwelling not having an attached garage.

In upholding the ordinance, the court commented as follows:

Has a municipality the right to impose minimum floor area requirements in the exercise of its zoning powers? Much of the proof adduced by the defendant township was devoted to showing that the mental and emotional health of its inhabitants depended on the proper size of their homes. We may take notice without formal proof that there are minimums in housing below which one may not go without risk of impairing the health of those who dwell therein. One does not need extensive experience in matrimonial causes to become aware of the adverse effect of overcrowding on the well-being of our most important institution, the home. Moreover, people who move into the country rightly expect more land, more living room, indoors and out, and more freedom in their scale of living than is generally possible in the city. City standards of housing are not adaptable to suburban areas and especially to the upbringing of children. But quite apart from these considerations of public health which cannot be overlooked, minimum floor-area standards are justified on the ground that they promote the general welfare of the community and, as we have seen in Schmidt v. Board of Adjustment of the City of Newark, 9 N.J. 405, 88 A.2d 607 (1952), *supra,* the courts in conformance with the constitutional provisions and the statutes hereinbefore cited take a broad view of what constitutes general welfare. The size of the dwellings in any community inevitably affects the character of the community and does much to determine whether or not it is a desirable place in which to live. It is the prevailing view in municipalities throughout the State that such minimum floor-area standards are necessary to protect the character of the community. A survey made by the Department of Conservation and Economic Development in 1951 disclosed that 64 municipalities out of the 138 reporting had minimum dwelling requirements. In the light of the Constitution and of the enabling statutes, the right of a municipality to impose minimum floor-area requirements is beyond controversy.

With respect to every zoning ordinance, however, the question remains as to whether or not in the particular facts of the case and in the light of all of the surrounding circumstances the minimum floor-area requirements are reasonable. Can a minimum of living floor space of 768 square feet for a one-story building; of 1,000 square feet for a two-story dwelling having an attached garage; and of 1,200 square feet for a two-story dwelling not having an attached garage be deemed unreasonable in a rural area just beginning to change to a suburban community? It is significant that the plaintiff admits that of the 100 houses in its development 30 met the minimum requirements when constructed and 20 more by voluntary additions of the owners to meet their individual needs have been enlarged to conform to the minimum requirements of the ordinance, and while this litigation has been pending 20 others have been constructed conforming to the ordinance. If some such requirements were not imposed there would be grave danger in certain parts of the township, particularly around the lakes which attract summer visitors, of the erection of shanties which would deteriorate land values generally to the great detriment of the increasing number of people who live in Wayne Township the year around. The minimum floor area requirements imposed by the ordinance are not large for a family of normal size. Without some such restrictions there is always the danger that after some homes have been erected giving a character to a neighborhood others might follow which would fail to live up to the standards thus voluntarily set. This has been the experience in many communities and it is against this that the township has sought to safeguard itself within limits which seem to us to be altogether reasonable.[7] [10 N.J. at 173-175, 89 A.2d at 697-698.]

Problems

33.1. A village zones property for "office building" use, permitting business and professional offices and accessory retail shops, apparently to protect a nearby shopping center from unwanted competition. A landowner who is restricted to the office building use tries to have the property rezoned for community store use in order to compete with the existing shopping center. Testimony establishes the land value as $350,000 if zoned community store but only $100,000 if zoned office building. Keeping in mind the stress in the *Lionshead* case on protecting against deterioration in land values, is the zoning valid? Should the outcome depend on whether the landowner purchased the tract before or after the zoning? See Pearce v. Village of Edina, 263 Minn. 553, 118 N.W.2d 659 (1962).

33.2. "The trial court found that the subject property has great value if used for rock, sand and gravel excavation but 'no appreciable economic value' for any other purpose . . . any suggestion that the property has economic value for any other use, including those uses for which it was zoned, 'is preposterous.' The planning commission approved, with certain recommended conditions, the plaintiffs' application for designation of their property as a "Rock and Gravel District," but the city council of Los Angeles denied the application. The plaintiffs contend that the city of Los Angeles has "taken" the plaintiffs' property without just compensation since it has left the plaintiffs with a valueless parcel of land. What decision? Consolidated Rock Products Co. v. City of Los Angeles, 370 P.2d 342, 57 Cal. 2d 515, 20 Cal. Rptr. 638, *appeal dismissed,* 371 U.S. 36 (1962).

---

7. See generally Comment, Snob Zoning—A Look at the Economic and Social Impact of Low Density Zoning, 15 Syracuse L. Rev. 507 (1964); Haar, footnote 3 *supra;* Note, Municipal Corporations—Protection of Property Values Held Sufficient Justification for Total Exclusion of Trailer Camps, 17 Rutgers L. Rev. 659 (1963), discussing *Vickers,* footnote 6 *supra;* Note, Minimum Lot Area Requirements in New York, 21 N.Y.U. Intra. L. Rev. 24 (1965).—EDS.

Note: Minimum Lot Size

The advantages enjoyed by those living in one family dwellings located upon an acre lot might be thought to exceed those possessed by persons living upon a lot of ten thousand square feet. More freedom from noise and traffic might result. The danger from fire from outside sources might be reduced. A better opportunity for rest and relaxation might be afforded. Greater facilities for children to play on the premises and not in the streets would be available. There may perhaps be more inducement for one to attempt something in the way of the cultivation of flowers, shrubs and vegetables. There may be other advantages accruing to the occupants of the larger lots. . . . [Simon v. Town of Needham, 311 Mass. 560, 563-564, 42 N.E.2d 516, 518 (1942).]

Courts generally have rejected attacks on minimum lot size requirements. See, e.g., Dilliard v. Village of North Hills, 276 A.D. 969, 94 N.Y.S.2d 715 (1950) (two acres); Senior v. Zoning Commission, 146 Conn. 531, 153 A.2d 415 (1959) (four acres); Honeck v. County of Cook, 12 Ill. 2d 257, 146 N.E.2d 35 (1957) (five acres). But see National Land & Investment Co. v. Kohn, 419 Pa. 504, 215 A.2d 597 (1965) (invalidating four acres). See generally Annot., 95 A.L.R.2d 716 (1964).

Note: Architectural Compatibility

State ex rel. Saveland Park Holding Corp. v. Wieland, 269 Wis. 262, 69 N.W.2d 217 (1955), considered the constitutionality of the following ordinance:

No building permit for any structure for which a building permit is required shall be issued unless it has been found as a fact by the Building Board by at least a majority vote, after a view of the site of the proposed structure, and an examination of the application papers for a building permit, which shall include exterior elevations of the proposed structure, that the exterior architectural appeal and functional plan of the proposed structure will, when erected, not be so at variance with either the exterior architectural appeal and functional plan of the structures already constructed or in the course of construction in the immediate neighborhood or the character of the applicable district established by Ordinance No. 117 [the general zoning ordinance of the village], or any ordinance amendatory thereof or supplementary thereto, as to cause a substantial depreciation in the property values of said neighborhood within said applicable district.

Subsequent sections of the ordinance provide that the building board shall consist of three residents of the village, two of whom shall be architects, and provide a method of appeal from the decision of the building board to the board of appeals of the village. In upholding the constitutionality of the ordinance, the Wisconsin Supreme Court said:

We have no difficulty in arriving at the conclusion that the protection of property values is an objective which falls within the exercise of the police power to promote the "general welfare," and that it is immaterial whether the zoning ordinance is grounded solely upon such objective or that such purpose is but one of several legitimate objectives. Anything that tends to destroy property values of the inhabitants of the village necessarily adversely affects the prosperity, and therefore the general welfare, of the entire village. Just because, in the particular case now before us, property values in a limited area only of the village are at stake does not mean that such threatened depreciation of property values does not affect the general welfare of the village as a whole. If relator is permitted to erect a dwelling house on its land of such nature as to substantially depreciate the value of surrounding property, there is danger that this same thing may be repeated elsewhere within the village, thus threatening property values throughout the village. [269 Wis. at 270-271, 69 N.W.2d at 222.]

In closing, the Wisconsin court said:

It is our considered judgment that ordinance No. 129 constitutes a valid exercise of the police power of the village of Fox Point, and its provisions are not so indefinite or ambiguous as to subject applicants for building permits to the uncontrolled arbitrary discretion or caprice of the Building Board.[8] [269 Wis. at 276, 69 N.W.2d at 224.]

Problems

33.3. In assessing the *Wieland* case, does it make any difference that Fox Point is an exclusive residential community along Lake Michigan containing homes in the $100,000-plus category?

33.4. City of West Palm Beach v. State ex rel. Duffey, 158 Fla. 863, 30 So. 2d 491 (1947), invalidated the following ordinance: "[T]he completed appearance of every new building or structure must substantially equal that of the adjacent buildings or structures in said subdivision in appearance, square foot area, and height." Can this case and the *Wieland* case be distinguished?

33.5. Is the *Wieland* case authority for the proposition that zoning may be predicated on aesthetic considerations, alone, or is it only authority that zoning may preserve property values? What is the difference?

Note: *Zoning for Purely Aesthetic Objectives*

Aesthetics is frequently the real basis behind a zoning ordinance, but courts frequently go to extreme lengths to uphold an ordinance on some

8. For another case that held that an architectural board did not act unreasonably in refusing to approve the design of a house, see Reid v. Architectural Board of Review, 119 Ohio App. 67, 192 N.E.2d 74 (1963). — EDS.

other ground, i.e., one of the four traditional predicates of the police power. The exclusion of billboards has probably given birth to the best examples of this type of "reasoning." Consider the following:

> The signboards and billboards upon which this class of advertisements are displayed are constant menaces to the public safety and welfare of the city; they endanger the public health, promote immorality, constitute hiding places and retreats for criminals and all classes of miscreants. They are also inartistic and unsightly. In cases of fire they often cause their spread and constitute barriers against their extinction; and in cases of high wind, their temporary character, frail structure and broad surface, render them liable to be blown down and to fall upon and injure those who may happen to be in their vicinity. The evidence shows and common observation teaches us that the ground in the rear thereof is being constantly used as privies and dumping ground for all kinds of waste and deleterious matters, and thereby creating public nuisances and jeopardizing public health; the evidence also shows that behind these obstructions the lowest form of prostitution and other acts of immorality are frequently carried on, almost under public gaze; they offer shelter and concealment for the criminal while lying in wait for his victim; and last, but not least, they obstruct the light, sunshine, and air, which are so conducive to health and comfort. [St. Louis Gunning Advertising Co. v. City of St. Louis, 235 Mo. 99, 145, 137 S.W. 929, 942 (1911).]

Compare United Advertising Corp. v. Metuchen, 42 N.J. 1, 198 A.2d 447 (1964), where "by stipulation of the parties, all of the stereotyped reasons ordinarily utilized to support the use of the police power in billboard cases were removed from consideration," i.e., each of the "reasons" given in St. Louis Gunning Advertising Co. v. City of St. Louis was agreed by the parties to be factually untenable.

Why are the courts afraid to admit aesthetics as a sole predicate for a zoning ordinance? Is this fear justified? Consider the following case.

PEOPLE v. STOVER

12 N.Y.2d 462, 191 N.E.2d 272, *appeal dismissed,* 375 U.S. 42 (1963)

FULD, J.

The defendants, Mr. and Mrs. Stover, residents of the city of Rye since 1940, live in a 2½-story 1-family dwelling, located in a pleasant and built-up residential district, on the corner of Rye Beach and Forest Avenues. A clothesline, filled with old clothes and rags, made its first appearance in the Stovers' front yard in 1956 as a form of "peaceful protest" against the high taxes imposed by the city. And, during each of the five succeeding years, the defendants added another clothesline to mark their continued displeasure with the taxes. In 1961, therefore, six lines, from which there hung tattered clothing, old uniforms, underwear, rags and scarecrows, were strung across the Stovers' yard — three from the porch across the front yard to trees along Forest Avenue and three from the porch across the side yard to trees along Rye Beach Avenue.

In August of 1961, the city enacted an ordinance prohibiting the erection and maintenance of clotheslines or other devices for hanging clothes or other fabrics in a front or side yard abutting a street (General Ordinances, §4-3.7). However, the ordinance provides for the issuance of a permit for the use of such clotheslines if there is "a practical difficulty or unnecessary hardship in drying clothes elsewhere on the premises" and grants a right of appeal to the applicant if a permit is denied.

Following enactment of the ordinance, Mrs. Stover, the record owner of the property, applied for a permit to maintain clotheslines in her yard. Her application was denied because, she was advised, she had sufficient other property available for hanging clothes and she was directed to remove the clotheslines which were in the yards abutting the streets. Although no appeal was taken from this determination and no permit ever issued, the clotheslines were not removed. Relying upon the ordinance, the city thereupon charged the defendants with violating its provisions. They were tried and convicted and their judgments of conviction have been affirmed by the County Court of Westchester County. Upon the trial the defendant Webster Stover disputed the sufficiency of the evidence to connect him with the erection or maintenance of the clotheslines but he does not do so here, urging instead that the ordinance, as it has been applied to him and his wife, is unconstitutional both as an interference with free speech and as a deprivation of property without due process.

It is a fair inference that adoption of the ordinance before us was prompted by the conduct and action of the defendants but we deem it clear that, if the law would otherwise be held constitutional, it will not be stricken as discriminatory or invalid because of its motivation. (Cf. Town of Hempstead v. Goldblatt, 9 N.Y.2d 101, 211 N.Y.S.2d 185, 172 N.E.2d 562, *affd.* 369 U.S. 590, 82 S. Ct. 987, 8 L. Ed. 2d 130.) Our problem, therefore, is to determine whether the law violates First Amendment rights or otherwise exceeds the police power vested in a city on the ground that it was enacted without regard to considerations of public health, safety and welfare.

The People maintain that the prohibition against clotheslines in front and side yards was "intended to provide clear visibility at street corners and in driving out of driveways, and thus avoid and reduce accidents; to reduce distractions to motorists and pedestrians; and to provide greater opportunity for access in the event of fires." Although there may be considerable doubt whether there is a sufficiently reasonable relationship between clotheslines and traffic or fire safety to support an exercise of the police power, it is our opinion that the ordinance may be sustained as an attempt to preserve the residential appearance of the city and its property values by banning, insofar as practicable, unsightly clotheslines from yards abutting a public street. In other words, the statute, though based on what may be termed aesthetic considerations, proscribes conduct which offends sensibilities and tends to debase the community and reduce real estate values.

There are a number of early decisions which hold that aesthetic considerations are not alone sufficient to justify exercise of the police power. But since 1930 this court has taken pains repeatedly to declare that the issue is an open and "unsettled" one in New York.

In addition, we have actually recognized the governmental interest in preserving the appearance of the community by holding that, whether or not aesthetic considerations are in and of themselves sufficient to support an exercise of the police power, they may be taken into account by the legislative body in enacting laws which are also designed to promote health and safety. "Aesthetic considerations," this court wrote in Dowsey v. Village of Kensington (257 N.Y. 221, 230, 177 N.E. 427, 430, *supra*), "are, fortunately, not wholly without weight in a practical world."

Once it be conceded that aesthetics is a valid subject of legislative concern, the conclusion seems inescapable that reasonable legislation designed to promote that end is a valid and permissible exercise of the police power. If zoning restrictions "which implement a policy of neighborhood amenity" are to be stricken as invalid, it should be, one commentator has said, not because they seek to promote "aesthetic objectives" but solely because the restrictions constitute "unreasonable devices of implementing community policy." (Dukeminier, Zoning for Aesthetic Objectives: A Reappraisal, 20 Law & Contemp. Prob. 218, 231.) Consequently, whether such a statute or ordinance should be voided should depend upon whether the restriction was "an arbitrary and irrational method of achieving an attractive, efficiently functioning, prosperous community—and *not* upon whether the objectives were primarily aesthetic." (Dukeminier, loc. cit.) And, indeed, this view finds support in an ever-increasing number of cases from other jurisdictions which recognize that aesthetic considerations alone may warrant an exercise of the police power. As Mr. Justice Douglas, writing for a unanimous court in *Berman* [Berman v. Parker] put it (348 U.S., at p. 33, 75 S. Ct., at p. 102):

> The concept of the public welfare is broad and inclusive. . . . The values it represents are spiritual as well as physical, aesthetic as well as monetary. It is within the power of the legislature to determine that the community should be beautiful as well as healthy, spacious as well as clean, well-balanced as well as carefully patrolled. . . . If those who govern the District of Columbia decide that the Nation's Capital should be beautiful as well as sanitary, there is nothing in the Fifth Amendment that stands in the way.

Cases may undoubtedly arise, as we observed above, in which the legislative body goes too far in the name of aesthetics (cf. Matter of Mid-State Adv. Corp. v. Bond, 274 N.Y. 82, 8 N.E.2d 286; Dowsey v. Village of Kensington, 257 N.Y. 221, 177 N.E. 427, *supra;* Dukeminier, Zoning for Aesthetic

Objectives: A Reappraisal, 20 Law & Contemp. Prob. 218, 231) but the present, quite clearly, is not one of them. The ordinance before us is in large sense regulatory rather than prohibitory. It causes no undue hardship to any property owner, for it expressly provides for the issuance of a permit for clotheslines in front and side yards in cases where there is practical difficulty or unnecessary hardship in drying clothes elsewhere on the premises. Moreover, the ordinance imposes no arbitrary or capricious standard of beauty or conformity upon the community. It simply proscribes conduct which is unnecessarily offensive to the visual sensibilities of the average person. It is settled that conduct which is similarly offensive to the senses of hearing and smell may be a valid subject of regulation under the police power (see, e.g., People v. Rubenfeld, 254 N.Y. 245, 172 N.E. 485, *supra*), and we perceive no basis for a different result merely because the sense of sight is involved.

Nor is there any warrant or justification for a charge — which seems to have been abandoned on this appeal — that the ordinance is being enforced solely against the defendants or that there is a pattern of discrimination consciously being practiced against them. As the court below noted, the building superintendent testified, without contradiction, that all applications for permits were checked and investigated, that other applications for permits had been denied and that the defendants were the only persons who refused to remove clotheslines violative of the ordinance.

Having concluded that the ordinance here in question is validly grounded on a proper exercise of the police power, we turn to the defendants' principal contention that it is invalid as applied to them because it constitutes an unconstitutional infringement of their freedom of speech. The defendants erected the six clotheslines on their property as a protest against their tax assessment. This form of nonverbal expression is, we shall assume, a form of speech within the meaning of the First Amendment. However, it is perfectly clear that, since these rights are neither absolute nor unlimited they are subject to such reasonable regulation as is provided by the ordinance before us. Although the city may not interfere with nonviolent speech, it may proscribe conduct which incites to violence or works an injury on property, and the circumstance that such prohibition has an impact on speech or expression, otherwise permissible, does not necessarily invalidate the legislation.

It must be borne in mind that the ordinance here in question is, in the language of a recent Supreme Court case (Edwards v. South Carolina, 372 U.S. 229, 236, 83 S. Ct. 680, 684, 9 L. Ed. 2d 697), a "precise and narrowly drawn regulatory statute evincing a legislative judgment that certain specific conduct be limited or proscribed." (See, also, Schneider v. State, 308 U.S. 147, 160-161, 60 S. Ct. 146, 84 L. Ed. 155.) As the court aptly observed in the Schneider case (308 U.S. 147, 160-161, 60 S. Ct. 146, 150, 84 L. Ed. 155, *supra*), "a person could not exercise [his freedom of speech] by taking his stand in the middle of a crowded street, contrary to traffic regulations, and maintain his position to the stoppage of all traffic; a group of distributors could not insist upon a constitutional right to form a cordon across the street and to allow no pedestrian to pass who did not accept a tendered leaflet; nor does the guarantee of freedom of speech or of the press deprive a municipality of power to enact regulations against throwing literature broadcast in the streets. Prohibition of such conduct would not abridge the constitutional liberty since such activity bears no necessary relationship to the freedom to speak, write, print or distribute information or opinion."

This reasoning is equally applicable to the case before us. The prohibition against clotheslines is designed to proscribe conduct which offends the sensibilities and tends to depress property values. The ordinance and its prohibition bear "no necessary relationship" to the dissemination of ideas or opinion and, accordingly, the defendants were not privileged to violate it by choosing to express their views in the altogether bizarre manner which they did. It is obvious that the value of their "protest" lay not in its message but in its offensiveness.

The judgment appealed from should be affirmed.

VAN VOORHIS, J. (dissenting).

DESMOND, C.J., and DYE, BURKE, FOSTER and SCILEPPI, JJ., concur with FULD, J.

Judgment affirmed.[9]

9. This case is discussed in the following notes: 28 Alb. L. Rev. 140 (1964); 13 Cath. U.L. Rev. 82 (1964); 64 Colum. L. Rev. 81 (1964); 49 Cornell L.Q. 304 (1964); 9 N.Y.U.L.F. 596 (1963); 38 N.Y.U.L. Rev. 1002 (1963); 15 Syracuse L. Rev. 33 (1963); 11 U.C.L.A.L. Rev. 859 (1964).

See generally Dukeminier, Zoning for Aesthetic Objectives: A Reappraisal, 20 Law & Contemp. Probs. 218, 225-227 (1955). See generally Agnor, Beauty Begins a Comeback: Aesthetic Considerations in Zoning, 11 J. Pub. L. 260 (1962); Note, Zoning: Aesthetics: The Chameleon of Zoning, 4 Tulsa L.J. 48 (1967); Note, Aesthetic Zoning: A Current Evaluation of the Law, 18 U. Fla. L. Rev. 430 (1965); Note, Aesthetic Control of Land Use: A House Built Upon the Sand? 59 Nw. U.L. Rev. 372 (1964); Note, Zoning for Aesthetics—A Problem of Definition, 32 U. Cin. L. Rev. 367 (1963).

The following is from the New York Times, Jan. 16, 1964, at 46, col. 2 (copyright © 1964 by The New York Times Company; reprinted by permission):

RYE, N.Y.,—Jan. 15—Dr. Webster Stover, 61-year-old former president of Arnold College, went to jail today in the latest chapter of his long-standing feud with authorities here.

He had spent the last few days in a Manhattan hotel room "working on my income taxes, due today" while Westchester County deputy sheriffs had sought him since Friday.

He was sentenced to a 30-day jail term in 1961 for flaunting clotheslines in the front yard of his home here as a protest against Rye taxes. He served 11 days then and was released on bail of $500 pending appeals that were carried in vain to the United States Supreme Court. He chose to surrender today to serve the 19 remaining days, rather than pay a $100 fine.

His wife, Marion, 62 years old, paraded in front of their big, red-brick colonial house today carrying picket signs protesting taxes in Rye and her husband's arrest.

"False Arrest in Rye" one sign read. "I put up all clotheslines to protest three illegal tax increases but Rye sends my husband to jail."

"Let them try to find a law against this," the slim, gray-haired woman snapped. "I'll march with these signs every day my husband is in jail."

—EDS.

Note: Aesthetic Ends Achieved by Elimination of Nuisances

When considering whether a valid zoning ordinance may be predicated solely on aesthetic considerations, note the somewhat similar problem of whether a court may enjoin an "eyesore" as a nuisance.

> The beauty of a fashionable residence neighborhood in a city is for the comfort and happiness of the residents, and it sustains in a general way the value of property in the neighborhood. It is therefore as much a matter of general welfare as is any other condition that fosters comfort or happiness, and consequent values generally of the property in the neighborhood. Why should not the police power avail, as well to suppress or prevent a nuisance committed by offending the sense of sight, as to suppress or prevent a nuisance committed by offending the sense of hearing, or the olfactory nerves? An eyesore in a neighborhood of residences might be as much a public nuisance, and as ruinous to property values in the neighborhood generally, as a disagreeable noise, or odor, or a menace to safety or health.[10]

Long before New York City enacted the first "comprehensive" zoning ordinance, in 1916, courts had been called upon to resolve discordant land uses through judge-made doctrines of private and public nuisance. Although this chapter is not generally concerned with the law of nuisance (not because it is unimportant but because we assume it is adequately handled in your torts course), nevertheless certain problems must be noted. We have already alluded to the problem of enjoining an "eyesore" as a nuisance. Two other problems need to be briefly mentioned. (1) May a use, although permitted under a valid zoning ordinance, nevertheless be enjoined as a common-law nuisance? (2) May a nonconforming use be enjoined as a common-law nuisance — i.e., to what extent is the nuisance doctrine an effective tool for rooting out and eliminating nonconforming uses?[11]

Generally, the fact that a use is permitted under a valid zoning ordinance does not preclude a court applying equitable principles from enjoining such use if it finds such use to constitute a nuisance in fact.[12]

---

10. State ex rel. Civello v. City of New Orleans, 154 La. 271, 283, 97 So. 440, 444 (1923). Compare Parkersburg Builders Material Co. v. Barrack, 118 W. Va. 608, 191 S.E. 368 (1937), with Feldstein v. Kammauf, 209 Md. 479, 121 A.2d 716 (1956) (long dictum on aesthetics as a basis for nuisance injunctions). See generally Noel, Unaesthetic Sights as Nuisances, 25 Cornell L.Q. 1 (1939). — Eds.

11. Discussion of the second question will be deferred until after we examine nonconforming uses from a zoning standpoint. See Note: Nonconforming Uses, page 1154 *infra*.

12. See generally Beuscher & Morrison, Judicial Zoning Through Recent Nuisance Cases, 1955 Wis. L. Rev. 440; Comment, Zoning Ordinances and Common-Law Nuisance, 16 Syracuse L. Rev. 860 (1965); Comment, Zoning and the Law of Nuisance, 29 Fordham L. Rev. 749 (1961); Comment, Real Property — The Effect of Zoning Ordinances on the Law of Nuisances, 54 Mich. L. Rev. 266 (1955).

The hotel and freight terminal are located at the boundaries of a district zoned for business and adjoin a district zoned for residences in which all the plaintiffs have their homes. The fact that the operation of certain kinds of commercial enterprises is permitted under a zoning ordinance is an important factor in determining whether the use being made of the land in conducting a particular enterprise goes beyond what is reasonable in view of the nature and character of the locality, the effect of the use upon those who live in the neighborhood, and the strength and force appropriately due to the various conflicting interests usually involved in the subject matter. But a zoning ordinance affords no protection to one who uses his land in such a manner as to constitute a private nuisance.[13]

Note: Zoning to Preserve Historic Landmarks (Herein Reference to Density Zoning)[14]

The use of zoning to control the density of the use which may be made of land is recognized. If the owner of one tract of land could transfer to another some portion of the density rights with respect to the owner's land, thereby increasing the density rights of such purchaser as to the purchaser's land and correspondingly lowering the density rights of such seller, the overall density use in the area would be the same. In an article entitled Development Rights Transfer: An Exploratory Essay, 83 Yale L.J. 75 (1973), Professor Costonis discusses the possibility of using such sales as a means of preserving low density landmark uses and low density pro-environmental uses, rather than using the police power or eminent domain to preserve landmarks and to prevent uses that may adversely affect the environment. See also Costonis, The Chicago Plan: Incentive Zoning and the Preservation of Urban Landmarks, 85 Harv. L. Rev. 574 (1972).

Penn Central Transportation Co. v. City of New York, which is set forth below, presented to the Court the question of whether a city may, as a part of a comprehensive program to preserve historic landmarks and historic dis-

---

13.   Weltshe v. Graf, 323 Mass. 498, 500, 82 N.E.2d 795, 796 (1948). Funeral parlor cases are clearly the most successful. Compare Bove v. Donner-Hanna Coke Corp., 236 A.D. 37, 258 N.Y.S. 229 (1932) (refusing to enjoin a use permitted under a zoning ordinance), with Sweet v. Campbell, 282 N.Y. 146, 25 N.E.2d 963 (1940) (the zoning ordinance permitted a funeral parlor in the district, subject to certain conditions, which were satisfied: "Nevertheless, even so, the right of plaintiffs to challenge, in an action in equity, the location of the funeral establishment and proposed use of the property on the ground that it constitutes a nuisance still remains.").—EDS.

14.   Courts generally have sustained architectural controls to preserve a neighborhood's "historic" appearance. See generally Note, The Police Power, Eminent Domain, and the Preservation of Historic Property, 63 Colum. L. Rev. 708 (1963); Comment, Aesthetic Zoning: Preservation of Historic Areas, 29 Fordham L. Rev. 729 (1961). Compare Manhattan Club v. Landmarks Preservation Commission, 51 Misc. 2d 556, 273 N.Y.S.2d 848 (Sup. Ct. 1966), with In re Trustees of Sailors' Snug Harbor v. Platt, 53 Misc. 2d 933, 280 N.Y.S.2d 75 (Sup. Ct. 1967).

tricts, place restrictions on the development of individual historic land-marks — in addition to those imposed by zoning ordinances — without effecting a "taking," requiring the payment of "just compensation." The case specifically concerned Grand Central Terminal in New York City.

PENN CENTRAL TRANSPORTATION CO. v. CITY OF NEW YORK
439 U.S. 883, 98 S. Ct. 2646 (1978)

Over the past 50 years, all 50 States and over 500 municipalities have enacted laws to encourage or require the preservation of buildings and areas with historic or aesthetic importance.[15] These nationwide legislative efforts have been precipitated by two concerns. The first is recognition that, in recent years, large numbers of historic structures, landmarks, and areas have been destroyed[16] without adequate consideration of either the values represented therein or the possibility of preserving the destroyed properties for use in economically productive ways.[17] The second is a widely shared belief that structures with special historic, cultural, or architectural significance enhance the quality of life for all. Not only do these buildings and their workmanship represent the lessons of the past and embody precious features of our heritage, they serve as examples of quality for today. "[H]istoric conservation is but one aspect of the much larger problem, basically an environmental one, of enhancing — or perhaps developing for the first time — the quality of life for people.[18]

New York City, responding to similar concerns and acting pursuant to a New York State enabling act, adopted its Landmarks Preservation Law in 1965. See New York City Charter and Administrative Code, ch. 8-A, §205-1.0 et seq. (1976). The city acted from the conviction that "the

15. See National Trust for Historic Preservation, A Guide to State Historic Preservation Programs (1976); National Trust for Historic Preservation, Directory of Landmark and Historic Commissions (1976). In addition to these State and municipal legislative efforts, Congress has determined that "the historical and cultural foundation of the Nation should be preserved as a living part of our community life and development in order to give a sense of orientation to the American people," National Historic Preservation Act of 1966, 80 Stat. 915, 16 U.S.C. §470(b), and has enacted a series of measures designed to encourage preservation of sites and structures of historic, architectural, or cultural significance. See generally Gray, The Response of Federal Legislation to Historic Preservation, 36 Law & Contemp. Prob. 314 (1971).

16. Over one half of the buildings listed in the Historic American Buildings Survey, begun by the Federal Government in 1933, have been destroyed. See Costonis, The Chicago Plan: Incentive Zoning and the Preservation of Urban Landmarks, 85 Harv. L. Rev. 574, 574 n.1 (1972), citing Huxtable, Bank's Building Sets Off Debate on "Progress," N.Y. Times, Jan. 17, 1971, §8, at 1, col. 2.

17. See, e.g., New York City Administrative Code, §205-1.0(a) (1976).

18. Gilbert, Introduction, Precedents for the Future, 36 Law & Contemp. Prob. 311, 312 (1971), quoting address by Robert Stipe, 1971 Conference on Preservation Law, Washington, D.C., May 1, 1971 (unpublished text, at 6-7).

standing of [New York City] as a worldwide tourist center and world capital of business, culture, and government" would be threatened if legislation were not enacted to protect historic landmarks and neighborhoods from precipitate decisions to destroy or fundamentally alter their character. §205-1.0(a). The city believed that comprehensive measures to safeguard desirable features of the existing urban fabric would benefit its citizens in a variety of ways: e.g., fostering "civic pride in the beauty and noble accomplishments of the past"; protecting and enhancing "the city's attraction to tourists and visitors"; "support[ing] and stimul[ating] business and industry"; "strengthen[ing] the economy of the city"; and promoting "the use of historic districts, landmarks, interior landmarks, and scenic landmarks for the education, pleasure and welfare of the people of the city." §205-1.0(b).

The New York City law is typical of many urban landmark laws in that its primary method of achieving its goals is not by acquisitions of historic properties[19] but rather by involving public entities in land use decisions affecting these properties and providing services, standards, controls, and incentives that will encourage preservation by private owners and users. While the law does place special restrictions on landmark properties as a necessary feature to the attainment of its larger objectives, the major theme of the Act is to ensure the owners of any such properties both a "reasonable return" on their investments and maximum latitude to use their parcels for purposes not inconsistent with the preservation goals.

The operation of the law can be briefly summarized. The primary responsibility for administering the Act is vested in the Landmarks Preservation Commission (Commission), a broad based, 11-member agency[20] assisted by a technical staff. The Commission first performs the function, critical to any landmark preservation effort, of identifying properties and areas that have "a special character or special historical or aesthetic interest or value as part of the development, heritage, or cultural characteristics of the city, state or nation." §207-1.0(n); see §207-1.0(h). If the Commission determines, after giving all interested parties an opportunity to be heard, that a building or area satisfies the ordinance's criteria, it will designate a

---

19. The consensus is that widespread public ownership of historic properties in urban settings is neither feasible nor wise. Public ownership reduces the tax base, burdens the public budget with costs of acquisitions and maintenance and results in the preservation of public buildings as museums and similar facilities, rather than as economically productive features of the urban scene. See Wilson & Winkler, The Response of State Legislation to Historic Preservation, 36 Law & Contemp. Prob. 329, 330-331, 339-340 (1971).

20. The ordinance creating the Commission requires that it include at least three architects, one historian qualified in the field, one city planner or landscape architect, one realtor, and at least one resident of each of the city's five boroughs. New York City Charter, §534 (1976). In addition to the ordinance's requirements concerning the composition of the Commission, there is, according to a former chairman, a "prudent tradition" that the Commission include one or two lawyers, preferably with experience in municipal government, and several laymen with no specialized qualifications other than concern for the good of the city. Goldstone, Aesthetics in Historic Districts, 36 Law & Contemp. Prob. 379, 384-385 (1971).

building to be a "landmark," §207-1.0(n),[21] situated on a particular "landmark site," §207-1.0(o)[22] or will designate an area to be a "historic district,"§207-1.0(h).[23] After the Commission makes a designation, New York City's Board of Estimate, after considering the relationship of the designated property "to the master plan, the zoning resolution, projected public improvements, and any plans for the renewal of the area involved," §207-2.0(g)(1), may modify or disapprove the designation, and the owner may seek judicial review of the final designation decision. Thus far, 31 historic districts and over 400 individual landmarks have been finally designated, and the process is a continuing one.

Final designation as a landmark results in restrictions upon the property owner's options concerning use of the landmark site. First, the Act imposes a duty upon the owner to keep the exterior features of the building "in good repair" to assure that the Act's objectives not be defeated by the landmark's falling into a state of irremediable disrepair. See §207-10.0(a). Second, the Commission must approve in advance any proposal to alter the exterior architectural features of the landmark or to construct any exterior improvement on the landmark site, thus ensuring that decisions concerning construction on the landmark site are made with due consideration of both the public interest in the maintenance of the structure and the landowner's interest in use of the property. See §§207-4.0 to 207-9.0.

In the event an owner wishes to alter a landmark site, three separate procedures are available through which administrative approval may be obtained. First, the owner may apply to the Commission for a "certificate of no effect on protected architectural features": that is, for an order approving the improvement or alteration on the ground that it will not change or affect any architectural feature of the landmark and will be in harmony therewith. See §207-5.0. Denial of the certificate is subject to judicial review.

Second, the owner may apply to the Commission for a certificate of "appropriateness." See §207-6.0. Such certificates will be granted if the Commission concludes—focusing upon aesthetic, historical, and architectural values—that the proposed construction on the landmark site would not unduly hinder the protection, enhancement, perpetuation, and use of

---

21. " 'Landmark.' Any improvement, any part of which is thirty years old or older, which has a special character or special historical or aesthetic interest or value as part of the development, heritage or cultural characteristics of the city, state or nation and which has been designated as a landmark pursuant to the provisions of this chapter." §207-1.0(n).

22. " 'Landmark site.' An improvement parcel or part thereof on which is situated a landmark and any abutting improvement parcel or part thereof used as and constituting part of the premises on which the landmark is situated, and which has been designated as a landmark site pursuant to the provisions of this chapter." §207-1.0(o).

23. " 'Historic district.' Any area which: (1) contains improvements which: (a) have a special character or special historical or aesthetic interest or value; and (b) represent one or more periods or styles of architecture typical of one or more eras in the history of the city; and (c) cause such area, by reason of such factors, to constitute a distinct section of the city; and (2) has been designated as a historic district pursuant to the provisions of this chapter." §207-1.0(h). The Act also provides for the designation of "scenic landmarks," see §207-1.0(w), and "interior landmarks." See §207-1.0(m).

the landmark. Again, denial of the certificate is subject to judicial review. Moreover, the owner who is denied either a certificate of no exterior effect or a certificate of appropriateness may submit an alternative or modified plan for approval. The final procedure — seeking a certificate of appropriateness on the ground of "insufficient return," see §207-8.0 — provides special mechanisms, which vary depending on whether or not the landmark enjoys a tax exemption,[24] to ensure that designation does not cause economic hardship.

Although the designation of a landmark and landmark site restricts the owner's control over the parcel, designation also enhances the economic position of the landmark owner in one significant respect. Under New York City's zoning laws, owners of real property who have not developed their property to the full extent permitted by the applicable zoning laws are allowed to transfer development rights to contiguous parcels on the same city block. See New York City, Zoning Resolution Art. I., ch. 2, §12-10 (1978) (definition of "zoning lot"). A 1968 ordinance gave the owners of landmark sites additional opportunities to transfer development rights to other parcels. Subject to a restriction that the floor area of the transferee lot may not be increased by more than 20% above its authorized level, the ordinance permitted transfers from a landmark parcel to propery across the street or across a street intersection. In 1969, the law governing the conditions under which transfers from landmark parcels could occur was liberalized, see New York City Zoning Resolutions, 74-79 to 74-793, apparently to

---

24. If the owner of a nontax-exempt parcel has been denied certificates of appropriateness for a proposed alteration and shows that he is not earning a reasonable return on the property in its present state, the Commission and other city agencies must assume the burden of developing a plan that will enable the landmark owner to earn a reasonable return on the landmark site. The plan may include, but need not be limited to, partial or complete tax exemption, remission of taxes, and authorizations for alterations, construction or reconstruction appropriate for and not inconsistent with the purposes of the Act. §207-8.0(c). The owner is free to accept or reject a plan devised by the Commission and approved by the other city agencies. If he accepts the plan, he proceeds to operate the property pursuant to the plan. If he rejects the plan, the Commission may recommend that the city proceed by eminent domain to acquire a protective interest in the landmark, but if the city does not do so within a specified time period, the Commission must issue a notice allowing the property owner to proceed with the alteration or improvement as originally proposed in his application for a certificate of appropriateness.

Tax exempt structures are treated somewhat differently. They become eligible for special treatment only if four preconditions are satisfied: (1) the owner previously entered into an agreement to sell the parcel that was contingent upon the issuance of a certificate of approval; (2) the property, as it exists at the time of the request, is not capable of earning a reasonable return; (3) the structure is no longer suitable to its past or present purposes; and (4) the prospective buyer intends to alter the landmark structure. In the event the owner demonstrates that the property in its present state is not earning a reasonable return, the Commission must either find another buyer for it or allow the sale and construction to proceed.

But this is not the only remedy available for owners of tax exempt landmarks. As the case at bar illustrates, see *infra,* if an owner files suit and establishes that he is incapable of earning a "reasonable return" on the site in its present state, he can be afforded judicial relief. See *infra.* Similarly, where a landmark owner who enjoys a tax exemption has demonstrated that the landmark structure, as restricted, is totally inadequate for the owner's "legitimate needs," the Act has been held invalid as applied to that parcel. See Lutheran Church v. City of New York, 35 N.Y.2d 121, 359 N.Y.S.2d 7, 316 N.E.2d 305 (1974).

ensure that the Landmarks Law would not unduly restrict the development options of the owners of Grand Central Terminal. See Marcus, Air Rights Transfers in New York City, 36 Law & Contemp. Prob. 372, 375 (1971). The class of recipient lots was expanded to include lots "across a street and opposite to another lot or lots which except for the intervention of streets or street intersections form a series extending to the lot occupied by the landmark building [, provided that] all lots [are] in the same ownership." New York City Zoning Resolution, §74-79 (emphasis deleted).[25] In addition, the 1969 amendment permits, in highly commercialized areas like midtown Manhattan, the transfer of all unused development rights to a single parcel. Ibid. . . .

The issues presented by appellants are (1) whether the restrictions imposed by New York City's law upon appellants' exploitation of the Terminal site effect a "taking" of appellants' property for a public use within the meaning of the Fifth Amendment, which of course is made applicable to the States through the Fourteenth Amendment, see Chicago B. & Q.R. Co. v. Chicago, 166 U.S. 226, 239, 17 S. Ct. 581, 585, 41 L. Ed. 979 (1897) and, (2) if so, whether the transferable development rights afforded appellants constitute "just compensation" within the meaning of the Fifth Amendment. We need only address the question whether a "taking" has occurred[26]. . . .

[The Supreme Court reviewed the factors that have shaped the jurisprudence of the fifth amendment injunction, and stated that "private property [shall not] be taken for a public use, without just compensation." It also examined each of the contentions that a taking had occurred in this case, concluding as follows:]

On this record we conclude that the application of New York City's Landmarks Preservation Law has not effected a "taking" of appellants' property. The restrictions imposed are substantially related to the promotion of the general welfare and not only permit reasonable beneficial use of the landmark site but afford appellants opportunities further to enhance not only the Terminal site proper but also other properties.[27]

---

25. To obtain approval for a proposed transfer, the landmark owner must follow the following procedure. First, he must obtain the permission of the Commission which will examine the plans for the development of the transferee lot to determine whether the planned construction would be compatible with the landmark. Second, he must obtain the approbation of New York City's Planning Commission which will focus on the effects of the transfer on occupants of the buildings in the vicinity of the transfer lot and whether the landmark owner will preserve the landmark. Finally, the matter goes to the Board of Estimate, which has final authority to grant or deny the application. See also Costonis, 85 Harv. L. Rev. 574, 585-586 (1972).

26. As is implicit in our opinion, we do not embrace the proposition that a "taking" can never occur unless Government has transferred physical control over a portion of a parcel.

27. We emphasize that our holding today is on the present record which in turn is based on Penn Central's present ability to use the Terminal for its intended purposes and in a gainful fashion. The city conceded at oral argument that if appellants can demonstrate at some point in the future that circumstances have changed such that the Terminal ceases to be, in the city counsel's words, "economically viable," appellants may obtain relief. See Tr. of Oral Arg. 42-43.

[Justice Rehnquist wrote a dissenting opinion and was joined therein by the Chief Justice and Justice Stevens.

A brief in support of the decision of the New York Court of Appeals was filed by the Department of Justice. Supporting briefs were also filed by the National League of Cities and the National Trust for Historic Preservation. Briefs advocating a contrary position were filed by the Real Estate Board of New York and the Pacific Legal Foundation. See N.Y. Times, Apr. 14, 1978, at B4.]

Note: The "Petaluma Plan" to Control the City of Petaluma's Rate of Growth

If a city's rate of growth is too rapid, a serious strain is put on the various utilities that are needed to provide for the city's population. The question is whether a city encounters any constitutional problems if it undertakes to control its rate of growth. The "Petaluma Plan," described in the case below, raises such constitutional problems.

CONSTRUCTION INDUSTRY ASSOCIATION v. CITY OF PETALUMA

522 F.2d 897 (1975), *cert. denied,* 424 U.S. 934 (1976)

The City [of Petaluma] is located in southern Sonoma County, about 40 miles north of San Francisco. In the 1950's and 1960's, Petaluma was a relatively self-sufficient town. It experienced a steady population growth from 10,315 in 1950 to 24,870 in 1970. Eventually, the City was drawn into the Bay Area metropolitan housing market as people working in San Francisco and San Rafael became willing to commute longer distances to secure relatively inexpensive housing available there. By November 1972, according to unofficial figures, Petaluma's population was at 30,500, a dramatic increase of almost 25 per cent in little over two years.

The increase in the City's population, not suprisingly, is reflected in the increase in the number of its housing units. From 1964 to 1971, the following number of residential housing units were completed:

1964	270	1968	379
1965	440	1969	358
1966	321	1970	591
1967	234	1971	891

In 1970 and 1971, the years of the most rapid growth, demand for housing in the City was even greater than above indicated. Taking 1970 and

1971 together, builders won approval of a total of 2000 permits although only 1482 were actually completed by the end of 1971.

Alarmed by the accelerated rate of growth in 1970 and 1971, the demand for even more housing, and the sprawl of the City eastward, the City adopted a temporary freeze on development in early 1971. The construction and zoning change moratorium was intended to give the City Council and the City planners an opportunity to study the housing and zoning situation and to develop short and long range plans. The Council made specific findings with respect to housing patterns and availability in Petaluma, including the following: That from 1960-1970 housing had been in almost unvarying 6000 square-foot lots laid out in regular grid patterns; that there was a density of approximately 4.5 housing units per acre in the single-family home areas; that during 1960-1970, 88 per cent of housing permits issued were for single-family detached homes; that in 1970, 83 per cent of Petaluma's housing was single-family dwellings; that the bulk of recent development (largely single-family homes) occurred in the eastern portion of the City, causing a large deficiency in moderately priced multi-family and apartment units on the east side.

To correct the imbalance between single-family and multi-family dwellings, curb the sprawl of the City on the east, and retard the accelerating growth of the City, the Council in 1972 adopted several resolutions, which collectively are called the "Petaluma Plan" (the Plan).

The Plan, on its face limited to a five-year period (1972-1977),[28] fixes a housing development growth rate not to exceed 500 dwelling units per year.[29] Each dwelling unit represents approximately three people. The 500-unit figure is somewhat misleading, however, because it applies only to housing units (hereinafter referred to as "development-units") that are part of projects involving five units or more. Thus, the 500-unit figure does not reflect any housing and population growth due to construction of single-family homes or even four-unit apartment buildings not part of any larger project.

The Plan also positions a 200 foot wide "greenbelt" around the City,[30] to serve as a boundary for urban expansion for at least five years, and with respect to the east and north sides of the City, for perhaps ten to fifteen years.

---

28.   The district court found that although the Plan is ostensibly limited to a five-year period, official attempts have been made to perpetuate the Plan beyond 1977. Such attempts include the urban extension line (*see* text *infra*) and the agreement to purchase from the Sonoma County Water Agency only 9.8 million gallons of water per day through the year 1990. This flow is sufficient to support a population of 55,000. If the City were to grow at a rate of about 500 housing units per year (approximately three persons per unit), the City would reach a population of 55,000 about the year 1990. The 55,000 figure was mentioned by City officials as the projected optimal (and maximum) size of Petaluma. See, e.g., R.T. at 135-43, 145-46.

29.   The allotment for each year is not an inflexible limitation. The Plan does provide for a 10 percent variance (50 units) below or above the 500 units annual figure, but the expectation of the Council is that not more than 2500 units will be constructed during the five-year period.

30.   At some points this urban extension line is about one-quarter of a mile beyond the present City limits.

One of the most innovative features of the Plan is the Residential Development Control System which provides procedures and criteria for the award of the annual 500 development-unit permits. At the heart of the allocation procedure is an intricate point system, whereby a builder accumulates points for conformity by his projects with the City's general plan and environmental design plans, for good architectural design, and for providing low and moderate income dwelling units and various recreational facilities. The Plan further directs that allocations of building permits are to be divided as evenly as feasible between the west and east sections of the City and between single-family dwellings and multiple residential units (including rental units),[31] that the sections of the City closest to the center are to be developed first in order to cause "infilling" of vacant area, and that 8 to 12 per cent of the housing units approved be for low and moderate income persons.

In a provision of the Plan, intended to maintain the close-in rural space outside and surrounding Petaluma, the City solicited Sonoma County to establish stringent subdivision and appropriate acreage parcel controls for the areas outside the urban extension line of the City and to limit severely further residential infilling.

[In commenting generally on the effect of the plan on the availability of housing, the court said:]

According to undisputed expert testimony at trial, if the Plan (limiting housing starts to approximately 6 per cent of existing housing stock each year) were to be adopted by municipalities throughout the region, the impact on the housing market would be substantial. For the decade 1970 to 1980, the shortfall in needed housing in the region would be about 105,000 units (or 25 per cent of the units needed). Further, the aggregate effect of a proliferation of the Plan throughout the San Francisco region would be a decline in regional housing stock quality, a loss of the mobility of current and prospective residents and a deterioration in the quality and choice of housing available to income earners with real incomes of $14,000 per year or less. If, however, the Plan were considered by itself and with respect to Petaluma only, there is no evidence to suggest that there would be a deterioration in the quality and choice of housing available there to persons in the lower and middle income brackets. Actually, the Plan increases the availability of multi-family units (owner-occupied and rental units) and low-income units which were rarely constructed in the pre-Plan days.

[In upholding the plan against the attacks on its constitutionality, the court concluded as follows:]

31. By providing for the increase of multi-family dwellings (including townhouses as well as rental apartments), the Plan allows increased density. Whereas, during the years just preceding the Plan, housing density was about 4.5 units per acre, under the Plan single-family housing will consist of not only low (4.5 units per acre) but also medium density (4.5 to 10 units per acre). And multi-family housing, to comprise about half of the housing under the Plan, will be built at a density of 10 or more units per acre.

We conclude therefore that . . . the concept of the public welfare is sufficiently broad to uphold Petaluma's desire to preserve its small town character, its open spaces and low density of population, and to grow at an orderly and deliberate pace.[32]

[The court also dismissed the claim that the plan unreasonably burdened interstate commerce.]

Note: Enterprise Zones

An enterprise zone is a locally nominated, federally designated, and economically deteriorated urban area into which commercial activity is to be attracted by means of a partial rollback of federal and local taxes and the elimination of local regulations. See Callies & Tamashiro, Enterprise Zones: The Redevelopment Sweepstakes Begins, 15 Urb. Law. 231 (1983).

Note: American Law Institute's Model Land Development Code

The American Law Institute's Model Land Development Code provides a model for legislation in the zoning area. In the Foreword to the Proposed Official Draft dated April 15, 1975, the director of the ALI said:

> The judgment is that total localism in the regulation of land has now become anachronistic but that resource to the State's authority should be confined to protecting defined values that ought not to be subordinated to competing local interests; and that even then reliance should be placed so far as possible on local agencies as organs of administration.

Note: Nonconforming Uses

When zoning laws were first enacted, it was generally assumed that nonconforming uses would eventually disappear. However, experience has

---

32. Our decision upholding the Plan as not in violation of the appellees' due process rights should not be read as a permanent endorsement of the Plan. In a few years the City itself for good reason may abandon the Plan or the state may decide to alter its laws delegating its zoning power to the local authorities; or to meet legitimate regional needs, regional zoning authorities may be established. See, e.g., Cal. Gov. Code §§66600 et seq. (San Francisco Bay Conservation and Development Commission); Cal. Gov. Code §§66801, 67000 et seq. (Tahoe Regional Planning Agency); Public Resources Code §§27000 et seq. (California Coastal Zone Conservation Commission). To be sure, housing needs in metropolitan areas like the San Francisco Bay Area are pressing and the needs are not being met by present methods of supplying housing. However, the federal court is not the proper forum for resolving these problems. The controversy stirred up by the present litigation, as indicated by the number and variety of amici on each side, and the complex economic, political and social factors involved in this case are compelling evidence that resolution of the important housing and environmental issues raised here is exclusively the domain of the legislature.

shown that this has not been the case. One major reason for this is that the nonconforming user receives a limited, geographic monopoly as a result of the zoning laws. The corner grocery store in a residentially zoned neighborhood, from which all other commercial uses have been excluded, is obviously quite a valuable piece of real estate and understandably is slow to disappear. Zoning ordinances usually provide for the termination of nonconforming uses if they are destroyed or substantially damaged. They frequently limit structural repairs and alterations, in the hope of hastening their demise. But nonconforming uses continue to thrive.

The nuisance injunction has not been very successful in rooting out or eliminating nonconforming uses, as such. The rules discussed at page 1144 *supra* as to the relationship of zoning to nuisance doctrines are generally applicable to nonconforming uses.[33]

The case which follows examines the nonconforming use problem.

HOFFMANN v. KINEALY
389 S.W.2d 745 (Mo. 1965)

A. P. Stone, Jr., Special Judge.

This is an appeal by Carl O. Hoffmann, Jr., and Mrs. Geraldine St. Denis (herein called relators), the owners of two adjoining lots (frequently referred to as the lots) in the 3100 block of Pennsylvania in the City of St. Louis, from the judgment of the Circuit Court of the City of St. Louis affirming, upon review by certiorari (V.A.M.S. §89.110), a decision of the board of adjustment sustaining a decision of the building commissioner which denied relators' application for a certificate of occupancy of the lots for a pre-existing lawful nonconforming use, to wit, for the open storage of lumber, building materials and construction equipment.

The lots have an aggregate width of 52½ feet, north and south, are 125 feet deep, east and west, and front on the west side of Pennsylvania, a north-south street, in a block bounded on the east by Pennsylvania, on the north by Juniata, on the west by Minnesota, and on the south by Wyoming. An east-west alley runs along the south side of the lots, and a north-south alley runs along their rear. Portions of the block, i.e., (1) that portion in which the lots are located, which is east of the north-south alley and fronts on Pennsylvania, and (2) that portion south of the east-west alley and fronting on Wyoming, are in a "B" two-family dwelling district, while the remainder of the block, i.e., that portion which is west of the north-south alley (and thus on the opposite side of the alley behind the lots) and fronts on Minnesota is in a "J" industrial district and is used for the operation of a planing mill and for open storage of lumber. A small building housing the general offices of

---

33. See, e.g., Robinson Brick Co. v. Luthi, 115 Colo. 106, 169 P.2d 171 (1946). See generally Comment, The Elimination of Nonconforming Uses, 1951 Wis. L. Rev. 685; Noel, Retroactive Zoning and Nuisances, 41 Colum. L. Rev. 457 (1941); Comment, Zoning—Abatement of Prior Nonconforming Uses: Nuisance Regulations and Amortization Provisions, 31 Mo. L. Rev. 280 (1966).

Hoffmann Construction Company, relators' business in connection with which the lots have been used, is located in the "B" two-family dwelling district on the south side of the east-west alley and just across the alley from the lots.

The exhibits presented at the hearing before the board of adjustment, and brought to us with the transcript on appeal, indicate that there are fourteen buildings in the same portion of the block in which the lots are situate, including a tavern on the southwest corner of Pennsylvania and Juniata, one three-family residence, eleven other residences, and at the rear of one residence a building identified on a plat as used for "tractor parts"; ten buildings in that portion of the block south of the east-west alley, including a grocery store on the northwest corner of Pennsylvania and Wyoming, eight residences (all owned by relators), and at the rear of one residence the above-mentioned office building of Hoffmann Construction Company; and that, on the other three corners of the intersection of Pennsylvania and Wyoming, there are two taverns and a cleaning and pressing shop.

Counsel for the city conceded at the hearing before the board of adjustment, and the subsequent finding of the board (not here disputed) was, that the lots were being used at the time of hearing for the open storage of lumber, building materials and construction equipment and that (in the language of the board's finding) "these premises have been used for this same purpose continuously since the year 1910." The front end of the lots is "landscaped" with a hedge and shrubbery, and the area used for open storage is enclosed with a high fence.

The first comprehensive zoning ordinance of the City of St. Louis became effective in 1926. On April 25, 1950, numerous sections of the zoning code were amended by Ordinance 45309. Section 5 A 1 of that ordinance provided that "No building or land shall be used for a use other than those permitted in the district in which such premises are located unless . . . such use existed prior to the effective date of this ordinance." Section 5 B of the same ordinance, insofar as here material, provided that "The use of land within any dwelling district . . . for purposes of open storage . . . which do not conform to the provisions of this ordinance shall be discontinued within six (6) years from the effective date of this ordinance."

About six years and three months later, to wit, on July 24, 1956, Ordinance 48007 was enacted, amending that portion of Section 5 B of Ordinance 45309, with which we are here concerned, to read as follows: "The use of land within any dwelling district for the purpose of open storage is hereby prohibited."

On April 12, 1961, Ordinance 50547 was approved amending Ordinance 45309, as amended, by repealing several sections, including Section 5 thereof, and enacting in lieu thereof several new sections. However, Section 5 A 1 as it appeared in Ordinance 45309 and Section 5 B as it appeared in Ordinance 48007 were carried forward verbatim in Ordinance 50547.

In May 1961 the provisions of Sections 5 A 1 and 5 B were codified in Sections 903.010 and 903.030 of "The Zoning Code" as a part of "The Revised Code of the City of St. Louis, 1960," in the following language:

Section 903.010. "No building or land shall be used for a use other than those permitted in the district in which such premises are located unless (a) such use is permitted by other provisions of this Chapter or by Chapter 915 (Use, Height, and Area Exceptions) or Chapter 916 (Board of Adjustment); or (b) such use existed prior to April 25, 1950."

Section 903.030. "The use of land within any dwelling district for the purpose of open storage is prohibited."

After relators had been notified on December 7, 1962, to cease the use of the lots for open storage, they filed with the building commissioner on December 21, 1962, an application for a certificate of occupancy of the lots for a pre-existing lawful nonconforming use, to wit, for the open storage of lumber, building materials and construction equipment. From the decision of the building commissioner denying that application, relators appealed to the board of adjustment which, after a public hearing and the taking of evidence, sustained the decision of the building commissioner. Upon review by certiorari, the circuit court accorded the parties a trial on the merits, considered the full record of prior proceedings including exhibits, and affirmed the findings and decision of the board of adjustment.

Relators' petition in the circuit court, upon which the writ of certiorari was issued, charged that Section 903.030 of the zoning code was unconstitutional, null and void and was of no effect as to relators' lots because, by prohibiting continuance of the pre-existing lawful nonconforming use of the lots, said section would impair, restrict and deprive relators of vested property rights and thereby would take and damage relators' private property for public use without just compensation in violation of Article 1, Section 26, Missouri Constitution of 1945, V.A.M.S. Likewise, that is the essence of relators' complaint upon this appeal.

Respondents' position is that, under the statutory grant of police power in municipal zoning and planning (V.A.M.S. §§89.020 and 89.040), the city was empowered to enact on April 25, 1950, Section 5 B of Ordinance 45309, a so-called "amortization" or "toleration" provision which required discontinuance within six years thereafter of the nonconforming use of land within any dwelling district for purposes of open storage, and that, such six-year "amortization" or "toleration" period having run in April 1956, the subsequent absolute prohibition of said nonconforming use of land by Ordinance 48007 enacted on July 24, 1956, thereafter reenacted by Ordinance 50547 on April 12, 1961, and codified in Section 903.030, was valid.

Relators reply that their right to continue their pre-existing lawful nonconforming use actually was taken, notwithstanding the fact that such taking was delayed, and that the constitutional interdiction against the taking of private property for public use without just compensation (Art. 1, Sec. 26, Mo. Const. of 1945) is absolute and subject to no exception as to a delayed or postponed taking. There has been and is no suggestion that relators' use of their lots constituted a nuisance.

The parties thus present, as a matter of first impression in the appellate courts of this state, the constitutionality of the "amortization" or "toleration" technique of eliminating pre-existing lawful nonconforming uses. It may be observed preliminarily that, although the six-year amortization provision in Section 5 B of Ordinance 45309 enacted in 1950 was not carried forward in Ordinance 48007 enacted in 1956 after the six-year term had run or in the 1960 codification in effect when this proceeding was instituted, we are of the opinion that the validity of Section 903.030 of the 1960 codification should be determined in the light of the 1950 ordinance.

In earlier days of zoning legislation, it generally was recognized and conceded that termination of pre-existing lawful nonconforming uses would be unconstitutional. The expressions by way of dicta in our cases suggest that this has been taken for granted in Missouri. In Women's Christian Ass'n. of Kansas City v. Brown, 354 Mo. 700, 709-710, 190 S.W.2d 900, 906, involving an attempted change of nonconforming use from a riding academy to a dance hall, this court said that: "*Nonconforming uses, existing at the commencement of zoning are of course permitted to continue as vested rights.* Zoning Law and Practice, Smith, §85." (All emphasis herein is ours.) The Enabling Act, under which the applicable Zoning Order of Jackson County had been enacted, specifically provided that "[t]he powers by this act given shall not be exercised so as to deprive the owner, lessee or tenant, of any existing property of its use or maintenance for the purpose to which it is then lawfully devoted. . . ." (Laws of 1941, p. 485), but that statute was not cited in connection with the quoted statement, which was immediately followed by this illuminating commentary upon the theory of zoning:

> "Within a period of another twenty years, a large number of such 'nonconforming' uses will have disappeared, either through the necessity of enlargement and expansion which invariably is forbidden or limited by ordinance, or by the owners realizing that it is unwise and uneconomic to be located in a district which probably is not suitable for the nonconforming purpose, or by obsolescence, destruction by fire or by the elements or similar inability to be used; so that many of these nonconforming uses will 'fade out,' with a resulting substantial and definite benefit to all communities." The Law of Zoning, Metzenbaum, p. 288.

When the same factual situation was presented a second time in Brown v. Gambrel, 358 Mo. 192, 198, 213 S.W.2d 931, 935(1), this court said, with respect to the prior lawful use of the building as a public stable or riding academy, that "*(s)uch use of such building was a priorly vested right of which the county by the institution* (April 26, 1943) *of its zoning plan could not deprive appellants.* Zoning Law and Practice, Smith, Sec. 85, p. 108; Women's Christian Ass'n. of Kansas City v. Brown, *supra;* In re Botz, 236 Mo. App. 566, 159 S.W.2d 367; . . . Laws of Missouri, 1941, page 485. . . ."

In State ex rel. Capps v. Bruns, Mo. App., 353 S.W.2d 829, relator sought a writ of mandamus directing issuance to him of a license to operate a junk yard, a pre-existing nonconforming use of his land. The Kansas City Court of Appeals wrote:

> "The general rule is that nonconforming structures and uses existing at the time of the effective date of a zoning ordinance or restriction may be continued." [8] McQuillin, Municipal Corporations, 3d Ed., page 464. Such use and the operation of such a business was continuance of a vested right of which the city could not deprive plaintiff. See Brown et al v. Gambrel et al, 358 Mo. 192, 213 S.W.2d 931, 935. In addition, General Ordinance 3162, Sec. 11-21, City of St. Joseph, squarely authorizes such continuing nonconforming use. [353 S.W.2d at 830.]

Again, the court pointed out: "In our case we have an applicant who for twenty years has conducted a junk yard at this particular location. *He has a vested right which zoning ordinances could not abrogate."* 353 S.W.2d at 831. Later in the opinion, we find this gratuitous observation, without discussion or citation of authority: "Many [?] ordinances limit the life of nonconforming uses to a period of years and such ordinances have been approved. There are apparently no such 'tolerance period' ordinances involved in our case." 353 S.W.2d at 832.

In considering their appellate jurisdiction in Bartholomew v. Board of Zoning Adjustment, Mo. App., 307, S.W.2d 730, 732, the Kansas City Court of Appeals stated:

> Plaintiffs do not question the general constitutionality of the zoning law. *It is rather their position that under the facts here, they proved a lawful nonconforming use amounting to a vested right, which both constitutions will preserve. If the evidence discloses such proof this court will protect such right and defendants do not contend otherwise.*

These statements from *Bartholomew, supra,* were quoted with approval by this court in a discussion of appellate jurisdiction in Dunbar v. Board of Zoning Adjustment, Mo., 380 S.W.2d 442, 444, where property owners were complaining of deprivation of "prior vested property rights."

So much for the dicta in this state. Obviously, none of the cited Missouri cases reached or ruled on the basic question before us here, but they indicate, so we think, that heretofore the validity of pre-existing lawful nonconforming uses has been recognized in this jurisdiction, as elsewhere.

Certainly, the spirit of zoning ordinances always has been and still is to diminish and decrease nonconforming uses (Brown v. Gambrel, *supra,* 358 Mo. at 199, 213 S.W.2d at 935-936; 8 McQuillin, Municipal Corporations (3d Ed.), §25.183, p. 473), and to that end municipalities have employed various approved regulatory methods such as prohibiting the resumption of a nonconforming use after its abandonment or discontinuance, prohibiting the rebuilding or alteration of nonconforming structures or structures occupied for nonconforming uses, and prohibiting or rigidly restricting a change from one nonconforming use to another. 2 Rathkopf, The Law of Zoning and Planning, Ch. 62, pp. 62-2 to 62-4 (1960). Even so, pre-existing lawful nonconforming uses have not faded out or eliminated themselves as quickly as had been anticipated, so zoning zealots have been casting about for other methods or techniques to hasten the elimination of nonconforming uses. In so doing, only infrequent use has been made of the power of eminent domain, primarily because of the expense of compensating damaged property owners, but increasing emphasis has been placed upon the "amortization" or "tolerance" technique which conveniently bypasses the troublesome element of compensation.

"Stated in its simplest terms, amortization contemplates the compulsory termination of a non-conformity at the expiration of a specified period of time, which period is equaled [sic] to the useful economic life of the non-conformity." Katarincic, Elimination of Non-Conforming Uses, Buildings, and Structures by Amortization—Concept v. Law, 2 Duquesne Univ. L. Rev. 1. "The basic idea is to determine the remaining normal useful life of a pre-existing nonconforming use. The owner is then allowed to continue his use for this period and at the end must either conform or eliminate it." Note, 44 Cornell L.Q. 450, 453 (1959). Courts approving the amortization technique as a valid exercise of the police power rationalize their holdings in this fashion:

> The distinction between an ordinance restricting future uses and one requiring the termination of present uses within a reasonable period of time is merely one of degree, and constitutionality depends on the relative importance to be given to the public gain and to the private loss. Zoning as it affects every piece of property is to some extent retroactive in that it applies to property already owned at the time of the effective date of the ordinance. The elimination of existing uses within a reasonable time does not amount to a taking of property nor does it necessarily restrict the use of property so that it cannot be used for any reasonable purpose. Use of a reasonable amortization scheme provides an equitable means of reconciliation of the conflicting interests in satisfaction of due process requirements. As a method of eliminating existing nonconforming uses it allows the owner of the nonconforming use, by affording an opportunity to make new plans, at least partially to offset any loss he might suffer. . . . If the amortization period is reasonable the loss to the owner may be small when compared with the benefit to the public. [City of Los Angeles v. Gage, 127 Cal. App. 2d 442, 274 P.2d 34, 44; Grant v. Mayor and City Council of Baltimore, 212 Md. 301, 129 A.2d 363, 368.]

Several cases in other jurisdiction have approved the termination of pre-existing nonconforming uses by the amortization technique. However, there are a number of decisions to the opposite effect, and it may be fairly said that there is "a decided lack of accord" in this area. 58 Am. Jur., Zoning, §148 (1964-65 Supp., p. 146); annotation 42 A.L.R.2d 1146.

With respect to some of the cases . . . in which the amortization technique has been employed, brief comments may not be inappropriate. As other courts have observed, the opinions in State ex rel. Dema Realty Co. v. McDonald, 168 La. 172, 121 So. 613, and State ex rel. Dema Realty Co. v. Jacoby, 168 La. 752, 123 So. 314, exhibit "a confusion between the objects of zoning and nuisance regulation" (Jones v. City of Los Angeles, 211 Cal. 304, 295 P. 14, 21; James v. City of Greenville, 227 S.C. 565, 88 S.E.2d 661, 671), and certainly the same properly may be said with respect to Livingston Rock & Gravel Co. v. County of Los Angeles, 43 Cal. 2d 121, 272 P.2d 4, where, under a rezoning ordinance providing an "automatic exception" to permit continuance of certain nonconforming uses but authorizing the revocation of any such exception where that could be done without impairment of "constitutional rights," it was found by the planning commission that " 'use of the property with a cement batching plant thereon' was 'being exercised in such a manner as to be detrimental to public health, and so as to be a nuisance.' " 272 P.2d at 7. Referring to the Dema Realty Company cases, *supra,* one writer has offered this caustic criticism: "The Louisiana decisions in this field . . . sound more like Cossack interpretations of Muscovite ukases than utterances of a court operating under the benign provisions of the Magna Carta." Fratcher, Constitutional Law — Zoning Ordinances Prohibiting Repair of Existing Structures, 35 Mich. L. Rev. 642, 644 (1937). And in Grant v. Mayor and City Council of Baltimore, *supra,* 129 A.2d at 367, it was frankly conceded that the opinions in the Dema Realty Company cases, *supra,* and in Standard Oil Co. v. City of Tallahassee, 5 Cir., 183 F.2d 410, were "not particularly persuasive in their reasoning," although the court was "impressed" with the decisions in Livingston Rock & Gravel Co. v. County of Los Angeles, *supra,* and City of Los Angeles v. Gage, *supra.* With respect to Standard Oil Co. v. City of Tallahassee, *supra,* a perspicacious student has pointed out that:

> Discontinuance was required in spite of the fact that many 'of the residences [in the area] are far below standard and many of them shacks. . . .' (87 F. Supp. 145, 149 (D.C. Fla. 1949)) Thus, it would seem, the court was sanctioning the use of 'amortization' provisions to redevelop an unsightly area. [Note, 44 Cornell L.Q. 450, 455 (1959).]

In Harbison v. City of Buffalo, 4 N.Y.2d 553, 176 N.Y.S.2d 598, 152 N.E.2d 42, frequently cited by advocates of the amortization technique, only two judges concurred in the principal opinion while the additional two included in the bare majority of four concurred in result "upon the principles stated in People v. Miller, 304 N.Y. 105, 108, 109, 106 N.E.2d 34, 35, 36." 176 N.Y.S.2d at 616, 152 N.E.2d at 54. The "principles stated" in People v. Miller, *supra,* were that "nonconforming uses or structures, in existence when a zoning ordinance is enacted, are, as a general rule, constitutionally protected and will be permitted to continue, notwithstanding the contrary provisions of the ordinance" (106 N.E.2d at 35(1); that, however, "the enforcement of a zoning regulation against a prior nonconforming use will be sustained where the resulting loss to the owner is relatively slight and insubstantial" (106 N.E.2d at 35 (3); that the principle permitting continuance of pre-existing nonconforming uses was "clearly inapplicable to a purely incidental use of property for recreational or amusement purposes only"; and that "an inconsequential use as that here involved — the harboring of pigeons as a hobby — (did) not amount to a 'vested right'" protected against termination by an amended zoning ordinance. 106 N.E.2d at 36. The author of a comprehensive note on Harbison v. City of Buffalo, *supra,* appropriately suggests that, since two of the four judges constituting the majority in that case concurred only in result on the basis of People v. Miller, *supra,* "it is doubtful if the Court of Appeals as a whole intended to move too far away from that decision and its fundamental principle that a prior nonconforming use can be terminated only where it is insubstantial." Note, 44 Cornell L.Q. 450, 457.

But, although the holdings in other jurisdictions may, in some instances, be enlightening and persuasive, it is neither our duty nor our inclination to rule a question of first impression in this state simply by counting foreign cases and then falling off the judicial fence on the side on which more cases can be found. Rather, our concern should be and is to determine the basic constitutional right of the matter, as we see it. Property is defined as including not only ownership and possession but also the right of use and enjoyment for lawful purposes. In fact, "[t]he substantial value of property lies in its use." It follows that: " '[t]he constitutional guaranty of protection for all private property extends equally to the enjoyment and the possession of lands. An arbitrary interference by the government, or by its authority, with the reasonable enjoyment of private lands is a taking of private property without due process of law, which is inhibited by the Constitution.' Tiedeman's Limitation of Police Powers, §122." Ex parte Davis, 321 Mo. 370, 375, 13 S.W.2d 40, 41. See 1 Lewis, Eminent Domain (3d Ed.), §65, p. 56.

Counsel for instant respondents would support and justify the amortization provision under consideration as constituting reasonable and permissible *regulation* of the use of property. Of course, every comprehensive zoning ordinance limits and thereby regulates the use of property prospectively. But we cannot embrace the doctrine espoused by advocates of the amortization technique that there is no material distinction between regulating the future use of property and terminating pre-existing lawful nonconforming uses.

The amortization provision under review would terminate and take from instant relators the right to continue a lawful nonconforming use of their lots which has been exercised and enjoyed since 1910 — a right of the character to which the courts traditionally have referred as a "vested right." To our knowledge, no one has, as yet, been so brash as to contend that such a pre-existing lawful nonconforming use properly might be terminated *immediately.* In fact, the contrary is implicit in the amortization technique itself which would validate a taking *presently* unconstitutional by the simple expedient of *postponing* such taking for a "reasonable" time. All of this leads us to suggest, as did the three dissenting justices in Harbison v. City of Buffalo, *supra,* 152 N.E.2d at 49, that it would be a strange and novel doctrine indeed which would approve a municipality taking private property for public use without compensation if the property was not too valuable and the taking was not too soon, and prompts us to repeat the caveat of Mr. Justice Holmes in Pennsylvania Coal Co. v. Mahon, 260 U.S. 393, 416, 43 S. Ct. 158, 160, 67 L. Ed. 322, 326, 28 A.L.R. 1321, that "[w]e are in danger of forgetting that a strong public desire to improve the public condition is not enough to warrant achieving the desire by a shorter cut than the constitutional way of paying for the change." In this connection, we note also the terse comment of Chief Judge Hutcheson dissenting in Standard Oil Co. v. City of Tallahassee, *supra,* 183 F.2d at 414, "that even in this age of enlightenment the Constitution still protects the citizen against arbitrary and unreasonable action" and that the majority opinion in that case left him "in no doubt" but that "a good general principle, the public interest in zoning, [had] been run into the ground, the tail of legislative confiscation by caprice [had] been permitted to wag the dog of judicial constitutional protection."

It had been suggested that perhaps some distinction should be made between the termination of pre-existing nonconforming uses of *land* and the termination of such uses of *buildings,* and that it might be constitutionally permissible to terminate uses in the first category but not in the second. However, such distinction would be not only illogical but also in utter disregard of the economic realities of modern urban life, for the use of vacant land often is more valuable than the use of buildings. E.g., older buildings frequently are torn down to make the underlying land available for more profitable uses such as used car lots or parking lots. In City of Seattle v. Martin, 54 Wash. 2d 541, 342 P.2d 602 (1959), involving an ordinance which limited application of the amortization technique to nonconforming uses of vacant land, defendant's counsel, in his unavailing plea of unconstitutionality, with understandable cynicism pointed out that: "A watchmaker in a $400.00 building could continue [a pre-existing nonconforming use]. A used car lot or a parking lot with no office would have to stop. If [defendant] had a $100.00 office building perhaps [he] could continue. Such distinctions are not reasonable." Katarincic, op. cit. *supra,* at p. 34. And the commentator, although of the amortization school, observes in the same vein as defendant's counsel that limitation of the ordinance to nonconforming uses of vacant land "suggests that the ordinance was motivated by aesthetic considerations" and that "[i]t would be difficult to imagine that a use would become any less or more compatible if it takes place in or outside a building." Katarincic, op. cit. *supra,* at p. 34. . . .

In declining to adopt the suggestion that there may be some valid distinction between the termination of pre-existing lawful nonconforming uses of land and the termination of such uses of buildings, we have not overlooked the discussion in the case of In re Botz, 236 Mo. App. 566, 159 S.W.2d 367, which did *not* concern the termination of pre-existing lawful nonconforming uses by the amortization technique but which pertained only to a provision of the then effective St. Louis zoning ordinance permitting the owner of a *building* to change from one pre-existing lawful nonconforming use "to another nonconforming use of the same or a more restricted classification," if no structural alterations were made. 236 Mo. App. at 574, 159 S.W.2d at 371. That the court, by way of dicta, thought it reasonable that the Board of Aldermen had not seen fit to extend to owners of *land* the same right to change from one nonconforming use to another is not, to us, persuasive here.

Although the record before us leaves much to be desired by way of detail, it is sufficient for the purposes of this opinion to say that the record adequately shows that instant relators' use of their lots may not be brushed aside and disregarded as "relatively slight and insubstantial." Contrast People v. Miller *supra,* 106 N.E.2d at 35, 36, involving the harboring of pigeons as a hobby. In our view of the matter, termination of relators' pre-existing lawful nonconforming use of their lots for the open storage of lumber, building materials and construction equipment would constitute the taking of private property for public use without just compensation in violation of Article 1, Section 26, Missouri Constitution of 1945 — a taking not to be justified as an exercise of the police power which is always subject to, and may never transcend, constitutional rights and limitations.

Accordingly, the judgment of the circuit court is set aside and the cause is remanded with directions to enter judgment ordering respondents, constituting the board of adjustment of the City of St. Louis, to issue, or cause to be issued, to relators a certificate of occupancy for continuance of the pre-existing lawful nonconforming use of relators' lots for the open storage of lumber, building materials and construction equipment.

All concur, except HYDE, J., who dissents in separate dissenting opinion filed.[34]

---

34. This case is discussed in the following Notes: 18 Ala. L. Rev. 186 (1965); 20 Ark. L. Rev. 202 (1966); 45 Neb. L. Rev. 636 (1966); 42 N.D.L. Rev. 245 (1966); 10 St. Louis L.J. 422 (1966); 3 San Diego L. Rev. 104 (1966); 44 Tex. L. Rev. 368 (1965); 34 U.M.K.C.L. Rev. 441 (1966); 11 Vill. L. Rev. 189 (1965).

See generally Graham, Legislative Techniques for the Amortization of the Non-Conforming Use: A Suggested Formula, 12 Wayne L. Rev. 435 (1966); Moore, The Termination of Non-Conforming Uses, 6 Wm. & Mary L. Rev. 1 (1965); Fell, Amortization of Non-Conforming Uses, 24 Md. L. Rev. 323 (1964); Anderson, Non-Conforming Use — A Product of Euclidean Zoning, 10 Syracuse L. Rev. 214 (1959); Note, Amortization of Non-Conforming Uses, 4 Tulsa L.J. 32 (1967); Note, Termination of Non-Conforming Uses — *Harbison* to the Present, 14 Syracuse L. Rev. 62 (1962); Note, The Abatement of Pre-Existing Non-Conforming Uses Under Zoning Laws: Amortization, 57 Nw. U.L. Rev. 323 (1962); Note, Elimination of Non-Conforming Uses: Alternatives and Adjuncts to Amortization, 14 U.C.L.A.L. Rev. 354 (1966); Comment, Principle of Retroactivity and Amortization of the Non-Conforming Use — A Paradox in Property Law, 4 Vill. L. Rev. 416 (1959). — EDS.

Note: Means of Providing Flexibility in Euclidean Zoning (Herein: Amendments, Variances, and Exceptions) and Beyond Euclidean Zoning (Herein: Floating Zones and Contract Zoning)[35]

You need not be an expert in land planning to realize that any attempt to zone an area as large as most counties or as varied as most cities would be an exercise in futility unless some "safety valve" is provided to take into account all the various existing shapes, sizes, topography, uses, and particular conditions of each lot. The agency originally set up to provide this safety valve from the rigidity of "comprehensive" zoning is the board of adjustment,[36] which is authorized to grant both variances and exceptions. Most enabling acts provide that the board of adjustment may grant relief by way of variance where the restrictions imposed by the zoning ordinance cause the landowner to suffer "practical difficulty" or "unnecessary hardship."[37] These two tests are quite different; the latter is usually applied when a use variance is sought, whereas the former is applied for any other type of variance, e.g., area or bulk.[38]

Exceptions have been variously called "special exceptions," "special permits," "special uses," or "conditional uses." Whatever they are called, they are uses permitted by the zoning ordinance only when specified facts and conditions enumerated in the zoning ordinance are found to exist by the board of adjustment. The assumption underlying their widespread adoption is that while certain uses may be compatible with other uses, their compatibility in any particular case depends upon the surrounding circumstances, i.e., the enumerated uses are not necessarily incompatible with other uses but might cause harm if not closely supervised.[39] Common examples are golf courses, certain institutions, and gas stations.

---

35. See generally the following: Makielski, Legal Theory and Political Practice, 45 J. Urb. L. 1 (1967); Bryden, Zoning: Frigid, Flexible or Fluid, 44 J. Urb. L. 287 (1966); Dukeminier & Stapleton, The Zoning Board of Adjustment: A Case Study in Misrule, 50 Ky. L.J. 273 (1962); Comment, Zoning Change: Flexibility v. Stability, 26 Md. L. Rev. 48 (1966); Comment, Administration of Zoning Flexibility Devices: An Explanation for Recent Judicial Frustration, 49 Minn. L. Rev. 973 (1965); Note: Administrative Discretion in Zoning, 82 Harv. L. Rev. 668 (1969).

36. See Standard State Zoning Enabling Act, section 7, published by the U.S. Department of Commerce (1926).

37. Donovan, Variance Administration in Almeda County, 50 Calif. L. Rev. 101 (1962); Hardy, Zoning: Nonconforming Uses, Accessory Uses and Variances, 46 Mass. L.Q. 3 (1961); Comment, Zoning Variances, 74 Harv. L. Rev. 1396 (1961); Comment, Zoning Amendments and Variances Subject to Conditions, 12 Syracuse L. Rev. 230 (1960); Note, Zoning Variances in New York City, 3 Colum. J.L. & Soc. Probs. 120 (1967).

38. See, e.g., Hoffman v. Harris, 17 N.Y.2d 138, 216 N.E.2d 326 (1966), where the landowner applied both for an area variance and a use variance; held: former allowed, latter denied.

39. Carson, Reclassification, Variances, and Special Exceptions in Maryland, 21 Md. L. Rev. 306 (1961); Green, Are "Special Use" Procedures in Trouble? 12 Zoning Dig. 73 (1960); Comment, Flexible Land Use Control: Herein of the Special Use, 59 Nw. U.L. Rev. 394 (1964).

The ordinance itself may be amended or changed from time to time. In theory, zoning amendments are to be made in response to substantial changes in environmental conditions since the adoption of the ordinance, i.e., when a change in the "comprehensive plan" is indicated. It is in form and in fact a rezoning and is subject to the same standards as an original zoning ordinance. Unfortunately, all too frequently amendments have been used to take care of limited changes in use, usually confined to a single lot — a technique that is called spot zoning.[40]

A "floating zone" is so called because it "floats" in the air until it is later fixed to the map. It is a zone provided for in the zoning ordinance to which no land is assigned on the zoning map until a landowner requests, and is granted, such zoning classification.[41] It is frequently called two-step zoning because of this two-step process of first defining a permitted use and second finding land upon which this use will be pinned.

Contract zoning is a situation in which a municipal zoning authority reclassifies land to a less restricted use while the applicant for rezoning agrees to subject the land to restrictions by covenants running in favor of the municipality — on use or area, etc. — greater than those imposed by the zoning ordinance.[42]

SECTION 2. EMINENT DOMAIN

The fifth amendment to the United States Constitution has two express limitations upon the exercise of government power in relation to private

---

40. Comment, Spot Zoning, 34 Rocky Mtn. L. Rev. 231 (1962); Comment, "Spot Zoning"—A Vicious Practice or a Community Benefit? 29 Fordham L. Rev. 740 (1961); Note, Spot Zoning as Use Control, 13 Hastings L.J. 390 (1962); Note, 15 Okla. L. Rev. 197 (1962).

41. Not permitted in Eves v. Zoning Board of Adjustment, 401 Pa. 211, 164 A.2d 7 (1960). Permitted in Rodgers v. Village of Tarrytown, 302 N.Y. 115, 96 N.E.2d 731 (1951); Beall v. Montgomery County Council, 240 Md. 77, 212 A.2d 751 (1965). See generally Mosher, Floating Zone: Legal Status and Application to Gasoline Stations, 1 Tulsa L.J. 149 (1964); Reno, Non-Euclidean Zoning: The Use of the Floating Zone, 23 Md. L. Rev. 105 (1963); Haar & Hering, The *Lower Gwynned* Case: Too Flexible Zoning or an Inflexible Judiciary, 74 Harv. L. Rev. 1552 (1961); Note, Delayed Zoning or Floating Zone? 67 Dick. L. Rev. 185 (1963).

42. 2 Rathkopf, The Law of Zoning and Planning 74-79 (3d ed. 1963); Trager, Contract Zoning, 23 Md. L. Rev. 121 (1963); Shapiro, The Case for Conditional Zoning, 41 Temple L.Q. 267 (1968); Schaffer, Contract Zoning and Conditional Zoning, 11 Prac. Law. 43 (1965); Comment, Use and Abuse of Contract Zoning, 12 U.C.L.A.L. Rev. 897 (1965). It has been approved in Pecora v. Zoning Commission, 145 Conn. 435, 144 A.2d 48 (1958); Sylvania Electric Products, Inc. v. City of Newton, 344 Mass. 428, 183 N.E.2d 118 (1962); Bucholz v. City of Omaha, 174 Neb. 862, 120 N.W.2d 270 (1963); Church v. Town of Islip, 8 N.Y.2d 254, 168 N.E.2d 680 (1960); Johnson v. Griffiths, 74 Ohio L. Abs. 482, 141 N.E.2d 774 (Ct. App. 1955). It has been disapproved in Harnett v. Austin, 93 So. 2d 86 (Fla. 1956); Baylis v. City of Baltimore, 219 Md. 164, 148 A.2d 429 (1959); Houston Petroleum Co. v. Automotive Products Credit Association, 9 N.J. 122, 87 A.2d 319 (1952).

property: "No person shall be . . . deprived of . . . property, without due process of law; nor shall private property be taken for public use without just compensation." Although the fifth amendment is not directly applicable to the states, the due process is repeated in the same language in the fourteenth amendment, which is applicable to the states. The latter clause, the eminent domain clause, is found in the constitutions of almost every state, and the Supreme Court of the United States has held that the due process clause of the fourteenth amendment "incorporates" the same requirements.[43]

The eminent domain clause, following its language, nicely divides itself into four separable questions. (1) What is "property"?[44] (2) What is a "taking"? (3) What is "public use"? (4) What is "just compensation"?[45] This section will consider only the second and the third questions.

Note: What Is a "Taking"?

Reread the quotation from Pennsylvania Coal Co. v. Mahon, set out at page 1115 *supra*, and ask yourself whether Justice Holmes would have considered New York's action, in the following case, a "taking" of property or mere "regulation" under the police power.

JENAD, INC. v. VILLAGE OF SCARSDALE
18 N.Y.2d 78, 218 N.E.2d 673 (1966)

DESMOND, C.J.

The Village of Scarsdale, pursuant to statute (Village Law, Consol. Laws, c.64, §179-k) has given its Planning Commission the authority to approve proposed plats for subdividing lands in the village. On this appeal the principal question of law, answered in the negative by the Appellate Divi-

---

43. Missouri Pacific Railway v. Nebraska, 164 U.S. 403, 417 (1896); Fallbrook Irrigation District v. Bradley, 164 U.S. 112, 158 (1896).

44. Where "property" is "taken" by eminent domain, the owner of the fee is not necessarily the only person entitled to "just compensation." "Property" includes all estates successive in time and all easements and similar rights in the land, provided they are rights which are capable of enforcement by the courts as against third persons. You have already seen the problem arise in the context of landlord-tenant relations; see page 470 *supra*. You have also encountered the problem in the preceding chapter, page 1053 *supra*. See also Annot., Eminent Domain: Restrictive Covenant or Right to Enforcement Thereof as Compensable Property Right, 4 A.L.R.3d 1147 (1965). Finally, you have encountered the problem in statutes which either limit or abolish the possibility of reverter and right of entry; see page 1054 *supra*. Would a statute that abolished existing rights of inchoate dower be constitutional? Such a statute was upheld in Opinion of the Justices, 337 Mass. 786, 151 N.E.2d 475 (1958).

45. See Kaltenbach, Just Compensation (a service with monthly supplements, indexed for the United States and each of the states); Hershman, Compensation—Just and Unjust: A Study in Eminent Domain, 21 Bus. Law. 285 (1966); Sargstock & McAuliffe, What Is the Price of Eminent Domain? An Introduction to the Problems of Valuation in Eminent Domain Proceedings, 44 J. Urb. L. 185 (1966).

sion, is this: was it valid for the village to authorize its planning board to require, as a condition precedent to the approval of subdivision plats which show new streets or highways, that the subdivider allot some land within the subdivision for park purposes or, at the option of the village planning board, pay the village a fee in lieu of such allotment? Our answer is in the affirmative. We hold, first, that section 179-*l* of the Village Law, empowering a village to require as to subdivision plats that there be set aside therein lands for parks, playgrounds or other recreational purposes, is valid and enforcible. Further, we hold that there is no constitutional or statutory ban against section 2, article 12, of the Rules and Regulations of the Planning Commission of defendant Village of Scarsdale as approved by the village trustees on September 24, 1957. These rules and regulations give the commission power to direct that, in lieu of such dedication of land, a charge or fee of $250 per lot be collected by the village "and credited to a separate fund to be used for park, playground and recreational purposes in such manner as may be determined by the Village Board of Trustees from time to time."

The facts of the particular controversy between plaintiff and the village are set out in full in the dissenting opinion and need not be repeated. We add some generally pertinent items. In at least five counties of this State there are cities, towns or villages which make it possible to insist on developers' paying cash in lieu of setting aside areas in their developments for parks, playground and similar purposes (information supplied by the New York State Office for Local Government). In Westchester County alone 16 or more local governments (among them several villages including Scarsdale) have "monies in lieu of land" regulations (this data received from Westchester County Department of Planning). As we shall see later on when we cite recent cases from Wisconsin and Montana, such rules exist and are upheld by courts in other States. There is conflict between a 1956 opinion of the State Attorney-General that a city has no such power under section 33 of the General City Law, Consol. Laws, c.21, and three separate opinions of the State Comptroller dated in 1954, 1961 and 1963 (1954 Op. St. Comp. No. 6836; 17 Op. St. Comp., 1961, p. 79; 19 Op. St. Comp., 1963, p. 3) which state that towns and villages could exact such fees under section 277 of the Town Law, Consol. Laws, c.62 and section 179-*l* of the Village Law.

We find in section 179-*l* of the Village Law a sufficient grant to villages of power to make such exactions. In specific terms the statute validates "in proper cases" requirements by village planning boards that a subdivision map, to obtain approval, must show "a park or parks suitably located for playground or other recreation purposes." There is, to be sure, no such specificity as to a village rule setting up a "money in lieu of land" system. However, section 179-*l* says that a village planning board, when the specific circumstances of a particular plat are such that park lands therein are not requisite, may "waive" provision therefor, "subject to appropriate conditions and guarantees." We agree with the above-cited opinions of the State

Comptroller that the phrase "appropriate conditions and guarantees" reasonably includes the kind of arrangement here made. That is, instead of allotting part of the subdivision itself for parks and play areas, the subdivider may be ordered to pay so much per lot into a separate village fund which is "to be used for park, playground and recreational purposes," in such manner as the village trustees may decide.

We turn our attention to the arguments advanced against the constitutionality of collecting such fees from developers. Plaintiff like the Appellate Division relies on Gulest Assoc. v. Town of Newburgh, 25 Misc. 2d 1004, 209 N.Y.S.2d 729, affd. 15 A.D.2d 815, 225 N.Y.S.2d 538, which held invalid a 1959 amendment to section 277 of the Town Law. The amendment specifically authorized towns (there is in the Village Law no such specific authorization) to demand money payments instead of assignment of subdivision lands for recreational uses. The Special Term opinion in *Gulest* turns on what the court thought was vagueness in the Town Law amendment at the point where it appeared to give a town planning board the privilege of using the money for "any recreational purpose." Even if the *Gulest* decision were correct—and we hold it is not—it would not apply here since by the Scarsdale rules and regulations the moneys collected as "in lieu" of fees are not only put into "a separate fund to be used for park, playground and recreational purposes" (there was no such reserve set up in *Gulest*) but, as provided by the board of trustees, expenditures from such fund are to be made only for "acquisition and improvement of recreation and park lands" in the village. There is nothing vague about that language.

Going beyond *Gulest* (*supra*), plaintiff (and amicus curiae) insist that what Scarsdale has imposed is an unconstitutional and unauthorized "tax" on plaintiff and others similarly situated, in that the payments are for general governmental purposes thus charged against subdivision developers. We think that this labeling distorts the purpose and meaning of the requirements. This is not a tax at all but a reasonable form of village planning for the general community good.

Scarsdale and other communities, observing that their vacant lands were being cut up into subdivision lots, and being alert to their responsibilities, saw to it, before it was too late, that the subdivisions make allowance for open park spaces therein. This was merely a kind of zoning, like set-back and side-yard regulations, minimum size of lots, etc., and akin also to other reasonable requirements for necessary sewers, water mains, lights, sidewalks, etc. If the developers did not provide for parks and playgrounds in their own tracts, the municipality would have to do it since it would now be required for the benefit of all the inhabitants.

But it was found, in some instances, that the separate subdivisions were too small to permit substantial park lands to be set off, yet the creation of such subdivisions, too, enlarged the demand for more recreational space in the community. In such cases it was just as reasonable to assess the subdividers an amount per lot to go into a fund for more park lands for the village or town. One arrangement is no more of a "tax" or "illegal taking" than the other.

In 1965 (Jordan v. Village of Menomonee Falls, 28 Wis. 2d 608, 137 N.W.2d 442) the Supreme Court of Wisconsin in a careful and convincing opinion upheld as against assertions of unconstitutionality a village ordinance or statute which, for present purposes, is identical with the one we are considering. The Wisconsin court noted that municipal planners agree that to create a good environment for dwellings there must be a minimum devotion of land to park and school purposes. It was held in the *Jordan* case that it was not necessary to prove that the land required to be dedicated for a park or school site was to meet a need solely attributable to the influx into the community of people who would occupy this particular subdivision. The court concluded that "a required dedication of land for school, park, or recreational sites as a condition for the approval of the subdivision plat should be upheld as a valid exercise of police power if the evidence reasonably establishes that the municipality will be required to provide more land for schools, parks, and playgrounds as a result of approval of the subdivision" (p. 618, 137 N.W.2d p. 448). As to the constitutionality of what was called an "equalization fee provision" the court said that the same reasons justify with equal force the land dedication requirement and the provision for an equalization fee, and that the equalization fee was not a tax imposed on the land as such but was a fee imposed on the transaction of obtaining approval of the plat (p. 622, 137 N.W.2d p. 449). In 1964 the Montana Supreme Court in Billings Props. Inc. v. Yellowstone County, 144 Mont. 25, 394 P.2d 182 passed on a State statute which required land to be dedicated for park and playground purposes as a condition precedent to approval of a subdivision plat and which statute authorized the county planning board to waive the requirement in appropriate cases. The Montana court remarked (p. 29, 394 P.2d p. 185) that: "Statutes requiring dedication of park and playground land as a condition precedent to the approval of plats are in force in one form or another in most all states." The court said this at page 33, 394 P.2d at page 187:

> Appellant does not deny the need for parks and playgrounds, however, it would require the city to purchase or condemn land for their establishment. But this court is of the opinion that if the subdivision creates the specific need for such parks and playgrounds, then it is not unreasonable to charge the subdivider with the burden of providing them. . . .

The order appealed from should be reversed and defendants' motion for summary judgment dismissing the complaint granted, with costs in this court and in the Appellate Division.

VAN VOORHIS, J. (dissenting).

The principle of decision in this case would constitutionally allow municipal officers to prohibit real estate development in cities, towns and villages

unless the newcomers pay whatever sums of money the local public authorities may decide arbitrarily to impose upon them for the privilege of moving
into the community, to be spent on schools, public buildings, police and fire
protection, parks and recreation or any other general municipal purpose
past, present or to come, and without relation to special benefits or assessed
valuation. The comment is apt by the late Chief Justice Vanderbilt, speaking
for the Supreme Court of New Jersey in Daniels v. Borough of Point
Pleasant (23 N.J. 357, 362, 129 A.2d 265, 267):

> The philosophy of this ordinance is that the tax rate of the borough should
> remain the same and the new people coming into the municipality should
> bear the burden of the increased costs of their presence. This is so totally
> contrary to tax philosophy as to require it to be stricken down; see Gilbert v.
> Town of Irvington, 20 N.J. 432, 120 A.2d 114 (1956). . . .

FULD, BERGAN and KEATING, JJ., concur with DESMOND, C.J.

VAN VOORHIS, J., dissents and votes to affirm in an opinion in which
BURKE and SCILEPPI, JJ., concur.[46]

Note: More on How to Define a Taking

Recall what was held not to constitute a taking in Penn Central Transportation Co. v. City of New York, 439 U.S. 883, 98 S. Ct. 2646 (1978), referred
to at page 1146 *supra.*

Loretto v. Teleprompter Manhattan CATV Corp., 458 U.S. 419, 102 S.
Ct. 3164 (1982), makes it clear that there will be a "taking" when the
consequence of the governmental action is the permanent physical occupation of a person's property by someone other than the owner. The Supreme
Court said: "We conclude that a permanent physical occupation authorized
by government is a taking without regard to the public interests that it may
serve. Our constitutional history confirms the rule, recent cases do not
question it, and the purposes of the Takings Clause compel its retention"
(102 S. Ct. at 3171). The Supreme Court recognized that the extent of the
occupation is a relevant factor in determining the compensation due:

> Our holding today is very narrow. We affirm the traditional rule that a
> permanent physical occupation of property is a taking. In such a case, the
> property owner entertains an historically-rooted expectation of compensa-
> tion, and the character of the invasion is qualitatively more intrusive than
> perhaps any other category of property regulation. We do not, however,

---

46. See Heyman & Gilhool, The Constitutionality of Imposing Increased Community
Costs on New Suburban Residents Through Subdivision Exactions, 73 Yale L.J. 119 (1964);
Comment, Money Payment Requirements as Conditions to Approval of Subdivision Maps:
Analysis and Prognosis, 9 Vill. L. Rev. 294 (1964).—EDS.

question the equally substantial authority upholding a State's broad power to impose appropriate restrictions upon an owner's use of his property. [102 S. Ct. at 3179.]

Justices Blackmun, Brennan, and White dissented in the *Loretto* case.

Was not the position in the *Village of Scarsdale* case — that there was no constitutional ban on a requirement that lands for parks, playgrounds, or other recreational use be set aside in order to obtain the approval of subdivision plats — an authorization of governmental action that would involve permanent physical occupation of the owner's property by others?

See generally Michelman, Property, Utility, and Fairness: Comments on the Ethical Foundation of "Just Compensation" Law, 80 Harv. L. Rev. 1165 (1967); Costonis, Presumptive and Per Se Takings: A Decisional Model for the Taking Issue, 58 N.Y.U.L. Rev. 466 (1983).

Note: Inverse Condemnation

Inverse condemnation is the popular description of a cause of action against a governmental defendant to recover the value of property which has been taken in fact by the governmental defendant, even though no formal exercise of the power of eminent domain has been attempted by the taking agency.[47]

The doctrine of inverse condemnation requires a court to make a factual finding of a taking when the government insists that none was intended. It is not a damage action, leaving the plaintiff as owner, but rather a forced purchase of the plaintiff's property. Hence the term "inverse condemnation," for the usual condemnation, is a forced sale and not a forced purchase.

The United States Supreme Court opened what some consider a Pandora's box when it held that frequent low flights by United States military aircraft, which were a direct and immediate interference with the enjoyment of land, amounted to a taking of an easement entitling the property owner to compensation within the meaning of the fifth amendment.[48]

Fifteen years later the Supreme Court held that simply because Congress had redefined "navigable airspace" so as to include that space necessary for take-off and landing[49] would not preclude a property owner from an inverse condemnation action based on low-flying aircraft — although the taking had occurred in this newly defined "navigable airspace."[50]

There is a split of authorities over whether there must be direct "over-

---

47. Thornburg v. Port of Portland, 233 Or. 178, 180 n.1, 376 P.2d 100, 101 n.1 (1962).
48. United States v. Causby, 328 U.S. 256, 66 S. Ct. 1062 (1946), printed in full in Chapter 36.
49. 49 U.S.C. §1301(24).
50. Griggs v. Allegheny County, 369 U.S. 84, 82 S. Ct. 531 (1962).

flights" to constitute a taking, or whether sound shock waves could also amount to a taking, although there had been no actual invasion of the airspace over the plaintiff's property. The federal courts require a direct overflight, emphasizing the need to place some limits on this action.[51] Some state courts refuse to so limit the doctrine.

> We are unable to accept the premise that recovery for interference with the use of land should depend upon anything as irrelevant as whether the wing tip of the aircraft passes through some fraction of an inch of the airspace directly above the plaintiff's land.[52] Although the two United States Supreme Court decisions involved direct overflights, the court's reasoning is easily extended to include flights which do not directly invade plaintiff's airspace.[53]

A zoning law that protects open areas from development may not deprive owners of their private land in violation of the Constitution. If, however, a taking is found to have taken place by such governmental action, rather than attack the zoning law as unconstitutional, could the owner treat this as a case of inverse condemnation and collect damages?

Agins v. City of Tiburon, 447 U.S. 255, 100 S. Ct. 2138 (1980), involved a zoning law that required that open spaces be left in the development of land for residential purposes. The court upheld the zoning law against an attack on its constitutionality, and thus there was no consideration of whether, as an alternative to holding the zoning law unconstitutional, this could be treated as a case of inverse condemnation and the landowner could be awarded damages for the taking. The Supreme Court observed as follows:

> The State Supreme Court determined that the appellants could not recover damages for inverse condemnation even if the zoning ordinances constituted a taking. The court stated that only mandamus and a declaratory judgment are remedies available to such land owner. Because no taking has occurred, we need not consider whether a state may limit the remedies available to a person whose land has been taken without just compensation. [447 U.S. at 263, 100 S. Ct. at 2143.]

See also in regard to this issue of damages for inverse condemnation, San Diego Gas & Electric Co. v. City of San Diego, 450 U.S. 621, 101 S. Ct. 1287 (1981), where the Supreme Court again refused to consider whether a landowner had a right to damages for inverse condemnation when there was a taking because the state court had not rendered a final judgment as to whether there was a taking.

---

51. Batten v. United States, 306 F.2d 580 (10th Cir. 1962); Avery v. United States, 330 F.2d 640 (Ct. Cl. 1964).

52. Martin v. Port of Seattle, 64 Wash. 2d 309, 316, 391 P.2d 540, 545 (1964); see also Thornburg v. Port of Portland, footnote 47 *supra.*—EDS.

53. See generally Note, Property: Inverse Condemnation A Growing Problem? 3 Tulsa L.J. 169 (1966); Annot., 77 A.L.R.2d 1355 (1961); Mandelker, Inverse Condemnation: The Constitutional Limits of Public Responsibility, 1966 Wis. L. Rev. 3.—EDS.

B. What Is a "Public Use" (with particular reference to urban renewal)?

Although the language of the fifth amendment is less than clear on what a public use is, it is well settled that the prohibition against the taking of property for public use without just compensation impliedly, but definitely, prohibits a taking of property for private use—even with just compensation. Consider the implications of a proposed amendment to the Connecticut constitution, which said: "No property shall be taken for public use unless the taking be necessary for such use, and then, only upon the payment of just compensation."[54] The former language is similar to that of the fifth amendment. As you read the cases which follow, ask yourself whether such an amendment is desirable and whether it adds anything to the present law.

BERMAN v. PARKER
348 U.S. 26, 75 S. Ct. 98 (1954)

Mr. Justice DOUGLAS delivered the opinion of the Court.

This is an appeal (28 USC §1253) from the judgment of a three-judge District Court which dismissed a complaint seeking to enjoin the condemnation of appellants' property under the District of Columbia Redevelopment Act of 1945, 60 Stat. 790, DC Code, 1951, §§5-701-5-719. The challenge was to the constitutionality of the Act, particularly as applied to the taking of appellants' property. The District Court sustained the constitutionality of the Act. 117 F. Supp 705.

By §2 of the Act, Congress made a "legislative determination" that "owing to technological and sociological changes, obsolete lay-out, and other factors, conditions existing in the District of Columbia with respect to substandard housing and blighted areas, including the use of buildings in alleys as dwellings for human habitation, are injurious to the public health, safety, morals, and welfare; and it is hereby declared to be the policy of the United States to protect and promote the welfare of the inhabitants of the seat of the Government by eliminating all such injurious conditions by employing all means necessary and appropriate for the purpose."

Section 2 goes on to declare that acquisition of property is necessary to eliminate these housing conditions.

Congress further finds in §2 that these ends cannot be attained "by the ordinary operations of private enterprise alone without public participation"; that "the sound replanning and redevelopment of an obsolescent or obsolescing portion" of the District "cannot be accomplished unless it be done in the light of comprehensive and coordinated planning of the whole of

---

54. Amendment to Conn. Const. art. 1, §11, rejected in a 1965 statewide referendum.

the territory of the District of Columbia and its environs"; and that "the acquisition and the assembly of real property and the leasing or sale thereof for redevelopment pursuant to a project area redevelopment plan . . . is hereby declared to be a public use."

Section 4 creates the District of Columbia Redevelopment Land Agency (hereinafter called the Agency), composed of five members, which is granted power by §5(a) to acquire and assemble, by eminent domain and otherwise, real property for "the redevelopment of blighted territory in the District of Columbia and the prevention, reduction, or elimination of blighting factors or causes of blight."

Section 6(a) of the Act directs the National Capital Planning Commission (hereinafter called the Planning Commission) to make and develop "a comprehensive or general plan" of the District, including "a land-use plan" which designates land for use for "housing, business, industry, recreation, education, public buildings, public reservations, and other general categories of public and private uses of the land." Section 6(b) authorizes the Planning Commission to adopt redevelopment plans for specific project areas. These plans are subject to the approval of the District Commissioners after a public hearing; and they prescribe the various public and private land uses for the respective areas, the "standards of population density and building intensity," and "the amount or character or class of any low-rent housing."§6(b).

Once the Planning Commission adopts a plan and that plan is approved by the Commissioners, the Planning Commission certifies it to the Agency. §6(b). At that point, the Agency is authorized to acquire and assemble the real property in the area. Id.

After the real estate has been assembled, the Agency is authorized to transfer to public agencies the land to be devoted to such public purposes as streets, utilities, recreational facilities, and schools, §7(a), and to lease or sell the remainder as an entirety or in parts to a redevelopment company, individual, or partnership. §7(b), (f). The leases or sales must provide that the lessees or purchasers will carry out the redevelopment plan and that "no use shall be made of any land or real property included in the lease or sale nor any building or structure erected thereon" which does not conform to the plan, §§7(d), 11. Preference is to be given to private enterprise over public agencies in executing the redevelopment plan. §7(g).

The first project undertaken under the Act relates to Project Area B in Southwest Washington D.C. In 1950 the Planning Commission prepared and published a comprehensive plan for the District. Surveys revealed that in Area B, 64.3% of the dwellings were beyond repair, 18.4% needed major repairs, only 17.3% were satisfactory; 57.8% of the dwellings had outside toilets, 60.3% had no baths, 29.3% lacked electricity, 82.2% had no wash basins or laundry tubs, 83.8% lacked central heating. In the judgment of the District's Director of Health it was necessary to redevelop Area B in the interests of public health. The population of Area B amounted to 5,012 persons, of whom 97.5% were Negroes.

The plan for Area B specifies the boundaries and allocates the use of the land for various purposes. It makes detailed provisions for types of dwelling units and provides that at least one-third of them are to be low-rent housing with a maximum rental of $17 per room per month.

After a public hearing, the Commissioners approved the plan and the Planning Commission certified it to the Agency for execution. The Agency undertook the preliminary steps for redevelopment of the area when this suit was brought.

Appellants own property in Area B at 712 Fourth Street, S.W. It is not used as a dwelling or place of habitation. A department store is located on it. Appellants object to the appropriation of this property for the purposes of the project. They claim that their property may not be taken constitutionally for this project. It is commercial, not residential property; it is not slum housing; it will be put into the project under the management of a private, not a public, agency and redeveloped for private, not public, use. That is the argument; and the contention is that appellant's private property is being taken contrary to two mandates of the Fifth Amendment — (1) "No person shall . . . be deprived of . . . property, without due process of law"; (2) "nor shall private property be taken for public use, without just compensation." To take for the purpose of ridding the area of slums is one thing; it is quite another, the argument goes, to take a man's property merely to develop a better balanced, more attractive community. The District Court, while agreeing in general with that argument, saved the Act by construing it to mean that the Agency could condemn property only for the reasonable necessities of slum clearance and prevention, its concept of "slum" being the existence of conditions "injurious to the public health, safety, morals and welfare." 117 F Supp 705, 724, 725.

The power of Congress over the District of Columbia includes all the legislative powers which a state may exercise over its affairs. We deal, in other words, with what traditionally has been known as the police power. An attempt to define its reach or trace its outer limits is fruitless, for each case must turn on its own facts. The definition is essentially the product of legislative determinations addressed to the purposes of government, purposes neither abstractly nor historically capable of complete definition. Subject to specific constitutional limitations, when the legislature has spoken, the public interest has been declared in terms well-nigh conclusive. In such cases the legislature, not the judiciary, is the main guardian of the public needs to be served by social legislation, whether it be Congress legislating concerning the District of Columbia or the States legislating concerning local affairs. This principle admits of no exception merely because the power of eminent domain is involved. The role of the judiciary in determining whether that power is being exercised for a public purpose is an extremely narrow one. Public safety, public health, morality, peace and quiet, law and order — these are some of the more conspicuous examples of the traditional application of the police power to municipal affairs. Yet they merely illustrate the scope of the power and do not delimit it. Miserable and disreputable housing conditions may do more than spread disease and crime and immorality. They may also suffocate the spirit by reducing the people who live there to the status of cattle. They may indeed make living an almost insufferable burden. They may also be an ugly sore, a blight on the community which robs it of charm, which makes it a place from which men turn. The misery of housing may despoil a community as an open sewer may ruin a river.

We do not sit to determine whether a particular housing project is or is not desirable. The concept of the public welfare is broad and inclusive. The values it represents are spiritual as well as physical, aesthetic as well as monetary. It is within the power of the legislature to determine that the community should be beautiful as well as healthy, spacious as well as clean, well-balanced as well as carefully patrolled. In the present case, the Congress and its authorized agencies have made determinations that take into account a wide variety of values. It is not for us to reappraise them. If those who govern the District of Columbia decide that the Nation's Capital should be beautiful as well as sanitary, there is nothing in the Fifth Amendment that stands in the way.

Once the object is within the authority of Congress, the right to realize it through the exercise of eminent domain is clear. For the power of eminent domain is merely the means to the end. Once the object is within the authority of Congress, the means by which it will be attained is also for Congress to determine. Here one of the means chosen is the use of private enterprise for redevelopment of the area. Appellants argue that this makes the project a taking from one businessman for the benefit of another businessman. But the means of executing the project are for Congress and Congress alone to determine, once the public purpose has been established. The public end may be as well or better served through an agency of private enterprise than through a department of government — or so the Congress might conclude. We cannot say that public ownership is the sole method of promoting the public purposes of community redevelopment projects. What we have said also disposes of any contention concerning the fact that certain property owners in the area may be permitted to repurchase their properties for redevelopment in harmony with the over-all plan. That, too, is a legitimate means which Congress and its agencies may adopt, if they choose.

In the present case, Congress and its authorized agencies attack the problem of the blighted parts of the community on an area rather than on a structure-by-structure basis. That, too, is opposed by appellants. They maintain that since their building does not imperil health or safety nor contribute to the making of a slum or a blighted area, it cannot be swept into a redevelopment plan by the mere dictum of the Planning Commission or the Commissioners. The particular uses to be made of the land in the project were determined with regard to the needs of the particular community. The experts concluded that if the community were to be healthy, if it were not to revert again to a blighted or slum area, as though possessed of a congenital disease, the area must be planned as a whole. It was not enough, they believed, to remove existing buildings that were unsanitary or unsightly. It was important to redesign the whole area so as to eliminate the conditions that cause slums — the overcrowding of dwellings, the lack of parks, the lack of adequate streets and alleys, the absence of recreational areas, the lack of light and air, the presence of outmoded street patterns. It was believed that the piecemeal approach, the removal of individual structures that were offensive, would be only a palliative. The entire area needed redesigning so that a balanced, integrated plan could be developed for the region, including not only new homes but also schools, churches, parks, streets, and shopping centers. In this way it was hoped that the cycle of decay of the area could be controlled and the birth of future slums prevented. Such diversification in future use is plainly relevant to the maintenance of the desired housing standards and therefore within congressional power.

The District Court below suggested that, if such a broad scope were intended for the statute, the standards contained in the Act would not be sufficiently definite to sustain the delegation of authority. 117 F Supp 705, 721. We do not agree. We think the standards prescribed were adequate for executing the plan to eliminate not only slums as narrowly defined by the District Court but also the blighted areas that tend to produce slums. Property may of course be taken for this redevelopment which, standing by itself, is innocuous and unoffending. But we have said enough to indicate that it is the need of the area as a whole which Congress and its agencies are evaluating. If owner after owner were permitted to resist these redevelopment programs on the ground that his particular property was not being used against the public interest, integrated plans for redevelopment would suffer greatly. The argument pressed on us is, indeed, a plea to substitute the landowner's standard of the public need for the standard prescribed by Congress. But as we have already stated, community redevelopment programs need not, by force of the Constitution, be on a piecemeal basis — lot by lot, building by building.

It is not for the courts to oversee the choice of the boundary line nor to sit in review on the size of a particular project area. Once the question of the public purpose has been decided, the amount and character of land to be taken for the project and the need for a particular tract to complete the integrated plan rests in the discretion of the legislative branch.

The District Court indicated grave doubts concerning the Agency's right to take full title to the land as distinguished from the objectionable buildings located on it. 117 F Supp 705, 715-719. We do not share those doubts. If the Agency considers it necessary in carrying out the redevelopment project to take full title to the real property involved, it may do so. It is not for the courts to determine whether it is necessary for successful consummation of the project that unsafe, unsightly, or unsanitary buildings alone be taken or whether title to the land be included, any more than it is the function of the courts to sort and choose among the various parcels selected for condemnation.

The rights of these property owners are satisfied when they receive that just compensation which the Fifth Amendment exacts as the price of the taking.

The judgment of the District Court, as modified by this opinion is Affirmed.

Note: Urban Renewal

Berman v. Parker gave considerable impetus to the use of eminent domain to bring about urban renewal. Miller v. City of Tacoma, set forth in part below, involved a challenge to the urban renewal law of the state of Washington. The court referred to Berman v. Parker, pointing out that that decision settled any question of public use or due process under the federal Constitution with regard to this type of legislation. There is still the question of how this legislation stands up under state constitutional provisions. The conclusion of the court in the *City of Tacoma* case and the appendix attached to the opinion are as follows.

MILLER v. CITY OF TACOMA
61 Wash. 2d 374, 378 P.2d 464 (1963)

An overwhelming majority of the courts of last resort in other jurisdictions have held that urban renewal laws, similar to the one before us, are for a "public use" and constitutional; hence, the expenditure of public funds is for a public purpose.

We agree.

Many of the cases are collected in an annotation: "Validity, construction, and effect of statutes providing for urban redevelopment by private enterprise," by C. C. Marvel, 44 A.L.R.2d 1414 (1955). The attached appendix, footnote 6, sets forth the leading cases on this subject in each jurisdiction. . . .

The judgment is affirmed.

FINLEY, HUNTER, HAMILTON and HALE, JJ., concur.

[Rosellini, J., filed a dissenting opinion, which was concurred in by Ott, C.J., and Hill & Donworth, JJ.]

APPENDIX . . .

4 — Constitutional provisions re eminent domain, public use, and protection of private property: Alabama, Art. I, §23; Arkansas, Art. II, §22;

Colorado, Art. II, §§14, 15 (very similar to Washington); Connecticut, Art. I, §11, C.G.S.A.: Delaware, Art. I, §8, Del. C. Ann.; Florida, Art. XVI, §29, F.S.A.; Illinois, Art. II, §13, S.H.A.; Indiana, Art. I, §21; Kansas, Art. XII, §4; Maine, Art. I, §21; Massachusetts, Art. X (Pt. 1), M.G.L.A.; Michigan, Art. XIII, §§1, 2; Minnesota, Art. I, §13; New Hampshire, Part. I, Art. XII; North Carolina, Art. I, §17; Ohio, Art. I, §19; Oregon, Art. I, §18; Pennsylvania, Art. I, §10 and Art. XVI, §3, P.S.; Rhode Island, Art. I, §16; South Carolina, Art. I, §17; Tennessee, Art. I, §21; Texas, Art. I, §17, Vernon's Ann. St.; Virginia, §58; Wisconsin, Art. I, §13, W.S.A.

5 — Urban Redevelopment Laws Held Constitutional under Specific Constitutional Provisions:

California: Redevelopment Agency of City and County of San Francisco v. Hayes, 122 Cal. App. 2d 777, 266 P.2d 105 (1954), *cert. den.* in Van Hoff v. Redevelopment Agency of the City and County of San Francisco, 348 U.S. 897, 75 S. Ct. 214, 99 L. Ed. 705 (1954); Babcock v. Community Redevelopment Agency of the City of Los Angeles, 148 Cal. App. 2d 38, 306 P.2d 513 (1957).

Georgia: Bailey v. Housing Authority of City of Bainbridge, 214 Ga. 790, 107 S.E.2d 812 (1959); Allen v. City Council of Augusta, 215 Ga. 778, 113 S.E.2d 621 (1960).

Maryland: Herzinger v. Mayor and City Council of Baltimore, 203 Md. 49, 98 A.2d 87 (1953).

Missouri: State on Information of Dalton v. Land Clearance for Redevelopment Authority of Kansas City, 364 Mo. 974, 270 S.W.2d 44 (1954).

New Jersey: Wilson v. City of Long Branch, 27 N.J. 360, 142 A.2d 837 (1958), *cert. den.* 358 U.S. 873, 79 S. Ct. 113, 3 L. Ed. 2d 104 (1958).

New York: Murray v. LaGuardia, 291 N.Y. 320, 52 N.E.2d 884 (1943), *cert. den.* 321 U.S. 771, 64 S. Ct. 530, 88 L. Ed. 1066.

6 — Redevelopment Laws Held Constitutional:

Alabama: Opinion of the Justices, 254 Ala. 343, 48 So. 2d 757 (1950); Blankenship v. City of Decatur, 269 Ala. 670, 115 So. 2d 459 (1959).

Arkansas: Rowe v. The Housing Authority of the City of Little Rock, 220 Ark. 698, 249 S.W.2d 551 (1952).

Colorado: Rabinoff v. District Court, 145 Colo. 225, 360 P.2d 114 (1961).

Connecticut: Gohld Realty Co. v. Hartford, 141 Conn. 135, 104 A.2d 365 (1954).

Delaware: Randolph v. Wilmington Housing Authority, 37 Del. Ch. 202, 139 A.2d 476 (1958).

District of Columbia: Schneider v. District of Columbia, 117 F. Supp. 705 (D.C. 1953), *affirmed as modified* by Berman v. Parker, 348 U.S. 26, 75 S. Ct. 98, 99 L. Ed. 27.

Florida: Grubstein v. Urban Renewal Agency of City of Tampa, (Fla.) 115 So. 2d 745 (1959).

Illinois: Zurn v. City of Chicago, 389 Ill. 114, 59 N.E.2d 18 (1945); People ex rel. Adamowski v. Chicago Land Clearance Comm., 14 Ill. 2d 74, 150 N.E.2d 792 (1958).

Indiana: Alanel Corp. v. Indianapolis Redevelopment Comm., 239 Ind. 35, 154 N.E.2d 515 (1958).

Kansas: State ex rel. Fatzer v. Urban Renewal Agency of Kansas City, 179 Kan. 435, 296 P.2d 656 (1956).

Kentucky: Miller v. City of Louisville, (Ky.) 321 S.W.2d 237 (1959).

Maine: Crommett v. City of Portland, 150 Me. 217, 107 A.2d 841 (1954).

Massachusetts: Papadinis v. City of Somerville, 331 Mass. 627, 121 N.E.2d 714 (1954); Worcester Knitting Realty Co. v. Worcester Housing Authority, 335 Mass. 19, 138 N.E.2d 356 (1956).

Michigan: In re Slum Clearance in City of Detroit, 331 Mich. 714, 50 N.W.2d 340 (1951).

Minnesota: Housing and Redevelopment Authority of City of St. Paul v. Greenman, 255 Minn. 396, 96 N.W.2d 673 (1959).

New Hampshire: Velishka v. City of Nashua, 99 N.H. 161, 106 A.2d 571, 44 A.L.R.2d 1406 (1954).

New Jersey: Redfern v. Board of Comm. of Jersey City, 137 N.J.L. 356, 59 A.2d 641 (1948).

North Carolina: Redevelopment Commission of Greensboro v. Security National Bank of Greensboro, 252 N.C. 595, 114 S.E.2d 688 (1960).

Ohio: State ex rel. Bruestle v. Rich, 159 Ohio St. 13, 110 N.E.2d 778 (1953).

Oregon: Foeller v. Housing Authority of Portland, 198 Or. 205, 256 P.2d 752 (1953).

Pennsylvania: Belovsky v. Redevelopment Authority of City of Philadelphia, 357 Pa. 329, 54 A.2d 277, 172 A.L.R. 953 (1947).

Rhode Island: Opinion to the Governor, 76 R.I. 249, 69 A.2d 531 (1949); Ajootian v. Providence Redevelopment Agency of City of Providence, 80 R.I. 73, 91 A.2d 21 (1952).

Tennessee: Nashville Housing Authority v. City of Nashville, 192 Tenn. 103, 237 S.W.2d 946 (1951).

Texas: Davis v. City of Lubbock, 160 Tex. 38, 326 S.W.2d 699 (1959).

Virginia: Hunter v. Norfolk Redevelopment and Housing Authority, 195 Va. 326, 78 S.E.2d 893 (1953).

Wisconsin: David Jeffrey Co. v. Milwaukee, 267 Wis. 559, 66 N.W.2d 362 (1954). . . .

Note: Direct Federal Intervention in Urban Renewal

If a state blocks urban renewal on the ground that it would involve a taking of private property for other than a public purpose, would a federal statute which authorized a federal agency to go into such state and take private property for compensation and make it available to private enterprise to develop so as to eliminate slum areas be constitutional? In considering this question, keep in mind the following provision of the fourteenth amendment of the federal Constitution: "Section 5. The Congress shall have power to enforce, by appropriate legislation, the provisions of this article."[55]

COURTESY SANDWICH SHOP, INC. v. PORT OF NEW YORK AUTHORITY

12 N.Y.2d 379, 190 N.E.2d 402, *appeal dismissed,* 375 U.S. 78
(1963)

BURKE, J.

Chapter 209 of the Laws of New York, 1962, McK. Unconsol. Laws, §6601 et seq., together with concurrent New Jersey legislation (Laws of N.J., 1962, ch. 8, N.J.S.A. 32:1-35.50 et seq.), authorizes the Port of New York Authority, through the appellant subsidiary, to effectuate a single port development project to consist of the present Hudson & Manhattan Railroad system and a new development to be known as the "World Trade Center," all on a site in lower Manhattan, part of which is now occupied by the existing Hudson & Manhattan Terminal. Appellant is authorized to condemn property to achieve this purpose and, under this power, instituted the condemnation proceeding here challenged by respondents, who have an interest in the subject property. Respondents argue that chapter 209 violates section 7 of article I of the New York Constitution and the United States Constitution (Matter of Hopper v. Britt, 203 N.Y. 144, 149, 96 N.E. 371, 372-373, 37 A.L.R., N.S., 825; Missouri Pacific Ry. v. Nebraska, 164 U.S. 403, 17 S. Ct. 130, 41 L. Ed. 489) in that it authorizes the taking of private property by eminent domain for other than a public use.

The proposed World Trade Center is defined by statute as that part of the unified project that is "a facility of commerce . . . for the centralized accommodation of functions, activities and services for or incidental to the transportation of persons, the exchange, buying, selling and transportation of commodities . . . in world trade and commerce . . . governmental services." It also states that as far as structures are concerned the World Trade Center also includes any such structure not devoted to railroad functions (thus preserving the distinction between the Hudson & Manhattan part of the project and the World Trade Center functions) even though portions of such structures are not functionally related to the project's purpose and are used solely for "the production of incidental revenue . . . for the expenses of all or part of the port development project" (ch. 209, §2).

---

55. In relation to the improvement of the living and the economic conditions of various members of our society, see also the following items: Note, Family Relocation in Urban Renewal, 82 Harv. L. Rev. 864 (1969); Note: Community Development Corporations: A New Approach to the Poverty Problem, 82 Harv. L. Rev. 644 (1969).

All of the Appellate Division Justices are agreed that the World Trade Center concept represents a public purpose. The majority found, however, the statute was on its face unconstitutional, in that the act granted a power to condemn property to be used for no other purpose than the raising of revenue for the expenses of the project, and for a class of tenants with a remote relationship with world trade. These conclusions were drawn from the inclusion in the definition of the term "incidental." The definition refers to "incidental" revenue and "functions . . . incidental to . . . the exchange, buying, selling . . . of commodities . . . in world trade and commerce." The dissent read the definition as not including the power to condemn any independent areas separately accommodating only incidental revenue tenants not related to the World Trade Center concept. Therefore, it found that revenue production was incidental and not the primary purpose of the taking.

The prime issue, then, is whether the language of the act must be interpreted so as to authorize condemnation for the production of revenue without subordination to any primary purpose. If that is so the act goes beyond what the cases authorized and beyond what can be constitutionally permitted. We think that the statute is valid.

The Appellate Division has stated that the concept of the World Trade Center is a public purpose. We understand this to mean that any use of the property sought to be condemned that is functionally related to the centralizing of all port business is unobjectionable even though private persons are to be the immediate lessees. The "concept" referred to by the Appellate Division can mean only that. It is the gathering together of all business relating to world trade that is supposed to be the great convenience held out to those who use American ports and which is supposed to attract trade with a resultant stimulus to the economic well-being of the Port of New York. This benefit is not too remote or speculative as to render the means chosen to achieve it patently unreasonable; nor is the benefit sought itself an improper concern of government. The history of western civilization demonstrates the cause and effect relationship between a great port and a great city. (See Pirenne, Economic and Social History of Medieval Europe, [Harcourt, Brace & Co., N.Y.].) Fostering harbor facilities has long been recognized by this court as the legitimate concern of government. (Matter of Mayor of City of N.Y., 135 N.Y. 253, 31 N.E. 1043.) Even the centralization of inland trade has supported the exercise of the power of eminent domain for the establishment of public markets wherein private merchants plied their trades. More recently the indirect benefits deriving from slum clearance and from a "plan to turn a predominantly vacant, poorly developed and organized area into a site for new industrial buildings" have justified condemnation. To retreat from the public importance of piers, markets and slum clearance, even esthetic improvements have been held to be a public purpose justifying condemnation (Berman v. Parker, 348 U.S. 26, 75 S. Ct. 98, 99 L. Ed. 27). No further demonstration is required that improvement of the Port of New York by facilitating the flow of commerce and centralizing all activity incident thereto is a public purpose supporting the condemnation of property for any activity functionally related to that purpose. Nor can it be said that the use of property to produce revenue to help finance the operation of those activities that tend to achieve the purpose of the project does not itself perform such a function, provided, of course, that there are in fact such other activities to be supported by incidental revenue production. The crux of the problem here, however, is that the statute has been read by the Appellate Division as allowing unfettered erection of structures that are solely revenue producing. As the dissent below maintains, this misreads the statute. The act was construed so as to raise rather than settle a constitutional question. We have said that where there are two possible interpretations the court will accept that which avoids constitutional doubts. The act may properly be read to authorize only incidental extensions of a site required for a public use. . . .

Even without resort to familiar canons of construction that control when a statute is called into question on constitutional grounds, the statute, it seems to us, allows only "portions" of structures otherwise devoted to project purposes to be used for "the production of incidental revenue . . . for the expenses of all or part of the port development project." Thus considered it does not vitiate the public purpose of the development as a whole. As to the fears expressed by the respondents that the Port Authority may illegally seize a particular piece of property for an unauthorized nonpublic use, it is sufficient to say that the condemnation procedures prescribed by statute fully protect the respondents and others in like position against any taking for nonpublic purposes in violation of the Port Development Project Law. . . .

The orders appealed from should be reversed, the orders of Special Term in the condemnation proceeding reinstated, a judgment rendered that chapter 209 of the Laws of 1962 is constitutional, and the certified question answered in the negative.

VAN VOORHIS, J. (dissenting).

This statute (L. 1962, ch. 209), as drafted, includes a great deal more than the sponsors of a World Trade Center were talking about, and renders it in my opinion subject to the constitutional defects which the Appellate Division has found. These provisions, as analyzed and criticized by the Appellate Division, appear to have been due to no inadvertence; they bear every indication of having been consciously and deliberately inserted so as to grant to the Port Authority extensive and uncontrolled governmental power to condemn and manage private real property for private purposes as a major object of the act. . . .

Disregard of the constitutional protection of private property and stigmatization of the small or not so small entrepreneur as standing in the way of progress has everywhere characterized the advance of collectivism. To hold a purpose to be public merely for the reason that it is invoked by a public body to serve its ideas of the public good, it seems to me, can be done only on the assumption that we have passed the point of no return, that the trade, commerce and manufacture of our principal cities can be conducted by private enterprise only on a diminishing scale and that private capital should progressively be displaced by public capital which should increasingly take over. The economic and geographical advantages of the City of New York have withstood a great deal of attrition and can probably withstand more, but there is a limit beyond which socialization cannot be carried without destruction of the constitutional bases of private ownership and enterprise. It seems to me to be the part of courts to enforce the constitutional rights of property which are involved here.

The orders of the Appellate Division appealed from should be affirmed.

DESMOND, C.J., and DYE, FULD, FOSTER and SCILEPPI, JJ., concur with BURKE, J.

Note: *The World Trade Center*

In May of 1967, the Port of New York Authority announced that New York City's nine television stations had agreed to move their transmitters from atop the Empire State Building to the World Trade Center. The television stations had been paying an annual rental of $1,250,000 to the Empire State Building owners, under a lease terminating in 1984, with renewal privileges. In order to induce the stations to make the move, the Port of New York Authority agreed to allow the stations the use of its facilities rent-free until 1984.[56]

Although we are not concerned with the question of what is "just compensation," does it matter in evaluating the principal case that under New York decisions it is settled that goodwill is a noncompensable item in a condemnation proceeding?

POLETOWN NEIGHBORHOOD COUNCIL v. CITY OF DETROIT

410 Mich. 616, 304 N.W.2d 455 (1981)

Per Curiam.

This case arises out of a plan by the Detroit Economic Development Corporation to acquire, by condemnation if necessary, a large tract of land to be conveyed to General Motors Corporation as a site for construction of an assembly plant. The plaintiffs, a neighborhood association and several individual residents of the affected area, brought suit in Wayne Circuit

---

56. N.Y. Times, May 19, 1967, at 1, col. 2.

Court to challenge the project on a number of grounds, not all of which have been argued to this Court. Defendants' motions for summary judgment were denied pending trial on a single question of fact: whether, under 1980 PA 87; M.C.L. §213.51 et seq.; M.S.A. §8.265(1) et seq., the city abused its discretion in determining that condemnation of plaintiffs' property was necessary to complete the project.

The trial lasted 10 days and resulted in a judgment for defendants and an order on December 9, 1980, dismissing plaintiffs' complaint. The plaintiffs filed a claim of appeal with the Court of Appeals on December 12, 1980, and an application for bypass with this Court on December 15, 1980.

We granted a motion for immediate consideration and an application for leave to appeal prior to decision by the Court of Appeals to consider the following questions:

Does the use of eminent domain in this case constitute a taking of private property for private use and, therefore, contravene Const. 1963, Art. 10, §2?

Did the court below err in ruling that cultural, social and historical institutions were not protected by the Michigan Environmental Protection Act?

We conclude that these questions must be answered in the negative and affirm the trial court's decision.

This case raises a question of paramount importance to the future welfare of this state and its residents: Can a municipality use the power of eminent domain granted to it by the Economic Development Corporations Act, M.C.L. §125.1601 et seq., M.S.A. §5.3520(1) et seq., to condemn property for transfer to a private corporation to build a plant to promote industry and commerce, thereby adding jobs and taxes to the economic base of the municipality and state?

Const. 1963, Art. 10, §2, states in pertinent part that "[p]rivate property shall not be taken for public use without just compensation therefor being first made or secured in a manner prescribed by law." Art. 10, §2 has been interpreted as requiring that the power of eminent domain not be invoked except to further a public use or purpose.[57] Plaintiffs-appellants urge us to distinguish between the terms "use" and "purpose," asserting they are not synonymous and have been distinguished in the law of eminent domain. We are persuaded the terms have been used interchangeably in Michigan statutes and decisions in an effort to describe the protean concept of public benefit. The term "public use" has not received a narrow or inelastic definition by this Court in prior cases.[58] Indeed, this Court has stated that "'[a] public use changes with the changing conditions of society'" and that "'[t]he right of the public to receive and enjoy the benefit of the use determines whether the use is public or private.'"[59]

57.   Shizas v. Detroit, 333 Mich. 44, 50, 52 N.W.2d 589 (1952).

58.   City of Center Line v. Michigan Bell Telephone Co., 387 Mich. 260, 196 N.W.2d 144 (1972); Gregory Marina, Inc. v. Detroit, 378 Mich. 364, 144 N.W.2d 503 (1966); and In re Slum Clearance, 331 Mich. 714, 50 N.W.2d 340 (1951).

59.   Hays v. Kalamazoo, 316 Mich. 443, 453-454, 25 N.W.2d 787, 169 A.L.R. 1218 (1947), quoting from 37 Am. Jur., Municipal Corporations, §120, pp. 734-735.

The Economic Development Corporations Act is a part of the comprehensive legislation dealing with planning, housing and zoning whereby the State of Michigan is attempting to provide for the general health, safety, and welfare through alleviating unemployment, providing economic assistance to industry, assisting the rehabilitation of blighted areas, and fostering urban redevelopment.

Section 2 of the act provides:

> There exists in this state the continuing need for programs to alleviate and prevent conditions of unemployment, and that it is accordingly necessary to assist and retain local industries and commercial enterprises to strengthen and revitalize the economy of this state and its municipalities; that accordingly it is necessary to provide means and methods for the encouragement and assistance of industrial and commercial enterprises in locating, purchasing, constructing, reconstructing, modernizing, improving, maintaining, repairing, furnishing, equipping, and expanding in this state and in its municipalities; and that it is also necessary to encourage the location and expansion of commercial enterprises to more conveniently provide needed services and facilities of the commercial enterprises to municipalities and the residents thereof. *Therefore, the powers granted in this act constitute the performance of essential public purposes and functions for this state and its municipalities.* [M.C.L. §125.1602; M.S.A. §5.3520(2). (Emphasis added.)]

To further the objectives of this act, the legislature has authorized municipalities to acquire property by condemnation in order to provide industrial and commercial sites and the means of transfer from the municipality to private users. M.C.L. §125.1622; M.S.A. §5.3520(22).

Plaintiffs-appellants do not challenge the declaration of the legislature that programs to alleviate and prevent conditions of unemployment and to preserve and develop industry and commerce are essential public purposes. Nor do they challenge the proposition that legislation to accomplish this purpose falls with the Constitutional grant of general legislative power to the legislature in Const. 1963, Art, 4, §51, which reads as follows:

> The public health and general welfare of the people of the state are hereby declared to be matters of primary public concern. The legislature shall pass suitable laws for the protection and promotion of the public health.

What plaintiffs-appellants do challenge is the constitutionality of using the power of eminent domain to condemn one person's property to convey it to another private person in order to bolster the economy. They argue that whatever incidental benefit may accrue to the public, assembling land to General Motors' specifications for conveyance to General Motors for its uncontrolled use in profit making is really a taking for private use and not condemnation.

The defendants-appellees contend, on the other hand, that the controlling public purpose in taking this land is to create an industrial site which will be used to alleviate and prevent conditions of unemployment and fiscal distress. The fact that it will be conveyed to and ultimately used by a private manufacturer does not defeat this predominant public purpose.

There is no dispute about the law. All agree that condemnation for a public use or purpose is permitted. All agree that condemnation for a private use or purpose is forbidden. Similarly, condemnation for a private use cannot be authorized whatever its incidental public benefit and condemnation for a public purpose cannot be forbidden whatever the incidental private gain. The heart of this dispute is whether the proposed condemnation is for the primary benefit of the public or the private user.

The Legislature has determined that governmental action of the type contemplated here meets a public need and serves an essential public purpose. The Court's role after such a determination is made is limited.

> The determination of what constitutes a public purpose is primarily a legislative function, subject to review by the courts when abused, and the determination of the legislative body of that matter should not be reversed except in instances where such determination is palpable and manifestly arbitrary and incorrect. [Gregory Marina, Inc. v. Detroit, 378 Mich. 364, 396, 144 N.W.2d 503 (1966).]

The United States Supreme Court has held that when a legislature speaks, the public interest has been declared in terms "well-nigh conclusive." Berman v. Parker, 348 U.S. 26, 32, 75 S. Ct. 98, 102, 99 L. Ed. 27 (1954).

The Legislature has delegated the authority to determine whether a particular project constitutes a public purpose to the governing body of the municipality involved.[60] The plaintiffs concede that this project is the type contemplated by the Legislature[61] and that the procedures set forth in the Economic Development Corporations Act have been followed.[62] This further limits our review.

In the court below, the plaintiffs-appellants challenged the necessity for the taking of the land for the proposed project. In this regard the city presented substantial evidence of the severe economic conditions facing the residents of the city and state, the need for new industrial development to revitalize local industries, the economic boost the proposed project would provide, and the lack of other adequate available sites to implement the project.

As Justice Cooley stated over a hundred years ago "the most important consideration in the case of eminent domain is the necessity of accomplishing some public good which is otherwise impracticable, and . . . the law does not so much regard the means as the need." People ex rel. Detroit & Howell R. Co. v. Salem Twp. Board, 20 Mich. 452, 480-481 (1870).

---

60. M.C.L. §125.1610(2); M.S.A. §5.3520(10)(2).
61. M.C.L. §125.1603(e); M.S.A §5.3520(3)(e).
62. M.C.L. §§125.1608, 125.1609; M.S.A. §§5.3520(8), 5.3520(9).

When there is such public need, "[t]he abstract right [of an individual] to make use of his own property in his own way is compelled to yield to the general comfort and protection of community, and to a proper regard to relative rights in others." Id. Eminent domain is an inherent power of the sovereign of the same nature as, albeit more severe than, the power to regulate the use of land through zoning or the prohibition of public nuisances.

In the instant case the benefit to be received by the municipality invoking the power of eminent domain is a clear and significant one and is sufficient to satisfy this Court that such a project was an intended and a legitimate object of the Legislature when it allowed municipalities to exercise condemnation powers even though a private party will also, ultimately, receive a benefit as an incident thereto.

The power of eminent domain is to be used in this instance primarily to accomplish the essential public purposes of alleviating unemployment and revitalizing the economic base of the community. The benefit to a private interest is merely incidental.

Our determination that this project falls within the public purpose, as stated by the Legislature, does not mean that every condemnation proposed by an economic development corporation will meet with similar acceptance simply because it may provide some jobs or add to the industrial or commercial base. If the public benefit was not so clear and significant, we would hesitate to sanction approval of such a project. The power of eminent domain is restricted to furthering public uses and purposes and is not to be exercised without substantial proof that the public is primarily to be benefited. Where, as here, the condemnation power is exercised in a way that benefits specific and identifiable private interests, a court inspects with heightened scrutiny the claim that the public interest is the predominant interest being advanced. Such public benefit cannot be speculative or marginal but must be clear and significant if it is to be within the legitimate purpose as stated by the Legislature. We hold this project is warranted on the basis that its significance for the people of Detroit and the state has been demonstrated.

II

Plaintiffs' complaint also alleged that the proposed project violates the Michigan Environmental Protection Act (MEPA), M.C.L. §691.1201 et seq.; M.S.A. §14.528(201) et seq., because it "will have a major adverse impact on the adjoining social and cultural environment which is referred to as Poletown." The trial court dismissed this claim, stating that " 'social and cultural environments' are matters not within the purview of the MEPA and outside its legislative intent." We agree.

M.C.L. §691.1202(1); M.S.A. §14.528(202)(1) permits maintenance of an action for declaratory and equitable relief against the state, its political subdivisions, or private entities, "for the protection of the *air, water, and other natural resources* and the public trust therein from pollution, impairment or destruction." (Emphasis supplied.) The reference to "air, water and other natural resources" is also made in other sections of the act and in its title. Given its plain meaning, the term "natural resources" does not encompass a "social and cultural environment." Moreover, under the principle of *ejusdem generis,* where a statute contains a general term supplementing a more specific enumeration, the general term will not be construed to refer to objects not of like kind with those enumerated. 2A Sutherland, Statutory Construction (4th ed.), §§47.18-47.19, pp. 109-114.

The decision of the trial court is affirmed.

The clerk is directed to issue the Court's judgment order forthwith, in accordance with GCR 1963, 866.3(c).

No costs, a public question being involved.

COLEMAN, C.J., and MOODY, LEVIN, KAVANAGH and WILLIAMS, JJ., concur.

FITZGERALD, J. (dissenting). . . .

The majority relies on the principle that the concept of public use is an evolving one; however, I cannot believe that this evolution has eroded our historic protection against the taking of private property for private use to the degree sanctioned by this Court's decision today. The decision that the prospect of increased employment, tax revenue, and general economic stimulation makes a taking of private property for transfer to another private part sufficiently "public" to authorize the use of the power of eminent domain means that there is virtually no limit to the use of condemnation to aid private businesses. Any business enterprise produces benefits to society at large. Now that we have authorized local legislative bodies to decide that a different commercial or industrial use of property will produce greater public benefits than its present use, no homeowner's, merchant's or manufacturer's property, however productive or valuable to its owner, is immune from condemnation for the benefit of other private interests that will put it to a "higher" use.[63] As one prominent commentator has written:

> It often happens that the erection of a large factory will be of more benefit to the whole community in which it is planned to build it than any strictly public improvement which the inhabitants of the place could possibly undertake; but even if the plan was blocked by the refusal of the selfish owner of a

___

63. It would be easy to sustain the proposed project because of its large size and the extent of the claimed benefits to flow from it. The estimate is that approximately 6150 persons would be employed in the factory itself, with the generation of substantial other employment, business activity, and tax revenue as a result. However, it must be remembered that the dislocations and other costs of the project are also massive. The project plan indicated that a total of 3438 persons will be displaced by the project, that it will require the destruction of 1176 structures, and that the cost of the project to the public sector will be nearly $200,000,000.

small but necessary parcel of land to part with it at any price, the public mind would instinctively revolt at any attempt to take such land by eminent domain. [2A Nichols, Eminent Domain §7.61[1] (rev. 3d ed.).

The condemnation contemplated in the present action goes beyond the scope of the power of eminent domain in that it takes private property for private use. I would reverse the judgment of the circuit court.

RYAN, J., concurs.

RYAN, J. (dissenting). . . .

Eminent domain is an attribute of sovereignty. When individual citizens are forced to suffer great social dislocation to permit private corporations to construct plants where they deem it most profitable, one is left to wonder who the sovereign is.

The sudden and fundamental change in established law effected by the Court in this case, entailing such a significant diminution of constitutional rights, cannot be justified as a function of judicial construction; the only proper vehicle for change of this dimension is a constitutional amendment. What has been done in this case can be explained by the overwhelming sense of inevitability that has attended this litigation from the beginning; a sense attributable to the combination and coincidence of the interests of a desperate city administration and a giant corporation willing and able to take advantage of the opportunity that presented itself. The justification for it, like the inevitability of it, has been made to seem more acceptable by the "team spirit" chorus of approval of the project which has been supplied by the voices of labor, business, industry, government, finance, and even the news media. Virtually the only discordant sounds of dissent have come from the minuscule minority of citizens most profoundly affected by this case, the Poletown residents whose neighborhood has been destroyed.

With this case the Court has subordinated a constitutional right to private corporate interests. As demolition of existing structures on the future plant site goes forward, the best that can be hoped for, jurisprudentially, is that the precedential value of this case will be lost in the accumulating rubble.

I would hold M.C.L. §125.1622; M.S.A. §5.3520(22) unconstitutional because it authorizes a taking of property for private use both facially and as applied.

Note: **Poletown Neighborhood Council**

The word "Poletown" is used in describing the neighborhood council because many of the inhabitants of the area are of Polish extraction. William Safire's New York Times essay Poletown Wrecker's Ball (N.Y. Times, Apr. 30, 1981, at A31, col. 5) discusses the *Poletown Neighborhood Council* case.

Note: Hawaii's Land Reform Act

Hawaii's land reform act has as its principal purpose the redistribution of residential land from a few large trusts and corporations to private landowners. This redistribution is to be accomplished by a state agency condemning the land of the large landowner and, after paying for it, reselling it to a private resident for residential purposes. The Hawaiian act was held unconstitutional in Midkiff v. Tom, 702 F.2d 788 (9th Cir. 1983), as a violation of the fifth and fourteenth amendments, in that the taking was not for a public purpose. The decision of the Ninth Circuit is before the Supreme Court of the United States. As of December, 1983, the case had been argued; a decision is expected early in 1984.

PART IX

RIGHTS INCIDENT TO OWNERSHIP OF LAND

CHAPTER 34

LATERAL AND SUBJACENT SUPPORT

Note: Meaning of the Terms "Lateral Support" and "Subjacent Support"

The following material is quoted from American Law of Property §28.36 (Casner ed. 1952):

> The right that land in its natural condition shall receive necessary support from adjoining and underlying geologic structures is incident to the lawful possession thereof. It is jure naturae and is a real property right that is appurtenant to and runs with the supported estate unless surrendered by deed or contract, or lost by prescription or estoppel. It is rarely classed as an easement, as it need not rest upon grant, express or implied, nor upon prescription, and is not subject to the common law rules applicable to easements. Rather it is a proprietary right, sometimes described as a third estate in land, that may be held or conveyed separately from either the surface or the minerals.
>
> The right to naturally necessary support is absolute. When such support is withdrawn and injury ensues, the responsible person is liable regardless of the care employed in his operations and notwithstanding the fact that some reduction in support might be necessary to put the supporting estate to any kind of beneficial use whatsoever. The rationale for the right is natural justice. Land in its improved state is held together by natural forces, any alteration or reduction of which seriously impairs its economic and utilitarian value. Accordingly, if coterminous landowners are to be ensured equality of enjoyment of their respective tracts, each must be accorded the right to require substantial maintenance of the natural support conditions.
>
> This natural right of absolute support has not attached to buildings and other artificially added superincumbent pressures, nor to soil which has been deprived of its natural cohesive characteristics. Pursuant to the rationale of the support rule that coterminous landowners have equality of enjoyment of their respective tracts, it follows that one landowner should not be allowed to increase the support burdens and limit the range of uses of his neighbor's

property by the prior erection of a building on his own. Rather the one who erects such a building near his boundary line should foresee possible injury thereto from the reasonable employment of the adjoining tract, and should either assume the risk of subsidence or take the precaution of securing voluntary easements of support by grant or contract from the owner of the naturally servient estate.

The right to have the surface of land supported by adjoining land is called lateral support. Removal of such support is actionable only when it produces subsidence of the agricultural surface, not when it merely endangers subsurface mining operations. Accordingly it has been held that a miner need not refrain from working a deposit to his boundary line in order to avoid injury to earlier mine workings on adjoining property.

The right to have land supported by underlying strata, severed in ownership by grant or reservation, is termed subjacent support. Unlike the servitude of lateral support, this right may not be limited to the protection of the superficial or agricultural surface. Rather the surface owner is entitled to the support of any strata above the alien mineral estate, the natural condition of which is necessary to hold water for the enjoyment of the surface land. Similarly, where several subsurface estates have been created, each has a right to support from all underlying estates and owes a duty of support to all above.

Lateral and subjacent support is discussed generally in American Law of Property §§28.36-28.54. See also Leesman, Significance of the Doctrine of Lateral Support as a Real Property Right, 16 Ill. L. Rev. 108 (1921).

Note: When Damage to Buildings as a Consequence of Removal of Lateral Support Is Recoverable

Prete v. Cray, 49 R.I. 209, 141 A. 609 (1928), describes the difference in views as to whether recovery for damage to buildings as a result of the removal of lateral support is dependent on establishment of negligence on the part of the person removing the lateral support:

> Between adjacent landowners the general principle in this regard is that each has an absolute property right to have his land laterally supported by the soil of his neighbor and if either in excavating on his own premises so disturbs the lateral support of his neighbor's land as to cause it, in its natural state, by the pressure of its own weight, to fall away or slide from its position the one so excavating is liable. This right of lateral support applies only to the land of the adjacent owner and does not include the right to have the weight of the building placed upon the land also supported. And when, upon an excavation made on his own land by an adjoining landowner, a building upon the adjacent land by its weight and pressure causes the building itself and the land upon which it stands to sink, then in the absence of negligence the one making the excavation is not liable for injury to the building resulting from its subsidence.

A condition sometimes arises where as the result of an excavation made on his own land by one adjoining landowner there is a disturbance of the lateral support to his neighbor's land due solely to the weight of the neighbor's land itself in its natural condition, and there has also been injury to a building on such neighbor's land resulting from the subsidence of the land, which subsidence cannot be ascribed in any degree to the pressure of the building upon the land.

In such circumstances some courts have applied the general rule as to damages and have held that, in the absence of negligence on his part, the landowner making the excavation is not liable for damages arising from injury to the building of his neighbor. A line of authority, however, has been developed which has regarded the condition we have named as calling for a qualification of the general rule, and it has been held by a number of courts that a landowner by building upon his land has not thereby lost his right to have his soil supported, and when that right is invaded by his neighbor and his land sinks he is entitled to compensation for the direct results of such breach of duty including any injury to buildings upon his land, when such injury is due to an interference with the lateral support of the soil, and cannot be ascribed to the weight and pressure of the buildings upon the land. Such is the rule enunciated in the English cases. Hunt v. Peake, 29 L.J. Eq. 785; Brown v. Robins, 4 H. & N. 186; Stroyan v. Knowles, 6 H. & N. 454. Upon this question there is a distinction in principle between liability and damage which appear to have been overlooked in cases holding contra to what we may call the English rule. This distinction may be stated as follows: there is no legal duty in the landowner A to furnish lateral support for the building of his neighbor B, and if without negligence on A's part B's soil falls away solely by reason of A's excavation on his own land and due in no respect to the weight of B's building, yet B's building is injured due to the subsidence of the soil under it, nevertheless, under the general rule A has committed no actionable wrong in respect to the injury to B's building, he has, however, committed an actionable wrong with respect to B's land, and under the general legal principle that a wrongdoer must make compensation in damages for all the direct results of his wrongdoing, B is entitled to recover compensation for the injury to his building solely because it is a part of his damage for the actionable wrong which A has committed. In the English case of Attorney-General ex rel. v. Conduit Colliery Co. (1895), 1 Q. B. 301 at 312, Collins, J. has commented upon this distinction as follows:

> That such is the true principle, — that is, that it is the subsidence and not the pecuniary loss which grounds the cause of action — is, I think, apparent from those decisions which establish that, on proof that the weight of a newly-erected house has not contributed to the subsidence, its value may be recovered by way of damage consequent on the original injury in an action against the adjoining owner who has withdrawn the support of the adjacent land; Brown v. Robins, 4 H. & N. 186; Hamer v. Knowles, 6 H. & N. 454. In these cases the fall of the house itself could give no cause of action, for there was no right to have it supported; therefore an injuria giving a right of action had to be shown before the consequential damage by reason of the falling of the house could be claimed; and such an injuria was shown on proof that the unincum-

bered soil would have subsided, although no pecuniary damage, even to the extent of a farthing, was suggested or proved had not the house been there.

A number of American decisions are in harmony with the principle just set forth. Sterns v. Richmond, 88 Va. 992, 14 S.E. 847; Farnandis v. Great Northern R. Co., 41 Wash. 486, 84 P. 18; Busby v. Holthaus, 46 Mo. 161; Riley v. Continuous Rail Joint Co., 110 App. Div. 787, 97 N.Y.S. 283, confirmed in 193 N.Y. 643, 86 N.E. 1132; Louisville & Nashville R.R. Co. v. Bonhayo, 94 Ky. 67, 21 S.W. 526; Langhorne v. Turman, 141 Ky. 809, 133 S.W. 1008. We approve the decisions in those cases as being sounder in principle and as placing upon one who commits a breach of duty full responsibility for his wrongful act.[1] [49 R.I. at 212-215, 141 A. at 611-612.]

Problems

34.1. A and B are the owners of adjoining tracts of land fronting on Long Island Sound. During a hurricane, the tidewaters washed out a sizable portion of A's seawall and the land in back of it, close to, but not immediately at, B's boundary line. A took no steps to replace the land washed away. As a result of the loss of support from the land washed away, B's land subsided, causing damage to the land and the building thereon. It is agreed that the pressure of the building did not cause the subsidence but that the land would have subsided in its natural state. B brings an action to obtain an injunction requiring A to replace the support and to recover for the damage already caused to B's land and building. Is B entitled to all or any part of the relief requested? In answering this question, consider whether it is material what position the jurisdiction takes in regard to the materiality of establishing negligence on the part of the one removing the support when there has been damage to a building on the adjacent land. See Carrig v. Andrews, 127 Conn. 403, 17 A.2d 520 (1941).

34.2. A owns a tract of land which is bounded on the north by a tract of land owned by B, and B's tract is bounded on the north by a tract of land owned by C. B worked out the coal beneath his land, leaving enough subjacent support so that there was no subsidence of his land or the tracts of land of A and C. C then worked out the coal beneath her land, thereby causing a subsidence of her land and the tracts of land of A and B. It is agreed that neither A's land nor B's land would have subsided as a result of C's action had it not been for the fact that B had removed coal from beneath his land. Advise A as to her rights. See Birmingham v. Allen, 6 L.R.-Ch. D. 284 (1877).

---

1. Can one gain an easement of support entirely by the passage of time that will go beyond the natural right of support in restricting the adjoining landowner in the use of his or her property? See Sullivan v. Zeiner, 98 Cal. 346, 33 P. 209 (1893), which answers this question in the negative. See also Mitchell v. Rome, 49 Ga. 19 (1873). See also Problem 34.4. — EDS.

34.3. A and B are the owners of adjoining tracts of land. A's land has a building on it which was placed there several years ago. B commenced excavating his lot, thereby causing the building on A's lot and the soil thereunder to start collapsing. It is agreed that B's excavations would have caused A's land to collapse even in its natural state. B immediately notified A of the situation and offered her free entry onto his land to brace the land and building. A refused to do anything. B is advised by his contractor that if the excavation proceeds, even with the utmost care, A's land and building will collapse completely and fall into the excavation unless steps are taken to brace and shore A's property. The cost of bracing and shoring A's property is substantial. Can B recover from A the money he expends in bracing and shoring A's property? See Braun v. Hamack, 206 Minn. 572, 289 N.W. 553 (1940).

34.4. A owns a tract of land. On part of this land she builds a house. A then sells to B part of the land, and on the part sold to B is situated the house. B builds a substantial addition to the house. A, some twenty years later, makes an excavation on her land, using due care. Nevertheless, the land granted to B caves in, thereby causing substantial damage to the house. It is agreed that B's land would not have caved in had it not been for the pressure of the original house on the land. Is A liable to B for the damage he has sustained? See Tunstall v. Christian, 80 Va. 1 (1885).

GORTON v. SCHOFIELD
311 Mass. 352, 41 N.E.2d (1942)

DOLAN, J. This is a bill in equity by which the plaintiff seeks to compel the defendant to rebuild or repair a retaining wall on the defendant's land which provides lateral support to the plaintiff's land. The judge entered an interlocutory decree overruling the defendant's exceptions to the master's report and confirming the same, and a final decree ordering the defendant to "provide adequate support to the plaintiff's land, at the rear thereof, adjoining the retaining wall . . . by strengthening the said retaining wall now existing, or by any other effective means which will provide adequate support to the plaintiff's land . . . (and enjoining the defendant) from doing any acts, or permitting any acts to be done, which will weaken further said retaining wall or in any way deprive the plaintiff's land of its present lateral support." Under the terms of the decree the defendant was further enjoined from removing props and beams supporting a portion of the retaining wall "until permanent support to the plaintiff's land is made," and the defendant was ordered to pay the plaintiff $15 (damages) and costs. The defendant's appeal from the final decree brings the case before us.

Material facts found by the master follow: The plaintiff is the owner of a parcel of land with a dwelling house thereon situated on the southerly side of Middle Street in Gloucester. The lot runs easterly along the street sixty-five and thirty-seven hundredths feet, southerly one hundred one and seventy-six hundredths feet, then westerly eighty-three and twenty hundredths feet and northerly one hundred and sixty-five hundredths feet.[2] The defendant's lot faces on Main Street which runs parallel to Middle Street and the rear of his lot adjoins and abuts the rear of the plaintiff's lot. The defendant's lot extends back from Main Street about one hundred sixty-six feet, the deeds describing it as running back as far as the Gorton lot. The retaining wall is erected on the rear line of the defendant's property and is "constructed entirely upon the Schofield land." The wall is three feet from the plaintiff's boundary line at the southeast corner of the Gorton lot and coincides with the boundary line at a point two feet from the southwest corner. On the top course of the wall there are five stones which project toward Middle Street. Three of these stones project a few inches over the Gorton line and are used as supports for perpendicular poles which are part of a wire fence constructed on the plaintiff's land along its rear boundary to a jog in the wall.

The wall, of granite construction, is approximately eighty-five feet long and fourteen feet high, and on its top at the easterly part thereof there is a brick wall four feet high and approximately fifty-five feet long. The granite wall is in disrepair and is not sufficiently strong to support the land of the plaintiff without being repaired or properly braced. The plaintiff's land has caved or fallen in, and is cracked to a greater or lesser degree along the entire rear line of her property. Originally the plaintiff's and the defendant's lands were on a "sloping ridge or hill, which sloped southerly from Middle Street down to the sea." The defendant's land, due to excavations, is now level, but the plaintiff's land still slopes down to the retaining wall. The plaintiff's and the defendant's respective lots "were never held by the same ownership."

Prior to 1937 there was standing on the defendant's property a stable built close up against and abutting the retaining wall. This building was erected prior to the year 1880. It was a substantial structure with upright timbers close up against the wall, and the roof of the easterly part of the stable was fastened directly to the wall. This building furnished support to the wall. In 1937, however, this stable was completely demolished, and in the spring of 1938 there was a sinking of the land in the rear of the plaintiff's lot forming a large hole four or five feet deep, ten or twelve feet wide, extending six or eight feet to a point about four feet from the rear of the plaintiff's house. Later other holes appeared.

To remedy this condition the plaintiff, with the defendant's permission shored and supported the most unstable part of the wall with wooden timbers and the parties stipulated that no admissions of liability or waiver were made by so doing. The wall, however, particularly the easterly part, is still unsafe, unstable and in danger of collapse. The master further found that the total amount expended by the plaintiff to the time of the hearing was

---

2. Through apparent inadvertent but immaterial error the directions of these bounds were stated incorrectly by the master.

$15, but that the cost of repair of the wall would be between $1,000 and $1,500. He also found that there had been no damage to the plaintiff's house.

The master found that here "was no evidence establishing the date, when, or the person by whom, this excavation of the defendant's land was made, or when or by whom the wall was built," but he also found on all the evidence and the reasonable inferences therefrom that the excavation had been made by a former owner of the defendant's land (between 1848 and 1876) and that the wall was constructed at that time by the same person to provide support for the plaintiff's land. . . .

The decisive question is what are the legal duties and responsibilities of the defendant with relation to the maintenance of the retaining wall built by a predecessor in title in the circumstances before set forth. The law with relation to lateral support is of ancient origin and is firmly established. "The right of an owner of land to the support of the land adjoining is jure naturae, like the right in a flowing stream. Every owner of land is entitled, as against his neighbor, to have the earth stand and the water flow in its natural condition . . . [and] in the case of land, which is fixed in its place, each owner has the absolute right to have his land remain in its natural condition, unaffected by any act of his neighbor; and, if the neighbor digs upon or improves his own land so as to injure this right, may maintain an action against him, without proof of negligence." Gilmore v. Driscoll, 122 Mass. 199, 201 et seq., and cases cited. Kronberg v. Bulle, 247 Mass. 325, 328, 142 N.E. 61. Triulzi v. Costa, 296 Mass. 24, 27, 4 N.E.2d 617. See cases cited in 50 Am. L.R. 486 et seq.

This being the basic law, the question in the case at bar is whether the defendant, the present owner of the land upon which the excavation was made and the wall built by a predecessor in title, is bound to maintain the wall in such condition as to prevent damage to the plaintiff's land. The plaintiff has not argued that the structure on her land is in danger of collapse as a result of the condition of the retaining wall, and hence we are not concerned with any question relating to the structures thereon. See, however, Gilmore v. Driscoll, 122 Mass. 199, 204, 205. There seems to be but little authority upon the precise question under discussion. The point does not seem to have been decided heretofore by this court. The plaintiff has cited in support of her position Lyons v. Walsh, 92 Conn. 18, 101 A. 488, Cavanaugh v. Weber, 11 Ky. Law Rep. 858, and Foster v. Brown, 48 Ont. Law Rep. 1. In the last case cited it appeared that an excavation had been made upon land by the predecessor in title of the defendant, and that the former had built a retaining wall for the purpose of providing support to the plaintiff's adjoining land; that this wall "got out of repair and failed to answer the purpose for which it was built" (page 3), and that from time to time as a result a subsidence of the plaintiff's land occurred after the defendant became the owner of the land upon which the wall had been erected, and the soil fell into the excavation. The court held, in substance, that the defendant was responsible for the damage that the plaintiff had sustained, saying, at pages 5-6, that it saw "no reason why, if a person who is in possession of land in which there is an excavation which is a source of danger to the public, although the excavation was not made by him but by a predecessor in title, is liable for the consequences of his permitting the dangerous condition to continue, the same rule should not be applied where a lateral support has been withdrawn by a predecessor in title, and the condition so caused has been permitted to remain and to cause injury to his neighbour, the owner of the land at the time the injury occurs should not be answerable for it." In that case the court pointed out that the consequences "of holding otherwise would be that where a land-owner had made an excavation in his land, and thereby removed the lateral support to which his neighbour is entitled, but had built a solid retaining wall to prevent subsidence, which, during his ownership, prevented it, and had then sold his land to another and that other to others, and, owing to a subsequent owner — it might well be fifty years after — permitting the retaining wall to decay and no longer to answer the purpose for which it was constructed, with the result that his neighbour's land has subsided, he would be liable to answer in damages for the injury, and the man whose failure to keep up the retaining wall was the effective cause of the injury would go scot free, and that too where the subsidence would not have occurred if the retaining wall had been kept in repair." And at page 6, Fry, L.J., expressing his concurrence said, in part: "I am unable to understand why the failure of a subsequent owner to provide the necessary support, and a fortiori where he suffers a retaining wall to decay, is not equally a continual or continued withdrawal of support. . . ." See 10 B.R.C. 918, and annotation.

These principles were recognized for the most part in Lyons v. Walsh, 92 Conn. 18, 101 A. 488, but it is true that in that case the court, while holding that the plaintiff was entitled to recover damages from a subsequent owner of the servient land, was of opinion that the equitable relief sought, that is, that the defendant should restore the wall to its original condition, should not be granted because the court was not satisfied that irreparable injury was "clearly enough disclosed to warrant the exercise of so drastic a power."

We have already said, in substance, in Foley v. Wyeth, 2 Allen, 131, and Gilmore v. Driscoll, 122 Mass. 199, that the right to lateral support of soil in its natural state is a property right which naturally attaches to and passes with the soil without any grant thereof. We concur in the reasoning in Foster v. Brown, 48 Ont. Law Rep. 1, which we have herein-before set forth at some length, and are of opinion that the burden of providing lateral support to the plaintiff's land in its natural condition is one of continued support running against the servient land.

The defendant has argued that the plaintiff's prayer for equitable relief should not have been granted by the judge because she has not shown irreparable damage. We do not sustain that contention. The findings of the master relative to subsidences in the plaintiff's land have already been recited. They have been occurring from time to time. They still occur "especially after heavy rains." It is a reasonable assumption that as time goes on they will continue to occur, and it follows that a mere award of expenses incurred by the plaintiff to the time of the trial would not give her adequate relief. Such an award would not prevent foreseeable future damage resulting from the failure of the defendant to continue to provide lateral support to the plaintiff's land. See Marcus v. Brody, 254 Mass. 152, 149 N.E. 673; Geragosian v. Union Realty Co., 289 Mass. 104, 109, 110, 193 N.E. 726, and cases cited. The only effective remedy that can be afforded the plaintiff and which will put an end to litigation is to require the defendant to conform to the terms of the final decree entered by the judge. See Simon v. Nance, 45 Tex. Civ. App. 480, 100 S.W. 1038; Thompson, Real Property, Sec. 559, and cases cited.[3]

Decree affirmed with costs.

Problems

34.5. A and B are the owners of adjoining tracts of land. A made an excavation on her land in order to obtain soil to fill in another tract of land which she owned. The removal of this soil did not affect B's land in any way at the time. Over the years, however, A's land kept crumbling and sliding into the hole made by her excavation, and finally, B's land began to fall away. Prior to the time B's land was affected, A had conveyed her land to C. B now seeks an injunction to compel C to restore the support to his land and damages for the loss already sustained. It is agreed that B's land would not have been damaged if the excavation had not been made originally by A. Is B entitled to recover? See Kansas City Northwestern R.R. v. Schwake, 70 Kan. 141, 78 P. 431 (1904); Noonan v. Pardee, 200 Pa. 474, 50 A. 255 (1901).

34.6. In the previous problem, if A's deed to C contains a covenant of general warranty, may C recover from A, for the breach of such covenant, the damage she sustains if she is compelled to restore the support to B's land and reimburse B for his loss?

34.7. If you are the attorney for the purchaser of land and you desire to avoid the problem of Gorton v. Schofield, how can you determine whether that problem may arise with respect to the land being purchased?

---

3. See Annot., Right of Owner of Land to Recover From Adjoining Owner Amount Expended by Former to Prevent Collapse of Building upon Latter's Land, or to Recover Damages Caused by Such Collapse, 129 A.L.R. 623 (1940); Annot., Duty and Liability of Owner in Respect of Lateral Support as Affected by Excavation by Predecessor in Title, 139 A.L.R. 1267 (1942). — EDS.

Note: Statutory Provisions Relating To Lateral and Subjacent Support

You must not overlook the possibility that your jurisdiction may have enacted legislation (state or municipal) concerning lateral or subjacent support. The provisions of the Ohio Revised Code Annotated set forth below are illustrative.

§723.49. *Damage from excavation.* If the owner or possessor of any lot or land in any municipal corporation digs, or causes to be dug, any cellar, pit, vault, or excavation, to a greater depth than nine feet below the curb of the street or streets on which such lot or land abuts, or, if there is no curb, below the established grade of the street or streets on which such lot or land abuts, or, if there is no curb or established grade, below the surface of the adjoining lots, and by such excavation he causes damage to any wall, house, or other building upon the lots adjoining thereto, such owner or possessor shall be liable, in civil action, to the party injured, to the full amount of such damage. When there is a curb or established grade, the depth of such excavation, at any point thereof, shall be measured downward from the pitch line projected laterally over the lot or land, from and between the corresponding points in the nearest curb or established grade opposite the ends of such pitch line.

§723.50. *Depth of excavation allowable.* The owner or possessor of any lot or land in any municipal corporation may dig, or cause to be dug, any cellar, pit, or excavation, to the full depth of any foundation wall of any building upon the adjoining lot or lots, or to the full depth of nine feet below the established grade of the street or streets on which such lot abuts, without reference to the depth of adjoining foundation walls, without incurring the liability prescribed in §723.49 of the Revised Code, and may, on thirty days' notice to adjoining owners, grade and improve the surface of any lot to correspond with the established grade of the street, streets or alleys upon which such lot or land abuts, without incurring liability.

CHAPTER 35

WATER RIGHTS[1]

Note: *Significance of Water Law in the Economic Development of the United States*

The great influence water has had on the industrial and agricultural development of the United States is known in a general way by all of us. Such general knowledge as we have, supplemented from time to time by more detailed information, is relevant in a consideration of the legal aspects of water rights because we are interested in ascertaining to what extent the legal doctrines in this field have kept pace with the times.

We are primarily concerned in this chapter with the rights an owner of land has in the water on or adjacent to his or her land, including not only the right to use such water but the right to prevent it from coming onto his or her land. Let your imagination ramble for a minute to see if you can visualize the problems which may arise and the factors which may be relevant in their solution.

Consider first the possible significance of the source of the water involved. The water may come from a navigable stream or lake which is one of the vital highways of the country. If such water is diverted to the use of adjoining landowners, the damage may be not only to other landowners on the water course but also to the economic development of the whole area. For example, the source may be a non-navigable stream, underground percolating water, or surface water which is following the natural drainage contours of the land.

Consider next the economic interests of the area and the importance of water in the furtherance of those interests. In highly industrialized regions, such as New England, water power has been of outstanding significance; in the arid sections of the West, irrigation has become of major importance to many activities. Estimate the basic soundness of a case in this field with due regard to its effect on the economic interests of the jurisdiction involved.

1. See generally American Law of Property §§28.55-28.68 (Casner ed. 1952) and all of Volume 41 of the Iowa Law Review for the winter of 1956.

Do not overlook the relevance of the date of a case. A policy which developed in a period when the particular area was largely rural and thinly populated may be entirely unsatisfactory when that same area has become urban and thickly settled. Furthermore, a liberal policy as to the use of water may be desirable in the pioneering days when every attraction is being offered to induce people to come and develop the natural resources of the state and be fatal to the welfare of the state after conditions have stabilized.

What are the typical problems that arise with respect to water? The following are suggestive:

1. Water is diverted from a stream by an upper riparian owner to irrigate such owner's land. The amount taken is such that a lower riparian owner is unable to use the stream for water power to run a mill.

2. An upper riparian owner drains his sewage into the stream, thus polluting it, and thereby a lower riparian owner is unable to use it for domestic purposes.

3. A lower riparian owner dredges the bed of the stream, thus increasing the speed of the flow of the water and thereby depriving the upper riparian owner of a use he or she otherwise might have made of the water.

4. A landowner blocks the natural flow of surface water from the land of a neighbor, thereby causing the latter substantial damage.

These and related problems are considered in this chapter. The materials presented here, however, are only introductory to a subject of vast current importance.

SECTION 1. NATURAL STREAMS AND LAKES

Note: Common-Law Rules Relating to Riparian Rights in Non-Navigable Waters

Gehlen Brothers v. Knorr, 101 Iowa 700, 70 N.W. 757 (1897), describes the riparian rights in non-navigable waters as follows:

> Broadly stated, the general rule is that the owner of the land through which a stream of water runs, has a right to have it flow over his land in the natural channel, undiminished in quantity, and unimpaired in quality, except in so far as diminution or contamination is inseparable from a reasonable use of such water. No statement can be made as to what is such reasonable use which will, without variation or qualification, apply to the facts of every case. But in determining whether a use is reasonable we must consider what the use is for; its extent, duration, necessity, and its application; the nature and size of the

stream, and the several uses to which it is put; the extent of the injury to the one proprietor, and of the benefit to the other; and all other facts which may bear upon the reasonableness of the use. Red River Roller Mills v. Wright, 30 Minn. 249, 15 N.W. Rep. 167, and cases cited. Washburn, page 379. Now, while one riparian proprietor may not divert the water of a stream so as to deprive a lower proprietor on the same stream of the benefit thereof, such upper proprietor may reasonably detain the water for proper purposes. The doctrine that such use by the upper proprietor may result in diminishing the quantity of water which will go down the stream, and may affect the current by retarding the flow to a reasonable extent, and still be consistent with the existence of a common right, was early held in this country, and has been constantly adhered to. If the general rule that each riparian proprietor is entitled to the flow of the stream according to its natural course, without interruption or diminution, should be strictly adhered to, it would result in a virtual abrogation of the well-settled doctrine that the rights of all proprietors of the stream are equal, and would "preclude the use of flowing waters in most cases; as where power is desired, the rule must yield to the necessity of gathering the water into reservoirs. It is lawful to do this where it is done in good faith, for a useful purpose, and with as little interference with the rights of other proprietors as is reasonably practical under the circumstances." Cooley, Torts (1st Ed.), page 584; Tyler v. Wilkinson [4 Mas. 397, F. Cas. No. 14,312]. In Dumont v. Kellogg [29 Mich. 420], it was held, in an action by a mill proprietor against one having a mill and dam above him, on the same stream, for damages caused by detention of the water, that it could not be said that such upper proprietor had no right to use the water to the prejudice of such lower proprietor; nor could it be held that such upper proprietor could not lawfully divert any of the water which would otherwise flow down the stream. The court said the real question was "whether, under all the circumstances of the case, the use of the water by one is reasonable, and consistent with a correspondent enjoyment of right by the other." In Bullard v. Manufacturing Co. [77 N.Y. 530], it is said that the fact that an injury results to other riparian owners from the construction and use of dams is not decisive upon the question as to whether such use is permissible. In that case the upper proprietor had interfered with the flow of water by collecting the water at times in a pond, and while it was so collecting, plaintiff had not sufficient water to use his mill. The court of appeals sustained a finding by the lower court that the detention of the water by the upper proprietor was not unreasonable. . . . We do not think that a detention of the water for two or three days by defendants, while their pond was filling, can be said to be an unreasonable detention. It is clear that the use of the water of the stream for any artificial use whatsoever by the defendants would require the erection of a dam, and the detention of the water long enough to fill the pond. If they had not the right to do this, they would not be placed upon an equality of right with the plantiffs as to the use of the water. If the contention of plaintiffs be sustained, the result would be that, in effect, they would be given rights in the water of the river superior to all persons above them, so far as artificial uses are concerned; and upper riparian owners would be deprived of all right to use the water for artificial purposes. Such a holding would not be in accord with the rules of law applicable to such cases, and would be most inequitable and unjust. These

parties are, by the law, placed upon an equality as to their right to use the water
of this stream, and neither may exercise his right as to unduly interfere with
the rights of the other; still both must put up with such slight disadvantages as
are indispensable to a reasonable use by the other. [101 Iowa at 704-710, 70
N.W. at 758-760.]

Scranton Gas & Water Co. v. Delaware Lackawanna & Western
Railroad, 240 Pa. 604, 88 A. 24 (1913), adds the following thoughts to the
common-law practice:

> It is settled law that riparian owners have no ownership of running water,
> nor have they any right to divert or sell it for general use, and are limited in
> their own use of it to ordinary purposes incident to the enjoyment of the
> riparian land, and in exceptional cases to what is called extraordinary uses
> upon the land itself, provided such extraordinary use does not materially
> diminish the flow of the stream or impair the quality of the water. But the
> extraordinary use must be upon the riparian land and this is the utmost limit
> to which our cases have gone. To further extend the doctrine would be to
> disregard settled principles of law. [248 Pa. at 610, 88 A. at 25.]

The effect on riparian rights of multiple occupancy of the riparian land is
treated in this excerpt from Filbert v. Dechert, 22 Pa. Super. 362 (1903):

> The right is a natural one, recognized as growing out of the natural wants of
> man; it is inherent in the ownership of the land, and is to be enjoyed by all who
> lawfully dwell upon the premises to the ownership of which it is an incident,
> without regard to the duration or purpose of such residence. All those who
> lawfully occupy the riparian lands have a right to the ordinary use of the water
> for the purpose of supplying their natural wants, including drinking, washing,
> cooking, and about their habitations for such things as are necessary to the
> preservation of life and health. This natural right is not dependent upon
> whether the dwellers by the stream occupy homes or hospitals, are sheltered by
> tents or live in the open. The state might lawfully ordain that the National
> Guard should encamp upon this tract of land and take water for their use,
> while there, from this stream. The ordinary use of the water, for the purpose of
> supplying the natural wants of those who inhabit the riparian lands, may
> involve an exhaustion of the stream without incurring liability to lower
> riparian proprietors: Attorney General v. Gt. Eastern Ry. Co., 23 L.T.N.S.
> 344. When the use is extraordinary, for the supply of artificial wants, such as
> manufactures, those whose supply of water is thereby sensibly diminished,
> have a right of action: Gould on Waters (3d ed.), sec. 205; Black's Pomeroy on
> Water Rights, secs. 138, 140, and cases there cited. [22 Pa. Super. at 368-369.]

Problems

35.1.   What is riparian land? Suppose O owns a tract of land bordering
on a stream and buys the adjoining tract, which adjoining tract does not

border on the stream. Is such adjoining land now riparian land? Suppose O's land is such that part of it is not within the watershed of the stream. Is the part beyond the watershed riparian land? See Watkins Land Co. v. Clements, 98 Tex. 578, 86 S.W. 733 (1905); American Law of Property §28.55 (Casner ed. 1952).

35.2. A owned land through which a stream flowed. A was in the business of raising cattle for commercial purposes. He had 2,000 head of cattle on his land. A diverted all the water from the stream for purpose of watering his cattle. B, a lower riparian owner, seeks an injunction against such action on A's part. Is B entitled to the injunction? See Cowell v. Armstrong, 210 Cal. 218, 290 P. 1036 (1930).

35.3. A, a riparian owner, diverted the course of a stream which ran through her land in order to have the stream pass through the part of the land where she kept cattle and thus enable her to provide water for the cattle more easily. Before the stream left her land, A provided for its return to its natural course. The acts of A do not change substantially the flow of the water to the lower riparian owners. B, a lower riparian owner, seeks to enjoin the diversion of the water from its natural course. Is B entitled to the injunction? See Mentone Irrigation Co. v. Redlands Electric Light & Power Co., 155 Cal. 323, 100 P. 1082 (1909).

35.4. A, a riparian owner, operated a sawmill and deposited the sawdust and other refuse from the mill in the stream flowing through A's land. B is a lower riparian owner and seeks to enjoin A from making such deposits in the stream because the sawdust and other refuse floats down the stream and clogs the flume and wheel of B's flouring mill. Discuss the relevance of the following factors in determining whether A should be enjoined:

a. A's sawmill is so constructed that its value as a waterpower mill is destroyed if sawdust and other refuse cannot be deposited in the stream.

b. It is the custom of others operating water-power sawmills to throw sawdust and other refuse in the streams.

See Red River Roller Mills v. Wright, 30 Minn. 249, 15 N.W. 167 (1883).

Note: The Doctrine of Prior Appropriation

The Massachusetts statutory provisions, usually referred to as "the Mill acts" are discussed in Smith v. Agawam Canal Co., 84 Mass. (2 Allen) 355 (1861):

> . . . But, under our statutes, any person may erect and maintain a water-mill, and a dam to raise water for working it, across any stream which is not navigable; and for this purpose may lawfully flood the lands of all persons over which the water will be caused to flow by keeping up and maintaining the dam. This privilege, however, is given subject to prescribed conditions and

restrictions; one of which, among many others, is, that no such dam shall be erected to the injury of any mill lawfully existing either above or below it on the same stream. Gen. Sts. c.149, Secs. 1, 2, & seq. Rev. Sts. c.116, St. 1795, c.74.

From these provisions it is an inevitable implication, that, although the right is given indiscriminately to all riparian proprietors, he who first erects and establishes his mill does, by his priority of occupation, acquire to that extent a title to the use of the water in the stream prior and superior to that of any other person, and a right to maintain his dam against all proprietors of lands both above and below his own. Cary v. Daniels, 8 Met. 466. Gould v. Boston Duck Co. ubi supra. But the right which is thus acquired is not so absolute as to give him the control of the whole stream, or to deprive other proprietors of the reasonable enjoyment of the privileges to which they are naturally entitled. They may still construct and maintain dams across the stream at any point either above or below his mill, for the purpose of raising a head of water to propel, operate and work mills of their own, erected on the adjoining land, provided that their arrangements are so made that they will not unreasonably withhold and detain the water above, nor throw it back from below, so as to affect, impede, delay or obstruct the movement and operation of the wheels and machinery of his previously existing mill. [84 Mass. (2 Allen) at 356.]

See Mass. Gen. Laws ch. 253 for the present wording of the Massachusetts Mill Acts.

The doctrine of prior appropriation which is operative under the Massachusetts Mill Acts, whereby the riparian owner who first appropriates the water to his use can prevent other riparian owners from using the water in such a manner as to interfere with his prior appropriation, has been particularly significant in the development of water law in the western and southwestern states. For an excellent discussion of the cases on prior appropriation in the western and southwestern states, see Wiel, Fifty Years of Water Law, 50 Harv. L. Rev. 252 (1936). See also Haar & Gordon, Riparian Water Rights vs. a Prior Appropriation System, 38 B.U.L. Rev. 207 (1958).

In Peabody v. City of Vallejo, 2 Cal. 2d 351, 40 P.2d 486 (1935), the following reference is made to the doctrine of prior appropriation:

> In adopting a policy modifying the long standing riparian doctrine of this state, California has done by constitutional amendment what many of the western states have done by statute or court decisions. Of the seventeen western states generally referred to as the irrigation states, nine now recognize the modified doctrine of riparian rights and eight have entirely abrogated the doctrine of riparian rights and recognize only the doctrine of appropriation. The nine are North Dakota, South Dakota, Nebraska, Kansas, Oklahoma, Texas, Washington, Oregon, and California; and the eight are Montana, Idaho, Wyoming, Nevada, Utah, Colorado, Arizona, and New Mexico. [2 Cal. 2d at 365-366, 40 P.2d at 490.]

The modified doctrine of riparian rights referred to in the quotation above is that prior appropriation is significant only if it occurred before the land bordering the stream passed out of the government. See American Law of Property §28.58 (Casner ed. 1952).

Under the common-law rule as to riparian rights, prior appropriation is not significant except as it may be a basis of acquiring a right by prescription.

Note: *The Iowa Water Statute*

Iowa Code ch. 455A sets forth a comprehensive statute establishing a permit system in regard to the use of water administered by a Water Commissioner. The Iowa statute is discussed in O'Connell, Iowa's New Water Statute — The Constitutionality of Regulating Existing Uses of Water, 47 Iowa L. Rev. 549 (1962).

Note: *Lakes Versus Streams*

A person whose land abuts on a lake or pond has the same rights and is subject to the same limitations as to the use of water as a riparian owner on a flowing stream. See American Law of Property §28.55 (Casner ed. 1952).

Note: *The Significance of Navigable Waters*

Up to this point, we have been concerned with riparian rights in non-navigable waters; we now turn our attention to the significance of navigable waters in the development of the substantive law.

UNITED STATES v. WILLOW RIVER POWER CO.

324 U.S. 499, 65 S. Ct. 761 (1945)

The basic doctrine of riparian rights in flowing streams prevails with minor variations in thirty-one states of the Union.[2] It chiefly was evolved to settle conflicts between parties, both of whom were riparian owners. Equal-

---

2. The other 17 have some form of the appropriative system. It is based on the principle of priority or seniority, under which rights accrue to users in the order in which they first put waters to beneficial use. The principle is not equal right of use but paramount right in the earlier user. The use is not limited to riparian tracts but may be diverted to sites remote from the stream, thus spreading the benefits beyond riparian lands, a considerable advantage to some arid regions. The beneficial use is more extensive and includes use for irrigation, mining, manufacturing as well as domestic uses, and the water may be permanently diverted and the stream thereby diminished to an extent not allowable under the riparian rights theory. See Bannister, Interstate Rights in Interstate Streams in the Arid West, 36 Harv. L. Rev. 960 (1923).

ity of right between such claimants was the essence of the resulting water law. "The fundamental principle of this system is that each riparian proprietor has an equal right to make a reasonable use of the waters of the stream, subject to the equal right of the other riparian proprietors likewise to make a reasonable use."[3] With this basic principle as a bench mark, particular rights to use flowing water on riparian lands for domestic purposes and for power were defined, each right in every riparian owner subject to the same right in others above and to a corresponding duty to those below.

The doctrine of riparian rights attained its maximum authority on non-navigable streams. No overriding public interest chilled the contest between owners to get the utmost in benefits from flowing streams. Physical conditions usually favored practical utilization of theoretical rights. In general non-navigable streams were small, shifted their courses easily and were not stable enough to serve as property lines as larger streams often do. They were shallow, could be forded and were no great obstacle to tillage or pasturage on two sides of the stream as a single operation. Such streams, like the lands, were fenced in, and while the waters might show resentment by carrying away a few spans of fence in the spring, the riparian owner's rights in such streams were acknowledged by the custom of the countryside as well as recognized by the law. In such surroundings and as between such owners equality of benefits from flowing waters was sought in the rule that each was entitled to their natural flow, subject only to a reasonable riparian use which must not substantially diminish their quantity or impair their quality . . . .

On navigable streams a different right intervenes. While riparian owners on navigable streams usually were held to have the same rights to be free from interferences of other riparian owners as on non-navigable streams, it was recognized from the beginning that all riparian interests were subject to a dominant public interest in navigation. The consequences of the latter upon the former have been the subject of frequent litigation.

Without detailing the long struggle between such conflicting interests on navigable streams, it may point out that by 1909 the lines had become sharply drawn and were then summarized by a leading author:[4] "The older authorities hold that such an owner has no private rights in the stream or body of water which are appurtenant to his land, and, in short, no rights beyond that of any other member of the public, and that the only difference is that he is more conveniently situated to enjoy the privileges which all the public have in common, and that he has access to the waters over his own land, which the public do not." "Access to and use of the stream by the riparian owner is regarded as merely permissive on the part of the public and liable to be cut off absolutely if the public sees fit to do so." And he quoted

---

3. Bannister, *supra,* at 960 [see footnote 2, *supra*]. Choice of the arid sections of the country of the appropriative in preference to the riparian system is cited in Cardozo, Growth of the Law 118, 119-120, as an example of "conscious departure from a known rule, and the deliberate adoption of a new one, in obedience to the promptings of a social need so obvious and so insistent as to overrun the ancient channel and cut a new one for itself."

4. 1 Lewis on Eminent Domain 116, 119 (3d ed. 1909).

another writer of standing:[5] "The owner of the bank has no jus privatum, or special usufructuary interest, in the water. He does not, from the mere circumstance that he is the owner of the bank, acquire any special or particular interest in the stream, over any other member of the public, except that, by his proximity thereto, he enjoys greater conveniences than the public generally. To him, riparian ownership brings no greater rights than those incident to all the public, except that he can approach the water more readily, and over lands which the general public have no right to use for that purpose. But this is a mere convenience, arising from his ownership of the lands adjacent to the ordinary high-water mark, and does not prevent the State from depriving him entirely of this convenience, by itself making erections upon the shore, or authorizing the use of the shore by others, in such a way as to deprive him of this convenience altogether, and the injury resulting to him therefrom, although greater than that sustained by the rest of the public, is 'damnum absque injuria.'" On the other hand, the author pointed out, there were cases holding that the riparian owners on navigable streams "have valuable rights appurtenant to their estates, of which they cannot be deprived without compensation." He considered this the better rule, and suggested that the courts indicated some tendency to adopt it.

However, in 1913 this Court decided United States v. Chandler-Dunbar Co., 229 U.S. 53, 33 S. Ct. 667. It involved the claim that water power inherent in a navigable stream due to its fall in passing riparian lands belongs to the shore owner as an appurtenant to his lands. The Court set aside questions as to the right of riparian owners on non-navigable streams and all questions as to the rights of riparian owners on either navigable or non-navigable streams as between each other. And it laid aside as irrelevant whether the shore owner did or did not have a technical title to the bed of the river which would pass with it "as a shadow follows a substance." It declared that "In neither event can there be said to arise any ownership of the river. Ownership of a private stream wholly upon the lands of an individual is conceivable; but that the running water in a great navigable stream is capable of private ownership is inconceivable." 229 U.S. at pages 62, 69, 33 S. Ct. at pages 671, 674. This Court then took a view quite in line with the trend of former decisions there reviewed, that a strategic position for the development of power does not give rise to right to maintain it as against interference by the United States in aid of navigation. We have adhered to that position. United States v. Appalachian Electric Power Co., 311 U.S. 377, 424, 61 S. Ct. 291, 307. The Chandler-Dunbar case held that the shore owner had no appurtenant property right in two natural levels of water in front of its lands or to the use of the natural difference between as a head for power production. In this case the claimant asserts a similar right to one natural level in front of his lands and a right of ownership in the difference between that and the artificial level of the impounded water of the Willow River. It constituted a privilege or a convenience, enjoyed for many years,

---

5.   Wood on Nuisances §592 (1st ed.)

permissible so long as compatible with navigation interests, but it is not an interest protected by law when it becomes inconsistent with plans authorized by Congress for improvement of navigation. . . .

Rights, property or otherwise, which are absolute against all the world are certainly rare, and water rights are not among them. Whatever rights may be as between equals such as riparian owners, they are not the measure of riparian rights on a navigable stream relative to the function of the Government in improving navigation. Where these interests conflict they are not to be reconciled as between equals, but the private interest must give way to a superior right, or perhaps it would be more accurate to say that as against the Government such private interest is not a right at all.

Among the many cases involving navigable waters, the following may prove to be of particular interest: Opinion of the Justices, 365 Mass. 681, 313 N.E. 2d 561 (1974) (rights in coastal land between high- and low-water line); Oregon ex rel. State Land Board v. Corvallis Sand & Gravel Co., 429 U.S. 363, 97 S. Ct. 582 (1977) (title to land which is the bed of a navigable river); Ohio v. Kentucky, 444 U.S. 335, 100 S. Ct. 588, *rehearing denied,* 445 U.S. 939, 100 S. Ct. 1307 (1980) (effect on state boundaries of change in course of river which was original boundary); Kaiser Aetna v. United States, 444 U.S. 164, 100 S. Ct. 383 (1979) (rights of public where private action produces navigable waters); Vaughn v. Vermillion Corp., 444 U.S. 206, 100 S. Ct. 399 (1979) (same); Colorado v. New Mexico, — U.S. —, 103 S. Ct. 539 (1982) (diversion of water in interstate river by one state as against another state); California v. United States, 457 U.S. 273, 102 S. Ct. 2432 (1982) (title to land underlying territorial sea as between state and federal government).

Note: The Chicago River

The Chicago River at one time flowed into Lake Michigan. An artificial channel was created causing the river to flow in the opposite direction, thereby diverting water from Lake Michigan. After the change in its direction, the river flowed through various tributaries into the Mississippi River. The litigation growing out of this situation was very extensive. Various states complained because the lowering of water in the Great Lakes was said to affect the riparian rights of the states bordering on the Great Lakes and their citizens. Finally the United States government became concerned at the amount of water being diverted from the Great Lakes because of the navigation problems presented. For the culminating litigation on this whole matter, see Sanitary District of Chicago v. United States, 266 U.S. 405, 45 S. Ct. 176 (1925); Wisconsin v. Illinois, 278 U.S. 367, 49 S. Ct. 163 (1929); Wisconsin v. Illinois, 281 U.S. 179, 50 S. Ct. 266 (1930). See also LaSalle

County Carbon Coal Co. v. Sanitary District of Chicago, Chapter 4, at page 82 *supra.*

SECTION 2. SURFACE WATER[6]

Note: *Common-Law Rule Versus Civil-Law Rule*

The common-law and civil-law rules relating to the rights of parties with respect to surface water are explained thus in Garland v. Aurin, 103 Tenn. 555, 53 S.W. 940 (1899):

> Two distinct rules have been administered in the various States of the Union with respect to the right of a lower proprietor to obstruct and repel surface water flowing from the land of a higher proprietor — one being called the common law rule and the other the civil law rule. Under what is known as the common law rule, the holding is that the right of the lower proprietor to occupy and improve his land in such manner and for such purposes as he may see fit, either by changing the surface or by the erection of buildings or other structures thereon, is not restricted or modified by the fact that such improvements or occupation will obstruct and repel surface water that would otherwise naturally flow thereon from adjacent and higher land, even though the land of the upper proprietor may be injured thereby.
>
> This rule is based largely upon the maxim, "Cujus est solum, ejus est usque ad coelum et ad infernos," and seems to be administered in the States of Connecticut, Indiana, Kansas, Maine, Massachusetts, Minnesota, Missouri, New Hampshire, New Jersey, New York, and perhaps in Texas (except as to railroads), Vermont, and Wisconsin.
>
> On the contrary, by the rule of the civil law, the proprietor of the lower land may not obstruct, by any means, the natural flow of surface water, and turn it back, to the injury of the higher lands of his neighbor, the latter owner having, by the law of nature, an easement or servitude of drainage over the lands of the former for the flow of surface waters. This rule is based partly upon the necessity of the situation and partly upon the maxim, "Sic utere tuo ut alienum non laedas," and appears to prevail in Arkansas, Alabama, California, Georgia, Illinois, Iowa, Kentucky, Louisiana, Maryland, Michigan, Nevada, North Carolina, Ohio, Pennsylvania, Tennessee, Texas (as to railroads), Virginia and West Virginia.
>
> There have seemingly been some changes from one rule to the other in Arkansas, Missouri, Iowa, New Hampshire, and some of the other States; and South Carolina appears to occupy a kind of middle ground between the two, allowing the lower owner to make any reasonable use of his land which may

---

6. See generally in regard to surface water American Law of Property §§28.61-28.64 (Casner ed. 1952).

not unreasonably injure adjacent property above. [103 Tenn. at 557-558, 53 S.W. at 940-941.]

In the following case, the Supreme Judicial Court of Massachusetts prospectively overrules the Massachusetts position.

TUCKER v. BADOIAN
376 Mass. 907, 384 N.E.2d 1195 (1978)

QUIRICO, J. The plaintiffs in these two actions seek to recover for damages that they claim were caused to their land and the house thereon by the alleged negligence of the defendants. The plaintiffs contend that the defendants negligently made certain physical changes to their own land, which abuts that of the plaintiffs, thereby causing large quantities of water to collect on the plaintiffs' lot and in the cellar of their house. The jury returned a verdict for the plaintiffs in the amount of $60,000 in each of the two actions. The defendants moved for a new trial, and, after a hearing thereon, the judge ordered a remittitur of $35,000. He allowed the verdict in each case to stand in the reduced amount of $25,000, and the plaintiffs assented. See Mass. R. Civ. P. 59(a), 365 Mass. 827 (1974).

The defendants appealed from the judgments thus entered for the plaintiffs. After hearing the parties, the Appeals Court held that the trial judge had erred in denying the motions of the defendant in each case for a directed verdict and ordered that the judgments for the plaintiffs be reversed. Tucker v. Badoian, 5 Mass. App. —[7], 370 N.E.2d 717 (1977). The plaintiffs then filed applications for further appellate review in these two cases, and we allowed them. See G.L. c. 211A, §11; Mass. R.A.P. 27.1, 367 Mass. 919 (1975). . . .

We hold, as did the Appeals Court, that in each of the two cases now before us, it was error for the judge to deny the defendant's motion for directed verdict, that the judgments for the plaintiffs should be reversed, and that judgments should be entered for the defendants. . . .

The plaintiffs adduced a variety of expert testimony during the trial. As we are passing on the judge's alleged error in denying the defendants' motions for directed verdicts, we summarize this testimony in the light most favorable to the plaintiffs. Alholm v. Wareham, 371 Mass. —, —[8], 358 N.E.2d 788 (1976). The flooding of the plaintiffs' basement was caused, at least in part, by the circumstance that the water table was higher than the floor of the basement. In addition, the high water table prevented proper effluent filtration in the leaching field of the septic system, with the result that raw sewage mixed with ground water and flowed into the cellar. The

7. Mass. App. Adv. Sh. (1977) 1294.
8. Mass. Adv. Sh. (1976) 2946, 2951-2952.

grading and filling operations on Morningside's land might have contributed to raising the water table under the plaintiffs' land and thereby contributed to the damage the plaintiffs concededly suffered. In addition, the water table would tend to follow the level of water in the pothole, and the jury could have found that Morningside raised that level by filling in a portion of the pothole on its own land.

1. The single issue of law before us is whether, on the evidence summarized above, the judge should have directed verdicts for the defendants. This court first considered the respective rights and obligations of landowners with respect to surface drainage in Luther v. Winnisimmet Co., 9 Cush. 171 (1851). In that case we approved, as being "well adapted to the case," jury instructions to the effect that one landowner is free to stop surface water from entering his land despite harm to his neighbor. Id. at 174-175. Since 1851, we have frequently held not only that a landowner may freely defend his land from encroaching surface water but also that he may with impunity grade and improve his land for a lawful purpose even though he thereby diverts surface water onto his neighbor's land. Canavan & Manning, Inc. v. Freedman, 353 Mass. 762, 232 N.E.2d 680 (1968) (embankment). Kuklinska v. Maplewood Homes, Inc., 336 Mass 489, 492, 146 N.E.2d 523 (1957) (grading for housing development). Maddock v. Springfield, 281 Mass. 103, 105, 183 N.E. 148 (1932) (sidewalk and fill). Gannon v. Hargadon, 10 Allen 106, 109-110 (1865) (blocking cart ruts). We have not distinguished between surface and ground water. Kennison v. Inhabitants of Beverly, 146 Mass. 467, 469, 16 N.E. 278 (1888). Cf. Belkus v. Brockton, 282 Mass. 285, 288, 184 N.E. 812 (1933) (measure of damages same whether caused by ground or surface water); Wilson v. New Bedford, 108 Mass. 261, 266 (1871) (no difference in character of injury).

The law of this Commonwealth was stated as follows in the *Gannon* case:

> The right of an owner of land to occupy and improve it in such manner and for such purposes as he may see fit, either by changing the surface or the erection of buildings or other structures thereon, is not restricted or modified by the fact that his own land is so situated with reference to that of adjoining owners that an alteration in the mode of its improvement or occupation in any portion of it will cause water, which may accumulate thereon by rains and snows falling on its surface or flowing on to it over the surface of adjacent lots, either to stand in unusual quantities on other adjacent lands, or pass into and over the same in greater quantities or in other directions than they were accustomed to flow. [10 Allen at 109.]

These same principles have governed liability for damage caused by percolating ground water.

Because of our decision in Gannon v. Hargadon, *supra,* commentators have considered Massachusetts to follow the "common enemy" approach to surface water problems. See e.g., 6A American Law of Property §28.63, at 189-190 (A. J. Casner ed. 1954). Taken to its logical conclusion, the doctrine forecloses distinctions based on how drainage water is diverted from one parcel to another. E.g., 5 R. Powell, Real Property par. 730, at 438.2-438.5 (P. J. Rohan rev. ed. 1977). We have instead held that a landowner may not use definite, artificial channels so as to harm his neighbor. E.g., Chesarone v. Pinewood Builders, Inc., 345 Mass. 236, 239-240, 186 N.E.2d 712 (1962); Cernak v. Kay-Vee Realty Co., 341 Mass. 315, 318, 169 N.E.2d 879 (1960); Deyo v. Athol Hous. Auth., 335 Mass. 459, 467, 140 N.E.2d 393 (1957). Liability may arise either from collecting water and then discharging it directly onto the land of another, as in *Chesarone,* or from accumulating channelled water and allowing it to back up onto the land of another. See Mahoney v. Barrows, 240 Mass. 378, 378-379, 134 N.E. 246 (1922). There is no liability however, without proof that the defendant caused surface water, which might otherwise have been absorbed or have flowed elsewhere, to be artificially channelled and discharged on the plaintiff's land in a place and quantity sufficient to entitle the plaintiff to relief. Kapayanis v. Fishbein, 344 Mass. 86, 87, 181 N.E.2d 653 (1962). Kuklinska v. Maplewood Homes, Inc., *supra,* 336 Mass. at 493, 146 N.E.2d 523. See also McNamara v. Westview Bldg. Corp., 4 Mass. App. —, —[9], 357 N.E.2d 777 (1976); Kattor v. Sabatini, 4 Mass. App. —[10], 351 N.E.2d 553 (1976); Howe v. DiPierro Mfg. Co., 1 Mass. App. 81, 84-85, 294 N.E.2d 495 (1973).

We recognize that the courts of several other States have recently abandoned rigid approaches like our own in favor of a more flexible "reasonable use" doctrine. E.g., Pendergrast v. Aiken, 293 N.C. 201, 210-211, 236 S.E.2d 787 (1977) (collecting cases); Butler v. Bruno, 115 R.I. 264, 274-275, 341 A.2d 735 (1975). If this is a trend, it is not unanimous. See Johnson v. Whitten, 384 A.2d 698, 700-701 (Me. 1978) (restating Maine law in terms compatible with our own law). Since the parties to these actions have not asked that we change the law of this Commonwealth in this area, we decide the present appeals on the basis of our long-standing rule as stated in the *Gannon* case. . . .

3. For the reasons stated above, we hold that the judge should have allowed the motions for directed verdicts in favor of Badoian and Morningside. The cases are remanded to the Superior Court Department with directions to enter judgments in favor of Badoian and Morningside.

So ordered.

KAPLAN, J. (with whom HENNESSEY, C.J., BRAUCHER, WILKINS, LIACOS and ABRAMS, JJ., join, concurring in the result).

The whole court is in agreement with the result reached in the foregoing opinion of Justice Quirico applying the "common enemy" rule. Those subscribing to the present concurrence, however, desire to state that for the future they intend a change of the doctrine.

The common enemy rule had only questionable support in the common

---

9. Mass. App. Adv. Sh. (1976) 1183, 1185.
10. Mass. App. Adv. Sh. (1976) 908.

law when it was first sponsored by this court in the mid-nineteenth century. Being assimilated to conceptions of property rather than tort, it exhibited from the beginning a deplorable rigidity. In its substance, however, it was anarchic. Perhaps a common enemy doctrine served originally a public purpose by stimulating or assisting entrepreneurship in the exploitation of land. But, as Brennan, J. (now Mr. Justice Brennan), intimated in Armstrong v. Francis Corp., 20 N.J. 320, 330, 120 A.2d 4 (1956), at a matured stage of the economy there is little reason why costs of land development "should be borne in every case by adjoining landowners rather than by those who engage in such projects for profit."

As might be expected, jurisdictions espousing the rule have civilized it in one way or another, not always with explicit recognition of what they were doing. This court allowed some "exceptions," and no doubt we often reached sensible results. A like process of adjustment or amelioration could be discerned with respect to an unsatisfactory "natural flow" rule in vogue in another group of jurisdictions. This started at the opposite end and imposed liability on a possessor for interfering to the detriment of his neighbor with the drainage of surface waters in their natural course.

In practice and application, then, if not in terms, both rules tended in some degree to reach a plane of reason. Still the formulary statements on either side confused the issues and impaired the results. Therefore, with encouragement from competent scholars, a respectable number of courts over the past thirty years and more have abandoned the polar positions and adopted, instead, a "reasonable use" standard which introduces, in the resolution of quarrels between landowners about surface waters, the considerations typical of the law of private nuisance.[11] On such lines the question was treated in the Restatement of Torts as promulgated in 1939.[12] The movement is described in 5 Waters and Water Rights, c. 26 (ed. R. E. Clark et al. 1972, with 1978 supplement); 5 R. Powell on Real Property pars. 729-732 (P. J. Rohan rev. ed. 1977); Maloney & Plager, Diffused Surface

---

11. In the *Armstrong* case, the matter is put in general terms thus (at 327, 330, 120 A.2d at 8, 10):

> [E]ach possessor is legally privileged to make a reasonable use of his land, even though the flow of surface waters is altered thereby and causes some harm to others, but incurs liability when his harmful interference with the flow of surface waters is unreasonable. . . . The rule of reasonableness has the particular virtue of flexibility. The rule of reasonableness or unreasonableness becomes a question of fact to be determined in each case upon a consideration of all the relevant circumstances, including such factors as the amount of harm caused, the foreseeability of the harm which results, the purpose or motive with which the possessor acted, and all other relevant matter. . . . It is, of course, true that society has a great interest that land shall be developed for the greater good. It is therefore properly a consideration in these cases whether the utility of the possessor's use of his land outweighs the gravity of the harm which results from his alteration of the flow of surface waters.

12. Sections 833, 822-831, spell out the detailed considerations, and the subject is renewed in Restatement (Second) of Torts: Tentative Draft No. 16, pp. 62-75, 131-158 (April 24, 1970); No. 17, pp. 22-47 (April 26, 1971); No. 18, pp. 1-6 (April 26, 1972).

Water: Scourge or Bounty?, 8 Natural Resources J. 72 (1968). Among the apostasies of the courts from the older orthodoxies, a reader might consult the New Jersey case cited and the recent decisions of Pendergrast v. Aiken, 293 N.C. 201, 236 S.E.2d 787 (1977), Butler v. Bruno, 115 R.I. 264 (1975), and State v. Deetz, 66 Wis. 2d 1, 224 N.W.2d 407 (1974).

It will be understood that, in indicating the intention to move to the standard of reasonable use, we are not committing ourselves in advance to follow in every detail the position elaborated by any other court or by the Restatement. The details of the standard will evolve and be determined in the usual way through the decisional process.

Ordinarily a change of decisional law falls into place and is applied to past as well as to subsequent transactions or occurrences. In the present situation, however, we propose to alter a rule of long standing on which parties may have relied. Accordingly we think the new standard should be reserved for prospective application, that is, for conduct occurring hereafter, excepting future conduct so related in a continuum with past conduct that it would be unjust to apply the new standard to it. We do not apply the new standard to the instant case (which would entail reversing the judgment appealed from and remanding the matter for further proceedings) because the parties did not raise the question of a departure from the existing rule and were content to litigate within its bounds.[13]

Problems

35.5. A is the owner of land in a jurisdiction which adopts the common-law rule. The drainage of surface water is from B's adjoining land to A's land. A raised the level of his land, and by so doing he caused the surface water from B's land to be diverted from its natural course of drainage and flow instead to the land of C. Is A liable to C for the damage to C's land which results from the surface water so diverted by A? See Jordan v. St. Paul, Minneapolis & Manitoba Railway, 42 Minn. 172, 43 N.W. 849 (1889).

35.6. A is the owner of land in a jurisdiction which adopts the civil-law rule. The drainage of surface water is from B's adjoining land to A's land. B lowered the level of her land, and by so doing she prevented the surface water from reaching A's land. A's land is damaged by being deprived of the surface water, and A seeks to recover damages from B. Is A entitled to recover? See Terry v. Heppner, 59 S.D. 317, 239 N.W. 759 (1931).

35.7. A is the owner of land in a jurisdiction which adopts the civil-law

---

13. In State v. Deetz, 66 Wis. 2d 1, 224 N.W.2d 407 (1974), the Wisconsin Court, in turning to the rule of reasonable use, said it would apply only to future conduct, with the exception that it would also govern the appeal under review. The change of doctrine, however, had been argued to the court. See Diaz v. Eli Lilly & Co., 364 Mass. 153, 167, 302 N.E.2d 555 (1973). Various other courts in adopting the new standard have not adverted to the question of retroactivity.

rule. The drainage of surface water is from B's adjoining land to A's land. B permitted garbage and other refuse to collect on her land, and the surface water carried most of the refuse to A's land. A raised the level of his land, thus preventing the surface water with the refuse from reaching his land. Is A's action justified? See Crossland v. Borough of Pottsville, 126 Pa. St. 511, 18 A. 15 (1889).

35.8. Since the right to obstruct the flow of surface water may be different from the right to obstruct the flow of a natural stream, and since the right to appropriate surface water may be different from the right to appropriate water in a natural stream, it may be important to determine whether particular water is surface water or water in a natural stream. What factors will be significant in making such determination? See 40 A.L.R. 839 (1926).

35.9. A builds a house on her land and at considerable expense installs solar heat. Subsequently, B, who owns the adjoining land, erects a structure that blocks the access of the sun to A's house. Is blocking the flow of the sun in this situation subject to the same rules as blocking the flow of surface water or blocking the flow of a stream? See Fontainebleau Hotel Corp. v. Forty-Five Twenty-Five, Inc., 114 So. 2d 357 (Fla. Dist. Ct. App. 1959) (a tall building that cut off light and air and interfered with the view from neighboring land); People ex rel. Hoogasian v. Sears Roebuck & Co., 52 Ill. 2d 301, 287 N.E.2d 677 (1972) (101-story building that interfered with television reception in neighboring areas).

Note: Littoral Drifting of Sand

Lummis v. Lilly, 385 Mass. 41, 429 N.E.2d 1146 (1982), involved two properties on that part of the shore of Buzzard's Bay on Cape Cod known as Sippewisset Beach. The plaintiff objected to the installation and maintenance of a stone groin by the defendants on their property which almost adjoins the plaintiff's littoral property. We now pick up excerpts from the court's opinion relating to this dispute.

> A groin was defined in one expert's affidavit as "a solid structure which lies generally perpendicular to the shoreline and extends from the backshore out across the foreshore of the beach. The function of a groin is to interrupt the littoral drifting of sand along the shore, thereby producing deposition of sand on the updrift side of the structure and widening the beach." According to the same expert the "[l]ittoral drifting continues on the downdrift side of the structure and since the sand which is transported away is not replaced by sand from the updrift side, the beach narrows on the downdrift side of the groin." The Lummis property is on the downdrift side and these conditions, as they affect the Lummis property, are precisely the damage alleged by the plaintiff.
>
> The narrow but important issue is whether we should apply the rule of "reasonable use" as most recently enunciated by this court in Tucker v.

Badoian, 376 Mass. 907, 384 N.E.2d 1195 (1978), to the rights of owners of oceanfront property. . . .

Our jurisprudence on the rule governing littoral rights is not abundant. Some cases are inapposite because they address the question of public against private rights. See Gray v. Bartlett, 20 Pick. 186 (1838); Commonwealth v. Alger, 7 Cush. 53 (1851); Commonwealth v. Roxbury, 9 Gray 451 (1857); Henry v. Newburyport, 149 Mass. 582, 22 N.E. 75 (1889); Butler v. Attorney Gen., 195 Mass. 79, 80 N.E. 688 (1907); Michaelson v. Silver Beach Improvement Ass'n, 342 Mass. 251, 173 N.E.2d 273 (1961); Opinion of the Justices, 365 Mass. 681, 313 N.E.2d 561 (1974); Boston Waterfront Dev. Corp. v. Commonwealth, 378 Mass. 623, 393 N.E.2d 356 (1979); Opinion of the Justices, — Mass. — Mass. Adv. Sh. (1981) 1361, 424 N.E.2d 1092. In Davidson v. Boston & Maine R.R., 3 Cush. 91 (1849), the court spoke to the rights of littoral owners, but within the context of a taking which interfered with the public interest in navigation and not with the plaintiff's private rights. The following language from Commonwealth v. Alger, 7 Cush. 53, 86-87 (1851), comes closer to the mark: "[A]ll real estate, inland or on the sea-shore, derived immediately or remotely from the government of the state, is taken and held under the tacit understanding that the owner shall so deal with it as not to cause injury to others; . . . when land is so situated, or such is its conformation, that it forms a natural barrier to rivers or tidal watercourses, the owner cannot justifiably remove it, to such an extent as to . . . destroy the valuable rights of other proprietors, both in the navigation of the stream, and in the contiguous lands. . . . [T]he object [of the colonial ordinance] seems to have been, to secure to riparian proprietors in general, without special grant, a property in the land, with full power to erect such wharves, embankments and warehouses thereon, as would be usually required for purposes of commerce, *subordinate only to a reasonable use of the same, by other individual riparian proprietors and the public,* for the purposes of navigation, through any sea, creeks or coves, with their boats and vessels" (emphasis supplied). Id. at 89.

A more recent case to address the problem directly is Jubilee Yacht Club v. Gulf Ref. Co., 245 Mass. 60, 140 N.E. 280 (1923), in which the plaintiff sought damages and injunctive relief because of the defendant's construction of a breakwater. The defendant in the present action relies heavily on *Jubilee,* in which the court denied the plaintiff relief because the defendant "merely exercised the ordinary rights of an owner in fee." Id. at 64, 140 N.E. 280. There, the court analogized the defendant's contruction of the concrete breakwater to "acts . . . committed by the owner of adjoining property away from the seashore. . . . The building of fences, walls or other structures, or making excavations on his own land ordinarily is within the absolute right of the owner of a fee without reference to the incidental injury which may thereby be caused to his neighbor." Id. at 62, 140 N.E. 280.

To the extent that the *Jubilee* decision approved of a rule applicable to littoral owners other than that of reasonable use we choose not to follow it. There is no sound reason for imposing the obligation of reasonable use on riparian owners, while permitting littoral owners to use their property without any limitations. See Mears v. Dole, 135 Mass. 508, 510 (1883). . . .

As to relief for damages sustained prior to the entry of judgment, it appears that the plaintiff's claim is founded more nearly on longstanding principles enunciated in connection with the rights of riparian owners than on principles similar to the rights of landowners concerned with surface water, recently announced prospectively in Tucker v. Badoian, *supra.* Cf. *Stratton, supra* at 89, 103 N.E. 87; Parker v. American Woollen Co., 215 Mass. 176, 182, 102 N.E. 360 (1913). On this record, we cannot determine what, if any, damages may be recoverable by the plaintiff.

The judgment dismissing the plaintiff's complaint is reversed and the case is remanded to the Superior Court for action consistent with this opinion.

So ordered. [385 Mass. at 43-47, 429 N.E.2d at 1148-1150.]

SECTION 3.   UNDERGROUND WATER[14]

Note: *The English Rule Versus the Rule of Reasonable Use*

Meeker v. City of East Orange, reproduced in part below, describes the English rule and the rule of reasonable use in regard to underground percolating water.

MEEKER v. CITY OF EAST ORANGE
77 N.J.L. 623, 74 A. 379 (1909)

The judgments under review are based upon the theory that the city has an absolute right to appropriate all percolating water found beneath the land owned by it, and to use the water for purposes entirely unconnected with the beneficial use and enjoyment of that land, to the extent, indeed, of making merchandise of the water and conveying it to a distance for the supply of the inhabitants of East Orange, and that although by such diversion the plaintiff's spring, well and stream are dried up, and his land rendered so arid as to be untillable, it is damnum absque injuria.

The judgments are attacked upon the ground that the law recognizes correlative rights in percolating subterranean waters; that each landowner is entitled to use such waters only in a reasonable manner and to a reasonable extent beneficial to his own land, and without undue interference with the rights of other landowners to the like use and enjoyment of waters percolating beneath their lands, or of water courses fed therefrom.

The law respecting the rights of property owners in percolating subterranean waters is of comparatively recent development, the first English

14.   See generally in regard to underground waters American Law of Property §§28.65-28.68 (Casner ed. 1952).

decision bearing directly upon the question having been rendered in 1843. Acton v. Blundell, 12 Mees. & W. 324; 13 L.J. Exch. 289. This was followed by Chasemore v. Richards (1859), 7 H.L. Cas. 349, 29 L.J. Exch. 81; 5 Jur. (N.S.) 873; 1 Eng. Rul. Cas. 729. These cases may be taken as establishing for that jurisdiction the rule upon which the judgments under review are based.

They were followed by a considerable line of decisions in this country in which the English rule was adhered to, and which will be found discussed in Washb. Easem. *363, *390; Ang. Waterc., Secs. 109-114, and 30 Am. & Eng. Encyl. L. (2d ed.) 310, 313.

The soundness of the English doctrine was, however, challenged by the Supreme Court of New Hampshire in a well-considered case decided in 1862 (Bassett v. Salisbury Manufacturing Co., 43 N.H. 569; 3 Am. L. Reg. (N.S.) 223 (O.S., Vol. 12); 82 Am. Dec. 179), where it was elaborately reasoned that the doctrine of absolute ownership is not well founded in legal principles, and is not so commended by its practical application as to require its adoption; that the true rule is that the rights of each owner being similar, and their enjoyment dependent upon the action of other landowners, their rights must be correlative and subject to the operation of the maxim sic utere &c., so that each landowner is restricted to a reasonable exercise of his own rights and a reasonable use of his own property, in view of the similar right of others. This decision was followed by Swett v. Cutts (1870), 50 N.H. 439, 9 Am. Rep. 276; 11 Am. L. Reg. (N.S.) 11, where the court again laid it down that the landowner has not an absolute and unqualified property in all such water as may be found in his soil, to do what he pleases with it, as with the sand and rock that form part of the soil, but that his right is to make reasonable use of it for domestic, agricultural and manufacturing purposes, not trenching upon the similar rights of others. . . .

But it is not too much to say that the rule adopted in Chasemore v. Richards, and the reasoning upon which it was rested, have not withstood the test of time, experience and ampler discussion, and it is entirely clear that the strong trend of more recent decisions in this country is in the direction of a repudiation of the English rule and the adoption of the doctrine that there are correlative rights in percolating underground waters; that no landowner has the absolute right to withdraw these from the soil to the detriment of other owners, and is limited to reasonable uses. . . .

Again, the denial of the applicability to underground waters of the general principles of law that obtain with respect to waters upon the surface of the earth is in part placed upon the mere difficulty of proving the facts respecting water that is concealed from view. But experience has demonstrated in a multitude of cases that this difficulty is often readily solved. When it is solved in a given case, by the production of satisfactory proof, this reason for the rule at once vanishes.

It is sometimes said that unless the English rule be adopted, landowners will be hampered in the development of their property because of the uncertainty that would thus be thrown about their rights. It seems to us that this reasoning is wholly faulty. If the English rule is to obtain, a man may discover upon his own land springs of great value for medicinal purposes or for use in special forms of manufacture, and may invest large sums of money upon their development; yet he is subject at any time to have the normal supply of such springs wholly cut off by a neighboring landowner, who may, with impunity, sink deeper wells and employ more powerful machinery, and thus wholly drain the subsurface water from the land of the first discoverer. . . .

Upon the whole we are convinced, not only that the authority of the English cases is greatly weakened by the trend of modern decisions in this country, but that the reasoning upon which the doctrine of "reasonable user" rests is better supported upon general principles of law and more in consonance with natural justice and equity.

We therefore adopt the latter doctrine. This does not prevent the proper use by any landowner of the percolating waters subjacent to his soil in agriculture, manufacturing, irrigation or otherwise, nor does it prevent any reasonable development of his land by mining or the like, although the underground water of neighboring proprietors may thus be interfered with or diverted. But it does prevent the withdrawal of underground waters for distribution or sale for uses not connected with any beneficial ownership or enjoyment of the land whence they are taken, if it results therefrom that the owner of adjacent or neighboring land is interfered with in his right to the reasonable user of sub-surface water upon his land, or if his wells, springs or streams are thereby materially diminished in flow, or his land is rendered so arid as to be less valuable for agriculture, pasturage or other legitimate uses.

Problems

35.10. A, owner of Blackacre, killed several of his cows which were diseased. He buried the cows at a remote point on his land. It is found that the carcasses polluted subterranean water which, unknown to A, flows toward B's adjoining land. As a result, B's well is contaminated. You are B's attorney. What would you advise B to do?

35.11. A desires to purchase Blackacre, and the main thing which attracts her about the land is the plentiful supply of water furnished by two springs, evidently fed by subterranean waters. If you are attorney for A and know that A would not buy the land if the two springs were not on it, what would you advise A to do in a jurisdiction following the English rule? Would your advice to A be different in a jurisdiction following the rule of reasonable use?[15]

---

15. The significance of prior appropriation of underground water in the western states is considered in Kirkwood, Appropriation of Percolating Water, 1 Stan. L. Rev. 1 (1948). See also Ziegler, Acquisition and Protection of Water Supplies by Municipalities, 57 Mich. L. Rev. 349 (1959).

Note: Oil and Gas

Problems similar to those that arise with respect to underground water are presented in connection with oil and gas. Is one landowner entitled to place wells on his or her land and draw off oil or gas from underneath the land of another? The answer to this question forms an important part of the law of oil and gas. As to the nature of a landowner's right in oil and gas, see American Law of Property §§10.5-10.8 (Casner ed. 1952).

CHAPTER 36

INVASION OF AIR SPACE

UNITED STATES v. CAUSBY
328 U.S. 256, 66 S. Ct. 1062 (1946)

Mr. Justice DOUGLAS delivered the opinion of the court.

This is a case of first impression. The problem presented is whether respondents' property was taken, within the meaning of the Fifth Amendment, by frequent and regular flights of army and navy aircraft over respondents' land at low altitudes. The Court of Claims held that there was a taking and entered judgment for respondents, one judge dissenting. 104 Ct. Cls. 342, 60 F. Supp. 751. The case is here on a petition for a writ of certiorari which we granted because of the importance of the question presented.

Respondents own 2.8 acres near an airport outside of Greensboro, North Carolina. It has on it a dwelling house, and also various outbuildings which were mainly used for raising chickens. The end of the airport's northwest-southeast runway is 2,220 feet from respondents' barn and 2,275 feet from their house. The path of glide to this runway passes directly over the property — which is 100 feet wide and 1,200 feet long. The 30 to 1 safe glide angle[1] approved by the Civil Aeronautics Authority[2] passes over this property at 83 feet, which is 67 feet above the house, 63 feet above the barn and 18 feet above the highest tree.[3] The use by the United States of this airport is pursuant to a lease executed in May, 1942, for a term commencing June 1, 1942 and ending June 30, 1942, with a provision for renewals until June 30, 1967, or six months after the end of the national emergency, whichever is the earlier.

---

1. A 30 to 1 glide angle means one foot of elevation or descent for every 30 feet of horizontal distance.
2. Military planes are subject to the rules of the Civil Aeronautics Board where, as in the present case, there are no Army or Navy regulations to the contrary. Cameron v. Civil Aeronautics Board, 140 F.2d 482 (1944).
3. The house is approximately 16 feet high, the barn 20 feet, and the tallest tree 65 feet.

Various aircraft of the United States use this airport—bombers, transports and fighters. The direction of the prevailing wind determines when a particular runway is used. The northwest-southeast runway in question is used about four percent of the time in taking off and about seven percent of the time in landing. Since the United States began operations in May, 1942, its four-motored heavy bombers, other planes of the heavier type, and its fighter planes have frequently passed over respondents' land and buildings in considerable numbers and rather close together. They come close enough at times to appear barely to miss the tops of the trees and at times so close to the tops of the trees as to blow the old leaves off. The noise is startling. And at night the glare from the planes brightly lights up the place. As a result of the noise, respondents had to give up their chicken business. As many as six to ten of their chickens were killed in one day by flying into the walls from fright. The total chickens lost in that manner was about 150. Production also fell off. The result was the destruction of the use of the property as a commercial chicken farm. Respondents are frequently deprived of their sleep and the family has become nervous and frightened. Although there have been no airplane accidents on respondents' property, there have been several accidents near the airport and close to respondents' place. These are the essential facts found by the Court of Claims. On the basis of these facts, it found that respondents' property had depreciated in value. It held that the United States had taken an easement over the property on June 1, 1942, and that the value of the property destroyed and the easement taken was $2,000.

I. The United States relies on the Air Commerce Act of 1926, 44 Stat. 586, 49 U.S.C., Sec. 171, as amended by the Civil Aeronautics Act of 1938, 52 Stat. 973, 49 U.S.C., Sec. 401. Under those statutes the United States has "complete and exclusive national sovereignty in the air space" over this country. 49 U.S.C., Sec. 176(a). They grant any citizen of the United States "a public right of freedom of transit in air commerce[4] through the navigable air space of the United States." 49 U.S.C. Sec. 403. And "navigable air space" is defined as "airspace above the minimum safe altitudes of flight prescribed by the Civil Aeronautics Authority." 49 U.S.C., Sec. 180. And it is provided that "such navigable airspace shall be subject to a public right of freedom of interstate and foreign air navigation." Id. It is, therefore, argued that since these flights were within the minimum safe altitudes of flight which had been prescribed, they were an exercise of the declared right of travel through the airspace. The United States concludes that when flights are made within the navigable airspace without any physical invasion of the property of the landowners, there has been no taking of property. It says that at most there was merely incidental damage occurring as a consequence of authorized air navigation. It also argues that the landowner does not own

---

4. "Air commerce" is defined as including "any operation or navigation of aircraft which directly affects, or which may endanger safety in, interstate, overseas, or foreign air commerce." 49 U.S.C., Sec. 401 (3) [repealed by Pub. L. No. 85-726, §1401(5), 72 Stat. 806 (1958)].

superadjacent airspace which he has not subjected to possession by the erection of structures or other occupancy. Moreover, it is argued that even if the United States took airspace owned by respondents, no compensable damage was shown. Any damages are said to be merely consequential for which no compensation may be obtained under the Fifth Amendment.

It is ancient doctrine that at common law ownership of the land extended to the periphery of the universe — Cujus est solum ejus est usque ad coelum.[5] But that doctrine has no place in the modern world. The air is a public highway, as Congress has declared. Were that not true, every transcontinental flight would subject the operator to countless trespass suits. Common sense revolts at the idea. To recognize such private claims to the airspace would clog these highways, seriously interfere with their control and development in the public interest, and transfer into private ownership that to which only the public has a just claim.

But that general principle does not control the present case. For the United States conceded on oral argument that if the flights over respondents' property rendered it uninhabitable, there would be a taking compensable under the Fifth Amendment. It is the owner's loss, not the taker's gain, which is the measure of the value of the property taken. United States v. Miller, 317 U.S. 369, 63 S. Ct. 276. Market value fairly determined is the normal measure of the recovery. Id. And that value may reflect the use to which the land could readily be converted, as well as the existing use. United States v. Powelson, 319 U.S. 266, 275, 63 S. Ct. 1047, and cases cited. If, by reason of the frequency and altitude of the flights, respondents could not use this land for any purpose, their loss would be complete.[6] It would be as complete as if the United States had entered upon the surface of the land and taken exclusive possession of it.

We agree that in those circumstances there would be a taking. Though it would be only an easement of flight which was taken, that easement, if permanent and not merely temporary, normally would be the equivalent of a fee interest. It would be a definite exercise of complete dominion and control over the surface of the land. The fact that the planes never touched the surface would be as irrelevant as the absence in this day of the feudal livery of seisin on the transfer of real estate. The owner's right to possess and exploit the land — that is to say, his beneficial ownership of it — would be destroyed. It would not be a case of incidental damages arising from a legalized nuisance such as was involved in Richards v. Washington Terminal Co., 233 U.S. 546, 34 S. Ct. 654. In that case, property owners whose lands adjoined a railroad line were denied recovery for damages resulting

---

5. 1 Coke, Institutes (19th ed., 1832), Chap. 1, Sec. 1(4a); 2 Blackstone, Commentaries (Lewis ed., 1902), p. 18; 3 Kent, Commentaries (Gould ed., 1896), p. 621.

6. The destruction of all uses of the property by flooding has been held to constitute a taking. Pumpelly v. Green Bay Co., 13 Wall. 166; United States v. Lynah, 188 U.S. 445, 23 S. Ct. 349; United States v. Welch, 217 U.S. 333, 30 S. Ct. 527.

from the noise, vibrations, smoke and the like, incidental to the operations of the trains. In the supposed case, the line of flight is over the land. And the land is appropriated as directly and completely as if it were used for the runways themselves.

There is no material difference between the supposed case and the present one, except that here enjoyment and use of the land are not completely destroyed. But that does not seem to us to be controlling. The path of glide for airplanes might reduce a valuable factory site to grazing land, an orchard to a vegetable patch, a residential section to a wheat field. Some value would remain. But the use of the airspace immediately above the land would limit the utility of the land and cause a diminution in its value.[7] That was the philosophy of Portsmouth Co. v. United States, 260 U.S. 327, 43 S. Ct. 135. In that case the petition alleged that the United States erected a fort on nearby land, established a battery and a fire control station there, and fired guns over petitioner's land. The Court, speaking through Mr. Justice Holmes, reversed the Court of Claims, which dismissed the petition on a demurrer, holding that "the specific facts set forth would warrant a finding that a servitude has been imposed."[8] 260 U.S. p. 330, 43 S. Ct. 135. And see Delta Air Corp. v. Kersey, 193 Ga. 862, 20 S.E. 2d 245. Cf. United States v. 357.25 Acres of Land, 55 F. Supp. 461.

The fact that the path of glide taken by the planes was that approved by the Civil Aeronautics Authority does not change the result. The navigable airspace which Congress has placed in the public domain is "airspace above the minimum safe altitudes of flight prescribed by the Civil Aeronautics Authority." 49 U.S.C., Sec. 180. If that agency prescribed 83 feet as the minimum safe altitude, then we would have presented the question of the validity of the regulation. But nothing of the sort has been done. The path of glide governs the method of operating—of landing or taking off. The altitude required for that operation is not the minimum safe altitude of flight which is the downward reach of the navigable airspace. The minimum prescribed by the Authority is 500 feet during the day and 1,000 feet at night for air carriers (Civil Air Regulations, Pt. 61, Secs. 61.7400, 61.7401, Code

---

7.   It was stated in United States v. General Motors Corp., 323 U.S. 373, 378, 65 S. Ct. 357, 359-360,

> The courts have held that the deprivation of the former owner rather than the accretion of a right or interest to the sovereign constitutes the taking. Governmental action short of acquisition of title or occupancy has been held, if its effects are so complete as to deprive the owner of all or most of his interests in the subject matter, to amount to a taking.

The present case falls short of the *General Motors* case. This is not a case where the United States has merely destroyed property. It is using a part of it for the flight of its planes.
   Cf. Warren Township School Dist. v. Detroit, 308 Mich. 460, 14 N.W.2d 134; Smith v. New England Aircraft Co., 270 Mass. 511, 170 N.E. 385; Burnham v. Beverly Airways, Inc., 311 Mass. 628, 42 N.E.2d 575.
   8.   On remand the allegations in the petition were found not to be supported by the facts. 64 Ct. Cls. 572.

Fed. Reg. Cum. Supp., Tit. 14, ch. 1), and from 300 feet to 1,000 feet for other aircraft, depending on the type of plane and the character of the terrain. Id., Pt. 60, Secs. 60.350-60.3505, Fed. Reg. Cum. Supp., supra. Hence, the flights in question were not within the navigable airspace which Congress placed within the public domain. If any airspace needed for landing or taking off were included, flights which were so close to the land as to render it uninhabitable would be immune. But the United States concedes, as we have said, that in that event there would be a taking. Thus, it is apparent that the path of glide is not the minimum safe altitude of flight within the meaning of the statute. The Civil Aeronautics Authority has, of course, the power to prescribe air traffic rules. But Congress has defined navigable airspace only in terms of one of them — the minimum safe altitudes of flight.

We have said that the airspace is a public highway. Yet it is obvious that if the landowner is to have full enjoyment of the land, he must have exclusive control of the immediate reaches of the enveloping atmosphere. Otherwise buildings could not be erected, trees could not be planted, and even fences could not be run. The principle is recognized when the law gives a remedy in case overhanging structures are erected on adjoining land.[9] The landowner owns at least as much of the space above the ground as he can occupy or use in connection with the land. See Hinman v. Pacific Air Transport, 84 F.2d 755. The fact that he does not occupy it in a physical sense — by the erection of buildings and the like — is not material. As we have said, the flight of airplanes, which skim the surface but do not touch it, is as much an appropriation of the use of the land as a more conventional entry upon it. We would not doubt that, if the United States erected an elevated railway over respondents' land at the precise altitude where its planes now fly, there would be a partial taking, even though none of the supports of the structure rested on the land.[10] The reason is that there would be an intrusion so immediate and direct as to subtract from the owner's full enjoyment of the property and to limit his exploitation of it. While the owner does not in any physical manner occupy that stratum of airspace or make use of it in the

---

9. Baten's Case, 9 Coke R. 53b; Meyer v. Metzler, 51 Cal. 142; Codman v. Evans, 89 Mass. 431; Harrington v. McCarthy, 169 Mass. 492, 48 N.E. 278. See Ball, The Vertical Extent of Ownership in Land, 76 U. Pa. L. Rev. 631, 658-671.

10. It was held in Butler v. Frontier Telephone Co., 186 N.Y. 486, 79 N.E. 716, that ejectment would lie where a telephone wire was strung across the plaintiff's property, even though it did not touch the soil. The court stated, pp. 491-492 of 186 N.Y., page 718 of 79 N.E.:

. . . an owner is entitled to the absolute and undisturbed possession of every part of his premises, including the space above, as much as a mine beneath. If the wire had been a huge cable, several inches thick and but a foot above the ground, there would have been a difference in degree, but not in principle. Expand the wire into a beam supported by posts standing upon abutting lots without touching the surface of plaintiff's land, and the difference would still be one of degree only. Enlarge the beam into a bridge, and yet space only would be occupied. Erect a house upon the bridge, and the air above the surface of the land would alone be disturbed.

conventional sense, he does use it in somewhat the same sense that space left between buildings for the purpose of light and air is used. The superadjacent airspace at this low altitude is so close to the land that continuous invasions of it affect the use of the surface of the land itself. We think that the landowner, as an incident to his ownership, has a claim to it and that invasions of it are in the same category as invasions of the surface.[11]

In this case, as in Portsmouth Co. v. United States, *supra*, the damages were not merely consequential. They were the product of a direct invasion of respondents' domain. As stated in United States v. Cress, 243 U.S. 316, 328, 37 S. Ct. 380, 385, ". . . it is the character of the invasion, not the amount of damage resulting from it, so long as the damage is substantial, that determines the question whether it is a taking."

We said in United States v. Powelson, *supra*, 319 U.S. at page 279, 63 S. Ct. at page 1054, that while the meaning of "property" as used in the Fifth Amendment was a federal question, "It will normally obtain its content by reference to local law." If we look to North Carolina law, we reach the same result. Sovereignty in the airspace rests in the State "except where granted to and assumed by the United States." Gen. Stats. 1943, Sec. 63-11. The flight of aircraft is lawful "unless at such a low altitude as to interfere with the then existing use to which the land or water, or the space over the land or water, is put by the owner, or unless so conducted as to be imminently dangerous to persons or property lawfully on the land or water beneath." Id., Sec. 63-13. Subject to that right of flight, "ownership of the space above the lands and waters of this State is declared to be vested in the several owners of the surface beneath. . . ." Id., Sec. 63-12. Our holding that there was an invasion of respondents' property is thus not inconsistent with the local law governing a landowner's claim to the immediate reaches of the superadjacent airspace.

The airplane is part of the modern environment of life, and the inconveniences which it causes are normally not compensable under the Fifth Amendment. The airspace, apart from the immediate reaches above the land, is part of the public domain. We need not determine at this time what those precise limits are. Flights over private land are not a taking, unless they are so low and so frequent as to be a direct and immediate interference with the enjoyment and use of the land. We need not speculate on that phase of the present case. For the findings of the Court of Claims plainly establish that there was a diminution in value of the property and that the frequent, low-level flights were the direct and immediate cause. We agree with the Court of Claims that a servitude has been imposed upon the land.

II. By Sec. 145(1) of the Judicial Code, 28 U.S.C. Sec. 250(1), the Court of Claims has jurisdiction to hear and determine "All claims (except for

---

11. See Bouve, Private Ownership of Navigable Airspace Under the Commerce Clause, 21 Amer. Bar Assoc. Journ. 416, 421-422; Hise, Ownership and Sovereignty of the Air, 16 Ia. L. Rev. 169; Eubank, The Doctrine of the Airspace Zone of Effective Possession, 12 Boston Univ. L. Rev. 414.

pensions) founded upon the Constitution of the United States or . . . upon any contract, express or implied, with the Government of the United States . . ."

We need not decide whether repeated trespasses might give rise to an implied contract. Cf. Portsmouth Co. v. United States, *supra.* If there is a taking, the claim is "founded upon the Constitution" and within the jurisdiction of the Court of Claims to hear and determine. See Hollister v. Benedict Mfg. Co., 113 U.S. 59, 67, 5 S. Ct. 717, 721; Hurley v. Kincaid, 285 U.S. 95, 104, 52 S. Ct. 267, 269; Yearsley v. Ross Construction Co., 309 U.S. 18, 21, 60 S. Ct. 413, 415. Thus, the jurisdiction of the Court of Claims in this case is clear.

III. The Court of Claims held, as we have noted, that an easement was taken. But the findings of fact contain no precise description as to its nature. It is not described in terms of frequency of flight, permissible altitude, or type of airplane. Nor is there a finding as to whether the easement taken was temporary or permanent. Yet an accurate description of the property taken is essential, since that interest vests in the United States. United States v. Cress, *supra,* 328-329, 37 S. Ct. 385, 386 and cases cited. It is true that the Court of Claims stated in its opinion that the easement taken was permanent. But the deficiency in findings cannot be rectified by statements in the opinion. United States v. Esnault-Pelterie, 299 U.S. 201, 205-206, 57 S. Ct. 159, 161, 162; United States v. Seminole Nation, 299 U.S. 417, 422, 57 S. Ct. 283, 287. Findings of fact on every "material issue" are a statutory requirement. 53 Stat. 752, 28 U.S.C. Sec. 288. The importance of findings of fact based on evidence is emphasized here by the Court of Claims' treatment of the nature of the easement. It stated in its opinion that the easement was permanent because the United States "no doubt intended to make some sort of arrangement whereby it could use the airport for its military planes whenever it had occasion to do so." That sounds more like conjecture rather than a conclusion from evidence; and if so, it would not be a proper foundation for liability of the United States. We do not stop to examine the evidence to determine whether it would support such a finding, if made. For that is not our function. United States v. Esnault-Pelterie, *supra,* 299 U.S. at page 206, 57 S. Ct. at page 162.

Since on this record it is not clear whether the easement taken is a permanent or a temporary one, it would be premature for us to consider whether the amount of the award made by the Court of Claims was proper.

The judgment is reversed and the cause is remanded to the Court of Claims so that it may make the necessary findings in conformity with this opinion.

Reversed.

Mr. Justice JACKSON took no part in the consideration or decision of this case.

Mr. Justice BLACK, dissenting. . . .

The Court's opinion seems to indicate that the mere flying of planes through the column of air directly above the respondents' land does not constitute a "taking." Consequently, it appears to be noise and glare, to the extent and under the circumstances shown here, which make the Government a seizer of private property. But the allegation of noise and glare resulting in damages, constitutes at best an action in tort where there might be recovery if the noise and light constituted a nuisance, a violation of a statute,[12] or were the result of negligence.[13] But the Government has not consented to be sued in the Court of Claims except in actions based on express or implied contract. And there is no implied contract here, unless by reason of the noise and glare caused by the bombers the Government can be said to have "taken" respondents' property in a constitutional sense. The concept of taking property as used in the Constitution has heretofore never been given so sweeping a meaning. The Court's opinion presents no case where a man who makes noise or shines light onto his neighbor's property has been ejected from that property for wrongfully taking possession of it. Nor would anyone take seriously a claim that noisy automobiles passing on a highway are taking wrongful possession of the homes located thereon, or that a city elevated train which greatly interferes with the sleep of those who live next to it wrongfully takes their property. Even the one case in this Court which in considering the sufficiency of a complaint gave the most elastic meaning to the phrase "private property be taken" as used in the Fifth Amendment, did not go so far. Portsmouth Co. v. United States, 260 U.S. 327, 43 S. Ct. 135. I am not willing, nor do I think the Constitution and the decisions authorize me, to extend that phrase so as to guarantee an absolute constitutional right to relief not subject to legislative change, which is based on averments that at best show mere torts committed by government agents while flying over land. The future adjustment of the rights and remedies of property owners, which might be found necessary because of the flight of planes at safe altitudes, should, especially in view of the imminent expansion of air navigation, be left where I think the Constitution left it, with Congress.

Nor do I reach a different conclusion because of the fact that the particular circumstance which under the Court's opinion makes the tort here absolutely actionable, is the passing of planes through a column of air at

---

12.   Neiswonger v. Goodyear Tire & Rubber Co., 35 F.2d 761.

13.   As to the damage to chickens, Judge Madden, dissenting from this judgment against the Government, said,

> When railroads were new, cattle in fields in sight and hearing of the trains were alarmed, thinking that the great moving objects would turn aside and harm them. Horses ran away at the sight and sound of a train or a threshing machine engine. The farmer's chickens have to get over being alarmed at the incredible racket of the tractor starting up suddenly in the shed adjoining the chicken house. These sights and noises are a part of our world, and airplanes are now and will be to a greater degree, likewise a part of it. These disturbances should not be treated as torts, in the case of the airplane, any more than they are so treated in the case of the railroad or public highway. [104 Ct. Cls. 342, 358.]

an elevation of eighty-three feet directly over respondent's property. It is inconceivable to me that the Constitution guarantees that the air space of this Nation needed for air navigation is owned by the particular persons who happen to own the land beneath to the same degree as they own the surface below.[14]. . .

The broad provisions of the congressional statute cannot properly be circumscribed by making a distinction, as the Court's opinion does, between rules of safe altitude of flight while on the level of cross-country flight and rules of safe altitude during landing and taking off. First, such a distinction cannot be maintained from the practical standpoint. It is unlikely that Congress intended that the Authority prescribe safe altitudes for planes making cross-country flights, while at the same time it left the more hazardous landing and take-off operations unregulated. The legislative history, moreover, clearly shows that the Authority's power to prescribe air traffic rules includes the power to make rules governing landing and take-off. Nor is the Court justified in ignoring that history by labeling rules of safe altitude while on the level of cross-country flight as rules prescribing the safe altitude proper and rules governing take-off and landing as rules of operation. For the Conference Report explicitly states that such distinctions were purposely eliminated from the original House Bill in order that the Section on air traffic rules "might be given the broadest possible construction by the . . . (Civil Aeronautics Authority) and the courts."[15] In construing the statute narrowly, the Court thwarts the intent of Congress. A proper broad

---

14.   The House in its report on the Air Commerce Act of 1926 stated:

The public right of flight in the navigable air space owes its source to the same constitutional basis which, under decisions of the Supreme Court, has given rise to a public easement of navigation in the navigable waters of the United States, regardless of the ownership of the adjacent or subjacent soil. [H. Rep. No. 572, 69th Cong., 1st Sess., p. 10.]

15.   The full statement reads:

The substitute provides that the Secretary shall by regulation establish air traffic rules for the navigation, protection, and identification of all aircraft, including rules as to safe altitudes of flight and rules for the prevention of collisions between vessels and aircraft. The provision as to rules for taking off and alighting, for instance, was eliminated as unnecessary specification, for the reason that such rules are but one class of air traffic rules for the navigation and protection of aircraft. Rules as to marking were eliminated for the reason that such rules were fairly included within the scope of air rules for the identification of aircraft. No attempt is made by either the Senate bill or the House amendment to fully define the various classes of rules that would fall within the scope of air traffic [sic] rules, as, for instance, lights and signals along airways and at air-ports and upon emergency landing fields. In general, these rules would relate to the same subjects as those covered by navigation laws and regulations and by various State motor vehicle traffic codes. As noted above, surplusage was eliminated in specifying particular air traffic rules in order that the term might be given the broadest possible construction by the Department of Commerce and the courts. [H. Rep. No. 1162, 69th Cong., 1st Sess., p. 12.]

That the rules for landing and take-off are rules prescribing "minimum safe altitudes of flight" is shown by the following further statement in the House Report: ". . . the minimum safe altitudes of flight . . . would vary with the terrene [terrain] and location of cities and would coincide with the surface of the land or water at airports." Id. at p. 14.

construction, such as Congress commanded, would not permit the Court to decide what it has today without declaring the Act of Congress unconstitutional. I think the Act given the broad construction intended is unconstitutional.

No greater confusion could be brought about in the coming age of air transportation than that which would result were courts by constitutional interpretation to hamper Congress in its efforts to keep the air free. Old concepts of private ownership of land should not be introduced into the field of air regulation. I have no doubt that Congress will, if not handicapped by judicial interpretations of the Constitution, preserve the freedom of the air, and at the same time, satisfy the just claims of aggrieved persons. The noise of newer, larger, and more powerful planes may grow louder and louder and disturb people more and more. But the solution of the problems precipitated by these technological advances and new ways of living cannot come about through the application of rigid constitutional restraints formulated and enforced by the courts. What adjustments may have to be made, only the future can reveal. It seems certain, however, that courts do not possess the techniques of the personnel to consider and act upon the complex combinations of factors entering into the problems. The contribution of courts must be made through the awarding of damages for injuries suffered from the flying of planes, or by the granting of injunctions to prohibit their flying. When these two simple remedial devices are elevated to a constitutional level under the Fifth Amendment, as the Court today seems to have done, they can stand as obstacles to better adapted techniques that might be offered by experienced experts and accepted by Congress. Today's opinion is, I fear, an opening wedge for an unwarranted judicial interference with the power of Congress to develop solutions for new and vital national problems. In my opinion this case should be reversed on the ground that there has been no "taking" in the constitutional sense.[16]

Mr. Justice BURTON joins in this dissent.

FERGUSON v. CITY OF KEENE
108 N.H. 409, 238 A.2d 1. (1968)

DUNCAN, J.

The defendant's airport, known as the Dillant-Hopkins airport, was established in 1942. In 1947, the plaintiff purchased certain real estate, including her residence, located southerly of the north-south runway of the airport. In 1956 the city took a part of the westerly portion of plaintiff's land

---

16. For a discussion of the problem of conflicting interests and of zoning as a possible solution, see Hunter, The Conflicting Interests of Airport Owner and Nearby Property Owner, 11 Law & Contemp. Probs. 539 (1946). See also Note: Inverse Condemnation, Chapter 33. — EDS.

in order to lengthen the runway, which in 1959 and 1962 was extended a distance of a thousand feet, so that its southerly end is now located a few hundred feet west of the plaintiff's house.

The writ alleges that the use of a "warmup apron" located opposite the plaintiff's house resulted in 1963 and 1964 in such noise and vibration as to cause windows in the house to break, and to make conversation or sleep in the house impossible and life therein generally "unbearable." The writ alleges that this use of the airport "constitutes a taking and appropriation" of the plaintiff's property for which the defendant has refused to compensate her.

It is the settled law of this jurisdiction that a municipality, like any property owner, is bound to use its property in a reasonable manner, and is liable if its use results in a private nuisance. O'Brien v. Derry, 73 N.H. 198, 204, 60 A. 843; Proulx v. Kenne, 102 N.H. 427, 430-431, 158 A.2d 455; Webb v. Town of Rye, 108 N.H. 147, 150, 230 A.2d 223. The defendant contends however that no taking of the plaintiff's property can properly be alleged, since she admits that the flight path of aircraft does not cross it, and damage alone without any actual taking requires no compensation. United States v. Willow River Power Co., 324 U.S. 499, 510, 65 S. Ct. 761, 89 L. Ed. 1101. The defendant further argues that its use of the airport is "proper," and that subjection of airports to liability for claims such as this would unduly impede the progress of air transportation in the state.

The plaintiff asserts that the allegations of its writ include all of the classic elements of nuisance (Restatement, Torts, s. 822; see McKinney v. Riley, 105 N.H. 249, 251, 197 A.2d 218) and also that the defendant's conduct of the airport gives rise to a cause of action for "inverse condemnation," even though no overflights occur. Thornburg v. Port of Portland, 233 Or. 178, 376 P.2d 100; Martin v. Port of Seattle, 64 Wash. 2d 309, 391 P.2d 540. See City of Charlotte v. Spratt, 263 N.C. 656, 140 S.E.2d 341; City of Jacksonville v. Schumann (Fla.), 167 So. 2d 95; State ex rel. Royal v. City of Columbus, 3 Ohio St. 2d 154, 209 N.E.2d 405.

Inverse condemnation is a term used to describe "a cause of action against a governmental defendant to recover the value of property which has been taken in fact by the governmental defendant, even though no formal exercise of the power of eminent domain has been attempted by the taking agency." City of Jacksonville v. Schumann, *supra,* 167 So. 2d 98; City of Charlotte v. Spratt, 263 N.C. 656, *supra,* 663, 140 S.E.2d 341. See Hillsborough County Aviation Auth. v. Benitez (Fla. App.), 200 So. 2d 194. While in this jurisdiction the doctrine may not have been adverted to under that name, it is not unknown to our jurisprudence. Eaton v. B.C. & M.R.R., 51 N.H. 504, 510-516. See Van Alstyne, Statutory Modification of Inverse Condemnation, 19 Stanford L. Rev. 727, 738-768; Mandelker, Inverse Condemnation. The Constitutional Limits of Public Responsibility, 1966 Wis. L. Rev. 3, 18-19.

Pertinent cases decided by the United States Supreme Court have not gone beyond the point of holding that there may be recovery in inverse condemnation for damages occasioned by direct flights of aircraft over a claimant's property. United States v. Causby, 328 U.S. 256, 66 S. Ct. 1062, 90 L. Ed. 1206; Griggs v. Allegheny County, 369 U.S. 84, 82 S. Ct. 531, 7 L. Ed. 2d 585. As was pointed out in Dunham, Griggs v. Allegheny County in Perspective: Thirty Years of Supreme Court Expropriation Law, 1962 Supreme Court Review 63:

> The question whether those [claimants] adjacent to airports, but not in any flight path, should be compensated thus remains an open one so far as the Supreme Court decisions are concerned. But the logic of *Causby* and its idea of fairness would seem to require compensation even where planes do not fly directly over the objector's land. [Id., 88.]

However, in Batten v. United States, 306 F.2d 580 (10th Cir. 1962) the Court of Appeals declined to extend the doctrine to a case where overflights did not occur, relying upon United States v. Willow River Power Co., 324 U.S. 499, 65 S. Ct. 761, 89 L. Ed. 1101, *supra,* and the proposition that the Federal Constitution requires compensation for a "taking" only. This decision the United States Supreme Court declined to review on certiorari. Batten v. United States, 371 U.S. 955, 83 S. Ct. 506, 9 L. Ed. 2d 502.

The courts of at least two states proceeding under their own constitutions, have permitted recovery in cases where overflights were not involved. Thornburg v. Port of Portland, 233 Or. 178, 376 P.2d 100, *supra;* Martin v. Port of Seattle, 64 Wash. 2d 309, 391 P.2d 540, *supra.* See also, Thornburg v. Port of Portland, 244 Or. 69, 415 P.2d 750; 2 Nichols on Eminent Domain (3d ed.) s. 5.781; Annot. 77 A.L.R.2d 1355. They do not agree however upon the standards to be applied in determining when a taking has occurred, and the cases have been critically received by some commentators. See Spater, Noise and the Law, 63 Mich. L. Rev. 1373, 1404-1406 (1965). Moreover the Constitution of the State of Washington requires compensation for a "damaging" of property as well as a "taking," in this respect differing from both the Constitution of the United States and that of New Hampshire. See, N.H. Const., Pt. I, Art. 12.

"Since there is hardly a government act which could not cause someone substantial damage, an arbitrary boundary line must be drawn between compensable and non-compensable injury." Spater, *supra,* 1385-1386. Under the Federal Constitution, the line has been drawn at compensation for a taking of property. "The Fifth Amendment . . . requires just compensation where private property is taken for public use . . . [but] does not undertake . . . to socialize all losses. . . ." United States v. Willow River Power Co., 324 U.S. 499, *supra,* 502, 65 S. Ct. 761, 764, 89 L. Ed. 1101. See Batten v. United States, 306 F.2d 580, *supra.* Thus compensation is limited to recovery for "direct and immediate interference with enjoyment and use" by frequent low-level overflights. United States v. Causby, 328 U.S. 256, 66

S. Ct. 1062, 90 L. Ed. 1206, *supra.* See, Avery v. United States, 330 F.2d 640, 165 Ct. Cl. 357, 1964; A. J. Hodges Industries, Inc., 355 F.2d 592, 174 Ct. Cl. 259, 1966. See also, Note, Airplane Noise, 65 Col. L. Rev. 1428, 1431, 1432.

A genuine distinction may reasonably be thought to exist between the nature of the injury suffered by the owner whose land is subjected to direct overflight, and that suffered by his neighbor whose land is not beneath the flight path. Only the former has lost the use of the airspace above his land, and he is subjected to risks of physical damage and injury not shared by the latter. Specter, *supra,* 1394-1395.

While our Constitution may not preclude application of the doctrine of inverse condemnation to cases not involving overflights (See Eaton v. B.C. & M.R.R., 51 N.H. 504, *supra*), the "difficult questions which have arisen from attempts to define the requisite elements of the taking bear witness to the unsuitability of dealing with the problem of airplane noise by enforcing constitutionally-based claims." Note, 65 Col. L. Rev. 1428, *supra,* 1447. In holding that where no property is appropriated there may be no recovery for consequential damage due to noise, smoke, and vibrations incident to proximity to a railroad, in Richards v. Washington Terminal Co., 233 U.S. 546, 555, 34 S. Ct. 654, 657, 58 L. Ed. 1088, the Court said: "The doctrine has become so well established that it amounts to a rule of property, and should be modified, if at all, only by the law-making power."

To what extent the nuisance of which the plaintiff complains is essential to the public use of the defendant's airport is a question which is not determinable at this stage of this litigation. The question whether a defendant in circumstances such as these should be compelled by inverse condemnation to acquire an "easement" and compensate the plaintiff therefor (See Causby v. United States, 75 F. Supp. 262, 109 Ct. Cl. 768, 1948) presents issues of social policy which might well be the subject of legislative study and appropriate enactment. See Van Alstyne, Statutory Modification of Inverse Condemnation, 19 Stanford L. Rev. 727 *supra,* 738 (1967).

For purposes of this case, we hold that the plaintiff's writ and declaration fail to state a cause of action in inverse condemnation for want of any claim of overflights, but that a cause of action in nuisance is sufficiently alleged.

Exception overruled; remanded.

GRIMES, J., dissented; the others concurred.

GRIMES, J. (dissenting).

The plaintiff's writ alleges that "the noise from the planes 'warming up' for take off, make such a great amount of noise that it is impossible for the people in the house to converse or talk on the telephone, the house vibrates and the glass in windows shake and that more than 20 panes of glass have been broken by said vibration in the winter of 1963-1964, that it is often times impossible to sleep and there is no peace or quiet in their home and that life has become unbearable because of said noise."

The majority of the court says this declaration does not set forth a cause of action based on inverse condemnation. I disagree.

Our court long ago decided that in our state at least, the term "property" refers to "the right of any person to possess, use, enjoy and dispose of a thing" and is not limited to the thing itself, and that a person's property is "taken" for public use so as to entitle him to "just compensation" under our constitution when a physical interference substantially subverts one of these rights even though the thing itself is not taken. Eaton v. B.C. & M.R.R., 51 N.H. 504, 511 (1872). The majority opinion recognizes that the Eaton case applied the principle of what is now called "inverse condemnation."

The *Eaton* case also holds that the plaintiff may recover whether he is being "wholly deprived of the use of his land or only partially deprived of it." Id. 512. Also under *Eaton,* the plaintiff's right of recovery is not defeated because the defendant's activities are "proper." Id. 515, 516.

Surely the sound waves invading the plaintiff's property in the case before us constitute as much of a physical interference with his use as the water which occasionally entered upon the plaintiff's land in the Eaton case. But in any event I think a distinction based upon the nature of the invasion rather than the effect of it is unjustified. Batten v. United States, 306 F.2d 580, 585 dissenting opinion. Even the majority in the *Batten* case recognizes this but would restrict recovery to cases involving complete deprivation of use, a doctrine which was rejected in *Eaton.*

The court cites Batten v. United States *supra,* but in my judgment our *Eaton* case answers every proposition upon which the majority opinion in *Batten* is based. In addition, *Eaton* establishes a right in the plaintiff under our own constitution quite independent of the Constitution of the United States upon which Mr. Batten relied.

The declaration in the case at bar alleges that the sound waves from the planes invade plaintiff's premises to the extent that conversation, telephoning and sleep are not only difficult but impossible and also that they cause actual physical damage to the house itself. Twenty window panes broken in one winter is no trivial interference and we have no way of knowing without evidence what the long-range effect of the vibration and shaking of the house will have upon it. Certainly the declaration alleges more than mere inconvenience or annoyance for which I agree no recovery can be had.

Here we have allegations of interference with use and enjoyment which unquestionably is "sufficiently direct, sufficiently peculiar, and of sufficient magnitude to cause us to conclude that fairness and justice, as between the State and the citizen, requires the burden imposed to be borne by the public and not by the individual alone." Batten v. United States *supra* (Murrah, Chief Judge, dissenting).

The difficulty in determining where to draw the line between such a substantial interference with use as to constitute a taking and that which does not should not deter us from permitting recovery in a clear case. Eaton

v. B.C. & M.R.R. *supra,* 51 N.H. 521. Nor should any policy consideration relating to the public need for airports affect our decision. I agree with Judge Smith when ninety-six years ago he said that great public convenience and benefit "may afford an excellent reason for taking the plaintiff's land in the constitutional manner, but not for taking it without compensation. If the work is one of great public benefit, the public can afford to pay for it." Eaton v. B.C. & M.R.R., *supra,* 518.

The plaintiff's right to compensation cannot be made to depend upon legislative benevolence, as the majority suggest, as it is a right to which he is entitled under the Constitution. Eaton v. B.C. & M.R.R., *supra,* 510, 511; New Hampshire Water Resources Board v. Pera, 108 N.H. 18, 226 A.2d 774.

I am unimpressed with the rationale of those cases which confine inverse condemnation to overflights. A person's property rights can be damaged as greatly by sound waves traveling horizontally as by those traveling vertically, and to draw a distinction is to ignore reality.

We are dealing here with an important and fundamental individual right, the roots of which reach back to Magna Carta. It is one which deserves to be stoutly defended and liberally construed. It is one which we should not deny to this plaintiff because the means by which her property was taken was neither known to nor foreseen by the Barons of England or the Framers of our Constitution.

The court while denying the constitutional right has at least recognized that the plaintiff has set forth a cause of action based on nuisance. This I think is a poor substitute from the standpoint of both parties.

Problems

36.1. A's country home is situated next to an airport. The prevailing wind is such that planes landing and taking off from the airfield pass over A's land at low altitudes, considerably below the minimum safe altitude prescribed for level flight. The planes pass over a section of A's land which is unused and at some distance from her house. The noise is irritating to occupants of the house but does not substantially impair their use and enjoyment of it. May A enjoin the low flights over her land? Smith v. New England Aircraft Co., 270 Mass. 511, 170 N.E. 385 (1930).

36.2. A sells a right-of-way to an electric company which begins to run a high-voltage, uninsulated power line 90 feet high along the right-of-way. The power line, if completed, will be in the line of approach to the main runway of an adjoining airfield. The Uniform State Law for Aeronautics is in force and provides as follows:

Section 4. Flight in aircraft over the lands and waters of this State is lawful, unless at such a low altitude as to interfere with the then existing use to which the land or water, or the space over the land or water, is put by the owner, or unless so conducted as to be imminently dangerous to persons or property lawfully on the land or water beneath. . . .

May the airport enjoin the construction of the power line? Capitol Airways, Inc. v. Indianapolis Power & Light Co., 215 Ind. 462, 18 N.E.2d 776 (1939).

What if an obstruction were erected by A solely to force the airport to buy A's land on A's terms? See United Airports Co. v. Hinman, 1940 U.S. Av. R. 1 (S.D. Cal. 1939).

PART X

TAXATION

CHAPTER 37

A-B-C OF TAXES FOR PROPERTY LAWYERS
(As of March 1984)

No one can wisely engage in an important property transaction today without considering the tax consequences with a view to determining whether unnecessary tax burdens are being assumed. With this in mind, we have concluded that you should have some picture of the impact of taxation on property dealings at the beginning of your law school course.

Do not get the idea that a reading of the material which follows qualifies you to advise on tax issues. Our purpose is not that. We aim only to acquaint you with the elements of the tax structure sufficiently to let you understand something about the tax aspects of the property problems we shall consider. Later, your course in taxation will give the comprehensive understanding that is a professional necessity.

Tax laws are statutes, enacted under constitutional restrictions, and interpreted by administrative bodies and the courts. For answers to specific questions, go to these sources and to the professional aids which are particularly abundant in this field. The federal tax laws with which this discussion deals are found in the United States Internal Revenue Code (IRC).

Two specific warnings are here appropriate. (1) Any statement about taxes may become obsolete before it can be printed. The tax laws are continually amended — more frequently than any other type of legislation. For example in recent years we have had the Tax Reform Act of 1969, the Revenue Act of 1971, the Tax Reduction Act of 1975, the Tax Reform Act of 1976, the Tax Reduction and Simplification Bill of 1977, the Technical Corrections Act of 1978, The Technical Corrections Act of 1979, the Crude Oil Windfall Profit Tax Act of 1980, the Economic Recovery Tax Act of 1981, the Tax Equity and Fiscal Responsibility Act of 1982 (TEFRA), the Subchapter S Revision Bill of 1982, the Technical Corrections Act of 1982, and the Technical Corrections Act of 1983. (2) In making a simplified statement we necessarily omit qualifications and exceptions essential to professional accuracy. We try not to mislead you, but a characteristic of tax law is the meticulous detail in which it is elaborated, and therefore any general statement can be misleading to a reader who does not keep this basic fact in mind. Also, we describe here the tax law as it is at the beginning of 1984; past property transactions would be governed by the tax law in effect when those transactions took place.

SECTION 1.   TAXATION AS A FUNCTION OF GOVERNMENT

A.   Purposes of Taxation

The principal purpose of taxation is to raise revenue to support various governmental activities. However, taxation can also be used, and has increasingly been used, as a means of attaining political, economic, and social ends — for example, protecting local industries against foreign competition, improving the competitive position of butter as against oleomargarine, reducing purchasing power to combat inflation, making tax cuts to stimulate the economy. There are those who believe that the level of revenue-raising taxation is stifling our system of private property and free enterprise and that regulatory taxation is compounding the damage. Others proclaim that capitalism is being saved from itself by wise taxation measures. You will have to find your place in this dispute after your knowledge of the subject is sufficiently comprehensive.

Our discussion deals with revenue-raising taxation, although it must be recognized that any graduated tax (i.e., a tax where the *rate* increases with the amount of income or property being taxed) has a politico-socioeconomic tendency to eliminate large fortunes and large incomes. Such graduated taxes tend to reduce concentration of economic power; they also tend to reduce individual incentive to put forth great efforts.

B.   Who Imposes Taxes?

The federal government is the biggest tax collector in the United States. The elephantine growth of federal taxes began in 1941 as we approached World War II and it has been nourished subsequent to World War II by high defense expenditures and foreign aid assistance in carrying out the responsibilities of world leadership which we have assumed.

Each state government has its own tax system to support the governmental activities of the state. State taxes have climbed appreciably, if not spectacularly, over the years. The current enormous expenditures by the federal government, however, have resulted in a tremendous upward surge of the power of the federal government, and by comparison a decline in the significance of the power of the states.

Municipal governments and agencies—cities, towns, school districts, drainage districts, etc.—raise revenue by taxation to support their local activities. Local taxes have also been on the upswing in recent years in most areas.

C. What Is Taxed?

The federal government obtains most of its revenue from the income tax. The balance of its revenue comes from estate taxes, gift taxes, and various excise taxes.

The state governments rely heavily for their revenue on taxes on sales, on income, and on gasoline.

Municipal governments support themselves mainly out of the taxes collected on real estate. A few cities in recent years have adopted a municipal income tax which has produced substantial revenue. Other typical municipal taxes which contribute to the local revenue are levies on personal property, licenses, franchises, sales, etc.

The above sketch of federal, state, and local taxation should make it apparent that it is difficult to spend a dollar without paying a tax of some sort. Many of these taxes are hidden, since the tax is paid by someone else who passes it on through an increased price. Other taxes reach the taxpayer in the form of specific bills which leave an all-too-clear imprint on the mind.

SECTION 2. INCOME TAXES—FEDERAL AND STATE, INDIVIDUAL AND CORPORATION

The Federal Individual Income Tax

This is a graduated tax on the net income of individuals. It raises the following questions:
A. What is returnable as an individual's gross income? (Special treatment is given to capital gains and losses.)
B. What is deductible from gross income to produce taxable income?
C. How is the tax computed?
D. How is the tax paid?

You will find the following discussion more illuminating if you get a copy of the current version of the U.S. individual income tax return, see how it is set up, and see where various items which we mention fit into the return. Such a return can be obtained at the office of any federal collector of internal revenue, and most banks can give you one.

A. What Is Income?

Generally what you earn through your efforts and what is yielded by your investments comprise your gross income. Thus, salaries, wages, royalties, profits from running a business, rents, dividends, and interest are all income.

Gifts are not income. Thus, what someone leaves you in a will or gives you inter vivos need not be included in your return. But of course dividends and interest earned by property which you have received by gift is income to you. So also is income (as distinguished from principal) of a trust that you receive from a trustee. You will learn in your course in taxation, however, that some distributions of principal by a trustee or executor of an estate will subject the distributee to an income tax. The complex problems of income taxation of beneficiaries of trusts and estates is beyond the scope of this presentation.[1]

Here are some borderline matters which arise quite frequently:

1. Bonuses paid to employees at the end of the year are income. So also are tips received by a waiter or taxi driver. These look like gifts but are so related to employment as to be treated as earnings. Voluntary payments made to the spouse of a deceased employee by the former employer may be income to such spouse.

2. Refrigerators, automobiles, boxes of candy, or anything else won in a radio or other similar contest are usually returnable as income by the winner at market value. Again these look like gifts; but some participation is usually required of the winner, and the tax authorities rule that the chance of winning is compensation for the participation and that the prizes are therefore earnings.

3. If an individual pays alimony to an ex-spouse in monthly installments, this is returnable by the payee and deductible by the payor. But there is no income to the payee or deduction for the payor where (a) alimony is paid in a lump sum, or (b) the payments are made as support for children, instead of alimony. It is obvious that financial arrangements upon a divorce must be negotiated and divorce decrees drafted with these distinctions in mind.

4. The amount by which gambling winnings exceed losses for the year is

---

1. Income taxation of estates and trusts is considered in Casner, Estate Planning chs. 4, 12 (4th student ed. 1979, Supp. 1982; 4th lawyers' ed. 1980, Supp. 1983).

returnable as income. Neglect of this principle is the reason for several highly publicized citizens becoming long-term boarders of Uncle Sam.

Is there any compensation or return from investments which is exempt? Yes. An example is the exclusion from gross income of a limited amount of compensation received because of personal injuries or sickness. However, the most important tax-exempt income comprises interest on bonds of the states, of municipalities, and of various units of state government like school districts, counties, and sanitary districts. These are in great demand among the wealthy, for, to a person with an income which puts him or her in a 50 percent tax bracket, it is obvious that a tax-exempt municipal bond with a 5 percent yield will give such a person more spendable income than a corporate bond with a 9 percent yield.

Can a person ever be required to include in his or her tax return income which has not been received and to which such person is not entitled? Yes indeed. Generally speaking this is true when a person has made a gift of property but has kept some strings on it. The reason for charging such a person with this income is apparent when you realize that the rate of income tax increases as the amount of income increases, so that the total tax on two separate $20,000 incomes is less than the tax on one $40,000 income. The following cases are typical:

1. *Assignment of income.* H (a husband) is earning $50,000 a year, and his son is earning $5,000. H assigns to his son the right to receive $20,000 of H's income for the next year. H hopes that the result will be that H will return an income of $30,000 and his son an income of $25,000—which would produce a much lower total tax than H returning $50,000 and his son $5,000. But the Internal Revenue Code does not permit this. H is still chargeable with the $20,000 of income he has assigned. This is referred to as an anticipatory assignment of income.

2. *Revocable trust.* W (a wife), having a large earned income and owning 1,000 shares of General Motors, transfers the GM stock to a trustee in trust to pay the income to her daughter, D, for life and then to distribute the principal to D's children. (If this were the whole transaction, W would pay a gift tax, but the GM dividends would thereafter be returnable as income by D.) W adds a provision in the trust to the effect that W may revoke the trust at any time. This causes the income from the GM stock to be chargeable to W even though she never revokes the trust, and D in fact receives all of it. Each payment of income to D is a completed gift from W for gift tax purposes. As long as W's power to revoke remains in existence, she will not have made a completed gift for gift tax purposes of the property held by the trustee.

3. *Short-term trust.* W, from the previous illustration, transfers the GM stock irrevocably to a trustee for five years, to pay the income during

those five years to D. Same result — it is still W's income. Do you see why W should not be allowed to escape income taxes by creating a short-term trust even though the trust is irrevocable for the term? If the trust income is irrevocably payable to D for ten years, the income will be taxable to D, not to W. This arbitrary ten-year period is fixed by statute.[2] Whether the trust is for five years or ten years, however, W will have made a completed gift for gift tax purposes of the value of the term interest under the trust. The income and gift tax consequences of a short-term trust should be contrasted with such tax consequences of an interest-free loan by W to D (the Supreme Court of the United States has held that the lender makes a gift for gift tax purposes when the lender makes an interest-free loan).[3]

If a trust is created by will, or by an inter vivos instrument in which the person creating it so divorces himself or herself from the transferred property that the income will not be taxed to him or her to whom is the income of the trust taxable? If a beneficiary is entitled to receive the income — and this is usual — the beneficiary must include it in the beneficiary's tax return; but if the trustee has discretion not to pay the income to the beneficiary and does not in fact pay it, then the income is returnable by the trustee, not by the beneficiary. If the income is returnable by the trustee, the tax may be considerably smaller, since the beneficiary may have substantial other income which would push income received from the trustee into a higher tax bracket, whereas the trust is a separate entity for income tax purposes and has no income but that of the trust. Suppose, however, the trustee distributes the accumulated income to the beneficiary in a later year. Will the beneficiary have to treat such accumulation distribution as income? The income tax law contains what is called a throwback rule to deal with this situation. Under the throwback rule, accumulated income, when distributed, is taxed to the beneficiary under special rules set out in the Internal Revenue Code that avoid all such income being bunched in one taxable year of the distributee (any tax previously paid by the trust on such income is, of course, taken into account in determining the net tax payable by the beneficiary, except in limited situations too complex to consider here, but if the tax paid by the trust exceeds the tax payable by the beneficiary on the accumulation distribution, no refund is allowed — either to the beneficiary or the trust). Prior to the passage of the Tax Reform Act of 1969, there were some exceptions to the throwback rule and the throwback applied only to income accumulated during the five preceding years. The Tax Reform Act of 1969 eliminated the exceptions and adopted an unlimited throwback rule. One of the exceptions to the throwback rule eliminated by the 1969 Act related to income accumulated before the birth of the beneficiary or before

---

2. Short-term trusts and their federal income tax consequences are examined in Casner, Estate Planning ch. 6 (4th ed.).

3. See id., ch. 6, Problem 6.8.

the beneficiary attained the age of 21. The Tax Reform Act of 1976 restored this exception (with a modification of limited application). Prior to the 1969 Act, undistributed capital gains realized on trust property were taxed to the trust and were not subject to the throwback rule when distributed to a beneficiary in a later year. The 1969 Act introduced a capital gains throwback rule, but it had a relatively short life as the 1976 Act repealed the capital gains throwback rule. Thus, the trust remains as a separate tax entity but eventually the tax for all the years of the trust will be paid by the distributees and at the rates attributable to the distributees, except the tax paid by the trust on realized capital gains and the tax paid by the trust on income accumulated before the birth of a beneficiary or before he attains the age of 21. What has just been said applies only to domestic trusts; foreign trusts are treated differently.

Capital Gains and Losses

If you buy 100 shares of stock at $60 a share and sell it at $70 a share, you have realized a capital gain of $1,000. If you sell the same stock at $50 a share, you have sustained a capital loss of $1,000. However, if the stock goes up on the market to 70 or down to 50 and you do not sell, no gain or loss has been realized for tax purposes; that is, the income tax takes no account of "paper" profits and losses.

The Internal Revenue Code draws a distinction between long-term gains and losses (where the property has been held more than one year) and short-term gains and losses (where the property has been held one year or less). The most important fact about capital gains and losses is this: long-term capital gains pay a maximum rate of tax that is significantly less than the maximum rate that may be applicable to a corresponding amount of ordinary income.

Where there are long-term and short-term transactions, some profitable and some unprofitable, over a series of years, the tax computation is a matter too complex for the present discussion. Generally speaking, an excess of gains over losses has to be returned as income; an excess of losses over gains can be taken as a deduction from ordinary income only to a limited extent.

Profit or loss is a relationship between selling price and cost. Usually the selling price is easy to determine; but the *cost basis* may present difficulties. If you buy stock at 60 and sell at 70, the cost basis is obviously 60. But what about the following cases?

1. H (a husband) buys stock at 60, then gives it to his son, S, at a time when the market is 80. S sells the stock at 70 — or at 50. The IRC provides that, for figuring a capital gain by S, the cost basis is the cost to H increased (but not above the fair market value of the property at

the time of the gift) by the amount of the gift tax paid that is
attributable to the net appreciation in the value of the gift (as to gifts
made before January 1, 1977, the increase was in the amount of the
gift tax paid); for figuring a capital loss, the cost basis is the same as for
figuring a capital gain or the market value at the time of the gift,
whichever is the lower. Does this discrimination against the taxpayer
shock you? Can you defend the discrimination by showing the
loophole that would exist if, for figuring a capital loss, a donee could
take the cost basis of his donor as to assets which had lost most of
their value at the time of the gift?

2. W (a wife) buys stock at 60 and holds it until her death. By her will she
bequeaths the stock to her daughter, D. The stock is worth 80 at W's
death; D sells it at 75. D would have obtained a new basis in the stock
equal to its fair market value on the date it is valued for federal estate
tax purposes (such date would be either the date on which W died or
the so-called alternate valuation date, which is the earlier of the date
the property is disposed of or six months after the date W died). In
our case, the stock would have a basis of 80 in D's hands. Thus D
would sustain a loss as a result of the sale of the stock at 75. The Tax
Reform Act of 1976 introduced a carry-over basis rule as to property
acquired from or passing from a decedent, which new rule originally
was applicable to decedents dying after December 31, 1976, but its
applicability was postponed to decedents dying after December 31,
1979; then it was repealed, with an election for a limited time in the
executor to apply it in the case of decedents dying in 1977 or before
November 7, 1978. Section 425(a) of the Economic Recovery Tax
Act of 1981 added section 1014(e) to the Internal Revenue Code.
This new section adopts a carry-over basis rule in a limited situation.
The limited situation is where appreciated property was acquired by
a decedent by gift during the one-year period ending on the date of
the decedent's death and such property is acquired from the decedent
by (or passes from the decedent to) the donor of such property (or the
donor's spouse). This new section is designed to prevent the obtaining of a basis advantage where a person owning property with a low
basis gives it to a person who is about to die and the donee gives it
back to the donor on the donee's death. The gift augments the
donee's gross estate for estate tax purposes, but no tax is payable due
to the donee's unified credit referred to later. If it were not for section
1014(e), the donor would get the property back from the donee with a
basis equal to its value in the donee's gross estate. This section applies
to property acquired after August 13, 1981, by donees who die after
December 31, 1981.

There is a one-time exclusion of a specified amount of gain from the sale of a
principal residence by an individual who has attained the age of 55. See
section 121 of the Internal Revenue Code; see also section 1034.

B. *What Is Deductible From Gross Income to Produce Taxable Income?*

We consider here that which can be subtracted from gross income in computing the income upon which a tax is levied.

Business expenses, of course, are deducted from the total receipts of a business which the taxpayer conducts, to determine the net profit or loss thereof. These expenses include reasonable wages and salaries of employees, cost of goods sold, depreciation, and the like.

An exemption is allowed for the individual taxpayer. This exemption had remained at $600 for many years but the Tax Reform Act of 1969 moved it up to $625 for 1970, to $650 for 1971, to $700 for 1972, and to $750 for years subsequent to 1972. The Revenue Act of 1971 changed these figures to $675 for 1971 and $750 thereafter. The Revenue Act of 1978 increased the figure to $1,000. The exemption amount (that is, the $1,000 figure referred to above) as defined in section 151(f) added by the Economic Recovery Tax Act of 1981, section 104(c), is $1,000 increased by an amount equal to $1,000 multiplied by the cost-of-living adjustment (as defined in section 1(f)(3)) for the calendar year in which the taxable year begins. If a joint return is filed by husband and wife, each is a taxpayer and is entitled to an exemption. If a separate return is filed by one spouse, and the other spouse has no gross income for the year and is not the dependent of another taxpayer, the taxpayer spouse is entitled to an additional exemption for the spouse. Additional exemptions are available to a taxpayer and for the taxpayer's spouse when the taxpayer or the spouse is over 65 or blind. An additional exemption is allowed to the taxpayer for each dependent whose gross income for the calendar year in which the taxable year of the taxpayer begins is less than the amount of the exemption, or who is a child of the taxpayer and under 19 or a student. In order for a person to be a dependent of the taxpayer such person must receive over half of his or her support from the taxpayer and must be related to the taxpayer in a defined way (descendant, father, mother, descendant of father or mother, etc.).

Encouragement of individual charitable giving has been a policy of the tax structure for a long time. This is carried out in the federal income tax laws by allowing a deduction from gross income for charitable gifts. The maximum income tax deduction that can be taken for charitable gifts is 50 percent of the "contribution base" (only gifts to certain specified charitable organizations qualify for the 50 percent ceiling and as to gifts to other charitable organizations the ceiling is 20 percent). The net cost to a taxpayer in the 50 percent income tax bracket of making a deductible gift of $1,000 to a charity is $500.

Interest paid on an indebtedness of the taxpayer is usually deductible. Thus if you buy a home and borrow a substantial part of the money to pay for it (usually by giving a mortgage as security), you can deduct the interest paid in each year on the loan.

Certain taxes are deductible — for example, the real estate taxes upon property which you own, and income taxes which you pay to the state in which you reside. The deductibility of the real estate tax and of mortgage interest (see the preceding paragraph) and the non-deductibility of rent which you pay for a residence or apartment means that there are certain tax advantages in owning a home rather than renting one. A current problem is the comparison of the tax consequences of owning stock in a cooperative apartment and owning the apartment under a condominium arrangement. A special provision of the Internal Revenue Code (section 216) permits tenant-stockholders to deduct as interest and as real property taxes portions of amounts paid to the cooperative housing corporation.

Certain other deductions are authorized — medical expenses to a specified extent, losses by casualty to some extent, such as a car smash-up, etc. — but the present discussion is not appropriate for elaborating on these.

Certain deductions are described in the Code as tax preference items (see sections 56 through 58). A special tax is imposed on these tax preference items under specified circumstances.

C. How Is the Tax Determined?

Certain persons pay no tax. That is because the sum of the exemptions allowable for them and their dependents plus available deductions exceeds the amount of their "adjusted gross income."

The method of computing the tax is described on the return and in printed instructions which are provided therewith. You make the computation of the tax of an individual on the basis of rates set forth in the rate schedule. The Economic Recovery Tax Act of 1981 reduced the top rate for all income to 50 percent for taxable years beginning in 1982 (prior to this change, the 50 percent top rate only applied to earned income) and made various other changes that have the effect of lessening the income tax payable by individuals. If income is unduly bunched in one year, income averaging is allowed within certain limits to avoid an undue amount of income being taxed in one year at the top rate. To offset somewhat the income-splitting available to married couples who file a joint return, single individuals are given some relief in the rate schedule applicable to them. Two-earner, married couples also get the benefit of a deduction that is designed to make the total tax payable somewhat nearer what it would be if they were single. A so-called head of a household also gets a break in the rate schedule applicable to him or her.

The most striking feature in the income tax structure is the split-income provision for husband and wife which was introduced by the Revenue Act of 1948. This permits a husband and wife to file a joint return and to compute the tax on one-half of their total income and then pay twice the amount of the tax so ascertained. Thus, where a wife has taxable income of $10,000 and neither she nor her husband has any other income, tax is paid on two $5,000 incomes instead of on one $10,000 income — a substantial saving in tax in view of the fact that the rate of tax rises with the size of the income. Husbands and wives who have substantially equal income get no benefit from this provision. It is a not inconsiderable federal subsidy of marriage. Prior to 1948, husbands and wives were able, generally speaking, to split their incomes for tax purposes in the few states which had the community property system; agitation to end this discrimination resulted in the country-wide split-income provision of the Revenue Act of 1948.

D. How Is the Tax Paid?

Since 1943 it has been a principle of income tax policy to have the tax paid as it is earned. This is accomplished by two methods: (1) Employers, with certain exceptions, are required to withhold a percentage of wages and salaries and pay the amounts withheld to the collector of internal revenue as a credit against the employee's tax; (2) Taxpayers must file a declaration of estimated tax, pay currently the estimated tax, and pay the balance (or get back any overpayment) on April 15 of the following year when a definitive return is filed. The estimated tax for a given year is payable in four installments: April 15, June 15, September 15, and the following January 15. There are provisions for amending the estimate, and penalties for certain underestimates.

E. Concurrent Interests

Income from concurrently owned property is taxable to the concurrent owners, each concurrent owner being taxable on the proportionate part of the income each one is entitled to receive. Local law will determine in the circumstances of each case who is entitled to the income and in what proportions. Interest on joint bank accounts and interest on jointly owned government bonds are taxable to the joint owners in the same proportion as each contributed to the cost of the joint arrangement because each can withdraw his or her contribution from the arrangement at any time.

F. The Federal Corporation Income Tax

The corporate tax rates established by the Revenue Act of 1978 are 17 percent on the first $25,000 of taxable income, 20 percent on the next

$25,000, 30 percent on the next $25,000, 40 percent on the next $25,000, and 46 percent on taxable income above $100,000. The Economic Recovery Tax Act of 1981 changed the 17 percent rate to 16 percent for taxable years beginning in 1982 and to 15 percent thereafter, and it changed the 20 percent rate to 19 percent for taxable years beginning in 1982 and to 18 percent thereafter.

From the point of view of the property lawyer and estate planner, the important feature of the corporation income tax is its double-taxation aspect. Where an individual owns shares in a corporation and the corporation conducts a profitable business, the federal government hits the business profits twice on their way to the stockholder's pocket. First it imposes a corporation income tax on the profits; then the dividends declared by the corporation out of what is left are again taxed to the stockholder as an individual, this time at the graduated rates of the individual income tax. Some relief from double taxation has been granted in the form of the exclusion from gross income of a specified amount of dividend income received from taxable domestic corporations. The Economic Recovery Tax Act of 1981 re-established the $100 dividend exclusion ($200 in the case of a joint return) for tax years beginning after December 31, 1981. The Crude Oil Windfall Profit Tax Act of 1980 had established a $200 interest and dividend exclusion ($400 on a joint return) for tax years beginning after 1980. An interest exclusion was adopted by the Economic Recovery Tax Act of 1981 effective for taxable years beginning after December 31, 1984 (see section 128). An interest exclusion for interest on a depository institution tax-exempt savings certificate applies to taxable years ending after September 30, 1981 (see section 128). Additional relief has been given to closely held corporations by allowing an election to be taxed like a partnership, which eliminates the tax at the corporate level. It should be obvious that a decision whether to incorporate a business or not must be made in the light of the wide-ranging tax considerations.

The complex business and accounting problems of the corporation income tax are not appropriate for discussion in this brief survey.

G. State Income Taxes

Some states have them and some do not. The number that have them is growing. Those that have them differ in various respects as to what income is taxed. Some states have flat rates of tax and some have graduated rates. The rates of tax are low in comparison with the federal levy. It is a common practice to vary the tax from year to year according to the fiscal needs of the state by making temporary additions to the tax or subtractions from the tax.

SECTION 3.   ESTATE, INHERITANCE, AND GIFT TAXES—FEDERAL AND STATE

A.   Estate and Gift Taxes Generally

The federal government imposes an estate tax on the estates of decedents and a gift tax on inter vivos gifts. Most states levy some kind of tax on the transfer of property upon death and some also have a gift tax. (Taxes upon death may be "estate" taxes—i.e., a single tax determined by the amount of the estate of the decedent; or "inheritance" taxes—i.e., a number of separate taxes, one on each benefit conferred on a devisee, legatee, or heir, the amount of each tax usually being determined by the size of the gift and the closeness of relationship of the person who receives it.) It is obvious that there is a close relationship between estate and inheritance taxes on the one hand and gift taxes on the other, for, if there were a heavy tax on transfers on death but no tax on transfers inter vivos, the tendency would be for large property owners to defeat the estate and inheritance taxes by making inter vivos gifts. Thus gift taxes buttress estate and inheritance taxes.

Gift taxes also help to maintain some balance in the operation of an income tax system under which the ownership of income-producing property carries with it the burden of an income tax on the income produced. If the ownership could be shifted around without any gift tax cost, the temptation would be to shift such ownership annually within the family unit so as to cause the income to be taxed each year in the lowest possible income tax bracket. Even though there is a gift tax, shifts of ownership for income tax purposes are made, but not on the wide-open basis which would obtain if there were no gift tax.

Prior to the Revenue Act of 1948, the estate and inheritance taxes imposed by the states were not a major concern in many cases because, in a substantial estate, all or nearly all of the state death tax was available as a credit against the federal tax; therefore, it was the size of the federal tax which determined the amount of estate shrinkage. However, the "marital deduction" provision of the Revenue Act of 1948, later discussed, gave new importance to the state levies and caused them to produce real increases in the shrinkage of an estate. The state death tax credit for a taxable estate of $500,000 is $10,000. This means that if a state does not impose a state death tax of at least $10,000 on a taxable estate of a decedent of $500,000, it is simply allowing money which could be diverted to the state to go to the federal government without decreasing the total death tax payable by the decedent's estate. States generally have enacted state death tax statutes that will at least sponge up the amount of the state death tax credit; hence the name frequently given to such state death tax statutes is the sponge tax.

Upon the death of a citizen or resident of the United States a federal estate tax is payable (nonresident aliens also may have to pay some estate tax). There is also payable a state tax to whatever state the decedent was domiciled in, if that state imposes an estate or inheritance tax. But there is a practical difficulty here, arising out of the facts that (1) the power of a state to tax the personal estate of a decedent is dependent upon whether the decedent was domiciled in that state at the decedent's death (a state also has jurisdiction to tax real property and tangible personal property located in the state, though the owner is domiciled elsewhere, (2) a rich person is likely to spend parts of the year in various states — e.g., New York, Maine, Florida, and (3) each of these states, through its courts, is entitled to determine for itself the question of fact whether the decedent was domiciled in that state. This has occasionally resulted in multiple taxation. For example, John T. Dorrance (of the Campbell's Soup fortune) died in 1930 with an estate of $115,000,000. The New Jersey courts ruled that he was domiciled in New Jersey and that a tax of $17,000,000 was due to New Jersey. The Pennsylvania courts ruled that he was domiciled in Pennsylvania and that a tax of $17,000,000 was due to Pennsylvania. Both taxes were collected, as also was a federal estate tax.[4] A still more extreme case was that of one Colonel Green, the son of an eccentric New England millionaire, Hetty Green. At his death, owning $42,000,000, four states (Texas, Florida, New York, and Massachusetts) claimed him as a domiciliary and threatened to levy taxes in a total amount exceeding the full value of the estate. This was so bad that it was good, a paradox that is explained in Texas v. Florida, 306 U.S. 398 (1938); only one tax was paid. The problem generally still exists but many states have statutes designed to provide a mechanism which may be used to resolve conflicting state claims as to domicile.

The actual payment of any federal estate tax is avoided to the extent of what is called the unified credit available to a decedent's estate. This credit is also available to eliminate the actual payment of any gift tax. The unified credit came into the picture with respect to transfers after December 31, 1976, and was increased in amount by the Economic Recovery Tax Act of 1981. If a comparable credit is not available with respect to state death taxes, the state death tax burden becomes the most significant death tax in estates that, due to the availability of the unified credit, pay no federal estate tax.

B. The Federal Gift Tax

The federal government imposes a graduated tax upon taxable gifts. The tax is payable by the donor but if the donor fails to pay the tax, the donee may be

---

4. For the references, see 302 U.S. 297. A substantial part of these state taxes — but not all by any means — was deductible from the federal estate tax, for, under the law as it stood at that time, state taxes up to 80 percent of the entire federal tax were deductible from the federal tax. If Dorrance had died after 1932, an additional federal tax would have been imposed that permitted no deduction for state taxes.

reached. With respect to gifts made prior to 1982, no gift tax return was required to be filed until the calendar quarter in which the taxable gifts for the year were more than $25,000. Once that figure was reached, a gift tax return had to be filed for each succeeding calendar quarter in which there were taxable gifts. If that figure was not reached for the year but there were taxable gifts for the year, the gift tax return for the year was due by April 15 of the following year. When a gift tax return was due for a calendar quarter, the return had to be filed on or before the fifteenth day of the second month following the end of the quarter, except the fourth-quarter return which was due April 15. The Economic Recovery Tax Act of 1981 changed the date for filing all gift tax returns to April 15 following the close of the calendar year in which the gift was made. This change is effective with respect to gifts made after December 31, 1981. The return for the calendar year that includes the date of the death of the donor shall not be later than the time for filing the estate tax return of the donor.

1. What Is a Gift?

The gratuitous transfer of $10,000, or a house and lot, or 100 shares of stock of the X Corporation — these, of course, are gifts. But there are some transactions which are less clean-cut than these. Some transactions that look like gifts are not so regarded; and others which do not look like gifts are held to be taxable. Generally speaking, the test is whether an economic benefit has been transferred gratuitously — but you should realize that this generalization is only a very rough description of the legal result; the IRC and the regulations are very specific as to each type of transaction that is likely to arise. The following are common types of cases:

1. *Revocable trust.* H (a husband) transfers $100,000 to a trustee in trust to pay the income to his son, S, for life, and after S's death to pay the principal to S's issue; H reserves a power to revoke the trust. At this point no gift has been made, for the reservation of H's power to revoke means that neither S nor S's issue has any real economic benefit. When the first income is earned on the trust fund and is paid to S, this constitutes a gift of the income from H to S; so also does each succeeding increment of income that is paid to S. If H should release the power of revocation, this release would constitute a gift to S of the income on the trust fund for the life of S (the value of which would be computed on the basis of mortality tables), and also a gift to S's issue of the principal as of the future date upon which (under the mortality tables) the average person of S's age is expected to die.

2. *Sale for inadequate consideration.* W (a wife) sells a house and lot worth $20,000 to her daughter, D, for $12,000. W has made a gift to D in the amount of $8,000. It is possible for a sale at less than the full value of the property involved to be made without the difference in the sale price and full value being a gift. For such a result to obtain, it

must be established that the sale was made in the ordinary course of business, that is, in a transaction which is bona fide, at arm's length, and free from donative intent.

2.   Non-Taxability of Charitable Gifts

Charitable gifts are not taxable as gifts, regardless of their amount. As will appear, the same is true under the estate tax as to charitable bequests and devises made by a decedent. However, you will recall that charitable gifts are deductible from income, under the federal income tax, only to the extent of a certain percentage of the "contribution base" of the donor. What gifts are "charitable" is a matter which is very carefully defined in the tax laws. The following examples may be helpful:

1. The Red Cross, the Community Fund, and similar organizations are charities.
2. Gifts for educational or religious purposes are "charitable." This includes a gift to your university — or to its law school.
3. Gifts to a city or town, a state, or the United States (Justice Oliver Wendell Holmes left the entire residue of his estate "to the United States of America") are "charitable."
4. A gift to a particular poor family whom you may happen to know about, to provide them with food and rent, is not a "charitable" gift. A general line is drawn in favor of public charity and against private charity.
5. Gifts to organizations which are designed to promote good government or world peace or to attain other political, economic, or social ends may or may not be "charitable." The organization cannot be "charitable" if a substantial part of its activities is carrying on propaganda, or otherwise attempting to influence legislation. It is customary for organizations to submit their charters and bylaws to the Treasury Department for a ruling on whether they comply with the requirements of the statutes as to what constitutes a "charity." On receiving a favorable ruling such organizations frequently include a statement that "Gifts are deductible for federal income, estate and gift tax purposes" in their solicitations of funds.

A split-interest charitable gift is one which gives the charity benefits for a term with remainder then to go to individuals or vice versa. In order to obtain a charitable deduction for such a gift, very technical rules must be observed.

3.   The Annual Exclusion for Each Donee

The Economic Recovery Tax Act of 1981 increased the annual exclusion from $3,000 to $10,000 with respect to transfers made after December 31,

1981. The Act also added a new section 2503(e), which provides that no amount shall be treated as a transfer of property for gift tax purposes if the amount is paid on behalf of an individual as tuition to an educational organization for education or training of such individual or to any person who provides medical care with respect to such individual as payment for such medical care. Such payments do not count against the $10,000. Section 2503(e) is applicable to transfers after December 31, 1981. H can give $10,000 to his son, S, each year without incurring any gift tax or being required to file any gift tax return. He can also give $10,000 in each year to each other child of his and to any other donees whether related to him or not. H's wife can make $10,000 annual gifts to the same donees. This exclusion does not apply to *future interests* — e.g., to a gift of $10,000 by H in trust to pay the principal to S at some future date.

4.   The Gift Tax Marital Deduction

The gift tax marital deduction came into the picture in 1948 to equalize to some extent the gift tax situation in community property states and non-community property states. In a community property state, the spouses attain half and half ownership of the community property without the imposition of a gift tax no matter which spouse produces the community property. In a non-community property state, the spouse who produces the property was, prior to 1948, subject to a gift tax without the benefit of any deduction if a gift of one-half such property was made to the other spouse. The original gift tax marital deduction cut the value of the gift to the other spouse in half. For example, a gift of $100,000 to the donor's spouse would be taxed as if it were a gift of $50,000. Thus, though the original gift tax marital deduction allowed the spouses in a non-community property state to reach the stage of half and half ownership with a lesser gift tax cost, a gift tax cost was not eliminated entirely, except to the extent that the combination of the annual exclusion and the gift tax marital deduction could eliminate any taxable gift, as when the gift from one spouse to the other did not exceed $6,000 (during the period that the annual exclusion was $3,000). The 1976 Tax Reform Act, however, provided for an unlimited gift tax marital deduction as to the first $100,000 of gifts from one spouse to the other spouse made after December 31, 1976. The next $100,000 of gifts was fully taxable and then a gift tax marital deduction of one-half the value of the gift operated after $200,000 of gifts. The Economic Recovery Tax Act of 1981 brought in an unlimited gift tax marital deduction for gifts from one spouse to the other spouse made after December 31, 1981.

The availability of the original gift tax marital deduction was significantly curtailed in relation to property that had a community property background. In this regard, keep in mind that spouses living in a non-community property state may own property that is community property. The curtailment, where the property that was the subject matter of a gift from one spouse to another had a community property background, was that the gift tax marital deduction was allowed only to the extent the transfer could be shown to represent a gift of property which was not, at the time of the gift, held as community property under the law of any state, possession of the United States, or any foreign country. The phrase "held as community property" was defined in the Internal Revenue Code (section 2523(f)) and encompassed certain separate property that was once community property. For example, if husband and wife converted community property to the separate property of each by dividing it into equal shares, the separate property thus acquired by each one was "held as community property" for purposes of the gift tax marital deduction, so that if thereafter one spouse gave some of such separate property to the other spouse, no gift tax marital deduction was available with respect to such gift. If, however, one spouse gave the other spouse all of his or her interest in community property, thereby making the donee spouse the owner of the entire interest in what was formerly their community property, though the donor spouse was not entitled to any gift tax marital deduction for such gift, the separate property thus acquired by the donee spouse in all of what was formerly community property was not deemed "held as community property" by the donee spouse for purposes of the gift tax marital deduction in relation to future gifts by that spouse to the other spouse. The complexity described above with respect to the operation of the gift tax where community property is involved is eliminated for gifts of community property from one spouse to the other made after December 31 1981. The adoption of an unlimited gift tax marital deduction by the Economic Recovery Tax Act of 1981 accomplished this.

In order for a gift from one spouse to another spouse to qualify for the gift tax marital deduction, the donee spouse must receive an interest that qualifies for the marital deduction. Normally, a qualified marital deduction gift is one that places the entire subject of the gift under the control of the donee spouse. The Economic Recovery Tax Act of 1981 added section 2523(f) which permits a qualified gift tax marital deduction gift to take the form of a life interest in the donee spouse with remainder to others even though the donee spouse has no control over the destination of the property on the death of the donee spouse. Such life interest in the donee spouse is referred to as a "qualified terminable interest" and in order for such gift to qualify for the gift tax marital deduction for the value of the property in which the life interest exists, an election to have it qualify must be made by the donor on the gift tax return that is filed.

5. Gift-Splitting by Spouses

Another change made in 1948, as part of the attempt to make the gift tax as applied in community property states somewhat the same as applied in non-community property states was the adoption of a so-called gift-splitting rule in connection with gifts by married persons to third persons. A gift by husband and wife of community property to their son or anyone else is inherently a gift by each spouse of one-half of the property, no matter which spouse produced the property. Hence a gift in 1981 of community property worth $6,000 to the son is not a taxable gift by either spouse because each one is giving the son only $3,000 and the annual exclusion available to each donor eliminates any taxable gift. In a non-community property state prior to the 1948 change, however, a gift to the son by the spouse who produced the subject matter of the gift, which gift was worth $6,000, resulted in a taxable gift by the donor spouse of $3,000 after taking out the annual exclusion of $3,000. The so-called gift-splitting change made in 1948 allows one-half of the value of the gift by the donor spouse to be treated as a gift by the non-donor spouse to the son, if the non-donor spouse consents, thereby attaining a gift tax result comparable to that in a community property state when community property is the subject matter of a gift to the son. The $3,000 figure referred to above can be $10,000 as to gifts made after December 31, 1981, and the $6,000 figure referred to above can be $20,000 as to gifts made after December 31, 1981. These changes are the result of the adoption by the Economic Recovery Tax Act of 1981 of a per donee annual gift tax exclusion of $10,000 for gifts of present interests.

6. The Unified Rate Schedule

Taxable gifts (i.e., gifts that exceed the deductions and the annual exclusion) are taxed under what is called the unified rate schedule which was adopted by the Tax Reform Act of 1976. This rate schedule is applicable to both taxable lifetime gifts and to taxable deathtime transfers. The schedule as adopted provided graduated rates starting with 18 percent of the first $10,000 of taxable transfers and increasing in stages to a top bracket of 70 percent on taxable transfers which when added to previous taxable transfers produce a total in excess of $5,000,000. The Economic Recovery Tax Act of 1981 reduced the top bracket of 70 percent to 50 percent on taxable transfers that, when added to previous taxable transfers, produce a total in excess of $2,500,000. This change, however, is phased in over a period covering 1982 (when the top rate is 65 percent on excess over $4,000,000), 1983 (when the top rate is 60 percent on excess over $3,500,000), and 1984 (when the top rate is 55 percent on excess over $3,000,000). Thus the gift tax cost of a gift of the first $10,000 of taxable gifts is less than the gift tax cost of the second $10,000 of taxable gifts. Furthermore, all post-1976 taxable transfers count in locating the applicable rate in the unified rate schedule for deathtime taxable transfers.

Though the unified rate schedule became applicable only to taxable gifts made after December 31, 1976, taxable gifts made prior to January 1, 1977, must be taken into account in determining the starting bracket in the unified rate schedule for post-1976 taxable gifts. Pre-1977 taxable gifts are determined on the basis of the gift tax law as it existed before the Tax Reform Act of 1976, so a knowledge of that preexisting law is essential to determine what are taxable gifts that must be taken into account in computing the tax on post-1976 taxable gifts. For example, suppose that O made pre-1977 taxable gifts totaling $150,000 and O makes a post-1976 taxable gift of $100,000. The gift tax on the $100,000 gift is computed by first determining the gift tax under the unified rate schedule on a gift of $250,000 (which is $70,800), and then determining the gift tax under the unified rate schedule on a gift of $150,000 (which is $38,800), and the difference is the gift tax on the post-1976 taxable gift of $100,000 (which is $32,000). When O dies, in determining the rate bracket in the unified rate schedule that will be the beginning bracket for O's deathtime transfers, the pre-1977 gifts do not count, though as noted above they did count in the computation of the gift tax. For example, if O's deathtime taxable estate totaled $150,000, we would compute the tax under the unified rate schedule on $250,000 ($150,000 plus post-1976 taxable gifts of $100,000) and then we would subtract from the amount of tax so determined the aggregate amount of tax payable with respect to taxable lifetime gifts made after December 31, 1976.

7. The Unified Credit

The gift tax computed as outlined above will not require the payment of any dollars until the amount of the gift tax exceeds what is called the unified credit. Each donor is given a credit to use against the gift tax, which grew to $47,000 by 1981. This is a lifetime credit, not an annual one. The gift tax lifetime credit was $6,000 for the first six months of 1977, and increased to $30,000 for the last six months of 1977, and increased to $34,000 for 1978, to $38,000 for 1979, and to $42,500 for 1980. Thus, if a donor made taxable gifts that used up $10,000 of the donor's credit for 1978 and made no other taxable gifts prior to 1981, in 1981 the donor would have $37,000 of the donor's lifetime credit left. A lifetime credit of $47,000 will eliminate the actual payment of any dollars on taxable gifts totaling $175,625. The Economic Recovery Tax Act of 1981 increased the unified credit to $192,800, the equivalent of a $600,000 exemption, but phases in the increase over a period covering 1982 (credit $62,800, exemption equivalent $225,000), 1983 (credit $79,300, exemption equivalent $275,000), 1984 (credit $96,300, exemption equivalent $325,000), 1985 (credit $121,800, exemption equivalent $400,000), 1986 (credit $155,800, exemption equivalent $500,000). It must be kept in mind, however, that to the extent the unified credit is used up on lifetime taxable gifts, it will not be available to use against deathtime taxable transfers.

A lifetime giving program that utilizes to the maximum gift-splitting by spouses, the unified credit that each spouse has, and the annual exclusion available for gifts of present interests, enables a donor to move to others than a spouse a considerable amount of family wealth without the actual payment of dollars in gift tax costs. The unlimited gift tax marital deduction makes it possible to divide the ownership of property between the spouses to whatever extent may be appropriate without any gift tax cost.

8. Concurrent Interests

Joint ownership of property with the right of survivorship is quite common, particularly by husband and wife. A completed gift may or may not result at the time such joint ownership is created. There will be no completed gift as long as the contribution made to the joint ownership is fully withdrawable by the contributor without the consent of the other joint owner. This is normally the case with respect to a joint bank account and jointly owned United States Savings Bonds. A completed gift, however, will be made if the contributor to the joint ownership arrangement cannot withdraw all the contributor's contribution without the consent of the other joint owner. This will be the case on the establishment of a joint tenancy or a tenancy by the entirety. Though a completed gift is made, it does not necessarily follow that such gift is a taxable gift for gift tax purposes.

A section of the Internal Revenue Code introduced by the Revenue Act of 1954 (section 2515) prevented any taxable gift on the creation of a tenancy by the entirety in *real property*. (For purposes of this provision of the Code, a "tenancy by the entirety" which can exist only between husband and wife includes a joint tenancy between husband and wife with the right of survivorship.) The Code, however, allowed the donor spouse to elect to have such creation treated as a gift. An election to do so required the filing of a gift tax return regardless of the amount involved. If no election was made and the tenancy by the entirety (or joint tenancy) was terminated other than by reason of the death of one of the spouses, the donor spouse had to get back the proportion of the former jointly held property that corresponded to the proportion of the property the donor spouse put into the jointly owned arrangement or the donor spouse would be treated as making a gift at the time of such termination. For example, if the tenancy by the entirety was originally acquired for $50,000 and the husband put in $30,000 and the wife $20,000 and the tenancy was terminated by a sale of the land for $100,000, the husband had to receive three-fifths of $100,000 and the wife two-fifths to prevent any gift from being made at the time of the termination. Notice this dispensation from gift taxation applied only to "real property." It was ruled that section 2515 was not applicable to a long-term lease from a cooperative housing corporation. It would be applicable, however, to a condominium arrangement. If an election was made under section 2515 by the donor spouse to treat the creation of the tenancy by the entirety (or joint tenancy) as a gift for gift tax purposes, how was the gift to the non-donor spouse valued and was that gift a gift of a present interest so that the annual exclusion would be available and did it qualify for the gift tax marital deduction?

The answer to the valuation question depended on whether the tenancy by the entirety (or joint tenancy) in real property was created on or after January 1, 1977, or before that date. The 1976 Tax Reform Act, applicable to such joint ownership arrangements created on or after January 1, 1977, eliminated the necessity of the use of any actuarial computation in valuing the interest of each spouse in a tenancy by the entirety (the interest of each spouse in a joint tenancy has always been one-half) so that each spouse would be deemed to own a one-half interest in the tenancy by the entirety. As to a tenancy by the entirety created prior to January 1, 1977, because of the indestructible right of survivorship which attaches to such form of ownership, the value of the gift to the non-donor spouse depended on the ages of the donor spouse and the non-donor spouse. Thus if a tenancy by the entirety in real property was created on or after January 1, 1977, and the tenancy was originally acquired for $50,000, and the husband put in $30,000 and the wife $20,000, and an election was made under section 2515 by the husband to treat the creation of the tenancy as a gift for gift tax purposes, the husband made a gift to the wife for gift tax purposes of $5,000.

Whether the gift of $5,000 from the husband to the wife was a gift of a present interest so as to qualify for the annual exclusion depended on the legal rights of a wife in a tenancy by the entirety in real property under the law of the state in which the real property was located. If she was entitled only to the right to become the sole owner of the real property if she survived her husband, she had only a future interest. (In regard to the legal rights of a wife in a tenancy by the entirety see Chapter 14.) If she had only a future interest in the tenancy by the entirety, the annual per donee gift tax exclusion was not available.

The $5,000 gift from the husband to the wife qualified for the gift tax marital deduction. Thus the amount, if any, of the taxable gift for gift tax purposes depended on the extent that the $5,000 gift was reduced by the gift tax marital deduction. If there was any taxable gift, whether any dollars had to be paid out depended on how much of the donor spouse's unified credit remained.

It must be kept in mind that section 2515 did not apply to a tenancy by the entirety (or joint tenancy) in personal property. The Revenue Act of 1978 added section 2515A of the Code, which, with one exception, provided that in the case of the creation (either by one spouse alone or by both spouses) of a joint interest of husband and wife in personal property with right of survivorship, the retained interest of each spouse shall be treated as one-half of the value of their joint interest. The one exception was described in section 2515A(b) of the Code.

The Economic Recovery Tax Act of 1981 repealed sections 2515 and 2515A, effective with respect to gifts made after December 31, 1981. As to such gifts, however, the unlimited gift tax marital deduction is available so no gift tax will be payable after 1981 by the creator of jointly owned property where donor is the spouse of the donee.

C. The Federal Estate Tax

A federal tax is imposed upon the estate of a decedent who dies owning a "taxable estate" as that term is defined in the Code. As has been pointed out, this is an estate tax and not an inheritance tax such as some of the states have. With reference to this tax it is necessary to discuss:

1. What property is includible in the decedent's "gross estate."
2. From the "gross estate" what amounts are deductible in determining the "taxable estate."
3. How the tax is computed.

1. The Gross Estate

Property which a person owns at death is, of course, included in the gross estate; but there are many other types of property that are so included even though the decedent does not "own" them. The general aim of the Code is to tax real transfers of economic benefit upon death, regardless of legal forms and you will readily observe that some of the following categories are clearly justified on this basis. Then again, the Congress, urged by those who administer the Code, has felt that, in the interest of preventing tax avoidance, certain types of inter vivos transfers ought to be brought into the "gross estate" even though the economic benefit transferred on death is nearly or entirely nonexistent. We now describe the principal categories of property which fall into the gross estate.

1. *Gifts made within three years of death.* We will first describe the law as it existed prior to the Economic Recovery Tax Act of 1981. The value of gifts made within three years of death, as well as the gift tax paid on such gifts, was automatically includible in the gross estate. This was true, however, only with respect to gifts made after December 31, 1976. The value of gifts made prior to that date was includible in the gross estate if the decedent died within three years after the gift only if the gift was made in contemplation of death, but all gifts made within three years of death were presumed to be in contemplation of death.[5] This presumption, however, could be rebutted.

---

5. The gift causa mortis is a gift made in *immediate* expectation or fear of death. Contrast this requirement with the three-year presumption for gifts "in contemplation of death"; it is quite unlikely that a gift made as much as three months before the donor died would be considered to be "in immediate expectation or fear of death." If a gift is causa mortis, (a) it is revocable, and (b) it is automatically revoked if the donor recovers from the illness or otherwise survives the immediate danger to life. The fact that a gift is made "in contemplation of death" merely makes it includible in the donor's gross estate; it does not make it revocable. See Chapter 5 for a consideration of gifts causa mortis.

The 1976 Tax Reform Act adopted the automatic three-year return rule; thereby, as to gifts made after December 31, 1976, the contemplation-of-death issue is eliminated. Under the automatic three-year return rule, not only is the value of the gift brought back, but also the amount of any gift tax paid on the gift is included in the gross estate of the decedent donor. The effect of the above-mentioned automatic inclusion was to subject any gift tax paid, though it was a credit against the estate tax, to an estate tax — a tax on the tax. There was an important exception to the automatic three-year return rule and that was that it did not apply to any gift to a donee during a calendar year if the decedent was not required to file any gift tax return in such year with respect to gifts to such donee (for example, a $3,000 present interest gift), but this exception did not apply to any gift of an insurance policy.

Still referring to the situation prior to the Economic Recovery Tax Act of 1981, if a married person made a gift to a third person and the non-donor spouse consented to gift-splitting and the donor spouse died within three years, the entire value of the gift was included in the donor spouse's gross estate, not just the one-half of the gift treated as the donor spouse's gift for gift tax purposes. However, any tax payable by the non-donor spouse was treated as a tax paid by the deceased donor spouse. Any part of the non-donor spouse's unified credit used up in connection with such gift was restored.

The Economic Recovery Tax Act of 1981 significantly affected the three-year automatic return rule with respect to decedents dying after 1981. The 1981 Act adds section 2035(d), which eliminates the three-year automatic return rule in all situations to which it was previously applicable. To the extent the situations to which it was previously applicable involved adjusted taxable gifts, the value of such gifts will continue to be relevant in determining the estate tax payable. The value attributable to a taxable gift in determining the estate tax payable is its value on the date of the gift, and the gift property retains its basis. If the value of a taxable gift is includible in the decedent's gross estate under the three-year automatic return rule, the value of the gift for estate tax purposes is its value on the date of death, or the alternate valuation date, and the property obtains a new basis under section 1014. Thus by excluding from the gross estate the taxable gifts made within three years of death, a significant change as to both valuation and basis is made. There are exceptions under section 2035(d) to this wholesale elimination of the three-year automatic return rule. If the transfer within three years of death is one that involves an interest in property that is included in the value of the gross estate under section 2036, section 2037, section 2038, or section 2042, or would have been included under any of such sections if such interest had been retained by the decedent, then section 2035(d) is not applicable. Furthermore, the three-year rule is retained to cause the inclusion in the gross estate of transfers previously subject to it in determining the applicability of sections 303(b), 2032A, 6166 and subchapter C of chapter 64. It is to be noted that the changes referred to above have no effect on section 2035(c), which causes the inclusion in a decedent's gross estate of the amount of any gift tax paid by the decedent or the decedent's estate on any gift made by the decedent or the decedent's spouse during the three-year period ending on the date of the decedent's death.

2. *Life insurance.* Proceeds of life insurance policies are included in the gross estate, if the insured-decedent possessed at death any of the "incidents of ownership" of the policies of insurance, or if the proceeds of the insurance are payable to the insured-decedent's estate. As noted above, if the insured transfers a life insurance policy within three years of the insured's death, the proceeds of the policy will be included in the insured's gross estate.

3. *Concurrent interests.* Concurrent interests with the right of survivorship are subject to some special rules in determining the amount includible in the gross estate of the first to die. Generally speaking, the so-called consideration-paid test is applied, which means that there is includible in the gross estate of the first to die that proportion of the value of the jointly owned property that corresponds to the proportion of the consideration furnished by the decedent for the jointly owned property. If the decedent furnished the entire consideration, the entire value goes into the gross estate, and if the decedent furnished none of the consideration, nothing goes into the gross estate, and if neither joint owner furnished any of the consideration (as when a third person gave the property to the joint owners), one-half the value of the jointly owned property goes into the gross estate of the first to die (assuming there are two joint owners).

The Tax Reform Act of 1976 made a limited change in the operation of the so-called consideration-paid test. This change relates to what is termed a qualified joint interest. As defined in the 1976 Act, a qualified joint interest is any interest in property held by the decedent and the decedent's spouse as joint tenants or tenants by the entirety, but only if—

a. such joint interest was created by the decedent, the decedent's spouse, or both; and

b. in the case of personal property, the creation of the joint interest constituted in whole or in part a gift for gift tax purposes; and

c. in the case of real property, an election was made under section 2515 by the donor spouse to treat the creation of the joint interest as a gift for gift tax purposes; and

d. in the case of a joint tenancy, only the decedent and the decedent's spouse are joint tenants; and

e. the joint interest was created after December 31, 1976.

With respect to qualified joint interests, one-half the value of the joint interest is included in the gross estate of the first to die of the spouses, regardless of where the consideration came from to acquire the joint interest. The Economic Recovery Tax Act of 1981 amended section 2040(b)(2), the definition of a qualified joint interest, in regard to estates of decedents dying after December 31, 1981. As amended, a qualified joint interest is any property held by the decedent and the decedent's spouse as tenants by the entirety or as joint tenants with right of survivorship (but only if the decedent and the spouse of the decedent are the only joint tenants). The effect of this amendment is to cause the inclusion in the gross estate of the first to die of one-half of the value of the jointly held property without regard to when the joint interest was created.

The Revenue Act of 1978 added section 2040(c), applicable to estates of decedents dying after December 31, 1978, which was designed to credit a spouse, who materially participated in a farm or other business held by the decedent and the decedent's spouse as joint tenants or tenants by the entirety, with contributing to the acquisition of such farm or other business in applying the consideration-paid test. The Economic Recovery Tax Act of 1981 repealed section 2040(c), effective as to decedents dying after December 31, 1981. This section is no longer needed in light of the new definition of a qualified joint interest.

In determining what is includible in the gross estate of the first to die of concurrent owners, you must distinguish those joint interests with the right of survivorship which are considered above from concurrent ownerships, such as a tenancy in common or community property, which do not have any built-in right of survivorship. As to a tenancy in common there is included in the gross estate of the first to die only such person's undivided interest in the tenancy in common. As to community property, there is included in the gross estate of the first to die of the spouses one-half the value of the community property.

An illustration of the statements made above in regard to concurrent interests in others than spouses may be helpful. H in his will devises Blackacre to his son, S, and his daughter, D, as joint tenants and not as tenants in common. S dies. One-half of the value of Blackacre will be included in S's gross estate and D will become the sole owner of Blackacre under the right of survivorship. If D then dies, the full value of Blackacre will be included in her gross estate. Some relief from the double taxation of one-half of Blackacre is given in this situation if D dies within ten years after S dies by allowing a credit against the tax imposed on D's estate of the tax on one-half the value of Blackacre in S's estate. This credit declines in amount every two years and is gone entirely after ten years.

The illustration in the previous paragraph assumed the joint tenancy was created by a gift from a person other than one of the co-owners. Assume now that H purchases Blackacre with his own funds and places the title in the names of himself and his son S as joint tenants and not as tenants in common. He will have made a gift to S of one-half the value of Blackacre, as we have seen, and may have paid a gift tax. Nevertheless, if H dies first, the full value of Blackacre will be included in his gross estate because he furnished all the consideration for it. Again, to avoid the double taxation, gift tax on one-half and estate tax on the whole, a credit is allowed against the estate tax on H's estate for the gift tax H paid in creating the joint ownership arrangement. In the situation considered above, if S dies first and H becomes the sole owner under the right of survivorship, no part of the value of Blackacre will be included in S's gross estate since he did not furnish any of the consideration for its acquisition.

4. *Revocable trusts.* Such trusts created by the decedent are includible in the gross estate. This is an obvious corollary to the rule that the creation of a revocable trust is not a gift for purposes of the gift tax. The substantial transfer of economic benefit takes place not when the trust is created but when the donor dies without revoking it.

5. *Trusts where the donor reserves the income for life.* Such trusts are includible, even though they are irrevocable. Also, irrevocable trusts, under which the donor retains the power to determine who will enjoy the trust property, will be includible in the donor's gross estate.

6. *Transfers intended to take effect in possession or enjoyment at or after the death of the donor.* Such trusts are includible. The italicized words are quoted from section 2037 of the Internal Revenue Code and have been in the estate tax law since its inception. They have raised many difficulties. In due time you will hear of the *Hallock* case, the *Spiegel* case, the *Church* case, and the amendments to the Code subsequent to these cases. But these are too complex for present discussion and should be reserved for your course on taxation.[6]

7. *Powers of appointment.* Powers of appointment raise this question: suppose H by will leaves a trust fund with directions to the trustee to pay the income to S for life and on S's death to pay the principal to such of S's children as S shall appoint. If S appoints the fund to his child, C, is the property in the trust includible in S's gross estate? Or, in technical language, is the property subject to the power of appointment includible in the gross estate of the donee of the power? The answer is that it depends principally on how broad the power of appointment is. If S is limited so that he cannot appoint to himself, or to his creditors, or to his estate, or to the creditors of his estate, then the answer is no. But if the power is broader, then the appointive property, subject to some exceptions, is includible. Generally speaking, it makes no difference whether S *exercises* the power; the property is includible or not, depending upon whether he *has* the power. The donee of a power of appointment may be treated as the owner of the appointive assets for gift tax purposes as well as for estate tax purposes. The legislative history in relation to estate and gift taxation of property subject to a power of appointment is essential background, because the date a power was created may have a bearing on the tax consequences of the exercise or nonexercise of the power. This legislative history will be developed in the courses on taxation and estate planning.

8. *Generation-skipping arrangements.* In the illustration given under 7 above, if the value of the property is not included in S's gross estate because his power of appointment does not permit him to appoint to himself, his estate, his creditors or creditors of his estate, then S will have enjoyed the income of the property for his life and will have quite broad discretion in determining where the property will go on his death, but the property will

---

6. The key cases are as follows: Helvering v. Hallock, 309 U.S. 106 (1940); Commissioner v. Estate of Church, 335 U.S. 632 (1949); Estate of Spiegel v. Commissioner, 335 U.S. 701 (1949).

escape estate taxation on S's death. This was the situation prior to the Tax Reform Act of 1976, and as you might expect, many transferors, such as H, set up such trust arrangements for their children, such as S, to skip a generation so far as the imposition of another estate tax was concerned. The Tax Reform Act of 1976 undertook to deal with these so-called generation-skipping arrangements by the imposition of a generation-skipping tax to operate somewhat as though S in our illustration owned the property in the trust at the time of his death. There are exceptions to the imposition of the generation-skipping tax. The subject is too complex for further considera-tion at this point. As of the beginning of 1984, the generation-skipping transfer tax is under reconsideration.

2. The Taxable Estate

There are a number of items which are deducted from the gross estate to produce the taxable estate, i.e., the figure upon which the tax is levied. The principal items are discussed below.

Debts, funeral expenses, expenses of administration and casualty losses incurred during settlement of estate not compensated for by insurance are deductible. Expenses of administration include executor's fees and counsel fees.

The estate tax marital deduction is a creature of the Revenue Act of 1948. It is a part of the attempt to equalize the tax situation in community property states and common law states to which reference has already been made. We will describe first the estate tax marital deduction as it existed prior to the Economic Recovery Tax Act of 1981. Property in a decedent's gross estate, up to 50 percent of his "adjusted gross estate," or $250,000, whichever was greater, which passed from the decedent to the decedent's spouse outright (or in a manner that is deemed the equivalent) was deduct-ible. A trust for life with a general power of appointment is treated the same as an outright gift. The ramifications of this matter are complex. It is obvious, however, that this provision of the 1948 Act was tremendously important in estate planning. You will hear much of this in your course on estate planning.[7] The estate tax marital deduction and the gift tax marital deduction previously considered should be compared. Both of them re-quired that the transfer by one spouse to the other spouse be outright or its equivalent. The gift tax marital deduction was normally one-half of the amount of the gift, but you will recall that the 1976 Tax Reform Act gave an unlimited gift tax marital deduction for the first $100,000 of gifts by one

---

7. See Casner, Estate Planning Under the Revenue Act of 1948, 62 Harv. L. Rev. 413 (1949); Casner, Estate Planning Under The Revenue Act of 1948 — The Regulations, 63 Harv. L. Rev. 99 (1949); Casner, Estate Planning ch. 13 (4th ed.).

spouse to the other spouse made after 1976. If a decedent had taken advantage of that unlimited gift tax marital deduction, there was a cut down of the estate tax marital deduction in an amount equal to 50 percent of the amount of the unlimited gift tax marital deduction that was used. For example, suppose the donor spouse gave the donee spouse $83,000 and took a gift tax marital deduction of $80,000 ($3,000 of the gift was eliminated by the annual exclusion). On the donor spouse's death, the maximum allowable estate tax marital deduction was reduced by the difference between $80,000 and one-half of $83,000, which difference is $38,500. As noted above, the maximum estate tax marital deduction, subject to the cut-down rule just mentioned, was the greater of one-half of the adjusted gross estate or $250,000. Unless the adjusted gross estate exceeded $500,000, the maximum allowable estate tax marital deduction was $250,000. In order to be entitled to the maximum allowable estate tax marital deduction, items in the decedent's gross estate had to pass outright (or its equivalent) to the surviving spouse in an amount equal to such maximum or the maximum allowable deduction was not available. Prior to the 1976 Tax Reform Act, the maximum allowable estate tax marital deduction was restricted to one-half the adjusted gross estate. The $250,000 alternative was added by the 1976 Reform Act and hence it was applicable only to decedents dying after December 31, 1976. A decedent's adjusted gross estate is his gross estate minus the deductions for debts, funeral expenses, expenses of administration and deductible casualty losses.

You will recall that some special rules were applicable in relation to the gift tax marital deduction where property with a community property background was involved. The same was true in regard to the estate tax marital deduction. If the decedent and the decedent's surviving spouse at any time held property as community property under the law of any state, or possession of the United States, or any foreign country, then the adjusted gross estate for estate tax marital deduction purposes was determined by subtracting from the entire value of the gross estate the sum of the following:

1. the value of property which at the time of the decedent's death was held as such community property; and
2. the value of property transferred by the decedent during the decedent's life, if at the time of such transfer the property was held as such community property; and
3. the amount receivable as insurance under policies on the life of the decedent, to the extent purchased with premiums or other considerations paid out of property held as such community property; and
4. an amount which bears the same ratio to the aggregate of deductions allowed under sections 2053 and 2054 (debts, funeral expenses, expenses of administration, and deductible casualty losses) which the value of the property included in the gross estate, diminished by the amount subtracted under items 1, 2 and 3 above, bears to the entire value of the gross estate.

The amount to be subtracted under items 1, 2, and 3 above could not exceed the value of the interest in the property described therein which was included in determining the value of the gross estate.

The key to applying the complex rules for determining the adjusted gross estate where property with a community property background was in the picture was understanding the meaning of the phrase "property held as such community property." This phrase was defined in the Internal Revenue Code (section 2056 (c)(2)(C)) and had the same meaning as the phrase "held as community property" previously considered in connection with the discussion of the gift tax marital deduction.

Once the adjusted gross estate was determined with respect to the community property situation, we knew that at least one-half thereof was available for an estate tax marital deduction and transfers from the decedent spouse to make up such one-half could be made out of any property in the gross estate without regard to whether it was community property or separate property. However, when would a larger marital deduction be available under the $250,000 alternative referred to above? Section 2056(c)(1)(C) spelled out the so-called community adjustment with respect to the $250,000 alternative in order to determine whether it was greater than one-half of the adjusted gross estate. The instructions given in that section were as follows:

a.   Go back to the instructions for ascertaining the adjusted gross estate and write down the total subtraction called for under items 1, 2, and 3 — assume that figure was $200,000.
b.   Determine the aggregate of the deductions allowed for debts, funeral expenses, expenses of administration and deductible casualty losses — assume that figure was $25,000 — and determine the excess of that figure over the figure used in item 4 in the instructions for determining the adjusted gross estate — assume such excess was $12,500.
c.   Reduce the $250,000 alternative by $200,000 minus $12,500 — such reduced figure is $62,500 and that was the alternative to one-half of the adjusted gross estate, the maximum allowable estate tax marital deduction being the greater of the $62,500 and one-half the adjusted gross estate.

It should be obvious from this discussion that the $250,000 alternative began to go down in amount if the decedent's gross estate contained property "held as such community property" and reached zero as soon as property "held as such community property" totaled $250,000 more than the deductions under sections 2053 and 2054 that were attributable to property in the gross estate that was "held as such community property."

Do you see the advantage community property would have had in the operation of the gift tax marital deduction and the estate tax marital deduction if the complex adjustments described had not been required?

The Economic Recovery Tax Act of 1981 made some significant changes in the estate tax marital deduction. These changes are generally applicable to estates of decedents dying after December 31, 1981, and the most important change is the adoption of an unlimited estate tax marital deduction. A new section 2056(b)(7) permits a gift to the surviving spouse in the form of a life interest with remainder to others to qualify for the estate tax marital deduction, if the deceased spouse's executor so elects. This type of disposition is referred to as a "qualified terminable interest." On the death of the surviving spouse, the full value of the property in which the life interest existed will be included in the surviving spouse's gross estate, if the executor elected to take a marital deduction for it when the donor spouse died (see section 2044). The preceding sentence does not apply to the extent that the surviving spouse has made a transfer of the spouse's life interest because that is treated as a gift of the entire property under section 2519. Also removed from the category of a disqualified terminable interest is the life interest of a donee spouse under a charitable remainder annuity trust and a charitable remainder unitrust, if the surviving spouse of a decedent is the only non-charitable beneficiary (see section 2056(b)(8)).

If
a. the decedent dies after December 31, 1981;
b. by reason of the death of the decedent property passes from the decedent or is acquired from the decedent under a will executed before the date which is 30 days after the date of the enactment (August 13, 1981) of this Act, or a trust created before such date, which contains a formula expressly providing that the spouse is to receive the maximum amount of property qualifying for the marital deduction allowable by federal law,
c. the formula referred to in paragraph b was not amended to refer specifically to an unlimited marital deduction at any time after the date which is 30 days after the date of enactment of this Act, and before the death of the decedent; and
d. the state does not enact a statute applicable to such estate which construes this type of formula as referring to the marital deduction allowable by federal law as amended to make available the unlimited marital deduction —

then the former maximum marital deduction allowable shall apply to such formula gift, not the new unlimited marital deduction.

The unlimited estate tax marital deduction made available by the Economic Recovery Tax Act of 1981 eliminates all of the complexity in regard to the estate tax marital deduction where community property is involved. The result is that as to decedents dying after December 31, 1981, there is no distinction between community property and separate property so far as the estate tax marital deduction is concerned.

Charitable gifts are deductible, but the word "charitable" is given the same rather artificial meaning that was discussed under the gift tax. In order for a split-gift, i.e., one that is part to an individual and part to a charity, to be deductible as to the part going to charity, very complex rules must be satisfied.

Computation of the Amount of the Estate Tax

The computation of the federal estate tax requires resort to the unified rate schedule appearing in the Code. This is the same rate schedule that we referred to in the discussion of the gift tax.

The computation of the amount of the estate tax under the unified rate schedule involves the following steps:

1. the ascertainment of the taxable estate, which is the gross estate minus the deductions;
2. the amount of the so-called adjusted taxable gifts (that is the taxable gifts made by the decedent after December 31, 1976, that are not included in the decedent's gross estate);
3. the computation of a tentative tax under the unified rate schedule on the total produced by adding the taxable estate and the adjusted taxable gifts;
4. the reduction of the tentative tax so computed by the aggregate amount of gift taxes payable with respect to gifts made by the decedent after December 31, 1976 (for this purpose, if gift-splitting was used with respect to any gifts made after December 31, 1977, and the entire amount of the gift, including the one-half charged to the non-donor spouse, is included in the donor-spouse's gross estate, the gift tax paid by the non-donor spouse will be includible in the amount of gift taxes payable with respect to gifts made by the decedent after December 31, 1976); the Economic Recovery Tax Act of 1981 amended section 2001(b)(2); which relates to the reduction in the tentative tax for the gift tax paid with respect to gifts made after December 31, 1976, to provide that the amount of the reduction shall be the amount of gift tax that would have been payable if the rate schedule in effect at the decedent's death had been applicable at the time of the gift; this amendment is applicable to decedents dying after December 31, 1981;
5. the unified credit (the same one discussed in relation to gift taxes) is then applied against the estate tax determined by steps 1 through 4 to obtain the amount of tax payable (you will recall that the unified credit was $47,000 by 1981 (the unified credit for estate tax purposes was $30,000 for all of 1977, and it increased to $34,000 for 1978, to $38,000 for 1979, and to $42,500 for 1980)); the Economic Recovery Tax Act of 1981 increased the unified credit to $192,800 (after 1986); this increase is phased in as follows: $62,800 for 1982, $79,300 for 1983, $96,300 for 1984, $121,800 for 1985, $155,800 for 1986; after 1986, the credit will be the equivalent of an exemption of $600,000;
6. the amount of tax payable as outlined in 5 may be further reduced by

other credits against the tax, such as the credit for state death taxes, the credit for tax on prior transfers, and the credit for foreign death taxes.

The credit for the tax on prior transfers is designed to give some protection against too rapid retaxation of the same property. A credit is allowed for the federal estate tax paid with respect to a prior transfer of property to the decedent from another person who died within ten years before the decedent. A 100 percent credit is allowed if the transferor died within two years of the decedent and the credit diminishes by 20 percent in each two-year period thereafter, so that in the last two years before the ten-year period is up, the credit is only 20 percent of the federal estate tax paid on previously taxed property. There are some limitations placed on the amount of this credit, with the result that, under some circumstances, the amount of the credit will not equal the federal estate tax previously paid. Can you explain why the credit, though it equals the federal estate tax previously paid, may not equal the amount of the federal estate tax imposed on the property previously taxed in the subsequent decedent's estate?

There are two areas of possible double taxation in rapid succession that are not protected by any credit. (1) If H (a husband) makes a gift to his son, S, and pays a gift tax and S dies shortly thereafter and an estate tax is imposed on the property given to S by H, no credit is available against the estate tax imposed on S's estate for the gift tax paid by H. (2) If H makes a gift to his son, S, and S dies shortly thereafter, and more than two years after S dies but less than three years from the date of the gift H dies, and if the value of the gift is included in H's gross estate for estate tax purposes as a gift within three years of his death, and the value of the gift to S is taxed in S's estate, neither estate will get a credit for the estate tax imposed on the other estate. H's estate, of course, will get a credit against the estate tax imposed for the gift tax H paid. The Economic Recovery Tax Act of 1981 added section 2035(d), which eliminated the three-year automatic return rule in regard to most outright gifts to S from H. The gift by H, however, if it is not included in H's gross estate, is an adjusted taxable gift that will be taken into account in calculating the estate tax payable on H's estate whenever H dies. The amount of the gift tax H paid on the gift to S will be includible in H's gross estate, if H dies within three years after the gift.

Property of a citizen or resident which is situated in a foreign country is not eliminated from the gross estate. Thus, if such property were subject to a death tax in the country where it is located and this fact were ignored in assessing the federal estate tax, double taxation of the same property would be the result. Relief from this is given by allowing, with certain limitations, a credit for foreign death taxes. There is also a similar credit in the income tax field. The Code, however, makes no provision for any credit for foreign gift taxes. Tax treaties have been negotiated by the United States with various foreign countries and where such a treaty exists, it must be examined to obtain the full story of the foreign tax credit.

It may be useful to work through the computation of the estate tax in a somewhat typical situation. Assume the following asset picture with respect to H (the values stated are the values that are controlling for estate tax purposes; the executor may elect date-of-death values for all assets or the so-called alternate valuation date (date an estate asset is disposed of or six months after death, whichever is earlier) for all assets):

Gross Estate (H died in 1983)

1.	Tangible personal property	$ 5,000
2.	Real property owned outright by H	20,000
3.	Real property owned jointly by H and W as tenants by the entirety, the consideration for the acquisition of the real property furnished entirely by H; one-half of the value of real estate jointly owned included in gross estate (full value of real property $100,000)	50,000
4.	Bank account with $10,000 in it in name of H and W, payable to the survivor, the money in the account all came from H	10,000
5.	Securities owned outright by H	100,000
6.	Securities owned by H and W as joint tenants with right of survivorship, H furnished the purchase money for these securities, value of securities $200,000, so only one-half of that value, or $100,000, is carried in value column as being in gross estate	100,000
7.	Life insurance on H's life, all incidents of ownership retained by H	200,000
	Value of H's gross estate	$485,000

Adjusted Gross Estate (a term no longer defined in the estate tax provisions of the Code)

The adjusted gross estate is the gross estate minus the funeral expenses, debts, expenses of administration, and deductible casualty losses.

1.	Gross estate	$485,000
2.	Funeral expenses, debts, and expenses of administration (no deductible casualty losses)	25,000
	Adjusted gross estate	$460,000

Items in gross estate that qualify for marital deduction

1.	Tangible personal property (assume H's will gave this property outright to W)	$ 5,000
2.	Real property owned outright by H (assume H's will gave this property outright to W)	20,000
3.	Real property owned jointly by H and W as tenants by the entirety (this property passed outright to W under the right of survivorship and qualifies for the marital deduction to the extent its value is included in H's gross estate)	50,000

4. Bank account in name of H and W, payable to survivor
    (this bank account passed outright to W under the right
    of survivorship and qualifies for the marital deduction
    to the extent its value is included in H's gross estate)   10,000
5. Securities owned by H and W as joint tenants with
    right of survivorship (these securities passed outright to
    W under the right of survivorship, and they qualify for
    the marital deduction to the extent their value is in-
    cluded in H's gross estate)   100,000
Note: Assume that the other items in H's gross estate were
           not disposed of in a manner that qualifies them for
           the marital deduction.
           ‛Total value of items that qualify for the marital
           deduction $185,000

Maximum allowable marital deduction (unlimited)

The maximum allowable marital deduction is the adjusted gross estate.
1. Adjusted gross estate $460,000
Note: The marital deduction gifts fall short of the maxi-
           mum allowable marital deduction by the amount
           of $275,000
           Though H could have disposed of his property so as
           to pick up this additional $275,000 deduction, he
           did not and thus it is lost.

Taxable estate

1. Gross estate $485,000
    Deductions:
    1. Funeral expenses, debts, and ex-
        penses of administration   25,000
    2. Marital deduction   185,000
              Total   210,000
    Taxable estate   275,000
    Adjusted taxable gifts (assume taxable
      gifts made by H in 1977 that are not
      includible in his gross estate) $225,000
    Total of taxable estate and adjusted taxable gifts $500,000
    Tentative tax under unified rate schedule on $500,000 $155,800
    Aggregate amount of gift taxes payable with respect to
      gifts made by H in 1977 $ 32,800
    Estate tax (amount by which $155,800 exceeds
      $32,800) $123,000
    Unified credit (in 1983)   79,300
    Estate tax payable $ 43,700
    State death tax credit (calculated on the basis of the
      taxable estate less $60,000) $ 3,000

The estate tax will be almost wiped out by the unified credit if H dies in 1985, when the credit will be $121,800. It would be more than wiped out in 1986, when the credit will be $155,800. This means that by 1986, on the same facts, H would have made estate tax marital deduction gifts to his spouse that exceeded what would be necessary to wipe out the payment of any estate tax. It may be undesirable from a tax standpoint to make estate tax marital deduction gifts that exceed what is necessary to eliminate the payment of any tax after taking into account the available unified credit because H will simply be increasing W's gross estate without any compensating estate tax benefit to his estate.

It should be noted that the $3,000 state death tax credit cannot exceed the amount of the estate tax imposed, as reduced by the amount of the unified credit. Thus, the $3,000 state death tax credit will disappear as soon as the unified credit eliminates the payment of any estate tax.

D. Estate and Inheritance Taxes of the States

Nearly all of the states impose some kind of tax upon the passage of property upon death, and there is considerable variety in the nature of these taxes. Three types are common:

1. The oldest type is the inheritance tax, also called a legacy tax or succession tax. This imposes a tax on the transfer to each heir or next of kin if the decedent dies intestate, or to each devisee or legatee if decedent leaves a will. The rate of tax depends upon whether the beneficiary is a relative and, if so, how close a relative; and it also depends upon the amount the beneficiary receives.

2. Some states have estate taxes of their own, usually modeled on the federal estate tax. New York has such a tax. Massachusetts changed from an inheritance tax to an estate tax as to persons who die on or after January 1, 1976.

3. Some states impose a tax which is simply a percentage of the federal tax and is dependent upon the federal tax return. States which have types 1 and 2 also usually have a supplementary tax, type 3, to take advantage of the credit for state taxes allowed under the federal estate tax, sometimes referred to as a "sponge tax." Thus, if the total of state inheritance or estate taxes is less than the credit for state taxes which would be allowed under the federal estate tax, an estate tax is levied in the amount of the difference. You will observe that this costs the estate nothing; it merely results in the state getting some tax money that would otherwise go into the United States Treasury. Notice that the so-called sponge tax is zero if the unified credit eliminates the payment of any estate tax. If state death tax laws do not recognize a marital deduction, or at least do not recognize an unlimited marital deduction, the state death tax bill becomes the most significant death

tax cost with respect to transfers from one spouse to another. Likewise, if the state death tax laws do not provide for a unified credit, or at least, do not provide for one that is as large as the federal unified credit, there may be a state death tax payment though not a federal estate tax payment.

If a person dies domiciled in state A and owning real and personal property in states A, B, C, and D, which state imposes estate or inheritance taxes? This is a combined problem of constitutional law and the provisions of the various statutes. Generally speaking, real estate and tangible personal property are taxed by the state in which the property is located and other property is taxed by the state in which the decedent was domiciled at the time of his death. But, as we have already mentioned, the determination of domicile is fraught with difficulties.

E. State Gift Taxes

California, Colorado, Delaware, Louisiana, New York, North Carolina, Oregon, Rhode Island, South Carolina, South Dakota, Tennessee, Vermont, Virginia, Washington, and Wisconsin have gift taxes. Puerto Rico also has a gift tax. There is no credit against the federal gift tax for gift taxes paid to a state. Oklahoma repealed its gift tax law effective January 1, 1982. Minnesota did the same.

The rates are usually geared to the state inheritance tax, but in some states a different rate schedule is established.

Of course, under the terms of the estate or inheritance tax laws of most states, many types of gifts are taxed at the death of the donor. These types include gifts in contemplation of death, gifts to take effect upon death, revocable gifts, and the like.

It must be kept in mind that state gift tax laws may not correlate with the federal gift tax laws in regard to the unlimited marital deduction, the annual exclusion, and the unified credit. This anomaly may result in the imposition of a state gift tax though no federal gift tax is payable.

SECTION 4. MUNICIPAL REAL ESTATE
TAXES AND OTHER PROPERTY
LEVIES

Cities, towns, counties, school districts, sanitary districts, and the like are financed by a wide variety of levies on various kinds of property. The number and nature of these taxes, the method of assessment and review, the manner of determining the rate, and the machinery of collection differ substantially. We do not attempt to make a comprehensive survey of all types of such taxes and other levies, nor to state the variations which will be found in the application of any one type. We do try to describe the types which are most universally important and to give a fairly typical statement as to how these types work. You should realize, however, that the following material describes typical situations which are by no means universal.

A. *The Real Estate Tax*

Municipal governments are principally supported by a tax which is levied upon the local real estate. It is a flat-rate tax dependent upon the value of the land and buildings. The amount of the tax which any piece of property pays is determined by two factors: (1) the amount at which the value of the property is assessed by the official assessors, and (2) the tax rate determined by the municipal body having fiscal authority. Thus, if a residential property is assessed at $20,000 and the tax rate is $35 per thousand, the owner must pay a tax of $700.

Assessment. The decision of the assessors is not final. If the owner feels that he or she is aggrieved, a reviewing authority is usually provided, with judicial review as a last resort. In many localities a fairly important segment of law practice is concerned with proceedings to abate land assessments.

The relationship between the salable value of property and the amount for which it is assessed varies greatly between communities. In most large cities property is assessed up to the hilt, and it is a common thing to find property selling for considerably less than the assessed value. On the other hand, in suburban communities it is common enough to find property assessed for as little as 50 or 60 percent of the price it would bring in a fairly active real estate market. This means that the "true" tax rate in a given town may be considerably less than the figure appearing on the town treasurer's bill; for if property is habitually assessed at two-thirds of its value, a nominal tax rate of $30 is a "true" tax rate of $20.

It is obvious that, if a particular municipal government has any tendency to corruption (and there have been such), the process of assessment for real estate taxes offers a fertile field for the work of the unscrupulous.

The tax rate. This is usually determined by a simple mathematical process. You take the valuation of all property in the town as determined by the assessors (less a reserve to absorb abatements of assessments which the assessors or a reviewing authority grant); then you take the appropriation for the current year (less taxes derived from other sources); you then, by a process of division, determine how many dollars per thousand of value must be collected in order to meet the municipal budget. That is the tax rate.

Machinery of collection. There is usually an assessment date — say May 1 — and within a fixed period after this date any petitions for abatement of the assessment must be filed. The date upon which the tax is payable is usually later; often the tax is payable in two installments. The tax is a lien on the property. If the tax is not paid, the property can be sold by the municipality. Provisions for redemption of property from tax sales are usually liberal.

B. Betterment Assessments

When a street is widened or paved, or a sidewalk is put in, or a sewer laid, some portion of the cost is assessed against each piece of property that is benefited by the improvement.

It is customary to spread the payment of a betterment assessment over a period of years representing roughly the life of the improvement. It is also commonly provided that the assessment shall be apportioned between landlord and tenant, or between life tenant and remainderman.

C. Water Charges and Special Assessments

Charges for municipal services, such as water supply and antipest spraying of trees, are usually made liens upon the land.

D. The Personal Property Tax

In most states there is a flat-rate personal property tax which is levied for the benefit of municipalities. Sometimes the tax is upon tangible personalty only, and sometimes it includes intangibles. In at least one state the tax on intangibles is determined by the income on the property, and it is therefore in substance an income tax.

SECTION 5. SOURCES OF TAX LAW

You have already been warned that this very brief survey has the sole purpose of sketching the general tax pattern as it affects the practice of property law. Something should be said as to how you can obtain detailed and accurate information as to the tax law on particular subjects. If you examine into these, we predict that you will conclude that you had better leave them alone until you are ready to devote adequate time and concentration to the subject in the systematic study of your course on taxation.

Official sources. All taxes are enacted by a *statute;* hence the statute is the starting point. As to the federal income, estate, and gift taxes, the Treasury Department issues *regulations* which have the status of administrative interpretation — not binding on the courts, but highly persuasive. Some state tax statutes also are supplemented by administrative regulations. The United States Tax Court, the United States Court of Claims, and the United States district courts are forums in which federal tax disputes are litigated.

Unofficial sources. Textbooks are numerous in the tax field, but up-to-the-minute knowledge is so important that loose-leaf tax services (Prentice-Hall and Commerce Clearing House) are the standard reference works — expensive but essential.

Bibliography. A brief list of references for the principal types of taxes dealt with in this discussion is as follows:

1. *Federal individual income tax* (all references are to sections of the Internal Revenue Code).
    Rates of tax — sections 1-5 and 11 and 12.
    Gross income — section 61.
    Deductions — section 161.
    Income from trust — sections 641-683.
2. *Federal gift tax* (all references are to sections of the Internal Revenue Code).
    What is a gift — section 2511.
    Rate of tax — section 2502.
    Deductions — sections 2521-2524.
3. *Federal estate tax* (all references are to sections of the Internal Revenue Code).
    Rate of tax — section 2001.
    Gross estate — sections 2031-2044.
    Taxable estate — sections 2051-2056.
    Credits — sections 2011-2016.
4. *Generation-skipping tax* — sections 2601-2602.
5. *State taxes.*
    State Tax Review (published by Commerce Clearing House).

Problems

37.1. "A state which refuses to enact any inheritance or estate tax is more a gratuity to the federal government than a benefit to the state's taxpayers." Explain this statement.

37.2. "The federal income tax structure has a strong tendency to induce men of substantial income to own their homes rather than to live in rented houses or apartments. The federal income tax is the father of the cooperative apartment." Explain this statement.

37.3. In 1970 H transferred $500,000 to a trustee in trust to pay the income to H for life and upon H's death to pay the principal to such persons as H should appoint, and in default of appointment to pay the principal to S; H reserved the right to revoke the trust. In 1982 H effectively released his power to revoke the trust. In 1983 H effectively released his power to appoint by will. In 1984 H died.

State the federal income, gift, and estate tax consequences of these various events.

37.4. Interest paid out by the taxpayer upon loans which are used, directly or indirectly, for the purchase of municipal bonds, is not deductible under the federal income tax.

Why should this be?

37.5. H, alumnus of a well-known law school, has subscribed $10,000 to its endowment fund. Four years ago, he bought stock for $2,000 which is now worth $10,000. His top income tax bracket is 50 percent. You, his attorney, learn that he is about to sell this stock for the purpose of putting himself in funds to pay his subscription to the endowment fund. Can you give him any advice which will save him any money? How much money?

37.6. In 1953, Charles E. Wilson, president of General Motors (known as "Engine Charlie," to distinguish him from Charles E. Wilson, "Electric Charlie," who was president of General Electric), was nominated by President Eisenhower as Secretary of Defense. Hearings were held by the Senate Armed Services Committee on the issue of confirmation. It there appeared that Wilson owned General Motors stock, which had cost him $500,000, with a market value of $2,500,000. The committee insisted that, to eliminate a conflict of interest, he sell this stock. Reluctantly he agreed. He invested the proceeds of the sale in municipal bonds. What are the income tax and estate tax consequences of this transaction, assuming that Wilson (age 62) would have held the General Motors stock until his death? Out of this episode came the following comment:

> The action of the Armed Services Committee in the Wilson case will defeat, not promote, the public interest if we assume (as the Committee must have assumed) that Mr. Wilson's financial well-being will affect his action as Secretary of Defense. National defense will not be hurt if General Motors is given some preference over its competitors for defense contracts. But when the Secretary of Defense is forced to invest his private funds in fixed income securities having no potential as hedges against inflation a very serious conflict of interest is created which might induce Wilson to adopt policies which could be disastrous.
>
> Do you agree?

37.7. H is married and has one daughter, age 26 and married. H has a top income tax bracket of 50 percent. H and his wife each own a car. The daughter divorces her husband and returns to H's home. She too owns a car. She has no income and is totally dependent on H for support. H asks you whether collision insurance should be carried on these cars. Advise him as to any aspect of the tax laws relevant to this question. Indicate any course of action that would be desirable, assuming full cooperation of the daughter.

37.8. "The federal corporation income tax is a sales tax in disguise. Furthermore, unlike most direct sales taxes, it does not discriminate between the necessaries of life and the most extreme luxury. Those who pose as friends of the common people in opposing reduction or elimination of the corporation income tax are unconscionable demagogues." Comment on this statement.

37.9. "If the federal tax on capital gains, in its present form, were now repealed, so that there was no tax on realized gains the result would be a break in the stock market which would make the Big Break of 1929-1930 look like a boom." Comment on this statement.

37.10. It is said that in California no one of consequence would be seen riding in anything less than a Cadillac, and that 90 percent of the Cadillacs are owned by corporations. Why should they be thus owned?

37.11. The Treasury has warned that it will carefully scrutinize expense accounts. Suppose the Treasury concludes that a "convention" in Florida is in fact a vacation for favored officers. What would be the tax consequences?

37.12. H, who owns $1,000,000 in securities, is told he is dying of cancer and may live less than six months. He proposes to leave everything to his daughter. He asks you whether he can effect any savings by making her a present gift of his securities instead of leaving them by will. What would you tell him?

37.13. H is 83 years old. His first wife died several years ago. He has just married a woman age 55. Twenty years ago he set up a revocable inter vivos trust (present value $160,000) to pay the income to himself for life, then the income to his only son for life, then to pay the principal to the son's issue. His other assets comprise $240,000; he has drafted a will in which he leaves this amount to trustees in trust (a) to pay the income to his widow for life, the trustees to have discretion to make payments to the widow out of principal for her health and comfort, (b) on the death of his widow to pay the principal to his surviving issue. He has two life insurance policies: $20,000 payable to the son, $15,000 payable to the widow. The second wife has substantially no assets of her own. He asks you whether this set-up makes sense taxwise. Advise him as to savings that are available to him and by what means he can achieve them.

37.14. What are the advantages and disadvantages of a carry-over basis with respect to property acquired from or passing from a decedent as compared with the new-basis-at-death rule?

TABLE OF CASES

1287

TABLE OF STATUTES

Quoted statutes and their page numbers appear in italics.

INDEX